Writer's Guide to Book Editors, Publishers, and Literary Agents

13th Edition

Writer's Guide to Book Editors, Publishers, and Literary Agents

13th Edition

Who They Are! What They Want!
And How to Win Them Over!

JEFF HERMAN

PRIMA PUBLISHING

Published by Prima Publishing, Roseville, California. Member of the Crown Publishing Group, a division of Random House, Inc.

PRIMA PUBLISHING and colophon are trademarks of Random House, Inc., registered with the United States Patent and Trademark Office.

ISBN: 0-7615-3735-X
ISBN 0-7615-3745-7 (CD-ROM Deluxe Edition)
ISSN: 1089 3369

02 03 04 05 BB 10 9 8 7 6 5 4 3 2 1
Printed in the United States of America

Thirteenth Edition

Visit us online at www.primapublishing.com

This edition is dedicated to the work-a-day writers who seek to expand their success and the quality of their craft.

The power to publish is the power to create or destroy. It is not for the publishers to issue the call; that is determined by a source beyond them. By merits granted or earned, some will be chosen. The gates should therefore never be sealed, and those with the power to publish always revealed.

—An Anonymous Literary Agent

About the Author

Jeff Herman is the founder of The Jeff Herman Literary Agency, LLC. One of the most innovative agents in the book business, he represents more than 100 writers and has sold more than 450 titles in the United States and internationally. Herman has been extensively written and talked about in numerous print publications and broadcast programs, and he speaks at writer's conferences around the country. He is the coauthor with Deborah Levine Herman of *Write the Perfect Book Proposal*. Be sure to visit his high-content Web site at www.jeffherman.com.

Contributors

Deborah Levine Herman is vice president of The Jeff Herman Literary Agency and coauthor of *Write the Perfect Book Proposal: 10 Proposals That Sold and Why* (John Wiley & Sons) and *Spiritual Writing* (Beyond Words).

William Hamilton is the publisher at University of Hawaii Press.

Greg Ioannou is director of the Editorial Centre in Toronto, Ontario, Canada.

Jamie M. Forbes is a publishing and media consultant based in New York.

Morris Rosenthal is an author and translator. His computer books have been published in Chinese and Spanish editions, and you can visit his internationally recognized Web site at www.daileyint.com.

Toni Robino is a wonderful writer who is always there to help others write. Visit her Web site at withflyingcolors.com.

Mark Schreiber is a successful author from Columbus, Ohio.

Contents

Acknowledgments

Every edition of this work creates a new trial of endurance for myself and my dedicated associates who help me with this endeavor.

They include:

Deborah Herman, still my honey.

Amanda White, for once again doing a stupendous job.

Toni Robino, for her adept ability to tackle last minute situations, and still be excellent.

Tara Joffe and David Richardson my Prima editors, who are among the best in the business.

My thanks to the staff of the Science Fiction and Fantasy Writers of America's Writer Beware for checking the agents in this book against their database and sharing information from their files. The Writer Beware Web site (http://www.sfwa.org/beware) provides information about literary scams, schemes, and other pitfalls that face aspiring writers.

Introduction

Dear Reader,

I am happy to say that several hundred thousand copies of the *Writer's Guide* are in print. What I also find to be personally gratifying is that everyone from novices to seasoned veterans claim this work to be one of the most valuable tools available for and about the book publishing business.

More than ten years ago, when I was a twenty-something and still new to this business of agenting, I did not like the obstacles, fixed attitudes, or sense of exclusionary elitism I experienced along the way. In many ways, the murky world of agents and editors struck me as being some kind of secret society. I felt like this was wrong on many levels. All people deserved a fair shot at being a part of our nation's publishing infrastructure, and the distribution of ideas and words needed to flow like flood waters without arbitrary dams. I was an idealist. Plus, I wanted a way to attract more clients.

Back then, and today, the mission of the *Writer's Guide* hasn't changed: To expose as many of the key publishing decision-makers as possible, provide clear information and directions for ways to challenge the abstract obstacles, and penetrate the entire process to the point of success. Because of this book, countless editors and agents have more work to do than they otherwise would have. But that has always been the point, and the results are good for all who participate.

This book is an opportunity for you to learn and grow as it relates to the special endeavors of writing and publishing. I will appreciate hearing about your experiences, comments, and (okay) submissions. Thank you.

Best wishes,

Jeffrey H. Herman

Jeffrey H. Herman

The Jeff Herman Literary Agency
332 Bleeker Street, Suite G-31, New York, NY 10014
212-941-0540   fax: 212-941-0614
www.jeffherman.com   (e-mail) jeff@jeffherman.com

Directory of Book Publishers and Editors

United States Publishers

2.13.61 PUBLICATIONS, INC.

PO Box 1910, Los Angeles, CA 90078
213-969-8043 (information hotline)
www.two1361.com

2.13.61 Publications offers new fiction and creative narratives, creative prose nonfiction, poetry, cultural events and critical works, photographic books, and audiovisual products. The house was founded in 1988.

Titles from 2.13.61 include *Smile, You're Traveling; Solipsist; Do I Come Here Often?; Black Coffee Blues; The First Five; See a Grown Man Cry; Get in the Van; Eye Scream*, all by Henry Rollins; *Letters to Rollins* by Rob Overton; *The Cowardice of Amnesia* by Ellyn Maybe; *Go Tell the Mountain* by Jeffrey Lee Pierce; *Reach* and *Boy in the Air* by Don Bajema; *Attack God Inside* by Tricia Warden; *The Consumer* by Michael Gira; *Fish in a Barrel* by Peter Milne; *Dream Baby Dream* by Stephanie Chernikowski; *Planet Joe* by Joe Cole; *Metallica* (photographs by Ross Halfin); *Rosey the Baby Killer* by Bill Shields.

Oh, incidentally: It's no big secret, but this operation is under the watchful eye of none other than poet-rocker Henry Rollins himself. Want to start a contest? Guess what 2.13.61 means; a fancy facsimile of Henry Rollins's birth certificate goes to the winner.

2.13.61 Publications, Inc., distributes to the trade through Publishers Group West. Query letters and SASEs should be directed to:

Carol Bua, Director

ABBEVILLE PUBLISHING GROUP

Abbeville Kids

Artabras

Canopy Books

Cross River

22 Cortlandt Street, New York, NY 10007
212-577-5555   fax: 212-577-5579
www.abbeville.com

A

Abbeville is renowned for finely produced, award-winning volumes in the areas of fine arts, art history, architecture, graphic arts, design, lifestyle, cuisine, handicrafts, nature, collectibles, popular culture, sports, and illustrated historical works. Abbeville also produces postcard books, stationery items, pop-up children's books, artists' portfolios, and titles in biography, letters, literature, and humor. Abbeville issues hardcover and trade paperback editions—all published with attention to quality in design, illustration, and production standards. Abbeville Publishing Group includes Abbeville Press, Abbeville Kids, Artabras, Edition Stemmle, Touring Club of Italy, Skira, Van der Meer, and Flammarion. Abbeville Kids is the house's children's imprint (see subentry). Tiny Folios is a line of small, handsome, reasonably priced gift volumes. Editions Abbeville is the house's enterprising French imprint. Artabras is a house imprimatur for specially priced promotional/premium volumes. Abbeville is the exclusive distributor for English-language publications, based in Zurich, and for the Touring Club of Italy, Skira, and Van der Meer. They are publishers of fine art and photographic books.

Abbeville Publishing Group is an international firm with offices in New York and Paris. Abbeville upholds a tradition of bookmaking established by the publisher Harry N. Abrams, who with his son Robert E. Abrams started Abbeville Press (in 1977) subsequent to the purchase of the eponymous publishing house Harry N. Abrams, Inc., by the Times Mirror Company (see entry for Abrams in this directory).

Representing the Abbeville list: *Wristwatch Annual 2002* (edited by Peter Braun); *Wine: A Practical Guide to Enjoying Your Selection* by Jens Priewe; *The Great Wall of China* by Michel Jan (photography by Roland and Sabrina Michaud); *In the Market: The Illustrated History of the Financial Markets* by Christopher Finch; *Treasures of the White House* by Betty C. Monkman; *The Belize and Honduras Dive Guide* by Roberto Rinaldi; *On Exhibit 2002: Art Lover's Travel Guide to American Museums* by Judith Swirsky; *Tibet* by Carroll Dunham and Ian Baker, with foreword by the Dalai Lama; *Vanishing Africa* by Kate Klippensteen.

Tiny Folios accents miniature books—for those who love gifts that come in small packages. Series titles: *Hugs & Kisses* by Mimi Coucher; *Dogs Up Close* by Vicki Croke; *100 Classic Cocktails* by Barry Shelby; *Frank Lloyd Wright: American Master Architect* by Kathryn Smith; *Treasures of the Museum of Fine Arts, Boston* (chapter introductions by Gillian Wohlauer); *Edgar Degas* by George T. M. Shackelford; *Treasures of the Hermitage* (introduction by Vitaly A. Suslov); *Provence* by Sonja Bullaty and Angelo Domeo.

Artabras (quality books at bargain prices) titles: *Norman Rockwell: 332 Magazine Covers* by Christopher Finch; *Ethnic Style: From Mexico to the Mediterranean* by Miranda Innes; *Cats Up Close* by Vicki Croke; *Piaget: Watches and Wonders Since 1874* by Franco Cologni and Giampiero Negretti; *Venetian Taste* by Adam Tihany.

Abbeville Press distributes its own books throughout the United States. Unsolicited manuscripts are rarely accepted, but query letters and SASEs can be directed to:

Susan Costello, Editorial Director—Gardening, nature, folk art, general

Christopher Lyon, Executive Editor—Fine arts, general

Kerrie Baldwin, Assistant Editor—Children's, general

Abbeville Kids

Abbeville Kids produces a lineup designed to introduce younger folk to the world of art and design—as well as to hone the tastes of younger artists and connoisseurs. Abbeville Kids offers breakthrough series of interactive, inquiry-based books designed to teach children about art by looking at the world and about the world by looking at art. Abbeville Kids also offers books with a broader scope that cover the finer pleasures of living and life.

Titles from Abbeville Kids: Abbeville Animals series; *Father and Daughter Tales* by Josephine Evetts-Secker (illustrated by Helen Cann); *Felix Activity Book* by Marc Tyler Nobleman and Leslie Mosely; *In the Paint* by Patrick Ewing and Linda L. Louis; *The Story of Chess* by Horacio Cardo; *Women of Camelot: Queens and Enchantresses at the Court of King Arthur* by Mary Hoffman. How Artists See . . . is a series from Abbeville Kids with such titles as *How Artists See Feelings, How Artists See the Elements, How Artists See People, How Artists See Families, How Artists See Work, How Artists See Animals* (all by Colleen Carroll).

ABRAMS

100 Fifth Avenue, New York, NY 10011
212-206-7715   fax: 212-645-8437
www.abramsbooks.com

Abrams publishes in the fields of fine art, architecture, design; anthropology, archaeology, ethnology, and culture; gardening and the home; literary and art criticism; world history; travel and the natural sciences; creative use of technology and new media.

The Abrams list accents fine illustrated volumes, mainly in hardcover, with some trade paperback editions and series, as well as a selection of works in electronic format. Many Abrams books are published in cooperation with institutions such as museums, foundations, or art galleries; these works bring together top-quality illustrative materials and expert text. Abrams publishes a strong seasonal list of new titles and maintains an extensive backlist.

Abrams was founded in 1949 as an independent house (then known as Harry N. Abrams, Inc.) and has been a subsidiary of the Times Mirror Company from 1977 to 1997. In that year, Abrams was acquired by Groupe Latingy (now La Martiniere Groupe). From its inception, the firm has been among the leaders in the field of fine bookmaking in the areas of art, design, and illustrated works.

From Abrams: *African Ceremonies* by Carol Beckwith and Angela Fisher; *African Rock Art* by Alec Campbell; *Art Nouveau 1890–1914* (edited by Paul Greenhalgh); *Chicken Run: Hatching the Movie* by Brian Shelby; *Colonial Williamsburg* by Philip Kopper; *Design and Detail in the Home* by David Linley; *Diego Rivera* by Pete Hamill; *Earth from Above* (photographs by Yann Arthur-Bertrand); *Flowers A to Z: Buying, Growing, Cutting, Arranging* by Cecilia Heffernan; *Giorgio Armani* by Germano Celant and Harold Koda; *Hearst Castle: The Biography of a Country House* by Victoria Kastner; *History of Art* by Anthony F. Janson; *Hollywood Candid,* with photographs by Murray

Garrett; *Hollywood Moms* (photographs by Joyce Ostin); *Home: A Collection of Poetry and Art* by Stan Tymorek; *How to Look at Everything* by David Finn; *Laurie Anderson* by Roselee Goldberg; *Leonardo da Vinci: The Complete Paintings* by Pietro Marani; *Loving Picasso: The Private Journal of Fernande Oliver; The Magic of M. C. Escher* (created by Joost Elffers and Andreas Landshoff); *Mark Pickford Rediscovered* by Kevin Brownlow; *Matisse: Father and Son* by John Russell; *Norman Rockwell: Pictures for the American People* (edited by Maureen Hart Hennessey and Anne Knutson); *Physics in the 20th Century* by Curt Suplee; *The Red Rose Girls* by Alice Carter; *Tiffany Jewels* by John Loring; *Valley of the Golden Mummies* by Zahi Hawass; *YES: Yoko Ono* by Alexandra Monroe, with John Hendricks.

Abrams children's books include *Babar and the Succotash Bird* by Laurent de Brunhoff; *Hello Kitty Hello World; Sally Goes to the Beach* by Stephen Huneck; *The Worst Band in the Universe* by Graeme Base.

Abrams trade paperback lines include Discoveries (books covering history, archaeology, natural history, culture, and the arts, over the full range of house subject areas of interest).

Titles here: *Alexander the Great* by Pierre Briant; *The Aztecs* by Serge Gnuzinski; *The Birth of Greece* by Pierre Leveque; *Einstein* by Francoise Balibar.

It should be noted that Abrams is a specialist house and acquires projects on a highly selective basis that gives particular weight to such factors as the national or international renown and credentials of participant artists, photographers, and writers.

Abrams distributes its own books in the United States and Canada.

Query letters and SASEs should be directed to:

Eric Himmel, Editor in Chief

Mark Magowan, Publisher

ACADEMY CHICAGO PUBLISHERS

363 West Erie Street, Chicago, IL 60610
312-751-7300, 800-248-7323   fax: 312-751-7306
www.academychicago.com   e-mail: academy363@aol.com

Academy Chicago publishes general nonfiction, art, history, and cultural studies, as well as fiction (including mysteries). The house also offers a line of classic reprints. Academy Chicago Publishers (established in 1975), a small press with an inspired list, is a major player in American letters.

Nonfiction from Academy Chicago includes popular works with an emphasis on contemporary culture, current events, and historical interpretation. Titles here: *Kings and Queens of Early Britain* by Geoffrey Ashe; *The Provincial Lady in Russia* by E. M. Delafield; *Before and After Zachariah: A True Story About a Family and a Different Kind of Courage* by Fern Kupfer; *Titanic: A Survivor's Story & the Sinking of the S.S. Titanic* by Colonel Archibald Gracie and John B. Thayer; *The Five Weeks of Giuseppe Zangara: The Man Who Would Assassinate FDR* by Blaise Picchi; *The Celtic and Scandinavian Religions* by J. A. MacCulloch; *Ireland: A Concise History from the Twelfth Century to the Present Day* by Paul Johnson; *Night Witches: The Amazing Story of Russia's Women Pilots in World War II* by Bruce Myles.

The Academy Chicago program in fiction and letters encompasses English-language originals, often with a historical or cultural hook; a solid number of these titles feature the mystery and suspense modes. Academy Chicago also publishes a variety of contemporary and vintage novels in translation.

Frontlist fiction includes *Cutter's Island* by Vincent Panella; *The Marquise & Pauline: Two Novellas* by George Sand (translated by Sylvie Charron and Sue Huseman); *Murder at Heartbreak Hospital* by Henry Slesar; *A Writer of Books* by George Paston (Emily Morse Symonds); *The Man Who Once Played Catch with Nellie Fox* by John Manderino; *Freedom in the Dismal* by Monifa A. Love; *Death and Blintzes* by Dorothy and Sidney Rosen; *Leone Leoni* by George Sand; *Homer's Daughter* by Robert Graves; *The Monkey's Paw: And Other Tales of Mystery and the Macabre* by W. W. Jacobs (compiled and with an introduction by Gary Hoppenstand); *In a Dark Wood Wandering: A Novel of the Middle Ages* by Hella S. Haasse (translated by Anita Miller); *Thirteen Uncollected Stories* by John Cheever (edited by Franklin H. Dennis); *Indiana* by George Sand (translated by George Burnham Ives); *The White Guard* by Mikhail Bulgakov (translated by Michael Glenny).

Representing the range of Academy Chicago fiction and literary works: *The Fat Woman's Joke* by Fay Weldon; *The Life and Times of Deacon A. L. Wiley* by Gregory Alan-Williams (drama/African American studies); *The Perfect Murder* by H. R. F. Keating. Academy Chicago is the American publisher of the successful British series of humorous and profound Miss Read novels, including *Fresh from the Country*.

Academy Chicago handles its own distribution. Query letters and SASEs should be directed to:

Anita Miller, Senior Editor

Jordan Miller, Vice President and Editor

ADAMS MEDIA CORPORATION

57 Littlefield Street, 2nd Floor, Avon, MA 02322
508-427-7100   fax: 508-427-6790
www.adamsmedia.com

Adams Media Corporation has experienced dramatic growth over the past few years and, looking to the future, is poised for even greater title acquisition, higher store presence, and increased marketing sales, and media clout. One of the fast-growing publishers in the country, the now midsized trade house publishes approximately 150 books per year. Adams has created a truly unique and distinct publishing universe, with magnificent cover designs, eye-catching trademark brands, high-quality content, and competitive retail packaging.

The Adams Editorial Group is now structured to accommodate both bestselling Single Titles and powerhouse Series Publishing programs for trade, mass-market, special sales, gift markets, library sales, and other burgeoning outlets and channels.

In the Single Title area, the publisher has had tremendous success in the areas of self-help/self-improvement, women's issues, relationships, spirituality, popular psychology, personal finance, business management, and pets. Adams also considers proposals with

A

broad popular appeal and unique marketing hooks in the areas of parenting, cooking, careers, fitness/leisure how-to, and sales/marketing how-to.

The highly commercial spring 2002 list features such lead titles as *Laura: America's First Lady, First Mother* by Antonia Felix; *Beef Busters: Less Beef, Better Health!* by Marissa Cloutier, M.S., R.D., Deborah S. Romaine, and Eve Adamson; *Healthy Foods, Healthy Kids: A Complete Guide to Nutrition for Children from Birth to Six Years Old* by Elizabeth M. Ward, M.S., R.D.; *The Birth Order: How to Better Understand Yourself and Others* by Cliff Isaacson and Kris Radish; *The Complete Guide to Pregnancy After 30* by Carol Winkelman; *25 Sales Skills They Don't Teach You in Business School* by Stephan Schiffman; *The Road to CEO* by Sharon Voros; *IT Sales Boot Camp: Sure-Fire Techniques for Selling Technology Products to Mainstream Companies* by Brian Giese; *Guerrilla Publicity* by Jay Conrad Levinson, Rick Frishman, and Jill Lublin.

Among the company's Single Title backlist hot sellers are *Selling to VITO, 2nd Edition* by Anthony Parinello; *The Verbally Abusive Relationship* by Patricia Evans; *A Cup of Comfort* by Colleen Sell; *God Is My CEO* by Larry Julian.

The Adams Series Publishing Program continues to yield unparalleled results and now has an in-house acquisitions and development team to keep up with the insatiable market demand. The staff is actively seeking professional writers to build upon the phenomenal success of the flagship Everything series, which now boasts over 160 titles in more than a dozen publishing categories, including parenting, cooking, hobbies, spirituality, New Age, personal finance, pets, weddings, relationships, careers, gardening, and more. Among the series' top sellers are *The Everything Pregnancy Book, The Everything Baby Names Book, The Everything Bartenders Book, The Everything Dreams Book, The Everything Money Book, The Everything Wedding Book, The Everything Etiquette Book, The Everything Cat Book, The Everything Astrology Book,* and *The Everything Barbecue Book.*

The series has also spawned two hugely successful spinoff series, Everything Kids' and Everything Mini. The Kids' books include *The Everything Kids' Baseball Book, The Everything Kids' Witches and Wizards Book, The Everything Kids' Online Book, The Everything Kids' Puzzle Book,* and *The Everything Kids' Nature Book.* Among the Minis are *The Everything Dreams Mini Book, The Everything Baby Names Mini Book, The Everything Bedtime Story Mini Book, The Everything Pregnancy Mini Book,* and *The Everything Get Ready for Baby Mini Book.*

While shorter in terms of title count than the Everything series, with five books, the Small Miracles franchise has sold millions of copies and continues to enlighten readers around the world. Authors Yitta Halberstam and Judith Leventhal have assembled an astonishing collection of remarkable coincidences in *Small Miracles, Small Miracles II, Small Miracles for Women, Small Miracles of Love and Friendship,* and *Small Miracles for the Jewish Heart.*

Among Adams's many other series are: Streetwise, which now features two dozen business books, ranging from *Streetwise Managing People* to *Streetwise Internet Business Plan; Heartwarmers* by Azriela Jaffe, now firmly established with a third title, *Heartwarmers of Spirit;* Fastread, a series for people with limited reading time; Knock Em' Dead, a series of career books by Martin Yate; as well as Job Banks, Adams Almanacs, The 100 Best (Stocks, Mutual Funds), Mr. Cheap's, and 365 Ways to . . . .

Adams orchestrates its own worldwide distribution network. In the United States, Adams distributes directly to bookstore chains and independents and also operates through wholesales and jobbers; in the United Kingdom and elsewhere in the world, the publisher distributes via overseas distributors.

Query letters with SASEs should be directed to:

Gary M. Krebs, Publishing Director—Handles a variety of trade properties, both in series and single title; will often pass to appropriate editors

Claire Gerus, Executive Editor—Wide-ranging nonfiction list

Jill Alexander, Editor—business titles

Bethany Brown, Everything series

Allison Carpenter, Everything series

ADDISON WESLEY LONGMAN PUBLISHING COMPANY

Addison Wesley is now strictly a textbook publisher.

ALGONQUIN BOOKS OF CHAPEL HILL
(A DIVISION OF WORKMAN PUBLISHING COMPANY)

PO Box 2225, Chapel Hill, NC 27515
919-767-0108
www.algonquin.com

This division of Workman Publishing Company has a primarily literary orientation in commercial nonfiction and fiction. The house list represents the American tradition, ranging from the homespun to the avant-garde. Algonquin Books of Chapel Hill presents its titles in hardcover and trade paper editions with a look and feel befitting the publisher's emphasis on both the classical and contemporary—books designed to be comfortably handled when read. The Algonquin editorial organization operates from both the Chapel Hill and New York Workman offices.

Algonquin nonfiction includes: *Return of the Osprey* by David Gessner; *Godforsaken Sea* by Derek Lundy; *Educating Esme* by Esme Raji Codell; *Sugar Pie & Jelly Roll* by Robbin Gourley; *Somehow Form a Family,* essays by Tony Earley.

Algonquin fiction and literary works: *Gap Creek* by Robert Morgan; *Tea* by Stacey D'Erasmo; *Fay* by Larry Brown; *In the Name of Salome* by Julia Alvarez; *A Perfect Arrangement* by Suzanne Berne.

Algonquin Books of Chapel Hill is distributed by the parent Workman Publishing Company.

Query letters and SASEs should be directed to:

Elisabeth Scharlatt, Publisher

Shannon Ravenel, Editorial Director, Shannon Ravenel Books

Duncan Murrell, Editor

A

Kathy Pories, Editor

Antonia Fusco, Editor

AMACOM (AMERICAN MANAGEMENT ASSOCIATION)

1601 Broadway, New York, NY 10019-7420
212-586-8100
www.amnet.org

AMACOM publishes business and management books, primarily for a professional readership. AMACOM trade nonfiction lines include works that cover the fields of accounting and finance, career, customer service, management issues, general business and management, human resources, management skills, international business, manufacturing, organization development, strategy, information and communication technology, personal finance, marketing, advertising and public relations, personal development, small business, supervision, sales and sales management, and training.

Managers in large and small companies are encouraged to use AMACOM books as an inexpensive and effective way to improve their effectiveness, make their organizations more competitive, keep up with current trends and thinking, energize their staff, and inspire employees at all levels. Titles from AMACOM: *The E-Aligned Enterprise* by Jac Fitz-enz; *The Business of Innovation* by Roger Bean and Russell Radford; *Leading at the Edge* by Dennis N. T. Perkins; *Bodacious* by Mary Foley, with Martha Finney; *Focal Point* by Brian Tracy; *Technical Analysis of Stock Trends* by Robert D. Edwards and John Magee; *Mobile Technology Question and Answer Book* by Ron Schneiderman; *The Ultimate Internet Developer's Sourcebook* by Jessica Keyes; *Innovations in Competitive Manufacturing* by Paul M. Swamidass; *The Ultimate Six Sigma* by Keki R. Bhote; *The Nokia Revolution* by Dan Steinbock; *Keeping the People Who Keep You in Business* by F. Leigh Branham; *The ePolicy Handbook* by Nancy Flynn; *Artful Persuasion* by Harry Mills; *Trainers in Motion* by Jim Vidakovich; *The Accidental Salesperson* by Chris Little; *Net Value* by Peter J. Clark and Stephen Neil; *Delivering Knock Your Socks Off Service* by Kristin Anderson and Ron Zemke; *The New Manager's Starter Kit* by Robert Crittendon; *Get Weird!* by John Putzier. Prospective writers might keep in mind the AMACOM readership profile (not to typecast, but rather to offer guidelines): AMACOM readers are definitely not mass-market consumers; they want specialized materials and information on business issues that concern them most. AMACOM book buyers want more than a quick fix. They crave in-depth ideas and practical approaches they can try out on the job. They like to be on the leading edge and get a jump on the competition. They do not want secondhand information. They want to go straight to the source.

AMACOM distributes its own products through multiple marketing channels, including retail trade, direct marketing, special sales, and international sales (through McGraw-Hill). Query letters and SASEs should be directed to:

Adrienne Hickey, Executive Editor—General and human resource management, organization development, leadership, strategy

Janice Meagher, Executive Editor—Multi-contributor, reference books

Ellen Kadin, Senior Acquisitions Editor—Career skills, sales and marketing, customer service, self-development

Jacquie Flynn, Senior Acquisitions Editor—Information technology applications, training, e-commerce

Neil Levine, Senior Acquisitions Editor—Manufacturing, supply chain management, operations management, facilities management

A

AMERICAN PSYCHIATRIC PUBLISHING, INC. (FORMERLY AMERICAN PSYCHIATRIC PRESS, INC.)

1400 K Street, NW, Washington, DC 20005
202-682-6262, 800-368-5777   fax: 202- 682-6341
www.appi.org

In March 2001, American Psychiatric Publishing, Inc. (APPI), will celebrate its 20th anniversary. By then, the APPI will have published more than 800 titles, launched five journals, and merged all publishing operations of the American Psychiatric Association into a single corporation entity known as American Psychiatric Publishing, Inc.

American Psychiatric Publishing, Inc., publishes professional, reference, and trade books, as well as college textbooks. The press's spheres of interest include the behavioral and social sciences, psychiatry, and medicine. The house publishes a midsized booklist in hardcover and trade paper and also produces a number of professional journals; selected reference works are issued in electronic formats (including diskettes and CD-ROMs).

Although by far the major portion of the American Psychiatric list is geared toward the professional and academic markets, the house catalogs a small number of books in the areas of patient information and books for the general public, among which are selected titles marketed through trade channels.

Representative of the American Psychiatric popular-interest list: *The Selfish Brain: Learning from Addiction* by Robert L. DuPont, M.D.; *Women's Health Research: A Medical and Policy Primer,* from the Society for the Advancement of Women's Health Research; *The Broken Connection: On Death and the Continuity of Life* by Robert Jay Lifton; *Lies! Lies! Lies! The Psychology of Deceit* by Charles V. Ford; *Bad Men Do What Good Men Dream* by Robert I. Simon; *Talking About Sex* by Derek C. Polonsky; *How to Help Your Child Overcome Your Divorce* by Elissa P. Benedek and Catherine F. Brown; *The Preteen's First Book About Love, Sex, and AIDS* by Michelle Harrison (illustrated by Lynn Beckstrom).

Professional titles from American Psychiatric: *The American Psychiatric Press Textbook of Psychiatry, 3rd Edition* (edited by Robert E. Hales, M.D., and Stuart C. Yudofaley, M.D.); *DSM-IV Casebook* by Spitzer et al.; *Psychodynamic Psychiatry in Clinical Practice, 3rd Edition* by Glen O. Gabbard, M.D.

Practice Guidelines (guidelines were formulated to improve patient care and to assist with clinical decision making) titles: *American Psychiatric Association Practice Guideline for the Treatment of Patients with Schizophrenia; American Psychiatric Association Practice Guideline for the Treatment of Patients with Nicotine Dependence; American Psychiatric Association Practice Guideline for the Treatment of Patients with Alzheimer's*

A

Disease and Other Dementias of Late Life; American Psychiatric Association Practice Guideline for the Treatment of Patients with Substance Use Disorders: Alcohol, Cocaine, Opioids; American Psychiatric Association Practice Guideline for Eating Disorders.

American Psychiatric Publishing is the publisher of the psychiatric profession's acknowledged clinical guidebook, *Diagnostic and Statistical Manual of Mental Disorders* (4th edition, text revision), also known as *DSM-IVTR.*

American Psychiatric Publishing distributes through several regional distribution services. Query letters and SASEs should be directed to:

Robert E. Hales, M.D., M.B.A., Editor in Chief

Claire Reinburg, Editorial Director

AMERICAN PSYCHOLOGICAL ASSOCIATION, INC.

750 First Street, NE, Washington, DC 20002-4242
202-336-5793   fax: 202-336-5502
www.apa.org   e-mail: order@apa.org

Areas of American Psychological Association publishing interest include virtually all aspects of the field of psychology: methodology, history, student aids, teaching, health, business strategies, violence, personality, and clinical issues. APA publications include books, journals, publishing resources, continuing-education/home-study programs, audiocassettes, videotapes, and databases.

The information resources produced by APA are grounded in a long publishing tradition of scholarly and professional works that encompass diverse topics and applications in the arena of human behavior, from basic research to practical therapies, including the teaching curriculum of psychology, as well as the contributions of psychology to progressive education, from personality disorders to implications for psychology of public policies. The American Psychological Association (founded in 1892) is the major psychological organization in the United States.

On the APA list: *Children of Depressed Parents: Mechanisms of Risk and Implications for Treatment; Emotion Focused Therapy: Coaching Clients to Work Through Their Feelings; The Origins of Human Nature: Evolutionary Developmental Psychology; The Suicidal Patient: Clinical and Legal Standards of Care, 2nd Edition; On the Consequences of Meaning Selection: Perspectives on Resolving Lexical Ambiguity; Self and Motivation: Emerging Psychological Perspectives; Great Psychologists and Their Times: Scientific Insights Into Psychology's History; Perfectionism: Theory, Research and Treatment; The Pyschodynamics of Gender and Gender Role; Self-Injurious Behavior: Gene Brain-Behavior Relationships.*

A publication of the American Psychological Association that has wide influence in all areas of scholarly publishing, especially the social and behavioral sciences, is the *Publication Manual of the American Psychological Association* (now in its 4th edition), a resource that guides writers and editors through manuscript preparation and production. Query letters and SASEs should be directed to:

Julia Frank-McNeil, Director, APA Books

AMERICAN SOCIETY FOR TRAINING AND DEVELOPMENT (ASTD) BOOKS

1640 King Street, PO Box 1443, Alexandria, VA 22313-2043
703-683-8100   fax: 703-683-1523
www.astd.org   e-mail: CustomerCare@astd.org

American Society for Training and Development (ASTD) Books is a business-information specialist. Among ASTD's major categories are workplace learning and performance, human resource development, training, management development, career development, workforce issues, consulting, teamwork, technology, games, and problem solving and creativity. In addition to books, ASTD offers training kits, diagnostic tools, presentation materials, games and simulations, videos, audiocassettes, and computer software.

ASTD Books (founded in 1944) is the book-publishing wing of American Society for Training and Development, a nonprofit membership organization. The house's professional books cover such areas as employee education, training, and development; human resource development; organization management; career development; and performance improvement. Within this business arena, ASTD strives to put forth a list that represents the most current topics, the most innovative techniques, and the most gifted authors in the field. ASTD publishes selected titles in conjunction with other business-oriented houses, such as Berrett-Koehler, Jossey-Bass, and McGraw-Hill.

Books listed in the ASTD catalog are reviewed and selected by a distinguished and professional peer group.

Titles from ASTD: *The Targeted Evaluation Process: A Performance Consultant's Guide* by Wendy L. Combs and Salvatore V. Falletta; *ISD from the Ground Up: A No-Nonsense Approach to Instructional Design* by Chuck Hodell; *Project Management for Trainers: Stop "Winging It" and Get Control of Your Training Projects* by Lou Russell; *Managing Web Based Training: How to Keep Your Program on Track and Make It Successful* by Alan L. Ellis, Ellen D. Wagner, and Warren R. Longmire; *In Action: Leading Knowledge Management and Learning* by Dede Bonner; *Interactive Distance Learning Exercises That Really Work!* by Karen Mantyla; *Distance Learning: A Step-by-Step Guide for Trainers* by Karen Mantyla and Rick Gividen; *The ASTD Media Selection Tool for Workplace Learning* by Raymond J. Marx; *Promoting Emotional Intelligence in Organizations* by Cary Cherniss and Mitchel Adler; *Consulting on the Inside* by Beverly Scott.

ASTD's new E-learning series includes: *Leading E-Learning* by William Horton; *Selling E-Learning* by Darin E. Harley; *Designing E-Learning* by Saul Carliner; *Evaluating E-Learning* by William Horton; *Using E-Learning* by William Horton.

Writers: If you are working on a book targeted to trainers that you think ASTD might like to publish, please contact 703-683-9205. Guidelines for submitting a book proposal are available upon request.

ASTD Books distributes its own list via a catalog, easy-ordering, and online store. Some ASTD books are available through other publishing houses. ASTD also distributes and copublishes books from a variety of other publishers, including McGraw-Hill, Jossey-Bass, Berrett-Koheler, and others. ASTD also distributes through Amazon.com.

Query letters and SASEs should be directed to:

Mark Morrow, Senior Acquisitions Editor

Ruth Stadius, Director of Publications

ANDREWS MCMEEL PUBLISHING

4520 Main Street, Kansas City, MO 64111-7701
816-932-6700   fax: 816-932-6749

Andrews McMeel Publishing (founded in 1970) is an Andrews McMeel Universal company that publishes a wide assortment of general trade nonfiction books and gift books, humor (including cartoon books), and calendars. Areas of interest include popular culture and lifestyles, psychology and self-help, health and medicine, New Age and inspiration, and women's issues. Andrews McMeel publishes over 100 calendars each year in day-to-day, wall, and desk-diary format.

Titles from Andrews McMeel: *Looking for Mr. Right* by Bradley Trevor Greive; *Open Your Mind, Open Your Life* by Taro Gold; *September 11, 2001* by the Poynter Institute; *Coast to Coast Ghosts* by Leslie Rule; *Nell Hill's Style at Home* by Mary Carol Garrity; *Teachers* by John Yow; *The Millionaire Mind* by Thomas J. Stanley, Ph.D.; *The Meaning of Life* by Bradley Trevor Greive; *The Last Editor* by James Bellows; *Life Messages* by Josephine Carlton; *Believing in Ourselves: A Celebration of Women* (edited by Nancy Carson); *Too Busy to Count the Years* by Suzanne Snyder Jacobson; *The Gathering* by William X. Kienzle; *DADisms and MOMisms* by Cathy Hamilton; *I Am the Greatest: The Best Quotations from Muhammad Ali* by Karl Evanzz; *Turn Three Shots into Two* by Bill Moretti and Mike Stachura; *She's Leaving Home: Letting Go As My Daughter Goes to College* by Connie Jones; *Bridesmaids* by M. B. Roberts; *1,003 Great Things About Moms* by Lisa Birnback, Patricia Marx, and Ann Hodgman; *When You're Hot, You're Hot: How I Laughed My Way Though Menopause* by Jan King; *How Not to Become a Little Old Lady* by Mary McHugh; *The Payne Stewart Story* by Larry Guest; *101 Things Teens Should Know* by Lindsay Jackson; *Yoga for Men* by Bruce Eric Van Horn; *The Little Book of Bliss: How to Reach Cloud Nine* by Patrick Whiteside.

From Andrews Gift Books: *The Blue Day Book* by Bradley Trevor Greive; *Mom, You Rule!* by Cate Holly; *Famous Black Quotes on Sisters* by Janet Cheatham Bell; *The Joy of Fatherhood* by Thomas Kinkade; *What? Another Birthday!!* by John McPherson; *Life Strategies from the Art of War* by Philip Dunn.

Tiny Tomes are tiny, of course—as well as topical, traditional, tactile, tempting, and targeted. These teeny books from Andrews and McMeel are less than half the size of the house's little gift books—the tactile allure of these palm-size volumes is said to be irresistible. Titles include *Mom: You're the Greatest; A Tiny Treasury of African Proverbs; Sex: A Book of Quotations; The Little Book of Coffee.*

Each volume in the Cader Unstamped Books line presents 16 sheets of exquisitely designed and printed stamps. Use them to personalize and decorate correspondence, collect them, or frame them. Titles here include *Nature Unstamped; Holidays Unstamped; Angels Unstamped.*

Agents, please query. No unsolicited manuscripts are accepted. Query letters should be directed to:

A

Christine Schillig, Vice President and Editorial Director—General nonfiction, all categories

Dorothy O'Brien, Assistant Vice President and Managing Director—Humor and general nonfiction

Patty Rice, Senior Editor and Editorial Director—Gift books and general nonfiction

Jean Lucas, Editor—General nonfiction, illustrated books, humor

Jennifer Fox, Editor—General nonfiction, gift books, humor

Education: B.A. in Journalism from University of Missouri-Columbia.

Employment history/editor career path: Began as an Editorial Assistant at Andrews McMeel in 1996.

Do you represent fiction? No.

Do you represent nonfiction? Yes.

Do you require book proposals? If so, what do you look for in evaluating a book proposal? Yes. Solid summary, outline of book, competition, author bio, and sample text.

What process do you use for making a decision? What is the process for acquisition; is there a committee? I usually get a couple of reads from other editors before taking it to an acquisitions meeting with the committee.

What kinds of nonfiction books do you want to see less of? Parenting, business, serious self-help.

Are you interested in work geared for the masses (readers of *People, The Star,* etc.)? Yes, very much so.

Are agents important? Why? Yes, they're great for screening the material and sending it to the right publishing houses. They are also helpful in dealing with difficult authors.

How should writers approach you? They should approach me with a hook—what makes their idea different and salable.

What are some common mistakes writers make? What really gets on your nerves? Writers who expect a great deal of attention and publicity for a small book. Writers who don't trust the publisher to make the right decisions. Writers who are too hands-on.

What have been some of your best experiences with writers or in your job? Working with talented, hard-working, and professional writers whose books actually succeed. Then, signing up more books with those authors.

Any advice for writers? Any way to improve the system for you? Any additional thoughts? I'm always looking for gift books, light self-help, pop culture, and humor books. Remember to get an agent.

THE ANONYMOUS PRESS, INC.

332 Bleecker Street, New York, NY 10014

The Anonymous Press specializes in high-velocity projects that tap the current cultural pulse. The house is on the lookout for commercial, inherently marketable nonfiction in such areas as investigative and journalistic accounts; issue-oriented human-interest stories; celebrity biographies and memoirs; ultimate conspiracies, exposés, and scandalous affairs; and popular reference works (including high-interest single-volume encyclopedias, personal and professional how-to, and awareness).

A

The Anonymous Press, Inc. (founded in 1996), is an independent publisher dedicated to open expression and individual liberty. This is viewed as an activist mission, not a statement of guaranteed privilege. People must take it upon themselves to carry the ongoing fight for their personal right to pursue the life that's best for them. The press publishes in recognition of the primary designs of the book-buying public: looking good, feeling good, making money.

The Anonymous Press featured as its initial release *Sleeping with the President: My Intimate Years with Bill Clinton* by Gennifer Flowers—a powerful personal memoir written as a riveting political love story. Another Anonymous hit, *The Elvis Cover-Up* by Gail Brewer-Giorgio, explores the secret life of Elvis Presley, his connection to United States government law-enforcement agencies, and his involvement with a deep-cover sting operation; Elvis may have hoaxed his own death to lead a new life underground. This brand-new investigatory biography follows the author's *Is Elvis Alive?* (multimillion-copy *New York Times* bestseller), several highly rated syndicated television specials and video documentaries, and *Orion* (bestselling pop-cultural fiction; dramatic story of a mercurial musical performer).

Anonymous wishes to break through old barriers to create new publishing frontiers; the house is open to a wide variety of creative projects that will inspire the publisher's marketing vision. It is essential that submitted materials be imaginatively conceived and in professional book-proposal format. Authors must demonstrate expertise in the chosen topic area and must offer thorough and credible documentation.

Do not send materials via registered mail, overnight express delivery, or any other means requiring a recipient's signature. Please query first.

Query letters and SASEs should be directed to:

(Mr.) Gilchrist (Chris) Bonner, Acquisitions

THE APEX PRESS

The Bootstrap Press

Council on International and Public Affairs
777 United Nations Plaza, Suite 3C, New York, NY 10017
914-271-6500
e-mail: cipany@igc.apc.org

Branch office:
Box 337, Croton-on-Hudson, NY 10520

Apex accents nonfiction titles in such fields as corporate accountability, grassroots and worker participation, and intercultural understanding. One special publishing focus is on economic and social justice, human rights, and the impact of technology on contemporary society.

The Apex Press (introduced in 1990) is an imprint of the nonprofit research, education, and publishing group Council on International and Public Affairs (CIPA). Apex publishes hardcover and paperback books that provide critical analyses of and new approaches to

A

significant economic, social, and political issues in the United States, other industrialized nations, and the Third World.

The Council on International and Public Affairs was founded in 1954 and is a nonprofit research, education, and publishing group. The Council seeks to further the study and public understanding of problems and affairs of the peoples of the United States and other nations of the world through conferences, research, seminars and workshops, publications, and other means.

From Apex Press: *Inhuman Rights: The Western System and Global Human Rights Abuses* by Winin Pereira; *Washington's New Poor Law: Welfare "Reform" and the Roads Not Taken, 1935–1996* by Sheila D. Collins and Gertrude Schaffner Goldberg; *The Good Neighbor Handbook: A Community-Based Strategy for Sustainable Industry* by Sanford J. Lewis; *Greenwash: The Reality Behind Corporate Environmentalism* by Jed Greer and Kenny Bruno; *Taking Care of Business: The Underbelly of the U.S. Economy: Joblessness and Pauperization of Work* by David Dembo and Ward Morehouse; *Nuclear Weapons Are Illegal: The Opinions and Story Behind the Historic Decision of the World Court* (edited by Ann Fagan Giner); *Nurtured by Knowledge: Learning by Doing Participatory Action-Research* (edited by Susan E. Smith and Dennis G. Willms, with Nancy A. Johnson); *When Workers Decide: Workplace Democracy Takes Root in North America* (edited by Len Krimerman and Frank Lindenfeld).

The Apex Press handles its own distribution; the house catalog includes books and additional resources (including videos) from a number of publishers worldwide.

The Bootstrap Press
Intermediate Technology Development Group of North America

Bootstrap's publishing interest focuses on social economics and community economic change; the house covers small-scale and intermediate-scale or appropriate technology in both industrialized and emerging countries, with an aim to promote more just and sustainable societies. Its books explore business and industry theory and how-to, gardening and agriculture, building and construction, and communications.

The Bootstrap Press (inaugurated in 1988) is an imprint of Intermediate Technology Development Group of North America (ITDG/North America) in cooperation with the Council on International and Public Affairs.

Titles from Bootstrap: *Greening Cities: Building Just and Sustainable Communities* by Joan Reolofs; *Building Sustainable Communities: Tools and Concepts for Self-Reliant Economic Change* by C. George Benello, Robert Swann, and Shann Turnbull; *Chicken Little, Tomato Sauce and Agriculture: Who Will Produce Tomorrow's Food?* by Joan Dye Gussow.

Titles of Intermediate Technology Publications (London), previously distributed by the Bootstrap Press, are now available through Stylus Publishing.

Bootstrap publications are distributed with those of sibling operation the Apex Press. Query letters and SASEs should be directed to:

Judi Rizzi, Publications Manager

Ward Morehouse, President

APPLAUSE THEATRE & CINEMA BOOKS

151 West 46th Street, 8th Floor, New York, NY 10036
212-575-9265   fax: 646-562-5852

Applause Theatre Book Publishers (established in 1983) produces a list geared to fields of stage, cinema, and the entertainment arts. Applause produces collections, compendiums, biographies, histories, resource books, reference works, and guides keyed to the needs of the house's wide readership of seasoned pros, rookies, and aficionados.

The Applause program covers hardback and paperback editions, among them a number of generously illustrated and well-produced works. Applause issues stage plays and screenplays (many in translation and many in professional working-script format) that run the gamut from the classical repertory to contemporary works in drama, comedy, and musicals. Applause also offers audio works and a video library. The publisher's backlist is comprehensive (it has never declared a single title out of print and goes back to press for as few as 500 copies of a backlist standby).

Special-production volumes encompass works that detail the background and history behind the creation of works for stage and screen, in addition to containing complete scripts.

Titles from Applause: *The Real Life of Laurence Olivier* by Roger Lewis; *An Actor and His Time* by John Gielgud; *Ralph Richardson: An Actor's Life* by Garry O'Connor; *Seats: The Insider's Guide to the Performing Arts and Sports in New York* by Sandy Millman; *The Other Way: An Alternative Approach to Acting and Directing* by Charles Morowitz; *Fundamental Acting: A Practical Guide* by Paul Kuritz; *Theatre on the Edge: New Visions, New Voices* by Mel Gussow; *The Smart Set: George Jean Nathan and H. L. Mencken* by Thomas Quinn Curtiss; *London Theatre Walks* by Jim DeYoung; *Paul Scofield* by Garry O'Connor; *An Actor's Dickens* by Beatrice Manley; *Stones in His Pockets* by Marie Jones; *Political Stages* (edited by Emily Mann and David Roessel); *This Man & Music* by Anthony Borgess; *More Power to You* by Robert Cohen.

For theatrical professionals and students as well, Applause offers: *Acting in Film* (from the Applause Acting Series) by Michael Caine; *Telling Moments: 15 Gay Monologues* by Robert C. Reinhart; *The Actor and the Text* by Cicely Berry; *The Secret of Theatrical Space* by Josef Svoboda.

Applause Theatre Books are distributed by Hal Leonard Corporation. Query letters and SASEs should be directed to:

Glenn Young, Publisher

Mark Glubke, President

ARCADE PUBLISHING

141 Fifth Avenue, New York, NY 10010
212-475-2633   fax: 212-353-8148
www.arcadepub.com   e-mail: info@arcadepub.com

Arcade Publishing (founded in 1988 by Jeannette and Richard Seaver) produces commercial and literary nonfiction and fiction, as well as selected poetry. Nonfiction standouts

A

include issue-oriented titles, contemporary human-interest stories, and cultural historical works. Arcade's fiction list includes entrants in such categories as mystery, suspense, and thrillers. Arcade's program leans toward learned and enlightened reading.

From Arcade: *Scrolling Forward* by David Levy; *Mercy Among the Children* by David Adams Richards; *A Dog Called Perth* by Peter Martin; *Duke of Egypt* by Margriet de Moor; *Bin Laden* by Adam Robinson; *Riot: A Love Story* by Shashi Tharoor; *Imperial Legend* by Alexis Troubetzkoy; *The Freemasons* by Jasper Ridley. Arcade Publishing is distributed by Little, Brown.

Prospective authors please note that Arcade does not accept unsolicited submissions. Query letters and SASEs should be directed to:

Calvert Barksdale, Senior Editor, Senior Vice President and General Manager—All areas of house interest

Jeannette Seaver, Executive Editor, Publisher, Marketing Director—Fiction: literary; Nonfiction: history, politics, literary criticism, cookbooks, illustrated books

Richard Seaver, President and Editor-in-Chief—Fiction: literary; Nonfiction: history, politics, literary criticism, illustrated books

Greg Comer, Editor

JASON ARONSON INC., PUBLISHERS

230 Livingston Street, Northvale, NJ 07647
201-767-4093
www.aronson.com

Jason Aronson Inc., Publishers, marks two main sectors of publishing concentration: One Aronson line comprises psychotherapy, offering professional books (as well as some trade-oriented titles) in psychiatry, psychoanalysis, counseling (including pastoral care), and the behavioral sciences. The other Aronson publishing arena is Judaica, covering contemporary thought as well as traditional works. (Please see Aronson listing in Directory of Religious, Spiritual, and Inspirational Publishers.) Aronson's strong backlist encompasses a wide range of publications well regarded in the fields of psychotherapy and Judaica.

Among Aronson highlights in psychotherapy: *101 More Favorite Play Therapy Techniques* by Heidi Kaduson and Charles Schafer; *Behavioral Management Guide: Essential Treatment Strategies for Adult Psychotherapy* by Muriel P. Warren; *Counseling the Defiant Child: A Basic Guide to Helping Troubled and Aggressive Youth* by John B. Mordock; *Fundamentals of an Integrated Model of Psychotherapy* by Peter Buirski and Pamela Haglund; *Managing Addictions: Cognitive, Emotive, and Behavioral Techniques* by F. Michler Bishop; *Men with Sexual Problems and What Women Can Do to Help Them* by Eva Margolies; *Personalities: Master Clinicians Confront the Treatment of Borderline Personality Disorders* by Gerben Hellingna, Bert van Luyn, and Henk-Jan Dalewijk; *Stress Response Syndromes, 4th Edition: Personality Styles and Interventions* by Mardi Horowitz; *The Psychotherapist as Healer* by T. Byram Karasu; *Therapeutic Strategies for Treating Addiction: From Slavery to Freedom* by Jerome Levin; *Transforming Aggression: Psychotherapy with the Difficult-to-Treat Patient* by Frank M. Lachmann; *Vulnerable Moments: Deepening the Therapeutic Process* by Martin S. Livingston.

A

Among Aronson highlights in Judaica: *A Women's Voice* by Marcella Bakur Weiner and Blema Feinstein; *Kabbalah and Alchemy: An Essay on Common Archetypes* by Arturo Schwarz; *Kabbalistic Metaphors: Jewish Mystical Themes in Ancient and Modern Thought* by Sanford Drob; *Rabbi Shlomo Ganzfried: His Kitur and His Life* by Jack E. Friedman; *Rise and Be Seated: The Ups and Downs of Jewish Worship* by Joseph A. Levine; *Sacred Fire: Torah from the Years of Fury 1932–1942* by J. Hershy Worch and Deborah Miller; *Soul of the Torah: Insights of the Chasidic Masters on the Weekly Torah Portions* by Victor Cohen; *The Symbols of the Kabbalah: Philosophical and Psychological Perspectives* by Sanford Drob.

Jason Aronson Inc., Publishers (started in 1965), oversees a distribution network that utilizes its own in-house services, as well as independent trade-fulfillment services. Aronson also features a direct-mail catalog that includes special-interest titles from other presses.

As of this printing, Aronson has ceased paying advances or publishing new works.

Arthur Kurzweil, Editor in Chief, Publisher (Judaica)

AVALON BOOKS

160 Madison Avenue, New York, NY 10016
212-598-0222   fax: 212-979-1862
www.avalonbooks.com   e-mail: avalon-books@att.net

Avalon Books produces fiction lines primarily for distribution to library and institutional markets on a subscriber basis. Avalon editions are wholesome family stories in the following categories: traditional mysteries; mainstream romance; career romance; historical romance, traditional genre Westerns. Avalon produces a line of literary classics in reprint (on the Airmont Classics imprint).

Avalon Books (a subsidiary of Thomas Bouregy & Company, founded in 1950) publishes a primarily hardcover fiction list. The house emphasis on new original novels caters to the tastes and preferences of the all-important library readership; stories should consist of those likely to be of high interest to the patrons of this core market.

From the Avalon list: *The Marshal's Destiny* by C. H. Admirand; *Save Your Heart for Me* by Joye Ames; *Painted Lady* by Lucinda Baker; *That Saturday Feeling* by Ingrid Betz; *Hannah and the Horseman* by Johnny D. Boggs; *The Night Next Door* by Charlene Bowen; *Chasing Charlie* by Kathy Carmichael; *Lights of Love* by Roni Denholtz; *Growing Season* by Mike Gaherty; *In a Wink* by Lacey Green; *Imperfect Together* by Amanda Harte; *Making the Call* by Pat Hines; *Forever and a Day* by Patricia Johnston; *Romantic Doctor* by Terry McDermid; *Emerald Sky* by Gerry O'Hara; *Lasting Love* by Tara Randel; *Coming Home* by Nadia Shworan; *The Secret of Spring Hollow* by Jan Weeks.

Distribution is primarily through library sales. Query letters and SASEs should be directed to:

Mira Son, Assistant Editor

Paula Decker, Editorial Assistant

Erin Cartwright, Senior Editor
  Born: January 20.
  Education: B.A., in English and History from University of Delaware.

A

Employment history/editor career path: I grew up in the Bahamas, and I always knew I wanted to be a novelist and live in New York City. I discovered that I liked to edit much more than I liked the actual writing, so I became an Editor. I started out at a small magazine company called *Details Magazine.* I moved from there to Simon & Schuster for five years and then to HarperCollins for two years. I have been a Senior Editor at Avalon Books for one year.

Personal interests: Biking, running, snow boarding, travel, writing.

What would you be doing if you were not an editor? Teaching.

What has been your most successful book that you have acquired to date? *The Vitamin E Factor* and *Worst Fears Realized,* both on the *New York Times* bestseller lists.

What books have you acquired that make you the most proud? What books that you have acquired reflect the types of books you like to represent? *Love Is Friendship Caught on Fire* by Guy Zona.

Do you represent fiction? If so, what do you look for? Yes. Romance, mysteries, Westerns. I look for good writing, good stories, believable characters, and something that has a different edge to it.

Do you represent nonfiction? No.

Do you require book proposals? If so, what do you look for in evaluating a book proposal? No book proposal, but I do ask for a brief synopsis and the first three chapters with an SASE. If I like what I see, I will then request the entire manuscript.

What process do you use for making a decision? What is the process for acquisition; is there a committee? There is not a committee, but I will give the manuscript to about two or three other people to read. If they agree that it is a good buy, we will then discuss it in more detail.

Are agents important? Why? Yes, they are important for people who have published multiple books. I think first-time authors don't necessarily need an agent; it's when you decide to move on with more books, to the bigger houses, with a complicated contract, that you need an agent.

Do you like new writers? What should new writers do to break into the business? Yes. Most of my authors are first- or second-time authors. I think it's always good to have a fresh voice. To break into the business, you should take writing classes, always write, never give up even when the rejections are pouring in, and have others read and critique your work.

How should writers approach you? Go to the LMP or similar resources and find out what my submission guidelines are. Always give away the ending to your story in your cover letter to me; you don't have to "hook" an editor.

What are some common mistakes writers make? What really gets on your nerves? I tend to see the same kind of romances over and over again. There are too many cowboy romance stories. I don't like when the characters get killed in car accidents in the stories. It bothers me when people don't do their homework and submit something outside of my guidelines.

What can writers do to get your attention and to avoid the slush pile? Follow my submission guidelines.

What have been some of your craziest experiences with submissions? I've gotten some pretty weird stuff from people in prison and manuscripts sent in from teenagers.

What have been some of your best experiences with writers or in your job? I have recently bought an author's first book—she's 80 years old! She just started writing about

A

10 years ago and was thrilled! This is the most wonderful feeling, to get to be the one to make someone's day.

What, if anything, makes you different from other editors? I am willing and happy to give anyone a chance. I will work with you even if everything is not perfect the first time around. If you have talent, but I don't feel I can buy your manuscript, I will take the time to suggest other editors who may like to take a look.

Is there anything you would like to see changed in the industry? I would like to see authors make more money.

Any advice for writers? Keep writing, do your homework, find out everyone's submission guidelines, and *never quit!* Keep writing and submitting until someone says "yes," because eventually someone will.

AVALON PUBLISHING GROUP

Thunder's Mouth Press

Marlowe & Company

Blue Moon Books

See also Carroll & Graf Publishers, Inc.

161 William Street, 16th Floor, New York, NY 10038
212-614-7880   fax: 212-614-7887 www.avalonpub.com

Avalon Travel Publishing

5855 Beaudry Street, Emeryville, CA 94608
e-mail: avalonpub@aol.com

The Avalon Publishing Group combines five unique firms, each component maintaining its own distinct publishing persons, and is distributed by Publishers Group West.

Thunder's Mouth Press publishes adult trade books in a variety of subject areas, concentrating most heavily on popular culture, film, music, current events, contemporary culture, biography/personality, fantasy, role-playing games, the arts, and popular reference. Thunder's Mouth Press copublishes, with Balliett and Fitzgerald, Adrenaline Books, which features a series of anthologies written about extreme adventure sports and stories, and Adrenaline Classics, reprints of adventure classics. Thunder's Mouth also collaborates with the National Institute on an imprint called Nation Books, which features selections from this premier independent magazine of politics and culture.

Marlowe & Company focuses on personal growth, spirituality, psychology, self-help, health, and healthful cooking. Marlowe & Company is involved in a copublishing venture with Balliett & Fitzgerald called Illumina Books, which draws therapy and self-help from the world's finest literature.

Blue Moon Books, founded by longtime Grove Press publisher Barney Rosset, publishes mass-market erotic fiction, with an emphasis on Victorian erotica and discipline.

Carroll & Graf publishes a combination of original and reprinted fiction and nonfiction. It has become known for its history and current affairs titles, as well as for high-quality fiction and mysteries.

Avalon Travel Publishing guides feature a combination of practicality and spirit, offering a unique traveler-to-traveler perspective perfect for an afternoon hike, around-the-world journey, or anything in-between. Avalon Publishing Group publishes many guides by Rick Steves.

Representative of Thunder's Mouth Press: *The Book of Rock* by Philip Dodd; *Requiem for a Dream* by Hubert Selby, Jr.; *Gangs of New York* by Herbert Asbury; *Dreams: The Art of Boris Vallejo* by Boris Vallejo; *The Outlaw Bible of American Poetry* (edited by Alan Daufman); *Miles Davis* by Ian Carr; *Rebel for the Hell of It* by Armond White; *Soft as Steel* by Julie Bell; *Black Beauty* by Ben Arogundade; *Lobotomy: Surviving the Ramones* by Dee Dee Ramone.

Representative of Adrenaline Books: *Storm: Stories of Survival from Land, Sea and Sky* (edited by Clint Willis); *Adrenaline: The Year's Best Stories of Adventure and Survival 2000* (edited by Clint Willis); *Explore: Stories of Survival from Off the Map* (edited by Jennifer Sehwamm); *Climb: Stories of Survival from Rock, Snow and Ice* (edited by Clint Willis).

Representative of Adrenaline Classics: *Shackleton's Forgotten Men* by Lennard Binckel; *Annapurna South Face* by Sir Chris Bonington; *A Slender Thread* by Stephen Venables.

Representative of Nation Books: *The Best of the Nation* (edited by Victor Navasky and Katrina Vanden Hueval); *Cinema Nation: The Best Writing on Film from* The Nation *1913–2000* (edited by Carl Bromley); *Burning All Illusions: Writing from* The Nation *on Race* (edited by Paula Giddings).

Representative of Marlowe & Company: *The Glucose Revolution* by Jennie Brand-Miller, Kaye Foster-Powell, Thomas M. S. Wolever, and Stephen Colagiuri; *The Parent's Tao Te Ching* by William Martin; *Beach: Stories by the Sand and Sea* (edited by Lena Lencek and Gideon Bosker); *Eating for IBS* by Heather Van Vorous; *Soul Mapping* by Nina Frost, Kenneth Ruge, and Richard Shoup; *Vastu Living* by Kathleen Cox; *When the Little Things Count and They Always Count* by Barbara Pachier, with Susan Magee; *Tofu Mania* by Brita Housez; *Best Food Writing 2000* (edited by Holly Hughes).

Representative of Illumina Books: *Heart: Stories of Learning to Love Again* by series Editor Thomas Dyja; *Cure: Stories of Healing the Mind and Body* by series editor Thomas Dyja; *Why Meditate? The Essential Book About How Meditation Can Enrich Your Life* (edited by Clint Willis).

Representative of Blue Moon Books: *The Blue Moon Erotic Reader* (edited by Barney Rosser); *Shoe Leather* by Stan Kent; *Gynecocracy* by Viscount Ladywood; *CyberWebs* by Niranda Reigns; *Shadow Land II: Return to Random Point* by Eve Howard; *Suburban Souls* by Anonymous.

Representative of Carroll & Graf: *Master Georgie* by Beryl Bainbridge; *Close to the Wind* by Pete Goss; *Stanley Kubrick: A Biography* by John Baxter; *Faust's Metropolis* by Alexandra Richie; *One of Us* by David Freeman; *The Well* by Katie Hafner; *The Mammoth Book of Unsolved Crime* (edited by Roger Wilkes); *Military Blunders* by Saul David.

Representative of Avalon Travel Publishing: *Rick Steves' Europe Through the Back Door* by Rick Steves; *Road Trip USA: Cross-Country Adventures on America's Two-Lane Highways* by Jamie Jensen; *Travelers' Tales Greece* (edited by Larry Habegger and Sean O'Reilly); *Hidden Baja* by Richard Harris; *Moon Handbooks: Yellowstone/Grand Tetons* by Don Pitcher; *Foghorn Outdoors: Colorado Camping* by Tom Stienstra; *Great American Motorcycle Tours* by Gary McKechnie.

A

Avalon Publishing Group is unable to accept unsolicited manuscripts or queries at this time. Query letters and SASEs should be directed to:

Neil Ortenberg, Thunder's Mouth Press

Matthew Lore, Marlowe & Company

Claiborne Hancock, Carroll & Graf

Heather Tidrick, Avalon Travel Publishing

BAEN PUBLISHING ENTERPRISES (BAEN BOOKS)

PO Box 1403, Riverdale, NY 10471
718-548-3100
www.baen.com

Baen publishes science fiction and fantasy writing. The house's new releases are generally published in mass-market paperback format, with targeted lead titles produced in trade paper and hardcover editions. Baen is a prominent publisher of series in science fiction and fantasy and also publishes a notable lineup of collections and anthologies geared to various subgenre traditions and the works of individual writers.

Baen Publishing Enterprises (founded in 1984) concentrates its concise list on its proven categories of publishing strength. Baen's roster of writers includes James P. Hogan, John Ringo, David Weber, Marion Zimmer Bradley, Lois McMaster Bujold, John Dalmas, Robert A. Heinlein, Mercedes Lackey, Anne McCaffrey, Eric Flint, Spider and Jeanne Robinson.

From Baen: *Agent of Vega* by James H. Schmitz; *The Anvil* by S. M. Stirling and David Drake; *Barrenlands* by Doranna Durgin; *Birds of Prey* by David Drake; *Bug Park* by James P. Hogan; *Falling Free* by Lois McMaster Bujold; *The Fire Rose* by Mercedes Lackey; *Forward the Mage* by Eric Flint and Richard Roach; *Master of Many Treasures* by Mary Brown; *The Mines of Behemoth* by Michael Shea; *Winning Colors* by Elizabeth Moon; *Wolf Time* by Lars Walker; *Rescued from Paradise* by Robert L. Forward and Julie Forward; *The Right to Arm Bears* by Gordon R. Dickson.

Baen Books is distributed by Simon & Schuster. Query letters and SASEs should be directed to:

James Baen, Editor in Chief

Toni Weisscoff, Executive Editor

THE BALLANTINE PUBLISHING GROUP
(A DIVISION OF RANDOM HOUSE)

Ballantine Books

Ballantine Reader's Circle

Del Rey

Del Rey/Lucas Books

Fawcett

Ivy

One World

Wellspring

1540 Broadway, New York, NY 10036

B

The Ballantine Publishing Group is a Random House division that publishes hardcover, trade paperback, and mass market paperback books. Founded in 1952, Ballantine was acquired by Random House in 1973.

Its imprints include Ballantine Books, Ballantine Reader's Circle, Del Rey, Del Rey/Lucas Books, Fawcett, Ivy, One World, and Wellspring.

Ballantine Books

Ballantine Books publishes commercial fiction and general nonfiction, including health, diet, psychology, history, and biography. Representative titles: *Sugar Busters!* by H. Leighton Steward; *Secrets of the Baby Whisperer* by Tracy Hogg; *Henry VIII: The King and His Court* by Alison Weir; *The Surgeon* by Tess Gerritsen; *The Manhattan Hunt Club* by John Saul; *Best Friends, Worst Enemies* by Michael Thompson. The Ballantine list also includes a growing number of literary novels and short story collections, such as *The Speed of Light* by Elizabeth Rosner and *Among the Missing* by Dan Chaon.

The mass market list includes such bestselling authors as John Case, Robert Crais, Fannie Flagg, Sue Grafton, Kristin Hannah, John Irving, Jonathan Kellerman, Richard North Patterson, Anne Rice, Edward Rutherfurd, John Saul, Stephen King, and Anne Tyler.

Ballantine Reader's Circle

Ballantine Reader's Circle was created in 1997 to enhance readers' experience with select Ballantine books, both fiction and nonfiction. Each book selected for BRC includes a discussion guide that features an author interview, discussion questions, author biographies, and excerpts from book reviews. Some fiction titles include *While I Was Gone* by Sue Miller; *Drowning Ruth* by Christina Schwarz; *Big Stone Gap* by Adriana Trigiani; *A Conspiracy of Paper* by David Liss; *The Dress Lodger* by Shari Holman. Representative nonfiction titles include *The Battle for God* by Karen Armstrong; *Reviving Ophelia* by Mary Pipher; *King David* by Jonathan Kirsch; and *All Souls* by Michael Patrick MacDonald.

Del Rey

Del Rey publishes science fiction, fantasy, and alternate history in hardcover, trade paper, and mass-market paperback formats. Titles in science fiction and fantasy include *The Amber Spyglass* by Philip Pullman; *The World of Shannara* by Terry Brooks; *Star Wars, The New Jedi Order: Star by Star* by Troy Denning. Alternate fiction titles: *Stars & Stripes in Peril* by Harry Harrison and *The Great War: Walk in Hell* by Harry Turtledove.

Del Rey/Lucas Books published the novelizations of the first three Star Wars films, plus an array of other Star Wars fiction and nonfiction titles. Since October 1997, Del Rey has been publishing novels of the films in the New Jedi Order fiction program and nonfiction books, in both the new and the classic Star Wars programs. Titles here are *Star Wars Episode I, The Phantom Menace* by Terry Brooks; *The New Jedi Order: Vector Prime* by R. A. Salvatore; *Star Wars: Cloak of Deception* by James Luceno.

Fawcett Books

Fawcett Books publishes a wide spectrum of fiction, with an emphasis in mysteries, thrillers, and suspense. Its mass-market paperback list includes such titles as *The Syndrome* by John Case; *Death of a PTA Goddess* by Leslie O'Kane; *Murder in Havana* by Margaret Truman; *The Alpine Obituary* by Mary Daheim; *Funeral in Blue* by Anne Perry.

Ivy

Ivy is a mass-market paperback imprint that publishes both fiction and nonfiction books, including Balantine's mass-market romance books. The fiction list includes titles such as *Kiss and Tell* by Cherry Adair; *Highland Bride* by Janet Bieber; *The Trials of Angela* by Millie Criswell. Nonfiction titles representative of Ivy are: *Utmost Savagery* by Col. Joseph H. Alexander; *Unnatural Death: Confessions of a Medical Examiner* by Michael M. Baden, M.D.; *Lest We Forget* by William C. Meacham; *A Return to Christmas* by Chris Heimerdinger.

One World

One World publishes multicultural titles, including subjects of African American, Asian, Latin, and Native American interest across all categories and formats. Representative titles are *Satisfy My Soul* by Colin Channer; *Bittersweet* by Freddie Lee Johnson III; *Bill Clinton and Black America* by DeWayne Wickham; and the trade paperback edition of *Whatever Happened to Daddy's Little Girl? The Impact of Fatherlessness on Black Women* by Jonetta Rose Barras.

Wellspring

Wellspring, the newest Ballantine imprint thus far, was formed in 1999. Wellspring publishes new titles and repackaged classics from Balantine's backlist in the categories of spirituality, health sciences, psychology, Eastern philosophy, holistic health, nutrition, yoga, and mythology. A representation of some new titles includes *The Herbal Epicure* by Carole Ottesen; *The Jesus Sutras* by Martin Palmer; *Barefoot on Holy Ground* by Gloria D. Karpinski; and *Jivamukti Yoga* by Sharon Gannon and David Life.

Query letters with SASEs should be directed to:

Cathy Repetti, Associate Publisher—Mass-market nonfiction: health, biographies, diet, popular culture

Anita Diggs, Senior Editor—One World Books

Dan Smetanka, Senior Editor—Literary fiction and nonfiction

Elisa Wares, Senior Editor—Fiction: commercial women's, Regency romances, some historicals

Joanne Wyckoff, Senior Editor—Nonfiction: history, women's issues, biography, current events; some literary fiction

Joe Blades, Executive Editor and Associate Publisher—Fiction: hardcover and mass-market originals; mysteries, suspense, espionage

Judith Curr, Publisher and Editor in Chief—Oversees entire hardcover and mass-market programs; wide range of how-to/self-help nonfiction titles; frontlist fiction

Leona Nevler, Editorial Director—Commercial fiction

Maureen O'Neal, Editorial Director, Trade Paperbacks—Upscale, commercial nonfiction; literary and commercial fiction; in charge of trade paperback program

Shana Summers, Senior Editor—Women's fiction and romance

Shelly Shapiro, Editorial Director—Science fiction and fantasy

Nancy Miller, Editor—General nonfiction and fiction

B

BANTAM DELL PUBLISHING GROUP (A DIVISION OF RANDOM HOUSE)

Bantam Hardcover

Bantam Trade Paperback

Bantam Mass Market

Fanfare

Spectra

Delacorte Press

The Dial Press

Delta

DTP (See Dearborn Trade Publishing)

Dell

Island

1540 Broadway, New York NY 10036
212-354-6500

Bantam Dell Publishing Group publishes a broad spectrum of adult fiction and nonfiction, including frontlist commercial category, literary works, specialty titles, and genre fiction.

Bantam is one of the largest mass-market paperback publishers and also publishes titles in hardcover and trade paperback.

Nonfiction titles include *It Doesn't Take a Hero* by General H. Norman Schwarzkopf; *Emotional Intelligence* by Daniel Goleman; *The Wisdom of Menopause* by Christiane Northrup; *Flags of Our Fathers* by James Bradley, with Ron Powers; *Hannah's Gift* by Maria Housden; *Advanced Cinematherapy* by Nancy Peske and Beverly West; *The*

Dream Dictionary by Tony Crisp; *Astrology for the Soul* by Jan Spiller; *Complete Book of Eye Laser Surgery* by Stephen G. Slade, M.D., Richard N. Baker, O.D., and Dorothy Kay Brockman; *American Sign Language Dictionary* by Elaine Costello, Ph.D.

Bantam's fiction list includes commercial novels, mysteries, thrillers, suspense, science fiction and fantasy, romance, women's fiction, and select literary works. Bantam's hardcover fiction list includes novelists Dean Koontz, Tom Robbins, Elizabeth George, Iris Johansen, Tami Hoag, Diane Mott Davidson, George R. R. Martin, Michael Palmer, and Luanne Rice. Bantam mass-market and trade paperback authors include Louis L'Amour, Maya Angelou, Jean Auel, Sandra Brown, Pat Conroy, Nora Roberts, Tom Wolfe, Kay Hooper, Lisa Gardner, and Rita Mae Brown. Representative titles in mass-market paperback include *The Border Hostage* by Virginia Henley; *The Cottage* by Danielle Steel; *My Spy* by Christina Skye; *River of Eden* by Glenna McReynolds; *The Man Who Ate the 747* by Ben Sherwood.

Fanfare

Fanfare publishes women's fiction and romance, featuring adventure, suspense, historical settings, and Westerns. Titles are produced in hardcover, paperback, and trade paperback. Representative titles include *To Kiss a Spy* by Jane Feather and *Dream Island* by Josie Litton.

Spectra

Spectra's slogan is Speculative Fiction, Speculative Fact. This imprint of the Bantam Dell Publishing Group publishes science fiction and fantasy books in trade paperback and mass-market paperback.

Titles indicative of this list: *Fool's Errand* and *Ship of Destiny* by Robin Hobb; *Beyond Belief* by Roy Johansen; *Passage* by Connie Willis; *Fortress Dragonis* by Michael Stackpole; *The Saints of the Sword* by John Marco; *Vectors* by Michael P. Kube-McDowell; *Dune: House Corrino* by Brian Herbert and Keven J. Anderson; *The Way of the Rose* by Valery Leith; *Warautumn* by Tom Deitz; *The Eye of Night* by Pauline Alama; *The Ocean of Years* by Roger MacBride Allen; *A Clash of Kings* by George R. R. Martin; *Spirit of the Stone* by Maggie Furey; *Devlin's Luck* by Patricia Bray; *Blood of Mystery* by Mark Anthony; *Empire of Bones* by Liz Williams; *The Last Harbor* by George Foy; *Summerblood* by Tom Deitz; *Hopscotch* by Kevin J. Anderson; *The Grand Ellipse* by Paula Volsky.

Delacorte Press

Delacorte Press focuses on hardcover frontlist releases. Delacorte's categories include self-help, self-actualization, popular psychology, child care, politics, true crime, and current issues and events.

Delacorte's trade paperback fiction includes commercial novels, romance, historical, mystery, and futuristic works.

Nonfiction: *Far Appalachia* by Noah Adams; *Aches & Pains* by Maeve Binchy; *For the Bride* by Colin Cowie; *The Promise of Sleep* by William C. Dement, M.D., Ph.D., and

Christopher Vaughn; *How to Think Like Leonardo Da Vinci* by Michael Gelb; *The Coalwood Way* by Homer Hickam; *More Grandmothers Are Like Snowflakes, No Two Are Alike* by Janet Lanese.

Fiction: *No Man's Mistress* by Mary Balogh; *A Summer to Remember* by Mary Balogh; *The Thief-Taker* by T. F. Banks, *Thief of Souls* by Ann Benson; *The Sibyl in Her Grave* by Sarah Caudwell; *Sometimes I Dream in Italian* by Rita Ciresi; *Gone for Good* by Harlan Coben; *Tell No One* by Harlan Coben; *The Palace of Tears* by Alev Lytle Croutier; *The Smoke Jumper* by Nicholas Evans; *Dragonfly in Amber* by Diana Gabaldon.

B

The Dial Press

The Dial Press, an imprint of Bantam Dell Publishing Group, publishes literary fiction and nonfiction, including works by Allegra Goodman, Caroline Knapp, Elizabeth McCracken, Michael Paterniti, David Schickler, and Katie Roiphe, among others.

Dial Press author Justin Cronin won the Hemingway Foundation/PEN Award for First Fiction for *Mary and O'Neil,* a collection of connected short stories. Elizabeth McCracken won the L. L. Winship/PEN New England Prize for her second novel, *Niagara Falls All Over Again,* published by The Dial Press.

Other titles indicative of this list: *American Chica* by Marie Arana; *Franklin Flyer* by Nicholas Christopher; *Crow Lake* by Mary Lawson.

Delta

Delta publishes nonfiction and fiction in trade paperback format. Nonfiction titles are often biographies or memoirs, whereas the fiction list leans toward literary and short story collections.

Fiction titles: *Giovanni's Room* by James Baldwin; *Paradise Park* by Allegra Goodman.

Dell

Dell is a long-standing leader in publishing adult fiction and nonfiction in trade paperback format. Dell is home to the bestselling female novelist Danielle Steel, who is published in Delacorte hardcover. Dell also publishes John Grisham. Other writers who are published in mass market by Dell include Thomas Harris, Nicholas Evans, Diana Gabaldon, Sara Paretsky, Belva Plain, Perri O'Shaughnessy, Harlan Coben, and Homer Hickam.

Island

Formerly Dell Island, this imprint publishes paperback fiction, with an emphasis on mystery, romance, and suspense. Titles include *City of Light* by Lauren Belfer and *A Woman of Passion* by Virginia Henley.

Query letters and SASEs should be directed to:

Ann Harris, Senior Editor—Nonfiction interests consistent with the house list

Anne Lesley Groell, Editor—Fiction: Bantam Spectra science fiction/fantasy imprint

Toni Burbank, Vice President and Executive Editor—Spirituality, addition/recovery, health

Wendy McCurdy, Senior Editor—Women's fiction, romance, commercial nonfiction, popular culture

Robin Michaelson, Editor—Nonfiction

Danielle Perez, Senior Editor—Spirituality, health

Kate Miciak, Executive Editor—Mysteries

BARRICADE BOOKS INC.

185 Bridge Plaza North, Suite 308-A, Fort Lee, NJ 07024
201-944-7600
www.barricadebooks.com

Barricade's publishing interests include arts and entertainment; how-to/self-help; biography, history, politics, and current events; humor; natural sciences; New Age, occult, and religion; psychology, health, and sexuality; recreation; and true crime.

Barricade Books was founded in 1991 by the veteran publisher Lyle Stuart, who had previously founded Lyle Stuart Inc. (Lyle Stuart Inc. was sold and eventually became the Carol Publishing Group before Carol closed its doors in late 1999.) Barricade Books was launched in order to continue the tradition begun in 1956 when Lyle Stuart became a publisher—to specialize in books other publishers might hesitate to publish because they were too controversial.

Barricade sought bankruptcy protection in 1999, due to an expensive libel suit against it by Las Vegas gambling tycoon Steve Wynn, but the firm continues full operations.

Barricade publisher Carole Stuart is the author of a number of successful books, including *I'll Never Be Fat Again* and *Why Was I Adopted?* She has worked in book publishing her entire adult life. Lyle Stuart is a former newspaper reporter who launched his career as a book publisher with $8,000 that he won in a libel action against Walter Winchell. Stuart sold that company three decades later for $12 million. The Barricade catalog expands this tradition with a roster of freethinking writers that is perhaps unrivaled in the international commercial publishing arena. Barricade's list is exemplary of publishing courage in action.

From Barricade: *Silent Justice: The Clarence Thomas Story* by John Greenya; *The Complete Book of U.S. Presidents, 2001 Edition* by William A. Gregorio; *The Design of Virtual Environments* by Rory Stuart; *The Violent Years: Prohibition and the Detroit Mobs* by Paul R. Kavieff; *Full-Time Gambler: An American Classic* by L. G. Holloway; *Except for One Little Problem* by Joan Denson; *The Complete Book of Dreams* by Leonard R. M. Ashley; *A German Tale: A Girl Surviving Hitler's Legacy* by Erika V. Shearin-Karres; *Celebrities in Hell* by Warren Allen Smith; *The New Bride Guide* by Judith Ann Graham; *Paul Pellicoro on Tango* by Paul Pellicoro; *Your Skin from A to Z* by Jerome Litt, M.D.

Query letters and SASEs should be directed to:

Carole Stuart, Publisher

BARRON'S/BARRON'S EDUCATIONAL SERIES, INC.

250 Wireless Boulevard, Hauppauge, NY 11788
631-434-3311   fax: 631-434-3723
www.barronseduc.com

B

Barron's hosts a broad publishing operation that encompasses books in business and finance; gift books; titles in cooking, family and health, gardening, nature, pets, and retirement lifestyle; as well as selected titles in arts, crafts, and hobbying. Barron's produces computer books and software. The house highlights a children's line.

Barron's (founded in 1941) was originally known for its comprehensive line of study notes and test-preparation guides in business, literature, languages, and standardized tests in individual subject and professional fields. The house offers a number of practical business series, retirement and parenting keys, programs on skills development in foreign languages (as well as in English), and specialty reference titles in allied areas of interest.

Barron's cookbooks address international cuisines as well as healthful cookery. Dictionaries of health-related terms and many other specialized topics are offered. Under the rubric of special-interest titles, Barron's produces series on arts and crafts techniques, biographies of well-known artists, and home and garden. Books on pets and pet care include numerous titles keyed to particular breeds and species of birds, fish, dogs, and cats.

Children's and young-adult books and books of family interest include series on pets, nature and the environment, dinosaurs, sports, fantasy, adventure, and humor. Many of these are picture storybooks, illustrated works, and popular reference titles of general interest.

Barron's children's and young adult titles include *101 Games for Spring* by Joseph M. Allue; *Bach* by Ann Rachlin and Tony Hart; *Bertie Bones* by Tim Wood; *By the Light of the Moon* by Gina Erickson, M.A., and Kelli C. Foster, Ph.D.; *Chunky Farm Horse* by Emily Bolam; *Dinosaurs* by Dougal Dixon; *Guess Who's Hiding!* by Ana Martin-Larranaga; *Into Space* by Kate Petty; *Penguins* by Judith Hodge and Susan Brocker; *Teatime Piglet* by Steve Bland.

Barron's offers an extensive general-interest series lineup of interest to students and educators: Masters of Music series, Megascope series, Bravo series, the History series, the Natural World series, and Literature Made Easy series.

Barron's Study Guides subjects include book notes, college review, easy-way series, English language arts, EZ-101 Study Keys, foreign language, law, literature, mathematics, philosophy/religion, science, social studies, study tips/reference, and test preparation.

From Barron's: *Entrepreneurship 101* by Jae K. Shim, Ph.D., and Joel G. Siegel, Ph.D., C.P.A.; *Economics* by Walter J. Wessels; *Dictionary of Business Terms* by Jack P. Friedman et al.; *Cooking with the Stars* by Rick Ameil; *The Tea Box* by Gilles Brochard; *The Joy of Grilling* by Joseph Famularo; *Baby Yoga* by Francoise Barbara Freedman; *Organic Living in 10 Simple Lessons* by Karen Sullivan; *The Perfect Life of Hunters* by Eric Joly; *Where They Fell* by Tim Newark; *Speed Reading the Easy Way* by Howard S. Berg and Marcus A. Conyers; *Student Success Secrets* by Jensen.

Barron's handles its own distribution. Send query letters with SASEs to:

Mark Miele, Managing Editor

Max Reed, Senior Editor

Linda Turner, Senior Editor

B

BEACON PRESS

25 Beacon Street, Boston, MA 02108

617-742-2110   fax: 617-742- 3097

www.beacon.org

Beacon is primarily a publisher of nonfiction works (along with some fiction). Beacon's areas of publishing interest include contemporary affairs; gender, ethnic, and cultural studies; the life of the mind and spirit; history; science; and the spectrum of global and environmental concerns. The publisher also hosts a short, strong list of titles in literary essays and poetry. The house no longer publishes children's titles. Beacon Press tenders an extensive backlist.

Beacon Press has been a light of independent American publishing since 1854, when the house was established by the Unitarian Universalist Church. The Beacon Press list is presented as a complement to corporate publishing's rapt attention to commercially correct topics and as a publishing platform for those whose search for meaning draws them to fresh points of view. Indeed, the house's estimable reputation thrives on the diversity and divergence of the ideas and stances advanced by Beacon authors.

Beacon titles: *Notes of a Native Son* by James Baldwin; *The Winged Serpent: American Indian Prose* (edited by Margo Astov); *All Souls* by Michael Patrick MacDonald; *An Autobiography: The Story of My Experiments with Truth* by Mohandas K. Gandhi, foreword by Sissela Bok; *Fist Stick Knife Gun: A Personal History of Violence in America* by Geoffrey Canada; *Talking About Death: A Dialogue Between Parent and Child* by Earl A. Grollman; *Thousand Pieces of Gold* by Ruthanne Lum McCunn; *Kindred* by Octavia Butler; *Transgender Warriors: Making History from Joan of Arc to Dennis Rodman* by Leslie Feinberg; *You Can't Be Neutral on a Moving Train: A Personal History of Our Times* by Howard Zinn; *Heretic's Heart* by Margot Adler; *Nature and Walking* by Ralph Waldo Emerson and Henry David Thoreau (introduction by John Elder); *The Poetics of Space* by Gaston Bachelard; *House of Light* by Mary Oliver; *A Buddhist Bible* (edited by Dwight Goddard); *Beyond God and Father: Toward a Philosophy of Women's Liberation* by Mary Daly; *Race Matters* by Cornel West.

Scholarly highlights: Beacon's new editions of *Gnostic Religion* by Hans Jonas; *The Woman in the Body: A Cultural Analysis of Reproduction* by Emily Martin; *The Ethnic Myth and Turning Back* by Stephen Steinberg; *Broken Spears: The Aztec Account of the Conquest of Mexico* by Miguel Leon-Portillo.

Writers, please note these Beacon titles that address themes in the writing life: *Ruined by Reading: A Life in Books* by Lynne Sharon Schwartz; *Writing as a Way of Healing: How Telling Our Stories Transforms Our Lives* by Louise DeSalvo; *The Thief of Happiness* by Bonnie Freidman.

Beacon Press is distributed to the trade by Houghton Mifflin. Query letters and SASE's should be directed to:

Editorial Department

B

PETER BEDRICK BOOKS

156 Fifth Avenue, New York, NY 10010
212-206-3738   fax: 212-206-4741
e-mail: bedrick@panix.com

Bedrick's list focuses on popular reference works in history, folklore and mythology, and women's studies; the Bedrick children's list accents highly illustrated nonfiction, including several ongoing series in world history and cultures and numerous educational titles.

Peter Bedrick Books was established in 1983, following the founder's long and successful association with Schocken Books. Today a midsized publishing house with a fetching swan logo, Bedrick still has a personal touch—evident from the first Bedrick list, which featured adult and children's books and introduced the initial three titles in the Library of the World's Myths and Legends.

Special from Bedrick: *The World of the Pirate* by Valerie Garwood (illustrated by Richard Berridge); *The World of Native Americans* by Marion Wood (illustrated by Antonella Pastorelli and Federico Michelli); *The Atlas of the Classical World* by Piero Bardi (illustrated by Paola Ravaglia and Matteo Chesi); *The Atlas of World Cultures* by Brunetto Chiarelli and Anna Lisa Bebi (illustrated by Paola Ravaglia); *Slavery: From Africa to the Americas* by Christine Hatt.

The Inside Story series offers titles filled with full-color cutaway illustrations and informative text. Notable entrants here: *The Roman Colosseum* by Fiona Macdonald (illustrated by Mark Bergin); *A Renaissance Town* by Jacqueline Morley (illustrated by Mark Peppe).

First Facts Series titles: *First Facts About the American Frontier* and *First Facts About the Ancient Romans* by Fiona Macdonald; *First Facts About the Ancient Egyptians* and *First Facts About the Vikings* by Jacqueline Morley.

Peter Bedrick Books has been acquired by NTC/Contemporary Publishing. The house does not accept any unsolicited manuscripts. Query letters and SASEs should be directed to:

Peter Bedrick, President and Publisher

MATTHEW BENDER & COMPANY, INC.

744 Broad Street, Newark, NJ 07102
973-820-2000   fax: 973-820-2007
www.bender.com

Bender produces works in the fields of law, accounting, banking, insurance, and related professions. Areas of Bender concentration include general accounting, administrative law, admiralty, bankruptcy, civil rights law, computer law, elder law, employment/labor, environmental, estate and financial planning, federal practice and procedure, government, health care, immigration, insurance, intellectual property, law-office management, personal injury/medico-legal, products liability, real estate, securities, taxation, and worker's compensation.

Matthew Bender (founded in 1887), a member of the Reed Elsevier plc group, is a specialist publisher of professional information in print and electronic format. Bender publishes general references as well as state-specific works. Bender produces treatises, textbooks, manuals, and form books, as well as newsletters and periodicals. Many Matthew Bender publications are available in the CD-ROM format (Authority CD-ROM libraries make available the most comprehensive and accurate information for the practice of law) on the Internet and on LexisNexis.

Matthew Bender has served professionals for more than 100 years and has achieved its unique status as a specialty publisher in diverse areas of the law. Matthew Bender combines in-house editorial talent and publishing ties with the foremost experts in the legal profession to produce a product that will fit its customers' needs. Practicing attorneys often serve as contributing legal writers in their areas of expertise. Matthew Bender is one of the world's leading publishers of legal analysis and case law and pours this experience and expertise into more than 500 publications in print and electronic formats and serves professionals in more than 160 countries.

Matthew Bender considers itself an essential partner with law professionals, providing integrated information, resources, and tools, and delivering that information in formats useful to its customers, to help them reach solutions with confidence.

Representative titles from Matthew Bender: *Computer Contracts* by Esther C. Roditt; *Cable Television Law: A Video Communications Practice Guide* by Charles D. Ferris, Frank W. Lloyd, and Thomas J. Casey; *Franchising* by Gladys Glickman; *The Law of Advertising* by George Eric Rosden and Peter Eric Rosden; *Business Organizations with Tax Planning* by Zolman Cavitch; *Employment Discrimination* by Lex K. Larson; *Moore's Federal Practice* by James William Moore and the Moore's Editorial Board; *Immigration Law and Procedure* by Charles Gordon, Stanley Mailman, and Stephen Yale-Loehr; *Responsibilities of Insurance Agents and Brokers* by Bertram Harnett; *World Patent Law and Practice: Patent Statutes, Regulations and Treaties* by John P. Sinnott and William Joseph Cotreau; *Environmental Law Practice Guide* by Michael B. Berrard (General Editor); *Environmental Law in Real Estate and Business Transactions* by David R. Berz and Stanley M. Spracker.

Matthew Bender handles its own distribution. Query letters and SASEs should be directed to:

George Bearese, Vice President and Editor in Chief

BERRETT-KOEHLER PUBLISHERS

235 Montgomery Street, Suite 650, San Francisco, CA 94104-2916
415-288-0260
www.bkconnection.com   e-mail: bkpub@bkpub.com

Berrett-Koehler's nonfiction program accents the areas of work and the workplace, business, management, leadership, career development, entrepreneurship, human resources, and global sustainability. Berrett-Koehler Publishers (instituted in 1992) is an independent press that produces books, periodicals, journals, newsletters, and audiocassettes.

The Berrett-Koehler booklist is produced in well-crafted, ecologically aware hardcover and paperback editions.

Berrett-Koehler stands for a commitment to produce publications that support the movement toward a more enlightened world of work and more free, open, humane, effective, and globally sustainable organizations. The house is committed to do publications that challenge conventional views of work and management, that create new lenses for understanding organizations, that pioneer new purposes and values in business, and that open up new sources of guidance for today's complex work world.

Berrett-Koehler's focus is seeking to make each book it publishes successful, which seems natural, yet goes against the prevailing "numbers game" model in conglomerate publishing: put out large numbers of titles and see which ones succeed with little support from the publisher. Unfortunately, most conglomerates' titles do not succeed and have only a short shelf life before they go out of print. Berrett-Koehler is committed to keeping books in print far longer than the big publishers' norm, and, in fact, none of its first five years' titles has yet gone out of print. Berrett-Koehler's key to making each book successful and keeping books in print is marketing through multiple channels in addition to bookstores (such as direct mail, corporate sales, and association sales), not only to support bookstore sales but also to provide an ongoing life for books when their bookstore shelf life is past.

Titles: *301 More Ways to Have Fun at Work* by Dave Hemsath; *Downshifting* by John D. Drake; *E-Supply Chain* by Charles C. Poirier and Michael J. Bauer; *Microshift* by Ervin Laszlo; *How to Succeed in Your First Job* by Elwood F. Holton, III, and Sharon S. Naquin; *Leadership and the New Science* by Margaret J. Wheatley; *Love 'Em or Lose 'Em* by Beverly Kaye and Sharon Jordan-Evans; *The 21 Success Secrets of Self-Made Millionaires* by Brian Tracy; *The Influence Edge* by Alan A. Vengel; *The New Super Leadership* by Charles C. Manz, Ph.D., and Henry P. Sims, Jr.; *Whistle While You Work* by Richard J. Leider and David A. Shapiro.

Bestselling titles from Berrett-Koehler include *Emotional Value* by Janelle Barlow and Dianna Maul; *When Corporations Rule the World* by David Korten; *Managing Your Own Learning* by James R. Davis and Adelaide B. Davis; *Future Search* by Marvin R. Weisbord and Sandra Janoff; *Identity Is Destiny* by Laurence D. Ackerman; *Results* by Richard A. Swanson and Elwood F. Holton, III.

Berrett-Koehler tends its own multichanneled distribution, through bookstores, direct-mail brochures, catalogs, a toll-free telephone-order number, book clubs, association book services, e-books, and special sales to business, government, and nonprofit organizations; the house is distributed to the trade via Publishers Group West. Query letters and SASEs should be directed to:

Jeevan Sivasubramaniam, Managing Editor

BLOOMBERG PRESS

100 Business Park Drive, PO Box 888, Princeton, NJ 08542-0888
609-279-7049, 800-388-2749   fax: 917-369-8288
www.bloomberg.com/books   e-mail: press@bloomberg.com

B

Bloomberg publishes books in finance, personal finance, business, economics, management, investments, financial planning, and related categories. House imprints and specialty lines include Bloomberg Professional Library (primarily for financial professionals), Bloomberg Personal Bookshelf (consumer-oriented personal finance and investing titles), and books on small businesses and entrepreneurship.

Bloomberg Press (founded in 1996) is part of Bloomberg L.P., a global, multimedia-based information service that combines news, data, and analysis for financial markets and businesses. The parent company runs a real-time financial information network, as well as a number of news-service operations (supplying news and stories to, among other clients, reporters, editors, and news bureaus), and radio, Web, and television enterprises (Bloomberg Radio, Bloomberg.com, Bloomberg Television).

The goal at Bloomberg Press has been to cut through the technical static of the markets and provide a clear picture. Bloomberg Press books pack a lot of practical information. They are designed to be functional as well as factual, organized to take the reader's busy schedule into account. Authors are prominent authorities and financial journalists. Bloomberg publishes books for brokers, traders, portfolio managers, analysts, money managers, CEOs, CFOs, bankers, and other professionals, as well as for small-business people, consultants, and sophisticated investors worldwide. Subject areas include investment intelligence, portfolio management, markets, financial analytics, and economic analysis of use to traders and other financial professionals.

Representative titles: *Best Practices for Financial Advisors* by Mary Rowland; *Thriving as a Broker in the 21st Century* by Thomas J. Dorsey; *New Thinking in Technical Analysis* (edited by Rick Bensignor); *Small Cap Dynamics* by Satya Pradhuman.

Categories for consumers include investing; managing personal wealth; choosing products and services, including insurance, health care, banking services, and real estate; personal-finance reference, education, use of personal computers for investment decisions, and online information; and other topics, from a personal-finance angle, such as credit, taxes, and estate planning.

Titles include *Investing in Small-Cap Stocks* by Christopher Graja and Elizabeth Ungar, Ph.D.; *Investing 101* by Kathy Kristof; *In Defense of Free Capital Markets* by David F. DeRosa; *The Pied Pipers of Wall Street* by Benjamin Cole.

Bloomberg markets its products and services internationally through a creative variety of outlets, including traditional print venues as well as electronic distribution. Bloomberg Press is distributed by W. W. Norton & Company.

Query letters and SASEs should be directed to:

Tracy Tait, Associate Editor

Kathleen Peterson, Senior Acquisitions Editor

BLUE MOON BOOKS
(A SUBSIDIARY OF THE AVALON PUBLISHING GROUP)

161 William Street, 16th Floor, New York, NY 10038
646-325-2570
www.avalonpub.com

Blue Moon's Web site contains a complete listing of available books and cover art. Blue Moon's erotica includes some of the finest novels and stories in the field. Blue Moon Books also publishes selected trade fiction and nonfiction. Blue Moon Books was established in 1987 by Barney Rosset, the trailblazing publisher who earlier founded Grove Press and developed that enterprise into a house of international literary, cultural, and commercial renown.

Blue Moon erotica: *Folies O'Amour* by Anne-Marie Villefranche; *Jennifer* by O. M. Perkins; *Incognito* by Lisabet Savai; *Sex Practice* by Ray Gordon; *Dark Star* by Michael Perkins; *Oyster Redux* by Anonymous; *Gardens of the Night* by Felicia Plessey; *Beauty in the Birch* by Anonymous; *The Man of Her Dream* by Briony Shilton; *Romance of Lust* by Anonymous; *Mistress of Instruction* by Christine Kerr; *Tutor's Bride* by Martin Pyx; *Blue Angel Nights* by Margarete von Falkenese; *Education of a Maiden* by Anonymous; *The Autobiography of a Flea* by Anonymous; *Love for Sale* by Celia St. Gogarty; *Best of Shadow Lane* by Eve Howard. In addition to fervid classical romances, Blue Moon offers erotic works with such contemporary themes as psychosexual suspense thrillers; the house offers a significant listing of erotic fiction by women.

Blue Moon Books oversees its own distribution. The house no longer accepts unsolicited submissions. All work must be submitted by literary agents.

BONUS BOOKS, INC.

160 East Illinois Street, Chicago, IL, 60611-3880
312-467-0580   fax: 312-467-9271
www.bonus-books.com   e-mail: bb@bonus-books.com

Bonus publishes general nonfiction, accenting titles in broadcasting, business and careers, collectibles, consumer, legal, self-help, health and fitness, cooking, autobiography and biography, books of regional interest (including the Chicago area), sports, gambling, and current affairs. Titles from the Precept Press imprint are written by and for fundraising professionals, physicians, and the broadcasting industry.

Bonus Books, Inc. (founded in 1985), had an original focus on sports titles and grew quickly into a trade book publisher with nationwide prominence. Strong Bonus growth categories have been sports books and gambling books. As Bonus publisher Aaron Cohodes remarked in a letter to booksellers, "I don't know what this says about our society, but perhaps that's just as well."

Bonus highlights include *Nutritional Care for High-Risk Newborns* (edited by Sharon Groh-Wargo, Melody Thompson, and Janice Hovas Cox); *Forever Crops* by Frank Scoblete; *Stock Car Champions* by Richard Huff; *Coin Collector's Survival Manual, 4th Edition* by Scott A. Travers; *The Continuing Journey* by William Sturtevant; *Get the Edge at Blackjack* by John May; *Million Dollar Mailings* by Denison Hatch; *Best Newspaper Writing 2001* (edited by Keith Woods); *A Few Marbles Left* by John Corcoran; *Get the Edge at Roulette* by Christopher Pawlicki; *Vascular Access for Hemodialysis VII* (edited by Mitchell L. Henry, M.D.); *Make It Memorable* by Bob Dotson.

Bonus's watershed title, *Ditka: An Autobiography* by Mike Ditka with Don Pierson, remains in print on a sturdy backlist. Other Bonus backlist favorites are *Beat the Crap*

Out of the Casinos by Frank Scoblete*; Break the One-Armed Bandits* by Frank Scoblete; *The Artful Journey* by William Sturtevant; *Writing Broadcast News* by Mervin Block; *Overlay, Overlay: How to Bet Horses Like a Pro* by Bill Heller; *A Little League Instructional Guide* by Jeff Burroughs; *The World's Greatest Wealth Builder* by Carleton Sheets.

Bonus Books distributes its own list and utilizes a number of national sales representatives. Query letters and SASEs should be directed to:

Erin Kahl, Acquisitions Editor

Marion Boyars Publishing
U.K. Office:
Marion Boyars Publishing, 24 Lacy Road, London SW15 INL, England, U.K.

Note: Marion Boyars's New York office at 237 East 39th Street, New York, NY 10016, is for publicity only. All editorial is handled in the U.K.

The Marion Boyars publishing program gives preeminence to fine writing and is open to considering the highest level of expression in virtually any category. Areas of particular Marion Boyars accomplishment are in the fields of fiction, belles lettres, memoirs, literary criticism, biography, music, theater, sociology, and travel. Marion Boyars Publishing (founded in 1978) has achieved international renown and commercial presence in letters with an individualist precision and personalized disposition. Marion Boyars releases a moderate-sized seasonal list; the house tends a strong backlist. Though not technically a United States publishing house (projects emanate editorially from the London base), Boyars presents writers whose works may have more of an international appeal than a strictly commercial-American flavor. The publisher acquires on the basis of enthusiasm for a given work—and this is not necessarily based on projections of huge initial sales. Indeed, Marion Boyars herself has remarked that overlooked books and translations are often the house's jewels.

A representative coup is the English-language publication of *Nip the Buds, Shoot the Kids* by Nobel Laureate Kenzaburo Oe. On the Marion Boyars list: *Waiting Period* by Hubert Selby, Jr.; *Father and I* by Carol Gebler; *Corpsing* by Toby Lift.

Marion Boyars Publishing is distributed by Consortium Saint Paul, MN. Query letters and SASEs should be directed to:

Cathy Kilgarriff, President, Editor in Chief—Fiction submissions accepted through literary agents only

Boyds Mills Press
(A Subsidiary of Highlights for Children)
815 Church Street, Honesdale, PA 18431
570-253-1164, 800-490-5111
www.boydsmillspress.com   e-mail: Admin@boydsmillspress.com

Boyds Mills produces books for children, picture books, novels, nonfiction, and poetry—nonsensical verse, as well as more serious fare. The press promotes a solid seasonal list of new titles and hosts a hefty backlist. Boyds Mills Press (founded in 1990) is a subsidiary of Highlights for Children.

Boyds Mills wants books that challenge, inspire, and entertain young people the world over. Boyds Mills has published such international bestsellers as Dougal Dixon's *Dinosaurs* (over a dozen editions in 10 languages, plus multivolume spinoffs).

Boyds Mills releases: *Bobcat: North America's Cat; Boy Who Swallowed a Rainbow; The Bus for Us; Coyote and Badger: Desert Hunters of the Southwest; Daisy the Firecow; Dear Mother, Dear Daughter: Poems for Young People; Emma Jo's Song; Grandfather's Day; Groover's Heart; Highlights Fun to Play Recorder Book; Horsepower: The Wonder of Draft Horses; The Itsy Bitsy Spider; Last Night at the Zoo; Lemonade Sun: And Other Summer Poems; Love Me, Love You; Mommy Poems; On the Trail of Sacagawea; Poison Dart Frogs; The Best of: Puzzlemania Mazes, Vol. 1; Sharks! Strange and Wonderful!; Sing of the Earth and Sky: Poems About Our Planet and the Wonders Beyond; Six Creepy Sheep; Storm Coming!; The Super Colossal Book of Hidden Pictures, Vol. 2; This Is the Ocean.*

Among featured Boyds Mills authors is Jane Yolen, award-winning author of more than 170 books. A sampling of her titles includes: *All in the Woodland Early: An ABC Book; Before the Storm; How Beastly! A Menagerie of Nonsense Poems; An Invitation to the Butterfly Ball: A Counting Rhyme; Jane Yolen's Mother Goose Songbook; Weather Report: A Book of Poems; Street Rhymes Around the World; Once Upon Ice; Water Music; Color Me a Rhyme.*

Boyds Mills Press handles its own distribution. Query letters and SASEs should be directed to:

Kent L. Brown, Jr., Publisher

Clay Winters, President

Larry Rosler, Editorial Director

Jan Cheripko, Assistant to the Publisher

Shirley Brinkerhoff, Publishing Assistant

Brassey's Inc.

22841 Quicksilver Drive, Dulles, VA 20166
703-661-1548   fax: 703-661-1547
www.brasseysinc.com

Brassey's Inc. is a leading publisher in history (especially military history), biography, defense, national and international affairs, foreign policy, military reference, and intelligence. The Brassey's Sports imprint publishes trade titles related to various sports topics.

Forthcoming Brassey's titles include *Silent Knights: Blowing the Whistle on Military Accidents and Their Cover-Ups* by Alan E. Diehl; *War of Words: Abraham Lincoln and the Civil War Press* by Harry J. Maihafer; *CIA, Inc.: Espionage and the Craft of Business Intelligence* by F. W. Rustmann, Jr.; *Sacred Secrets: How Soviet Intelligence Operations*

B

Changed American History by Jerrold and Leona Schecter; *Cold War Submarines: U.S. and Soviet Design and Flattop from Keel to Mast, 1934–46* by Robert J. Cressman; *Military Strategy: Principles, Practices, and Historical Perspectives* by John M. Collins; *Baseball Prospectus: 2002 Edition* by Joseph Sheehan et al.; *Tennis Confidential: Today's Greatest Players, Matches, and Controversies* by Paul Fein; *Playing Hurt: Evaluating and Treating the Warriors of the NFL* by Pierce E. Scranton, Jr., M.D.; *Blue Ribbon College Football Yearbook: 2002 Edition* (edited by Christ Dortch); *Basketball's Most Wanted: The Top 10 Books of Hoops' Outrageous Dunders, Incredible Buzzer-Beaters, and Other Oddities* by Floyd Connor.

Query letter with SASE should be directed to:

Donald Jacobs, Senior Assistant Editor

Don McKeon, Vice President and Publisher
    Born: April 15, 1952.
    Education: B.A., English, College of Holy Cross.
    Employment history/editor career path: My editorial career path had several detours, but the route was basically as follows: bookstore Clerk, Proofreader and Copy Editor, Managing Editor of a monthly defense and foreign affairs magazine, and then Publishing Manager of what was then Pergamon-Brassey's International Defense Publishers, Inc. I have been with Brassey's for 14 years.
    Personal interests: Reading (of course), volleyball, and motorcycling.
    What would you be doing if you were not an editor? I'd possibly be working in international development. I served in the Peace Corps in West Africa after college.
    What has been your most successful book that you have acquired to date? *Baseball Prospectus* by Chris Kahrl et al., a highly praised and entertaining annual analysis of baseball statistics, from the major league level down to the lowest minor leagues. Sales have improved each year, and now we're developing a *Football Prospectus* and a *Hockey Prospectus.*
    What books have you acquired that make you the most proud? What books that you have acquired reflect the types of books you like to represent? I'm most proud of our books that make a real contribution to the literature, such as *Dien Bien Phu: The Epic Battle America Forgot* by Howard R. Simpson and *One War at a Time: The International Dimensions of the American Civil War* by Dean B. Mahin. Other books that reflect the types of books I like to represent include *Baseball Prospectus* by Chris Kahrl et al.; *Military Geography* by John M. Collins; *A Mind in Prison: The Memoir of a Son and Soldier of the Third Reich* by Bruno Manz; *A Chain of Events: The Government Cover-Up of the Black Hawk Incident and the Friendly-Fire Death of Lt. Laura Piper* by Joan L. Piper; *The Outpost War: The U.S. Marine Corps in Korea, 1952* by Lee Ballenger. I should add that I am now seeking more titles that can be used in courses at the military academies, in ROTC units, and at the military postgraduate schools.
    Do you represent fiction? Brassey's no longer publishes fiction.
    What do you want to see less of? Since we no longer publish fiction, I'd naturally like to see no more proposals for novels. Also, with all due respect to veterans, I'd like to see fewer proposals for unremarkable wartime memoirs. They must be unique and well written.
    Do you represent nonfiction? Brassey's publishes nonfiction in the following areas: history (especially military history), world and national affairs, foreign policy, defense,

intelligence, and biography. In addition, Brassey's is now developing books about transportation (especially automobiles) and about the personalities and events of national and international athletic competition.

Do you require book proposals? If so, what do you look for in evaluating a book proposal? We do require book proposals. We ask for a one-page synopsis, a table of contents or outline, one or two sample chapters, authors' thoughts on the book's market and competition, their qualifications, and photocopies of any sample photos. In evaluating proposals, besides deciding whether the topic itself interests us, we look for clarity and organization and for relevance in the author's credentials.

Are certain aspects of a book proposal given more weight than others? A proposal by an author with a strong publishing record will certainly get our attention.

What process do you use for making a decision? What is the process for acquisition; is there a committee? The first hurdle, I reject perhaps 95 percent of submissions out of hand. The rest are discussed at an editorial meeting, where the decision is made whether to have the proposal or manuscript read by outside experts. We regularly consult an informal network of authorities in our publishing areas.

Are you interested in work geared for the masses (readers of *People, The Star,* etc.)? We are interested to some degree in work geared to the masses, but only if it's somehow related to our core list. For example, this year we're publishing an account by a mother whose daughter, an Air Force officer, was killed in a friendly-fire incident and who fought government bureaucracies for years for accountability. Stories such as this have broad general appeal.

Are agents important? Why? Agents are important to publishers because they presumably don't waste their time on projects of little value, and the better agents know what kind of projects will be of interest to specific publishers.

Do you like new writers? What should new writers do to break into the business? We've had a lot of success with first-time authors, although it's usually easier to work with an author who already knows the game. I'm not sure what to suggest to new authors who want to break into the business except that perhaps they should find a new angle on a topic of broad interest and be able to summarize their project in 25 words or less.

How should writers approach you? By mail or e-mail, although we do not open unsolicited attached files. Please note that our new address is 22841 Quicksilver Drive, Dulles, VA 20166. I can be reached by e-mail at Don@BooksIntl.com.

What are some common mistakes writers make? What really gets on your nerves? Perhaps the biggest mistake I see is some authors' compulsion to use all the information dredged up during the book's research. They just cannot bring themselves to throw anything away. Authors should continually ask themselves how important each fact is to their thesis. What does it add? As to what really gets on my nerves, I'd have to say authors who don't make deadlines, who are disorganized, and who don't fact-check their own work.

What can writers do to get your attention and to avoid the slush pile? Potential authors could provide me with their proposal in a brief, clear, concise cover letter that tells me what the book is about, why it would be important, why it would sell, and why they are the proper person to write it.

What have been some of your craziest experiences with submissions? I can't think offhand of any particular example of a crazy submission experience, but we do occasionally receive those kinds of proposals on which every marginless page is completely filled with tiny handwriting and contains references to an extremely personal relationship with God.

What have been some of your best experiences with writers or in your job? My best publishing experiences have been with authors of memoirs—people who have led exemplary, sometimes courageous lives—some of whom I now consider friends.

What, if anything, makes you different from other editors? Although I've never been an author, I believe I have the ability to look at the publishing process from the author's perspective and can empathize with that individual. I wouldn't be doing my job if I always agreed with the authors, of course, but I'm patient, and many authors have said they enjoy working with me. Brassey's prides itself on its repeat authors.

Is there anything you would like to see changed in the industry? I wouldn't mind if the industry were more lucrative at the lower editorial and production levels so that it attracted and retained more bright young people.

Any advice for writers? Any way to change the system for you? Any additional thoughts? I would advise authors to remember who their main audience is and to write for that group, but also to try to get feedback from people who would not normally read their kind of book. Different perspectives can be valuable.

GEORGE BRAZILLER, INC.

171 Madison Avenue, New York, NY 10016
212-889-0909

George Braziller accents fine editions in art and design, architecture, and art movements and history. The house also publishes selected literary titles, as well as philosophy, science, history, criticism, and biographical works. The house hosts a solid backlist.

George Braziller, Inc. (founded in 1955), is perhaps most widely known for original fine books in the fields of art and architecture. Much of Braziller's fiction and poetry is foreign literature in translation, although the publisher does publish original literary novels (such as works by Janet Frame) and works in the English language that have received initial publication elsewhere.

Braziller also has a strong interest in literary criticism and writing relating to the arts, in addition to a small selection of contemporary and modern poetry. Essential Readings in Black Literature is a Braziller series that features world-class writers from around the globe. Other Braziller series include Library of Far Eastern Art and New Directions in Architecture.

From Braziller: *Impressionism: Reflections and Perceptions* by Meyer Schapiro; *Painted Prayers: The Book of Hours in Medieval and Renaissance Art* by Roger S. Wieck; *Picturing Hong Kong: Photography 1855–1910* by Roberta Wue, Edwin K. Lai, and Joanna Waley-Cohen; *The Gallery of Maps in the Vatican* by Lucio Gambi (translated by Francoise Pouncey Chiarini); *Georgia O'Keeffe: A Celebration of Music and Dance* by Katherine Hoffman; *Dreamings: The Art of Aboriginal Australia* (edited by Peter Sutton).

Great Frescoes of the Italian Renaissance series (10 volumes of the world's major fresco cycles from the early 14th–17th centuries): *Giotto: The Schrovegnia Chapel, Padua* by Bruce Cole; *The Brancacci Chapel, Florence* by Andrew Ladis; *Raphael: The*

Stanza Della Segnatura, Rome by James Beck; *Ambrogio Lorenzetti: The Palazzo Pubblico, Siena* by Randolph Starn; *Andrea Mantegna: Padua and Mantua* by Keith Christiansen; *Piero Della Francesca: San Francesco, Arezzo* by Marilyn Aronberg Lavin; *Annibale Carracci: The Farnese Gallery, Rome* by Charles Dempsey; *Fra Angelico: San Marco, Florence* by William Hood; *Luca Signorelli: The San Brizio Chapel, Orvieto* by Jonathan B. Riess; *Michelangelo: The Sistine Chapel Ceiling, Rome* by Loren Partridge.

Braziller titles are distributed by W. W. Norton & Co. Query letters and SASEs should be directed to:

George Braziller, Publisher—All areas consistent with publisher description

BROADWAY BOOKS (A DIVISION OF RANDOM HOUSE INC.)
1540 Broadway, New York, NY 10036
212-782-6500

Broadway was recently reorganized as Doubleday/Broadway Books. It generates commercial nonfiction in celebrity autobiography and biography; historical, political, and cultural biography and memoirs; politics and current affairs; multicultural topics; popular culture; cookbooks, diet, and nutrition; consumer reference, business, and personal finance; popular psychology, spirituality, and women's issues. The house also provides selective commercial/literary frontlist fiction, primarily by established or highly promotable authors.

Broadway's emporium strategy involves publishing unique, marketable books of the highest editorial quality by authors who are authorities in their field and who use their credibility and expertise to promote their work.

Broadway Books began operation in mid-1995, with a mission to publish high-quality nonfiction hardcovers and trade paperbacks. In 1999 it was merged with Doubleday to form the Doubleday Broadway Publishing Group, with Stephen Rubin as the group's publisher.

The publishing house's namesake street and logo (a diagonally bisected letter B) are emblematic of the publisher's mandate. Broadway is New York's oldest thoroughfare and runs obliquely through the diversity of Manhattan's multicultural neighborhoods, from the original harbor and the financial district, along the city's centers of government, literature, music, theater, communications, retail shops, and educational and medical institutions.

Representative of Broadway's titles: *The O'Reilly Factor* by Bill O'Reilly; *Bella Tuscany in Tuscany* by Frances Mayes; *Fair Ball* by Bob Costas; *The Corner: A Year in the Life of an Inner-City Neighborhood* by David Simon and Edward Burns; *Life Makeovers* by Cheryl Richardson; *Smart Women Finish Rich* by David Bach; *Webonomics: Nine Essential Principles for Growing Your Business on the World Wide Web* by Evan I. Schwartz; *Under the Tuscan Sun* by Frances Mayers; *A Walk in the Woods* by Bill Bryson; *Vegetarian Cooking for Everyone* by Deborah Madison; *Simple to Spectacular* by Jean Georges Vongerichten; *The Minimalist Cooks at Home* by Mark Bittman; *Life Makeovers* by Cheryl Richardson; *If Life Is a Game, These Are the Rules* by Cherie Carter-Scott; *A Year by the Sea* by Joan Anderson; *Close to Shore* by Michael Capuzzo; *Falling Leaves* by Adeline Yen Mah; *Smart Couples Finish Rich* by David Bach; *Jemima J* by Jane Green; *The No Spin Zone* by Bill O'Reilly.

Broadway's general nonfiction program includes kitchen arts and lifestyle; relationships, parenting, and the family; popular business; popular issues; humor; and popular psychology, inspirational, parenting and self-help/self-awareness works.

Please query the house's acquisition stance prior to submitting projects—Broadway wishes to receive no unsolicited manuscripts; only agented works will be considered. Query letters and SASEs should be directed to:

Jennifer Josephy, Executive Editor—Cookbooks

Ann Campbell, Editor—Narrative nonfiction, women's history, women's fiction, health and fitness, spirituality

Charles Conrad, Vice President and Executive Editor—New nonfiction projects: popular culture, social history, literary nonfiction; contemporary literary and quality fiction; in charge of trade-paperback reprints

Suzanne Oaks, Senior Editor—Commercial nonfiction, investigative and other business stories

Gerald Howard, Editorial Director—Narrative nonfiction and literary fiction

Patricia Medved, Senior Editor—Parenting, self-help, consumer reference, and health

BURNHAM PUBLISHERS

111 North Canal Street, Suite 955, Chicago, IL 60606
312-930-9446

Burnham (formerly Nelson-Hall) publishes college textbooks in political science, sociology, and mass communications.

Samples of recent Burnham titles include *Living Off Crime* by Ken Tunnell; *Three Black Generations at the Crossroads* by Lois Benjamin; *Cities in the Third Wave* by Leonard Ruchelman; *History of Nazi Germany* by Joseph Bendersky. Virtually all of our authors are college professors at various institutions around the nation.

Burnham handles its own distribution and welcomes manuscript submissions (please write directly to Burnham for proposal guidelines). Query letters and SASEs should be directed to:

Richard Meade, General Manager

CAREER PRESS

New Page Books

3 Tice Road, PO Box 687, Franklin Lakes, NJ 07417
201-848-0310   fax: 201-848-1727
www.careerpress.com, www.newpagebooks.com

Career Press is established as a hard-driving, entrepreneurial publisher of essential career, business, reference, and personal finance titles. The still-independent company celebrated its 15th anniversary in March 2000. The year 2000 also saw a new Career Press imprint called New Page Books, which features general nonfiction books centered in these categories: weddings, Judaica, New Age, self-help, and health.

Between the two imprints, Career Press has published 65 titles in 2000. There is an active backlist of more than 200 strong-selling and well-promoted titles. The publisher promotes aggressively and resourcefully and stocks booksellers with titles geared to receive major nationwide publicity.

Career Press highlights for 2002: *Money Mastery: How to Control Your Spending, Eliminate Debt and Maximize Your Savings* by Alan M. Williams, Peter Jeppson, and Sanford Botkin; *Business Etiquette, 2nd Edition* by Ann Marie Sabath; *Comfort Zone Investing* by Gillette Edmunds; *Deliberate Success: Realize Your Vision with Purpose, Passion and Performance* by Eric Allenbaugh, Ph.D.; *Great Toasts* by Andrew Fronthingham; *Business Letters for Busy People, 4th Edition* by John A. Carey; *Bulletproof Presentations* by G. Michael Campbell; *Be the Boss Your Employees Deserve* by Ken Lloyd; *50 Powerful Ideas You Can Use to Keep Your Customers, 3rd Edition* by Paul R. Timm, Ph.D.; *Seize the Day: 7 Steps to Achieving the Extraordinary in an Ordinary World* by Danny Cox and John Hoover; *Inc. Yourself: How to Profit by Setting Up Your Own Corporation* by Judith H. McQuown; *Surviving Job Stress* by John B. Arden, Ph.D.; *Clutter Proof Your Business* by Mike Nelson; *Master Math: Trigonometry* by Debra Ross; *Last Minute Term Papers* by Ron Fry; *Companies with a Conscience, 2nd Edition* by Mary Scott and Howard Rothman.

New Page highlights for 2002: *Tarot for Your Self* by Mary K. Greer; *How to Be a Couple and Still Be Free, 3rd Edition* by Tina B. Tessina, Ph.D., and Riley K. Smith, M.A.; *Clan of the Goddess* by C. C. Brondwin; *Karmic Tarot, 3rd Edition* by William Lammey; *Celebrate Your Dreams* by Joyce Chapman; *The Practical Pagan: Common Sense Guidelines for Modern Practitioners* by Dana Eilers; *Secrets of the Ancient Incas: A Modern Approach to Ancient Ritual and Practice* by Michael Peter Langevin; *Diane Warner's Great Parties on Small Budgets* by Diane Warner; *The Haindl Tarot, Revised Edition* by Rachel Pollack; *The Cyber Spellbook* by Sirona Knight and Patricia Telesco; *Celtic Astrology: How the Mystical Power of the Druid Tree Signs Can Transform Your Life* by Phyllis Vega; *Dreams of the Goddess* by Scarlett Ross; *A Witch's Guide to Ghosts and the Supernatural* by Gerina Dunwich; *Faery Magick* by Sirona Knight; *Animal Spirit* by Patricia Telesco and Rowan Hall; *No More Panic Attacks* by Jennifer Shoquist, M.D., and Diane Stafford.

Go to careerpress.com for complete information. Career Press distributes its own list. Query letters and SASEs should be directed to:

Ronald Fry, President

CAROL PUBLISHING GROUP

This large and respected independent house went bankrupt and permanently shut its doors in late 1999. It is missed.

CARROLL & GRAF PUBLISHERS, INC.
161 William Street, New York, NY 10038
212-627-8590   fax: 212-627-8490
www.pgw.com

Carroll & Graf publishes commercial trade nonfiction and literary and commercial fiction (including a strong list in mystery and suspense). Carroll & Graf (founded in 1983) is a compact house with a catalog as select and well targeted as it is diverse. In addition to its original titles, Carroll & Graf reprints American classics and genre works, along with foreign literature in translation. The house issues a full raft of genre-specific anthologies. Carroll & Graf produces hardcover, trade paper, and mass-market paperback editions.

Carroll & Graf nonfiction emphasizes contemporary culture, current events, and issue-oriented perspectives (including investigative accounts, political and historical works, and top-end true crime); business, finance, and economics; self-improvement; humor and games; and high-interest topical reference.

In fiction and the literary arts, Carroll & Graf produces mainstream novels; tales of the supernatural, fantasy, and science fiction and is particularly adventuresome in suspense categories, publishing an array of titles that runs from traditional mysteries to future-horror crime thrillers with a literary bent.

Titles from Carroll & Graf: *According to Queeny; Angelica's Grotto; April Rising; Baby Boomer's Guide to Getting It Right the Second Time Around; The Barrens; Bloody Mary's Martyrs; The Book of Cain; Clint; Cozy; Creative Loveplay; Dead Secret; Death by Horoscope; Death of Kings; The Devil's Oasis; Dr. Mortimer and the Barking Man Mystery; The Dragon Syndicates; Fairness; A Few Minutes Past Midnight; The Flight of the Maidens; A Good Man in Evil Times; The House of Death; In the Heat of the Night; Kids' Letters to Harry Potter; The Last Battle; The Mammoth Book of UFOs; The Mammoth Book of Astounding Puzzles; The Mammoth Book of Legal Thrillers; Mouthing the Words; The Oppermanns; The Orange Curtain; A Prize for Princess; Pulp Masters; A Pure Clear Light; A Purple Thread for Sky; Russia's Heroes; The Sea Warriors; Soldier Sahibs; Star-Spangled Eden; Time; The Transfer Agreement; The Well; Within the Dark Man Calls; With a Gem-Like Flame.*

Mammoth Books is a line from Carroll & Graf that accents quantity as well as quality: The Mammoth list includes literary anthologies, works of topical appeal, and specialist interests. Titles here: *The Mammoth Book of New Sherlock Holmes Adventures* (edited by Mike Ashley); *The Mammoth Book of the Third Reich at War* (edited by Michael Veranov); *The Mammoth Book of Chess* by Graham Burgess; *The Mammoth Book of Carnival Puzzles* by David J. Bodycombe; *The Mammoth Book of Fortune Telling* by Celestine.

Carroll & Graf books is now completely owned by its distributor, Publishers Group West. Kent Carroll will be leaving the firm in early 2001, though his good name will continue to grace the firm he cofounded with Herman Graf.

Carroll & Graf Publishers no longer accepts unsolicited submissions. The house only accepts agented submissions. Query letters and SASEs should be directed to:

Philip Turner, Editor

CATBIRD PRESS

16 Windsor Road, North Haven, CT 06473
203-230-2391
e-mail: catbird@pipeline.com

Catbird Press (founded in 1987) is a small publisher with concentration in the areas of literary fiction, sophisticated humor, and Central European literature.

Fiction, humor, and titles with a literary appeal: *Performing Without a Stage: The Art of Literary Translation* by Robert Wechsler; *The Poetry of Jaroslav Seifert* (edited by George Gibian, translated from the Czech by Ewald Osers), the largest English-language collection of poetry by the Nobel Prize–winning poet; *It Came with the House* (short stories) by Jeffrey Shaffer; *A Double Life* (novel) by Frederic Raphael; *Labor Day* (novel) by Floyd Kensher; *Lovers and Murderers* (novel) by Vladimir Paral, translated from the Czech by Craig Cravens.

Catbird epitomizes small-press savvy in its continuing success in garnering industry publicity and promotion. Catbird Press is distributed to the trade by Independent Publishers Group. Proposals and SASEs should be directed to:

Robert Wechsler, Publisher

CCC PUBLICATIONS

9725 Lurline Avenue, Chatsworth, CA 91311
818-718-0507   fax: 818-718-0655

CCC Publications accents nonfiction trade books in crisply targeted categories: relationships, self-help/how-to, humor, inspiration, humorous inspirational titles, age-related and over-the-hill titles, games and puzzles, party books, cartoon books, gift books and merchandise, gag and blank books—and a group of titles mischievously cataloged as On the Edge. CCC publishes a number of books by bestselling author Jan King.

CCC produces primarily trade paperbacks, smaller gift-size editions, accessories (such as bags and bookmarks), and a line of audio works (including collections of answering-machine messages and sound effects).

In addition to books, CCC Publications also has a sidelines division: CCC Novel Tease Apparel Co. is one of the largest producers of embroidered occasion merchandise. Our themes include Bridal, New Parent, Baby, Age-Related, Anniversary, Over-the-Hill, Maternity, Graduation & Prom, and novelty items. Our fiber-optic design division is producing light-up caps and jackets for numerous major accounts.

On the CCC list: *Golfaholics* by Bob Zahn; *So, You're Getting Married* by Fred Sahner (illustrated by Lennie Peterson); *The Last Diet Book: You'll Ever Need!* by Dr. David Fisch; *Why God Makes Bald Guys* by Lennie Peterson; *Are We Dysfunctional Yet?* by Randy Glasbergen; *You Know He's a Two-Timing, Egomaniacal, Womanizing, Slimeball When . . .* by Jon Michaels; *Technology Bytes!* by Randy Glasbergen; *Love Dat Cat: 150 Wonderful Things You Can Do for Your Cat* by Jill Kramer; *How to Survive a Jewish*

Mother: A Guilt-Ridden Guide by Steven Arnold; *Red-Hot Monogamy in Just 60 Seconds a Day* by Patrick T. Hunt, M.D.; *50 Ways to Hustle Your Friends* by Jim Karol.

From On the Edge: *Men Are Pigs, Women Are Bitches* by Jerry King; *The Definitive Fart Book* by Desmond Mullan; *The Very Very Sexy Adult Dot-to-Dot Book* by Tony Goffe; *The Complete Wimp's Guide to Sex* by Jed Pascoe.

Jan King books: *Over the Hill . . . Deal with It!; Ladies, Start Your Engines: The Secrets for Restoring Romance, Passion and Great Sex in Your Relationship; Why Men Don't Have a Clue; Hormones from Hell; Killer Bras (and Other Hazards of the 50s).*

CCC (founded in 1983) orchestrates its own distribution. Query letters and SASEs should be directed to:

Cliff Carle, Editorial Director

Mark Chutick, Publisher

CHAPMAN AND HALL

Wolters-Kluwer Academic Publishers has purchased Chapman and Hall. The Chapman and Hall office has been closed.

CHAPTERS PUBLISHING

222 Berkeley Street, Boston, MA 02116
617-351-3855

Chapters specializes in books on cooking and nutrition, health and fitness, gardening, nature, country living, and home and family (including a series of weekend-projects books). The house offers a line of calendars with themes linked to its overall publishing interests. Chapters productions are recognized for their excellent book design and feature top-quality paper and binding.

Chapters Publishing (founded in 1991) publishes a select number of new titles each season and tends toward larger print runs; many Chapters titles enjoy sales through established book clubs. Chapters' evolution as a small commercial press has been markedly winning; and writers might note that the publisher's advances are generally comparable with those expected of large houses.

On the Chapters list: *The Joy of Coffee: The Essential Guide to Buying, Brewing and Enjoying* by Corby Kummer; *The New Games Treasury: More Than 500 Indoor and Outdoor Favorites with Strategies, Rules and Traditions* by Merilyn Dimonds Mohr; *The Complete Italian Vegetarian Cookbook: 350 Essential Recipes for Inspired, Everyday Eating* by Jack Bishop; *Mission Furniture You Can Build: Authentic Techniques and Designs for the Home Woodworker* by John Wagner; *Passing Strange: True Tales of New England Hauntings and Horrors* by Joseph A. Citro; *Eating Thin for Life: Food Secrets and Recipes from People Who Have Lost Weight and Kept It Off* by Anne M. Fletcher, M.S., R.D.; *Just the Weigh You Are: How to Be Fit and Healthy, Whatever Your Size* by Steven Jonas, M.D., and Linda Konner; *Tender Roses for Tough Climates* by Douglas Green; *Hummingbird Gar-*

dens: Attracting Nature's Jewels to Your Backyard by Nancy L. Newfield and Barbara Nielsen; *Orchid Simplified: An Indoor Gardening Guide* by Henry Jaworski.

Among Chapters series: Simply Healthful Cookbooks (recipes for tasty, healthful dishes without a lot of fuss and bother); How to Spot . . . (books written by professional naturalists that give a thorough description of a specific animal's habitat, range, diet, and breeding habits to increase amateur naturalists' enjoyment of animal watching).

The Curious Naturalist Series promotes works (in handsome trade paperback editions) from some of North America's finest naturalist writers, such as Peter Mathiessen, R. D. Lawrence, Adrian Forsyth, and Sy Montgomery. Titles here include *A Natural History of Sex: The Ecology and Evolution of Mating Behavior* by Adrian Forsyth; *Birds of Tropical America* by Steven J. Hilty; *Nature's Everyday Mysteries: A Field Guide to the World in Your Backyard* by Sy Montgomery; *Shark! Nature's Masterpiece* by R. D. Lawrence; *The Wind Birds: Shorebirds of North America* by Peter Mathiessen.

Chapters is distributed in the United States by W. W. Norton; Canadian distribution is handled by Key Porter Books. Chapters Publishing is now part of Houghton Mifflin Company. Query letters and SASEs should be directed to:

Lori Galvin-Frost, Assistant Managing Editor—Cookbooks

CHELSEA GREEN PUBLISHING COMPANY

205 Gates-Briggs Building, PO Box 428, White River Junction, VT 05001
802-295-6300   fax: 802-295-6444
www.chelseagreen.com

Chelsea Green publishes trade nonfiction in natural gardening and food, energy and shelter, nature and the environment, and regional books (including travel, social issues, history, and culture). Chelsea Green projects include a publishing co-venture with Real Goods Trading Company, designated by the imprimatur *Real Goods Independent Living Book.*

Chelsea Green Publishing Company (founded in 1984) is a compact, independent firm of individualistic spirit; the house continues to hone its publishing program through a small number of new seasonal releases (in hardcover and trade paper formats) and a hardy backlist. Chelsea Green's goal is to improve the visibility of sustainability by showing that even a small, home-based business can be instrumental in bringing about social change on a global scale.

On the Chelsea Green list: *The Neighborhood Forager: A Guide for the Wild Food Gourmet* by Robert Henderson; *The Natural House: Energy Efficient Environment Homes* by Daniel Chiras; *The Good Woodcutter's Guide: Chainsaws, Portable Sawmills, and Woodlots* by Dave Johnson; *The NEW Independent Home: People and Houses That Harvest the Sun* by Michael Potts; *The Straw Bale House* by Athena Swentzell Steen, Bill Steen, and David Bainbridge with David Eisenberon; *The Apple Grower: A Guide for the Organic Orchardist* by Michael Phillips; *The Blooming Lawn: Creating a Flower Meadow* by Yvette Verner; *The Earth-Sheltered House: An Architect's Sketchbook* by Malcolm Wells; *Bamboo Rediscovered* by Victor Cusack; *Gaviotas: A Village to Reinvent the World* by Alan Weisman; *Hammer. Nail. Wood.: The Compulsion to Build* by Thomas

P. Glynn; *The Bread Builders: Hearth Loaves and Masonry Ovens* by Daniel Wing and Alan Scott; *Global Spin: The Corporate Assault on Environmentalism* by Sharon Beder.

Chelsea Green handles its own distribution and distributes for a number of other small, innovative independent presses such as Green Books, Ltd.; Orwell Cove; OttoGraphics; Ecological Design Press; Harmonious Press; and Seed Savers Exchange. Query letters and SASEs should be directed to:

Hannah Silverstein, Production Editor

Stephen Morris, President and Publisher

Alan Berolzheimer, Acquisitions Editor

Jim Schley, Editor in Chief (Editor off the Grid)
   Born: November 13, 1956.
   Education: I went to Dartmouth College and have a B.A. in Literature and Creative Writing, a minor in Native American studies, and an M.A. in Poetry from Warren Wilson College.
   Employment history/editor career path: I have always loved books, so I knew early on that I wanted to teach or be involved in publishing. I started as an intern at *New England Review* magazine and climbed very quickly up the ladder to become an Editor.
   Personal interests: Reading, books, being outside, hiking, camping, activist politics; I built my house from scratch.
   What would you be doing if you were not an editor? It's impossible for me to imagine, but I would probably be teaching or doing some kind of freelance work.
   What has been your most successful book that you have acquired to date? *The Straw Bale House* by Athena Stein et al.
   What books have you acquired that make you the most proud? What books that you have acquired reflect the types of books you like to represent? *Gaviotias* by Alan Weisman.
   Do you represent fiction? If so, what do you look for? Yes. *Hammer. Nail. Wood* by Thomas Glynn; *Toyle,* which is a diary of someone working construction.
   Do you represent nonfiction? Yes, unusual how-to books, gardening, building.
   Do you require book proposals? If so, what do you look for in evaluating a book proposal? Yes, I need something written. In some cases I can help the author to do this, but in most I would expect to see an outline, writing samples, and so on.
   What process do you use for making a decision? What is the process for acquisition; is there a committee? Yes, there is a committee made up of the publisher, editor in chief, acquiring editor, and the production and marketing team.
   What kinds of nonfiction books do you want to see less of? I would like to see fewer submissions of material that we do not handle. We publish books that are related to ecology in some way. It needs to have something to do with environmentalism for us to take a look at it.
   Are you interested in work geared for the masses (readers of *People, The Star,* etc.)? No.
   Are agents important? Why? Yes, I think they are important. I've learned a lot about agents over the last couple of years; due to higher advances, they seem to be around more and more. Agents are very editor-savvy, they can think editorially and have good market-

ing skills. In most cases they are more sophisticated about the publishing business than the author, which helps to make the process go as smoothly as possible.

Do you like new writers? What should new writers do to break into the business? Yes, we publish many first-time authors. To break into the business, an author should learn how to write. Start out by getting something published in magazines, newspapers, and so on.

How should writers approach you? Look at our Web site, chelseagreen.com, for our guidelines. To approach me, send me a letter or an e-mail. I would rather have something in writing than a phone call.

What are some common mistakes writers make? What really gets on your nerves? Writers concentrate so much sometimes on their subject, they forget about all the other aspects of writing. To be a writer, you need to have more than a good idea and it takes more than saying, "Everyone I know loves this idea!"

What can writers do to get your attention and to avoid the slush pile? Our slush pile is quite thin. But to avoid it, be clear and articulate and have a unique idea. We're a writer-friendly house and try to keep the slush to a minimum.

What have been some of your craziest experiences with submissions? Someone once brought me an idea for a book that was all about using human feces as fertilizer.

What have been some of your best experiences with writers or in your job? I love being an editor and working with my colleagues. I love the working relationship between the author and the editor. The editor gets to learn all aspects of a writer, that individual's strengths, weaknesses, and so on. Some authors turn into your best friends.

What, if anything, makes you different from other editors? I'm a very literary person, I read on my own time, I bring the skills of being a literary editor to a practical level.

Is there anything you would like to see changed in the industry? I can't answer what I would change, but I can tell you what *not* to change. What I would not like to see is the intimacy that reading represents for some people being lost.

Any advice for writers? Be clear, be inventive, and take pleasure in the task.

C

CHELSEA HOUSE PUBLISHERS
(A SUBSIDIARY OF HAIGHTS CROSS COMMUNICATIONS)

1974 Sproul Road, Suite 400, Broomall, PA 19008-0914
610-353-5166   fax: 610-359-1439
www.chelseahouse.com   e-mail: Sales@Chelseahouse.com
The entire Chelsea House catalog is available on the Internet's World Wide Web.

Chelsea House produces books for older children and young adults, as well as books for elementary school students. The Chelsea House program accents the educational and institutional market in history, young-adult nonfiction, reference works, and literary criticism, as well as some works of broader appeal. Books on the Chelsea House list are most often produced in library-bound hardcover volumes, with some titles offered in trade paperback editions.

The editorial focus is on biography, culture, and history (American and worldwide). Broad interest areas include multicultural studies, social studies, literary criticism/English, general biography, mythology, sports, science, health/drug education, Spanish-language books, art, economics/business and personal finance, and law.

This approach is underscored by developmental marketing of such series as the Asian American Experience, Folk Tales and Fables, the Immigrant Experience, Lives of the Physically Challenged, Milestones in Black American History, Mysterious Places, Pop Culture Legends, Science Discoveries, and Sports Legends.

Chelsea House Publishers was originally instituted (founded in 1967) as a small press (then located in New York City) devoted to trade and reference titles on American history and popular culture. The company was bought in 1983 by Main Line Book Company, a library distributor based in suburban Philadelphia—whereupon the house's emphasis turned toward nonfiction for a young-adult readership.

Chelsea House series and highlights:

Famous Figures of the Civil War Era: *Jefferson Davis; Frederick Douglas; Ulysses S. Grant; Robert E. Lee; Abraham Lincoln; Children of the World; Civil War Leaders; Egyptian Kings and Queens; Classical Deities; Good Luck Symbols and Talismans; Greetings of the World.*

Cats and Dogs: A Basic Training, Caring, and Understanding Library: *Kittens & Cats; Skin Care for Cats; The Myth & Magic of Cats; The Well Trained Dog; Adopting a Dog; The Perfect Retriever; Traveling with Dogs; Puppy Training.*

Funtastic Science Activities for Kids: *Sound Fundamentals; Electricity & Magnetism Fundamentals; Heat Fundamentals.*

Major World Nations: *Albania, Argentina, Australia, Vietnam, West Bank, West Indies, Zimbabwe.*

Overcoming Adversity: *Tim Allen; Jim Carrey; James Earl Jones; Abraham Lincoln; William Penn.*

Superstars of Film: *Robert DeNiro; Johnny Depp; Brad Pitt; Keanu Reeves; John Travolta.*

They Died Too Young: *Kurt Cobain; Jimi Hendrix; Bruce Lee; John Lennon; Elvis Presley.*

Great Disasters: *Reforms and Ramifications; The Bombing of Hiroshima; The Exxon Valdez; Pearl Harbor; Three Mile Island; The Titanic.*

Male/Female Sports Stars: *Baseball Legends: Roger Clemens, Randy Johnson, Chipper Jones, Mark McGwire, Larry Walker; Superstars of Men's Figure Skating; Superstars of Men's Track and Field; Superstars of Women's Golf; Superstars of Women's Tennis; Superstars of Women's Gymnastics.*

The Illustrated Living History Series: *Tall Ships of the World; Woodland Indians; Revolutionary Medicine; Homebuilding and Woodworking in Colonial America.*

Women of Achievement: *Madeleine Albright; Hillary Rodham Clinton; Diana, Princess of Wales; Rosie O'Donnell; Elizabeth Taylor; Barbara Walters.*

Women Writers of English and Their Words: *Native American Women Writers; Jewish Women Fiction Writers; Asian-American Women Writers; British Women Fiction Writers of the 19th Century.*

Explorers of New Worlds: *Daniel Boone, Vasco de Gama; Lewis and Clark; Juan Ponce de Leon; The Viking Explorers.*

Crime, Justice, and Punishment: *Detectives, Private Investigators, and Bounty Hunters; Hate Crimes; The Jury System.*

Administrative, editorial, and warehousing facilities are currently located in the Philadelphia area. Query letters and SASEs should be directed to:

Sally Cheney, Editor in Chief

Kim Shinners, Director of Production

Pamela Loos, Manufacturing Manager

Sara Davis, Art Director

CHRONICLE BOOKS

Chronicle Children's Books

85 Second Street, 6th Floor, San Francisco, CA 94105
415-537-3730, 415-537-4441   fax: 415-537-4470
www.chroniclebooks.com   e-mail: customerfrontdesk@chroniclebooks.com

It was announced in late 1999 that this respected, independent firm was acquired from its corporate parent by the Associate Publisher, Nion McEvoy. McEvoy is the great-grandson of Michel de Young, who cofounded the *San Francisco Chronicle* with his brother Charles in 1865.

Founded in 1968, Chronicle Books publishes 300 new titles each year across its three divisions—Adult Trade, Children's, and Gift—in the subject areas of food, photography, art, architecture, interior design, gardening, pop culture, and fiction. It also distributes the publishing programs of the Princeton Architectural Press, North South Books, and innovative KIDS.

Chronicle's areas of interest include architecture and fine arts, design, photography, history and popular culture, the outdoors lifestyle (cuisine, pets, travel, home, and family), business and finance, and sports; the house issues a separate catalog for its children's books and for the gift list.

Chronicle Books was best known initially for its glossy paperback series of illustrated theme cookbooks. Since that era, Chronicle has gradually ventured further afield and currently publishes general nonfiction in both hardback and paperback. Chronicle Books also publishes selected fiction and literary works.

The Chronicle program features many selections of California regional interest (food, architecture, outdoors), with a focus on San Francisco and the Bay Area in particular (on both frontlist and backlist). The publisher has expanded its regional scope: Chronicle is open to an increasing variety of titles keyed to areas and travel destinations worldwide. Chronicle scored major bestseller hits with Nick Bantock's Griffin & Sabine fiction trilogy: *Griffin & Sabine, Sabine's Notebook,* and *The Golden Mean.*

Representative Chronicle titles: *Rolling Stones: The Decades of Rock & Roll; The Art of Monsters, Inc.; The Wildlife of Star Wars; World Architecture 1900–2000 Canada and US; Collapsible: The Genius of Space-Saving Design; Anti-Bride Guide: Tying the Knot Outside of the Box; The Knot Book of Wedding Gowns; The Il Fornaio Banking Book; Sweet and Savory Recipes from the Italian Kitchen; The Big Book of Soups and Stews; Living Modern: Bringing Modernism Home; United We Stand: Flying the American Flag; The Campus Guides: University of California Berkeley; Twin Towers Recovered.*

Chronicle Children's Books

Chronicle's children's lineup has a reputation for high quality and innovation in traditional and not-so-traditional formats. From the Chronicle children's list: *Hush Little Baby* by Sylvia Long; *If I Had a Horse* by Jonathan London (illustrated by Brooke Scudder); *Desert Dwellers: Native People of the American Southwest* by Scott Warren; *The Clubhouse Crew's Joker's Bag of Tricks* by Anne Civardi and Ruth Thomson (illustrated by Mark Oliver); *The Merchant of Marvels and the Peddler of Dreams* by Frederick Clement; *Beneath the Sea in 3-D* by Mark Blum; *Star Wars, The Empire Strikes Back, and Return of the Jedi* by John Whitman (illustrated by Brandon McKinney); *A Rainbow at Night: The World in Words and Pictures by Navajo Children* by Bruce Hucko.

Query letters and SASEs should be directed to:

Victoria Rock, Director and Associate Publisher—Children's books

Alan Rapp, Associate Editor—Adult Trade

Bill LeBlond, Editorial Director—Cookbooks

Christine Carswell, Associate Publisher—Adult Trade

Jay Schaefer, Editorial Director—Literature

Leslie Jonath, Senior Editor—Gardening, crafts, lifestyle

Sarah Malarky, Executive Editor—Popular culture: all areas

Mikyla Brunder, Editor—Craft/lifestyle

Kerry Tessaro, Editor—Gift

Leigh Anna Mendenhall, Editor—Children's, calendars

Lisa Campbell, Editorial Assistant—Adult Trade

Lisa McGuinness, Associate Editor—Children's

Samantha McFerrin, Editorial Assistant—Children's

Amy Treadwell, Editorial Assistant—Adult Trade

Ann Wilson, Managing Editor—Gift

Anne Bunn, Assistant Editor—Adult Trade

Beth Weber, Managing Editor—Children's

Brenda Modliszewski, Editorial Assistant—Gift

Doug Ogan, Editorial Assistant—Adult Trade

Jodi Davis, Assistant Editor—Adult Trade

Bill LeBlond, Editor—Cookbooks

CITY LIGHTS PUBLISHERS

261 Columbus Avenue, San Francisco, CA 94133
415-362- 8193   fax: 415-362-4921
www.citylights.com   e-mail: staff@citylights.com

City Lights publishes literary essays and criticism, biography, philosophy, literary fiction (including first novels) and poetry, and books on political and social issues, as well as artistically ecumenical volumes featuring both words and visual images.

City Lights Booksellers and Publishers (founded in 1953 by the poet-publisher Lawrence Ferlinghetti) is a San Francisco treasure, its bookstore a North Beach landmark and, above all else, a resolute cultural institution and self-embodied tradition. City Lights initially featured the Pocket Poets series, which introduced to a wider audience such writers as Gregory Corso, Allen Ginsberg, Jack Kerouac, and other Beats. Since then, as successive literary generations have commenced and terminated, City Lights remains most assuredly commercially viable.

Highlights from City Lights: *Book of Dreams* by Jack Kerouac; *San Francisco Beat: Talking with the Poets* (edited by David Meltzer); *Stories of Mr. Keuner by Bertolt Brecht* (translated from the German and with an afterword by Martin Chalmers); *Points of Departure: New Stories from Mexico* (edited by Monica Lavin, translated by Gustavo Segade); *Landscapes of War: From Sarajevo to Chechnya* by Juan Goytisolo (translated from the Spanish by Peter Bush); *Whose Song? And Other Stories* by Thomas Glave. The City Lights backlist embraces many of this publishing house's classic publications, such as *Howl and Other Poems* by Allen Ginsberg (available in the original Pocket Poets format, as well as in lavish trade-paper reprint); *Gasoline* (poetry) by Gregory Corso; *Scripture of the Golden Eternity* (literary writings) by Jack Kerouac; *William S. Burroughs's Yage Letters* (creative essays and imaginative correspondence with Allen Ginsberg); *Shock Treatment* (monologues from performance artist Karen Finley). Each fall, the publisher issues *City Lights Review: Annual Journal of Literature and Politics,* which brims with original poetry, essays, and fiction.

City Lights is distributed by Consortium Book Sales and Distribution and has its own in-house mail-order fulfillment department. Query letters and SASEs should be directed to:

Elaine Katzenberger, Acquisitions Editor—Latin American literature, women's studies, fiction

James Brook, Acquisitions Editor—Nonfiction

Nancy J. Peters, Publisher and Executive Editor

Robert Sharrard, Acquisitions Editor—Poetry and literature

CLEIS PRESS

PO Box 14684, San Francisco, CA 94114
415-575-4700

Cleis Press publishes books on sexual politics and self-help, lesbian and gay studies and culture, feminism, fiction, erotica, humor, and translations of world-class women's literature. Cleis titles cross-market from niches of gender and sexuality to reach the widest possible audiences.

Projects from Cleis Press (founded in 1980) garner numerous awards and reviews—and include many bestselling books. The house is committed to publishing the most original, creative, and provocative works by women (and a few men) in the United States and Canada.

From the Cleis list: *Sexually Speaking* by Gore Vidal; *The New Good Vibrations Guide to Sex: Tips and Techniques from America's Favorite Sex Toy Store* by Cathy Winds and Anne Semans; *Whole Lesbian Sex* by Felice Newman.

Cleis fiction includes: *Memory Mambo* by Achy Obejas; *A Ghost in the Closet* (mystery featuring Nancy Clue and the Hardly Boys) by Mabel Maney; *Best Gay Erotica* (published annually; series editor Richard Labonté); *Best Lesbian Erotica* (published annually; series editor Tristan Taormino).

Cleis Books is represented to the book trade by Publishers Group West. Query letters and SASEs should be directed to:

Felice Newman, Publisher and Acquisitions Editor

Frédérique Delacoste, Publisher and Acquisitions Editor

CLEVELAND STATE UNIVERSITY POETRY CENTER

1983 East 24th Street, Cleveland, OH 44115-2440
216-687-3986, 888-278-7473   fax: 216-687-6943
www.csuohio.edu/poetrycenter   e-mail: poetrycenter@csuohio.edu

Cleveland State University Poetry Center was begun in 1962 at Fenn College (which became Cleveland State in 1964); the center initiated its book-publishing program in 1971. The press publishes poets of local, regional, and international reach, generally under the aegis of one or another of the center's ongoing series. Under its flying-unicorn logo, CSU Poetry Center most often publishes trade paper editions, but has also offered some titles in hardbound. The press generally produces a limited number of new titles each year. In addition, the house maintains a full backlist.

CSU Poetry Center presents a variety of styles and viewpoints—some with evident sociopolitical bent, others with broadly inspirational themes, and others notable for their strong individualistic inflections. The Poetry Center sponsors the Poetry Forum workshop and presents programs of public readings.

The center sponsors an annual poetry contest; please contact the CSU Poetry Center for submission guidelines.

Before the Blue Hour, by Deirdre O'Connor, was selected by Marie Howe from 856 manuscripts as the contest winner in the 2001 competition. The competition is extremely tough, and the Poetry Center recommends that poets publish some individual poems in magazines and literary journals before submitting to this series. It is also recommended that prospective entrants review some of the work that the Poetry Center publishes.

Recent books from the Poetry Center: *The Largest Possible Life* by Alison Luterman; *The Book of Orgasms* (Imagination series) by Nin Andrews; *Attendant Ghosts* by George Looney; *A Short History of Pets* by Carol Potter. Shorter volumes and chapbooks: *Almost Home* by Susan Grimm; *The Book of Snow* by Mary Moore; *Troubled by an Angel* by Elizabeth Murawski; *Enough Light to Steer By* by Steven Reese.

The full range of publications from CSU Poetry Center Press includes award-winning volumes from established poets and releases from accomplished new writers. On the CSU list: *Blood Stories* by Martha Ramsey; *Hurdy-Gurdy* and *Hammerlock* by Tim

Seibles; *Order, or Disorder* by Amy Newman; *Refinery* by Claudia Keelan; *Fugitive Colors* by Chrystos; *Lives of the Saints and Everything* by Susan Firer; *The Long Turn Toward Light* by Cleveland poet and artist Barbara Tanner Angell; *At Redbones* by Thylias Moss; *The Sioux Dog Dance: Shunk ah weh* by Red Hawk.

Poetry Center books are distributed through Partners Book Distributing, Ingram, and Spring Church Book Company.

The Poetry Center accepts manuscripts only from November 1 to February 1 in connection with the Center's annual competition ($20 entry fee; full manuscripts only). For complete guidelines, send request plus SASE, or visit www.csuohio.edu/poetrycenter.

SASEs should be directed to:

Ted Lardner, Director

Rita Grabowski, Director

COBBLEHILL BOOKS

See Penguin Putnam, Inc.

COFFEE HOUSE PRESS

27 North Fourth Street, Suite 400, Minneapolis, MN 55401
612-338-0125   fax: 612-338-4004
www.coffeehousepress.org

Coffee House produces contemporary poetry, short fiction, and novels. The press is a source of contemporary writing that is challenging and thought-provoking, funny and furious, wildly diverse, even downright wacky, vibrant, and lyrical.

Coffee House Press is a nonprofit publisher dedicated to presenting visionary books of contemporary literature by diverse authors. The mission of Coffee House Press is to promote exciting, vital, and enduring authors of our time; to delight and inspire readers; to increase awareness of and appreciation for the traditional book arts; to enrich our literary heritage; and to contribute to the cultural life of our community. Coffee House Press publishes books that advance the craft of writing; books that present the dreams and ambitions of people who have been underrepresented in published literature; books that help build a sense of community; and books that help to shape our national consciousness.

Coffee House descends from what was originally (in the 1970s) a letterpress specialty firm, with a small list and an intimate circle of readers. The publisher then introduced titles geared toward an expanded readership; happily, conviviality and craft remain in strong evidence. Coffee House Press (established in 1984) is a publisher of trade titles and fine editions in a program that features a creative approach to the publishing arts. The house colophon is a steaming book, which is chosen to let the reader know (as the Coffee House motto runs) "where good books are brewing."

Titles from Coffee House: *Distance and Direction* by Judith Kitchen; *The Old Ballerina* by Ellen Cooney; *Shiny Pencils at the Edge of Things; Bird at My Window* by Rosa Guy; *Notes on the Possibilities and Attractions of Existence: Selected Poems 1965–2000* by Anselm Hollo; *Circle K Cycles; Vow to Poetry; Necessary Distance; The Man Who Swam with Beavers* by Nancy Lord; *Earliest Words; The Impossible* by Laird Hunt; *The Complexities of Intimacy* by Mary Caponegro; *That Kind of Sleep; Maraca; The Cotillion; Club Reservation.*

Coffee House books are printed on acid-free paper stock and have sewn bindings for long life and comfortable reading—as well they might, for the house features a comprehensive and enduring backlist.

Coffee House Press oversees its own marketing and sales network with the assistance of regional representatives; trade distribution is handled by Consortium. Query letters and SASEs should be directed to:

Allan Kornblum, Editor and Publisher

Christopher Fischbach, Managing Editor

Anitra Budd, Editorial Assistant

COLLECTOR BOOKS
(A DIVISION OF THE SCHROEDER PUBLISHING COMPANY)

5801 Kentucky Dam Road, Paducah, KY 42001
270-898-6211   fax: 270-898-8890
www.collectorbooks.com   e-mail: editor@collectorbooks.com

Mailing address:
PO Box 3009, Paducah, KY 42002-3009

Collector Books produces books for collectors in such fields as Depression glass, glassware, pottery and porcelain, china and dinnerware, cookie jars and salt shakers, stoneware, paper collectibles, Barbie dolls, dolls, toys, quilts, tools and weapons, jewelry and accessories, furniture, advertising memorabilia, bottles, Christmas collectibles, cigarette lighters, decoys, doorstops, and gas station memorabilia.

Collector Books (founded in 1969) is a division of Schroeder Publishing Company. Collector Books is dedicated to bringing the most up-to-date information and values to collectors in an attractive, high-quality format. Books are designed to be practical, easy-to-use tools that assist dealers and collectors in their pursuit of antiques and collectibles. Collector's publications are liberally illustrated editions, generally filled with histories, production facts and lore, research sources, and identification information. Collector Books also produces inventory ledgers for professional dealers and avid collectors.

The house produces a midsized list of new offerings each year and maintains a sizable backlist. Springing from its original principles of offering quality products, customer satisfaction, giving customers the most for their dollar and one-day sudden service, Collector Books has grown from 1 title on fruit jars to over 500 titles, and from a firm of 2 employees to over 70. Fueled by strong customer support, the publisher's list of new releases continues its recent growth.

Every August, Collector publishes *Schroeder's Antiques Price Guide,* which features more than 50,000 listings and hundreds of photographs for identification and current values, as well as background and historical information.

Sample titles: *Collector's Guide to Ideal Dolls, Identification & Values, 2nd Edition* by Judith Izen; *Collector's Guide to Children's Books, 1850–1950, Volume 2* by Diane McClure Jones and Rosemary Jones; *Dugan & Diamond Carnival Glass, 1909–1931* by Carl O. Burns; *B. J. Summers' Guide to Coca-Cola* by B. J. Summers; *Pocket Guide to Depression Glass and More (1920s–1960s)* (12th edition); *Stemware Identification Featuring Cordials with Values, 1920s–1960s* by Gene Florence; *McCoy Pottery: Collector's Reference and Value Guide* by Bob Hanson, Craig Nissen, and Margaret Hanson; *Antique and Collectible Buttons: Identification and Values* by Debra J. Wisniewski; *Antique and Vintage Clothing: A Guide to Dating and Valuation of Women's Clothing, 1850–1940* by Diane Snyder-Haug; *The Standard Knife Collector's Guide, 3rd Edition* by Roy Ritchie and Ron Stewart; *Garage Sale and Flea Market Annual, 9th Edition* by Bob and Sharon Huxford; *Schroeder's Collectible Toys* by Bob and Sharon Huxford; *Collector's Guide to Lunch Boxes* by Carole Bess White and L. M. White; *Flea Market Trader* by Bob and Sharon Huxford; *Collectible Glassware from the 40s 50s & 60s* by Gene Florence; *Collecting Blue Willow* by M. A. Hoffman; *Toy Car Collector's Guide* by Dana Johnson; *Vintage Golf Collectibles* by Ronald John; *Anchor Hocking's Fire King & More* by Gene Florence; *Standard Encyclopedia of Fiesta* by Bob and Sharon Huxford; *McDonald's Collectibles* by Gary Henriques and Audre DuVall; *Modern Guns, ID & Value Guide* by Russell and Steve Quertermous; *Racing Collectibles* by Diane McClure; *Indian Artifacts of the Midwest* by Lar Hothem.

Collector Books looks for its authors to be knowledgeable people who are considered experts within their fields. Writers who feel there is a real need for a book on their collectible subject and have available a large comprehensive collection are invited to contact the publisher at the house's mailing address.

Collector Books distributes its own list, targeting particularly bookstore buyers and antiques-trade professionals. Collector Books operates an especially strong mail-order program and purveys selected works from other publishers, including out-of-print titles in the collectibles and antiques field. Query letters and SASEs should be directed to:

Billy Schroeder, Publisher

Lisa Stroup, Editor

COMPUTE BOOKS

Compute Books (a computer-book specialist founded in 1979) is no longer doing business.

CONARI PRESS

2550 Ninth Street, Suite 101, Berkeley, CA 94710
510-649-7185
www.conari.com

Conari Press (founded in 1987) accents works in relationships, self-awareness, spirituality, and the family. In addition to books, Conari produces a select line of audiocassettes, project packets, buttons, and posters. The house began as a small press and has grown step by step, expanding cogently on its strong backlist base. Conari is one of the most successful regional independent publishers.

Conari titles: *The Food Revolution* by John Robbins; *Take It Personally* by Anita Roddick; *Once and Future Myths* by Phil Couslheam; *Mystics, Master Saints and Sages* by Bob and Judith Ullman; *The Way We Pray* by Maggie Oman Shannon; *Doctors Killed George Washington* and *Dracula Was a Lawyer,* both by Jack Mingo and Erin Barrett. Conari Press seeks to be a catalyst for profound change by providing enlightening books on topics that range from spirituality and women's issues to sexuality, relationships, and personal growth. Conari values integrity, process, compassion, and receptivity, in publishing projects as well as in the house's internal workings.

Conari is distributed to the trade by Publishers Group West; gift store distribution is handled through Sourcebooks, Inc.

Query letters and SASEs should be directed to:

Julie Kessler, Editorial Assistant

CONTEMPORARY BOOKS (A DIVISION OF MCGRAW-HILL)

2 Penn Plaza, New York, NY 10021
212-512-2000

Contemporary offers a general nonfiction lineup that accents the areas of self-improvement, personal finance, health, popular biography, and lifestyle. The list is particularly strong in sports, parenting, cooking, New Age, spirituality, relationships, and personality and historical profiles. Jamestown Publishing is a line that accents the educational market. Contemporary Books also has a major concentration in materials for adult education.

Originally an independent press, Contemporary Books (established in 1947) was part of the Tribune New Media organization and an imprint of NTC/Contemporary Publishing Company. The Tribune's book group was bought by McGraw-Hill in 2000. Contemporary has branched out from a former emphasis on sports titles to a program broad in scope that includes hardcover and trade paperback editions.

From Contemporary: *Lost on Everest: The Search for Mallory and Irving* by Peter Firstbrook; *Stages of the Soul* by Father Paul Keenana; *Coaching Yourself to Success* by Talane Miedaner; *Lapsing into a Comma* by Bill Walsh; *Unbelievably Good Deals and Great Adventures You Absolutely Can't Get Unless You're Over 50* by Joan Heilman (which is coming out in its 12th edition).

Contemporary's series of discount guides—*Buying Retail Is Stupid!*—is geared toward buying everything at up to 80 percent off retail; works include information on all aspects of discount shopping (mail order, outlets, resale stores, auctions, government surplus sales).

Contemporary Books handles its own distribution and also distributes books for the American Diabetes Association; FASA; Lowell House, which it now owns; and the *Sporting News.*

Query letters and SASEs should be directed to:

Judith McCarthy, Senior Editor—General trade and reference

Matthew Carnicelli, Senior Editor—General trade and nonfiction

CONTINUUM INTERNATIONAL PUBLISHING GROUP

370 Lexington Avenue, New York, NY 10017-6550
212-953-5858 fax: 212-953-5944
www.continuumbooks.com

Continuum's Web site contains details on forthcoming, current, and previously published titles, as well as links to Chiron Publications, Daimon Publications, Spring Publications, and Paragon House.

Continuum International publishes general trade books, texts, scholarly monographs, and reference works in the areas of literature and the arts, psychology, history and social thought, women's studies, and religion. Continuum offers more than 250 new publications a year, as well as 3,500 established backlist titles.

Continuum's broad focus integrates the fields of literature and criticism, psychology and counseling, religion, women's studies, and social issues of contemporary public interest. The house is known for its select line of books in popular and scholarly approaches to religion and philosophy. The Frederick Ungar imprint specializes in literature, film, and the performing arts.

Continuum and Crossroad Publishing Company were editorially independent components of the Crossroad/Continuum Publishing Group from 1980 into the early 1990s, since which time Continuum has pursued its own independent publishing trajectory now with a London office of former Cassell Academic and religion titles. (For Crossroad Publishing, see entry in the Directory of Religious, Spiritual, and Inspirational Publishers.)

From the Continuum trade list: *The Religious Art of Andy Warhol* by Jane Daggett Dillenberger; *Breaking the Fine Rain of Death: African American Health Issues and the Womanist Ethic of Care* by Emilie M. Townes; *The Family and HIV Today: Recent Research and Practice* (edited by Robert Bor and Jonathan Elford); *Legal Queeries* (edited by Leslie Moran, Sarah Beresford, and Daniel Monk); *The Lesbian and Gay Christian Movement: Campaigning for Justice, Truth and Love* (edited by Sean Gill); *Love Does No Harm: Sexual Ethics for the Rest of Us* by Marie M. Fortune; *Text and Psyche: Experiencing the Scripture Today* by Schuyler Brown; *The Way of Compassion: Survival Strategies for a World in Crisis* (edited by Martin Rowe); *Genetic Knowledge, Human Values, and Responsibility: An Essential Guidebook to the Moral and Scientific Issues in Gene Therapy* (edited by Jacquelyn Kegley); *Beyond the Human Species: The Life and Work of Sri Aurobindo and the Mother* by Georges Van Vrekham. Continuum's Hollywood-related titles: *Gielgud: A Threatened Life* by Jonathan Croall; *Fever* by Emanuel Levy; *Toms, Coons, Mulattoes, Mummies and Bucks: An Interpretation History of Blacks in American Films, 4th edition* by Donald Bogie; *Broadway the Golden Years* by Robert Emmet Long; *Robert Altman: Hollywood Survivor* by Daniel O'Brien; *The Cinema of Oliver Stone* by Norman Kagan; *The Cinema of Stanley Kubrick* by Norman Kagan; *Steven Spielberg: The Man, His Movies, and Their Meaning* by Philip M. Taylor.

Continuum is distributed through Books International. Continuum also distributes the distinguished publishing programs of Chiron Publications, Daimon Publications, Spring Publications, and Paragon House. Query letters and SASEs should be directed to:

Evander Lomke, Vice President and Managing Editor—Psychological counseling, history and the arts, literary criticism, current affairs, women's studies

Frank Oveis, Vice President and Senior Editor—Academic religious and biblical studies, world religions, spirituality

David C. Cook Publishing Company

See listing for Chariot/Victor in Directory of Religious, Spiritual, and Inspirational Publishers.

Copper Canyon Press

PO Box 271, Port Townsend, WA 98368
360-385-4925 or 877-501-1393   fax: 360-385-4985
coppercanyonpress.org

The Copper Canyon mission is to publish poetry distinguished in both content and design, within the context of belief that the publisher's art—like the poet's—is sacramental. Copper Canyon Press (founded in 1972) publishes in hardcover and paperback.

Within this ambitious vision, there are limitations; Copper Canyon generally does not sign many new writers. The house assigns its resources to furthering its established roster. The publisher's success in its aim is proven through abundant and continuing recognition of its authors via honors, awards, grants, and fellowships.

Copper Canyon Press publishes a list with such titles as these: *Always Beginning* by Maxine Kumin; *Armored Hearts* by David Bottoms; *August Zero* by Jane Miller; *Below Cold Mountain* by Joseph Stroud; *Black Iris* by Denise Levertov; *The Book of Questions* by Pablo Neruda; *Carrying Over* by Carolyn Kizer; *Communion* by Primaus St. John; *Cool, Calm, & Collected* by Carolyn Kizer; *Daughter's Latitude* by Karen Swenson; *Death Son* by Thomas McGrath; *East Window* by W. S. Merwin; *Exiled in the Word* by Jerome Rothenberg and Harris Lenowitz; *Heart of Bamboo* by Sam Hamill; *Iris of Creation* by Marvin Bell; *Like Underground Water* by Edward Lueders; *The Leaf Path* by Emily Warn; *Moment to Moment* by David Budbill; *Nightworks* by Marvin Bell; *On Poetry and Craft* by Theodor Roethke; *Rivers of Sale* by Shirley Kaufman; *The Sea and the Bells* by Pablo Neruda; *Selected Essays and Reviews* by Hayden Carruth; *The Steel Cricket* by Stephen Berg; *The Mercy Seat* by Norman Dubie; *The Wandering Border* by Jann Kaplinski; *Words for My Daughter* by John Balaban.

Copper Canyon distributes to the trade via Consortium.

Manuscripts for first, second, or third books are considered only in conjunction with the Hayden Carruth Award. Contact the press with an SASE for the entry form in September; submissions are accepted during the month of November, and the winner will be announced in February. The winner of the first Hayden Carruth Award is Sascha Feinstein, for his poems *Blues Departures*. Visit our Web site at www.ccpress.org for details.

All queries must include an SASE. We do not accept manuscript queries by e-mail. Copper Canyon generally does not sign many new writers. Query letters and SASEs should be directed to:

Sam Hamill, Editor

Michael Wiegers, Managing Editor

Thatcher Bailey, Publisher

Mary Jane Knecht, Associate Publisher

CRAIN BOOKS

See The McGraw-Hill Companies, Inc.

CRISP PUBLICATIONS

1200 Hamilton Court, Menlo Park, CA 94025
650-323-6100

Crisp Publications produces nonfiction business books and media packages; topic areas include management, personal improvement, human resources and wellness, communications and creativity, customer service, sales, small businesses, financial planning, adult literacy and learning, careers, and retirement and life planning. The house is known for a number of successful lines: 50-Minute Book, series in small-business ventures, and business titles keyed to use of new media.

Crisp Publications (founded in 1985) is a specialist in target business publishing and is equally expert at marketing the resultant product. Crisp offers an extensive selection of training programs (including self-study formats) that incorporate books, manuals, and audiovisual materials. The house's aim is to provide high-quality, cost-effective books and videos that can help business organizations succeed in competitive times.

The 50-Minute Book is Crisp's signature designation for books produced with the concept of being concise, easily read, and readily understood through personal involvement with exercises, activities, and assessments. Other Crisp lines are the Quick Read Series, the Small Business and Entrepreneurship Series, and the Crisp Management Library.

Highlights from Crisp: *Organizing Your Workspace* by Odette Pollar; *Measure and Manage Stress* by Herbert Kindler and Marilyn Ginsburg; *Motivating at Work: Empowering Employees to Give Their Best* by Twyla Dell; *Preventing Job Burnout* by Beverly A. Potter; *Preventing Workplace Violence* by Marianne Minor; *The Art of Communicating* by Bert Decker; *The New Supervisor* by Elwood N. Chapman; *Training Managers to Train* by Brother Herman Zaccarelli; *A Legal Guide for Small Business* by Charles Lickson.

Crisp Publications distributes through a commission sales force. Query letters and SASEs should be directed to:

George Young, Editor

CROWN PUBLISHING GROUP (PART OF RANDOM HOUSE)

Bell Tower

Clarkson Potter/Publishers

Crown Books

Crown Business

Harmony Books

Prima Publishing

Shaye Areheart Books

Three Rivers Press

299 Park Avenue, New York, NY 10171

Crown publishes a variety of trade-oriented fiction and nonfiction titles in hardcover and paperback. Crown (acquired by Random House in 1988) incorporates a number of Random House imprints and acquisitions that together make up the Crown Publishing Group. Crown imprints include Harmony Books, the Crown imprint, Crown Business, Clarkson Potter, Shaye Areheart Books, Three Rivers Press, Prima Publishing, and Bell Tower.

Three Rivers Press is a new designation for what was formerly Crown Trade Paperbacks. The imprint has branched out to include trade paperback originals. Titles include *Our Dumb Century* from The Onion Web site; *Business Plan for the Body* by Jim Karas; *Nine Steps to Financial Freedom* by Suze Orman; *Kick Me* by Paula Feig; *Black Rubber Dress* by Lauren Henderson; *We Got the Neutron Bomb* by Mark Spitz; *The New York Times Parent's Guide to the Best Books for Children* by Eden Ross Lipson; *The Latina's Bible* from former *Latina* magazine Senior Editor Sandra Guzman.

The House of Collectibles line of books is the definitive leader in price guides for a broad spectrum of collectibles, from coins to teacups to bottles. It includes the *Official Beckett Price Guides* to sports cards.

Crown fiction includes commercial novels across the trade spectrum, including mystery and suspense. Shaye Areheart books embraces a typically more vanguard literary tone.

Crown's fiction list and works of cultural and literary interest are exemplified by *Another City, Not My Own: A Novel in the Form of a Memoir* by Dominick Dunne; *When Elephants Dance* by Tess Uriza Holthe; *Sloppy Firsts* by Megan McCafferty; *Guenevere* by Rosalind Miles; *Nappily Ever After* by Trisha R. Thomas; Jean Auel's *Shelter's of Stone.*

Shaye Areheart Books includes such quality fiction as Chris Bohjalian's *Buffalo Soldiers* and Jeanne Ray's *Step, Ball, Change.*

Cuisine and lifestyle are areas of Clarkson Potter emphasis, most notably their beautiful four-color design books. Releases here include Martha Stewart's coffee-table editions and *The Barefoot Contessa* books by Ina Garten, the contemporary and innovative hostess guru of the Hamptons. Clarkson Potter has also recently published Melinda and Robert Blanchard's *A Trip to the Beach.*

The Crown Group's nonfiction encompasses popular titles in biography, history, art, pop-culture, contemporary culture, crime, sports, travel, popular and literary science, languages, spirituality, cookbooks, and self-help/how-to, antiques and collectibles, as well as popular-reference works.

Harmony's solid literary nonfiction list includes Deepak Chopra's *How to Know God;* Tara Bennett-Goleman's *Emotional Alchemy;* Stephen Mitchell's translation of *Bhagavad Gita;* Suzanne Finstad's biography of Natalie Wood, *Natasha;* Stephen Jay Gould's *I Have Landed;* Douglas Adams' *The Salmon of Doubt;* Roger Housden's *Ten Poems to Change Your Life.*

From the Crown imprint's nonfiction: *IBM and the Holocaust* by Edwin Black; *Tupac Shakur* by the editors of *VIBE Magazine,* foreword by Quincy Jones, introduction by

Danyl Smith; *Blinded by the Right* by David Brock; *The Intelligence Edge: How to Profit in the Information Age* by George Friedman, Meredith Friedman, John S. Baker, Jr., and Colin Chapman; Gene Simmons's *Kiss and Make-Up; Justice* by Dominick Dunne; *Lest We Forget: The Passage from Africa to Slavery and Emancipation* by Graham Hancock and Robert Bauval; as well as Suzanne Sommer's diet and fitness series.

Crown Business publishes both traditional and cutting-edge business books, such as *The Deviant Advantage: How Fringe Ideas Become Mass Market* by Ryan Mathews and Watts Walker; *Customers.com* by Patricia Seybold; *Execution: The Discipline of Getting Things Done* by Larry Bossidy and Ram Charan.

Please note that Harmony Books and Shaye Areheart Books do not accept manuscripts without agent representation.

Query letters and SASEs should be directed to:

Doug Pepper, Vice President and Senior Editor—Literary fiction and issue-oriented nonfiction

Kristin Kiser, Senior Editor—Thrillers and literary fiction; special interests, popular culture, music, sports, popular science, and narrative nonfiction

Pete Fornatale, Associate Editor—Adult trade fiction and nonfiction; does not accept unsolicited manuscripts

Rachel Kahan, Associate Editor—Historical fiction, narrative nonfiction, contemporary fiction

Steve Ross, Senior Vice President and Editorial Director—Adult trade fiction and nonfiction; also oversees Times Books and Times Business Imprints; does not accept unsolicited manuscripts

Emily Loose, Executive Editor

Chris Jackson, Senior Editor

Caroline Sincerbeaux, Assistant Editor

Stephanie Higgs, Editorial Assistant

Jonathan Slonim, Editorial Assistant

Kate Donovan, Editorial Assistant

Dorianne Steele, Editorial Assistant

Claudia Gable, Editorial Assistant

Clarkson Potter/Publishers

Clarkson Potter is a leader in nonfiction, beautifully illustrated books about cookery, gardening, and interior design. Its authors include Martha Stewart, Mario Batali, Chris Casson Madden, and Ina Garten. Titles indicative of this list are *Decorating with Color: The Best of Martha Stewart Living; Paraiso Mexicano Gardens, Landscapes, and Mexican Soul* by Marie-Pierre Colle; *The Fourth Star* by Leslie Brenner; *Eden on Their Minds: American Gardeners with Bold Visions* by Starr Ockenga; *Santa Fe Houses* by Christine Mather, with Sharon Woods; *The Babbo Cookbook* by Mario Batali; *Dim Sum* by Ellen

Leong Blonder; *Kaffeehaus* by Rick Rodgers; *Terence Conran Kitchens: The Hub of the Home* by Terence Conran; *The Art of Expecting* by Veronique Vienne.

Annetta Hanna, Senior Editor—Design, gardening, biography, popular culture, how-to style and decorating books

Lauren Shakely, Senior Vice President and Editorial Director—How-to style and decorating books, art books, gardening, biography

Margot Schupf, Associate Editor

Pam Krauss, Vice President and Executive Editor—Cooking and food, how-to style and decorating books, gardening, narrative nonfiction

Roy Finamore, Editor and Special Projects—Cooking and food, design and architecture, special projects, style and decorating, biography, popular culture

Katie Workman, Senior Editor—Cooking and food, popular culture, how-to style and decorating books

Born: March 11, 1968.

Education: Major in British American Literature; Minor in Psychology and Minor in Philosophy from George Washington University.

Employment history/editor career path: I am a rare case; I started working at Clarkson Potter right out of college and have been here ever since—10 years.

Personal interests: Cooking, food related things, volunteer work, working out, and I have a new baby.

What would you be doing if you were not an editor? Something in the food world or doing volunteer work. Maybe working on the Internet.

What has been your most successful book that you have acquired to date? The *Pillsbury* series; we just published the ninth one. Probably the most successful was *The Pillsbury Best of the Bake-Off*. This sold more than one million copies.

What books have you acquired that make you the most proud? What books that you have acquired reflect the types of books you like to represent? *Almost Vegetarian* by Diana Shaw (sold 200,000) copies; *The Blue Ribbon Country Cookbook* by Diane Roupe (it has more than 1,000 recipes from more than 10 years of award-winning blue ribbon food in Iowa).

Do you represent fiction? No.

Do you represent nonfiction? Yes, mostly branded books (company-connected books), such as Pillsbury, Omaha Steaks, and so on.

Do you require book proposals? If so, what do you look for in evaluating a book proposal? Yes. The right balance of editorial integrity, must have a strong emphasis on the market for the book, who the audience is, and what is your competition.

What process do you use for making a decision? What is the process for acquisition; is there a committee? We have an editorial meeting once a week with all the editors, sales, and marketing people at Clarkson.

Are you interested in work geared for the masses (readers of *People, The Star,* etc.)? Yes.

Are agents important? Why? Yes, they are part of the screening process.

Do you like new writers? What should new writers do to break into the business? It's tough to break into this business. I think getting an agent helps. Go to the bookstore and read books similar to the one you are proposing to write, read the acknowledgments section of the book to find the agents acknowledged. This is a good way to find an agent who obviously represents work in your field. Put together a good proposal and use all of your contacts that you know.

How should writers approach you? I look at everything that comes to me; do your homework and know what I like to see and then mail me something (snail mail).

What are some common mistakes writers make? What really gets on your nerves? Lateness. Authors who cannot meet deadlines. When querying me, don't tell me that no one has written a book like yours; chances are, if you do your research, someone has.

What can writers do to get your attention and to avoid the slush pile? Write a good concise cover letter telling me why you should be the person to write this book. Do your homework!!

What have been some of your best experiences with writers or in your job? Some of my authors have become really good friends of mine. The Pillsbury relationship has been wonderful. I love when something unique happens with a book.

What, if anything, makes you different from other editors? I do think of things from a sales and marketing perspective. I like to be involved with all aspects of the book, not just editing.

Is there anything you would like to see changed in the industry? We should all remember that the focus of book publishing is on the authors and books themselves. I would like to see everyone in the industry having more fun and enjoying the publishing process.

Crown Business

Crown Business is one of the leading publishers of business titles, whose authors include Charles Schwab, Suze Orman, Ram Charan, Patricia Seybold, and Michael Hammer. Representative titles include *The Secret Code of the Superior Investor: How to Be a Long-Term Winner in a Short-Term World* by James K. Glassman; *A Good Hard Kick in the Ass* by Rob Adams; *Love Is the Killer App* by Tim Sanders; *The Provocateur* by Larry Weber.

John Mahaney, Executive Editor Crown Business

Harmony Books

Harmony Books publishes literary fiction and a variety of nonfiction categories, including spirituality, health, and psychology, as well as memoir, science, and general nonfiction. Its authors include Stephen Jay Gould, Carolyn Myss, Deepak Chopra, and Suzanne Finstad. Titles indicative of this list are *Mozart's Brain and the Fighter Pilot: Unleashing Your Brain's Potential* by Richard Restak, M.D.; *The Salmon of Doubt* by Douglas Adams; *Simple Spells for Hearth and Home* by Barrie Dolnick.

Bell Tower (a division of Harmony Books) publishes titles from many sacred traditions—"books that nourish the soul, illuminate the mind, and speak to the heart." Authors include Stephen Levine, Bernie Glassman, Ram Dass, and Rabbi Joseph Telushkin.

Queries and SASEs should be directed to:

Linda Loewenthal, Vice President, Executive Editorial Director, Harmony Books and Three Rivers Press—Narrative nonfiction, spirituality, psychology

Jake Morrissey, Senior Editor, Harmony—Literary nonfiction, science, literary fiction

Shaye Areheart, Vice President, Editorial Director, Shaye Areheart Books/Harmony Books—Literary fiction, biographies, humor, wide general nonfiction interests

Toinette Lippe, Editorial Director, Bell Tower—Spirituality and inspiration (not reincarnation, astrology, crystals, and the like)

Prima Publishing

3000 Lava Ridge Court, Roseville, CA 95661
916-787-7000   fax: 916-787-7001
www.primapublishing.com

Prima Publishing was founded in 1984 with its first self-published book, *Travel Free.* Ben and Nancy Dominitz began this venture in their home, and it soon grew to be one of the largest independent book publishers in North America, reaching $100 million in annual sales by 1999. By concentrating on topics such as health, business, parenting and education, homeschooling, current affairs, technology, and electronic games, Prima established itself as an authority in these chosen areas of expertise.

In late March of 2001, the Crown Publishing Group under Random House acquired Prima Publishing. With a fluid and innovative list, Prima Publishing's trade group publishes books in a wide variety of categories, including business, current affairs, parenting and education, weddings, gift, spirituality, inspiration, network marketing, pets, crafts, health, writing and reference, and travel. Prima is also the publisher of the book you are now reading, *Writer's Guide to Book Editors, Publishers, and Literary Agents, 13th Edition: Who They Are! What They Want! And How to Win Them Over!* by Jeff Herman.

Representative titles include *Walt Disney World with Kids* by Kim Wright Wiley; *Wave 3* and *Wave 4* by Richard Poe; *Your First Year in Network Marketing* by Mark Yarnell and Rene Reid Yarnell; *The Homeschooling Book of Answers* by Linda Dobson; *Ultimate Smoothies, Ultimate Juicing* and *Summer Smoothies* by Donna Pliner Rodnitzky; *Opening the Xbox* by Dean Takahashi; *The Ultimate History of Video Games* by Steven L. Kent; *The Wealthy Barber* by David Chilton; *The Frugal Bride* by Cynthia Clumeck Muchnick; *The Servant Leader* by James A. Autry; *The Complete Book of Triathlons* by Sally Edwards; *Encyclopedia of Natural Medicine* by Michael Murray, N.D., and Joseph Pizzorno, N.D. Prima also has a strong list of highly successful book series, including the POSITIVE DISCIPLINE series by Jane Nelsen, Ed.D.; A GIRL'S WORLD series by A Girl's World Productions Inc.; the COACHING GIRLS series; RELOCATING series; THE NATURAL PHARMACIST series, edited by Steve Bratman, M.D.; the NEW HOPE health series; and THE ABSOLUTE BEGINNER'S GUIDES.

Forum, Prima's serious nonfiction imprint, covers topics such as current affairs, public policy, libertarian/conservative thought, high-level management, individual empowerment, and historical biography. Recent titles include *bin Laden: The Man Who Declared War on America* by Yossef Bodansky; *The Age of Reagan, 1964–1980* by Steven F. Hayward; *The Secret History of the CIA* by Joseph J. Trento; *The New Thought Police* by Tammie Bruce; *Triumph* by H. W. Crocker III; *Let Us Talk of Many Things* by William F.

Buckley, Jr.; and the latest in the ON LEADERSHIP series, *Jack Welch on Leadership* by James A. Robinson.

Prima Venture gives entrepreneurs and executives the tools to thrive in the New Economy, with professional books on growing and innovating businesses. Venture titles include *The Complete M&A Handbook* by Tom Taulli; *Successful Energy Sector Investing* by Joe Duarte; *The Power of Cult Branding* by Matthew W. Ragas and B. J. Bueno; *The Complete Guide to Employee Stock Options* by Frederick Lipman; *The Internet and E-Commerce Legal Handbook* by Scott Pink.

Query letters and SASEs for Prima Publishing should be directed to:

Alice Feinstein, Editorial and Publishing Director

Dan Foster, Managing Editor—Biography, entertainment, history, and collectibles

David Richardson, Editor, Prima Forum and Prima Venture—current affairs, business, management, marketing, finance, and investing

Denise Sternad, Editor—Weddings, preteen and teen girls, sports and fitness, home, pets, and crafts

Jamie Miller, Editor—Parenting and education, homeschooling, health, and family travel

Jennifer Basye Sander, Senior Editor—Cookbooks, small business and home office, women's issues, natural medicine, network marketing, and current affairs

Shaye Areheart Books

Shaye Areheart Books is devoted to contemporary literary and commercial fiction. Authors include Chris Bohjalian, Craig Nova, Jeanne Ray, John Smolens, Sheri Reynolds, and Maggie Estep.

Shaye Areheart, Vice President, Editorial Director, Shaye Areheart Books/Harmony Books—Literary fiction, biographies, humor; wide general nonfiction interests

Three Rivers Press

Three Rivers Press is the trade paperback imprint of the Crown Group. It publishes reprints of books issued initially in hardcover by the other Crown imprints, as well as original softcover titles. Titles exemplary of its original list are *Our Dumb Century* by Scott Dikkers; *Black Planet* by David Shields; *I Hope You Have a Good Life* by Campbell Armstrong; *Aha!* by Jordan Ayan.

Three Rivers Press is also a strong force in the area of antiques and collectibles books. It is the home of Ralph and Terry Kovel, as well as the popular guides from the House of Collectibles.

Query letters and SASEs should be directed to:

Linda Loewenthal, Vice President, Executive Editorial Director, Harmony Books and Three Rivers Press—Narrative nonfiction, spirituality, psychology

Becky Cabaza, Executive Editor, Three Rivers Press—Health, fitness, parenting, humor, business, pop science, narrative nonfiction

Carrie Thornton, Editor, Three Rivers Press—Pop culture, music, humor, gay and lesbian, dating and relationships, film

Jennifer Kasius, Editor, Three Rivers Press—Pop-culture, narrative nonfiction, health, dating and relationships, trade fiction, and parenting

---

DALKEY ARCHIVE PRESS

Illinois State University, Campus Box 4241, Normal, IL 61790-4241
309-438-7555   fax: 309-438-7422
www.dalkeyarchive.com   e-mail: cwpost@dalkeyarchive.com

Dalkey Archive (founded in 1984) is dedicated to breakthrough artistic expression in fiction. Dalkey's writers are among the most influential stylists on the printed page. Dalkey Archive Press is a division of the Center for Book Culture.

From the Dalkey Archive list: *The Age of Wire and String* by Ben Marcus; *Take Five* by D. Keith Mano; *Cigarettes* by Harry Mathews; *Tlooth,* also by Harry Mathews; *Excitability* by Diane Williams; *A Short Rhetoric for Leaving the Family* by Peter Dimock; *The Polish Complex* by Tadeusz Konwicki (introduction by the translator Richard Lourie); *The Dick Gibson Show* by Stanley Elkin; *Pushkin House* by Andrei Bitov; *Chromos* by Felipe Alfau; *Odile* by Raymond Queneau; *The Engineer of Human Souls* by Josef Skvorecky (translated by Paul Wilson).

Dalkey Archive distributes through Chicago Distribution Center. Query letters and SASEs should be directed to:

Chad Post, Editor

DAW BOOKS, INC.

375 Hudson Street, New York, NY 10014
212-366-2096
www.dawbooks.com

DAW Books publishes science fiction, fantasy, science fantasy, future fiction and future fantasy, dark suspense, and horror. DAW publishes mass-market paperbound originals and reprints, as well as hardcovers and trade paperbacks.

The DAW line includes masterful genre-keyed anthologies that showcase some of the most respected writers in their respective literary provinces. DAW typically produces a medium-sized seasonal list of new titles. The DAW backlist is replete with successful individual titles, along with a host of perennially selling series.

DAW Books (founded in 1971) is at the forefront of the literary categories and genres in which it specializes. The house is affiliated with Penguin Putnam, Inc.

Now, more than 25 years and more than a thousand titles later, DAW has a well-deserved reputation for discovering and publishing the hottest talents in the industry. Many stars of the science fiction and fantasy field made their debuts in the pages of a DAW book, including Ted Williams, C. J. Cherryh, Mercedes Lackey, Melanie Rawn, C. S. Friedman, Jennifer Robertson, and Tanith Lee.

From DAW Books: *Takes a Thief: A Novel of Valdemar* by Mercedes Lackey; *The Dragons of the Cuyahoga* by S. Andrew Swann; *The Lion Throne* by Jennifer Robertson; *Past Imperfect* (edited by Martin H. Greenberg and Larry Segriff); *The Sea of Silver Light* by Tad Williams.

DAW distribution is through an affiliation with Penguin USA. Query letters and SASEs should be directed to:

Peter Stampfel, Submissions Editor

DEACONESS PRESS
See Fairview Press.

DEARBORN TRADE PUBLISHING (A KAPLAN PROFESSIONAL COMPANY)

155 North Wacker Drive, Chicago, IL 60606-1719
312-836-4400   fax: 312-836-1021
www.dearborn.com

Dearborn Trade Publishing is the nation's premier provider of personal finance, investment, real estate, general business, and management resources for consumers and professionals. In 2001 Dearborn launched a list dedicated to sales and marketing topics.

Dearborn has constantly been redefining and refining its direction ever since the trade division started actively publishing practical how-to books for consumers and investors in 1986. Prior to that, the company (founded in 1967) focused on training for financial professionals in real estate, insurance, and securities. Dearborn remains the premier provider—worldwide—of prelicensing, continuing professional education, and training in the financial services and real estate industries. Dearborn Trade publishes titles intended for individual book buyers, whether they are general consumers or CEOs of corporations. Specific topics include personal finance, securities, trading, tax issues, estate planning, consumer real estate, general management, corporate biographies, business leader biographies, entrepreneurship, sales, and marketing.

From Dearborn: *The Power of DFSS* by Subir Chowdhury; *Blues Clues for Success* by Diane Tracy; *Always Think Big* by Thomas N. Duening and John M. Ivancevick; *Low Risk Real Estate Investments* by Peter Conti and David Finku; *Best Intentions* by Victoria Collins and Colleen Barney.

Query letters and SASEs should be directed to

Don Hull, Editorial Director—Finance and investing

Mary B. Good, Acquisitions Editor—Consumer real estate and entrepreneurship

Jean Iversen, Senior Acquisitions Editor—Management and general business
Born: September 21.
Education: B.A. in Journalism from Columbia College, Chicago, Illinois.
Employment history/editor career path: I was a magazine Editor and writer before coming to the book publishing industry. I was an Acquisitions Editor at Publications

International, a consumer book Publisher in the suburbs of Chicago, for three years before coming to Dearborn, where I have been for almost two years now. I love being back in the city!

Personal interests: Reading, of course. I also do some freelance writing for local newspapers and music publications on rock and entertainment in general. My original major was piano performance, and I sung/played in rock bands for over 10 years. About 5 years ago I discovered scuba diving and have since been to Mexico, the Bahamas, and Bonaire. It's one of those incredible experiences in life.

What would you be doing if you were not an editor? On the other side of the fence—writing. Or an underwater photographer.

What has been your most successful book that you have acquired to date? A couple of titles: *Web Rules* by Tom Murphy, which chronicles the return of power to the consumer via the Internet; and *Handy Ma'am,* a how-to home repair and decorating guide by PBS's femme fatale Beverly DeJulio.

What books have you acquired that make you the most proud? What books that you have acquired reflect the types of books you like to represent? *Lightning in a Bottle* by author David Baum, a collection of over 60 stories and anecdotes on the subject of corporate change. It's David's first book, and we received so much positive feedback when it came out. It was humorous and enlightening, captivating and compelling—all the things we were trying to be. And because we succeeded, it's been a very positive and fulfilling book to be a part of. I've actually attracted very credible authors who saw and read the book and wanted to be a part of the Dearborn fold.

Do you represent fiction? No.

What do you want to see less of? Too many proposals are on dated topics or written from an unoriginal perspective.

Do you represent nonfiction? Yes. Management/general business.

Do you require book proposals? If so, what do you look for in evaluating a book proposal? Generally, I prefer a completed proposal and either one sample chapter or relevant writing samples. However, a query letter with a detailed description and compelling book synopsis can also be effective. In evaluating proposals, I look for timely topics or topics with a fresh spin or perspective on them. The author *must* be shedding new light on the subject. I also look for authors who are aggressive promoters and who bear impressive credentials.

Are certain aspects of a book proposal given more weight than others? Obviously, the ability of authors (or ghostwriters) to write, but also their credentials and name recognition.

What process do you use for making a decision? What is the process for acquisition; is there a committee? We are a small house, so the process is probably quicker than most; though, because we are small, each project is scrutinized very carefully. I generally present each project to our editorial committee, which consists of key sales, marketing, and editorial staff. Based on the feedback at this meeting, I will make an offer to the author. Our current president lets us acquire projects on our own, thereby giving us the autonomy we need to function as a growing, innovative publishing house.

What kinds of nonfiction books do you want to see less of? Ones that tell the same old story that we heard last year, the year before, and so on. Tell us something new!

Are you interested in work geared for the masses (readers of *People, The Star,* etc.)? No. We're a business publisher. Though one of our books, *Rags to Riches,* did get excerpted in the *National Enquirer*!

Are agents important? Why? Yes, especially for first-time authors. I see many proposals that are good, but way too rough, and suggest that the writer contract an agent or editorial adviser to help out in the proposal process. A good agent can also help an author through the contract negotiation process, as some authors need an objective party to explain the terms. I wouldn't say that every author needs an agent, but it is crucial in many cases.

Do you like new writers? What should new writers do to break into the business? I sign new writers and repeat writers. I've been very successful with many new writers. Because they are new to the process, it can be a lot of fun to work with them and be creative and guide them through the process. It's nice to hear, at the end of the development process, that they'd like to do another book with us and that they enjoyed the process. Writing a book can certainly be a very grueling process.

How should writers approach you? Either a query letter or a completed proposal with a sample chapter or relevant writing samples. I've gotten phone calls from referrals, and that can be okay, too, because I've already heard about their idea and they've been referred to me, but those are exceptions. Maybe it's just me, but I don't like it when authors or agents e-mail unsolicited proposals to me.

What are some common mistakes writers make? What really gets on your nerves? If you misspell my name or anything in your query letter, then you're representing yourself as unprofessional and I can't take you very seriously. Also, proposals on topics that we would obviously never publish. Please read our catalogs, visit our Web site, or do some research at the bookstore or library. Get to know us before you send us a proposal.

What can writers do to get your attention and to avoid the slush pile? Again, propose timely topics with a fresh spin that are consistent with our publishing program. Present yourself as a credible, promotable author. If your writing is weak, get help—from the proposal stage on up. Convince us that we can't afford to not publish your title, and be realistic. Editors see through hyperbole more than anyone else.

What have been some of your craziest experiences with submissions? I received a submission for a book on *How to Start Your Own Organic Farm.*

What have been some of your best experiences with writers or in your job? Some of my best experiences have been with writers who were very willing collaborators and found creative ways to either write/organize or promote their books and saw their book as one piece of their professional portfolio.

What, if anything, makes you different from other editors? This can only be told by those who have worked with me! I have been told, however, that I involve myself quite a bit more than other editors and truly assist in the development of the manuscript, rather than putting the rubber stamp of approval on their first draft and pushing it on the copyeditor. I take a personal interest in every detail of each author's book and do my best to help all authors realize their fullest potential.

Is there anything you would like to see changed in the industry? It is, of course, extremely tough to be in an industry where almost all of your product is sold on a consignment basis. That said, I think the evolution of electronic publishing is crucial to being competitive in this marketplace and should be developed in a way that is fruitful to both authors and publishers.

Any advice for writers? Do your homework. Research publishers. Know your topic inside and out—you want to be perceived as the "expert" on your topic. And seek editorial assistance—whether you're a published author or not—because too many authors work in a vacuum and become myopic in the development of their work.

DELACORTE PRESS
See Bantam Dell Publishing Group.

DELL PUBLISHING (A DIVISION OF BANTAM DELL PUBLISHING)
See Bantam Dell Publishing Group.

THE DERRYDALE PRESS
4720 Boston Way, Lanham, MD 20706
fax: 301-429-5748
www.derrydalepress.com

The Derrydale Press was founded in 1927 by Eugene V. Connett III and then quickly became America's preeminent publisher of books on outdoor sports. An avid sportsman himself, Connett sought out manuscripts by the leading sportsmen and sportswomen of his generation, for whom he published books of the highest quality materials.

The Derrydale Press currently has over 150 titles in print and continues to publish in the areas of fishing, hunting, equestrian sports, sporting art, the outdoors, and other aspects of nature. The Derrydale Press is an imprint of the Rowman & Littlefield Publishing Group, whose sister company, National Book Network (NBN), is responsible for the distribution of Derrydale books.

Please direct query letters with SASEs to:

Stephen Driver, Associate Editor

DIOGENES PUBLISHING
PO Box 40, Sutter Creek, CA 95685
209-296-6082   fax: 209-296-6082
www.diogenespublishing.com   e-mail: sales@diogenespublishing.com

Diogenes is a small-sized house specializing in social commentary, philosophy, psychology, humor, and satire. Diogenes is committed to publishing honest and truthful writing that evaluates any facet of contemporary society, including its values, beliefs, families, media, and celebrities. Diogenes does NOT publish self-help, spiritual, or inspirational material. Instead, the house promotes independent thinking and represents writers who offer alternative and unpopular points of view. Diogenes is more concerned with the quality than the quantity of its publications, opting for works that appeal to a thoughtful and critical—if small—audience.

Most recent publication: *Happiness and Other Lies* by Mary Massaro. Diogenes distributes to the trade through Ingram, Book People, and Quality Books. Its Web site links to Amazon and Barnes & Noble.

Query letters should be directed to:

Mary Gillissie, President

THE DOUBLEDAY BROADWAY PUBLISHING GROUP
(A DIVISION OF RANDOM HOUSE)

D

Broadway Books (See separate listing.)

Currency

Doubleday

Doubleday Religious Publishing

Doubleday/Image

Main Street Books

Nan A. Talese

Harlem Moon

1540 Broadway, New York, NY 10036
212-354-6500

The Doubleday Broadway Publishing Group is known for its strong commercial lists in both fiction and nonfiction. This group has experienced numerous changes over the past few years, but continues to maintain its strong presence in the marketplace. One of the notable changes is that Anchor Books has joined with Vintage Books to create Vintage Anchor, currently part of the Knopf Publishing Group. (See The Knopf Publishing Group for more details.) Meanwhile, Broadway Books, a relatively new imprint, is quickly becoming a well-known division with both writers and book buyers. The Doubleday Broadway Publishing Group publishes titles in hardcover, paperback, and audio formats.

Direct queries and SASEs to:

Jennifer Josephy, Executive Editor—Cookbooks

Ann Campbell, Editor—Narrative nonfiction, women's history, spirituality, health and fitness

Charles Conrad, Vice President and Executive Editor—New nonfiction projects: popular culture, social history, literary nonfiction; contemporary literary and quality fiction; in charge of trade-paperback reprints

Suzanne Oaks, Editor—Commercial nonfiction, investigative and other business stories

Gerald Howard, Editorial Director—Narrative nonfiction and literary fiction

Eric Major, Director, Religious Publishing—Scholarly and popular works on religion and spirituality; titles likely to provoke religious controversy; books covering a wide range of religious thought, including Hinduism and Buddhism; Judaica

Trace Murphy, Editor, Religious Publishing—Scholarly and popular works on religion and spirituality

Deb Futter, Executive Editor—Fiction and general nonfiction

Amy Scheibe, Senior Editor—Fiction and general nonfiction

Janet Hill, Executive Editor, Harlem Moon Imprint—African American subjects

Currency

Currency publishes hardcover business books in a variety of categories, including business narrative and biography, general business, marketing/sales, careers, personal finance and investing, leadership, and entrepreneurship.

Titles indicative of this list are *Creative Destruction: Why Companies That Are Built to Last Underperform the Market—And How to Successfully Transform Them* by Richard Foster and Sarah Kaplan; *TheStreet.com Guide to Smart Investing in the Internet Era: Everything You Need to Know to Outsmart Wall Street and Select Winning Stocks* by Dave Kansas and the writers of TheStreet.com; *The Art of Innovation: Lessons in Creativity from IDEO, America's Leading Design Firm* by Thomas Kelley, with Jonathan Littman; *The Anatomy of Buzz: How to Create Word of Mouth Marketing* by Emanuel Rosen; *Maximum Success: Changing the 12 Behavior Patterns That Keep You from Getting Ahead* by James Waldroop, Ph.D., and Timothy Butler, Ph.D.; *Zoom: How 12 Exceptional Companies Are Navigating the Road to the Next Economy* by Jim Citrin; *The One to One B2B Customer Relationship Management Strategies for the Real Economy* by Don Peppers and Martha Rogers, Ph.D.

Send query letters with SASEs to:

Roger Scholl, Editor

Doubleday

Doubleday, now with more than a century in the publishing business, remains one of the world's most renowned houses. Perhaps best known for its strong commercial list in fiction and nonfiction, Doubleday continues to be a dominating force in mainstream popular nonfiction, in addition to books of literary note.

Representative titles in Doubleday fiction are *The Summons* by John Grisham; *Vine of Desire* by Chitra Divakaruni; *Three Weeks in Paris* by Barbara Taylor Bradford; *Palladio* by Jonathan Dee; *Choke* by Chuck Palahniuk; *Free, Short Stories* by Anika Nailah; *The Treatment* by Mo Hayder; *The Hostage* by Robert Crais; *Beacon Street Mourning* by Diane Day; *Cold and Pure and Very Dead* by Joanne Dobson; *Shackling Water* by Adam Mansbach.

Doubleday nonfiction categories run as broad as they run deep, including biography and autobiography, artists and photographs, current affairs, political science, public affairs, philosophy, ethics, family, marriage, sports and recreation, health, history, home and garden, and self-help.

Recent titles indicative of Broadway's nonfiction list are *The Natural: The Misunderstood Presidency of Bill Clinton* by Joe Klein; *The Good, the Bad & the Difference: How to Tell the Right from Wrong in Everyday Situations* by Randy Cohen; *The Mountain of the Women: Memoirs of an Irish Troubadour* by Liam Clancy; *When Katie Wakes: A Memoir* by Connie May Fowler; *The Autobiography of Quincy Jones* by Quincy Jones; *Crowns: Portraits of Black Women in Church Hats* by Michael Cunningham and Craig Marberry; *I Like Being Married: Treasured Traditions, Rituals, and Stories* by Michael Leach and Therese Borchard; *A-Game Golf* by John Anselmo.

Doubleday Religious Publishing

Doubleday Religious Publishing produces select titles in hardcover, as well as makes some books available as e-books. Categories cover spirituality and religions, including Christianity, Buddhism, and Judaism.

Indicative titles of this list: *The Living Christ* by Harold Fickett; *Religions for Peace* by Francis Cardinal Arinze; *Angels & Dragons* by Molly Wolf; *The Divine Hours* by Phyllis Tickle; *It's a God Thing* by Luis Palau; *The Mountain of Silence* by Kyriacos C. Markides; *Soul Survivor* by Philip Yancey; *God Underneath* by Edward L. Beck; *Spiritual Survival Guide* by Charles Shields and Cynthia Ferrell; *Befriending Life,* edited by Beth Porter; *Hail, Holy Queen* by Scott Hahn; *Exploring Jewish Tradition* by Rabbi Abraham B. Witty and Rachel J. Witty.

Doubleday/Image

For more than 50 years, Image Books has been producing quality, enduring religious books. Titles representative of this list are: *Rabbi Jesus* by Bruce Chilton; *Wounded Prophet* by Michael Ford; *Deliberate Acts of Kindness* by Meredith Gould; *The Messenger* by Joseph F. Girzone; *A Cry for Mercy* by Henri J. Nouwen; *The Living Christ* by Harold Fickett.

Main Street Books

Main Street Books publishes a wide array of nonfiction and select fiction titles in hardcover and trade paperback format.

Titles indicative of Main Street Books' fiction list: *Dead Solid Perfect* by Dan Jenkins; *The Green* by Troon McAllister; *Compass of the Heart: A Novel of Discovery* by Priscilla Cogan; *J. Crewd: A Parody* by Justin Racz; *Outside Providence* by Peter Farrelly; *A Crack Up at the Race Riots* by Harmony Korine.

Nonfiction titles representative of Main Street Books include *How to Make Your Child a Reader for Life* by Paul Kropp; *10 Natural Remedies That Can Save Your Life* by James F. Balch, M.D.; *Family Circle 2000 Hints & Tips: Great Ideas for Managing Your Time, Your Home, Your Self* by Family Circle Editors; *Where They Ain't: The Fabled Life and Untimely Death of the Original Baltimore Orioles, the Team That Gave Birth to Modern Baseball* by Burt Solomon; *Healing Signs: The Astrological Guide to Wholeness and Well-Being* by Ronnie Gale Dreyer; *Kosher Sex: A Recipe for Passion and Intimacy* by Shmuley Boteach; *The Wedding Dress Diet: Lose Weight and Look Great on Your Wedding*

Day and Beyond by Robyn Flipse and Jacqueline Shannon; *Writing to Win: The Legal Writer* by Steven D. Stark; *Teaching Tolerance: Raising Open-Minded Empathetic Children* by S. Bullard; *Four Magic Moves to Winning Golf* by Joe Dante.

Nan A. Talese

1540 Broadway, 18th Floor, New York, NY 10036
212/782-8918

Nan A. Talese/Doubleday, formed in 1990, is committed to publishing quality fiction and nonfiction, both in terms of its authors and the production of its books.

This literary trade paperback imprint is known for its new authors of fiction and nonfiction, as well as for the authors Mrs. Talese has published for many years. Nan Talese is a Senior Vice President of Doubleday and the Publisher and Editorial Director of Nan A. Talese/Doubleday.

Among its writers are Peter Ackroyd, Margaret Atwood, Pinckney Benedict, Thomas Cahill, Kevin Canty, Lorene Cary, Pat Conroy, Jennifer Egan, Mia Farrow, Antonia Fraser, David Grand, Nicola Griffith, Aleksandar Hemon, Thomas Keneally, Alex Kotlowitz, Robert MacNeil, Ian McEwan, Gita Mehta, George Plimpton, Edvard Radzinsky, Mark Richard, Nicholas Shakespeare, Barry Unsworth, and Gus Van Sant.

Representative titles: *Good Bones and Simple Murders* by Margaret Eleanor Atwood; *London* by Peter Ackroyd; *Alias Grace* by Margaret Atwood; *Desert Queen: The Extraordinary Life of Gertrude Bell: Adventurer, Advisor to Kings, Ally of Lawrence of Arabia* by Janet Wallach.

Earlier titles include *How the Irish Saved Civilization* by Thomas Cahill; *Beach Music* by Pat Conroy; *There Are No Children Here* by Alex Kotlotwitz; *Amsterdam* by Ian McEwan; *Sacred Hunger* by Barry Unsworth.

Talese does not accept unagented/unsolicited submissions. Query letters and SASEs should be directed to:

Sean McDonald, Editor—smcdonald@randomhouse.com

Lorna Owen, Assistant Editor—lowen@randomhouse.com

Amy Ostergaard, Administrative Assistant—aostergaard@randomhouse.com

ENTREPRENEUR PRESS

2445 McCabe Way, 4th Floor, Irvine, CA 92614
949-261-2325   fax: 949-261-7729
www.smallbizbooks.com   e-mail: jcalmes@entrepreneur.com

Entrepreneur Press, a division of Entrepreneur Media, Inc., publishes trade books offering practical advice and inspirational success stories for business owners and aspiring entrepreneurs. Our areas of expertise include instructional business books, motivational, management, marketing, new economy, e-commerce, and personal finance titles that appeal to a broad spectrum of the business book–buying audience. Steady sellers include *Start Your Own Business,* the *Entrepreneur* magazine's Start-Up Series; *Power Tools for*

Women in Business: 10 Ways to Succeed in Life and Work; At Work with Thomas Edison: 10 Business Lessons from America's Greatest Innovator.

Entrepreneur Press books are distributed to the trade by NBN. Query letters and SASEs should be directed to:

Jere Calmes, Editorial Director

M. Evans & Company, Inc.
216 East 49th Street, New York, NY 10017
212-688-2810   fax: 212-486-4544
e-mail: editorial@mevans.com

The M. Evans frontlist features high-profile offerings in topical issues; investigative stories in politics, business, and entertainment; and popular biography. The core Evans program accents popular nonfiction books in the areas of health and fitness, human relationships, business and finance, and lifestyle and cuisine. Evans also issues a small list in popular fiction. The house tends a strong and varied backlist.

M. Evans and Company (founded in 1963) thrives as a selective trade publisher (in hardcover and trade paperback) with a clear, constantly honed commercial focus in its favored market niches.

Evans fiction is exemplified by *Private Heart* (An Art Harding mystery) by Robert Bailey; *Down the Common* by Ann Baer. Nonfiction titles include *Parent School* by Jared L. Biederman; *Dr. Atkins' New Diet Revolution; Baby Love and The Mighty Toddler* by Robin Barke.

M. Evans books are distributed to the trade via National Book Network. Query letters and SASEs should be directed to:

George C. de Kay, President and Publisher—Popular psychology, health, cookbooks, commercial fiction

(Ms.) PJ Dempsey, Senior Editor—Health, parenting, biography, cookbooks

Marc Baller, Associate Editor—Current affairs, humor, personalities

Facts On File
132 West 31st Street, 17th Floor, New York, NY 10001
212-967-8800   fax: 212-967-9196
www.factsonfile.com   e-mail: Custserv@factsonfile.com

Facts On File specializes in reference and information titles in a broad popular range, including science, nature, technology, world history, American history, business, popular culture, fashion, design, sports, health, current affairs and politics, and the environment—in addition to general reference works. Facts On File offers a broad selection of historical and cultural atlases, dictionaries, and encyclopedias geared toward professional as well as popular interests and is one of the pioneers of the electronic multimedia–publishing frontier.

Facts On File (founded in 1940) is a dynamic popular-reference publisher. The house has a full skein of award-winning titles to its credit, and many Facts On File publications feature an innovative production approach. The publisher is extremely well tuned to specific category markets, which it targets with marked commercial consistency.

Facts On File has made a renewed commitment to its goal of becoming the premier print and electronic reference publisher in the industry. It is striving to be a beacon and a guide for librarians, teachers, students, parents, and researchers to look to for award-winning materials, cutting-edge trends, and innovative products. This is the publisher you seek when the requirements are nebulous and the transitions are turbulent.

The year 1998 brought the launch of the trade imprint Checkmark Books. It was created to provide booksellers and consumers with quality resources focused on topics such as business, careers, fitness, health and nutrition, history, nature, parenting, pop culture, and self-help.

Facts On File titles include *The History of Archaeology; Vice Presidents; Working in America; Encyclopedia of African History and Culture; Capital Punishment; Chronology of American Indian History; Encyclopedia of Cold War Politics; The Facts on File Handbook of Earth Science; Plate Tectonics; Animal Habitats; Elephants; Alien Encounters; The Facts on File Dictionary of Astronomy; The Encyclopedia of Child Abuse; New Complete Book of Herbs, Spices & Condiments; The Encyclopedia of Schizophrenia and Other Psychotic Disorders; British English from A to Zed; Edgar Allan Poe A to Z; The Literary 100; Words to Rhyme With; Career Opportunities for Writers; The Executors' Handbook; Best Baby Names in World; Black Belt Tae Kwon Do; Forbidden Films; Athletic Scholarships; Career Ideas for Kids Who Like Money.*

On File is an award-winning collection of reference materials. Spanning virtually every subject in the middle- and high-school curricula, each On File contains hundreds of images that visually depict complex subjects in a way that will both engage and inform young people. Even students at the elementary and college levels will find the material useful. Filled with hundreds of exciting hands-on activities, projects, exercises, and experiments, On File volumes encourage critical thinking and allow students to actively participate in their educational process.

Facts On File utilizes individualized marketing and distribution programs that are particularly strong in the areas of corporate, institutional, and library sales. Query letters and SASEs should be directed to:

Anne Savarese, Editor—Reference books: language and literature

Laurie Likoff, Editorial Director—Family, parenting, trade books, science, music, history

Nicole Bowen, Executive Editor—Reference books: American history and culture, multicultural; and nonfiction young-adult reference books about military history, sports, American culture and history, music, women's issues

Jim Chambers, Editor—Trade books, entertainment subjects, TV, and reference books on entertainment subjects, TV, movies, Broadway, sports, and health

Frank Darmstadt, Senior Editor—Reference books, science, technology, nature

Claudia Schrab, Editor—World history, religion

Owen Lancer, Editor in Chief—Reference books, geography, military, politics and government, law, history

FAIRVIEW PRESS

2450 Riverside Avenue, Minneapolis, MN 55454
612-672-4180   fax: 612-672-4980
www.fairviewpress.org

Fairview Press publishes books and related materials that educate individuals and families about their physical, emotional, and spiritual health and motivate them to seek positive changes in themselves and their communities.

Fairview Press (formerly Deaconess Press; founded in 1988) is a division of Fairview Health Services, a community-focused health system affiliated with the University of Minnesota.

Imprints of Fairview Press include Fairview Publications (medical/technical) and the Center for Spirituality and Healing (integrative medicine and spirituality).

On the Fairview list: *Karma and Happiness: A Tibetan Odyssey in Ethics, Spirituality, and Healing* by Miriam E. Cameron, Ph.D., R.N.; *At Grandmother's Table: Women Write about Food, Life, and the Enduring Bond Between Grandmothers and Granddaughters* (edited by Ellen Perry Berkeley); *Staying Strong: A Senior's Guide to a More Active and Independent Life* (edited by Lorie A. Schleck, M.A., P.T.); *Choices at the End of Life: Finding Out What Your Parents Want Before It's Too Late* by Linda Norlander, R.N., M.S., and Kerstin McSteen, R.N., M.S.; *The New Nursing Homes: A 20 Minute Way to Find Great Long-Term Care* by Marilyn Rantz, Ph.D., Lori Popejoy, R.N., and Mary Zwygart-Stauffacher, Ph.D.; *The Cancer Poetry Project: Healing Poems by Cancer Patients and Those Who Love Them* (edited by Karin B. Miller); *Navigating Through a Strange Land: A Book for Brain Tumor Patients and Their Families* (edited by Tricia Ann Roloff); *Drawing Together to Develop Self-Control* by Marge Heegaard; *Living Well with Heart Disease* by Fairview Health Services; *Daily Comforts for Caregivers* by Pat Samples; *The Family Handbook of Hospice Care* by Fairview Health Services; *Caring for You and Your Baby: From Pregnancy Through the First Year of Life* by Fairview Health Services; *Help Me Say Goodbye: Activities for Helping Kids Cope When a Special Person Dies* by Janis Silverman; *The Book of Positive Quotations,* compiled and arranged by John Cook; *When Men Grieve: Why Men Grieve Differently and How You Can Help* by Elizabeth Levan, Ph.D.; *Cry Until You Laugh: Comforting Guidance for Coping with Grief* by Richard J. Obershaw, M.S.W., L.I.CS.W.

Fairview Press operates through a variety of sales venues; the press is distributed to the trade through National Book Network. Query letters and SASEs should be addressed to:

Lane Stiles, Director

Stephanie Billecke, Editor

FANTAGRAPHICS BOOKS

7563 Lake City Way NE, Seattle, WA 98115
206-524-1967, 800-657-1100   fax: 206-524-2104
www.fantagraphics.com

Fantagraphics produces comics and comic art. The house accents a list of mainstream, classic, and borderline offerings in this specialty arena and also purveys a strong line of erotic comics and books. Fantagraphics Books (inaugurated in 1976) produces trade paperbacks, hardbound editions, and quality fine-art album editions of graphic productions, in addition to comic books, comics-related magazines, and a line of gift items dedicated to this most accessible literary form.

The Fantagraphics catalog lists, in addition to its own lines, products from additional publishers of comics and books, as well as audio, video, and multimedia works.

The Fantagraphics roster features some of the finest cartoonists of America and around the world—underground masters, political satirists, artists in the realms of science fiction and fantasy, and reprints of classic newspaper comic-strip series—as well as works from the emerging young Turks in the field.

Comics creators cataloged by Fantagraphics include Peter Bagge, Vaughn Bode, Daniel Clowes, Guido Crepax, Robert Crumb, Dame Darcy, Kim Deitch, Julie Doucet, Jules Feiffer, Frank Frazetta, Drew Friedman, Rick Geary, Los Bros. Hernandez, Peter Kuper, Terry LeBan, Douglas Michael, Joe Sacco, Gilbert Shelton, Art Spiegelman, Ralph Steadman, Basil Wolverton, and Wallace Wood.

Fantagraphics projects: *Whoa, Nellie! Graphic Novel* by Jaime Hernandez; *Tales of Terror—The Complete EC Compendium* by Grant Geissman and Fred von Bernewitz; *Complete Crumb Comics Volume 14; The Early 80's and WEIRDO Magazine* by Robert Crumb; *Palestine* by Joe Sacco; *Blab! Volume 12* by Mark Mothersbaugh; *Skin Deep* by Charles Burns; *Schizophrenia* by Vaughn Bode. Fantagraphics also offers Burne Hogarth's set of art-instruction books.

Fantagraphics distributes its own list and catalogs selections from a number of other comics- and graphics-oriented publishers, in addition to audio CDs, computer CD-ROMs, videotapes, and books, posters, and calendars. Query letters should be accompanied by short, carefully selected samples.

Michael Dowers, Submissions Editor

FARRAR, STRAUS & GIROUX

Farrar, Straus & Giroux Books for Young Readers

Hill and Wang

North Point Press

Faber and Faber Inc.

19 Union Square West, New York, NY 10003
212-741-6900   fax: 212-206-5340

Farrar, Straus & Giroux was founded in 1946 by Roger W. Straus. The firm is renowned for its international list of literary fiction, nonfiction, poetry, and children's books. Farrar, Straus & Giroux authors have won extraordinary acclaim over the years, including numerous National Book Awards, Pulitzer Prizes, and 21 Nobel Prizes in literature. Nobel Prize winners include Knut Hamsun, Hermann Hesse, T. S. Eliot, Par Lagerkvist, Francois Mauriac, Juan Ramon Jimenez, Salvatore Quasimodo, Nelly Sachs, Czeslaw Milosz, Elias Canetti, William Golding, Wole Soyinka, Joseph Brodsky, Camilo Jose Cela, Nadine Gordimer, Derek Walcott, and Seamus Heaney.

Poetry has always played a pivotal role on the Farrar, Straus & Giroux list, which boasts some of the greatest names in modern verse, ranging from Elizabeth Bishop, Ted Hughes, and Phillip Larkin to John Ashbery, Thom Gunn, and Les Murray.

Fiction has an even greater international reach, distinguished by Rosellen Brown, Jim Crace, Michael Cunningham, Jonathan Franzen, Carlos Fuentes, Peter Hoeg, Jamaica Kincaid, Bernard Malamud, Alice McDermott, Peter Nadas, Walker Percy, Richard Powers, Susan Sontag, Scott Turow, Mario Vargas Llosa, Tom Wolfe, and Lois-Ann Yamanaka.

History, art history, natural history, current affairs, and science round out a strong list in nonfiction, represented by Thomas Friedman, Philip Gourevitch, Roy Jenkins, Gina Kolata, Ben Macintyre, Louis Menaud, Giles Milton, and John McPhee, among others.

FSG's sales catalog and promotional endeavors include services for a number of smaller houses with literary orientations, such as Soho Press, Aperture, Harvill Press, and Graywolf Press.

Query letters and SASEs should be directed to:

Jonathan Galassi, President—Fiction, nonfiction, art history, belles lettres, business, and poetry

John Glusman, Editor in Chief—Literary fiction, history, biography, science, politics, current events

Elisabeth Sifton, Vice President and Senior Editor—History, politics, current events and issues, biography, and literary fiction; oversees Hill and Wang program

Ayesha Pande, Senior Editor—Fiction, narrative nonfiction, memoirs, multicultural projects

Rebecca Saletan, Senior Editor—Fiction, nonfiction, personal memoir

Paul Ellie, Editor—Literary nonfiction, music, religion, translation

Farrar, Straus & Giroux Books for Young Readers

The FSG juvenile program Books for Young Readers publishes quality picture books and novels for children and young adults. Award-winning authors include Jack Gantos, Madeleine L'Engle, Louis Sacbar, Uri Shulevitz, Peter Sis, David Small, William Steig, and Sarah Stewart.

Query letters and SASEs should be directed to:

Frances Foster, Publisher, Frances Foster Books

Margaret Ferguson, Vice President, Associate Publisher, and Editorial Director

Wes Adams, Senior Editor

Melanie Kroupa, Publisher, Melanie Kroupa Books

Hill and Wang

Hill and Wang focuses on hard- and softcover books of academic interest for both the trade market and the college (supplemental reading for courses) market. The list is strong in American history, world history, and politics. Among its authors are Roland Barthes, Michael Burleigh, William Cronon, Langston Hughes, Robert Wiebe, and Elie Wiesel.

Query letters and SASEs should be directed to:

Elisabeth Sifton, Publisher—American history, politics, public-policy issues

Thomas Levine, Editor

North Point Press

The North Point Press specializes in hard- and softcover literary nonfiction, with an emphasis on natural history, travel, ecology, music, food, and cultural criticism. Authors past and present include Peter Matthiessen, Evan Connell, Beryl Markahm, A. J. Liebling, Margaret Visser, Wendell Berry, and M. F. K. Fisher.

Query letters and SASEs should be directed to:

Ethan Nosowsky, Editor

Rebecca Saletan, Editorial Director

Faber and Faber Inc.

Faber and Faber Inc. offers a unique list of drama, film, poetry, and books of cultural interest and counts the Pulitzer Prize–winning playwrights David Auburn and Margaret Edson, as well as the British dramatists Tom Stoppard and David Hare, among its authors.

Query letters and SASEs should be directed to:

Linda Rosenberg, Editor

Denise Oswald, Editor

F

FOUR WALLS EIGHT WINDOWS

39 West 14th Street, Suite 503, New York, NY 10011
212-206-8965   fax: 212-206-8799
www.4w8w.com   e-mail: edit@4w8w.com

Four Walls Eight Windows offers a select seasonal list in creative nonfiction and literary fiction oriented toward topical issues and current culture. The house is known for journalistic forays into progressive politics; experimental fiction that features a stylistic and intellectual edge (including illustrated narrative); American and world culture expressed and portrayed through the essay; penetrating literary and critical studies; and individualistic poetry.

This is a publisher with a list far from the norm: Four Walls Eight Windows catalogs cultural artifacts in book form. The house hosts a healthy backlist laden with critically acclaimed, accomplished sellers, as well as an array of literary reprints.

Four Walls Eight Windows (established in 1987) was founded by John Oakes and Daniel Simon. Repeat: Contrary to speculation, when Dan Simon split to found the independent press Seven Stories (in early 1995; see separate entry for Seven Stories in this directory), John Oakes did not even contemplate a name change to Two Walls Four Windows.

Representative titles from Four Walls include *How Wall Street Created a Nation* by Ovidio Diaz Espino; *Desert Survivor: An Adventurer's Guide to Exploring the Great*

American Desert by John Annerino; *The Thank You Book* by Carole Stuart (illustrated by Arthur Robins); *The Choices We Made: Twenty-Five Women and Men Speak Out About Abortion* by Angela Bonavoglai; *Jane Sexes It Up: True Confessions of Feminist Desire* by Merri Lisa Johnson; *The Jaguar Hunter* by Lucas Shepard; *The Cornelius Quartet* by Michael Moorcock; *Headbanger* by Hugo Hamilton; *The Angel Quickest for Flight* by Steven Kotler; *Here Comes the Bride* by Jaclyn Geller; *The Autobiography of Abbie Hoffman* by Abbie Hoffman; *Before the Big Bang: The Origins of the Universe and the Nature of Matter* by Ernest J. Sternglass; *Sizzling Chops and Devilish Spins* by Jerome Charyn; *The Prisoners of Cabrera* by Denis Smith; *Death in Paradise* by Tony Blache and Brad Schreiber; *Synners* by Pat Cadigan; *The Bone Museum* by Wayne Grady; *The Jaguar Hunter* by Lucius Shepard; *The Thank You Book* by Carole Stuart.

Four Walls Eight Windows books are distributed to the trade by Publishers Group West; foreign rights are administered by Writers House. Query letters and SASEs should be directed to:

Jofie Ferrari-Adler, Associate Editor

FOXROCK, INC.

61 Fourth Avenue, New York, NY 10003
fax: 212-673-1039
www.foxrock.com   e-mail: foxrock@mail.com

Foxrock was formed in 1994 by Barney Rosset, John G. H. Oakes, and Dan Simon. Since operations began in 1994, Foxrock has published books and distributed videotapes. Foxrock, Inc., features fine writing in both hardcover and paperback. Foxrock hosts literary anthologies, poetic works, shorter and longer fiction, as well as general trade titles.

On the Foxrock list: *Stirrings Still* by Samuel Beckett; *The Man Sitting in the Corridor* (fiction) by Marguerite Duras; *The Correct Sadist* (novel) by Terence Sellers; *Lament: A Novel About How the West Was Blown* by David (Sunset) Carson; *The Ghost Ship* (poetry) by Henry Hart; *Triangulation from a Known Point* (poetry) by Ruth Danon; *New and Selected Poems 1930–1990* by Richard Eberhart; *The Colors of Infinity* (poetry) by Donald E. Axinn; *Two Dogs and Freedom: The Open School in Soweto* (schoolchildren from South Africa's Open School speak out); *Sitting Shiva* by Elliot Feldman; *Jew Boy* by Alan Kaufman.

The Foxrock Line has republished a number of classic literary compilations: *The Olympia Reader* and *The New Olympia Reader* (edited by Maurice Girodias) are filled with ribald and erotic writings first published in Paris by the germinal publisher of Olympia Press, Maurice Girodias; these volumes feature the work of such authors as Jean Genet, Henry Miller, Chester Himes, Lawrence Durrell, William S. Burroughs, Gregory Corso, George Bataille, John Cleland, Pauline Réage, Samuel Beckett, and the Marquis de Sade. Blue Moon publisher, Barney Rosset, along with associates, has edited *Evergreen Review Reader 1957–1966,* featuring selections from *Evergreen,* America's fabled journal of literary provocateurism.

Beginning in the spring of 2001, Foxrock plans on expanding its list of books to include important new works, as well as classic literary titles that have been unavailable for many years.

Query letters and SASEs should be directed to:

Barney Rosset, President

Astrid Myers, Publisher's Assistant

FREE SPIRIT PUBLISHING

217 Fifth Avenue North, Suite 200, Minneapolis, MN 55401-1299
612-338-2068   fax: 612-337-5050
www.freespirit.com   e-mail: help4kids@freespirit.com

Free Spirit Publishing produces trade nonfiction arenas keyed to parenting, child and adolescent development, the family, education, and relationships. Areas of special concentration: self-help for kids, self-help for teens, gifted and talented education, learning differences (LD), creative learning, parenting and teaching, social action, service learning, school success. Free Spirit Publishing offers creative learning materials that enrich the lives of children and teens.

Free Spirit publications include issue-focused guides for students, educators, parents, mental health professionals, children, and teens. The publisher (founded in 1983) has been particularly successful with its Self-Help for Kids and Self-Help for Teens lines of books and educational materials. Free Spirit also catalogs posters and other creative learning wares.

Free Spirit highlights: *The Gifted Kid's Survival Guide for Ages 10 & Under* by Judy Galbraith, M.A.; *Jump Starters: Quick Classroom Activities That Develop Self-Esteem, Creativity and Cooperation* by Linda Nason McElhern, M.A.; *Cliques, Phonies, and Other Baloney* by Trevor Romain; *I'm Like You, You're Like Me: A Child's Book About Understanding and Celebrating Each Other,* written and illustrated by Cindy Gainer; *The Bully Free Classroom: Over 100 Tips and Strategies for Teachers K–12* by Allan Beane, Ph.D.; *How to Handle a Hard-to-Handle Kid: A Parent's Guide to Understanding and Changing Problem Behaviors* by C. Drew Edwards, Ph.D.; *School Power* by Jeanne Shay Schumm, Ph.D.; *What Kids Need to Succeed* by Peter Benson, Ph.D., Judy Galbraith, M.A., and Pamela Espeland; *Teaching Gifted Kids in the Regular Classroom* by Susan Winebrenner; *How Rude!* by Alex Packer; *Cool Women, Hot Jobs* by Tina Schwager, P.T.A., A.T.C., and Michele Schuerger.

Free Spirit's distribution is through the trade market, as well as direct to schools and other youth-serving venues. Query letters and SASEs should be directed to:

Sid Farrar, Executive Editor

W. H. FREEMAN AND COMPANY PUBLISHERS

Computer Science Press

Scientific American Books

41 Madison Avenue, New York, NY 10010
212-576-9400, 800-903-3019   fax: 212- 689-2383
www.whfreeman.com

W. H. Freeman accents mathematics and the sciences; the house roster features trade titles of general interest, textbooks, and professional books. Areas of trade interest include anthropology, astronomy, current issues, nature and the environment, health and medicine, life sciences, parenting, and psychology.

W. H. Freeman represents a tradition of outstanding and innovative publishing in the sciences. Freeman books—especially the popular works—often display superb graphics and fine design. W. H. Freeman and Company (established in 1946) is a subsidiary of Scientific American, Inc. The house logs a trusty backlist.

From Freeman: *Universe: Stars and Galaxies* by Roger Freedman and William Kaufmann; *Universe: The Solar System* by Roger Freedman and William Kaufmann; *Astronomy Online* by Timothy Slater; *Biochemistry* by Jeremy M. Berg, John L. Tymoczko, and Lubert Stryer; *BioStats Basics* by James L. Gould; *Modern Genetic Analysis* by Anthony Griffiths, William Gelbart, Richard Lewontin, and Jeffrey Miller; *General Chemistry* by American Chemical Society; *Physical Chemistry* by Peter Atkins and Julio DePaula; *Chemical Principles* by Peter Atkins and Loretta Jones; *Bridging to the Lab* by Loretta Jones and Roy Tasker; *The Practice of Chemistry* by Donald J. Wink, Sharon Fetzer-Gislason, and Sheila McNicholas; *EarthInquiry: Recurrence Intervals of Floods* by American Geological Institute and Robert Ridky; *World Regional Geography* by Lydia Mihelic Pulsipher; *The Basics of Abstract Algebra* by Paul Bland; *College Algebra* by COMAP; *Linear Algebra* by Ted Shifrin and Malcolm Adams.

From Scientific American Library, a line of trade-oriented books authored by celebrated scientists, come titles geared to particular fields, in addition to works of general-readership appeal. Sample titles: *Visual Computing* by Richard Mark Friedhoff and Mark S. Peercy; *Gravity's Fatal Attraction: Black Holes in the Universe* by Mitchell Begelman and Martin Rees; *Investigating Disease Patterns: The Science of Epidemiology* by Paul S. Stolley and Tamar Lasky; *The Origin of Modern Humans* by Roger Lewin.

A special coproduction of Infon, Inc., Scientific American, and W. H. Freeman is *Molecular Cell Biology* (CD-ROM).

W. H. Freeman oversees its own distribution. Query letters and SASEs should be directed to:

Michelle Julet, Acquisitions Editor—Chemistry

Nicole Folchetti, Sponsoring Editor—Life Science

Richard Bonacci, Acquisitions Editor—Mathematics

Sara Tenney, Senior Editor—Life Science

Erika Goldman, Senior Editor—Narrative nonfiction

John Michael, Executive Editor—Trade areas of house interest
   Education: B.A., Physics.
   Employment history/editor career path: After college I worked for about a year and a half in a marketing position and then decided I wanted to get into publishing. I started working at HarperCollins, and I have been with W. H. Freeman for 3 years. I have 17 years of experience in the publishing industry.

F

Personal interests: I have a son who's eight and a half years old.

What would you be doing if you were not an editor? I would be teaching English (poetry) to jocks or to people who didn't want to learn it.

Do you represent fiction? No.

Do you represent nonfiction? Yes, exclusively science.

Do you require book proposals? If so, what do you look for in evaluating a book proposal? Yes. I look for an extraordinary topic and a good writer.

Are certain aspects of a book proposal given more weight than others? The way it's written.

What process do you use for making a decision? What is the process for acquisition; is there a committee? Yes, we have a small and informal "committee." We will come together and discuss manuscripts, but we don't really have an official meeting.

What kinds of nonfiction books do you want to see less of? Repeat books. Books that are already out there.

Are agents important? Why? I do believe they are important, but they are not necessary for everyone. They are familiar with the business and know how to help authors get more money and get the best deal with the best house for their book. They will fight for the authors' rights.

Do you like new writers? What should new writers do to break into the business? Breaking into the business is like trying to find an apartment in Manhattan. You need to pull out all of the stops, talk to everyone you know, and find and make connections.

How should writers approach you? With a 30-page proposal that states up front what the book is about and can get my attention within a couple of pages.

What are some common mistakes writers make? What really gets on your nerves? It gets on my nerves when authors tell me how to do my job, how to do the marketing, how to publish the book, and so on.

What can writers do to get your attention and to avoid the slush pile? Get referred by someone and you will avoid the slush pile. To get my attention, have a good title and opening page.

What have been some of your craziest experiences with submissions? I once had a guy (when I worked at Harper) who submitted his book *Charlotte's Web* and said that E. B. White had stolen his book and that he wanted all rights and royalties to be reverted to him at once, and he also wanted to be booked on the Carson show right away. I also had a guy once come to the office and tell me that he had a book that was going to save the world; the entire book was on 5×7 index cards.

What have been some of your best experiences with writers or in your job? I had an author that I worked with follow me to three different houses, just so I could be the editor for his material. We worked together for 10 years and finally finished the project, which won the John Burroughs award.

What, if anything, makes you different from other editors? I have a willingness and a desire to work closely with the author. I do all forms of editing, starting with the down and dirty line editing.

Is there anything you would like to see changed in the industry? I would like to see all of the conglomerates broken up into tiny houses. "When will they realize this is a cottage business?" (Francis Lindley).

Any advice for writers? Write for yourself, don't write for fame (you will be disappointed). Don't fall into the John Kennedy Toole trap.

Susan Brennan, Executive Editor/Publisher

Born: September 1961.

Education: B.A., in Medieval History from Cornell University.

Employment history/editor career path: After college I went into retail, working as an Assistant Buyer for A&S department stores; went to Prentice Hall as a sales rep. And shortly afterward was promoted to an Editor.

Personal interests: Theater; I have two children, aged nine months and three years, and my husband. Restaurants, jogging, hiking.

What would you be doing if you were not an editor? I never really thought about it. I feel lucky that I happened to end up in this position.

What has been your most successful book that you have acquired to date? *Abnormal Psychology* book by Rathus and Nevid, 1st edition, around 1990.

What books have you acquired that make you the most proud? What books that you have acquired reflect the types of books you like to represent? Innovative books. In college publishing you are always publishing for a particular market; college professors don't change quickly. Freeman is an innovative publisher.

Do you represent fiction? If so, what do you look for? No.

Do you represent nonfiction? Yes.

Do you require book proposals? If so, what do you look for in evaluating a book proposal? Yes. Most textbooks that we sign, it's something that we have been pursuing. It's not like trade publishing where you get hundreds of submissions per day. Proposals are usually joint adventures between the publisher and the author for textbooks.

Are certain aspects of a book proposal given more weight than others? Yes. Do you have an idea that will set your book apart from other books? The quality of the author. How well do you understand your market and competition?

What process do you use for making a decision? What is the process for acquisition; is there a committee? No committees. I read the material and I then send the material out to the people who teach that specific course to review. We get the responses from the reviews and send them to the author and try to revise the book from there.

What kinds of nonfiction books do you want to see less of? Vanilla-flavored textbooks—you can't tell why it is different from the books that are already there.

Are agents important? Why? No. Once in a blue moon. I don't like working with an agent; I like to work directly with the author.

How should writers approach you? Contact me directly by e-mail or mail. Don't call.

What are some common mistakes writers make? What really gets on your nerves? Everyone's book is too long, constantly trying to rein it in. Having to spend a lot of time cutting out material.

What have been some of your craziest experiences with submissions? Schizos from prison who will send you handwritten material that is really crazy. Crazy times for us are when we are involved in a competitive signing and end up doing things that we never thought we would do to obtain the deal.

F

What have been some of your best experiences with writers or in your job? When you are working with an author and something "clicks." You know when you are right on target. It's very rewarding when you sell a lot of books.

What, if anything, makes you different from other editors? Authors love to work with me. I'm straight with my authors; I tell them exactly what I think the issues are, how these should be addressed, and so on. I am in contact with them a lot, and I think a lot of other authors have problems with this; they feel neglected.

Is there anything you would like to see changed in the industry? I don't like the high cost of textbooks for the students.

Computer Science Press

Computer Science Press publishes in computer science and information technology, with an eye on emerging areas within these quick-moving fields. The house offers introductory- to advanced-level college texts in computer sciences, telecommunications, and computer mathematics, as well as related areas.

Computer Science Press, founded in 1974, became an imprint of W. H. Freeman in 1988. Query letters and SASEs should be directed to:

Richard Bonacci, Publisher

F

FULCRUM PUBLISHING

16100 Table Mountain Parkway, Suite 300, Golden, CO 80403-5093
303-277-1623, 800-992-2908
www.fulcrum-books.com

Fulcrum publishes general trade nonfiction books, with emphasis in gardening, nature, and the outdoors; food; travel guides; business and the environment; Colorado and the Rockies; parenting; health; humor; and American history, world history, and cultural history.

Fulcrum imprints and lines include the Library of Congress series of Americana, educational books (for children and adults), and the Starwood line of books and calendars; the house also issues selected audiocassettes on the Fulcrum Audio Book imprint. Native American writers and subjects are a vital part of the Fulcrum program.

Fulcrum Publishing (founded in 1984) is a growing firm with an ambitious list. It is the Fulcrum vision to produce works that provide a link to the experiences and wisdom of the past. This image fits in neatly with the publisher's characterization of the editorial relationship:

In his autobiography, Anthony Trollope wrote, "Of all the needs that a book has, the chief need is that it be readable." When that happens, it is due to excellent writers and professional and understanding editors. It is difficult and sometimes lonely being a writer, but a good editor is a supporter, a confidant, a representative of the reader, and often can assist the writer in producing a book far better than the writer is capable of creating alone. Sometimes the changes are obvious, sometimes subtle, but they are always aimed at making the book readable. Bob Baron, Publisher, would like to praise and thank Fulcrum's dedicated editors who have made all of its 250 books possible and who have tried to achieve the standards of Trollope.

This is good news for Fulcrum readers, and good news for writers, too. Fulcrum supports a hefty backlist.

Special Fulcrum projects: *The Book in America* by Richard Clement, who used the vast resources in the Library of Congress to trace the history of the American book. *All the World's a Stage,* a volume that combines writing from William Shakespeare with the calligraphy and full-color illustrations of Dorothy Boux. Fulcrum is working with colleagues in England to celebrate the building of the new Globe Theatre in London. *Faces of a Nation: The Rise and Fall of the Soviet Union, 1917–1991,* is a photo essay featuring Dmitri Daltermants, Russia's most famous photographer, with text by noted historian Theodore H. Von Laue.

On the Fulcrum list: *All the Sincerity in Hollywood: Selections from the Writings of Fred Allen* by Stuart Hample*; American Nature Writing: 2002* by John A. Murray; *Bitterbrush Country: Living on the Edge of the Land* by Diane Josephy Peavey; *Bold Visions for the Garden* by Richard Hartlage; *Growing Up True: Lessons from a Western Boyhood* by Craig S. Barnes; *Gunfight at the O.K. Corral* by Thom Ross; *The June Rise: The Apocryphal Letters of Joseph Antoine Janis* by William Tremblay; *Lewis and Clark: Doctors in the Wilderness* by Bruce C. Paton, M.D.; *RVs—Getting Out and STAYING Out* by Alan and Barbara Lidstone; *Six-Legged Sex: The Erotic Lives of Bugs* by James K. Wangberg, illustrations by Marjorie C. Leggitt; *Wilderness and Humanity: The Global Issue* (edited by Vance G. Martin and M. A. Parthy Sarathy); *America's Prairies and Grasslands: Guide to Plants and Animals* by Marianne D. Wallace; *That's Weird! Awesome Science Mysteries* by Kendall Haven.

Children's titles: *Keepers of the Earth: Native American Stories and Environmental Activities for Children; Keepers of the Animals: Native American Stories and Wildlife Activities for Children; Keepers of Life: Discovering Plants Through Native American Stories and Earth Activities for Children* by Michael J. Caduto and Joseph Bruchac; *From Butterflies to Thunderbolts: Discovering Science with Books Kids Love* by Anthony D. Fredericks (illustrated by Rebecca Fredericks); *Do Bees Sneeze? And Other Questions Kids Ask About Insects* by James K. Wangberg (illustrated by Ellen Parker).

Fulcrum Publishing handles its own distribution. Query letters and SASEs should be directed to:

Bob Baron, President and Publisher

Charlotte Baron, Vice President

Dianne Howie, Vice President

Nancy Blessing, Editor in Chief

Daniel Forrest-Bank, Managing Editor

Susan Zernial, Editor—Education

T. J. Baker, Acquisitions Editor—Projects consistent with the house list

Naomi Horii, Acquisitions Editorm, Fulcrum Resources
350 Indiana Street, Suite 350, Golden, CO 80401-5093
800-992-2908

F

Sign: Capricorn.

Education: B.S. in Journalism; M.A. in Literature.

Employment history or editor career path: Editor at Scientific Publishing House; Editor at *Many Mountains Moving,* a literary journal; Editor at Fulcrum.

Personal interests: Literature, writing, nature.

What would you be doing if you were not an editor? I'd be a teacher.

What has been your most successful book that you have acquired to date? I've acquired poetry, fiction, essays, and art for *Many Mountains Moving,* an internationally distributed literary journal that has had work reprinted in *Best American* and the *Pushcart Prize* anthology. I've worked with some of the world's best writers—Sherman Alexie, Allen Ginsberg, Naomi Shihab Nye, and many more.

What books that you have acquired reflect the types of books you like to represent? I acquired a book on teaching poetry, which I love.

Do you represent fiction? If so, what do you look for? We are considering fiction geared to grades 3 to 8. I look for an engaging voice and a story that stays with me long after I've finished the last page.

What do you want to see less of? I would like to see less work that talks down to young readers.

Do you represent nonfiction? Yes.

Do you require book proposals? If so, what do you look for in evaluating a book proposal? We do require book proposals. In evaluating them, I want to know that authors have carefully thought out the concept and audience of their book. I also like to see sample chapters.

Are certain areas of a book proposal given more weight than others? The main thing I evaluate in a book proposal is whether the topic seems like something that people would be interested in.

What process do you use for making a decision? What is the process for acquisition, is there a committee? I immediately reject about 90 percent of the proposals that come in. The other 10 percent I will reread and perhaps pass on to other members of our publishing team for a second opinion.

What kinds of nonfiction books do you want to see less of? Less therapy books.

Are you interested in work geared for the masses (readers of *People, The Star,* etc.)? Yes, as long as it is intelligently written and not dumbed down for the lowest common denominator.

Are agents important? Why? I try to read all manuscripts with an open mind, whether or not the author has an agent. But good agents can be invaluable to an author to help find appropriate forums for the manuscript and to help make things go smoothly for the author.

Do you like new writers? What should new writers do to break into the business? I always keep an eye out for new writers and encourage them to submit work. The most important advice I would give new writers is to know the market. Before even thinking about sending a piece to a certain publishing house, the writer should be familiar with the kinds of books that house has published. To send submissions blindly is a waste of everyone's time.

How should writers approach you? I prefer that writers simply send in a book proposal and a sample chapter with a brief cover letter.

What are some common mistakes writers make? What really gets on your nerves? I dislike manuscripts that write down to readers, whether they be children or adults. I loathe overly cutesy manuscripts.

What can writers do to get your attention and to avoid the slush pile? I try to read every manuscript that comes through the door with equal attention. A good manuscript will always get my attention.

What have been some of your craziest experiences with submissions? I have read for a number of publishers and have read the same manuscript for three different publishing houses. I've also had authors become irate when we've turned down their work.

What have been some of your best experiences with writers or in your job? I delight in discovering new writers, but I also love to work with any authors who care passionately about their work.

Is there anything you would like to see changed in the industry? In general, I think that sometimes the market, or the perceived market, dictates what is published. The book industry, as well as Hollywood, has been ruled too long by what some executives think will sell. I think it's important that publishers publish what is good and then decide how they will market or sell that material, rather than trying to figure out whether or not it will sell. There's always room for good material.

Any advice for new writers? My advice to writers is to know your market and to not be discouraged. Some of the books that have become classics were initially rejected by numerous publishers.

GARRETT PUBLISHING

384 South Military Trail, Deerfield Beach, FL 33442
954-480-8543   fax: 954-698-0057
www.garrettpub.com

Garrett's focus is on books in business, finance, law, and personal finance. Garrett books are practical, often featuring a self-help/how-to approach that highlights sample forms, ready-to-use templates, checklists, instructions, resources, and informative examples. A major Garrett imprint is E-Z Legal Books.

Garrett Publishing (founded in 1990) is on the lookout for authors with marketable projects: authors who are expert in their fields and know how to get their point across clearly and enthusiastically. Garrett's marketing department is staffed with professionals skilled in publicity, promotions, advertising, and editorial services. Garrett promotes its authors' books through print advertising, television appearances, and radio spots. The house offers competitive advances and royalties.

With sales representatives located strategically across the United States, Garrett's books are available in the giant trade bookseller chains and are obtainable from major wholesalers and distributors. Over the past several seasons, the publisher has expanded its retail distribution.

Representative of the Garrett program: *Asset Protection Secrets; How to Settle with the IRS—For Pennies on the Dollar, 2nd Edition; Building Your Financial Fortress: How to Protect Your Assets from the 10 Deadly Threats to Your Wealth!; The Limited Partnership Book.*

Garrett Publishing distributes through its own house operation, as well as via such outlets as Quality Book Distributors, Ingram, and Baker and Taylor. Query letters and SASEs should be directed to:

Arnold Goldstein, Editor/Owner

GENERAL PUBLISHING GROUP

This young West Coast start-up fell victim to the harsh realities of independent publishing and closed shop.

THE GLOBE PEQUOT PRESS

246 Goose Lane #200, PO Box 480, Guilford, CT 06437-0833
203-458-4500, 888-249-7586   fax: 800-508-8938
www.globe-pequot.com   e-mail: info@globe-pequot.com

Globe Pequot Press (founded in 1947) is a specialist in travel and outdoor recreation, with additional interest in cooking, personal finance, and home-based business. The publisher accents titles marketed to both trade and specialty market slots.

Within this program, Globe Pequot looks for works in a number of important categories: travel books—regional and special-interest travel guides; family adventure guides; travel annuals, accommodations guides, itinerary-format guides, and travel how-to's; outdoor recreation—any outdoor sport, how-to, and where-to guides; and home-based business. Authors should have firsthand experience running the featured home-based business.

In the travel arena, Globe Pequot is well regarded for several bestselling series and also distributes for a number of travel-specialist houses. Among Globe Pequot lines: Quick Escapes (weekend and day trips keyed to metropolitan areas or regions); Romantic Days and Nights; Recommended Bed & Breakfasts; Fun with the Family Guides; Cadogan Guides to destinations worldwide for the discriminating traveler; and the popular Off-the-Beaten-Path series. Globe Pequot also updates a variety of annuals, among them Europe by Eurorail. Globe Pequot's regionally keyed books also cover such interest areas as biking, hiking, mountaineering, skiing, and family activities in the wilderness and on the beach.

Globe Pequot representative titles: *The Seasons of a Fisherman; Hiking Arizona, 2nd Edition; Practical Outdoor Projects; Caribbean Hiking; LL Bean Upland Bird Hunting Handbook; Insider's Guide to Salt Lake City, 3rd Edition; Globetrotter Golfer's Guide Scotland; 100 Best All Inclusive Resorts of the World, 2nd Edition; Texas Off the Beaten Path, 4th Edition; Country Houses and How to Build Them; Wilderness Mother—The Chronicle of a Modern Pioneer; Essential Tennis; Men Who Ride Mountains: Incredible True Tales of Legendary Surfers; Passion for Golf; The Essential Cyclist; Fishing Yellowstone Hatches; Trout & Salmon—The Greatest Fly Fishing For Trout and Salmon Worldwide.*

Globe Pequot was purchased in early 1997 by Morris Communications Corporation, a privately held company (founded in 1795) with nationwide, diversified holdings in newspaper and magazine publishing, radio, outdoor advertising, and computer services. Query letters and SASEs should be directed to:

G

Lafe Low, Acquisitions Editor—Outdoor submissions

Shelley Wolf, Submissions Editor—General submissions

Laura Strom, Executive Editor—Travel submissions
Born: April 24.
Education: B.A., English Literature.
Employment history/editor career path: I started out in an unrelated industry out of college, but shortly after that I worked in an entry-level position at a vanity press and then shortly after that I moved to Connecticut and got an editorial/proofreading position. Four years later Globe Pequot was hiring, and I have been with the company for 11 years.
Personal interests: Traveling, swing dancing, gardening, being outdoors.
What would you be doing if you were not an editor? I would be a farmer.
What has been your most successful book that you have acquired to date? A companion book to a PBS genre on legendary lighthouses (fall 1998); it's been back to press four times.
What books have you acquired that make you the most proud? What books that you have acquired reflect the types of books you like to represent? The companion book is one of them, also a book titled *New York Neighborhoods,* which is a food lovers' guide to the ethnic community by Elenor Berman (1999). I also developed a romantic travel book called *Romantic Days and Nights.*
Do you represent fiction? If so, what do you look for? No.
Do you represent nonfiction? Yes. In our specific areas (travel).
Do you require book proposals? If so, what do you look for in evaluating a book proposal? Yes. First I look to see if it's something we actually publish; well-credentialed authors; new ideas that can be sold into nontrade; any previous writing experience.
Are certain aspects of a book proposal given more weight than others? We look for excellent writing, the marketability and promotability of the author.
What process do you use for making a decision? What is the process for acquisition; is there a committee? We do have a committee that meets every couple of weeks and the Acquisitions Editors usually present the new ideas to the committee. The committee is made up of sales representatives, as well as our administration and editorial staff. We discuss new ideas that we have, and if everyone agrees, we do a thorough competition search, and so on.
What kinds of nonfiction books do you want to see less of? Motor home travel books.
Do you think that agents are important? Why? Yes, agents are really important. They tend to represent some of the better authors. We also work with unagented authors or previous authors of ours.
Do you like new writers? What should new writers do to break into the business? Yes, especially for our regional guidebooks. New writers are often very enthusiastic.
How should writers approach you? With a query letter via snail mail.
What are some common mistakes writers make? What really gets on your nerves? Query letters that sound like they are a sales pitch or gimmick.
What can writers do to get your attention and to avoid the slush pile? Be polite, undemanding, do periodic follow-ups by e-mail or through the mail. No phone calls.

G

What have been some of your best experiences with writers or in your job? Working with authors who really know how to write.

What, if anything, makes you different from other editors? I really care about my authors.

DAVID R. GODINE, PUBLISHER, INC.

9 Hamilton Place, Boston, MA 02108
617-451-9600   fax: 617-350-0250
www.godine.com   e-mail:info@godine.com

Godine publishes trade nonfiction in such areas as history and criticism, typography and graphic arts, art and architecture, horticulture, cooking, Americana, and regional-interest books. The house also publishes fiction (including mysteries), literature and essays, and poetry, as well as children's books. Godine offers a line of classic works in reprint, as well as works in translation.

The Godine program is committed to quality. Godine specializes in attentively produced hardcover and trade paperback editions. The house issues a small catalog of new titles each year, while maintaining an active backlist. Godine's imprints include Country Classics, Double Detectives, and Nonpareil Books.

David R. Godine, Publisher (founded in 1969), was started in an abandoned cow barn, where David R. Godine both worked and lived; the expanding operation later moved to Boston.

Godine has intentionally kept itself small, the list eclectic, and the quality consistently high, with a stronger concentration on titles with backlist potential (particularly nonfiction). The house maintains its fortunate position of being able to ask: What do we really believe is superior? rather than, What are we confident will sell? The editors at Godine have learned to trust their instincts. By staying small, this house is lucky enough to have kept most of its goals attainable. It does not need to sell 10,000 copies of a book to make money. It does not need to put authors on tour or to indulge in massive hype. Good books, like water, find their own levels. It sometimes takes years, but it is inevitable.

In short, David R. Godine, Publisher, remains what it was 30 years ago: a true cottage industry, surviving on a very small budget, and doing what it does and what it knows best: publishing books that matter for people who care.

Titles from Godine: *Aubrey's Brief Life* by Sir John Aubrey; *Mefisto and the Newton Letter* by John Banville; *The Decline and Fall of Practically Everybody* by Will Cuppy; *It's Only Rock and Roll* by Janice Eidus; *Beyond* by Albert Goldbarth; *Bright Stars, Dark Trees, Clear Water* by Wayne Grady; *Talking in the Dark* by Wesley McNair; *The Autobiography of Michel de Montaigne* by Michel de Montaigne; *A Tally of Types* by Stanley Morison; *The Disobedience of Water* by Sena Jeter Naslund; *We Didn't Mean to Go to Sea* by Arthur Ransom; *Six Israeli Novellas* by Gershon Shaked; *Woodcut Art of J. J. Lankes* by Welford Dunaway Taylor; *Fields of Peace* by George Tice; *The Philosopher's Diet* by Richard Watson; *The Sacrificial Years* by Walt Whitman.

Query letters and SASEs should be directed to:

The Editorial Department

GRAYWOLF PRESS

2402 University Avenue, Suite 203, Saint Paul, MN 55114
651-641-0077   fax: 651-641-0036
www.graywolfpress.org

Graywolf publishes poetry, fiction, nonfiction, and essays. Graywolf produces works by writers past and present, with particular emphasis on the scene of contemporary international letters, as well as a line of literary anthologies and reissues. Graywolf hosts a solid backlist of featured titles.

About the Graywolf Press trade motto: Creative writing for creative reading. This distinctive approach to publishing signifies Graywolf Press as an independent, not-for-profit publisher dedicated to the creation and promotion of thoughtful and imaginative contemporary literature essential to a vital and diverse culture.

Graywolf backs up its authors and its literary claims with publishing prowess: the Graywolves have been successful in finding an audience for their works, and the Graywolf Press list has been augmented, confirming the achievement of a program that runs contrary to the stream of contemporary commercial publishing.

Begun in 1974, Graywolf Press exemplifies the small-scale independent American literary house. The publisher's wolf pack logo marks a list rippling with award-winners and critical endorsement.

The Graywolf Forum series was launched with the publication of Graywolf Forum One: *Tolstoy's Dictaphone: Technology and the Muse,* a collection of new essays edited by Sven Birkerts (author of the hotly debated *Gutenberg Elegies*).

General-interest trade books include *If You Want to Write: A Book About Art, Independence and Spirit* by Brenca Ueland; *Burning Down the House: Essays on Fiction* by Charles Baxter; *The Outermost Dream: Literary Sketches* by William Maxwell; *Diary of a Left-Handed Birdwatcher* by Leonard Nathan.

Graywolf fiction and literary works: *War Memorials* by Clint McCown; *Otherwise: New & Selected Poems* by Jane Kenyon; *A Four-Sided Bed* by Elizabeth Searle; *Pastoral* by Carl Phillips; *Domestic Work* by Natasha Trethewey; *Some Ether* by Nick Flynn; *The Way It Is: New and Selected Poems* by William Statford; *Ana Imagined* by Perrin Ireland.

Graywolf Press utilizes a network of regional sales representatives; books are proffered to the trade through Consortium Book Sales and Distribution. Query letters and SASEs should be directed to:

Katie Dublinski, Editor—Fiction

Anne Czarniecki, Executive Editor—Fiction and nonfiction

Daniel Kos, Publishing Assistant

Fiona McCrae, Publisher

G

GROVE/ATLANTIC, INC.

Atlantic Monthly Press

Grove Press

841 Broadway, New York, NY 10003
212-614-7850   fax: 212-614-7886

Grove/Atlantic publishes trade nonfiction and fiction; these works often display a contemporary cultural bent or an issue-oriented edge. Grove Press and Atlantic Monthly Press, two previously independent houses, are united under the Grove/Atlantic, Inc., corporate crest. Grove/Atlantic operates from the former Grove headquarters on Broadway (with Atlantic having relocated from its previous digs at nearby Union Square West). Grove/Atlantic operates essentially as one house, while maintaining the distinction of two major imprints. (See separate subentries further on for both Atlantic Monthly Press and Grove Press.)

Grove/Atlantic holds a tradition of publishing arresting literature—from the writing of Samuel Beckett and William S. Burroughs to Jean Genet and Marguerite Duras, from John Kennedy Toole and J. P. Donleavy to Henry Miller and Jeanette Winterson. The house initiated an aggressive program to repackage these modern classics, as well as to return to print the work of such celebrated writers as Terry Southern, Robert Coover, Jerzy Kosinski, Frederick Barthelme, Patricia Highsmith, Aharon Appelfeld, Barry Hannah, and Kenzaburo Oe. In a marketplace it sees as increasingly dominated by ephemera, Grove/Atlantic is committed to publishing serious books that last and to introducing classic books to a new generation of readers.

Subsequent to the previously noted Grove/Atlantic merger—with Atlantic most decidedly the major partner—speculation was that Atlantic had bought Grove essentially for Grove's extensive, internationally renowned backlist; Atlantic would presumably vampirize Grove's backlist, then cast aside the dry husk of Grove Press to any interested bidders. Happily, such tiresome prognostications have not come to pass; the publishing image of Grove/Atlantic is, if anything, more finely honed under the auspices of the umbrella house.

Titles from Grove/Atlantic include *About Harry Towns; Big Girls Don't Cry; Barrow's Boys; The CEO of the Sofa; The Dark Clue; Elvissey; Fair Warning; A Good Scent from a Strange Mountain; Indian Country; The Last Stand of Mr. America; The Magic of Blood; A Quiet Life; The Raw and the Cooked; A Son of Thunder; Talleyrand; The Zygote Chronicles.*

Grove/Atlantic books are distributed by Publishers Group West. Grove/Atlantic does not accept unsolicited manuscripts. Query letters and SASEs should be directed to:

Amy Hundley, Editor

Brendan Cahill, Editor

Daniel Maurer, Assistant Editor

Atlantic Monthly Press

Atlantic Monthly Press paces the spectrum of commercial categories, publishing hardcover and trade paperback editions in memoirs, belles lettres, history, social sciences, current affairs, natural history, ethnology, lifestyle, fashion, and cuisine, in addition to literary and popular fiction. AMP authors have over the years garnered an enormous

G

wealth of recognition for their work, including Pulitzers, Nobels, and National Book Awards. The AMP Traveler series encompasses nonfiction works that offer unstinting looks at nations, cultures, and peoples of the world.

Atlantic Monthly Press has long been representative of the highest aims of American publishing—with a list that features quality writing, fine production, and strong commercial presence. Atlantic Monthly Press was inaugurated originally (in 1917) to be primarily a book-publishing vehicle for writers associated with *Atlantic Monthly* magazine. From 1925 through 1984, the press was an imprint of Boston's Little, Brown. Atlantic Monthly Press was bought by Carl Navarre in 1985, and under current owner-publisher Morgan Entrekin (who bought out Navarre in 1991), AMP (now in consort with Grove) continues as a leading force in American letters.

Prospective authors please note that Grove/Atlantic no longer accepts unsolicited material.

Grove Press

Grove Press accents trade nonfiction and fiction with a sharp cultural consciousness and literary flair. The house continues to expand on its powerful backlist base by engaging at the forefront of publishing trends: Grove publishes a line of feature-film screenplays and has instituted a new poetry series.

Grove Press was founded in 1951 by literary trailblazer Barney Rosset, who established a tradition of enterprising lists that featured some of the finest and most fearless writing from around the globe. This literary institution was purchased by Ann Getty in 1985; in league with the British-based house of Weidenfeld & Nicholson, the publisher (briefly) operated under the sobriquet Grove Weidenfeld. With the early retreat of the Weidenfeld interests, the fate of Grove was a popular topic of publishing tattle—rumored by some to be perpetually on the block, both prior and subsequent to the house's merger with Atlantic Monthly Press.

Throughout these corporate shifts, Grove nevertheless extended its distinguished reputation, with a masterly mix of backlist offerings, as well as with commercially successful and stimulating new titles—as befits the Grove tradition.

The Grove nonfiction list covers biography and memoirs, popular culture worldwide, literary criticism, history, and politics.

Grove/Atlantic Monthly editors acquire in all areas consistent with house description. Prospective authors please note that Grove/Atlantic no longer accepts unsolicited material. However, you may still send a query or (occasionally) talk directly with an editor before sending a manuscript. Query letters and SASEs should be directed to:

Joan Bingham, Executive Editor

Morgan Entrekin, Publisher

G

GULF PUBLISHING COMPANY

All operations ceased in 2000.

HARCOURT INC.

Harcourt Trade Children's Books

Harvest Books

San Diego office:

525 B Street, Suite 1900, San Diego, CA 92101-4495
619-231-6616

New York office:
15 East 26th Street, New York, NY 10010

The Harcourt trade division publishes the gamut of nonfiction categories, as well as some serious and commercial fiction, in hardcover and paperback editions. Special lines include Harcourt's Judaica backlist, literary works in translation, the Harvest imprint (which accents American and international literature and culture in trade paper originals and reprints), Gulliver Books (popular works in hardcover and trade paper for readers of all ages).

Harcourt (founded in 1919) has through the decades evolved into a publishing house of prodigious reach. Harcourt's multidimensional sprawl encompasses offices in such diverse locations as Chicago, Orlando, San Diego, Toronto, and New York. Although the trade-publishing program was trimmed markedly through the late 1980s into the early 1990s, Harcourt (formerly Harcourt Brace Jovanovich) remains particularly potent in the arena of educational materials and texts, as well as professional reference.

Among Harcourt subsidiaries are Academic Press, Johnson Reprint (scholarly and special-interest titles), W. B. Saunders (professional and academic medical publications), and Holt, Rinehart & Winston (focusing on the educational market from elementary through university levels).

On the Harcourt list: *Riddle of the Compass* by Amir D. Aczel; *Double Down* by Frederick and Steven Barthelme; *A Hole in the Earth* by Robert Bausch; *Advent of the Algorithm* by David Berlinski; *Presidential Inaugurations* by Paul. F. Boller, Jr.; *Devil's Valley* and *Rights of Desire* by Andre Brink; *Spytime* and *Elvis in the Morning* by William F. Buckley, Jr.; *An Honorable Defeat* by William C. Davis; *Allegiance* by David Detzer; *Slammerkin* by Emma Donoghue; *Peppered Moth* by Margaret Drabble; *Under the Skin* by Michael Faber; *Troy* by Adele Geras; *Talking in the Dark* by Laura Glen Louis; *The Other Statue* by Edward Gorey; *At End of the Day* by George V. Higgins; *Soulcatcher* by Charles Johnson; *Unwinding the Clock* by Jonsson Bodil; *Painter of Birds* by Lidia Jorge; *Head Game* by Roger Kahn; *Blue Bedspread* by Raj Damal Jha; *A Case of Curiosities* by Allen Kurzweil; *America's Undeclared War* by Daniel Lazare; *Tales from Earthsea* by Ursula K. Le Guin; *Six Figures* by Fred G. Leebron; *Stolen Words* by Thomas Mallon; *Hunters* by Claire Messud; *Knick Knack Paddy Whack* by Ardal O'Hanlon; *Home Run* by George Plimpton; *Mermaids Explained* by Christopher Reid; *Lost Legends of New Jersey* by Rederick Reiken; *Rails Under My Back* by Jeffery Renard Allen; *Scandalmonger* by William Safire; *Journey to Portugal* by Jose Saramago; *Nebula Awards Showcase 2001* by Robert Silverberg; *Jumping Fire* by Murray A. Taylor; *Confessions of Mycroft Holmes* by Marcel Theroux; *Half Empty, Half Full* by Susan C. Vaughan; *Why We Hurt* by Frank

T. Vertosick, Jr.; *Word Count* by Barbara Wallraff; *Secret Lives of Word* by Paul West; *One Man's Justice* by Akira Yoshimura.

Harcourt handles its own distribution. Send query letters with SASEs to:

Walter Bode, Senior Editor—Literary fiction and nonfiction

Ann Patty, Executive Editor—Literary fiction, women's fiction

Daniel H. Farley, Vice President and Publisher (New York and San Diego)—Adult trade books

Jane Isay, Editor in Chief (New York)—Nonfiction books; hardcover originals; also works intended for the Harvest trade paper line

Drenka Willen, Editor (New York)—Literary fiction, translations; some poetry

Harcourt Trade Children's Books

Gulliver Books
Gulliver Green
Red Wagon Books

Harcourt children's categories include picture books, easy readers, nonfiction, fiction, poetry, big books, older readers, and reference books.

Harcourt produces a full offering of children's books in hardcover and paperback. Many Harcourt titles are presented as books for all ages—intended to embrace a wide readership range.

The house features several distinct imprints for young readers. Among them: Gulliver Books, Gulliver Green, Gulliver Books in Paperback, Red Wagon Books, Magic Carpet Books, Harcourt Big Books, Harcourt Creative Curriculum Connections, and the paperback lines Odyssey and Voyager Books—along with a lineup of author videos. Libros Viajeros is the Voyager line of Spanish-language books.

On the Harcourt children's list: *Lou Gehrig* by David A. Adler; *Baby Duck's New Friend* by Frank and David Asch; *Stella's Dancing Days* by Sandy Asher; *Little Green* by Keith Baker; *Twinnies* by Eve Bunting; *Marco's Run* by Wesley Cartier; *Miles Away from Home* by Joan Vcottle; *Splash!* by Driane and Aruego Jose Dewey; *Deep Wizardry* by Diane Duane; *Lizards, Frogs and Polliwogs* and *Kipper and the Egg* by Mick Inkpen.

Unsolicited manuscripts are no longer accepted. Editors now work exclusively through literary agents.

Harvest Books

Harvest Books, the trade paperback imprint of Harcourt Inc. offers the best from the house's illustrious 77-year publishing history, as well as from its distinguished present.

Harvest Books publishes fiction, nonfiction, and poetry by some of the most exciting writers and celebrities. Many Harcourt hardcovers are published simultaneously in paperback by Harvest Books. Representative titles include *The Years with Laura Diaz* by Carlos Fuentes; *Reading Magic* by Mem Fox; *Jell-O: A Biography* by Carolyn Wyman; *The Only Investment Guide You'll Ever Need* by Andrew Tobias; *The Tao of Elvis* by David

H

Rosen; *Field Guide* by Gwendolen Gross; *The Columnist* by Jeffrey Frank; *Snow Mountain Passage* by James D. Houston.

Although Harcourt has greatly reduced its acquisitions of commercially oriented titles, the house is still active in the trade arena. Query letters and SASEs should be directed to:

André Bernard, Editor in Chief, Harvest Books

Katie Hesford, Editor

Jen Charat, Editor

HARLEQUIN BOOKS/SILHOUETTE BOOKS

Red Dress Ink

300 East 42nd Street, 6th Floor, New York, NY 10017
212-682-6080

Harlequin and Silhouette publish romance novels, love stories, and women's fiction. With commanding emphasis on these interrelated categories, the publisher is always experimenting with inventive, distinctive lines that explore new approaches to the age-old tradition of tales of amour.

The Harlequin Books New York office issues several Harlequin series; the rest of the list is published from the Harlequin Enterprises base in Ontario, Canada (please see directory of Canadian publishers and editors), and the house's United Kingdom branch (contact information for which is listed under the Harlequin listing in the Canadian section). Silhouette Books (a division of Harlequin with editorial offices in New York) is profiled in a separate subentry further on.

Both Harlequin and Silhouette provide editorial guidelines for writers who wish to submit manuscripts for publishing consideration. Included in these materials are series requirements—including tips for authors regarding plot and character (some of which are applicable to other fiction-genre areas), as well as nuts-and-bolts advice pertaining to the preferred physical properties of manuscripts they review.

Harlequin Books

Harlequin Books is an innovator—not only in the romance category field, but also in defining and refining the market for women's fiction in general. The Harlequin enterprise continues to access that important market sector through venues that range from direct marketing to discount-department-store wire racks to the woodgrained shelves of major book-chain superstores.

A précis of the Harlequin Books American lines follows.

Harlequin American Romance is an exciting series of passionate and emotional love stories—contemporary, engrossing, and uniquely American. These are longer, satisfying novels of conflict and challenge, stories of modern men and women dealing with life and love in today's changing world. Harlequin American Romance offers a lineup of contemporary, upbeat, action-packed novels, set in a world where everything is possible—not problem-based or introspective. These stories feature a characteristically self-assured, perceptive American woman as heroine. The hero is a dynamic American man who is irresistible, whether he's rough around the edges, earthy, slick, or sophisticated. Sizzling repartee and one-upmanship are hallmarks of the characters' attraction.

Because romance is all about mystery . . . Harlequin Intrigue offers something unique in the world of romance fiction: a compelling blend of romance, action, and suspense. These complex contemporary stories are chock-full of dynamic drama in the finest Harlequin tradition. Harlequin Intrigue is an exciting presentation of romance within such genre formats as a hidden identity, a woman-in-jeopardy, who did its, and thrillers. The love story is central to the mystery at the level of the novel's premise. The heroine and her hero must be indispensable in solving the mystery or completing whatever adventure they undertake. Their lives are on the line, as are their hearts.

Harlequin Historicals are tales of yesterday written for today's women. This distinctly different line delivers a compelling and quickly paced love story with all the scope of a traditional historical novel. Passionate romance and historical richness combine to give Harlequin Historicals a unique flavor. Harlequin Historicals are conceived as sweeping period romances and range from Medieval sagas to lighthearted Westerns and everything in-between. These romance titles should be authentically detailed and realistic (to provide atmosphere, rather than a history lesson). Heroes and heroines are equally strong-willed, with their relationship the focus of the story. The writing should be rich and evocative, with the characters bringing the material alive so that the reader may connect with and appreciate the attributes of the historical setting. The story focus is on the heroine and how one man changes her life forever; the stories must have depth and complexity: Subplots and important secondary characters are necessary items here.

Length of manuscript and level of sensuality vary from series to series; contact Harlequin for detailed editorial guidelines. When corresponding with Harlequin, please specify the series for which your manuscript is intended. Query letters and SASEs should be directed to:

Denise O'Sullivan, Associate Senior Editor, Harlequin Intrigue

Melissa Endlich, Associate Editor

Melissa Jeglinski, Associate Senior Editor, Harlequin American Romance

Tara Gavin, Editorial Director

Tracy Farrell, Senior Editor/Editorial Coordinator, Harlequin Historicals and Steeple Hill Love Inspired

Ann Leslie Tuttle, Associate Editor

Kim Nadelson, Associate Editor

Tina Colombo, Associate Editor

Priscilla Berthiaume, Associate Editor

Silhouette Books

Silhouette Books publishes adult category romances set in a contemporary milieu. Authors must indicate with their submissions for which series their work is intended. Silhouette Books was previously a major competitor of Harlequin Enterprises, its current parent company. A summary of the Silhouette romance lines follows.

Silhouette Romance is the house's original line of romance fiction. Silhouette Romance novels are contemporary, tender, emotional stories for today's reader, featuring the challenges and changes that occur as a couple falls in love. The wonder of a reassuring romance is that it can touch every woman's heart, no matter her age or experience. Although the hero and the heroine do not make love unless married, continuing sexual tension and a strong romantic and emotional awareness keep the reader engaged. Silhouette encourages writers to come up with fresh twists to classic themes, as well as innovative, original stories. New writers are always welcome.

Silhouette Desire is a passionate, powerful, and provocative series with a strong emotional impact. Built on believable situations about how two people grow and develop, the plots capture the intensity of falling in love and explore the emotional and physical aspects of a meaningful relationship. Silhouette Desire accents the sensuous side of romance. These books are written for today's woman, whether innocent or experienced. The conflict should be emotional, springing naturally from within the characters. The characters do not have to be married to make love, but lovemaking is not taken lightly. New slants on classic formulas are welcome. Secondary characters and subplots must blend with the core story.

Silhouette Special Edition novels are substantial, contemporary romances that explore issues that heighten the drama of living and loving through true-to-life characters and compelling, romantic plots. Sophisticated and packed with emotion, these novels are for every woman who dreams of building a home with a very special man. With grace, courage, and determination, each of these vivacious heroines is empowered to be all that she can—lover, wife, mother—as she makes her dreams come true. Sensuality may be sizzling or subtle. The plot can run the gamut from the wildly innovative to the comfortably traditional. The novel's depth and emotional richness should contribute to the overall effect of a very special romance between unforgettable, fully developed characters.

Silhouette Intimate Moments features characters swept into a passionate world that is larger than life. These novels explore new directions by setting the core romance within the framework of today's mainstream novels: glamor, melodrama, suspense, and adventure, even occasionally paranormal. Let your imagination be your guide. Excitement is the key to a successful intimate moment novel. Your reader should be swept along with your characters as emotions run high against the backdrop of a compelling, complex, and always dramatic plot. Manuscript length and other series requirements vary; detailed editorial guidelines are available from the publisher. When querying, please specify the series for which your work is intended. Query letters and SASEs should be directed to:

Gail Chasan, Editor

Joan Marlow Golan, Senior Editor, Silhouette Desire

Karen Taylor Richman, Senior Editor, Silhouette Special Edition

Leslie Wainger, Executive Senior Editor, Silhouette Intimate Moments

Lynda Curnyn, Editor

Mary Theresa Hussey, Senior Editor, Silhouette Romance

Tara Gavin, Editorial Director

Julie Barnett, Editor

Allison Lyons, Assistant Editor

Shannon Degen, Assistant Editor

Mavis Allen, Editor

Stephanie Maurer, Assistant Editor

Patience Smith, Associate Editor

Stacy Boyd, Associate Editor

Margaret O'Neill Marbury, Associate Senior Editor, Red Dress Ink
   The Editorial Staff, Harlequin/Silhouette/Mills and Boon/Steeple Hill
   Born/Sign: Editorial age range is from early 20s to over 50, and we include every sign of the zodiac.
   Employment history/editor career path: It varies with the editor. Some of the senior editorial staff have been with the company over 20 years; some of the junior and senior staff have worked at other publishing houses, both in romance publishing and other genres.
   Personal interests: Responses include reading (of course!); walking; aerobics; fishing; salsa dancing; squash; art and sculpture; theater; architecture; interior design; dining out; psychology; travel; photography; watching television and movies; kids; playing the stock market.
   What would you be doing if you were not an editor? Responses include unhappy accountant who reads romance at every opportunity; personal trainer and fitness instructor; veterinarian; archaeologist; film camera person; architect; classical actress or drama coach; librarian; teacher; bookstore employee; researcher; or producer for a Web site.
   What has been your most successful book that you have acquired to date? We are proud of the success of a wide variety of authors who write or have written category romances for one or more of our various series and imprints and of the dedication to their readership that has led to many of our original authors, including some who've gone on to major mainstream success to continue to contribute to our category lines. The honors garnered by our authors include positions on the *New York Times*, *USA Today,* and *Publishers Weekly* bestseller lists, as well as numerous awards such as the coveted RITA awards bestowed by the Romance Writers of America.
   What books have you acquired that make you the most proud? What books that you have acquired reflect the types of books you like to represent? We're proud of all our books, and we're especially proud that in order to satisfy the demands of our readership—to be something beloved and familiar they can rely on, as well as something fresh and unique that will capture their imagination—we've more than doubled our output of incremental offerings during the past 10 years and increased the number of series as well. These devoted readers can count on our books to both celebrate their values and provide a respite from the daily stress and demands of their lives, reinvigorating their spirit. Harlequin celebrated its 50th anniversary in 1999; Silhouette is celebrating its 20th anniversary in 2000; and Mills & Boon has been publishing romance novels for more than 7 decades. Our category publishing activity has steadily increased and continues to be vibrant in 24 languages in more than 100 international markets.
   Do you represent fiction? If so, what do you look for? Yes. We are always looking for writers with a distinctive, appealing, and upbeat voice who can create vivid, sympathetic

H

characters and offer fresh approaches to the classic romance themes, along with compelling storytelling.

What do you want to see less of? It's not what you do, but how you do it—but keep in mind that we are a romance publisher. A happy ending is a must. Also, while there may be other elements in our romance novels, like a mystery or secondary plot, the focus must be on the love story between the hero and heroine. Please note that we do not accept e-mailed submissions or multiple submissions.

Do you represent nonfiction? No. We publish category romance, including inspirational romance, all of which is fiction.

Do you require book proposals? If so, what do you look for in evaluating a book proposal? Yes. We ask for a query letter that includes a word count and pertinent facts about the author as a writer, including familiarity with the romance genre and publishing history, and what series the project is appropriate for, as well as a brief synopsis (no more than two single-spaced pages). When we request a submission, we want to see a complete manuscript from unpublished authors and a proposal consisting of the first three chapters and an outline from published authors. We look for a clear idea of both plot and characters and an exciting new author voice.

Are certain aspects of a book proposal given more weight than others? A distinctive, appealing voice and compelling characterization are distinguishing factors that often get an editor's attention.

What process do you use for making a decision? What is the process for acquisition; is there a committee? If the proposal works for us, we ask to see the complete manuscript from unpublished authors and an outline and three sample chapters from previously published authors. The submission may be sent to an outside reader for evaluation before being considered in house. Both an acquiring editor and the senior editor of the series for which the work is targeted have to read and approve the submission in order for it to be bought.

Are you interested in work geared for the masses (readers of *People, The Star,* etc.)? With romance novels comprising close to half of all mass-market books sold, the romance genre continues its decades-long domination of the marketplace. As the world's largest publisher of category romance novels, Harlequin, with its imprints Harlequin, Silhouette, Steeple Hill, Mills & Boon, and its foreign language imprints, constantly strives to meet the needs of its growing marketplace.

Are agents important? Why? Harlequin/Silhouette/Mills & Boon are looking for romance authors with fresh, compelling voices. An agent is not necessary—we consider each and every submission, whether it comes in over the transom or from an agent—but we urge interested authors to research the genre fully and write in for our current guidelines before sending us any material. For over 15 years, most of our lines have requested unagented authors to send query letters with SASEs, while agented authors skip the query letter stage in favor of complete manuscripts (new authors) and proposals (published authors). Both methods have resulted in publication and long-term careers with us for large numbers of authors.

Do you like new writers? What should new writers do to break into the business? Yes! We publish new authors all the time within all of our series. A talented writer will bring her own special magic to whatever type of romance she writes, and a talented editor will discern it.

How should writers approach you? After reviewing our submission requirements on our Web site, eHarlequin.com, or sending in an SASE and request for our guidelines, please send a query letter and 2-page synopsis to the romance series you're targeting. Information can also be obtained from libraries, which often carry writers' guides, and some authors join writers' organizations—one specifically focused on romance writers and writing is Romance Writers of America (RWA).

What are some common mistakes writers make? What really gets on your nerves? Some new writers take too long to get into their story, whereas ideally the reader should be hooked from page one. If the most compelling material is "saved" for chapter 3 or 4, it's too late. Within the shorter category romances, new writers sometimes neglect to focus on the hero and heroine and allot too many pages to minor characters. Too often writers are not aware of our guidelines or lack an understanding of category romance and submit manuscripts that are inappropriate for our series. Swooning, passing-out heroines are a thing of the past and are not welcome. We do publish "bodice rippers." New writers will sometimes stagnate because they can't put aside a rejected manuscript and start writing a new one. Be aware that many category writers experience a few rejections before they make their first sale. Our biggest headaches are the result of contracted manuscripts not being delivered in a timely fashion, especially when we aren't given adequate notice of delays.

What can writers do to get your attention and to avoid the slush pile? Read widely in the series you've targeted. Research our books before submitting your manuscript. All of our guidelines are available at our Web site, eHarlequin.com. Keep in mind, too, that ultimately it is the emotional appeal of a given story, not its trendiness or lack thereof, that makes it a reader's favorite.

What have been some of your best experiences with writers or in your job? We are proud that authors who were among the original authors for each of our imprints are still writing for us and that close to 100 of our current authors have published 20 or more books with Harlequin/Silhouette, Mills & Boon, or both. We value as well the many letters we get from readers telling us how much our books mean to them and the ways in which our authors' stories have touched and even changed their lives.

What, if anything, makes you different from other editors? The strength of our brand allows us to acquire never-before-published authors and publish them effectively. And while our titles must, of course, always meet our readers' expectations, because we are a unique publisher, we can let authors experiment with stories that never would have been published at a midlist house. We also publish many authors and many books from each author and, therefore, work with her editorially to develop her voice and a successful career. Within category romance, we offer our authors a variety of options to accommodate their particular talents and styles—their books may be contemporary or historical; tender or sexy; short enough to be read in one sitting or longer and more complex; pure romance or romance with elements of mystery, suspense, or paranormal; stand-alone books or miniseries; and in addition to category romance, we also offer authors the opportunity to contribute to short story anthologies and to write single titles that often evolve from a popular miniseries.

H

Is there anything you would like to see changed in the industry? We'd like to see a heightened perception of the romance genre and an elimination of negative bias against romance. In terms of author relations, we would like to see a timely delivery of manuscripts, as well as a willingness to work with the publisher to find effective solutions to problems.

Any advice for writers? Any way to improve the system for you? Any additional thoughts? Please keep in mind that inadequately thought-through or unsalable submissions take up significant editorial time and lengthen response time. Authors who are responsive to reader tastes and present polished, professionally presented material avoid this.

HARPERCOLLINS PUBLISHING GROUPS

HarperCollins General Books Group

HarperCollins Children's Books Group

Zondervan (See separate entry in Religious Publishers)

10 E. 53rd Street, New York, NY 10022-5299
212-207-7000
www.harpercollins.com

HarperCollins Publishing Groups produces a broad variety of commercial, trade, professional, academic, and mass-market books in hardcover, paperback, and multimedia editions. As one of the largest English-language publishers in the world, HarperCollins is a subsidiary of News Corporation, which is owned by the Australia media giant Rupert Murdock. The main office is in New York, but publishing groups are also located in Canada, the U.K., and Australasia, and imprints of various groups can be found across the United States.

HarperCollins' holdings include Fox Broadcasting, Twentieth Century Fox, *TV Guide,* more than 128 newspapers, and other media interests worldwide.

Submissions: HarperCollins Publishers is willing to consider material submitted by literary agents and previously published authors, as well as submissions accompanied by a positive assessment from a manuscript assessment agency. Please note that 12 weeks or more may elapse before the editors are able to respond to your proposal.

If the previous criteria are met, the following guidelines apply:

For fiction, send a full manuscript. For nonfiction, send a full proposal and two sample chapters. HarperCollins requires all submitted materials to be typed in double spacing on A4 paper. Avoid elaborate binding or stapling. Do not send an electronic version of your manuscript (including computer disks, e-mailed files, or Web site proposals)—the editors will request one if they decide to publish the book.

Include an SASE that is large enough for the return of your manuscript and that bears sufficient postage to cover costs. Please make sure you keep a copy, and never send original illustrations.

Subject to the previous criteria, HarperCollins Publishers will consider fiction, nonfiction, and children's books aimed at a general trade market. The house is not currently looking for poetry or academic books.

These guidelines apply to all submissions across the range of imprints.

HarperCollins General Books Group

Amistad Press
Avon
Cliff Street Books
Ecco Press
Eos
HarperBusiness
HarperCollins
HarperEntertainment
HarperResource
HarperSanFrancisco
Perennial
PerfectBound
Quill
RAYO
ReganBooks
William Morrow

From romance to religion, pop culture to perennial classics—in traditional print, audio, and e-books—HarperCollins imprints have it all. Please see individual subentries for more information.

Amistad Press

Amistad Press publishes works by and about people of African descent and subjects and themes that have significant influence on the intellectual, cultural, and historical perspectives of a world audience. Formats include hardcover and paperback.

Representative nonfiction titles: *The Amistad Pictorial History of the African American Athlete: Collegiate* by Francis C. Harris; *It's All Good Hair: The Definitive Guide to Styling and Grooming Black Children's Hair* by Michele N-K Collison; *The House That Jack Built: My Life As a Trailblazer in Broadcasting and Entertainment* by Hal Jackson, et al.; *Essence Brings You Great Cooking* by Jonell Nash; *Not Guilty: Twelve Black Men Speak Out on Law, Justice, and Life* by Jabari Asim (Editor); *Lighten Up: The Healthquest 30-Day Weight-Loss Program* by Therman Evans (Contributor), et al.; *The Warrior Method: A Program for Rearing Healthy Black Boys* by Raymond A. Winbush.

Titles indicative of the fiction list: *Love the One You're With* by James Earl Hardy; *Black Heat* by Norman Kelley and Norma Kelly; *A Phat Death: A Nina Halligan Mystery* by Norman Kelley.

Avon Books

Avon Books, founded in 1941, is the second-oldest paperback publishing house in the United States. Recently acquired by the HarperCollins Publishing Groups, Avon Books

H

publishes titles for adults and young readers. Avon is recognized for pioneering the historical romance category and continues to produce commercial literature for the broadest possible audience in mass-market paperback format.

Titles indicative of Avon Romance: *Dancing at Midnight* by Julia Quinn; *Heaven, Texas* by Susan Elizabeth Phillips; *On a Wicked Dawn* by Stephanie Laurens; *An Affair to Remember* by Karen Hawkins; *Her Highness, My Wife* by Victoria Alexander; *Man at Work* by Elaine Fox; *Black Silk* by Judith Ivory; *The Maiden Warrior* by Mary Reed McCall; *Marry Me* by Susan Kay Law; *Tempt Me with Kisses* by Margaret Moore.

Representative titles of Avon Mystery: *The Hanging Valley* by Peter Robinson; *Fatal Truth* by Robin Burcell; *The House of Seven Mables: A Jane Jeffry Mystery* by Jill Churchill; *Paradise Lost: A Joanna Brady Mystery* by J. A. Jance; *SEALs Sub Rescue: Operation Endurance* by S. M. Gunn; *Splendor in the Glass: A Den of Antiquity Mystery* by Tamar Myers; *The Bounty Hunters* by Elmore Leonard; *Hombre* by Elmore Leonard; *Lord of the Silent: A Novel of Suspense* by Elizabeth Peters; *Yesterday's Shadow* by Jon Cleary; *A Killing Season* by Jessica Speart.

Avon Romance Submission Guidelines

Avon does not read unsolicited manuscripts or proposals, but it does have a submissions process in place for budding romance writers and encourages them to send their query letters and synopses. Avon is currently looking for romances in the areas of historical romance, African American romance, and contemporary romance, including romantic suspense.

The following is from the publisher's own Web site.

Historical Romance

(100,000 words/approximately 400 ms. pages)

A man and a woman meet—she's like no other woman he's ever known. She tantalizes him in ways he never thought possible . . . and he'll stop at nothing to make her his—forever.

At Avon, we're seeking deliciously romantic historical novels for all parts of the list—Avon Romance, Avon Treasure, and Avon Superleader. These are love stories set primarily in Great Britain and the United States before 1900, and they are filled with all the promise—and passion—that Avon readers expect.

Contemporary Romance

(100,000 words/approximately 400 ms. pages)

When Avon contemporary romance came on the scene, the face of romance was changed forever. If you'd like to be part of this explosion, don't hesitate to send your manuscript to us!

We seek stories of emotional complexity, written by authors with unique voices. Books with humor, drama, romantic suspense—all types and tones can be right for Avon. If your manuscript is exciting, electrifying, and exceptional, then we want to see it.

AFRICAN AMERICAN ROMANCE

(90,000 words/approximately 380 pages)

We have listened to many of our readers and are actively seeking romance with African American heroes and heroines. These should be contemporary love stories of approximately 90,000–100,000 words, set in the United States. This is not a "line." Each author will be packaged, and developed, individually. So, if your manuscript has the unforgettable emotion, irresistible characters—especially the hero—and sizzling sensuality that are hallmarks of Avon romance, please send it right away.

HOW TO SUBMIT A MANUSCRIPT

To submit your historical or contemporary romance, please *query first. We strongly urge you to query by e-mail.* Your query should be brief, no more than a two-page description of your book. Do not send chapters or a full synopsis at this time. You will receive a response—either a decline or a request for more material—in approximately one to two weeks.

Please e-mail your query to avonromance@harpercollins.com.

Direct your electronic query to:

(Ms.) Carrie Feron, Executive Editor—Commercial nonfiction and mass-market fiction

Patricia Lande Grader, Executive Editor—General nonfiction

Lucia Macro, Senior Editor—Romance

Cliff Street Books

Cliff Street Books publishes distinct, high-concept books that speak to a wide audience. This imprint, named for the house where the four Harper Brothers published Melville, Poe, Twain, Dickens, James, and Trollope, publishes select titles in literary fiction and a broad range of books in the categories of self-help, inspiration, social commentary, style, and fashion. Formats include hardcover, paperback, and multimedia.

Titles representative of the nonfiction list: *The Public Ivies: America's Flagship Public Universities* (Greene's Guides to Educational Planning) by Howard Greene, et al.; *The Grrl Genius Guide to Life: A 12 Step Program on How to Become a Grrl Genius, According to Me!* by Cathryn Michon; *Stroke-Free for Life: The Complete Guide to Stroke Prevention and Treatment* by David O. Wiebers; *Murder in Spokane: Catching a Serial Killer* by Mark Fuhrman; *Tournament Week: Inside the Ropes and Behind the Scenes on the PGA Tour* by John Strege; *The Placebo Response: How You Can Release the Body's Inner Pharmacy for Better Health* by Howard Brody, Daralyn Brody (Contributor); *Racing the Antelope: What Animals Can Teach Us About Running and Life* by Bernd Heinrich.

Fiction titles indicative of Cliff Street Books' list: *The Width of the Sea* by Michelle Chalfoun; *The Blind Side of the Heart* by Michael C. White; *A Dream of Wolves: A Novel* by Michael C. White; *Past Forgetting: My Memory Lost and Found* by Jill Robinson; *One of the Guys* by Robert Clark Young.

H

Ecco Press

The Ecco Press currently publishes 60 titles per year by such critically acclaimed authors as John Ashbery, Paul Bowles, Italo Calvino, Gerald Early, Louise Glück, Robert Hass, Zbigniew Herbert, Erica Jong, Cormac McCarthy, Czeslaw Milosz, Joyce Carol Oates, Josef Skvorecky, Mark Strand, and Tobias Wolff. The Press has also created a number of literary series that today enjoy a special celebrity in the world of book publishing.

Titles in literature and fiction on this list include *Middle Age: A Romance* by Joyce Carol Oates; *Wide Open* by Nicola Barker; *Memoir of the Hawk* by James Tate; *Crocodile Soup* by Julia Darling; *Oyster* by John Biguenet; *The Seven Ages* by Louise Glück; *The Torturer's Apprentice* by John Biguenet; *Now That My Father Lies Down Beside Me: New & Selected Poems, 1970–2000* by Stanley Plumly.

Books indicative of the cooking, food, and wine category are *Salt: Grain of Life* by Pierre Laszlo; *A Short History of Wine* by Rod Phillips; *Cuisines of India: The Art and Tradition of Regional Indian Cooking* by Smita Chandra and Sanjeev Chandra; *Writing at the Kitchen Table: The Authorized Biography of Elizabeth David* by Artemis Cooper; *Kitchen Confidential: Adventures in the Culinary Underbelly* by Anthony Bourdain; *Madhur Jaffrey's Step-by-Step Cooking: Over 150 Dishes from India and the Far East, Including Thailand, Vietnam, Indonesia, and Malaysia* by Madhur Jaffrey.

Titles representative of Ecco Press memoirs and biographies include *Until Death Do Us Part: My Struggle to Reclaim Colombia* by Ingrid Betancourt and Steven Rendall; *Skating to Antarctica: A Journey to the End of the World* by Jenny Diski; *Pushkin: A Biography* by Elaine Feinstein; *Man Flies: The Story of Alberto Santos-Dumont, Master of the Balloon, Conqueror of the Air* by Nancy Winters.

Query letters and SASEs should be directed to:

Daniel Halpern, Vice President and Editorial Director

Eos

H

Eos, founded in 1998, has already gained a positive reputation for its progressive editorial style, not to mention its bold, "break the rules" packaging and innovative promotional campaigns. Named for the Greek goddess of the dawn, Eos is committed to "bringing new life to science fiction and fantasy." Bestselling Eos authors include Raymond E. Feist, Anne McCaffrey, and Gregory Benford.

Titles representative of this list: *The Watch* by Dennis Danvers; *Wheel of the Infinite* by Martha Wells; *The Annunciate* by Severna Park; *The Great Book of Amber: The Complete Amber Chronicles, 1–10* by Roger Zelazny; *Acorna's Search* by Anne McCaffrey; *Elizabeth Ann Scarborough, Child of Venus* by Pamela Sargent; *Hammerfall* by C. J. Cherry; *The Isle of Battle: Book Two of the Swans' War* by Sean Russell; *The Longest Way Home* by Robert Silverberg; *Metaplanetary: A Novel of Interplanetary War* by Tony Daniel; *Year's Best Fantasy* by David G. Hartwell; *Icebones* by Stephen Baxter; *Light Music* by Kathleen Ann Goonan; *Year's Best Science Fiction* by David G. Hartwell (Editor); *The King of Dreams: The King of Dreams, a Majipoor Novel* by Robert Silverberg; *Memory of Fire: Book One of the World Gates* by Holly Lisle; *Schild's Ladder* by Greg Egan; *Destiny: Book Three of the Blending Enthroned* by Sharon Green; *Longtusk* by Stephen Baxter; *The Visitor* by Sheri S. Tepper; *The Mask and the Sorceress: The House of the Pandragore* by Dennis Jones; *Bones of the Earth* by Michael Swanwick; *The Fresco* by Sheri S. Tepper; *The Beyond* by Jeffrey Ford; *Peril's Gate (Wars of Light and Shadow, Book 6)* by Janny Wurts.

HarperBusiness

HarperBusiness produces innovative ideas and distinctive voices in the categories of general business, leadership, finances, entrepreneurship, and corporate strategies.

Titles representative of this list include *Money for Life* by Robert Sheard; *The Money Trap* by Ron Gallen; *Die Broke: Complete Book of Money* by Stephan M. Pollan; *Built to Last: Successful Habits of Visionary Companies* by James C. Collins and Jerry I. Porras; *Trading with the Enemy: Seduction and Betrayal on Jim Cramer's Wall Street* by Nicholas W. Maier; *The E-Myth Revisited: Why Most Small Businesses Don't Work and What to Do About It* by Michael E. Gerber; *Good to Great: Why Some Companies Make the Leap . . . and Other's Don't* [abridged] by James C. Collins, Jim Collins (Reader) (Audio CD); *Crossing the Chasm: Marketing and Selling High-Tech Products to Mainstream Customers* by Geoffrey A. Moore and Regis McKenna; *The Innovator's Dilemma: The Revolutionary National Bestseller That Changed the Way We Do Business* by Clayton M. Christensen; *The 22 Immutable Laws of Marketing: Violate Them at Your Own Risk* by Al Ries and Jack Trout; *Value Rx: How to Make the Most of Your Organization's Assets and Relationships* by Edward J. Giniat and Barry D. Libert; *Living on the Fault Line: Managing for Shareholder Value in Any Economy* by Geoffrey A. Moore; *The Cycle of Leadership: How Great Leaders Teach Their Companies to Win* by Noel M. Tichy; *Secrets of Six-Figure Women: Surprising Strategies to Up Your Earnings and Change Your Life* by Barbara Stanny; *The Chasm Companion* by Paul Wiefels and Geoffrey A. Moore; *The Engaged Customer: Using the New Rules of Direct Marketing to Create Profitable Customer Relationships* by Hans Peter Brondmo.

Send query letters with SASEs to:

David Conti, Editor

HarperCollins

HarperCollins produces adult hardcover books, trade paperbacks, and mass-market paperback editions that cover the breadth of trade publishing categories, including feature biographies (celebrities, sports, and historical), business books, mysteries and thrillers, popular culture, humor, inspiration, and how-to (including cookbooks and health), in addition to works across most popular reference categories. HarperStyle specializes in illustrated works keyed to contemporary lifestyle, design, and culture.

Representative of HarperCollins's popular titles in general nonfiction: *Throwing the Elephant: Zen and the Art of Managing Up* by Stanley Bing; *Turning Toward the Mystery: A Dharma Life* by Stephen Levine; *The Art of the Sports Car: The Greatest Designs of the 20th Century* by Dennis Adler; *Beautiful Child* by Torey L. Hayden; *Raising Blaze: Bringing Up an Extraordinary Son in an Ordinary World* by Debra Ginsberg; *The Marriage*

Problem: How Our Culture Has Weakened Families by James Q. Wilson; *The Making of a Philosopher: An Insider's Journey Through Twentieth Century Philosophy* by Colin McGinn; *50 Ways to Save Our Children: Small, Medium, and Big Ways You Can Change a Child's Lif*e by Cheryl Saban; *Not Always So: Practicing the True Spirit of Zen* by Shunryu Suzuki, Edward Espe Brown (Editor); *HarperCollins Spanish-English, English-Spanish Dictionary* by Teresa A. Garcia (Editor); *Statecraft: Strategies for a Changing World* by Margaret Thatcher.

HarperCollins offers fiction and literary works in a diversified program that includes commercial novels and standout category titles, in addition to select literary works. HarperCollins has published such authors as Anne Rivers Siddons, Ursula K. Le Guin, Sue Miller, Len Deighton, Allen Ginsberg, Barbara Taylor Bradford, Oscar Hijuelos, Tony Hillerman, Leon Uris, and William Lashner.

Titles from HarperCollins's literature and fiction list: *Barracoon* by Zora Neale Hurston; *The Blacker the Berry: Poems* by Joyce Carol Thomas, et al.; *African Stories* by Donna Washington and James Ransome; *Flight Lessons* by Patricia Gaffney; *Law of Gravity* by Stephen Horn; *Saved* by Kate Morgenroth; *Big Mouth and Ugly Girl* by Joyce Carol Oates; *Triggerfish Twist: A Novel* by Tim Dorse; *Savannah Blues* by Mary Kay Andrews; *The Season of Lillian Dawes* by Katherine Mosby; *Chameleon: A Novel* by Mark Burnell; *The House of Blue Mangoes* by David J. Davida; *Resurrection Club* by Christopher Wallace.

Direct queries and SASEs to:

Carolyn Marino, Vice President, Editorial Director—Commercial fiction, including mysteries, suspense, and women's fiction

David Hirshey, Executive Editor—Popular culture, celebrity books, politics, current affairs

Gladys Justin Carr, Associate Publisher—Fiction: literary and commercial; nonfiction: biographies and memoirs, military and general history, nutrition, medicine, celebrity stories, popular culture, true crime, sports, current events, business

Harriet Bell, Editor—Cookbooks

Hugh Van Dusen, Executive Editor, HarperPerennial—History, biography, spirituality, self-help; fiction and nonfiction reprints and originals in quality paperback

Mauro DiPreta, Executive Editor, HarperEntertainment—Nonfiction: pop culture, humor, commercial nonfiction

Megan Newman, Editor—General nonfiction, how-to, self-help trade paperback originals

Susan Friedland, Executive Editor—Food, cookbooks, literary history

Edwin Tan, Associate Editor—Business and other nonfiction narratives, business and general humor, motivation/self-help/advice, the arts, sex and sexuality, social studies, and general fiction

Tim Duggan, Senior Editor—Serious nonfiction, literary fiction

Tom Dupre, Senior Editor—Rock biographies, comic novels

Dan Conaway, Executive Editor

HarperEntertainment

HarperEntertainment lays claim to being "your #1 media source," for television, movies, celebrities, sports, and music, from *Seinfeld* to new franchises like Mystic Knights. HarperEntertainment boasts an all-star cast of brand-name products, including NASCAR, NBA, *The X-Files,* and *Titanic.*

HarperResource

HarperResource publishes leading names and brands in the practical nonfiction and reference categories. With an emphasis on books of enduring quality that educate, inform, and motivate, HarperResource produces a wide range of resource books and reference guides, including college guides, field guides, Spanish dictionaries, film encyclopedias, and etiquette guides.

The Postal Service Guide to U.S. Stamps; Chi Fitness: A Workout for Body, Mind, and Spirit by Sue Benton and Drew Denbaum; *Emily Post's the Gift of Good Manners: A Parent's Guide to Raising Respectful, Kind, Considerate Children* by Peggy Post and Cindy Post Senning; *Kids Are Worth It: Giving Your Child the Gift of Inner Discipline* by Barbara Coloroso; *The Total Back Book* by Jennifer Sutcliffe; *HarperCollins Pocket Thesaurus* by HarperCollins UK (Editor); *HarperCollins Pocket Webster's Dictionary* by HarperCollins UK (Editor); *The Highly Selective Dictionary of Golden Adjectives: For the Extraordinarily Literate* by Eugene Ehrlich; *Thyroid Power: Ten Steps to Total Health* by Richard L. Shames and Karilee Halo Shames; *Happily Ever After* by Wendy Paris; *What Makes Flamingos Pink?* by Bill McLain; *Jane's Submarines* by Robert Hutchinson.

Direct queries and SASEs to:

Toni Sciarra, Editor

HarperSanFrancisco

353 Sacramento Street, Suite 500, San Francisco, CA 94111-3653
415-477-4400   fax: 415-477-4444
www.harpercollins.com/sanfran   e-mail: hcsanfrancisco@harpercollins.com

HarperSanFrancisco strives to be the preeminent publisher of titles on religion, spirituality, mind, body, and spirit, in hardcover and mass-market paperback. This imprint is dedicated to "publishing books that both illuminate diverse religious traditions and spiritual journeys and offer paths toward personal growth and well-being."

Titles representative of this list: *Choices: Taking Control of Your Life and Making It Matter* by Melody Beattie; *The 100 Simple Secrets of Successful People* by David Niven; *Stretching Lessons: The Daring That Starts from Within* by Sue Bender; *Just Shy of Harmony* by Philip Gulley; *The Secret of the Shadow: The Power of Owning Your Whole Story* by Debbie Ford; *Forgive for Good* by Dr. Fred Luskin; *Lives of the Saints: From Mary and Francis of Assisi to John XVIII and Mother Teresa* by Richard P. McBrien; *Dialogues with Silence: Prayers & Drawings* by Thomas Merton and Jonathan Montaldo; *A New Christianity for a New World: Why Traditional Faith Is Dying and What Should Take Its Place* by John Shelby Spong; *The Soul of Rumi: A New Collection of*

H

Ecstatic Poems by Jalal Al-Din Rumi and Coleman Barks; *The Monk Downstairs* by Tim Farrington; *The Things I Know Best: A Novel* by Lynne Hinton; *One Dharma: The Emerging Western Buddhism* by Joseph Goldstein; *Up from Here: A Guide to Transforming Emotions into Power and Freedom* by Iyanla Vanzant.

Query letters and SASEs should be directed to:

David Hennessy, Associate Editor

Elizabeth Perle, Editor at Large—Psychology/self-help; women and family, biography, alternative and complementary health; Buddhist and Jewish spirituality; lesbian and gay studies; multicultural studies

Gideon Weil, Associate Editor

Born: August 16, 1971.

Education: Vassar College—English Major.

Employment history/editor career path: I started out working in the newspaper business at the *New York Press*. I then worked at Witherspoon Associates as a literary agent for four years, and I have now been at HarperSanFrancisco for two years.

Do you represent fiction? We do acquire fiction.

Do you represent nonfiction? Yes, inspiration, self-help, narrative nonfiction.

Do you require book proposals? If so, what do you look for in evaluating a book proposal? Yes, I like to see the structure of the book, sample chapters, outline. Tell me where it fits in the marketplace.

Are certain aspects of a book proposal given more weight than others? Sample chapters.

What process do you use for making a decision? What is the process for acquisition; is there a committee? Yes, it consists of the publisher, editorial staff, and marketing and sales people.

What kinds of nonfiction books do you want to see less of? Random memoirs with no direction.

Are you interested in work geared for the masses (readers of *People, The Star,* etc.)? Yes.

Are agents important? Why? Yes. Good agents make the process run smoothly.

Do you like new writers? What should new writers do to break into the business? Yes. Be confident in writing for an audience and know who your audience is. Read books. Know how to effectively get your point across to the reader. Take your time. Know why you are writing. Sell yourself in two paragraphs.

How should writers approach you? Through agents.

What are some common mistakes writers make? What really gets on your nerves? Laziness, putting little thought into something.

What can writers do to get your attention and to avoid the slush pile? Write good, clear, concise cover letters. Put your best foot forward.

What have been some of your craziest experiences with submissions? After I have rejected a project, having family members call and try to convince me of why I am making a mistake.

What have been some of your best experiences with writers or in your job? Developing a productive author and editor relationship is the most fulfilling part of the job.

What, if anything, makes you different from other editors? I make myself available to the author, I'm conscientious, I come from the agent side so I know what is important to authors. I can negotiate and know what the common problems are that writers have and know how to effectively solve them.

Any advice for writers? Be aggressive, sell yourself, get an agent. Nothing will happen if you are passive in this business; be aggressive, but don't nag.

John V. Loudon, Executive Editor—Religious studies, biblical studies, psychology/ personal growth, inspiration, Eastern religions, Buddhist and Christian spirituality.

Renee Sedliar, Associate Editor

Born: October 28, 1970.

Education: B.A., English and Liberal Arts; M.A., Fine Arts and Creative Writing from the University of Michigan.

Employment history/editor career path: I have been at HarperSanFrancisco for five years.

Personal interests: Reading, writing, poetry, working out, sports.

What would you be doing if you were not an editor? I would teach creative writing on a high school or undergraduate level.

What has been your most successful book that you have acquired to date? I've worked with Lynne Hinton, author of *Friendship Cake, The Things I Know Best,* and *Garden of Faith.*

What books have you acquired that make you the most proud? What books that you have acquired reflect the types of books you like to represent? *Fruitflesh: Seeds of Inspiration for Women Who Write; The Monk Downstairs: A Novel; Mediation Secrets for Women.*

Do you represent fiction? If so, what are you looking for? We're starting to do more fiction here—it must have a spiritual angle. Recent titles in fiction include Lynne Hinton's books: *The Treasure of Montsegur, The Monk Downstairs.*

Do you represent nonfiction? Yes—it must have a spiritual or inspirational tone.

Do you require book proposals? If so, what do you look for in evaluating a book proposal? Yes. I look for clarity, directness of purpose, creativity, how well authors know what they want to do (where they are going), author credentials, and sample material.

Are certain aspects of a book proposal given more weight than others? It's on a per-project basis—author credentials, sample chapters, timeliness of topic.

What process do you use for making a decision? What is the process for acquisition; is there a committee? Yes, we have weekly meetings with a committee composed of the editorial staff, publicity, marketing, and the publisher.

Are you interested in work geared for the masses (readers of *People, The Star,* etc.)? Yes, as long as it has a spiritual/inspirational element.

Are agents important? Why? Yes, they make the whole publishing process go much smoother. They know which editors to send what projects to, and they help authors to understand the publishing business.

Do you like new writers? What should new writers do to break into the business? Yes, I champion the underdog. I would say to break into the business, you need to get a good agent and pay attention to the market.

H

How should writers approach you? A query letter, sample chapters, outline with SASE.

What are some common mistakes writers make? What really gets on your nerves? Lack of knowledge about their material or the market. Lack of knowledge about what we publish. General sloppiness (typos in cover letters don't make a good impression).

What can writers do to get your attention and to avoid the slush pile? Have a topic that catches my attention or write about something that appeals to me. If it doesn't appeal to me but I know of a colleague to whom it does, I will pass it on to that person. I do try to read everything that comes across my desk.

What have been some of your craziest experiences with submissions? I've received some proposals with strangely creative content, making outrageous claims along the lines of things you would find in the tabloids/*Weekly World News.*

What have been some of your best experiences with writers or in your job? Simply meeting and working with so many amazing, creative, and intelligent people.

Any advice for writers? Be conscientious, be neat and careful, pay attention to the market and to whom you are sending material, don't waste valuable time, and realize that there is a lot of work involved in writing a book.

Perennial

Perennial publishes fiction and nonfiction originals and reprints in trade paperback format. Perennial's broad range includes everything from Matt Groening's *The Simpsons* to Thomas Moore's *Care of the Soul.*

Recent titles indicative of the nonfiction list: *African Blood* by Alex Shoumatoff; *Mars and Venus in Touch* by John Gray; *Daughters of Britannia: The Lives and Times of Diplomatic Wives* by Katie Hickman; *The American Dream: Stories from the Heart of Our Nation* by Dan Rather; *Venus Envy: Power Games, Teenage Vixens, and Million-Dollar Egos on the Women's Tennis Tour* by L. Jon Wertheim; *Frida: A Biography of Frida Kahlo* by Hayden Herrera; *The Cheating of America: How Tax Avoidance and Evasion by the Super Rich Are Costing the Country Billions—And What You Can Do About It* by Charles Lewis and Bill Allison; *Happy Hours: Alcohol in a Woman's Life* by Devon Jersild; *Heart: A Natural History of the Heart-Filled Life* by Gail Godwin; *Reconstruction: America's Unfinished Revolution, 1863–1877* (Perennial Classics) by Eric Foner, et al.; *Who Owns Death?: Capital Punishment, the American Conscience, and the End of Executions* by Robert Jay Lifton and Greg Mitchell.

Titles representative of Perennial's literature and fiction list: *About the Author* by John Colapinto; *Suicide's Girlfriend: A Novella and Short Stories* by Elizabeth Evans; *Too Many Men* by Lily Brett; *Watch by Moonlight* by Kate Hawks; *Where We Lived: Short Stories* by Christina Fitzpatrick; *The Catsitters* by James Wolcott; *Edgewater: Poems* (The National Poetry Series) by Ruth L. Schwartz; *I Wish I Had a Red Dress* by Pearl Cleage; *The Justus Girls* by Evelyn "Slim" Lambright; *The Shape of Things to Come* by Maud Casey.

PerfectBound

PerfectBound, the new e-book imprint at HarperCollins, publishes a diverse list of titles. Many of the e-book titles have special features that are unavailable in other editions.

Quill

Quill reprints previously published books in mass-market paperback format.

RAYO

RAYO publishes books that exemplify the diversity within the Latino community, in both English and Spanish-language editions in hardcover and paperback. RAYO's mission is to "connect culture with thought, invigorating tradition with spirit."

Titles representative of RAYO's select list include *Thirteen Senses, a Memoir* by Victor Villaseñor; *The Hispanic Condition: The Power of a People* by Ilan Stavans; *The Twelve Gifts of Birth* by Charlene Costanzo; *El Cucuy De LA Manana/My Life in Radio's Fast Lane* by Renan Almendarez Coello; *One Hot Summer* by Carolina Aguilera Garcia and Carolina Garcia-Aguilera; *Let Their Spirits Dance* by Stella Pope Duarte; *The Republic of East LA: Stories* by Luis J. Rodriguez; *Does a Kangaroo Have a Mother Too? El Canguro Tiene Mama* by Eric Carle (Illustrator), Teresa Mlawer (Translator); *The Mexicans: A Personal Portrait of a People* by Patrick Oster; *The Wise Women of Havana* by Jose Raul Bernardo.

ReganBooks

This imprint is known for its informal slogan "Not Just the Same Old Story."

From politics to pop culture, health and fitness, to hot new fiction—wherever there's a zeitgeist, there's a Regan publishing campaign. ReganBooks boasts a stable of phenomenal and diverse bestselling authors, including Wally Lamb, Jackie Collins, Howard Stern, Robert Bork, Christopher Darden, Marilu Henner, and Dr. Barry Sears. The imprint was founded by one of publishing's most dynamic personalities, Judith Regan.

Titles indicative of the fiction list: *The Power of a Teacup: A Story of Art, Love, and Sacred Gardens* by Lissi Kaplan; *Sorcerers of the Nightwing* (The Ravenscliff Series, Book 1) by Geoffrey Huntington; *Dark City Dames: The Wicked Women of Film Noir* by Eddie Muller; *The Return of the Sacred* by F. David Peat.

Nonfiction titles representative of ReganBooks: *Testimony: My Life on the Edge* by Mathew Hoffman; *500 Questions to Ask Before You Ask Them to Bed: Finding the Right Mate by Asking the Right Questions* by Laurie L. Seale; *Boat Bastard: A Memoir of Love and Hate* by Deborah van Rooyen; *Child No More: A Memoir* by Xaviera Hollander; *The 24-Hour Turnaround: 8 Total Life Changes to Improve Your Body, Your Health, and Your Life—Today!* by Jay Williams; *The Dirt: Confessions of the World's Most Notorious Rock Band* by Tommy Lee, et al.; *Puppy Parenting: Everything You Need to Know About Your Puppy's First Year* by Jan Greye and Gail Smith.

Direct queries and SASEs to:

Judith Regan, Publisher

Calvert Morgan, Editorial Director

Conor Risch, Editor

William Morrow

William Morrow, now part of HarperCollins Publishing, is one of the nation's leading publishers of general trade books, including bestselling fiction, nonfiction, and cookbooks. Morrow continues its history of publishing quality books and remains committed to bringing the best of commercial hardcover literature to the broadest possible audience, with acclaimed authors such as Sidney Sheldon, Mary Stewart, Robert Pirsig, Emeril Lagasse, and Cokie Roberts.

Titles in the biographies and memoirs category that show William Morrow's breadth: *Authorized Biography of Christopher Isherwood* by Peter Parker; *Michael Jordan* by Richard Brenner; *Famous* by Anthony Haden-Guest; *Back Then: Two Lives in 1950s New York* by Anne Bernays and Justin Kaplan; *One Perfect Op: An Insider's Account of the Navy Seal Special Warfare Teams* by Dennis C. Chalker, et al.; *Zoya's Story: An Afghan Woman's Struggle for Freedom* by John Follain (Contributor) and Rita Cristofari (Contributor).

Titles indicative of William Morrow's literature and fiction list: *Tishomingo Blues: A Novel* by Elmore Leonard; *Enough Rope: Collected Stories* by Lawrence Block; *The Middle Ages* by Jennie Fields; *The Transplanted Man* by Sanjay Nigam; *The Last Phoenix* by Richard Herman; *Sleepyhead* by Mark Billingham; *Breathing Room* by Susan Elizabeth Phillips; *Angels* by Marian Keyes; *The Shadows of Power: A Novel* by James W. Huston; *Sons of Heaven* by Terrence Cheng; *One More for the Road: A New Short Story Collection* by Ray Bradbury; *The Body in the Bonfire: A Faith Fairchild Mystery* by Katherine Hall Page; *The Dream Room* by Marcel Moring and Stacey Knecht; *Enemy Women* by Paulette Jiles; *Buried at Sea* by Paul Garrison; *Unholy Order: A Paul Devlin Mystery* by William Heffernan.

Direct queries and SASEs to:

Carolyn Marino, Vice President, Editorial Director—Commercial fiction, including mysteries, suspense, and women's fiction

David Hirshey, Executive Editor—Popular culture, celebrity books, politics, current affairs

Gladys Justin Carr, Associate Publisher—Fiction: literary and commercial; nonfiction: biographies and memoirs, military and general history, nutrition, medicine, celebrity stories, popular culture, true crime, sports, current events, business

Harriet Bell, Editor—Cookbooks

Hugh Van Dusen, Executive Editor, HarperPerennial—History, biography, spirituality, self-help; fiction and nonfiction reprints and originals in quality paperback

Mauro DiPreta, Executive Editor, HarperEntertainment—Nonfiction: pop culture, humor, commercial nonfiction

Megan Newman, Editor—General nonfiction, how-to, self-help trade paperback originals

Susan Friedland, Executive Editor—Food, cookbooks, literary history

Edwin Tan, Associate Editor—Business and other nonfiction narratives, business and general humor, motivation/self-help/advice, the arts, sex and sexuality, social studies, and general fiction

Tim Duggan, Senior Editor—Serious nonfiction, literary fiction

Tom Dupre, Senior Editor—Rock biographies, comic novels

Dan Conaway, Executive Editor

HarperCollins Children's Books Group

Avon

Greenwillow Books

HarperCollins Children's Books

HarperFestival

HarperTrophy

Joanna Cotler Books

Laura Geringer Books

Tempest

10 E. 53rd St., New York, NY 10022
212-207-7000

Avon

Avon Books is home to some of the most popular fiction being published for young readers in library binding and paperback formats. Romance, mystery, high adventure, and fantasy titles dominate this imprint's list. Avon also boasts successful series like Making Out, Animal Emergency, Get Real, and Enchanted Hearts. Authors representative of Avon are Bruce Coville, Beatrice Sparks, and Dave Duncan. Avon describes its list as a "kid-friendly bestselling commercial powerhouse."

Representative titles in the 4–8 age group: *Get Well, Gators* by Joanna Cole; *Bravo, Amelia Bedelia!* by Herman Parish and Lynn Sweat (Illustrator). In Young Adult: *Gwyneth and the Thief* (An Avon True Romance) by Margaret Moore; *Anna and the Duke* (An Avon True Romance) by Kathryn Smith.

Greenwillow Books

Greenwillow, founded in 1974, publishes books for children of all ages in hardcover, library binding, and paperback formats. This imprint says, "We hope that at the heart of each book there is honesty, emotion, and depth—conveyed by an author or artist who has something that is worth saying to children and who says it in a way that is worth reading." Titles indicative of Greenwillow include *McKendree* by Sandra Belton; *Praying to A.L.* by Judith Casely; *The Queen of Attolia* by Megan Whalen Turner; *Tippy-Toe Chick, Go* by George Shannon, Laura Dronzek (Illustrator); *The Boy Who Writes Poems and Plays* by Rebecca Piatt Davidson, Anita Lobel (Illustrator); *The High-Rise Private Eyes: The Case of the Sleepy Sloth* by Cynthia Rylant, G. Brian Karas (Illustrator); *Mr. Moon* by Rachel Isadora; *Scranimals* by Jack Prelutsky, Peter Sis (Illustrator).

H

HarperCollins Children's Books

HarperCollins Children's Books is known worldwide for its tradition of publishing quality books for children, from toddlers through teens, in hardcover, library binding, and paperback. This imprint also boasts several successful series, such as I Can Read, Math Start, and Let's Read and Find Out.

Recent titles representative of this list: *Ten Go Tango* by Arthur Dorros; *But I Waaannt It!* by Dr. Laura Schlessinger; *I'm Not Going to Chase the Cat Today!* by Jessica Harper. In books for toddlers: *Big Bear Ball* by Joanne Ryder, Steven Kellogg (Illustrator); *The Firebird* by Jane Yolen, Vladimir Vasilevich Vagin (Illustrator); *Danny and the Dinosaur Go to Camp* (I Can Read Book) by Syd Hoff (Illustrator); *Good for You!: Toddler Rhymes for Toddler Times* by Stephanie Calmenson, Melissa Sweet (Illustrator). Ages 4–8: *My Grandson Lew* by Charlotte Zolotow; *The Bee-Man of Orn* by Frank R. Stockton, Maurice Sendak (Illustrator); *Betsy Who Cried Wolf* by Gail Carson Levine, Scott Nash (Illustrator). Ages 9–12: *Carnivorous Carnival* (Series of Unfortunate Events [Lib], 9) by Lemony Snicket, Brett Helquist (Illustrator); *Dork on the Run* by Carol Gorman; *The Good Liar* by Gregory Maguire. Teen titles: *The Hunting of the Last Dragon* by Sherryl Jordan; *Teen Sunshine Reflections: Words for the Teen Soul* by June Cotner (Compiler); *All the Old Haunts* by Chris Lynch; *Flight of the Raven* by Stephanie S. Tolan; *Wurst Case Scenario* by Catherine Clark.

Query letters, manuscripts, and SASEs regarding novels should be directed to:

Alix Reid, Executive Editor

Joanna Cotler, Senior Vice President and Publisher, Joanna Cotler Books

Kate Morgan Jackson, Senior Vice President, Associate Publisher, Editor in Chief

Laura Geringer, Senior Vice President and Publisher, Laura Geringer Books

Emily Brenner, Editorial Director, HarperFestival

Phoebe Yeh, Editorial Director

Robert Warren, Editorial Director

Elise Howard, Vice President and Director of Paperback Publishing

Susan Hirschman, Senior Vice President and Publisher, Greenwillow Books

Barbara Lalicki, Senior Vice President and Editorial Director

HarperFestival

HarperFestival is home to books, novelties, and merchandise for very young children, from infants up to about 6-year-olds. Classic board books, such as *Goodnight Moon* and *Runaway Bunny,* established this list a decade ago. Today, Festival boasts programs such as HarperGrowing Tree and Heidi Murkoff's What to Expect Kids, as well as character-based programs such as Biscuit and Paddington Bear. A few titles indicative of this list: *Pepperidge Farm Goldfish Counting Fun Book* by Barbara Barbieri McGrath; *Prudence's Get Well Book* by Alona Frankel; *Let's Go, Baby-O!* by Marcia Leonard.

HarperTrophy

HarperTrophy is a leading paperback imprint for children, producing original fiction and nonfiction, as well as paperback reprints of previously published titles. Currently with more Newbery and Caldecott winners than any other publisher, Harper has good reason to be proud. From picture books by Maurice Sendak to novels by Laura Ingalls Wilder, E. B. White, Katherine Paterson, and Beverly Cleary, Trophy continues its tradition of offering a broad list of the old and the new. A few recent titles representative of this list: *Tumble Bumble Story* and full-color pictures by Felicia Bond; *Betsy-Tacy* by Maud Hart Lovelace; *Cowboy Ghost* by Robert Newton Peck.

Joanna Cotler Books

Joanna Cotler Books publishes literary and commercial picture books and fiction for all ages. Authors and illustrators include award winners, bestsellers, and luminaries such as Clive Barker, Francesca Lia Block, Sharon Creech, Jamie Lee Curtis, Laura Cornell, Patricia MacLachlan, Barbara Robinson, Art Spiegelman, Jerry Spinelli, and William Steig.

A few recent titles indicative of Joanna Cotler's list are *The Wanderer* by Sharon Creech; *Penelope Jane* by Rosanne Cash; *Cindy Ellen* by Susan Lowell.

Laura Geringer Books

Laura Geringer Books was founded in the early 1990s to provide children with award-winning, bestselling, and innovative authors and artists who "push the envelope" and set new standards of excellence. Authors on this list include William Joyce, Laura Numeroff Joyce, Felicia Bond, Bruce Brooks, Richard Egielski, and Sarah Weeks.

Titles indicative of this list: *Guy Time* by Sarah Weeks; *Throwing Smoke* by Bruce Brooks; *If You Give a Pig a Pancake Big Book* by Laura Numeroff.

Tempest

Tempest produces previously published books in both hardcover and paperback formats, as well as some original titles for young adults, better known today as "teens." Tempest's commitment is to publish "Great books for real teens, with characters, settings, and stories relevant to their own lives, minds, and spirits."

Titles indicative of this list are *Truth or Dairy* by Catherine Clark; *3 NBs of Julian Drew* by James M. Deem; *Welcome to the Ark* by Stephanie S. Tolan.

H

THE HARVARD COMMON PRESS

535 Albany Street, Boston, MA 02118
617-423-5803   fax: 617-695-9794
www.harvardcommonpress.com   e-mail: orders@harvardcommonpress.com

Harvard Common Press accents trade nonfiction in the areas of food, home and the family, small-business guides, travel, and lifestyle, and in addition offers a select list of children's books.

The Harvard Common Press (founded in 1976) is a smaller house devoted to the publication of general nonfiction books in hardcover and trade paperback; the press maintains a solid backlist. The company colophon features a representation of a classical javelin thrower on the run—emblematic of the house's athletic publishing vigor.

Harvard Common issues the Best Places to Stay series as part of its travel line; the Gambit Books imprint covers how-to business titles geared to starting up and operating enterprises such as small restaurants, small newspapers, and small theaters, as well as alternative careers for teachers. Parenting and the family are sectors where Harvard Common shows particular traditional success.

Titles: *Mediterranean Vegetables* by Clifford A. Wright; *The Soup Mix* by Diane Phillips; *Nine Months and a Day: A Pregnancy, Labor, and Delivery Companion* by Adrienne B. Lieberman and Linda Hughey Hold, M.D., F.A.C.O.G.; *Essential Exercises for Breast Cancer Survivors: How to Live Stronger and Feel Better* by Amy Halverstadt and Andrea Leonard; *The Birth Partner: Everything You Need to Know to Help a Woman Through Childbirth, 2nd Edition* by Penny Simkin, P.T.; *Cast Your Net: A Step-by-Step Guide to Finding Your Soul Mate on the Internet* by Eric F. Fagan. The Harvard Common Press is represented to the trade by National Book Network. Query letters and SASEs should be directed to:

Bruce Shaw, President

Pam Hoenig, Executive Editor

Valerie Cimino, Managing Editor

Jodi Marchowsky, Production Editor

H

HEALTH COMMUNICATIONS, INC.

3201 Southwest 15th Street, Deerfield Beach, FL 33442
954-360-0909   fax: 954-360-0034
www.hci-online.com

Health Communications features nonfiction trade titles in relationships, spirituality, health, empowerment, self-help, inspiration, esteem, and psychology. The publisher has achieved notable success with topical approaches to personal growth, women's issues, addiction and other compulsive behaviors, abuse and trauma, family relationships, and healing.

Health Communications (founded in 1976) publishes with the intent to provide direction for the journey of living. The publisher's issue-orientation is apparent in a list that addresses a family spectrum of interest, encompassing books geared to be read by early readers through adults, as well as targeted market interest segments. Health Communications publishes books in affordable hardcover and trade paperback editions and also produces a line of audiobooks.

Health Communications operates in tandem with sister companies U.S. Journal and U.S. Journal Training. The program brings together professional caregivers and the broader community in a publishing forum that embraces books, journals, pamphlets, and conferences.

Exemplifying the Health Communications list: *Addictive Relationships: Reclaiming Your Boundaries* by Joy Miller; *An Adult Child's Guide to What's Normal* by John Friel, Ph.D., and Linda Friel, M.A.; *Before It's Too Late: Helping Women in Controlling an Abusive Relationship* by Robert J. Ackerman, Ph.D., and Susan E. Pickering; *Healing the Human Condition* by Charles L. Whitfield; *Healing the Child Within: Discovering and Recovery for Adult Children of Dysfunctional Families* by Charles L. Whitfield; *Gentle Reminders for Co-Dependents* by Mitzi Chandler; *From the First Bite: A Complete Guide to Recovery from Food Addiction* by Kay Sheppard; *Learning to Love Yourself* by Sharon Wegscheider-Cruise; *Lifeskills for Adult Children* by Janet Woitlitz, Ed.D., and Alan Gurner, M.A.; *Perfect Daughters: Adult Daughters of Alcoholics* by Robert J. Ackerman; *Time for Joy* by Ruth Fishel; *Eternal Blessings* by Brahma Kurmaris; *Pearls of Wisdom* by Dadi Janki; *The Soulful Money Manual: 9 Keys to Being Effective, Happy and at Peace with Money* by Richard Mitz; *Becoming a Father* by John L. Hart, Ph.D.; *Fun Facts About Cats* and *Fun Facts About Dogs* by Richard Torregrossa; *How to Change Your Life* by Ernest Holmes and Michael Beckwith; *Lives Charmed: Intimate Conversations with Extraordinary People* by Linda Sivertsen; *Taste Berries for Teens* by Bettie B. Youngs, Ph.D., and Jennifer Leigh Youngs; *Struggle for Intimacy* by Janet C. Woitiz; *The Lost Boy* by Dave Pelzer; *Healing Shame That Binds You* by John Bradshaw; *The Flying Boy: Healing the Wounded Man* by John Lee; *Choicemaking: For Spirituality Seekers, Co-Dependents and Adult Children* by Sharon Wegscheider-Cruise; *A Child Called It: An Abused Child's Journey from Victim to Victor* by Dave Pelzer; *The 7 Worst Things Parents Do* by John C. Friel, Ph.D., and Linda D. Friel, M.A.; *Bradshaw On: The Family, Revised Edition* by John Bradshaw.

Health Communications published *Chicken Soup for the Soul: 101 Stories to Open the Heart and Rekindle the Spirit* (written and compiled by Jack Canfield and Mark Victor Hansen), an entertaining, uplifting work that features selections from a wide variety of writers. As this book goes to press, the original *Chicken Soup* has been an international bestseller for several years. This book has spawned a number of successful *Chicken Soup* collections. Indeed, if imitation is the sincerest form of flattery, the number of works with allied themes that currently appear under other publishers' imprints is a genuine tribute from the industry to this popular genre originated by the authors and Health Communications. More titles in this series: *Chicken Soup for the Christian Soul: 101 Stories to Open the Heart and Rekindle the Spirit* by Jack Canfield, Mark Victor Hansen, Patty Aubery, and Nancy Mitchell; *Chicken Soup for the Woman's Soul: 101 Stories to Open the Hearts and Rekindle the Spirits of Women* by Jack Canfield, Mark Victor Hansen, Jennifer Read Hawthorne, and Marci Shimoff; *Condensed Chicken Soup for the Soul* by Jack Canfield, Mark Victor Hansen, and Patty Hansen; *Chicken Soup for the Soul at Work: 101 Stories of Courage, Compassion & Creativity in the Workplace* by Jack Canfield, Mark Victor Hansen, Martin Rutte, Maida Rogerson, and Tim Clauss.

Health Communications distributes its own list. Query letters and SASEs should be directed to:

H

Allison Janse, Senior Editor

Lisa Drucker, Senior Editor

Susan Tobias, Editor

Christine Belleris, Editorial Director
Sign: Leo.
Education: B.A., Journalism, from the University of Colorado.
Employment history/editor career path: I have always been interested in reading and writing. After I graduated from college, I was a Legislative Assistant for a U.S. congressman in Washington, D.C., for about four years. I decided I didn't want to stay in politics, so I started doing freelance work for the *Colorado Statesman.* I then moved to Boca Raton, Florida, and started working at SIRS, publishing research material. I then came to Health Communications, where I have been employed for eight years.
Personal interests: Reading, writing, running, bicycling; I have a two-year-old and a new baby on the way.
What would you be doing if you were not an editor? I would be a travel writer.
What has been your most successful book that you have acquired to date? *The Schwarz bein Principle.*
What book have you acquired that makes you the most proud? What books that you have acquired reflect the types of books you like to represent? *The Immune Spirit* and *Not Just One in Eight.*
Do you represent fiction? If so, what do you look for? Yes, we do occasionally, but not much. Visionary fiction, New Age.
Do you represent nonfiction? Yes, self-help, books for teenagers, books on healthy aging, and anything that is new and different.
Do you require book proposals? If so, what do you look for in evaluating a book proposal? Yes, I look for two sample chapters, a table of contents, a detailed profile of the author, and marketing ideas. It has to be well written, neat, and follow our guidelines.
Are certain aspects of a book proposal given more weight than others? It helps if the authors are experts in their field, but we use a strategy known as HERT. H stands for healing. E, the author is an expert. R stands for whether the material is readable. T is timely. We need the proposal to meet all of these categories.
What process do you use for making a decision? What is the process for acquisition; is there a committee? We use the HERT system and, yes, we have a committee. The committee meets once a month and consists of staff from sales, marketing, e-public relations, and the editorial department.
What kinds of nonfiction books do you want to see less of? Personal memoirs that can't help a general audience.
Are you interested in work geared for the masses (readers of *People, The Star,* etc.)? Yes.
Are agents important? Why? Yes, they are very important. They bring a higher caliber of authors and manuscripts to us. They can "weed-out" all the material that is not what we're looking for.

Do you like new writers? What should new writers do to break into the business? Yes, we're always looking for new writers. I would say to join a writers group and try to publish some work in periodicals.

How should writers approach you? First, send me a query letter in the mail. If I like the material, I will call you to request the manuscript.

What are some common mistakes that writers make? What really gets on your nerves? When people call after you've asked them not to call. Most authors don't realize just how busy editors are. When authors don't do their homework and send me material that we don't even publish (i.e., poetry). When authors send unsolicited material without an SASE and expect that we will return it. We read unsolicited material as a courtesy, not an obligation.

What can writers do to get your attention and to avoid the slush pile? The way to get my attention is to send a professional-looking package with a well-written proposal inside.

What have been some of your craziest experiences with submissions? Getting gifts with the submissions. I've gotten everything from cookies, to stuffed animals, gum, rocks, you name it. A colleague of mine once received a dozen red roses.

What have been some of your best experiences with writers or in your job? Getting to know people. I always have good professional advice in this profession (diet, therapy). I'm always learning new things and I love to develop a wonderful relationship with the authors.

What, if anything, makes you different from other editors? I'm a good listener and am good at compromise. It's important in this job and business that you are willing to "bend" a little.

Is there anything that you would like to see changed in the industry? I would like to see less consolidation of bookstores; I like the independent bookstores.

Any advice for writers? Be persistent. Don't get discouraged because one person turns you down, and get many different viewpoints.

H

THE HEARST BOOK GROUP

The entire Hearst Book Group was acquired by HarperCollins in late 1999.

HENRY HOLT AND COMPANY
(PART OF THE VERLAGSGRUPPE GEORG VON HOLTZBRINCK)

Henry Holt for Young Readers

Edge Books

Redfeather Books

Owlets Paperbacks

Henry Holt Reference

John Macrae Books
Metropolitan Books
Owl Books
Times Books
21st Century Books

115 West 18th Street, New York, NY 10011
212-886-9200
www.henryholt.com

Henry Holt is one of the oldest publishers in the United States and is known for publishing high-quality books, including works by such authors as Erich Fromm, Robert Frost, Hermann Hesse, Norman Mailer, Robert Louis Stevenson, Ivan Turgenev, and H. G. Wells. Currently, the publication program focuses on American and international fiction; biography, history and politics; science, psychology and health; and books for children. The firm was purchased by the German-based Holtzbrink Group several years ago and merged with other recently purchased U.S. publishers.

Titles indicative of Henry Holt's nonfiction list: *American Road: The Story of an Epic Transcontinental Journey at the Dawn of the Motor Age* by Pete Davies; *American Son: A Portrait of John F. Kennedy, Jr.* by Richard Blow; *A Death in Texas: A Story of Race, Murder and a Small Town's Struggle for Redemption* by Dina Temple-Raston; *Balsamic Dreams: A Short but Self-Important History of the Baby Boomer Generation* by Joe Queenan; *Below Another Sky: A Mountain Adventure in Search of a Lost Father* by Rick Ridgeway; *Borrowed Finery: A Memoir* by Paula Fox; *The Bridge at No Gun Ri: A Hidden Nightmare from the Korean War* by Charles J. Hanley, Martha Mendoza, and Sang-hun Choe; *Bury My Heart at Wounded Knee: An Indian History of the American West* by Dee Brown; *Day of Infamy 60th Anniversary: The Classic Account of the Bombing of Pearl Harbor* by Walter Lord; *Dr. Eckener's Dream Machine: The Great Zeppelin and the Dawn of Air Travel* by Douglas Botting; *For Women Only: A Revolutionary Guide to Overcoming Sexual Dysfunction and Reclaiming Your Sex Life* by Dr. Jennifer Berman, Dr. Laura Berman, and Elisabeth Bumiller; *Home Lands: Portrait of the New Jewish Diaspora* by Larry Tye.

Titles representative of Henry Holt fiction: *Accidents in the Home* by Tessa Hadley; *Desert Burial* by Brian Littlefair; *The Bear in the Attic* by Patrick F. McManus; *Eva Moves the Furniture* by Margot Livesey; *Field Guide* by Gwendolen Gross; *The Good German* by Joseph Kanon; *Great American Plain* by Gary Sernovitz; *Greetings from the Golden State* by Leslie Brenner; *He Sleeps* by Reginald McKnight; *Iced* by Jenny Siler.

Direct query letters and SASEs to:

Laura Godwin, Associate Publisher

David Sobel, Editorial Director, Times Books—Science travel adventure, business, personal finance, parenting

Elizabeth Stein, Editor—History, biography, current events, military history

Jennifer Barth, Editor in Chief, Holt—Commercial and literary fiction, biography, memoir, narrative nonfiction

H

Sara Bershtel, Associate Publisher, Metropolitan Books—Individualistic nonfiction and literary fiction

Tom Bissell, Associate Editor, Holt—Literary fiction and nonfiction

Riva Hocherman, Editor, Metropolitan

Henry Holt and Company Books for Young Readers

Henry Holt and Company Books for Young Readers publishes a wide range of children's books, from picture books for preschoolers to fiction for young adults. Imprints include Edge Books, Redfeather Books, and Owlets Paperbacks.

Representative titles in the 0–3 age group: *Humphrey's Bedtime* by Sally Hunter (Illustrator); *A Christmas Tree in the White House* by Gary Hines, Alexandra Wallner (Illustrator). In the 4–8 age group: *Air Show* by Anastasia Suen, Cecco Mariniello (Illustrator); *Army Ant Parade* by April Pulley Sayre, Rick Chrustowski (Illustrator); *Badger's New House* by Robin Muller (Illustrator); *Bug Cemetery* by Frances Hill, Vera Rosenberry (Illustrator); *Cat in the Manger* by Michael Foreman (Illustrator). In the 9–12 age group: *Ark in the Park* by Wendy Orr, Kerry Millard (Illustrator); *The Circus Lunicus* by Marilyn Singer; *The Copper Treasure* by Melvin Burgess, Richard Williams (Illustrator); *A Dog's Gotta Do What a Dog's Gotta Do: Dogs at Work* by Marilyn Singe; *The Dollhouse Magic* by Yona Zeldis McDonough, Diane Palmisciano (Illustrator); *The Number Devil: A Mathematical Adventure* by Hans Magnus Enzensberger, et al.; *Ola's Wake* by B. J. Stone.

John Macrae Books

Nonfiction titles representative of John Macrae Books: *Vermeer: A View of Delft* by Anthony Bailey; *Among the Bears: Raising Orphaned Cubs in the Wild* (edited by Benjamin Gray Kilham); *Eisenhower: The Making of a Commander* by Carlo D'Este; *Eye of the Albatross: Views of the Endangered Sea* by Carl Safina; *The Artist's Wife* by Max Phillips.

Direct queries and SASEs to:

John Macrae, Associate Publisher

Metropolitan Books

Metropolitan Books, established in 1995, publishes fiction and nonfiction of the highest quality, both American and international. This Henry Holt imprint is open to various genres, unconventional points of view, controversial opinions, and new voices. From short stories to social science, award-winning novels to American politics, foreign fiction to cutting-edge history and current affairs, Metropolitan is committed to diversity, distinction, and surprise.

Authors published by Metropolitan Books include Ann Crittenden, Mike Davis, Barbara Ehrenreich, Susan Faludi, Orlando Figes, Michael Frayn, Eduardo Galeano, Atul Gawande, Todd Gitlin, Arlie Russell Hochschild, Michael Ignatieff, Orville Schell, and Tom Segev.

H

Titles representative of Metropolitan's nonfiction list: *Black Earth City: When Russia Ran Wild (and So Did We)* by Charlotte Hobson; *Complications: A Surgeon's Notes on an Imperfect Science* by Atul Gawande; *Dr. Tatiana's Sex Advice to All Creation* by Olivia Judson; *Elvis in Jerusalem: Post-Zionism and the Americanization of Israel* by Tom Segev and Haim Watzman; *Media Unlimited: How the Torrent of Images and Sounds Overwhelms Our Lives* by Todd Gitlin; *The Mind of Egypt: History and Meaning in the Time of the Pharaohs* by Jan Assmann and Andrew Jenkins; *The Wannsee Conference and the Final Solution: A Reconsideration* by Mark Roseman.

Titles indicative of Metropolitan fiction: *The Beholder* by Thomas Farber; *Spies* by Michael Frayn; *The Appointment* by Herta Muller, et al.; *Housebroken: 3 Novellas* by Yael Hedaya, et al.; *Afterimage* by Helen Humphreys; *Dugan Under Ground* by Tom De Haven; *I Dreamed I Was a Ballerina* by Anna Pavlova and Edgar Degas.

Owl Books

Owl Books publishes much of Henry Holt's nonfiction in trade paperback format, as well as producing original titles.

Titles indicative of the Owl list: *Om: Yoga for Mothers and Babies* by Laura Staton and Sarah Perron; *The Battle of Savo Island* by Richard F. Newcomb; *The Bear-Proof Investor: Prospering Safely in Any Market* by John F. Wasik; *Blue Frontier: Saving America's Living Seas* by David Helvarg; *The Evolutionists: The Struggle for Darwin's Soul* by Richard Morris, Ph.D.; *The Genie in the Bottle: 64 All New Commentaries on the Fascinating Chemistry of Everyday Life* by Joe Schwarcz; *Iwo Jima* by Richard F. Newcomb; *The Joy of Writing Sex: A Guide for Fiction Writers* by Elizabeth Benedict.

Times Books

Times Books, launched in 2001, is the result of a copublishing agreement between Holt and the *New York Times;* its nonfiction list focuses on science, business, and current events.

Titles representative of this list: *The Big Questions: Probing the Promise and Limits of Science* by Richard Morris, Ph.D.; *Courting Disaster: The Supreme Court and the Dangerous Unmaking of American Law* by Martin Garbus; *The Dependent Gene: The Fallacy of "Nature vs. Nuture"* by David S. Moore; *Future Evolution: An Illuminated History of Life to Come* by Peter Ward and Alexis Rockman; *Grover Cleveland* (The American Presidents Series) by Henry Graff and Arthur M. Schlesinger, Jr.; *Healing the Brain* by Curt Freed, M.D., and Simon LeVay, Ph.D.; *How Race Is Lived in America: Pulling Together, Pulling Apart* by Correspondents of the *New York Times:* Joseph Lelyveld, James Madison, Garry Wills, and Arthur M. Schlesinger, Jr.; *John Quincy Adams* by Robert V. Remini and Arthur M. Schlesinger, Jr.; *The New Rules of Personal Investing: How to Prosper in a Changing Economy* by Allen R. Myerson, Floyd Norris, and Gretchen Morgenson; *Portraits: 9/11/01: The Collected "Portraits of Grief"* from the *New York Times; The Power of Babel: A Natural History of Language* by John McWhorter; *Sex: A Natural History* by Joann Ellison Rodgers; *The Tangled Wing: Biological Constraints on the Human Spirit* by Melvin Konner; *The Tending Instinct: How Nurturing Is Essential to Who We*

Are and How We Live by Shelley E. Taylor; *The Turtle and the Stars: Observations of an Earthbound Astronomer* by Arthur Upgren, Ph.D.; *Writers on Writing: Collected Essays from the New York Times* by John Darnton.

HILL STREET PRESS, LLC

191 East Broad Street, Suite 209, Athens, GA 30601-2848
fax: 706-613-7204
www.hillstreetpress.com

Hill Street Press was founded in May 1998 and currently has 50 titles in print. Hill Street Press is a publisher of regional focus and international interest. We plan to increase our number of literary and popular fiction titles, ranging from the hard-edged to the home-spun, as our backlist grows. HSP is particularly interested in nonfiction titles of various kinds, particularly contemporary issues. We do not publish poetry, children's or juvenile literature, science fiction, or romance. We are nationally and internationally distributed through LCP/InBook and Source Books and sell to all major chains and independents, as well as through the major e-commerce outlets.

Representative titles include *Before Scarlet: Girlhood Writings of Margaret Mitchell* by Margaret Mitchell; *Bevelyn Blair's Everyday Cakes* by Bevelyn Blair; *Special Kay: The Wisdom of Terry Kay* by Terry Kay; *Celestine Sibley: A Granddaughter's Reminiscence* by Celestine Sibley Fleming; *Southern Belly: The Ultimate Food Lover's Companion to the South* by John T. Edge; *The Total View of Taftly* by Scott Morris; *Flannery O'Connor: A Celebration of Genius* by Sarah Gordon; *Fatal Flowers* by Rosemary Daniell; *The Crackers: Early Days of Atlanta Baseball* by Tim Darnell.

Please direct query letters with SASEs to:

Patrick Allen, Senior Editor

H

HIPPOCRENE BOOKS

171 Madison Avenue, New York, NY 10016
212-685-4371   fax: 212-779-9338
www.hippocrenebooks.com   e-mail: hippocre@ix.netcom.com

Hippocrene accents history, military science, international literature, music, travel, cuisine, and scholarly Judaica and Polonica. The house offers selected works in the areas of current affairs and popular culture, in addition to a comprehensive line of foreign-language dictionaries. The house publishes dictionaries and instruction books in over 100 languages. Hippocrene Books (founded in 1971) publishes hardcovers and trade paperbacks.

Hippocrene has undertaken publication of the works of Polish writer Henryk Sienkiewicz (1905 Nobel Laureate in literature) in English translation.

Hippocrene titles for the general trade: *You Can't Do Business (or Most Anything Else) Without Yiddish* by Leon H. Gildin; *Wedded Strangers: The Challenges of Russian-American Marriages, Expanded Edition* by Lynn Vision; *Jews in Old China, Expanded Edition* by Sidney Shapiro; *Greece: An Illustrated History* by Tom Stone; *China: An Illustrated History* by Yong Ho.

Hippocrene Books prides itself on being the foremost United States publisher of international cookbooks and foreign-language dictionaries.

International cookbook titles: *Taste of Latvia* by Siri Lise Doub; *The Indian Spice Kitchen* by Monisha Bharadwaj; *Afghan Food & Cookery* by Helen Saberi; *The Best of Croatian Cooking* by Liliana Pavicic and Gordana Pirker-Mosher; *Hungarian Cookbook: Old World Recipes for New World Cooks* by Yolanda Nagy Fintor; *Imperial Mongolian Cooking: Recipes from the Kingdoms of Genghis Khan* by Marc Cramer.

Hippocrene's Bilingual series titles include *Swahili Practical Dictionary* by Nicholas Awde; *Japanese Dictionary & Phrasebook* by Evgeny Steiner; *Croatian Dictionary & Phrasebook* by Ante Susnjar; *Beginner's Italian* by Joseph Privitera; *Beginner's Slovak* by Elena Letnanova.

Hippocrene offers practical and concise dictionaries, as well as unabridged and comprehensive dictionaries, specialty dictionaries, proverbs dictionaries, and standard dictionaries in over 100 languages.

Mastering Advanced . . . guides make up a line that offers the student reasonably priced, contemporary foreign-language instruction. The Hippocrene Beginner's series is designed for students with little or no background in a foreign language. The goal of each volume is to provide readers with a basic knowledge to travel independently, speak and understand, and read and write essential words.

Hippocrene distributes its own list. Query letters and SASEs should be directed to:

Carol Chitnis-Gress, Managing Editor—Oversees international cooking, travel, library of world folklore, and general history titles

George Blagowidow, President and Editorial Director

Paul Simpson, Associate Editor—Oversees illustrated histories, series, international proverbs

Caroline Gates, Associate Editor—Oversees all foreign-language dictionaries and learning guides

H

HOUGHTON MIFFLIN COMPANY

Clarion Books

College Division

Great Source

Houghton Mifflin Books for Children

International Division

McDougal Littell

Riverside Publishing Company

School Division

Sunburst Technology

Trade and Reference Division

Boston office:
222 Berkeley Street, Boston, MA 02116-3764
617-351-5000
www.houghtonmifflinbooks.com

New York office:
215 Park Avenue South, New York, NY 10003
212-420-5800

Houghton Mifflin produces general trade nonfiction and fiction in hardcover and paper-back, as well as a strong general-reference list. Mariner is a trade-paperback imprint covering house interests in fiction and nonfiction. Children's divisions include Houghton Mifflin Books for Children and the editorially independent juveniles' imprint Clarion Books (see subentries further on). The backlist of formerly independent Ticknor & Fields has been incorporated into the core Houghton Mifflin catalog.

Houghton Mifflin (founded in 1832) is one of the grand names of the American publishing tradition. The house's renowned leaping-dolphin emblem embellishes a distinguished list.

Houghton Mifflin nonfiction encompasses mainstream titles in such areas as current events, international affairs, business, journalism, lifestyle and travel, and natural history.

Reference works from Houghton Mifflin include *American Heritage Dictionary of the English Language* (an excellent resource for American writers); *The Columbia Encyclopedia* (copublished with Columbia University); *Cannon's Concise Guide to Rules of Order.*

Also on the Houghton Mifflin list are travel and nature series that include the Peterson Field Guides and Best Places to Stay Guides. Houghton Mifflin is known for publishing the ever popular *American Heritage Dictionary.*

Popular Houghton Mifflin nonfiction: *Building Big* by David Macaulay; *Carson McCullers: A Life* by Josyane Savigneau; *A Life in the Twentieth Century: Innocent Beginnings* by James Carroll; *Fast Food Nation: The Dark Side of the All American Meal* by Eric Schlosser; *Surviving Galeras* by Stanley Williams and Fen Montaigne; *The Perfect Recipe* by Pam Anderson; *Birds of North America* by Kenn Kaufman; *Sober for Good* by Anne M. Fletcher; *The Ultimate Workout Log* by Suzanne Schlosberg; *The Algeria Hotel* by Adam Nossister; *Beyond Innocence* by Jane Goodall; *The Ultimate Baseball Book: The Classic Illustrated History of the World's Greatest Game* (edited by Daniel Okrent and Harris Lewine).

Fiction and works with literary and cultural scope: *Gathering Blue* by Lois Lowry; *The Best American Mystery Stories of the Century* by Tony Hillerman; *Taps* by Willie Morris; *Sheba* by Nicholas Clapp; *The Far Field* by Edie Meidav; *The Silmarillion* by J. R. R. Tolkien; *The Lord of the Ring* by J. R. R. Tolkien; *All We Know of Heaven* by Remy Rougeau; *Hotel Honolulu* by Paul Theroux; *Dupont Circle* by Paul Kafka-Gibbons; *The Dying Animal* by Philip Roth; *Doghouse Roses* by Steve Earle; *Interpreter of Maladies* by Jhumpa Lahiri.

H

The publisher also issues selected works of poetry, including *Time & Money: New Poems* by William Matthews; *Nature: Poems Old and New* by May Swenson.

Houghton Mifflin distributes its own list. Query letters and SASEs should be directed to:

Eamon Dolan, Executive Editor (New York)—Business, technology, nonfiction; travel guides

Elaine Pfefferbilt, Editor at Large (New York)—Philosophy, history, biography, general nonfiction; literary fiction; nonfiction consistent with the house list

Eric Chinski, Senior Editor (New York)—Philosophy, history, Jewish studies, biography, general

Harry L. Foster, Jr., Senior Editor (Boston)—Nature and history

Janet Silver, Vice President, Associate Publisher and Editor in Chief (Boston)—Literary nonfiction and fiction; nonfiction: biographies, arts and culture, women's issues; focus on developing writers

Laura van Dam, Science Editor (Boston)—Hard science, medicine, technology; practical nonfiction

Pat Strachan, Executive Editor (New York)—Poetry, literary fiction and nonfiction, gardening, general reference works

Rex Martin, Senior Editor (Boston)—Cooking, health, self-help, poetry, biography, literary nonfiction

Wendy Strothmann, Executive Vice President (Boston)

Anton Mueller, Senior Editor (Boston)—Literary fiction, political/cultural nonfiction

Susan Canavan, Manager, Mariner Paperbacks, Editor (Boston)—Sports, health, southern fiction

Brandy Vickers, Assistant Manager, Mariner Paperbacks (Boston)

Heidi Pitlor, Editor (Boston)—Literary fiction

Lori Galvin-Frost, Assistant Managing Editor (Boston)—Cookbooks

Lisa White, Associate Director (Boston)—Field guides

Deanne Urmy, Senior Editor—Science, nature, serious nonfiction

Frances Tenenbaum, Imprint Editor/Senior Editor Houghton Mifflin (Boston)—Gardening books; oversees Taylor gardening guides and Tasha Tudor books

Education: University of Michigan and Columbia School of Journalism.

Employment history/editor career path: I have worked here for over 25 years. I started as a journalist and then moved on to work for a small publisher. I then worked for a small book club and was writing a book on gardening and wildflowers. Soon after, I moved out of Long Island and came to work for Houghton Mifflin.

Personal interests: Gardening, nonfiction editing, I love editing—don't like writing.

What would you be doing if you were not an editor? I don't know—I don't even want to think about it.

What has been your most successful book that you have acquired to date? *Tasha Tudor's Garden* by Tovah Martin and Richard Brown. It's a large, beautiful book that is full of color. It was published in 1994 and is in its ninth printing. I am also the editor of a whole series of gardening books called *The Tailor's Guide to Gardening.*

What books have you acquired that make you the most proud? What books that you have acquired reflect the types of books you like to represent? I am the Editor for three of Henry Mitchell's books, who is a late columnist of the *Washington Post.* He is one of the most opinionated writers in gardening.

Do you represent nonfiction? Yes.

Do you require book proposals? If so, what do you look for in evaluating a book proposal? Yes, from people I don't know. Subject is the first thing, writing is the second. What is the salability of the project? It must have a unique voice.

What process do you use for making a decision? What is the process for acquisition; is there a committee? Because I'm the "expert" on gardening at Houghton Mifflin, I'm the one who usually reads the gardening books. I might go to other people who may be interested, such as the sales/marketing division. We do have an acquisitions committee.

Are agents important? Why? Yes and no. I work with some agents, and I also work with people who do not have agents.

How should writers approach you? Not by phone.

What are some common mistakes writers make? What really gets on your nerves? When writers tell me that their project is unique, when I know that it's not. I don't like books that are rehashes, the same thing over and over again. I also don't like books that are manufactured in the author's head. As far as gardening books, it gets on my nerves when people have just taken it up, and they want to tell everyone else about it.

What can writers do to get your attention and to avoid the slush pile? If you write it directly to me, it doesn't go to the slush pile.

What have been some of your craziest experiences with submissions? My assistant usually goes through everything first, so she sees most of the "crazy" submissions.

What have been some of your best experiences with writers or in your job? I have some wonderful writers who turned out to be my best friends. I have recently found out that an organization that is giving a book party for one of my authors is actually giving the party for both of us. That's never happened to me before.

Is there anything that you would like to see changed in the industry? Yes, the whole industry.

Clarion Books

215 Park Avenue South, 10th Floor, New York, NY 10003
212-420-5800

Clarion publishes books geared for the youngest readers up through the early teen years. Clarion Books is an award-winning children's book division that is editorially independent of Houghton Mifflin's other lines.

On Clarion's list in fiction and picture books: *The Three Pigs* by David Wiesner; *Riding the Tiger* by Eve Bunting (illustrated by David Frampton); *A Pocketful of Poems* by Nikki Grimes (illustrated by Javaka Steptoe); *The Secrets of Ms. Snickle's Class* by Laurie Miller Hornik (illustrated by Debbie Tilley); *A Single Shard* by Linda Sue Park; *Sigmund Freud:*

Pioneer of the Mind by Catherine Reef; *Heroine of the Titanic: The Real Unsinkable Molly Brown* by Elaine Landau.

Query letters and SASEs should be directed to:

Dinah Stevenson, Vice President and Editorial Director

Jennifer Greene, Associate Editor

Julie Strauss-Gabel, Associate Editor

Michele Coppola, Editor

Houghton Mifflin Books for Children

The Houghton Mifflin children's-book division stands out with a broad list that addresses topics of wide import; at all reading levels, the Houghton program accents works of thematic complexity and emotional depth. Imprints and lines include Walter Lorraine Books (illustrated and novelty titles) and Sandpiper Paperbacks.

Houghton Mifflin Books for Children publishes hardcover and paperback titles from picture books for the youngest readers to fiction for young adults, audio products, foldout books, boardbooks, lift-the-flap books—and the house showcases a brace of successful authors as well. Caldecott and Newbery medallions abound in the tradition of Houghton Mifflin Books for Children.

Representing Houghton Mifflin titles: Picture books: *Score One for the Sloths* by Helen Lester, illustrated by Lynn Munsinger; *The Strange Egg* by Mary Newell DePalma, illustrated by the author; *The Race of the Birkebeiners* by Lisa Lunge-Larsen, illustrated by Mary Azarian; *I Live in Tokyo: A Japanese Calendar* by Mari Takabayashi; *Animals in Flight* by Robin Page, illustrated by Steve Jenkins. Novels: *Breaking Through* by Francisco Jimenez; *Goose Chase by* Patrice Kindl; *When I Was Older* by Garret Freymann-Weyr.

Query letters and SASEs should be directed to:

Margaret Raymo, Acquisitions Editor (Boston)

H

HUMANICS PUBLISHING GROUP

Humanics Learning

PO Box 7400, Atlanta, GA 30357
404-874-2176   fax: 404-874-1976
e-mail: humanics@mindspring.com

The Humanics publishing program covers the categories of self-help, how-to, psychology, human relations, health and nutrition, creative expression (in art, crafts, literature), education, humor, and spirituality. Special emphasis is on subjects such as personal growth, love and relationships, environment, peace, and Taoism. Market areas of concentration include elementary child and child development, teachers' resource books, child care, and the family.

Humanics produces children's books under the Humanics Children's House imprint. The Humanics line of teachers' resource books and materials in child development is directed in part to colleges and institutional markets; popular works in this arena are published under the Humanics Learning imprint.

Humanics Publishing Group (founded in 1976) publishes a small- to medium-sized list of paperback trade books, a line of special fine editions, and audiocassettes.

Humanics titles: *The Millennium Myth: The Ever-Ending Story* by Sean O'Shea and Meryl Walker; *Garden of the Sufi: Insights into the Nature of Man* by Jim Aghevli; *While You Are Expecting: Your Own Prenatal Classroom* by F. Rene Van DeCarr and Marc Lehrer, M.D.; *The Adlerian Primer: How to Manage Children at Home and in the Classroom* by Alex Chew, Ed.D.; *The Way of Virtue: The Ancient Wisdom of Confucius Adapted for a New Age* by James Vollbracht; *Many Paths, One Truth: The Common Thread* by Carole Addlestone; *The Magic of Zen* by Inez D. Stein; *The I Ching of Management* by William E. Sadler; *Inner Bridges: A Guide to Energy Movement and Body Structure* by Fritz Frederick Smith, M.D.; *All Presidents' Sexual Styles* by John Berice.

The Humanics Tao series offers a variety of titles: *The Tao of Recovery: A Quiet Path to Wellness* by Jim McGregor; *The Creative Tao: Lao Tzu's Tao Te Ching Adopted for a New Age* by Pamela Metz; *The Tao of Design: Taoist Elements for Designers* by Carl Garant; *The Tao of Leadership* by John Heider, Ph.D.; *The Tao of Women* by Pamela Meets and Jacqueline Tobin; *The Tao Te Ching: A New Approach—Backward Down the Path* by Jerry Dalton; *The Tao of Sailing* by Ray Grigg.

Humanics oversees its own distribution. Query letters and SASEs should be directed to:

Arthur Bligh, Acquisitions Editor—Adult trade books

Humanics Learning

The accent at Humanics Learning is on original stories and tales targeted for younger readers, in a program geared primarily toward illustrated works. The Fun E. Friends series is one of the house's successful lines. Humanics produces guides for caregivers and educators under the Humanics Learning logo.

On the Humanics Learning list: *Bottle Cap Activities: Recycled Crafts for All Ages* by Kathy Cisneros; *Homespun Curriculum: A Developmentally Appropriate Activities Guide* by Denise Theobold; *Cambio Chameleon* by Mauro Magellan; *The Planet of the Dinosaurs* by Barbara Carr (illustrated by Alice Bear); *The Adventure of Paz in the Land of Numbers* by Miriam Bowden; *Giggle E. Goose, Fibber E. Frog, Fraid E. Cat,* and *Greb E. Dog* by Al Newman (illustrated by Jim Doody).

Titles for teachers and caregivers under the Humanics Learning imprint: *Science, Math and Nutrition for Toddlers: Setting the Stage for Lifelong Skills* by Rita Schrank; *The Planet of the Parental Classroom: A Parent's Guide for Teaching Your Baby in the Womb* by Rene Van De Carr and Marc Lehrer; *Teaching Terrific Twos* by Terry Graham and Linda Camp; *The Infant and Toddler Handbook* by Kathryn Castle; *Toddlers Learn by Doing* by Rita Schrank.

Query letters and SASEs should be directed to:

Arthur Bligh, Humanics Learning

H

HUMAN KINETICS

1607 North Market Street, PO Box 5076, Champaign, IL 61825-5076
217-351-5076   fax: 217-351-1549
www.humankinetics.com

Human Kinetics produces works in recreational and competitive sports, physical education, sports medicine, and fitness. Human Kinetics (founded in 1974) offers a list of trade and academic works (including college textbooks) that covers a wide range of athletic pursuits, with books geared for professional-level coaches, trainers, and participants, in addition to serious leisure-time athletes. Human Kinetics has established the Human Kinetics Foundation to issue grants promoting youth sports and school physical education.

A notable HK imprint is YMCA of America Books. Human Kinetics books are issued primarily in trade paperback editions, with special editions in hardcover. The press also publishes a number of periodicals in its areas of interest. Human Kinetics bills itself as the premier publisher for sports and fitness.

New textbooks from HK include *Evaluating Worksite Health Promotion; Neuromuscular Aspects of Physical Activity; Kinetic Anatomy; Life Span Motor Development—3rd; Ethics in Sports; Adapted Physical Education and Sport—3rd; Contemporary Issues in Sociology of Sport; Therapeutic Exercise for Athletic Injuries; Neuromechanics of Human Movement—3rd; Classics in Movement Science.*

Human Kinetics oversees its own distribution. Query letters and SASEs should be directed to:

Rainer Martens, Publisher and President

Holly Gilly, Vice President of Publication

Leigh LaHood, Managing Editor

Coree Schutter, Editorial Coordinator

Jennifer Walker, Editorial Coordinator

H

HYPERION

Disney Press

Hyperion Books for Children

Miramax Books

ABC Daytime Books

Theia

77 W. 66th Street, New York, NY 10023-6298
212-456-0100

Hyperion Books for Children offices:
114 Fifth Avenue, New York, NY 10011-5690
212-633-4400

Hyperion (founded in 1991) publishes commercial fiction, literary works, and frontlist nonfiction in the areas of popular culture, health and wellness, business, current topical interest, popular psychology and self-help, and humor. The house publishes books in hardcover, trade paperback, and mass-market paperback formats. Hyperion operates a strong children's program that encompasses Hyperion Paperbacks for Children and Disney Press (see subentry for Hyperion Books for Children further on). Miramax Books (see separate subentry further on) concentrates on projects that tie in with the world of film.

Hyperion is part of Disney—the transnational corporate entity noted for its bountiful theme parks, hotels, and resorts, as well as its considerable ledger of film and television enterprises (including ABC, ESPN, Touchstone, Miramax, and Disney studios). Disney launched Hyperion as a full-fledged, well-funded book-publishing division, and the house's top-of-the-line reputation commenced with its initial well-chosen list.

Representing Hyperion: *Lucky Man* by Michael J. Fox; *Still Woman Enough* by Loretta Lyn; *It's Not Business, It's Personal* by Ronna Lichtenberg; *My Country Versus Me* by Wen Ho Lee, with Helen Zia; *Outsmarting Female Fatigue* and *Outsmarting the Female Fat Cell—After Pregnancy* by Debra Waterhouse, M.P.H., R.D.; *Simplify Your Work Life* by Elaine St. James; *Around the World in a Bad Mood* by Rene Foss; *In Every Kid There Lurks a Tiger* by Rudy Duran and Rick Lipsey; *In the Company of Angels* by N. M. Kelby; *The Knitting Goddess* by Deborah Bergman; *Tracy Porter's Home Style* by Tracy Porter; *Dr. Timothy Johnson's On Call Guide to Men's Health* by Dr. Timothy Johnson; *How to Become a Great Boss* by Jeffry J. Fox; *ESPN "The Magazine" Presents Answer Guy* by Answer Guy; *The Lifetime Love and Sex Quiz Book* by Dr. Pepper Swartz; *The Memory Bible* by Gary Small, M.D.; *Sam Choy's Polynesian Kitchen* by Sam Choy; *The Art of Deception* by Ridley Pearson; *Girls Will Be Girls* by JoAnn Deak, Ph.D., with Teresa Barker.

Hyperion hardcover and trade paperback books are distributed to the trade by Little, Brown; Warner Books handles special sales, as well as the mass-market paperback list.

Hyperion is not currently accepting unsolicited manuscripts. Any materials received will be returned without review.

Gretchen Young, Senior Editor

Jennifer Lang, Associate Editor

Katherine Brown Tegen, Editor in Chief—Hyperion Books for Children

Leigh Haber, Executive Editor

(Ms.) Leslie Wells, Executive Editor

Michael DiCapua, Publisher, Michael DiCapua Books, a new imprint within Hyperion's Children's Program, formerly an imprint at HarperCollins

Peternelle Van Arsdale, Executive Editor

Will Schwalbe, Editor in Chief

Mary Ellen O'Neill, Senior Editor

H

Hyperion Books for Children

Hyperion Paperbacks for Children
Disney Press

The children's book division of Hyperion publishes titles for younger readers through young adult via a number of series, imprints, and lines. On the Hyperion children's division list are volumes that are finely designed and luxuriously produced in hardcover and paperback.

Hyperion Books for Children produces illustrated fairy tales, picture storybooks, poetry, illustrated fiction, calendars, and activity books—many of which are lavish, inventively presented works. Disney Press concentrates on illustrated works that tie in with Disney children's cinema classics, old and new—including series novelizations and books with cinematically conceived formats.

From Hyperion Books for Children: *McDuff and the Baby* by Rosemary Wells (illustrated by Susan Jeffers); *Dinorella: A Prehistoric Fairytale* by Pamela Duncan Edwards (illustrated by Henry Cole); *Pat the Beastie Hand Puppet* by Henrik Drescher; *Breakfast at the Liberty Diner* by Daniel Kirk; *The Secret of the Lost Kingdom* by Michael Bolton (illustrated by David Jermann); *William Wegman Puppies* by William Wegman; *The Peacock's Pride* by Melissa Kajpust (illustrated by Jo Anne Kelly); *The Bone Man: A Native American Modoc Tale* by Laura Simms (illustrated by Michael McCurdy); *Phoebe and the Spelling Bee* by Barney Saltzberg; *The Little Mermaid* by Hans Christian Anderson (illustrated with Disney Archival Art); *Teddy's Christmas: A Pop-up Book with Mini Christmas Cards* by Margie Palatini (illustrated by Mike Reed); *El Arbol de Navidad/The Christmas Tree* by Alma Flor Ada (illustrated by Terry Ybañez); *The Farolitos of Christmas* by Rudolfo Anaya (illustrated by Edward Gonzalez); *Armadillos Sleep in Dugouts: And Other Places Animals Live* by Pam Muñoz Ryan (illustrated by Diane deGroat); *The Buried City of Pompeii: What It Was Like When Vesuvius Exploded* by Shelley Tanaka (illustrated by Greg Ruhl); *The Wonder Worm Wars* by Margie Palatini; *Sons of Liberty* by Adele Griffin; *Wolf Shadows* by Mary Casanova.

Other noteworthy titles: *Tim Burton's Vincent* by Tim Burton; illustrated by the author (his first picture book, which he wrote and illustrated, was *The Nightmare Before Christmas*); *Anastasia's Album* by Shelley Tanaka (edited by Hugh Brewster; the true story of the youngest daughter of Czar Nicholas II of Russia and her incredible life, told through her own snapshots, diaries, and letters); *On Board the Titanic: An I Was There Book* by Shelly Tanaka (illustrated by Ken Marschall; true-story account of the famous ocean liner's fate told through the eyes of two young survivors).

Fiendly Corners by E. W. Leroe is a new Hyperion series that features paperback originals with eye-popping die-cut covers: *Fiendly Corners No. 1: Monster Vision; Fiendly Corners No. 2: Pizza Zombies; Fiendly Corners No. 3: Revenge of the Hairy Horror; Fiendly Corners No. 4: Nasty the Snowman.*

Hyperion is proud to announce an ongoing series of FamilyPC books designed to grow as families grow. The FamilyPC book series is intended as the absolute best option for parents who want to get the most productivity and fun out of their home computers—in tandem with the Editors of award-winning *FamilyPC* magazine. Titles: *The FamilyPC Guide to Homework* by Gregg Keizer and the Editors of *FamilyPC; The FamilyPC Soft-*

H

ware Buyer's Guide by Kurt Carlson, Valle Dwight, and the Editors of *FamilyPC; The FamilyPC Guide to Cool PC Projects* by Sam Mea and the Editors of *FamilyPC.*

Disney Press produces a lineup that includes picture books, boardbooks, pop-up books, novels, and activity books. Many of these works are derived from such successful Disney cinematic productions as *101 Dalmatians, The Hunchback of Notre Dame, The Lion King, Beauty and the Beast, James and the Giant Peach, Aladdin, Pocahontas, Lady and the Tramp, Bambi, The Mighty Ducks,* and *The Little Mermaid.*

Special Hyperion project: *Since the World Began: Walt Disney World's First 25 Years* by Jeff Kurtti. This work celebrates the 25th anniversary of the Disney World theme park. The book is a lavish, entertaining, and absolutely unique history of Walt's city of dreams—and the world's most popular tourist destination.

Hyperion Books for Children and products from Disney Press are distributed to the trade by Little, Brown.

Hyperion Books for Children is not currently accepting unsolicited manuscripts. Any materials received will be returned without review.

Andrea Cascardi, Associate Publisher

Gretchen Young, Editor—Also works with core Hyperion adult-trade list

Ken Geist, Associate Publisher

Lisa Holton, Vice President and Publisher

Wendy Lefkon, Executive Editor—Disney-related projects; has own Disney imprint

Miramax Books

Miramax Books accents titles keyed to cinema—as a profession, industry, lifestyle, or avocation. The Miramax imprint develops a wide range of markets within this interest area. The Miramax list includes select original fiction (usually with a high-concept media link, or at least a halfway-celebrity author), reprints of novels that serve as the basis for films, and other movie tie-in projects.

From Miramax Books: *From Dusk Till Dawn* (a script by Quentin Tarantino); *The Last of the High Kings* (novel keyed to a film project) by Ferdia MacAnna; a currently untitled dark-comic novel by David Lipsky (author of *The Pallbearer*); *The Piano* (a script by Jane Campion); *The Postman* (a script by Antonio Skarmeta); *Jane Eyre* by Charlotte Brontë (classic fiction produced in a film tie-in reprint edition); *Pulp Fiction* (a script by Quentin Tarantino and Roger Avary).

Miramax Books is not currently accepting unsolicited manuscripts. Any materials received will be returned without review.

Susan Costello, Vice President of Publishing—Film-related projects

I

INDUSTRIAL PRESS

200 Madison Avenue, New York, NY 10016
212-889-6330, 888-528-7852   fax: 212-545-8327
www.industrialpress.com   e-mail: induspress@aol.com

Industrial Press produces scientific works, technical handbooks, professional guides, and reference books in the areas of engineering, manufacturing processes and materials, design engineering, and quality control. In addition to professional books, Industrial Press produces basic textbooks in its fields of interest.

Industrial Press (founded in 1883) is a leading specialist house in the professional, scientific, and scholarly publishing arenas. The publisher typically offers about a dozen handpicked new titles a year, in addition to its ongoing backlist of established sellers.

Industrial Press continues to offer its classic *Machinery's Handbook* by Erik Oberg, Franklin D. Jones, Holbrook L. Horton, and Henry H. Ryffel (elaborated from the Green-McCauley original in both print and CD-ROM), along with a companion guidebook (in fully revised formats).

Representative of the Industrial Press list: *Interpretation of Geometric Dimensioning and Tolerancing* by Daniel E. Puncochar; *Engineering Formulas, Conversions, Definitions, and Tables* by Frank Sims; *CNC Machining Handbook* by James Madison; *Setup Reduction Through Effective Workholding* by Edward G. Hoffman; *Blueprint Reading Basics, 2nd edition* by Warren Hammer; *Plastic Component Design* by Paul Campbell; *Why Systems Fail: And How to Make Sure Yours Doesn't* by David A. Turbide; *Purchasing for Manufacturing* by Harry E. Hough; *Lubrication for Industry* by Kenneth E. Bannister; *The Handbook of Maintenance Management* by Joel Levitt; *Microbiologically Influenced Corrosion Handbook* by Susan Watkins Borenstein; *Welding Essentials* by William Galvery and Frank Marlow, and *Pipefitter's Handbook* by Forrest R. Lindsey.

Industrial Press handles its own distribution.

Industrial Press is expanding its list of professional and educational titles and also starting a new program in electronic publishing. For guidelines and suggestions regarding submitting proposals, check out the Web site or contact John Carleo.

John F. Carleo, Marketing Director and Editor

ISLAND PRESS

Editorial office:
1718 Connecticut Avenue, NW, Suite 300, Washington, DC 20009
202-232-7933   fax: 202-234-1328
www.islandpress.org   e-mail: info@islandpress.org

West Coast operations:
58440 Main Street, PO Box 7, Covelo, CA 95428
fax: 707-983-6414
service@islandpress.org

Island Press issues books for resource conservation professionals and activists. The Island Press list is keyed to topics and issues in ecology, conservation, nature, regional studies, science (including biology and natural sciences), landscape architecture, land use, education, policy and planning, economics, and reference. Island publishes hardcover and trade paperback editions. The Shearwater Books imprint accents books of mainstream trade appeal and topical interest in hardbound and trade paper.

Island Press (founded in 1979; a subsidiary of Center for Resource Economics) pronounces itself "the environmental publisher." Many Island Press books are authored in association with research groups, funds, and institutes with environmental focus.

From Island Press: *Climate Change Policy* by Stephen H. Schneider; *Conservation Directory 2002* by the National Wildlife Federation; *Ecotourism and Certification* by Martha Honey; *Energy* by Robert Bent Randall Baker; *Engineering the Farm* by Britt Bailey; *Epicurean Simplicity* by Stephanie Mills; *The Farm as Natural Habitat* by Dana L. Jackson; *Fatal Harvest* by Andrew Kimbrell; *Fire, Native Peoples, and the Natural Landscape* by Thomas R. Vale; *The Forgotten Founders* by Stewart L. Udall; *The Good in Nature and Humanity* by Stephen R. Kellert; *An Introduction to Coastal Zone Management, 2nd Edition* by Timothy Beatley; *The Limitless City* by Oliver Gillham; *Solving Sprawl* by F. Kaid Benfield; *Welfare Ranching* by George Wuerthner; *Wildlife Restoration* by Michael L. Morrision; *World's Water 2002–2003* by Peter H. Gleick.

Titles from Shearwater: *Fishcamp: Life on an Alaskan Shore* by Nancy Lord (illustrated by Laura Simonds Southworth); *Kinship to Mastery: Biophilia in Human Evolution and Development* by Stephen R. Kellert; *The Value of Life: Biological Diversity and Human Society* by Stephen R. Kellert; *The Others: How Animals Made Us Human* by Paul Shepard.

Island Press handles its own distribution.

Acquisitions are made primarily through the Washington office. Initial contact names and locations should be confirmed prior to any query. Query letters and SASEs should be directed to:

Barbara Dean, Executive Editor—Biology, environmental restoration, ecosystem management, forestry, and sustainable agriculture books that are written for practitioners, scholars, undergraduate and graduate students, and general readers

Dan Sayre, Vice President and Publisher

Jonathon Cobb, Executive Editor, Shearwater Books

Todd Baldwin, Senior Editor—Marine affairs, energy policy, local governance, climate change

Heather Boyer, Editor—Human Habitat List—Landscape, architecture

James Nuzum, Assistant Editor

Laura Carrithers, Editorial Assistant

J

JOSSEY-BASS, INC., PUBLISHERS (A WILEY COMPANY)
Pfeiffer & Company

989 Market Street, San Francisco, CA 94103
415-782-3196   fax: 415-433-1711
www.pfeiffer.com

Jossey-Bass, Inc., Publishers (established in 1967), produces nonfiction in professional and advanced trade categories covering business, management, and administration in public and nonprofit sectors, as well as issues in psychology, social and health sciences, religion, and education. Major Jossey-Bass divisions include Pfeiffer & Company. The house sustains an extensive backlist and publishes specialist journals in fields allied to editors.

The firm was acquired by John Wiley & Sons in 1999.

Pfeiffer & Company is a formerly independent business-and-workplace specialist press acquired by Jossey-Bass in 1996 (see subentry for Pfeiffer & Company).

Jossey-Bass has an editorial commitment to provide useful, leading-edge resources grounded in research and proven in practice. These works present substantive ideas that will help individuals and organizations to learn, develop, and improve their effectiveness.

The Jossey-Bass publishing niche accents theory-to-practice books for thinking professionals, often in larger corporations, who are progressive and curious and who are in a position to influence their organizations. Most J-B books are grounded in primary research by the authors and are aimed at the twin concerns of development of the organization as a whole, as well as of the individuals within the organization.

Jossey-Bass sells via a half-dozen channels; about 20 to 25 percent of J-B business and management titles get general-market trade-bookstore distribution, while the balance is sold through direct mail, direct to corporations, via catalog companies, through agency bookstore accounts (mostly large, independent professional booksellers), and for use in college-level courses.

Titles: *A New Beginning for Pastors and Congregations: Building an Excellent Match Upon Your Shared Strengths* by Kennor L. Callahan; *On Becoming a Servant Leader: The Private Writings of Robert K. Greenleaf* by Don M. Frick and Larry C. Spears; *Our Lives as Torah: Finding God in Our Own Stories* by Carol Ochs; *Living with Paradox: Religious Leadership and the Genius of Double Vision* by Newton Malony; *Jewish Spiritual Guidance: Finding Our Way to God* by Carol Ochs and Kerry Olitzky; *Reaching for Higher Ground in Conflict Resolution* by E. Ranklin Dukes, Marina A. Piscolish, and John B. Stephens; *Resolving Personal and Organizational Conflict* by Kenneth Cloke and John Goldsmith; *Narrative Mediation: A New Approach to Conflict Resolution* by John Winslade and Gerald Monk; *Peace Skills* by Alice Frazer Evans, Robert A. Evans, and Ronald S. Kraybill; *Collaborating: Finding Common Ground for Multiparty Problems* by Barbara Gray; *Work and Motivation* by Victor H. Vroom; *Working Scared: Achieving Success in Trying Times* by Kenneth N. Wexley and Stanley B. Silverman; *Working with Family Businesses: A Guide for Professionals* by David Bork, Dennis T. Jaffe, Sam H. Lane, and Leslie Dashew; *Visionary Leadership: Creating a Compelling Sense of Direction for Your Organization* by Burt Nanus; *Telecommuting: A Manager's Guide to Flexible Work Arrangements* by Joel Kugelmass; *Thought Leaders: Insights on the Future of Business* by Joel Kurtzman; *Strategic Pay: Aligning Organizational Strategies and Pay Systems* by Edward E. Lawler; *Smart Alliances: A Practical Guide to Repeatable Success* by John R. Harbison and Peter Pekar; *Spirit at Work: Discovering the Spirituality in Leadership* by Jay A. Conger.

A representative Drucker Foundation Future series book: *The Leader of the Future: New Visions, Strategies, and Practices for the Next Era* (edited by Frances Hesselbein, Marshall Goldsmith, and Richard Beckhard; foreword by Peter F. Drucker). This Drucker Foundation Future series book asks the leaders of today to imagine the leadership of tomorrow.

Books from Warren Bennis Executive Briefing series: *The 21st Century Organization: Reinventing Through Reengineering* by Warren Bennis and Michael Mische; *Why Leaders Can't Lead: The Unconscious Conspiracy Continues* by Warren Bennis; *Fabled Service: Ordinary Acts, Extraordinary Outcomes* by Betsy Sanders; *The Absolutes of Leadership* by Philip B. Crosby.

Query letters and SASEs should be directed to:

Susan Williams, Editor—Business management/leadership

Lesley Iura, Senior Editor—Education

Alan Rinzler, Executive Editor—Psychology/self-improvement

Julianna Gustafson, Editor—Self-improvement with a spirituality component

Mark Kerr, Editor—Education books, religion, anything related to the evangelical Christian marketplace

Cedric Crocker, Executive Editor—Global business, strategy, and e-business models

Kathe Sweeney, Editor—Creativity/innovation, entrepreneurship (especially women), growing companies, post start-up, high-tech management, women in business, communications, transitions, third age, leadership development (CCL), and work/life balance

Pfeiffer & Company

Pfeiffer's trade business list targets such areas as career/personal development and general business/management. Pfeiffer also produces a dynamic array of training games, simulation/experiential-learning leader's manuals, computer software/CD-ROMs, and audio- and videocassettes.

Pfeiffer & Company (formerly an independent business-and-workplace specialist press acquired by Jossey-Bass in 1996) is an international house that specializes in business topics directed particularly toward trainers, consultants, and managers. With offices in Amsterdam, Johannesburg, London, Sydney, and Toronto, in addition to its former United States home in San Diego, the Pfeiffer & Company scope is adamantly global. As an imprint of Jossey-Bass, Inc., Publishers, Pfeiffer & Company offers innovative products for Human Resource Development.

From Pfeiffer & Company: *Getting Together: Icebreakers and Group Energizers* by Lorraine L. Ukens; *Feeding the Zircon Gorilla and Other Team Building Activities* by Sam Sikes; *Team Players and Teamwork: The New Competitive Business Strategy* by Glenn M. Parker; *The Skilled Facilitator: Practical Wisdom for Developing Effective Groups* by Roger M. Schwarz; *Leading with Soul: An Uncommon Journey of Spirit* by Lee G. Bolman and Terrence E. Deal; *Empowerment Takes More Than a Minute* by Ken Blanchard, John P. Carlos, and Alan Randolph.

Query letters and SASEs should be directed to:

Matt Holt, Editor—Practical materials in human resource development and management; organization development

Susan Rachmeier, Associate Editor—Management, careers, training

J

KENSINGTON PUBLISHING CORPORATION

Pinnacle Books

Zebra Books

Dafina Books

Citadel Books

Citadel Press

850 Third Avenue, 16th Floor, New York, NY 10022-6222
212-407-1500
www.kensingtonbooks.com

The Kensington, Zebra, and Pinnacle programs cover all major categories of commercial and popular trade nonfiction and fiction. Kensington nonfiction is strong in issue-oriented investigatory works of topical interest, humor, health, self-help and awareness, true crime, and popular biography. Areas of fiction concentration include romance fiction (historical and contemporary), horror, mystery and suspense, thrillers, and women's fiction.

Kensington is one of the largest independently owned book publishers. Kensington Publishing Corporation is home to such divisional imprints as Kensington Books (primarily hardcover and trade paperback originals), along with Zebra and Pinnacle (mainly mass-market paperback editions, as well as selected hardcovers). Long a leader in the paperback category arena, the house has expanded its publishing emphasis along the commercial spectrum; under the Kensington and Zebra/Pinnacle banners, the house is a vital hardcover presence. Kensington recently bought the Carol Publishing Group's backlist.

The Kensington mass-market imprint publishes quality and commercial fiction and nonfiction, both original titles and reprints.

Zebra Books (founded in 1975) and its sibling house Pinnacle Books (acquired in 1987) publish a colossal list of mass-market paperback originals that spans the spectrum of mainstream and genre categories. Zebra and Pinnacle also produce mass-market reprints of hardcover originals, as well as fiction and nonfiction in trade paper and designated high-profile titles in original hardcover editions.

The paperback-originals division of the house maintains a firm backlist of books—however, in keeping with mass-market rack tradition, titles that don't move are soon gone.

Kensington continues its romance program under such imprints, series, and lines as Bouquet Romance, Regency Romance, Historical Romance, and Arabesque (a line of multicultural romances).

Sample Kensington titles: *Other Girls* by Diane Ayres; *Mayo Clinic on Vision and Eye Health: Hypoglycemia* by Jeraldine Saunders and Dr. Harvey M. Ross, M.D.; *Kentucky Heat* by Fern Michaels; *Halfway Home* by Mary Sheldon; *Dating Can Be Murder* by Jennifer Apodaca; *Double Date* by Barbara Taylor McCafferty and Beverly Taylor Herald; *Face Down Under the Wych Elm* by Kathy Lynn Emerson; *Can't Buy Me Love* by Chris Kenry; *Cathedral City* by Gregory Hinton; *Cubans in America* by Alex Anton and Roger E. Hernandez.

Representative Zebra titles: *After Dark* by Beverly Barton; *A Scandalous Connection* by Hayley Ann Solomon; *A Kiss for Papa* by Jo Ann Ferguson, Valerie King, and Jeanne Savery; *A Gentleman at Heart* by Barbara Pierce; *A Princess Born* by Sandra Madden; *Bride*

K

and Groom by Deborah Johns, Linda Madl, and Patricia Waddell; *As Night Falls* by S. K. McClafferty; *Annie's Rainbow* by Fern Michaels; *Completely Smitten* by Kristine Crayson; *Dance on the Wind* by Brenda K. Jernigan; *Dear Emily* by Fern Michaels; *Flight of Fancy* by Tracy Cozzens; *Flowers for Mama* by Mona Gedney, Cindy Holbrook, and Mary Kingsley.

From Pinnacle: *Love Me to Death* by Steve Jackson; *Code Name: Coldfire* by William W. Johnstone; *Crimson Night* by Trisha Baker; *At the Edge* by David Dun.

Kensington oversees its own distributional operations. All listed Kensington editors have a wide range of interests in fiction and nonfiction; some of their personal specialties are noted as follows. Query letters and SASEs should be directed to:

Ann LaFarge, Executive Editor, Kensington and Zebra Books and Citadel Press—Women's fiction, thrillers, Westerns, commercial nonfiction

John Scognamiglio, Editorial Director, Fiction—Historical romance, Regency romance, women's contemporary fiction, gay fiction and nonfiction, mysteries, suspense, mainstream fiction

Karen Thomas, Editorial Director, Dafina/Arabesque—African American fiction and nonfiction

Kate Duffy, Editorial Director, Romance and Women's fiction—Historical romance, Regency romance, Brava erotic romance, women's contemporary fiction

Lee Heiman, Consulting Editor—Alternative health

Bruce Bender, Managing Director, Citadel Press—Popular nonfiction, film, television, wicca, gambling, current events

Margaret Wolf, Senior Editor, Citadel Press—Psychology, women's issues, women's health, entertainment, current events, cookbooks

Bob Shuman, Senior Editor, Citadel Press—politics, military, wicca, business, Judaica, sports

Amy Garvey, Consulting Editor—Historical romance, Regency romance, women's fiction

Michael Hamilton, Editor in Chief—Thrillers, mysteries, mainstream fiction, true crime, current events

Elaine Sparber, Senior Editor—Health, alternative health, pets, New Age, self-help

Richard Ember, Editor, Citadel Press—Biography, film, sports, New Age, spirituality

Miles Lott, Assistant Editor—Mainstream fiction, thrillers, horror, women's fiction, general nonfiction, popular culture, entertainment

Lisa Filippattos, Consulting Editor—Contemporary and historical romance, Regency romances, Brava erotic romance, women's fiction, thrillers

---

KIVAKÍ PRESS, INC.

PO Box 1053, Skyland, NC 28776
828-274-7941   fax: 828-274-7943
www.kivakipress.com

Kivakí Press is a small house with a focus on three editorial areas: environmental restoration, community renewal and education, and personal and holistic healing. Kivakí exists to provide people with practical strategies for restoring their ecosystems, for reconnecting with their places and local cultures, and for renewing their bodies holistically. Kivakí addresses academic, holistic health, and environmental book markets. Located in the mountains of North Carolina, the press produces a small number of new titles on a seasonal basis to add to a strong backlist.

Indicative of Kivakí interest: *A Wilder Life: Essays from Home* by Ken Wright; *The Company of Others: Essays in Celebration of Paul Shepard* (edited by Max Oelschlaeger); *Look to the Mountain: An Ecology of Indigenous Education* by Gregory Cajete; *Seasons of Change: Growing Through Pregnancy and Birth* by Suzanne Arms; *Restoration Forestry: An International Guide to Sustainable Forestry Practices* (edited by Michael Pilarski); *Flora of the San Juans: A Field Guide to the Mountain Plants of Southwestern Colorado* by Sue Komarek; *Sacred Land Sacred Sex: Rapture of the Deep—Concerning Deep Ecology and Celebrating Life* by Dolores Lachapelle; *Deep Powder Snow* by Dolores Lachapelle; *Igniting the Sparkle: An Indigenous Science Education Model* by Gregory Cajete; *David Johns: On the Trail of Beauty* by Lois and Jerry Jack.

Kivakí oversees its own distribution, including direct mail-order, and a trade distribution network that utilizes the facilities of several national fulfillment and distribution firms. Query letters and SASEs should be directed to:

Fred Gray, Publisher

THE KNOPF PUBLISHING GROUP (A DIVISION OF RANDOM HOUSE)

Alfred A. Knopf

Everyman's Library

Pantheon Books

Schocken Books

Vintage Anchor Publishing

Anchor Books

299 Park Avenue, New York, NY 10171
212-751-2600

Alfred A. Knopf

Alfred A. Knopf was founded in 1915 by Alfred and his wife, Blanche. Knopf, well-known as a publisher of distinguished hardcover fiction and nonfiction, is also known well by its logo, the running dog, officially referred to as a "coursing Borzoi." Knopf was quoted to say, "The coursing Borzoi has always been our trademark. . . . From the very beginning we have frequently been asked the meaning of the word *Borzoi* and what it has to do with books. When I started in business, the publisher I admired most was London's William Heinemann, and the sign of a Heinemann book was a windmill. . . . Since a windmill obviously had nothing to do with books, I saw no reason why we could not adopt the Borzoi as our mark." Knopf nonfiction categories include biography, history, nature, travel, cooking, and select poetry. Knopf also publishes the National Audubon Field Guides and the illustrated culture and travel companions, the Knopf Guides and the Knopf City Guides.

Nonfiction titles here include *American Sphinx* by Joseph Ellis; *How We Die* by Sherwin B. Nuland; *Lincoln's Virtues* by William Lee Miller; *The River's Tale* by Edward A. Gargan; *Paperboy: Confessions of a Future Engineer* by Henry Petroski; *Kurt Weill on Stage: From Berlin to Broadway* by Foster Hirsch; *Breaking Clean* by Judy Blunt; *Soros: The Life and Times of a Messianiac Billionaire* by Michael T. Kaufman; *Genes, Girls, and Gamow: After the Double Helix* by James D. Watson; *Somewhere for Me: A Biography of Richard Rodgers* by Meryle Secrest; *The Camera My Mother Gave Me* by Susanna Kaysen; *The Northern Lights* by Lucy Jago; *Mark Twain: An Illustrated Biography* by Geoffrey C. Ward, Dayton Duncan, and Ken Burns; *The Roosevelt Cousins: Growing Up Together, 1882–1924* by Linda Donn; *Dreamland: Europeans and Jews in the Aftermath of the Great War* by Howard M. Sachar; *A Is for American: Letters and Other Characters in the Newly United States* by Jill Lepore; *Soldiers: Fighting Men's Lives, 1901–2001* by Philip Ziegler; *Temperament: The Idea That Solved Music's Greatest Riddle* by Stuart M. Isacoff; *The Reel Civil War: Mythmaking in American Film* by Bruce Chadwick; *Art: A Field Guide* by Robert Cumming.

Representative fiction titles include *Century's Son* by Robert Boswell; *The Dive from Clausen's Pier* by Ann Packer; *All I Could Get* by Scott Lasser; *By the Lake* by John Mcgahern; *Burning Marguerite* by Elizabeth Inness-Brown; *The Rotters' Club* by Jonathan Coe; *A Multitude of Sins* by Richard Ford; *Me Times Three* by Alex Witchell; *Rapture* by Susan Minot; *Basket Case* by Carl Hiaasen; *Hateship, Friendship, Courtship, Loveship, Marriage* by Alice Munro.

Send query letters and SASEs to:

Ann Close, Editor—Literary fiction, geography, social and cultural history

Gary Fisketjon, Editor—Literary fiction; varied serious nonfiction interests

Jane Garrett, Editor—United States history, some European and Middle Eastern history, craft and hobby books

Jonathan Segal, Senior Editor—Twentieth-century history, contemporary events and issues

Judith Jones, Senior Editor and Vice President—Literary fiction, cookbooks, cultural history, the arts

Ken Schneider, Assistant Editor—Contemporary fiction; nonfiction: cultural history, the arts (drama, music, ballet); works with Judith Jones

Robin Desser, Senior Editor—Contemporary fiction; works with international/multicultural outlook; narrative nonfiction, including literary travel

Susan Ralston, Editorial Director of Schocken, Senior Editor of Knopf

Victoria Wilson, Senior Editor—Nonfiction: biography and memoir; cultural and social history; performing and creative arts, including film; literary fiction

Deb Garrision, Poetry Editor at Knopf, Senior Editor of Pantheon

K

Everyman's Library

Everyman's Library publishes a series of world literature classics. The series has grown to hundreds of volumes and also includes lines of Children's Classics and Pocket Poets.

Pantheon Books

Pantheon accents nonfiction books in current events, international affairs, contemporary culture, literary criticism and the arts, popular business, psychology, travel, nature, science, and history. The house has a strong list in contemporary fiction, poetry, and drama. Pantheon also offers the Fairytale and Folktale Library.

Pantheon was founded in 1942 by Helen and Kurt Wolff, refugees from Nazi Germany. "Building on its tradition of publishing important works of international fiction in translation and groundbreaking works of social policy, Pantheon now publishes quality fiction and nonfiction in a wide range of areas."

Representative titles include *Waiting* by Ha Jin; *Sap Rising* by Christine Lincoln; *Hidden Power: Presidential Marriages That Shaped Our Recent History* by Kati Marton; *The Bear's Embrace* by Patricia Van Tighem; *Red: Passion and Patience in the Desert* by Terry Tempest Williams; *Life Turns Man Up and Down: High Life, Useful Advice, and Mad English* (edited by Kurt Thometz); *Power, Politics, and Culture: Interviews with Edward W. Said* (edited by Gauri Viswanathan); *The Dark Room* by Rachel Seiffert; *The Diagnosis of Olaf Olaffson* by Alan Lightman; *The Feast of Love* by Charles Baxter.

Schocken Books

Schocken publishes titles in Judaica; cultural, religious, and women's studies; science and health; literature; and the social sciences. With a firm footing in both commercial and academic publishing, Schocken produces books in hardcover and trade paperback formats.

Salman Schocken, Zionist, bibliophile, and head of a department store, founded Schocken Books in Germany in 1931. Schocken began publishing in the United States in 1945 and became part of Random House, Inc., in 1987. In addition to its historic commitment to publishing Judaica, Schocken also produces fiction and nonfiction books that are of interest to the Jewish, as well as the general, audience.

Representative list titles: *Living a Life That Matters* by Harold Kushner; *The Conversion* by Aharon Appelfeld; *On the Mystical Shape of the Godhead* by Gershom Scholem; *The Jewish Holiday Kitchen* by Joan Nathan; *How to Be a Jewish Parent* by Anita Diamant with Karen Kushner; *A Guide to Jewish Prayer* by Adin Steinsaltz; *Letters to Auntie Fori* by Martin Gilbert; *Perfect Match* by Anistatia R. Miller and Jared M. Brown; *A Book That Was Lost* by S. Y. Agnon; *Tevye the Dairyman and the Railroad Stories* by Sholom Aleichem; *On Judaism* by Martin Buber; *The Trial* by Franz Kafka; *Conversations with Elie Wiesel* by Elie Wiesel and Richard D. Heffner.

Proposals and SASEs should be directed to:

Altie Karper, Editor

Cecelia Cancellaro, Editor

Susan Ralston, Editorial Director

Vintage Anchor Publishing

Vintage Anchor Publishing is the trade paperback arm of the Knopf Publishing Group and consists of Vintage Books and Anchor Books.

Vintage Books' publishing list includes a wide range, from world literature to contemporary fiction and distinguished nonfiction, featuring such writers as William Faulkner, Vladimir Nabokov, Albert Camus, Ralph Ellison, Dashiell Hammett, William Styron, A. S. Byatt, Philip Roth, Richard Ford, Cormac McCarthy, Alice Munro, David Guterson, and Arthur Golden.

Nonfiction titles include *The Beauty of the Husband: A Fictional Essay in 29 Tangos* by Anne Carson; *Quarrel & Quandary* by Cynthia Ozick; *Christ* by Jack Miles; *History on Trial* by Gary Nash, Charlotte Crabtree, and Ross E. Dunn; *The Global Soul* by Pico Iyer; *About Face* by James Mann.

Fiction titles: *Charlotte Gray* by Sebastian Faulks; *DelCorso's Gallery* by Philip Caputo; *The Vintage Book of Contemporary Chinese Fiction* (edited by Carolyn Choa and David Su Li-qun); *After the Banquet* by Yukio Mishima; *On the Yankee Station* by William Boyd; *Call If You Need Me* by Raymond Carver.

Send query letters and SASEs to:

Martin Asher, Editor in Chief

Anchor Books

Anchor Books is the oldest trade paperback publisher in America. It was founded in 1953 by Jason Epstein, with the goal of making inexpensive editions of modern classics widely available to college students and the adult reading public. Today, Anchor's list boasts award-winning history, science, women's studies, sociology, and quality fiction. Authors published by Anchor Books include Susan Sontag, Natalie Angier, Thomas Cahill, Ian McEwan, Anne Lamott, and Margaret Atwood.

Fiction titles indicative of this list include *Balzac and the Little Chinese Seamstress* by Dai Sijie; *The No. 1 Ladies' Detective Agency* by Alexander McCall Smith; *Tears of the Giraffe* by Alexander McCall Smith; *Ella Minnow Pea* by Mark Dunn; *Highwire Moon* by Susan Straight; *Look at Me* by Jennifer Egan; *Only in London* by Hanan al-Shaykh; *Swift as Desire* by Laura Esquivel; *Doctor Glas* by Hjalmar Soderberg; *Juno & Juliet* by Julian Gough.

Representative nonfiction titles: *Marie Antoinette* by Antonia Fraser; *The Radical Center* by Ted Halstead and Michael Lind; *Red Dust* by Ma Jian; *Searching for Certainty* by Darrell Bricker and Ed Greenspon; *Kids* by Meredith Small; *Wuhu Diary* by Emily Prager; *Carnage and Culture* by Victor Davis Hanson; *At Home in the Heart of Appalachia* by John O'Brien; *An Autumn of War* by Victor Davis Hanson; *To Touch a Wild Dolphin* by Rachel Smolker; *A Field Guide to Germs* by Wayne Biddle.

KRAUSE PUBLICATIONS

700 East State Street, Iola, WI 54990-0001
888-457-2873, 715-445-2214   fax: 715-445-4087
www.krause.com

Krause is a large publisher of trade nonfiction, with a concentration in antiques, collectibles, sewing, ceramics, and crafts and hobbies, as well as technical and professional topics (in such areas as engineering). Series include Contemporary Quilting, Creative Machine Arts, and a full lineup of consumer/trade titles that lists current market values for a wide range of antiques and collectibles (usually in periodically updated editions).

Representative of the list: *Standard Catalog of Sports Memorabilia; Standard Guide to American Muscle Cars; Ultimate Auto Album; The Gun Digest Book of the 1911; Machine Guns; Standard Catalog of World Coins Spain, Portugal and the New World; Woman's Depression Glass Field Guide; Arnold Grummer's Complete Guide to Paper Casting; Classic Muscle Car Advertising; 2002 Standard Catalog of Firearms; Standard Catalog of Mustang 1964–2001; 100 Legendary Knives; Standard Catalog of Hard Times Tokens 1832–1844; GMC; Got Tape?; Character Wreaths; Standard Guide to Small-Size U.S. Paper Money, 1928 to Date; Standard Catalog of Imported Cars 1946–2000; The Potter's Guide to Ceramic Surfaces; Marilyn Memorabilia; The Knitting Stitch Bible; Woman's Coins and Paper Money.*

Query letters and SASEs should be directed to:

Deb Faupel, Editor, Book Division

Don Johnson, Vice President of Publishing, Magazines and periodicals

LATIN AMERICAN LITERARY REVIEW PRESS

PO Box 17660, Pittsburgh, PA 15235
412-824-7903   fax: 412-824-7909
www.lalrp.org   e-mail: latin@angstrom.net

Latin American Literary Review Press produces reference books, trade books, and specialty publications in Latin American interest and studies. The press produces books in art, architecture, literature, and poetry; history, biography, and natural science; country studies (Spain, Europe, United States, Latin America); and children's books.

Latin American Literary Review Press (founded in 1980) is an independent house that is particularly vigorous in such fields as Latin American literature in English translation, Spanish-language art books, and literary criticism in Spanish. The press also publishes the journal *Latin American Literary Review,* the only journal in the United States devoted solely to the study of Latin American literature.

Representative titles in fiction and literature: *Clara* by Luisa Valenzuela (translated by Andrea G. Labinger); *Ceremonial Songs* by Chilean Nobel Laureate Pablo Neruda (translated by Maria Jacketti); *The Island of Cundeamor* by Rene Vazquez Diaz (translated by David E. Davis); *The Medicine Man* by Francisco Rojas Gonzalez (translated by Robert Rudder and Gloria Arjona); *Scent of Love* by Edla Van Steen (translated by David S. George); *Strange Forces* by Leopoldo Lugones (translated by Gilbert Alter-Gilbert); *People on the Prowl* by Jaime Collyer (translated by Lillian Lorca de Tagle); *Melodious Women* by Jarjorie Agosin (edited by Croi L. Gabbard, translated by Monica Bruno Galmozzi); *Bebbeh* by Sabina Berman (translated by Andrea G. Labinger); *Yo-Yo Boing!* by Giannina Braschi; *Beer Cans in the Rio de la Plata* by Jorge Stamadianos (translated by

L

Leland Chambers); *Maria de Estrada, Gypsy Conquistadora* by Gloria Duran; *The Cuban Mile* by Alejandro Hernandez Diaz (translated by Dick Cluster); *Sultry Moon* by Mempo Giardinelli.

Nonfiction and critical works: *XVIII Century Spanish Music Villancicos of Juan Francés de Iribarren* by Marta Sánchez; *Mexican American Theater: Legacy and Reality* by Nicolás Kanellos; *The Art of Mariano Azuela* by Eliud Martínez.

Latin American Literary Review Press has its own in-house distribution operation; in addition, the house markets through direct-mail catalog dissemination and utilizes a variety of national and regional distribution houses. Major markets include public libraries, trade booksellers, and university and college libraries. Latin American Literary Review Press handles distribution for a number of domestic and international presses. Query letters and SASEs should be directed to:

Yvette E. Miller, President and Editor in Chief

Maria G. Trujillo, Assistant Editor

LEARNING EXPRESS

900 Broadway, Suite 604, New York, NY 10003
212-995-2566   fax: 212-995-5512
www.learnatest.com

Learning Express is a leading publisher of print and online test preparation, career guidance, and basic skills materials. LearnATest.com/Library, its online interactive resource, offers practice tests and exercises for academic and career exams. Books are distributed by Delmar/Thomson Learning.

Query letters and SASEs should be directed to:

Jennifer Farthing, Senior Editorial Producer

LEISURE BOOKS

276 Fifth Avenue, Suite 1008, New York, NY 10001
212-725-8811

Leisure's publishing program centers on mass-market paperback originals in fiction, with a short list of hardcover reprints. Leisure's category fiction embraces historical romance, horror, technothrillers, thrillers, and Westerns.

Leisure hosts a fine list from established genre writers and also offers works from newer authors; the house publishes several brand-name category series and issues a notable number of deluxe double editions. The innovative Love Spell line has defined new market territory with experimental marketing slates in paranormal, futuristic, time travel, legendary lovers, perfect heroes, and faerie tale romance. Love Spell is developing a new line of humorous contemporary romance and also launched a new line of gothic romances. Leisure Books (founded in 1970) and Love Spell are divisions of Dorchester Publishing Company.

L

Indicative of Leisure Books interest: *Spirit's Song* by Madeline Baker; *The Cowboys: Sean* by Leigh Greenwood; *Savage Joy* by Cassie Edwards; *Pirate* by Connie Mason; *Lark* by Norah Hess; *The Bewitched Viking* by Sandra Hill; *Mine to Take* by Dara Joy; *Two Sixes* by Max Brand; *Danger Ridge* by Tim McGuire; *The Halloween Man* by Douglas Clegg; *Drawn to the Grave* by Mary Ann Mitchell.

Leisure is distributed by Hearst Distribution Group. Query letters and SASEs should be directed to:

Alicia Condon, Editorial Director

Christopher Keeslar, Senior Editor

Don D'Auria, Senior Editor

Leah Hultenschmidt, Editorial Assistant

Ashley Kuehl, Editorial Assistant

Kate Seaver, Associate Editor

LIFELINE PRESS (AN IMPRINT OF REGNERY PUBLISHING)

See also Regnery Publishing, Inc.

One Massachusetts Avenue NW, Washington, DC 20001
202-216-0600   fax: 202-216-0612

LifeLine Press is a new imprint of Regnery Publishing, which is dedicated to health, wellness, and child care. The press is committed to publishing the latest ground-breaking medical research in the fields of alternative health, nutrition, wellness, and child development. LifeLine's mission is "to provide timely and accurate information for consumers concerned about their health." LifeLine Press is committed to building a successful partnership with authors that could lead to the publication of not only the authors' first books, but their second and third books as well.

Query letters and SASEs should be directed to:

Mike Ward, Associate Publisher

LITTLE, BROWN AND COMPANY (PART OF TIME WARNER)

Back Bay Books

Bulfinch Press

Arcade Publishing (See separate entry)

Little, Brown and Company Books for Children and Young Adults

New York office:
Time & Life Building, 1271 Avenue of the Americas, New York, NY 10020
212-522-8700   fax: 212-522-2067

Boston office: (Bulfinch Press)
3 Center Plaza, Boston, MA 02108
617-227-0730   fax: 617-263-2857

L

Little, Brown publishes commercial trade nonfiction and fiction. Nonfiction interests encompass popular and literary biography, history, travel, art, medicine and allied health education, law, science, cuisine and lifestyle, reference, inspiration, and keepsake volumes/gift books. Little, Brown also produces commercial and literary fiction, essays, and memoirs; cultural, literary, and art criticism; and selected poetry. Little, Brown publishes in hardcover, trade paper, and mass-market paperback editions and produces selected deluxe editions of bestselling works, coffee-table volumes, and a line of calendars.

Little, Brown and Company (founded in 1837) originated as an independent house with a Boston home base. Little, Brown earned renown as a publisher with a dynamic, commercially successful line, as well as an outstanding literary list. Little, Brown, now a subsidiary of Time Warner, functions autonomously, primarily from within the Time & Life building (where its main trade offices reside), and releases titles under its stately colophon image of an eagle-topped column. Bulfinch Press (a division still based in Boston; see subentry) is one of the leading houses to specialize in fine-arts publishing and illustrated volumes.

Little, Brown popular works: *The Pregnancy Book* by William Sears, M.D., and Martha Sears, R.N.; *Stokes Beginner's Guide to BATS, Stokes Beginner's Guide to BIRD-FEEDING, Stokes Beginner's Guide to DRAGONFLIES,* and *Stokes Beginner's Guide to HUM-MINGBIRDS* by Donald and Lillian Stokes; *The Sailor's Handbook* by Halsey C. Herreshoff; *The Dream Workbook* by Jill Morris; *As Always, Jack: A Wartime Love Story* by Emma Sweeney; *Bad Boy Brawly Brown* by Walter Mosley; *City of Bones* by Michael Connelly; *How to Be Your Dog's Best Friend* by the Monks of New Skete; *In the Walled Gardens* by Alice Sebold; *The Perfect Store: Inside eBay* by Adam Cohen; *Simple Recipes: Stories* by Madeleine Thien; *A Young Athlete: A Sports Doctor's Complete Guide for Parents* by Jordan D. Metzl, M.D., with Carol Shookhoff.

Little, Brown maintains an extensive backlist, which is especially strong in literary fiction and nonfiction. Little, Brown distributes its own titles, as well as those of a changing list of other publishing houses both large and small, including Arcade Publishing, Bilingual Books, Food and Wine, Hyperion Books, and Miramax.

Please note: There are currently no Little, Brown adult-trade editors in Boston full time. Query letters and SASEs should be directed to these New York editors:

Judy Clain, Senior Editor—Literary and commercial fiction; serious nonfiction

Michael Pietsch, Vice President and Editor in Chief—Literary fiction and thrillers; general nonfiction, music biography, and autobiography; authors published or under contract include Peter Blanner, Michael Connelly, John Feinstein, Peter Guralnick, Joe McGinnis, Rick Moody, Walter Mostley, and the Neville Brothers

Terry Adams, Vice President and Director, Trade Paperbacks

Bill Phillips, Bill has spent more than 35 years with Little Brown and is one of the most acclaimed editors of our time. Although he retired last year, Bill continues to work for Little, Brown as a Consulting Editor. Bill works out of his home, and queries can be addressed to him at william.phillips@aol.wbg.com.

Geoff Shandler, Executive Editor

Deborah Baker, Senior Editor

Reagan Arthur, Senior Editor

L

Linda Biagi, Vice President and Rights Director

Ryan Harbage, Assistant Editor—Narrative nonfiction, business books and fiction

Asya Muchnick, Associate Editor

Emily Salkin, Assistant Editor, Back Bay Books

Mary Tondorf-Dick, Senior Managing Editor

Back Bay Books

Back Bay Books is a Little, Brown trade paperback imprint that accents contemporary fiction; Back Bay titles are generally cataloged with the core Little, Brown list. Little, Brown and Company Books for Young Adults is among the strongest and most respected imprints in its field.

Representative titles for Back Bay include *All The Finest Girls: A Novel* by Alexandra Styron; *ATOM: A Single Atom's Odyssey from the Big Bang to Life on Earth . . . And Beyond* by Lawrence M. Krauss; *Believing It All: Lessons I Learned from My Children* by Marc Parent; *Black Mischief: A Novel* by Evelyn Waugh; *The Cabal and Other Stories* by Rick Moody; *Fire in the Lake: The Vietnamese and the Americans in Vietnam* by Frances FitzGerald; *The Glory* by Herman Wouk; *Purple America* by Rick Moody; *Shooting the Moon* by David Harris; *Tip O'Neill and the Democratic Century* by John A. Farrell; *The Unwanted: A Memoir of Childhood* by Kien Nguyen; *Where Dead Voices Gather* by Nick Tosches.

Bulfinch Press

Bulfinch Press is a Little, Brown and Company division (based in Boston) that specializes in fine arts, architecture, photography, and design, as well as in finely produced collections of literary classics and illustrated volumes with a historical, cultural, or geographical accent. The house produces lush hardcover and paperback volumes, as well as merchandise lines, including posters and calendars.

Representative of the Bulfinch list: *Allure* by Diana Vreeland; *Antarctica: A Year at the Bottom of the World* by Jim Mastro; *The Breathing Field: Yoga as Art* by Wyatt Townley; *Cape Light* by Joel Meyerowitz; *Colefax & Fowler's Interior Inspirations* by Roger Banks-Pye; *Dorothea Lange: The Heart and Mind of a Photographer* by Pierre Borhan; *Earthly Bodies: Irving Penn's Nudes, 1949–50* by Irving Penn; *The Epicurean Collector* by Patrick Dunne and the Editors of Southern Accents.

Little, Brown and Company Books for Children and Young Adults

Three Center Plaza, Boston, MA 02108
617-227-0730

Little, Brown's children's books division (headquartered in Boston) produces picture books, boardbooks, pop-up and lift-the-flap editions, chapter books, and general fiction and nonfiction titles for middle- and young-adult readers.

This division also issues resource guides and reference titles in careers, social issues, and intellectual topics for higher grade levels and the college-bound. Marc Brown's Arthur books and Matt's Christopher sports series are especially successful. The house offers volumes in Spanish language and in dual Spanish/English editions and is on the lookout for multicultural titles.

Sample titles: Caldecott winner *Saint George and the Dragon* (illustrated by Trina Schart Hyman); Newbery winner *Maniac Magee* by Jerry Spinelli; *Toot & Puddle* by Holly Hobbie; *Daisy and the Egg* by Jane Simmons; *Kevin and His Dad* by Irene Smalls; *Go Away, Big Green Monster!* by Ed Emberley; *Animal Crackers* by Jane Dyer; *The Jolly Pocket Postman* by Janet and Allen Ahlberg.

Little, Brown and Company recently added the imprint Megan Tingley Books to its children's division. (See entry for Megan Tingley Books.) The house distributes the publications of Disney Press and Hyperion Books for Children.

Prospective authors please note: Little Brown's children's division does not accept unsolicited manuscripts directly from authors. Manuscripts must go through an agent to:

Children's Editorial Dept.

LODESTAR BOOKS (AN IMPRINT OF DUTTON)

See Penguin Putnam, Inc.

LONELY PLANET PUBLICATIONS

150 Linden Street, Oakland, CA 94607
510-893-8555   fax: 510-893-8563
www.lonelyplanet.com   e-mail: info@lonelyplanet.com

Lonely Planet specializes in travel guides, phrasebooks, maps, atlases, restaurant guides, activity guides, and other specialist travel series, covering every country in the world and with options for a full range of budgets and styles. There are over 600 Lonely Planet publications produced in offices in Melbourne, Australia, Oakland, California, London, and Paris.

Lonely Planet's "shoestring guides" are the world's best-selling budget guides. Designed for the long-haul independent traveler, "shoestrings" cover either entire continents or large sections of entire continents.

"Travel Guides" are in-depth country or regional guides and include options and budget information for all types of travelers.

"Condensed Guides" are ideal pocket guides when time is tight, with quick-view maps, full-color throughout, top sights, and the best places to stay, eat, and shop, all in a pocket-sized format.

"CitySync" is Lonely Planet's series of digital city guides for Palm and other PDAs. The series is currently available as a download, on CD-ROM, or as a Handspring module and a Palm "Travel Pak" card.

"Walking Guides" are for those who believe the best way to see the world is on foot, from family strolls to difficult treks, with reliable maps and essential travel information.

L

"Cycling Guides" map out the best bike routes, long and short, in day-to-day detail. Includes advice on staying healthy, bike maintenance, places to stay and eat, bike shops, and innovative maps with detailed cues to each ride and elevation charts.

"Watching Wildlife" guides are packed with advice on where, when, and how to view a region's wildlife, with photos of more than 300 species and engaging insights into their lives and environments.

"Pisces" guides explore the world's great diving and snorkeling areas and include full-color photos throughout, practical information on activities above and below the water, and listings of diving services and resorts. Each guide also includes health and safety tips and site details such as depth, visibility, levels of difficulty, and marine life you're likely to see.

"Phrasebooks" cover essential words and phrases, two-way dictionaries, local script for easy reference, and much more in pocket-sized format.

Lonely Planet also produces a limited series of hardcover, beautifully designed and produced, illustrated gift books on travel. Titles in this series include *Chasing Rickshaws; Sacred India and the Shape of Perfection; Buddhist Stupas in Asia.*

Other series from Lonely Planet include Read This First, Healthy Travel, City Maps, World Foot, Out to Eat, as well as videos, calendars, and other merchandise.

Lonely Planet's Web site includes over 300 Destinations Profiles, well-researched, and up-to-date reports on countries, cities, islands, and regions and complete with maps and photographs. In addition, www.lonelyplanet.com's "Thorn Tree" has become the center of the independent travel community, with over 5,000 postings a day on hundreds of travel topics.

The people at Lonely Planet (founded in 1975) strongly believe that travelers can make a positive contribution to the countries they visit, both through their appreciation of the countries' culture, wildlife, and natural features and through the money they spend. In addition, Lonely Planet makes a direct contribution to the countries and regions it covers. Since 1986 a percentage of the income from each book has been donated to ventures such as famine relief in Africa, aid projects in India, agricultural projects in Central America, Greenpeace's efforts to halt French nuclear testing in the Pacific, and Amnesty International.

As the publisher's message suggests: "I hope we send the people out with the right attitude about travel. You realize when you travel that there are many different perspectives about the world, so we hope these books will make people more interested in what they see. These are guidebooks, but you can't really guide people. All you can do is point them in the right direction."

Lonely Planet produces an anecdotal and informative travel newsletter and distributes its own list in America through its United States office. The Lonely Planet Publications editorial division is located in Australia—though manuscripts and proposals are given preliminary consideration at the stateside contact address. Query letters and SASEs should be directed to:

Eric Kettunen, U.S. Manager (at United States office)

LONGMEADOW PRESS USA

Longmeadow Press, begun in 1984, is no longer operating as a publisher. The house was a proprietary publishing division of the powerful retail-bookstore chain WaldenBooks.

LONGSTREET PRESS

2140 Newmarket Parkway, Suite 122, Marietta, GA 30067
770-980-1488, 800-927-1488   fax: 770-859-9894
www.longstreetpress.com   e-mail: info@longstreetpress.net

Longstreet publishes general nonfiction and fiction (often with a Southern regional accent), self-help, gardening, sports, health, photography and art, gift books, and calendars.

Titles from Longstreet include *A Girl's Guide to a Guy's World* by Jennifer Babbit and Samantha Bank; *Small Blessings: A Book of Prayers for Children* by Don Harp; *Trees for the South* by Don Hastings; *Sweet Words to God* by Rabbi Arnold Goodman; *Forever Green: A History and Hope of the American Forest* by Chuck Leavell*; Family Estrangements: How They Begin, How to Mend Them, How to Cope with Them* by Barbara LeBey; *The Thank You Book* and *The Thank You Book for Kids* by Ali Lauren Spizman; *Bobby Jones: Extra!* (compiled by Sidney L. Matthew); *Down the Fairway* by Robert T. Jones and O. B. Keeler; *Voices from the Edge: Life Lessons from the Cancer Community* by Michael Hayes Samuelson; *Get Ahead: Scovil's 7 Rules for Success in Management* by Roger Scovil; *True Women* by Janice Woods Windle; *Tips for Good Living with Arthritis* by the Arthritis Foundation; *The Arthritis Foundation's Guide to Good Living with Fibromyalgia; Even a Geek Can Speak* by Joey Asher; *The Wolf Camera Guide to Taking Better Pictures* by Wolf Camera Staff; *Angel in the Front Room, Devil Out Back* by Stanford Diehl.

Longstreet publishes the popular Jeff Foxworthy's *You Might Be a Redneck If . . . ,* which now has more than one million copies in print. Other Foxworthy books include *Red Ain't Dead; Games Rednecks Play; Check Your Neck; You're Not a Kid Anymore; Redneck Classic; The Final Helping of You Might Be a Redneck If . . . .*

Longstreet oversees its own distribution. Please note that due to a recently downsized acquisitions department, Longstreet currently is not accepting unsolicited or unagented manuscript submissions.

Query letters and SASEs should be directed to:

Ann Lovet, Editorial and Publicity Assistant

Scott Bard, Publisher and President

LOOMPANICS UNLIMITED

Box 1197, Port Townsend, WA 98368
360-385-2230   fax: 360-385-7785
www.loompanics.com   e-mail: editorial@loompanics.com

Loompanics Unlimited produces books of nonfiction trade interest, in addition to professional and special-interest nonfiction. The Loompanics list accents practical self-help and how-to, contemporary and historical culture, and sociopolitical and issue-oriented works. The house offers a selective fiction list (primarily, reprints of hitherto overlooked masterworks).

Loompanics offers books in such categories as underground economy, tax "avoision," money-making opportunities, individual privacy, fake identification, Big Brother is

L

watching you, conducting investigations, crime and police science, locks and lock-smithing, self-defense, revenge, guns, weapons, bombs and explosives, guerrilla warfare, murder and torture, survival, self-sufficiency, head for the hills, gimme shelter, health and life extension, paralegal skills, sex, drugs, rock and roll, intelligence increase, science and technology, heresy/weird ideas, anarchism and egoism, work, mass media, censorship, reality creation, self-publishing—and an enigmatic category of works classified solely as miscellaneous.

Since its foundation in 1973, Loompanics titles have been among the most controversial and unusual publications available, and the publishing program has produced recognized classics in a number of fields.

Many Loompanics publications test the edge of the free-speech envelope—and often do so with humorous subversiveness and literary zest; some of the more treacherous materials are clearly intended exclusively for amusement, informational, or scholarly reference purposes.

Loompanics features: *Secrets of Methamphetamine Manufacture* by Uncle Fester; *The Outlaw's Bible* by E. X. Boozhie; *Take No Prisoners: Destroying Enemies with Dirty and Malicious Tricks* by Mack Nasty; *Gaslighting: How to Drive Your Enemies Crazy* by Victor Santoro; *Poison Pen Letters* by Keith Wade; *Identity Theft: The Cyber Crime of the Millennium* by John Q Newman; *Sex, Drugs & the Twinkie Murders* by Paul Krassner; *Anarchic Harmony: The Spirituality of Social Disobedience* by William J. Murray; *Principia Discordia: Or How I Found the Goddess and What I Did to Her When I Found Her* by Malaclypse the Younger; *How to Sneak into the Movies* by Dan Zamudio; *Practical LSD Manufacture* by Uncle Fester; *Secondhand Success: How to Turn Discards into Dollars* by Jordan L. Cooper; *Uberhaker! How to Break into Computers* by Carolyn Meinel; *The Politics of Consciousness: A Practical Guide to Personal Freedom* by Steve Kubby; *Stoned Free: How to Get High Without Drugs* by Patrick Wells, with Douglas Rushkoff; *You Are Going to Prison* (a survival guide) by Jim Hogshire.

From the arena of literary fiction: *The Gas* (another classic literary work in reissue) by Charles Platt.

Some backlist Loompanics hits: *Bad Girls Do It! An Encyclopedia of Female Murderers* by Michael Newton (author of *Serial Slaughter: What's Behind America's Murder Epidemic?*); *Still At Large: A Casebook of 20th Century Serial Killers and Psychedelic Shamanism* by Jim DeKorne; *Secrets of a Superhacker* by an incognito information superhighwayman known as the Knightmare; *Shadow Merchants: Successful Retailing Without a Storefront* by Jordan L. Cooper; *The Art & Science of Dumpster Diving* by John Hoffman (with original comix by Ace Backwords); *Community Technology* by Karl Hess; *How to Obtain a Second Passport and Citizenship and Why You Want To* by Adam Starchild; *The Rape of the American Constitution* by Chuck Shiver; *The Wild and Free Cookbook* by Tom Squire; *Travel-Trailer Homesteading Under $5,000* by Brian D. Kelly; *Screw the Bitch: Divorce Tactics for Men* by Dick Hart; *Natural Law: Or Don't Put a Rubber on Your Willy* by Robert Anton Wilson.

Special Loompanics compilations: *Loompanics' Greatest Hits: Articles and Features from the Best Book Catalog in the World* (edited by Michael Hoy); *Loompanics Unlimited Live! in Las Vegas* (edited by Michael Hoy).

Loompanics Unlimited is editorially a reclusive house. Writers who wish to work with Loompanics should note that its business is the printed word, and potential authors should

L

approach Loompanics through the printed word (via mail—do not telephone or e-mail proposals or submissions). The publisher also notes that the press tends toward small advances and works through literary agents only on occasion.

The Loompanics Unlimited direct-order catalog (emblazoned with the publisher's free-booter-spaceship colophon) depicts a wealth of titles from its own list, as well as select offerings from other houses, in a luscious newsprint format that includes graphics, essays, and short fiction, along with blurbs from reviewers and satisfied customers testifying to the potency of the house's list and the efficacy of the Loompanics distribution and fulfillment services.

Query letters and SASEs should be directed to:

Michael Hoy, President

Gia Cosindas, Editor

LOWELL HOUSE

Lowell House was acquired as part of McGraw-Hill's acquisition of parent company Contemporary Books. The Lowell House backlist will be maintained, but there will be no new title acquisitions and the office has been closed.

THE LYONS PRESS

123 West 18th Street, New York, NY 10010
212-620-9580   fax: 212-929-1836

The Lyons Press produces trade nonfiction, especially books on country living, horses, fly fishing, adventure, travel, military history, natural history, and outdoor recreation and sports; the house also produces works aimed at regional interests worldwide, selected literary fiction and essays, and reference.

From Lyons Press: *Hemingway on Fishing* (edited by Nick Lyons); *Bacchus & Me* by Jay McInerney; *Some Horses* by Thomas McGuane; *The Faraway Horse* by Buck Brannaman; *Toro* by Mark Sundeen; *Last Flight Out* by Randy Wayne White; *Twelve Days of Terror* by Richard G. Fernicola; *A Life Worth Living* by Jack Hemingway; *The Greatest Dog Stories Ever Told* (edited by Patricia M. Sherwood); *The Last Posse* by Gale Christianson; *My Faraway Home* by Mary Maynard; *Cougar Attacks!* by Kathy Etling; *Advanced Fly Tying* by A. K. Best; *The Hunter, the Hammer, and Heaven* by Robert Young Pelton; *Ill Nature* by Joy Williams; *The Greatest Baseball Stories Ever Told* (edited by Jeff Silverman); *L. L. Bean Fly Fishing Handbook* by Dave Whitlock; *Pocket Waters* by William Tappley; *The Quotable Traveler* (edited by Deborah McHugh); *The Long Walk* by Slavomir Rawicz; *We Die Alone* by David Howarth. The Lyons Press has ongoing series with the Nature Conservancy, L. L, Bean, *Field & Stream,* the Orvis Company, *Outdoor Life,* Outward Bound, and the *New York Times.*

Fiction and literature: *Ice Hunter* (mystery) by Joseph Heywood; *Dry Rain* (stories) by Pete Fromm; *Travers Corners* (stories about the Lake Wobegon of fly fishing) by Scott Waldie.

L

The company logo shows a leaping trout poised gracefully midair over the publisher's ingenious LP colophon. Lyons Press produces a midsize roster of new titles and keeps a substantial backlist.

The Lyons Press is now an imprint of the Globe Pequot. Query letters and SASEs should be directed to:

Tony Lyons, Publisher—Adventure, military history

Jay Cassell, Senior Editor—Hunting, fishing, history

Enrica Gadler, Senior Editor—Horses, nature writing, memoirs

Becky Koh, Senior Editor—Sports and fitness, adventure and exploration, country living

Tom McCarthy, Editor—Sports

Jonathan J. McCullough, Editor—Fishing, adventure, narrative nonfiction

Brando Skyhorse, Editor—Narrative nonfiction, military history, travel and adventure

Ann Triestman, Editor—Country living, sports

Lisa Purcell, Assistant Editor—History, gardening, cooking, pets, travel

Mark Weinstein, Assistant Editor—Sports, history, military history

Lilly Golden, Editor at Large—Literary fiction, essays

Bill Bowers, Managing Editor—Fly fishing

Nick Lyons, Editorial Consultant—Essays, literary fiction

M & T Books

M & T has been acquired by IDG, which has been renamed Hungry Minds.

Masquerade Books

Has discontinued its publishing operations.

McFarland & Company, Inc., Publishers

Box 611, Jefferson, NC 28640-0611
336-246-4460   fax: 336-246-5018
www.mcfarlandpub.com   e-mail: info@mcfarlandpub.com

McFarland & Company, Inc., Publishers is an independent nontrade publisher specializing in general reference, performing arts (especially film, radio, television, and theater), baseball, popular culture, automotive history, chess, Appalachian studies, history (U.S., Civil War, world), international studies, criminal justice, women's studies, and African American studies. Publishes nonfiction only, around 200 titles a year.

Query letters and SASEs should be directed to:

Robert Franklin, President and Editor in Chief

Virginia Tobiassen, Editor

M

Steve Wilson, Senior Editor

Born: November 27, 1968.

Education: B.A., summa cum laude, in English, UNC-Chapel Hill, 1991.

Employment history/editor career path: Started at McFarland as Assistant Editor shortly after college; no prior publishing experience.

Personal interests: Automotive history, Southern literature, woodworking, scale automotive modeling.

What books have you acquired that make you the most proud? What books that you have acquired reflect the types of books you like to represent? Two works, both coincidentally on North Carolina history, come to mind: Fred Mallison's *The Civil War on the Outer Banks* and R. G. (Hank) Utley and Scott Verner's *The Independent Carolina Baseball League, 1936–1938: Baseball Outlaws.* They're both labors of love, the kind of lifelong research efforts that can only be accomplished by someone deeply involved with the subject material. Moreover, they're both charming and fascinating. Both books also represent unknown marketing quantities that performed well.

Do you represent fiction? No.

Do you represent nonfiction? Yes, exclusively.

Do you require book proposals? If so, what do you look for in evaluating a book proposal? If the manuscript is complete when the author first contacts us, we generally invite the entire manuscript if it sounds plausible. At the opposite extreme, we're willing to launch a discussion based on nothing more than an idea, particularly if we have worked with the author before. At some point prior to a contract offer, we do need a proposal, though—preferably an outline, length estimate, draft of introduction or preface, two sample chapters, and description of special elements such as illustrations or appendices. We look for authoritative and complete coverage of a subject that is not already exhausted, competent research and organization, and reliability (we don't want to be forced to verify absolutely every fact and spelling).

Are certain aspects of a book proposal given more weight than others? Yes, but they vary according to the type of book. In a work of film reference, for example, we look hard at the depth of filmographic data; in a biography, the freshness of the material tends to be a key factor; in a book of library cartoons, the question is whether they're funny.

What process do you use for making a decision? What is the process for acquisition; is there a committee? All members of our editorial staff are involved in acquisitions. Proposals are distributed as they arrive, and the editors meet once a week to discuss the new proposals they've received.

What kinds of nonfiction books do you want to see less of? We do not publish devotional works, stories of personal triumph over adversity, theories about the functioning of the cosmos (a very frequent offering), or children's books, all of which are proposed to us regularly.

Are you interested in work geared for the masses (readers of *People, The Star,* etc.)? Generally, no. Our market consists of (1) libraries and (2) individuals with a strongly focused interest in any of several specialty subjects (film, old-time radio, baseball, chess, automotive history, and others).

Are agents important? Why? From our perspective, no. We use a standard contract that does not vary from book to book, so an agent has no real negotiating role in signing a contract with us. Communication with an author is smoother, too, when it is direct.

M

Do you like new writers? What should writers do to break into the business? We do like new writers. Perhaps as many as half our authors had not published a book before coming to McFarland, and many have gone on to publish several successful books with us. (We enjoy a very high rate of repeat authors.) For breaking in with a publisher like us, the best advice to a new author is to find a fresh, interesting subject and produce a fairly substantial sample before contacting us. Our Web site lists some useful guidelines.

How should writers approach you? The traditional query letter, followed up by a formal proposal if we express interest, is hard to beat. We accept queries by telephone or even by e-mail (no attachments please), but a letter tends to make the best impression.

What are some common mistakes writers make? What really gets on your nerves? Writers are better off not phoning every few days to see if we've looked at a proposal yet. We're really quite prompt—we respond inside of two weeks in most cases, and it almost never takes us more than a month—but some authors can't stand even that wait. The innocent "Have you gotten to my proposal yet" question is almost impossible to answer by phone. We receive too many proposals to remember them all instantly (especially before actually looking through them), and a given proposal may be with any of four or five of us. An author who phones two or three times in the short period before we can reply signals a possible "personality problem."

What have been some of your craziest experiences with submissions? Authors re-proposing previously rejected manuscripts three or four times or writing us under a different name after a rejection. One or two have refused to reveal the subject of the manuscript without a commitment of interest and a written confidentiality agreement.

What have been some of your best experiences with writers or in your job? Well, there's really nothing more satisfying than a happy author. Editors sometimes forget the sheer work that goes into a manuscript. When an author's long labor has produced something really good, we've done our job right and turned out a beautiful book, and the author senses that we've made the manuscript better, I feel good. That sense of productive partnership is enormously rewarding.

The McGraw-Hill Companies, Inc.

Glencoe/McGraw-Hill

McGraw-Hill/Osborne Media

McGraw-Hill Professional

Access Med Books

Business McGraw-Hill

International Marine

Ragged Mountain Press

Schaum's McGraw Hill

Wright Group/McGraw-Hill (see separate entry)

2 Penn Plaza, New York, NY 10121
212-512-2000   fax: 212-904-6096

M

For over 100 years, McGraw-Hill has been publishing nonfiction titles in a wide range of categories. In addition to a long list of fiction titles, McGraw-Hill operates specialty programs in a variety of professional, business, and educational fields such as health care, law, high-tech industries, and textbooks for primary school through college. This house publishes books for professional, institutional, and trade markets; journals geared to core areas of interest; and seminar and group workshop materials; it issues a broad selection of electronic products, including e-books and CD-ROMs.

While still geared toward business and professional titles, McGraw-Hill continues to venture into the broader range of commercial trade arenas, including aviation, careers, cooking, computing, engineering, architecture, foreign language, general and self-help, medical, science, mathematics, sports, recreation, and telecommunications.

McGraw-Hill distributes for all its divisions. Query letters and SASEs should be directed to:

Barry Neville, Editor—General business

McGraw-Hill/Osborne Media

2600 Tenth Street, 6th Floor, Berkeley, CA 94710

McGraw-Hill/Osborne Media produces self-paced computer training materials, including user and reference guides, titles on business and technology, and high-level but practical titles on networking, programming, and Web development tools. McGraw-Hill/Osborne Media is the official press of Oracle, Corel, Global Knowledge, J. D. Edwards, Intuit, and RSA Security, Inc., and has a strategic publishing relationship with ComputerWorld. McGraw-Hill/Osborne Media is focusing on consumer support, emerging technologies, and innovative applications for developing future computer books.

McGraw-Hill/Osborne Media is known for its series, including The Complete Reference Series, A Beginners Guide Series, All in One Series, and Certification Press Series.

Titles indicative of this list: *C# Programming Tips & Techniques* by Charles Wright and Kris Jamsa; *Learn to Program with Visual Basic.NET* by John Smiley; *Oracle 9i New Features* by Robert Freeman; *Mike Meyers' Network+ Certification Passport* by Michael Meyers and Nigel Kendrick; *OCP Oracle9i Database New Features for Administrators Exam Guide* by Daniel Benjamin; *DSL Survival Guide* by Lisa Lee; *Home Networking Survival Guide* by David Strom; *FrontPage 2002 Virtual Classroom* by David Karlins.

Direct query letters and SASEs to:

Scott Rogers, Editor in Chief—Scott_Rogers@mcgraw-hill.com

McGraw-Hill Professional

McGraw-Hill Professional focuses on professional, reference, and trade publishing. This division produces general-interest books, study guides, software, multimedia, and online products.

This broad list includes titles in business and economics, computers, education, family and relationships, foreign language study, health and fitness, history, language arts and disciplines, mathematics, medical, nature, nonclassifiable, psychology and psychiatry, science, self-help, social science, sports and recreation, technology and engineering, and transportation and travel.

General titles span the categories of art; body, mind, and spirit; cooking; crafts and hobbies; family and relationships; gardening; health and fitness; history; house and home; humor; music; nature; performing arts; photography; and self-help.

Titles indicative of McGraw-Hill Professional: *Fit from Within: 101 Simple Secrets to Change Your Body and Your Life—Starting Today and Lasting Forever* by Victoria Moran; *The No-Cry Sleep Solution: Gentle Ways to Help Your Baby Sleep Through the Night* by Elizabeth Pantley; *Model Mommy: Vendela's Plan for Emotional Support, Exercise, and Eating Right After Having a Baby* by Vendela Kirsebom; *Dealing with People You Can't Stand: How to Bring Out the Best in People at Their Worst* by Rick Brinkman and Rick Kirschner; *Beating Depression: The Journey to Hope* by Maga Jackson-Triche, Kenneth Wells, and Katherine Minnium; *Ten Secrets of Successful Men That Women Want to Know* by Donna Brooks and Lynn Brooks; *The September 11 Syndrome: Seven Steps to Getting a Grip in Uncertain Times* by Harriet Braiker; *Teach Yourself World Faiths, New Edition* by Paul Oliver; *Teach Yourself Film Making* by Tom Holden; *Table for One Chicago* by Michael Kaminer and Amy LaBan.

Aviation titles: *Safe Air Travel Companion* by Dan McKinnon; *Once a Fighter Pilot* by Jerry Cook; *Rescue Pilot* by Dan McKinnon; *Profit Strategies for Air Transportation* by George Radnoti; *Handling In-Flight Emergencies* by Jerry Eichenberger; *Ace the Technical Pilot Interview* by Gary Bristow.

Career titles: *Ace the IT Resume!* by Paula Moreira and Robyn Thorpe; *201 Best Questions to Ask on Your Interview* by John Kador; *101 Best Resumes to Sell Yourself* by Jay Block; *The Career Survival Guide Making Your Next Career Move* by Brian O'Connell; *Occupational Outlook Handbook, 2002–2003 Edition* by U.S. Department of Labor; *Ace the Technical Pilot Interview* by Gary Bristow.

Engineering and Architecture titles representative of this list: *McGraw-Hill's National Electrical Safety Code Handbook* by David Marne; *Master Handbook of Video Production* by Jerry Whitaker; *Lineman's and Cableman's Handbook* by Thomas Shoemaker and James Mack; *Architects on Architects* by Susan Gray; *Interior Design Handbook of Professional Practice* by Cindy Coleman of *Interior Design Magazine; TAB Electronics Build Your Own Robot Kit* by Myke Predko and Ben Wirz; *Build a Remote-Controlled Robot* by David Shircliff; *Structures of Our Time: 31 Buildings That Changed Modern Life* by Roger Shepherd.

Direct query letters and SASEs to:

Judy Bass—Telecommunications; judy_bass@mcgraw-hill.com

Shelley Carr—Aviation, technical trades; shelley_carr@mcgraw-hill.com

Steve Chapman—Electrical engineering, telecommunications, video/audio; steve_chapman@mcgraw-hill.com

Scott Grillo—TAB electronics, embedded systems, electrical wiring; scott_grillo @mcgraw-hill.com

Larry Hager—Civil engineering, industrial engineering, quality engineering, construction; larry_hager@mcgraw-hill.com

Ken McCombs—Chemical engineering, environmental engineering, mechanical engineering, fire science; kenneth_mccombs@mcgraw-hill.com

Marjorie Spencer—Telecommunications, networking; marjorie_spencer@mcgraw -hill.com

Cary Sullivan—Architecture, landscape architecture, interior design, urban design; cary_sullivan@mcgraw-hill.com

Access Med Books

2 Penn Plaza, 12th Floor, New York, NY 10121-2298
fax: 212-904-6045

Access Med Books produces select medical titles. A few representative titles include *Cosmetic Dermatology Principles and Practice* by Leslie Baumann; *Spine Surgery: A Practical Atlas* by F. Todd Wetzel and Edward Hanley, Jr.; *Harrison's Internet Edition* by Eugene Braunwald, Anthony Fauci, Dennis Kasper, Stephen Hauser, Dan Longo, and J. Jameson; *Cardiology at a Glance* by Johnny Lee and Paul Lee; *Operative Obstetrics* by Larry Gilstrap, F. Cunningham, and J. Peter VanDorsten; *Goodman & Gilman's: The Pharmacological Basis of Therapeutics* by Joel Hardman, Lee Limbird, and Alfred Gilman.

   Direct query letters and SASEs to:

Martin Wonsiewicz, Publisher—Specialty: Clinical medicine; martin_wonsiewicz @mcgraw-hill.com

Jack Farrell, Publisher and Sales Manager—Specialty: Medical education products; jack_farrell@mcgraw-hill.com

Mikael Engebretson, Publisher—Specialty: Online publishing (including Harrison's Online); mikael_engebretson@mcgraw-hill.com

Business McGraw-Hill

2 Penn Plaza, New York, New York 10121
212-512-2000   fax: 212-904-6096

Business McGraw-Hill publishes trade and professional titles in business, finance, entrepreneurship, marketing, training, human resources, investing, management, advertising, sales, and communication.

   Representative of the Business McGraw-Hill list: *Financial Planning for the Utterly Confused* by Joel Lerner; *Short Cycle Selling: Beating Your Competitors in the Sales Race* by Jim Kasper; *Valuing Wall Street* by Andrew Smithers and Stephen Wright; *Software Rules: How the Next Generation of Enterprise Applications Will Increase Strategic Effectiveness* by Mark Barrenechea; *Investing in Separate Accounts* by Erik Davidson and Kevin Freeman; *The Rumsfeld Way: The Leadership Wisdom of a Battle-Hardened Maverick* by Jeffrey Krames; *Character Counts* by John Bogle; *Six Sigma for Managers* by Greg Brue; *The Welch Way* by Jeffrey Krames; *Streetsmart Guide to Managing Your Portfolio* by Frank Yao, Bret Xu, Kenneth Doucet, and Patrick Adams.

   Direct query letters and SASEs to:

Mary E. Glenn, Editor—Management and management theory, self-help with a business focus, some marketing and sales; topical books with global appeal that can cross over into serious nonfiction

Philip Ruppel, Publisher—All areas indicated in house description, including marketing, management, quality, human resources, training, operations management

Richard Narramore, Senior Editor—Training and development, organizational development, management

Barry Neville, Editor—General business

International Marine

PO Box 220, Camden, ME 04843-0220
207-236-4837   fax: 207-236-6314
www.internationalmarine.com

International Marine has been publishing books about boats since 1970. Located near the Rockport and Camden harbors of midcoast Maine, IM has published more than 200 titles covering everything from boat and engine maintenance, to boat handling and seamanship, to nautical adventures that are stranger than fiction. This division's slogan is "The best books about boats."

Titles representative of this list: *The Ship and the Storm: Hurricane Mitch and the Loss of the Fantome* by Jim Carrier; *The Boat Doctor: A Boating Magazine Book* by Allen Berrien; *One Minute Guide to the Nautical Rules of the Road* by Charlie Wing; *The Voyager's Handbook: The Essential Guide to Bluewater Cruising* by Beth A. Leonard.

Direct query letters and SASEs to:

Jon Eaton, Editorial Director—jonathan_eaton@mcgraw-hill.com

Alex Barnett, Acquisitions—alex_barnett@mcgraw-hill.com

Ragged Mountain Press

PO Box 220, Camden, ME 04843-0220
207-236-4837   fax: 207-236-6314
www.raggedmountainpress.com

Ragged Mountain Press publishes informative titles on outdoor activities and pursuits from fly fishing to outdoor cooking, sea kayaking to survival techniques, survival methods to RV living.

This division produces between 20 and 23 books each year. Titles indicative of this list: *The Backpacker's Handbook* by Chris Townsend; *The Baffled Parents' Guide to Great Baseball Drills* by Jim Garland; *The Essential Outdoor Gear Manual: Equipment Care, Repair, and Selection* by Annie Getchell, et al.; *The Essential Wilderness Navigator: How to Find Your Way in the Great Outdoors* by David Seidman; *Great Basketball Drills: A Baffled Parent's Guide* by James Garland; *Scuba Diving: A Woman's Guide* by Claire Walter; *The Last Log of the Titanic* by David G. Brown (digital).

Direct query letters and SASEs to:

Jon Eaton, Editorial Director—jonathan_eaton@mcgraw-hill.com

Alex Barnett, Acquisitions—alex_barnett@mcgraw-hill.com

MEADOWBROOK PRESS

5451 Smetana Drive, Minnetonka, MN 55343
952-930-1100, 800-338-2232   fax: 952-930-1940
www.meadowbrookpress.com

Meadowbrook publishes books with a family outlook, encompassing the areas of pregnancy and child care, parenting, health, the environment, business, travel, cooking, reference, party-planning, and children's activity books. Meadowbrook Press (established in 1975) is a small trade-oriented house that has particular success pinpointing such specialty markets as baby names, family humor, and the facts of life.

Frontlist releases: *The Children's Busy Book* by Trish Kuffner; *Smart Start for Your Baby* by Penny Warner; *Long Shot* by Timothy Tocher; *The Mocktail Bar Guide* by Frank Thomas and Karen L. Brown; *The Aliens Have Landed!* by Kenn Nesbitt; *Free Stuff for Kids 2002* by the Free Stuff Editors; *Pregnancy, Childbirth, and the Newborn* (Revision) by Penny Simkin, Janet Whalley, and Ann Keppler; *Our Bundle of Joy* by Bruce Lansky. From the Meadowbrook backlist: *The Joy of Sisters* by Karen Brown; *Free Stuff for Kids* (in periodically updated editions) by the Free Stuff Editors; *Eating Expectantly* by Bridget Swinney; *The Toddler's Busy Book* by Trish Kuffner; *Storybook Parties* by Penny Warner; *The Best Bachelorette Party Book* by Becky Long; *Pregnancy, Childbirth and the Newborn* by Penny Simkin and Janet Whalley; *52 Romantic Evenings* by Liya Lee Oertel.

Meadowbrook Press is distributed by Simon & Schuster. Query letters and SASEs should be directed to:

Bruce Lansky, Publisher

MECKLERMEDIA CORPORATION

Mecklermedia (founded in 1971; earlier known as Meckler Publishing) is no longer publishing. The house was a specialist publisher with emphasis on informational books, directories, and databases keyed to a wide range of subjects and applications.

MEGAN TINGLEY BOOKS
(AN IMPRINT OF LITTLE, BROWN AND COMPANY)

Three Center Plaza, Boston, MA 02108

Megan Tingley Books, an imprint of Little, Brown and Company, publishes mainly picture books, with some fiction and nonfiction for middle-grade and young adult readers. This imprint does not consider "genre" novels for publication (including mystery, romance, and science fiction).

Titles from Megan Tingley include *Look Alikes* by Joan Steiner; *Just Like a Baby* by Rebecca Bond; *The Girls' Guide to Life* by Catherine Dee; *Define Normal* by Anne Peters; *This Land Is Your Land* by Woody Guthrie and Kathy Jakobsen; *You Read to Me, I'll Read to You* by Mary Ann Hoberman and Michael Emberley; *It's Okay to Be Different* by Todd Parr; *Twin Tales: The Magic and Mystery of Multiple* by Donna M. Jackson.

M

While the submission guidelines for Megan Tingley Books remain the same as Little Brown's, unpublished authors may submit one-page query letters for fiction and nonfiction. Please mark the envelope "Query" and address to:

Alvina Ling, Editorial Assistant, Megan Tingley Books, Little, Brown and Company, Three Center Plaza, Boston, MA 02108; include an SASE for response

Mary Gruetzke, Assistant Editor

Mercury House, Inc.

PO Box 192850, San Francisco, CA 94119-2850
fax: 415-626-7875
www.mercuryhouse.org

Mercury House produces a list strong in contemporary fiction, world literature in translation, literary classics, Asian literature and philosophy, cultural studies, film and performing arts, current affairs, nature and environment, and general nonfiction. The press issues hardcovers and trade paperbacks.

Mercury House (a nonprofit corporation founded in 1984) is a publisher guided by literary values. Categories of house interest encompass quality fiction; biographies and autobiographies; history and narrative nonfiction; multiethnic and cross-cultural literary expression (including essays and true-life narratives, as well as fiction); arts and entertainment; literary travel. The Mercury House logo is a graphic representation of a winged manuscript scroll in flight.

From Mercury House: *Pharmakol Poeia: Plant Teachers and the Poison Path* by Dale Pendell; *Narrow Road to the Deep North: A Journey into the Interior of Alaska* by Katherine McNamara; *House with the Blue Bed* by Alfred Arteaga; *The House by the Sea: A Portrait of the Holocaust in Greece* by Rebecca Fromer; *In the Ring of Fire: A Pacific Basin Journey* by James D. Houston; *A Girl with a Monkey: New and Selected Stories* by Leonard Michaels.

Mercury House distributes through Consortium. Please check its Web site for information about submissions policies at www.mercuryhouse.org.

K. Janene-Nelson, Executive Director

Microsoft Press

One Microsoft Way, Redmond, WA 98052-6399
206-882-8080, 800-677-7377
http://mspress.microsoft.com

Microsoft Press specializes in solution-oriented computer books—especially those relating to the corpus of Microsoft products, the Microsoft operating system, and selected titles pertaining to the Apple Macintosh world. Microsoft Press lists titles in general personal-computer applications, programming, and general-interest computing areas. The house brochure features books, book-and-software packages (including diskettes and CD-ROMs), and training videos. Microsoft Press (founded in 1983) is a product unit within the Microsoft

Corporation and a leading source of comprehensive self-paced learning, training, evaluation, and support resources designed to help everyone from developers and IT professionals to end users get the most from Microsoft technology. Users can choose from more than 250 current titles in print, multimedia, and network-ready formats—learning solutions made by Microsoft. More information is available at http://mspress.microsoft.com.

Microsoft Press titles are constantly updated and released in newly revised versions in order to anticipate advances in hardware and software systems, as well as the underlying technology to which they pertain. The house aims to produce information that is reliable, timely, and easy to use so that readers can get their work done faster and without frustration.

Series from Microsoft Press include At a Glance Series (get answers in a picture, not a thousand words); Step by Step (self-paced training); Running (in-depth reference and inside tips from the software experts); Field Guide (quick, easy answers); WYSIWYG (What You See Is What You Get—books for beginners); Best Practices (candid accounts of the new movement in software development—highly readable accounts of what works in the real world); Microsoft Professional Editions (technical information straight from the source); Microsoft Programming (the foundations of software development); Solution Developer (expert development strategies for creating custom business solutions).

The Mastering series is a line of CD-ROM–based interactive training titles created to help intermediate and advanced developers' master tasks and concepts for writing sophisticated solutions with Microsoft tools.

A representative general reference work is *Microsoft Press Computer Dictionary.*

Microsoft Press distributes its own books; the list is also available through electronic mail via CompuServe. Query letters and SASEs should be directed to:

Alex Blanton, Acquisitions Editor—Bookidea@microsoft.com

MILKWEED EDITIONS

Milkweeds for Young Readers

1011 Washington Avenue South, Suite 300, Minneapolis, MN 55415
612-332-3192   fax: 612-215-2550
www.milkweed.org and www.worldashome.org

Milkweed publishes fiction, essays and literature, poetry anthologies, and poetry, as well as literary nonfiction about the natural world in its the World as Home publishing program. Milkweeds for Young Readers is the house's children's line. Milkweed Editions (instituted in 1984) presents a personalized small-house approach that accents high standards of content and production.

Milkweed was founded (in 1979) as a nonprofit literary press, publishing with the intention of making a humane impact on society, in the belief that literature is a transformative art uniquely able to convey the essential experiences of the human heart and spirit. The house presents distinctive voices of literary merit in handsomely designed, visually dynamic books, exploring the ethical, cultural, and aesthetic issues that free societies must continually address.

Under Emilie Buchwald (Publisher/CEO), the house maintains its position to make a humane impact on society. Milkweed Editions offers an award-winning list of distinctive

M

literary voices, with a line of handsomely designed, visually dynamic volumes that address ethical, cultural, and aesthetic issues.

Milkweed publishes diverse, nonhomogeneous literary books that take artistic and financial risks and that give readers access to the richness, aliveness, and possibilities afforded by the written word. Milkweed exists to publish, promote, and keep alive this important literature for readers today and in the future.

The company's continued marketing success augments the publisher's stance in support of exceptional books with appeal to discerning readers. Milkweed Editions hosts a substantial backlist of hardcovers, paperbacks, and chapbooks.

Poetry: *Turning Over the Earth* by Ralph Black; *Song of the World Becoming: Poems New & Collected 1981–2001* by Pattiann Rogers; *The Porcelain Apes of Moses Menoelssohov* by Jean Nordhaus.

Nonfiction about the natural world: *Ecology of a Cracker Childhood* by Janisse Ray; *Swimming with Giants* by Anne Collet; *Brown Dog of the Yaak* by Rick Bass; *Boundary Waters: The Grace of the Wild* by Paul Gruchow.

Milkweed fiction titles: *Thirst* and *Pu-239 and Other Russian Fantasies* by Ken Kalfus; *Falling Dark* by Tim Tharp; *My Lord Bag of Rice* by Carol Buy; *Hell's Bottom, Colorado* by Laura Pritchett; *Montana 1948* by Larry Watson.

Milkweed is the publisher of Susan Straight's acclaimed *Aquaboogie: A Novel in Stories* (among a number of novels-in-stories projects). Contact the editorial department for information pertaining to the Milkweed Prize for Children's Literature and the Milkweed National Fiction Prize.

Books from Milkweed Editions are available via direct order from the publisher; the house's titles are distributed to the trade through Publishers Group West.

Milkweeds for Young Readers

Milkweeds for Young Readers produces children's books of literary merit that embody humane values. Books that ask the most of young readers, the publisher maintains, have the staying power to influence them for a lifetime. Milkweed also produces a series of teaching guides.

Titles from Milkweed's children's program: *The $66 Summer* by John Armistead; *The Ocean Within* by V. M. Caldwell; *The Secret of the Ruby Ring* by Yvonne MacGrory; *Behind the Bedroom Wall* by Laura E. Williams.

Query letters and SASEs should be directed to:

Elisabeth Fitz, First Reader

Emilie Buchwald, Publisher

Greg Larson, Fiction Editor

THE MOUNTAINEERS BOOKS

1001 Southwest Klickitat Way, Suite 201, Seattle, WA 98134
206-223-6303, 800-553-4453   fax: 206-223-6306
www.mountaineerbooks.org   e-mail: mbooks@mountaineers.org

The Mountaineers produces adventure narratives, mountaineering histories and guides, hiking and rock climbing books, and instructional guides to the outdoors and winter trekking, focused on the Pacific Northwest.

The Mountaineers (founded in 1906) is a conservation and outdoor-activity group with a mission to explore, study, preserve, and enjoy the natural beauty of the outdoors.

The Mountaineers Books was founded in 1961 as a nonprofit publishing program of the club. The Mountaineers sponsors the Barbara Savage/Miles from Nowhere Memorial Award competition for outstanding unpublished nonfiction adventure-narrative manuscripts. The initial title offered by Mountaineers Books, *Mountaineering: The Freedom of the Hills,* is still in print in a fully revised edition.

Series from Mountaineers: 100 Hikes, 100 Classic Hikes, Hiking Geology, Best Short Hikes, State Parks, Afoot and Afloat, Exploring Wild Areas. Mountaineers titles: *Kiss or Kill, Confessions of a Serial Climber* by Mark Twight; *Where the Pavement Ends, One Woman's Bicycle Trip Through Mongolia,* and *China & Vietnam* by Erika Warmbrunn; *Rock and Ice Goldline: Stories of Climbing Adventure and Tradition* by Gregory Crouch; *Extreme Rock and Ice, 25 of the World's Great Climbs* by Garth Hattingh; *Everest, Eighty Years of Triumph and Tragedy, 2nd Edition* by Peter and Leni Gillman; *River Running, 2nd Edition* by Verne Huser; *Hiking the Triple Crown* by Karen Berger; *Fearless on Everest: The Quest for Sandy Irvine* by Julie Summers; *Conquistadors of the Useless: From the Alps to Annapurna* by Lionel Terray.

Winners of the Barbara Savage "Miles from Nowhere" competition (biennial award for a previously unpublished adventure narrative manuscript): *Himalayan Passage: Seven Months in the High Country of Tibet, Nepal, China, India, and Pakistan* by Jeremy Schmidt (photographs by Patrick Morrow); *American Discoveries: Scouting the First Coast-to-Coast Recreational Trail* by Dudley and Seaborg. Winners of Barbara Savage award include *Where the Pavement Ends* by Erika Warmbrunn; *Spirited Waters: Soloing South Through the Inside Passage* by Jennifer Hahn.

The Mountaineers Books distributes its list via direct orders and also utilizes the services of regional and national wholesalers and trade representatives. The American Alpine Club Press is now distributed by the Mountaineers Books.

Query letters and SASEs should be directed to:

Laura Drury, Acquisitions Assistant

David Emblidge, Editor in Chief

Cassandra Conyers, Acquisitions Editor

Christine Hosler, Assistant Acquisitions Editor

MOYER BELL LIMITED

54 Phillips Street, Wickford, RI 02852
401-294-0106   fax: 401-294-1076
www.moyerbell.com   e-mail: info@moyerbell.com

Moyer Bell Limited specializes in literary works, reference works, and books in art and design. Many general-interest nonfiction works from this smaller house evidence a

M

high-interest cultural or public-issues slant. Within this specialty arena, Moyer Bell produces original titles, reprints, and translations. The house also maintains a strong commitment to poetry. The Asphodel Press imprint was founded as a nonprofit organization in 1990 and concentrates on fine literary titles.

Moyer Bell Limited was established in 1984 by Jennifer Moyer and Britt Bell; this notably independent house (with a U.K. base in London, in addition to its U.S. operations) has received worldwide accolades for its roster of fine writers and stylish product.

Moyer Bell nonfiction: *Writing in Time: A Political Chronicle* by Jonathan Schell; *The Art Book of Lucien Pissarro* by Lora Urbanelli; *Don't Look Back: A Memoir* by Patrick O'Connor; *Walking to LaMilpa: Living in Guatemala with Armies, Demons, Abrazos, and Death* by Marcos McPeek Villatoro; *The New Genetics: Challenges for Science, Faith, and Politics* by Roger L. Shinn; *In the Wake of Death: Surviving the Loss of a Child* by Mark Cosman; *Rebirth of Thought: Light from the East* by Ruth Nanda Anshen; *A Trifle, a Coddle, a Fry: An Irish Literary Cookbook* by Veronica Jane O'Mara and Fionnuala O'Reilly.

Fiction and literary titles: *The Only Piece of Furniture in the House* by Diane Glancy; *The Orchard on Fire* by Shena Mackay; *The Raven: With the Philosophy of Composition* by Edgar Allan Poe (poetry and essay; illustrated by Alan James Robinson); *Peace Breaks Out, Private Enterprise,* and *The Demon in the House* by Angela Thirkell (granddaughter of Edward Burne-Jones and a cousin of Rudyard Kipling); *Peony* by Pearl S. Buck.

On Moyer Bell's reference book list is the periodically revised *Grant Seekers Guide* by James McGrath Morris and Laura Adler. From Asphodel Press: *Directory of Literary Magazines* (updated annually) by the Council of Literary Magazines and Presses.

Moyer Bell Limited books are distributed to the trade by Publishers Group West.

Britt Bell, Editor and Publisher

MUSEUM OF NEW MEXICO PRESS

Deliveries and physical address:
228 East Palace Avenue, Santa Fe, NM 87501
505-827-6454   fax: 505-827-5741

Mailing address:
PO Box 2087, Santa Fe, NM 87504-2087
e-mail: mwachs@oca.state.nm.us, agallegos@oca.state.nm.us

Museum of New Mexico Press is a nationally distributed publisher affiliated with the Museum of New Mexico. Museum of New Mexico Press publishes high-quality illustrated books on the arts and culture of the Southwest, such as Native America, the Hispanic Southwest, 20th-century fine art, folk art from around the world, Latin American arts, nature and gardening, architecture and style, folklore.

Query letters and SASEs should be directed to:

Mary Wachs, Editorial Director

Anna Gallegos, Director

Mustang Publishing Company

PO Box 770426, Memphis, TN 38177
901-684-1200   fax: 901-684-1256
e-mail: MustangPub@aol.com

Mustang produces trade nonfiction books in hardcover and paperback. Mustang is especially successful with its lines of specialty how-to's and titles in the fields of humor, games, outdoor recreation, sports, travel, and careers. Mustang Publishing Company (founded in 1983) is a modest-sized house with a concise publishing vision and compactly tailored list.

Representative frontlist titles: *101 Classic Jewish Jokes: Jewish Humor from Groucho Marx to Jerry Seinfeld* by Robert Menchin (illustrated by Joel Kohl); *Dear Elvis: Graffiti from Graceland* by Daniel Wright; *Lucky Pants and Other Golf Myths* by Joe Kohl; *The Complete Book of Golf Games* by Scott Johnston; *How to Be a Way Cool Grandfather* by Verne Steen.

Mustang's specialty books include those geared to expansive lifestyles. Titles here: *Paintball! Strategies and Tactics* by Bill Barnes with Peter Wrenn; *Bet on It! The Ultimate Guide to Nevada* by Mary Jane and Greg Edwards; *The Hangover Handbook: 101 Cures for Humanity's Oldest Malady* by Nic van Oudtshoorn. There's also the immensely popular *The Complete Book of Beer Drinking Games* by Andy Griscom, Ben Rand, and Scott Johnson—as well as *Beer Games II: The Exploitative Sequel.*

The For Free series is a godsend for people scared by the high cost of travel and for everyone who loves a bargain. Each book describes hundreds of terrific things to do and see, and nothing costs one single penny, lire, franc, or pfennig. Titles: *Europe for Free, London for Free,* and *DC for Free* by Brian Butler; *The Southwest for Free* by Mary Jane and Greg Edwards; *Hawaii for Free* by Frances Carter; *Paris for Free (or Extremely Cheap)* by Mark Beffart.

The touring and travel list also includes: *Festival Europe! Fairs and Celebrations Throughout Europe* by Margaret M. Johnson; *The Nepal Trekker's Handbook* by Amy R. Kaplan, with Michael Keller; *Europe on 10 Salads a Day* by Mary Jane and Greg Edwards; plus, the hilariously revised and expanded edition of *Let's Blow Thru Europe: How to Have a Blast on Your Whirlwind Trip Through Europe* by Thomas Neenan and Greg Hancock.

A solid group of Mustang books targets a higher education–bound audience, including series for students and graduate-school applicants, often geared toward particular professional curricula: *The One Hour College Applicant* by Lois Rochester and Judy Mandell; *Medical School Admissions: The Insider's Guide* by John A. Zebala and Daniel B. Jones.

The Essays That Worked series inspires thousands of students to write the best essays they can. There's also lots of practical advice on the application process. Titles: *Essays That Worked for College Applicants* and *Essays That Worked for Business Schools* (edited by Boykin Curry and Brian Kasbar); *Essays That Worked for Law Schools* (edited by Boykin Curry).

Representative career title: *Working in T.V. News: The Insider's Guide* by Carl Filoreto, with Lynn Setzer; *Medical School Admissions: The Insider's Guide, 4th Edition* by John Zebala, Daniel Jones, and Stephanie Jones.

Mustang also offers Alan and Theresa von Altendorf's general reference *ISMs: A Compendium of Concepts and Beliefs from Abolitionism to Zygodactylism.*

Writers should note that Mustang welcomes book proposals on almost any nonfiction topic. The publisher prefers to see an outline and two to three sample chapters—and urges authors to be sure to enclose a self-addressed stamped envelope (the ubiquitous SASE) with each submission. No phone calls, please.

Mustang's books are distributed through National Book Network. Query letters and SASEs should be directed to:

Rollin A. Riggs, President and Publisher

THE NAIAD PRESS

PO Box 10543, Tallahassee, FL 32302
850-539-5965   fax: 850-539-9731
www.naiadpress.com

Naiad publishes lesbian and feminist fiction, essays, poetry, short stories, humor, translations, and bibliographies. The Naiad emphasis in category fiction includes stylish and traditional mysteries, espionage thrillers, adventure yarns, science fiction, fantasy, romances, historical fiction, erotica, and Westerns. Naiad Press (established in 1973) remains joyously the oldest and largest lesbian publishing company in the world, going from one title to being the publisher of more than 400 books.

Naiad has been particularly innovative among book-publishing operations in the development of specialized target-marketing techniques. The house has expanded its media presence to become active in the wider arena of audio books, videos, and theatrical film. The romantic fiction *Claire of the Moon,* by Nicole Conn (writer and director of the feature film of the same name), represents a groundbreaking Naiad project that embraces documentary, music, and storytelling in cinema, video, audiocassette, CD, and print. Naiad Books maintains a comprehensive backlist.

Nonfiction from Naiad: *Sapphistory* by Pat Califia; *For Love and for Life* and *Intimate Portraits of Lesbian Couples* by Susan Johnson; *Sex Variant Women in Literature* by Jeanette H. Foster; *There's Something I've Been Meaning to Tell You* by Loralee MacPike; *The Loving Lesbian* by Claire McNabl; *Parents Matter* by Ann Muller; *Before Stonewall* by Weiss and Schiller.

Sample Naiad fiction and belles lettres: *Both Sides* by Saxon Bennett; *Claire of the Moon* by Nicole Conn; *Curious Wine* by Katherine V. Forrest; *Greener Than Grass* by Jennifer Fulton; *City Lights Country Candles* by Penny Hayes; *Car Pool* by Karin Kallmaker; *Cherished Love* by Evelyn Kennedy; *Dawn of the Dance* by Marianne Martin; *Window Garden* by Janet McClellan; *Yes I Said Yes I Will* by Judith McDaniel; *The Finer Grain* by Denise Ohio; *The Other Woman* by Ann O'Leary; *Endless Love* by Lisa Shapiro; *The Drive* by Trisha Todd; *Piece of My Heart* by Julia Watts.

The women of Naiad Press continue in pursuit of their essential goal—which is to make sure that someday, any woman, anyplace, can recognize her lesbianism and be able to walk into a bookstore and pick up a book that says to her: "Yes, you are a lesbian and you are wonderful." With that aim in mind, Naiad has adopted the following slogan for use in its potent mailing-list campaigns: Lesbians always know; if it's a book by Naiad Press, it's a book you want to own.

Naiad Press books are available directly from the publisher via a toll-free telephone-order number and from the following distributors as well: Bookpeople, LPC Group, Borders, and Ingram.

Query letters and SASEs should be directed to:

Barbara Grier, Chief Executive Officer

N

NATIONAL GEOGRAPHIC SOCIETY BOOKS

1145 17th Street Northwest, Washington, DC 20036
202-857-7000   fax: 202-429-5727

National Geographic Society Books' motto is "to diffuse geographic knowledge." Books are distributed by Simon & Schuster. National Geographic Society Books is interested in any type of book written from a geographic perspective.

Query letters and SASEs should be directed to:

Kevin Mulroy, Vice President and Director of Book Division

NAVAL INSTITUTE PRESS

United States Naval Institute, 118 Maryland Avenue, Annapolis, MD 21402-5035
410-268-6110   fax: 410-269-7940
www.usni.org

Naval Institute Press features trade books, in addition to the house's targeted professional and reference titles. Areas of NIP interest include how-to books on boating and navigation, battle histories, and biographies, as well as occasional selected titles in fiction (typically, with a nautical adventure orientation). Specific categories encompass such fields as seamanship, naval history and literature, the Age of Sail, aviation and aircraft, World War II naval history, World War II ships and aircraft, current naval affairs, naval science, and general naval resources and guidebooks. Bluejacket Books is a trade-paperback imprint that includes time-honored classics as well as original titles. Naval Institute Press also publishes a line of historical and contemporary photographs and poster art.

Naval Institute Press, situated on the grounds of the United States Naval Academy, is the book-publishing imprint of the United States Naval Institute, a private, independent, nonprofit professional society for members of the military services and civilians who share an interest in naval and maritime affairs. USNI was established in 1873 at the Naval Academy in Annapolis; the press inaugurated its publishing program in 1898 with a series of basic guides to United States naval practice.

Titles from Naval Institute Press: *Green Berets in the Vanguard: Inside Special Forces 1953–1963* by Chalmers Archer, Jr.; *Punk's War* (novel) by Ward Carroll; *Death on the Hellships: Prisoners at Sea in the Pacific War* by Gregory F. Michno; *Reluctant Allies: German–Japanese Naval Relations in World War II* by Hans-Joachim Krug, et al.; *Shield*

N

and Sword: The United States Navy and the Persian Gulf War by Edward J. Marolda and Robert Schneller Jr.; *The Eagle Mutiny* by Richard Linnett and Roberto Loiederman; *Nelson Speaks: Admiral Lord Nelson in His Own Words* by Joseph F. Callo; *Matthew Calbraith Perry: Antebellum Sailor and Diplomat* by John H. Schroeder; *Three Days to Pearl: Incredible Encounter on the Eve of War* by Peter J. Shepherd; *The Co-Vans: U.S. Marine Advisors in Vietnam* by John Grider Miller.

Fighter Squadron at Guadalcanal by Max Brand is a lost classic, published 50 years after the author's death. Now after more than 50 years and a string of fortunate coincidences, Brand's stirring firsthand account of the 212th Marine Fighter Squadron's operations at Guadalcanal in 1942 has been published.

The Naval Institute Guide to the Ships and Aircraft of the U.S. Fleet (17th edition) by Norman Polmar is indispensable to anyone needing technical data and program information on the contemporary U.S. Navy.

Bluejacket Books is an exciting series of fiction and nonfiction titles available in affordable paperback editions. Titles: *Around the World Submerged: The Voyage of the Triton* by Edward L. Beach; *Midway: The Battle That Doomed Japan, the Japanese Navy's Story* by Mitsuo Fuchida and Masatake Okumiya; *A Country Such As This* by James Webb; *Reminiscences* by Douglas MacArthur; *Teddy Roosevelt's Great White Fleet* by James R. Reckner.

Naval Institute Press handles its own distribution. Query letters and SASEs should be directed to:

Eric Mills, Acquisitions Editor

Thomas J. Cutler, Senior Acquisitions Editor

Paul Wilderson, Executive Editor

NEW CENTURY BOOKS

PO Box 7113, The Woodlands, TX 77387-7113
936-295-5357

New Century publishes several lines of nonfiction books (New Century was established in 2000).

Its first list includes the Exceptional Lives series. Titles include *A Desert Daughter's Odyssey: For All Those Whose Lives Have Been Touched by Cancer—Personally, Professionally or Through a Loved One* by Sharon Wanslee; *The Man Who Was Dr. Seuss: The Life and Work of Theodor Seuss Geisel; The Man Who Was Walter Mitty: The Life and Work of James Thurber.*

In its Communication, Culture and Literature Series, New Century has *Writing Solutions: Beginnings, Middles & Endings,* and others.

The imprint Sharon's Books is devoted to women's health/women's issues, women's memoirs, children, pets, religious, and multicultural (Hispanic).

New Century is also developing a series of "Top Secret" books.

New Century is interested in autobiographies and biographies, business and personal success, communication/journalism, current affairs, parenting, popular culture, history, multicultural (Hispanic), how-to, Southwestern and mountain states subjects, sports, trends, women's issues/women's health, and perhaps a selected few children's books and mysteries.

New Century is not interested in computer books, gothic romances, horror, poetry, sci-fi, screenplays, Westerns, or anything of a non-book-length nature. Note: The house's list will likely continue to be 99 percent nonfiction.

New Century Books are available in hardcover, trade paperback, and "palm reader" versions.

New Century Books pays royalties. The rate varies. The house pays monthly and plans 5–15 books per year. Queries and SASEs should be directed to:

Thomas Fensch, Publisher

New Horizon Press

Small Horizons

34 Church Street, Liberty Corner, NJ 07938
908-604-6311   fax: 908-604-6330
www.newhorizonpressbooks.com   e-mail: nhp@newhorizonpressbooks.com

Mailing address:
PO Box 669, Far Hills, NJ 07931

New Horizon Press: Real people . . . incredible stories. That's right. The New Horizon list accents true-life events with narrative nonfiction accounts told by actual participants. In its broader program, the house addresses topics of social concern, including corporate and professional responsibility, behavioral diversity, and politics, as well as personal self-help, how-to, and mainstream business books.

New Horizon Press (established in 1983) was originally an imprint of Horizon Press. Now a separate publishing entity, New Horizon Press is remarkable for its pinpoint commercial vision in the arena of nonfiction stories of courageous individuals. These incredible tales of real people display an intense human-interest appeal and often embody an investigative journalistic stance that probes related public issues. The house maintains a solid backlist that is particularly strong in self-help titles.

New Horizon is configured as a small press: Projects are often initiated with restrained author advances; more money accrues to the writer through subsequent sales. The publisher has had conspicuous success in expanding the scope of its projects via targeted promotion, advertising, touring, and subsidiary rights, both in print via book-club selections and in the electronic arena in the form of related television docudramas, talk show appearances by authors, and feature items on television journals.

From the New Horizon list: *Grave Accusations; CastOff; Whispers of Romance, Threats of Death; ER—Enter At Your Own Risk: How to Avoid Dangers Inside the Emergency Room; Swallowing a Bitter Pill: How Prescription and Over-the-Counter Drug Abuse Is Ruining Lives—My Story; Breadwinner Wives and the Men They Marry: How to Have a Successful Marriage While Outearning Your Husband; 60 Second Sleep-Ease:*

Quick Tips to Get a Good Night's Rest; 60 Second Anger Management: Quick Tips to Handle Explosive Feelings.

New Horizon Press is distributed by National Book Network, Inc. Query letters and SASEs should be directed to:

Joan S. Dunphy, Editor in Chief
  Sign: Leo/Virgo.
  Education: Ph.D., from Miami University; English, Psychology, and Philosophy.
  Employment history/editor career path: Assistant Professor at Rutgers University.
  Personal interests: Reading, rock specimens.
  What would you be doing if you were not an editor? Teaching English at a college level and writing.
  What has been your most successful book that you have acquired to date? *Black Widow/False Arrest.*
  What books have you acquired that make you the most proud? What books that you have acquired reflect the types of books you like to represent? *In Africa with Schweitzer; My Life on the Streets.*
  Do you represent fiction? No.
  What do you want to see less of? Nonfiction generalized manuscripts on the educational system, life, and so forth, and so on.
  Do you represent nonfiction? Yes.
  Do you require book proposals? If so, what do you look for in evaluating a book proposal? A subject matter that matters.
  Are certain aspects of a book proposal given more weight than others? The plot and whether the author is the prime mover of the action.
  What process do you use for making a decision? What is the process for acquisition; is there a committee? No committee, but we meet to discuss the merits, or lack of, on manuscripts we feel deserve attention.
  Are you interested in work geared for the masses (readers of *People, The Star,* etc.)? Yes. I believe as Virgil said: Oftentimes the common people see "rightly."
  Are agents important? Why? At times, very. Often an agent can recognize and send us the real essence of a true story, whereas the author who has lived it may not recognize its significance.
  Do you like new writers? What should new writers do to break into the business? Since we are geared toward finding modern heroes who've made a difference, changing the status quo and present problems, we like new writers and subjects.
  How should writers approach you? In writing, send: query, chapter synopsis, and at least two chapters. Please don't call.
  What are some common mistakes writers make? What really gets on your nerves? Trying to get the editor's attention by diffuse methods (i.e., My story is the most dramatic, heartrending tale ever written, and then not saying what it is).
  What can writers do to get your attention and to avoid the slush pile? Tell the story. In a synopsis tell us why it's important and make sure it is.
  What have been some of your craziest experiences with submissions? The niece of Mary Phagan, a young girl murdered in the South, whose death brought back the KKK,

sent a one-pager with red ink stains in the shape of tears. However, her story became the basis for a strong book and Emmy Award–winning mini-series.

What have been some of your best experiences with writers or in your job? Meeting brave and significant people who have fought for what they believe in.

What, if anything, makes you different from other editors? I look for true stories with social issues, and we are willing, if we find them, to do heavy rewriting in house.

Is there anything you would like to see changed in the industry? First and foremost: more diversity. I would like to see more interdisciplinary accords between film, Internet, and print so that the publishing industry does not vanish.

Any advice for writers? Any way to improve the system for you? For writers: Do not embellish, simplify. For the critics: Remember, the books that have transcended their times were often ridiculed or overlooked in them. And for our industry: "Change is here; it's not going away, it's gonna keep on happening; so, let's find a way to adapt to it."

Small Horizons

Small Horizons is an imprint offering self-help books for children, written by teachers and mental-health professionals. Small Horizons Self-Help Books for Children: *The Stick Family: Helping Children Cope with Divorce* by Natalie Reilly; *I Am So Angry, I Could Scream: Helping Children Deal with Anger* by Laura Fox; *The Boy Who Sat by the Window: Helping Children Cope with Violence* by Chris Loftis; *There's a Skunk in My Bunk: Teaching Children Tolerance for Others* by Dr. Joseph McCann.

NEWMARKET PRESS

18 East 48th Street, New York, NY 10017
212-832-3575   fax: 212-832-3629
www.newmarketpress.com   e-mail: mailbox@newmarketpress.com

Newmarket concentrates on general nonfiction, accenting such categories as contemporary issues, history and biography, psychology, parenting, health, nutrition, cooking, personal finance, and business. A major Newmarket program salutes classic literary figures, other media, and performing arts, featuring titles in film (including shooting scripts) and music. Newmarket also issues occasional works of high-interest fiction (the house was the original publisher of the hardcover edition of Michael Blake's novel *Dances with Wolves*).

Newmarket Press (founded in 1981) is a division of Newmarket Publishing and Communications Company. The house produces books in hardcover, trade paper, and mass-market paperback editions.

General trade titles: *The West Wing Script Book* by Aaron Sorkin; *Fly Away Home* by Patricia Hermes, Robert Rodat, and Vincent McKewin; *Kids and Sports* by Eric Small, M.D., FAAP; *Submerged* by Daniel Lenihan; *Tea Chings* by Ron Rubin, Stuart Avery Gold, and the Republic of Tea; *The Antioxidant Save-Your-Life Cookbook* by Jane Kinderleher and Daniel A. Kinderleher, M.D.; *The Totally Awesome Business Book for Kids* by Adriane G. Berg and Arthur Berg Bochner; *Whose Body Is It Anyway?* by Joan Kenley, Ph.D. (edited by John C. Arpels); *The Matrix* by Larry Wachowski and Andy

N

Wachowski; *How Do We Tell the Children?* by Dan Schaefer and Christine Lyons; *My Feelings, My Self* by Lynda Madaras and Area Madaras; *The Blackstone Book of Magic and Illusion* by Harry Blackstone, with Charles Reynolds and Regina Reynolds. Special Newmarket editions: *The Words of Gandhi* (selected and introduced by Sir Richard Attenborough); *The Words of Albert Schweitzer* (selected and introduced by Norman Cousins); *The Words of Martin Luther King, Jr.* (selected and introduced by Coretta Scott King).

Film-related books: *A Beautiful Mind* by Akiva Goldsman; *Cast Away,* screenplay and introduction by William Broyles, Jr.; *Making Tootsie* by Susan Dworkin; *Traffic,* screenplay by Stephen Gaghan; *Erin Brockovich,* screenplay and introduction by Susannah Grant; *Snatch,* screenplay and introduction by Guy Ritchie; *The Jaws Log* by Carl Gottlieb (introduction by Peter Benchley); *Crouching Tiger, Hidden Dragon.*

Newmarket distributes its list through W. W. Norton & Company. No children's titles. Query letters and SASEs should be directed to:

Keith Hollaman, Executive Editor

Esther Margolis, President and Publisher

Shannon Berning, Assistant Editor

THE NOBLE PRESS

The Noble Press is no longer doing business.

NOLO.COM

950 Parker Street, Berkeley, CA 94710
510-549-1976
www.nolo.com

Nolo.com, formerly Nolo Press, presents a glittering array of self-help titles in law and business. The house promotes a related list in lifestyle, recreation, travel, and retirement. Nolo also produces law-form kits, legal software, electronic books, and videotapes.

Nolo's consumerist perspective encompasses homeowners, landlords, and tenants; going to court; money matters; estate planning and probate; business; legal reform; patents, copyrights, and trademarks; employee rights and the workplace; family matters; immigration; research and reference; older Americans; and humor titles.

Nolo.com is the pioneer publisher of self-help legal books and software. The house (started in 1971) was founded by two Legal Aid lawyers who were fed up with the public's lack of access to affordable legal information and advice. Convinced that with good, reliable information, Americans could handle routine legal problems without hiring an attorney, they began writing plain-English law books for the general readership.

Nolo led off its first list with *How to Do Your Own Divorce in California* and has been going strong since, with a steady stream of titles addressing consumer needs in a wide range of general and specialist areas. Whereas lawyers have historically sold information only to the few who can afford their services, Nolo aims to provide comprehensive low-cost information to the public at large.

The Nolo Web site (www.nolo.com) is an award-winning destination for consumers, businesspersons, and not a few lawyers. The *Nolo Encyclopedia,* available free on the site, gives plain English answers to commonly asked questions. All of Nolo's books and software can be downloaded from the site or ordered in hard copy. Nolo also offers "e-Guides," "e-Form Kits," and "Web Forms," which are electronic products that allow users to buy legal information and tools "by the drink."

All Nolo publications are regularly revised and are issued in updated editions, and the publisher maintains a hardy backlist. Most Nolo titles are written by practicing attorneys who are specialists in their fields of authorship. A major portion of the Nolo list exhibits a national orientation, while some titles are specifically geared to regional markets.

Representative titles: *License Your Invention: Take Your Great Idea to Market with a Solid Legal Agreement* by Attorney Richard Stim; *Every Landlord's Legal Guide* by Marcia Stewart and attorneys Ralph Warner and Janet Portman; *WillMaker,* 50-state estate-planning software; *Patent It Yourself* (revised edition) by Attorney David Pressman.

Social, community, career, lifestyle, and issue-oriented titles: *Get a Life: You Don't Need a Million to Retire Well* by Ralph Warner; *The Copyright Handbook: How to Protect and Use Written Works* by Stephen Fishman; *How to Buy a House in California* by Attorney Ralph Warner, Ira Serkes, and George Devine; *Stand Up to the IRS* by Frederick W. Daily; *Dog Law* by Mary Randolph; *Neighbor Law: Fences, Trees, Boundaries & Noise* by Cora Jordan; *A Legal Guide for Lesbian and Gay Couples* by Hayden Curry, Denis Clifford, and Robin Leonard; *The Independent Paralegal's Handbook* (revised edition) by Attorney Ralph Warner; *How to Mediate Your Dispute: Find a Solution You Can Live with Quickly and Cheaply Outside the Courtroom* by Peter Lovenheim.

Some humor: *29 Reasons Not to Go to Law School* by Ralph Warner, Toni Ihara, and Barbara Kate Repa; *Poetic Justice: The Funniest, Meanest Things Ever Said About Lawyers* (edited by Jonathan and Andrew Roth); *The Devil's Advocates: The Unnatural History of Lawyers* by Andrew and Jonathan Roth.

Nolo.com distributes its own books to the trade (along with selected titles from other publishers) and also utilizes several distribution services; in addition, Nolo sells to consumers via direct mail and from its Web site and operates its own bookstore in Berkeley. Query letters and SASEs should be directed to:

Janet Portman, Publisher—Books and software

W. W. NORTON AND COMPANY, INC.

Countryman Press/Backcountry Publications

500 Fifth Avenue, New York, NY 10110
212-354-5500   fax: 212-869-0856
www.wwnorton.com

Norton publishes trade nonfiction and belles lettres, as well as works for professional and academic markets. W. W. Norton (founded in 1923) offers prime-caliber publications in all areas of its trade program; the house is equally esteemed for its line of college texts and professional reference titles.

W. W. Norton produces hardcover and trade paperback editions under its celebrated gliding-seagull colophon, as well as through a variety of imprints, including Liveright and Countryman. Norton nourishes a comprehensive backlist of books in all areas of its publishing interest.

Norton nonfiction accents trade titles in topics of current interest, with a range of works featuring the popular as well as scholarly approach to fields, including cultural criticism, biography, psychology, history, economics, politics, natural history, the sciences, fine arts and design, photography, and lifestyle. Norton also offers a line of books for enthusiasts of sailing and publishes Blue Guide travel books.

Nonfiction from Norton: *America's Black Architects and Builders* by Stephen A. Kliment; *The Country Houses of David Adler* by Steven M. Salny; *New York for New Yorkers, 2nd edition* by Liza M. Greene; *Between Lives: An Artist and Her World* by Dorothea Tanning; *Basil Street Blues: A Memoir* by Michael Holroyd; *The Life of Jung* by Ronald Hayman; *Next: The Invisible Revolution* by Michael Lewis; *Latinos: A Biography of the People* by Earl Shorris; *The Bush Dyslexicon* by Mark Crispin Miller; *Something Under the Sun: An Environmental History of the Twentieth Century World* by J. R. McNeill; *Vital Signs 2001: The Environmental Trends That Are Shaping Our Future* by Worldwatch Institute; *Stone in the Garden: Inspiring Designs and Practical Projects* by Gordon Hayward; *The Body Silent: The Different World of the Disabled* by Robert F. Murphy; *Around America: A Tour of Our Magnificent Coastline* by Walter Cronkite; *Children of the West: Family Life on the Frontier* by Cathy Luchetti; *Ariel's Gift: Ted Hughes, Sylvia Plath, and the Story of Birthday Letters* by Erica Wagner; *The Pushcart Prize XXV: Best of the Small Presses, 2001 Edition* by Bill Henderson, Editor, with the Pushcart Prize Editors; *How Can We Keep from Singing: Music and the Passionate Life* by Joan Oliver Goldsmith.

In fiction and literary writing, Norton publishes novels, poetry (including the Norton Anthologies series), and short story collections—from established, distinguished scribes and from a select few marketable new voices. In addition, the house publishes critical essays, biographies, and literary histories. The Norton fiction list covers classical, modern, contemporary, and experimental styles, as well as novels showing a mainstream commercial profile; the Norton program also encompasses mystery and suspense fiction.

Examples from the Norton fiction list: *Babe in Paradise* by Marisa Silver; *The Edge of Marriage Stories* by Hester Kaplan; *Glue* by Irvine Welsh; *Hussein: An Entertainment* by Patrick O'Brian; *The Partnership* by Barry Unsworth; *Strange Fire* by Melvin Jules Bukiet; *Strangers on a Train* by Patricia Highsmith; *A Suspension of Mercy* by Patricia Highsmith; *The Miracle Life of Edgar Mint* by Brady Udall.

Norton poetry includes *Blackbird Singing: Lyrics and Poems, 1963–1999* by Paul McCartney; *Collected Poems 1951–1971* by A. A. Ammons; *Landscape with Chainsaw: Poems* by James Lasdum; *Last Blue: Poems* by Gerald Stern; *The Making of a Poem: A Norton Anthology of Poetic Forms* (edited by Mark Strand and Eavan Boland); *A Mayan Astronomer in Hell's Kitchen: Poems* by Martin Espada; *Worldly Hopes: Poems* by A. R. Ammons.

Works of speculative literary configuration: *The Coral Sea* (poetry, fiction, and essay) by Patti Smith; *In Short: A Collection of Brief Creative Nonfiction* (edited by Judith Kitchen and Mary Paumier Jones); *Sudden Fiction (Continued): 60 New Short-Short Stories* (edited by Robert Shepard and James Thomas); *When the Air Hits Your Brain: Tales of Neurosurgery* by Frank Vertosick; *Wise Women: Over 2,000 Years of Spiritual Writing by Women* (edited by Susan Cahill); *Holy Land: A Suburban Memoir* by D. J. Waldie.

W. W. Norton distributes its own list and handles distribution for its subsidiaries and imprints, as well as for a number of other publishers. Norton's distribution network includes Chapters Publishing, Countryman Press, Ecco Press, Liveright Publishing Corporation, New Directions Books, the New Press, Pushcart Press, the Taunton Press, Thames and Hudson, and Verso.

Query letters and SASEs should be directed to:

Alane Mason, Editor—Serious nonfiction for a general audience, particularly cultural and intellectual history; some illustrated books; literary fiction and memoir

Amy Cherry, Senior Editor—History, biography, women's issues, African American, health, fiction

Angela von der Lippe, Senior Editor—Trade nonfiction; serious works in behavioral sciences, earth sciences, astronomy, neuroscience, education

Carol Houck Smith, Editor at Large—Literary fiction, travel memoirs, behavioral sciences, nature

Edwin Barber, Senior Editor—Acquires for the full range of house interests

Jill Bialosky, Senior Editor—Literary fiction, biographies, memoirs, poetry

Jim Mairs, Senior Editor—History, illustrated books, photography

Robert Weil, Executive Editor—Literature in translation, intellectual history, social science, German and Jewish interests

Starling Lawrence, Editor in Chief—Acquires for the full range of house interests

W. Drake McFeely, President—Nonfiction of all kinds, particularly science and social science

Maria Guarnaschelli, Senior Editor—Cookbooks, serious nonfiction

Countryman Press/Backcountry Publications

New England office:
PO Box 748, Woodstock, VT 05091
fax: 802-457-1678

Countryman specializes in travel, regional history, recreation, gardening, nature, environment, how-to, regional hiking, walking, bicycling, fishing, cross-country skiing, and canoeing guides. Imprints include Countryman Press and Backcountry Guides.

Countryman (founded in 1973) has been on the cusp of the small, regional press initiative that has enriched the North American publishing scene through editorial acumen and niche-marketing panache. Now affiliated with W. W. Norton & Company, Countryman remains editorially independent.

Representative Countryman titles: *Maine: An Explorer's Guide* by Chris Tree; *The Soul of Vermont* by Richard Brown; *The Granite Kiss* by Kevin Gardner; *American Rock* by Don Moller; *The King Arthur Flour Cookbook* by Brita Sands; *The Battered Stars* by Howard Coffin.

Backcountry Guides: *50 Hikes in the Lower Hudson Valley* by Stella Green and Neil Zimmerman*; Sea Kayaking the Maine Coast* by Dorcas Miller; *Back Road Bicycling in Connecticut* by Ann-Marie Fusco.

Sales and distribution for Countryman are handled by the parent corporation, W. W. Norton. Query letters and SASEs should be directed to:

Kermit Hummel, Editorial Director

OAK TREE PRESS

915 W. Foothill Blvd., Suite 411, Claremont, CA 91711-3356
fax: 909-624-3930
OakTreeBooks.com

Oak Tree Press is an independent publisher of a wide variety of fiction and nonfiction, with a concentration on the mystery genre. Founded in 1998 to offer a counterpoint to shrinking publishing opportunities, Oak Tree maintains its welcoming attitude toward new authors. Since 1999, the publisher has sponsored the Dark Oak Mystery Contest and published the winning entry. Timeless Love, an imprint for romance novels, was introduced in July 2001.

Oak Tree policies include dynamic cover design, aggressive outreach, strong backlist promotion, and an open editorial policy. We will consider almost any subject—so long as there is no gratuitous violence against women.

Trade fiction titles include *Tulsa Time* by Letha Albright; *The Damned Never Die* by J. McKay; *Callie and the Dealer* and *A Dog Named Jake* by Wendy Howell Mills; *An Affinity for Murder* by Anne White. In addition, Oak Tree is re-releasing a number of classic out-of-print titles from Odie Hawkins, beginning with *Ghetto Sketches* in spring 2001.

Under the new Timeless Love imprint: *Hearts Across Forever* by Mary Montague Sikes.

Nonfiction titles include *Of Weeds and Views* by Frances U. Crain; *Mid-Life Mojo: A Guide for the Newly Single Male* by Robert M. Davis, Ph.D.; *Business Buyer's Handbook* by Jim Calkins.

In spring of 2001, Oak Tree made an entry into the audio and music realm through its sister company, WEGOTSKILLZ music, which will distribute and produce the work of independent artists.

Oak Tree Press handles its own marketing, sales, and distribution. Query letters with SASEs should be directed to:

Billie Johnson, Publisher

Sarah Wasson, Editorial Assistant

THE OVERLOOK PRESS

141 Wooster Street, New York, NY 10012
845-679-6838   fax: 845-679-8571
www.overlookpress.com   e-mail: overlook@netstep.net

Overlook focuses on general nonfiction and offers a respected line in fiction, belles lettres, and poetry. The nonfiction purview encompasses biography, crafts, how-to, fine arts, architecture and design, Hudson Valley regionals, cookbooks, and natural history. The house releases a limited number of titles directed toward the young reader.

The Overlook Press was founded in 1971 by Peter Mayer (until recently also Chief Executive of the Worldwide Penguin Group) and his father. Overlook is a smaller publisher with a diverse and select list. Under its enigmatic logo (a mythical beast in cartouche that calls to mind a winged elephantine species), Overlook produces books in special fine editions, hardcover, and trade paperback. The house nurtures a thriving backlist that features such titles as the business-martial arts classic *Book of Five Rings* by Miyamoto Musashi (translated by Victor Harris); *The Gormenghast Trilogy* by Mervyn Peake; *Tiny Houses* by Lester Walker.

Overlook was founded with the intent to publish against the grain. Here was a new publishing company that did not exactly imitate the policies of large companies. The editors did not pursue bestsellers; they wanted good-sellers. And they believed in the backlist. They did not want to be a niche publisher, just a small general publisher. They wanted to publish books that very likely had been "overlooked" by larger houses— although the Overlook name actually came from a mountain in Woodstock, New York.

Overlook made a name by publishing useful books in areas where none existed. It published the first book on wood stoves in the early 1970s, anticipating a major trend; when the house produced the first book on Kendo published in the United States (*A Book of Five Rings*)—who knew it would become famous as a metaphor for business strategy?

In 1977, Overlook launched the Ivory Press to publish unusual books in the visual arts, joining Tusk paperbacks in the Overlook family of imprints.

Overlook's authors roster is one of the finest in the land. Fiction: Paul West, Geoff Nicholson, Steve Weiner, Richard Foreman, Robert Schneider, David Shapiro, and Paul Auster. Film books: Howard Koch, Peter Bogdanovich, Ian McKellen, Derek Jarman, Ang Lee, Guin Turner, Rose Troche, Michael Ritchie, Cyril Collard, and Bruce Robinson. Nonfiction: Buckminster Fuller, Erving Goffman, Martin Esslin, Armond White, and Howard Jacobson. Design: Milton Glaser, Raymond Loewy, Terence Conran, Osborne and Little, Judith Miller, and Caroline Wrey.

Overlook titles include *The Complete Book of the Winter Olympics* by David Wallechinsky; *Jitney* by August Wilson; *Their First Time in the Movies* by Les Krantz; *The Royal Physician's Visit* by Per Olav Enquist; *The Destruction of the Bismark* by David Bercuson and Holger Herwig; *The Reconstructionist* by Josephine Hart; *The Girl from the Golden Horn* by Kurban Said; *Secret Agent* by David Stafford; *Green* by Benjamin Zucker; *The King of Limbo* by Adrianne Harun; *Deception in War* by Jon Latimer; *Shardik* by Richard Adams; *Wilson* by David Mamet; *Film Posters of the 80's* (edited by Tony Nourmand and Graham Marsh); *The Yellow Sailor* by Steve Weiner; *The Poetry and Life of Allen Ginsberg* by Ed Sanders; *Freddy Goes Camping* by Walter R. Brooks; *Zombie00* by Brad Gooch; *Chanel* by Amy de la Haye; *Coney* by Amram Ducovny; *Love in the Days of Rage* by Lawrence Ferlinghetti; *The English* by Jeremy Paxman; *A Brief History of the Future* by John Naughton; *Getting Away with Murder* by Howard Engel.

Overlook Press is distributed by Penguin Puntam, Inc. Query letters and SASEs should be directed to:

Peter Mayer, Publisher

Tracy Karns, Editor

P

PALADIN PRESS

Paladin Enterprises, PO Box 1307, Boulder, CO 80306
303-443-7250   fax: 303-442-8741
www.paladin-press.com

Paladin issues new titles and reprints in such categories as new identity and personal freedom, espionage and investigation, weapons, military science, revenge and humor, special forces, survival, martial arts, action careers, sniping, knives and knife fighting, locksmithing, self-defense, police science, silencers, and history and culture relating to the previous fields, as well as selected general-interest books. Paladin also purveys a video library. Paladin Press (established in 1970) is a division of Paladin Enterprises.

Certain Paladin titles exhibit a markedly subversive approach and are intended as high-edge, satiric amusement. It should be further noted that particular works on the Paladin list contain material that may be restricted in some jurisdictions and are sold for academic, research, or informational reference purposes only.

Frontlist catalog entrants: *Cowboy Action Pistol Shooting: Secrets of Fast and Accurate Gunplay* by Charles K. Stephens; *The Jeet Kune Do Experience: Understanding Bruce Lee's Ultimate Martial Art* by Jerry Beasley, Ed.D.; *The Logic of Steel: A Fighter's View of Blade and Shank Encounters* by James LaFond; *No Waiting: How to Get What You Want, When You Want It* by Andy Kane; *Stopping Power: A Practical Analysis of the Latest Handgun Ammunition* by Evan P. Marshall and Edwin J. Sanow; *Surviving Street Patrol: The Officer's Guide to Safe and Effective Policing* by Steve Albrecht; *The Passport Report: Over 100 Ways and Many Good Reasons to Obtain a Second Foreign Passport* by Dr. W. G. Hill; *The Perpetual Traveler 2: A Coherent Plan for a Stress-Free, Healthy and Prosperous Life Without Government Interference, Taxes or Coercion* by Dr. W. G. Hill; *The Moment of Truth: How to Physically, Mentally, and Legally Survive a Street Fight* by Lucianao Silveria; *Secrets of Back-Alley ID Man: Fake ID Construction Techniques Underground; How to Become a Professional Con Artist; Freeware Encryption and Security Programs: Protecting Your Computer and Your Privacy; Surgical Speed Shooting: How to Achieve High-Speed Marksmanship in a Gunfight; Overseas Americans: The Essential Guide to Living and Working Abroad; Tactical Medicine: An Introduction to Law Enforcement Care.*

Highlights from the backlist (including all-time Paladin hits): *Protect Your Assets: How to Avoid Falling Victim to the Government's Forfeiture Laws* by Adam Starchild; *Running a Ring of Spies: Spycraft and Black Operations in the Real World of Espionage* by Jefferson Mack; *SWAT Battle Tactics: How to Organize, Train, and Equip a SWAT Team for Law Enforcement or Self-Defense* by Pat Cascio and John McSweeney; *Body for Sale: An Inside Look at Medical Research, Drug Testing, and Organ Transplants and How You Can Profit from Them* by Ed Brassard.

Paladin Press looks for original manuscripts on combat shooting, firearms and exotic weapons, personal and financial freedom, military science, and other action topics. For more information, call or write the publisher for a copy of the Author Style Guide and *Insider Newsletter.*

Paladin Press distributes its own list and in addition services individual orders via toll-free ordering numbers, mail order, and its Web site. Query letters and SASEs should be directed to:

Jon Ford, Editorial Director

PATHFINDER PRESS

410 West Street, New York, NY 10014
212-741-0690   fax: 212-727-0150
e-mail: pathfinderpress@compuserve.com

The Pathfinder program catalogs such fields as black and African studies; women's rights; the Cuban revolution in world politics; revolutionaries and working-class fighters; fascism, big business, and the labor movement; Russia, Eastern Europe, and the Balkans; scientific views of politics and economics; trade unions: past, present, and future; United States history and political issues; Latin America and the Caribbean; the Middle East and China; and art, culture, and politics. Pathfinder titles often suggest such streams of thought as populism, internationalism, utopianism, socialism, and communism.

Pathfinder Press (established in 1940) issues books, booklets, pamphlets, posters, and postcards keyed to issues affecting working people worldwide. Pathfinder produces titles in English, Spanish, French, Swedish, Farsi, Greek, Icelandic, and Russian. Pathfinder distributes the journal *New International.*

The Pathfinder Mural that once adorned the company's editorial and manufacturing digs in Manhattan's Far West Village featured a depiction of a gargantuan printing press in action, as well as portraits of revolutionary leaders whose writings and speeches are published by Pathfinder; this community cultural icon represented the work of more than 80 artists from 20 countries.

Representative Pathfinder books: *Episodes of the Cuban Revolutionary War, 1956–58* by Ernesto Che Guevara (firsthand account of the military campaigns and political events that culminated in the January 1959 popular insurrection that overthrew the U.S.-backed dictatorship in Cuba); *Lenin's Final Fight: Speeches and Writings, 1922–23* by V. I. Lenin; *In Defense of Marxism: The Social and Political Contradictions of the Soviet Union* by Leon Trotsky; *The Second Declaration of Havana* by Fidel Castro.

On Pathfinder's staunch backlist: *Bolivian Diary* by Ernesto (Che) Guevara; *Peru's Shining Path: Anatomy of a Reactionary Sect* by Martín Koppel; *Lenny Bruce: The Comedian as Social Critic and Secular Moralist* by Frank Kofsky; *The Revolution Betrayed: What Is the Soviet Union and Where Is It Going?* by Leon Trotsky; *The Politics of Chicano Liberation* (edited by Olga Rodriguez); *Polemics in Marxist Philosophy* by George Novack; *The Communist Manifesto* by Karl Marx and Frederick Engels; *Cuba's Internationalist Foreign Policy, 1975–80* by Fidel Castro; *To Speak the Truth: Why Washington's "Cold War" Against Cuba Doesn't End* by Fidel Castro and Che Guevara; *How Far We Slaves Have Come! South Africa and Cuba in Today's World* by Nelson Mandela and Fidel Castro; *Che Guevara: Economics and Politics in the Transition to Socialism* by Carlos Tablada.

Pathfinder's *New International* is a magazine of Marxist politics and theory. Many of the articles that appear in *New International* are available in Spanish, French, and Swedish. The magazine is a numbered series in trade paperback format.

Special Pathfinder series include *Malcolm X: Speeches and Writings,* as well as written works and spoken words from James P. Cannon, Eugene V. Debs, Farrell Dobbs, Carlos Fonseca, Mother Jones, Rosa Luxemburg, Nelson Mandela, Fidel Castro, and Ernesto (Che) Guevara; the house also publishes the works of Karl Marx, Frederick Engels, V. I. Lenin, and Leon Trotsky.

P

A number of bookstores around the world distribute Pathfinder's titles and offer membership in a readers' club for an annual fee (entitling members to enjoy special Pathfinder discounts); individual orders are payable via Visa and MasterCard. Pathfinder Press distributes its own publications in the United States and worldwide primarily through its own fulfillment centers.

Query letters and SASEs should be directed to:

Michael Taber, Editorial Director—Projects consistent with the Pathfinder list

---

PEACHPIT PRESS (A DIVISION OF PEARSON EDUCATION)

1249 Eighth Street, Berkeley, CA 94710
510-524-2178, 800-283-9444   fax: 510-524-2221
www.peachpit.com

Peachpit is a specialist computer-publishing house with a list in personal computing and desktop publishing for business and recreational users. Peachpit publishes books and book/software packages (including CD-ROM products) that tackle basic practical tasks and troubleshooting, as well as advanced applications.

Peachpit covers a number of categories: general introductory works on computing, general works about the Macintosh computer system, Macintosh Bible series, Visual Quick Start series, On the Web series, the Real World series, the Non-Designer's series, desktop publishing, graphics, Windows and Windows applications, word processing, and related topics. Many Peachpit releases are keyed to particular proprietary products.

Visual Quick Start Guides provide exactly what the title implies: a fast, simple way to get up and running with a new program—which is perhaps the secret to the popularity of this successful line.

Peachpit's editorial approach is to make the computing world relevant, make it dramatic, and make it fun. Peachpit authors are at the forefront of ongoing technological developments and trends in computer hardware and software development and are masterful at teasing out the nuances of end-user potential in print.

Publisher's statement: Peachpit is not only in the book business and not only a player on the computer-business stage; Peachpit is also in the teaching business. In addition to trade bookstores and computer venues, Peachpit hits a variety of market sectors, such as schools and educational enterprises (including evening classes and adult education); library, institutional, and corporate consumers; and end-user and professional groups.

Peachpit Press (founded in 1986) was acquired by Addison-Wesley in late 1994, and the house is now a division of Pearson Education. Within this corporate structure, Peachpit maintains its independent editorial stance and gains financial and distributional leverage from the new ownership to the benefit of Peachpit's worthy list.

Titles from Peachpit: *Adobe Acrobat 5 Master Class; After Effects 5.5 Hands-On Training; Excel X for Mac OS X: Visual Quickstart Guide; Illustrator 10 for Windows and Macintosh: Visual QuickStart Guide; Mac 911; Macromedia Flash ActionScripting: Advanced Training from the Source; The Painter 7 Wow! Book; Real World Adobe Illustrator 1.0; Stop Stealing Sheep and Find Out How Type Works, 2nd Edition; REALbasic for Macintosh: Visual Quickstart Guide.*

Peachpit Press is distributed through the parent company Pearson Education. Query letters and SASEs should be directed to:

Nancy Aldrich-Ruenzel, Publisher

Marjorie Baer, Executive Editor

Cliff Colby, Associate Managing Editor

Nancy Davis, Managing Editor

Victor Gavenda, Senior Technical Editor and Producer

Rebecca Gulick, Editor

Becky Morgan, Editor

Jill Lodwig, Editor

P

PEACHTREE PUBLISHERS, LTD.

Peachtree Children's Books

1700 Chattahoochee Avenue, Atlanta, GA 30318-2112
404-876-8761   fax: 404-875-2578

Peachtree publishes children's books and general trade and offers a substantial and growing children's list. Peachtree has a concentration in markedly innovative books in self-help, self-awareness, health, and parenting. A special area of Peachtree publishing interest encompasses regional topics, including the American South in general and the state of Georgia in particular.

Peachtree Publishers (established in 1978) is a midsize house that produces books in hardcover and trade paperback editions. Peachtree hosts a hardy backlist.

From Peachtree: *Cheap Psychological Tricks: What to Do When Hard Work, Honesty, and Perseverance Fail!* by Perry Buffington. Standout Peachtree projects: *Out to Pasture* by Ellie Leland Wilder (a five-volume series of tales from FairAcres Retirement Home); *To Dance with the White Dog* by Terry Kay; *Hiking Trails of the North Georgia Mountains* by Tim Homan; *Cooking in the New South: A Modern Approach to Traditional Southern Fare* by Anne Bryn; *Margaret Mitchell & John Marsh: The Love Story Behind Gone with the Wind* by Marianne Walker; *A Modern Southern Reader: Major Stories, Drama, Poetry, Essays, Interviews and Reminiscences from the Twentieth-Century South* (edited by Ben Forkner and Patrick Samway); *The Single Mother's Book: A Practical Guide to Managing Your Children, Career, Home, Finances and Everything Else* by Joan Anderson; *Helping with the Child Who Doesn't Fit In* by Stephen Nowicki, Jr., and Marshall Duke, Ph.D.

Peachtree distributes its own list to the trade with the assistance of regional sales representatives. Query letters and SASEs should be directed to:

Helen Harriss, Editorial Department

Peachtree Children's Books

Children's editions from Peachtree encompass award-winning illustrated storybooks for younger readers, as well as a select group of works directed toward parents. Peachtree Jr.

is a line of chapter books targeted for ages 8 years and up. The AllStar SportStory series combines contemporary tales with sports history and statistics. Freestone is a line of novels for today's teenagers, ages 12 to 16.

Standout Peachtree Children's Books: *The Yellow Star, Library Dragon,* and *Agatha's Feather Bed* by Carmen Agra Deedy; *Crossing Jordan* by Adrian Fogelin; *Eleanor's Story: An American Girl in Hitler's Germany* by Eleanor Ramrath Garner; The Misfits series by Mark Delaney; *Seaman: The Dog Who Explored the West with Lewis and Clark* by Gail Langer Karwoski; *The Horned Toad Prince* and *Three Armadillies Tuff* by Jackie Hopkins; *While You Were Sleeping* and other books by John Butler.

Query letters and SASEs should be directed to:

Helen Harriss, Editorial Department

P

PELICAN PUBLISHING COMPANY

PO Box 3110, Gretna, LA 70054-3110
504-368-1175, 800-843-1724 (orders)   fax: 504-368-1195
www.pelicanpub.com   e-mail: editorial@pelicanpub.com

Pelican Publishing Company (founded in 1926) produces a general trade list with special interests in travel and lifestyle guides, Americana, cookbooks, art and architecture, photography, humor, sports, and motivational and inspirational titles. Many Pelican titles offer a regional or cultural perspective in such areas as the American South, Civil War history, Louisiana and the New Orleans environs, and Irish and Scottish American heritage. Pelican produces a short menu of children's books and offers a select group of fiction works, many of which have a regional or historical twist.

Pelican's travel series include the Maverick Guides (for the independent traveler— these guides include history, customs, language, and attractions, as well as current prices and recommendations for accommodations, dining spots, etc.), the Marmac Guides (up-to-date information on population, services, recreation, accommodations, and restaurants in various American cities), At Cost Travel Guide series (for the value-conscious traveler), and the Pelican Guide series (designed to give the discriminating traveler insight into some of the most interesting locations within the United States).

Other Pelican series include the Majesty Architecture series, the New Orleans Architecture series, the Best Editorial Cartoons of the Year series, the Editorial Cartoonists series, the Cruising Guides series, and the Clovis Crawfish Series for kids.

From Pelican: *Ghost Army of World War II* by Jack M. Kneece; *The Warlord's Beads* by Virginia Walton Pilegard (illustrated by Nicholas Debon); *Mardi Gras Treasures: Float Designs of the Golden Age* by Henri Schindler. Pelican's Top-30 list includes *See You at the Top* by Zig Ziglar; *The Justin Wilson Cook Book, The Justin Wilson Gourmet and Gourmand Cookbook,* and *Justin Wilson's Outdoor Cooking with Inside Help* all by Justin Wilson.

Representing the Pelican's children's list favorites: *Pennsylvania Dutch Night Before Christmas* by Chet Williamson (illustrated by James Rice); *Why Cowgirls Are Such Sweet Talkers* by Laurie Lazzaro Knowlton (illustrated by James Rice); *Lucky O'Leprechaun Comes to America,* written and illustrated by Jana Dillon.

Pelican Publishing Company handles its own distribution. Query letters and SASEs should be directed to:

Nina Kooij, Editor in Chief

PENGUIN PUTNAM INC. (AN AFFILIATE OF THE PENGUIN GROUP INTERNATIONAL, PART OF PEARSON)

Adult Division

Avery

Berkley Books Group

BlueHen Books

Dorling Kindersley

Dutton

HP Books

Jeremy P. Tarcher

New American Library/NAL

Penguin

Perigee Books

Plume

Price Stern Sloan

Prime Crime

Putnam

Riverhead Books

Viking

Penguin Putnam Books for Young Readers (See separate entry)

375 Hudson Street, New York, NY 10014
212-366-2000

Penguin Putnam is a leading U.S. adult and children's trade book publishing group, formed in 1996 as a result of the merger between Penguin Books USA and the Putnam Berkley Group. The Penguin Group, headquartered in the United Kingdom, is owned by Pearson plc, an international media group.

Penguin Putnam publishes under a broad range of imprints and trademarks, among them Berkley Books, Dutton, Grosset & Dunlap, New American Library, Penguin, Philomel, G. P. Putnam's Sons, Riverhead Books, and Viking.

The company possesses a distinctive list of bestselling authors, including Dorothy Allison, Melissa Bank, Saul Bellow, A. Scott Berg, Harold Bloom, Sylvia Browne, Tom Clancy, Robin Cook, Patricia Cornwell, Catherine Coulter, Clive Cussler, the Dalai Lama, Dick Francis, Sue Grafton, W. E. B. Griffin, Jan Karon, Robert Ludlum, James McBride, Terry McMillan, Arthur Miller, Jacqueline Mitchard, Toni Morrison, Kathleen

Norris, Joyce Carol Oates, Suze Orman, Robert Parker, Nora Roberts, Maeve Binchy, John Sandford, Carol Shields, John Steinbeck, Amy Tan, Eric Jerome Dickey, Kurt Vonnegut, and Neale Donald Walsch.

Penguin Putnam is also a global leader in children's publishing, through its Books for Young Readers, with imprints such as Dial Books, Dutton, Grosset & Dunlap, Philomel, Puffin, G. P. Putnam's Sons, Viking, and Frederick Warne. These imprints are home to Ludwig Bemelmans, Jan Brett, Eric Carle, Roald Dahl, Tomie dePaola, Hardie Gramatky, Eric Hill, Brian Jacques, A. A. Milne, and Tasha Tudor. Grosset & Dunlap issues such perennial favorites as *The Little Engine That Could* and the Nancy Drew and Hardy Boys series. (See separate entry for Penguin Putnam Books for Young Readers.)

Penguin Putnam recently launched Penguinclassics.com, an online community devoted to classic titles. The company also launched Penguin Lives, a series of short biographies about well-known historical and cultural figures, written by some of today's most respected authors. In addition, Penguin Putnam resumed its Pelican Shakespeare series, one of the bestselling editions of Shakespeare's plays since it was first published in the mid-1960s.

P

Avery

Avery's publishing program is dedicated primarily to complementary medicine, nutrition, and healthful cooking. It was established in 1976 as a college textbook publisher specializing in niche areas. Through a series of alliances, most notably with Hippocrates Health Institute, Avery began a program of health books by such authors as Ann Wigmore and Michio Kushi, whose work on macrobiotics helped propel the Avery list in the health food and alternative markets. The firm was acquired by the Penguin Group in 2000.

In addition to producing original titles in hardcover and paperback formats, Avery has a backlist of several hundred titles in trade and mass-market formats that includes works by pioneers in alternative healing, scientists, and health-care professionals involved in cutting-edge research.

Titles representative of the Avery list: *Dare to Lose: 4 Simple Steps to a Better Body* by Shari Lieberman, Ph.D., Nancy Bruning (Contributor); *The Edge: Ben and Joe Weider's Guide to Ultimate Strength, Speed, and Stamina* by Ben Weider, et al.; *Natural Highs: Supplements, Nutrition, and Mind/Body Techniques to Help You Feel Good All the Time* by Hyla Cass and Patrick Holford; *Aromatherapy: Essential Oils for Vibrant Health and Beauty* by Roberta Wilson; *Dangerous Grains: Why Gluten Cereal Grains May Be Hazardous to Your Health* by James Braly, M.D., and Ron Hoggan M.A.; *Natural Asthma Relief: Comprehensive, Drug-Free Solutions for the Treatment and Prevention of Asthma and Allergies* by C. Leigh Broadhurst, Ph.D., and Vladimir Badmaev, M.D.; *Secrets from a Healthy Asian Kitchen* by Ying Chang and Ying Chang Compestine; *Natural Therapy for Your Liver: Herbs and Other Natural Remedies for a Healthy Liver* by Christopher Hobbs; *Prescription for Herbal Healing: An Easy-to-Use A–Z Reference to Hundreds of Common Disorders and Their Herbal Remedies* by Phyllis A. Balch; *Sin-Free Chocolate Smoothies: A Chocolate Lover's Guide to 70 Nutritious Blended Drinks* by Gabriel Constans; *Stopping Scoliosis: The Whole Family Guide to Diagnosis and Treatment* by Nancy Schommer and Nancy Hooper; *The Whole Family Guide to Natural Asthma Relief: Comprehensive Drug Free Solutions for the Treatment and Prevention of Asthma and Allergies* by C. Leigh Broadhurst, Ph.D., and Vladimir Badmaev; *Women at Risk: The HPV Epidemic and Your Cervical Health* by Gregory Henderson M.D., Ph.D., et al.

Direct query letters and SASEs to:

John Duff—Publisher, Vice President, and Senior Editor

Laura Shepherd, Editor

Berkley Books Group

Ace

Berkley

Boulevard

Jove

Ace Books

Ace Books, founded in 1953 by A. A. Wyn, is the oldest continuously operating science fiction publisher in the United States. In 1982, Ace, which had been part of Grosset & Dunlap, was acquired by G. P. Putnam's Sons (later known as the Putnam Berkley Group), and Ace soon became Berkley's science fiction imprint.

The combined backlists of Ace and Berkley made a powerful presence in the science fiction field, with Frank Herbert's bestselling *Dune* series, T. H. White's classic Arthurian novel *The Once and Future King* (basis for the musical *Camelot*), and much of Robert A. Heinlein's adult fiction, including *Stranger in a Strange Land.* More recent important authors include Joe Haldeman, winner of the 1998 Hugo and Nebula awards for *Forever Peace,* and William Gibson, whose *Neuromancer* is credited with having introduced the concept of cyberspace.

Ace produces original titles in hardcover and mass-market paperback, as well as reprints previously published in hardcover and trade paperback fiction. Titles indicative of the Ace list: *Chindi* by Jack McDevitt; *Behind Time* by Lynn Abbey; *The Black Chalice* by Marie Jakober; *Channeling Cleopatra* by Elizabeth Ann Scarborough; *Deathday* by William C. Dietz; *Chasm City* by Alastair Reynolds; *Another Fine Myth, Myth Conceptions* by Robert Asprin; *Chronospace* by Allen M. Steele; *Burnt Offerings* (Anita Blake, Vampire Hunter) by Laurell K. Hamilton; *California Sorcery* by William Nolan (Editor), et al.; *The Chalice* (*The Sword, the Ring, and the Chalice,* Book 3) by Deborah Chester.

Direct query letters and SASEs to:

Susan Allison, Editor in Chief of Ace Books

Berkley Books

Berkley Books, under the leadership of President and Publisher Leslie Gelbman, publishes more than 500 titles a year under the Berkley, Jove, and Ace imprints, in mass-market paperback, trade paperback, hardcover, audiocassettes, and audio CD-ROM formats. Berkley publishes some of the country's bestselling authors, including Tom Clancy, Robin Cook, Patricia Cornwell, Catherine Coulter, and Nora Roberts.

P

Representative nonfiction titles on the Berkley Books list: *Alternate Gettysburgs* by Brian Thomsen and Martin H. Greenberg*; Americans Remember the Home Front: An Oral Narrative of the World War II Years in America* by Roy Hoopes; *Angels at Dawn: The Los Banos Raid* by Edward M. Flanagan Jr.; *The Art of Thinking* by Allen F. Harrison, et al.; *Blood Type A: Food, Beverage and Supplement Lists from Eat Right for Your Type* by Peter J. D'Adamo and Catherine Whitney; *Conspiracies and Cover Ups* by David Alexander; *Counterfire* (Seal Team Seven, 16) by Keith Douglass.

Fiction titles indicative of Berkley Books include *The Boy Next Door* by Josie Lloyd and Emlyn Rees; *Caliente* by J. H. Blair (Editor); *Cape Light* by Thomas Kinkade and Katherine Spencer; *An Empire of a Woman* by Karen Shepard; *Across Five Aprils* by Irene Hunt.

Direct query letters and SASEs to:

Leslie Gelbman, Publisher, President, and Editor in Chief for Berkley—Wide range of projects in commercial fiction and nonfiction. Works with such authors as Nora Roberts, Laura Kinsale, and Erich Segal

Sara Carder, Editor

Denise Silvestro, Senior Editor—Women's fiction and nonfiction, health, self-help, popular culture, inspirational, and New Age books

Gail Fortune, Editor—Women's fiction, romance, mystery

Christine Zika, Senior Editor—Commercial nonfiction; business subjects

Judith Palais, Senior Editor—Women's fiction, general fiction, commercial/literary works, romance

Natalie Rosenstein, Vice President, Senior Executive Editor—General fiction, mystery

Susan Allison, Vice President, Editor in Chief, Ace Books—Science fiction, fantasy, horror

Tom Colgan, Senior Editor—Wide range of commercial nonfiction and fiction; nonfiction: history, business, inspiration, biography; fiction: suspense, mysteries, thrillers, adventure, police, espionage

Allison McCabe, Senior Editor—General fiction and nonfiction, commercial/literary works

BlueHen Books

BlueHen Books, established by Frederick Ramey and Greg Michalson, was launched in March 2000 and presented its debut list in summer 2001. BlueHen is "dedicated to introducing writers of quality fiction to a broad audience." "Bluehen" is the breeder's term for a thoroughbred mare that produces a long line of competitors. BlueHen is looking for books with compelling stories that are artfully told.

Titles indicative of this growing list: *The Deadwood Beetle* by Mylène Dressler; *The Webster Chronicle* by Daniel Akst; *Any Small Thing Can Save You: A Bestiary* by Christina Adam.

Direct query letters and SASEs to:

Fred Ramey, Editor

Greg Michalson, Editor

Dorling Kindersley

Dorling Kindersley is an international publishing company specializing in the creation of high-quality, illustrated information books; interactive software; TV programs; and online resources for children and adults. Founded in London in 1974, DK now has offices in the United Kingdom, United States, Australia, South Africa, India, France, Germany, and Russia.

In May 2000 DK was acquired by Pearson plc, an international media company. This acquisition saw DK join the Penguin Group, as Peter Kindersley stepped down from his executive role at DK and Anthony Forbes Watson became Chief Executive of both DK and Penguin UK.

DK is one of the world's premier publishers of illustrated reference books. Aiming to be a "complete 'cradle to grave' publisher that families can grow up with," DK produces books for children of all ages and books for adults covering a wide variety of subjects, including child care, health, gardening, food and wine, travel, business, and sports. DK produces books in hardcover, trade paperback, and CD-ROM.

Titles representative of the DK list: *Anatomy for the Artist* by Sarah Simblet; *Art of Calligraphy* by David Harris; *Sister Wendy's Story of Painting* (Second Edition) by Sister Wendy Beckett; *An Introduction to Art Techniques* by Ray Smith, James Horton, and Michael Wright; *John Hedgecoe's New Book of Photography* by John Hedgecoe; *Pure Style Living* by Jane Cumberbatch; *Bathroom* by Suzanne Ardley; *The Weekend Decorator* by Amy Dawson and Gina Moore; *Decorating Hints & Tips* by Peter Parham and Julian Cassell; *Delia Smith's How to Cook* by Delia Smith; *Ultimate Beer: A Visual Guide to Appreciating and Drinking 450 Classic Brews* by Michael Jackson; *Sophie Grigson's Sunshine Food,* a companion book to the PBS Television series *Great Food; Garden Masterclass* by John Brookes; *Fitness for Life* by Matt Roberts; *American Horticultural Society Plants for Places, Natural Landscapes* by John Brookes; *Pilates: Body in Motion* by Alycea Ungaro; *Eyewitness Travel Phrase Book: European Italian in Three Months; Birth Your Way* by Sheila Kitzinger; *Love, Laughter & Parenting: Enjoying the Precious Years from Birth to Six* by Steve and Sharon Biddulph; *New Complete Dog Training Manual* by Dr. Bruce Fogle; *The Complete Aquarium* by Peter Scott; *Smithsonian Handbooks: Mammals; Hot Bikes* by Hugo Wilson; *Hyperspace: The Universe and Its Mysteries* by John Gribbin.

DK also produces the Essential Science Series and Eyewitness Top 10 Travel guides. DK books are produced in-house.

Dutton

Dutton dates back to 1852, when Edward Payson Dutton founded a book-selling firm in Boston, E. P. Dutton. Dutton currently publishes about 50 hardcover titles a year.

Dutton authors include Maeve Binchy (*Scarlet Feather*), John Jakes (*On Secret Service*), Sylvia Browne (*Life on the Other Side* and *Past Lives, Future Healing*), Eric Jerome Dickey (*Between Lovers*), John Lescroart (*The Hearing*), Wendy Northcutt (*The Darwin Awards*), Darin Strauss (*Chang and Eng*), Barbara Parker (*Suspicion of Vengeance*), Dave Pelzer (*Help Yourself*), Randall Robinson (*The Debt*), and Tracy Chevalier (*Girl with a Pearl Earring* and *Falling Angels*).

Titles indicative of the Dutton list: *Hoping for Hope* by Lucy Clare; *Himalayan Dhaba* by Craig Joseph Danner; *The Impressionist* by Hari Kunzru; *Love Don't Live Here Anymore* by Denene Millner and Nick Chiles; *The Oath* by John T. Lescroart; *One-Hit Wonder* by Lisa Jewell; *Pen Pals* by Olivia Goldsmith; *Picture Maker* by Penina Keen Spinka; *The Real McCoy* by Darin Strauss; *The Trouble with Catherine* by Andes Hruby.

Direct query letters and SASEs to:

Brian Tart, Editorial Director, Vice President

Laurie Chittenden, Senior Editor—Popular and commercial works in nonfiction; occasional fiction

Mitch Hoffman, Editor—Mysteries, thrillers, narrative nonfiction, and humor

HPBooks

HPBooks, acquired by the Penguin Putnam Group as part of the purchase of Price Stern Sloan, originated in Tucson, Arizona, as publishers of nonfiction books in the categories of cooking, automotive, photography, gardening, health, and child care. HPBooks now specializes in cooking and automotive titles, publishing about a dozen books a year in trade paperback and a few in hardcover. Among the stars of this list, Mable Hoffman's *Crockery Cookery* recently celebrated its 20th year in print with more than 5 million copies sold.

Recent titles representative of this list include *The Book of Jewish Cooking* by Denise Phillips, David Murray (Photographer); *Celebrations: A Joyous Guide to the Holidays from Past to Present* by Jim McCann and Jeanne Benedict; *The Chevy S-10/GMC S-15 Handbook* by *Trucking Magazine* (Editor); *A Fan's Guide to Circle Track Racing: Facts, Tracks, and Stats on NASCAR, Busch, Craftsman Truck, ARCA, ASA, World of Outlaws, and Other Regional Racing* by Tony Sakkis; *Fondues and Hot Pots: From Appetizers to Desserts—A Complete Guide to Preparing Fondues, Hot Pots and Asian One-Pot Dishes, Right at the Table* by Susan Fuller Slack; *Glow: A Prescription for Radiant Health and Beauty* by Christina Pirello; *How to Maintain and Repair Your Jeep: Covers (1945–1986) and Wrangler (1987–1995) Models* by Rob Reaser, et al.; *Lowrider Handbook* by *Lowrider Magazine* (Editor); *The Mediterranean Vegan Kitchen: Meat-Free, Egg-Free, Dairy-Free Dishes from the Healthiest Place Under the Sun* by Donna Klein; *Mustang Performance Engine Tuning* by *Muscle Mustang* (Editor) and *Fast Ford Magazine* (Editor).

Direct query letters and SASEs to:

John Duff, Publisher, Vice President, and Senior Editor

Michael Lufty, Editorial Director

Jeremy P. Tarcher

Jeremy P. Tarcher publishes some 50 titles annually, in both hardcover and paperback, covering a broad spectrum of topics that ranges from current affairs, social commentary, literary nonfiction, and creativity, to spirituality/religion, health, psychology, parenting, business, and other topics. It has had numerous national bestsellers, including *Drawing on the Right Side of the Brain* and *Seven Years in Tibet*.

Titles representative of this list: *The Artist's Way* by Julie Cameron; *Women Who Love Too Much* by Robin Norwood; *The Hard Questions: 100 Essential Questions to Ask*

Before You Say "I Do" by Susan Piver; *Trust Us, We're Experts: How Industry Manipulates . . .* by Sheldon Rampton and John Stauber; *Quarterlife Crisis* by Alexandra Robbins and Abby Wilner; *365 Buddha: Daily Meditations* by Jeff Schmidt; *Alchemical Psychology: Old Recipes for Living in a New World* by Thom F. Cavalli; *The American Soul: Rediscovering the Wisdom of the Founders* by Jacob Needleman; *Awakening the Mind: A Guide to Mastering the Power of Your Brain Waves* by Anna Wise; *Beauty in the Beasts: True Stories of Animals Who Chose to Do Good* by Kristin Von Kreisler, et al.; *Beyond the Words: The Three Untapped Sources of Creative Fulfillment for Writers* by Bonni Goldberg; *Come to the Quiet: The Principles of Christian Meditation* by John Michael Talbot; *Crew of One: The Odyssey of a Solo Marlin Fisherman* by Carlos Bentos; *Doing Nothing* by Steven Harrison; *The Entrepreneurial Parent* by Paul Edwards, et al.; *Get a Grip: A Take-Charge Approach to Living with Arthritis* by Joe Layden; *God and the Evolving Universe: The Next Step in Personal Evolution* by James Redfield, et al.; *God's Dictionary: Divine Definitions for Everyday Enlightenment* by Susan Corso; *Great with Child: Reflections on Faith, Fullness and Becoming a Mother* by Debra Rienstra; *Hallucinogens: A Reader* by Charles S. Grob; *Headache Survival: The Holistic Medical Treatment Program for Migraine, Tension* by Robert S. Ivker and Todd H. Nelson; *Hope's Edge: The Next Diet for a Small Planet* by Frances Moore Lappe and Anna Lappe.

Tarcher also produces paperback reprints of previously published titles. Direct query letters and SASEs to:

Joel Fotinos, Publisher

Sara Carder, Editor

Mitch Horowitz, Senior Editor—Focuses on new trends in spirituality, science, social thought, and personal growth

Wendy Hubbert, Senior Editor—Focuses on science, psychology, narrative nonfiction, and memoir

New American Library/NAL (A Division of Penguin Putnam, Inc.)

Onyx

Signet

Roc

New American Library—popularly known as NAL—publishes a diverse and exciting range of paperback books, including *New York Times* bestsellers by Maeve Binchy, Stuart Woods, John Lescroart, and Ken Follett. Under the Signet, Onyx, and NAL imprints, NAL publishes fiction and nonfiction and has recently expanded its trade paperback and hardcover programs in addition to the core mass-market format.

As part of NAL's ongoing efforts to initiate new developments in areas of commercial fiction and nonfiction, its editors are looking for strong, innovative authors who offer distinctive voices and original ideas. We encourage writers to submit their work through an agent.

The NAL editorial staff includes:

Leslie Gelbman, President

Kara Walsh, Publisher

Claire Zion, Editorial Director

Ellen Edward, Executive Editor

Laura Ann Gilman, Executive Editor, Roc

Audrey LaFehr, Executive Editor

Doug Grad, Senior Editor

Dan Slater, Senior Editor

Cecilia Oh, Editor

Genny Ostertag, Editor

Jen Heddle, Editor

Jen Jahner, Assistant Editor

Onyx

Onyx produces mass-market and trade paperbacks, both reprints and originals. Titles representative of the list include *Breach of Confidence* by Eben Paul Perison; *Death Rites* by Bruce Elliot; *Chasing Darkness* by Danielle Girard; *The Edge of Heaven* by Teresa Hill; *Final Justice* by Nancy Kopp; *Hometown Girl* by Mary Jane Meier; *Hush* by Anne Frasier; *Insomnia* by Robert Westbrook; *Manhattan South* by John MacKie; *Saving Souls* by Lucy Taylor; *Some Survive* by James Preston Girard.

Roc

Roc publishes reprints and originals, in both trade paperback and mass-market paperback formats. Titles indicative of this list: *Angry Lead Skies* by Glen Cook; *Belarus* by Lee Hogan; *The Darker Side* by John Pelan (Editor); *The Disappeared* by Kristine Kathryn Rusch; *The Dragon Delasangre* by Alan F. Troop; *Drinking Midnight Wine* by Simon R. Green; *Fallen Host* by Lyda Morehouse; *Nebula Awards Showcase 2002: The Year's Best SF and Fantasy* by Kim Stanley Robinson (Editor); *Orbis* by Scott Mackay; *Season of Sacrifice* by Mindy L. Klasky.

Signet

This imprint produces mass-market paperback reprints, as well as some original titles in mass-market paperback format. Titles representative of this list: *Always in My Heart* by Catherine Anderson; *The Alamosa* by Ralph Compton; *The Banished Bride* by Andrea Pickens; *Bloody Brazos* (Trailsman, 245) by Jon Sharpe; *Caywood Valley Feud* by Judson Gray; *Dead Man's Ghost* by Peter King; *Hazard* by Jo Beverly.

Direct query letters and SASEs to:

Kara Welsh, Vice President, Publisher of New American Library

Penguin

Penguin produces numerous nonfiction and fiction trade paperback reprints, as well as publishing original titles in trade paperback format. Covering subjects such as literature, biography, memoir, history, science, business, psychology, popular reference, and self-help, the Penguin list now has more than 3,000 books in print in the United States.

Two series, Penguin Classics and Penguin Twentieth-Century Classics, comprise more than 1,300 titles, making Penguin the largest publisher of ancient and modern classic literature in the English-speaking world.

The Penguin list continues to grow, to embrace new writers, and to keep in print the works of some of the world's most important authors. Titles indicative of this list: *The Adventures of David Simple* by Sarah Fielding, Linda Bree (Editor); *Aromatherapy: Essential Oils for Vibrant Health and Beauty* by Roberta Wison; *Arthur's Britain* by Leslie Alcock; *At War at Sea* by Ronald H. Spector; *Better Day Coming* by Adam Fairclough; *Captivate Your Kids* by Dr. John E. Whitcomb; *As Ever* by Joanne Kyger.

Direct query letters and SASEs to:

Jane von Mehren, Editor in Chief and Associate Publisher—Health and social issues, self-help, child care and parenting, nature, memoir, history, popular culture, and personal stories, as well as contemporary and historical literary fiction

Caroline White, Editor—Literary fiction, women's issues, memoirs, sociology, religion, film and television, popular culture, Penguin Classics

Kathryn Court, Publisher—Literary and commercial fiction, including Third World and European fiction; nonfiction interests include humor, travel writing, biography, current affairs, business, nature, women's issues, true crime

Laurie Walsh, Assistant Editor—Literary and commercial fiction

Michael Millman, Senior Editor—Oversees the Penguin Classics and Twentieth-Century Classics, the Viking Portable Library, and the Penguin Nature Classics series

Sarah Baker, Senior Editor—Nonfiction paperback originals with backlist potential in several areas; popular culture, music, humor, current events, environment; also hardcover and paperback originals for the Arkana imprint, which publishes spiritual literature

Perigee Books

Perigee Books, originally created as the trade paperback imprint for G. P. Putnam's Sons, has featured an eclectic range of titles from practically every category of publishing, both fiction and nonfiction in hardcover and trade paperback format.

Among the bestsellers are *The Complete Guide to Prescription and Nonprescription Drugs; The Perigee Visual Dictionary of Signing*; *The Out-of-Sync Child; The Lyle Official Antiques Review.* Featured Perigee authors include Heloise, Vicki Iovine, and JoAnna Lund.

Titles representative of this list: *The 6 Secrets of a Lasting Relationship* by Mark Goulston and Philip Goldberg; *Bridging the Gap: Raising a Child with Nonverbal Learning Disorder* by Rondalyn Varney Whitney; *Calm Mother, Calm Child* by Paul Wilson and Tania Wilson; *Cancer Has Its Privileges: Stories of Hope and Laughter* by Christine Clifford and Carole Maggio; *Facercise* by Carole Maggio and Mike Gianelli; *Cooking Healthy with a Man in Mind* by Joann M. Lund, et al.; *Crossword for the Connoisseur Omnibus* by Charles Preston; *Facebuilder for Men* by Carole Maggio and Mike Gianelli; *Fearless Living* by Rhonda Britten; *Fibromyalgia: Fact vs. Fiction: As Explained by an*

American Authority by Don L. Goldenberg; *Fuel Up: Using the Principles of Sports Nutrition to Train Like a Pro* by Eric Sternlicht, Neil Feineman (Contributor); *Getting Through to Your Kids: Talking to Children About Sex, Drugs and Alcohol, Safety, Violence, Death, Smoking, Self-Esteem, and Other Critical Issues* by Michael Popkin, Ph.D., and Robyn Freedman Spizman; *Giving Birth: A Journey with Midwives* by Catherine Taylor; *A Goddess Is a Girl's Best Friend: A Divine Guide to Finding Love, Success, and Happiness* by Laurie Sue Brockway; *How to Make Your Man Look Good: Without Making Him Feel Bad* by Nancy Butcher; *In Our Humble Opinion* by Tom Magliozzi and Ray Magliozzi; *Run for Your Life: A Book for Beginning Women Runners* by Deborah Reber; *Sexual Fitness* by Hank C. K. Wuh, M.D., and Meimei Fox.

Direct query letters and SASEs to:

John Duff, Publisher, Vice President, and Senior Editor of Perigee, HPBooks, and Avery. Duff is also a Vice President and Senior Editor for G. P. Putnam's Sons

Jennifer Repo, Editor—Spirituality, women's issues, health, relationships, and pop culture

Sheila Curry Oakes, Executive Editor—Spirituality, general nonfiction, health, and fitness

Plume

Plume, founded in 1970 as the trade paperback imprint of New American Library, is now recognized as one of the preeminent trade paperback imprints. Throughout its history, Plume has been dedicated to giving an opportunity to voices previously neglected by mainstream publishing. The pioneering program in multicultural literature, which began with Toni Morrison and Jamaica Kincaid, has expanded to include ground-breaking works by Latino, African American, and Asian American authors. Plume publishes such writers as Julia Alvarez (*In The Name of Salomé*), Bernice McFadden (*Sugar*), Gish Jen (*Typical American*), Charles Johnson (*Middle Passage*), Gus Lee (*China Boy*), and August Wilson (*Fences*). Plume was also a pioneer in gay publishing, with Edmund White's *A Boy's Own Story* and Andrew Holleran's *Dancer from the Dance.*

Plume's literary fiction boasts many bestselling and prize-winning authors, including Dorothy Allison (*Bastard Out of Carolina*), Pat Barker (*Regeneration*), E. L. Doctorow (*Ragtime*), Diane Johnson (*Le Divorce*), Joyce Carol Oates (*We Were the Mulvaneys*), Cathleen Schine (*The Evolution of Jane*), and Tracy Chevalier (*Girl with a Pearl Earring*). Quality nonfiction is another area in which Plume takes special pride, publishing Dave Pelzer (*A Man Named Dave*), Mary Catherine Bateson (*Composing a Life*), Russell Baker (*Growing Up*), Robert Coles (*The Moral Intelligence of Children*), Dr. James Comer (*Maggie's American Dream*), Mark Mathabane (*Kaffir Boy*), and Bill McKibben (*The Age of Missing Information*), among others.

Plume's backlist is diverse, including Ayn Rand's *The Fountainhead; The Joy of Cooking; Todd Wilbur's Top Secret Recipes.* The business and personal finance list is a mix of the classic and the cutting-edge, featuring everything from Gary Hamel's *Leading the Revolution* to Jason Kelley's *Neatest Little Guide to Investing.* The diet and health category leads with Dr. Rachael Heller and Dr. Richard Heller's *Carbohydrate Addict's Life-Span Program,* with more than 1.5 million copies sold.

Titles representative of this list: *After Hours: A Collection of Erotic Writing by Black Men* by Robert Fleming (Editor); *Backpack* by Emily Barr; *Bitch Goddess: A Novel* by

Robert Rodi; *The Darwin Awards* by Wendy Nothcutt; *Farm Fatale: A Comedy of Country Manors* by Wendy Holden; *The Fed* by Martin Mayer; *How to Settle an Estate* by Charles K. Plotnick and Stephan R. Leimberg; *The Imp of the Mind: Exploring the Silent Epidemic of Obsessive Bad Thoughts* by Lee Baer, Ph.D.

Direct query letters and SASEs to:

Trena Keating, Editor in Chief—Health, popular psychology, spirituality

Price Stern Sloan

Price Stern Sloan produces humor, novelty formats, and children's books. (See entry for Penguin Putnam Books for Young Readers.) The company had tremendous success with a number of proprietary brands, among them *Mad Libs.* Price Stern Sloan was purchased by the Putnam Berkley Group in 1993, and in 1997 the offices were moved to New York. PSS also produces a list of desk calendars.

Direct query letters and SASEs to:

Jon Anderson, Publisher

Prime Crime

Prime Crime produces original fiction crime titles in hardcover, trade, and mass-market paperback format. It also publishes paperback reprints. Titles representative of the Prime Crime list: *The Bloodied Cravat* by Rosemary Stevens; *The Clerk's Tale* by Margaret Frazer; *A Crossword to Die For* by Nero Blanc; *Death Lurks in the Bush* by Kate Grilley; *Death a L'Orange* by Nancy Fairbanks; *Decorated for Murder* by M. T. Jefferson; *The Devil and Lou Prophet* by Peter Brandvold; *The Etruscan Chimera: An Archaeological Mystery* by Lyn Hamilton; *Garden View* by Mary Freeman; *Gunpowder Green* by Laura Childs; *The Ironclad Alibi* by Michael Kilian; *Murder Will Travel* by Emily Toll.

Putnam

Putnam produces a broad range of nonfiction and fiction titles that spans categories across the board. Formats for original titles include hardcover, trade paperback, and audio cassette. Putnam also publishes paperback reprints.

Titles representative of Putnam's list: *Acid Row* by Minette Walters; *Adelita of the Kitchen: A Mexican Cinderella Story* by Tomie dePaola; *Alt Ed* by Catherine Atkins; *Anyway: The Paradoxical Commandments—Finding Personal Meaning in a Crazy World* by Kent M. Keith; *Aromatherapy: Essential Oils for Vibrant Health and Beauty* by Roberta Wison; *The Arraignment* by Steve Martini; *Baroque-A-Nova* by Kevin Chong; *The Burying Field* by Kenneth Abel; *By Way of Water* by Charlotte Gullick; *A Clean Kill* by Mike Stewart; *The Commander* by Patrick A. Davis; *Criminal Intent* by Sheldon Siegel; *Flashover* by Suzanne Chazin; *Flint's Law* by Paul Eddy; *From Wall to Wall* by Susan Kuklin; *A Game of Spies* by John Altman; *Hush* by Jacqueline Woodson; *Fragrant Harbor* by John Lanchester.

Direct query letters with SASEs to:

Christine Pepe, Senior Editor—Fiction: mysteries, thrillers, horror; nonfiction: business

David Highfill, Senior Editor—Fiction: mysteries and mainstream novels; commercial nonfiction

John Duff, Vice President and Senior Editor—Nonfiction, self-help, popular reference (see also listing for John Duff under Perigee Books)

Laura Mathews, Senior Editor—Serious women's fiction and nonfiction

Neil Nyren, Publisher, G. P. Putnam's Sons—Serious and commercial fiction and nonfiction

Hillery Borton, Editor—Literary fiction and serious biography

Riverhead Books

Riverhead Books produces quality fiction and groundbreaking nonfiction in hardcover and trade paperback format.

This past year the house helped usher Nick Hornby's third novel, *How to be Good,* onto the *New York Times* bestseller list; it launched the fiction debut of the memoirist Nuala O'Faolain, *My Dream of You,* also a *New York Times* bestseller, as well as a critically acclaimed first memoir by Rebecca Walker, *Black White and Jewish;* and it has kept alive its tradition of publishing the works of today's most prominent spiritual leaders, with Thich Nhat Hanh's *Anger* and Ghelek Rimpoche's *Good Life, Good Death.* As Riverhead enters the 21st century, it continues to extend its vision to help readers enlarge their understanding of the world and their place in it.

Riverhead is quickly gaining a reputation as the house to watch for up-and-coming fiction writers. So far, Riverhead has launched Jennifer Belle (*Going Down; High Maintenance*), Junot Díaz (*Drown*), Alex Garland (*The Beach; The Tesseract*), Nick Hornby (*High Fidelity; About a Boy; How to Be Good*), Danzy Senna (*Caucasia*), Aryeh Lev Stollman (*The Far Euphrates; The Illuminated Soul*), and Sarah Waters (*Tipping the Velvet; Affinity; Fingersmith*).

In February 2002, Riverhead published McBride's much-anticipated first novel, *Miracle at St. Anna.* Other significant nonfiction *New York Times* bestsellers from Riverhead include Rachel Remen's inspiring *Kitchen Table Wisdom;* Harold Bloom's magnum opus *Shakespeare: The Invention of the Human,* which was a finalist for the National Book Award and the National Book Critics Circle Award; and two major *New York Times* bestsellers from financial guru Suze Orman, *The Road to Wealth* and the number-one, million-copy bestseller *The Courage to Be Rich.*

Riverhead published the Dalai Lama's *The Art of Happiness* and *Ethics for the New Millennium.* Other spiritual books on Riverhead's list include Kathleen Norris's *The Cloister Walk* and *Amazing Grace,* also *New York Times* bestsellers; Stephen Batchelor's *Buddhism Without Beliefs;* Thich Nhat Hanh's three Buddhist classics, *Living Buddha, Living Christ; Going Home; Anger;* as well as Robert Thurman's *Inner Revolution.*

Recent Riverhead acquisitions include *Blue Shoe* by Anne Lamott and *Lessons in Becoming Myself* by Ellen Burstyn. Nonfiction titles indicative of this list: *All Girls* by Karen Stabiner; *Benedict's Dharma* by Patrick Henry (Editor); *Blessing* by David Spangler; *The Box Children* by Sharon Wyse; *Crossing the Unknown Sea* by David Whyte; *Dark Night of the Soul: St. John of the Cross* by Mirabai Starr (Translator); *Darwin, His Daughter, and Human Evolution* by Randal Keynes; *The Eat Right for Your Type Complete Blood Type Encyclopedia* by Peter J. D'Adamo, Catherine Whitney (Contributor); *How to Prevent and Treat Cancer with Natural Medicine* by Dr. Michael Murray, et al.

Representative titles on the fiction list: *Dream of Scipio* by Iain Pears; *Fingersmith* by Sarah Waters; *The Fruit of Stone* by Mark Spragg; *Losing Gemma* by Katy Gardner; *No Place, Louisiana* by Martin Pousson; *The Pact* by Samson Davis, et al.; *Sister India* by Peggy Payne; *What Harry Saw* by Thomas Moran; *The Good Men* by Charmaine Craig.

Direct query letters and SASEs to:

Susan Petersen Kennedy, Riverhead Books Publisher, President, Penguin Putnam Inc., Chairman, Viking Penguin, Plume, and Studio Books

Julie Grau, Co-Editorial Director

Cindy Spiegel, Co-Editorial Director

Viking

Viking, founded in 1925, currently publishes approximately 100 books a year, both non-fiction and fiction, in hardcover. The firm's name and its logo, a Viking ship drawn by Rockwell Kent, were chosen as symbols of enterprise, adventure, and exploration.

The house issues a broad range of literary titles, as well as commercial titles. Viking is recognized for "increasing the visibility of its established and more prominent authors, while orchestrating the successful launch of new and relatively unknown writers."

Titles representative of Viking's nonfiction list: *America and Americans and Selected Nonfiction* by John Steinbeck, et al.; *Bamboozled at the Revolution: How Big Media Lost Billions in the Battle for the Internet* by John Motavalli; *Black Livingstone: A True Tale of Adventure in the Nineteenth-Century Congo* by Pagan Kennedy; *Brown: The Last Discovery of America* by Richard Rodriguez; *The Career As a Path to the Soul* by David Rottman; *The Fall of Berlin 1945* by Antony Beevor; *From a Victorian Garden: Creating the Romance of a Bygone Age Right in Your Own Backyard* by Michael Weishan and Cristina Roig.

Titles indicative of Viking's fiction list: *Annie Dunne* by Sebastian Barry; *Between* by Jean Thesman; *Ariel's Crossing* by Bradford Morrow; *City of Names* by Kevin Brock-meier; *The Clubhouse* by Anastasia Suen, et al.; *Emporium: Stories* by Adam Johnson; *The Escher Twist: A Homer Kelly Mystery* by Jane Langton; *Evil River* by William S. Burroughs; *Forty-Seven Roses* by Peter Sheridan; *Fox Girl* by Nora Okja Keller; *Girl from the South* by Joanna Trollope; *Journey to the Well* by Vashti Murphy McKenzie; *Last Things* by David Searcy; *Must Love Dogs: A Novel* by Claire Cook; *Red Rain* by Michael Crow; *Women About Town* by Laura Jacobs.

Viking also produces illustrated titles through its imprint, **Viking Studio.** Titles on Viking Studio's list: *Blue Dog; The Secret Language of Birthdays; King: The Photobiography of Martin Luther King* by Charles Johnson; *Vanity Fair's Hollywood;* the *Pennyroyal Caxton Bible,* illustrated by Barry Moser.

Direct query letters and SASEs to:

Rick Kot, Senior Editor—Commercial works in nonfiction; some fiction

Paul Slovak, Vice President Viking Publishing, Senior Editor, Assistant Publisher—Poetry, literary fiction, beat work (Kerouac and the like), intellectual nonfiction

Carolyn Carlson, Senior Editor—Narrative nonfiction, cultural history, biography, women's issues, commercial nonfiction, commercial and literary fiction, mysteries

Clare Feraro, President—Commercial fiction and nonfiction

Janet Goldstein, Executive Editor—Spirituality, health, psychology, narrative nonfiction

Pamela Dorman, Executive Editor—Commercial fiction, especially women's fiction and suspense; Nonfiction interests include self-help and psychology, investigative stories and narrative nonfiction, popular inspiration, popular reference, and women's issues

Wendy Wolf, Senior Editor—Nonfiction, especially music, culture, humor

PENGUIN PUTNAM BOOKS FOR YOUNG READERS

AlloyBooks

Dial Books for Young Readers

Dutton Children's Books (Dutton, Grosset & Dunlap)

Frederick Warne

G. P. Putnam's Sons Books for Young Readers

Grosset & Dunlap

Philomel Books

Phyllis Fogelman Books

Price Stern Sloan

Puffin Books

Viking Children's Books

375 Hudson Street, New York, NY 10014
212-366-2000

Penguin Putnam Books for Young Readers produces titles for children of all ages and also young adults. This house offers a wide array of distinctive divisions, imprints, and affiliates of Penguin Putnam Inc.'s component houses, including Alloy Books, Dial Books for Young Readers, Frederick Warne, Grosset & Dunlap, Philomel, Phyllis Fogelman Books, Price Stern Sloan, Puffin Books, and Viking Children's Books,

Each imprint publishes a broad assortment of titles in a variety of formats, and each children's house is a recognized name in the industry. Together, these imprints form a powerhouse in the young-reader arena.

AlloyBooks

AlloyBooks is a new Penguin Putnam imprint aimed at teens. Headed by Tracy Tang, Alloy released its first four nonfiction titles in August 2000, including *Slam,* a unique poetry anthology; *DIY Beauty,* a do-it-yourself beauty guide; *Dreams,* a funky dream interpretation manual; and . . . *Any Advice?* a book packed with advice for teens from Alloy.com's advice experts. Subsequent lists have included *Spiritualized,* a personalized look at teen spirituality across the country; *This Book Is About Sex,* a frank and honest exploration of teen sexuality and advice on sex; *Who Do You Think You Are?: 12 Methods for Analyzing the True You,* a fun collection of self-analysis methods ranging from astrology to chakras to body types; two great quiz books, *Is Your Crush Crushing Back?: 20 Love Quizzes to Set Your Heart Straight* and *What's Your Pop Culture IQ?: 20 Quizzes About Music, Movies, TV and More; Have a Nice Life,* a funny, offbeat fiction series by Scarlett MacDougal.

Direct query letters and SASEs to:

Tracy Tang, Publisher

Dial Books for Young Readers

Dial Books for Young Readers is a hardcover trade children's book division publishing 50 titles a year for children from preschool through young adult.

This Penguin Putnam Inc. imprint traces its roots to 1880 and the founding of *The Dial,* a monthly literary magazine that published such literary giants as e.e. cummings, T. S. Eliot, D. H. Lawrence, and Gertrude Stein. Since the children's list was launched in 1961, Dial has been known for books of high literary merit and fine design for readers of all ages. It has pioneered books for the young, including the first quality boardbooks published in the United States. Dial introduced its Easy-to-Read series in 1979 to publish full-color early readers with popular children's book authors and artists, including James Marshall, creator of the "Fox" series.

Today, Dial continues its tradition of literary and illustrative excellence, publishing talented picture-book creators such as Steven Kellogg, Tedd Arnold, Emily McCully, and Mary GrandPre. Dial's award-winning novelists include Nikki Grimes, whose *Jazmin's Notebook* was a recent Coretta Scott King Honor Book, and Richard Peck, winner of the 2001 Newbery Medal for his novel *A Year Down Yonder.*

Direct query letters and SASEs to:

Nancy Paulsen, President and Publisher

Lauri Hornik, Editorial Director

Dutton Children's Books

Dutton Children's Books is one of the oldest continually operating children's publishers in the United States. Edward Payson Dutton opened the doors of his Boston bookshop in 1852 and shortly thereafter began to release "fresh and entertaining" books for young readers. Nearly 150 years later, Dutton's tagline, "Every book a promise," reflects the imprint's mission to create high-quality books that will transport young readers. The Dutton list of today looks very different, but its commitment to excellence, freshness, and entertainment has not changed. Today's novelty list includes bestselling single titles such as *Wheels on the Bus* by Paul O. Zelinsky and *Dinosaur Roar!* by Paul Stickland, and licensed books published with such partners as DreamWorks/SKG, Hallmark-owned Interart's Holly Pond Hill, Radio Flyer, and Little Souls. Approximately 100 new titles, hardcover, novelty, and licensed, are published every year. Nonfiction for children of all ages remains a strength for Dutton, with award-winning writers such as Albert Marrin and Milton Meltzer and innovative author-photographers such as Charles R. Smith, Jr., and Ellen Senisi.

Direct query letters and SASEs to:

Stephanie Owens Lurie, President and Publisher

Frederick Warne

Frederick Warne was founded in 1865 by a bookseller turned publisher who gave his own name to the firm. The hallmarks of the publishing program are beautifully produced editions of historic original works, such as *Beatrix Potter,* plus lively spin-off books ranging from baby record books and treasuries to boardbooks and novelty titles.

G. P. Putnam's Sons Books for Young Readers

G. P. Putnam's Sons Books for Young Readers publishes about 50 trade hardcover books a year for children, including lively, accessible picture books and some of today's strongest voices in fiction. This house publishes popular novels and picture books from some of the top names in children's books today.

G. P. Putnam's Sons is the home of celebrated picture-book creators Tomie dePaola, Jan Brett, Eric Hill, Rachael Isadora, Maira Kalman, Keiko Kasza, and Peggy Rathmann. Award-winning authors for older readers include Joan Bauer, Paula Danziger, Jean Fritz, Vicki Grove, Suzy Kline, Robin McKinley, Jacqueline Woodson, and Laurence Yep.

G. P. Putnam's Sons, Books for Young Readers is accepting manuscripts.

GUIDELINES FOR MANUSCRIPT SUBMISSIONS TO
G. P. PUTNAM'S SONS, BOOKS FOR YOUNG READERS

Picture Books

We accept full picture book manuscripts for review. Art should not be sent until specifically requested.

Fiction (middle-grade, chapter books, young adult)

Please send a query letter before submitting fiction. Please include a synopsis and one to three sample chapters. Your query letter and sample chapters will be circulated among the editors and the entire work will be requested upon interest.

Nonfiction

Please send a query letter before submitting nonfiction. Please include a synopsis and one or two sample chapters, as well as a table of contents. Your query letter and sample chapters will be circulated among the editors and the entire work will be requested upon interest.

Direct all submissions to:

Putnam Children's Editorial, Manuscript Editor, 14th Floor, 345 Hudson Street, New York, NY 10014

Grosset & Dunlap

Grossett & Dunlap produces about 125 mass-market children's books each year in hardcover, paperback, library binding, and other formats. Since the 1940s, in addition to the original Nancy Drew and Hardy Boys series, Grosset has published the Illustrated Junior Library. This collection of hardcover editions of *Little Women, Tom Sawyer,* and more than 20 other classics is a mainstay of practically every bookstore selling children's books.

Known for originality, quality, and value, Grosset & Dunlap currently publishes many well-known book lines, including the ALL ABOARD READING series of leveled paperback readers and READING RAILROAD paperback 8 x 8s. Another Grosset series that continues to sell well is THE ZACK FILES, a chapter book series by humorist Dan Greenburg. This series is now a TV show and launched the first TV tie-in book in March 2002.

Grosset & Dunlap recently launched two new series. The first one is SMART ABOUT ART, an innovative new way to bring nonfiction subjects to life for kids ages 5 to 9. These books are written in the voice of a young student in the format of a school report. The books, many of which are about famous artists, relate events from the artist's life and offer insights about his or her work. Illustrated with childlike drawings and reproductions of the artist's paintings in scrapbook-style layouts, both the stories and the text are lively.

The other new series is WHO WAS . . . ? a biography series for kids 8 to 11. Grosset says, "Each book is written by well-regarded kid-friendly authors who know how to make really famous dead people come alive!"

Titles representative of this list include *All God's Little Creatures* (Sticker Stories) by Christine Powers (Illustrator); *Annie's Journey* (The Fairy Diaries) by Louise Bradley (illustrated by Broeck Steadman); *Anyone but Me* (Katie Kazoo Switcheroo) by Nancy Krulik; *Baby Animals* (Little Engine That Could) by Watty Piper (illustrated by Cristina Ong); *Baby Dinosaurs* (Dino Days) by Dino Don Lessem, et al.; *Be Brown!* by Barbara Bottner (illustrated by Barry Gott); *Bear Cub* (All Aboard Reading Level 2) by Pam Pollack, et al.; *The Best Easter Basket Ever* (Glitter Tattoos), edited by Mara Conlon (illustrated by Lucinda McQueen); *Bible Sticker Stories, Bible Songs and Rhymes* (Doyle and Fossey) by Stephanie Peterson (Illustrator); *Biggest Dinosaurs* (Dino Days) by Dino Don Lessem, et al.; *Bless My Little Friends* (Christian Mother Goose) by Marjorie Ainsborough Decker (illustrated by Benton Mahan); *Boiling Point* (Dish #3) by Diane Muldrow (illustrated by Barbara Pollak); *Boss for a Day* (All Aboard Reading. Level 1) by Tomie De Paola; *Busy Ballet School: With 20 Glitter Tattoos* (Glitter Tattoos) edited by Emily Sollinger (illustrated by Stacey Lamb); *Butterflies and Moths* (Nature Sticker Stories Book) edited by Mara Conlon (illustrated by Roberta Collier-Morales); *Cats Go* by Annie Horwood; *Chitter Chatter* (Chatterbooks) by David Crossley (Illustrator); *Christian Mother Goose & Friends: A Giant Lift-The-Flap* (Christian Mother Goose) by Marjorie Ainsborough Decker, et al.; *Claude Monet: Sunshine and Waterlilies* (Smart About Art) by True Kelley.

Direct query letters and SASEs to:

Debra Dorfman, President and Publisher

Philomel Books

Philomel Books was created in the early 1980s from World Publishing Books for Young People, by Editor and Publisher Ann Beneduce. Ms. Beneduce was a pioneer in choosing books that would sell to both trade and institutional markets, so for the new list she chose the name *Philomel,* a term for an English nightingale that literally means "love of learning." The name implied that these books would be distinguished, beautiful in concept and form, fine enough to be sought as gifts, and original and handsome enough to be bought by libraries and schools. Titles are published in hardcover, as well as with school and library binding.

Philomel published Caldecott-winners *Owl Moon* by Jane Yolen and John Schoenherr, and *Lon Po Po* by Ed Young. Philomel became the primary publisher of popular artist-author Patricia Polacco, who created *Pink and Say, Chicken Sunday,* and many other biographical folk-like tales. Philomel was honored with *New York Times* Best Illustrated Awards for *Cats Are Cats* by Ed Young and *Fox's Dream* by Tejima.

The Philomel list has also included popular and respected novels. In the late 1980s it became a leader in the field of fantasy with Brian Jacques's Redwall books, a series now 11 books deep and growing. The trend toward quality fiction continues, with such titles as *The Lost Years of Merlin* by T. A. Barron; *The Lost Flower Children* by Janet Taylor Lisle; *I Am Mordred* by Nancy Springer.

Other worlds, of one form or another, have always been of interest to Philomel. Hence its publishing of historical fiction, such as Sally Keehn's *I Am Regina;* Stephen Menick's *The Muffin Child.* The imprint supports books with a social conscience, such as *Be Good to Eddie Lee* by Virginia Fleming and Floyd Cooper, and *Choosing Up Sides* by John H. Ritter, recipient of the 1999 International Reading Award for Older Readers. Publishing books and ideas that celebrate a child's potential—indeed, human potential—in worlds past and present is Philomel's goal.

Titles indicative of this list: *One Rainy Day* by Valeri Gorbachev; *I Invited a Dragon to Dinner: And Other Poems to Make You Laugh Out Loud* by Chris L. Demarest (Illustrator); *Tanya and the Red Shoes* by Patricia Lee Gauch, Satomi Ichikawa (Illustrator); *Elefantina's Dream* by X. J. Kennedy, Graham Percy (Illustrator); *Anna Sunday* by Sally M. Keehn; *The Tribes of Redwall: Badgers* (The Tribes of Redwall Series) by Brian Jacques, Peter Standley (Illustrator); *Things Not Seen* by Andrew Clements; *The Kingfisher's Gift* by Susan Williams Beckhorn; *Birdbrain Amos* by Michael Delaney; *Point Blank: An Alex Rider Adventure* by Anthony Horowitz; *The Girl in the Cage* by Jane Yolen and Robert J. Harris.

Direct query letters and SASEs to:

Patricia Lee Gauch, Publisher and Editorial Director

Phyllis Fogelman Books

Phyllis Fogelman Books was announced in September 1998, when Ms. Fogelman, previously the Publisher of Dial Books for Young Readers, was given her own imprint. The new imprint, which was launched in Fall 1999, publishes 5 to 20 high-quality, well-designed books for children from preschool age through young adult. Ms. Fogelman continues to work with a number of the award-winning authors and artists she published and edited during her long career at Dial; they include Caralyn and Mark Buehner, Tom Feelings, Julius Lester, Marianna Mayer, Jerry and Gloria Jean Pinkney, Mildred Taylor, and Jean Van Leeuwen.

Titles indicative of the Fogelman list: *Amanda Pig and the Awful Scary Monster* by Jean Van Leeuwen, Ann Schweninger (Illustrator); *The Amazing Air Balloon* by Jean Van

Leeuwen, Marco Ventura (Illustrator); *Animals of the Bible* by Mary Hoffman, Jackie Morris (Illustrator); *Chimp and Zee and the Big Storm* by Catherine Anholt and Laurence Anholt; *The Color of Home* by Mary Hoffman, Karin Littlewood (Illustrator); *The Doomspell* (All Aboard Reading Level 2) by Cliff McNish, Geoff Taylor (Illustrator); *Dreaming in Black and White* by Reinhardt Jung and Anthea Bell; *The Great Googlestein Museum Mystery* by Jean Van Leeuwen, R. W. Alley (Illustrator); *The Handle and the Key* by John Neufeld; *Lucky Socks* by Carrie Weston, Charlotte Middleton (Illustrator).

Direct query letters and SASEs to:

Phyllis Fogelman, Vice President and Publisher

Price Stern Sloan

Stern Sloan was founded in Los Angeles in the early 1960s to publish the Mad Libs series that Roger Price and Leonard Stern had concocted during their stint as writers for Steve Allen's *Tonight Show.* Along with their partner Larry Sloan, they expanded the company into a wide variety of publishing categories, especially children's books, novelty formats, and humor. The company had tremendous success with a number of proprietary brands, many of which flourish to this day; among them, *Mad Libs, Wee Sing, Mr. Men & Little Miss, Serendipity, Crazy Games,* and *Doodle Art.*

The company was purchased by the Putnam Berkley Group in 1993, and in 1997 the offices were moved to New York. With about 75 titles per year, Price Stern Sloan continues to publish successfully its proprietary brands, as well as titles that fall into the preschool children's mass merchandise categories. PSS also produces a successful annual list of desk calendars and occasional humor titles for the adult market.

Among PSS authors are Pamela Beall, Arthur Bloch, Stephen Cosgrove, Dan Greenburg, Roger Hargreaves, Susan Nipp, Jan Pienkowski, and Charles Reasoner.

Titles indicative of this list: *Aladdin* by Melissa Tyrrell, et al.; *Amazing Alphabet Maze Book* by Patrick Baldus (Illustrator); *The Ants Go Marching* (Wee Sing Board Books) by Susan Hagan, et al.; *The Big Burger Book* by Jocelyn Jamison; *Cinderella* (Hank the Cowdog, 40) by Melissa Tyrrell, et al.; *The Dinosaur Store* (Welcome to Eurekaville) by Sylvia Branzei, et al.; *Easter Treats* by Leigh Harris; *Five Little Ghosts* by William Boniface, Jerry Smath (Illustrator); *The Ghost Hunter's Handbook* by Rachel Dickinson; *Haunted Mad Libs* by Roger Price, et al.; *The Hokey Pokey* (Wee Sing Board Books) by Pamela Conn Beall, et al.; *How to Be a Pig* by Ima Swine, Shelly Meredith (Illustrator); *The Mighty Big Book of Travel Games* by Dina Anastassio, et al.; *Muffin Dragon* by Stephen Cosgrove, Robin James (Illustrator).

In addition to producing original titles, Stern Sloan also reissues previously published books. Direct query letters and SASEs to:

Jon Anderson, Publisher

Puffin Books

Puffin Books was founded on a strong literary tradition and a commitment to publishing a successful mix of classic children's fiction, as well as some of the best new literature for children. Over the years, Puffin has transformed from a small, yet distinguished, paperback house into one of the largest, most diverse, and successful children's publishers in business, publishing everything from picture books to ground-breaking middle grade and teen fiction. In addition to publishing new editions of quality literary fiction, Puffin has started several original series with broad commercial appeal.

During the 1980s, Puffin Books produced quality paperback editions of Viking titles, aggressively acquired titles for paperback publication from outside publishing houses, reprinted Puffin UK titles, and maintained a backlist packed with award-winning children's literature, including Robert McCloskey's Caldecott Medal–winner *Make Way For Ducklings;* Ludwig Bemelmans's beloved Caldecott Honor book *Madeline;* Don Freeman's classic *Corduroy.*

In 1988, Penguin merged with New American Library and Dutton, creating a new powerhouse Puffin list. Incorporating titles from three hardcover imprints, Viking Children's Books, Dial Books for Young Readers, and Dutton Children's Books, Puffin drew on the strength of its expanded list to launch the Puffin Easy-to-Read series, as well as—in a major joint venture with Puffin UK—a newly redesigned Puffin Classics series. The 1996 merger of Penguin Books with the Putnam Berkley Group, and the subsequent incorporation of Putnam's PaperStar imprint into Puffin, cemented Puffin's long-standing position as one of the leading children's paperback publishers in the business.

Publishing about 225 titles a year, Puffin produces titles for young readers in every age group: lift-the-flaps and picture books for young children, Puffin Easy-to-Reads for first-time readers, Puffin Chapters and the best in historical and contemporary fiction for middle-graders, and critically acclaimed novels for older readers.

Recently, Puffin Books published several *New York Times* and *Publishers Weekly* bestsellers, including the fantasy romp *Which Witch* by Eva Ibbotson; the Newbery Honor book *Rules of the Road* by Joan Bauer; Richard Peck's Newbery Honor book *A Long Way From Chicago;* Tomie dePaola's first chapter book and recipient of a Newbery Honor, *26 Fairmount Avenue;* and Laurie Halse Anderson's National Book Award Finalist and Printz Honor Book, *Speak.* Lost classics like Elizabeth Goudge's *The Little White Horse,* M. M. Kaye's *The Ordinary Princess,* and Walter R. Brooks's Freddy the Pig series are finding a new generation of fans in Puffin. And Jon Scieszka's hilarious Time Warp Trio series keeps middle-grade readers in stitches, as Puffin's highly addictive original fiction series Sweep breaks new ground for teen readers.

Puffin is also expanding its list of original books for younger children. The Timothy Goes to School Get Set for Kindergarten! series features Rosemary Wells's beloved characters and ties in with PBS's popular Saturday morning programming block, *The Bookworm Bunch.* Younger children love Claire Masurel and Susan Calitri's adorable bunny Emily, star of such charming lift-the-flaps as *Emily's Dance Class, Emily and Her Baby-Sitter,* and the new book and doll set *Emily's Ballet Box.*

Noted Puffin picture book authors and illustrators include *Madeline* author Ludwig Bemelmans, *The Gingerbread Boy* illustrator Jan Brett, *The Very Hungry Caterpillar*'s Eric Carle, *Strega Nona* creator Tomie dePaola, *Miss Fannie's Hat*'s Jan Karon, *The Snowy Day*'s Ezra Jack Keats, *Make Way For Ducklings* author Robert McCloskey, *Max and Ruby* creator Rosemary Wells, and Caldecott Medal– and Honor–winner Paul O. Zelinsky.

Middle-graders and teen readers devour books by Puffin's fiction authors, who include Lloyd Alexander, author of *Time Cat* and *The Chronicles of Pyrdain; Charlie and the Chocolate Factory* author, Roald Dahl; *The Cat Ate My Gymsuit* author and Amber Brown creator, Paula Danziger; award-winning historical fiction author Jean Fritz; *The Outsider*'s S. E. Hinton; *Pippi Longstocking* creator, Astrid Lindgren; *Lyddie*'s Katherine Paterson; Newbery Honor– and Newbery Medal–winner Richard Peck; *Roll of Thunder, Hear My Cry*'s author, Mildred D. Taylor; and *Miracle's Boys'* award-winning author, Jacqueline Woodson.

Direct query letters and SASEs to:

Kristin Gilson, Executive Editor

Sharyn November, Senior Editor

Viking Children's Books

Viking Children's Books, founded in 1933, publishes approximately 60 titles a year, ranging from books for very young children, such as board and lift-the-flap books, to sophisticated fiction and nonfiction for teenagers.

The current Viking list is known for such classic characters as *Madeline, Corduroy, Pippi Longstocking,* Roald Dahl's *Matilda,* Rosemary Wells's *Max & Ruby, The Stinky Cheese Man, Cam Jansen,* and *Froggy.* Viking publishes the entire works of Ezra Jack Keats, including *The Snowy Day,* winner of the Caldecott Medal; and Robert McCloskey, author of *Make Way for Ducklings,* a Caldecott winner, and *Homer Price.*

Throughout Viking's history, it has been known for innovation as well as for a dedication to quality books that has created the rich backlist the house enjoys. Viking has published 10 Newbery Medal–winners and 10 Caldecott Medal–winners, more than any other publishing house, as well as 27 Newbery Honor books, 33 Caldecott Honor books, and an American Book Award winner. Sixteen Viking books have been recognized as *New York Times* Best Illustrated Books. Two Viking books have received the Coretta Scott King Award, two have been Batchelder Honor books, four have received the Christopher Medal, and two authors, S. E. Hinton and Richard Peck, have received the Margaret A. Edwards Award for bodies of work that included Viking titles. Among the ground-breaking titles published by Viking are *The Outsiders* (1969), still the bestselling young adult book ever published; *The Snowy Day* (1963), which brought multicultural books mainstream recognition; and *The Stinky Cheese Man* (1992), widely hailed for its innovative design. In 2000, *Book of the Lion* by Michael Cadnum was one of five finalists for the National Book Award.

In 1985, Viking won the Carey Thomas Award for creative publishing, the first children's list to receive this award. Viking has been nominated twice for the LMP Award for Best Children's list.

Direct query letters and SASEs to:

Regina Hayes, Publisher

Gerard Mancini, Associate Publisher

P

THE PERMANENT PRESS/SECOND CHANCE PRESS

4170 Noyac Road, Sag Harbor, NY 11963
fax: 631-725-1101

Founded in 1978 by copublishers Judith and Martin Shepard, the Permanent Press produces expressive, vital, and exciting nongenre fiction. The sine qua non here for titles is that they be artfully written. The Permanent Press publishes 12 books a year in cloth editions only. Selected out-of-print books are released in reprint under the Second Chance Press imprint.

Judith and Martin Shepard have endeavored to bring out quality writing, primarily fiction, without regard to authors' reputations or track records. The publisher presents a handpicked list in which it firmly believes. Such dedication is not without payoff: Permanent Press titles generate considerable and favorable word of mouth among readers and booksellers and reap the kinds of reviews that pique wide interest (particularly in the realm of subsidiary rights).

While publishing only 12 books a year, Permanent Press has, since 1986, gained 49 literary awards for its titles (including an American Book Award and a National Book Award finalist). The press has launched the careers of such novelists as Bill Albert, Larry Duberstein, David Galef, Andrew Klavan, Howard Owen, Sandra Scofield, and William Browning Spencer. Permanent has published a Nobel Prize–winner (Halldor Laxness) and a Nobel Prize–nominee (Berry Fleming). This is the house that gave a fresh start to Clifford Irving after his misadventures involving the Howard Hughes "autobiography," by publishing Irving's account of that episode (*The Hoax*).

To celebrate Permanent's 20th year, the list presents 20 titles (8 more than it has ever done before) selected from the more than 8,000 submissions received: 16 novels, 3 works of nonfiction, and a short-story collection.

Fiction on the Permanent Press list: *Marginalia* by Doran Larsen; *Natural Bridges* by Debbie Lynn McCampbell; *The Trap* by Rink van der Velde (originally published in the Netherlands in 1966); *Geometry of Love* by Joan Fay Cuccio; *Up, Down, & Sideways* and *Life Between Wars* by Robert H. Patton; *The Deer Mouse* by Ken Grant; *The Speed of Light* by Susan Pashman; *Bending Time* by Stephen Minot (short stories); *Queen of the Silver Dollar* by Edward Hower; *Apology for Big Rod* by Charles Holdefer; *They Don't Play Stickball in Milwaukee* by Reed Farrel Coleman; *Going to Chicago* by Rob Levandoski.

Nonfiction titles: *So's Your Old Man: A Curmudgeon's Words to His Son* by Peter Cross; *Fishing in the Stars: The Education of Namory Keita* by Donald Lawder; *Home to India* by Jacqueline Singh (originally published in New Delhi by Penguin, India).

News from the subrights front: *Résumé with Monsters* (science fiction), by William Browning Spencer, has garnered foreign rights in at least two countries—Germany and Italy. The film option for *An Occasional Hell* (mystery), by Randall Silvis, became an official purchase when the cameras started to roll.

The house has also brought back all the original works (and some new ones) by Marco Vassi—works that gained Vassi a reputation as the best erotic writer of his generation. The Vassi Collection is a 10-volume offering of erotic fiction that has hitherto been long out of print and generally unavailable. Titles in the Vassi Collection: *The Stoned Apoca-*

lypse; Mind Blower; The Gentle Degenerate; The Saline Solution; Contours of Darkness; The Devil's Sperm Is Cold; The Sensual Mirror; Slave Lover. More from Vassi: *A Driving Passion; The Erotic Comedies; The Other Hand Clapping.*

Permanent Press handles its own distribution. Query letters and SASEs should be directed to:

Judith Shepard, Editor and Copublisher

PERSEA BOOKS, INC.

171 Madison Avenue, New York, NY 10016
212-779-7668
www.perseabooks.com

Persea produces a discriminating list in trade and reference nonfiction, fiction and belles lettres, and poetry. Persea's categories include essays, memoirs, literary criticism, novels and stories, fine arts and art history, scholarly works, social sciences, and gender and cultural studies.

Persea Books (founded by Michael Braziller in 1975) is an independently owned press. The house's titles in the arts are brought out in handsomely designed and produced editions. Persea's contemporary literature has an international cast of eminent writers.

Entrants from the Persea program: *Living on the Margins* (edited by Hilda Raz); *On Leaf and Flower* (edited by Charles Dean and Clyde Wachsberger); *Promise Hill* by Helen Falconer; *The Holocaust Kid* by Sonia Pileer; *A Man and a Woman and a Man* by Savyon Liebrecht; *Fishing for Chickens* (edited by Jim Heynen); *The Return of Felix Nogara* by Pablo Medina.

Persea shares office space with and is distributed by W. W. Norton & Company. Query letters and SASEs should be directed to:

Karen Braziller, Editorial Director

Gabriel Fried, Associate Editor

PERSEUS BOOKS GROUP

Basic Books

Basic Civitas Books

Counterpoint Press

Da Capo Press

Fisher Books

Perseus Publishing

Public Affairs

Westview Press

Perseus Books Group (Headquarters)
10 E. 53rd Street, New York, NY 10022

Massachusetts office:
11 Cambridge Center, Cambridge, MA 02142

The Perseus Books Group was founded in 1997 on the ideal of creating a new publishing model that allows more "quality" titles to be published, without forgoing financial success. This group has eight member publishers, each with a distinct focus and individual strengths. Each Perseus Books Group member company is editorially independent and individually focused, although they each share the common mission of "publishing books that matter."

Perseus Books Group publishes major nonfiction works, as well as literary fiction. It has also developed a backlist in a wide variety of categories.

P

Basic Books

387 Park Avenue South, New York, NY 10016-8810

Basic Books has survived the half-century mark and continues to thrive throughout the turbulence of changes, most recently becoming a member of the Perseus Books Group in 1997. Known for its titles in psychology, history, philosophy, politics, sociology, and anthropology, Basic Books prides itself on "taking the most exciting thinkers of our time and introducing them to a wider reading audience." This house produces serious nonfiction in hardcover and trade paperback formats, often authored by pioneers, scholars, or leaders in respective fields.

Representative titles include *A Problem from Hell: America and the Age of Genocide* by Samantha Power; *Heartbreak: The Political Memoir of a Feminist Militant by* Andrea Dworkin; *The Tsar's Last Armada* by Constantine Pleshakov; *So Others Might Live* by Terry Golway; *The Mystery of Capital: Why Capitalism Succeeds in The West and Fails Everywhere Else* by Hernando de Soto; *The Dawn of Universal History* by Raymond Aron; *The Health of the Country: How American Settlers Understood Themselves and Their Land* by Conevery Bolton Valencius; *The Psychology of the Sopranos: Love, Death, Desire and Betrayal in America's Favorite Gangster Family* by Glen O. Gabbard; *The Company of Critics, Reissue* by Michael Walzer; *Little Red Riding Hood Uncloaked: Ten Moral Tales from the Forest* by Catherine Orenstein; *Three Roads to Quantum Gravity* by Lee Smolin; *Acquiring Genomes: A Theory of the Origins of Species* by Lynn Margulis; *Significant Others* by Craig Stanford; *High Noon: 20 Global Issues, 20 Years to Solve Them* by Jean-François Rischard; *The Other Path* by Hernando de Soto; *Sunlight at Midnight St. Petersburg* and *The Rise of Modern Russia* by W. Bruce Lincoln.

Direct queries and SASEs to:

Liz Maguire, Editor—Cultural history and current affairs

Jo Ann Miller, Editor—Psychology, law, women's studies and current affairs

William Frucht, Editor—Science, economics, technology, and social change

Don Fehr, Editor—History and religion

Vanessa Mobley, Editor: Politics and current affairs, with a special interest in investigative reporting

John Donatich: Publisher

Basic Civitas Books

10 E. 53rd Street, New York, NY 10022-5299
212-207-7600   fax: 212-207-7703

Directed by Henry Louis Gates, Jr., Basic Civitas Books is devoted to publishing original voices in a broad range of African and African American studies. Titles are produced in hardcover and trade paperback formats.

Recent titles indicative of this list: *The Cornel West Reader* by Cornel West; *Africana: The Encyclopedia of the African and African American Experience* by Kwame Anthony Appiah, Henry Louis Gates, Jr. (Editor); *The Hip Hop Generation: The Crisis in African American Culture* by Bakari Kitwana; *Out There: Mavericks of Black Literature* by Darryl Pinckney; *Freedom: Freedom in the Making of Western Culture* by Orlando Patterson.

Counterpoint Press

1627 I Street NW, Suite 500, Washington, DC 20006
202-887-0363, 202-393-8088

Counterpoint Press is the "original" member of the Perseus Books Group and is well-known for its literary fiction and essays from new and established voices, including Wendell Berry, Frederick Barthelme, Evan Connell, Gary Snyder, and James Salter. Counterpoint Press publishes serious literary work, with an emphasis on natural history, science, philosophy and contemporary thought, history, art, poetry, and fiction. Counterpoint produces books in hardcover as well as paperback format.

Although short in years, Counterpoint is already long in awards. Authors published under this imprint have received the PEN/Faulkner Award, the National Book Critics Circle Award, the Bollingen Poetry Prize, the T. S. Eliot Award, the PEN Translation Prize, the Bay Area Book Reviewers Award, the Robert Kirsch Lifetime Achievement Award from the *Los Angeles Times,* the Lannan Lifetime Achievement Award, and the Harold Morton Landon Prize from the Academy of American Poets.

Fiction titles representative of this list include *Bending Heaven: Stories* by Jessica Francis Kane; *The Moth Diaries: A Novel* by Rachel Klein; *Sparrow Nights* by David Gilmour; *Stanley Park* by Timothy Taylor; *Three Short Novels* by Wendell Berry; *The Memory Room* by Mary Rakow; *Running After Antelope* by Scott Carrier; *Odds* by Patty Friedmann; *Cassada* by James Salter.

Nonfiction titles indicative of this list: *Critical Injuries* by Joan Barfoot; *On the Wing: A Young American Abroad* (memoir) by Nora Sayre; *The Room Lit by Roses: A Journal of Pregnancy and Birth* by Carole Maso; *Watershed: The Undamming of America* by Elizabeth Grossman; *With Bold Knife and Fork* by M. F. K. Fisher; *Castaways of the Image Planet: Movies, Show Business, Public Spectacle* by Geoffrey O'Brien; *Reporting Back: Notes on Journalism* by Lillian Ross; *Works on Paper: The Craft of Biography and*

Autobiography Writing by Michael Holroyd; *Body Toxic: An Environmental Memoir* by Suzanne Antonetta; *Following the Sun: From Andalusia to the Hebrides* by John Hanson Mitchell.

Counterpoint Press does not accept unsolicited manuscripts. Query letters and SASEs should be directed to:

Editorial and Publicity, 717 D Street NW, Suite 203, Washington, DC 20004 (202-393-8088; fax 202-393-8488)

Jack Shoemaker, Publisher

Trish Hoard, Executive and Editorial Associate

Da Capo Press

11 Cambridge Center, Cambridge MA 02142
617-252-5200

Da Capo, founded in 1975, has begun moving into original publishing, in addition to continuing its tradition of publishing key reprints in the areas of music and history. Da Capo became a member of the Perseus Books Group in 1999 and maintains offices in Cambridge, Massachusetts, and Manhattan. The house has earned acclaim for its titles in music, particularly jazz, but also classical, pop, rock, blues, and Celtic. Other nonfiction categories, published in hardcover and paperback, are American and world history, film, dance, theater, literature, art and architecture, sports, and African American studies.

Representative titles in general history, American history, European history, and military history include *Crazy Rhythm* by Leonard Garment; *Zin: The History and Mystery of Zinfandel* by David Darlington; *A History of Celibacy* by Elizabeth Abbott; *The Salem Witch Trials Reader* by Frances Hill; *A Delusion of Satan: The Full Story of the Salem Witch Trials* by Frances Hill; *My Day: The Best of Eleanor Roosevelt's Newspaper Columns; Allies for Freedom & Blacks on John Brown* by Benjamin Quarles; *The Last Madam: A Life in the New Orleans Underworld* by Christine Wiltz; *The Templars: The Dramatic History of the Knights Templar* by Piers Paul Read; *A Rum Affair: A True Story of Botanical Fraud* by Karl Sabbagh; *A History in Fragments: Europe in the 20th Century* by Richard Vinen; *The Sisters of Henry VIII* by Maria Perry; *Allies: Pearl Harbor to D-Day* by John S. D. Eisenhower; *Foot Soldier: A Combat Infantryman's War in Europe* by Roscoe C. Blunt.

Titles indicative of Da Capo's rich music list include *Like Young: Jazz, Pop, Youth, and Middle Age* by Frances Davis; *The Da Capo Jazz and Blues Lover's Guide* by Christiane Bird; *Satchmo: The Genius of Louis Armstrong* by Gary Giddins; *Kind of Blue* by Ashley Kahn; *Backbeat: Earl Palmer's Story* by Tony Scherrman; *Jazz in the Bittersweet Blues of Life* by Wynton Marsalis and Carl Vigeland; *The Dylan Companion* by Elizabeth Thomson and David Gutman; *A Cure for Gravity: A Musical Pilgrimage* by Joe Jackson; *Beat Punks* by Victor Bockris; *Can't You Hear Me Calling? The Life of Bill Monroe, Father of Bluegrass* by Richard D. Smith; *My First 79 Years* by Isaac Stern; *Celtic Music: A Complete Guide* by June Skinner Sawyers; *Hank Williams, Snapshots from the Lost Highway* by Colin Escott and Kira Florita.

Other nonfiction titles on this list: *Sports Guy* by Charles P. Pierce; *Friday Night Lights* by H. G. Bissinger; *What a Time It Was: The Best Sportswriting of W. C. Heinz; The Leaf and the Cloud* by Mary Oliver; *The Nick Tosches Reader; The Autobiography of Joseph Stalin* by Richard Lourie; *About Town:* The New Yorker *and the World It Made* by Ben Yagoda; *Endangered Species: Writers Talk About Their Craft, Their Visions, Their Lives* by Lawrence Grobel.

Authors on Da Capo's eclectic backlist include Duke Ellington, Harrison Salisbury, Walker Evans, Gary Giddins, Loretta Lynn, Groucho Marx, Nick Tosches, Diana Vreeland, Louis Armstrong, Eleanor Roosevelt, Peter Guralnick, Mary Oliver, H. G. Bissinger, Nat Hentoff, Ned Rorem, Joe Jackson, John S. D. Eisenhower, Albert Murray, Dore Ashton, Jonathan Schell, and Donald Spoto.

Da Capo Press accepts unsolicited manuscripts. Please send your query letter, SASEs, and/or manuscript to:

John Radziewicz, Publisher

Andrea Schultz, Executive Editor

P

Fisher Books

Fisher Books, the most recent addition of the Perseus Books Group, publishes nonfiction guides to pregnancy and parenting, as well as popular guides to health and nutrition, in hardcover and paperback format.

Titles representative of this list include *Baby and Toddler Learning Fun: 50 Interactive and Developmental Activities to Enjoy with Your Child* by Sally R. Goldberg, Ph.D.; *Getting the Lead Out: The Complete Resource for Preventing and Coping with Lead Poisoning* by Irene Kessel, et al.; *Custom Auto Interiors* by Don Taylor and Ron Mangus; *Your Pregnancy Questions & Answers* by Glade B. Curtis, M.D., et al.; *Dr. Paula's Good Nutrition Guide for Babies, Toddlers, and Preschoolers: Answers to Parents' Most Common Questions Plus Help for Coping with Fussy Eaters* by Paula M. Elbirt, M.D.; *Living with Anxiety: A Clinically Tested Step-by-Step Plan for Drug-Free Management* by Bob Montgomery and Laurel Morris; *Your Pregnancy After 35* by Glade B. Curtis M.D., et al.; *The Mediterranean Heart Diet: How It Works and How to Reap the Health Benefits, with Recipes to Get You Started* by Helen V. Fisher, et al.; *Being Happy Being Married: A Guide to Building a Better Relationship* by Lee Schnebly, M.Ed.; *Raising Confident Boys: 100 Tips for Parents and Teachers* by Elizabeth Hartley; *Fiber and Your Health* by Jeanette Parsons Egan; *Nurturing Yourself and Others: Learn How to Fill Your Life with Happiness* by Lee Schnebly; *Landscape Plants for Dry Regions: More Than 600 Species from Around the World* by Warren D. Jones and Charles Sacamano.

Direct queries and SASEs to:

Helen Fisher, Publisher

Perseus Publishing

Perseus Publishing was created when the Perseus Books Group acquired Addison Wesley's trade list. Perseus has made a name for itself with titles published in the categories of health, pregnancy and parenting, business, and technology. It also produces select titles in self-help, psychology, fitness, and general nonfiction.

Titles indicative of this list include (Business): *Anytime, Anywhere: How the Best Bricks-and-Clicks Businesses Deliver Seamless Service to Their Customers* by Robert Spector; *Work 2.0: Rewriting the Contract* by Bill Jensen; *New Ideas About New Ideas: Insights on Creativity from the World's Leading Innovators* by Shira P. White with G. Patton Wright; (Science): *Linked, The New Science of Networks* by Albert-László Barabási; *Flatterland: Like Flatland Only More So* by Ian Stewart; *The Dragon Seekers: How an Extraordinary Circle of Fossilists Discovered the Dinosaurs and Paved the Way for Darwin* by Christopher McGowan; (Health & Fitness): *Your Genetic Destiny: Know Your Genes and Save Your Life* by Aubrey Milunsky, M.D., D.Sc.; *Jonny Bowden's Shape Up! The 8-Week Program to Turn Around Your Body, Your Health, Your Life* by Jonny Bowden, M.A., C.N.; *Hot Point Fitness: The Revolutionary New Program for Fast and Total Body Transformation* by Steve Zim and Mark Laska; (Psychology and Self Help): *Out of Its Mind, Psychiatry in Crisis: A Call for Reform* by J. Allan Hobson and Jonathan A. Leonard; *Not Your Mother's Life: Changing the Rules of Work, Love, and Family* by Joan K. Peters; (Parenting & Pregnancy): *Toilet Trained for Yale: Adventures in 21st Century Parenting* by Ralph Schoenstein; *The Secure Child: Helping Children Feel Safe and Confident in an Insecure World* by Stanley I. Greenspan, M.D.; *Make Your Own Preschool Games: A Personalized Play and Learn Program* by Sally R. Goldberg, Ph.D.; (General Interest): *A Twentieth Century Journey in Science and Politics* by Edward Teller and Judith Shoolery; *A Faceless Enemy: The Origins of Modern Terrorism* by Carole Dorsch Schweitzer.

Perseus Publishing accepts proposals in the areas of business, science, parenting, psychology, health, and general nonfiction. Please send a cover letter and sample chapter with SASE to:

Nicholas Philipson, Executive Editor—Business subjects

Marnie Cochran, Senior Editor—Health, parenting, general self-help/how-to

Amanda Cook, Senior Editor—Popular science

Public Affairs

250 West 57th Street, Suite 1321, New York, NY 10107
212-397-6666

Public Affairs publishes original nonfiction works by field experts from journalists and politicians, to political dissidents and leaders in the arts. Perhaps it is most well-known for the success of *The Tiananmen Papers,* which made front-page news due to its exposition of the force used by Chinese leaders during protests in 1989.

Public Affairs produces titles from authors such as Jane Alexander, Jim Lehrer, Boris Yeltsin, Vladimir Putin, Garrick Utley, and Andy Rooney.

Titles indicative of this list: *Gracefully Insane: The Rise and Fall of America's Premier Mental Hospital* by Alex Beam; *The Cat from Hue* by John Laurence; *Booknotes* by Brian Lamb; *Henry Ford and the Jews* by Neil Baldwin; *The Oligarchs* by David E. Hoffman; *First Job* by Rinker Buck; *JFK, Nixon, Oliver Stone and Me* by Eric Hamburg; *Washing-*

ton by Meg Greenfield, et al.; *What Dying People Want: Practical Wisdom for the End of Life* by David Kuhl; *The Courage of Strangers: Coming of Age with the Human Rights Movement* by Jeri Laber; *A Soldier of the Revolution* by Ward S. Just; *Bold Women, Big Ideas: Learning to Play the High-Risk Entrepreneurial Game* by Kay Koplovitz, Peter Israel (Contributor); *Horse of a Different Color: A Tale of Breeding Geniuses, Dominant Females, and the Fastest Derby Winner Since Secretariat* by Jim Squires; *A Great, Silly Grin: The British Satire Boom of the 1960s* by Humphrey Carpenter; *The Terrible Gift: The Brave New World of Genetic Medicine* by Rick J. Carlson and Gary Stimeling; *The Underboss: The Rise and Fall of a Mafia Family* by Gerard O'Neill, et al.; *Vietnam, Now: A Reporter Returns* by David Lamb.

Direct query letters and SASEs to:

Kate Darnton, Editor—Current events, biographies, memoirs, women authors

Darrell Jones, Assistant to Publisher

Paul Golob, Executive Editor

Westview Press

5500 Central Avenue, Boulder, CO 80301-2877
303-444-3541

Westview Press, formerly part of HarperCollins, remains a major presence in academic publishing under its new publishing group, Perseus Books. Westview, now in its third decade of publishing, is known for its textbooks and academic monographs. It also publishes some trade titles in politics, history, religion, philosophy, sociology, art history, anthropology, and area studies.

This press was founded in 1975 by Frederick A. Praeger and Maurice B. Mitchell in the basement of their Boulder, Colorado, home on Westview Drive. Though its first list published only 9 books, four years later the list had grown to 169 and kept right on growing. In 1981 all departments were relocated to the present location on Central Avenue. Under the direction and leadership of Fred Praeger, and guided by the motto "Books That Matter," Westview Press continues to grow and prosper. According to Praeger, "We see our future as a sort of knowledge supermarket, where service is enthusiastic, efficient, fast, and highly professional, handling knowledge and information produced by the scholarly and scientific community."

Westview Press produces a wide array of academic and professional books, in addition to undergraduate- and graduate-level texts in the social sciences and humanities. The meat of its broad political science program is the Dilemmas in American Politics, Dilemmas in World Politics, and Transforming American Politics series, which include valuable contributions to these fields, such as Susan Tolchin's *The Angry American;* Paula McClain and Joseph Stewart, Jr.'s *Can We All Get Along?*; Gareth Porter and Janet Welsh Brown's *Global Environmental Politics;* Ted Gurr and Barbara Harff's *Ethnic Conflict in World Politics;* and Sandy Maisel's *The Parties Respond.* The sociology publishing program at Westview is also among the best in academia. Westview has published classics like Jay MacLeod's *Ain't No Makin' It;* David Wagner's *Checkerboard Square,* winner of the 1993 C. Wright Mills Award; and Charles Lemert's *Sociology After the Crisis.*

Westview is particularly well known for its titles in area studies literature, with best-selling texts like *Latin American Politics and Development,* edited by Howard J. Wiarda and Harvey F. Kline; *A History of the Modern Middle East* by William Cleveland; *A Concise History of the Middle East* by Arthur Goldschmidt, Jr.; *Modern Japan: A Historical Survey* by Mikiso Hane; *Latin America: Its Problems and Its Promise*, edited by Jan Knippers Black. Westview's history list is highlighted by historian William McNeill, who is series editor for Westview's Essays in World History series. Series advisers in military history, another Westview strength, include Arther Ferrill, James M. McPherson, and Kenneth Hagan.

In 1997, Westview acquired IconEditions, a respected HarperCollins art criticism and art history list under the direction of Cass Canfield, Jr. These impeccably produced volumes are now known as WestviewPress/IconEditions, and Westview will continue to offer the classic Icon backlist titles, as well as take the list forward to publish new works of quality and scholarship.

In recent years, Westview has become a recognizable and respected force in trade and general nonfiction publishing, with the release of titles like Joel Dyer's *Harvest of Rage,* Stansfield Turner's *Caging the Nuclear Genie,* Nina Sutton's *Bettelheim: A Life and a Legacy,* Sheila Tobias's *Faces of Feminism,* and Peggy McCarthy's *Breast Cancer? Let Me Check My Schedule!* New titles like *The Double-Edged Sword* by Robert Shogan, *The Freshmen* by Linda Killian, and *Rigoberta Menchu and the Story of All Poor Guatemalans* by David Stoll are "books that matter," and Westview is committed to publishing these books and others like them as the press dances on the cutting edge of nonfiction trade publishing.

Westview's success, according to founder Fred Praeger, "will be measured by the contribution we can make to the harmony, the balance, and the survivability of this world."

Westview Press is not accepting any unsolicited packages or letters. Query letters and book proposals may be sent electronically to wvproposal@perseusbooks.com.

Holly Hodder, Vice President and Publisher

Jill Rothenberg, Senior Editor—Sociology, current affairs, gender studies

Karl Yambert, Senior Editor—Anthropology, archaeology, area studies

Sarah Warner, Senior Editor—Film studies, religion, philosophy

---

PETERSON'S

202 Carnegie Center, PO Box 2123, Princeton, NJ 08540
609-243-9111   fax: 609-243-9150
www.petersons.com

Peterson's is the country's largest educational information/communications company, providing the academic, consumer, and professional communities with books, software, and online services in support of lifelong education access and career choice. Peterson's, founded in 1966, publishes such well-known references as its annual guides to graduate and professional job hunting programs, colleges and universities, financial aid, private schools, standardized test-prep, summer programs, international study, executive education, job hunting, and career opportunities, as well as a full line of software offering career guidance and information for adult learners. Many of Peterson's reference works are updated annually. Peterson's is a Thomson company.

Peterson's markets strongly to libraries and institutions, as well as to the corporate sector.

Newly authored frontlist titles include *The Ultimate College Survival Guide* by Janet Farrar Worthington and Ronald Farrar; *The Ultimate Job Search Guide* by Paul L. Dyer; *The Ultimate New Employee Survival Guide* by Ed Holton; *The Ultimate Home Office Survival Guide* by Sunny Baker and Kim Baker. Authored backlist titles include *The Colorblind Career* by Ollie Stevenson; *Portfolio Power* by Martin Kimeldorf; *How to Write a Winning Personal Statement for Graduate and Professional School* by Richard J. Seltzer; *Paralegal* by Barbara Bernardo; *Virtual College* by Pam Dixon; *Financing Graduate School* by Patricia McWade; *Smart Parents' Guide to College* by Dr. Ernest Boyer and Paul Boyer.

Query letters and SASEs should be directed to:

Eileen Fiore, Executive Assistant, Research and Editorial Development—Interests consistent with house list

Ian Gallagher, Senior Editor—Test preparation

P

PFEIFER-HAMILTON PUBLISHERS & WHOLE PERSON ASSOCIATES

210 West Michigan Street, Duluth, MN 55802-1908
218-727-0500, 800-247-6789   fax: 218-727-0505
www.wholeperson.com   e-mail: books@wholeperson.com

Pfeifer-Hamilton produces publications in self-awareness, motivation, and improvement; inspirational works; books on peace and healing; and select children's titles. Additional Pfeifer focus is on gift books and books that celebrate the special beauty and unique lifestyle of the North Country.

This house offers books that awaken your senses, excite your imagination, make you laugh, make you cry, touch your heart, and give you hope; books that inspire creativity, critical thinking, inner change, and personal growth.

Whole Person Associates, which was founded in 1977, develops a noteworthy lineup of stress-management and wellness training materials, including books, audiotapes, and videotapes. The house has achieved increasing market penetration. P-H's marketing strategy is to concentrate promotional efforts regionally prior to inaugurating national campaigns.

Titles by Sam Cook, Pfeifer-Hamilton's first author: *If This Is Mid-Life, Where's the Crisis?; Up North; Quiet Magic; CampSights* (illustrated by Bob Cary).

On the Pfeifer-Hamilton list: *Connections & Reflections: Mothers & Daughters in Their Own Light, in Their Own Words* by Catherine Koemptgen; *Christmas Song of the North* by Marsha Bonicatto (watercolors by Karlyn Holman); *Time at the Lake: A Minnesota Album* by William Albert Allard; *Not Now—I'm Having a No-Hair Day: Humor and Healing for People with Cancer* by Christine Clifford (illustrated by Jack Lindstrom); *Journey of the Heart: Spiritual Insights on the Road to a Transplant* by Beth

P

Bartlett; *Kicking Your Holiday Stress Habits* by Donald A. Tubesing and Nancy Loving Tubesing (W.P.A.); *Our Family Has Cancer, Too!* by Christine Clifford (illustrated by Jack Lindstrom*); Building Community* by Kent Curtis, George Manning, and Steve McMillen; *Desktop Yoga* by Julie Lusk; *Parenting on the Go* by L. Tobin.

Whole Person Associates develops and publishes stress-management and wellness-promotion training and self-care resources for health professionals, counselors, trainers, therapists, consultants, educators, and group leaders. Titles here: *Instant Icebreakers: 50 Powerful Catalysts for Group Interaction and High-Impact Learning* by Sandy Stewart Christian and Nancy Loving Tubesing; *Sleep Secrets for Shift Workers & People with Off-Beat Schedules* by David Morgan; *Don't Get Mad, Get Funny!: A Light-Hearted Approach to Stress Management* by Leigh Anne Jasheway (illustrated by Geoffrey M. Welles); *Working with Groups to Overcome Panic, Anxiety, & Phobias: Structured Exercises in Healing* by Shirley Babior and Carol Goldman.

Whole Person Associates also offers a wide variety of relaxation and healing audiotapes, as well as videotapes on achieving healthful lifestyles and managing job stress. On the video list: *Team Esteem Overview; Building Communication in the Workplace; Empowerment and Wellness in the Workplace; Developing Mission and Purpose; Putting Team Esteem to Work.*

Pfeifer-Hamilton Publishers oversees its own distribution. Query letters and SASEs should be directed to:

Carlene Sippola, Publisher, Whole Person Associates

PLENUM PUBLISHING GROUP

The entire Plenum program was acquired in 1999 by the independent Perseus Group. Its frontlist acquisition program is being reorganized. The Spring Street offices have been closed.

POCKET BOOKS/ATRIA BOOKS

1230 Avenue of the Americas, New York, NY 10020
212-698-7000

Pocket Books, which is now strictly a paperback publisher and which was founded in 1939, was America's first publisher of paperback books. Today, Pocket is producing general-interest fiction and nonfiction books in mass-market paperback, trade paperback, and hardcover format.

Recent titles that Pocket has published in hardcover include *The Cat and the Tao* by Kwong Kuen Shan; *The Summerhouse* by Jude Deveraux; *Untitled Vince Flynn #5* by Vince Flynn; *The Camino* by Shirley MacLaine; *The Astrology of Time* by Gary Goldschneider; *The Intelligencer* by Leslie Silbert; *Good in Bed* by Jennifer Weiner.

Other titles representative of Pocket Books: *Maggody and the Moonbeams* by Joan Hess; *Untitled Tally Nowata Book* by Hannah Nyala; *Larousse French English Dictionary Canadian Edition* by Larousse; *Mercy* by Julie Garwood; *Bad Boy: The Influence of Sean "Puffy" Combs on the Music Industry* by Ronin Ro; *The Core* by Dean Wesley Smith.

Pocket Books was recently reorganized into autonomous hardcover and paperback programs. To help give the hardcover program a distinct identity, it has been given a new imprint, Atria Books. The imprint will continue the Pocket tradition of publishing commercial mass market titles.

Direct query letters and SASEs to:

Amanda Ayers, Associate Editor

Amy Pierpont, Senior Editor

Caroline Tolley, Senior Editor—Historical romances

Emily Bestler, Vice President and Executive Editorial Direction, Atria Books—Commercial fiction and nonfiction

George Lucas, Senior Editor, Atria Books—Thrillers, commercial male-oriented fiction and nonfiction

Brenda Copeland, Editor

Jason Kaufiran, Senior Editor

Kate Collins, Editor

Kim Kanner, Editor, Atria Books—Memoir, spirituality, literary and commercial fiction, health and wellness, narrative nonfiction, Asian voices

Kip Hakala, Associate Editor

Marco Palmieri, Editor

Mitchell Ivers, Senior Editor—Commercial fiction and celebrity nonfiction

Maggie Crawford, Vice President and Editorial Director—Women's fiction

Tracy Bernstein, Editor—Health, pop psychology, general nonfiction

Jessica McGivney, Associate Editor—Science fiction

Greer Kessel-Hendricks, Senior Editor, Atria Books—Literary and commercial fiction, narrative nonfiction, memoir, lifestyle

Tracy Behar, Vice President and Editorial Direction, Atria Books—Spirituality, Buddhism, narrative nonfiction (especially science and history), self-help and personal development, health, family

Rosemary Ahern, Vice President, Director of Washington Square Press—Literary fiction and narrative nonfiction in areas of history, women's studies, cultural issues

Malaika Adero, Senior Editor, Atria Books—Literary fiction, narrative nonfiction, health and fitness, spirituality, memoir, biography, African American interests, art, culture

Luke Dempsey, Senior Editor, Atria Books—Narrative nonfiction, sports (especially baseball and golf), popular culture, literary and commercial fiction, popular history

Sarah Branham, Associate Editor, Atria Books—Commercial fiction, memoir, biography, history, health, personal and family development

Brenda Copeland, Associate Editor, Atria Books—Literary and commercial fiction (especially Canadian voices), narrative nonfiction, practical self-help and personal development, astrology

Suzanne O'Neill, Assistant Editor, Atria Books—Literary fiction, humor, human interest, narrative nonfiction, memoir, pop culture, social issues.

Wendy Walker, Assistant Editor, Atria Books—Narrative nonfiction (especially true crime), popular culture, literary and commercial fiction.

POMEGRANATE COMMUNICATIONS, INC.

Box 6099, Rohnert Park, CA 94927
707-586-5500, 800-227-1428   fax: 707-586-5518
www.pomegranatecommunications.com   e-mail: info@pomegranate.com

Pomegranate publishes an attractive array of graphically lavish books and specialty items geared to interests such as fine art, contemporary art, architecture, travel, ethnic culture, and crafts. Pomegranate is among the premier publishers of calendars of all types and stripes, posters and poster art, note cards, games and puzzles, specialty sets, and popular topical card decks.

Sample titles include *Sunday Afternoon, Looking for the Car: The Aberrant Art of Barry Kite* by Alan Bisbort; *Cultivating Sacred Space: Gardening for the Soul* by Elizabeth Murray; *CatDreams* by B. Kliban; *Maxfield Parrish: A Retrospective* by Laurence S. Cutler and Judy Goffman Cutler; *Edward Hopper's New England* by Carl Little; *The Collectible Art of Susan Seddon Boulet.* The Little Wright Books Series showcases the work of Frank Lloyd Wright, with each volume focusing on a particular topic. Titles by Carla Lind: *Frank Lloyd Wright's California Houses; Frank Lloyd Wright's First Houses; Frank Lloyd Wright's Public Buildings; Frank Lloyd Wright's Prairie Houses; Frank Lloyd Wright's Lost Buildings; Frank Lloyd Wright's Fireplaces; Frank Lloyd Wright's Dining Rooms.*

Pomegranate is an independent house and operates its own distributional network, including foreign representation worldwide. Query letters and SASEs should be directed to:

Submissions Department

PRENTICE HALL DIRECT (PART OF PEARSON EDUCATION GROUP)
Prentice Hall Press

At press time, the Prentice Hall trade program was terminated.

PRESIDIO PRESS

PO Box 1764, Novato, CA 94948-1764
415-898-1081   fax: 415-898-0383

Presidio is known for works in such areas as general military history, American history, aviation, biography and memoirs, world wars, Korean War, Vietnam, African American studies, military theory, and professional studies. Presidio also issues a small number of superior fiction titles that favor a military-historical milieu.

Presidio Press (founded in 1974) is America's foremost publisher of military history. The house emphasizes both popular and scholarly works, especially those with potential for backlist endurance. Presidio publishes in hardcover and quality paperback editions.

Nonfiction from Presidio: *Shadow Flights: America's Secret Air War Against the Soviet Union: A Cold War History* by Curtis Peebles; *Black Sheep One: The Life of Gregory "Pappy" Boyington* by Bruce Gamble; *With the Old Corps in Nicaragua* by George B. Clark; *Formidable Enemies: The North Korean and Chinese Soldier in the Korean War* by Kevin Mahoney; *Carlson's Raid: The Daring Assault on Makin* by George W. Smith; *Spirit, Blood, and Treasure: The American Cost of Battle in the 21st Century* (edited by Donald Vandergriff); *Somalia on Five Dollars a Day: A Soldier's Story* by Martin Stanton; *Beyond the Rhine: A Screaming Eagle in Germany* by Donald R. Burgett; *A Few Good Men: The Fighting Fifth Marines: A History of the USMC's Most Decorated Regiment* by Ronald J. Brown; *His Time in Hell: A Texas Marine in France: The World War I Memoir of Warren R. Jackson* (edited by George B. Clark); *What They Didn't Teach You About the 60's* by Mike Wright; *Afternoon of the Rising Sun: The Battle of Leyte Gulf* by Kenneth I. Friedman*; By Their Deeds Alone: America's Combat Commanders on the Art of War* (edited by Richard D. Hooker, Jr.).

Presidio's Gulf War memoir *She Went to War: The Rhonda Cornum Story* by flight surgeon Rhonda Cornum, as told to Peter Copeland, garnered considerable subsidiary-rights interest—including a high-profile television-movie.

Presidio Press titles, as well as those associated imprints (such as British military publisher Greenhill Books), are distributed to the book trade in the United States and Canada through National Book Network. Query letters and SASEs should be directed to:

E. J. McCarthy, Executive Editor

PROFESSIONAL PUBLICATIONS, INC.

1250 Fifth Avenue, Belmont, CA 94002-3863
650-593-9119
www.ppi2pass.com

Professional Publications publishes titles in engineering, architecture, and interior design, as well as works aimed toward the broader business and professional trade arena. The house produces books and educational aids (such as audiocassettes, videos, software, and study guides) for the professional market.

Professional Publications (established in 1981) earned initial success with examination-preparation packages (reference manuals, ancillary workbooks, sample exams, and solved problem books) for the professional engineering license examination given to applicants in the major engineering disciplines. Once this niche market was secured, the house branched into wider publishing territory.

On the Professional Publications list: *FE Review Manual, Civil Engineering Reference Manual,* and *Mechanical Engineering Reference Manual,* all by Michael R. Lindeburg; *Interior Construction and Detailing for Designers and Architects* and *Interior Design Reference Manual,* both by David K. Ballast.

Professional Publications oversees its own distribution. Query letters and SASEs should be directed to:

Aline S. Magee, Acquisitions Editor

PROMETHEUS BOOKS

59 John Glenn Drive, Amherst, NY 14228-2197
716-691-0133, 800-421-0351   fax: 716-564-2711
www.prometheusbooks.com   e-mail: editorial@prometheusbooks.com

Prometheus catalogs works with challenging stances on contemporary issues. The house is particularly strong in popular science, science and the paranormal, biblical criticism, religion and politics, politics and current events, consumer health and fitness, philosophy, humanism, free thought, sports, human sexuality and sexual autobiography, literature and literary history, popular culture, creation versus evolution, religion, and education, as well as reference works in allied fields and occasional works of fiction. Prometheus also publishes books for young readers, produces a line of titles on human aging, and serves the educational market with several series of modestly priced classics in reprint (including Great Books in Philosophy, Literary Classics, and Great Minds). The house offers select works in electronic format.

Prometheus Books (established in 1969) produces an ambitious frontlist that embraces a wide range of perennially popular nonfiction topics; more enduring titles are backlisted indefinitely.

Prometheus also publishes the following periodicals: *Scientific Review of Alternative Medicine* (a peer-reviewed medical journal providing objective, scientific assessments of the treatments, methods, and hypotheses of unconventional medicine—the realm of acupuncture, homeopathy, herbal therapies, therapeutic touch, "miraculous" cancer treatments, and more); *Nutrition Forum* (bimonthly newsletter on the frontline of the anti–health fraud movement); *The Journal for the Critical Study of Religion, Ethics, and Society* (articles in the area of religious studies and scholarly assessments of society, ethics, and culture that have a bearing on the understanding of religion; the journal seeks to promote a broadly humanistic understanding of culture).

On the Prometheus list: *A Solstice Tree for Jenny* by Karen Shragg; *A Treatise on Painting* by Leonardo da Vinci, translated by John Francis Rigaud; *Abnormal Pap Smears* by Lynda Rushing, M.D., and Nancy Joste, M.D.; *Air Rage* by Anonymous and Andrew R. Thomas; *Awakening of a Jehovah's Witness* by Diane Wilson; *Catholic Power vs. American Freedom* by Fr. George La Piana and John M. Swomley; *Civic Justice* by Peter Murphy; *Classic Tales and Fables for Children* by Leo Tolstoy; *Cosmic Discoveries* by David H. Levy and Wendee Wallach-Levy; *Decisions, Decisions* by David A. Welch; *Defining Dialogue* by Geoffrey Rockwell; *Demons of the Modern World* by Malcolm McGrath; *Don't Get Dumped!* by Dr. Larry M. Forness; *Down and Out in Silicon Valley* by Mel Krantzler, Ph.D., and Patricia Biondi Krantzler, M.A.; *Ecohumanism* (edited by Robert B. Tapp); *False Start* by Henry Wassermann; *Great Quotations on Religious Freedom* (compiled and edited by Albert J.

Menendez and Edd Doerr); *Is Nature Supernatural?* by Simon L. Altmann; *Jews Without Judaism* by Rabbi Daniel Friedman; *Life and Death on Your Own Terms* by L. L. Basta, M.D.; *Patriotism* (edited by Igor Primoratz); *Pornography, Sex and Feminism* by Alan Soble; *Radioactive Substances* by Marie Curie; *The Philosophy of the Present* by George Herbert Mead; *The Zaddik* by Elaine Grudin Deholtz; *Virtue Ethics* by Richard Taylor.

Prometheus Books introduces the Literary Classics line. This is a series of attractive, moderately priced paperback editions of classic authors (in both poetry and prose) whose works embody free inquiry and free thought. Titles here: *The Turn of the Screw: The Lesson of the Master* by Henry James; *The Awakening* by Kate Chopin; *Main Street* by Sinclair Lewis; *The Confidence Man* by Herman Melville.

Please note: Though known primarily as a house that operates on an advance/royalty arrangement, Prometheus has on occasion offered agreements to authors through which the author invests cooperatively in the costs and thus subsidizes publication.

Prometheus distributes its own list. Query letters and SASEs should be directed to:

Steven L. Mitchell, Editorial Director

Mark Hall, Ph.D., Managing Editor/Creative Marketing Coordinator
   Born/sign: May 29, 1952; Gemini.
   Education: Ph.D. from the University of Pennsylvania in Ancient Near Eastern Studies; B.A. in Classics from the University of New York in Buffalo.
   Employment history/editor career path: I originally went to grad school for ancient history with the intent of teaching on a university level. I found out while in school that few positions were available in the area that I specialized in; nonetheless, I finished the degree. In 1990 I applied to Prometheus Books and got the job. I started as the Production Manager and then went on to edit trade books. The production demand to edit trade books was much too high for me, so I eventually left and went to marketing. I also do freelance medical editing for John Wiley & Sons in the department of psychology.
   Personal interests: Ancient Near Eastern History, archaeology, history of the Bible, following modern fiction. I used to write poetry, so I try to keep up with that.
   What would you be doing if you were not an editor? If there had been good opportunities in academics, I would love to be in that field.
   What has been your most successful book that you have acquired to date? Prometheus is known for its midlist books.
   What books have you acquired that make you the most proud? What books that you have acquired reflect the types of books you like to represent? *End of Days* by Erna Paris, which is a story of expulsion of the Jews in Spain at the time of Ferdinand and Isabella. She is a wonderful presenter and can do so in a way that is in great detail and has very interesting twists.
   Do you represent fiction? If so, what do you look for? Prometheus doesn't publish much fiction.
   What do you want to see less of? Works that tend to be narcissistic, self-indulgent, or that talk about boredom of the wealthy.
   Do you represent nonfiction? Yes.
   Do you require book proposals? If so, what do you look for in evaluating a book proposal? Yes. I look for a good, brief synopsis of what the book is about, a table of

P

contents, a sample chapter, who is the competition. I don't usually like to see the entire manuscript.

What process do you use for making a decision? What is the process for acquisition, is there a committee? The Editor in Chief looks at almost every serious submission. We have recently hired two Acquisitions Editors to present material to the committee.

What kinds of nonfiction books do you want to see less of? Self-help, psychology, diet books, New Age, committed scientific evaluations.

Are agents important? Why? Agents are a fact of life in this business. They bring important authors to my attention.

Do you like new writers? Sometimes.

How should writers approach you? With a simple query letter. I would advise authors that sending a proposal on the first attempt is totally inappropriate.

What can writers do to get your attention and to avoid the slush pile? Do your homework.

What have been some of your craziest experiences with submissions? I once received a submission from a man who was recounting his experience 25 years ago in the Himalayas. He was searching for the meaning of life and went up the mountain and almost died. He was then rescued by a hermit and the hermit revealed to him the secrets of the universe.

What have been some of your best experiences with writers or in your job? Steve Allen, who wrote *Dumbth,* has been wonderful to work with. Peter Ustinov has also been a great joy to work with.

What, if anything, makes you different from other editors? My background in ancient eastern history.

Is there anything you would like to see changed in the industry? I would like to see less of a tendency to go with the conglomerates. The rise of Barnes & Noble and Borders, limiting the bookselling markets.

PUSHCART PRESS

Box 380, Wainscott, NY 11975
631-324-9300

Pushcart Press (established in 1972) is a small, personalized house that is emblematic of the mission to provide useful as well as entertaining trade books and reference volumes directed primarily toward writers, editors, small publishers, and literary aficionados; Pushcart Press is also a dedicated forum for fiction and nonfiction works of literary merit, and the house list includes many award-winning volumes.

Pushcart is known as the house that issues the established annual literary anthology *The Pushcart Prize: Best of the Small Presses,* in addition to the classic *The Publish-It-Yourself Handbook: Literary Tradition and How-to Without Commercial or Vanity Publishers* (both works edited by Pushcart Publisher Bill Henderson). *The Pushcart Book of Essays* (edited by Anthony Brandt) expands the house's line of exemplary writing collections.

Ongoing Pushcart Press publishing projects include the Literary Companion series and the Editors' Book Award series.

Titles from Pushcart: *To a Violent Grave: An Oral Biography of Jackson Pollock* by Jeffrey Potter; *Yeshua: The Gospel of St. Thomas* by Alan Decker McNary; *Garden State: A Novel* by Rick Moody; *Imagine a Great White Light* by Sheila Schwartz; *Writing for Your Life* by Sybil Steinberg; the anonymous *Autobiography of an Elderly Woman* (with an afterword by Doris Grumbach); *The Tale of the Ring: A Kaddish* by Frank Stiffel.

Pushcart Press is distributed by W. W. Norton. Query letters and SASEs should be directed to:

Bill Henderson, President

RANDOM HOUSE, INC.

Random House Audio Publishing Group

Random House Children's Books

The Random House Information Group

Random House Trade Group

Random House Ventures

1540 Broadway, New York, NY 10036
212-354-6500

Random House Inc., a division of the Bertelsmann Book Group of Bertelsmann AG, is the world's largest English-language general trade book publisher. Founded in 1925, Random House has grown into an intricate web of divisions, publishing groups, and imprints. The span of this house's titles runs both wide and deep, including a broad array of categories in both commercial fiction and nonfiction. Random House publishes titles in hardcover, trade paperback, mass-market paperback, audio, electronic, and digital, for adults, young adults, and children.

When Random House, Inc., was acquired by Bertelsmann in 1998, the imprints of the former Random House, Inc., and those of the former Bantam Doubleday Dell were joined to form the Bantam Dell Publishing Group. Random House, Inc.'s other publishing groups include Ballantine Books, the Crown Publishing Group, the Doubleday Broadway Publishing Group, the Knopf Publishing Group, the Random House Audio Publishing Group, Random House Children's Books, the Random House Diversified Publishing Group, the Random House Information Group, the Random House Trade Publishing Group, and Random House Ventures.

Random House accepts only manuscripts submitted by an agent. It does not accept unsolicited submissions, proposals, manuscripts, or submission queries via e-mail at this time. Direct queries to:

Ann Godoff, Publisher—Nonfiction: contemporary issues; commercial and literary fiction

Katie Hall, Senior Editor—Wide range of interests consistent with the house list

Jonathan Karp, Vice President, Executive Editor

Lee Boudreau, Editor—Fiction and narrative nonfiction

Random House Children's Books

Random House Children's Books consists of two editorial divisions and their respective imprints, series, and licenses: the Knopf Delacorte Dell Young Readers Group and the Random House Young Readers Group:

Knopf Delacorte Dell Young Readers Group

Alfred A. Knopf

Bantam

Crown

David Fickling Books

Delacorte Press

Dell Dragonfly

Dell Laurel-Leaf

Dell Yearling Books

Doubleday

Wendy Lamb Books

Random House Young Readers Group

Beginner Books

Disney

Sesame Workshop

Picturebacks

Step into Reading

Stepping Stones

LucasBooks

Landmark Books

First Time Books

Random House Children's Books produces books for preschool children through young adult readers, in all formats from boardbooks to activity books to picture books and novels.

Random House Children's Books publishes the mega-selling Dr. Seuss Books (more than 400 million copies) and other well-known licenses, such as Arthur, the Berenstain Bears, Disney, Sesame Workshop, and Thomas the Tank Engine.

Random House also publishes many of young readers' favorite authors, including Judy Blume, Robert Cormier, Madeleine L'Engle, Leo Lionni, Mary Pope Osborne, Gary Paulsen, Tamora Pierce, Philip Pullman, Faith Ringgold, and Jerry Spinelli. Random House is the publisher of Christopher Paul Curtis's novel *Bud, Not Buddy,* winner of the 2000 John Newbery Medal and the Coretta Scott King Author Award, and David Almond's novel *Kit's Wilderness,* winner of the 2001 Michael L. Printz Award.

In August 2001, Random House, Inc., acquired all the book-publishing properties of Golden Books Family Entertainment, which produces storybooks, coloring and activity books, puzzle books, educational workbooks, reference books, novelty books, and chapter books. The Golden Books publishing program features *Blue's Clues, Rugrats, Bob the Builder,* and *Barbie,* and the Little Golden Books series publishes classic favorites such as *Pat the Bunny,* and *The Poky Little Puppy.* Random House Children's Books is currently integrating the Golden Books publishing program into its own.

Other recent news at Random House includes a promising venture with Disney Publishing Worldwide to create a new line of books based on Disney properties and featuring characters like Mickey Mouse, Winnie the Pooh, and Cinderella. This new imprint, **Disney Books for Young Readers**, was launched in January of 2001 and features a wide array of books that includes coloring and activity books, storybooks, novelty books, and early readers. All of these books draw upon classic Disney films such as *The Little Mermaid, The Lion King, Atlantis,* and *Monsters, Inc.*

Random House has a number of book series specifically designed for young readers, including the Stepping Stones first chapter book series, Marvin Redpost and A to Z Mysteries, the Magic Tree House, and Junie B. Jones series. Replica, Dinoverse, and Francine Pascal's SVH Senior Year are popular series aimed at middle-grade and young adult readers.

In addition to series, Random House Children's Books publishes popular fiction such as *Anne of Green Gables, Where the Red Fern Grows,* and *The Phantom Tollbooth,* as well as Newbery Honor– and Medal–winning books such as *The Watsons Go to Birmingham—1963, Lily's Crossing, Holes, A Wrinkle in Time, The Giver, The Dark-Thirty,* and *Shabanu.* The Random House list also features Caldecott Honor– and Medal–winning books, such as *Tar Beach, Time Flies, Song and Dance Man,* and the late Leo Lionni's *Frederick, Swimmy,* and *Alexander and the Wind-Up Mouse.*

Query letters and SASEs should be directed to:

Diana Capriotti, Senior Editor, Bantam

Janet Schulman, Vice President, Knopf/Crown

Nancy Siscoe, Executive Editor, Knopf/Crown

Nancy Hinkel, Editor, Knopf/Crown

Mallory Loehr, Editor in Chief, Random House

Jim Thomas, Editor, Random House

Courtney Devon Silk, Editor, Random House, mass market

Dennis Shealy, Senior Editor, Disney Books

Random House Information Group

Fodor's Travel Publications

Living Language

Princeton Review

Prima Games

Random House Español

Random House Puzzles & Games

Random House Reference Publishing

A division of Random House, Inc., the Information Group publishes a well-developed list of consumer reference and dictionary titles, language study courses and academic test preparation titles. For a full list of Random House Information Group titles, please visit the Random House Web site at www.randomhouse.com.

Fodor's Travel Publications, the world's largest English-language travel information publisher, has more than 440 travel titles to destinations worldwide. Fodor's Travel Publications is a unit of Fodor's LLC, a subsidiary of Random House, Inc., and its parent company, Bertelsmann AG, one of the world's largest media companies. For more information about Fodor's, visit the Web site at www.fodors.com. For information about other recent releases from Fodor's, visit the press center at www.fodors.com/company/press.html.

Fodor's publishes niche market travel guidebooks, as well as more traditional guides that offer practical information on popular destinations worldwide. Fodor's publishes over 14 different series to address every type of travel experience imaginable. These include the flagship Gold Guides series, Fodor's FYI, Escape, Around the City with Kids, To Go, and Fodor's Road Guides USA.

Living Language is one of the most well-known names in both foreign-language and English-language instruction. Publishing courses that meet a variety of needs, Living Language offers a wide range of programs, including Complete Basic Courses; the All-Audio, Ultimate, In-Flight, and English for New Americans series; and the popular Daily Phrase & Culture Calendars. The Living Language line includes books, cassettes, CDs, and videos in 23 languages.

The world's leader in electronic entertainment publishing, **Prima Games** publishes strategy guides for PC and console games. For a full list of titles, visit the Prima Games Web site at www.primagames.com. If you're an experienced strategy guide author or an expert gamer who loves to write, please send a resume and writing sample to Prima Games, 3000 Lava Ridge Court, Roseville, CA 95661.

Random House Español publishes Spanish- language books covering many subjects, including biography, history, health care, reference, self-help, spiritual and astrological, and practical how-to books. Further augmenting these offerings, Random House Español distributes titles from the diverse publishing programs of Random House's affiliate Spanish-language publishing companies: Plaza & Jans in Spain and Mexico, as well as Sudamericana in Argentina. With this combined strength, Random House Español offers one of the largest and most diverse lists of Spanish language books available in the United States.U.S.

Random House Puzzles & Games publishes crossword puzzle books, including those drawn from the pages of the *Los Angeles Times,* the *Boston Globe,* and the *New York Times.* The imprint recently added a line of Dell Crossword puzzle books, as well as trivia books on baseball by Jeffrey and Doug Lyons.

The Princeton Review imprint publishes books that help students sharpen their academic skills, prepare for standardized tests, and gain entrance into college and graduate school. Representative titles include *Cracking the SAT, The Best 331 Colleges,* and *Word Smart,* the flagship title of the Princeton Review's "Smart" series.

Random House Reference Publishing is a leading publisher of reference works in both print and electronic formats. Its lexicography program is highly regarded for its inclusion of new words in the English language earlier than most other reference publishers. Classic titles include *Random House Webster's College Dictionary, Random House Webster's Unabridged Dictionary, Random House Roget's College Thesaurus,* and *Random House Historical Dictionary of American Slang.* Random House Reference also publishes a line of trade reference titles such as *Verbal Advantage* by Charles Elster, *Finding a Place Called Home: A Guide to African-American Genealogy and Historical Identity* by Dr. Dee Parmer Woodtor, and *The Random House Treasury of Best-Loved Poems.* In 2002, the Random House Reference group will be publishing a completely new edition of the *Random House Webster's Unabridged Dictionary.*

The Random House Trade Publishing Group

Random House Trade Books

Villard Books

The Modern Library

Random House Trade Paperbacks

Random House Trade Books

Random House Trade Books publishes trade fiction and nonfiction covering a broad scope of literary and commercial appeal. Since 1995, it has published three of the best-selling books of all time: *My American Journey* by Colin Powell, *Midnight in the Garden of Good and Evil* by John Berendt, and *The Greatest Generation* by Tom Brokaw. This group has also become a showcase for fiction and nonfiction authors publishing for the first time. Representative titles from this group include *The God of Small Things* by Arundhati Roy; *Amy and Isabelle* by Elizabeth Strout; *White Teeth* by Zadie Smith; *Seabiscuit* by Laura Hillenbrand.

Villard Books

201 E 50th Street, New York, NY 10022

Villard Books publishes a general nonfiction and fiction list that is known for its titles in sports, personal narrative, new-voice fiction, and cooking.

Nonfiction hardcover titles include *Mysterious Stranger* by David Blaine; *Motherhood and Hollywood* by Patricia Heaton; *Hold the Enlightenment* by Tim Cahill; *The Elvis Treasures* by Robert Gordon; *The Territory of Men* by Joelle Fraser; *Dear Rhonda* by Demitri Kornegay.

Nonfiction trade paperbacks include *Miss Vera's Cross-Dress for Success* by Veronica Vera; *The Phytogenic Hormone Solution* by Saundra McKenna, C.N.M.; *A Homeopathic Handbook of Natural Remedies* by Laura Josephson, C.C.H., R.S.Hom.; *The Travel Detective Flight Crew Confidential* by Peter Greenberg; *Los Barrios Family Cookbook* by Diana Barrios Trevino.

Hardcover fiction titles: *Neva Hafta* by Edwardo Jackson; *Cubicles* by Camika Spencer; *Married but Still Looking* by Travis Hunter; *April Witch* by Majgull Axelsson; *I'll Let You Go* by Bruce Wagner; *Hand-Me-Down Heartache* by Tajuana "TJ" Butler; *The Holy Road* by Michael Blake.

Trade paperback fiction titles: *No More Mr. Nice Guy* by C. Kelly Robinson; *Bliss* by Gabrielle Pina; *Ever After* by Edwardo Jackson; *Dream in Color* by Darlene Johnson; *Promises to Keep* by Gloria Mallette; *Slave to Fashion* by Rebecca Campbell; *Meant to Be* by Rita Coburn Whack; *Sittin' in the Front Pew* by Parry "Ebony Satin" Brown.

Villard Books recently introduced **Strivers Row**, a new series committed to publishing African American fiction and nonfiction in trade paperback format. Strivers Row titles include *Sorority Sisters* by Tajuana "TJ" Butler; *The Hearts of Men* by Travis Hunter; *Black Coffee* by Tracy Price-Thompson; *Rich Minds, Rich Rewards* by Valorie Burton; *Between Brothers* by C. Kelly Robinson.

Bruce Tracy, Editorial Director

Melody Guy, Associate Editor

Pamela Cannon, Editor

The Modern Library

The Modern Library, known for publishing American classics, has expanded its program to include trade paperbacks and series of classics in various subject areas with distinguished guest editors. These include Jon Krakauer's Exploration Series, Caleb Carr's War Series, Martin Scorsese's Movie Series, Steve Martin's Humor and Wit Series, and Ruth Reichl's Food Series.

RED WHEEL/WEISER

368 Congress Street, 4th Floor, Boston, MA 02210
617-542-1324   fax: 617-482-9676
www.redwheelweiser.com

Red Wheel/Weiser's traditional interests are self-transformation, alternative healing methods, meditation, metaphysics, consciousness, magic, astrology, tarot, astral projection, Kabbalah, earth religions, Eastern philosophy and religions, Buddhism, t'ai chi, healing, and Tibetan studies.

The publisher has observed the many paths that lead to personal transformation and strives to publish books to help many different people find the path that is right for them. Red Wheel/Weiser specializes in books relating to all facets of the secret and hidden teachings worldwide.

This distinguished publisher of occult and spiritual books was purchased last year. Its newest incarnation promises much of the familiar, with a more commercial flair.

Frontlist titles include *Love, Light, and Laughter* by Monte Farber and Amy Zerner; *Sex with Spirit* by Michelle Pauli; *The Old Girls' Book of Spells* by Cal Garrison; *Crappy to Happy* by Randy Peyser; *Dirt Farmer Wisdom* by JoJo Jensen; *The Green Man* by John

Matthews; *Reality Works* by Chandra Alexander; *Intuition @ Work & at Home and Play* by James Wanless; *The Wise Earth Speaks to Your Spirit* by Janell Moon; *Beginner's Guide to Mediumship* by Larry Dreller; *Spirit Allies* by Christopher Penczak; *Gypsy Magic* by Patrinella Cooper; *Wiccan Wisdomkeepers* by Sally Griffyn; *Kitchen Witchery* by Marilyn Daniel; *The Virtual Pagan* by Lisa McSherry; *Everyday Tarot* by Gail Fairfield; *Tea Cup Reading* by Sasha Fenton; *Dreaming with the Archangels* by Linda Miller-Russo and Peter Miller Russo.

Red Wheel/Weiser handles its own distribution and distributes selected titles from other houses; the Red/Wheel Weiser distribution catalog lists titles from more than 200 publishers.

Query letters with SASEs should be directed to:

Jan Johnson, Publisher

Robyn Heisey, Associate Publisher

REGNERY PUBLISHING, INC.

One Massachusetts Avenue, NW, Washington, DC 20001
202-216-0600, 800-462-6420
www.regnery.com

Areas of Regnery publishing interest include contemporary politics, current events, public issues, biography, history, and alternative health; the house is open to projects with broad trade appeal by promotable authors with strong media CVs.

Regnery Publishing Inc. (formerly Regnery Gateway, founded in 1947) is a growing, midsize house that produces primarily nonfiction projects in hardcover and quality paper editions. Regnery Gateway was acquired by Phillips Publishing International and is part of Phillips's Eagle Publishing subsidiary, which produces public-policy periodicals and operates the Conservative Book Club. A major accent of Regnery's program is to feature books that offer a Washington-insider purview. The house is also traditionally strong in paperbound reprints for the college market. Regnery Publishing supports a strong backlist. In 1997, Regnery launched LifeLine Press, which will concentrate on alternative health books.

The Phillips corporate connection enables Regnery to promote titles through such venues as Phillips's *Human Events* newspaper and to take advantage of the parent company's expertise in direct-mail and special-market sales.

From the Regnery Publishing trade list: *Gods, Guns, and Rock & Roll* by Ted Nugent; *Absolute Power* by David Limbaugh; *At Any Cost* by Bill Sammon; *Bias* by Bernard Goldberg.

Indicative of this house's heritage is founder Henry Regnery's choice of his publisher's mark—the gateway that serves as colophon for books published by Regnery. This gateway is a graphic representation of the Porta Nigra in Trier, Germany, a Roman gate constructed about A.D. 300, when Trier was a colonial capital city of the Roman Empire. As such, the gateway symbolizes the passage from barbarous realms into the world of civilization.

Regnery Publishing is distributed to the trade by National Book Network. Query letters and SASEs should be directed to:

Mike Ward, Associate Publisher—Lifeline Press

Harry Crocker, Executive Editor

RENAISSANCE BOOKS

Audio Renaissance

Renaissance Books was purchased in 2001 by Holtzbrink. Its book-publishing program was terminated, and it is now solely an audio publisher.

RIZZOLI INTERNATIONAL PUBLICATIONS

300 Park Avenue South, New York, NY 10010-5399

212-982-2300

Rizzoli catalogs titles in fine arts, architecture, crafts, culinary arts, decorative arts, design, fashion, the home, gardens, landscaping, travel, and photography. Rizzoli also offers selected titles in sports and the performing arts.

The Rizzoli catalog offers titles from additional publishers in the arts and literary arena, including Angel City Press, Collectors' Press, Vendome, PBC International, Villegas Editores, Ipso Facto, and Merrell.

Rizzoli International (founded in 1976) is one of the exclusive set of cosmopolitan publishers renowned for finesse in the bookmaking craft. The house interest embraces artistic realms worldwide, throughout history as well as in the contemporary arena.

Rizzoli's consummately produced volumes feature graphics of the highest quality and are offered in hardback and trade paperback editions. (Please see entry for Universe Publishing.)

Titles from Rizzoli: *Fifth Avenue: The Best Address* by Jerry Patterson; *The Sensual Home* by Ilse Crawford (photographs by Martyn Thompson); *John Galliano: Romantic, Realist and Revolutionary* by Colin McDowell; *Architectural Glass Art: Form and Technique in Contemporary Glass* by Andrew Moor; *German Expressionism: Art and Society* by Stephanie Barron and Wolf-Dieter Dube; *East Meets West: Global Design for Contemporary Interiors* by Kelly Hoppen (photographs by Bill Batten); *Secret Gardens of Santa Fe* by Sydney LeBlanc (photographs by Charles Mann); *Living by Design: A Country House & Garden* by John Stefanidis (photographs by Fritz von der Schulenburg); *Diving: The World's Best Sites* by Jack Jackson.

PBC International titles: *New American Style* by Mike Strohl; *Kitchens: Lifestyle and Design* by James W. Krengel and Bernadette Baczynski; *Designing with Light: The Creative Touch* by Dr. Carol Soucer King, Ph.D.; *Color: Details and Design* by Terry Trucco; *Magazines Inside and Out* by Steven Heller and Teresa Fernandes.

Rizzoli International Publications is distributed to the trade in the United States by St. Martin's Press; Canadian distribution is handled through McClelland & Stewart.

The house acquires new projects only on an extremely selective basis. Query letters and SASEs should be directed to:

Isabel Venero, Editor—Art and general trade books

Liz Sullivan, Senior Editor—Art, culinary arts

David Morton, Senior Editor—Architecture

RODALE, INC.

33 East Minor Street, Emmaus, PA 18098-0099
610-967-5171, 800-813-6627
www.rodalepress.com

Rodale, Inc. (founded in 1932) specializes in books on health and wellness; sports and fitness; gardening and organic lifestyles; home arts such as cooking, quilting, and sewing; practical spirituality and inspiration; self-improvement; and selected general interest titles. Rodale, Inc., publishes hardcover and trade paperback books and some video products.

Rodale, Inc., publishes several award-winning magazines, including *Men's Health, Prevention, Organic Gardening, Runner's World, Bicycling,* and *Backpacker.*

Rodale, Inc., published two *New York Times* bestsellers in 2000: Dr. Shapiro's *Picture Perfect Weight Loss* by Dr. Howard Shapiro and *The Wrinkle Cure* by Dr. Nicholas Perricone.

Other recent books from Rodale include *Ann Lovejoy's Organic Garden Design School* by Ann Lovejoy; *Try and Make Me* by Ray Levy, Ph.D., and Bill O'Hanlong, with Tyler Norris Goode; *The Immunity Pleasure Connection* by Carl Chametski, Ph.D., and Francis Brennan, Ph.D.; *Run with the Champions* by Marc Bloom; *Another Shot* by Joe Kita; *The Green Pharmacy Anti-Aging Prescription* by Dr. James A. Duke; *The Joint Health Prescription* by James Rippe, M.D.

Rodale, Inc., distributes books through multiple channels: direct mail, retail sales, book clubs, and so on. St. Martin's Press distributes Rodale titles to the book trade. Query letters and SASEs should be directed to:

Jennifer Kusher, Associate Editor

Stephanie Tade, Editor

Tami Booth, Vice President and Editor in Chief—Self-help, psychology, narrative nonfiction, women's health, health-related fiction

Ellen Phillips, Executive Editor—Home arts, tips, pets

Anne Egan, Executive Editor—Cooking

Mary South, Deputy Editor—Narrative nonfiction, psychology, emotional and mental health, healing, sociology

Jeremy Katz, Editor—Men's health

Margot Shupf, Editor—Organic living

Anne Gaudinier, Senior Editor—Direct rights acquisitions for direct mail sales

Susan Berg, Editor—Senior health, herbal remedies, natural health, nutrition

Lou Cinquino, Senior Editor—Parenting, history

Sharon Faelten, Senior Editor—Women's health and conditions, fitness

Mariska van Aalst, Associate Editor—Self-help, psychology, women's health issues, narrative nonfiction, health-related fiction

Karen Bolesta, Editor—Quilting, knitting

Kathy Everleth, Associate Editor—Cooking

ROUTLEDGE (AN IMPRINT OF TAYLOR & FRANCIS BOOKS)

29 West 35th Street, New York, NY 10001-2299
212-216-7800   fax: 212-564-7854
www.routledge.com

Routledge accents current events, communications and media, cultural studies, education, self-improvement, world political and cultural studies, philosophical thought, economics, feminist theory, gender studies, history, and literary criticism. The house produces trade nonfiction and academic works.

Routledge produces adult nonfiction in the humanities and social sciences. Routledge specialties include projects that give a vanguard twist to topical issues. Routledge imprints include Theatre Arts Books.

Founded as Methuen Inc. (in 1977), and then as part of Routledge and Chapman and Hall (as a subsidiary of International Thompson Organization), the house held to the overall profile of a commercial publisher, abreast of trends in scholarship and general public interest, as it issued strong lines of trade and academic books. Routledge (with a concentration in the contemporary trade arena) is now separate from Chapman and Hall, which was purchased by Wolters-Kluwer Academic Publishers and has since been closed. Routledge is now an imprint of Taylor & Francis Books.

Routledge titles: *Me Against My Brother* by Scott Peterson; *New Labour, New Language?* by Norman Fairclough; *The Almanac of British Politics, 6th Edition* by Robert Waller and Bryon Criddle; *Vespasian* by Barbara Levick; *Handwriting of the Twentieth Century* by Rosemary Sassoon; *Liquid Pleasures: A Social History of Drinks in Modern Britain* by John Burnett; *Lost Innocents: A Follow-Up Study of Fatal Child Abuse* by Peter Reder and Sylvia Duncan; *Twin and Triplet Psychology: A Professional Guide to Working with Multiples* by Audrey Sandbank; *Punk Rock: So What? The Cultural Legacy of Punk Rock* by Roger Sabin; *TV Living: Television Culture and Everyday Life* by David Gauntlett and Anneaen Hill; *The Atlantic* by Paul Butel; *101 Philosophy Problems* by Martin Cohen.

Query letters and SASEs should be directed to:

Linda Hollick, Vice President and Publisher

Bill Germano, Vice President and Publisher, Director—Humanities

Sylvia Miller, Publishing Director—Reference

Eric Nelson, Editor—Politics

Ilene Kalish, Editor—Sociology and women's studies

Anne Davidson, Senior Editor—Literary studies

Richard Carlin, Executive Editor—Music and dance

Joseph Miranda, Editor—Education

David McBride, Editor—Geography/urban studies

Nick Street, Editor—Religion

Damon Zucca, Associate Editor—Philosophy and religion

Karen A. Wolny, Publishing Director—Social sciences and history

Matthew Byrnie, Associate Editor—Media

George Zimmer, Executive Editor—Behavioral science

Emily Epstem, Associate Editor—Behavioral science

RUNNING PRESS BOOK PUBLISHERS

Running Press Books for Children

125 South 22nd Street, Philadelphia, PA 19103-4399
215-567-5080   fax: 215-568-2919
www.runningpress.com

Running Press shows flair in the areas of popular culture and arts, lifestyle, popular science, hobby how-to, and popular-interest reference titles. Running Press produces a singular line of specialty items that include bookstore-counter impulse-sale wares, striking free-standing exhibition units for kids' books, and a gleaming array of display and promotional titles (especially on the Courage Books imprint).

Running Press Book Publishers (founded in 1972) publishes hardcover and paperback trade books in general nonfiction. The house, in addition, issues audiocassettes, stylized journals, diaries, bookplates, Miniature Editions, generously appointed educational-entertainment kits, and postcard books. Running Press products are associated with sleek production, as well as a sometimes humorous or insouciant air. Running Press maintains a solid backlist.

Sample Running Press titles: *Free to Be . . . You and Me* and *Free to Be . . . a Family (a 25th Anniversary Celebration: Stories, Songs and Poems for Children and Adults to Enjoy Together),* conceived by Marlo Thomas, with introductions by Gloria Steinem and Letty Cottin Pogrebin; *Strange Fruit* by David Margolick; *I Feel Great* and *110%* by Pat Croce; *My Soul Has Grown Deep* by John Edgar Wideman; *Ceviche!* by Guillermo Pernot with Aliza Green; *Danny Boy* by Malachy McCourt; *On the Shoulders of Giants* by Stephen Hawking.

Running Press Miniature Edition books are delightful little books that fit in the palm of your hand; more than 32 million copies have been sold worldwide. The list covers an astonishing range of subjects: *Love: Quotations from the Heart; Passion; Quotable Cats; You Are Special: Neighborly Wit and Wisdom from Mister Rogers; African-American Wisdom; The Winning Woman; Angels; Irish Blessings; The Kiss.* Running Press has developed minis with such brand names as *Joy of Cooking, 7 Habits of Highly Effective People, One Up on Wall Street, Disney, Star Wars, Free to Be . . . ,* For Dummies Books, *Wine Spectator, Cigar Aficionado, Rolling Stone, Silver Palate Cookbook, Moosewood Cookbook,* and Beverly Clark.

Running Press Miniature Editions has recently expanded to include book-plus-product kits. These latest palm-sized kits are fun and interactive, and they make great gifts! Titles include *The Serenity Kit; Wishing Stones; Mini Sunflower Garden; The Ornamental Grass Kit; The Art of the Love Letter; The Mini Bonsai Kit; The Mini Fondue Kit; The Mini Origami Kit; The Mini Voodoo Kit; The Sushi Box.*

Courage Books is the promotional imprint of Running Press, producing eye-catching volumes that can be advertised by booksellers as attractive, reasonably priced items. Sample Courage titles: *Grill It!* by Annete Yates; *Harley Davidson: The Ultimate Machine* by Tod Rafferty; *Tiger Woods: A Pictorial Biography* by Hank Gola; *Diana: The People's Princess* by Peter Donnelly; *Mother Teresa: The Pictorial Biography; Streisand: The Pictorial Biography* by Diana Karanikas Harvey and Jackson Harvey; *The Flowering of American Folk Art 1776–1876* by Joan Lipman and Alice Winchester; *Mothers: A Loving Celebration* (edited by Tara Ann McFadden, with contributions from Mark Twain and Toni Morrison); *The Good Sex Book* by Dr. Paul Brown and Christine Kell.

Running Press participates in a joint publishing program with M. Shanken Communications, Inc., publishers of *Wine Spectator* and *Cigar Aficionado* magazines. Titles available: *California Wine: A Comprehensive Guide to the Wineries, Wines, Vintages and Vineyards of America's Premier Winegrowing State* by James Laube; *Ultimate Guide to Buying Wine; Guide to Great Wine Values $10 and Under; Buying Guide to Premium Cigars.*

Running Press distributes its own list. Query letters and SASEs should be directed to:

Carlo DeVito, Associate Publisher

Jennifer Worick, Editorial Director

Stuart Teacher, President

Running Press Books for Children

Running Press Books for Children features finely engineered pop-up books, foldouts, small-format editions, kits, coloring books, and how-to's—in stand-alone editions and numerous series.

Running Press created the Fit-a-Shape series (books for preschoolers that teach basic concepts using three-dimensional objects that fit matching shapes); the Gem series (captivating, fact-filled titles, each with vast amounts of information in a handy format); Five-Minute Mysteries (that test your powers of observation and deductive reasoning); Treasure Chests (expeditions into ancient cultures); Action Books (informative texts and components for exploring science and creating projects); Discovery Kits (read about a specific subject, such as a radio; then build your own); Book Buddy, created by Penny Dann (each title in this series features a die-cut corner where a soft-fabric Book Buddy lives); and Start Collecting (each title includes a guide that explains the history of the category, famous specimens, a poster, and tips on how to begin collecting).

ST. MARTIN'S PRESS (A DIVISION OF THE HOLTZBRINCK PUBLISHING GROUP)

St. Martin's Press Trade

St. Martin's Paperbacks

St. Martin's Reference Group

175 Fifth Avenue, New York, NY 10010
212-674-5151
www.stmartins.com

Founded in 1952, St. Martin's Press is one of the ten largest general publishers in the United States and an important publisher of trade, mass-market, college, and global academic titles. St. Martin's Press is an international publisher with a broad and comprehensive program. St. Martin's is now part of the German-based international communications conglomerate Verlagsgruppe Georg von Holtzbrinck. Within its framework, St. Martin's enjoys its long-standing tradition of editorial independence, as it operates from its historic environs in Manhattan's famed Flatiron Building.

St. Martin's publishes across the spectrum of trade nonfiction and hosts a wide range of popular and literary fiction. The house is particularly strong in a number of special areas, some with associated lines and imprints (including popular culture, international arts and letters, relationships, multicultural topics, science, business, and professional). St. Martin's is known for a strong list of scholarly and reference titles and offers a solid lineup of college textbooks. St. Martin's produces hardcover, trade paperback, and mass-market paper editions and also offers a line of calendars. The press includes a few works for young readers.

Queries and SASEs should be directed to:

Charles Spicer, Senior Editor—Commercial fiction: crime, suspense, mysteries; nonfiction: true crime, biography, history; titles include *The Other Mrs. Kennedy* by Jerry Oppenheimer; *Topping from Below* by Laura Reese; *The Rise and Fall of the British Empire* by Lawrence James

Corin See, Associate Editor—reference; first novels; collection of comics; film

Michael Connor, Assistant Editor—Pop culture, general nonfiction

Elizabeth Beir, Editor—General nonfiction

George Witte, Editor in Chief for St. Martin's Press—Quality literary fiction and nonfiction of literary or intellectual interest; titles include *Farewell, I'm Bound to Leave You* by Fred Chappell; *In the Deep Midwinter* by Robert Clark; *The River Beyond the World* by Janet Peery

Heather Jackson, Editor—Commercial nonfiction of all stripes: health, nutrition, parenting, child care, popular reference, popular culture, psychology/self-help; titles include *The Ten Commandments of Pleasure* by Susan Block, *The Kitchen Klutz* by Colleen Johnson

Hope Dellon, Senior Editor—Fiction: mysteries, serious historical novels; nonfiction: parenting, women's issues, psychology, biography; titles include *Mary Queen of Scotland and the Isles* by Margaret George; *The Sculptress* by Minette Walters; *Beyond Jennifer and Jason* by Linda Rose

Jennifer Weis, Executive Editor—Commercial fiction: women's, thrillers, romance; commercial nonfiction: people books, narrative nonfiction, cookbooks, self-help, health and parenting, humor, popular culture; projects include *Aaron Spelling: A Prime-Time Life* by Aaron Spelling

John Sargent, Chairman, Editorial Director—Bestseller fiction, controversial current affairs

Keith Kahla, Editor—Gay and lesbian interest, mystery and suspense, literary fiction, cartoon books, anthologies; projects include *Murder on the Appian Way* by Steven Saylor; *Pawn to Queen Four* by Louis Eighner

S

Kelley Ragland, Associate Editor—Commercial and serious nonfiction; literary nonfiction, especially related to women's or racial issues; also including parenting, psychology, biography; essays; popular and literary fiction: a wide range of mysteries, thrillers, suspense

Mark Resnick, Editor

Marian Lizzi, Editor—Nonfiction: popular culture, women's issues, popular history, self-improvement, and an occasional cookbook; titles include *Funk: The Music, the People, and the Rhythm of the One* by Rickey Vincent; *Welcome to the Jungle* by Geoffrey Holtz

Matthew J. Shear, Vice President and Publisher, Mass-Market Division—All mass-market categories in fiction and nonfiction

Michael Denneny, Senior Editor—Literary nonfiction and fiction; gay and lesbian subjects

Sally Richardson, President and Publisher, Trade Division; President, Mass Market Division

Jennifer Enderlin, Senior Editor—Women's fiction, psychological suspense, general commercial fiction; commercial nonfiction (sex, relationships, psychology); projects include *To Build the Life You Want, Create the Work You Love* by Marsha Sinetar

   Born: June 10, 1967.

   Education: B.A. in English from University of New Hampshire.

   Employment history/editor career path: Started at Putnam/Berkley in 1989; moved to NAL/Dutton in 1991; moved to SMP in 1993.

   Personal interests: Travel.

   What would you be doing if you were not an editor? I'd still be reading if I weren't an editor. But maybe only 10 books a week. I'd like to work in a spa—it's the nurturing side of me.

   What has been your most successful book that you have acquired to date? *High Five* by Janet Evanovich; *Never Be Lied to Again* by Dr. David Lieberman.

   Do you represent fiction? If so, what do you look for? Yes. Commercial women's fiction.

   Do you represent nonfiction? Yes.

   Are agents important? Why? Yes. I love agents! They bring me great projects and they work hard. After all, they have to do the two hardest things on earth, seek (projects) and sell (projects).

   Do you like new writers? What should new writers do to break into the business? Writers are some of the most hilarious, wonderful, inventive, intelligent people around. I feel privileged that I can work with them. On the downside, they can often be insecure, needy, unappreciative, and arrogant! But I'm sure they would say the same thing about editors.

   Is there anything you would like to see changed in the industry? I would change dismal entry-level publishing salaries so that we don't lose the best and the brightest to the Internet.

   Any additional thoughts? I love the fact that I get to read for a living! I love discovering new writers. I love seeing a book I've fought for, work in the marketplace. I hate the fact that every single weekend is occupied by work. People don't seem to understand that I do not read or edit in the office. Every submission is read at home, every bit of editing is done on the weekends. "Part 2" of my job begins weeknights at 7:30 P.M. and for 8 to 10 hours per day on the weekends.

St. Martin's Press Trade

Bedford Books

Minotaur

Palgrave

Picador USA

Renaissance

Stonewall Inn Editions

Thomas Dunne Books

Tor, Forge, & Orb

175 Fifth Avenue, New York, NY 10010
212-674-5151   fax: 212-674-3179

Bedford

Bedford is a college publisher specializing in the humanities. Book categories include communication, English, history, music, religion, culture and linguistics, and business and technical writing.

Recent titles indicative of this list include *England's Glorious Revolution and the Origins of Liberalism* by Pincus; *Research and Documentation in the Electronic Age* by Diana Hacker and Barbara Fister; *Thinking and Writing About Philosophy* by Hugo Bedau; *The Investigative Reporter's Handbook: A Guide to Documents, Databases and Techniques* by Brant Houston, et al.; *The Bedford Guide for College Writers* by X. J. Kennedy, et al.; *A Writer's Reference* by Diana Hacker.

S

Minotaur

175 5th Avenue, New York, NY 10010
fax: 212-674-6132

Minotaur is a mystery imprint created by St. Martin's Press in 1999. The name was suggested by editor Ruth Cavin, who says she loves the symbolism of the Greek mythological figure the Minotaur, a creature who guarded the fabled labyrinth and devoured anyone who entered (except for Theseus, of course).

Minotaur publishes mystery books with an emphasis on thrillers that range from very soft to very hard. Many of these books are police procedural, historical nonfiction, and true crime.

Titles representative of Minotaur's list include *The Pillow Book of Lady Wisteria* by Laura Joh Rowland; *In the Bleak Midwinter* by Julia Spencer-Fleming; *A Mist of Prophecies* by Steven Saylor; *Blackwater Sound* by James W. Hall; *The Bawdy Basket* by Edward Marston; *Blood Lies* by Marianne MacDonald; *Buttons and Foes* by Dolores Johnson; *The Corporal Works of Murder* by Carol Anne O'Marie; *The Devil's Hawk* by Ray Sipherd; *Hard Freeze: A Joe Kurtz Novel* by Dan Simmons; *Here Comes the Corpse* by Mark Richard Zubro; *The Irish Sports Pages* by Les Roberts; *Last Scene Alive* by Charlaine Harris; *Medusa* by Skye Kathleen Moody.

Palgrave

175 Fifth Avenue, New York, NY 10010
212-982-3900   fax: 212-777-6359

Palgrave, created in October 2000 and formerly known as St. Martin's Press Scholarly and Reference Division, publishes sophisticated trade books for the general educated reader or scholar, monographs, and upper-level and graduate-level texts. It was created when St. Martin's Press Scholarly and Reference and Macmillan Press (UK) united their global publishing operations.

Palgrave publishes a wide range of nonfiction books in the humanities and social sciences. The list contains original works by many of the foremost academic writers and editors in the world, including several Nobel laureates. Books include specialized monographs that make original contributions to scholarship in their disciplines, upper-division supplemental texts and readers designed for classroom use, and trade titles written for a broad, educated, but nonacademic audience. Categories include history, politics, literature and cultural studies, medieval studies, theater studies, education, religion, gender studies, anthropology, and Latino and Latin American studies.

St. Martin's Press and Macmillan Press (UK) are members of the Holtzbrinck Group of companies. Holtzbrinck, headquartered in Stuttgart, Germany, also owns Scientific American; Farrar, Straus and Giroux; Henry Holt and Company; and Handelsblatt, among other media properties.

Titles indicative of this list: *A History of Censorship in Islamic Societies* by Trevor Mostyn; *A New Democracy* by Harry Shutt; *A Revolutionary Year* by Wm. Roger Louis and Roger Owen; *Arabia of the Bedouins* by Marcel Kurpershoek; *Dialogue of Civilizations* by Majid Tehranian and David W. Chappell; *Diplomacy and Murder in Tehran* by Lawrence Kelly; *Dracula by Bram Stoker* (edited by John Paul Riquelme); *Political Intellectuals and Public Identities in Britain Since 1850* by Julia Stapleton; *Postcolonial International Relations* by L. H. M. Ling; *The Cognition of Geographic Space* by Rob Kitchin and Mark Blades; *The Cult of Ivan the Terrible in Stalin's Russia* by Maureen Perrie; *The Effectiveness of EU Business Associations* by Justin Greenwood.

Palgrave is also the U.S. distributor of the following U.K. publishers: Manchester University Press, I. B.Tauris, and Zed Books.

Direct query letters and SASEs to:

Michael Flamini, Vice President, Editorial Director

Picador USA

175 5th Avenue, New York, NY 10010
212-674-5151   fax: 212-253-9627

Picador USA was founded by St. Martin's Press in 1994. With an international cast of world-class authors, Picador (and its sibling Picador United Kingdom imprint) publishes hardcover and paperback editions, highlighting original titles as well as reprints.

Recent Picador USA titles include *See Under Love* by David Grossman; *Elegy for Iris* by John Bayley; *Father of the Four Passages* by Lois-Ann Yamanaka; *The Adversary* by Emmanuel Carrere; *Lost Geography* by Charlotte Bacon; *The Love of Stones* by Tobias

Hill; *Notes from the Hyena's Belly* by Nega Mezlekia; *An Unexpected Light* by Jason Elliot; *The God Who Begat a Jackal* by Nega Mezlekia.

Query letters and SASEs should be directed to:

Frances Coady, Publisher

Diane Higgins, Editor

Renaissance Books

This St. Martin's Press imprint produces hardcover and paperbacks in nonfiction, as well as select literary titles.

Representative titles include *Science, Sense, and Soul* by Casey Blood; *Blood and Bone Brigade* by Jana Abrams Karam; *One Bird, One Stone: American Zen Stories* by Sean Murphy; *17 Lies That Are Holding You Back & the Truth That Will Set You Free* by Steve Chandler; *Discovering Colorado* by Elizabeth P. Linebaugh; *Healing Hands and a Soldier's Heart: A Year in the Trenches with EMS* by Jana Abrams Karam; *The 90/10 Weight Loss Plan* by Joy Bauer; *Hollywood 101: The Film Industry* by Frederick Levy; *Reading Monarchs' Writing: The Poetry of Henry VIII, Mary Stuart, Elizabeth I, and James VII* by Peter C. Herman (Editor); *Gayellow Pages, East and South Edition: 2001–2002.*

Stonewall Inn Editions

Stonewall Inn Editions publishes works with a lesbian and gay cultural slant in hardcover and paperback editions. The house addresses such trade areas as current events and public interest, reference works, cultural affairs, literary anthologies, Stonewall Inn Studio Books (featuring graphically lavish and luxuriously produced gift volumes), and the Stonewall Inn Mysteries line. The scope of St. Martin's lesbian- and gay-interest list is not limited to works issued under the Stonewall Inn imprint.

Featured Stonewall Inn authors have included such lights as Quentin Crisp, Larry Kramer, Paul Monette, Ethan Mordden, Denise Ohio, Randy Shilts, Edmund White, and Mark Richard Zubro.

Popular titles from Stonewall Inn: *The Violet Quill Reader: The Emergence of Gay Writing After Stonewall* (edited by David Bergman); *Sportsdykes: Stories from On and Off the Field* by Susan Fox Rogers; *Dark Wind: A True Account of Hurricane Gloria's Assault on Fire Island* by John Jiler; *Another Dead Teenager* (a Paul Turner mystery) by Mark Richard Zubro; *Sacred Lips of the Bronx* (a love story) by Douglas Sadonick; *End of the Empire* (visionary romance-adventure) by Denise Ohio; *Drama Queen: A Gay Man's Guide to An Uncomplicated Life* by Patrick Price; *Dirty Pictures: Tom of Finland, Masculinity, and Homosexuality* by Micha Ramakers; *Half-Moon Scar* by Allison Green.

Thomas Dunne Books

In Thomas Dunne's more than 25 years at St. Martin's Press, he has published virtually every kind of book, from runaway bestsellers such as *The Shell Seekers* by Rosamunde Pilcher and *River God* by Wilbur Smith, to the critically acclaimed nonfiction of Robert Kaplan and Juliet Barker. The Thomas Dunne imprint produces roughly 150 titles per year and covers a wide array of interests that include commercial fiction, mysteries, military histories, biographies, divination systems, politics, philosophy, humor, literary fiction, and current events.

Titles representative of this list: *Arousal: The Secret Logic of Sexual Fantasies* by Dr. Michael J. Bader; *Barbara Bush: Matriarch of a Dynasty* by Pamela Kilian; *Tigers of the Snow: How One Fateful Climb Made the Sherpas Mountaineering Legends* by Jonathan Neale; *You Don't Need Meat* by Peter Cox; *101 Damnations: The Humorists' Tour of Personal Hells* by Michael J. Rosen (Editor); *Alcohol: A History* by Griffith Edwards; *Soul Picnic: The Music and Passion of Laura Nyro* by Michele Kort; *The Way of Zen* by David Scott, et al.

Select titles from Dunne's fiction list: *Area 7* by Matthew Reilly; *From the Heart of Covington* by Joan A. Medlicott; *Bronx Boy* by Jerome Charyn; *Flip-Flopped* by Jill Smolinski; *Drop Dead Gorgeous* by Anna Cheska; *Looking for Mary Gabriel* by Carole Lawrence; *A Week in Winter* by Marcia Wilett.

Queries and SASEs should be directed to:

Thomas L. Dunne, Vice President, Executive Editor, Publisher, A Thomas Dunne Book for St. Martin's Press—Eclectic interests; projects have covered commercial women's fiction, mysteries, military histories, biographies, divination systems, politics, philosophy, humor, literary fiction, current events

Peter Wolverton, Senior Editor and Associate Publisher, A Thomas Dunne Book for St. Martin's Press—Fiction: Commercial and popular literature, genre mysteries; nonfiction: Wide range consistent with the Thomas Dunne list; sports—golf, football

Ruth Cavin, Senior Editor; Associate Publisher, A Thomas Dunne Book for St. Martin's Press—Crime fiction, contemporary fiction, anecdotal science, and medicine novelties (quotation books). Titles include *The Beekeeper's Apprentice* by Laurie R. King; *Whoever Fights Monsters* by Robert Ressler; *Four Hands* by Paco Ignacio Taibo II

Sign: Libra.

Employment history/editor career path: St. Martin's Press, 1988 to present; Walker Books 1979–1988; Two Continents Publishing, 1975–1979, freelance writer, Editor, author.

Personal interests: Theater, travel, children/grandchildren, people.

What would you be doing if you were not an editor? I would travel. I would probably also write. But I intend to keep my day job, because I love it. They will have to throw me or carry me out.

What has been the most successful book that you have acquired to date? I would have to look at the numbers, but what comes to mind is: Nonfiction: *Whoever Fights Monsters,* Robert K. Ressler and Tom Shachtman; Fiction: *A Grave Talent,* Laurie King.

What books have you acquired that make you the most proud? What books that you have acquired reflect the types of books you like to represent? I'm proud of a great many of them. I publish almost 50 books a year and have done so for the last dozen years; it would be too difficult to list them all. The only ones I'm considerably less proud of are those that were mistakes in judgment, in the sense that I saw potential I thought could be realized but wasn't, because the author and I could not agree, or the author was not able to do what I expected. But there are only a few of those. There are also books that I am certainly not ashamed of, but that I publish because I know people want them rather than that I would give them "A for Excellence." The types of books I like to represent are anything as varied, very well written, and imaginative as *Charles Todd: A Test of Wills* or *Afterzen* by Janwillem van de Wetering or *Volcano Cowboys* by Dick Thompson. I look for good books, fiction or nonfiction, that I feel are well worth reading, that others will enjoy, and that have a reasonable chance of commercial success.

Do you represent fiction? Yes, I publish fiction. Some mainstream novels, but it is difficult to launch a new mainstream novel unless something about it will help to sell it; if the author is known for something else, or if the house is very high on it and will spend money promoting it. David Corn's first novel, *Deep Background,* sold well because it's a terrific book; David had published a successful nonfiction book previously; his name is known as the longtime Washington editor of *The Nation;* he knows people whose "blurb" will impress bookstores and readers; it got terrific reviews; and David himself is a familiar on political talk shows. And even then, the book did only moderately well—but well above the usual for a first novel. Yet hope springs eternal, and if there is a wonderful book of fiction like *This Is Graceanne's Book* by P. L. Whitney or *Jenny Rose* by Mary Anne Kelly or *My Darling Elia* by Eugenie Melnyk, I publish it. Of course, all three authors had been published as mystery writers before. I have published novels from some "names"—for example, Herbert Gold, Jerome Charyn. You do keep trying if you believe in the book and the author understands not to give up that day job. Category books like mysteries are easier than mainstream novels to get out there when the author is unknown, because people who follow the category are actively looking for new writers and protagonists. I look for individuality, imagination, a fresh voice.

What do you want to see less of? Mysteries just like a hundred others.

Do you represent nonfiction? Yes, I publish nonfiction.

Do you require book proposals? If so, what do you look for in evaluating a book proposal? I require something, either a proposal, an outline, a writing sample, or a full manuscript. I will buy nonfiction on a proposal if the subject is one I think will find an audience, the author has some kind of credentials for writing about that subject, and I have an outline and enough writing sample to be confident about the author's style. I will not buy fiction on a proposal except from authors whose work I have published previously and know well, but if an author or agent wants to submit an outline and three chapters I will be able to tell whether I want to see the complete manuscript.

Are certain aspects of a book proposal given more weight than others? I suppose in nonfiction the subject/the content. But the outline and the writing style are very important.

What process do you use for making a decision? What is the process for acquisition, is there a committee? I read the proposal or manuscript. I sometimes ask colleagues for an opinion, although I don't always. I ask for the author's track record; other books published and sales and subrights figures if any, reviews, other writing background, publicity possibilities. (A good agent gives you these without being asked.) I then discuss the book and its attributes with my boss, Tom Dunne, and we arrive at a figure for an offer, with some knowledge of what to include in any necessary negotiation. If the money is more than usual, we get an estimated P & L from sales, production, and accounting and also consult our publisher and others in the house.

What kinds of nonfiction books do you want to see less of? I want to see nothing of inspirational, religious, psychological self-help, beauty, slimming diet, celebrity bios, all that commercial stuff that I know brings in a lot of money, but isn't for me.

Are you interested in work geared for the masses (readers of *People, The Star,* etc.)? No way.

Are agents important? Why? Yes, because the good ones winnow out the chaff and also know which editor is interested in what kinds of books. They understand the business and can be easier than an inexperienced author to deal with. But I also look at non-agented work.

Do you like new writers? What should new writers do to break into the business? It's not a question of like or not like. It's harder, of course; they have no following. But if their books are good and I feel they have a chance of selling, I'll be delighted. If new writers want to write fiction, they have a better shot for publication by writing category books than mainstream, but they have to listen to their own desires.

How should writers approach you? Send a proposal or manuscript addressed to me. Be prepared to wait for an answer; I get hundreds of submissions. Do not call and ask if I've read it; when I've read it, you'll know. The call just puts it off further, when it is one of many. Do not send a query letter and nothing else for a work of fiction, there's no way I can judge fiction from a query letter unless the plot description is so incredibly awful, it rules out any desire to see the rest. It's easy to describe a plot, but a book made from that story can be dreadful or marvelous and there's no way a letter can indicate that.

What are some common mistakes writers make? What really gets on your nerves? If you mean in the actual writing, I can't say, except if they don't use some imagination instead of the same old same old. Some of the physical details really get on my nerves. Such as, giving me a pitch on how this book is going to be the grandest blockbuster of a bestseller I've ever published. Sending cover designs along. Not numbering the pages consecutively (numbering each chapter separately instead). Single-spacing. Sending the book in a heavy and unwieldy binder, using expensive paper that makes the manuscript twice as heavy as good old copier paper. (Editors have to schlep the books around—home, to the baseball game, anywhere they can find a little time to read it.) Not keeping a copy for themselves in case we lose the one they sent.

What can writers do to get your attention and to avoid the slush pile? If a submission is addressed to me by my name, it will not land in the slush pile. I don't guarantee to read it all the way through, but it will get a read of a large-enough section to let me know whether or not it is something I want to pursue further.

What have been some of your craziest experiences with submissions? Annoying and funny: A woman who had the whole U.S. postal system looking for a manuscript we returned, not because she didn't have a copy (that would just have been a tragedy) but because she was sure that we had stolen it and were going to make a fortune by publishing it under our name. (This, I shall say gently, was highly unlikely even if we were inclined to cheat an author.) Sad: The factory worker who drove all the way overnight from somewhere in the Midwest to deliver by hand a (quite promising) six-page or so proposal for a memoir and was then going back that night so he could go to work the next day.

What have been some of your best experiences with writers or in your job? Above all, working for and with Tom Dunne. Meeting wonderful, very generous, interesting, and varied authors, so many that I can't start naming them here.

What, if anything, makes you different from other editors? Old age.

Is there anything you would like to see changed in the industry? Yes. I would like to see the publishers take the $27,000 they spend on a full-page ad in the *New York Times* to tell us about a book that already has six million copies out and use the money to bring some fine authors to the attention they are not getting and that they deserve. I'd like to find a way of convincing the reading public how their lives will be enriched if they raise their standards of and demands for good writing.

Any advice for writers? Writing a book is more than putting words down on paper; it requires a lot of thinking, a lot of discernment, constant observation of the way people behave, reading but not aping, and the primary motive: you must want to write that book. Wanting to have a published book is not enough, and wanting to make a fortune with a bestseller is adolescent and a futile way to go about it. Don't give up your day job.

Tor

This imprint, created in 1981, is known for its science fiction/fantasy list, including the bestselling Sword of Truth series by Terry Goodkind. *Tor* is an English word indicating an outcropping, butte, promontory, summit, peak, or high hill, which is representative of this list's goals and successes.

Titles indicative of this list: *Ender's Shadow* by Orson Scott Card; *Appleseed* by John Clute; *Argonaut* by Stanley Schmidt; *The Baron War* by Jory Sherman; *Beast Master's Ark* by Andre Norton and Lyn McConchie; *Blood Diamonds* by Jon Land; *Burning the Ice* by Laura J. Mixon; *Conan and the Spider God* by L. Sprague De Camp; *Dance of Knives* by Donna McMahon; *Daughter of Ireland* by Juilene Osborne-McKnight.

The Official Tor Submissions Guidelines, *from the Web site.*

1. Submissions should be sent to Tor Books, 175 Fifth Avenue, New York NY 10010. Do not submit work on disk, tape, or other electronic media; do not submit work by e-mail.
2. Address unsolicited science fiction and fantasy submissions to **Patrick Nielsen Hayden** and unsolicited mainstream submissions to **Melissa Singer.**
3. Submit only the first three chapters of your book and a synopsis of the entire book. (We're not big on query letters, since we can't tell whether we'll like the book until we see a chunk of the manuscript.) And please make sure you send the first three chapters. No matter how good your synopsis is, it's difficult for us to get a good sense of the book from chapters 4, 17, and 32.
4. Your cover letter should state the genre of the submission and previous sales or publications, if relevant.
5. Never send us the only copy of your book. The U.S. Post Office is no more perfect than the rest of us, and things do get lost in the mail. Always put your name and address on the manuscript. In addition, your name, the manuscript title, and the page number should appear on every page of the manuscript. If you wish your manuscript to be returned, enclose a stamped, self-addressed envelope large enough to hold your submission; publishers are not responsible for returning submissions unaccompanied by return postage. If you do not wish your manuscript to be returned, please say so in the cover letter, and enclose a stamped, self-addressed, business-sized envelope for our reply. If you enclose a stamped, self-addressed postcard, we will return it to verify receipt of the manuscript.
6. Type your manuscript on plain white paper, double-spaced, using only one side of the page. Do not staple or otherwise bind your manuscript; a paper clip will suffice.

If you use a computer and printer, do not submit low-resolution dot matrix print-outs; they will not be read. Please do not use a fancy font (this is almost as difficult to read as the palest dot matrix), and please make sure you use a font large enough to read easily. Please turn off margin justification and proportional spacing; pages with ragged right margins are easier for us to read and easier for our production department to set.

7. Please indicate italics by underlining and indicate boldface by drawing a wavy line beneath the affected characters. Copy to be typeset needs to be marked in very specific ways, and if you use italics or boldface in the manuscript, they will still need to be marked up by production.

8. Please allow at least four to six months for your manuscript to be considered. If you haven't heard from us after four months and wish to make sure your manuscript got here, please write a letter stating the genre, the date of submission, and the title of the manuscript, rather than calling. We will respond promptly.

9. We do not accept simultaneous submissions.

Forge Books

Forge Books publishes nonfiction, thrillers, suspense, mystery, historicals, and Westerns, targeted to the mainstream audience. Forge was created in 1993 as a new imprint to market contemporary books.

Among the books currently appearing under the Forge imprint are bestsellers like Harold Robbins's *The Predators;* technothrillers like Michael Cassutt's *Missing Man;* and legal thrillers like Junius Podrug's *Presumed Guilty;* as well as mysteries like Kate Flora's *Death at the Wheel* and Bill Eidson's *The Guardian.* Its strong list of historical titles includes the bestselling *1916,* Morgan Llewelyn's novel of the Irish Troubles; distinguished historical novelist Cecelia Holland's *Railroad Schemes;* and works ranging from such Americana as Fred Bean's Civil War novel *Lorena; The Wages of Fame* by Thomas Fleming; *The Way to Bright Star* by Dee Brown (author of *Bury My Heart at Wounded Knee*); to "H. N. Turteltaub's" (i.e., Harry Turtledove's) brilliant Byzantine epic *Justinian.*

Orb Books

In 1992, Tom Doherty Associates created Orb Books in response to complaints from readers and booksellers that some of their favorite science fiction and fantasy backlist titles were no longer available. Consequently, Orb publishes trade paperbacks that have previously been published in Tor mass-market editions.

St. Martin's Paperbacks (mass market)

Griffin Trade Paperbacks

Griffin, a St. Martin's imprint, publishes trade paperbacks, with a strong emphasis in "how to" nonfiction, contemporary fiction, travel, biography, and current culture.

Titles indicative of Griffin's nonfiction list: *Just How Smart Are You?* by Terry Stickels and Abbie F. Salny; *The Guide to Getting In* by Harvard Student Agencies; *How to Play*

Bass Guitar by Laurence Canty; *Label Launch: A Guide to Independent Record Recording, Promotion, and Distribution* by Veronika Kalmar; *The New York Times Guide to Coin Collecting* by Ed Reiter; *In the Shadows of the Net: Breaking Free of Compulsive Online Sexual Behavior* by Patrick Carnes (Editor), et al.

Titles representative of the fiction list: The Griffin & Sabine Trilogy Boxed Set: *Griffin & Sabine/Sabine's Notebook/The Golden Mean* by Nick Bantock; *Under Fire* by W. E. B. Griffin; *Boogie Woogie* by Danny Moynihan; *Dispensing with the Truth* by Alicia Mundy; *Dr. Johnson's London* by Liza Picard; *The Key* by James N. Frey; *The Secrets of My Life* by Kathy McCoy.

St. Martin's Reference Group

Let's Go Travel Guides

Golden Guides and Golden Field Guides

Encarta

Let's Go Publications

67 Mount Auburn Street, Cambridge, MA 02138
www.letsgo.com

Let's Go is a budget travel series that prides itself in being the "only guidebook publisher that updates its entire series each year." As a wholly owned subsidiary of Harvard Student Agencies, all Let's Go guides are written by full-time, degree-seeking Harvard students.

Golden Guides and Golden Field Guides

Golden Guides are a series of small "guidebooks" on various aspects of nature. Printed in 5" × 6" format, these guides are basic enough for beginners and informative enough for seasoned amateurs.

Titles include *Endangered Animals* by George S. Fichte; *Tropical Fish: A Guide for Setting Up and Maintaining an Aquarium for Tropical Fish and Other Animals* (Golden Field Guide Series.) by Bruce W. Halstead, et al.; *Exploring Space* by Mark R. Chartrand and Ron Miller (Photographer); *Poisonous Animals* (Golden Field Guide Series) by Edmund D. Brodie, et al.; *Bird Life: A Guide to the Behavior and Biology of Birds* by Stephen W. Kress, Ph.D., and John D. Dawson (Illustrator); *Dinosaurs* by Eugene S. Gaffney and John Dawson; *North American Indian Arts* by Andrew Hunter Whiteford, et al.; *Mammals: A Guide to Familiar American Species* by Herbert S. Zim, Ph.D., et al.; *Planets* by Mark R. Chartrand and Ron Miller (Illustrator); *Wildflowers: A Guide to Familiar American Wildflowers* by Herbert S. Zim, Ph.D., et al.; *The Sky Observer's Guide: A Handbook for Amateur Astronomers* by R. Newton Mayall, et al.; *Geology* by Frank H. T. Rhodes and Raymond Perlman.

Encarta

Encarta publishes the *Encarta World Dictionary* in a variety of languages.

S

SASQUATCH BOOKS

615 Second Avenue, Suite 260, Seattle, WA 98101
206-467-4300   fax: 206-467-4301
www.sasquatchbooks.com   e-mail: books@sasquatchbooks.com

Sasquatch specializes in books on travel, regional interest, gardening, guidebooks, nature, the outdoors, and food and wine. Sasquatch is broadening its Pacific Northwest regional concentration to include California. Additional areas of Sasquatch interest include literary nonfiction, especially in subject areas related to the house's core interests.

Sasquatch Books (founded in 1979) is known for a string of small-press successes. Among these: the Best Places travel series (Northwest Best Places; Northern California Best Places), the Cascadia Gardening series, and the Art Wolfe photo books.

Books from Sasquatch: *Watertrail: The Hidden Path Through Puget Sound* by Joel W. Rogers; *The Garden in Bloom: Plants & Wisdom for the Year-Round Gardener in the Pacific Northwest* by Ann Lovejoy; *Native Peoples of Alaska: A Traveler's Guide to Land, Art, and Culture* by Jan Halliday, with Patricia J. Petrivelli and the Alaska Native Heritage Center; *Inside Passage Walking Tours: Exploring Major Ports of Call in Southeast Alaska* by Julianne Chase; *Field Guide to North American Bison: A Natural History and Viewing Guide to the Great Plains Buffalo* by Robert Stellquist; *Slug Tossing and Other Adventures of a Reluctant Gardener* by Meg Descamp.

Titles in the Best Places series: *Inside Out Oregon: A Best Places Guide to the Outdoors* by Terry Richard; *Northwest Budget Traveler: Cheap Eats, Cheap Sleeps, Affordable Adventure* (edited by Nancy Leson); *The Northwest Best Places Cookbook: Recipes from the Outstanding Restaurants and Inns of Washington, Oregon, and British Columbia* by Cynthia Nims and Lori McKean.

Sasquatch Books is distributed through a network of regional sales representatives. Jennie McDonald can be reached at Sasquatch Books, 1563 Solano Avenue, Box 364, Berkeley, CA, 94707. Query letters and SASEs should be directed to:

Gary Luke, Editorial Director

Jennie McDonald, Senior Editor

Kate Rogers, Senior Editor

SCHOLASTIC, INC.

Orchard Books

555 Broadway, New York, NY 10012
212-343-6100

Scholastic publishes quality hardcover picture books, middle-grade and young adult fiction, and some nonfiction.

The house publishes not only trade hardcover, but also educational lines in hardcover and paperback editions, and owns a solid niche in electronic publishing. In addition, Scholastic, Prep. (founded in 1920), issues magazines, operates classroom book clubs, and offers computer software.

Scholastic's high-end hardcover imprints include Blue Sky Press, Scholastic Press, and Acedina Books. Cartwheel publishes boardbooks and novelties for pre-K.

Scholastic created the Literacy Place and Solares lines: These two core-curriculum reading and language-arts programs are for English and Spanish languages. Scholastic spent six years developing these programs because the publishers believe that teachers and children need and deserve a coherent plan of skills development (including phonics), better assessment, and, of course, the best children's literature.

Wiggleworks and Wiggleworks Español for grades K–2 (a complete early literacy system) are geared to raise reading scores. These programs use books and other educational technology that help emerging readers develop fluency, confidence, and control by reading, writing, listening, and speaking.

Solares is an innovative K–6 reading and language program in Spanish. Children read a wide variety of quality fiction that includes works originally written in Spanish, as well as classics translated from English and other languages. Solares provides a solid foundation for literacy through a program of explicit, intentional skills instruction that includes phonics.

Scholastic handles its own distribution.

FYI, here's the standard response "UNs" (Unagented/unsolicited writers) might encounter from Scholastic and other over-burdened presses.

Dear Writer,

Due to the overwhelming volume of submissions Scholastic Press receives, we regret that we are unable to accept any unsolicited manuscripts at this time. Scholastic Press considers only requested material or submissions from agented and/or previously published authors. Individual editors may also consider manuscripts from writers they meet at SCBWI conferences.

All solicited/requested submissions should by typed, double-spaced copies of your original work and accompanied by an SASE for return. Please allow 4–6 months for review.

Sincerely,
The Editors

Picture book manuscripts, query letters, and SASEs should be directed to:

Liz Szabla, Editorial Director

Dianne Hess, Executive Editor

Tracy Mack, Executive Editor

Lauren Thompson, Senior Editor

Orchard Books

557 Broadway, New York, NY 10012-3999
212-951-2649

Orchard Books produces mainstream trade children's fiction books, many of them illustrated works—and here again, award-winning titles and authors abound. Storybooks, boardbooks, novelty books, picture books, and middle grade and young adult novels are among areas of particular house emphasis.

Orchard emphasizes individual trade titles. Representative titles: *Clem's Chances* by S. Levitin; *Mouse in Love* by Kraus/Arvego/Dewey; *Stepping Out with Grandma Mac* by Grimes/Angelo; *Flora's Blanket* by Glori; *One Monday* by A. Huntington; *Born in the Breezes* by Lasky/Krudoz; *Case Closed: The Real Scoop on Detective Work* by Meltzer.

Query letters and SASEs should be directed to:

Ken Geist, Vice President and Editorial Director

Amy Griffin, Senior Editor

Seal Press

3131 Western Avenue, Suite 410, Seattle, WA 98121-1041
206-283-7844   fax: 206-285-9410
www.sealpress.com

Seal Press is dedicated to promoting the work of women writers. It is currently focusing its acquisitions in women's nonfiction titles (see the list that follows); in the past, it has published a wide range of fiction; poetry; and titles in women's studies, lesbian studies, sports and the outdoors, popular culture, parenting, self-help, and health.

Seal Press books enjoy a reputation for high literary quality, and the list often features finely designed, well-produced editions in hardcover and trade paperback. Seal Press supports a hardy backlist.

Founded in 1976, Seal is a smaller house that has leaped into its third decade of publishing with the same enthusiasm and mission that inspired the first book bearing the Seal name. More than 150 books later, the publishing business, as well as the cultural climate surrounding feminism, has changed considerably. Seal remains editorially agile and responsible to the industry's current challenges. Recent Seal books evidence the shifting signposts of feminism and an ever-expanding range of women's interests.

Seal is currently focusing its acquisitions in two successful series in its publishing program: the Adventura and Live Girls series. The Adventura line contains lively outdoor/adventure and travel books; the Live Girls series features both fiction and nonfiction, with a focus on third-wave feminism concerns.

The Live Girls series was launched in 1995 with the publication of *Listen Up: Voices from the Next Feminist Generation* (edited by Barbara Findlen, and recently released in a new expanded edition). The series includes such recent titles as *Yentl's Revenge: The Next Wave of Jewish Feminism* (edited by Jill Corral and Lisa Miya-Jervis); *Breeder: Real Life Stories from the New Generation of Mothers* (edited by Ariel Gore and Bee Lavender); *Valencia* by Michelle Tea; *Cunt: A Declaration of Independence* by Inga Muscio. This line features edgy writing by young women who wield their own brands of modern feminism and apply their realities to an established, yet necessarily fluid, movement for social change.

Adventura Books is a series that captures women's outdoor and travel experiences with some of the finest writing of its kind. Adventura blazes a literary trail and encourages the spirit of adventure in every woman. Some Adventura series titles: *Dream of a Thousand*

Lives: A Sojourn in Thailand by Karen Connelly; *Journey Across Tibet* by Sorrel Wilby; *A Woman Alone: Travel Tales from Around the Globe* (edited by Faith Conlon, Christina Henry de Tessan, and Ingrid Emerick); *The Unsavvy Traveler: Women's Comic Tales of Catastrophe* (edited by Rosemary Caperton, Anne Mathews, and Lucie Ocenas); *Girl in the Curl: A Century of Women in Surfing* by Andrea Gabbard; *Pilgrimage to India: A Woman Revisits Her Homeland* by Pramila Jayapal; *No Hurry to Get Home: The Memoir of the* New Yorker *Writer Whose Unconventional Life and Adventures Spanned the Twentieth Century* by Emily Hahn.

For an up-to-date listing of Seal Press's current acquisitions focus and editorial needs, please see Seal Press's submission guidelines and calls for submissions at www .sealpress.com.

Seal Press is distributed to the trade by Publishers Group West. Query letters and SASEs should be directed to:

Faith Conlon, Publisher and Editor

Leslie Miller, Senior Editor

Anne Mathews, Managing Editor

SELF-COUNSEL PRESS

1704 North State Street, Bellingham, WA 98225
360-676-4530   fax: 360-676-4549

Vancouver editorial office:
1481 Charlotte Road, North Vancouver, BC Canada V7J 1H1
604-986-3366

Self-Counsel produces business how-to, legal reference, self-help, and practical popular psychology. Topical areas include entrepreneurship, the legal system and you, business training, the family, and human resources development and management. The house also produces titles geared to lifestyles and business and legal issues in Florida, Oregon, and Washington.

Self-Counsel Press (founded in 1977) is a smaller house dedicated to providing well-researched up-to-date books (primarily trade paperbacks), as well as cassettes and work kits. The company's trade motto is "Our business is helping business people succeed." Self-Counsel's expertly written books do not just tell people what to do; they show them—step by step—how to do it. Kick Start Guides is a lineup of pocket-size titles designed for business travelers. The Start and Run list shows how to start and run a number of different kinds of small-business ventures.

Self-Counsel books cover everything from business to finance, legal matters to family matters, in language that everyone can understand. Self-Counsel prides itself on delivering concise, easy-to-understand books and audio, offering the practical information you need, whether it is for helpful legal tips, succeeding in business, or personal self-help issues.

Self-Counsel also offers legal books covering national issues, as well as books that cover legal matters in Florida, Oregon, and Washington. Other topics include retirement, personal self-help, and lifestyles.

S

From Self-Counsel: *So You Wanna Buy a Car . . . Insider Tips for Saving Money and Your Sanity* by Bruce Fuller and Tony Whitney; *Start and Run a Profitable Mail-Order Business* by Robert W. Bly; *Start and Run a Profitable Tour Guiding Business* by Barbara Braidwood, Susan Boyce, and Richard Cropp; *First-Time Sales Rep: Sound Like a Pro, Act Like a Pro, Sell Like a Pro!* by Wayne Vanwyck; *Study Smarter, Not Harder: Your Guide to Successful Learning and Studying in Any Situation* by Kevin Paul; *A Small Business Guide to Doing Big Business on the Internet* by Brian Hurley and Peter Birkwood.

Kick Start Guides is a series of handy, pocket-size guides developed for the business traveler. Each guide is written for a specific country and is designed to help readers kick-start themselves into action as soon as they arrive at their destination. The Guides are also helpful tools for entrepreneurs on the lookout for overseas business opportunities.

The Start and Run series offers step-by-step business plans and shows how to set up shop, sell products or services, hire employees, get financing, design marketing strategies, and identify legal considerations for a variety of different enterprises. The Start and Run Series includes titles keyed to bed-and-breakfast, the crafts business, freelance writing, secondhand bookstores, student-run businesses, and the gift-basket business.

Self-Counsel Press operates its own distribution services. Query letters and SASEs should be directed to:

Diana R. Douglas, President (Vancouver Office)

Ruth Wilson, Managing Editor (Vancouver Office)

S

SEVEN STORIES PRESS

140 Watts Street, New York, NY 10013
212-226-8760
www.sevenstories.com

Seven Stories publishes trade nonfiction, commercial literature, and popular reference works. The house's signature is a provocative edge in literature, current events, contemporary culture, biography/personality and memoirs, and inventive writing of all stripes (including classic reprints). In 2000, a Spanish-language imprint, Siete Cueulos Editorial, was founded.

Seven Stories Press was founded by publisher Dan Simon in 1996. Simon was previously cofounder (with John Oakes) of Four Walls Eight Windows (see separate entry). Seven Stories' publishing assets include backlist properties formerly catalogued by Four Walls.

Some titles from Seven Stories: *Grand Central Winter: Stories from the Street* by Lee Stringer; *The Man with the Golden Arm* from *Nonconformity: Writing on Writing* by Nelson Algren; *Dark Alliance: The CIA, the Contras and the Crack Cocaine Explosion* by Gary Webb; *Profit Over People* by Noam Chomsky; *The Zinn Reader* by Howard Zinn; *Borrowed Hearts: New and Selected Stories* by Rick DeMarinis; *Like Shaking Hands with God: A Conversation About Writing* by Kurt Vonnegut and Lee Stringer; *Get Healthy Now! With Gary Null* by Gary Null; *Scandals of '51: How the Gamblers Almost Killed College Basketball* by Carley Rosen; *The Undiscovered Chekhov: Thirty-Eight New Stories* by Anton Chekhov; *Shame* by Annie Ernaux; *The Open Media Pamphlet Series.*

Distribution to the trade for Seven Stories is handled by Publishers Group West. Query letters and SASEs should be directed to:

Jill Schoolman, Associate Editor

M. E. SHARPE

80 Business Park Drive, Armonk, NY 10504
914-273-1800   fax: 914-273-2106
www.mesharpe.com

Sharpe publishes across the range of social and political sciences, including law, literature, area studies, women's studies, multicultural studies, business, comparative politics, and international and developmental economics. Special Sharpe focus is on Asian studies, Slavic and Eastern Europe studies, business (international and domestic), Latin American studies, economics, political science, history, sociology, comparative public-policy analysis, and studies of the former Soviet Union.

M. E. Sharpe (founded in 1959) is a privately held company that produces trade books, reference books, scholarly and academic works, business books, and professional books in hardcover and paperback.

M. E. Sharpe has long been known for its area studies program covering Russia, Eastern Europe, and Asia. Expanding on that excellent publishing tradition, Sharpe has inaugurated programs in Latin American studies, American studies, African studies, and European studies, as well as related disciplines of comparative studies, women's studies, and literature, to provide a comprehensive understanding of today's world.

M. E. Sharpe chooses titles and authors that will define future debates about the political, economic, and social issues faced by various global regions and their peoples. Titles are selected by the editors to represent the most innovative and critical thinking in their respective disciplines.

Along with the primarily scholarly works, M. E. Sharpe publishes major single and multivolume reference works under the Sharpe Reference imprint; books aimed at the professional market are generally under the Sharpe Professional stamp.

The Sharpe list thus encompasses original research, policy studies, translations, reference compendiums, popular literature and classic reprints, and books that lend themselves to slots in the trade market. Sharpe started as a publisher of academic and professional journals and by the late 1970s had begun expansion into book publishing.

Books from Sharpe: *The Making of Modern Economics: The Lives and Ideas of the Great Thinkers* by Mark Skousen; *The Negotiation Handbook* by Patrick J. Cleary; *Consumer Economics: A Practical Overview* by Steven Soderlind; *An Introduction to the Policy Process: Theories, Concepts, and Models of Public Policy Making* by Thomas A. Birkland; *New York Politics: A Tale of Two States* by Edward Schneier and John Brian Murtaugh; *Russian Wondertales I. Tales of Heroes and Villains: Volume 3 of the Complete Russian Folktale* by Editor Jack V. Haney; *The Alternative Principles of Economics* by Stanley Bober; *The Ancient Americans: A Reference Guide to the Art, Culture, and History of Pre-Columbian North and South America* by Juan Schobinger; *Dictionary of the Political Thought of the People's Republic of China* by Henry Yuhuai He; *Elite Politics in Contemporary China* by Joseph

Fewsmiht; *Eyewitness to Massacre: American Missionaries Bear Witness to Japanese Atrocities in Najing* by Editors Kaiyan Zhang and Martha Lund Smally; *The Negotiation Handbook* by Patrick J. Cleary; *A Rainbow in the Desert: An Anthology of Early Twentieth Century Japanese Children's Literature* by Yuki Ohta; *Soldiers of Fortune: The Rise and Fall of the Chinese Military-Business Complex, 1978–1998* by James Charles Mulvenon.

It also highlights titles of the practical how-to variety on its Sharpe Professional list. Sharpe sells and promotes its titles both nationally and internationally; the house is a recognized industry leader in worldwide distribution. A large portion of Sharpe's sales comes from direct marketing; in addition, the house pursues a variety of means to sell its list, such as libraries, universities, trade and institutional bookstores, and catalogs.

M. E. Sharpe orchestrates its own distribution network, including stateside regional sales representatives, library-market specialists, and international wholesalers and reps. Query letters and SASEs should be directed to:

Patricia Loo, Editorial Director and Executive Editor—Asian studies

Patricia A. Kolb, Executive Editor—European and Russian studies, political science

Peter M. Labella, Executive Editor—American studies and history

Elizabeth Granda, Editor—Economics

Harry Briggs, Executive Editor—Management and public administration

---

SIERRA CLUB BOOKS
Sierra Club Books for Children

85 Second Street, San Francisco, CA 94105
415-977-5500   fax: 415-977- 5792
www.sierraclub.org/books

Sierra Club publishes works in the categories of nature, appropriate technology, outdoor activities, mountaineering, health, gardening, natural history, travel, and environmental issues. Sierra Club series include the Adventure Travel Guides, Sierra Club Totebooks, Naturalist's Guides, Natural Traveler, the John Muir Library, and Guides to the Natural Areas of the United States. Sierra Club Books has a strong division that publishes works geared to children and young adults (see subentry for Sierra Club Books for Children).

Founded in 1892 by John Muir, the membership of the Sierra Club has for more than a century stood in the forefront of the study and protection of the earth's scenic, environmental, and ecological resources; Sierra Club Books is part of the nonprofit effort the club carries on as a public trust. The house publishes hardcover and paperback books, many of them finely illustrated.

Sierra Club Books has the proud tradition of publishing books that are worldwide messengers for the Sierra Club mission: "To explore, enjoy and protect the wild places of the Earth; to practice and promote the responsible use of the Earth's ecosystems and resources; to educate and enlist humanity to protect and store the quality of the natural and human environment; and to use all lawful means to carry out these objectives."

The books represent the finest in outdoor photographic artistry; fervent and thought-provoking discussions of ecological issues; literary masterworks by the highest-caliber naturalist authors; authoritative handbooks to the best recreational activities the natural world can offer. Today, the need to protect and expand John Muir's legacy is greater than ever—to help stop the relentless abuse of irreplaceable wilderness lands, save endangered species, and protect the global environment.

On the Sierra Club list: *Wild L.A.: A Celebration of the Natural Areas in and Around the City* by James Lawrence; *Breaking Gridlock: Moving Toward Transportation That Works* by Jim Motavalli; *Where Vultures Feast: Shell, Human Rights and Oil in the Niger Delta* by Ike Okonta and Oronto Douglas; *My Story as Told by Water: Confessions, Druidic Rants, Reflections, Bird-Watchings, Fish Stalkings, Visions, Song and Prayers Refracting Light from Living Rivers in the Age of the Industrial Dark* by David James Duncan; *Forward Drive: The Race to Build "Clean" Cars for the Future* by Jim Motavalli (foreword by Ed Begley, Jr.); *The Stations of Still Creek* by Barbara J. Scott.

Sierra Club Books are distributed to the book trade by University of California Press. Query letters and SASEs should be directed to:

Danny Moses, Editor in Chief—Nature writing; environmental issues; nonfiction literary works dealing with nature, environment, cultural anthropology, history, travel, and geography; fiction and poetry that are clearly related to natural or environmental themes

Linda Gunnarson, Senior Editor—Areas consistent with house list

Sierra Club Books for Children

Sierra Club Books for Children publishes primarily nonfiction, along with selected fiction keyed to subject areas that generally reflect the overall Sierra Club house emphasis.

Titles here: *Desert Dog* by Tony Johnston (full color paintings by Robert Wentherford); *The Waterfall's Gift* by Joanne Ryder (illustrated in full color by Richard Jesse Watson).

Sierra Club Books for Children are distributed to the trade by Gibbs Smith, Publisher. We are currently not accepting proposals or manuscripts.

S

SIMON & SCHUSTER (PART OF VIACOM INC.)

Simon & Schuster Adult Publishing Group

Archway

Baen Books

PB Press

Pimsleur

Scribner

Simon & Schuster

Simon & Schuster Trade Paperbacks

Simon & Schuster Children's Publishing

1230 Avenue of the Americas, New York, NY 10020
212-698-7000

Simon & Schuster, the publishing operation of Viacom Inc., is a global leader in the field of general-interest publishing, dedicated to providing the best in fiction and nonfiction for consumers of all ages, across all printed, electronic, and multimedia formats. Its divisions include the Simon & Schuster Adult Publishing Group, Simon & Schuster Children's Publishing, Simon & Schuster New Media, Simon & Schuster Online, Simon & Schuster U.K., and Simon & Schuster Australia.

The Simon & Schuster Adult Publishing Group was formed when the Simon & Schuster Trade Division was combined with Pocket Books. Two publishing units were formed out of what was previously Pocket Books: PB Press took its place alongside the other hard-cover-only imprints in the Adult Publishing Group—Simon & Schuster, Scribner, the Free Press, and Simon & Schuster Source—and Pocket Books will now publish primarily in the mass-market and original trade paperback formats. As this program now moves forward as PB Press, the house is expected to extend the range of books that it publishes and increase its output, while maintaining its track record as a commercial publishing house.

Today, Simon & Schuster publishes a wide variety of bestsellers across all formats and has more than 50,000 backlist titles and 52 Pulitzer Prize–winners. In 1999, Simon & Schuster published 59 *New York Times* bestsellers, including Bob Woodward's *Shadow;* Barbara Delinsky's *Coast Road* and *Lake News;* Stephen King's *The Girl Who Loved Tom Gordon* and *Hearts in Atlantis;* Frank McCourt's *'Tis;* Iyanla Vanzant's *Yesterday I Cried.* By June 2000, Simon & Schuster already had 31 titles on the *New York Times* best-sellers list, including Dave Eggers's *A Heartbreaking Work of Staggering Genius,* Mary Higgins Clark's *We'll Meet Again,* and Jeffery Deaver's *The Devil's Teardrop.*

Simon & Schuster has formed lasting relationships with top-selling authors such as Stephen King and Clive Cussler, creating innovative deals that promise maximum profit potential and that are revolutionary departures from the traditional economics of the publishing industry. Simon & Schuster has also tapped MTV Network's youth-oriented audience with several publishing programs. Pocket Books and MTV: Music Television joined forces to create the MTV Books imprint in 1995, which has produced several *New York Times* bestsellers.

Archway

Archway produces titles in digital format. Titles indicative of this growing list include *Heath Ledger: The Heath Is On!* by Nancy Krulik; *Marion Jones: The Fastest Woman in the World* by Bill Gutman; *Night of the Pompon* by Sarah Jett; *Viking Claw* by Michael Dahl.

Baen Books

Baen Books produces science fiction and fantasy titles in hardcover, trade paperback, and mass-market paperback.

Titles representative of this list: *Between the Strokes of Night* by Charles Sheffield; *The Black Throne* by Fred Saberhagen and Roger Zelazny; *Fallen Angels* by Larry Niven, Jerry Pournelle, and Mike Flynn; *March to the Sea* by David Weber and John Ringo; *Resurgence* by Charles Sheffield; *Skylock* by Paul Kozerski; *Bolo Strike* by William H. Keith; *Kaspar's Box* by Jack L. Chalker; *Seas of Venus* by David Drake; *The Tide of Vic-*

tory by Eric Flint and David Drake; *War of Honor* by David Weber; *Beyond This Horizon* by Robert A. Heinlein; *Conrad's Time Machine* by Leo Frankowski; *Eternal Frontier* by James H. Schmitz (edited by Eric Flint); *Field of Dishonor* by David Weber; *Flag in Exile* by David Weber; *Foreign Legions* by Eric Flint (edited by David Drake, with David Weber); *Miles Errant* by Lois McMaster Bujold.

Send query letters with SASEs to:

James Baen, Editor in Chief

Toni Weisscoft, Executive Editor

The Free Press

The Free Press publishes nonfiction cutting-edge works in social thought, politics, current affairs, history, science, psychology, religion and spirituality, music, and a much broader business list than it has previously published. It also produces college textbooks. Titles are produced in hardcover format.

Titles indicative of this list: *Origin of the American Revolution* by Bernard Knollenberg; *Pension Fund* by Peter Dietz; *Changing the Rules: Adventures of a Wall Street Maverick* by Muriel Siebert and Aimee Lee Ball; *American: Beyond Our Grandest Notions* by Chris Matthews; *A Century of Triumph: The History of Aviation* by Christopher Chant, illustrated by John Batchelor; *Confessions of a Political Anarchist: Why the Two Party System Doesn't Work—And How We're Going to Fix It* by Bill Hillsman; *How to Fix (Just About) Everything: Step-by-Step Instructions for Everything from Curing a Hangover to Repairing a Toilet to Removing Gum from Hair* by Bill Marken; *Piano Notes: The Hidden World of the Pianist* by Charles Rosen; *The Prophets: Who They Were, What They Are* by Norman Podhoretz; *Origins of Existence: How Life Emerged in the Universe* by Fred Adams, illustrated by Ian Schoenherr.

Direct query letters and SASEs to:

Martha K. Levin, Vice President, Publisher

Fred Hills, Editor—General business, motivation, spirituality, current issues, history

Dominick Anfuso, Editor—General nonfiction

Rachel Klayman, Editor—Current events

Bruce Nichols, Vice President, Senior Editor—Serious nonfiction

Scribner

Scribner produces fiction and nonfiction titles in hardcover format. Categories include general fiction, history, military, social science, popular culture, and self-help.

Titles indicative of this list include *Mistress to An Age: A Life of Madame De Stael* by J. Christopher Herold; *Bow's Boy: A Novel* by Richard Babcock; *Four Sisters of Hofei: A History* by Annping Chin; *Odysseus in America: Combat Trauma and the Trials of Homecoming* by Jonathan Shay; *White Christmas: The Story of an American Song* by Jody Rosen; *Romancing the Ordinary: A Year of Simple Splendor* by Sarah Ban Breathnach; *Blood on the Tongue: A Crime Novel* by Stephen Booth.

Send query letters with SASEs to:

Beth Wareham, Editor—Cookbooks

Gillian Blake, Senior Editor—Commercial and literary fiction and nonfiction consistent with the Scribner list; projects include *For Colored Girls Who Have Considered Suicide/When the Rainbow Is Enuf* by Ntozake Shange

Lisa Drew, Publisher, Lisa Drew Books—Commercial nonfiction, including high-interest history, celebrity biographies, and current affairs; popular fiction; titles include *George Bush: The Life of a Lone Star Yankee* by Herbert S. Parmet; *Michael and Natasha: The Life and Love of Michael II, the Last of the Romanov Tsars* by Rosemary and Donald Crawford

Nan Graham, Vice President and Editor in Chief—American literary fiction; fiction about clashing cultures, Third World and European; nonfiction interests include contemporary social and political issues, women's studies, historical and literary biography, and biographies of artists

Susan Moldow, Publisher—Areas consistent with house interest; projects include *The Illusionist* by Dinitia Smith; *The Color Code* by Taylor Hartman, Ph.D.; *Three Gospels* by Reynolds Price

Susanne Kirk, Vice President/Senior Editor, Scribner/Simon & Schuster—Mystery and suspense fiction; titles include *Déjà Dead* by Kathy Reichs; *Dreaming of the Bones* by Deborah Crombie; *Tequila Mockingbird* by Paul Bishop; *Final Jeopardy* by Linda Fairstein; *Death on a Vineyard Beach* by Philip R. Craig

Simon & Schuster

Simon & Schuster publishes fiction and nonfiction in hardcover format.

Titles representative of this list: *Apples of Gold in Settings of Silver, Stories of Dinner As a Work of Art* by Carolin C. Young; *The Conquerors: Roosevelt, Truman and the Destruction of Hitler's Germany* by Michael R. Beschloss; *Down by the River: Drugs, Money, Murder, and Family* by Charles Bowden; *Ghost Image: A Novel* by Joshua Gilder; *Going with the Grain: A Wandering Bread Lover Takes a Bite Out of Life* by Susan Seligson; *The Gold Swan: A Novel* by James Thayer; *The Greatest Minds and Ideas of All Time* by Will Durant; *An Illustrated Dictionary of Tatting* by Judith Connors; *More Glass Painting Designs* by Janet Eadie.

Send query letters with SASEs to:

Amanda Murray, Editor—Hardcover nonfiction, both narrative and practical; subjects include (but aren't limited to) popular reference, beauty, fashion, entertainment, mind/body/health, and general women's interest

Constance Herndon, Editor—General fiction and nonfiction

Alice Mayhew, Editorial Director, Simon & Schuster Trade Division—Politics, current events, contemporary biographies and memoirs; projects include *Making the Most of Your Money* by Jane Bryant Quinn; *Pillar of Fire* by Taylor Branch; *In Love with Daylight* by Wilfrid Sheed; *Taking Charge* by Michael Bechloss

Bill Rosen, Simon & Schuster Editions—Vice President and Associate Publisher for Illustrated Books for the Simon & Schuster Group; in charge of illustrated books and special projects

Charles F. Adams, Senior Editor—Commercial fiction and nonfiction; titles include *No Regrets* by Caroline Seebohm; *Armadillos & Old Lace* by Kinky Freidman; *Ray Had an Idea About Love* by Eddie Lewis; *Off Stage* by Betty Comden

Geof Klosker, Editor, Nonfiction—Serious nonfiction

Jeff Neuman, Senior Editor—Sports stories and biographies; humor; titles include *Year of the Cat* by Scott Fowler and Charles Chandler; *Under the Lone Star Flagstick* by Melanie Hauser; *Postcard from Hell* by Rex Dancer

Mary Sue Rucci, Senior Editor—Commercial fiction and nonfiction; projects include *Women Make the Best Friends* by Lois Wyse; *Shed 10 Years in 10 Weeks* by Julian Whitaker and Carol Colman; *Divided Lives: The Public and Private Struggles of Three Accomplished Women* by Elsa Walsh

Michael Korda, Editor in Chief—Commercial fiction and nonfiction; *Flood Tide* by Clive Cussler; *Comanche Moon* by Larry McMurtry. With Charles Adams: *Climbing the Mountain* by Kirk Douglas; *Footnotes* by Tommy Tune

Robert Bender, Senior Editor—Popular psychology, natural history, health and fitness, literary biography; wide commercial interests (excluding New Age and celebrity stories); titles include *Sophia Loren* by Warren G. Harris; *Curing Cancer* by Michael Waldholtz

Simon & Schuster Trade Paperbacks

Fireside

Scribner Paperbacks

Sonnet

Touchstone

TV Books

Simon & Schuster Trade Paperbacks division is comprised of several imprints, including Fireside, Scribner, and Touchstone Books.

Fireside

Fireside publishes nonfiction titles in trade paperback format, as well as reissuing paperback books previously published in hardcover format. Categories include crafts and hobbies, self-help, motivational, health and fitness, healing, games and word puzzles, humor, political, and other general nonfiction.

Titles representative of this list: *2003 American Guide to U.S. Coins: The Most Up-to-Date Coin Prices Available* by Charles F. French, Scott Mitchell (Editor); *The Accidental Gourmet: Weeknights* by Sally Sondheim and Suzannah Sloan; *Always My Child: A Parent's Guide to Understanding Your Gay, Lesbian, Bisexual, Transgendered, or Questioning Son or*

Daughter by Kevin Jennings, Pat Shapiro (Contributor); *American Yoga Association Beginner's Manual* by Alice Christensen; *Ask a Nurse: From Home Remedies to Hospital Care* by American Association of Colleges (Editor) and Geraldine Bednash; *Best Alternative Medicine* by Dr. Kenneth Pelletier, et al.; *Clients for Life: Evolving from an Expert for Hire to an Extraordinary Advisor* by Jagdish N. Sheth and Andrew Sobel; *Dream Big!: A Roadmap for Facing Life's Challenges and Creating the Life You Deserve* by Deborah Rosado Shaw; *Finding Hope When a Child Dies: What Other Cultures Can Teach Us* by Sukie Miller; *A Passion for Knitting: Step-by-Step Illustrated Techniques, Easy Contemporary Patterns, and Essential Resources for Becoming Part of the World of Knitting* by Ilana Rabinowitz and Nancy Thomas; *Every Day I Pray: Prayers for Awakening to the Grace of Inner Communion* by Iyanla Vanzant; *More George W. Bushisms: More of Slate's Accidental Wit and Wisdom of Our 43rd President* by Jacob Weisberg; *Simon & Schuster Super Crostics Book #6* (edited by Thomas H. Middleton); *The Journey: A Road Map to the Soul* by Brandon Bays.

Send query letters with SASEs to:

Caroline Sutton, Senior Editor—Interests include psychology and self-help, health and medicine, American history, nature, humor, and language; also acquires originals for Fireside and Touchstone; projects include *Beyond the Battlefield,* sponsored by the U.S. Civil War Center, and *Blonde Like Me* by Natlia Ilyin

Cherise Grant, Editor—Major interests include the craft of writing, branded nonfiction, career development, education, health, self-help, American history, illustrated books, humor, pop/youth/hip hop culture, personal memoir, and home decorating; titles include *Conquering Chaos at Work* by Harriet Schechter

Doris Cooper, Senior Editor—Interests include narrative nonfiction, women's issues, psychology and self-help, sports and fitness (especially the outdoors), health, quirky business, relationships (from romantic to familial), and literary fiction; she is also interested in clever branded books

Lisa Considine, Senior Editor—Has a deep and abiding interest in psychology and self-help, health, science and nature, American history, business—particularly titles related to new media—and literary fiction

Matt Walker, Associate Editor—Major interests include movies, rock, pop culture; literary fiction, and literate nonfiction for Gen-X readers; chess, crosswords, and games; and offbeat science and history

Trish Todd, Vice President and Editor in Chief—Interests include humor, self-help, child care, health, and psychology

Marcela Landres, Associate Editor—Marcela is seeking mysteries for the Manolo Blahnik crowd, commercial fiction, gay/lesbian, relationships, sexuality, inspiration, New Age, pop culture, reader-centric, results-oriented self-help, and multicultural—particularly, Latina—fiction and nonfiction

Touchstone

Touchstone publishes nonfiction trade paperbacks in all categories of history, politics, military, political science, biography, and autobiography.

Titles indicative of Touchstone's list: *The Story of World War II: Revised, Expanded, and Updated from the Original Text by Henry Steele Commager* by Henry Steele Commager and Donald L. Miller; *Hemingway on Fishing* by Ernest Hemingway (edited by Nick Lyons); *The Kennedy White House: Family Life and Pictures, 1961–1963* by Carl Sferrazza Anthony; *Reaching for Glory: The Johnson White House Tapes, 1964–1965* by Michael R. Beschloss; *No More Words: A Journal of My Mother, Anne Morrow Lindbergh* by Reeve Lindbergh; *On Seas of Glory: Heroic Men, Great Ships, and Epic Battles of the American Navy* by John Lehman; *The Rehnquist Choice: The Untold Story of the Nixon Appointment That Redefined the Supreme Court* by John W. Dean; *Dixie: A Personal Odyssey Through Events That Shaped the Modern South* by Curtis Wilkie; *President Nixon: Alone in the White House* by Richard Reeves.

Simon & Schuster Children's Publishing

AAA Books

Aladdin Paperbacks

Atheneum Books for Young Readers

Little Simon

Margaret K. McElderry

Minstrel

Nick Jr.

Simon & Schuster Books for Young Readers

Simon Pulse

Simon Spotlight

Send query letters with SASEs to:

Kristina Peterson, President and Publisher

Robin Corey, Vice President and Publisher—Novelty and media tie-ins

AAA Books

AAA Books publishes titles for children of all ages, from babies through teens, in hardcover and paperback formats. A few titles representative of this list include *The Easter Chicken* by Lisa Funari Willever, et al.; *Chumpkin* by Lisa Funari Willever, et al.; *Early Poems* by A. F. Moritz.

Aladdin Paperbacks

Aladdin Paperbacks publishes juvenile fiction and nonfiction in mass-market paperback.

Titles indicative of Aladdin's list: *Albert's Birthday* by Leslie Tryon; *A Boy at War: A Novel of Pearl Harbor* by Harry Mazer; *Brave Norman* by Andrew Clements, illustrated by Donald Cook; *The Hideout* by Peg Kehret, illustrated by Paul Casale; *Mistletoe Mystery* (Nancy Drew #169) by Carolyn Keene; *Mush, Part II* by Daniel Pinkwater, illustrated by Jill Pinkwater; *Mutiny!* by Brad Strickland and Tom Fuller, illustrated by Dominic Saponaro; *Raggedy Ann and Andy and the Nice Police Officer* by Johnny Gruelle, illustrated by Jan Palmer; *Ringo Saves the Day!* by Andrew Clements, illustrated by Donald Cook.

Send query letters with SASEs to:

Ellen Krieger, Vice President, Associate Publisher and Editorial Director

Atheneum Books for Young Readers

Atheneum produces new titles in fiction, nonfiction, and poetry for preschool to high school age children. Formats include hardcover and paperback. Categories include history, action/adventure, social situations, family, military and wars, humor, friendship, and general. Atheneum also reissues top-sellers and classics.

Titles indicative of this list: *Blubber* by Judy Blume; *The Last of the Mohicans* by James Fenimore Cooper, illustrated by N. C. Wyeth; *Red Badge of Courage* by Stephen Crane, illustrated by Wendell Minor; *The Annoyance Bureau* by Lucy Frank; *Blizzard's Wake* by Phyllis Reynolds Naylor; *Fields of Fury: The American Civil War* by James M. McPherson; *The Mixed-Up Files of Mrs. Basil E. Frankweiler: 35th Anniversary Edition* by E. L. Konigsburg; *Herbie's Secret Santa* by Petra Mathers, illustrated by Petra Mathers; *Horace and Morris Join the Chorus* by James Howe, illustrated by Amy Walrod; *The House of the Scorpion* by Nancy Farmer.

Send query letters with SASEs to:

Caitlyn Dlouhy, Senior Editor

Jonathan Lanman, Editor at Large

Ginee Seo, Vice President and Associate Publisher

Marcia Marshall, Executive Editor

Little Simon

Little Simon produces nonfiction and novelty books for juveniles in hardcover and mass-market paperback formats.

Titles representative of this list: *1 Is One* by Tasha Tudor, illustrated by Tasha Tudor; *The House That Mack Built* by Susanna Hill, illustrated by Ken Wilson-Max; *What on Earth Can It Be?* by Roger McGough, illustrated by Lydia Monks; *'Twas the Day After Thanksgiving: A Lift-the-Flap Story* by Mavis Smith, illustrated by Mavis Smith; *Chanukah Bugs* by David A. Carter, illustrated by David A. Carter; *A Charlie Brown Christmas* by Charles M. Schulz, illustrated by Charles M. Schulz; *Eight Nights of Chanukah Lights* by Dian Curtis Regan, illustrated by Dawn Apperley; *Message for Santa* by Patricia Hall, illustrated by Alison Winfield.

Send query letters with SASEs to:

Cindy Alvarez, Editorial Director

Erin Molta (née McCormack), Senior Editor

Margaret K. McElderry Books

1230 Sixth Avenue, New York, NY 10020

Margaret K. McElderry Books publishes fiction and nonfiction for young children and juveniles in hardcover format. Titles indicative of this list: *Happy Christmas, Honey!* (Happy Honey #4) by Laura Godwin, illustrated by Jane Chapman; *Musical Beds* by Mara Bergman, illustrated by Marjolein Pottie; *Storm Cats* by Malachy Doyle, illustrated by Stuart Trotter; *Was That Christmas?* by Hilary McKay, illustrated by Amanda Harvey; *Hello Benny! What It's Like to Be a Baby?* by Robie H. Harris, illustrated by Michael Emberley; *Loose Threads* by Lorie Ann Grover; *Skeleton Hiccups* by Margery Cuyler, illustrated by S. D. Schindler; *Twelve Hats for Lena: A Book of Months* by Karen Katz; *Cow* by Malachy Doyle, illustrated by Angelo Rinaldi.

Send query letters with SASEs to:

Emma K. Dryden, Executive Editor

Margaret K. McElderry, Vice President and Publisher

Minstrel

1230 Avenue of the Americas, New York, NY 10020

Minstrel publishes fiction and nonfiction for readers aged 8–12 in mass-market paperback, school and library binding, and digital formats. Titles representative of this list include *The Broadway Ballplayers #4: Sideline Blues* by Maureen Holohan; *Bub Moose* by Carol Wallace, et al.; *Camp Hide-a-Pet* (Full House: Michelle and Friends, No .39) by Cathy East Dubowski; *The Case of the Twin Teddy Bears* by Carolyn Keene; *The Castle Conundrum* by Franklin W. Dixon; *The Chinese New Year Mystery* by Carolyn Keene, Jan Naimo Jones (Illustrator); *Chomps, Flea, and Gray Cat (That's Me!)* by Carol Wallace, et al.; *Circus Act: The Clues Challenge* by Carolyn Keene; *Crime in the Cards* by Franklin W Dixon.

Nick Jr.

Nick Jr. is a new line of preschool and young adults books, associated with Nickelodeon. The creation of Nick Jr. was the largest licensing launch in children's publishing history.

Simon & Schuster Books for Young Readers

Simon & Schuster Books for Young Readers publishes fiction and nonfiction titles for children of all ages, from preschool through teens, in hardcover format.

Titles representative of this nonfiction list include *Apolo Anton Ohno: My Story* by Apolo Anton Ohno, with Nancy Richardson; *Elizabeth Taylor's Nibbles and Me* by Elizabeth Taylor; *Parker Picks* by Deb Levine, illustrated by Pedro Martin; *Let's Try It Out with Freezing and Melting* (Let's Try It Out #7) by Seymour Simon and Nicole Fauteux, illustrated by Doug Cushman.

S

Fiction titles in this house span the spectrum from social situations and self-esteem, to animals and pets, action and adventure, holidays and festivals, science fiction, fantasy, African American, and other ethnic stories. Titles indicative of the fiction list include *Because of Anya* by Margaret Peterson Haddix; *Eloise Takes a Bawth* by Kay Thompson, illustrated by Hilary Knight; *Henry and Mudge and the Tall Tree House* by Cynthia Rylant; *Please, Baby, Please* by Spike Lee and Tonya Lewis Lee, illustrated by Kadir Nelson; *Puppy Mudge Takes a Bath* by Cynthia Rylant, illustrated by Isidre Mones; *Soul Searching: Thirteen Stories About Faith and Belief* (edited by Lisa Fraustino); *Taking Liberty: The Story of Oney Judge, George Washington's Runaway Slave* by Ann Rinaldi; *Chicken Soup by Heart* by Esther Hershenhorn, illustrated by Rosanne Litzinger; *Deaf Child Crossing* by Marlee Matlin; *Four Friends at Christmas* by Tomie dePaola; *Justin Morgan Had a Horse* by Marguerite Henry, illustrated by Wesley Dennis; *The Light of Christmas* by Richard Paul Evans, illustrated by Dan Craig; *Riding the Flume* by Patricia Curtis Pfitsch, cover by David Bowers; *Tithe: A Modern Faeire Tale* by Holly Black, cover by Greg Spalenka; *Big Al and Shrimpy* by Andrew Clements, illustrated by Yoshi Kogo; *Class Pets* (Work 1) by Frank Asch; *Everything I Know About Monsters: A Collection of Made-Up Facts, Educated Guesses, and Silly Pictures About Creatures of Creepiness* by Tom Lichtenheld.

Send query letters with SASEs to:

David Gale, Editorial Director—Middle-grade and young-adult novels, primarily; looks for sharp writing and fresh voices; does not want to consider standard young-adult problem novels or romances, but is interested in more unusual, hard-hitting, and literary young-adult novels

Kevin Lewis, Editor—Picture books (both short texts for younger readers and longer texts for older readers), interesting and fresh nonfiction for all age groups, and middle-grade novels with a distinctive voice

Jessica Schulte, Editor

Stephen Geck, Vice President, Associate Publisher

Simon Pulse

Simon Pulse produces juvenile fiction titles in mass-market paperback and hardcover formats. Many of this imprint's books have movie or television tie-ins, such as: *Buffy the Vampire Slayer Script Book Season 2, Vol. 3.*

Categories include historical and medieval fiction, espionage, family, siblings, social situations, and self-esteem, among others. Titles representative of Simon Pulse include *Betrayed* (Fearless #24) by Francine Pascal; *Dark Vengeance* by Diana G. Gallagher; *The Queen of Everything* by Deb Caletti; *Endangered Species* by Nancy Holder and Jeff Mariotte; *From the Mixed-Up Files of Mrs. Basil E. Frankweiler* by E. L. Konigsburg; *Hounded by Baskervilles* (Sabrina the Teenage Witch #45) by Mercer Warriner; *Probably Still Nick Swansen* by Virginia Euwer Wolff, cover by Bruce Katz.

Simon Spotlight

Simon Spotlight publishes hardcover and mass-market paperback fiction books tied to Viacom properties such as *Rugrats* and *The Busy World of Richard Scarry.*

Other titles indicative of Simon Spotlight's list: *Little Bill's Big Book of Jokes* by Susan Gaber; *Look and Find!* by Susan Kantor, illustrated by Joe Ewers; *The Wild Thornberrys Movie* by Cathy East Dubowski; *Bob* by Lauryn Silverhardt, illustrated by Barry Goldberg; *Bob's Big Story Collection* by various authors and illustrators; *A Comfy, Cosy Thanksgiving* by Kiki Thorpe; *Scoop* by Lauryn Silverhardt, illustrated by Barry Goldberg; *Curse of the Werewuff* by David Lewman, illustrated by Sharon Ross, Anastasios Gionis, and Carl A. Braxton.

Send query letters with SASEs to:

Jenny Miglis, Senior Editor

Jennifer Koch, Editorial Director

Sheri Tan, Executive Editor

GIBBS SMITH, PUBLISHER

PO Box 667, Layton, UT 84041
801-544-9800
www.gibbs-smith.com

Gibbs Smith publishes general trade nonfiction, including interior decorating, Western lifestyle, architecture, and nature. Gibbs Smith also produces a line of children's outdoor activity books and picture books. The house has a strong emphasis on home and health literature of the Western United States, including cowboy humor and poetry. The publisher's architecture program features a new work on *The Blacker House* by Randell Makinson.

The house produces books in fine hardcover and trade paper editions and offers distinctive lines of gift books keyed to the publisher's interest areas.

Gibbs Smith, Publisher (founded in 1969), is a house with a resourceful spirit. Company mission statement: To enrich and inspire humankind. Gibbs Smith looks for new projects that contribute to and refresh this spirit. Gibbs Smith believes that the single most important quality for both writer and publisher is passion: a sense of great purpose; an unusually heightened interest in the subject matter and in the task—whether it be writing or publishing. As Gibbs M. Smith writes: "It is a great privilege to work from our old barn office in the Rocky Mountains and have our books enter the literary bloodstream of the world."

High on the Gibbs Smith list: *The Lesson* by Carol Lynn Pearson (illustrated by Kathleen Peterson); *French by Design* by Betty Lou Phillips; *Camps and Cottages* by Molly Hyde English; *Bungalow Bathrooms* by Jane Powell.

Gibbs Smith publishes a seasonal-holiday sampler modeled on Moore's classic "Night Before Christmas." Subjects include teachers, grandmas, grandpas, dads, cats, dogs, fishermen, and golfers, in Texas, Chicago, Seattle, Florida, and California.

Of interest to children and family: *Bullfrog Pops!* by Rick Walton (illustrated by Chris McAllister); *Fishing in a Brook* by Lawson Drinkard (illustrated by Fran Lee); *Trekking on a Trail* by Linda White (illustrated by Fran Lee).

Gibbs Smith, Publisher, distributes its own list and utilizes a network of regional sales representatives. Query letters and SASEs should be directed to:

Madge Baird, V. P. Editorial—Interior design, Western, architecture

Suzanne Taylor, Senior Editor—Interior design, children's, gift books

Glenn Law, Editor—Nature, outdoor activities

SOHO PRESS

853 Broadway, New York, NY 10003
212-260-1900

Soho publishes trade nonfiction and fiction. Nonfiction covers areas such as literary criticism, international affairs, and memoirs. This compact house is also distinguished for its formidable list of contemporary fiction (often with a literary bent), which includes mysteries and historical reprints. The Soho train of interest also verges into travel, autobiography, and the social sciences.

Soho Press (founded in 1986) publishes a superior roster of hardcover and softcover trade books. Many of the house's titles have achieved marked critical and commercial success, including Oprah winner and National Book Award nominee Edwidge Danticat, author of *The Farming of Bones* and *Breath, Eyes and Memory.*

Fiction and literary arts from Soho: *Gloria* by Keith Maillard; *The Gravity of Sunlight* by Rosa Shand; *Death of a Red Heroine* by Qiu Xialong; *The Sixteen Pleasures* by Robert Hellenga; *The Twins* by Tessa De Loo; *Adrian Mole: The Cappuccino Years* by Sue Townsend.

Soho mysteries: *The Amsterdam Cops* by Janwillem van de Wetering; *The Vault* and *The Reaper* by Peter Lovesey; *The Tattoo Murder Case* by Akimitsu Takagi (translated by Deborah Boehm); *The Whispering Wall* and *The Souvenir* by Patricia Carlon.

The Hera Series presents reprints of historical fiction that feature strong female characters. Hera series titles: *Lady of the Reeds* by Pauline Gedge; *Stealing Heaven: The Love Story of Heloise and Abelard* by Marion Meade.

Soho Press books are distributed to the trade by Farrar, Straus & Giroux. Query letters and SASEs should be directed to:

Juris Jurjevics, Publisher

SOURCEBOOKS, INC.

Sourcebooks Casablanca

Sourcebooks Hysteria

Sourcebooks Landmark

Sourcebooks Media Fusion

Sphinx Publishing

Illinois office:
1935 Brookdale Road, Suite 139, Naperville, IL 60563
fax: 630-961-2168

Connecticut office:
955 Connecticut Avenue, #5310, Bridgeport, CT 06607
203-333-9399   fax: 203-367-7188

Founded in 1987, Sourcebooks' mission is to reach as many people as possible with books that will enlighten their lives. In 2000, Sourcebooks was named one of the fastest-growing private companies by *Inc.* magazine in its *Inc.* 500 list. Sourcebooks is the only publisher on this year's list. Sourcebooks also won the 2000 Blue Chip Enterprise Award.

Sourcebooks has strong distribution into the retail market—bookstores, gift shops, and specialty stores whose primary product is something other than books—and provides tremendous editorial, sales, marketing, and publicity support for its authors. The house follows a somewhat out-of-date model for book publishing that makes its passion for books central. In short, Sourcebooks believes in authorship. The house works with authors to develop great books that find and inspire a wide audience. Sourcebooks believes in helping to develop authors' careers and recognizes that a well-published, successful book is often a cornerstone. The company seeks authors who are as committed to success as it is.

Its fiction imprint, Sourcebooks Landmark, publishes a variety of titles. It is interested first and foremost in books that have a story to tell. Sourcebooks is currently reviewing only agented fiction manuscripts.

For nonfiction, Sourcebooks is interested in books that will establish a unique standard in their area. The house looks for books with a well-defined, strong target market. Its publishing list includes most nonfiction categories, such as entertainment, sports, general self-help/psychology, business (particularly small business, marketing, and management), parenting, health and beauty, reference, biographies, gift books, and women's issues.

Sourcebooks is not currently publishing children's books, but it does keep an active list of artists and illustrators.

Please direct query letters with SASEs to Sourcebooks, Editorial Submissions, PO Box 4410, Naperville, IL 60567-4410:

Hillel Black, (CT) Executive Editor—Commercial and literary fiction, thrillers, suspense, love stories, historical fiction, and mysteries; in nonfiction, history, biography, autobiography, science, medicine, relationship books

Deborah Werksman, (CT) Editorial Manager Gift Books—Humor, love, dating, relationships, wedding books, self-help, women's interest, parenting, gift books

Jennifer Fusco, (IL) Editor—Parenting, self-help, history, politics/current affairs, cookbooks, psychology and health, women's fiction, literary fiction, family sagas

Alex Lubertozzi, (IL) Editor—Acquires books for Sourcebooks MediaFusion and Sourcebooks Landmark; media components (audio CDs, DVDs); historical, cultural, and sports stories; all genres of fiction

Dianne Wheeler, (IL)—Division Manager of Sphinx Publishing; titles that cover legal topics to interest the lay customer

S

STACKPOLE BOOKS

5067 Ritter Road, Mechanicsburg, PA 17055-6921
717-796-0411   fax: 717-796-0412

Stackpole specializes in nature and the outdoors, crafts and hobbies, fly fishing, sporting literature, history (especially military history), military reference, and works geared to the Pennsylvania region.

Stackpole Books publishes editions that are created lovingly, with striking design. When selecting projects to produce, the publisher determines what readers need and how these needs will be met through a proposed project's fresh perspective. Stackpole signs expert authors, juggles production schedules, and commits the personalized verve to make the dream real. Stackpole believes in perfectionism and care—when focused upon the practical—as keys to successful publishing.

Stackpole Books was established in 1933 as Stackpole & Sons, a small family-owned publishing enterprise. The house acquired the Military Service Publishing Company in 1935 and has continued to grow into additional publishing areas, while remaining attuned to its original publishing vision.

On the Stackpole list: *Around the World on a Bicycle* by Thomas Stevens (with an introduction by Thomas Pauly); *The Barrier Islands* by Curtis K. Badger and Rick Kellam; *Civil War Firsts: The Legacies of America's Bloodiest Conflict* by Gerald S. Henig and Eric Niderost; *The Complete Guide to New Zealand Trout Lures* by Derek Quilliam; *From Blue to Gray: The Life of Confederate General Cadmus M. Wilcox* by Gerard A. Patterson; *Pop Flyes: Bob Popovic's Approach to Saltwater Fly Design* by Ed Jaworowski and Bob Popovics; *Rocky Mountain: A Visitor's Companion* by George Wuerthner (illustrated by Douglas W. Moore); *Mountain Biking* by Susanna and German Mills; *Senator* by Samuel J. Martin; *Underground Railroad in Pennsylvania* by William J. Switala; *Whitewater Rafting* by Graeme Addison; *Bird Sounds: How and Why Birds Sing, Call, Chatter and Screech* by Barry Kent MacKay; *Homeward Bound: The Demobilization of the Union and Confederate Armies 1865–1866* by William B. Holberton; *Captain Marryat: Seaman, Writer and Adventurer* by Tom Pocock; *County Courthouses of Pennsylvania: A Guide* by Oliver Williams; *Falling Stars: A Guide to Meteors and Meteorites* by Michael Reynolds; *Guide to Military Installations, 6th Edition* by Dan Cragg; *Swamp Doctor: The Diary of a Union Surgeon in the Virginia and North Carolina Marshes* by Thomas Lowry; *A Good Horse Has No Color: Searching Iceland for the Perfect Horse* by Nancy Marie Brown; *The Guide and the CEO* by M. David Detweiler; *Real Alaska: Finding Our Way in the Wild Country* by Paul Schullery; *The Half Not Told: The Civil War in a Frontier Town* by Preston Filbert.

From the Who's Who in British History series: *Who's Who in Tudor England, 1485–1603, Volume 1* by C. R. N. Routh; *Who's Who in Victorian Britain, 1851–1901, Volume 1* by Roger Ellis; *Who's Who in Early Medieval England* by Christopher Tyermand; *Who's Who in Late Medieval England* by Michael Hicks.

From the Pennsylvania Trail of History Guides: *Erie Maritime Museum and U.S. Brig Niagara; Brandywine Battlefield; Pennsbury Manor; Conrad Weiser Homestead; Hope Lodge; Mather Mill.*

Exploring the Appalachian Trail series titles: *Hikes in Northern New England* by Michael Kodas, Andrew Weegar, Mark Condon, and Glenn Scherer; *Hikes in Southern New England* by David Emblidge; *Hikes in the Mid-Atlantic States* by Glenn Scherer and Don Hopes; *Hikes in the Virginias* by David Lillard and Gwyn Hicks; *Hikes in the Southern Appalachians* by Doris Gove.

Stackpole distributes its own books, as well as a list of titles from U.K. and U.S. publishers. Query letters and SASEs should be directed to:

Ed Skender, Editor—Military reference

Judith Schnell, Editorial Director—Outdoor sports; fly fishing

Kyle Weaver, Editor—Pennsylvania

Leigh Ann Berry, Editor—History

Mark Allison, Editor—Nature
Born: 1964.
Education: B.A., English, Penn State University.
Employment history/editor career path: Started as an Editorial Assistant at Stackpole after working as a writer and Proofreader.
Personal interests: Photography; reading books out of my line.
What books have you acquired that make you the most proud? What books that you have acquired reflect the types of books you like to represent? Books with a long shelf life. We want to keep an author's work in print forever.
Do you represent fiction? No.
What do you want to see less of? Imitations of successful titles, *Harvey's Penick's Little Red Book*–style treatments for subjects other than golf.
Do you represent nonfiction? Yes, exclusively.
Do you require book proposals? If so, what do you look for in evaluating a book proposal? I require a proposal or a sample chapter with a cover letter, no magic formula. I look for demonstrated expertise in the subject matter, demonstrated skill as a writer, and evidence of commitment to the project.
Are certain aspects of a book proposal given more weight than others? The writing itself and the description of what the book is all about—which must be well thought out, exact, and clearly presented.
What process do you use for making a decision? What is the process for acquisition; is there a committee? (1) Investigation and research by the editor. (2) Input from sales and marketing. (3) Review and discussion by the editorial board.
What kinds of nonfiction books do you want to see less of? Books that are heavy on design and photography/art, but skimpy on content.
Are you interested in work geared for the masses (readers of *People*, *The Star*, etc.)? Our readers usually have a keen interest in the activities or subject matter our lines cover: birding, fly fishing, Civil War history, and so on.
Are agents important? Why? We usually deal directly with authors, but have good working relationships with a few agents who know our lines. We sometimes get proposals from agents that are so far out of our lines that I wonder what purpose they are serving.

Do you like new writers? What should new writers do to break into the business? We publish a number of new writers, who should establish their expertise and perhaps an audience by writing for magazines and newspapers before tackling a book.

How should writers approach you? Query and proposal or query and sample chapter are the best ways. I personally don't like e-mail queries.

What are some common mistakes writers make? What really gets on your nerves? Focus on design and presentation of the book, instead of on the content.

What can writers do to get your attention and to avoid the slush pile? Straightforward presentation of the project in our line, author expertise.

What have been some of your craziest experiences with submissions? A querying author once refused to reveal the subject matter of his "top secret" project until a contract was signed.

Any advice for writers? Try to stay enthusiastic and realistic and remember that the author and publisher should be working toward the same goal.

STERLING PUBLISHING COMPANY

387 Park Avenue South, New York, NY 10016-8810
212-532-7160

Sterling emphasizes general popular reference and information books, science, nature, arts and crafts, architecture, home improvement, history, humor, health, self-help, wine and food, gardening, business and careers, social sciences, sports, pets, hobbies, drama and music, psychology, occult, New Age, and military-science books. Sterling also publishes games, puzzles, and children's books.

The current scope of the Sterling Publishing Company program includes a wide range of nonfiction practical approaches, including informative how-to books in gardening, crafts, and woodworking; books on military history; art and reference titles; and activity and puzzle books for the kids. The house (founded in 1949) hosts a formidable backlist.

Representative Sterling titles: *Body Shaping with Free Weights: Easy Routines for Your Home Workout* by Stephenie Karony and Anthony L. Ranken; *Golf Mistakes & How to Correct Them* by Oliver Heuler; *200 Perplexing Chess Puzzles* by Martin Freif; *The Little Giant Encyclopedia of Mazes* by the Diagram Group; *Space Mazes* by Roger Moreau; *Challenging False Logic Puzzles* by Norman D. Willis; *Weight Training Basics* by Robert Kennedy (publisher of *MuscleMag International*); *Gemstones of the World* by Walter Schumann; *Romantic Massage* by R. J. Nikola, L.M.T.; *Zen Wisdom: Daily Teaching from the Zen Masters* by Timothy Freke; *The Truth About Alien Abductions* by Peter Hough and Moyshe Kalman; *The Mystic Grail: The Magical World of the Arthurian Quest* by John Matthew.

On the Sterling children's book list: *Science Crafts for Kids: 50 Fantastic Things to Invent & Create* and *Nature Crafts for Kids: 50 Fantastic Things to Make with Mother Nature's Help* by Gwen Diehn and Terry Krautwurst; *The Great Rubber Stamp Book: Designing, Making, Using* by Dee Gruenig; *Cat Crafts: More Than 50 Purrfect Projects* by Dawn Cusick; *Dog Crafts: More Than 50 Grrreat Projects* by Bobbe Needham.

Query letters and SASEs should be directed to:

Acquisitions Department

STEWART, TABORI & CHANG

115 West 18th Street, New York, NY 10111
212-519-1200   fax: 212-519-1230

Stewart, Tabori, & Chang publishes luxuriously produced titles about love, food, spirituality, divination, history, comic art, music, and Christmas. The house offers topnotch specialty merchandise such as calendars, cards, journals, and engagement books. Terrail is an imprint in collaboration with Editions Terrail that publishes a line of art books at reasonable prices. The Essential Gardens library is a line accenting a wide range of topical-interest editions. The publisher offers a solid list of new seasonal titles and supports an impeccably select backlist.

Stewart, Tabori & Chang books are produced in hardcover and trade paperback editions. Booksellers especially appreciate the quality product signified by the publisher's prancing-bison trade logo—these books on display in a bookstore can draw significant point-of-purchase interest from customers. House trade motto: "The heart and soul of illustrated books."

Stewart, Tabori & Chang (founded in 1981 by Andy Stewart, Lena Tabori, and Nai Chang), recently part of the publishing stable of Peter Brant (owner of the magazines *Interview, Art in America,* and *Antiques*), is now a division of U.S. Media Holdings, Inc.

From Stewart, Tabori & Chang: *Colors of Provence* by Michel Bicha (photographs by Heinz Angermayr); *Quick Cooking with Pacific Flavors* by Hugh Carpenter and Teri Sandison; *Goddess: A Celebration in Art and Literature* (edited by Jalaja Bonheim); *Little Moments of Happiness* by Elisabeth Brami and Philippe Bertrand; *I Ching: A Spiritual Guide* by Frits Blok; *Tangram: The Ancient Chinese Puzzle* by Joost Elffers and Michael Schuyt; *Native Americans: A Portrait, the Art and Travels of Charles Bird King, George Catlin, and Karl Bodmer* by Robert J. Moore, Jr.; *Heart & Soul: A Celebration of Black Music Style in America 1930–1978* by Bob Merlis and Davin Seay; *The Jewish Spirit: A Celebration in Stories and Art* (edited by Ellen Frankel); *The Discovery of the Nile* by Gianni Guadalupi; *Ancient Greece: The Dawn of the Western World* by Furio Durando.

The Essential Garden Library series encompasses gardening titles covering a variety of subjects and formats. Each book in the series features Stewart, Tabori & Chang quality in writing, photography, and production. Numbered chronologically, these books are uniform in height and width to stand next to one another in the reader's garden library. Some titles: *Herbs* by George Carter (photographs by Marianne Marjerus); *Getting Ready for Winter and Other Fall Tasks* by Stephen Bradley.

Stewart, Tabori & Chang distributes to the trade via Publishers Resources; in addition, the house uses a network of independent regional sales representatives. Query letters and SASEs should be directed to:

Alexandra Childs, Assistant Editor

Linda Sunshine, Editorial Director

Mary Kalamaras, Editor

SYBEX, INC.

1151 Marina Village Parkway, Alameda, CA 94501
510-523-8233   fax: 510-523-1766
www.sybex.com   e-mail: info@sybex.com

Sybex was founded in 1976 and is the oldest publisher of computer books, as well as the largest independent computer book publisher. Sybex also publishes a wide range of computer-based training and Web-based training products. It publishes trade computer books for all levels and all types of users. Sybex offers high-quality tutorials and references in all main software areas, including certification, programming, graphics, business applications, operating systems, and games. The company has wide distribution in all major retail bookstores, mass-market outlets, and warehouse clubs and enjoys superior worldwide distribution.

The Sybex catalog features certification titles for technical professionals; the Mastering series for beginning, intermediate, and advanced users; Strategies and Secrets for gamers; I Didn't Know You Could Do That! for intermediate users; Complete for beginning to intermediate users; Developer's Guides for professional programmers and developers; and Jumpstart and Visual Jumpstart for beginners.

Recent bestsellers include *CCNA Study Guide* by Todd Lammle; *Mastering Windows 2000 Server,* 3rd edition, and *The Complete PC Upgrade and Maintenance Guide, 11th Edition* by Mark Mianasi; *MCSE Window 2000 Core Requirements Study Guides* by James Chellis and other authors; *Pokemon Gold and Silver Pathways to Adventure* by Jason Rich.

Sybex handles its own distribution. Query letters and SASEs should be directed to:

Jordan Gold, Vice President and Publisher—He will direct you to the appropriate associate publisher and acquisitions editor who is responsible for the particular product or topic area; any book or series idea may be directed to his attention. He will also help you in any publishing-related matter.

THE TAUNTON PRESS (PART OF PUBLISHER'S GROUP WEST)

63 South Main Street, PO Box 5506, Newtown, CT 06470-5506
203-426-8171   fax: 203-426-3434
www.taunton.com

The Taunton Press is known for its high-quality, authentic books and magazines. For more than 20 years, it has published leading magazines, such as *Fine Woodworking* and *Fine Gardening.* Taunton started out publishing woodworking books, but then grew to include fiber arts, home design, building and remodeling, gardening, and cooking. Taunton is a small publishing company, but has a strong market reach through its parent company, Publisher's Group West. Taunton currently publishes 35–40 frontlist titles each year, with an active backlist of more than 250 books.

Query letters and SASEs should be directed to:

Jim Childs, Publisher

TAYLOR PUBLISHING COMPANY

1550 West Mockingbird Lane, Dallas, TX 75235
214-819-8501

Taylor presents frontlist trade books and targeted-interest practical titles in the areas of celebrity biography, health and fitness, gardening, home improvement, lifestyle, parenting, popular culture, regional, sports, and coffee-table/gift books. Taylor Publishing Company (founded in 1980) is an innovative house that is particularly adept at hitting specialty-interest areas and international gift-book/display markets.

Titles from Taylor: *ESPN: The Uncensored History* by Michael Freeman; *Koufax* by Ed Oruver; *The Depressed Child* by Dr. Douglas Riley; *The Bully Pulpit: A Teddy Roosevelt Book of Quotations* (edited by H. Paul Jeffers); *The Moonlit Garden* by Scott Ogden; *The Stan DeFreitas Garden Answer Book* by Stan DeFreitas.

Backlist hits: *Spielberg: The Man, the Movies, the Mythology* by Frank Santello; *Patty Sheehan on Golf* by Patty Sheehan and Betty Hicks; *A Winning Edge* by Bonnie Blair with Greg Brown (illustrated by Doug Keith); *Count Me In, Never Give Up* by Cal Ripken, Jr.

Taylor Publishing distributes its own list and handles distribution for a variety of other houses. Query letters and SASEs should be directed to:

Lynn A. Brooks, Publisher and Editorial Director

Michael Emmerich, Acquisitions Director

T

TEN SPEED PRESS/CELESTIAL ARTS

Celestial Arts

Tricycle Press

PO Box 7123, Berkeley, CA 94707
510-559-1600   fax: 510-524-1052
www.tenspeed.com

Ten Speed/Celestial Arts publishes practical nonfiction in cooking, business and careers, women's issues, parenting, health, self-discovery, leisure and lifestyle, humor, outdoors, house crafts, and popular reference. Tricycle Press (please see subentry) is Ten Speed/Celestial's children's division. Ten Speed Press/Celestial Arts publishes hardcover and paperback titles; the house also produces a line of posters and novelty items.

Ten Speed Press (founded in 1971) gained success with *Anybody's Bike Book* by Tom Cuthbertson—the first book the publisher produced; this classic work has been revised and updated several times and is emblematic of the type of reference book that Ten Speed Press publishes so well. With the acquisition of the Celestial Arts subsidiary (see subentry), the house obtained the midsize status that set the platform for subsequent expansion of the list. Throughout this growth, Ten Speed has been renowned for its small press publishing savvy.

Ten Speed/Celestial is selective in acquiring new works and procures in part on the basis of projected endurance: The hardy backlist and announcements of revised editions read as fresh and bright as many houses' new releases.

Ten Speed is noted for the individualist expression of the American culture as voiced by the house's authors. Many Ten Speed titles feature unconventional approaches to the subject matter at hand—making creativity an enduring Ten Speed/Celestial Arts hallmark. Among its perennial sellers, Ten Speed publishes *What Color Is Your Parachute?* and other career-related works by Richard Bolles; *The Moosewood Cookbook* by Mollie Katzen; *How to Shit in the Woods* by Kathleen Meyer.

Ten Speed titles: *Charlie Trotter Cooks at Home* by Charlie Trotter; *Mushrooms Demystified* by David Arora; *The Village Baker* by Joe Ortiz; *White Trash Cooking* by Ernest Matthew Mickler; *Why Cats Paint* by Burton Silver and Heather Busch; *Mustards Grill Napa Valley Cookbook* by Cindy Pawlcyn; *Caprial Cooks for Friends* by Caprial Pence; *Terra: Cooking from the Heart of Napa Valley* by Hiro Sone and Lissa Doumani; *Cool Colleges* by Don Asher; *Man Eating Bugs* by Peter Menzel and Faith D'Aluisio.

Ten Speed Press/Celestial Arts handles its own distribution. Query letters and SASEs should be directed to:

Kirsty Melville, Publisher

Lorena Jones, Editorial Director

Celestial Arts

The Celestial Arts program homes toward titles in self-discovery, nutrition and fitness, general health, spirituality, popular psychology, relationships and healing, pregnancy and parenting, gay and lesbian issues, practical how-to, kitchen arts, and general trade nonfiction.

Celestial Arts was founded as an independent house in 1966 and was acquired by Ten Speed Press in 1983. The house produces an individual line of hardcover and trade paperback books, along with calendars, maps, poster art, personal journals, and engagement books.

On the Celestial Arts roster: *Bestfeeding* by Mary Renfrew, Chloe Fisher, and Suzanne Arms; *Living Juicy* by Sark; *Uncommon Sense for Parents with Teenagers* by Mike Riera; *Natural Superwoman* by Rosamon Richardson; *Hit Below the Belt: Facing Up to Prostate Cancer* by F. Ralph Berberich, M.D.; *Natural Alternatives to HRT Cookbook* by Marilyn Glenville; *Positively Gay* (edited by Betty Berzon, Ph.D.); *The Detox Diet* by Elson M. Haas, M.D.

Celestial Arts is distributed by Ten Speed Press/Celestial Arts. Query letters and SASEs should be directed to:

Jo Ann Deck, Publisher

Tricycle Press

Tricycle is devoted to books and posters for kids and their grown-ups. Tricycle Press was started in 1993 to unify and expand the house's children's list (previously divided between parent Ten Speed and sister Celestial Arts). Tricycle Press, in addition to its own roster of originals, catalogs appropriate backlist selections from Ten Speed and Celestial Arts.

Tricycle is committed to publishing projects that reflect the creative spirit of the parent company, Ten Speed Press, and its publishing partner, Celestial Arts.

Titles from Tricycle: *Q Is for Quark and G Is for Googol* by David Schwartz; *Pretend Soup* and *Honest Pretzels* by Mollie Katzen; *Hey Little Ant* by Phillip and Hannah Hoose; *The Pumpkin Blanket* by Deborah Turney Zagwyn; *We Can Work It Out: Conflict Resolution for Children* by Barbara K. Polland*; Crashed, Smashed, and Mashed: A Trip to Junkyard Heaven* by Joyce Slayton Mitchell and Steven Borns.

No query letters please. Manuscript guidelines can be found online at www.tenspeed.com. Send complete picture book manuscripts, and sample chapters and outlines for middle-grade novels or other longer works, making sure to include an SASE, care of:

Nicole Geiger, Publisher

THAMES AND HUDSON

500 Fifth Avenue, New York, NY 10110
212-354-3763   fax: 212-398-1252
www.thamesandhudsonusa.com

Thames and Hudson publishes popular and scholarly works, as well as college texts in the fine arts, archaeology, architecture, biography, crafts, history, mysticism, music, photography, and the sciences.

Thames and Hudson (founded in 1977) is an international producer of well-crafted nonfiction trade books in hardcover and trade paperback under its double-dolphin logo. Though a portion of the publisher's list is originated through the New York editorial office, the greater part of Thames and Hudson's titles are imports via the house's United Kingdom branch.

From Thames and Hudson: *The Most Beautiful Villages and Towns of the South; The Golden Age of Dutch Art; Looking Back at Francis Bacon; Living in the Highlands; Techno Architecture; The Dalai Lama's Secret Temple; William Blake: The Complete Illuminated Books; Practically Minimal; Chronicle of the Maya Kings and Queens; The World of King Arthur.*

Thames and Hudson is distributed to the trade by W. W. Norton. The house also offers an 800 ordering number and has in-house fulfillment services for purchases by individual consumers.

Query letters and SASEs should be directed to:

Peter Warner, President

T

THEATRE COMMUNICATIONS GROUP, INC.

355 Lexington Avenue, New York, NY 10017-0217
212-697-5230

Theatre Communications Group is interested in theater-related works.

TIMBERWOLF PRESS

PO Box 266, Allen, TX 75013
972-644-7098
www.TwolfPress.com   e-mail: info@twolfpress.com

Founded in 1994 by Patrick Seaman, Timberwolf Press started out as a software company, publishing a Windows Database version of the bestselling trade reference, the *Insider's Guide to Book Editors, Publishers, and Literary Agents* by Jeff Herman. The software was called *Writer's Desktop Database for Windows* and is now in its fourth annual release.

In 1995, Patrick became affiliated with the premiere Internet broadcasting company AudioNet (http://www.AudioNet.com). While searching for content to broadcast on AudioNet, Seaman asked a writing acquaintance, Jim Cline, to produce an audio version of a novel that Jim was working on at the time. In late 1995, this project gave birth to the first serialized audio-novel on the Internet. Thanks to the Internet, it received fan mail from around the world.

In 1997, Timberwolf Press expanded from a software and multimedia publishing company to the world of print publishing when it released Jim Cline's epic military science fiction novel in a hardback edition: *A Small Percentage*.

A sequel to *A Small Percentage* is in the works, as well as other science fiction and techno-thriller titles.

Query letters and SASEs should be directed to:

Eve McClellen, Senior Editor

Jennifer Mikhail, Editor at Large

Patrick Seaman, Publisher

TIME WARNER TRADE BOOK PUBLISHING GROUP

Warner Books

Little, Brown and Company (see separate entry)

Mysterious Press

Time Warner Audio Books

Warner Aspect

Warner Faith

Warner Business

Time & Life Building, 1271 Avenue of the Americas, New York, NY 10020
212-522-7200
www.twbookmark.com

Warner Books publishes trade nonfiction and commercial fiction. Warner produces mass-market, trade paperback, and hardcover originals, as well as reprints. Among Warner's nonfiction categories are biography, business, cooking, current affairs, history, house and home, humor, popular culture, psychology, self-help, sports, games books, and general reference. Warner fiction accents the popular approach and includes frontlist commercial novels and works in the categories of mystery and suspense, fantasy and science fiction, action thrillers, horror, and contemporary and historical romance.

Warner Aspect is an imprint that specializes in future fiction, science fiction, and fantasy. Warner Vision books are generally high-profile mass-market releases. Books on cassette are the domain of Time Warner AudioBooks. The formerly independent Mysterious Press publishes a distinguished list of mystery, suspense, and crime novels, as well as selected crime nonfiction and reference.

Warner Books (founded in 1961) is a division of Time Warner Communications.

From the Warner list: *Cancer Schmancer* by Fran Drescher; *Mortal Allies* by Brian Haig; *Rush Home Road* by Lori Lansens; *The Black Veil: A Memoir with Digressions* by Rick Moody; *West Point: The First 200 Years; Long Lost* by David Morrell; *If Looks Could Kill* by Kate White; *Five Past Midnight in Bhopal* by Dominique Lapierre and Jaview Moro; *The Faber Report* by David Faber with Ken Kurson; *Yet a Stranger: Why Black Americans Still Don't Feel at Home* by Deborah Mathis; *All That Lives* by Melissa Sanders-Self; *Can't Be Satisfied: The Life and Times of Muddy Waters* by Robert Gordon; *The PGA Manual of Golf* by Rick Martino, PGA of America with Don Wade; *Open and Shut* by David Rosenfelt; *The Beach House* by James Patterson and Peter de Jonge; *High on a Hill* by Dorothy Garlock; *A Conversation with the Mann* by John Ridley; *Only Son: A Memoir* by John Johnson with Jeff Coplon; *Raising Abel* by W. Michael Gear and Kathleen O'Neal Gear; *The Road South: A Memoir* by Shelley Stewart with Nathan Hale Turner, Jr.; *A Bend in the Road* by Nicholas Sparks.

Warner Books handles its own distribution and distributes book products from other publishers.

Query letters and SASEs should be directed to:

Amy Einhorn, Executive Editor, Warner Trade Paperbacks—Popular culture, business, fitness, and self-help

Betsy Mitchell, Executive Editor—Science fiction

Caryn Karmatz Rudy, Senior Editor—Fiction, general nonfiction, and popular culture

Diana Baroni, Senior Editor—Fitness/health, general fiction, nonfiction

T

Dan Ambrosio, Associate Editor—Business Subjects

Jamie Raab, Senior Vice President/Publisher, Warner hardcovers—General nonfiction and fiction

John Aherne, Associate Editor—Popular culture, fiction, general nonfiction

Les Pockell, Associate Publisher—General nonfiction

Rick Horgan, Vice President and Executive Editor—General nonfiction; fiction: thrillers

Rob McMahon, Senior Editor—Business, fiction, sports

Beth de Guzman, Editorial director—Mass market (fiction and nonfiction)

Sara Ann Freed, Editor in Chief, Mysterious Press—Mysteries and suspense

Jackie Joiner, Associate Editor—Commercial fiction, spiritual/New Age, memoir/biography

Rolf Zettersten, Executive Editor, Warner Faith

Rick Wolff, Vice President, Executive Editor, Warner Books—General nonfiction and fiction
>   **Born:** July 14, 1951.
>   **Education:** Harvard, 1973; Long Island University, M.A., 1985.
>   **Employment history/editor career path:** Warner books for the last seven years; Macmillan Books seven years before that; and Alex Hamilton Institute eight years before that.
>   **Personal interests:** I'm fairly eclectic—everything from sports to psychology to reading books. But most of my spare time is devoted to my wife and our three children. Our lives revolve around them.
>   **What would you be doing if you were not an editor?** Probably writing books instead of editing them.
>   **What has been your most successful book that you have acquired to date?** *Politically Correct Fairy Tales*—a humorous hardcover that was on the *NYT* list for close to two years and was number one for a few weeks. That book sold more than four million copies worldwide. The author was James Finn Garner. *How I Play Golf* by Tiger Woods; *The Rich Dad, Poor Dad* books by Roger Kiyosaki.
>   **What books have you acquired that make you the most proud? What books that you have acquired reflect the types of books you like to represent?** *Pros and Cons: The Criminals Who Play in the NFL* (Warner, 1999). Also, *You Gotta Have Wa* by Robert Whiting, about the Japanese obsession with baseball (Macmillan, 1987*). Rich Dad, Poor Dad,* which is on the list right now. Financial advice from Robert Kiyosaki.
>   **Do you represent fiction? If so, what do you look for?** Yes. Strictly big-time commercial fiction. Warner has a very short fiction list, so whatever we acquire, it has to smell like a bestseller.
>   **What do you want to see less of?** Can't say. After all, *Politically Correct Fairy Tales* came in the slush pile.
>   **Do you represent nonfiction?** Yes—I handle business, sports, humor, psychology, biography, finances, and so on.
>   **Do you require book proposals? If so, what do you look for in evaluating a book proposal?** A book proposal is a *must.* I don't have the time to chat about "ideas" for a book over the phone or in e-mail.

T

Are certain aspects of a book proposal given more weight than others? It has to be well written by an author with top credentials, who is committed to promoting the book, and the idea behind the book has to be fresh and different.

What process do you use for making a decision? What is the process for acquisition; is there a committee? If a proposal gets past my review, I take it to the general editorial meeting to get more readings. If it makes the cut there, I take it to the publisher's review meeting for a determination of whether we should pursue it and for how much.

What kinds of nonfiction books do you want to see less of? At Warner, which is a major frontlist house, unless the book can break out in a major way for us, it probably isn't right for us. That usually means most general midlist nonfiction won't work for us.

Are you interested in work geared for the masses (readers of *People, The Star,* etc.)? Depends on the star and how popular they are.

Are agents important? Why? Of course. To help develop proposals, to help the author understand the publishing process, and to work with the editor to make sure the book is a success.

Do you like new writers? What should new writers do to break into the business? Write for newspapers and magazines. Build from that.

How should writers approach you? Through an agent. I wish I had more time to chat with writers who aspire to be published, but unfortunately, I just don't.

What are some common mistakes writers make? What really gets on your nerves? Not promoting their books. Assuming that they can place demands on their editor and other people in the publishing house.

What can writers do to get your attention and to avoid the slush pile? Get an agent.

What have been some of your craziest experiences with submissions? I once put a clause in a contract with the author, a woman in her early 20s, that she couldn't lose her virginity until her book was published. And she signed the contract.

What have been some of your best experiences with writers or in your job? Most of them become lifelong friends and trusted colleagues. That's a major part of the job.

What, if anything, makes you different from other editors? I'm smarter and better looking than my editorial colleagues.

Is there anything you would like to see changed in the industry? I wish the production process could be speeded up with books. It seems silly to have to wait eight or nine months to get a book published after the manuscript is completed.

Any additional thoughts? One of the great aspects of book publishing is that you never know when a new talent is going to be discovered. That's what drives me—I'm always on the lookout for that next great writer.

J. N. TOWNSEND, PUBLISHING

4 Franklin Street, Exeter, NH 03833
603-778-9883   fax: 603-772-1980
www.jntownsendpublishing.com   e-mail: jntown@mediaone.net

J. N. Townsend is a small publisher with a successful line of titles about pets, wildlife, nature, and country living. Townsend (founded in 1986) initially published in softcover format only and issued its first hardcover title in 1994. The house has thrived on the basis of short press runs and by keeping titles alive on a full backlist.

From Townsend: *Duffy: Adventures of a Collie* by Irving Townsend; *Goat Song: My Island Angora Goat Farm* by Susan Basquin; *A Cat's Life: Dulcy's Story,* as told to Dee Ready; *Who Ever Heard of a HORSE in the HOUSE?* by Jacqueline Tresl; *The Ugly Dachshund* (6th printing) by G. B. Stern; *Regards, Rodeo: The Mariner Dog of Cassi* (2nd printing) by Alan Armstrong (illustrations by Martha Armstrong).

J. N. Townsend Publishing presents the latest book by Era Zistel, *The Good Year;* she writes about her life with animals in the Catskill Mountains of New York. Other Zistel titles: *Gentle People; Wintertime Cat; Orphan; A Gathering of Cats; Good Companions.*

Celebrating a third printing is *Separate Lifetimes: A Collection* by Irving Townsend (illustrated by Judith Roberts-Rondeau); this collection of essays is particularly cherished by readers who have suffered the loss of an animal companion. *Separate Lifetimes* was the first book published by the press in 1986 as a memorial to the publisher's father.

Distributed to the trade by Alan C. Hood and Company. Query letters and SASEs should be directed to:

Terri Fyler, Editor

TURNER PUBLISHING, INC.

Turner Publishing has officially gone out of business.

TUTTLE PUBLISHING

153 Milk Street, 5th Floor, Boston, MA 02109
617-951-4080   fax: 617-951-4045

Tuttle Publishing is America's leading independent publisher of Asian-interest books and maps and the premier publisher of English-language books in Japan. Tuttle's imprints strive to span the East and West with market-leading books on cooking, martial arts, Eastern philosophy, spiritual development, Asian culture, design, and language learning.

Its publications include such renowned books as: *The New Nelson Japanese-English Dictionary; Bruce Lee's Striking Thoughts,* compiled and annotated by John Little; *The Henna Body Art Kit* by Aileen Marron; *Japan's Big Bang: The Deregulation and Revitalization of the Japanese Economy* by Declan Hayes; *Zen Flesh, Zen Bones* by Nyogen Senzaki and Paul Reps.

Query letters with SASEs should be directed to:

Ed Walters, Publishing Director

Ashley Benning, Associate Editor

Jennifer Lantagne, Associate Publisher

Ben Gleason, Assistant Editor

UNITED PUBLISHERS GROUP/UPG

Hastings House

Gates & Bridges

Judd Publishing

50 Washington Street, Norwalk, CT 06854
203-838-4083   fax: 203-838-4084
www.upub.com   e-mail: info@upub.com

United Publishers Group/UPG produces a number of trade nonfiction lines and selective fiction through several affiliated imprints. The group includes Hastings House (Daytrips travel guides), Gates & Bridges (works with multicultural/global themes), Judd Publishing (illustrated editions), and Rosset-Morgan Books (books with a literary or cultural perspective).

United Publishers Group (founded in 1996) and its imprints conduct their programs from offices in several locations, including Connecticut; Washington, D.C.; and Manhattan. UPG is a subsidiary of the German-based Peter Leers Group, a privately held real-estate and insurance amalgamate.

Henno Lohmeyer (UPG publisher) opened the house in fine style by acquiring several previously independent publishing firms and by securing the U.S. rights to a number of international publishing properties. Plans are to build the publishing group through a number of robust boutique imprints, rather than by combining editorial operations.

From Hastings House: *The Truth About Fiction Writing* by William Appel and Denise Sterrs; *Test Your Bible Power* by Jerry Agel; *Passion for Wine: The Ultimate Guide* by Paul Lirette.

Gates & Bridges is a new imprint that features works that exemplify the essential image: "gates to new worlds . . . bridges between continents." From G&B: *Land of the Ascending Dragon: Rediscovering Vietnam* (photoessay) by Paul Martin (photographs by Steven Raymer); *The Opera Quiz Book: Everything You Always Wanted to Know About the Greatest Art Form Ever Invented by Mankind* by Michael Walsh (photographs by Henry Grossman).

United Publishers Group distributes through Publishers Group West. Initial queries to UPG may be directed to the main-entry address. Query letters and SASEs should be directed to:

Henno Lohmeyer, Publisher and Editor, Gates and Bridges—Works from an international perspective; regional markets; commercial and trade nonfiction

Hy Steirman, Editor in Chief, Hastings House—Presides over Hastings House (now featuring Daytrips travel guides)

Ruina W. Judd, Editor in Chief, Judd Publishing—Illustrated books

U

UNIVERSE PUBLISHING

Children's Universe

300 Park Avenue South, New York, NY 10010-5399
212-982-2300

Universe produces books in art history and appreciation, architecture and design, photography, fashion, sports, alternative culture, and performing arts. Universe Publishing also takes on selected high-interest projects in literary writing and criticism, and the occasional human- or social-interest title in illustrated format. The Universe Publishing emphasis (through individual titles and a number of successful series) is on works of popular, as well as scholarly, interest in the arts worldwide and the arts and artists of the Western and European tradition from prehistoric to contemporary times.

Universe Publishing (founded in 1956; formerly a wing of Phaidon Universe) is an affiliate division of Rizzoli International. Imprints and associated publishers include Universe, Children's Universe, Universe Calendars, Vendome, and Universe Publishing. Among Universe's products are illustrated gift books, children's books, children's paper products, calendars, address books, and diaries.

Universe titles: *The Internet Design Project: The Best of Graphic Art on the Web* by Patrick Burgoyne and Liz Faber; *All-American: A Tommy Hilfiger Style Book* by Tommy Hilfiger, with David A. Keeps; *Secrets of Skating* by Oksana Baiul; *Gymnastics: Balancing Acts* by Christina Lessa; *Camera Ready: How to Shoot Your Kids* by Arthur Elgort; *Intimate Landscapes: The Canyon Suite of Georgia O'Keeffe* by Dana Self, in association with the Kemper Museum of Contemporary Art & Design; *The Romance of California Vineyards* by Molly Chappellet (photographs by Daniel D'Agostini); *Weekends with the Impressionists: A Collection from the National Gallery of Art, Washington* by Carla Brenner.

Universe Publishing and Vendome Press combine on special series lines: Universe of Fashion; Universe of Design; Universe of Art. Beautifully printed and designed—and reasonably priced—these books are geared to appeal equally to novice and expert.

Universe of Fashion offerings are introduced by Grace Mirabella (of magazine fame); each volume deals with the works of great 20th-century couturiers. These books connect the worlds of art, couture, and society with stories of legendary designers. Titles: *Coco Chanel* by Francois Baudot; *Dior* by Marie-France Pocha; *Yves Saint Laurent* by Pierre Bergé; *Valentino* by Bernadine Morris; *Versace* by Richard Martin.

From Universe of Design: *Ferrari and Pininfarina* by Lionel Froissard; *Cartier* by Philippe Trétiack.

The Universe of Art series features shifting, distinctive approaches. Some titles focus on an important facet in the work of an individual legendary master, generally a period or place that encapsulates the essence of a lifetime's work. Titles: *Matisse in Nice* by Xavier Girard; *Renoir's Nudes* by Isabelle Cahn; *Degas Backstage* by Richard Kendall; *Cézanne in Provence* by Denis Coutagne. Other titles in this series feature celebrity authors writing on celebrated artists: *Jasper Johns* by Leo Castelli; *Andy Warhol* by Bob Colacello.

From Vendome: *House & Garden Book of Country Rooms* by Leonie Highton; *Secrets of the Harem* by Carla Coco; *Treasures from Italy's Great Libraries* by Lorenzo Crinelli;

Churches of Rome by Pierre Grimal (photographs by Caroline Rose); *The Grand Canal* by Umberto Franzoi (photographs by Mark Smith).

Universe is distributed to the trade by St. Martin's. Query letters and SASEs should be directed to:

Charles Miers, Publisher—Calendars, graphic products; Children's Universe projects

Elizabeth Johnson, Senior Editor—Art, architecture, women's studies

Children's Universe

Children's Universe produces a variety of inventive products, ranging from book-and-toy packages to storybooks, to hide-and-seek books (with moveable parts), cut-out puppets, posters, masks, and make-it-yourself gift boxes. These are finely designed books and are produced in sturdy editions to withstand carefree handling.

Books from Children's Universe: *Skateboard Monsters* by Daniel Kirk; *Ravita and the Land of Unknown Shadows* (story by Marietta and Peter Brill; illustrated by Laurie Smollett Kutscera); *Head Trips* by Sara Schwartz; *First Steps in Paint: A New and Simple Way to Learn How to Paint* by Tom Robb; *Dinosaur Cowboys Puppet Theatre* by Judy Lichtenstein; *The ABC's of Art* (with a wall frieze version) by the National Gallery of Art, London (with flash cards by the National Gallery of Art, Washington, D.C.).

Van Nostrand Reinhold

Van Nostrand Reinhold was purchased by John Wiley in 1997 and disbanded as an independent publisher.

Verso, Inc.

New York office:
180 Varick Street, New York, NY 10014-4606
212-807-9680   fax: 212-807-9152
www.versobooks.com

U.K. Office (Verso/New Left Books):
6 Meard Street, London W1S 0EG
0171-437-3546   fax: 0171-734-0059
e-mail: 100434.1414@compuserve.com

Verso accents trade nonfiction and literary fiction. Areas of Verso scope include contemporary issues and culture; history and biography; investigative works; world literature and thought in translation; continental, postmodernist, and deconstructivist philosophy and criticism; humor. Verso produces hardcover and trade paperback editions, as well as occasional special merchandise lines such as calendars and cards.

Verso, Inc. (founded in 1968), is an international house; the United Kingdom head-quarters operates from London offices; the downtown New York wing is responsible for Stateside promotion, marketing, sales, and distribution; the major editorial acquisitions program is centered in the United Kingdom; over the past several seasons the U.S. list has gained increasing presence.

Titles from Verso: *The World Is Not for Sale: Farmers Against Junk Food* by Jose Bove and Francoix Dufour; *Merchants and Revolution: Commercial Change, Political Conflict, and London's Overseas Traders, 1550–1653* by Robert Brenner; *Close Up: Iranian Cinema: Past, Present and Future* by Hamid Dabashi; *The Murder of Lumumba* by Ludo De Witte; *The No Nonsense Guide to Globalisation* by Wayne Ellwood; *Virtuality Check: Power Relations and Alternative Strategies in the Information Society* by Fran-cois Fortier; *The Trial of Henry Kissinger* by Christopher Hitchens; *Flying Sparks: Growing Up on the Edge of Las Vegas* by Odette Larson; *Hollywood Flatlands: Animation, Critical Theory and the Avant-Garde* by Esther Leslie; *Mother Millett* by Kate Millett; *The No Nonsense Guide to Fair Trade* by David Ransom; *Wanderlust: A History of Walking* by Rebecca Solnit; *Rock Til' You Drop* by John Strausbaugh; *Private Warriors* by Ken Silverstein; *High Art Life: British Art in the 1990's.*

Verso distributes to the trade through W. W. Norton (U.S.); Penguin Canada (Canada); and Marston Book Services (U.K. and the rest of the world).

Query letters and SASEs for the United States concerns and interests of Verso, Inc., should be directed to **Managing Editor** at the New York address**.** Otherwise, contact U.K. offices.

WALKER & COMPANY

Walker & Company Books for Young Readers

435 Hudson Street, New York, NY 10014
212-727-8300   fax: 212-727-0984

Walker publishes trade nonfiction and mystery fiction. Nonfiction emphasis includes science, history, health, nature, self-help, business, and entrepreneurship. Frontlist fiction accents mysteries. Walker produces a list of large-print Judaica and Christian inspirational titles; books for children range from preschool picture books to books for young adults (please see subentry for Walker & Company Books for Young Readers).

Walker & Company (established in 1959) is a concentrated powerhouse with a hard-hitting, diverse list; especially strong are Walker's market niches in history and science, health, mysteries, large-print religious and inspirational titles, and children's books that complement a broad, carefully chosen selection of adult nonfiction titles.

Walker operates on the publishing credo that what often separates the success of one book from another is the ability to execute an effective marketing strategy; what then separates one house from another is the ability to execute many such strategies—often simultaneously—season upon season.

Walker & Company was founded by the intrepid Sam Walker, who expressed the view "there cannot be a surfeit of good taste." Such faith in editorial content remains at the heart of the firm today, under the current leadership of publisher George Gibson. Underlying the house's publishing strategy is a commitment to quality of product. This two-pronged assault on the marketplace thus relies on compositional and literary depth, as well as on the ability to capitalize on the potential appeal of such works.

Walker nonfiction titles: *Longitude: The True Story of a Genius Who Solved the Greatest Scientific Problem of His Time* and *Galileo's Daughter* by Dava Sobel; *Cod: A Biography of the Fish That Changed the World* by Mark Kurlansky; *Monitor: The Story of the Legendary Civil War Ironclad and the Man Whose Invention Changed the Course of History* by James Tertius deKay; *Overcoming Overspending: A Winning Plan for Spenders and Their Partners* by Olivia Mellan with Sherry Christie; *The Joy of Pi* by David Blatner; *Fermat's Enigma: The Epic Quest to Solve the World's Greatest Mathematical Problem* by Simon Singh; *E = MC2: A Biography of the World's Most Famous Equation* by David Bodanis; *Burnelleschi's Dome* by Ross King.

In fiction, Walker is admired for its standout approach to category books (a significant number of which are first novels) in mysteries. (Walker discontinued its lines in such genres as Western thrillers, romances, and adventure novels.)

On the Walker list in mystery: *Killing Cassidy: A Dorothy Martin Mystery* by Jeanne M. Dams; *Eye of the Cricket: A Lew Griffin Mystery* by James Sallis; *The Wrong Dog: A Rachel Alexander and Dash Mystery* by Carol Lea Benjamin; *The Ice Pick Artist: A Carl Wilcox Mystery* by Harold Adams; *Five Card Stud: A Jake Hines Mystery* by Elizabeth Gunn.

Walker's guidelines for manuscript submission to its genre lists include valuable hints for fiction authors in general and category writers in particular; the sheet for Walker mysteries notes such tips as the editorial view that the mystery novel is a game between author and reader, an entertaining puzzle to be savored and solved; the mystery must be primary (with such nuances as romantic interest secondary); the mystery-novel story line must be rooted in the real world (and not imbued with supernatural overtones); and manuscripts should in general respect the conventions of the genre.

Authors please note: Materials submitted without a self-addressed stamped envelope (SASE) will not be returned.

Walker handles marketing, sales, and distribution for its own list. Query letters and SASEs should be directed to:

George Gibson, Publisher—Nonfiction in all Walker areas, including science, nature, parenting, education, business, health, sourcebooks

Jacqueline Johnson, Editor—Nonfiction

Michael Seidman, Editor—Mysteries; no romantic suspense or horror stories

Walker and Company Books for Young Readers

Walker and Company Books for Young Readers maintains a backlist in addition to its seasonal offerings of new books. The house caters to a variety of young-reader markets from preschooler picture books to fiction and nonfiction for young adults.

Walker titles for young readers: *Snow Day* by Moira Fain; *The Milkman's Boy* by Donald Hall (illustrated by Greg Shed); *Velcome* by Kevin O'Malley; *Grand Canyon: A Trail Through Time* by Linda Vieria (illustrated by Christopher Canyon); *Naming the Cat* by

Laurence Pringle (illustrated by Katherine Potter); *Until I Met Dudley: How Everyday Things Really Work* by Roger McGough (illustrated by Chris Riddell); *Trapped by the Ice: Shackleton's Amazing Antarctic Adventure* by Michael McCurdy; *The Keeping Room* by Anna Myers.

Query letters and SASEs should be directed to:

Emily Easton, Publisher

Jim Travaglini, Editor

The previous two editors acquire children's books. They are especially interested in young science, photoessays, historical fiction for middle grades, biographies, current affairs, and young-adult nonfiction.

THE WASHINGTON SQUARE PRESS

1230 Avenue of the Americas, New York, NY 10020
212-698-7000

The Washington Square Press publishes quality fiction and nonfiction in both hardcover and trade paperback.

Fiction titles span the categories of general fiction, humorous, historical, performing arts, and literary. Titles indicative of this list: *A Little Yellow Dog: An Easy Rawlins Mystery* by Walter Mosley; *The Royal Physician's Visit: A Novel* by Per Olov Enquist; *White Butterfly: An Easy Rawlins Mystery* by Walter Mosley; *Mercy Among the Children* by David Richards; *Forrest Gump* by Winston Groom; *The Third Witch* by Rebecca Reisert; *Devil in a Blue Dress: An Easy Rawlins Mystery* by Walter Mosley; *The Book of Fred: A Novel* by Abby Bardi; *Alexander: The Ends of the Earth* by Valerio Massimo Manfredi; *The New Yorker Book of Literary Cartoons* by Bob Mankoff.

Washington Square Press nonfiction focuses on current affairs and includes literary autobiographies and biographies. Recent titles include *Afterwords to Come,* compiled by the Editors of Salon.com; *Still Waters* by Jennifer Lauck.

This house also reissues titles by Shakespeare such as *The Taming of the Shrew* (edited by Barbara A. Mowat).

Direct query letters and SASEs to:

Rosemary Ahern, Vice President and Editorial Director

WATSON-GUPTILL PUBLICATIONS

770 Broadway, New York, NY 10001
646-654-5500

Watson-Guptill produces titles in art instruction and technique, graphic design, fine arts, photography, crafts, environmental and interior design, lifestyle, popular culture, architecture, music, theater, and film. Manuals and handbooks abound on the Watson-Guptill booklist, as do annual design reviews geared to these specialized fields.

Watson-Guptill's imprints include Whitney Library of Design, Amphoto, Billboard Books, Back Stage Books, and RAC Books. The publisher maintains an extensive backlist and is a leading publisher in its areas of interest. Watson-Guptill Publications (founded in 1937) is a division of Billboard Publications.

The Watson-Guptill imprint addresses art instruction and graphic design, architecture, interior design, and planning. Amphoto produces instructional volumes from leading photographers. Whitney Library of Design issues selected titles in architecture and planning. Billboard Books vends authoritative, up-to-the-minute books on every aspect of music and entertainment. Back Stage Books purveys informative reference and instruction books in the performing arts. RAC Books offers a complete line of titles for radio amateurs.

Watson-Guptill distributes its own list. Query letters and SASEs should be directed to:

Bob Nirkind, Senior Acquisitions Editor, Billboard Books—Music, film, television

Candace Raney, Senior Acquisitions Editor—Fine art, art technique, cartooning, and comic book art

Alison Hagge, Editor—Crafts and interior design

Victoria Craven, Senior Editor, Amphoto and Lifestyle

Julie Mazor, Editor—Children's books

JOHN WILEY & SONS
Wiley Children's Books

605 Third Avenue, New York, NY 10158-0012
212-850-6000, 800-225-5945   fax: 212-850-6088
www.wiley.com (Wiley's Web site has the latest information on new books, journals, and other publications, along with special promotions and publicity.)

Wiley is best known in the areas of (in alphabetical order): architecture and design, biography, black interests, business and management, careers, children's and young adult nonfiction, computers, finance, health, history, hospitality, investment, nature, parenting, psychology, science, and tax. The publisher maintains a reputation for publishing top-drawer professional and popular works, in addition to academically oriented works in business and the sciences. Wiley publishes in hardcover and trade paperback editions.

John Wiley & Sons (founded in 1807) is an independent, global publisher of print and electronic products, specializing in textbooks and educational materials for colleges and universities, scientific and technical books and journals, and professional and consumer books and subscription services. The company has publishing, marketing, and distribution centers in the United States, Canada, Europe, Asia, and Australia.

From the Wiley trade list: *The Book of Business Wisdom: Classic Writings by the Legends of Commerce & Industry* (edited by Peter Krass); *Forbes Great Minds of Business* (edited by Gretchen Morgenson, Senior Editor, *Forbes*); *Plain Talk: Lessons from a Business Maverick* by Ken Iverson; *The Rich and Famous Money Book: Investment Strategies of Leading Celebrities* by Jean Sherman Chatzky; *Against the Gods: The Remarkable Story of Risk* by Peter L. Bernstein; *The Nordstrom Way: The Inside Story of America's*

No. 1 Customer Service Company by Robert Spector and Patrick D. McCarthy; *Women of the Street: Making It on Wall Street in the World's Toughest Business* by Sue Herera; *Back from the Brink: The Greenspan Years* by Steven K. Beckner; *The Education of a Speculator* by Victor Niederhoffer; *Jacqueline Bouvier: An Intimate Memoir* by John H. Davis; *Jerusalem in the Twentieth Century* by Martin Gilbert; *Superchefs: Signature Recipes from America's New Royalty* by Karen Gantz Zahler; *Would-Be Worlds: Breaking the Complexity Barrier with the New Science of Simulation* by John L. Casti; *Sister Power: How Phenomenal Black Women Are Rising to the Top in a Race-Conscious Society* by Patricia Reid-Merritt; *Goodbye, Descartes: The End of Logic and the Search for a New Cosmology of the Mind* by Keith Devlin.

John Wiley & Sons handles its own distribution. Query letters and SASEs should be directed to:

Airie Dekidjiev, Sr., Editor—Narrative nonfiction, business marketing, business biography, business history

Larry Alexander, Publisher—Business/management

Bob Ipsen, Publisher—Computer books; technology-related topical nonfiction

Gerard Helferich, Publisher—General interest books

Carole Hall, Editor in Chief—African American books

Debra Englander, Editor—Financial and investment subjects

Hana Umlauf Lane, Senior Editor—History, biography

Jeanne Glasser, Senior Editor—E-finance

Mike Hamilton, Senior Editor—Career development, small businesses, real estate

Tom Miller, Executive Editor—Health, self-improvement, spirituality

Chip Rosetti, Senior Editor—Reference, biography, history, narrative nonfiction, writing

Steven Power, Executive Editor—Science

Matthew Holt, Executive Editor

Jeff Golick, Editor—Science and reference

Elizabeth Zack, Editor—Health

Wiley Children's Books

Wiley Children's Books shows the house motto: "Discovering the world up close." Wiley children's titles offer an in-depth approach to subjects at hand, be it the natural world, science and technology, or witty fun-and-game experimental projects. Branches in the Wiley children's family include the Earth-Friendly series, Janice VanCleave's science lines (including the Science for Every Kid series), Flying Start, the House of Science, and "Spend the Day" series.

Some titles: *The Mash and Smash Cookbook: Fun and Yummy Recipes Every Kid Can Make* by Marian Buck-Murray; *What Makes the Grand Canyon Grand? The World's Most Awe-Inspiring Natural Wonders* by Spencer Christian and Antonia Felix; *Science in*

Seconds with Toys: Over 100 Experiments You Can Do in Ten Minutes or Less by Jean Potter; *Janice VanCleave's Insects and Spiders: Mind-Boggling Experiments You Can Turn into Science Fair Projects* by Janice VanCleave; *The New York Public Library Amazing African American History* by Diane Patrick Wexler.

Query letters and SASEs should be directed to:

Kate Bradford, Senior Editor, Professional and Trade Division—Science, nature, children's nonfiction

---

WILLIAMSON PUBLISHING COMPANY

1355 Church Hill Road, PO Box 185, Charlotte, VT 05445
802-425-2102   fax: 802-425-2199
e-mail: info@williamsonbooks.com

Williamson's books help children succeed by helping them to discover their creative capacity. Kids Can!, Little Hands, Kaleidoscope Kids, Quick Starts for Kids, and Good Times books encourage curiosity and exploration with irresistible graphics and open-ended instruction. The house publishes hands-on learning books in science and nature, arts and craft, math and history, cooking, social studies and more, featuring new Kaleidoscope Kids and Kids Can! titles. Its publishing program is committed to maintaining excellent quality while providing good value for parents, teachers, and children.

Williamson Publishing Company (founded in 1983) is known for a wide variety of works and viewpoints, united through an enthusiastic, upbeat, purposeful how-to approach. Williamson typically produces 16 new titles each year and commands a comprehensive backlist.

Titles from Williamson: *Who Really Discovered America?: Unraveling the Mystery & Solving the Puzzle* by Avery Hart; *The Kids' Guide to First Aid: All About Bruises, Burns, Stings, Sprains & Other Ouches* by Karen Gale, R.N.; *Skyscrapers!: Super Structures to Design and Build* by Carol A. Johmann; *Real-World Math* by Cindy A. Littlefield; *Make Your Own Birdhouses & Feeders* by Robyn Haus; *The Kids' Book of Weather Forecasting* by Mark Breen and Kathleen Friestad; *Wow! I'm Reading!* by Jill Frankel Hauser; *Draw Your Own Cartoons!* by Don Mayne; *Around-the-World Art & Activities* by Judy Press; *Easy Art Fun!* by Jill Frankel Hauser.

Williamson Publishing prides itself on publishing books that are acclaimed by teachers, kids, parents, and those in the publishing industry. A few of the many awards the house has won include *Mexico!* (American Bookseller Pick of the Lists); *Kids Make Music!* (Parents' Choice Gold Award; Benjamin Franklin Best Juvenile Nonfiction Award); *Fun with My 5 Senses* (Parents' Choice Gold Award); *Gizmos & Gadgets* (Benjamin Franklin Best Education/Teaching Book Award; 2000 American Institute of Physics Science Writing Award; American Bookseller Pick of the Lists).

Williamson Publishing distributes its own list and works through a number of regional book sales representatives. Query letters and SASEs should be directed to:

Susan Williamson, Editorial Director

WILLOW CREEK PRESS

PO Box 147, 9931 Highway 70 West, Minocqua, WI 54548
800-850-9453   fax: 715-358-7010
e-mail: books@willowcreekpress.com

Willow Creek Press is a fast-growing, small press company that publishes high-quality books mainly related to pets, the outdoors, wildlife, hunting, fishing, and cooking. The house is also interested in videos and calendars.

Query letters and SASEs should be directed to:

Tom Petrie, Publisher

Andrea Donner, Managing Editor

WORKMAN PUBLISHING COMPANY

Artisan

Greenwich Workshop Press

See also Algonquin Books of Chapel Hill

708 Broadway, New York, NY 10003-9555
212-254-5900   fax: 212-254-8098
www.workmanweb.com

Workman publishes commercial nonfiction with an accent on lifestyle areas of cooking, food and wine, health and exercise, how-to, sports, pregnancy and child care, cats, and related popular reference. The house is known for a precisely targeted selection of games and puzzles, cartoon books, and specialty merchandise such as gift books, calendars, journals, and diaries. General trade nonfiction hits the high points of most how-to/self-help categories; business, careers, and personal finance; and quirky works that strike a contemporary note in the popular culture. Workman hosts an outstanding line of children's books.

Workman also lists titles in popular science, satire and humor, self-discovery, fun and games, hobbies and handicrafts, gardening and the home, and travel. Workman imprints and divisions include Artisan and Greenwich Workshop Press (which stress lifestyle, crafts, and design). (See subentry.) In 1988 Workman acquired Algonquin Books of Chapel Hill, which specializes in American fiction and belletristic nonfiction.

Workman Publishing Company (started in 1967) is adept at a marketing, sales, and promotional style that features such results as eye-catching counter displays for booksellers and racks devoted entirely to Workman lines.

Highlights from Workman: *The Silver Palate Cookbook* by Julee Rosso and Sheila Lukins; *Non Compus Mentors* by Anders Henriksson; *Desperation Dinners! Home-Cooked Meals for Frantic Families in 20 Minutes Flat* by Beverly Mills and Alicia Ross; *Children Learn What They Live* by Dorothy Law Nolte, Ph.D., with Rachel Harris, Ph.D. Calendars and diaries are often theme-keyed to other arenas of Workman publishing interest. Many calendar lines tie in with Workman's successful series in lifestyle, inspiration, nature, games and puzzles, humor, sports, cats, and dogs.

W

Of interest to young readers and the family: *Brain Quest* and *The Magic Locket* by Elizabeth Koda-Callan; *Peek-A-Boo, Lizzy Lou! A Daytime Book and Muppet Puppet* by Lauren Attinelo (illustrated by author; puppet by Rolie Krewson); *Barnyard Dance* by Sandy Boynton.

Workman Publishing Company handles its own distribution. Query letters and SASEs should be directed to:

Peter Workman, President—Oversees entire program; acquires in all areas consistent with list

Susan Bolotin, Editor in Chief—Acquires in all areas consistent with list

Suzanne Rafer, Editor—Cookbooks, humor, family issues; children's activity books

Artisan
Greenwich Workshop Press

Workman's Artisan division specializes in lifestyle titles; the Artisan list includes titles from the Greenwich Workshop Press imprint (crafts and the arts), as well as calendars and other specialty merchandise. Artisan and Greenwich Workshop Press together accent crafts, home, garden, and design, each with its own distinctive editorial approach and publishing lines.

On the Artisan list: *Pierre Franey Cooks with His Friends* by Pierre Franey with Claudia Franey Jensen (photographs by Martin Brigdale and Jean Cazals); *French Tarts: 50 Savory and Sweet Recipes* by Linda Dannenberg (photographs by Guy Bouchet; illustrated by Vavro); *Portobello Cookbook* (mushroom recipes) by Jack Czarnecki (photographs by Alexandra Maldonado); *Fresh Cuts: Arrangements with Flowers, Leaves, Buds & Branches* by Edwina von Gal (photographs by John Hall; foreword by Ken Druse); *Picasso's One-Liners* (single-line drawings by Pablo Picasso); *Cowgirl Rising* (paintings by Donna Howell-Sickles; text by Peg Streep; introduction by Teresa Jordan); *The Glory of Flight: The Art of William S. Phillips* (paintings by William S. Phillips; text by Edwards Park; introduction by Stephen Coonts).

Artisan is the publisher of the Audubon Society's calendar line and distributes books for Eating Well Books (from *Eating Well* magazine).

Ann Bramson, Editor

WRIGHT GROUP/MCGRAW-HILL

19201 120th Avenue, NE, Bothell, WA 98011
800-345-6073, 800-523-2371
www.wrightgroup.com

Wright Group/McGraw-Hill (founded in 1980) is a leading publisher of educational books for elementary school and junior high curricula. Wright series lines include SUNSHINE Foundations, Heritage Readers, Woodland Mysteries, the Writing Project, Visions: African American Experiences, the Evangeline Nicholas Collection, Story Vine, Fast Track Reading, and Doors to Discovery.

Wright Group/McGraw-Hill publishers believe that after the parents' role, teachers are the most important people in the life of a child. The teacher who empowers a child to read fulfills the greatest purpose.

Wright educational tools feature the "whole language" approach to reading; Wright hosts a wide range of books in science and social studies, as well as professional books for educators. The house has a full slate of books geared to the Spanish-language market.

The SUNSHINE program is a core instructional reading program with more than 1,000 books for children. SUNSHINE includes fiction, nonfiction, poetry, plays, collections, traditional tales, and more. SUNSHINE features a mix of talented authors and illustrators from cultures and countries around the world. SUNSHINE is also available in Spanish.

The Foundations program introduces a powerful intervention system for use by classroom teachers. Foundations offers immediate intervention for children who are having problems learning to read and write.

Heritage Readers is an integrated literature and language-arts program for K–8 students. Heritage Readers are illustrated by renowned artists from the past and present and feature stories from the classic literary legacies of many cultures.

Woodland Mysteries is a collection of 30 high-interest novels designed especially for discouraged readers and ESL students.

The Writing Project complements and extends any language-arts program. Using their own life experience, students structure their writing from authentic writing models that incorporate various styles, forms, and functions.

Visions: African American Experiences is a guide-reading program for young students that brings together a collaborative team of African American educators, authors, and illustrators.

The Evangeline Nicholas Collection introduces students to rich multi-ethnic characters and true-to-life urban settings. Story Vine is a line that weaves tales of the American continent. These multicultural books include contemporary stories, traditional stories, and a memoir.

Wright Group/McGraw-Hill also offers professional books for teachers: *Think Big! Creating Big Books with Children* by Cynthia Johnson; *Whole Learning: Whole Child* by Joy Cowley; *Student Portfolios: A Practical Guide to Evaluation* by Lindy Vizyak; *Literacy Learning: A Revolution in Progress* by David B. Doake; *The Spelling Teacher's Book of Lists* by Joe Phenix.

Wright Group/McGraw-Hill handles its own distribution. Please check our Web site for current submission acceptance status.

THE WRITER, INC.

Plays, Inc., Publishers

120 Boylston Street, Boston, MA 02116-4615
617-423-3157   fax: 617-423-2168
www.channel1.com/thewriter/

The Writer, Inc., publishes a selection of books in hardcover and paperback on all phases of writing and selling the written work; these publications are written and edited by experienced and successful authors.

Since 1887, both aspiring and professional writers have looked to *The Writer* magazine ("the pioneer magazine for literary workers") as a practical guide to instruct, inform, and inspire them in their work. *The Writer* is renowned for the annually updated reference resource *The Writer's Handbook* (edited by Sylvia K. Burack). The house also publishes *Plays: The Drama Magazine for Young People,* with an attendant list in books.

Frontlist offerings: *Practical Playwriting* by David Copelin; *How to Write Your Novel* by Margaret Chittenden; *Write on Target* by Dennis E. Hensley and Holly G. Miller; *The Elements of Mystery Fiction* by William G. Tapply; *Writing & Revising Your Fiction* by Mark Wisniewski.

Reference books for writers: *The Writer's Handbook* (edited by Sylvia K. Burack); *The Thirty-Six Dramatic Situations* by Georges Polti; *Dictionary of Fictional Characters* by Martin Seymour-Smith; *The Writer's Rhyming Dictionary* by Langford Reed; *Writing Poetry: Where Poems Come from and How to Write Them* by David Kirby; *Preparing Your Manuscript* by Elizabeth Preston; *Guide to Fiction Writing* by Phyllis A. Whitney; *Writing Books for Young People* by James Cross Giblin; *How to Write and Sell Your Articles* (edited by Sylvia K. Birrade).

The Writer distributes its own books. Query letters and SASEs should be directed to:

Sylvia K. Burack, Editor

Plays, Inc., Publishers

Plays, Inc., Publishers is a wing of the Writer that targets younger performers in theater. This imprint's list also includes a solid slate of resource materials of value to professionals who work in the theater with children.

From Plays, Inc.: *Lively Plays for Young Actors* by Christine Hamlett; *Great American Events on Stage, Thirty Plays from Favorite Stories,* and *The Big Book of Skits* (edited by Sylvia E. Kamerman); *Plays from African Tales* and *Plays from Hispanic Tales* by Barbara Winther; *Costume: An Illustrated Survey from Ancient Times to the 20th Century* by Margot Lister; *The Puppet Book* by Claire Buchwald (illustrated by Audrey Jacubiszyn); *Mime: Basics for Beginners* by Cindie and Mathew Straub (photographs by Jeff Blanton).

WRITER'S DIGEST BOOKS

4700 E. Galbraith Road, Cincinnati, OH 45236
513-531-2222   fax: 513-531-4744

Writer's Digest produces books to help writers, poets, artists, songwriters, and photographers develop their talent, hone their professional skills, and—of course—sell their work. The publisher pursues this mission by issuing a list of guidebooks, how-to, reference, and professional titles in hardcover and paperback editions.

Writer's Digest Books (founded in 1919) is a division of F&W Publications, publisher of *Writer's Digest Magazine.* The firm was bought in 2000 by Citibank. Writer's Digest Books offers a classic and expansive list for the professional, as well as the aspiring, writer.

Query letters and SASEs should be sent to:

Donya Dickerson, Editor

University Presses

The University As Publisher

From Academic Press to Commercial Presence

WILLIAM HAMILTON

You nod as you glance at the ads in the book reviews, you are aware of the spots you heard or saw on radio and late-night television, and you recognize the authors from television interviews and radio call-in shows. So you know that today's university presses publish much more than scholarly monographs and academic tomes.

Although the monograph is—and will always be—the bread and butter of the university press, several factors over the past quarter century have compelled university presses to look beyond their primary publishing mission of disseminating scholarship. The reductions in financial support from parent institutions, library-budget cutbacks by federal and local governments, and the increasing scarcity of grants to underwrite the costs of publishing monographs have put these presses under severe financial pressure. The watchword for university presses, even in the 1970s, was survival.

While university presses were fighting for their lives, their commercial counterparts also experienced difficult changes. The commercial sector responded by selling off unprofitable and incompatible lists or merging with other publishers; many houses were bought out by larger concerns. Publishers began to concentrate their editorial and marketing resources on a few new titles that would generate larger revenues. Books that commercial publishers now categorized as financial risks were seen by university presses as means of entry into new markets and opportunities to revive sagging publishing programs.

Take a look through one of the really good bookstores in your area. You'll find university press imprints on regional cookbooks, popular fiction, serious nonfiction, calendars, literature in translation, reference works, finely produced art books, and a considerable number of upper-division textbooks. Books and other items normally associated with commercial publishers are now a regular and important part of university press publishing.

There are approximately 100 university presses in North America, including U.S. branches of the venerable Oxford University Press and Cambridge University Press. Of the largest American university presses—California, Chicago, Columbia, Harvard, MIT,

Princeton, Texas, and Yale—each publishes well over 100 books per year. Many of these titles are trade books that are sold in retail outlets throughout the world.

The medium-sized university presses—approximately 20 fit this category—publish between 50 and 100 books a year. Presses such as Washington, Indiana, Cornell, North Carolina, Johns Hopkins, and Stanford are well established as publishers of important works worthy of broad circulation.

All but the smallest university presses have developed extensive channels of distribution, which ensure that their books will be widely available in bookstores and wherever serious books are sold. Small university presses usually retain larger university presses or commissioned sales firms to represent them.

UNIVERSITY PRESS TRADE PUBLISHING

The two most common trade areas in which university presses publish are (1) nonfiction titles that reflect the research interests of their parent universities and (2) regional titles.

For example, University of Hawaii Press publishes approximately 30 new books a year with Asian or Pacific Rim themes. Typically, 8 to 10 of these books are trade titles. Recent titles have included Japanese literature in translation, a lavishly illustrated book on Thai textiles, books on forms of Chinese architecture, and a historical guide to ancient Burmese temples. This is a typical university press trade list—a diverse, intellectually stimulating selection of books that will be read by a variety of well-informed, responsive general readers.

For projects with special trade potential, some of the major university presses enter into copublishing arrangements with commercial publishers—notably in the fields of art books and serious nonfiction with a current-issues slant—and there seems to be more of these high-profile projects lately.

Certain of the larger and medium-sized university presses have in the past few years hired editors with experience in commercial publishing to add extra dimensions and impact to the portion of their program with a trade orientation.

It's too early to know whether these observations represent trends. Even if so, the repercussions remain to be seen. Obviously, with the publishing community as a whole going through a period of change, it pays to stay tuned to events.

UNIVERSITY PRESS AUTHORS

Where do university press authors come from? The majority of them are involved in one way or another with a university, research center, or public agency, or they are experts in a particular academic field. Very few would list their primary occupation as author. Most of the books they write are the result of years of research or reflect years of experience in their fields.

The university press is not overly concerned about the number of academic degrees following its trade book authors' names. What matters is the author's thoroughness in addressing the topic, regardless of his or her residence, age, or amount of formal education.

A rigorous evaluation of content and style determines whether the manuscript meets the university press's standards.

UNIVERSITY PRESS ACQUISITION PROCESS

Several of the other essays in this volume provide specific strategies for you to follow to ensure that your book idea receives consideration from your publisher of choice—but let me interject a cautionary note: The major commercial publishers are extremely difficult to approach unless you have an agent, and obtaining an agent can be more difficult than finding a publisher!

The commercial publishers are so overwhelmed by unsolicited manuscripts that you would be among the fortunate few if your proposal or manuscript even received a thorough reading. Your unagented proposal or manuscript will most likely be read by an editorial assistant, returned unread, or thrown on the slushpile unread and unreturned.

An alternative to the commercial publisher is the university press. Not only will the university press respond, but also the response will generally come from the decision maker—the acquisitions editor.

Before approaching any publisher, however, you must perform a personal assessment of your expectations for your book. If you are writing because you want your book to be on the bestseller list, go to a medium to large commercial press. If you are writing to make a financial killing, go to a large commercial publisher. If you are writing in the hope that your book will be a literary success, contribute to knowledge, be widely distributed, provide a modest royalty, and be in print for several years, you should consider a university press.

SHOULD A UNIVERSITY PRESS BE YOUR FIRST CHOICE?

That depends on the subject matter. It is very difficult to sell a commercial publisher on what appears on the surface to be a book with a limited market. For example, Tom Clancy was unable to sell *The Hunt for Red October* to a commercial publisher because the content was considered too technical for the average reader of action-adventure books. Clancy sent the manuscript to a university press that specialized in military-related topics. Naval Institute Press had the foresight to see the literary and commercial value of Clancy's work. As they say, the rest is history. Tom Clancy created the present-day technothriller genre and has accumulated royalties well into the millions of dollars. Once Clancy became a known quantity, the commercial publishers began courting him. All of his subsequent books have been published by commercial houses.

How do you find the university press that is suitable for you? You must research the university press industry. Start by finding out something about university presses. In addition to the listings in the directory of publishers and editors appearing in this book, most university presses are listed in *Literary Market Place*.

A far better and more complete source is *The Association of American University Presses Directory*. The AAUP directory offers a detailed description of each AAUP member press, with a summary of its publishing program. The directory lists the names and responsibilities of each press's key staff, including the acquisitions editors. Each press states its editorial program—what it will consider for publication. A section on submitting manuscripts provides a detailed description of what the university press expects a proposal to contain. Another useful feature is the comprehensive subject grid, which identifies more than 125 subject areas and lists the university presses that publish in each of them.

An updated edition of *The Association of American University Presses Directory* is published every fall and is available for a nominal charge from the AAUP central offices in New York City or through its distributor, University of Chicago Press.

Most university presses are also regional publishers. They publish titles that reflect local interests and tastes and are intended for sale primarily in the university press's local region. For example, University of Hawaii Press has more than 250 titles on Hawaii. The books—both trade and scholarly—cover practically every topic one can think of. Books on native birds, trees, marine life, local history, native culture, and an endless variety of other topics can be found in local stores, including the chain bookstores.

This regional pattern is repeated by university presses throughout the country. University of Washington Press publishes several titles each year on the Pacific Northwest and Alaska. Rutgers University Press publishes regional fiction. University of New Mexico Press publishes books on art and photography, most dealing with the desert Southwest. Louisiana State University Press publishes Southern history and literature. Nebraska publishes on the American West.

Almost all university presses publish important regional nonfiction. If your book naturally fits a particular region, you should do everything possible to get a university press located in that region to evaluate your manuscript.

Do not mistake the regional nature of the university press for an inability to sell books nationally—or globally. As mentioned earlier, most university presses have established channels of distribution and use the same resources that commercial publishers use for book distribution. The major difference is that the primary retail outlets for university press books tend to be bookstores associated with universities, smaller academic bookstores, specialized literary bookstores, and independent bookstores that carry a large number of titles.

Matching books to buyers is not as difficult as you might think. Most patrons of university press bookstores know these stores are likely to carry the books they want.

Traditionally, very few university press titles are sold through major chain bookstores outside their local region. Even so, this truism is subject to change. Some of the biggest bookstore chains are experimenting with university press sections in their large superstores.

WHAT TO EXPECT AT A UNIVERSITY PRESS

You should expect a personal reply from the acquisitions editor. If the acquisitions editor expresses interest, you can expect the evaluation process to take as long as 6 to 8 months. For reasons known only to editorial staffs—commercial, as well as those of university presses—manuscripts sit and sit and sit. Then they go out for review, come back, and go out for review again!

Once a favorable evaluation is received, the editor must submit the book to the press's editorial board. It is not until the editorial board approves the manuscript for publication that a university press is authorized to publish the book under its imprint.

A word about editorial boards: The imprint of a university press is typically controlled by an editorial board appointed from the faculty. Each project presented to the editorial board is accompanied by a set of peer reviews, the acquisitions editor's summary of the reviews, and the author's replies to the reviews. The project is discussed with the press's management and voted upon.

Decisions from the editorial board range from approval, through conditional approval, to flat rejection. Most university presses present to the editorial board only those projects they feel stand a strong chance of acceptance—approximately 10 to 15 percent of the projects submitted annually. So if you have been told that your book is being submitted to the editorial board, there's a good chance that the book will be accepted.

Once a book has been accepted by the editorial board, the acquisitions editor is authorized to offer the author a publishing contract. The publishing contract of a university press is quite similar to a commercial publisher's contract. The majority of the paragraphs read the same. The difference is most apparent in two areas—submission of the manuscript and financial terms.

University presses view publishing schedules as very flexible. If the author needs an extra 6 to 12 months to polish the manuscript, the market is not going to be affected too much. If the author needs additional time to proofread the galleys or page proofs, the press is willing to go along. Why? Because a university press is publishing for the long term. The book is going to be in print for several years. It is not unusual for a first printing of a university press title to be available for 10 or more years. Under normal circumstances the topic will be timeless, enduring, and therefore of lasting interest.

University presses go to great lengths to ensure that a book is as close to error-free as possible. The academic and stylistic integrity of the work is foremost in the editor's mind. Not only the content but also the notes, references, bibliography, and index should be flawless—and all charts, graphs, maps, and other illustrations perfectly keyed.

It does not matter whether the book is a limited-market monograph or serious nonfiction for a popular trade. The university press devotes the same amount of care to the editorial and production processes to ensure that the book is as accurate and complete as possible. Which leads us to the second difference—the financial terms.

Commercial publishers follow the maxim that time is money. The goal of the organization is to maximize shareholder wealth. Often the decision to publish a book is based solely on financial considerations. If a book must be available for a specific season in order to meet its financial goals, pressure may be applied to editorial by marketing, and editorial in turn puts pressure on the author to meet the agreed-upon schedule. This pressure may result in mistakes, typos, and inaccuracies—but will also assure timely publication and provide the publisher with the opportunity to earn its expected profit. At the commercial publishing house, senior management is measured by its ability to meet annual financial goals.

University presses are not-for-profit organizations. Their basic mission is to publish books of high merit that contribute to universal knowledge. Financial considerations are secondary to what the author has to say. A thoroughly researched, meticulously documented, and clearly written book is more important than meeting a specific publication date. The university press market will accept the book when it appears.

Do not get the impression that university presses are entirely insensitive to schedules or market conditions. University presses are aware that certain books—primarily textbooks and topical trade titles—must be published at specific times of the year if sales are to be maximized. But less than 20 percent of any year's list would fall into such a category.

University Presses and Author Remuneration

What about advances? Royalties? Surely, university presses offer these amenities—which is not to suggest they must be commensurate with the rates paid by commercial houses.

No and yes. No royalties are paid on a predetermined number of copies of scholarly monographs—usually 1,000 to 2,000.

A royalty is usually paid on textbooks and trade books. The royalty will be based on the title's sales revenue (net sales) and will usually be a sliding-scale royalty, ranging from as low as 5 percent to as high as 15 percent.

As with commercial publishers, royalties are entirely negotiable. Do not be afraid or embarrassed to discuss them with your publisher. Just remember that university presses rarely have surplus funds to apply to generous advances or high royalty rates. However, the larger the university press, the more likely you are to get an advance for a trade book.

Never expect an advance for a monograph or supplemental textbook.

When Considering a University Press

When you're deciding where to submit your manuscript, keep the following in mind. University presses produce approximately 10 percent of the books published in the United States each year. University presses win approximately 20 percent of the annual major book awards. Yet university presses generate just 2 percent of the annual sales revenue.

So if you want to write a book that is taken seriously, that will be carefully reviewed and edited; if you want to be treated as an important part of the publishing process and want your book to have a good chance to win an award; and if you are not too concerned about the financial rewards—then a university press may very well be the publisher for you.

Cambridge University Press

40 West 20th Street, New York, NY 10011-4211
212-924-3900, 800-872-7423   fax: 212-691-3239

The Cambridge list includes hardcover and paperback titles of topical contemporary general interest, as well as academic import, in the fields of literature, art, music, religion, history, philosophy, economics, the classics, mathematics, and the behavioral, biological, physical, social, and computer sciences. One of publishing's old guard, Cambridge University Press (founded in 1534) is now a major international operation that holds fast to a long commitment to quality.

Cambridge University Press is the printing and publishing house of the University of Cambridge. It is a charitable enterprise required by University Statute to devote itself to printing and publishing in the furtherance of the acquisition, advancement, conservation, and dissemination of knowledge in all subjects; to the advancement of education, religion, learning, and research; and to the advancement of literature and good letters.

Special imprints include Cambridge Film Classics and the popularly priced Canto line. Cambridge also produces some titles for young readers and publishes a full range of academic and popular reference works. Cambridge is strong in the reprint area, offering editions of anthologies and compilations, as well as individual classic works.

Cambridge publishes more than 2,000 new titles each year.

The house hosts a strong reference list, including *The Cambridge International Dictionary of English* (edited by Paul Procter).

Cambridge University Press handles its own distribution.

Query letters and SASEs should be directed to:

Adam Black, Editor—Physical sciences

Roger Astley, Editor—Mathematics

Beatrice Rehl, Editor—Arts and classics

Andrew Winnard, Editor—Linguistics

Deborah Goldblatt, Senior Editor—ESL (English as a second language) books

Ellen Carlin, Editor—Engineering

Frank Smith, Publishing Director—Social sciences

Alan Harvey, Editor—Mathematics and computer science

Lewis Bateman, Editor—Political science

Lothlorien Homet, Editor—Computing

Mary Child, Editor—Social sciences

Mary Vaughn, Publishing Director—ESL (English as a second language) books

Matt Lloyd, Editor—Earth sciences

Katrina Halliday, Editor—Life science

Philip Laughlin, Editor—Psychology

Scott Parris, Editor—Economics

Terry Moore, Publishing Director—Humanities

COLUMBIA UNIVERSITY PRESS

61 West 62nd Street, New York, NY 10023
212-459-0600

Columbia hosts a roster of trade and specialty titles, including distinguished lines in Asian studies, literary studies, social work, history, earth sciences, and film and media studies. Columbia's publishing interests also include current events, public issues, popular culture and fine arts, gay and lesbian studies, history, the sciences, literature, religion, and Asian studies. Columbia University Press (established in 1893) publishes a slate of general-interest titles in addition to its established list of scholarly, academic, and scientific works. Also on the roster is a number of standard reference works geared for the institutional and academic market. The press produces books in hardcover and trade paperback editions and nurtures a healthy backlist.

Among Columbia highlights: *Acre* by Thomas Phillip; *The Assault on Social Society* by William Roth; *Beyond the Ivory Tower* by Joseph Lepgold and Miroslav Nincic; *Chinese Fossil Vertebrates* by Spencer Lucas; *Colonial Effects* by Joseph A. Massad; *The Compromise of Liberal Environmentalism* by Steven Bernstein; *Consumer Politics in Postwar Japan* by Patricia L. Maclachlan; *Democracy* (edited by Ricardo Blaug and John Schwarzmantel); *Exceptional Fossil Preservation* by David J. Bottjer, Walter Etter, James W. Hagadorn, and Carol M. Tang; *Fluid Boundaries* by William F. Fisher; *The Fine Art of Copyediting,* Second Edition, by Elsie Myers Stainton; *Gendering World Politics* by J. Ann Tickner; *Milton and the Rabbis* by Jeffrey Shoulson; *New Immigrants in New York* (edited by Nancy Foner); *Palatable Poison* (edited by Laura Doan and Jay Prosser); *Piracy, Slavery & Redemption* (edited by Daniel J. Vitkus); *The Poetry of Sylvia Plath* (edited by Claire Brennan); *Practicing Religion in the Age of the Media* (edited by Stewart M. Hoover and Lynn Schofield Clark); *Shaky Ground* by Alice Echols; *Travels in Manchuria and Mongolia* by Yosano Akiko; *Up from Invisibility* by Larry Gross; *Voices of Revolution* by Rodger Streitmatter; *Wondrous Difference* by Alison Griffiths.

From Columbia reference: *The Columbia Encyclopedia* (edited by Jay Parini); *The Columbia Guide to Standard American English* by Kenneth G. Wilson.

Columbia University Press distributes its own list and handles distribution for a number of other academically oriented publishers, including East European Monographs, Edinburgh University Press, and Kegan Paul International.

Query letters and SASEs should be directed to:

Wendy Lochner, Senior Executive Editor—Religion, medieval studies, and anthropology

Robin C. Smith, Senior Executive Editor—Science

Jennifer Crewe, Editorial Director—Literature, film, and Asian studies

John Michel, Senior Executive Editor—Social work, journalism

Peter Dimock, Senior Executive Editor—History and political science

James Warren, Executive Editor—Reference

CORNELL UNIVERSITY PRESS

Sage House, 512 East State Street, Ithaca, NY 14850
607-277-2338
www.cornellpress.cornell.edu

Cornell publishes trade nonfiction, in addition to a wide berth of academic and scholarly titles. The press's Comstock Books series continues a tradition of excellence in natural history. The ILR Press imprint focuses on labor and workplace issues. Cornell University Press (begun in 1869) is the oldest university press in the United States.

Representing the Cornell program: *Knowing the Past: Victorian Literature and Culture* by Suzy Anger; *The Early Slavs: Culture and Society in Early Medieval Eastern Europe* by P. M. Barford; *I'm Not a Racist, But . . . : The Moral Quandary of Race* by Lawrence Blum; *Amphibians of Central and Southern Africa* by Alan Channing; *Sex Drives: Fantasies of Fascism in Literary Modernism* by Laura Frost; *Ariadne's Thread: A Guide to International Tales Found in Classical Literature* by William Hansen; *Korean Workers: The Culture and Politics of Class Formation* by Koo Hagen; *The Real World of Employee Ownership* by John Logue, Jacquelyn Yates, and William Greider; *The Victorian Homefront: American Thought and Culture, 1860–1880* by Louise L. Stevenson; *The Countryside in the Age of the Modern State: Political Histories of Rural America* by Catherine McNicol Stock and Robert D. Johnston; *Claiming the City: Politics, Faith and the Power of Place in St. Paul* by Mary Lethert Wingerd.

Cornell University Press distributes its own list.

Query letters and SASEs should be directed to:

Bernhard Kendler, Executive Editor—Literary criticism, classics, drama and film studies, art history, archaeology

Catherine Rice, Editor—Women's studies, music, philosophy, race studies, gay and lesbian studies, and political theory

Frances Benson, Editor in Chief—Labor, business, sociology, anthropology

John Ackerman, Director—European history, medieval studies

Peter Prescott, Editor—Life sciences, natural history, plant science, animal science, ecology, entomology, geology, zoology

Roger Haydon, Editor—philosophy, history of science, U.S. politics, international relations, Asian and Slavic studies

Sheryl Englund, Editor—American History, American studies, law, religion

DUKE UNIVERSITY PRESS

PO Box 90660, Durham, NC 27708-0660
919-687-3600   fax: 919-688- 4574
www.duke.edu/web/dupress

Areas of Duke publishing scope include cultural studies; literary studies; Latin American and Caribbean studies; legal studies; history; East European, Soviet, and post-Soviet studies; German studies; environmental studies; and history of economics. Post-Contemporary Interventions is a series that features imaginative world-class thinkers on culture, media, and global society.

Duke University Press (founded in 1921) publishes scholarly, trade, and textbooks in hardcover and trade paperback editions and maintains a strong backlist. Duke also publishes a number of academic journals, including *MLQ: Modern Language Quarterly.*

On the Duke list: *Telling to Live: Latina Feminist Testimonials* by the Latina Feminist Group; *Gender and Sexuality in Latin America* by Gilberty M. Joseph; *Women on the Verge: Japanese Women, Western Dreams* by Karen Kelsky; *An Absent Presence: Japanese Americans in Postwar American Culture, 1945–1960* by Caroline Chung Simpson; *Millennial Japan* by Tomiko Yoda and Harry Harootunian; *Orientations: Mapping Studies in the*

Asian Diaspora by Kandace Chuh and Karen Shimakawa; *Harbin and Manchuria: Place, Space and Identity* by Thomas Lahusen; *Labors Appropriate to Their Sex: Gender, Labor and Politics in Urban Chile 1900–1930* by Elizabeth Quay Hutchinson; *The Grooves of Change: Eastern Europe at the Turn of the Millennium* by J. F. Brown; *Crime and Punishment in Latin America: Law and Society Since Late Colonial Times* by Ricardo D. Salvatore, Carlos Aguirre, and Gilbert M. Joseph; *Publishing the Family* by June Howard.

Duke University Press oversees its own distribution.

Query letters and SASEs should be directed to:

Kenneth A. Wissoker, Editor in Chief

Fiona Morgan, Senior Editorial Assistant

Christine K. Habermass, Senior Editorial Assistant

J. Reynolds Smith, Executive Editor

Sharon Parks Torian, Senior Editorial Assistant

Valerie Millholland, Editor

Raphael Allen, Editor

THE FEMINIST PRESS AT THE CITY UNIVERSITY OF NEW YORK

365 Fifth Avenue, New York, NY 10016
212-360-5790

The publishing horizon at the Feminist Press includes biographies, cross-cultural studies, fiction, reprints, history/sociology, interdisciplinary texts, literary anthologies, resources and reference works, educational materials, middle grade and young adult books, and women's studies (including several notable series). The house hosts a reprint program but does not publish original fiction or poetry. It also supports a feminist journal, *Women's Studies Quarterly.* The Feminist Press publishes in hardcover and paperback editions and moves a backlist both heady and deep through special sales, including holiday mailings.

The Feminist Press maintains its aim to express and celebrate differences within the cultural context of humanity; in so doing, the house has held the publishing forefront with a series of important works that brings fresh dimensions to the attention of readers. Founded in 1970 at the crest of the second wave of American feminism, the press led off with a list that concentrated on a program to reestablish hitherto overlooked women's literary classics, aligned with an additional focus on literature of United States working-class women. The house's agenda has expanded gradually to encompass such themes as growing up female, women artists, and the family, as well as the publication of academic and general-interest works with an international cast of authors in varied disciplines and literary forms.

Highlights from Feminist Press: *Among the White Moon Faces: An Asian-American Memoir of Homelands* by Shirley Geok-lin Lim; *The New Lesbian Studies: Into the 21st Century* (edited by Bonnie Zimmerman and Toni A. H. McNaron); *Families As We Are: Conversations from Around the World* by Perdita Huston; *Women of Color and the Multicultural Curriculum* (edited by Liza Fiol-Matta and Miriam K. Chamberlain).

In fiction and literature: *Paper Fish* by Tina De Rosa; *Winter's Edge* by Valerie Miner; *Changes* by Ama Ata Aidoo; *Songs My Mother Taught Me* by Wakako Yamauchi; *Unspeakable Women* (edited and translated by Robin Pickering-Iazzi); a bilingual edition of *The Answer/La Repuesta* by Sor Juana Inéz de la Cruz; *What Did Miss Darrington See? An Anthology of Feminist Supernatural Fiction* (edited by Jessica Amanda Salmonson).

A special-production volume from Feminist Press is *Long Walks and Intimate Talks,* with stories and poems by Grace Paley and paintings by Vera B. Williams.

The Feminist Press list is distributed to the trade in the United States via Consortium Book Sales & Distribution.

Submission guidelines can be found at www.feministpress.org.

Query letters and SASEs should be directed to:

Molly Vaux, Senior Editor

GALLAUDET UNIVERSITY PRESS

800 Florida Avenue NE, Washington, DC 20002-3695
202-651-5488 fax: 202-651-5489
http://gupress.gallaudet.edu

Gallaudet offers titles in categories such as communication, language arts, deaf culture and history, employment and law, audiology and speechreading, instructional materials, literature, parenting, and professional books, as well as a special concentration in sign language (including American Sign Language). The publisher maintains an extensive backlist.

Imprints of Gallaudet University Press include Clerc Books and Kendall Green Publications. Among areas of current publishing emphasis are audiology, sociolegal issues in special education, English as a second language (ESL), and signed children's books in English; the house also markets a line of videotapes.

The publishing program of Gallaudet University Press (founded in 1968) exemplifies the educational impulse of Gallaudet University through an accent on issues pertinent to deafness. Gallaudet University Press publishes scholarly, educational, and general-interest titles, as well as children's books.

Among Gallaudet features: *Baby's First Signs* and *More Baby's First Signs* by Kim Votry and Curt Waller; *A Mighty Change: An Anthology of Deaf American Writing, 1816–1864* by Christopher Krentz; *Language in Hand: Why Sign Came Before Speech* by William C. Stokoe; *Orchid of the Bayou: A Deaf Woman Faces Blindness* by Cathryn Carroll and Catherine Hoffpauir Fischer; *Inner Lives of Deaf Children* by Martha Sheridan; *Linguistics of American Sign Language* by Clayton Valli and Ceil Lucas; *Context, Cognition, and Deafness* by M. Diane Clark, Marc Marschark, and Michael Karchmer; *Signed Languages: Discoveries from International Research* by Valerie Dively, Melanie Metzger, Sarah Taub, and Anne Marie Baer.

Gallaudet University Press books are distributed via Chicago Distribution Center.

Query letters and SASEs should be directed to:

Ivey Wallace, Assistant Director, Editorial

G

HARVARD BUSINESS SCHOOL PRESS

60 Harvard Way, Boston, MA 02163
617-783-7636 fax: 617-783-7489

New York office:
509 Madison Avenue, 15th Floor, New York, NY 10022
212-873-9280
www.hbsp.harvard.edu

Our mission at Harvard Business School Press is straightforward: to be the source of the most influential ideas and conversations that shape business worldwide. Yet it addresses an enormous ambition. We understand that our books, however thoughtful, provocative, and enlightening, will become influential only when their ideas are brought to bear on our daily business activities. No matter how savvy the marketing, attractive the packaging, or aggressive the sales force, at the end of the day only the ideas themselves can make a difference in the thoughts, practice, and conversations of business book readers.

As the publishers of landmark books in strategy, general management, the digital economy, technology and innovation, and human resources, among other disciplines, we take a broad look at the questions businesspeople face every day and provide the answers that will have a profound impact on their lives and work. Among our titles: *The Company of the Future: How the Communications Revolution Is Changing Management* by Frances Cairncross; *Leading Quietly: An Unorthodox Guide to Doing the Right Things* by Joseph L. Badaracco; *Managing Across Borders* by Christopher A. Bartlett and Sumantra Ghoshal; *Developing Global Executives* by Morgan W. McCall Jr. and George P. Hollenbeck; *The Money of Invention* by Paul A. Gompers and Josh Lerner; *Information Markets: What Businesses Can Learn from Financial Innovation* by William J. Wilhelm Jr. and Joseph D. Downing; *The Harvard Business School Guide to Careers in Finance 2002; Harvard Business Review on Turnarounds; The Loyalty Effect: The Hidden Force Behind Growth, Profits, and Lasting Value* by Frederick F. Reichheld; *The Infinite Asset: Managing Brands to Build New Value* by Sam Hill and Chris Lederer; *Marketing Moves: A New Approach to Profits, Growth and Renewal* by Philip Kotler, Dipak C. Jain, and Suvit Maesincee; *The Elephant and the Flea: Reflections of a Reluctant Capitalist* by Charles Handy; *Total Access: Giving Customers What They Want in an Anytime, Anywhere World* by Regis McKenna.

Established in 1984, the Press currently has more than 300 titles in print. Our publishing program combines the high standards of a university press with the aggressive marketing of a trade publisher to deliver the best of contemporary thinking in business and management to the widest possible audience. Manuscripts considered for publication by the Press are reviewed by peers, a process unique in trade publishing that ensures the quality and relevance of books that carry the Harvard Business School Press imprint.

Harvard Business School Press titles are consistently recognized by publishing industry awards and annual "best book" round-ups, among them, the *Financial Times*/Booz, Allen & Hamilton Best Business Book of 1997 for *The Innovator's Dilemma* by Clayton Christensen; *Business Week*'s Ten Best Books of the Year awards; *Library Journal*'s Best

Books of the Year awards; and Soundview Executive Book Summaries' Thirty Best Books of the Year. In 1994, *Business Week* hailed *Competing for the Future* by Gary Hamel and C. K. Prahalad the "year's best management book."

Harvard Business School Press titles regularly garner significant national media attention in publications such as *Business Week;* the *Economist; Fortune, Inc.; Wired;* the *New York Times;* the *Financial Times; USA Today;* and the *Wall Street Journal.* Several books have appeared on the national *Business Week* Bestseller List, including *Competing for the Future, The Loyalty Effect, Leading Change, Net Gain, Real Time, Unleashing the Killer App, Net Worth,* and *The Innovator's Dilemma.* Press titles also regularly appear on many regional bestseller lists, including the *Denver Post, Philadelphia Inquirer,* and *San Francisco Chronicle.*

Harvard Business School Press is a business unit of Harvard Business School Publishing, a wholly owned, not-for-profit subsidiary of the Harvard Business School that is headquartered in Boston, Massachusetts. Harvard Business School Publishing offers material in a variety of platforms and delivery methods that reflect its extension of the educational mission of the Harvard Business School and its access to leading authors and companies. Other business units of Harvard Business School Publishing include Harvard Business Review, Academic Cases & Reprints, Conferences, e-Learning, and Newsletters, which publishes *Harvard Management Update, Harvard Management Communications Letter,* and *The Balanced Scorecard Report.*

Query letters and SASEs should be sent to:

Carol Franco, Vice President, HBS Publishing, Director, HBS Press

Hollis Heimbouch, Editorial Director

Kirsten D. Sandberg, Executive Editor (NY)

Melinda Adams Merino, Senior Editor

Jacqueline Murphy, Senior Editor

Suzanne Rotondo, Senior Editor (NY)

Jeff Kehoe, Editor

H

HARVARD UNIVERSITY PRESS

79 Garden Street, Cambridge, MA 02138
617-495-2480, 800-448-2242   fax: 617-495-5898, 800-962-4983
www.hup.harvard.edu

Harvard's publishing categories include current events, cultural affairs, the arts, history, psychology, literary studies (including selected poetry), the sciences, legal studies, and economics. Harvard's special series have included such lines as the Twentieth Century Fund, the Global AIDS Policy Coalition, and the Developing Child series.

Harvard University Press (started in 1913) is currently the largest academic press in the United States. Harvard University Press produces a large number of trade-oriented, general-interest books for an eclectic readership, while maintaining its core program to provide a balanced offering of scholarly works in a range of academic fields. Harvard's extensive list is published in hardcover and trade paperback editions.

Featured Harvard titles: *Semblance's of Sovereignty: The Constitution, the State and American Citizenship* by Alexander T. Aleinkoff; *Minding the Laws* by Anthony Amsterdam; *Fiction in the Age of Photography: The Legacy of British Realism* by Nancy Armstrong; *The Arcades Project* by Walter Benjamin; *The Rise of Southern Republicans* by Earl Black; *On Histories and Stories: Selected Essays* by A. S. Byatt; *Creative Industries: Contacts Between Art and Commerce* by Richard E. Caves; *The Questions of Tenure* by Richard P. Chait; *What Price Fame?* by Tyler Cowen; *Look Homeward: A Life of Thomas Wolfe* by David Donald; *Gaylaw: Challenging the Apartheid of the Closet* by William N. Eskridge; *History's Memory: Writing America's Past 1880–1980* by Ellen Fitzpatrick; *Japan Encyclopedia* by Louis Frederic; *American Agriculture in the Twentieth Century* by Bruce L. Gardner; *Unequal Freedom: How Race and Gender Shaped American Citizenship and Labor* by Evelyn Nakanao Glenn; *Teaching in America: The Slow Revolution* by Gerald Grant; *Separation of Church and State* by Philip Hamburger; *The Union Divided: Party Conflict in the Civil War North* by Mark E. Neelym Jr.; *The Book of Korean Shijo* by Kevin O'Rourke; *Law and Social Norms* by Eric A. Posner; *The Problem of Perception* by A. D. Smith; *Travels in the Genetically Modified Zone* by Mark L. Winston; *Tears of Longing: Nostalgia and the Nation in Japanese Popular Song* by Christine R. Yano.

Harvard University Press handles its own distribution.

The publisher will not consider unsolicited poetry or fiction.

Query letters and SASEs should be directed to:

Elizabeth Knoll, Senior Editor for the Behavioral Sciences—Behavioral sciences, earth sciences, astronomy, neuroscience, education

Elizabeth Suttell, Senior Editor—East Asian studies

Joyce Seltzer, Senior Executive Editor—History, contemporary affairs. Contact Joyce Seltzer at: 150 Fifth Avenue, Suite 625, New York, NY 10011, 212-337-0280.

Lindsay Waters, Executive Editor for the Humanities—Literary criticism, philosophy, film studies, cultural studies

Margaretta Fulton, General Editor for the Humanities—Classics (including Loeb Classics), religion, music, art, Jewish studies, women's studies

Michael A. Aronson, Senior Editor, Social Sciences—Economics, political science, sociology, law, some business

Michael Fisher, Executive Editor for Science and Medicine—Medicine, science (except astronomy), neuroscience

Stephanie Gouse, Paperbacks and Foreign Rights

Kathleen McDermott, Senior Editor—History and social sciences

H

HOWARD UNIVERSITY PRESS

2225 Georgia Avenue NW, #720, Washington, DC 20059
202-238-2575   fax: 202-588-9849
www.founders.howard.edu/hupress

Customer service:
PO Box 50283, Baltimore, MD 21211
410-516-6947, 800-537-5487

The Howard University Press publishing scope addresses the conditions, concerns, and contributions of African Americans, other African diasporic populations, and other people of color worldwide—including cultural expressions, geopolitical topics, and historical studies. Howard University Press (founded in 1972) produces scholarly and general non-fiction works in the areas of history, biography, economics, sociology, political science, education, contemporary affairs, communications, the arts, and literature. Howard University Press generally publishes a select group of new titles per year in hardcover and trade paperback editions. The press maintains a diverse backlist.

Indicative of the Howard University Press publishing program: *Barbara C. Jordan: Selected Speeches* (edited by Sandra Parham, with a foreword by Ann Richards); *Singular Like a Bird: The Art of Nancy Morejon* (edited by Miriam DeCosta-Willis); *A History of the Black Press* by Armistead Pride and Clint C. Wilson II; *Othello: New Essays by Black Writers* (edited by Mythili Kaul); *Mordecai—The Man and His Message: The Story of Mordecai Wyatt Johnson* by Richard I. McKinney; *The Jamaican Crime Scene: A Perspective* by Bernard Headley; *Basic Currents of Nigerian Foreign Policy* by Mae C. King; *We Paid Our Dues: Women Trade Union Leaders of the Caribbean* by A. Lynn Bolles; *African Americans and U.S. Policy Toward Africa* by Elliott P. Skinner; *Captain Paul Cuffe's Logs and Letters, 1808–1817: A Black Quaker's "Voice from Within the Veil"* (edited by Rosalind Wiggins); *An African Victorian Feminist: The Life and Times of Adelaide Smith Casely Hayford, 1869–1960* by Adelaide Cromwell; *Manichean Psychology: Racism and the Minds of People of African Descent* by Camara Jules P. Harrell; *Cocoa and Chaos in Ghana* by Gwendolyn Mikell.

On the literary, cultural, and artistic front: *Social Rituals and the Verbal Art of Zora Neale Hurston* by Lynda Marion Hill; *The Dramatic Vision of August Wilson* by Sandra Shannon; *Ancient Songs Set Ablaze: The Theatre of Femi Osofisan* by Sandra L. Richards; *Black Drama in America* (edited by Darwin T. Turner); *Modern Negro Art* by James A. Porter; *The New Cavalcade: African American Writing from 1700 to the Present* (edited by Arthur P. Davis, J. Saunders Redding, and Joyce Ann Joyce).

Howard University Press handles distribution through its own in-house marketing department; fulfillment is handled through Johns Hopkins University Press.

The publisher will not consider unsolicited fiction or poetry. Please contact Howard University Press Editorial Department prior to sending any correspondence, including queries.

D. Kamili Anderson, Director of the Press

H

INDIANA UNIVERSITY PRESS

601 North Morton Street, Bloomington, IN 47404-3797
812-855-8817, 800-842-6796   fax: 812-855-8507
www.iupress.indiana.edu   e-mail: iupress@indiana.edu

Indiana University Press (founded in 1950) publishes books of serious trade interest, as well as titles directed toward scholarly and academic audiences. The press addresses such subjects as African and Afro-American studies, Russian studies, music, philosophy, regional and cultural studies, military history, political science and international affairs, popular culture and the arts, semiotics, science and technology, environmental issues and natural history, Jewish studies, paleontology, Middle East studies, classics, anthropology, and gender studies. Indiana University Press also publishes fiction in translation. IUP produces hardcover and paperback editions.

Indiana University Press issues a number of prestigious series, among them Middle East Studies, Studies in Continental Thought, Theories of Contemporary Culture, Blacks in the Diaspora, Arab and Islamic Studies, and Medical Ethics. The house is home to a variety of academic journals, including *Africa Today, Jewish Social Studies,* and a number of journals in feminist studies.

On the IUP list: *Fortress Conservation; Literary Culture in Colonial Ghana; Readings in African Popular Fiction; The Rise of an African Middle Class; Haitian Revolutionary Studies; Fictions of U.S. History; Sex and Humor; My Life in Stalinist Russia; The Voice of Harriet Taylor Mill; The Grand Scribe's Records; The Monuments of Ancient Egypt; Fortress Conservation; Female, Jewish and Educated; Painted in Words; Together and Apart in Brzezany; Mothers of the Nation; Guitar Towns; Singing, Acting, and Movement in Opera; Becoming John Dewey; Gaining Ground; King of the Crocodylians; Derrida and Husserl; A Short History of African Philosophy; The Puzzle Instinct; Monon; Uncle Sam's Locomotives; Russian Women, 1698–1917; When Hens Crow; Pilgrims of Love; Social Change and Sustainable Transport.*

Indiana University Press distributes its own list, as well as books produced by the Indiana Historical Society and the British Film Institute; IUP also serves as regional sales representative for several other university presses.

Query letters and SASEs should be directed to:

Janet Rabinowich, Editorial Director—Russian and East European studies, African studies, Middle Eastern and Judaic studies, philosophy

Robert Sloan, Senior Sponsoring Editor—Science, military history, U.S. history, African American studies, and religion

Roberta Diehl, Sponsoring Editor—Gardening, regional topics, and railroads

Marilyn Grobschmidt, Sponsoring Editor—Medical ethics, philanthropy, women's studies (history and social science), politics, and international studies

Michael Lundell, Sponsoring Editor—Classical studies, ancient history, medieval and Renaissance studies, film, folklore, and literature

I

Dee Mortensen, Sponsoring Editor—African studies, Caribbean and Black diaspora studies, philosophy, and women's studies (literary and cultural)

Gayle Sherwood, Sponsoring Editor—Music

Rebecca Tolen, Assistant Sponsoring Editor—Anthropology

THE JOHNS HOPKINS UNIVERSITY PRESS

2715 North Charles Street, Baltimore, MD 21218-4363
410-516-6900
www.press.jhu.edu

The Johns Hopkins University Press (founded in 1878) issues a strong list of contemporary-interest titles and academic trade books, as well as scholarly, technical, and professional works and select course books, reference books, and books of regional interest. The Press publishes in such diverse academic areas as literary criticism, ancient studies, religious studies, political science, and history of and current trends in medicine, science, and technology.

Johns Hopkins titles: *My House Is Killing Me! The Home Guide for Families with Allergies and Asthma* by Jeffrey C. May; *Zeppelin! Germany and the Airship, 1900–1939* by Guillame de Syon; *Saving the Bay: People Working for the Future of the Chesapeake* by Ann E. Dorbin (photographs by Richard A. K. Dorbin); *The Universities of the Italian Renaissance* by Paul F. Grendler; *The Tradition of the Trojan War in Homer and the Epic Cycle* by Jonathan Burgess; *The Rule of Law in America* by Ronald A. Cass; *Higher Education Law: The Faculty* by Steven G. Poskanzer; *Trauma and Its Representations: The Social Life of Mimesis in Post-Revolutionary France* by Deborah Jenson.

Johns Hopkins produces a number of specialty lines, such as the American Moment series of undergraduate course books in American history, the American Land Classics series of facsimile reprint editions, and Complete Roman Drama in Translation. The Johns Hopkins University Press handles its own distribution with the support of regional sales representatives.

The press will not consider unsolicited poetry or fiction.

Query letters and SASEs should be directed to:

James D. Jordan, Director—Science

Trevor Lipscombe, Editor in Chief—Physics and astronomy

Henry Y. K. Tom, Executive Editor—Sociology, religious studies, economics, development, European history, sociology, political science

Jacqueline C. Wehmueller, Executive Editor—Trade medical books for an educated general audience, books in higher education, history of medicine, reference books

Wendy Harris, Medical Editor—Medicine (hard science for medical professionals), public health, bioethics

Robert Brugger, History Editor—American history, history of science and technology, regional titles, documentary editions

J

Maura E. Burnett, Humanities Editor—Humanities, literary theory and criticism, classics and ancient studies, film studies, American studies, theater

George F. Thompson, Project Editor—Geography and environmental studies, Anabaptist studies, urban planning

---

LOUISIANA STATE UNIVERSITY PRESS

PO Box 25053, Baton Rouge, LA 70894-5053
3990 West Lakeshore Drive, Baton Rouge, LA 70803
225-578-6294, 225-578-6618   fax: 225-578-6461
www.lsu.edu

Areas of Louisiana State University Press interest include Southern history, the American Civil War, African American history, United States history, Latin American history, European history, philosophy and politics, art, architecture and design, photography, literary voices of the South, American literature, general criticism and European literature, music, natural history, and medicine. LSU offers a wide variety of regional books (not limited to Louisiana environs), as well as concentrations in contemporary fiction, poetry, and literary criticism. The house produces hardcover and trade paperback editions and maintains a solid backlist. Louisiana State University Press (founded in 1935) publishes a primarily academic and scholarly list, along with a good number of general-interest titles.

From LSU Press: *My Diary North and South* by Eugene H. Berwanger; *Grant, Lee, Lincoln and the Radicals: Essays on Civil War Leadership* by Grady McWhiney; *Autumn of the Heartland: The Army of Tennessee, 1861–1862* by Thomas Lawrence Connelly; *Gardening in the Humid South* by Edmund N. O'Rourke Jr. and Leon C. Standifer; *Peter Taylor: A Writer's Life* by Hubert H. McAlexander; *Birds of the Gulf Coast* by Brian K. Miller and William R. Fontenot; *An Honorable Estate: My Time in the Working Press* by Louis D. Rubin Jr.; *John Marshall and the Heroic Age of the Supreme Court* by R. Kent Newmyer; *New Orleans Yesterday and Today: Third Edition* by Walter G. Cowan et al.; *Our People and Our History: Fifty Creole Portraits* by Rodolphe Lucien Desdunes; *Along the River Road: Revised and Expanded Edition* by Mary Ann Sternberg.

Fiction and poetry from LSU: *Dixiana Moon* by William Price Fox; *The Annunciation* by Ellen Gilchrist; *A Recent Martyr* by Valerie Martin; *Set in Motion* by Valerie Martin; *A Sacrificial Zinc* by Matthew Cooperman; *Strangers to Their Courage* by Alice Derry; *Icon and Evidence* by Margaret Gibson; *Anvil, Clock & Last* by Paulette Roeske; *A Word in Your Ear* by Monroe Spears.

Louisiana State University Press oversees a distributional network that uses the services of regional university presses and book-distribution companies, as well as independent sales representatives. The Press will not consider unsolicited poetry or any original fiction.

Query letters and SASEs should be directed to:

Maureen G. Hewitt, Associate Director and Editor in Chief—All subject areas

John Easterly, Executive Editor—Literary studies

L

Sylvia Frank Rodrigue, Acquisitions Editor—American Civil War history, Southern history, civil rights studies

Gerry Anders, Editor/Electronic Editing Coordinator

Nicola Mason, Editor—All subject areas

George Roupe, Editor—All subject areas

THE MIT PRESS

5 Cambridge Center, Cambridge, MA 02142
617-253-5646

The MIT Press publishes nonfiction titles in the forefront of such fields as contemporary art, architectural studies, science, environmental studies, computer science and artificial intelligence, cognitive science and neuroscience, linguistics, and economics and finance. The house produces scholarly and professional works, in addition to educational textbooks and books for general audience. The MIT Press was founded in 1961 as the publishing wing of the Massachusetts Institute of Technology.

Representative titles from MIT Press include *A Ghost's Memoir* by John McDonald; *Advances in Neural Information Processing Systems 14* by Thomas G. Dietterich, Suzanna Becker, and Zoubin Ghahramani; *American Economic Policy in the 1990s* by Jeffrey A. Frankel and Peter R. Orszag; *Architectural Encounters with Essence and Form in Modern China* by Peter G. Rowe and Seng Kuan; *The Arts at Black Mountain College* by Mary Emma Harris; *Barriers to Riches* by Stephen L. Parente and Edward C. Prescott; *Belief's Own Ethics* by Jonathan E. Adler; *Borders and Brethren* by Brenda Shaffer; *The Dynamic Neuron* by John Smythies; *Each Wild Idea: Writing, Photography, History* by Geoffrey Batchen; *Engendering International Health* by Gita Sen, Asha George, and Piroska Ostlin; *The Favored Circle* by Garry Stevens; *Flexibility Principles in Boolean Semantics* by Yoad Winter; *Framing Production* by Paul Rosen.

The MIT Press also publishes 40-odd specialist journals such as *The Drama Review, The Washington Quarterly,* and *October.* The Bradford Books imprint accents titles representing the frontiers of cognitive science and neuroscience.

The MIT Press distributes its own list and handles distribution for several other publishers (including Zone Books and AAAI Press).

Query letters and SASEs should be directed to:

Tom Stone, Linguistics and Cognitive Science Editor

Clay Morgan, Environmental Science Editor

Douglas Sery, Computer Science Editor

Larry Cohen, Editor in Chief

Barbara Murphy, Neurosciences Editor

Robert Prior, Computer Science Editor

Roger Conover, Architecture and Design Editor

Elizabeth Murry, Economics, Finance, and Business Editor

John Covell, Economics, Finance, and Business Editor

New York University Press

853 Broadway, 3rd Floor, New York, NY 10003-4812

212-998-2575   fax: 212-995-3833

www.nyupress.nyu.edu   e-mail: nyupress.feedback@nyu.edu

New York University Press covers the fields of law and politics, history, American history, religion and Jewish studies, psychology, gender studies, sociology, cultural studies, media studies, literary criticism, urban studies, anthropology, race and ethnic studies, business, and New York regional affairs.

New York University Press (founded in 1916) offers a list laden with works of wide contemporary appeal for the general reader; NYU also maintains a strong presence in the scholarly and professional arena. Major series include titles catalogued under Fast Track (general-interest contemporary issues and affairs): *Critical America; Sexual Cultures: New Directions from the Center for Gay and Lesbian Studies; Cultural Front; The World of War;* The Religion, Race and Ethnicity series; *New Perspectives on Jewish Studies; Essential Papers in Jewish Studies; Essential Papers in Psychoanalysis;* and *Qualitative Studies in Psychology.* NYU publishes hardcover and paperback editions and supports a vigorous backlist.

From the NYU program: *Black Gay Man* by Robert Reid-Pharr; *Lure of the Sinister: The Unnatural History of Satanism* by Gareth J. Medway; *The Practical Guide to Aging* by Christine K. Cassel; *TechniColor: Race, Technology, and Everyday Life* (edited by Alondra Nelson, Thuy Linh N. Tu, Alicia Headlman Hines); *Reflections: The Life and Writings of a Young Blind Woman in Post-Revolutionary France* by Therese-Adele Husson (translated by Catherine Kudlick and Zina Weygand); *The Encyclopedia of Jewish Life Before and During the Holocaust* (edited by Shmuel Spector and Geoffrey Wigoder); *Inventing the 19th Century: 100 Inventions That Shaped the Victorian Age, from Aspirin to the Zepplin* by Stephen van Dulken; *The Best Pitcher in Baseball: The Life of Rube Foster, Blackball Giant* by Robert Charles Cottrell; *Rebels on the Air: An Alternative History of Radio in America* by Jesse Walker; *One Nation Underground* by Kenneth D. Rose.

NYU Press is the exclusive North American distributor for Berg Publishers, Monthly Review Press, Lawrence & Wishart, and Rivers Oram (Pandora).

NYU Press Prize winners include *The Marvelous Adventures of Pierre Baptiste: Father and Mother, First and Last* (fiction) by Patricia Eakins and *The Alphabet of Desire* (poetry) by Barbara Hamby.

New York University Press handles distribution through its own sales office, as well as a network of regional sales and marketing representatives.

Query letters and SASEs should be directed to:

Eric Zinner, Editor in Chief—Literary criticism and cultural studies, media studies, history, anthropology

Jennifer Hammer, Editor—Religion and psychology

Stephen Magro, Editor—Sociology and politics

Alison Waldenberg, Editor—Literary nonfiction and fiction

OHIO UNIVERSITY PRESS

Scott Quadrangle, Athens, OH 45701
740-593-1155   fax: 740-593-4536
www.ohiou.edu/oupress

Ohio University Press areas of interest encompass literary criticism, philosophy, African studies, history, international, regional and cultural studies, and Frontier Americana; the press also publishes fiction reprints and anthologies. Poetry issued through the Swallow Press imprint certifies the house's outstanding presence in this literary niche.

Ohio University Press (established in 1964) produces scholarly and academic works, as well as a line of general-interest titles. OU Press publishes in hardcover and paperback. The house backlist is comprehensive.

On the OU Press list: *Dared and Done: The Marriage of Elizabeth Barrett and Robert Browning* by Julia Markus; *Death and Taxes: The Complete Guide to Family Inheritance Planning* by Randell C. Doane and Rebecca G. Doane; *Deprived of Unhappiness* by Sam Pickering; *Brave Are My People: Indian Heroes Not Forgotten* by Frank Waters (foreword by Vine Deloria Jr.); *RFD* by Charles Allen Smart (foreword by Gene Logsdon); *The Watchers* by Memye Curtis Tucker; *Ruskin's Mythic Queen: Gender Subversion in Victorian Culture* by Sharon Aronofsky Weltman; *The Absent Man: The Narrative Craft of Charles W. Chesnutt; The Complete Works of Robert Browning, Volume XVI: With Variant Readings and Annotations* (edited by Susan Crowl and Roma A. King Jr.); *Word Play Place: Essays on the Poetry of John Matthias* (edited by Robert Archambeau); *The Green Archipelago: Forestry in Preindustrial Japan* by Conrad Totman (foreword by James L. A. Webb Jr.); *Theory of Objective Mind: An Introduction to the Philosophy of Culture* by Hans Freyer (translated and with an introduction by Steven Grosby); *Es'kia Mphahlele: Themes of Alienation and African Humanism* by Ruth Obee; *Herero Heroes: A Socio-Political History of the Herero of Namibia, 1890–1923* by Jan-Bart Gerwald; *Theater and Martial Arts in West Sumatra: Randai and Silek of the Minangkabau* by Kirstin Pauka.

Ohio University Press oversees its own sales and distribution.

Query letters and SASEs should be directed to:

Gillian Berchowitz, Senior Editor

OXFORD UNIVERSITY PRESS

198 Madison Avenue, New York, NY 10016
212-726-6000

Oxford's list is especially prominent in the subject areas of life science, world history (both ancient and modern), United States history, law, philosophy, religion, psychology, classics, literature, engineering, politics, sociology, economics, finance, business and management, and music.

Oxford University Press is the world's largest university press. It publishes 3,000 new books a year and has a presence in more than 50 countries. Founded in 1478, Oxford is an international publisher of trade, scholarly, professional, and reference titles in the humanities, the arts, science, medicine, and social studies in hardcover and paperback editions. OUP also publishes college textbooks, English as a second language educational materials, and children's books, as well as a number of journals.

Oxford titles include *Inroads into Burma* by Gerry Abbott; *Sport in Australian History* by Daryl Adair; *Tourism and Spatial Transformation* by G. J. Ashworth; *Tourism in Spain* by M. Barke; *The Oxford Companion to the Wines of North America* by Bruce Cass; *Rome* by Amanda Claridge; *Spain* by Roger Collins; *The Temple Tiger and More Man-Eaters of Kumaon* by Jim Corbett; *World Leisure Participation* by G. Cushman; *The Classical Cookbook* by Andrew Dalby; *The A–Z of Sailing Terms,* Second Edition, by Ian Dear; *Traditional Chinese Clothing* by Valery M. Garrett; *Trends in Outdoor Recreation, Leisure and Tourism* by W. C. Gartner; *Sou' West in Wanderer IV* by Eric C. Hiscock; *Budapest* by Michael Jacobs; *Travelers' India* by H. K. Kaul; *The Oxford Companion to Ships and the Sea* by Peter Kemp; *Yangtze River* by Madeleine Lynn; *Destinations* by Jan Morris; *The Holy Land,* Fourth Edition, by Jerome Murphy O'Connor; *Oxford History of Board Games* by David Parlett*; The Oxford Book of Australian Travel Writing* by Roslyn Pesman; *Eisenhower and the Cold War* by Robert A. Divine; *Narrative of the Life of Frederick Douglass, and American Slave* by Frederick Douglass; *The American Pacific* by Arthur P. Dudden; *Them Dark Days* by William Dusinberre.

Oxford's New York office is editorially independent of the British home office and handles distribution of its own list, as well as titles originating from Oxford's branches worldwide.

Query letters and SASEs should be directed to:

Niko Pfund, Academic Publisher

Joan Bossert, Associate Publisher—Science and professional books

Catharine Carlin, Associate Publisher—Psychology

Martha Cooley, Editor—Business

Paul Donnelly, Executive Editor—Business, finance, economics

Dedi Felman, Editor—Politics, criminology, law, sociology

Susan Ferber, Editor—American and world history, art history

Kirk Jensen, Executive Editor—Life sciences

Susan Lee, Editor—Earth sciences, food services, physics, atmospheric science, agronomy, geography, crop/soil science, physical science, archaeology

Sharon Liu, Associate Editor—Chemistry

Stephen McGroarty, Associate Editor—Economics

Elissa Morris, Editor—Literary studies, classics, media studies, cultural studies, gay/lesbian studies, literature, African American studies

Peter Ohlin, Editor—Linguistics, philosophy

Cynthia Read, Senior Editor—Religion

Peter Ginna, Trade Editorial Director—American history

Tim Bartlett, Senior Editor—Political science, sociology, current events

Elda Rotor, Editor—Literature, cultural studies, art, photography, architecture

Nancy Toff, Editorial Director—Children's and young adult books

Jeff House, Executive Editor—Medicine

Fiona Stevens, Senior Editor—Psychiatry, medicine, neuroscience

Donald Kraus, Executive Editor—Bibles

PRINCETON UNIVERSITY PRESS

41 William Street, Princeton, NJ 08540
609-258-4900
www.pup.princeton.edu

U.K. office:
3 Market Place, Woodstock, Oxfordshire OX20 1SY, U.K.
(011) 44-1993-814500

Princeton University Press has a particularly strong focus in such areas as popular culture and fine arts, current affairs, literary biography, European history, political science, economics, and natural history. Princeton University Press (founded in 1905) publishes trade and general-interest books, in addition to a list of scholarly and scientific works that spans the academic spectrum. Popular Princeton lines include the Bollingen series and Princeton Science Library. Princeton publishes hardcover and paperback editions and hosts a comprehensive backlist.

Princeton titles: *Charles Taylor* by Ruth Abbey; *Sexual Identities, Queer Politics* (edited by Mark Blasius); *Financing the American Dream: A Cultural History of Consumer Credit* by Lendol Calder; *Diplomacy of Conscience: Amnesty International and Changing Human Rights Norms* by Ann Marie Clark; *Asset Pricing* by John H. Cochrane; *The Secular Mind* by Robert Coles; *Winslow Homer and the Critics: Forging a National Art 1870's* by Margaret C. Conrads; *Home Team: Professional Sports and the American Metropolis* by Michael N. Danielson; *Learning and Expectations in Macroeconomics* by George W. Evans and Seppo Honkapohja; *How the Leopard Changed Its Spots: The Evolution of Complexity* by Brian Goodwin; *The Color of School Reform, Race, Politics, and the Challenge of Urban Education* by Jeffrey R. Henig, Richard C. Hula, Marion Orr, and Desiree S. Pedescleaux; *The Necessary Nation* by Gregory Jusdanis; *The Story of Mathematics* by Richard Mankiewicz; *Suburban Warriors: The Origins of the New American Right* by Lisa McGirr; *William Blake: The Creation of the Songs from Manuscript to Illuminated Printing* by Michael Phillips.

The Bollingen Series, established in 1941, is sponsored by the Bollingen Foundation and has been published by Princeton since 1967. Bollingen titles are works of original scholarship, translations, and new editions of classics. An ongoing Bollingen project is Mythos: The Princeton/Bollingen series in world mythology. Titles include *Psychology of Kundalini Yoga* by C. G. Young; *On the Laws of the Poetic Art* by Anthony Hecht; *The Survival of the Pagan Gods: The Mythological Tradition and Its Place in Renaissance Humanism and Art* by Jean Seznec.

Books from the Princeton Science Library include *Infinity and the Mind* by Rudy Rucker; *A Natural History of Shells* by Geerat J. Vermeij; *Total Eclipses of the Sun* by J. B. Zirker.

Princeton University Press handles distribution through the offices of California/Princeton Fulfillment Services, as well as regional sales representation worldwide.

Query letters and SASEs should be directed to:

Mary Murrell, Anthropology Editor and Literary Studies

Peter Dougherty, Economics Editor and Publisher

Walter Lippincott, Director

Sam Elworthy, Science Editor/Science Group Manager—Biology, earth science, and trade science

Nancy Grubb, Executive Editor—Fine arts and art history

Robert Kirk, Senior Editor—Natural history

Thomas LeBien, American Studies Editor—Pre-twentieth-century American history, American studies, and American religion

Ian Malcolm, Philosophy, Political Theory, and Sociology Editor

Chuck Myers, Political Science, Law, and Classics Editor

Brigitta van Rheinberg, Senior Editor—History and Religion Editor—Twentieth-century American history, non-American history, and religion (Jewish and Asian studies)

Terry Vaughn, Editor in Chief

Joe Wisnovsky, Executive Editor—Physical sciences and trade science

Richard Baggaley (U.K. office), European Publishing Director—Finance and economics

David Ireland (U.K. office), Applied Math Editor

Fred Appel, Associate Editor—Music, anthropology, and literature

Vickie Kearu, Senior Editor—Mathematics

RUTGERS UNIVERSITY PRESS

100 Joyce Kilmer Avenue, Piscataway, NJ 08854
732-445-7762
http://rutgerspress.rutgers.edu

Rutgers subject areas include African American studies, American history, anthropology, art and architecture, Asian American studies, environment and ecology, European history, gay and gender studies, geography, health and medicine, history of medicine and science, literature and literary criticism, media studies, multicultural studies, New Jerseyana, peace studies, poetry, religion, and sociology.

Rutgers University Press (founded in 1936) publishes a list of general-interest trade books in addition to scholarly titles in the humanities and social sciences, as well as books with a regional American bent.

Representing the nonfiction Rutgers list: *Midnight Dreary: The Mysterious Death of Edgar Allan Poe* by John Evangelist Walsh; *Talking Leadership: Conversations with Powerful Women* (edited by Mary S. Hartman); *The Truth That Never Hurts: Writings on Race, Gender, and Freedom* by Barbara Smith; *Surviving Modern Medicine: How to Get the Best from Doctors, Family and Friends* by Peter Clarke and Susan H. Evans; *Mortal Men: Living with Asymptomatic HIV* by Richard MacIntyre (foreword by Stephen Lacey); *Heresy in the University: The Black Athena Controversy and the Responsibilities of American Intellectuals* by Jacques Berlinerblau; *How Jews Became White Folks and What That Says About Race in America* by Karen Brodkin; *Consuming Environments: Television and Commercial Culture* by Mike Budd, Steve Craig, and Clay Steinman; *Evaluating Alternative Cancer Therapies: A Guide to the Science and Politics of an Emerging Medical Field* by David Hess; *In Praise of Difference: The Emergence of a Global Feminism* by Rosiska Darcy De Oliveira; *Gone Fishin': The 100 Best Spots in New Jersey* by Manny Luftglass and Ron Bern; *Anatomy of a Miracle: The End of Apartheid and the Birth of the New South Africa* by Patti Waldmeir.

Rutgers features the Touring North America guidebook series, which offers an accent on regional landscape. Titles: *Beyond the Great Divide: Denver to the Grand Canyon; Megalopolis: Washington, DC, to Boston.*

New Jerseyana from Rutgers includes *Roadside New Jersey* by Peter Genovese; *Murdered in Jersey* by Gerald Tomlinson; *Teenage New Jersey, 1941–1975* (edited by Kathryn Grover); *The New Jersey State Constitution: A Reference Guide* by Robert F. Williams; *New Jersey Parks, Forests, and Natural Areas* by Michael P. Brown.

Rutgers University Press handles its own distribution.

Query letters and SASEs should be directed to:

David Myers, Editor—Social sciences

Helen Hsu, Senior Editor—Sciences

Leslie Mitchner, Associate Director and Editor in Chief—Humanities, literature, film, communications

Suzanne Kellam, Associate Editor in the Humanities—History

STANFORD UNIVERSITY PRESS

Stanford, CA 94305-2235

415-723-9598

Stanford produces a notable line of titles in the fields of new technology, the global political and natural environment, postmodern philosophy and psychology, gender studies, and international issues, as well as a number of books (many in translation) dealing with current cultural and literary theory. A major Stanford publishing concentration is in the Asian American and Pacific Rim fields of studies.

Stanford University Press (started in 1925) produces trade and scholarly books in literature, the social sciences, religion, history, political science, anthropology, and natural science in hardcover and paperback editions.

Highlights from Stanford: *Taking Our Pulse: The Health of America's Women* by Iris F. Litt, M.D.; *The Cable Car in America* by George W. Hilton; *The Fall of the Packard Motor Car Company* by James A. Ward; *From Immigrant to Ethnic Culture: American Yiddish in South Philadelphia* by Rakhmiel Peltz; *Caught by History: Holocaust Effects in Contemporary Art, Literature, and Theory* by Ernst Van Alphen; *Desiring Women Writing: English Renaissance Examples* by Jonathan Goldberg; *The Mottled Screen: Reading Proust Visually* by Mieke Bal; *Psychoanalyzing: On the Order of the Unconscious and the Practice of the Letter* by Serge Leclaire (translated by Peggy Kamuf); *The Queer Afterlife of Vaslav Nijinsky* by Kevin Kopelson; *A Sense for the Other: The Timeliness and Relevance of Anthropology* by Marc Augé (translated by Amy Jacobs); *Freedom and Religion in the Nineteenth Century* (edited by Richard Helmstadter); *The Price of Redemption: The Spiritual Economy of Puritan New England* by Mark A. Peterson; *Traces of Dreams: Landscape, Cultural Memory, and the Poetry of Basho* by Haruo Shirane; *The Will to Orthodoxy: A Critical Genealogy of Northern Chan Buddhism* by Bernard Faure (translated by Phyllis Brooks); *Space Between Words: The Origin of Silent Reading* by Paul Saenger.

Stanford University Press books are distributed by Cambridge University Press Distribution Center.

Query letters and SASEs should be directed to:

Helen Tartar, Assistant Director—Philosophy, literary criticism and theory

John Feneron, Managing Editor—Asian literature

Muriel Bell, Senior Editor—Asian studies, political science, anthropology

Norris Pope, Director—Latin American studies, history, Victorian studies, natural sciences

SYRACUSE UNIVERSITY PRESS

621 Skytop Road, Suite 110, Syracuse, NY 13244-5290
315-443-5534   fax: 315-443-5545
e-mail: talitz@syr.edu

Syracuse University Press (founded in 1943) hosts a publishing program that accents scholarly, general, and regional (New York and New England) nonfiction interests, as well as literature and criticism. Syracuse has a particular presence in Irish studies, Iroquois studies, Middle Eastern studies, studies in peace and conflict resolution, history of the medieval period, and historical American utopianism and communitarianism.

On the Syracuse list: *Crossing Highbridge: A Memoir of Irish America* by Maureen Waters; *Under the Spell of Arabia* (photographs by Mathias Oppersdorff); *Gertrude Bell: The Arabian Diaries, 1913–1914* (edited by Rosemary O'Brien); *Women in Muslim Fam-*

ily Law by John L. Esposito with Natana DeLong-Bas; *The Gatekeeper: My 20 Years as a TV Censor* by Alfred R. Schneider with Kaye Pullen; *Prime Time Authorship: Works About and by Three TV Dramatists* by Douglas Heil; *Gustav Stickley's Craftsman Farms: The Quest for an Arts and Crafts Utopia* by Mark Alan Hewitt; *Masterpieces of American Furniture from the Munson-Williams-Proctor Institute* (edited by Anna Tobin D'Ambrosio); *My Self, My Muse* (edited by Patricia Boyle Haberstroh); *Reading Roddy Doyle* by Caramine White; *The Scottish Connection: The Rise of English Literary Study in Early America* by Franklin E. Court; *Pleasure Zones: Bodies, Cities, Spaces* (edited by David Bell); *Does Your Government Measure Up? Basic Tools for Local Officials and Citizens* by William D. Coplin and Carol Dwyer; *The President Is at Camp David* by W. Dale Nelson; *The Man Who Stopped the Trains to Auschwitz* by David Kranzler; *Diary of an Adulterous Woman* by Curt Leviant; *TV Creators: Conversations with America's Top Producers of Television Drama* by James L. Longworth Jr.; *Catching Dreams: My Life in the Negro Baseball Leagues* by Frazier "Slow" Robinson with Paul Bauer; *A Room of His Own: In Search of the Feminine in the Novels of Saul Bellow* by Gloria Cronin.

Titles in the Reader's Guide series: *A Reader's Guide to Walt Whitman* by Gay Wilson Allen; *A Reader's Guide to Joseph Conrad* by Frederick R. Karl; *A Reader's Guide to William Butler Yeats* by John Unterecker; *A Reader's Guide to Dylan Thomas, A Reader's Guide to James Joyce,* and *A Reader's Guide to Finnegan's Wake* by William York Tindall; *A Reader's Guide to Samuel Beckett* by Hugh Kenner.

Syracuse University Press distributes its list via its own in-house offices and utilizes a variety of distribution services worldwide.

Syracuse University Press does not wish to receive unsolicited manuscripts.

Mary Shelden Evans, Executive Editor; e-mail: msevans@syr.edu

TEXAS A&M UNIVERSITY PRESS

John H. Lindsey Building, Lewis Street, College Station, TX 77843-4354
979-458-3975   fax: 979-847-8752
www.tamu.edu/upress/   e-mail: d-vance@tamu.edu

Texas A&M University Press (founded in 1974) publishes scholarly nonfiction, regional studies, art, economics, government, history, environmental history, natural history, social science, United States–Mexican borderlands studies, veterinary medicine, women's studies, and military studies. A special portion of the Texas A&M list accents Texas photography, history, and literature.

Texas A & M nonfiction: *Land of the Desert Sun: Texas' Big Bend Country* by D. Gentry Steele; *Wild Edens: Africa's Premier Game Parks and Their Wildlife* by Joseph James Shomon; *Planetary Astronomy: From Ancient Times to the Third Millennium* by Ronald A. Schorn; *Stirring Prose: Cooking with Texas Authors* by Deborah Douglas; *Tejano Empire: Life on the South Texas Ranchos* by Andres Tijerina; *The Plains Indians* by Paul H. Carlson; *Sailing Ship Elissa* by Patricia Bellis Bixel; *Coercive Military Strategy* by Stephen J. Cimbala; *Shaping and Signaling Presidential Policy: The National Security Decision Making of Eisenhower and Kennedy* by Meena Bose; *Under Ice:*

Waldo Lyon and the Development of the Arctic Submarine by William M. Leary; *East of Chosin: Entrapment and Breakout in Korea, 1950* by Roy E. Appleman; *Galveston and the Great West* by Earle B. Young.

Texas A&M University Press manages its own distribution network and handles distribution for several other regional, academically oriented presses.

Query letters and SASEs should be directed to:

Mary Lenn Dixon, Editor in Chief; e-mail: mary-dixon@tamu.edu

Shannon Davies, Senior Editor; e-mail: smdavies@aol.com

Jim Sadkovich, Acquisitions Editor; e-mail: j-sadkovich@tamu.edu

---

UNIVERSITY OF ARIZONA PRESS

355 South Euclid, Suite 103, Tucson, AZ 85719
520-621-1441   fax: 520-621-8899
www.uapress.arizona.edu

University of Arizona Press (founded in 1959) publishes works of general as well as academic interest, related primarily to the scholarly emphasis of the university's programs in Southwest regional culture and natural history. Fields of publishing concentration include general nonfiction about Arizona, the American West, and Mexico; wider categories encompass the American Indian and Latin America, anthropology, and archaeology.

From the Arizona program: *Homol'ovi: An Ancient Hopi Settlement Cluster* by E. Charles Adams; *Backcountry Pilot: Flying Adventures with Ike Russell* by Thomas Bowen; *Moving from the Margins: A Chicana Voice on Public Policy* by Adela de la Torre; *Western Pueblo Identities* by Andrew Duff; *Mexican Americans and the U.S. Economy* by Arturo Gonzalez; *Beyond Chaco: Great Kiva Communities on the Mogollon Rim Frontier* by Sarah A. Herr; *Language Shift Among the Navajos* by Deborah House; *The Lessening Stream: An Environmental History of the Santa Cruz River* by Michael F. Logan; *The Devil's Workshop* by Demetria Martinez; *The Truth About Alicia and Other Stories* by Ana Consuelo Matiella; *Gender, Law and Resistance in India* by Erin P. Moore; *Spanish American Saints and the Rhetoric of Identity, 1600–1810* by Ronald J. Morgan; *The Desert Smells Like Rain: A Naturalist in O'odham Country* by Gary Paul Nabhan.

University of Arizona Press handles its own distribution and also distributes titles originating from the publishing programs of such enterprises and institutions as Oregon State University Press, the Arizona State Museum, and other archaeological and environmental consulting firms.

Query letters and SASEs should be directed to:

Christine Szuter, Director

Judith Wesley Allen, Managing Editor

Al Schroder, Assistant Managing Editor

Nancy Arora, Editor

Patti Hartmann, Editor

Yvonne Reineke, Editor
Julie Blackwell, Editorial Assistant

UNIVERSITY OF ARKANSAS PRESS

201 Ozark Avenue, Fayetteville, AR 72701
501-575-3246, 800-626-0090   fax: 501-575-6044
www.uapress.com   e-mail: UAPRINFO@cavern.uark.edu

University of Arkansas Press (begun in 1980) features titles in Middle Eastern studies, civil rights studies, poetry, literary criticism, history, regional studies, natural science, political science, and popular culture. The house issues a moderate list of new books each season (in hardcover and paperback editions), while tending a hardy backlist.

Indicative of the Arkansas list: *Sports Wars: Athletes in the Age of Aquarius* by David W. Zang; *The Artificial Southerner: Equivocations and Love Songs* by Philip Martin; *Blood in Their Eyes: The Elaine Race Massacres of 1919* by Grif Stockley; *A Beautiful Sickness: Reflections on the Sweet Science* by Thomas Hauser; *The Ozarks: Land and Life,* Second Edition, by Milton D. Rafferty; *Stars at Noon: Poems from the Life of Jacqueline Cochran* by Enid Shomer; *Changeable Thunder, Poems* by David Baker; *Roads to Dystopia: Sociological Essays on the Postmodern Condition* by Stanford M. Lyman; *The Apple That Astonished Paris* by Billy Collins.

University of Arkansas Press distributes its own list.

Query letters and SASEs should be directed to:

John Coghlan, Acting Director and Production Manager
Lawrence S. Malbey, Director and Editor

UNIVERSITY OF CALIFORNIA PRESS

2120 Berkeley Way, Berkeley, CA 94720

Branch office:
1600 Hershey Hall South Annex, UCLA, CA 90095
510-642-4247   fax: 510-643-7127
www.upress.edu

University of California Press (founded in 1893) publishes a solid general-interest list, in addition to its substantial contribution in academic publishing. The house maintains a broad program that encompasses scholarly and classical studies, humanities and the arts, medicine and science, the environment, popular historical and contemporary culture and issues, and language and linguistics. The press has major concentrations in such specialty areas as California and the West; the Pacific Ocean region, including the Pacific Rim; Asian studies; Oceania; and Latin America. University of California Press also produces literary fiction, letters, and poetry.

University of California titles include *Food Politics: How the Food Industry Influences Nutrition and Health* by Marion Nestle; *Empire and Revolution: The Americans in Mexico Since the Civil War* by John Mason Hart; *Passionate Uncertainty: Inside the American Jesuits* by Peter McDonough and Eugene C. Bianchi; *What It Means to Be 98% Chimpanzee: Apes, People, and Their Genes* by Jonathan Marks; *The Private Life of a Masterpiece* by Monica Bohm-Duchn; *The Paintings of Joan Mitchell* by Jane Livingston; *Nathan Oliveira* by Peter Selz; *Ruth Harriet Louse and Hollywood Glamour Photography* by Robert Dance and Bruce Robertson; *Sundance to Sarajevo: Film Festivals and the World They Made* by Kenneth Turan; *The Civilization of Angkor* by Charles Hingham; *Sexual Selections: What We Can and Can't Learn About Sex from Animals* by Marlene Zuk; *Colored White: Transcending the Racial Past* by David R. Roediger; *Global Community: The Role of International Organizations in the Making of the Contemporary World* by Akira Iriye; *The Red Count: The Life and Times of Harry Kessler* by Laird M. Easton; *The Art of Calligraphy in Modern China* by Gordon S. Barrass; *Sleeping with the Dictionary* by Harryette Mullen.

University of California Press distributes its own list.

Query letters and SASEs should be directed to:

Deborah Kirshman, Editor—Fine arts

Doris Kretchmer, Executive Editor—Natural history, biology

Lynne Withey, Editor—Middle Eastern studies, world history

Kate Toll, Editor—Classics

Monica McCormick, Editor—African studies and American studies

Naomi Schneider, Executive Editor—Sociology, politics, gender studies, ethnic studies, Latin American studies

Sheila Levine, Editorial Director—Asian studies and European history, food

Stan Holwitz, Assistant Director—Anthropology

Stephanie Fay, Editor—Fine arts

Mary Francis, Editor—Music

Blake Edgar, Editor—Environmental science, biology, archaeology, viticulture

Eric Smoodin—Film, philosophy

Reed Malcom—Religion, political science

UNIVERSITY OF CHICAGO PRESS

1427 East 60th Street, Chicago, IL 60637-2954
773-702-7700   fax: 773-702-9756
www.press.uchicago.edu   e-mail: marketing@press.uchicago.edu

University of Chicago Press (founded in 1891) specializes in the arts, humanities, and social sciences. Above all a scholarly and academic house, Chicago nonetheless has a noteworthy list of books intended for a wider readership. Major areas of Chicago publishing interest are history, regional Chicago and Illinois books, literary studies, philosophy and linguistics, anthropology, archaeology, art, architecture, music, religion, business and economics, media studies, political science, sociology, psychology, education, legal studies, gender studies, popular culture, and publishing, along with selected titles in the biological and physical sciences.

Titles from University of Chicago Press: *Making Patriots* by Walter Berns; *Free to Die for Their Country: The Story of the Japanese American Draft Resisters in World War II* by Eric L. Muller; *Dancing at Armageddon: Survivalism and Chaos in Modern Times* by Richard G. Mitchell Jr.; *The Rules of the Global Game: A New Look at US International Economic Policymaking* by Kenneth W. Dam; *For the Love of Mike: More of the Best of Mike Royko* by Mike Royko; *The Moment of Complexity: Emerging Network Culture* by Mark C. Taylor; *Why Architecture Matters: Lessons from Chicago* by Blair Kamin; *On My Honor: Boy Scouts and the Making of American Youth* by Jay Mechling; *Love Stories: Sex Between Men Before Homosexuality* by Jonathan Ned Katz; *All the Rage: The Story of Gay Visibility in America* by Suzanna Danuta Walters; *The Votes That Counted: How the Court Decided the 2000 Presidential Election* by Howard Gillman; *Rock of Ages, Sands of Time* by Warren Allmon (paintings by Barbara Page); *With Strings* by Charles Bernstein; *A Guide to Chicago's Murals* by Mary Lackritz Gray.

University of Chicago Press distributes its own list.

Query letters and SASEs should be directed to:

Alan Thomas, Editor—Literary criticism and theory, religious studies

Christie Henry, Editor—Biological science

Douglas Mitchell, Editor—Sociology, history, gay and lesbian studies

Geoffrey Huck, Editor—Economics, linguistics, classics

John Tryneski, Editor—Political science, law, education

Kathleen Hansell, Editor—Music

Linda Halorson, Editor—Reference

Penelope Kaiserlian, Associate Director—Geography

Susan Abrams, Editor—History of science

Susan Bielstein, Editor—Art, architecture, classics, women's studies

T. David Brent, Editor—Anthropology, philosophy, psychology

UNIVERSITY OF GEORGIA PRESS

330 Research Drive, Athens, GA 30602-4901
706-369-6130   fax: 706-369-6131
www.uga.edu/ugapress

University of Georgia Press (established in 1938) publishes a solid list of mainstream-interest books, in addition to its specialized roster of academic, scholarly, and scientific publications. Georgia trade-book titles accent fiction and literature, biography and memoirs, history, current affairs, and regional titles; the house academic emphasis overlaps these areas of concentration in a program that features scholarly nonfiction, poetry, short fiction, regional studies, and novels. The press publishes hardcover and trade paperback editions.

Representative of the Georgia list: *Ozark Wildflowers; The Violence of the Morning; Another Beauty; Apalachee; Two Cities; "Wild Apples" and Other Natural History Essays; Remembering Heaven's Face; Canada and the United States; Essays on Nature and Landscape; God and the Imagination; Seas of Gold, Seas of Cotton; Nations Divided; The Riddle Song and Other Rememberings; The Necessary Grace to Fall; Memories of a Georgia Teacher; Fleshing Out America; South to the Future; Camera Man's Journey; We Shall Not Be Moved; UGA Press Subject Catalog: Photography.*

Backlist favorites: *American Plants for American Gardens: Plant Ecology—The Study of Plants in Relation to Their Environment* by Edith A. Roberts and Elsa Rehmann; *Why the South Lost the Civil War* by Richard E. Beringer, Herman Hattaway, Archer Jones, and William N. Still Jr.

The New Georgia Guide is filled with essays, tours, maps, and other resources keyed to Georgia's heritage and culture.

University of Georgia Press sponsors the Flannery O'Connor Award for Short Fiction. (Please write for entry requirements and submission guidelines.)

University of Georgia Press oversees its own distribution.

Query letters and SASEs should be directed to:

Barbara Ras, Executive Editor

Emily Montjoy, Assistant Editor

Erin McElroy, Acquisitions Editorial Assistant

UNIVERSITY OF HAWAII PRESS

2840 Kolowalu Street, Honolulu, HI 96822-1888
808-956-8257   fax: 808-988-6052
www.uhpress.hawaii.edu

Areas of University of Hawaii Press publishing interest include cultural history, economics, social history, travel, arts and crafts, costume, marine biology, natural history, botany, ecology, religion, law, political science, anthropology, and general reference; particular UHP emphasis is on regional topics relating to Hawaii, and scholarly and academic books on East Asia, South and Southeast Asia, and Hawaii and the Pacific.

University of Hawaii Press (started in 1947) publishes books for the general trade, as well as titles keyed to the academic market. UHP also issues a series of special-interest journals. The house maintains an established backlist.

On the University of Hawaii list: *My Brother Hideo Kobayashi* by Junko Takamizawa; *Hawaii Under the Rising Sun: Japan's Plans for Conquest After Pearl Harbor* by John J. Stephan; *Stories from the Marshall Islands: Bwebwenato Jan Aelon Kein* by Jack A. Tobin; *From the Spider Bone Diaries: Poems and Songs* by Richard Hamasaki; *Queen Salote of Tonga: The Story of an Era, 1900–1965* by Elizabeth Wood Ellem; *An Anthropologist in Papua: The Photography of F. E. Williams 1922–1939* by Michael Young and

Julia Clark; *Remaking the Chinese City: Modernity and National Identity 1900–1950* by Joseph W. Esherick; *Secret Places: New Writing from Nepal* (edited by Frank Stewart and Upadhyay Samrat); *Other Oceans* by Thomas Farber; *Listen to Your Body: The Wisdom of Dao* by Bisong Guo and Andrew Powell; *The Moneylenders of Late Medieval Kyoto* by Suzanne Gay; *Sea Turtles of Hawaii* by Patrick Ching; *Asian Media Productions* by Brain Moeran; *Birthing the Pacific: Beyond Tradition and Modernity* by Vicki Lukere and Margaret Jolly; *ABC Dictionary of Chinese Proverbs* (edited by John S. Rohsenow).

A notable UHP series is Talanoa: Contemporary Pacific Literature, which makes writing of Pacific Islanders available to a wider audience. Sample titles: *Deep River Talk: Collected Poems* by Hone Tuwhere; *Once Were Warriors* by Alan Duff; *Leaves of the Banyan Tree* by Albert Wendt.

The University of Hawaii Press handles its own distribution via a network that includes in-house fulfillment services, as well as independent sales representatives.

Query letters and SASEs should be directed to:

Keith Leber, Acquisitions Editor—Natural history and science of Hawaii and the Pacific; e-mail: kleber@ hawaii.edu

Pamela Kelley, Acquisitions Editor—Pacific studies, Southeast Asian studies, and Asian literature; e-mail: pkelley@hawaii.edu

Patricia Crosby, Executive Editor—East Asia history, philosophy, religion, art history, and social sciences; e-mail: pcrosby@hawaii.edu

Masako Ikeda, Acquisitions Editor—Hawaiiana, Pacific literature, and Asian American studies; e-mail: masakoi@hawaii.edu

William Hamilton, Director

UNIVERSITY OF ILLINOIS PRESS

1325 South Oak Street, Champaign, IL 61820
217-333-0950   fax: 217-244-8082
www.press.uillinois.edu   e-mail: uipress@uillinois.edu

University of Illinois Press (founded in 1918) publishes books of general and scholarly nonfiction, with strong emphasis on American studies (especially history, literature, music), communications, film studies, folklore, gender studies, African American studies, regional studies, law and political science, religion and philosophy, labor studies, and athletics. The press also publishes poetry (submissions accepted in February only).

Representative of the University of Illinois program: *African American Mayors; American Opera; Ancient Records of Egypt; Bluegrass Odyssey; Chicago and the Old Northwest; Damnedest Radical; Desirable Body; Early Encounter with Tomorrow; Elliot Coues; Enemies Within; Gold and the American Country Club; Graying of America; Haunting Violations; Holding Up More Than Half the Sky; House of Poured Out Waters; Lessons in Progress; Love, War, and the 96th Engineers; Masculine Women in America 1890–1935; Mormons and Mormonism; Salt Hour; Science or Pseudoscience; Shaping Losses; Spirit of Youth and the City Streets; Tomorrow's Eve; Vacation Stories; Zion in the Courts.*

U

The University of Illinois Press has been chosen as one of the publishers for the National Poetry Series. New poetry titles: *Grazing* by Ira Sadoff; *Walt Whitman Bathing* (poems) by David Wagoner; *To the Bone* (new and selected poems) by Sydney Lea; *The Tracks We Leave: Poems on Endangered Wildlife of North America* by Barbara Helfgott Hyett (illustrated by Robert W. Treanor); *The Broken World* (poems) by Marcus Cafagna; *Dance Script with Electric Ballerina* (poems) by Alice Fulton; *Bruised Paradise* (poems) by Kevin Stein.

Of literary note: *"I Cease Not to Yowl": Ezra Pound's Letters to Olivia Rossetti Agresti* (edited by Demetres P. Tryphonopoulos and Leon Surette); *Unbought Spirit: A John Jay Chapman Reader* (edited by Richard Stone); *The Urban Sublime in American Literary Naturalism* by Christophe Den Tandt; *Taking It Home: Stories from the Neighborhood* by Tony Ardizzone; *Flights in the Heavenlies* by Ernest J. Finney; *The New World* by Russell Banks; *Walter Burley in America* (photographs and essay by Mati Maldre; essay, catalog, and selected bibliography by Paul Kruty).

University of Illinois Press distributes its own list, as well as books from other university publishers, including Vanderbilt University Press.

Query letters and SASEs should be directed to:

Joan Catapano, Associate Director and Editor in Chief—Women's studies, history, African American studies, film

Ann Lowry, Journals Manager and Senior Editor—Literature

Elizabeth G. Dulany, Editor—Western Americana, religious studies, archaeology, anthropology

Judith M. McCulloh, Executive Editor—Music, folklore, pop culture

Richard J. Martin, Executive Editor—Political science, sociology, law, philosophy, architecture, economics

Richard L. Wentworth, Editor—American history, Black history, communications, sports history, and regional books

Willis G. Regier, Director—Literature, Near Eastern studies, foodways

U

UNIVERSITY OF IOWA PRESS

100 Kuhl House, Iowa City, IA 52242-1000
319-335-2000   fax: 319-335-2055
www.uiowa.edu/~uipress

University of Iowa Press (established in 1938) produces a solid list in selected categories that includes scholarly works, general-interest nonfiction, and regional titles in the areas of archaeology, anthropology, and history. The house also produces short stories, literary criticism, creative nonfiction, and poetry.

Iowa series include American Land and Life, Sightline Books: The Iowa series in literary nonfiction, Kahl House Poets, and publications from studies in Theatre History and Culture, the annual Iowa Poetry Prize competition.

Iowa nonfiction: *King James and Letters of Homoerotic Desire* by David M. Bergeron; *Of Cabbages and Kings County: Agriculture and the Formation of Modern Brooklyn* by Marc Linder and Lawrence S. Zacharias; *Soldier Boy: The Civil War Letters of Charles O. Musser, 29th Iowa* (edited by Barry Popchock); *Sickness, Recovery, and Death: A History and Forecast of Ill Health* by James C. Riley; *After the West Was Won: Homesteaders and Town-Builders in Western South Dakota* by Paula M. Nelson; *China Dreams: Growing Up in Jewish Tientsin* by Isabelle Maynard (foreword by Albert E. Stone); *Okoboji Wetlands: A Lesson in Natural History* by Michael J. Lannoo; *Fourteen Landing Zones: Approaches to Vietnam War Literature* (edited by Philip K Jason); *Beyond Homelessness: Frames of Reference* by Benedict and Jeffrey Giamo.

Iowa fiction and literature: *Shiny Objects* by Dianne Benedict; *Friendly Fire* by Kathryn Chetkovich; *Old Wives' Tales* by Susan M. Dodd; *Igloo Among Palms* by Rod Val Moore; *Traps* by Sondra Spatt Olsen; *The Black Velvet Girl* by C. E. Poverman; *Between the Heartbeats* (poems and prose by nurses; edited by Cortney Davis and Judy Schaefer); *Uncertainty and Plenitude: Five Contemporary Poets* by Peter Stitt.

Literary criticism and the arts are areas in which Iowa has traditionally produced a strong list. Titles: *Metafiction: A Community of Writers* by Paul Engle and the Iowa Writer's Workshop; *Interpreting the Theatrical Past: Essays in the Historiography of Performance* by Thomas and Bruce A. Postlewait; *Bearing the Bad News: Contemporary American Literature and Culture* by Sanford Pinsker; *Self-Consciousness in African American Literature* by Madelyn Jablon; *Notations of the Wild: Ecology in the Poetry of Wallace Stevens* by Gyorgyi Voros; *Textual and Theatrical Shakespeare: Questions of Evidence* (edited by Edward Pechter).

Winners of the Iowa Poetry Prize include *Wake* by Bin Ramke; *The Oval Hour* by Kathleen Peirce; *Try* by Cole Swensen.

University of Iowa Press books are distributed by the University of Chicago Distribution Center.

Query letters and SASEs should be directed to:

Holly Carver, Director and Editor

Prasenjit Gupta, Humanities Editor

UNIVERSITY OF MICHIGAN PRESS

839 Greene Street, PO Box 1104, Ann Arbor, MI 48106-1104
734-764-4388, 734-936-0456
www.press.umich.edu

University of Michigan publishes trade nonfiction and works of scholarly and academic interest. Topic areas and categories include African American studies, anthropology, archaeology, Asian studies, classical studies, literary criticism and theory, economics, education, German studies, history, linguistics, law, literary biography, literature, Michigan and the Great Lakes region, music, physical sciences, philosophy and religion, poetry, political science, psychology, sociology, theater and drama, women's studies, disability studies, and gay and lesbian studies.

University of Michigan Press (founded in 1930) executes a major program to publish an abundant list of textbooks, monographs, academic literature, undergraduate texts, and a wide variety of books for general readers. Subject areas here encompass disciplines within the behavioral sciences, as well as the humanities. University of Michigan Press publishes in hardcover and paperback editions. Ann Arbor Paperbacks is an imprint geared toward the general trade market.

From the Michigan list: *Tony Kushner in Conversation* (edited by Robert Vorlicky); *Approaching the Millennium: Essays on Angels in America* (edited by Deborah R. Geis and Steven F. Kruger); *Health Benefits at Work: An Economic and Political Analysis of Employment-Based Health Insurance* by Mark V. Pauly; *Purchasing Population Health: Paying for Results* by David A. Kindig; *The Body and Physical Difference: Discourses of Disability in the Humanities* (edited by David Mitchell and Sharon Snyder); *Law and the Postmodern Mind: Essays on Psychoanalysis and Jurisprudence* (edited by David Gray Carlson and Peter Goodrich); *The Cat and the Human Imagination: Feline Images from Beast to Garfield* by Katharine M. Rogers; *John Coltrane: His Life and Music* by Lewis Porter.

University of Michigan Press handles distribution through a worldwide network of independent sales representatives.

Query letters and SASEs should be directed to:

Ellen McCarthy, Senior Editor—Economics, anthropology, social issues

Kelly Sippell, English as a Second Language Manager—ESL, applied linguistics, regional studies, sports titles

LeAnn Fields, Executive Editor—Literature, performance studies, gender studies, disability studies

Mary Erwin, Assistant Director—Regional studies

Phil Pochoda, Director

Collin Ganio, Acquisitions Editor—Classics, archaeology, medieval history, Renaissance history, German studies

Jeremy Shine, Acquisitions Editor—Political science and law

Chris Hebert, Acquisitions Editor—Music and distributed titles

University of Minnesota Press

111 Third Avenue South, Suite 290, Minneapolis, MN 55401-2520
612-627-1970
www.upress.umn.edu

The University of Minnesota Press (founded in 1927) is a not-for-profit publisher of academic books for scholars and selected general interest titles. We do not publish original fiction or poetry. Areas of emphasis include American studies, anthropology, art and aesthetics, cultural theory, film and media studies, gay and lesbian studies, geography, literary theory, political and social theory, race and ethnic studies, sociology, and urban studies. The Press also maintains a long-standing commitment to publishing books that focus on Minnesota and the Upper Midwest, including regional nonfiction, history, and natural science.

Recent notable titles: *The Dubious Spectacle; A Queer Mother for the Nation; Being Political; Reading Autobiography; The Unfinished System of Nonknowledge; Bodies in Technology; Christopher and His Kind; My Guru and His Disciple; Cyberculture; American Studies in a Moment of Danger; Time Passages; Deep Mexico, Silent Mexico; On Your Marx; Sex and Money; On the Rim; Views on the Mississippi; The Unmaking of Fascist Aesthetics; Mothering Across Cultures; Civilization and Violence; Change Mummified; An American Family; Scenes from Postmodern Life; The Tilted Arc Controversy.*

University of Minnesota Press orders are filled by the Chicago Distribution Center and in the U.K. and Europe by Plymbridge Distributors, Ltd.

Query letters and SASEs should be directed to:

Richard Morrison, Acquisitions Editor—American studies, cultural theory, gay and lesbian studies, humanities

Carrie Mullen, Executive Editor—Anthropology, art and aesthetics, film and media studies, geography, Native American studies, political and social theory, race and ethnic studies, sociology, urban studies

---

UNIVERSITY OF MISSOURI PRESS

2910 LeMone Boulevard, Columbia, MO 65201
573-882-7641   fax: 573-884-4498
www.system.missouri.edu/press   e-mail: upress@umsystem.edu

The University of Missouri Press accents scholarly books, general-interest trade titles, fiction, and regional works. Specific areas within the UMP publishing range include African American studies, cultural studies, folklore, gender studies, intellectual history, journalism, and photography. University of Missouri Press (founded in 1958) publishes in hardback and trade paper editions.

Highlights of the Missouri line: *Mark Twain: Social Philosopher* by Louis J. Budd; *The Soledades, Gongora's Masque of the Imagination* by Marsha A. Collins; *A Consuming Faith: The Social Gospel and Modern American Culture* by Susan Curtis; *Writing the Pioneer Woman* by Janet Floyd; *Boys Keep Being Born* by Joan Frank; *The Unforeseen Self in the Works of Wendell Berry* by Janet Goodrich; *Above Time: Emerson's and Thoreau's Temporal Revolutions* by James Guthrie; *My Favorite Lies: Stories* by Ruth Hamel; *Deep River: A Memoir of a Missouri Farm* by David Hamilton; *James G. Blaine and Latin America* by David Healy; *Elston and Me: The Story of the First Black Yankee* by Arleen Howard with Ralph Wimbish; *Thomas Merton and the Inclusive Imagination* by Ross Labrie; *Missouri: Then and Now,* New and Enlarged Edition, by Perry McCandless and William E. Foley; *A Gift of Meaning* by Bill Tammeus; *Fiction Rivals Science: The French Novel from Balzac to Proust* by Allen Thiher; *The Magic Kingdom: Walt Disney and the American Way of Life* by Steven Watts.

U

University of Missouri Press handles its own distributional services.
Query letters and SASEs should be directed to:

Beverly Jarrett, Director and Editor in Chief

Clair Willcox, Acquisitions Editor

Jane Lago, Managing Editor

John Brenner, Editor

Sara Davis, Editor

Gary Kass, Editor

Julie Schroeder, Editor

Sharon M. McDaniel, Editorial Assistant

UNIVERSITY OF NEBRASKA PRESS

233 North 8th Street, Lincoln, NE 68588-0255
402-472-3581   fax: 402-472-6214
http://nebraskapress.unl.edu   e-mail: pressmail@unl.edu

The program at University of Nebraska Press encompasses anthropology, environmental studies, history, literature and criticism, Native American studies, philosophy, wildlife and environment, and general reference works. The house further accents the literature and history of the Trans-Missouri West, the American Indian, contemporary and modern literary trends, sports, and the environment (especially emphasizing Western United States and American Indian tie-in topics).

University of Nebraska Press (founded in 1941) publishes general trade titles in hardcover and paperback, as well as selected scholarly nonfiction. Many UNP titles and subject areas overlap categories and are thus provided wider marketing exposure. University of Nebraska Press has successfully established niches in each of its targeted market sectors; a solid showcase of Nebraska titles has garnered book-club sales in both mainstream and specialty venues.

The University of Nebraska literary horizon features leading-edge criticism and theory, works keyed to the American West and the American Indian, and historical as well as current writers worldwide, including European women and French literature in translation; the house offers a strong selection of scholarly writings on the life and works of Willa Cather.

University of Nebraska Press produces the Women in the West series, Western history and literature, American Indian topics, and the great outdoors. Bison Books is Nebraska's imprint for popularly oriented trade titles.

Nebraska's American Indian studies include biography and memoirs, literature and legend, society and culture, and history, as well as a line of titles for young readers. Series listed in this area are American Indian Lives, Sources of American Indian Oral Literature, Studies in the Anthropology of North American Indians, Indians of the Southeast, and

The Iroquoians and Their World. The press offers the North American Indian Prose Award, in conjunction with the Native American Studies Program at the University of California, Berkeley. (Detailed information is available from the publisher upon request.) A recent winner of this award is *Boarding School Seasons* by Brenda Child.

Representative of the Nebraska publishing program: *Thoughts from a Queen-Sized Bed* by Mimi Schwartz; *How Nancy Jackson Married Kate Wilson and Other Tales of Rebellious Girls and Daring Young Women* by Mark Twain (edited by John Cooley); *Standing Up to the Rock* by T. Louise Freeman-Toole.

The Bison Frontiers of Imagination Series features reprints of classic speculative fiction, ranging from Edgar Rice Burroughs's *Land That Time Forgot* to Wylie and Balmer's *When Worlds Collide*.

Query letters and SASEs should be directed to:

Steve Hilliard, Interim Director

Gary Dunham, Editor in Chief

UNIVERSITY OF NEW MEXICO PRESS

1720 Lomas Boulevard, NE, Albuquerque, NM 87131-1591
505-277-2346   fax: 505-277-9270
e-mail: unmpress@unm.edu

University of New Mexico Press (begun in 1929) is a publisher of general, scholarly, and regional trade books in hardcover and paperback editions. Among areas of strong New Mexico interest are archaeology, folkways, literature, art and architecture, photography, crafts, biography, women's studies, travel, and the outdoors. New Mexico offers a robust list of books in subject areas pertinent to the American Southwest, including native Anasazi, Navajo, Hopi, Zuni, and Apache cultures; Nuevomexicano (New Mexican) culture; the pre-Columbian Americas; and Latin American affairs. UNMP also publishes works of regional fiction and belles lettres, both contemporary and classical. The press commands a staunch backlist.

Representative of the University of New Mexico Press list: *"Sin Nombre" Hispana and Hispano Artists of the New Deal Era* by Tey Marianna Nun; *Navajo Trading: The End of an Era* by Willow Roberts Powers; *Salt Dreams: Land and Water in Low-Down California* by William deBuys and Joan Myers; *Coal Camp Days: A Boy's Remembrance* by Ricardo L. Garcia; *Crossing Guadalupe Street: Growing Up Hispanic and Protestant* by David Maldonadao Jr.; *Finding the West: Explorations with Lewis and Clark* by James P. Ronda; *The Great Maya Droughts: Water, Life and Death* by Richardson B. Gill; *Joseno: Another Mayan Voice Speaks from Guatemala* (edited by James D. Sexton); *Leslie Marmon Silko: A Collection of Critical Essays* (edited by Louise K. Barnett and James L. Thorson); *Going Native* by Tom Harmer; *True Tales from Another Mexico* by Sam Quinones; *Tina Modotti: Image, Texture, Photography* by Andrea Noble; *Orozco in Gringoland: The Years in New York* by Alejandro Anreus.

U

New Mexico fiction/poetry titles: *Poetry Lover* by Gary Soto; *Losers and Keepers in Argentina: A Work of Fiction* by Nina Barragan; *Miracles of Sainted Earth* (poems) by Victoria Edwards Tester; *Cavern* by Jake Page.

University of New Mexico Press is home to the literary journal *Blue Mesa Review*. The Pasó por Aquí series makes available texts from the Nuevomexicano literary heritage (many editions in bilingual format). Diálogos is a series in Latin American studies, specializing in books with crossover potential in both academic and general markets.

University of New Mexico Press handles distribution for its own list and also works through regional sales representatives.

Query letters and SASEs should be directed to:

David V. Holtby, Associate Director and Editor—Latin American studies

Evelyn Schlatter, Acquisitions Editor

Luther Wilson, Director

University of North Carolina Press

PO Box 2288, Chapel Hill, NC 27515-2288
919-966-3561   fax: 919-966-3829
www.uncpress.unc.edu   e-mail: uncpress@unc.edu

University of North Carolina Press (founded in 1922) publishes works of general nonfiction, scholarly titles, and regional books, as well as a selection of general-interest trade titles. The house has a broad array of books on a firm backlist.

University of North Carolina Press publishing interest encompasses African American studies, American studies, British history, business history, Civil War, folklore, Latin American studies, literary studies, anthropology, nature, political science, social issues, legal history, sports and sports history, and gender studies.

North Carolina highlights: *Working the Garden* by William Conlogue; *A World of Its Own* by Matt Garcia; *Conflicting Missions* by Piero Gleijeses; *The Mormon Question* by Sarah Barringer Gordon; *Scientists, Business and the State, 1890–1960* by Patrick J. McGrath; *A Blessed Company* by John K. Nelson; *Black Identity and Black Protest in the Antebellum North* by Patrick Rael; *Forged Genealogies* by Carol Rigolot; *Visiones de Estereoscopio* by Maria Soledad Fernandez Utrera.

University of North Carolina Press handles its own distribution with the assistance of regional sales representatives.

Query letters and SASEs should be directed to:

David Perry, Assistant Director and Editor in Chief—History, regional trade, Civil War

Kate Douglas Torrey, Director—Gender studies

Mark Simpson-Vos, Associate Editor and Assistant to the Editor in Chief

Chuck Grench, Assistant Director and Senior Editor—History, classics, economics and business history, law and legal studies, political science

UNIVERSITY OF OKLAHOMA PRESS

1005 Asp Avenue, Norman, OK 73019-6051
405-325-2000

University of Oklahoma Press highlights the fields of Americana, regional topics (especially the American West), anthropology, archaeology, history, military history, political science, literature, classical studies, and women's studies. University of Oklahoma Press series include the Western Frontier Library, the American Indian Literature and Critical Studies series, and the Bruce Alonzo Goff Series in Architecture.

University of Oklahoma Press (founded in 1928) publishes a wide range of scholarly nonfiction, with crossover trade titles primarily in popular history and the arts; the house's prowess is particularly renowned in the arena of the native cultures of North, Central, and South America—the extensive backlist as well as new and current offerings in these fields embrace a wellspring of over 250 titles.

On Oklahoma's nonfiction list: *A Son of the Sun; A Walk Toward Oregon; Along Route 66; American Indians; An Archaeological Guide to Central and Southern Mexico; Between Indian and White Worlds; Biodiversity and Native America; Cavalier in Buckskin; Chahta Anumpa; Choctaw Language and Culture; Circle of Women; Common and Contested Ground; Comparing Cowboys and Frontiers; Esther Ross, Stillaguamish Champion; General Crook and Western Frontier; I Hear the Train; Improving on American Indian Health Care; King of the Wood; Last Hurrah of the James-Younger Gang; Letters from the Dust Bowl; Maya Wars; Mexico's Indigenous Past; Mixedblood Messages; Navajo Lifeways; Silver Horn; The Art of Political Warfare.*

Fiction and literary titles: *Nightland; War Women; El Indio Jesus; Chancers; Cherokee Dragon.*

The University of Oklahoma Press distributes its own books and those of the University Press of Colorado, Vanderbilt University Press, and Geoscience Press, with the assistance of regional sales representatives.

Query letters with SASEs should be directed to:

Jean Hurtado, Acquisitions Editor—Western history, political science

Joann Reece, Acquisitions Editor—Native American studies, Latin America

John N. Drayton, Director—Literature and literary studies, natural history

Daniel Simon, Acquisitions Editor—Paperbacks

U

UNIVERSITY OF SOUTH CAROLINA PRESS

937 Assembly Street, 8th Floor, Carolina Plaza, Columbia, SC 29208
803-777-5243   fax: 800-868-0740

University of South Carolina Press covers Southern studies, military history, contemporary and modern American literature, maritime history, religious studies, and speech and communication. University of South Carolina Press (founded in 1944) publishes a strong academic and scholarly list, with some crossover general trade titles. The press publishes in hardcover, as well as trade paperback, and maintains an extensive backlist.

Indicative of the South Carolina program: *Before Gatsby: The First Twenty-Six Stories by F. Scott Fitzgerald* (edited by Matthew J. Bruccoli, with the assistance of Judith S. Baughman); *Between North and South: The Letters of Emily Wharton Sinkler, 1842–1865* (edited by Anne Sinkler Whaley LeClercq); *Charleston in My Time: The Paintings of West Fraser* by West Fraser; *The Duchess of Malfi's Apricots, and Other Literary Fruits* by Robert Palter; *The Guns of Meeting Street: A Southern Tragedy* by T. Felder Dorn; *John Among the Gospels,* Second Edition, by D. Moody Smith; *A Memoir of the Last Year of the War for Independence in the Confederate States of America* by Jabul A. Early, with a new introduction by Gary W. Gallagher; *A Portion of the People: Three Hundred Years of Southern Jewish Life* (edited with an introduction by Theodore Rosengarten); *Rhett: The Turbulent Life and Times of a Fire-Eater* by William C. Davis; *Stateside Soldier: Life in the Women's Army Corps, 1944–1945* by Aileen Kilgore Henderson.

University of South Carolina Press oversees its own distribution.

Query letters and SASEs should be directed to:

Linda Fogle, Assistant Director—Trade titles

Barry Blose, Acquisitions Editor—Literary studies, rhetoric, religious studies, studies in social work

Alex Moore, Acquisitions Editor—Southern history, regional studies, Civil War studies, maritime history

---

UNIVERSITY OF TENNESSEE PRESS

110 Conference Center Building, Knoxville, TN 37996-4108
865-974-3321   fax: 865-974-3724

The University of Tennessee Press publishes scholarly and general interest books in American studies in the following subdisciplines: African American studies, Appalachian studies, literature, religion (history, sociology, anthropology, biography), folklore, history, architecture, material culture, and historical archaeology. Submissions in other fields, and submissions of poetry, textbooks, and translations, are not invited.

The University of Tennessee Press (founded in 1940) has earned a national reputation for excellence, with titles representing both traditional and cutting-edge scholarship. The press's editorial point of view reflects an awareness of social and quality-of-life issues and results in books that inform thought and policy, as well as contribute to scholarship.

Recent books published by UT Press include *A Separate Circle: Jewish Life in Knoxville, Tennessee* by Wendy Lowe Besmann; *Thinking Confederates: Academia and the Idea of Progress in the New South* by Dan R. Frost; *Rac(e)ing to the Right: Selected Essays of George S. Schuyler* (edited by Jeffrey B. Leak); *Spiritual Merchants: Religion, Magic and Commerce* by Carolyn Long; *Bound to Be a Soldier: The Letters of Private James T. Miller, 111th Pennsylvania Infantry, 1861–1864* (edited by Jedediah Mannis and

Galen R. Wilson); *The African American Aeneas: Classical Origins of the American Self* by John C. Shields; *Ralph Emerson McGill: Voice of Southern Conscience* by Leonard Ray Teel; *Tennessee's New Deal Landscape* by Carroll Van West; *She Left Nothing in Particular: The Autobiographical Legacy of Nineteenth-Century Women's Diaries* by Amy L. Wink.

Books from the University of Tennessee Press are distributed by the Chicago Distribution Center.

Query letters and SASEs should be directed to:

Joyce Harrison, Acquisitions Editor

UNIVERSITY OF TEXAS PRESS

PO Box 7819, Austin, TX 78713-7819
512-471-7233   fax: 512-232-7178
www.utexas.edu/utpress   e-mail: utpress@uts.cc.utexas.edu

Areas of University of Texas Press publishing scope include international and regional studies, gender studies, Latin America, American Southwest, Native America, Texana, Mesoamerica, applied language and Latino literature (including Latin American and Middle Eastern works in translation), the environment and nature, art and architecture, classics, film studies, social sciences, and humanities.

University of Texas Press (founded in 1950) is among the largest of American university presses. UTP publishes in a wide range of general nonfiction fields, offering titles of popular interest and for scholarly and academic readers produced in hardcover and trade paperback.

On the UTP list: *Planning the Family in Egypt; Staying Sober in Mexico City; The Collected Poems and Selected Prose; Imagining Texas; The Purple Martin; Latin Politics, Global Media; The Last Battle of the Civil War; Mixing Rice, Mixing Culture; Driving Visions; Sista, Speak!; The Brave Bulls; Narrative Threads; Being Rapoport; Once Upon a Time in Texas; The Behavior of Texas Birds; The Human Cost of Food; Television Talk; Sugar's Life in the Hood; A Rainbow of Gangs; The Medium of the Video Game.*

University of Texas Press handles its own distribution.

Query letters and SASEs should be directed to:

Jim Burr, Sponsoring Editor—Classics and ancient world, film and media studies, Middle East studies, Old World archaeology, architecture

William Bishel, Sponsoring Editor—Texana, ornithology, botany, marine science, natural history, geography, environmental studies

Theresa May, Editor in Chief—Latin American studies, Chicano/a studies, Native American studies, anthropology, New World archaeology, applied language, art

Allison Faust, Associate Editor: Assistant to Theresa May

Wendy Moore, Assistant Editor: Assistant to William Bishel and Jim Burr

U

University of Washington Press

PO Box 50096, Seattle, WA 98145-5096
206-543-4050   fax: 206-543-3932
www.washington.edu/uwpress/   e-mail: uwpord@u.washington.edu

The program at University of Washington Press is particularly strong in some of the fields of the publisher's major academic concentrations, which encompass fine arts (including a special interest in the arts of Asia), regional America (with an emphasis on Seattle and the Pacific Northwest), and Native American studies. University of Washington Press maintains a solid backlist.

University of Washington Press (established in 1920) is a midsize house with a primarily scholarly list that features select titles geared toward the general-interest trade market. The house produces books in hardcover and paperback (including reprint editions) and distributes adjunct visual resources (including videotapes, films, and filmstrips). University of Washington also handles a line of scholarly imports (primarily fine arts titles). UWP enters into joint-publication projects with a variety of museums and cultural foundations and produces a large number of fine arts books and exhibition catalogs.

On the Washington list: *Afghanistan's Endless War: State Failure and Regional Politics* by Larry P. Goodson; *The Art of Xu Bing: Words Without Meaning, Meaning Without Words* by Britta Erickson; *Color-Line to Borderlands: The Matrix of American Ethnic Studies* (edited by Johnnella E. Butler); *Findings: The Jewelry of Romona Solberg* by Vicki Halper; *Fire: A Brief History* by Stephen Pyne; *For the Century's End: Poems, 1900–1999* by John Haines; *Forest Giants of the Pacific Coast* by Robert Van Pelt; *Gaylen Hansen* by Vici Halper; *Kimono: Fashioning Culture* by Liza Crihfield Dalby; *Landscape Traveled by Coyote and Crane: The World of the Schitsu'umsh* by Rodney Frey; *Mending Fences: The Evolution of Moscow's China Policy from Brezhnev to Yeltsin* by Elizabeth Wishnick; *Saving the Reservation; Joe Garry and the Battle to Be Indian* by John Fahey; *Ways of Being Ethnic in Southwest China* by Stevan Harrell; *Women in Pacific Northwest History,* Revised Edition (edited by Karen J. Blair); *The Woven Coverlets of Norway* by Katherine Larson.

Weyerhaeuser Environmental Books series (under the general editorship of William Cronon) titles: *Landscapes of Promise: The Oregon Story, 1800–1940* by William Robbins; *World Fire: The Culture of Fire on Earth* and *Fire in America: A Cultural History of Wildland and Rural Fire,* both by Stephen J. Pyne.

University of Washington Press handles its own distribution via its home office and a number of regional sales representatives, as well as distributes for a number of other specialist publishers and arts institutions, including the Tate Gallery, Asian Art Museum of San Francisco, Reaktion Books, the Columbus Museum of Art, National Portrait Gallery of the Smithsonian Institution, Exhibitions International, and the Idaho State Historical Society.

Query letters and SASEs should be directed to:

Michael Duckworth, Acquisitions Editor—Asian studies, Middle East studies, Russian and East European studies

U

Naomi Pascal, Associate Director and Editor in Chief—Western studies, Asian American studies, Western history, regional history

UNIVERSITY OF WISCONSIN PRESS

1930 Monroe Street, 3rd Floor, Madison, WI 53711-2059
608-263-1110   fax: 608-263-1120
www.wisc.edu   e-mail: uwiscpress@uwpress.wisc.edu

University of Wisconsin Press catalogs such fields as African studies, autobiography, art, American studies, anthropology and folklore, biography, contemporary issues, classical studies, environmental studies, European studies, gay studies, geography, history, criminology, Latin American studies, law, literature and criticism, medicine, music, poetry, sociology, Wisconsin regional studies, and women's studies. The press hosts a steadfast backlist.

Titles from UWP: *An Aran Keening* by Andrew McNeillie; *The Autobiographical Documentary in America* by Jim Lane; *The Craft of Old-Master Drawings* by James Watrous; *A Deeper Freedom* by Charles W. Anderson; *The Fire Stays in Red* by Ronny Someck; *Glenway Wescott Personally (A Biography)* by Jerry Rosco; *Landscape, Nature, and the Body Politic* by Kenneth Olwig; *Purity in Print* by Paul S. Boyer; *Surviving Madness: A Therapist's Own Story* by Betty Berzon; *Thoughtful Wanderings* by Douglas Hill; *First, Do No Harm: Power, Oppression and Violence in Healthcare* (edited by Nancy L. Diekelmann); *The Wedding in Ancient Athens* by John H. Oakley and Rebecca H. Sinos; *Festivals of Attica* by Erika Simon.

University of Wisconsin Press (founded in 1937) is a midsize house that specializes in nonfiction and scholarly books and journals, with a growing and vigorous list of crossover titles geared to mainstream trade interest.

Distribution for University of Wisconsin Press publications is through the Chicago Distribution Center; trade sales are garnered nationwide by the press's formidable lineup of regional field representatives.

Query letters and SASEs should be directed to:

Raphael Kadushin, Acquisitions Editor—Gay and lesbian studies, autobiography, film studies, classics, environmental studies, history, Holocaust studies, dance, and performance art

Sheila McMahon Moermond, Acquisitions Assistant

VANDERBILT UNIVERSITY PRESS

Box 1813, Station B, Nashville, TN 37235-0001
615-322-3585   fax: 615-343-8823
www.vanderbilt.edu/vupress   e-mail: vupress@vanderbilt.edu

Founded in 1940, Vanderbilt University Press is the publishing arm of one of the nation's leading research universities. The Press publishes intellectually provocative and socially

Y

significant books in the humanities, health care, social sciences, education, and regional studies for both academic and general audiences.

Notable titles include *Singing in the Saddle: A History of the Singing Cowboy* by Douglas B. Green; *Invisible Work* by Efrain Kristal; *Cervantes in Algiers: A Captive's Tale* by Maria Antonia Garces; *Reading Novels* by George Hughes; *The Holocaust and Other Genocides* (edited by Helmut Walser Smith); *The Clinton Wars: The Constitution, Congress and War Powers* by Ryan C. Hendrickson; *To Give Their Gifts: Health, Community, and Democracy* by Richard A. Couto with Stephanie C. Eken; *Fatherhood Arrested: Parenting from Within the Juvenile Justice System* by Anne M. Nurse; *Families at Work: Expanding the Bounds* (edited by Naomi Gerstel, Dan Clawson, and Robert Zussman).

Warehousing and worldwide order fulfillment are provided by the University of Oklahoma Press in Norman, Oklahoma.

Query letters and SASEs should be directed to:

Michael Ames, Director

YALE UNIVERSITY PRESS

302 Temple Street, New Haven, CT 06511
PO Box 209040, New Haven, CT 06520-9040
203-432-0960   fax: 203-432-0948
www.yale.edu/yup/   e-mail: yupmkt@yalevm.cis.yale.edu

The Yale publishing program offers both trade and academically oriented titles in the fields of the arts, the humanities, and the social sciences. Particular general-interest areas include contemporary issues, culture, and events; architecture, art criticism, and art history; history of America (with additional focus on the American West); literature and literary criticism; and political science, economics, and military studies. Yale produces hardcover and trade paper editions.

Yale University Press sponsors the annual Yale Younger Poets Competition and publishes the winning manuscript. Yale series include Composers of the Twentieth Century and Early Chinese Civilization.

Yale University Press (established in 1908) is at the forefront of university publishing. The house is one of the major academic houses, and Yale's commercial presence is evident in the catalogs of book clubs, as well as on national, regional, and specialty bestseller lists.

Notable titles from Yale: *The Archaeology of Athens; You Look Beautiful Like That; The Art of Mu Xin; The Tumultuous Fifties; The Battle for Realism; Candace Wheeler; Great British Paintings from American Collections; Queen Anne (A Biography); Selected Letters of Robert Louis Stevenson (A Biography); Household and City Organization at Olynthus; The Five "Confucian" Classics; Loss of Happiness in Market Economies; Corporate Irresponsibility; Yale French Studies 100; The Elements of Learning; Making Good Citizens; Moral Questions in the Classroom; Forests in a Full World; Heart Attack!; Writing, Speaking, and Communication Skills for Health Professionals; Paper Before Print; Unearthing Gotham; Affairs of Honor; The History of the European Family;*

Y

Divided Jerusalem; Divergent Jewish Cultures; Grammar of Classical Arabic; The Art of Non-Conversation; Christian Perspectives on Legal Thought; Our Unsettled Constitution; First Nights; Gadamer in Conversation; What Is Philosophy?; The Strange Death of American Liberalism; Ethnic Conflict and Civic Life; An Unconventional Family; Spanish Rome; The Coldest March; The Fragile Middle Class; Red Lines, Black Spaces.
    Yale University Press handles its own distribution.
    Query letters and SASEs should be directed to:

Jean E. Thomson Black, Acquisitions Editor—Science and medicine

Jonathan Brent, Editorial Director—Literature, literary studies, theater, Slavic studies

Robert T. Flynn, Acquisitions Editor—Religion, law, and philosophy

Susan C. Arellano, Acquisitions Editor—Psychology, education, child development, psychiatry, sociology, and anthropology

Lara Heimert, Senior Editor—History, intellectual history, women's studies

Alex Schwartz, Senior Editor—Reference

John Kulka, Senior Editor—Literature, philosophy, and political science

Religious, Spiritual, and Inspirational Publishers

The Writer's Journey
Themes of the Spirit and Inspiration

DEBORAH LEVINE HERMAN

If you have decided to pursue writing as a career instead of as a longing or a dream, you might find yourself falling into a pattern of focusing on the goal instead of the process. When you have a great book idea, you may envision yourself on a book-signing tour or as a guest on *Oprah* before you've written a single word.

It's human nature to look into your own future, but too much projection can get in the way of what the writing experience is all about. The process of writing is like a wondrous journey that can help you cross a bridge to the treasures hidden within your own subconscious. Some people believe that it's a way for you to link with the collective or universal consciousness, the storehouse of all wisdom and truth, as it has existed since the beginning of time.

Many methods of writing bring their own rewards. Some people can produce exceptional prose by using their intellect and their mastery of the writing craft. They use research and analytical skills to help them produce works of great importance and merit.

Then there are those who have learned to tap into the wellspring from which all genius flows. They are the inspired ones who write with the intensity of an impassioned lover. They are the spiritual writers who write because they have to. They may not want to, they may not know how to, but something inside them is begging to be let out. It gnaws away at them until they find a way to set it free.

Although they may not realize it, spiritual writers are engaged in a larger spiritual journey toward ultimate self-mastery and unification with God.

Spiritual writers often feel as if they're taking dictation. It is as though their thoughts have a life of their own, and the mind is merely a receiver. Some people refer to this as "channeling" and believe disembodied spirits take over and write through them. Although I sincerely doubt that Gandhi or other notables have authored as many channeled books as people have claimed, truly spiritual writing does have an otherworldly feeling and can often teach writers things they would otherwise not have known.

Writing opens you up to new perspectives, much like self-induced psychotherapy. Although journals are the most direct route for self-evaluation, fiction and nonfiction also serve as vehicles for a writer's growth. Writing helps the mind expand to the limits of the imagination.

Anyone can become a spiritual writer. There are many benefits from doing so, not the least of which is the development of your soul. On a more practical level, it is much less difficult to write with flow and fervor than it is to be bound by the limitations of logic and analysis. If you tap into the universal source, there is no end to your potential creativity.

The greatest barrier to becoming a spiritual writer is the human ego. We treat our words as if they were our children—only we tend to be neurotic parents. Children are not owned by parents, but rather must be loved, guided, and nurtured until they can carry on, on their own.

The same is true for our words. If we try to own and control them like property, they will be limited by our vision for them. We will overprotect them and will not be able to see when we may be taking them in the wrong direction for their ultimate well-being.

Another ego problem that creates a barrier to creativity is our need for constant approval and our tendency toward perfectionism. We may feel the tug toward free expression but will erect blockades to ensure appropriate style and structure. We write with a "schoolmarm" hanging over our shoulders, waiting to tell us what we are doing wrong.

Style and structure are important to ultimate presentation, but that is what editing is for. Ideas and concepts need to flow like water through a running stream.

The best way to become a spiritual writer is to relax and have fun. If you are relaxed and are in a basically good mood, you'll be open to intuition. Writers tend to take themselves too seriously, which causes anxiety, which exacerbates fear, which causes insecurity, which diminishes our self-confidence and leads ultimately to mounds of crumpled papers and lost inspiration.

If you have faith in a Supreme Being, the best way to begin a spiritual writing session is with the following writer's prayer:

> Almighty God (Jesus, Allah, Great Spirit, etc.), Creator of the Universe, help me to become a vehicle for your wisdom so that what I write is of the highest purpose and will serve the greatest good. I humbly place my (pen/keyboard/Dictaphone) in your hands so that you may guide me.

Prayer helps connect you to the universal source. It empties the mind of trash, noise, and potential writer's blocks. If you are not comfortable with formal prayer, a few minutes of meditation will serve the same purpose.

Spiritual writing as a process does not necessarily lead to a sale. The fact is that some people have more commercial potential than others, no matter how seemingly unimportant their message may be. Knowledge of the business of writing will help you make a career of it. If you combine this with the spiritual process, it can also bring you gratification and inner peace.

If you trust the process of writing and allow the journey to take you where it will, it may bring you benefits far beyond your expectations.

ABINGDON PRESS

Dimensions for Living

Kingswood Books

201 Eighth Avenue South, PO Box 801, Nashville, TN 37202-0801
615-749-6290
www.Abingdonpress.com

Abingdon Press is the book-publishing division of the United Methodist Publishing House (founded in 1789). Abingdon produces hardcover, trade paperback, and mass-market paperback editions, covering a wide range of religious specialty, religious trade, and popular markets. Areas of concentration include professional reference and resources for the clergy, academic and scholarly works in the fields of religious and biblical history and theory, inspirational and devotional books, and titles with contemporary spiritual and ethical themes intended for a wider readership. Abingdon's publishing presence includes software and works on CD-ROM.

Abingdon also issues several series of books for children, in addition to resources for Sunday school and general Christian education, as well as church supplies (posters, calendars, certificates, maps, buttons, music, and dramatic scripts). Dimensions for Living is an Abingdon imprint dedicated to titles with a popular orientation (see separate subentry following). Abingdon reprints a number of its bestselling titles in mass-market paperback editions and tends a formidable backlist.

On the Abingdon list: *An Introduction to Christian Theology* by Zaida Meldondo Perez; *And You Welcomed Me* by Amy Oden; *Counseling Families Across the Stages of Life* by George Harold Koenig, Linda Revilla, and Andrew Weaver; *Her Own Story* by Paul Chilcote; *John Wesley on Christian Beliefs* by Kenneth Cain Kinghorn; *Pastor* by William H. Willimon; *Public Reading of Scripture* by Clay Schmit; *New Tools for a New Century* by John Jewell; *Nurturing Faith in Families* by Jolene Rochlkepartain; *A Day of Rest* by Martha W. Hickman; *Abingdon Clergy Income Tax Guide 2002* by Webster, Chamberlin, Bean and Charles Watkins; *Addiction* by Bucky Dann; *African American History Month* by Sheron Patterson; *The Poor and the People Called Methodists* by Richard Heifzenrater; *The Ten Commandments* by John Holbert; *The Web of Preaching* by Richard Eslinger; *The Wesleyan Tradition* by Paul Chilcote.

The Grand Sweep series by Ellsworth Kalas is a bible study program that moves in canonical sequence, based on Ellsworth Kalas's book *365 Days from Genesis Through Revelation*. Titles: *The Grand Sweep: Bible Study for Individuals and Groups; The Grand Sweep: Daily Response Book; The Grand Sweep: Sermon Ideas for 52 Weeks.*

Body & Soul: A Disciplined Approach to a Healthy Lifestyle is a series of programs for Christians seeking a healthful lifestyle. Body & Soul focuses on the spiritual, physical, mental, emotional, and social aspects of persons for a powerful approach to behavior change. Titles: *Health Yourself; Second Helpings; Wonderfully Healthy; Caring & Sharing; Stepping Forward.*

In addition to distributing its own books, Abingdon Press handles the lists of several other smaller religious publishers. Query letters and SASEs should be directed to:

Dr. Rex D. Matthews, Editor, Academic Books—Books for Sunday and parochial schools and seminaries

Jack Keller, Editor, Professional Books and Reference Books—Methodist doctrine and church practices for clergy and laity. Dictionaries and general reference guides relevant to Methodist history and policy

Mary Catherine Dean, Editor, Trade Books—Nonfiction books that help families and individuals live Christian lives; contemporary social themes of Christian relevance

Dimensions for Living

Dimensions for Living is an Abingdon imprint devoted to general-interest religious trade books on practical Christian living. Dimensions for Living publishes in the popular categories of inspiration, devotion, self-help, home, and family, as well as gift volumes. The concept behind the Dimensions for Living imprint—"quality books that celebrate life"—was developed in response to market research. The editorial approach is to combine contemporary themes with mainstream Christian theology.

Titles from Dimensions for Living: *A Day of Rest* by Martha Hickman; *African Prayers* by Robert Van De Weyer; *Blessings for Today* by Susan Skinner; *From Eve to Esther* by Nell Mohney; *From Mary to Lydia* by Nell Mohney; *God Sightings* by Bass M. Mitchell; *God Was Here and I Went Out to Lunch* by James W. Moore; *Lord of the Evening* by Frank Topping; *Personal Prayers for Seniors* by Alan W. Schreiber; *Personal Prayers for Women* by Grace Simpson.

Query letters and SASEs should be directed to:

Sally Sharpe, Editor, Dimensions for Living—Quality books that celebrate life and affirm the Christian faith

Kingswood Books

Kingswood books is an Abingdon imprint that publishes scholarly works in all areas of Methodists and Wesleyan studies. The imprint honors John Wesley's lifelong commitment to the Christian lifestyle. This commitment, which took expression in his extensive writing and publishing, took form in his establishment of the Kingswood School near Bristol, England.

New titles from Kingswood include: *Politics in the Order of Salvation* by Theodore Weber; *Trinity, Community and Power* by Douglas Meeks; *The Episcopacy of American Methodism* by James E. Kirby; *Methodism and the Shaping of American Culture* by John H. Wigger and Nathan O. Hatch.

AMERICAN FEDERATION OF ASTROLOGERS

6535 South Rural Road, PO Box 22040, Tempe, AZ 85285-2040
480-838-1751   fax: 480-838-8293
www.astrologers.com   e-mail: AFA@msn.com

American Federation of Astrologers (founded in 1938) is a specialist publisher of books in astrology for everyone from the beginner to the professional; the house also offers astrological software, charts, and other astrological aids, but does not publish these.

As an organization, American Federation of Astrologers aims to further astrological education and research. AFA is an astrological membership organization, as well as a major publisher and distributor of astrological books and related supplies. AFA books are written by a variety of talented astrologers from all over the globe.

AFA encourages and promotes the science and art of astrology and advocates freedom of thought and speech in the astrological arena; the house offers a monthly membership bulletin, *Today's Astrologer,* and hosts periodic conventions. The organization's publishing program generally produces a short list of new titles each year and supports an extensive publications backlist.

From American Federation of Astrologers: *You in a Modern World* by Doris Chase Doane; *First Survive, Then Thrive: The Journey from Crisis to Transformation* by John F. Eddington and Beth Rosato; *Phases of the Moon* by Marilyn Busteed and Dorothy Wergin; *Freudian Astrology; Lilith; Libido* by Elizabeth Greenwood; *Zodiac Explorer's Handbook* by Helene Hess; *The Living Stars* by Dr. Eric Morse; *Sun Sign Success* by Joseph Polansky; *Cosmopsychology: Engine of Destiny* by Marc Robertson; *The Book of Lovers* by Carolyn Reynolds.

Authors please note: American Federation of Astrologers wishes to consider for publication completed manuscripts only—and does not wish to consider queries, outlines, samples, or proposals. Manuscripts may be submitted along with copies on diskette (other than Macintosh), in text format.

American Federation of Astrologers distributes its own list, as well as publications of other houses.

Send completed manuscripts to:

Kris Brandt Riske, Production Manager

JASON ARONSON INC., PUBLISHERS

230 Livingston Street, Northvale, NJ 07647
201-767-4093
www.aronson.com

Jason Aronson Inc., Publishers (founded in 1965) produces a strong list of works in the field of Jewish interest, covering contemporary currents of Jewish thought, as well as traditional Judaica. The house interest embraces popular, scholarly, and literary works—original titles and reprints. The well-nurtured Aronson backlist includes a lineup of established classics. (For Aronson's program in psychotherapy, please see U.S. Publishers section.)

Representative of the Aronson list: *Holy Brother: Inspiring Stories and Enchanted Tales About Rabbi Shlomo Carlebach* by Yitta Halbertstam Mandelbaum; *Pathways: Jews Who Return* by Richard H. Greenberg; *Piety and Fanaticism: Rabbinic Criticism of Religious Stringency* by Sara Epstein Weinstein; *American Torah Toons: 54 Illustrated Commentaries* by Lawrence Bush; *Ascending Jacob's Ladder: Jewish Views of Angels, Demons,*

A

and Evil Spirits by Ronald H. Isaacs; *The Jokes of Sigmund Freud: A Study in Humor and Jewish Identity* by Elliott Oring; *Einstein's God: Albert Einstein's Quest as a Scientist and as a Jew to Replace a Forsaken God* by Robert N. Goldman; *Restoring the Jews to Their Homeland: Nineteen Centuries in the Quest for Zion* by Joseph Adler; *Easy Kosher Cooking* by Rosalyn F. Manesse; *Forest of the Night: The Fear of God in Early Hasidic Thought* by Niles Elliot Goldstein; *The Faith and Doubt of Holocaust Survivors* by Reeve Robert Brenner; *Waiting for the Messiah: Stories to Inspire Jews with Hope* by Mordechai Staiman; *The Puzzle of the 613 Commandments and Why Bother* by Philip J. Caplan; *Above the Zodiac: Astrology in Jewish Thought* by Matityahu Glazerson; *The Dead Sea Scrolls: Understanding Their Spiritual Message* by Steven Fisdel; *God's Presence in History: Jewish Affirmations and Philosophical Reflections* by Emil L. Fackenheim.

Aronson supervises its own distribution, which, in addition to a network of regional and national trade-fulfillment services, features a direct-mail catalog operation. Aronson also oversees the operations of the Jewish Book Club. As of this printing, Aronson has ceased paying advances or publishing new works.

Arthur Kurzweil, Editor in Chief

AUGSBURG FORTRESS PUBLISHING

Fortress Press

100 South Fifth Street, Suite 700, Minneapolis, MN 55402
612-330-3300, 800-426-0115   fax: 612-330-3455
www.augsburgfortress.org

Mailing address:
PO Box 1209, Minneapolis, MN 55440-1209

Augsburg Fortress publishes titles in popular and professional religious categories. The Augsburg Fortress list accents works of interest to general readers, in addition to books that appeal primarily to a mainstream religious readership and a solid selection of works geared to professional clergy and practitioners of pastoral counseling.

Categories include theology and pastoral care, biblical and historical academic studies, the life and tradition of Martin Luther, self-improvement and recovery, and books for younger readers from nursery and preschoolers through young adult.

The Fortress Press imprint accents issues of contemporary cultural, theological, and political impact. In addition, Augsburg Fortress produces computer software, recordings, artwork, and gift items. Augsburg Fortress also vends a line of liturgical vestments and supplies. The house is widely known for its full range of Bibles, produced in a variety of edition styles.

Augsburg Fortress's ecumenical emphasis enables the house to address a broad range of issues and views within a diversified booklist. Augsburg Fortress Publishing (founded in 1890) is a subsidiary of the Publishing House of the Evangelical Lutheran Church in America.

Representative of the Augsburg list: *Jesus' Lonely Road* by Robert C. Bankhead; *At the Cross with Jesus* by Carl B. Rife; *The First Step Bible* by Mack Thomas; *The Rhyme Bible Storybook* by L. J. Sattgast; *Welcome Aboard* by Tim Wright; *Acts of Faith 2: Dramas for*

God's People by Brad Kindell; *Everyone Who Is Thirsty, Come!* by Jay Beech; *The Gifts of Lent* by Donald H. Neidigk; *Conversations with the Savior* by Donald H. Neidigk; *Gathering at Golgotha* by Katherine Bailey Babb; *Thespian Theology* by John A. TenBrook.

Children's selections include the line of Good News Explorers Sunday School Curriculum series, the Rejoice series, and the Witness series, as well as individual titles. Samples here: *Swamped!* by Nathan Aaseng; *So I Can Read* by Dandi Mackall (illustrated by Deborah A. Kirkeeide); *Ms. Pollywog's Problem-Solving Service* by Ellen Javernick (illustrated by Meredith Johnson).

Authors should note: Augsburg Fortress prefers to receive a proposal rather than a completed manuscript. The house receives over 3,000 submissions per year—a finely honed book proposal may therefore be considered essential.

Augsburg Fortress has a potent distribution network with sales representatives operating via offices nationwide.

Fortress Press

Fortress Press focuses on the ever-changing religious worldview of the contemporary world. The Fortress list is keyed to issues of topical interest, tackled with vision and precision. These works address political and cultural issues and are often on the cusp of current religious debate. The Fortress market orientation tilts toward both the general trade and the religious trade.

Titles from Fortress Press: *God Beyond Gender: Feminist Christian God Language* by Gail Ramshaw; *The Crucifixion of Jesus: History, Myth, Faith* by Gerard S. Sloyan; *The Paradoxical Vision: A Public Theology for the Twenty-First Century* by Robert Benne; *The Spirituality of African Peoples: The Search for a Common Moral Discourse* by Peter J. Paris; *Theology for a Scientific Age: Being and Becoming—Natural, Divine, and Human* by Arthur Peacocke; *Womanism and Afrocentrism in Theology* by Cheryl J. Sanders; *X-odus: An African-American Male Journey* by Garth Kasimu Baker-Fletcher.

Query letters and SASEs should be directed to:

Marshall Johnson, Editorial Director

Robert Klausmeier, Senior Acquisitions Editor

BAKER BOOK HOUSE

Chosen Books

Fleming H. Revell

Spire Books

Twin Brooks Industrial Park, 6030 East Fulton Road, Ada, MI 49301
616-676-9185   fax: 616-676-9573
www.bakerbooks.com

Mailing address:
PO Box 6287, Grand Rapids, MI 49516-6287

B

Baker Book House (founded in 1939) produces works across the spectrum of general religious subject areas (from Protestant and ecumenical perspectives). Baker Book House is a preeminent distributor in the religious-publishing field. Baker Book House distributes its own list (including its diverse imprints).

The publishing division of Baker Book House issues titles of general trade interest, as well as a wide selection of books for ministers, students, schools, libraries, and church workers.

Highlighting the Baker program: *Ruth Bell Graham's Collected Poems* by Ruth Bell Graham; *Messenger of Hope: Becoming Agents of Revival for the Twenty-First Century* by David Bryant; *Willing to Believe: The Controversy Over Free Will* by R. C. Sproul; *Yearning Minds and Burning Hearts: Rediscovering the Spirituality of Jesus* by Glendion Carney and William Long; *A Time to Heal: John Perkins, Community Development, and Racial Reconciliation* by Stephen E. Berk; *Masterpieces of the Bible: Insights into Classical Art of Faith* by Keith White; *Teaching in Tough Times* by Judy Nichols; *Treasured Friends: Finding and Keeping True Friendships* by Ann Hibbard; *Turning Points: Decisive Moments in the History of Christianity* by Mark A. Noll; *Jehovah-Talk: The Mind-Control Language of Jehovah's Witnesses* by David A. Reed.

Query letters and SASEs should be directed to:

Rebecca Cooper, Assistant Editor

Chosen Books
Fleming H. Revell
Spire Books

This Baker wing specializes in spiritually oriented works for the popular religious audience, including a wide range of fiction. Offerings from the Revell program include the Treasury of Helen Steiner Rice line of inspirational titles. The Chosen Books imprint produces evangelical Christian books for personal growth and enrichment. Spire accents an inspirational list of personal stories told through autobiography and memoir.

From Revell: *The New Birth Order Book* by Dr. Kevin Lemani; *The Menopause Manager: Balancing Medical Knowledge and Botanical Wisdom for Optimal Health* by Mary Ann and Joseph L. Mayo; *Happily Ever After: And 21 Other Myths About Family Life* by Karen Scalf Linamen; *Love Busters: Overcoming the Habits That Destroy Romantic Love* by Willard F. Harley, Jr.; *What Kids Need Most Is Mom* by Patricia H. Rushford; *When Your Best Is Never Good Enough: The Secret of Measuring Up* by Kevin Leman; *Women of Grace* by Kathleen Morgan.

Chosen titles include: *Twilight Labyrinth: Why Does Spiritual Darkness Linger Where It Does?* by George K. Otis, Jr.; *The Love Every Woman Needs: Intimacy with Jesus* by Jan McCray; *I Give You Authority* by Charles H. Kraft; *Blessing or Curse* by Derek Prince.

On the Spire roster: *Jonathan, You Left Too Soon* by David B. Biebel; *Getting the Best of Your Anger* by Les Carter; *Making Peace with Your Past* by H. Norman Wright; *Those Turbulent Teen Years* by Jeenie Gordon.

Baker Book House does not accept unsolicited manuscripts. We recommend that you submit your work to First Edition, an online service of the Evangelical Christian Publishers' Association, and The Writer's Edge. We subscribe to both these services and regularly review the proposals posted there. You may contact these organizations at these addresses:

First Edition: www.ecpa.org/FE/ or e-mail: FirstEdition@ECPA.org
The Writer's Edge: www.writersedgeservice.com or
e-mail: info@WritersEdgeService.com
PO Box 1266, Wheaton, IL 60189

B

BETHANY HOUSE PUBLISHERS

11400 Hampshire Avenue South, Bloomington, MN 55438
952-829-2500   fax: 952-829-2572
www.bethanyhouse.com

Bethany House Publishers (founded in 1956) issues hardcover and trade paperback titles in evangelical Christian fiction (with an accent on historicals) and nonfiction, as well as a powerful youth lineup. Areas of Bethany House nonfiction interest include devotional works, relationships and family, and biblical reference.

Bethany's fiction authors include such bestselling names as Janette Oke, Judith Pella, and Gilbert Morris. The program accents titles with American prairie and Western themes, historical romances, and works with contemporary settings; the house also offers boxed series sets. Among Bethany fiction features are the series by the father/daughter writing team Lynn Morris and Gilbert Morris.

The house's trade credo is "God's light shining through good books." Bethany's traditional devotion to bookmaking is evident in its enduring backlist.

Nonfiction from Bethany: *Into the Depths of God* by Calvin Miller; *Becoming a Vessel God Can Use* by Donna Partow; *Telling Yourself the Truth* by William Backus; *How to Save Money Every Day* by Ellie Kay; *Contemplating the Cross* by Tricia McCary Rhodes; *Life Keys: Discovering Who You Are, Why You Are Here, What You Do Best* by Jane A. G. Kise, David Starks, and Sandra Krebs Hirsh; *Becoming Friends with God* by Leith Anderson; *Empty Womb, Aching Heart: Hope for Those Struggling with Infertility* by Mario Schalesky; *Why Revival Tarries* by Leonard Ravenhill; *Deepening Your Conversation with God* by Ben Patterson.

Bethany adult fiction includes *Sanctuary* by Beverly and David Lewis; *The Meeting Place* by Janette Oke and T. Davis Bunn; *Some Wildflowers in My Heart* by Jamie Langston Turner; *Eve's Daughter* by Lynn Austin; *Wild Grows the Heather in Devon* by Michael Phillips; *While Mortals Sleep* by Jack Cavanaugh; *Written on the Wind* by Judith Pella; *City of Angels* by Tracie Peterson and James Scott Bell; *A Dream to Follow* by Lauraine Snelling; *The Swan House* by Elizabeth Musser; *The Rose Legacy* by Kristen Heitzmann.

Nonfiction for children and young adults: *What Children Need to Know When Parents Get Divorced* by William L. Coleman; *Hero Tales: A Family Treasury of True Stories from the Lives of Christian Heroes* by Dave and Neta Jackson; *Girl Talk: 61 Questions from Girls Like You!* by Sandra Byrd; *Pray Hard* (Early Teen Discipleship series) by Kevin Johnson.

Children's and young adult fiction: *The Birthday Present Mystery* (Young Cousins Mysteries) by Elspeth Campbell Murphy; *About Face Space Race* (AstroKids series) by Robert Elmer; *Cross My Heart* (The Hidden Diary series) by Sandra Byrd; *Promise Breaker* (Promise of Zion series) by Robert Elmer.

Bethany House distributes to the trade through Ingram, Baker & Taylor and other wholesalers.

Bethany House Publishers will no longer accept unsolicited manuscripts and book proposals. We will continue to accept queries, proposals, and manuscripts through established literary agents, recognized manuscript services, and writers' conferences attended by BHP editorial staff. We will also accept one-page-only facsimile proposals directed to Adult Nonfiction, Adult Fiction, or YA/children editors. Check our Web site for current numbers.

Query letters and SASEs should be directed to:

Donna Birky, Administrative Editorial Assistant

Sharon Madison, Acquisitions Editor

COOK COMMUNICATIONS

Victor Books

Faith Marriage

Faith Parenting

Faithful Woman

Lion Publishing

Faith Kids Books

Faith Kids Toys & Media

4050 Lee Vance View, Colorado Springs, CO 80918
719-536-3271   fax: 719-536-3296

Cook Communications produces mainstream Christian religious titles in books and other media. Divisions include: Victor Books, Faith Marriage, Faith Parenting, Faithful Woman, Lion Publishing, Faith Kids Books, and Faith Kids Toys & Media.

Cook Communications and its imprints reflect the merger (in July of 1996) of Chariot Family Publishing and Scripture Press Publications/Victor Books, along with the operation's relocation from Illinois to Colorado.

The house mission is to assist in the spiritual development of people by producing and distributing consumer-driven, centrist Christian products that foster discipleship, increase understanding of the bible, and promote the application of Christian values in everyday life.

Cook Communications products are prayerfully crafted to fit its prime audience. They are inspirational, fun, and creative and provide sound Christian education. They are easy and simple for parents, teachers, and others to use effectively. The nature of the house product and its marketing will encourage linking church and home.

Cook Communications markets lines that target broad sectors of the market: youth (primarily from the Faith Kids Brand), adult (Victor Books, Faith Marriage, Faith Parenting, and Faithful Woman), and general religious trade (Lion Publishing).

Cook Communications distribution utilizes a network of field representatives and services that includes its own in-house catalog and marketing operations.

Faith Kids Books & Toys

Faith Kids produces a strong list of titles with a religious orientation in the publishing areas of juvenile fiction, inspirational and devotional, reference (most of them are works for young readers), as well as works for a general religious readership. Chariot markets a line of illustrated bibles and illustrated inspirational and devotional readings.

As the editors of Faith Kids Books note: "We have been called by Christ to foster the spiritual development of children. That is why first, through Faith Kids Books & Toys, we focus on training children in and through the family. We exist to help parents evangelize and discipline their children as a part of everyday life as commanded in Deuteronomy 6:5–9. We will facilitate family discipleship by providing an organized Christian growth program of market-sensitive, exemplary products."

Faith Kids Books offers a wide range of reading materials for ages birth to teen. Faith Kids Toys offers gift and educational items that are inspirational and fun—toys, games, and gift products for ages birth to teen. Each book/product contains a Faith Building or Faith Parenting Guide that is designed to help children understand God's word through sight, sound, and touch/action.

Lion Publishing

Lion Publishing produces works for the religious trade and serious general trade markets.

Through the Lion imprint, the publisher strives to reach the spiritually inquisitive or "seeker" directly or through outreach gift giving. Such books do not presuppose any prior Christian or biblical understanding. Instead, seeker adult and children's books facilitate the spiritual development process, primarily at preevangelism and evangelism levels.

Query letters and SASEs should be directed to:

Lion Publishing
Peter's Way
Sandy Lane West
Oxford, OX4 5HG, England

Victor Books

Victor Books (founded in 1934) offers a wide range of books keyed to spiritual, religious, philosophical, and social topics for the adult, as well as educational materials and supplies.

Categories of publishing interest include family spiritual growth, women's spiritual growth, books of the bible, bible characters, group builder resources, and general topics.

The Victor Books imprint marks the trade-directed portion of the program. Victor is the imprint that marks games and gifts for adults.

The Victor product line meets various personal needs of the market. Victor reaches evangelicals with the purpose of aiding the intended audience in its spiritual formation. Victor adult fame and media adult products facilitate fun learning of bible truths through adult group and family interaction with such items as games, puzzles, and activities.

More than just entertaining, Cook Communications hopes to inspire you to fulfill the great commandment: to love God with all your heart, soul, mind, and strength and your neighbor as yourself. Toward that end, many of our books contain a personal note from the author.

Query letters and SASEs should be directed to:

Karen Athen, Secretary Department Head, Product

Faith Marriage

Faith Marriage seeks to help married men and women grow together in their relationship with Jesus Christ by providing materials specifically aimed at deepening couples' spiritual lives. Faith Marriage seeks to build up Christian marriage so that the partners will be equipped to meet the many challenges of modern married life.

Faith Parenting

Faith Parenting is designed to help parents with the biblical mandate of passing on their Christian faith to their children. Central to this effort are books that encourage family devotions, such as the *Family Night Tool Chest Line.*

Faithful Woman

Faithful Woman speaks to women through their specific spiritual needs as women. As ministries by and for women have become more and more prevalent, Cook Communications saw the need for a line of books that would address the special needs that women experience in their Christian walk. Faithful Woman aims to assist women in fulfilling their unique calling as members of the body of Christ.

COUNCIL OAK BOOKS

1290 Chestnut Street, Suite 2, San Francisco, CA 94109
fax: 415-931-5353
www.counciloakbooks.com   e-mail: kevincob@pacbell.net

Council Oak Books, founded in 1984, is a publisher of distinguished nonfiction books based in personal, intimate history (letters, diaries, memoir); Native American history and spiritual teachings; African American history and contemporary experience; small illustrated inspirational gift books; and unique vintage photo books and Americana. We're looking for those unique, eloquent voices whose history, teachings, and experiences illuminate our lives. No fiction, poetry, or children's books. Check our Web site at: www .counciloakbooks.com.

Titles from Council Oak: *Strongman* (edited by Robert Mainardi); *Of Unknown Origin* by Debra Levi Holtz; *Vow* by Kay Leigh Hagan; *No Word for Time: The Way of the Algonquin People* by Evan T. Pritchard; *Beyond Fear: A Toltec Guide to Freedom and Joy, The Teachings of Don Miguel Ruiz,* as recorded by Mary Carroll Nelson; *Secrets from an Inventor's Notebook* by Maurice Kanbar; *When the Night Bird Sings* by Joyce Sequichie Hifler; *A Cherokee Feast of Days* by Joyce Sequichie Hifler; *Fools Crow: Wisdom and Power* by Thomas E. Mails; *The Hoop and the Tree* by Chris Hoffman; *Bloodland: A True Story of Oil, Greed, and Murder on the Osage Reservation* by Dennis McAuliffe.

Send a brief query letter describing your book, with SASE, or a full proposal including table of contents or chapter outline, sample chapter, and author bio, with either sufficient postage for return or a notation that the material may be recycled if declined. Unsolicited manuscripts cannot be returned. Query or proposal should be directed to:

Kevin Bentley, Editor in Chief

THE CROSSING PRESS

1201 Shaffer Road, Suite B, Santa Cruz, CA 95060
831-420-1110   fax: 831-420-1114
www.crossingpress.com   e-mail: crossing@crossingpress.com

The Crossing Press publishes a wide range of hardcover and trade paperback editions and is dedicated to publishing books, videos, and audios on natural healing, spirituality, alternative healing practices, pet care, general nonfiction, and cookbooks. Our subjects include astrology, aromatherapy, body image, meditation, shamanism, and women's issues, to name a few. It is our hope that the power of information is a catalyst for change and development, not only for the self but for the global community as well.

The Crossing Press was established in upstate New York in 1972 as a modest, indeed a veritable cottage press, run from the farmhouse of the founders, Elaine Goldman Gill and John Gill, who were teaching at Cornell University at this time. Relocated to the central California coastal region in the 1980s, the Crossing Press retains its personalized editorial touch and small press savvy.

Titles from the Crossing Press include *A Magical Guide to Love & Sex: How to Use Rituals, Spells, and Nature's Energies to Bring Love into Your Life* by Cassandra Eason; *Explorations in Consciousness* by Atala Dorothy Toy; *Understanding and Overcoming Depression* by Tony Bates; *Inner Radiance, Outer Beauty* by Ambika Wauters; *Stein's Guide to Goddess Craft* by Diane Stein; *Healing Spirits* by J. Joslow Rodewald and P. West Barker.

The Crossing Press distributes through Publisher's Group West. The Crossing Press accepts unsolicited manuscripts. Query letters, proposals, and manuscripts (SASEs included) should be directed to:

Caryle Hirshberg, Managing Editor

Elaine Gill, Acquisitions Editor

CROSSROAD PUBLISHING COMPANY
Crossroad Herder

481 Eighth Avenue, Suite 1550, New York, NY 10001
fax: 212-868-2171
www.crossroadpublishing.com

Crossroad Publishing Company (founded in 1980) publishes scholarly and general-interest titles in religion, philosophy, spirituality, and personal improvement. Crossroad offers books in spirituality, religion, and counseling for general and popular religious markets. The Crossroad Herder imprint publishes books in theology, religious studies, and religious education for professionals and active members of Catholic and mainline Protestant churches.

Crossroad and sibling imprint Crossroad Herder (formerly Herder & Herder) is a United States–based wing of the international firm Verlag Herder (founded in 1798). The programs of Crossroad and Crossroad Herder offer books by some of the most distinguished authors in the United States and abroad in the fields of theology, biblical studies, spirituality, religious education, women's studies, world religions, psychology, and counseling. Crossroad supports a strong backlist.

Crossroad and Continuum, now two completely separate entities sharing the same address, were corporate affiliates within the Crossroad/Continuum Publishing Group from 1980 through the early 1990s. Even through the dual-house years, each publisher retained its distinct identity. (For Continuum, please see the entry in the U.S. Publishers section.)

Crossroad is an entrepreneurial house of modest size, with a tightly focused program that takes advantage of diverse marketing channels; as such, this publisher provides an excellent environment for authors looking for personalized and long-term publishing relationships.

Titles from Crossroad: *Beyond the Mirror: Reflections of Life and Death* by Henri J. Nouwen; *Finding My Way Home: Pathways to Life and the Spirit* by Henri J. Nouwen; *Beyond the Empire* by Desmond O'Grady; *The Christian Family Toolbox* by David Robinson; *Intimacy with God* by Thomas Keating; *Eyes on the Cross: A Guide for Contemplation* by Michael Kennedy; *On the Body: A Contemporary Theology of Sexuality* by Maria Carlo Martini; *The Doctors of the Church* by Bernard McGinn; *All Saints: Daily Reflections on Saints, Prophets and Witnesses for Our Time* by Robert Ellsberg; *Post Traumatic Stress Disorder: The Victim's Guide to Healing and Recovery* by Raymond B. Flannery, Jr.; *Spiritual Passages: The Psychology of Spiritual Development "For Those Who Seek"* by Benedict Groeschel, Jr.; *Educating for Life: A Spiritual Vision for Every Teacher and Parent* by Thomas Groome; *Consider Jesus: Waves of Renewal in Contemporary Christology* by Elizabeth Johnson; *Heaven in Stone and Glass: Experiencing the Spirituality of Great Cathedrals* by Robert Barron; *Rhythms and Cycles: Sacred Patterns in Everyday Life* by Nancy Bruning; *The Rule of St. Benedict* by Joan Chittister; *The Splendor of Faith: The Theological Vision of Pope John Paul II* by Avery J. Dulles; *Mary: Art, Culture and Religion Through the Ages* by Caroline H. Ebertshauser; *Violence Unveiled: Humanity at the Crossroads* by Gil Bailie; *And Now I See . . .* by Robert Barron; *Beauty for Ashes: Spiritual Reflections on the Attack on America* by John Farina.

An ongoing Crossroad line is the Adult Christian Education Program, which issues series titles in scripture study, theology and church history, Christian living, and world religious traditions.

Crossroad has sponsored the Crossword Women's Studies Award and the Crossroad Counseling Book Award, both of which bestow publication under the house imprimatur. (Details are available upon request from the publisher.) Crossroad distributes via Spring Arbor Distributing.

Query letters and SASEs should be directed to:

Alison Donohue, Editor

Paul McMahon, Editor

C

Crossroad Herder

Books published under the Crossroad Herder imprint mark the cutting edge of theology. Each volume presents fresh perspectives on a topic of interest, expands discussion on an issue of concern, and is accessible to the theologian and interested readers alike.

Titles from Crossroad Herder: *The Mystical Thought of Meister Eckhart* by Bernard McGinn; *Christian Hope and Christian Life* by Rowan A. Greer; *Paul in Chains* by Richard J. Cassidy; *She Who Is, Tenth Anniversary Edition* by Elizabeth A. Johnson; *The Dictionary of Popes and the Papacy* (edited by by Steimer and Parker); *The Ethical Thought of Hans Urs von Balthasar* by Christopher W. Steck; *Catholics and American Culture* by Mark Massa, S.J.

Query letters and SASEs should be directed to:

Michael Parker, Editor

CROSSWAY BOOKS (A DIVISION OF GOOD NEWS PUBLISHERS)
1300 Crescent Street, Wheaton, IL 60187-5883
630-682-4300   fax: 630-682-4785

Crossway produces a small list of books with an evangelical Christian perspective aimed at both the religious and general audience, including issue-oriented nonfiction, evangelical works, inspiration, and fiction. Crossway Books (founded in 1938) is a division of Good News Publishers.

From the Crossway nonfiction list: *Seeing and Savoring Jesus Christ* by John Piper; *God's Lesser Glory* by Bruce A. Ware; *Holiness by Grace* by Bryan Chapell; *Soul Satisfaction* by Debra Evans; *The Organized Home Schooler* by Vicki Caruana.

Representative Crossway fiction: *The Chairman* by Harry Kraus; *Fools' Gold* by Stephen Bly; *The Hawk and the Dove* by Penelope Wilcock.

Sample children's books: Lewis and Clark Squad series by Stephen Bly; *You Are Mine* by Max Lucado.

Crossway Books is interested in nonfiction areas of books on the deeper Christian life, issue-oriented books, and a select number of academic and professional volumes. It feels called to publish fiction works that fall into these categories: historical, youth/juvenile, adventure, action, intrigue, thriller, and contemporary and Christian realism.

Crossway handles its own distribution. Crossway Books invites query letters regarding works written from an evangelical Christian perspective. Please send a synopsis (one to two pages, double-spaced) and no more than two chapters. No entire manuscripts; such submissions will be returned. Query letters and SASEs should be directed to:

Marvin Padgett, Vice President, Editorial

DISCIPLESHIP RESOURCES

Delivery address:
1908 Grand Avenue, Nashville TN 37212

Mailing address:
PO Box 340003, Nashville, TN 37203
800-814-7833
www.discipleshipresources.org   e-mail: discipleshipresources@gbod.org

Discipleship Resources (founded in 1951) is the publishing component of the General Board of Discipleship, of the major program boards of the United Methodist Church. Areas of publishing interest encompass United Methodist history, doctrine, and theology, as well as bible study, Christian education, ethnic church concerns, evangelism, ministry of the laity, stewardship, United Methodist men, and worship.

Discipleship Resources issues a varied inventory, including books, booklets, manuals, audiovisuals, packets, and supplies directed to local church members and leaders, lay and clergy, men and women, children, youth, and adults—as well as to district and conference leaders and others serving the congregation. Some resources guide the leader of an area of work or particular program, while others are aimed toward individual study and enrichment.

Titles from Discipleship Resources: *Finding Christ, Finding Life*: *How to Live as a Christian in a Non-Christian World* by Von W. Unrub; *Hand in Hand: Growing Spiritually with Our Children* by Sue Downing; *Emmanuel! Celebrating God's Presence with Us* by Timothy L. Bias; *Come on the Feast: Inspirational Evangelism* by Roberto Escamilla; *Graceship* by Hoyt L. Hickman; *Couples Who Care* by Jane P. Ives; *Growing in Faith: United in Love* by Barb Nardi Kurtz; *Living Our Beliefs: The United Methodist Way* by Bishop Ken White; *The Faith-Sharing Congregation* by Roger K. Swanson and Shirley F. Clement.

Discipleship handles its own distribution. Writers who wish to submit materials to Discipleship Resources for publishing consideration may acquire editorial guidelines upon request from the publisher. The guide includes versatile tips that are broadly applicable to manuscript preparation in general. Query letters and SASEs should be directed to:

Mary Gregory, Business and Operations Director

WILLIAM B. EERDMANS PUBLISHING COMPANY

Eerdmans Books for Young Readers

255 Jefferson Avenue SE, Grand Rapids, MI 49503
616-459-4591
www.eerdmans.com

Eerdmans publishes books of general interest; religious, academic, and theological works; books for young readers; regional history; and American religious history. The Eerdmans publishing reach offers a Christian handle on such areas as anthropology, biblical studies, and in religious approaches to biography, African American studies, church administration, music, philosophy, psychology, science, social issues, current and historical theology, and women's interests.

The Eerdmans catalog also highlights general reference works, such as bible commentaries and theological dictionaries, as well as titles in Old and New Testament studies.

William B. Eerdmans Publishing Company (founded in 1911) is one of the largest independent nondenominational Christian religious publishers in the United States.

On the Eerdmans list: *The Confessions of St. Augustine* (edited by Carolinne White); *Women in Scripture* (edited by Carol Meyers); *Building a Healthy Culture* (edited by Don Eberly); *Religions of the Hellenistic-Roman Age* by Antonia Tripolitis; *Eerdmans Dictionary of the Bible* (edited by David Noel Freedman); *The Book of Marriage* (edited by Dana Mack and David Blankenhorn); *What Did the Biblical Writers Know and When Did They Know It?* by William Dever; *David's Secret Demons* by Baruch Halpern; *A Dream of the Tattered Man* by Randolph Loney.

A special Eerdmans project is the beautifully produced *The Leningrad Codex: A Facsimile Edition* (Astrid B. Beck, Managing Editor; David Noel Freedman, General Editor; James A. Sanders, Publication Editor).

Query letters and SASEs should be directed to:

Charles van Hof, Managing Editor

Jon Pott, Editor in Chief

Eerdmans Books for Young Readers

Eerdmans Books for Young Readers, an imprint of William B. Eerdmans Publishing Company founded in 1995, seeks to publish beautifully written and illustrated books that nurture children's faith in God and help young people to explore and understand the wonder, joy, and challenges of life. The house considers manuscripts that address spiritual themes in authentic and imaginative ways without being didactic.

Some recent titles include picture books *The Song of the Whooping Crane* by Eileen Spinelli (illustrated by Elsa Warnick); *What Does the Sky Say* by Nancy White Carlstrom (illustrated by Tim Ladwig); and *Jesus,* written and illustrated by Brian Wildsmith. Two recently published young adult novels include *Secrets in the House of Delgado* by Gloria Miklowitz and *Maggie in the Morning* by Elizabeth Van Steenwyk.

Eerdmans Books for Young Readers publishes between 12 and 16 books a year, with about 5 to 10 percent from first-time authors. The subcategories of books include picture books, novels, biographies, and bible stories.

Query letters and SASEs should be directed to:

Judy Zylstra, Editor-in-Chief

FELDHEIM PUBLISHERS

200 Airport Executive Park, Nanuet, NY 10954
845-356-2282   fax: 845-425-1908
www.feldheim.com

Feldheim Publishers (founded in 1954) is among the leading houses in areas of publishing activity that include works of contemporary authors in the field of Orthodox Jewish thought, translations from Hebrew of Jewish classical works, dictionaries and general reference works, textbooks, and guides for Sabbaths and festivals, as well as literature for readers ages three and up (Young Readers Division). The Feldheim publishing program is expanding, and the house releases an increasing number of new titles each season. Feldheim retains a comprehensive backlist.

From Feldheim: *Malka's Kosher Cookbook* by Malka Padwa-Engel; *In the Beginning* by Rosie Einhorn and Sherry Zimmerman; *Of Times Past* by Arlene Chavel and Sara Farkas; *No Different Than You* by Yehudis Bogartz; *Heartbeats; Salt, Pepper and Eternity* by Shaindel Weinbach; *Queen of Bais Yaakov* by Miriam Zakon; *The Lost Treasure of Tikun Hamiddos Island* by Baruch Chait.

Feldheim Publishers handles its own distribution, as well as offers books of additional publishers such as American Yisroel Chai Press and Targum Press. Query letters and SASEs should be directed to:

Yitzchak Feldheim, President

FRIENDSHIP PRESS

475 Riverside Drive, Room 860, New York, NY 10115-0050
212-870-2496   fax: 212-870-2550
www.osiem.org/ospre.enhanced/friendshippress.htm

The Friendship list encompasses religious books, as well as mainstream trade titles in the public-interest realm that address contemporary topics, including cultural pluralism, the media, global awareness, health and wholeness, technology and the environment, human rights, and world peace. Friendship also produces ecumenical religious, spiritual, inspirational, and educational program materials intended for the use of adults, youths, and children. The house offers several lines of videos, maps, notecards, and informational posters.

Friendship Press was established in 1902 as a missionary education movement in the United States and Canada. Now part of the National Council of the Churches of Christ

USA, Friendship Press is a leading ecumenical publisher of educational materials for schools and parishes.

Noted Friendship authors include Margaret Mead, Pearl Buck, Joseph Diescho, Wole Soyinka, Rogoberta Menchu, John R. Mott, Phillip Potter, Leslie Newbigin, Masao Takenaka, and Emilio Castro. Friendship Press books have been reviewed by the *New York Times* and *Publishers Weekly* and are recommended in colleges, universities, and seminars.

Friendship Press distributes its own list. Friendship Press publishes a limited number of new titles per season—most of which are commissioned additions to the house's ongoing curriculum series. Friendship is, however, open to considering manuscripts by authors written from an embracing global cultural perspective. Query letters and SASEs should be directed to:

Mary Byrne Hoffman, Editor

GLENEIDA PUBLISHING GROUP

See Baker Book House and Liguori Publications.

GOSPEL LIGHT PUBLICATIONS

Regal Books

Renew Books

2300 Knoll Drive, Ventura, CA 93003
805-644-9721, 800-235-3415

G

Founded in 1933 by Dr. Henrietta Mears, Gospel Light is committed to providing effective resources for evangelism, discipleship, and Christian education through Sunday school and Vacation Bible school curricula, videos, children's music, and Regal and Renew Books. Divisions of Gospel Light include Regal Books (founded in 1965) specializes in needs-oriented books and building efforts; Renew Books (founded in 1997) serves the fastest-growing segment of the church worldwide—those experiencing awakening and renewal with an expectancy for revival.

The mission of Gospel Light is to know Christ and make Him known; to provide His Church with effective bible teaching and learning resources for use in making disciples, empowering them for godly living, and equipping them for ministry and the evangelism of the world. Gospel Light is headquartered in Ventura, California, with distribution facilities in Cincinnati, Ohio.

Regal titles: *What the Bible Is All About* by Henrietta Mears; *Communication: Key to Your Marriage* by H. Norman Wright; *Always Daddy's Girl* by H. Norman Wright; *Victory Over the Darkness* by Neil Anderson; *Moments Together for Couples* by Dennis and Barbara Rainey; *Churchquake!* by Peter Wagner; *Prayer Shield* by Peter Wagner; *Intercessory Prayer* by Dutch Sheets; *God's Dream Team* by Tommy Tenney; *God's Secret to Greatness* by Tommy Tenney and David Cape; *Boiling Point* by George Barna; *The Habits of Highly*

Effective Churches by George Barna; *The Measure of a Man* by Gene Getz; *Fasting for Spiritual Breakthrough* by Elmer Towns; *The Five Star Church* by Stan Toler and Alan Nelson; *So, What's the Difference?* by Fritz Ridenour; *The Voice of God* by Cindy Jacobs; *Doing Church as a Team* by Wayne Cordeior; *Pure Desire* by Ted Roberts; *Beauty Restored* by Me Ra Koh; *I'll Hold You in Heaven* by Jack Hayford.

Renew titles: *Beyond the Veil* by Alice Smith; *Informed Intercession* by George Otis; *Becoming a Prayer Warrior* by Elizabeth Alves; *The River of God* by Dutch Sheets; *Moving the Apostolic* by John Eckhardt; *Prophetic Intercession* by Barbara Wentroble; *The Fire of His Holiness* by Sergio Scataglini; *Into the Fire* by Che Ahn; *The Last Great Anointing* by Moris Cerullo; *Developing Your Prophetic Gifting* by Graham Cooke; *How to Cast Out Demons* by Doris Wagner; *Fire on the Horizon* by Winkie Pratney; *Future Worship* by LaMar Boschman; *Experiencing the Spirit* by Robert Heidler; *End Time Warriors* by John Kelly; *Prayer Takes Wings* by Thetus Tenney; *The Future War of the Church* by Chuck Pierce and Rebecca Wagner; *Revolution!* by R. T. Kendall; *Step into the Water* by Peg Rankin; *Experience the Blessing* by John Arnott; *Shaking the Heavens* by Ana Mendez; *A Lifestyle of Worship* by David Morris.

On the Regal list of children's and youth books: *Stomping Out the Darkness* by Neil Anderson and Dave Park; *Stomping Out Depression* by Neil Anderson and Dave Park; *Surviving Adolescence* by Jim Burns; *What Hollywood Won't Tell You About Love, Sex and Dating* by Susie Shellenburger and Greg Johnson; *Getting Ready for the Guy/Girl Thing* by Susie Shellenburger and Greg Johnson; *O. Whillikers in the Hall of Champions* by Jay Carty.

Gospel Light overseas its own distribution. Unsolicited manuscripts are not accepted. Query letters and SASEs should be directed to:

Kyle Duncan, Acquisitions

H

HARPERSANFRANCISCO

353 Sacramento Street, Suite 500, San Francisco, CA 94111-3653
415-477-4400   fax: 415-477-4444
www.harpercollins.com/sanfran   e-mail: hcsanfrancisco@harpercollins.com

HarperSanFrancisco strives to be the preeminent publisher of the most important books across the full spectrum of religion and spiritual literature, adding to the wealth of the world's wisdom by respecting all traditions and favoring none. It publishes books in the areas of spirituality, religion, and inspiration from the full family of religious and spiritual traditions.

HSF focuses on books that inspire and nurture the mind, body, and spirit; explore the essential religious, spiritual, and philosophical questions; present the rich and diverse array of cultures and their wisdom traditions; and support readers in their ongoing personal discovery and enrichment.

It is the policy of HarperSanFrancisco to publish books that represent important religious groupings, express well-articulated thought, combine intellectual competence and felicitous style, add to the wealth of religious literature irrespective of creedal origin, and aid the cause of religion without proselytizing for any particular sect.

HSF has featured works by Martin Luther King, Jr., Huston Smith, Billy Graham, Mother Teresa, Marcus Borg, John Shelby Spong, the Dalai Lama, C. S. Lewis, Richard Foster, Philip Gulley, John Dominic Crossan, Diana Eck, and Melodie Beattie. The house is corporately affiliated with the editorially independent Zondervan, subsidiary of Harper-Collins (see separate Zondervan listing), which focuses on books for the evangelical Christian market.

HarperSanFrancisco is a division of the international HarperCollins corporate family of publisher HarperCollins Adult Trade Division (which includes imprints emanating from the HarperCollins New York offices; see HarperCollins in the U.S. Publishers section). HarperSanFrancisco benefits directly from core HarperCollins marketing, sales, and power and retains its editorial and marketing independence and identity.

Frontlist trade books from HarperSanFrancisco: *The Invitation* and *The Dance* by Oriah Mountain Dreamer; *Celebration of Discipline* by Richard Foster; *The Measure of a Man* by Sidney Poitier; *The Legacy of Luna* by Julia Butterfly Hill; *A New Christianity for a New World* and *Why Christianity Must Change or Die* by John Shelby Spong; *The Alchemist* by Paulo Coelho; *The Historical Jesus* and other Jesus books by John Dominic Crossan; *Why Religion Matters* and *The World's Religions* by Huston Smith; *The Soul of Rumi* and *The Essential Rumi,* translated by Coleman Barks; *Mere Christianity* and other classics by C. S. Lewis; *Catholicism* by Richard McBrien; *Everyday Zen* by Jako Beck; *The Tibetan Book of Living and Dying* by Sogyal Rinpoche; *The Jew in the Lotus* by Roger Kamenetz; *The Gospel of Thomas,* translated by Marvin Meyer; *The Divine Conspiracy* by Dallas Willard.

HarperSanFrancisco titles are distributed by HarperCollins Publishers in Scranton, Pennsylvania. HSF does not accept unsolicited manuscripts. Query letters and SASEs should be directed to:

Elizabeth Perle, Editor at Large—Psychology/self-help; women and family, biography, alternative and complementary health; Buddhist and Jewish spirituality; lesbian and gay studies; multicultural studies

Gideon Weil, Editor—Literary spiritual fiction and nonfiction, self-help, inspiration

John V. Loudon, Executive Editor—Religious studies, biblical studies, psychology/personal growth, inspiration, Eastern religions, Buddhist and Christian spirituality

Renee Sedliar, Associate Editor—Literary inspirational fiction and nonfiction, popular inspiration

H

HARVEST HOUSE PUBLISHERS

Harvest House Books for Children and Young Adults

990 Owen Loop North, Eugene, OR 97402
541-343-0123   fax: 541-302-0731

Harvest House produces religious-oriented nonfiction and fiction, bible study and theological thought, and educational and devotional resources. Harvest House frontlist titles address topics of current interest, often with widespread implications on the social-religious front. Subjects include media, technology, politics; parenting, youth, relationships, and the family; Christian living and contemporary values; cults and the occult; personal awareness, inspiration, and spiritual growth; Christian history and heritage; and humor.

The publisher's nondenominational list features many works that offer an evangelical Christian perspective and includes a number of notably individualist author voices. Harvest House publishes books in hardcover, trade paperback, and mass-market paperback editions.

The house issues a number of strong lines directed toward the children's-and-youth market (please see separate subentry following). Harvest House also produces books in the Spanish language, as well as audiobooks, calendars, and daily planners.

Harvest House Publishers (founded in 1974) holds the following credo for books and other product lines: "Helping people grow spiritually strong."

Nonfiction titles: *A Sanctuary for Your Soul* by Kay Arthur; *Heaven Sent* by Kathryn Andrews Fincher; *A Garden Full of Love* by Sandra Kuck; *Friends of the Heart* by Emilie Barnes and Donna Otto; *Whispers of Prayer* by Emilie Barnes; *How Big Is God's Love* by David and Helen Haidle; *Moms Who Have Changed the World* by Lindsey O'Connor; *Just Enough Light for the Step I'm On* by Stormie Omartian; *Unquenchable Love* by David and Heather Kopp; *Hidden Agendas for the New Millennium* by Dave Hunt; *Foreshadows of Wrath and Redemption* by William T. James; *Bruce and Stan's Guide to the End of the World* by Bruce Bickel and Stan Jantz; *What Every Catholic Should Ask* by Jim McCarthy; *A Friend Like You* by D. Morgan; *Hats Off to You* by Sandy Lynam Clough; *Stepping Out* by Pam Farrel; *A Romantic Treasury of Love* by Gay Talbott Boassy; *Celebrating Our Family* by Ruthann Winans and Linda Lee; *God Is Your Hope: His Love Never Fails* by Marie Shropshire; *Decorating Dreams on a Budget* by Yoli Brogger.

Special Harvest House project: *Simpler Times* by Thomas Kinkade, an artist renowned for light-infused paintings of nostalgic, heartwarming scenes, who combines his visual talents with thoughtful narrative in this exquisitely designed gift book. More than 20 full-color paintings are accompanied by Thomas Kinkade's thoughts on living in a complex age, keeping perspective, and creating balance. Additional titles in the Lighted Path Collection include *Home Is Where the Heart Is, Glory of Creation, I'll Be Home for Christmas, Romantic Hideaways,* and *Beyond the Garden Gate.*

Fiction from Harvest House includes mainstream novels with a religious accent, historical adventure tales, bible-based stories, books geared toward a women's readership (including romances), occult thrillers, mystery and suspense fiction, and futuristic works.

Biblical and historical fiction from Harvest House: *The Princess* by Lori Wick; *Island Bride* by Linda Chaikin; *Magnolia Dreams* by Virginia Gaffney; *Promise Me Tomorrow* by Lori Wick; *The Moment I Saw You* by Lisa Samson; *Captive Heart* by Linda Chaikin.

Harvest House manages its own distributional network.

H

Harvest House Books for Children and Young Adults

Harvest House produces a selection of books directed toward a youthful readership, as well as titles of interest to teachers and parents. The solid list encompasses boardbooks, picture books, storybooks, interactive books, joke books, general nonfiction, and novels (including a number of successful series).

On the Harvest House children's-and-youth list: *Let's Make Something Fun* by Emilie Barnes; *Nighty Night, Sleep Tight* (boardbook) by Michael Sparks; *The Bondage Breaker Youth Edition* by Neil T. Anderson and Dave Park; *Extremely Good Clean Jokes for Kids* by Bob Phillips.

Harvest House no longer accepts unsolicited query letters.

HAZELDEN PUBLISHING AND EDUCATIONAL SERVICES

Hazelden Foundation

15251 Pleasant Valley Road, PO Box 176, Center City, MN 55012-0176
612-257-4010
www.hazelden.org

Hazelden publishes books for a consumer and professional readership in such areas as recovery, personal and spiritual growth, self-help, spirituality, substance abuse, and compulsive behaviors. The house's backlist represents all areas of the Hazelden publishing program.

The Hazelden publications and marketing vision encompass books, pamphlets, audiocassettes and videocassettes, computer software, calendars, and books for young readers, along with a gift line.

Hazelden: A Mission in Motion. When Hazelden opened its doors 50 years ago, the mission seemed simple: to rehabilitate clients and restore self-worth and dignity to their lives. Hazelden still commits to this mission as a multidimensional organization involved in public policy, research, education, evaluation, and many other areas of chemical dependency. Hazelden has become a respected leader in the chemical-dependency field and the premier publisher of bibliotherapy. As a pioneer in addiction research and education, Hazelden's clinical expertise is reflected in educational materials that cover a wide range of topics in the treatment of chemical dependency and other additions. Core to the success of the treatment process, Hazelden materials interact with clients. This matrix of materials reinforces important information to clients. Most of all, these materials are a concrete way for clients to retain the concepts they learn in treatment.

Hazelden was established as a publishing operation (in 1954, as Hazelden Educational Materials) with the hardcover release of *Twenty-Four Hours a Day* by Richmond Walker (still in print in hardcover and paperback editions). Hazelden is a division of the Hazelden Foundation, which also operates a network of recovery centers. The publisher has a major concentration in materials related to the 12-Step approach.

In early 1994, Hazelden purchased CompCare and Parkside, two former niche publishers (both with strong backlists) in areas consistent with Hazelden's publishing range—particularly in treatment and recovery titles, as well as in the broader general-interest trade arena. Hazelden also bought Johnson Institute, a publisher that specialized in prevention issues related to chemical dependency. These titles address parenting topics, K–12 educational needs, and recovery issues.

H

In addition to the aforementioned *Twenty-Four Hours a Day,* Hazelden's bestselling trade entrants include *Codependent No More* and *The Language of Letting Go*, both by Melody Beattie, and *Each Day a New Beginning.*

From Hazelden: *More Language of Letting Go* by Melody Beattie; *Alcohol: Cradle to Grave* by Eric Newhouse; *Timeless Wisdom* by Karen Casey; *Igniting the Spirit at Work* by Marilyn Mason; *A Bar on Every Corner* by Jack Erdman with Larry Kearney; *Writing to Save Your Life* by Michele Weldon; *A Parent's Guide to Sex, Drugs, and Flunking Out* by Joel Epstein; *Cybersex Unhooked* by David Delmenico, Elizabeth Griffen, and Joseph Moriarty; *A Biography of Mrs. Marty Man* by Sally Brown and David R. Brown; *Love's Way* by Brenda Schaeffer; *Radical Acts of Love* by Susan Skog.

Hazelden furnishes its titles to the bookstore trade directly and has made inroads into the gift-distribution world. Additional marketing avenues for Hazelden trade titles include the house's direct-to-the-consumer mail-order business. Hazelden books are popular items worldwide, with a foreign distribution network that includes Russia and Canada.

Other areas to which Hazelden markets include structured care (Hazelden develops and markets print, audio, and visual materials for treatment centers, hospitals, and professional markets); prevention, education, and professional training (the publisher accesses the markets of primary and secondary schools, counselor-training programs, and community prevention and treatment programs); and corrections (the publisher addresses the needs of county, state, and federal corrections facilities).

Query letters and SASEs should be directed to:

Rebecca Post, Editorial Director

Deb Fautsch, Manuscript Coordinator

HEBREW PUBLISHING COMPANY

PO Box 222, Spencertown, NY 12165
518-392-3322   fax: 518-392-4280

Hebrew Publishing Company (established in 1901) offers a wide range of titles in such categories as reference and dictionaries; religion, law, and thought; Rabbinic literature; literature; history and biography; children's books; Hebrew-language textbooks and Hebrew culture; Yiddish; bible, Hebrew/English; bible, English only; prayers and liturgy: daily, Hebrew only, and Hebrew/English; prayers and liturgy: Sabbath, high holidays, and festivals; prayers and liturgy: memorial; prayers and liturgy: Purim; general prayers and liturgy; Hanukkah items; Haggadahs; educational materials; sermons and aids of the rabbi; and calendars. The house publishes a limited number of new titles and maintains an established backlist.

On the HPC list: *Yom Kippur* by Philip Birnbaum; *Judaism as a Civilization* by Mordecai Kaplan; *Acharon Hamohikanim* (The Last of the Mohicans) by James Fenimore Cooper; *Business Ethics in Jewish Law* (Jung/Levine); *Encyclopedia of Jewish Concepts* by Philip Birnbaum; *Rahel Varnhagen: The Life of a Jewess* by Hannah Arendt; *Torah and Tradition* by Orenstein and Frankel; *Jewish Tales and Legends* by Menachem Glen.

Hebrew Publishing Company oversees its own distribution, utilizing services of independent fulfillment and distribution firms. Query letters and SASEs should be directed to:

Charles Lieber, Editor in Chief

HEBREW UNION COLLEGE

3101 Clifton Avenue, Cincinnati, OH 45220-2488
513-221-1875
www.huc.edu/press   e-mail: hucpress@huc.edu

Hebrew Union publishes scholarly Judaica, along with some frontlist titles of broader appeal. Within the Hebrew Union College scope are books representing a variety of divisions, institutions, and programs: Klau Library, Skirball Museum, Kuntresim (Hebrew texts copublished with Ben-Zion Dinur Center of the Hebrew University), the journals *Hebrew Union College Annual* and *American Jewish Archives,* and special-interest projects (such as books and videotapes) from HUC-UC Ethics Center.

Hebrew Union College Press (founded in 1921) publishes a select list of new titles covering a full range of its list, while tending a full backlist. HUC engages in copublishing projects with other institutions, including Harvard University Press, KTAV Publishing House, University of Alabama Press, and Yale University Press.

From Hebrew Union College Press: *To Reveal Our Hearts: Jewish Women Writers in Tsarist Russia* by Carole Balin; *A Letter That Has Not Been Read: Dreams in the Hebrew Bible* by Shaul Bar; *In the Service of the King: Officialdom in Ancient Israel and Judah* by Nili S. Fox; *Modern Jewish Mythologies* by Glenda Abramson; *Profane Scriptures* by Ruth Kartun-Blum; *Beyond Survival and Philanthropy* by Allon Gal and Alfred Gottschalk; *The Jew in the Medieval World: A Source Book* by Jacob Rader Marcus; *German Jews Beyond Judaism* by George L. Mosse; *Theology and Poetry: Studies in the Medieval Plyyot* by Jakob J. Petuchowski.

Hebrew Union College Press is distributed by Wayne State University Press. HUC welcomes the submission of scholarly manuscripts in all areas of Judaica. For further information, contact Professor Michael Meyer, Chair, Publications Committee, at the publisher's address. Query letters and SASEs should be directed to:

Barbara Selya, Managing Editor

H

HORIZON PUBLISHERS, NOW PART OF CORNERSTONE

50 South 500 West, PO Box 490, Bountiful, UT 84011-0490
fax: 801-295-0196
www.horizonpublishers.com   e-mail: horizonp@burgoyne.com

Horizon Publishers (founded in 1971) was purchased in August 2000 by Cornerstone Publishing and Distribution, Inc. Cornerstone will continue to distribute Horizon's list and use the Horizon Publishers imprint on selected works. The combined companies form a smaller house that produces hardcover and paperback works with emphasis in the areas of religion, inspiration, youth and adult fiction, cooking and food storage, emergency preparedness, outdoor living, music and art, marriage and family, children's books, and crafts (especially cross-stitch).

Cornerstone is a privately owned corporation with no ecclesiastical ties. The main readership of the house's theological works is Latter-Day Saint (Mormon), so most of its religious works are compatible with that doctrinal perspective, but many are aimed at a wider Christian audience. Cornerstone/Horizon's publishing interest encompasses books on doctrine and church history, children's religious teaching, inspirational and doctrinal talk tapes, religious music, and art. Its list includes religious humor, faith-promoting experiences, historical works, biographies of well-known leaders, doctrinal studies, and fiction for middle-grade, young adult, and adult readers.

Representative of the Cornerstone/Horizon list: *Organize My Kingdom: A History of Restored Priesthood* by John A. Tvedtnes; *How Greek Philosophy Corrupted the Christian Concept of God* by Richard R. Hopkins; *Prophecy: Key to the Future* by Duane S. Crowther; *One in a Billion* by Sharlee Mullins Glenn (illustrated by Rachel Hoffman-Bayles); *The Latter Day Girl Collection,* with stories for middle readers by Carol Lynch Williams and Laurel Stowe Brady*; Let's Cook Dutch! A Complete Guide for the Dutch Oven Chef* by Robert L. Ririe; *Favorite Utah Pioneer Recipes* by Marla Rawlings; *You Can Stay Alive: Wilderness Living and Emergency Survival* by Larry J. Wells and Roger G. Giles; *Journeys Beyond Life: True Accounts of Next World Experiences* by Arvin S. Gibson.

Fiction titles: *Thy Kingdom Come, Volume 1: Prodigal Journey* by Linda Paulson Adams; *Singled Out* by Eric Samuelsen; *The Wise Man in the Checkered Shirt* by Michael Drake; *Crescendo* by Terry J. Moyer.

Family-oriented books: *How to Raise Kids Without Climbing the Walls* by Larry G. Brady, Ph.D.; *Making Marriage Magnificent* by Reed and Lorena Markham; *Family Home Evenings for Dads* by Dianne Friden, Carolyn Seimers, and Barbara Thackeray.

Cornerstone/Horizon handles its own distribution. The house's guidelines for authors are filled with apt advice for all writers. Query letters and SASEs should be directed to:

The Editorial Board

I

INNER TRADITIONS INTERNATIONAL, BEAR AND COMPANY

One Park Street, Rochester, VT 05767
802-767-3174   fax: 802-767-3726
www.InnerTraditions.com   e-mail: (contact name)@gotoit.com

Inner Traditions publishes across such subject areas as acupuncture, anthroposophy, aromatherapy, the arts, astrology, bodywork, cookbooks, crafts, cultural studies, earth studies, Egyptian studies, gemstones, health and healing, homeopathy, indigenous cultures, African American traditions, inner traditions of the West and the East, myth and legend, massage, natural medicine, self-transformation, sacred sexuality, spirituality, and travel.

Inner Traditions International (founded in 1975) produces hardcover trade books and trade paperbacks, illustrated gift books, and mass-market paperback editions, as well as a line of audioworks and selected videotapes. The house also packages specialty items such as boxed sets and tarot decks.

Special imprints include Destiny Books, Destiny Recordings, Healing Arts Press, and Park Street Press. Inner Traditions en Español is a line published in the Spanish language. Inner Traditions India issues works aimed at the Indian market. The house has announced a forthcoming slate of multimedia titles in the works. Inner Traditions International publishes a medium-sized list each year and maintains a strong backlist.

The Inner Traditions imprint accents works that represent the spiritual, cultural, and mythic traditions of the world, focusing on inner wisdom and the perennial philosophies.

Inner Traditions imprint titles: *The Celtic Wisdom of Tarot* by Caitlin Matthews; *The Lost Treasure of the Knights Templar: Solving the Oak Island Mystery* by Steven Sora; *Sacred Woman, Sacred Dance: Awakening Spirituality Through Movement and Ritual* by Iris J. Stewart; *A Yoga of Indian Classical Dance: The Yogini's Mirror* by Roxanne Kamayani Gupta; *The Heart of Yoga: Developing a Personal Practice* by T. K. V. Desikachar; *Transfigurations* by Alex Greg; *Pilates on the Ball* by Colleen Craig; *Advanced Bach Flower Therapy: A Scientific Approach to Diagnosis and Treatment* by Gotz Blome, M.D.

Destiny Books are contemporary metaphysical titles for a popular audience, with special emphasis on self-transformation, the occult, and psychological well-being. Destiny Recordings are cassettes and compact discs of spiritual and indigenous music traditions. Destiny Audio Editions include Inner Traditions books on tape, as well as original spoken-word cassettes.

Healing Arts Press publishes works on alternative medicine and holistic health that combine contemporary thought and innovative research with the accumulated knowledge of the world's great healing traditions.

Park Street Press produces books on travel, psychology, consumer and environmental issues, archaeology, women's and men's studies, and fine art.

Inner Traditions en Español is the house's Spanish-language publishing program, in cooperation with Lasser Press of Mexico City. This line includes popular titles from a variety of Inner Tradition imprints.

Bear and Company titles: *The Lost Book of Enki* by Zecharia Sitchin; *Catastrophobie* by Barbara Hand Clow; *Time and the Technoscope* by Jose Arguelles; *Gods of Eden* by Andrew Collins.

Selections from the Inner Traditions en Español list: *Secretos Sexuales* (Sexual Secrets) by Nik Douglas and Penny Slinger; *El Cáñamo para la Salud* (Hemp for Health) by Chris Conrad.

Kits and gift packages from Inner Traditions: *The Lakota Sioux Sweat Lodge Cards* by Chief Archie Fire Lame Deer and Helene Sarks; *Leela: The Game of Self-Knowledge* by Harish Johari.

Inner Traditions supervises its own distribution. Query letters and SASEs should be directed to:

Jon Graham, Acquisitions Editor

I

INNISFREE PRESS

136 Roumfort Road, Philadelphia, PA 19119-1632
215-247-4085, 800-367-5872   fax: 215-247-2343
www.innisfreepress.com   e-mail: InnisfreeP@aol.com

Innisfree is a creative publishing forum for books that feature the areas of personal growth with spiritual and feminine dimensions. The editorial sphere encompasses self-discovery, relationships, nutrition, writing and journaling, healing and inspiration, transition and renewal, bible study, and meditation. Innisfree acquired LuraMedia in late 1996.

From the Innisfree list: *Braided Streams; Bridge to Wholeness; Call to the Soul; Circle of Stones; The Circle Continues; Dream Theatres of the Soul; Family Puzzles; The God Between Us; God's Forgotten Daughter; Guerrillas of Grace; I Asked for Intimacy; I Sit Listening to the Wind; The Job Hunter's Spiritual Companion; Just a Sister Away; Leading Ladies; Mother Love; My Heart in My Mouth; Nobody Owns Me; Prayers to Sophia; Raising Up Queens; Red Fire; Return to the Sea; Sabbath Sense; Seasons of Friendship; Silence; Slow Miracles; Spiritual Lemons; The Star in My Heart; The Tao of Eating; This Is My Body; Tracks in the Straw; Whole Earth Meditation; The Wisdom of Daughters; Woman's Book of Money and Spiritual Vision; The Woman Who Found Her Voice; The Woman Who Lost Her Heart; Wrestling the Light; Writing and Being.*

LuraMedia, Inc. (founded in 1982), was known as a small house that undertook to select, design, produce, and distribute its list with care and flair; the publisher's stated goal was to provide materials that foster healing and hope, balance and justice. Effective November 15, 1996, LuraMedia was sold to Innisfree Press in Philadelphia, Pennsylvania, and the San Diego office of LuraMedia closed. LuraMedia books are available through the new company.

Innisfree distributes to the trade via Consortium. Query letters and SASEs should be directed to:

Marcia Broucek, Publisher

INTERVARSITY PRESS

InterVarsity Christian Fellowship of the USA, PO Box 1400, Downers Grove, IL 60515
630-734-4000   fax: 630-734-4200
www.ivpress.com   e-mail: mail@ivpress.com

InterVarsity Press publications embrace the main fields of bible study guides, reference books, academic and theological books, and issue-oriented books of general interest to educated Christians.

Nonfiction categories in areas of contemporary religious interest include titles in self-improvement, spirituality, and interpersonal relations. The house also produces humor.

InterVarsity Press (founded in 1947) is the publishing arm of InterVarsity Christian Fellowship of the USA. The press operates within IVCF's framework and publishes interdenominational books (in hardback and paperback) under the banner "Heart. Soul. Mind. Strength."

Indicative of the InterVarsity Press nonfiction frontlist: *Making Life Work* by Bill Hybels; *The Wedge of Truth* by Phillip E. Johnson; *Soul Craft* by Douglas Webster; *Habits of the Mind* by James W. Sire; *The Holy Spirit* by Donald Bloesch; *The Challenge of Jesus* by N. T. Wright; *Church Next* by Eddie Gibbs; *Love, Honor & Forgive* by Bill and Pam Fanel; *Never Beyond Hope* by J. I. Packer.

LifeGuide Bible Studies introduces new titles that focus on particular scriptural areas and specific books of the bible. Other bible studies are published each year.

A full set of guidelines for manuscript submission to InterVarsity Press is available upon request from the publisher. Query letters and SASEs should be directed to:

Andrew T. Le Peau, Editorial Director

JEWISH LIGHTS PUBLISHING

PO Box 237, Sunset Farm Offices, Route 4, Woodstock, VT 05091
802-457-4000   fax: 802-457-4004
www.jewishlights.com

Jewish Lights Publishing shows a vigorous approach to titles "for people of all faiths, all backgrounds." Its books cover Jewish spirituality, life cycle, self-help/healing, theology, history, and contemporary culture, all within the trade motto "Words for the soul—made in Vermont." Jewish Lights offers books in hardcover, quality paperback, and gift editions.

Jewish Lights features authors at the forefront of spiritual thought. Each voice is unique, and each speaks in a way readers can hear. Jewish Lights books are judged as successful not only by whether they are beautiful and commercially successful but also by the difference they make in their readers' lives.

Jewish Lights Publishing (founded in 1990), a division of LongHill Partners, Inc., describes itself as a publisher of books that reflect the Jewish wisdom tradition for people of all faiths and all backgrounds. Its books really focus on the issue of the quest for the self, seeking meaning in life. They are books that help you understand who you are and who you might become as a Jewish person, or as a person who is part of a tradition that has its roots in the Judeo-Christian world. The books deal with issues of personal growth and issues of religious inspiration.

Jewish Lights' principal goal is to stimulate thought and help all people learn about who the Jewish People are, where they come from, and what the future can be made to hold. Although people of diverse Jewish heritage are the primary audience, Jewish Lights books speak to people in the Christian world as well and will broaden their understanding of Judaism and the roots of their own faith.

Jewish Lights seeks out materials about the unity and community of the Jewish people and the relevance of Judaism to everyday life. To help in these efforts, respectful of the rich diversity of the Jewish heritage, the publisher has established an Advisory Board, representing a broad range of Jewish perspectives. The Advisory Board helps seek out new material and provides insights into the publishing needs of the Jewish community.

The press publishes the award-winning Kushner series, *Classics of Modern Jewish Spirituality* by Lawrence Kushner. A related special-edition project is *The Book of Letters: A Mystical Hebrew Alphabet* (designed by Lawrence Kushner).

J

From Jewish Lights: *The Book of Words: Talking Spiritual Life, Living Spiritual Talk* by Lawrence Kushner; *Eyes Remade for Wonder,* also by Lawrence Kushner; *Finding Joy: A Practical Spiritual Guide to Happiness* by Daniel L. Schwartz, with Mark Hass; *How to Claim the Spiritual Meaning of Your Bar or Bat Mitzvah; Moses—The Prince, the Prophet: His Life, Legend & Message for Our Lives* by Rabbi Levi Meier, Ph.D.; *Parenting as a Spiritual Journey: Deepening Ordinary & Extraordinary Events into Sacred Occasions* by Rabbi Nancy Fuchs-Kreimer; *Tears of Sorrow, Voices from Genesis: Guiding Us Through the Stages of Life* by Norman J. Cohen; *The Year Mom Got Religion: One Woman's Midlife Journey into Judaism* by Lee Meyerhoff Hendler; *Embracing the Covenant: Converts to Judaism Talk About Why & How* (edited by Rabbi Allan Berkowitz and Patti Moskovitz).

The Art of Jewish Living series from the Federation of Jewish Men's Clubs provides the following titles: *A Time to Mourn, a Time to Comfort: A Guide to Jewish Bereavement and Comfort; The Shabbat Seder;* and *Hanukkah* by Dr. Ron Wolfson.

The Jewish Thought series from Israel's MOD Books is distributed exclusively by Jewish Lights. A part of Israel's Broadcast University series, the books are written by leading experts and authors in their respective fields. Titles are published jointly by Tel Aviv University, the Chief Education office of the IDF, and IDF Radio. Selected series offerings: *Jerusalem in the 19th Century* by Yehoshua Ben-Arieh; *Jewish Reactions to the Holocaust* by Yehuda Bauer; *Lectures on the Philosophy of Spinoza* by Professor Yosef Ben-Shlomo; *The Spiritual History of the Dead Sea Sect* by David Flusser; *The World of the Aggadah* by Avigdor Shinan; *Human Rights in the Bible and Talmud* by Haim H. Cohn.

Children's titles and books for the family from Jewish Lights: *A Prayer for the Earth: The Story of Naamah, Noah's Wife* by Sandy Eisenberg Sasso (illustrated by Bethanne Andersen); *When a Grandparent Dies: A Child's Own Workbook for Dealing with Shiva and the Year Beyond* by Nechama Liss-Levenson; *The New Jewish Baby Book: A Guide to Choices for Today's Families* by Anita Diamant.

Jewish Lights Publishing handles its own distribution. Query letters and SASEs should be directed to:

Stuart M. Matlins, Editor in Chief

THE JEWISH PUBLICATION SOCIETY

2100 Arch Street, 2nd Floor, Philadelphia, PA 19103
215-832-0609   fax: 215-568-2017
www.jewishpub.org   e-mail: Jewishbook@aol.com

The Jewish Publication Society specializes in hardcover and trade paperback books of Jewish interest, especially traditional religious works (including the Torah), as well as relevant commentaries and resources for Jewish life.

The Jewish Publication Society (founded in 1888) upholds a commitment to the English-speaking Jewish community by publishing works of exceptional scholarship, contemporary significance, and enduring value. The publisher traditionally assumes a demanding balancing act among the various denominations of Jewish institutional life, between academic and popular interests, and between past and present visions of Judaism.

Recently published: *Swimming in the Sea of Talmud: Lessons for Everyday Living* by Michael Katz and Gershon Schwartz; *Entering the High Holy Days: A Complete Guide to the History, Prayers and Themes* by Reuven Hammer; *Matters of Life and Death: A Jewish Approach to Modern Medical Ethics* by Elliot N. Dorff; *Adoption and the Jewish Family: Contemporary Perspectives* by Shelley Kapnek Rosenberg; *A Time to Be Born: Jewish Birth Customs and Traditions* by Michele Klein, Ph.D.; *Reading Levinas/Reading Talmud: An Introduction* by Ira F. Stone; *The Language of Truth: The Torah Commentary of the Sefat Emet* (translated and interpreted by Arthur Green); *The Shema: Spirituality and Law in Judaism* by Norman Lamm; *Engendering Judaism* by Rachael Adler; *Genesis: The Beginning of Desire* by Avivah Gottlieb Zornberg.

Indicative of JPS nonfiction: *In the Year 1096: The First Crusade and the Jews* by Robert Chazen; *Reclaiming the Dead Sea Scrolls* by Lawrence Schiffman; *On the Possibility of Jewish Mysticism in Our Time* by Gershom Scholem; *On Family and Feminism* by Blu Greenberg; *Blessings* (a prayer book) by Melanie Greenberg.

The Jewish Publication Society is a not-for-profit educational institution that distributes its own list and, through its book club, offers to its membership Judaica from other publishers as well.

Query letters and SASEs should be directed to:

Jewishbook@jewishpub.org Attn: Acquisitions

KAR-BEN COPIES

6800 Tildenwood Lane, Rockville, MD 20852
301-984-8733, 800-4-KARBEN   fax: 301-881-9195
www.karben.com   e-mail: karben@aol.com

Kar-Ben Copies (founded in 1976) offers an expansive Jewish library for young children and families, as well as teachers. The Kar-Ben list encompasses presentations keyed to high holidays, Sabbath, culture and tradition, and general-interest concepts.

Kar-Ben's children's books are handsomely produced volumes that often incorporate fine illustrative work. The Kar-Ben catalog highlights books especially for toddlers, as well as a reference line for youngsters (the "All About" Jewish Holiday series). The house also offers audiocassettes and calendars.

Kar Ben's list of over 95 books on Jewish themes include such recent titles as *The Hardest Word* by Jacqueline Jules; *The Shabbat Box* by Lesley Simpson; *Hanukkah Cat* by Chaya Burnstein; and *Clap and Count—Jewish Action Rhymes* by Jacqueline Jules. Bestsellers include the six popular Sammy Spider books for Hanukkah, Passover, Purim, Tubshevar, Rosh Hashanah, and Sabbat.

A special Kar-Ben line consists of book-and-cassette packages, with accompanying leader's guides for family services keyed to the high holidays (Selichot, Rosh Hashanah, and Yom Kippur). These works are written by Judith Z. Abrams, designed and illustrated by Katherine Janus Kahn, with original music by Frances T. Goldman.

Kar-Ben welcomes comments, kudos, and manuscripts. Query letters and SASEs should be directed to:

Madeline Wikler, Editor in Chief

K

H. J. Kramer, Inc.

Starseed Press

PO Box 1082, Tiburon, CA 94920
415-435-5367   fax: 415-435-5364

Kramer covers spiritual life, interpersonal relationships, resources for good health, and self-awareness and guidance. The Starseed Press imprint publishes books for younger readers (see subentry following). Kramer books are finely produced editions in trade paperback and hardcover. The house typically issues a small number of new titles seasonally and sustains a strong backlist.

The books H. J. Kramer publishes are contributions to an emerging world based on co-operation rather than on competition, on affirmation of the human spirit rather than on self-doubt, and on the certainty that all humanity is connected. The goal of the publishers is to touch as many lives as possible with a message of hope for a better world.

H. J. Kramer, Inc. (founded in 1984 by Hal and Linda Kramer) holds a commitment to publishing books that touch the heart and open us to spirit. Kramer books, old and new, are intended to support the reader's personal vision. A number of Kramer books sell exceedingly well in the mainstream market and garner translation rights worldwide, as well as domestic book-club sales.

From Kramer: *The Last of the Dream People* by Alice Anne Parker; *Reclaiming Our Health: Exploding the Medical Myth and Embracing the Source of True Healing* by John Robbins; *Diet for a New America: How Your Food Choices Affect Your Health, Happiness, and the Future of Life on Earth,* also by John Robbins; *Way of the Peaceful Warrior: A Book That Changes Lives* by Dan Millman; *The Laughing Classroom: Everyone's Guide to Teaching with Humor and Play* by Diane Loomans and Karen Kolberg; *Personal Power Through Awareness: A Guidebook for Sensitive People* by Sanaya Roman; *Guardians of Hope: The Angels' Guide to Personal Growth* by Terry Lynn Taylor; *Soul Love: Awakening Your Heart Centers* by Sanaya Roman; *Into a Timeless Realm: A Metaphysical Adventure* by Michael J. Roads; *The Laws of Spirit: Simple, Powerful Truths for Making Life Work* by Dan Millman; *The Awakened Heart: Finding Harmony in a Changing World* by John Robbins and Ann Mortifee Biowing; *Zen* by Ray Brooks; *Moments of Union* by Hal Kramer.

The Earth Life series by Sanaya Roman, channel for Orin, is a course in learning to live with joy, sense energy, and grow spiritually. Titles include *Living with Joy: Keys to Personal Power and Spiritual Transformation; Personal Power Through Awareness: A Guidebook for Sensitive People; Spiritual Growth: Being Your Higher Self.*

A Kramer hallmark is Dan Millman's renowned set of writings (including *Way of the Peaceful Warrior*) that, in addition to audiocassette rendering, has now branched into a children's series. Kramer has also published a number of works on José Silva's mind-control method.

Prospective authors please note: Kramer's list is selective and is, generally speaking, fully slated several publishing seasons in advance. Kramer and Starseed are thus essentially closed to unsolicited submissions.

The company does not accept any submissions via fax. Query letters and SASEs should be directed to:

K

Hal Kramer, President

Linda Kramer, Publisher

Starseed Press

Starseed Press children's books from H. J. Kramer are award-winning children's books that build self-esteem, inspire nonviolence, and encourage positive values. The imprint produces illustrated works slated for trade as well as educational markets.

Starseed books embody the principles of education through the power of story and incorporate myths, legends, fables, fairy tales, folklore, and original author visions into volumes of contemporary appeal.

Titles here: *Where Does God Live?* by Holly Bea (illustrated by Kim Howard); *The Lovables in the Kingdom of Self-Esteem* by Diane Loomans (illustrated by Kim Howard); *Grandfather Four Winds and Rising Moon* by Michael Chanin (illustrated by Sally J. Smith).

The Peaceful Warrior children's series by Dan Millman (illustrated by T. Taylor Bruce) includes these titles: *Secret of the Peaceful Warrior* and *Quest for the Crystal Castle*. The series adapts the characters, lessons, and spirit of Dan Millman's international bestseller *Way of the Peaceful Warrior.*

Backlist benchmarks include *The Land of the Blue Flower* by Frances Hodgson Burnett (author of *The Secret Garden* and *The Little Princess*), in an edition illustrated by Judith Ann Griffith.

Starseed Press's mission statement reads as follows: "All children are seeds from the stars who look to adults for love, inspiration, guidance, and the promise of a safe and friendly world. We dedicate Starseed Press to this vision and to the sacred child in each of us."—Hal and Linda Kramer, publishers.

KTAV PUBLISHING HOUSE

900 Jefferson Street, PO Box 6249, Hoboken, NJ 07030-7205
201-963-9524   fax: 201-963-0102
www.ktav.com   e-mail: questions@ktav.com

KTAV Publishing House (founded in 1924) features books of Jewish interest, including scholarly Judaica, sermonica, textbooks, and books for a younger readership. KTAV also markets religious educational materials (including books), as well as gifts and decorative items. Many KTAV titles in the scholarly vein relate the history of Jewish thought and culture within the context of broader issues—some of global scope—and are of appeal to the interested general reader.

KTAV's catalog embraces the categories of Judaica, Biblica, Torah study, Jewish law, contemporary Halachic thought, sermonica, Jewish history, Jewish thought, contemporary Jewry, and Torah and science.

Titles from KTAV: *The Third How to Handbook for Jewish Living* by Kerry Okitzky; *Blessings of Freedom: Chapters in American Jewish History* by Michael Feldberg; *Thinking*

K

God: The Mysticism of Rabbi Kadok Hakohen Oflubin by Alan Brill; *The World of Jewish Learning* by Rabbi Aharon Lichtenstein; *Charlie Reminisces: The Stories of Charles H. Bendheim* by Charles Bendheim; *The Jewish Experiential Book* by Bernard Reisman; *Understanding the Talmud: A Dialogic Approach* by Jacob Neusner; *Walking Humbly with God* by Cohen; *Holocaust Hero: The Untold Story of Solomon Schonfeld, An Orthodox British Rabbi* by David Kranzler; *Judaism and Healing* by David Bleich; *Worship of the Heart: Essays on Jewish Prayer* by Joseph B. Soloveitchik; *Vatican Diplomacy and the Jews During the Holocaust, 1939–1943* by John Morley; *Family Redeemed: Essays on Family Relationships* by Rabbi Joseph B. Soloveitchik; *I Will Not Let You Go Until You Bless Me: Memoirs of a Reform Rabbi* by Harold Silver; *Jews of Kaifeng China* by Xu Xin; *Jewish Arguments and Counter Arguments* by Steven Bayme; *Out of the Whirlwind: Essays on Suffering, Mourning, and the Human Condition* by Joseph B. Soloveitchik; *Principals of Jewish Activism* by Avi Weiss.

KTAV distributes its own list; in addition, the house distributes the books of Yeshiva University Press. Query letters and SASEs should be directed to:

Bernard Scharfstein, Publisher

LIGUORI PUBLICATIONS

Liguori Triumph Books

One Liguori Drive, Liguori, MO 63057-9999
636-464-2500, 800-325-9526
www.liguori.org

Liguori Publications and its trade imprint Liguori Triumph Books represent a twofold approach to religious publishing. Liguori (run by Redemptionist priests) produces books and pamphlets focused on the needs of specialized religious-bookstore markets and Catholic parishes and publishes *Liguorian* magazine. Liguori Triumph Books publishes for the mainstream religious-trade-book market. Under the rubric of Liguori Faithware, the publisher supplies computer resources for Catholics.

Liguori initiated its book program in 1968 and met with immediate success with *Good Old Plastic Jesus* by Earnest Larsen and *Keeping Your Balance in the Modern Church* by Hugh O'Connell.

Though Liguori, America's largest producer of Catholic publications, is assuredly a business, it is primarily a ministry. Through publications—in print and through electronic media—Liguori is able to reach people in ways that are not available in ordinary day-to-day ministry.

Liguori titles: *Angels All Around Us: The Catholic Belief and Experience; Daily Strength: One Year of Experiencing the Psalms* by Victor M. Parachin; *For Men Only: Strategies for Living Catholic* by Mitch Finley; *In the Womb of God: Creative Nurturing for the Soul* by Celeste Snowber Schroeder; *A Call to Peace: 52 Meditations on the Family Pledge of Nonviolence* by James McGinnis; *Out of the Ordinary: Awareness of God in the Everyday* by Peter Verity; *The Essential Catholic Handbook: A Summary of Beliefs, Practices, and Prayers* (compiled by pastors and preachers of the Redemptionist Order);

L

Living Advent: A Daily Companion to the Lectionary by Julia Dugger; *Revisiting the Journey: Adult Faith-Sharing with the Catechism of the Catholic Church* (a Redemptorist Pastoral Publication); *The Light of the World* by David Fielding.

Highlights from Liguori include *Mother Teresa: In My Own Words* by Mother Teresa; *Family Planning: A Guide for Exploring the Issues* by Charles and Elizabeth Balsam; *Sex and the Christian Teen* by Jim Auer.

Liguori Publications promotes and markets through such vehicles as catalog mailings and listings in *Liguorian* magazine, circulates bookstore and parish newsletters, and utilizes flyers and self-mailers. Authors interested in Liguori or Triumph may request from the publisher a brochure covering submission guidelines. Query letters and SASEs should be directed to:

Rev. Harry Grile, Publisher, Editor in Chief, Book and Pamphlet Department

Liguori Triumph Books

Liguori Triumph Books emphasizes an ecumenical perspective in the religious trade market. Liguori Triumph reaches a wide readership through books in a variety of areas, including psychology, spirituality, inspiration, awareness, theology, and Christian living.

Liguori Triumph Books asserts the impact of social and cultural developments on readers' values and religious faith and reflects this stance in its selection of new titles. The publishing program accents topics of contemporary controversy and debate. Liguori Triumph was formerly part of Gleneida Publishing Group.

From Liguori Triumph: *Jesus: An Unconventional Biography* by Jacques Duquesne; *Shaking a Fist at God: Struggling with the Mystery of Undeserved Suffering* by Katharine Dell; *Happy Are They . . . Living the Beatitudes in America* by Jim Langford; *On Living Simply: The Golden Voice of John Chrysostom* (compiled by Robert Van de Weyer); *Lift Up Your Heart: A Guide to Spiritual Peace* by Fulton J. Sheen; *From a Monastery Kitchen* by Brother Victor-Antoine D'Avila-Latourrette; *A Human Search: Reflections on My Life* by Father Bede Griffiths (edited by John Swindells); *Where Does God Live? Questions and Answers for Parents and Children* by Rabbi Marc Gellman and Monsignor Thomas Hartman; *Divine Energy: God Beyond Us, Within Us, Among Us* by Donal Dorr; *Life Doesn't Get Any Better Than This: The Holiness of Little Daily Dramas* by Robert A. Alper; *Short Prayers for the Long Day* (compiled by Giles and Melville Harcourt).

Query letters and SASEs should be directed to:

Judy Bauer, Managing Editor

LLEWELLYN PUBLICATIONS

PO Box 64383, St. Paul, MN 55164-0383
651-291-1790, 800-The-Moon   fax: 651-291-1908
www.llewellyn.com   e-mail: lwlpc@llewellyn.com

Traditional areas of Llewellyn publishing concentration include astrology, magic, the occult, self-improvement, self-development, spiritual science, alternative technologies, nature religions and lifestyles, spiritist and mystery religions, divination, phenomena, and tantra. These works are brought out under the lustrous Llewellyn logo: a crescent moon. Llewellyn's trade motto—"New worlds of mind and spirit"—indicates the publisher's openness to explore new territory.

Llewellyn Publications (established in 1901) is a venerable house with a historical emphasis on the practical aspects of what today may be termed New Age science—how it works and how to do it.

Llewellyn catalogs a full stock of new seasonal releases, along with a prolific backlist in hardcover, trade paper, and mass-market editions. Llewellyn also issues tarot decks and divination kits. The house's expanded program includes Spanish-language trade paperbacks.

New titles from Llewellyn: *The Art of Predictive Astrology* by Carol Rushman; *Nostradamus, World War III, 2002* by David Montaigne; *Ostara* by Edain McCoy; *Charting Your Spiritual Path with Astrology* by Stephanie Clement; *Ayurvedic Balancing* by Joyce Bueker; *Nocturnal Witchcraft* by Konstantinos; *Seeker's Guide to Self-Freedom* by Guy Finley; *Pendulum Magic for Beginners* by Richard Webster; *The Sacred Round* by Elen Hawke; *Astrology of Intimacy, Sexuality & Relationships* by Noel Tyl.

Backlist favorites from Llewellyn include *Astrology for the Millions* by Grant Lewi; *Auras: See Them in Only 60 Seconds!* by Mark Smith; *The Intimate Enemy: Winning the War Within Yourself* by Guy Finley and Ellen Dickstein, Ph.D.; *In the Presence of Aliens: A Personal Experience of Dual Consciousness* by Janet Bergmark; *Magical Gardens: Myths, Mulch and Marigolds* by Patricia Monaghan; *Feng Shui for Beginners: Successful Living by Design* by Richard Webster; *Peaceful Transition: The Art of Conscious Dying & the Liberation of the Soul* by Dr. Bruce Goldberg; *How to Develop and Use Psychic Touch* by Ted Andrews; *Strange but True: From the Files of* FATE *Magazine* (edited by Corine Kenner and Craig Miller); *100 Days to Better Health, Good Sex & Long Life: A Guide to Taoist Yoga* by Eric Steven Yudelove; *Experiencing the Kabbalah: A Simple Guide to Spiritual Wholeness* by Chic Cicero and Sandra Tabatha Cicero; *Enochian Magic for Beginners: The Original System of Angel Magic* by Donald Tyson; *Twelve Faces of Saturn: Your Guardian Angel Planet* by Bil Tierney; *Inner Passages, Outer Journeys: Wilderness, Healing and the Discovery of Self* by David Cumes, M.D.; *Women at the Change: The Intelligent Woman's Guide to Menopause* by Madonna Sophia Compton; *Your Pet's Horoscope* by Diana Nilsen.

Llewellyn has produced a limited number of fiction titles. Among them: *Visions of Murder* by Florence Wagner McClain; *Lilith* by D. A. Heeley; *Cardinal's Sin: Psychic Defenders Uncover Evil in the Vatican* by Raymond Buckland; *Walker Between the Worlds* by Diane DesRochers; *The Holographic Dollhouse* by Charlotte Lawrence; *Beneath a Mountain Moon* by Silver Ravenwolf.

Llewellyn is a specialty house and looks for projects (books and audiotapes, as well as videos and computer software) that will have extended sales viability. Llewellyn is not geared toward academic or scholarly publishing, and its products are aimed at general audiences without specialist knowledge or training. Authors may request the house's writers' guidelines, which contain valuable tips generally applicable to structuring and proposing publishing projects.

L

To request a copy of the Llewellyn Writers' Guidelines for book publication, send an SASE to Nancy Mostad, Acquisitions Manager. Only writers who request and adhere to the writers' guidelines will be considered for publication.

An aggressive marketer and promoter, Llewellyn publications and authors are given full house support, including the areas of arranging author interviews and appropriate advertising and subsidiary rights—often incorporated into the schedule is placement in Llewellyn's magazine (*New Times*) and primarily promotional venues (*New Worlds*). Llewellyn's marketing network encompasses distributional arrangements worldwide.

Query letters and SASEs should be directed to:

Nancy J. Mostad, Acquisitions Manager

Barbara Wright, Acquisitions Editor—Tarot and kits

LOTUS PRESS (A DIVISION OF LOTUS BRANDS, INC.)

PO Box 325, Twin Lakes, WI 53181
262-889-8561   fax: 262-889-8591

Lotus Brands, Inc.

PO Box 325, Twin Lakes, WI 53181

Lotus Press produces works in the fields of health, yoga, and Native American and New Age metaphysics. Lotus Press (founded in 1981) is a division of Lotus Brands, Inc.

On the Lotus Press list: *The Healing Power of Grapefruit Seed* by Shalila Sharamon and Bodo J. Baginski; *The Healing Power of Essential Oils* by Rololphe Balz; *Abundance Through Reiki* by Paula Horan; *Ayurveda Secrets of Healing* by Maya Tiwari; *Reiki: Way of the Heart* by Walter Lubeck; *New Eden: For People, Animals, Nature* by Michael W. Fox (illustrated by Susan Seddon Boulet); *Rainforest Remedies: One Hundred Healing Herbs of Belize* by Rosita Arvigo and Michael Balick; *Stargazer: A Native American Inquiry into Extraterrestrial Phenomena* by Gerald Hausman.

Lotus Press distributes primarily through special product outlets such as health-food stores and spiritual-interest booksellers. Query letters and SASEs should be directed to:

Cathy Hoselton

LURAMEDIA, INC.

See listing for Innisfree Press.

MESORAH PUBLICATIONS

4401 Second Avenue, Brooklyn, NY 11232
718-921-9000
www.artscroll.com   e-mail: listproc@virtual.co.il

M

M

Mesorah Publications produces books of contemporary Jewish interest written by authors with sophisticated firsthand knowledge of Orthodox religious practices, history, and culture. It is also noted for its works in traditional Judaica, bible study, Talmud, liturgical materials, Jewish history, and juvenile literature. Founded in 1976, Mesorah Publications, Ltd., remains true to tradition in all of its publications, as expressed in its motto: "Mesorah Publications . . . helping to preserve the heritage, one book at a time."

From Mesorah: *Schottenstein Daf Yomi Edition of the Talmud-English Makkos: Patience: Formulas, Stories and Insights* by Rabbi Zelig Pliskin; *The Jewish People: A Light unto the Nations* by Rabbi Berel Wein; *Wisdom Each Day* by Rabbi Abraham J. Twerski; *Understanding Judaism* by Rabbi Mordechai Katz; *A Look Back* by Dr. Gershon Kranzler; *Calculated Risk* by Yair Weinstein; *Take Me to the Holy Land* by Tsivia Yanofsky; *The Jewish Experience: 2000 Years* by Rabbi Nachman Zakon.

Mesorah catalogs books from such other houses as Shaar Press, Tamar Books, and OU/NCSY Publications. Query letters and SASEs should be directed to:

Charlotte Friedland, Acquisitions Editor

MOODY PRESS

820 North LaSalle Boulevard, Chicago, IL 60610-3284
312-329-2101, 800-678-8812
www.moodypress.org   e-mail: pressinfo@moody.edu

In addition to general-interest religious titles (bible-based interdenominational), Moody produces a list that includes bibles, books for children and youths, novels, biographies, educational resources, and works for religious professionals. Moody's books are issued in clothbound editions, trade paper, and mass-market paperback. Moody also catalogs computer software, audiotapes, and videocassettes. Moody Press (founded in 1894) serves as the publishing ministry of Moody Bible Institute.

Moody produces a number of targeted and successful lines that encompass the spectrum of the house's publishing interests. This portion of the Moody program offers such series as Men of Integrity, Moody Acorns, Golden Oldies, Healing for the Heart, Quiet Time Books for Women, and Salt & Light Pocket Guides.

Representative Moody titles: *Seven Words to Change Your Family . . . While There's Still Time* by James MacDonald; *Sought by Grace* by R. Kent Hughes; *Totally Saved: Understanding, Experiencing and Enjoying the Greatness of Your Salvation* by Tony Evans; *Unlocking Your Legacy: 25 Keys for Success* by Paul J. Meyer; *With All Their Heart* by Christine Yount; *Holy Ambition: What It Takes to Make a Difference for God* by Chip Ingram; *If God Should Choose: The Authorized Story of Jim and Roni Bowers* by Kristen Stagg; *Life Changing Relationships* by James T. Meeks; *Not Guilty* by John P. Kee; *Outbreak: Creating a Contagious Youth Ministry Through Viral Evangelism* by Greg Stier; *Prophecy in Light Today* by Charles Dyer; *Cries from the Cross: A Journey into the Heart of Jesus* by Erwin W. Lutzer; *Embraced by the Cross: Discovering the Principles of Christian Faith and Life* by L. E. Maxwell; *Encounter Christ Through the Dramatic*

Story of Vinegar Boy by Alberta Hawse; *Just a Taste of Honey* by Norline H. Rendall; *Light Reflections* by Alma Barkman; *Love Talks for Couples* and *Love Talks for Families* by Gary Chapman and Ramon Presson; *A 30 Day Walk with God in the Psalms* by Nancy Leigh DeMoss; *A Place of Quiet Rest* by Nancy Leigh DeMoss; *The Battle Is the Lord's: Waging Victorious Spiritual Warfare* by Tony Evans; *The Best Is Yet to Come* by Tony Evans; *Bread from My Oven* by Marjorie Parker; *Building Unity in the Church of the New Millennium* by Dwight Perry.

Northfield Publishing, an imprint of Moody Press, is a line of books for non-Christians in your life, those who are exploring the Christian faith or acquaintances who identify themselves as Christians but may not be active in a local church. While the books remain true to biblical principles, certain Christian wording and scripture book references are eliminated to avoid reader confusion. Covering such areas as finances, relationships, and business, Northfield authors are professionals in their field who write with relevance and offer wide-ranging perspectives.

Some Northfield titles: *The Five Love Languages: How to Express Heartfelt Commitment to Your Mate* by Gary Chapman; *Reinventing Your Career: Surviving a Layoff and Creating New Opportunities* by Stephen P. Adams; *The Relaxed Parent: Helping Your Kids Do More As You Do Less* by Tim Smith.

Fiction from Moody includes historicals, high-tech espionage, and contemporary mysteries. Larry Burkett Products is a line of books and tapes accenting the social/financial sphere.

Query letters and SASEs should be directed to:

Jim Bell, Executive Editor

MOORINGS

As of spring 1996, Random House/Ballantine ceased publishing under the Moorings imprint.

MULTNOMAH PUBLISHERS

204 West Adams Avenue, PO Box 1720, Sisters, OR 97759
541-549-1144   fax: 541-549-2044

Multnomah covers the major categories of Christian trade publishing in general nonfiction and fiction.

Multnomah produces books and audiocassettes with a contemporary verve in Christian living and family enrichment, as well as lines of devotional titles and gift books.

Multnomah also offers a strong list of fiction, including contemporary and historical novels.

Multnomah is currently not accepting unsolicited manuscripts, proposals, or queries. Queries will be accepted through agents and at writer's conferences in which a Multnomah representative is present. Query letters and SASEs should be directed to the Editorial Department or to:

David Webb, Editorial Director

N

THOMAS NELSON PUBLISHERS

Tommy Nelson

501 Nelson Place, PO Box 141000, Nashville, TN 37214-1000
615-889-9000
www.thomasnelsonpublishers.com

Thomas Nelson Publishers is an editorially independent product group of Thomas Nelson, Inc. (founded in Scotland in 1798 and purchased by Sam Moore in 1969). Thomas Nelson Publishers produces Christian trade books in hardcover and trade paperback in the areas of health, inspiration, self-help, psychology, family concerns, parenting, charismatic interest, leadership and motivation, contemporary issues and interest, and healing and recovery. Oliver-Nelson is a trade-oriented imprint.

Already among the major players in the religious publishing arena, Nelson enjoys its current phase of corporate exuberance. The house bought Here's Life Publishers from Campus Crusade for Christ and expanded its evangelism and discipleship markets.

Titles from Thomas Nelson: *A Thousand Goodbyes* by Jim Huber; *Edge of the Wilderness: A Novel* by Stephanie Grace Whitson; *Forever Ruined for the Ordinary* by Joy Dawson; *The One: A Realistic Guide to Choosing Your Soul Mate* by Ben Young; *What If Jesus Had Never Been Born?* by D. James Kennedy; *Attack on America: New York, Jerusalem, and the Role of Terrorism in the Last Days* by John Hagee; *The Blood of the Moon: Understanding the Historic Struggle Between Islam and Western Civilization* by George Grant; *Trust and Tragedy: Encountering God in Times of Crisis* by Tommy Tenney; *When Tragedy Strikes* by Dr. Charles Stanley; *The Red Sea Rules* by Robert J. Morgan; *Let Love Change Your Life: Growing in Intimacy, Growing in Love* by Becky Tirabassi; *Islam Revealed: A Christian Arab's View of Islam* by Anis Shorrosh; *Financially Secure: An Easy-to-Follow Money Program for Women* by Deborah McNaughton; *Heart of the Sandhills: A Novel* by Stephanie Grace Whitson; *He Came First: Following Christ to Spiritual Breakthrough* by Rod Parsley.

Bestsellers from Thomas Nelson: *The 17 Indisputable Laws of Teamwork* and *The 17 Essential Qualities of a Team Player* by John C. Maxwell; *Beside Still Waters: A Devotional* by Thomas Kinkade; *Falling Forward: How to Make the Most Out of Your Mistakes* by John C. Maxwell; *How to Live Through a Bad Day: Seven Powerful Insights from Christ's Words on the Cross* by Jack Hayford; *Into His Presence: An In Touch Devotional* by Dr. Charles Stanley; *Kingdom Come: A Novel* by Larry Burkett; *Lord, I Want to Be Whole: The Power of Prayer and Scripture in Emotional Healing* by Stormie Omartian; *On the Brink: Breaking Through Every Obstacle into the Glory of God* by Rod Parsley; *The God Catchers: Experiencing the Manifest Presence of God* by Tommy Tenney; *Under Cover: The Key to Living in God's Provision and Protection* by John Bevere.

Thomas Nelson Publishers does not accept unsolicited query letters, proposals, or manuscripts.

Tommy Nelson

Tommy Nelson is a children's publishing division geared toward the youngest readers up through young adults. Launched as the new home for the highly successful Word Kids! and Nelson Jr. product lines, the Tommy Nelson list features such bestselling authors as Max Lucado, Frank Peretti, and Bill Myers. Tommy Nelson is particularly strong in fiction and novelty items. Series include the Itty Bitty Books line.

Nelson also issues a line of titles for young readers (currently accenting the Tommy Nelson division). The house offers a strong, select list of adult and young-adult fiction. Thomas Nelson produces magazines and journals and is among the largest publishers of Bibles and scriptural commentary in the United States. Nelson addresses the growing Christian Spanish readership in the United States and abroad through its Editorial Caribe and Editorial Betania divisions (both acquired in 1994). Thomas Nelson also owns the editorially independent Word Publishing (see separate main entry in this directory). The overall corporate banner for the various divisions in this enterprise is Nelson Word Publishing Group.

Thomas Nelson's publishing philosophy: To grow through fairness and integrity in distinctive service to all. Thomas Nelson's purpose: To publish, produce, and market products that honor God and serve humanity and to enhance shareholder value.

Representative titles: *The Crippled Lamb* by Max Lucado; *The Legend of Annie Murphy* by Frank Peretti; *The Parable of the Sunflower* by Liz Curtis Biggs; *Whose Eyes Are These?* by Elizabeth Burman; *Cyber: The Pharaoh's Tomb* by Sigmund Brouwer; *God Loves You* (a pop-up book) by Vlasta Van Kempen.

Thomas Nelson handles its own distribution. Query letters and SASEs should be directed to:

Laura Minchew, Editor for Tommy Nelson

NEWCASTLE PUBLISHING COMPANY

Newcastle Publishing Company has been purchased by Career Press.

NEW LEAF PRESS

Master Books

PO Box 726, Green Forest, AR 72638
870-438-5288   fax: 870-438-5120
e-mail: nlp@newleafpress.net.

Areas of New Leaf publishing include Christian living, prophecy and eschatology, theology, applied Christianity, bible study, family/home/marriage, friendship and love, education, evangelism, devotional works (including daily readings), and humor. Master Books is the house's imprint for its children's, as well as creation science, titles. The house has a solid backlist.

New Leaf Press (founded in 1975) publishes primarily for the Christian religious market, with some trade religious crossover titles. New Leaf produces in hardcover and paperback (trade paper and mass-market); many New Leaf books are priced economically.

On the New Leaf list: *First Comes Love, Then Comes Money* by Roger Gibson; *First Thing Monday Morning* by Dianna Booher; *Reasons for Believing: A Seeker's Guide to Christianity* by Frank Harper; *Recapturing Your Dreams* by David Shibley; *Bible Comes Alive,* Volume 2, by Drs. Clifford and Barbara Wilson; *The Fragrance of Christmas* by Dan and Dave Davidson; *A Cup of Devotion with God* by Dan and David Davidson; *Success Without Guilt* by Robert Strand; *When Hollywood Says Yes, How Can America Say No?* by Gene Wolfenbarger; *Alike in Love: When Opposites Attract* by Tim and Beverly LaHaye; *The Pursuit of Beauty* by Katie Luce; *Wounded Soldier* by John Steer; *Swept Away* by Ron Auch.

Master titles: *Buried Alive* by Dr. Jack Cuozzo; *The Great Alaskan Dinosaur Adventure* by Buddy Davis, Mike Liston, and John Whitmore; *Darwin's Enigma: Ebbing the Tide of Naturalism* by Luther Sunderland; *Fossils Facts & Fantasies* by Joe Taylor; *Bombus Finds a Friend* and *A Bombus Creativity Book* by Elsie Larson and Elizabeth Haidle; *Skeletons in Your Closet* by Dr. Gary Parker; *The Great Dinosaur Mystery Solved!* by Ken Ham; *That Their Words May Be Used Against Them* by Henry Morris.

New Leaf Press distributes its own list; New Leaf also provides distribution services for other publishers with related market outlooks. Query letters and SASEs should be directed to:

Roger Howerton, Acquisitions

Onjinjinkta Publishing

909 SE Everett Mall Way A120, Everett, WA 98208
fax: 425-290-7789
www.onjinjinkta.com

Onjinjinkta Publishing has ceased acquiring new titles.

Paulist Press, Inc.

997 Macarthur Boulevard, Mahwah, NJ 07430
201-825-7300   fax: 201-825-6921
www.paulistpress.com   e-mail: info@paulistpress.com

Paulist Press publishes Roman Catholic as well as ecumenical titles in bible study, biography, women's studies, spirituality, current issues, self-help and personal growth, Catholicism, liturgy, theology, philosophy, ethics, Jewish–Christian relations, world religions, youth ministry, and education. The Paulist list ranges from popularly oriented traditionalist works to provocative frontiers of religious thought. In addition to books, Paulist offers a multimedia line.

Titles from Paulist Press include *The 10 Commandments: Words of Wisdom from the Bible,* retold by Lois Rock; *A Lighthearted View of Wisdom in the Bible: How to Read Inspired Books* by James A. Fischer; *Abraham Miguel Cardozo: Selected Writings,* translated and introduced by David J. Halperin, preface by Elliot R. Wolfson; *Anglo-Saxon Spirituality: Selected Writings,* translated and introduced by Robert Boenig; *C. S. Lewis: Creator of Narnia* by Elaine Murray Stone; *Circling the Center: One Woman's Encounter with Silent Prayer* by Susan M. Tiberghien; *Confronting the Truth: Conscience in the Catholic Tradition* by Linda Hogan; *Journey of the Spirit: Meditations for the Spiritual Seeker* by Trevor Hudson with Morton Kelsey; *Living Catholicism* by Roderick Strange; *Living the Hospitality of God* by Lucien Richard; *The Myth of More and Other Lifetraps That Sabotage the Happiness You Deserve* by Joseph R. Novello; *Pilgrim Journey: John Henry Newman 1801–1845* by Vincent Ferrer Blehl.

Query letters and SASEs should be directed to:

Rev. Lawrence Boadt, CSP, Editorial Director

Susan Heyboer O'Keefe, C.S.P., Children's Book Editor

P

THE PILGRIM PRESS

See also: United Church Press
700 Prospect Avenue, East Cleveland, OH 44115-1100
216-736-3764   fax: 216-736- 2207
www.pilgrimpress.com   e-mail: pilgrim@ucc.org

Pilgrim Press is a Christian-related imprint that focuses on three areas: theological ethics (including science, technology, and medicine); human identity, relationships, and sexuality (including feminist and gay/lesbian issues); and activist spirituality (having a social dimension).

Pilgrim Press (begun in 1608 and established in the United States in 1895) is the book-publishing banner of the publishing wing of the United Church of Christ. United Church Press is a Pilgrim imprint geared primarily toward the inspirational readership.

Pilgrim's trade motto: Books at the Nexus of Religion and Culture.

The house has a tradition of publishing books and other resources that challenge, encourage, and inspire, crafted in accordance with fine standards of content, design, and production.

Indicative of the Pilgrim list: *Amistad: The Slave Uprising Aboard the Spanish Schooner* by Helen Kromer; *Celebrating Her: Feminist Ritualizing Comes of Age* by Wendy Hunter Roberts; *Crossing the Soul's River: A Rite of Passage for Men* by William O. Roberts, Jr.; *Now That You're Out of the Closet, What About the Rest of the House?* by Linda Handel; *Forgiving Our Grownup Children* by Dwight Lee Wolter; *Prayers for the Common Good* by A. Jean Lesher; *Just Peacemaking: Ten Practices for Abolishing War* by Glen Stassen; *Meditations on the Way of the Cross* by Mother Teresa of Calcutta and Brother Roger of Taize; *The Wealth or Health of Nations: Transforming Capitalism from Within* by Carol Johnston; *Sacred Texts and Authority* by Jacob Neusner; *The Great Commandment: A Theology of Resistance and Transformation* by Eleanor H. Haney.

The Pilgrim Library of World Religions is a series designed for both classroom and general use, written by authorities in each tradition. The series addresses how five great world religions—Judaism, Hinduism, Buddhism, Islam, and Christianity—approach a certain critical issue. Titles include *God* (edited by Jacob Neusner). Projected titles include *Evil and Suffering; Women and Families; Death and the Afterlife; Sacred Texts and Authority.* A representative title from Pilgrim Library of Ethics: *Abortion: A Reader* (edited by Jacob Neusner).

The Pilgrim Press oversees its own distribution. Query letters and SASEs should be directed to:

Timothy Staveteig, Publisher

PRESBYTERIAN PUBLISHING CORPORATION

100 Witherspoon Street, Louisville, KY 40202
502-569-5060   fax: 502-569-5113
www.pcusa.org/ppc/

The Presbyterian Publishing Corporation, denominational publisher of the Presbyterian Church (USA), publishes under the imprints Westminster/John Knox Press (see separate listing) and Geneva Press. PPC's three primary objectives are: (1) To develop and publish high-quality, useful resources for congregations, both within the PC (USA) and ecumenically; (2) To expand the scope of the Westminster/John Knox Press academic publishing program in order to better facilitate the training of clergy and scholars; and (3) To publish books for lay and general readers that "contribute to the broader conversation about religion, society, and moral values."

With a publishing heritage that dates back over 160 years, PPC publishes more than 100 new works each year, while maintaining a backlist of more than 1,000 titles sold around the world. PPC, located in Louisville, Kentucky, and with offices in the United Kingdom and the Netherlands, characterizes its publishing program with the theme "Challenging the Mind, Nourishing the Soul."

Query letters and SASEs should be directed to:

Angela Jackson, Editor

RED WHEEL/WEISER BOOKS

PO Box 612, York Beach, ME 03910-0612
207-363-4393   fax: 207-363-5799
e-mail: weiser@weiserbooks.com

See entry under U.S. Publishers.

REGAL BOOKS

See Gospel Light Publications.

ST. ANTHONY MESSENGER PRESS AND FRANCISCAN COMMUNICATIONS

28 West Liberty Street, Cincinnati, OH 45210
513-241-5615   fax: 513-241-1197
www.AmericanCatholic.org

Areas of St. Anthony Messenger publishing interest include Franciscan topics, Catholic identity, family life, morality and ethics, parish ministry, pastoral ministry, prayer helps, sacraments, saints and Christian heroes, scripture, seasonal favorites, small-group resources, spirituality for every day, children's books, and youth ministry. The house produces books (hardcover and paperback, many in economically priced editions), magazines, audiotapes, and videocassettes, as well as educational programs and an award-winning Web site.

St. Anthony Messenger Press (founded in 1970) and Franciscan Communications publishes Catholic religious works and resources for parishes, schools, and individuals. The house also owns the video/print imprints Ikonographics and Fischer Productions.

Titles: *A Retreat with John the Evangelist: That You May Have Life* by Raymond E. Brown, S.S.; *A Retreat with Mark: Embracing Discipleship* by Stephen C. Doyle, O.F.M.; *Living God's Word: Reflections on the Weekly Gospels: Cycle A* by David Knight; *Thresholds to Prayer* by Kathy Coffey; *Jesus of the Gospels: Teacher, Storyteller, Friend, Messiah* by Arthur E. Zannoni; *Jesus' Plan for a New World: The Sermon on the Mount* by Richard Rohr, O.F.M., with John Bookser Feister; *Following Francis of Assisi: A Spirituality for Daily Living* by Patti Normile; *Journeys into Matthew: 18 Lessons of Exploration and Discovery* by Raymond Apicella; *Marriage and the Spirituality of Intimacy* by Leif Kehrwald; *God Is Close to the Brokenhearted: Good News for Those Who Are Depressed* by Rachael Callahan, C.S.C., and Rea McDonnell, S.S.N.D.; *Harvest Us Home: Good News As We Age* by Rachel Callahan, C.S.C., and Rea McDonnell, S.S.N.D.; *The Blessing Candles: 58 Simple Mealtime Prayer-Celebrations* by Gaynell Bordes Cronin and Jack Rathschmidt, *Thomas Merton's Paradise Journey: Writings on Contemplation* by William H. Shannon; *The Lay Contemplative: Testimonies, Perspectives, Resources* (edited by Virginia Manss and Mary Frolich); *Twelve Tough Issues: What the Church*

Teaches—And Why by Archbishop Daniel E. Pilarczyk; *The Sun and Moon over Assisi: A Personal Encounter with Francis and Clare* by Gerard Thomas Straub; *Can You Find Jesus? Introducing Your Child to the Old Testament* and *Can You Find Followers? Introducing Your Child to Disciples* by Philip D. Gallery and Janet L. Harlow; *Mary's Flowers: Gardens, Legends and Meditations* by Vincenzina Krymow.

A special St. Anthony Messenger Press project is A Retreat with . . . , a series that features the words of such historical figures as Thomas Merton, Gerard Manley Hopkins, and Hildegard of Bingen. Did you ever wonder what it would be like to make a retreat with some great holy person from history? Authors weave the mentor's own words into seven days of prayer, dialogue, and deepening acquaintance. Selected titles: *A Retreat with Edith Stein: Trusting God's Purpose* by Patricia L. Marks; *A Retreat with Pope John XXIII: Opening the Windows to Wisdom* by Alfred McBride, O. Praem.; *A Retreat with Francis de Sales, Jane de Chantal and Aelred of Rievaulx: Befriending Each Other in God* by Wendy M. Wright; *A Retreat with Francis and Clare of Assisi: Following Our Pilgrim Hearts* by Murray Bodo, O.F.M., and Susan Saint Sing; *A Retreat with Thomas Merton: Becoming Who We Are* by Dr. Anthony T. Padovano.

St. Anthony Messenger Press also offers music CDs, computer software, videos, and audiocassettes.

St. Anthony Messenger Press distributes books through Ingram, Spring Arbor, Riverside Distributors, Appalachian Inc., Baker & Taylor, and ABS/Guardian. Query letters and SASEs should be directed to:

Lisa Biedenbach, Managing Editor

S

SHAMBHALA PUBLICATIONS

PO Box 308, Boston, MA 02117
617-424-0030   fax: 617-236-1563
www.shambhala.com   e-mail: editors@shambhala.com

Shambhala publishes hardcover and paperback titles in creativity, philosophy, psychology, medical arts and healing, mythology, folklore, religion, art, literature, cooking, martial arts, and cultural studies. Shambhala generally issues a modest list of new titles each year and tends a flourishing backlist; the house periodically updates some of its perennial sellers in revised editions.

The house packages a number of distinct lines, including gift editions and special-interest imprints. Shambhala Dragon Editions accents the sacred teachings of Asian masters. Shambhala Centaur Editions offers classics of world literature in small-sized gift editions. The New Science Library concentrates on titles relating to science, technology, and the environment. Shambhala copublishes C. G. Jung Foundation Books with the C. G. Jung Foundation for Analytical Psychology. Shambhala Redstone Editions are fine-boxed sets composed of books, postcards, games, art objects, and foldouts. Shambhala Lion Editions are spoken-word audiotape cassette presentations.

Shambhala Publications is a foremost representative of the wave of publishers specializing in the arena of contemporary globalized spiritual and cultural interest. Since Shambhala's inception (the house was founded in 1969), the field has blossomed into a still-burgeoning readership, as underscored by the many smaller independent presses and large corporate houses that tend this market.

Titles from Shambhala: *Buddha of Infinite Light* by D. T. Suzuki; *Imagery in Healing: Shamanism and Modern Medicine* by Jeanne Acherberg; *Lady of the Lotus-Born: The Life and Enlightenment of Yeshe Tsogyal* by Gyalwa Changchub and Namkhai Nyingpo (translated by Padmakara Translation Group); *Lightning at the Gate: A Visionary Journey of Healing* by Jeanne Achterberg; *The Myth of Freedom and the Way of Meditation* by Chogyam Trungpa; *Toward a Psychology of Awakening: Buddhism, Psychotherapy, and the Path of Personal and Spiritual Transformation* by John Welwood; *Twilight Goddess: Spiritual Feminism and Feminine Spirituality* by Thomas Cleary and Sartaz Aziz; *Being Zen: Bringing Meditation to Life* by Ezra Bayda; *The Five Wisdom Energies: A Buddhist Way of Understanding Personality, Emotions, and Relationships* by Irini Rockwell; *Infinite Circle: Teachings in Zen* by Bernie Glassman; *Spacecruiser Inquiry: True Guidance for the Inner Journey* by A. H. Almaas; *Turning Suffering Inside Out: Buddhist Wisdom for Living with Physical and Emotional Pain* by Darlene Cohen.

Shambhala distributes to the trade via Random House. Shambhala services individual and special orders through its own house fulfillment department. Query letters and SASEs should be directed to:

Peter Turner, President and Executive Editor

Sam Bercholz, Chairman and Editor in Chief

Mai Shaikhanuar-Cota, Managing Editor

Emily Hilburn-Sell, Senior Editor

Kendra Crossen Burroughs, Editor

Joel Segel, Associate Editor

Emily Bower, Editor

Eden Steinberg, Associate Editor

Beth Frankl, Associate Editor

Kerrie-Beth Mello, Production Editor

Jael Riordan, Editorial Assistant

S

SIGNATURE BOOKS

564 West 400 North Street, Salt Lake City, UT 84116-3411
801-531-1483   fax: 801-531-1488

The Signature list emphasizes contemporary literature, as well as scholarly works relevant to the Intermountain West. Signature Books (established in 1981) publishes subjects that range from outlaw biographies and Mormonism to speculative theology, from demographics to humor. In addition to a wide range of nonfiction, Signature publishes novels and collections of poetry. The common objective of the selections on Signature's roster is to provide alternatives to the institutional agendas that underlie many of the publications in the region.

Indicative of Signature nonfiction: *Salamander: The Story of the Mormon Forgery Murders* by Linda Sillitoe and Allen Roberts (George J. Throckmorton, forensic analysis); *Remembering Brad: On the Loss of a Son to AIDS* by H. Wayne Schow; *The Sanctity of Dissent* by Paul James Toscano; *Waiting for the World's End: The Diaries of Wilford Woodruff* (edited by Susan Staker); *A Sculptor's Testimony in Bronze and Stone: Sacred Sculpture of Avard T. Fairbanks; "Wild Bill" Hickman and the Mormon Frontier* by Hope A. Hilton.

Representative of Signature fiction and popular literature: *Aspen Marooney* by Levi S. Peterson; *The Backslider* by Levi S. Peterson; *Beyond the River: A Novel* by Michael Fillerup; *Bright Angels and Familiars: Contemporary Mormon Stories* (edited by Eugene England); *Canyon Interludes: Between White Water and Red Rock* by Paul W. Rea; *An Environment for Murder* by Rod Decker; *Imagination Comes to Breakfast: Poems* by Kathy Evans; *Love Chains: Stories* by Margaret Blair Young; *My New Life* by Ron Molen; *Secrets Keep: A Novel* by Linda Sillitoe; *Stone Spirits: Poems* by Susan Elizabeth Howe; *Washed by a Wave of Wind: Science Fiction from the Corridor* (edited by M. Shayne Bell); *The Tabernacle Bar* (novel) by Susan Plamer; *The Way We Live: Stories by Utah Women* (edited by Ellen Fagg); *No Man Knows My Pastries: The Secret (Not Sacred) Recipes of Sister Enid Christensen; Marketing Precedes the Miracle: More Cartoons* by Calvin Grondahl.

Signature Publications oversees distribution of its titles via in-house ordering services and a national network of wholesalers. Signature Books does not accept unsolicited manuscripts. Query letters and SASEs should be directed to:

Ron Priddcs, Director

T

TYNDALE HOUSE PUBLISHERS

351 Executive Drive, Carol Stream, IL 60188
630-668-8300   fax: 630-668-3245
www.tyndale.com

Tyndale offers a comprehensive program in Christian living (devotional, inspirational, and general nonfiction, from a nondenominational evangelical perspective). The house publishes the bestselling LEFT BEHIND series. Tyndale's publishing interest also encompasses religious fiction. The house offers a strong line of bibles. Tyndale House Publishers (founded in 1962) produces hardcover, trade paperback, and mass-market paperback originals, as well as reprints. Tyndale also catalogs audio and video products.

New titles from Tyndale: *130 Questions Children Ask About War and Terrorists* by Stephen Arterburn and David Stoop; *How to Study the Bible and Enjoy It* by Skip Heitzig; *Loving Your Body* by Deborah Newman; *Mama Says . . . Cookies Cure a Lot of*

Things by Rita Maggart; *The Never Alone Church* by David Ferguson; *No Fear Guide for First Time Parents* by Focus; *The No-Brainer's Guide to How Christians Live* and *The No-Brainer's Guide to What Christians Believe* by Stan Campbell and James S. Bell, Jr.; *Protecting Your Child in an X-rated World* by Frank York and Jan LaRue; *Rag Baby* by Karyn Henley; *Sacred Journeys* by Wendy Murray Zoba; *Why Believe?* by Greg Laurie; *Why You Can't Stay Silent* by Tom Minnery; *First Century Diaries: The Gaius Diary* by Gene Edwards; *Heart to Heart Series: Heart to Heart Stories for Sisters* by Joe Wheeler.

In a publishing partnership with the American Association of Christian Counselors, Tyndale offers books written by leading Christian counselors that integrate counseling principles and biblical theology as they offer authoritative analysis and research for the Professional Counseling Library. Titles: *Counseling Children Through the World of Play* by Daniel Sweeney, Ph.D.; *Psychology, Theology, and Spirituality in Christian Counseling* by Mark R. McMinn; *Counseling Through the Maze of Divorce* by George Ohlschlager; *Treating Sex Offenders* by Daniel Henderson; *Brief Counseling* by Gary J. Oliver; *Treating Victims of Sexual Abuse* by Diane Langberg.

Tyndale fiction includes mainstream novels, as well as a number of inspirational romance series, including works set in Revolutionary War and Civil War milieus. The house is interested in evangelical Christian-theme romance in other historical periods (including Regency), as well as those with a humorous twist.

Tyndale fiction list: *Looking for Cassandra Jane* by Melody Carison; *They Shall See God* by Athol Dickson; *Heartquest: English Ivy* by Catherine Palmer.

The Tyndale program of books for children and young adults is in a transitional phase; currently, the house is not interested in fiction geared for this younger age group.

Tyndale House oversees its own distribution. Tyndale also distributes books from Focus on the Family. Tyndale does not accept unsolicited manuscripts. For manuscript submissions, send SASE to the Manuscript Review Committee, requesting a copy of the committee's writers' guidelines—and query first. Query letters and SASEs should be directed to:

Ginny Williams—Children's and gift

Linda Washington—Adult nonfiction and fiction

Jan Stob—Adult fiction

Anne Goldsmith—Women's fiction and romance

U

Union of American Hebrew Congregations/UAHC Press

Union of American Hebrew Congregations, 633 Third Avenue,
  New York, NY 10017-6778
212-650-4121   fax: 212-650-4119
http://uahcpress.com   e-mail: press@uahc.org

Union of American Hebrew Congregations/UAHC Press publishes in the areas of religion (Jewish), Reform Judaism, textbooks, audiovisual materials, social action, biography, and life cycles and holidays. In trade categories, UAHC Press accents juvenile fiction and adult nonfiction books, as well as titles in basic Judaism and inspirational works. The house catalogs books, audiocassettes, videotapes, and multimedia products.

The UAHC Press provides the highest quality in religious educational materials and has done so for well over 100 years. The publications of the press are suitable for all ages, from preschool through adult, for use in both the classroom and at home. The publishers are committed to providing their readers with the foremost in materials and service, to be a continuing resource for books, publications, audiocassettes, videotapes, and multimedia.

Founded in 1873, UAHC Press is a division of Union of American Hebrew Congregations. The UAHC Press publishing program includes the *Reform Judaism* magazine.

Indicative of UAHC Press interest: *The Torah: A Modern Commentary* (edited by W. Gunther Plaut); *The Book of Genesis* by W. Gunther Plaut and Chaim Stern; *Meeting at the Well: A Jewish Spiritual Guide to Engagement* by Daniel Judson and Nancy Wiener; *Mishlei: A Modern Commentary on Proverbs* (edited and translated by Leonard S. Kravitz and Kenny M. Olizky); *Heads and Tales: Stories of the Sages to Enlighten Our Minds* by Edwin Goldberg; *Aleph Isn't Enough* by Linda Motzkin; *The Art of Cantillation, Volume 2: A Step-by-Step Guide to Chanting Haftarot and M'gilot* by Marshall Portnoy and Josee Wolff; *The High Holy Days* by Camille Kress; *Finding God: Selected Responses (Revised Edition)* by Rifat Sonsino and Daniel B. Syme; *Jewish U: A Contemporary Guide for the Jewish College Student* by Scott Aaron; *Repairing Our World from the Inside Out: An Adult Ethics Program Packet* by Michelle Shapiro Abraham.

Children's titles from UAHC: *Good Night, Lilah Tov* by Michelle Shapiro Abraham; *The High Holy Days* by Camille Kress; *Good Morning Boker Tov* by Michelle Shapiro Abraham; *Night Lights: A Sukkot Story* by Barbara Kiamond Goldin; *Holy Days, Holy Ways* by Sharon D. Halper; *The Atlas of Great Jewish Communities: Voyage Through Jewish History* by Sandra Leiman; *The Gift of Wisdom* by Steven E. Steinback;

UAHC Press handles its own distribution. Query letters and SASEs should be directed to:

Kenneth Gesser, Publisher

Rabbi Hara Person, Editor

VEDANTA PRESS

Vedanta Society of Southern California, 1946 Vedanta Place, Hollywood, CA 90068
323-960-1736
www.vedanta.com   e-mail: info@vedanta.com

Vedanta's publishing interest includes meditation, religions and philosophies, and women's studies. In addition to its list of titles imported from the East (primarily from Indian publishers), Vedanta's program embraces works of Western origin. The publisher catalogs titles from other publishers and also sells audiotapes and videotapes.

The house publishes books on the philosophy of Vedanta, with an aim to engage a wide variety of temperaments, using a broad spectrum of methods, in order to attain the realization of each individual personality's divinity within. Vedanta Press (founded in 1947) is a subsidiary of the Vedanta Society of Southern California.

Backlist from the press: *How to Know God: The Yoga Aphorisms of Patanjali* (translated by Swami Prabhavananda and Christopher Isherwood); *The Upanishads: Breath of the Eternal* (translated by Swami Prabhavananda and Frederick Manchester); *Women Saints: East and West* (edited by Swami Ghanananda and Sir John Stewart-Wallace); *The Sermon on the Mount According to Vedanta* by Swami Prabhavananda; *Seeing God Everywhere: A Practical Guide to Spiritual Living* by Swami Shraddhananda; *Six Lighted Windows: Memories of Swamis in the West* by Swami Yogeshananda. Vedanta publishes many classic Vedic works in a variety of editions and translations. Among them: *Bhagavad Gita: The Song of God* (translated by Swami Prabhavananda and Christopher Isherwood, introduction by Aldous Huxley).

Vedanta Press handles its own distribution.

Vedanta's books originate in house, though the publisher is open to considering additional projects that may fall within its program. Vedanta does not wish to receive unsolicited manuscripts. Before you submit a query letter, be sure your book is within their niche. They don't do personal spiritual biographies and subjects outside the Vedanta tradition. Please do your research before writing to them or, for that matter, any publisher. Query letters and SASEs should be directed to:

Bob Adjemian, Manager

WESTMINSTER/JOHN KNOX PRESS

Presbyterian Church (USA), 100 Witherspoon Street, Louisville, KY 40202-1396
502-569-5060   fax: 502-569-5113
www.wjkacademic.com

Westminster/John Knox publishes general-interest religious trade books, as well as academic and professional works in biblical studies, theology, philosophy, ethics, history, archaeology, personal growth, and pastoral counseling. Among Westminster/John Knox series are Literary Currents in Biblical Interpretation, Family Living in Pastoral Perspective, Gender and the Biblical Tradition, and the Presbyterian Presence: The Twentieth-Century Experience.

Westminster/John Knox Press represents the publications unit of the Presbyterian Church (USA). The house unites the former independents Westminster Press and John Knox Press, which were originally founded as one entity in 1838, then separated into distinct enterprises, and again merged as WJK following the reunion of the Northern and Southern Presbyterian Churches in 1983.

Selected titles from Westminster/John Knox: *Dark the Night, Wild the Sea* by Robert McAfee Brown; *Speaking the Truth in Love: Prophetic Preaching to a Broken World* by J. Philip Wogaman; *Our Testament Wisdom: An Introduction* (revised and enlarged) by James L. Crenshaw; *Theology of the Prophetic Books: The Death and Resurrection of Israel* by Donald E. Gowan; *Honor and Shame in the Gospel of Matthew* by Jerome H.

W

Neyrey; *Jesus as a Figure in History: How Modern Historians View the Man from Galilee* by Mark Allan Powell; *Athena's Disguises: Mentors in Everyday Life* by Susan Ford Wiltshire; *Both Feet Planted in Midair: My Spiritual Journey* by John McNeill; *Equipping the Saints: Teacher Training in the Church* by Sara Covin Juengst; *Survival or Revival: Ten Keys to Church Vitality* by Carnegie Samuel Calian; *We Have Seen the Lord!: The Passion and Resurrection of Jesus Christ* by William Barclay.

WJK's Studies in the Family, Religion, & Culture series offers informed and responsible analyses of the state of the American family from a religious perspective and provides practical assistance for the family's revitalization. Titles: *For the Love of Children: Genetic Technology and the Future of the Family* by Ted Peters; *Religion, Feminism, and the Family* (edited by Anne Carr and Mary Steward Van Leeuwen); *Faith Traditions and the Family* (edited by Phyllis D. Airhart and Margaret Lamberts Bendroth).

Westminster/John Knox distributes its list through Spring Arbor. The house also represents titles from other publishers, including Orbis Books, Pilgrim Press, Saint Andrew Press of Scotland, and Presbyterian Publishing Corporation.

Query letters and SASEs should be directed to:

Angela Jackson, Assistant Editor

WISDOM PUBLICATIONS

199 Elm Street, Somerville, MA 02144
617-776-7416   fax: 617-776-7841
www.wisdompubs.org   e-mail: info@wisdompubs.org

Wisdom Publications, a not-for-profit publisher, is dedicated to making available authentic Buddhist works for the benefit of all. The house publishes translations of the sutras and tantras, commentaries and teachings of past and contemporary Buddhist masters, and original works by the world's leading Buddhist scholars. Wisdom Publications was named one of the top 10 fastest-growing small publishers in the country (the company has been in the United States since 1989) by *Publishers Weekly* (November 18, 1996).

Wisdom titles are published in appreciation of Buddhism as a living philosophy and with the commitment to preserve and transmit important works from all the major Buddhist traditions. Wisdom products are distributed worldwide and have been translated into a dozen foreign languages.

Wisdom publishes the celebrated Tibetan Art Calendar, containing 13 full-color reproductions of the world's finest Indo-Tibetan thangka paintings, accompanied by detailed iconographical descriptions.

Wisdom highlight: *The Good Heart: A Buddhist Perspective on the Teachings of Jesus* by the Dalai Lama (introduced by Fr. Laurence Freeman).

Wisdom Publications is distributed to the trade in the United States and Canada by National Book Network (NBN). Query letters and SASEs should be directed to:

Timothy J. McNeill, Publisher

WORD PUBLISHING

Word Publishing is now an imprint of Thomas Nelson.

ZONDERVAN PUBLISHING HOUSE

5300 Patterson Avenue SE, Grand Rapids, MI 49530
616-698-6900   fax: 616-698-3454
www.zondervan.com

Zondervan Publishing House (founded in 1931) became a division of HarperCollins in 1988. Zondervan publishes both fiction and nonfiction books that have a strong emphasis in Christianity. Zondervan is the number one publisher worldwide of the bible and has held at least 5 (and as many as 10) out of the top 10 positions on the Christian Booksellers bestseller lists since 1995.

Although Zondervan specializes in publishing bibles and books, the house also produces a wide variety of resources, including audio books, eBooks, videos, CD-ROMs, and inspirational gifts. Zondervan has six primary product-group departments. These include: Bibles; Books; New Media, which publishes electronic format books, bibles, and software products; Zonderkidz; Inspirio; and Vida Publishers, Zondervan's multilingual publishing and distribution unit.

In 2000, Zondervan released the industry's first two e-Books, including the first Christian book published exclusively in electronic format, Leonard Sweet's *The Dawn Mistaken for Dusk.* Also in 2000, Zondervan launched its gift program, Inspirio, specializing in inspirational gift products.

Zonderkidz was formed in 1998 to represent the children's and juvenile division at Zondervan. Zonderkidz is now the leading publisher of children's bibles, children's Christian books, and other related products.

As the world's largest bible publisher, Zondervan holds exclusive publishing rights to the New International Version of the bible—the most popular translation of the bible—and has distributed more than 150 million copies worldwide. Zondervan publishes approximately 50 bible products, 150 books, 80 gifts, and 50 new media products each year.

Bestsellers from Zondervan include: *The Case for Christ* and *The Case for Faith* by Lee Strobel; *Emerald Windows* by Terri Blackstock; *He's Been Faithful* by Carol Cymbala; *How People Grow* by Dr. Henry Cloud and Dr. John Townsend; *If You Want to Walk on Water, You've Got to Get Out of the Boat* by John Ortberg; *The Life God Blesses* by Jim Cymbala, Stephen Sorenson, and Amanda Sorenson; *Mere Christianity* by C. S. Lewis; *Streams in the Desert* by James Reimann; *The Strongest Strong's Exhaustive Concordance* by James Strong, John R. Kohlenberger, and James A. Swanson; *Women of the Bible* by Jean Syswenda.

Zondervan distributes its own titles to the general market, the book trade, and the CBA. Zondervan asks that interested authors write to request submissions guidelines before submitting manuscripts or other material.

Canadian Publishers

Canadian Book Publishing and the Canadian Market

GREG IOANNOU

Canadian and U.S. writers who consider submitting inquiries to Canadian publishers should keep a few important points in mind. In most cases, Canadian book publishers are looking for material of Canadian interest. However, this does not mean they are not interested in queries from writers who reside in or are native to other countries.

Indeed, a rich current in the Canadian publishing stream features the Canadian experience from outlander or expatriate perspectives. Canadian reader interests are also keyed into a number of broader market sectors, such as North American pop culture or British Commonwealth concerns.

Appropriate queries (see the listings for these publishers) will be considered. Keep in mind the markets, as well as the mandates, of each house.

Publishing in Canada is markedly different from the industry in the United States. A large percentage of Canadian-owned publishing houses are small- to medium-sized, with net sales that may seem low to those accustomed to the standards of the U.S. marketplace. (Remember, the English-language Canadian market is only one-tenth the size of the U.S. market.)

Canada *is* a separate market, and some writers are able to sell the Canadian rights to their books separately from the U.S. rights. Before you sign a contract for "North American rights," consider whether your book would likely sell enough copies in Canada that it would be of interest to a Canadian publisher.

Don't just blithely sell the Canadian rights to a hockey book or a biography of a Canadian celebrity (such as Faye Wray, Neil Young, or Peter Jennings) to a U.S. publisher for the blanket "foreign rights" or "world English-language rights" rate—the Canadian rights alone may be worth more than the U.S. or the rest of the worldwide rights!

The Canadian government directly subsidizes the book industry to help ensure that Canadian writers get their works published domestically and to keep the national market from being overwhelmed by the publishing giants to the south. The government grant system makes possible a greater independence on the part of Canadian-owned houses, which comprise the creative heart of publishing in Canada.

Never send an unsolicited manuscript to a Canadian publisher. Many Canadian publishers will send them back unopened because of a court ruling that forced Doubleday Canada to pay a writer thousands of dollars in compensation for losing the only copy of an unsolicited manuscript. Send query letters only!

It is a nice touch for American writers to remember that Canada is *not* part of the United States, so Canadian publishers cannot use U.S. stamps to return anything you send them. Use International Reply Coupons (available at any post office) instead.

ANVIL PRESS

Correspondence address: MPO Box 3008, Vancouver, BC V63 3X5, Canada
Location: 175 East Broadway, Suite 204-A, Vancouver, BC V5T 1W2, Canada
604-876-8710
www.anvilpress.com

Anvil Press began in 1988 as the publisher for *sub-TERRAIN Magazine*. In 1991, it expanded into the book-publishing field with the mandate to discover and nurture new talent in Canada. It now publishes 8–12 titles a year and sponsors the International Novel Contest every Labour Day long weekend (more information about the contest is available on its Web site: www.anvilpress.com). Although it does occasionally publish nonfiction, Anvil specializes in contemporary literary fiction, poetry, and drama; it does not publish genre fiction.

Recent Anvil titles include *Snatch* by Judy Macinnes Jr.; *Skin* by Bonnie Bauman; and Lyle Neff's book of poetry, *Full MagPie Dodge*.

For fiction/nonfiction submissions, Anvil requests a brief, one-page synopsis of the entire manuscript and 20–30 pages of the manuscript itself. For poetry, 8–12 poems should be submitted. Anvil requests the entire manuscript for works of drama, unless excessively long. Anvil publishes only Canadian authors. Only manuscripts accompanied by an SASE will be considered. Query letters and SASEs should be directed to:

Brian Kaufman, Publisher

BEACH HOLME PUBLISHING

226-2040 West 12th Avenue, Vancouver, BC V6J 2G2, Canada
604-733-4868
www.beachholme.bc.ca

Beach Holme Publishing, so-named in honor of the owner's house, is a small Vancouver publisher with a mandate "to promote indigenous creative writing to the wider Canadian public." Its literary roots began with its former incarnation, Press Porcepic, which published such renowned authors as Dorothy Livesay and James Reaney. Porcepic Books continues as an imprint of Beach Holme and has built its own niche in the Canadian literary heritage with newer talents like Evelyn Lau and Jane Urquhart. Novels, plays, poetry, and short fiction are all featured under the Porcepic Books imprint. Beach Holme also publishes young adult fiction (Sandcastle Books).

Titles typical of the list: *What the Small Day Cannot Hold* by Susan Musgrave; *Tiger in Trouble* by Eric Walters; *Viking Quest* by Tom Henighan; *Hail Mary Corner* by Brian Payton; *Cold Clear Morning* by Lesley Choyce; *The Self-Completing Tree* by Dorothy Livesay.

Under its new imprint, Prospect Books, Beach Holme publishes creative nonfiction. Beach Holme Publishing produces only work by Canadian authors resident in Canada; foreign manuscripts will not be considered and should be directed elsewhere. Query letters and SASEs should be directed to:

Michael Carroll, Publisher

CORMORANT BOOKS

RR 1, Dunvegan, ON K0C 1J0, Canada
613-527-3348   fax: 613-527-2262
www.cormorant.com   e-mail: cormorant@glen-net.ca

Cormorant Books publishes a small, select list of literary fiction and trade nonfiction. This small press also produces several works of fiction in translation.

Notables from the Cormorant catalog: *Lives of the Saints* by Nino Ricci; *Kitchen Music* by Charles Foran; *Gaff Topsails* by Patrick Kavanagh; *The Good Body* by Bill Gaston; *Purple Forsky* by Carol Bruneau; *Drowning in Darkness* by Peter Oliva.

Recent nonfiction titles: *Living in the World as If It Were Home* by Tim Lilburn; *A Very Large Soul: Selected Letters from Margaret Laurence to Canadian Writers* (edited by J. A. Wainwright); *Invisible Among the Ruins: Field Notes of a Canadian in Ireland* by John Moss.

Query letters and SASEs should be directed to:

Barbara Glen, Assistant to the Publisher

Jan Geddes, Publisher

COTEAU BOOKS

401, 2206 Dewdney Avenue, Regina, SK S4R 1H3, Canada
306-777-0170   fax: 306-522-5152
www.coteaubooks.com   e-mail: coteau@coteaubooks.com

Coteau Books publishes a range of Canadian works, with a particular focus on the literary genres—novels, short fiction, poetry, drama, and juvenile fiction. Coteau presents an annual list that reflects literary quality across the country, including First Nations authors, with a focus on prairie voices of all kinds. Nonfiction work, especially memoir, is a growing interest as well.

D

Coteau has recently launched a new poetry series called Open Eye, with the intent to feature new, young poetic voices and attract a broad readership to the genre.

The Coteau list features such titles as the international short fiction anthology *Two Lands Two Visions* (edited by Janice Kulyk Keefer and Solomea Pavlychko); Open Eye poetry title *My Flesh the Sound of Rain* by Heather MacLeod; and *The Intrepid Polly McDoodle,* the second in a juvenile novel series by Edmonton author Mary Woodbury.

Recent titles include Governor-General's Award–winner Anne Szumigalski's greatest hits, *On Glassy Wings,* which received the Canadian Authors Association Poetry Prize; Barbara Nickels's first poetry book, *The Gladys Elegies,* which was awarded the Pat Lowther Memorial Prize as the best book of poetry by a woman; and the short fiction collection *In the Misleading Absence of Light* by Regina author Joanne Gerber (which has received five national and provincial awards to date).

Coteau also publishes the annual daybook *Herstory: The Canadian Women's Calendar,* compiled annually by the Saskatoon Women's Calendar Collective.

Queries and SASEs should be directed to:

Nik Burton, Managing Editor, Regina

DOUGLAS & MCINTYRE PUBLISHERS

Douglas & McIntyre Children's Division

Firefly Books

1615 Venables Street, Vancouver, BC V5L 2H1, Canada
604-254-7191

Toronto office:
585 Bloor Street West, 2nd Floor, Toronto, ON M6G 1K5
416-537-2501

Douglas & McIntyre Publishers (founded in 1964) offers a publishing program with Canadian emphasis—often with a specifically British Columbian inflection. The house produces hardcover and paperback books in both fiction and nonfiction. Nonfiction areas of interest include native art, current affairs, history, travel, and nature studies. Douglas & McIntyre fiction tends toward literary works, serious popular fiction, and tales of mystery and suspense.

Nonfiction titles: *Haida Art* by George F. MacDonald; *Cold as Charity: The Truth Behind the High Cost of Giving* by Walter Stewart; *Politically Speaking* by Judy Rebick and Kiké Roach; *HeartSmart Chinese Cooking* by Stephen Wong and the Heart & Stroke Foundation of Canada; *Working Dollars: The VanCity Savings Story* by Herschel Hardin; *Mike Harcourt: A Measure of Defiance* by Michael Harcourt, with Wayne Skene; *The Immortal Beaver: The World's Greatest Bush Plane* by Sean Rossiter; *Bishop's: The Cookbook* by John Bishop; *Back to the Front: An Accidental Historian Walks the Trenches of World War I* by Stephen O'Shea; *Toni Cavelti: A Jeweller's Life* by Max Wyman.

Fiction and literary works: *Bachelor Brothers' Bedside Companion* by Bill Richardson (illustrated by Rose Cowles); *eye wuz here: 30 women writers under 30* (edited by

Shannon Cooley); *The Lesser Blessed* by Richard VanCamp; *Let the Drums Be Your Heart: New Native Voices* (edited by Joel T. Maki); *Local Colour: Writers Discovering Canada* (edited by Carol Martin); *A Story as Sharp as a Knife: An Introduction to Classical Haida Literature* by Robert Bringhurst; *Notes from the Century Before: A Journal from British Columbia* by Edward Hoagland (illustrated by Claire Van Vliet).

The Greystone Books imprint offers travel guides, one-day getaways, regional histories, sports books (especially hockey), and titles in hiking, camping, and outdoor recreation. Representative titles from Greystone: *Cowgirls* by Candace Savage; *British Columbia: A Natural History* by Richard Cannings and Sydney Cannings; *Hockey the NHL Way: The Basics* by Sean Rossiter; *The Nature of Shorebirds: Nomads of the Wetlands* by Harry Thurston; *The Nature of Penguins: Birds of Distinction* by Jonathan Chester; *Orca: Visions of the Killer Whale* by Peter Knudtson; *Courting Saskatchewan: A Celebration of Winter Feasts, Summer Loves and Rising Brooks* by David Carpenter; *Day Trips from Vancouver* by Jack Christie; *Fishing in the West* by David Carpenter; *52 Weekend Activities Around Vancouver* by Sue Lebrecht and Judi Lees.

Douglas & McIntyre handles its own distribution, as well as purveys books from additional houses and institutions, including Canadian Museum of Civilization, the Mountaineers, the New Press, Sierra Club Books, and Thames and Hudson.

Query letters and SASEs should be directed to the **Acquisitions Editor;** correspondence will be redirected in house.

Douglas & McIntyre Children's Division

Within its children's division, Douglas & McIntyre offers several special imprints. Groundwood Press publishes titles for preschoolers through young adults. Earthcare Books is an environmental series for middle-grade readers, which includes *For the Birds,* written by Canadian novelist Margaret Atwood. First Discovery is a series of nature books for toddlers and early readers. Rounding out Douglas & McIntyre's juveniles list are fiction for young adults, picture books, the Walker imprint's nonfiction and picture books (some of which are targeted for appeal to the entire family), and Meadow Mouse paperbacks.

On the list: *So You Love to Draw: Every Kid's Guide to Becoming an Artist* by Michael Seary (illustrated by Michel Bisson); *Jade and Iron: Latin American Tales from Two Cultures* (translated by Hugh Hazelton; edited by Patricia Aldana; illustrated by Luís Garay); *A Completely Different Place* by Perry Nodelman (fiction for ages 10–13); *Mary Margaret's Tree* by Blair Drawson (picture book for ages 3–6); *Beaver the Tailor: A How-to Picture Book* by Lars Klinting (for ages 5–7); *The Rooster's Gift* by Pam Conrad (illustrated by Eric Beddows) (picture book for ages 4–8); *Steel Drums and Ice Skates* by Dirk Mclean (illustrated by Ho Che Anderson) (picture book for ages 6–9); *Sarah and the People of Sand River* by W. D. Valgardson (illustrated by Ian Wallace) (picture book for ages 5–9); *Enchantment in the Garden* by Shirley Hughes (ages 8 and up).

Query letters and SASEs should be directed to the **Acquisitions Editor;** correspondence will be redirected in house. The Toronto office handles fiction and children's books; the rest of the Douglas & McIntyre list is issued from the Vancouver office.

D

Firefly Books

3680 Victoria Park Avenue, Willowdale, ON M2H 3K1, Canada
416-499-8412, 800-387-5085

Firefly produces trade nonfiction in areas that include popular biography, popular science, lifestyles, the natural world, hobbies and crafts, gardening, food, sports, recreation, and health.

Representative of the Firefly list: *All Fired Up! Year Round Grilling and Barbecuing* by John and Margaret Howard; *The Wild Food Gourmet: Fresh and Savory Food from Nature* by Anne Gardon; *Clueless in the Kitchen: A Cookbook for Teens and Other Beginners* by Evelyn Raab; *The Art of Perennial Gardening: Creative Ways with Hardy Flowers* by Patrick Lima (photographs by John Scanlan); *Dry-Land Gardening: A Xeriscaping Guide for Dry-Summer Cold-Winter Climates* by Jennifer Bennett; *Butterflies of the World* by Valerio Sbordoni and Saverio Forestiero; *High Above the Canadian Rockies: Spectacular Aerial Photography* by Russ Heinl; *Restoring Houses of Brick and Stone* by Nigel Hutchins; *Caring for Your Parents in Their Senior Years: A Guide for Grown-Up Children* by William Molloy, M.D.; *Coaching: Winning Strategies for Every Level of Play* by Dave Chambers.

Firefly Books handles its own distribution. Query letters and SASEs should be directed to:

Lionel Koffler, President

FITZHENRY & WHITESIDE LTD.

195 Allstate Parkway, Markham, ON L3R 4T8, Canada
905-477-9700, 800-1387-9776   fax: 905-477-9179, 800-260-9777

Fitzhenry & Whiteside Ltd. (founded in 1966) specializes in trade nonfiction and children's books. The firm also offers a textbook list and a small list of literary/fiction works.

Fitzhenry & Whiteside nonfiction titles range throughout Canadian history, biography, native studies, nature, and antiques and collectibles. The children's book list includes early readers, picture books, and middle-grade and young adult novels. Markets include trade, school, library, professional and reference, college, mail order, and specialty.

From Fitzhenry & Whiteside nonfiction: *Trees in Canada* by John Laird Farrar; *What Time of Day Was That?* by Dale Patterson; *Under Sydenham Skies* by Cornelia Baines; *The Canadian Geographic Quiz Book* by Doug MacLean.

Fitzhenry & Whiteside fiction and literature: *The Poetry of Lucy Maud Montgomery* (edited by Kevin McCabe and Alexandra Heibron); *North with Franklin* by John Wilson; *New Canadian Poetry* (edited by Evan Jones).

On the children's list: *We'll All Go Sailing* by Maggee Spicer and Richard Thompson (illustrated by Kim La Fave); *Number 21* by Nancy Hundal (illustrated by Brian Deines); *The Adventures of Baby Bear* by Aubrey Lang (photographs by Wayne Lynch).

Fitzhenry & Whiteside distributes its own list and provides distribution services in Canada for a number of U.S. publishers.

Query letters and SASEs should be directed to:

Sharon Fitzhenry, President and Publisher

Gail Winskill, Children's Book Publisher

GOOSE LANE EDITIONS

469 King Street, Fredericton, NB E3B 1E5, Canada
506-450-4251   fax: 506-459-4991

Goose Lane Editions is a small Canadian publishing house that specializes in literary fiction, poetry, and a select list of nonfiction titles. It does not publish commercial fiction, genre fiction, or confessional works of any kind. Occasionally, one of its books will appeal to young adults, but it does not publish books specifically for that market, nor does it publish books for children.

Recent Goose Lane titles: *16 Categories of Desire* by Douglas Glover; *The Painted House of Maud Lewis: Conserving a Folk Art Treasure* by Laurie Hamilton; *Frank: The Life and Politics of Frank McKenna* by Philip Lee; *Conversations* by Hermenegilde Chiasson (translated by Jo-Anne Elder and Fred Cogswell).

As a member of the Literary Press group, Goose Lane Editions has a Canada-wide sales force serving the book trade. In addition, the company employs several regional sales representatives to nontraditional outlets such as gift stores. Academic sales are handled by Irwin Publishing. General Distribution Services takes care of order fulfillment.

Goose Lane considers submissions from outside Canada only rarely, and only when both the author and the material have significant Canadian connections and the material is of extraordinarily high interest and literary merit. Writers should submit a synopsis, outline, and sample (30–50 pages) with an SASE if in Canada; international authors should include an SASE and international reply coupons with submission. Please query by mail or phone before submitting; direct queries to:

Laurel Boone, Editorial Director

H

HARLEQUIN ENTERPRISES LIMITED

Worldwide Library

225 Duncan Mill Road, Don Mills, ON M3B 3K9, Canada
416-445-5860

The Harlequin Enterprises home base in Ontario, Canada, issues the greater portion of Harlequin Books series, while the New York office issues several Harlequin series, as well as the Silhouette list (please see listing for Harlequin Books in the directory of United States publishers and editors). Harlequin Enterprises Limited also publishes the Worldwide Library, which accents titles in the mystery/suspense and thriller mode.

Harlequin Books (Canada)

The Harlequin series of romance novels published in Canada, like their American counterparts, each stake out particular market-niche segments of reader interest within the overall categories of romance fiction and women's fiction.

The editorial acquisitions departments for Harlequin Romance and Harlequin Presents are located at the operation's United Kingdom offices (the address for which is listed farther on). Following are overviews of some of the editorial guidelines supplied to authors:

"MIRA Books is dedicated to mainstream single-title women's fiction in hardcover and mass-market paperback editions. MIRA titles assume no particular genre designation, though the works are considered to be of interest to a primarily women's readership. MIRA Books hosts a wide variety of authors and approaches.

"Harlequin Temptation introduces strong, independent heroines and successful, sexy heroes who overcome conflict inherent to their heated relationships and in the end decide to marry. The books in this series are known for their wit, as well as for emotional strength.

"Harlequin Temptations are sensuous romances about choices . . . dilemmas . . . resolutions . . . and, above all, the fulfillment of love. The most highly charged and most sensual Harlequin series.

"Harlequin Superromance is a line of longer, contemporary romance novels. Realistic stories with emotional depth and intensity . . . more involving plots . . . more complex characters. Superromance women are confident and independent, yet eager to share their lives.

"Harlequin Superromances are the longest books of the Harlequin series (approximately 350 manuscript pages) and therefore require a more complex plot and at least one fully developed subplot. This series is generally mainstream in tone, with romance, of course, being the propelling theme. Love scenes may be explicit, so long as they exhibit good taste."

Detailed information is available upon request from the publisher. Harlequin will send prospective authors full editorial guidelines with suggested heroine and hero profiles, as well as information pertaining to manuscript length, setting, and sexual approach and content.

Make sure your query is clear as to which line it is intended for: Harlequin Romance, Harlequin Presents, Harlequin Temptation, Harlequin Superromance, or Harlequin Duets.

Query letters and SASEs should be directed to:

Amy Moore-Benson, Editor, MIRA Books

Birgit Davis Todd, Senior Editor, Harlequin Temptation

Brenda Chin, Editor, Harlequin Temptation, Duets

Dianne Moggy, Editorial Director, MIRA Books

Laura Shin, Editor, Harlequin Superromance

Bev Sotelov, Editor, Harlequin Superromance

Paula Eykelhof, Senior Editor, Harlequin Superromance

Susan Sheppard, Editor, Harlequin Temptation, Duets

Zilla Soriano, Editor, Harlequin Superromance

Martha Keenan, Associate Editor, MIRA Books

Valerie Gray, Editor, MIRA Books

Harlequin Mills & Boon
Harlequin Presents
Harlequin Romance
Mills & Boon/Harlequin Enterprises Ltd.

Eton House, 18-24 Paradise Road, Richmond, Surrey TW9 1SR, United Kingdom

Acquisitions for Harlequin Romance and Harlequin Presents are through the United Kingdom offices. Query the offices to request a set of editorial guidelines supplied to prospective authors.

Harlequin Romance is the original line of romance fiction, the series that started it all—more than 35 years ago. These are warm, contemporary novels, filled with compassion and sensitivity, written by world-famous authors.

Harlequin Presents is overall the bestselling Harlequin line, published in 16 different languages and sold in almost every country in the world. This line features heartwarming romance novels about bright, capable women who are taking charge of their own lives, set in exotic locales.

To query the U.K. divisions, write (and enclose SASE) in care of the Editorial Department (especially to request guidelines), or direct inquiries to the following individual editors:

Lesley Stonehouse, Senior Editor—Silhouette

Karin Stoecker, Editorial Director—All Mills & Boon series

Linda Fildew, Senior Editor—Historical Romance and MIRA

Samantha Bell, Senior Editor—Mills and Boons Enchanted and Harlequin Romance

Sheila Hodgson, Senior Editor—Medical

Tessa Shapcott, Senior Editor—Harlequin Presents (contemporary romances)

Worldwide Library
Worldwide Mystery
Gold Eagle Books

The Worldwide Library division of Harlequin Enterprises hosts two major imprints, Worldwide Mystery and Gold Eagle Books. Worldwide Library emphasizes genre fiction in the categories of mystery and suspense, action-adventure, futuristic fiction, war drama, and post-holocaust thrillers. The house gives its titles (primarily mass-market paperbacks) solid marketing and promotional support.

The Worldwide Mystery imprint specializes in mainstream commercial mystery and detective fiction in reprint. This imprint has not been issuing previously unpublished,

H

original fiction; however, Worldwide is not to be overlooked as a resource regarding potential reprint-rights sales in this field. The house generally keeps lines of popular writers' ongoing series in print for a number of seasons, sometimes indefinitely.

Titles in reprint at Worldwide: *Zero at the Bone* by Mary Willis Walker; *Time of Hope* by Susan B. Kelly; *The Hour of the Knife* by Sharon Zukowski; *Murder Takes Two* by Bernie Lee; *Hard Luck* by Barbara D'Amato; *A Fine Italian Hand* by Eric Wright.

Gold Eagle Books is known for a fast-and-furious slate of men's action and adventure series with paramilitary and future-world themes. Series include Deathlands, the Destroyer, the Executioner, and Stony Man. Gold Eagle also publishes Super Books keyed to the various series—longer novels with more fully developed plots. Prospective authors should be familiar with the guidelines and regular characters associated with each series.

Query letters and SASEs should be directed to:

Feroze Mohammed, Senior Editor and Editorial Coordinator—Gold Eagle Books

Heather Locker, Associate Editor

HOUSE OF ANANSI PRESS

895 Don Mills Road, 400-2 Park Centre, Toronto, ON M3C 1W3, Canada
416-445-3333   fax: 416-445-5967
www.anansi.ca

House of Anansi Press is a literary press, founded in 1967 by Dennis Lee and David Godfrey, with a mandate to publish innovative literary works in fiction, nonfiction, and poetry by Canadian writers. Anansi acquired a reputation early on for its editors' ability to spot talented writers who push the boundaries and challenge the expectations of the literary community. This continues to be a part of the press's mandate, while it also maintains its rich backlist and keeps important works by Canadian writers in print.

Anansi has published works by such Canadian authors as Northrop Frye, Margaret Atwood, Michael Ondaatje, and Dennis Lee. The house emphasizes literary fiction, trade nonfiction, poetry, politics, philosophy, social thought, literary criticism, theory, autobiography, biography, and women's studies. Anansi also publishes *Alphabet City,* an annual journal of cultural theory, literature, philosophy, and architecture.

Representative of the list: *The Real World of Technology* by Ursula M. Franklin; *Becoming Human* by Jean Vanier; *Mean* by Ken Babstock; *The Plight of Happy People in an Ordinary World* by Natalee Caple; *Ruin and Beauty* by Patricia Young.

Query letters and SASEs should be directed to:

Adrienne Leahey, Editor

Martha Sharpe, Publisher

Andrew Heintzman

Gordon Johnston

Janice Kulyk Keefer

Esta Spalding

INSOMNIAC PRESS

192 Spadina Avenue, Suite 403, Toronto, ON M5T 2C2, Canada
416-504-6270   fax: 416-504-9313
www.insomniacpress.com

Insomniac Press publishes a small, eclectic list of books, most of which have an experimental bent. Though focused primarily on literary fiction, Insomniac also produces select nonfiction and popular trade titles. The Press celebrated its 10th anniversary in 2002.

Poetry and graphic novels round out the catalog of this unique press. Nonfiction areas of interest include architecture, social commentary, political science, business, personal finance, travel and food, Black studies, and pop culture. Insomniac also publishes literature of gay and lesbian interest and is celebrated for its high-caliber spoken word anthologies.

Works representative of the nonfiction list: *The New Investment Frontier* by Howard Atkinson and Donna Green; *Highs and Lows: A Personal Approach to Living with Diabetes* by Michael Twist; *Iced* (edited by Kerry Schooley and Peter Sellers); *This Is Not a Rave: In the Shadow of a Subculture* by Tara McCall; *At Last There Is Nothing Left to Say* by Matthew Good.

A sampler of titles from the literary line-up: *Loving This Man* by Althea Prince; *Endless Knot* by Mathew Styranka; *Gentle Fictions* by Sherwin Tjia; *Awful Gestures* by Adrienne Weiss; *Lost Sanity* by Brad Kelln.

Insomniac does not accept unsolicited manuscripts; send queries and SASEs to:

Mike O'Connor, Publisher

KEY PORTER BOOKS LTD.

70 The Esplanade, 3rd Floor, Toronto, ON M5E 1R2, Canada
416-862-7777   fax: 416-862-2304

Key Porter Books Ltd. (founded in 1981) is a midsize house that publishes a primarily nonfiction list with a Canadian twist. Key Porter produces titles in current affairs, science and health, travel, the environment, ecology, politics, sports, and a solid line of money books and entrepreneurial guides. In addition, the house offers coffee-table and gift editions, as well as occasional fiction and literary works.

Frontlist Key Porter titles are provided full promotional support that spotlights targeted review venues, national media exposure, magazine advertising (including co-op arrangements), and foreign-rights sales. The house maintains a strong backlist.

Among Key Porter highlights: *Walking on Land* by Farley Mowat; *Can Asians Think?* by Kishore Mahbubani; *The Hiding Place* by Trezza Azzopardip; *The Dog Rules* by William Thomas; *When Eve Was Naked* by Josef Skvorecky; *The Truth About Love* by Patrick Roscoe; *The Jasmine Man* by Lola Lemire Tostevin; *Always Give a Penny to a*

K

Blind Man by Eric Wright; *Odjig: The Art of Daphne Odjig 1966–2000* by Daphne Odjig with Carol Podedworny; *Civilians* by Felipe Fernandez-Armstrong.

Susan Renouf, President and Editor in Chief

Key Porter Fiction
Patrick Crean Editions
L&OD Editions

Key Porter's fiction program lies under three imprints: Key Porter Fiction, Patrick Crean Editions, and L&OD Editions. The list includes acclaimed Canadian and international writers such as Joan Barfoot, George Bowering, Don DeLillo, Sylvia Fraser, Zsuzsi Gartner, Cynthia Holz, Thomas Keneally, Ian McEwan, Erika Ritter, Leon Rooke, Josef Skvorecky, Susan Swan, William Trevor, Tim Wynveen, and Yevgeny Yevtushenko.

Key Porter Kids

Key Porter Kids is an imprint that specializes in works for younger readers, including pop-ups, board books, storybooks, novels, and reference works. The house publishes science books for children under the imprint Greeyde Pencier/Books from Owl. Some titles from this division are cross-cataloged with the house's core list.

Titles include *Bubblegum Delicious Alligator Pie* (collector's edition) and *Jelly Belly* by Dennis Lee; *The Deep Cold River Story* by Tabatha Southey (illustrated by Sue Savor); *New Animal Discoveries* by Ronald Orenstein (foreword by Jane Goodall); *Ancient Adventures for Modern Kids* (illustrated by John Mardon and Vesna Krstanovich); *The Little Women Pop-Up Dollhouse.*

Key Porter Kids also publishes the Young Readers' Classics Series, which includes: *Heidi; The Secret Garden; Anne of Green Gables; Little Women; Black Beauty* (retold by Barbara Greenwood and illustrated by Rennie Benoit).

Key Porter handles its own distribution.

McGill-Queen's University Press

Montreal office:
McGill University, 3430 McTavish Street, Montreal, QC H3A 1X9, Canada
514-398-3750

Kingston office:
Queen's University, Kingston, ON K7L 3N6, Canada
fax: 613-533-6822
e-mail: mqup@post.queensu.ca

Publications from McGill-Queen's University Press include works in architecture, biography, British studies, business history, Canadian history, Canadian politics, economics,

M

environment, French history, housing policy, international history, Irish history, Judaica, literature and literary criticism, Loyalist history, native studies, philosophy, political economy, psychology, Quebec history, sociology, urban geography, women's studies, poetry, and general-interest works, primarily in areas of current interest in international and cultural affairs. McGill-Queen's publishes no hard sciences.

McGill-Queen's University Press (founded in 1969) produces trade books with scholarly market crossover, as well as titles geared specifically for the academic market. The press is a conjoint publishing endeavor of Queen's University (Kingston) and McGill University (Montreal). Many McGill-Queen's books have a Canadian subject slant; in addition, the house is strong in a variety of fields in the international arena, as well as in the social sciences and humanities. McGill-Queen's publishes in the English language and occasionally in French.

On the McGill-Queen's list: *Marguerite Bourgeoys and Montreal 1640–1665* by Patricia Simpson; *Canada Enters the Nuclear Age: A Technical History of Atomic Energy of Canada Limited as Seen from Its Research Laboratories* by E. Critoph et al.; *Degrees of Freedom: Canada and the United States in a Changing World* (edited by Keith Banting, George Hoberg, and Richard Simeon); *The Secession of Quebec and the Future of Canada* by Robert A. Young; *A Long Way from Home: The Tuberculosis Epidemic Among the Inuit* by Pat Sandiford Grygier; *The Virtual Marshall McLuhan* by Donald F. Theall; *Stranger Gods: Salman Rushdie's Other Worlds* by Roger Y. Clark; *The Distant Relation: Time and Identity in Spanish American Fiction* by Eoin S. Thomson; *Canada, Latin America, and the New Internationalism* by Brian J. R. Stevenson; *Bullets on the Water: Canadian Refugee Stories* by Ivaylo Grouev; *French Socialists Before Marx* by Pamela Pilbeam; *The Future of NATO* by Charles-Philippe David and Jacques Levesque; *English Immigrant Voices* by Wendy Cameron; *Alejandro Melaspina: Portrait of a Visionary* by John Kendrick.

The McGill-Queen's literary purview embraces criticism, memoir, biography, and letters. *Lying About the Wolf: Essays in Culture and Education* by David Solway; *Aesthetics* by Colin Lyas; *African Exploits: The Diaries of William Stairs 1887–1892* (edited by Roy MacLaren); *The Cassock and the Crown: Canada's Most Controversial Murder Trial* by Jean Monet; *Cold Comfort: My Love Affair with the Arctic* by Graham W. Rowley; *Mapping Our Selves: Canadian Women's Autobiography* by Helen M. Buss; *The Birth of Modernism: Ezra Pound, T. S. Eliot, W. B. Yeats, and the Occult* by Leon Surette.

Distribution for McGill-Queen's University Press is handled by General Distribution Services in Canada and by Cornell University Press (Cup Services) in the United States.

Query letters and SASEs should be directed to:

Donald H. Akenson, Senior Editor (Kingston)

Joan Harcourt, Editor (Kingston)

Roger Martin, Editor (Kingston)

Philip J. Cercone, Executive Director of Press and Senior Editor (Montreal)

Aurele Parisien, Editor (Montreal)

John Zucchi, Editor (Montreal)

N

McGraw-Hill Ryerson Limited

300 Water Street, Whitby, ON L1N 9B6, Canada
905-430-5116

McGraw-Hill Ryerson Limited prides itself on being one of the "liveliest Canadian publishers." Though founded on its educational division, McGraw-Hill Ryerson also has a thriving trade arm. This division publishes general interest books by, about, and for Canadians.

Notable from the McGraw-Hill list: *Canadian Consumer Alert: 101 Ways to Protect Yourself and Your Money* by Pat Foran; *On Course with Mike Weir* by Mike Weir; *Make Sure It's Deductible* by Evelyn Jacks.

McGraw-Hill Ryerson concentrates on personal finance, management, and small business books.

Query letters and SASEs should be directed to:

Lynda Walthert, Assistant to the Publisher

NC Press Limited

345 Adelaide Street West, Toronto, ON M5V 1R5, Canada
416-593-6284

NC Press publishes a broad range of topics covering the spectrum of general trade interest in areas such as cooking, health, Canadian history, politics, poetry, art and performance, literature and literary criticism, folkways and lifeways, the natural world, self-help, and popular psychology.

NC Press Limited (incorporated in 1970) is a trade publisher of Canadian books dedicated to the social, political, economic, and spiritual health of the human community. This is a small press—currently publishing a frontlist of 6 to 10 new books each year—with an expansive vision: "To make a difference." NC Press thus strives to present complex ideas in ways accessible to a wide readership. Among NC Press books are numerous literary-award winners. The press has served as agent for non-Canadian publishers and catalogs a substantial backlist.

In 1988, Gary Perly, president of Perly's Maps, purchased a majority interest in NC Press Limited; the house now produces the Perly's map and atlas series, which offers a strong line of urban atlases and street guides to such environs as Toronto, Montreal, and Quebec City.

NC Press nonfiction: *Ninety-Nine Days: The Ford Strike in Windsor in 1945* by Herb Colling; *Living and Learning with a Child Who Stutters: From a Parent's Point of View* by Lise G. Cloutier-Steele; *Eating Bitterness: A Vision Beyond Prison Walls* by Arthur Solomon; *A Woman in My Position: The Politics of Breast Implant Safety* by Linda Wilson, with Dianne Brown.

Literary and works of cultural note: *Voices from the Odeyak* by Michael Posluns; *Folktales of French Canada* by Edith Fowke; *One Animal Among Many: Gaia Goats and Garlic* by David Walter-Toews; *Images: Thirty Stories by Favorite Writers* (compiled and with paintings by Len Gibbs).

NC Press books are distributed via the publisher's network, which involves independent sales representatives worldwide and the fulfillment services of University of Toronto Press.

Query letters and SASEs should be directed to:

Caroline Walker, President and Publisher

ORCA BOOK PUBLISHERS

PO Box 5626, Station B, Victoria, BC V8R 6S4, Canada
250-380-1229   fax: 250-380-1892
www.orcabook.com   e-mail: orca@orcabook.com

Orca publishes an eclectic mix of children's picture books, chapter books, and juvenile and young adult fiction. At the present, Orca considers only manuscripts by Canadian authors.

Pick of the Orca list: *Before Wings* by Beth Goobie; *Ballerinas Don't Wear Glasses* by Ainslie Manson; *In the Clear* by Anne Carter; *Red Moon Follows Truck* by Stephen Eaton Hume; *Daughter of Light* by Martha Attema.

Orca is accepting picture book manuscripts in the following areas: stories derived from the author's own childhood experiences, carefully researched historical tales, and modern stories situated within Canada, but with universal appeal. Manuscripts should be limited to 1,500 words in length.

In the juvenile and young adult fiction genres, Orca seeks manuscripts that meet the following criteria: regional stories, challenging language and themes, stories based on historical subjects, or contemporary stories that are issue-oriented. These manuscripts should be between 20,000 and 45,000 words in length. Chapter books should be between 8,000 and 15,000 words in length.

For picture books, submit a manuscript without artwork unless you are a trained artist; do not send any originals. For juvenile or young adult projects, send a query first, along with a synopsis and the first few chapters. All submissions should include an SASE. Do not query by e-mail or fax.

These and other guidelines can be found on the Orca Web site.

Query letters and SASEs should be directed to:

Maggie deVries, Children's Book Editor—Picture books, chapter books, juvenile fiction

Bob Tyrrell, Publisher—Teen fiction

PENGUIN BOOKS CANADA LIMITED

10 Alcorn Avenue, Suite 300, Toronto, ON M4V 3B2, Canada
416-925-2249
www.penguin.ca

Penguin Books Canada Limited operates independently of its American affiliate Penguin/Putnam USA. Founded in 1974, Penguin Canada's mandate is to publish Canadian authors; the house does so with fine style, covering a mother lode of original trade nonfiction, as well as a golden seam of mainstream and category fiction and literary works.

Penguin Canada purveys, via its catalog and distribution network, featured titles from the parent company's various international divisions, including Penguin USA, Viking Australia, and Viking UK. The house also distributes for W. W. Norton and Faber and Faber UK. The Viking Canada and Penguin Puffin and Viking are the house's juvenile imprints.

From the Penguin Canada list: *Kit's Law* by Donna Morrissey; *The Girl in the Picture* by Denise Chong; *Titans* by Peter C. Newman; *Paper Shadows* by Wayson Choy; *Parenting with Wit & Wisdom* by Barbara Coloroso; *Notes from the Hyena's Belly* by Nega Mezlekia; *Dagmar's Daughter* by Kim Echlin; *Cold Is the Grave* by Peter Robinson; *The Saratine Mosaic* by Guy Gavriel Kay; *Home from the Vinyl Café* by Stuart McLean.

Penguin Books Canada's titles are distributed by Canbook Distribution.

Query letters and SASEs should be directed to:

Barbara Berson, Children's Books and Fiction Editor

Cynthia Good, Publisher/President

Diane Turbide, Editorial Director

Michael Schellenberg, Editor—Genre fiction, general nonfiction

PLAYWRIGHTS CANADA PRESS

54 Wolseley Street, Toronto, ON M5T A5, Canada
416-703-0201   fax: 416-703-0059
e-mail: angela@puc.ca

Playwrights Canada Press is an award-winning drama publisher. The press publishes 12 to 15 titles annually, specializing in Canadian plays and selected drama theory and history.

Playwrights Canada Press accepts submissions to its editorial committee all year round. Plays submitted must have had at least one professional production in the past 10 years. Include first production information, including cast and crew, with the manuscript.

Recent titles include *The Drawer Boy* by Michael Healey; *It's All True* by Jason Sherman; *Perfect Pie* by Judith Thompson; *The Duchess* by Wallace Simpson.

The U.S. Distributor is Theatre Communications Group.

Query letters and SASEs should be directed to:

Angela Reberio, Publisher/Editor

POLESTAR BOOK PUBLISHERS

1011 Commercial Drive, 2nd Floor, Vancouver, BC V5L 3X1, Canada
604-251-9718   fax: 604-251-9738

Polestar Book Publishers produces literary and commercial titles aimed at a wide readership. Polestar encourages "culturally significant writing" through its First Fiction series, which publishes the work of new authors. Polestar also maintains a poetry list. Popular nonfiction rounds out the Polestar catalog, with an emphasis on sports, dogs, science, and food.

Books representative of the trade list: *Country on Ice* by Doug Beardsley; *Home Run* by Michael McRae; *Great Canadian Scientists* by Barry Shell. Literary line-up: *Love*

Medicine by Gregory Scofield; *Diss/Ed Banded Nation* by David Nandi Odhiambo; *Pool-Hopping* by Anne Fleming.

Polestar publishes Canadian authors only. It does not accept illustrated children's books. Query letters and SASEs should be directed to:

Lynn Henry, Managing Editor

Sirius Books

Sirius Books, an imprint of Polestar Book Publishers, is a collection of books for dog lovers.

The first Sirius Book titles are *Good Dog!: Positive Dog Training Techniques* by Deborah Wolfe; *One in a Million* by Nicholas Read.

THE PORCUPINE'S QUILL

68 Main Street, Erin, ON N0B 1T0, Canada
519-833-9158
www.sentex.net/~pql/new.html

The Porcupine's Quill is a leading Canadian small press producing a handpicked list of literary works (short story collections, novels, juvenile fiction, and poetry) by both emerging and veteran writers. The press is proud to have produced several books that have been shortlisted for awards, including the prestigious Governor General's Award. The Porcupine's Quill also produces a selection of trade and critical works, as well as a handful of books on the visual arts.

The Porcupine's Quill roster includes *A Kind of Fiction* by P. K. Page; *An Artist's Garden* by G. Brender a Brandis; *Done Legend* by Richard Outram; *Southern Stories* by Clark Blaise.

Now a popular destination for submissions, The Porcupine's Quill is swamped with manuscripts; as such, it does not accept unsolicited work. Instead, The Porcupine's Quill often seeks out writers whose work has appeared in literary magazines such as *The New Quarterly*. All submissions should include an SASE, short biography, and bibliography. They should be directed to:

John Metcalf, Senior Editor

Tim Inkster, Publisher

RAINCOAST BOOKS

8680 Cambie Street, Vancouver, BC V6P 6M9, Canada
604-323-7100   fax: 604-323-2600
www.raincoast.com   e-mail: info@raincoast.com

Raincoast Books publishes intelligent, topical, and beautifully designed books of a regional, national, and international nature in the areas of food, travel, creative nonfiction,

R

picture books, arts and photography, pop culture, biography, and the outdoors. Raincoast also has launched a new national fiction imprint publishing Canadian novels, short fiction, and young adult.

Raincoast has recently acquired Polestar Books, which will remain an imprint and continue to publish literary fiction, poetry, feminist works, and sports titles.

Titles published by Raincoast: *Harry Potter I–III* by J. K. Rowling; *Fire into Ice* by Verne Frolick; *The Mermaid's Muse* by Dave Bouchard; *Shocking Beauty* by Thomas Hobbs; *Zest for Life* by Diane Clement; *The Sensualist* by Barbara Hodgson.

Queries and SASEs should be directed to:

Lynn Henry, Executive Editor

Joy Gugeler, Editorial Director—Fiction

Michelle Benjamin, Associate Publisher

RANDOM HOUSE CANADA

One Toronto Street, Suite 300, Toronto, ON M5C 2V6, Canada
416-364-4449
www.randomhouse.ca

A division of Random House of Canada Limited, Random House Canada produces a select list of trade fiction and nonfiction. Publications include Canadian and international titles, with a major concentration on books that appeal to the Canadian market.

Nonfiction areas include popular topical interest and current events, cooking, lifestyle and the arts, history and politics, biography and memoir, travel narrative, popular science, and business and economics. Nonfiction titles include *The Water in Between* by Kevin Patterson; *Bones* by Elaine Dewar; *The Lion, the Fox, and the Eagle* by Carol Off; *Hot Sour Salty Sweet* by Jeffrey Alford and Naomi Duguid; *The Nature of Economies* by Jane Jacobs; *Anti Diva* by Carole Pope.

The Random House Canada fiction program is known for its mix of established literary titans and exciting new talent. The list includes Canadian authors such as Douglas Coupland, Katherine Govier, Paul Quarrington, John MacLachlan Gray, Elyse Friedman, Billie Livingston, and Pulitzer Prize–winner Carol Shields. Internationally, Random House Canada publishes authors who include Julian Barnes, Peter Carey, Eleanor Bailey, Barry Lopez, Graham Swift, and Booker Prize–winners Graham Swift and Arundhati Roy.

Query letters and SASEs should be directed to:

Anne Collins, Vice President and Publisher

SOMERVILLE HOUSE BOOKS LIMITED

24 Dinnick Crescent, Toronto, ON M4N 1L5, Canada
416-489-7769
www.sombooks.com   e-mail: sombooks@goodmedia.com, somer@sympatico.ca

Somerville House specializes in interactive books and kits for young readers. In 1997, Somerville House announced a joint-venture partnership with Penguin Putnam Inc. In 1999, Somerville House became the official youth publisher of the NHL. These new efforts continue to produce the same kind of fun and educational children's titles typical of the Somerville list.

Titles: *The Holographic Night Sky Book & Kit* by Kenneth Hewitt-White; *The Titanic Book and Submersible Model* by Susan Hughes and Steve Santini; *A Century of Hockey Heroes* by James Duplacey and Eric Zweig; *Chess for Kids* by Kevin F. R. Smith and Daniel C. Macdonald; *The Tiny Perfect Dinosaur Series: Tyrannosaurus Rex* by John Acorn and Dale Russell; *The Bones Book & Skeleton* by Stephen Cumbaa.

Children's nonfiction submissions are welcome. Please include an SASE. Due to the volume of submissions, Somerville House discards materials after three months if insufficient postage is enclosed. Direct all queries to:

Harry Endrulat, Manager, Editorial and Product Development

STODDART PUBLISHING COMPANY LTD.

34 Lesmill Road, Don Mills, ON M3B 2T6, Canada
416-445-3333

Stoddart Publishing maintains a hold on the mainstream of commercial publishing. Stoddart nonfiction categories include humor, history, military history, politics, hockey, finance, biography, environment, nutrition, and business and consumer guides. Stoddart also features a solid fiction line that publishes only literary fiction, not poetry. Stoddart Publishing (founded in 1984) is the trade-publishing arm of General Publishing Company. The house produces a wide range of titles with a Canadian orientation or by Canadian authors.

Nonfiction from Stoddart: *Water* by Marc DeVillers; *From Naked Ape to Superspecies* by David Suzuki and Holly Dressel; *Ultimate Hockey* by Trans Weir, Jeff Chapman, and Glenn Weir; *Ortona: Canada's Epic World War II Battle* by Mark Zuehlke.

Stoddart fiction and literature: *Olivo Oliva* by Phillippe Poloni; *The Long Stretch* by Linden MacIntyre; *Visible Amazement* by Gale Zoe Garnett.

Stoddart orchestrates its own distributional network worldwide and handles distribution for books issued by a number of other houses, including House of Anansi Press, the Boston Mills Press, and Cormorant Books. In the United States, Stoddart distributes to the trade through General Distribution Services, Inc.

Stoddart does not accept complete manuscripts. However, it will consider submission of up to two chapters. Query letters and SASEs should be directed to:

Don Bastian, Managing Editor

Stoddart Juveniles

Stoddart publishes a children's program with an emphasis on Canadian works. Stoddart's young-adult paperbacks list includes the Gemini and Junior Gemini lines. Stoddart Young

Readers are for preschoolers through young adults and include picture books, pop-up books, fairy tales, and science titles for young adults.

UNIVERSITY OF BRITISH COLUMBIA PRESS

2029 West Mall, Vancouver, BC V6T 1Z2, Canada
604-822-4161
www.ubcpress.ubc.ca   e-mail: info@ubcpress.ubc.ca

Categories of UBC Press interest include Canadian culture and history, political science, Asian studies, Native studies with emphasis on the Northwest Coast, gender studies, Pacific Rim studies, global geography, fisheries and forestry, environmental studies, Northern studies, and Canadian sociology.

UBC Press (founded in 1971) publishes academic books, as well as general-interest works, with an emphasis on Canadian subjects.

On the UBC Press list: *Couture and Commerce: The Transatlantic Fashion Trade in the 1950s* by Alexandra Palmer; *Planning the New Suburbia: Flexibility by Design* by Avi Friedman; *Wired to the World, Chained to the Home* by Penny Gursteing; *Hobnobbing with a Countess and Other Okanagan Adventures: The Diaries of Alice Barrett Parke 1891–1900; Preserving What Is Valued: Museums and First Nations* by Miriam Clavir; *The Transforming Image: Painted Arts of Northwest Coast First Nations* by Bill McLennan and Karen Duffek; *Prometheus Wired: The Hope for Democracy in the Age of Network Technology* by Darrin Barney; *Academic Freedom and the Inclusive University* (edited by Sharon E. Kahn and Dennis Pavlich); *Chinese Democracy After Tiananmen* by David Ding; *Cycling into Saigon: The Conservative Transition in Ontario* by David R. Cameron and Graham White; *Sustaining the Forests of the Pacific Coast: Forging Truces in the War in the Woods* and *Families, Labour, and Love: Family Diversity in a Changing World* by Maureen Baker.

UBC Press distribution is handled by Raincoast Books (e-mail: custserv@raincoast.com).

Query letters and SASEs should be directed to:

Jean Wilson, Associate Director, Editorial

U

UNIVERSITY OF TORONTO PRESS

10 Saint Mary Street, Suite 700, Toronto, ON M4Y 2W8, Canada
416-978-2239   fax: 416-978-4738

University of Toronto Press publishes in a range of fields, including history and politics; women's studies; health, family, and society; law and crime; economics; workplace communication; theory/culture; language, literature, semiotics, and drama; medieval studies; Renaissance studies; Erasmus; Italian-language studies; East European studies; classics; and nature. The list includes topical titles in Canadian studies, native studies, sociology, anthropology, urban studies, modern languages, and music, as well as travel and touring guides.

University of Toronto Press produces titles for the general trade, as well as academic works. UTP issues a series of specialist journals of note, including *Scholarly Publishing*. The house produces no original contemporary fiction or poetry.

Representing the University of Toronto nonfiction list: *The Butterflies of Canada* by Ross A. Layberry, Peter W. Hall, and J. Donald Lafontaine (with specimen plates by John T. Fowler); *Working for Wildlife: The Beginning of Preservation in Canada* by Janet Foster; *The Illuminated Page: Ten Centuries of Manuscript Painting in the British Library* by Janet Backhouse; *Conduct Unbecoming: The Story of the Murder of Canadian Prisoners of War in Normandy* by Howard Margolian; *The Socially Concerned Today* by John Kenneth Galbraith; *Kaiser and Führer: A Comparative Study of Personality and Politics* by Robert G. L. Waite; *Werewolf! The History of the National Socialist Guerrilla Movement 1944–1946* by Perry Biddiscombe; *The Science of War: Canadian Scientists and Allied Military Technology During the Second World War* by Donald H. Avery; *The Mystery of the Eye and the Shadow of Blindness* by Rod Michalko; *Into the Daylight: A Wholistic Approach to Healing* by Calvin Morrisseau; *Unfinished Dreams: Community Healing and the Reality of Aboriginal Self-Government* by Wayne Warry; *Looking White People in the Eye: Gender, Race, and Culture in Courtrooms and Classrooms* by Sherene H. Razack; *Making Work Making Trouble: Prostitution as a Social Problem* by Deborah R. Brock.

Publications in the arts and literature: *Power to Rise: The Story of the National Ballet of Canada* by James Neufeld; *Painting Place: The Life and Work of David B. Milne* by David P. Silcox; *Modern Furniture in Canada 1920–1970* by Virginia Wright; *Paths of Desire: Images of Exploration and Mapping in Canadian Women's Writings* by Marlene Goldman; *Allusion: A Literary Graft* by Allan H. Pasco; *Discoveries of the Other: Alterity in the Work of Leonard Cohen, Hubert Aquin, Michael Ondaatje, and Nicole Brossard* by Winifred Siemerling; *The Logic of Ecstasy: Canadian Mystical Painting 1920–1940* by Ann Davis; *Northern Voices: Inuit Writing in English* (edited by Penny Petrone); *Sounding Differences: Conversations with Seventeen Canadian Women Writers* by Janice Williamson; *The Political Writings of Mary Wollstonecraft* (edited by Janet Todd).

University of Toronto Press oversees a distributional network encompassing offices and sales agents worldwide; the house handles titles from other book publishers, as well as for institutions such as Royal Ontario Museum and Canadian Museum of Nature.

Query letters and SASEs should be directed to:

Gerald Hallowell, Editor—Canadian history and Canadian literature

Joan Bulger, Editor—Art and classics, architecture

Kieran Simpson, Editor—Department of Directories

Ron Schoeffel, Senior House Editor—Romance languages, native languages, religion and theology, education, philosophy

Suzanne Rancourt, Editor—Medieval studies, medieval and Old English literature

Virgil Duff, Executive Editor—Social sciences, scholarly medical books, law and criminology, women's studies

WHITECAP BOOKS

351 Lynn Avenue, North Vancouver, BC V7J 2C4, Canada
604-980-9852   fax: 604-980-8197
www.whitecap.ca

Whitecap Books, established in 1977, was created with one thing in mind: survival. As such, Whitecap Books is a commercial press, with a strong marketing program to showcase its publications.

Whitecap produces trade nonfiction, with a strong focus on cookbooks by chefs, gardening, large-format photography, and books on local interest subjects. Whitecap also maintains a children's list of nonfiction and fiction.

Representative titles include *The Lazy Gourmet* by Susan Mendelson; *The Blooming Great Gardening Book* by Steve Whysall; *Secret Coastline* by Andrew Scott; *Hiking Ontario's Heartland* by Shirley Teasdale.

Books from the children's list: *Whose House Is This?* by Wayne Lynch; *Gilbert de la Frogponde* by Jennifer Rae (illustrated by Rose Cowles).

Query letters and SASEs should be directed to:

Leanne McDonald, Foreign Rights and Acquisitions Associate

W

PART TWO

Directory of
Literary Agents

What Makes This Agent Directory Special?

Jeff Herman

No other listing of literary agents comes anywhere close to this one. We don't just tell you who the agents are and where to find them; we get the agents to actually talk to you and reveal a slice of their personalities as well. These surveys also reveal what agents want to represent (and don't want to), when and where they were born and educated, their career history, and their agenting track record. Memorize some of these tidbits and you can be something of a gossip.

About 200 exceptionally well-qualified agents are included in this listing. Each year I invite the 200-plus members of the Association of Author Representatives, as well as a couple dozen excellent nonmember agents, to be in the book. As you might expect, many of the most successful agents are not overly hungry for unsolicited new submissions, and some of them therefore do not wish to participate. We listed no agents against their wishes, and we allowed all agent contributors to be as terse or expansive as they pleased. I made the best effort to include only legitimate agencies. Please let me know about any negative experiences you encounter, though I hope there won't be any.

AEI ATCHITY EDITORIAL/ENTERTAINMENT INTERNATIONAL

9601 Wilshire Boulevard, Box 1202, Beverly Hills, CA 90210
323-932-0407   fax: 323-932-0321
www.AEIonline.com   e-mail: webAEI@aol.com

Agents: Literary Manager: Kenneth Atchity; Chi-Li Wong, President; Andrea McKeown, Executive Vice President; Brenna Lui, Vice President of Development; Jennifer Pope, Submissions; Felippe Marques, Associate Manager.

Born: Atchity: Eunice, Louisiana. Marques: March 22, 1969, Rio de Janeiro, Brazil.

Education: Atchity: B.A., Georgetown; Ph.D. in Comparative Literature, Yale. Marques: B.A., Hampden—Sydney College; M.S. in Environmental Policy and Science, Georgia Institute of Technology.

Career history: Atchity: Professor of comparative literature (classics, medieval, Renaissance), Occidental College (1970–1987); Instructor, UCLA Writer's Program (1970–1987). Author of 13 books, including *Joe Somebody,* starring Tim Allen (Fox 2000-New Regency), *Life or Something Like It,* starring Angelina Jolie and Ed Burns (New Regency); *A Writer's Time: A Guide to the Creative Process, from Vision Through Revision* (Norton), *The Mercury Transition: Career Change Through Entrepreneurship* (Longmeadow), and *Writing Treatments That Sell* (with Chi-Li Wong; Owl Books). Producer of 20 films for video, television, and theater, including *Champagne for Two* and *The Rose Café* (Cinemax-HBO), *Amityville: The Evil Escapes* (NBC), *Shadow of Obsession* (NBC), and *Falling Over Backwards.* Marques: Manager, Corporate Environmental Affairs, The Coca-Cola Company, Atlanta, GA (1993–1997); Sales/Marketing Manager for Servicios Protecao Ecologico, Lisbon, Portugal (1997); Director of Film Acquisitions and Distribution, IN Pictures, Los Angeles, CA (1998–2000); President, F.M.A. Independent Film Distribution Consulting, Los Angeles, CA (2000–present).

Hobbies/personal interests: Atchity: Collecting autographed editions, pitchers; tennis; travel. Marques: Travel, rock climbing, baseball, music.

Areas most interested in agenting: Atchity: Nonfiction: Strong mainstream nonfiction, especially true and heroic stories with TV or film potential; business books, especially with entrepreneurial orientation; self-help, inspirational, intelligent narrative nonfiction, women's issues, previously published books with solid sales records. Fiction: Mainstream commercial novels (action, horror, thrillers, suspense, mainstream romance, espionage, outstanding science fiction with strong characters) that can also be made into TV or feature films. Scripts: For TV: strong female leads. For film: All kinds, especially action, romantic comedy, thrillers, science fiction, and horror, screenplays adapting classics; hip, young novels; pop culture, pop music, celebrity biographies. We're dying to discover the next Hispanic American, Asian American, and African American novelists. Marques: Spanish language/Latino market in the United States for both fiction and nonfiction. Nonfiction: pop culture, music books and music-related films, celebrity biographies. Fiction: mystery, thrillers, action, strong fiction and nonfiction that can be made into TV or feature films.

Areas not interested in agenting: Atchity: Drug-related, fundamental religious, category romance, category mystery or Western, poetry, children's, "interior" confessional fiction. Marques: Cookbooks, fundamental religious, poetry, sci-fi, horror.

A

If not agenting, what would you be doing? Atchity: If I weren't a literary manager, writer, and producer, I'd be doing the same thing and calling it something else. Marques: If I weren't a literary manager/producer, I would be traveling and writing.

Best way to initiate contact: Query letter with SASE, or through "submission" button on our site: www.AEIonline.com.

Client representation by category: Nonfiction, 55%; Fiction, 29%; Textbooks, 1%; Scripts, 25%.

Commission: 15% of all domestic sales, 25–30% foreign. If we exercise our option to executive produce a project for film or television, commission on dramatic rights sale is refunded.

Number of titles sold last year: 22.

Rejection rate (all submissions): 95%.

Most common mistakes authors make: The most costly and time-consuming mistake is remaining ignorant of where your work fits into the market and of whom your reader might be. Sending the kind of work (romances, light mysteries, episodic scripts) we're specifically not looking for.

What can writers do to enhance their chances of getting you as an agent? Persist, heighten their self-expectation and ambition, perfect their writing, and, most of all, read commercial novels and see commercial films.

Description of the client from Hell: Clients from Hell are so self-impressed that it's impossible to provide constructive criticism; they make their package impossible to open, are abusive to our staff, and provide a return envelope too small to be used.

Description of a dream client: Dream clients come in with outstanding novels that are both high concept and castable, plus outlines for two more; are considerate of our time; and are delighted to take commercial direction on the writing and the career.

Why did you become an agent? Nearly two decades of teaching comparative literature and creative writing at Occidental College and the UCLA Writers Program, reviewing for the *Los Angeles Times* Book Review, and working with the dreams of creative people through DreamWorks (which I co-founded with Marsha Kinder) provided a natural foundation for this career. I made the transition from academic life through producing, but continued my publishing-consulting business by connecting my authors with agents. As I spent more and more time developing individuals' writing careers, as well as working directly with publishers in my search for film properties, it became obvious that literary management was the next step. True or fiction, what has always turned me on is a good story.

What were your favorite films last year? *Almost Famous, The Dao of Steve, Legally Blonde, Nurse Betty, Charlie's Angels, Snatch, Fight Club, Bridget Jones' Diary.*

Do you watch the *Sopranos?* Yes.

Comments: My most exciting experience is discovering that I'm reading what could be a bestselling proposal or manuscript. Everything else pales into insignificance compared with this moment of discovery. The only "bad feeling" that equals this high feeling is finding out that the writer has just signed with someone else. When you send a query, don't make a decision without letting us know you're about to!

Representative titles: *The Myth of Tomorrow* by Dr. Gary Buffone (McGraw Hill); *Choking on the Silver Spoon* by Dr. Gary Buffone (Regan Books); *The Art of Seduction* by Mary Taylor (Three Rivers); *Getting Loaded: What Every Young Person Should Know About Becoming a Millionaire by Age 40* by Peter Bielegus (NAL); *The Jeffy Diet* by Dr. Gregory Jeff (Dragon Door); *When I Loved Myself Enough* by Alison McMillan (St. Martin's Press). Fiction: *Prometheus* by John Robert Marlow (TOR); *The Danger Zone, The Trade* by Brien Palmer (MIRA); *Henry's List of Wrongs, Eulogy for Joseph Way, Layover* by John Scott Shepherd (Rugged Land); *Gold Fever* by Dr. Tom Stern (AEI-Titan); *Morafuriaum* by April Christofferson (Forge).

ALTAIR LITERARY AGENCY

141 Fifth Avenue, Suite 8N, New York, NY 10010
212-505-3320

Agents: Nicholas Smith, Andrea Pedolsky

Born: Smith: 1952, St. Louis, Missouri. Pedolsky: 1951, New York, New York.

Education: Smith: Languages, Vassar, 1973–1974; Arts Management, SUNY/Purchase, 1985. Pedolsky: B.A. in American Studies, CUNY/Queens College; M.S. in Library Science, Columbia University.

Career history: Smith: Bookseller, Editor, Publisher, Marketing and Sales Manager (publishing), Director, New Product Development (packager/agency); Independent Agent; Agent/Co-Founder Altair Literary Agency. Pedolsky: Editor, reference and professional books, Neal Schuman Publishers, 1978–1988; Acquisitions Editor, Director of Editorial Development and Production, Amacom Books; Executive Editor (created and launched) Peterson's/Pacesetter Books, 1994–1996; Agent/Co-Founder Altair Literary Agency. Also, Editor/Co-Editor/Co-Author of *Continuing Education for Businesspeople, The Small Business Sourcebook,* and *Creating a Financial Plan.*

Hobbies/personal interests: Smith: Music, reading, museums (art, science, and natural history exhibitions), travel, history. Pedolsky: Art, reading, walking, travel, old cities.

Areas most interested in agenting: Smith: American history (only pre-twentieth century); biography (historical figures only); exploration, history (a wide variety of eras, subjects, and places); illustrated books (topic-centered); museum exhibition–related books (science, natural history, history, and other museum topics); music (only history, biography, or reference); science and invention (especially history of); style and design books. Fiction: Literary historical fiction and historical mysteries (only pre-twentieth century settings for both categories). Literary children's books: Activity books only, and only those covering science, natural history, nature, or technology. (Especially interested in formats such as clue books, pop-ups, science you can do, die-cuts, reveals, puzzles, etc.). Pedolsky: Art (biography, history of), biography (prominent and historical figures); contemporary issues, gardening, illustrated books, multicultural topics, personal finance, religion and spirituality (history of, new ideas about), sports (women's and men's), women's issues. IMPORTANT: All prospective authors MUST have expertise in their topic.

Areas not interested in agenting: Smith: True crime, memoir, romance. Pedolsky: Children's, true crime, mystery, memoir, romance, cookbooks, fitness.

A

Best way to initiate contact: Nonfiction: A well-thought out and composed query letter, citing your related credentials and why you are the best person to write your book, and/or a complete proposal. We will only respond and/or return materials when you include an SASE. Fiction: A query letter, including a brief, compelling synopsis of the story, and a bio/c.v. with writing credits. We will only respond and/or return materials when you include an SASE.

Client representation by category: Smith: Nonfiction, 85%; Fiction (historical only), 10%; Children's (activity only), 5%. Pedolsky: Nonfiction, 95%; Fiction, 5%.

Commission: 15% domestic; 20% foreign.

Rejection rate (all submissions): 90%.

Most common mistakes authors make: Not demonstrating, either through your proposal or synopsis, that you have the background, knowledge, savvy, and ability to write your proposed book. Also, failing to understand and demonstrate how you can help your potential publisher to take advantage of the marketplace for your book. Another common mistake is querying by telephone or fax.

Description of the client from Hell: There have not been many. Those who come to mind have little or no understanding of the book marketplace and require too much handholding.

Description of a dream client: First and foremost, be a great writer and storyteller. Be someone who has the knowledge, skill, creativity, and expertise to write and support your book; who understands the collaborative aspects of working with an agent and editor; who takes responsibility for meeting deadliness; and who has a sense of humor.

Why did you become an agent? Smith: I love ideas and books, enjoy encountering interesting authors with both, and particularly like to bring authors and editors together over a great book—then mediate the process to everyone's benefit. Pedolsky: When I was an editor, I had to confine and align my acquiring efforts to a particular house's list and interests. It became clear to me that if I wanted to work with a variety of authors with unique voices, styles, and concerns, being an agent was the way to go.

Representative titles: Smith: *Solar System* by Christine Malloy, with the American Museum of Natural History (Chronicle Books); *Blue Whale* by Christine Malloy, with the American Museum of Natural History (Chronicle Books); *National Genealogical Society's Guides to . . .* (Genealogy series) by NGS and co-authors (Rutledge Hill Press). Pedolsky: *Crazy Wise* by Geri Larkin (Tuttle Publishing); *Triathlete Magazine's Complete Guide to Triathlon* by Matt Fitzgerald/*Triathlete Magazine* (Warner Books); *Making Her Mark: Firsts and Milestones in Women's Sports* by Ernestine Miller (Contemporary); *Essential Musical Intelligence* by Louise Montello (Quest Books).

MIRIAM ALTSHULER LITERARY AGENCY

53 Old Post Road North, Red Hook, NY 12571
845-758-9408   fax: 845-758-3118

Agent: Miriam Altshuler
Born: New York, New York.

Education: B.A., Middlebury College.

Career history: Agent for 11 years at Russell & Volkening. Started my own agency in 1994.

Hobbies/personal interests: Skiing, horses, the outdoors, my children, reading.

Areas most interested in agenting: Literary and commercial fiction, narrative nonfiction, popular culture.

Areas not interested in agenting: No sci-fi, Westerns, romance, horror, genre mysteries.

Best way to initiate contact: Query letter with SASE.

Reading-fee policy: No reading fee.

Client representation by category: Nonfiction, 50%; Fiction, 50%.

Commission: 15% books and movies; 20% foreign; 17.5% England.

AMICUS LITERARY AGENCY

3202 East Greenway, Suite 1307-182, Phoenix, AZ 85032

602-569-2481   fax: 602-569-2265

e-mail: bookwoman@qwest.net

Agent: Rose Stadler

Education: B.S.W., University of Minnesota, 1979; M.S.W., Arizona State University, May 1997.

Career history: More than 20 years in social work, counseling, college instructor.

Hobbies/personal interests: Writing, camping, photography, amateur astronomy.

Areas most interested in agenting: Mainstream, good literary fiction, mysteries/thrillers, current events, and nonfiction.

Areas not interested in agenting: No cookbooks, poetry, Westerns, or science fiction. Absolutely no pornography or satanic trash. No longer take children's literature.

If not agenting, what would you be doing? Stand-up comedy, teaching social work, teaching writing, more social work, counseling or being a therapist; writing, writing, and more writing.

Best way to initiate contact: A good query letter and the first 50 pages or first 3 chapters, with SASE for fiction. Query letter only for nonfiction with SASE. No bubble-wrap packaging, as I live in Arizona, and it results in melted plastic slime. Use a sturdy box and always enclose SASE. No SASE, no response. OK to e-mail me, but not more than one page; no attachments, please.

Reading-fee policy: No reading fee.

Client representation by category: Fiction, 50%; Nonfiction, 50%.

Commission: 15% domestic, 20% foreign.

Rejection rate (all submissions): 95%.

Most common mistakes authors make: Several come to mind. Don't call me at four in the morning and expect me to remember your name, much less anything coherent. Don't send me something that I don't handle; it's a waste of my time and yours. Don't convince me that I will absolutely love something if I read it all the way through. Don't

A

beg, don't grovel, and don't slip me something under the stall door if you see me at a conference. Please don't tell me that I absolutely, have to, must read it because if I don't, you will stop taking your medication, and it will be my fault when you do your swan dive off a storage shed. Don't send unsolicited manuscripts. Always include an SASE if you want a response. Please put your name, address, and phone number on the query letter.

Description of the client from Hell: CFHs are arrogant bullies, know-it-alls, overly concerned about advances and royalties, like to yell at agents and publishers, threaten bodily harm and lawsuits if their work doesn't sell, won't take criticism, don't meet deadlines, call daily for updates, become depressed and/or suicidal, need a financial adviser or marriage counselor, list the agent on a loan application, are selfish, are antisocial, or may have their own page in the *DSM-IV-R*. Since this is a self-imposed career, I do not have to work with unpleasant individuals and will send them packing should they become annoying, demanding, hysterical, or unethical.

Description of a dream client: Dream clients are persistent, tenacious, have an unsinkable attitude, get the work done on time, don't give me excuses or delays, provide copies and appropriate samples when needed, believe in their work, and are pleasant to work with. I respect and admire the people I work with, and we share mutual goals; therefore, we utilize a teamwork approach to see their work published.

How did you become an agent? One of my students sat on my front porch for three days and begged. At the same time, someone happened to write an article about writing in the local paper, and I returned the phone call. The next day there were 87 messages. I saw a need in Phoenix and took it from there. I discovered that I don't have to live in Los Angeles or New York to make things happen.

Why did you become an agent? For someone with an unquenchable thirst for books and a 20-year affair with the literary world, it was the right thing to do at the time. Besides, I love a good challenge.

What can writers do to enhance their chances of getting you as an agent? Make me laugh, convince me that you're better than the average bear. The three Ps—polished, professional, and proofread—are most important.

How would you describe what you actually do for a living? Interesting question: Days vary from picking up the mail, hauling it to my car by camel, schlepping it to my house by mule, piling it up in the living room, reading, answering mail, logging in mail, logging out mail, sitting at the computer for days, waiting in line at the post office to return packages; answering my e-mails, faxing phone lines, making calls, listening to bad music while on hold, talking to clients, talking to editors, calling publishing houses, getting more mail, answering more calls, writing letters and proposals, writing columns and/or articles, attending conferences and seminars, teaching several courses at the local community college, being a guest speaker for various groups, chatting, talking, writing, corresponding, handholding, buffering rejections, jumping for joy with a sale, negotiating advances and royalties (income), promoting authors, arranging book signings and tours, handling contracts, reading and answering more mail, more reading, traveling, schmoozing, more chatting, more promotions, and getting to wear blue jeans most of the days I don't leave the house. Some days I don't get home before midnight. Nothing is routine about this job, but I love it and can't see myself doing anything different. I'm a self-starter and I like it that way.

A

Betsy Amster Literary Enterprises

PO Box 27788, Los Angeles, CA 90027-0788
323-662-1987

Agent: Betsy Amster

Education: B.A., University of Michigan.

Career history: Before opening my agency in 1992, I spent 10 years as an Editor at Vintage Books and Pantheon and two years as Editorial Director of the Globe Pequot Press.

Hobbies/personal interests: Reading, movies, art, swimming, hiking, poking into odd corners of Los Angeles

Areas most interested in agenting: Literary fiction; narrative nonfiction (social issues, history, adventure, travel); psychology and self-help; women's issues; health; parenting; popular culture; clever gift books by illustrators who can also write.

Areas not interested in agenting: Children's or YA titles; commercial women's fiction; category romance, science fiction, fantasy, Westerns, horror; genre mysteries; computers; poetry.

If not agenting, what would you be doing? I'd be a lawyer.

Best way to initiate contact: No phone calls or faxes. For fiction, please send the first three pages of your manuscript; for nonfiction, please send a query letter or your proposal. No response without an SASE.

Reading-fee policy: No reading fee.

Commission: 15% domestic; 20% foreign.

Number of titles sold last year: 25.

Most common mistakes authors make: Nonfiction: Failing to research the competition. Fiction: Submitting a first draft.

Description of a dream client: Writes well, takes direction gracefully, moves easily from book to book. Meets deadlines. Rises to the challenge of helping the publisher promote the book. Knows the difference between a big problem and a little one. Calls and faxes only during business hours. Likes to laugh. A mensch!

Why did you become an agent? I can't keep my nose out of books.

What can writers do to enhance their chances of getting you as an agent? If you're writing nonfiction, read the books on how to write a book proposal. If you're writing fiction, join (or start) a writers' group to get feedback on your work. Study story structure. Be prepared to go through drafts and drafts. Ripeness is all.

How would you describe what you actually do for a living? I'm constantly on the lookout for writers whose work moves or enlightens me, which means I read everything in sight. Once I take writers on, I work with them to make sure that their proposal or manuscript is polished and persuasive. I keep track of which editors are doing what types of books and make sure that I understand their taste. I jump up and down on the phone with editors (or in their offices or over lunch) to share my enthusiasm for my clients' work. I nudge publishers as required, to see that they live up to their promises.

Representative titles: *Driving to Garden City* by Robin Chotzinoff (Algonquin); *The Victoria's Secret Catalog Never Stops Coming . . . and Other Lessons I Learned from*

Breast Cancer by Jennie Nash (Scribner); *Etiquette for Outlaws* by Rob Cohen and David Wollock (HarperCollins); *The Backbone of the World: A Portrait of the Vanishing West Along the Continental Divide* by Frank Clifford (Broadway); *The Souvenir: A Daughter Discovers Her Father's War* by Louise Steinman (Algonquin); *The Memory Room* by Mary Rakow (Counterpoint); *Esperanza's Box of Saints* by Maria Amparo Escandon (Scribner); *The Green Suit* by Dwight Allen (Plume); *The Road to Esmeralda* by Joy Nicholson (St. Martin's); *Cautionary* by Sharon Montrose (Viking Studio); *The Highly Sensitive Child* by Elaine N. Aron (Broadway); *The 24-Hour Pediatrician: Doctors from the Country's Leading Children's Hospitals Offer Parents Their Best Tips for Making Kids Feel Better Faster* by Christina Elston (Crown); *Casa Yucatan* by Karen Witynski and Joe Carr (Gibbs Smith).

MARCIA AMSTERDAM AGENCY

41 West 82nd Street, New York, NY 10024
212-873-4945

Agent: Marcia Amsterdam
   Education: B.A. in English and Journalism, Brooklyn College.
   Career history: Editor; agent (1960–present).
   Hobbies/personal interests: Reading, theater, movies, art, travel, discovering wonderful new writers.
   Areas most interested in agenting: An eclectic list of mainstream and category fiction and popular nonfiction. I enjoy medical and legal thrillers, character-driven science fiction, mysteries, horror, historical romance, contemporary women's fiction, and quality young-adult fiction.
   Areas not interested in agenting: Children's books, poetry, short stories, technical books, thrillers about drug cartels.
   If not agenting, what would you be doing? Reading published books more, traveling more.
   Best way to initiate contact: A query letter (with SASE).
   Reading-fee policy: No reading fee.
   Client representation by category: Nonfiction, 20%; Fiction, 70%; Children's, 10%.
   Commission: 15% domestic; 20% on foreign sales and movie and television sales (split with subagents); 10% on screenplays.
   Number of titles sold last year: A fair number.
   Rejection rate (all submissions): Alas, most.
   Most common mistakes authors make: Spelling and grammar still count, as does a comfortable, legible typeface.
   Description of the client from Hell: I wouldn't know. I've never had one.
   Description of a dream client: One who trusts the reader, is professional, is adaptable, has a sense of humor, and has confidence in my judgment.
   Why did you become an agent? When I was an editor, other editors often came to me for suggestions about books they were working on. I found that I enjoyed giving editorial

and career advice. One editor said, "You keep selling my books. Why don't you become an agent?" So I did.

Representative titles: *China Dome* (Kensington); *Flash Factor* (Kensington); *Moses Goes to School* (Farrar, Straus & Giroux); *Rosey in the Present Tense* (Walker & Co.); *The Haunting* by Ruby Jean Jensen (Kensington).

THE ANDERSON LITERARY AGENCY

395 Riverside Drive, Suite 12AH, New York, NY 10025
fax: 646-414-7639
e-mail: gilesa@rcn.com

Agent: Giles Anderson

Born: March 23, 1973, Princeton, New Jersey.

Education: B.A. in Philosophy and the History of Math and Science, St. John's College, Annapolis, Maryland.

Career history: Giles Anderson began his publishing career at Boston Zephyr Press, a small publisher of Russian and Ukrainian literature in translation, editing the works of such noted writers as Oksana Zabuzhko, Yuri Andrukhovych, and Yevehen Pashkovsky. He then served as an Assistant at the Curtis Brown Literary Agency and in 1997 joined Scott Waxman to found the Scott Waxman Agency. In September 2000, he left to form the Anderson Literary Agency.

Areas most interested in agenting: Narrative nonfiction, biography, science, memoir, spirituality (ABA and CBA material), books in translation, and literary fiction.

Areas not interested in agenting: Romance, science fiction, Westerns, genre mystery, and most children's material.

Best way to initiate contact? Brief e-mail query only.

Client representation by category: Nonfiction, 90%; Fiction, 10%.

Commission: 15% domestic, 25% foreign.

Number of titles sold last year: 20.

Rejection rate (all submissions): 99%.

Common mistakes authors make: Excessive calling and verbal pitching.

Why did you become an agent? I came to New York looking for an editorial job and learned about this side of the business. It appealed to me immediately and I called agencies until I was offered a job.

If not agenting, what might you be doing? Probably something else entrepreneurial, or perhaps I'd work in a fundraising capacity for a nonprofit cultural institution.

How did you become an agent? I had the good fortune to help an agent (Scott Waxman) set up his own agency, and he encouraged me to pursue my own clients while acting as his assistant.

What were your favorite films last year? *Momento, Sexy Beast.*

Do you watch the *Sopranos*? Sometimes, but in general I'm not exercised by Mafia-related stories.

A

Representative titles: *Silent Fire* by James Connor (Crown); *The Knight's Tour* by J. C. Hallman (St. Martin's); *The Art Is Long* by John Simmons (Houghton Mifflin); *Plain Business* by Louise Stoltzfus and Jo Tyler (Rutledge Hill); *The Long Marriage* by Maxine Kumin (Norton); *Desire and Ice* by David Brill (National Geographic); *The Most Unlikely Convert* by David Downing (Intervarsity); untitled novel by James Connor (Welcome Rain).

AUTHENTIC CREATIONS LITERARY AGENCY

875 Lawrenceville-Suwanee Road, Suite 310-306, Lawrenceville, GA 30043
770-339-3774   fax: 770-339-7126
www.authenticcreations.com   e-mail: Ron@authenticcreations.com

Agents: Mary Lee Laitsch, Ronald E. Laitsch
   Born: Mary Lee: Baraboo, Wisconsin. Ronald: Milwaukee, Wisconsin.
   Education: Mary Lee: B.S. in Education, University of Wisconsin. Ronald: J.D., University of Wisconsin Law School; B.S., University of Wisconsin School of Business.
   Career history: Mary Lee: Taught library science. Established my literary agency in 1995. Ronald: Attorney. Established literary agency in 1995.
   Hobbies/personal interests: Mary Lee: Family, reading, crafts, sewing. Ronald: Golf, reading, gardening.
   Areas most interested in agenting: Mary Lee: Fiction: Adventure, historical, murder mysteries, romance, suspense, and, of course, literary fiction. Nonfiction: Business, crafts, how-to, humor, political, sports, true crime, and women's issues. Ronald: Fiction: Adventure, murder mysteries, suspense, mainstream, and literary fiction. Nonfiction: Business, how-to, political, sports, true crime, and ethnic works.
   Areas not interested in agenting: Mary Lee: Poorly crafted works. Ronald: Projects that are not well written.
   If not agenting, what would you be doing? Mary Lee: I totally enjoy what I am doing and cannot imagine getting into any other line of work.
   Best way to initiate contact: Query letter with SASE.
   Reading-fee policy: No reading fee.
   Client representation by category: Nonfiction, 30%; Fiction, 65%; Children's, 5%. Ronald: Nonfiction, 50%; Fiction, 50%.
   Commission: 15% domestic, 20% foreign.
   Number of titles sold last year: Mary Lee: The exact number of manuscripts sold varies from year to year. The only constant is that each year has seen a steady increase over the number of manuscripts sold during the previous year. Ronald: 18.
   Rejection rate (all submissions): 99%.
   Description of the client from Hell: Mary Lee: We have clients from all over the world, but none of them, to our knowledge, comes from Hell. We attempt to treat all of our clients as the unique and talented artists they are and in return expect them to respect our professional opinion on how to get their books published. So far this system has worked out well for us. Ronald: One whose writing is wonderful but who is impossible to work with to the point we have to part company.

Description of a dream client: Mary Lee: A talented writer who has carefully proof-read the manuscript before submitting it to us. Ronald: A person who loves to write and lets the agent do the selling.

Most common mistakes authors make? Ronald: Not providing sufficient information about their project or their qualifications to write the manuscript.

Why did you become an agent? Mary Lee: I enjoy working with new writers to develop their initial works into publishable manuscripts.

What can authors do to enhance their chances of getting you as an agent? Mary Lee: I like working with enthusiastic writers. Let that show through in your query letter.

How would you describe what you actually do for a living? Ronald: I view the role of the agent as working with the author to perfect a marketable manuscript and then matching that manuscript with a publisher capable of maximizing the sales of the ensuing book.

How did you become an agent? Ronald: From a frustrated writer to a person in a position to remove that frustration for other writers. I know from experience how hard it is to write a good manuscript. I enjoy being in a position to help a writer get that effort into a published book.

What do you think about editors? Ronald: Good editors make all the difference between a successful book and a large number of remainders in a discount bookstore. They are the key to a successful writing career.

Do you watch the *Sopranos?* Ronald: Who watches television when there are so many great books to read?

Comments: Mary Lee: It takes an enormous amount of dedication and effort to write a marketable manuscript. It takes the same effort by the literary agent to find just the right publisher. We prefer to establish a long-term relationship with those authors who appreciate and respect the contributions made by each half of what will become a successful partnership. Ronald: An agent and a writer are a partnership with the same goal—to get the manuscript published. Each has to trust the other to get the job done or the project is doomed to failure. Placing and selling a manuscript takes time and perseverance. The author must have the patience while the agent carries out his end of the partnership with a minimum amount of contact. If the agent spends all his time on the phone with the author, then he can't be on the phone with the editor, who is the person in position to offer a publishing contract.

Representative titles: *Frankenstein: The Legacy* by Christopher Schildt (Simon & Schuster); *Night of Dracula* by Christopher Schildt (Simon & Schuster); *This Is the Zodiac Speaking* by Michael Kelleher (Greenwood).

LORETTA BARRETT BOOKS, INC.

101 Fifth Avenue, 11th Floor, New York, NY 10003
212-242-3420

Agent: Loretta Barrett
　Education: B.A./M.A., University of Pennsylvania.
　Career history: Social Studies teacher, then Editor in Chief of Anchor Books and Vice President and Executive Editor at Doubleday & Co., and a literary agent since 1990.

Hobbies/personal interests: Skiing, traveling, reading.

Areas most interested in agenting: Nonfiction: Spirituality, biography, popular science, self-help, health/fitness, psychology, narrative, women's issues, ethnic issues. Fiction: Mainstream contemporary, ethnic, family saga, mystery/suspense, contemporary romance, thriller/espionage.

Areas not interested in agenting: Science fiction, fantasy, cookbooks, poetry, children's books.

Best way to initiate contact: Send a well-written query letter with an SASE.

Client representation by category: Nonfiction, 70%; Fiction, 30%.

Commission: 15%.

Rejection rate (all submissions): 95%.

Most common mistakes authors make: Not providing enough background information on their own writing, work, or experience.

How did you become an agent? I was an Executive Editor at Doubleday and decided I wanted to work more directly with authors. I have been doing so for more than 10 years and love it.

Why did you become an agent? I love working directly with writers and helping them develop their projects.

What can writers do to enhance their chances of getting you as an agent? For nonfiction, submit a detailed marketing plan and as much background information as possible. For fiction, provide background information, not just a synopsis of the manuscript.

How would you describe what you actually do for a living? I would describe what I do as being a midwife. I help authors give life to their books and help find homes for them.

What do you think about editors? Good editors are worth their weight in gold.

What do you think about publishers? It concerns me that so many American publishers are owned by conglomerates, which means fewer houses for authors to approach for publication, and it also seems to limit competition. I also think good publishers are worth their weight in gold.

Representative titles: *The Shadow Negotiation: How Women Can Master the Hidden Agendas That Determine Bargaining Success* by Deborah Kolb and Judith Williams, Ph.D. (Simon & Schuster); *Terrible Honesty: Mongrel Manhattan in the 1920s* by Ann Douglas (Farrar, Straus & Giroux); *The Age of Spiritual Machines* by Ray Kurzweil (Viking); *Line of Sight* by Jack Kelly (Hyperion); *If You Can't Be Free, Be a Mystery: Myths and Meanings of Billie Holiday* by Farah Griffin (Free Press); *The Last Lover* by Laura Van Wormer (Mira); *Voices Carry* by Mariah Stewart (Pocket); *Inviting God to Your Wedding* by Martha Williamson (Harmony); *Witness to Hope: The Biography of Pope John Paul II* by George Weigel (HarperCollins).

THE WENDY BECKER LITERARY AGENCY

530-F Grand Street, Suite 11-H, New York, NY 10002
voice/fax: 212-228-5940
e-mail: dulf86a@prodigy.com, DanWen@prodigy.net

Agent: Wendy Becker

Career history: Associate Editor, McGraw-Hill. Editor, John Wiley & Sons. Agency begun in 1994.

Areas most interested in agenting: Nonfiction (trade): business, biography, history, current events, parenting/psychology.

Areas not interested in agenting: Poetry, literary fiction, short stories, children's books, anything in the college market.

Best way to initiate contact: Query letter (with SASE), to include outline, table of contents, author resume, and up to three sample chapters. Do not call. Do not send complete manuscripts.

Reading-fee policy: No reading fee.

Client representation by category: Nonfiction, 80%; Fiction, 20%.

Commission: 15%.

Most common mistakes authors make: Never approach an agent initially via telephone, because there is no way to properly evaluate authors without seeing their work.

MEREDITH BERNSTEIN LITERARY AGENCY, INC.

2112 Broadway, Suite 503A, New York, NY 10023
212-799-1007, 212-799-1145

Agents: Meredith Bernstein, Elizabeth Cavanaugh

Born: Bernstein: July 9, 1946, Hartford, Connecticut; Cavanaugh: October 16, 1962.

Education: Bernstein: B.A., University of Rochester, 1968; Cavanaugh: B.A. in Literature and Creative Writing, Ohio University (Athens).

Career history: Bernstein: Many jobs before becoming an agent: freelance reader, story editor; worked for another agency for five years before starting my own in 1981. Cavanaugh: Before working in publishing, I held a number of positions that were "book"-related, including working for a period as a librarian; began in publishing with the Bernstein Agency in the mid-1980s and was instrumental in the development of our foreign rights activity.

Hobbies/personal interests: Bernstein: I am a collector of vintage and contemporary costume jewelry and clothing, so fashion is a strong interest; sports of all kinds; almost any cultural event (I'm an avid theatergoer); spending time with friends; travel, adventure, and personal-growth work. Cavanaugh: I am interested in all forms of art and love museums, movies, dance, music (I studied the violin for 10 years), and, of course, reading. I am also an avid cook, love gardening, and am currently renovating a 70-year-old house. I am a strong environmentalist and love animals and nature, and enjoy camping, hiking, and canoeing.

Areas most interested in agenting: Bernstein: Nonfiction: Psychology, self-help, health/fitness, memoir, current events, business, biography, celebrity. Cavanaugh: Narrative nonfiction, parenting, pop-science, general nonfiction, mysteries, literary fiction, mainstream fiction.

Areas not interested in agenting: Bernstein: Children's books, Westerns (men's), sci-fi. Cavanaugh: Science fiction, children's, poetry, screenplays.

If not agenting, what would you be doing? Bernstein: (1) Curating the American Craft Museum; (2) Replacing Oprah; (3) Running a top fashion house in Paris. Cavanaugh: It would most likely involve some aspect of books or publishing (maybe editing or even writing), or perhaps be as far afield as environmental science or catering.

Best way to initiate contact: A query letter with SASE.

Reading-fee policy: No reading fee.

Client representation by category: Nonfiction, 50%; Fiction, 50%.

Commission: 15% domestic; 20% on foreign sales (split with subagents).

Number of titles sold last year: A lot!

Rejection rate (all submissions): Unsure, but probably fairly high because we must truly believe in the projects we represent and, therefore, are selective about what we request to see.

Most common mistakes authors make: Bernstein: Poor presentation, no SASE. Cavanaugh: Poorly researched projects (which includes not knowing the market in terms of what is already on the shelves for the type of book they are writing), sloppy presentation.

Description of the client from Hell: Bernstein: Pushy, demanding, inflexible, calls too much, sloppy presentation of material, egomaniacal. Cavanaugh: Those who do not take a professional approach to their career and who do not appreciate the role of an agent.

Description of a dream client: Bernstein: Professional, courteous; dream clients see our relationship as teamwork, respect how hard I work for them. Cavanaugh: Great writers whose talent and passion for their work bring the project to life and who want us to work together to reach their potential.

How did you become an agent? Bernstein: Sold my first book overnight(!) almost 25 years ago.

Why did you become an agent? Bernstein: I was born to do this! Cavanaugh: As an agent, the diversity of projects I represent allows me to work within the creative process in many different genres and with many different publishers.

How would you describe what you actually do for a living? Bernstein: I actualize the experience of the authors' dreams.

What do you think about editors? Bernstein: I wish they would stop becoming agents!

What do you think about publishers? Bernstein: This is a long conversation that I'd be happy to have over drinks!

Comments: Bernstein: The saddest thing for me about publishing today is that "the bottom line is king." I see so many beautiful pieces of work that I am told are "too small." In the old days, there was "a wing and a prayer"—the loss of that belief system is a failure to envision.

Representative titles: *Romances* by Smeron Sale a.k.a. Dinah McCau, Ana Leigh, Sandra Hill, and Janis Reems Hudson; *When Broken Glass Floats* by Chanrithy Him (W. W. Norton); *The Bone Density Diet* by Dr. Kessler (Ballantine); *The Nature of Animal Healing* by Dr. Martin Goldstein (Knopf); *The Whole Truth* by Nancy Pickard (Pocket); *Hormone Deception* by Lindsay Berkson (Contemporary); *The Swampwalker's Journal* by David Carroll (Houghton-Mifflin).

DANIEL BIAL AGENCY

41 West 83rd Street, Suite 5-C, New York, NY 10024
212-721-1786
e-mail: dbialagency@juno.com

Agent: Daniel Bial

Education: B.A. in English, Trinity College.

Career history: Editor for 15 years, including 10 years at HarperCollins. Founded agency in 1992.

Hobbies/personal interests: Travel, cooking, music, parenting.

Areas most interested in agenting: Nonfiction: Popular reference, business, popular culture, science, history, humor, Judaica, sports, psychology, cooking. Fiction: Quality fiction, mysteries.

Areas not interested in agenting: Nonfiction: Academic treatises, crafts, gift books. Fiction: Romances, horror, medical thrillers, children's books, poetry, novels by authors with no publishing credits.

Best way to initiate contact: Query letter with SASE. I accept e-mail queries, without attached files.

Reading-fee policy: No reading fee.

Client representation by category: Nonfiction, 90%; Fiction, 10%.

Commission: 15% domestic; 25% foreign.

Number of titles sold last year: 18.

Most common mistakes authors make: A surprising number of writers devote time in their query letter to telling me about their previous failures. They essentially reject themselves.

What gets you excited? Savvy writers research their field and rate the competition's strengths and weaknesses. They highlight why their book will be new, different, better. They explain why they are the best writer on the topic. And they display an enthusiasm that suggests it will survive all the ups and downs of the publishing process.

Description of the client from Hell: Clients from Hell are almost always wrapped up in private grievances and needs. They talk when they should listen, try force when they should use tact, and get involved in personal gamesmanship when much of publishing calls for team play. They suspect the worst and often cause crises simply through their own closed-mindedness.

Description of a dream client: Dream clients produce trim, tight, ready-to-sell material. They know the business and how to get ahead. They recognize the importance of marketing and know that good intentions don't sell books—hard work does. They take pride in their work and their relationships.

Why did you become an agent? I became an agent for the same reason I first became an editor: because I loved the discovery of new authors and books, loved helping create a sellable project, and loved negotiating big advances. I switched desks because I wanted to be my own boss.

Comments: While I am always looking for authors who write beautifully without any outside help, I am also an experienced book doctor. As a former editor, I can be demanding of some authors, insisting that they rework and rewrite their proposal until it represents the best book they can write. I will also work with less experienced writers to help them prepare their work for others to agent.

DAVID BLACK LITERARY AGENCY

156 5th Avenue, Suite 608, New York, NY 10010
212-242-5080   fax: 212-924-6609

Agents: David Black, Gary Morris, Susan Raihofer, Laureen Rowland, Joy E. Tutela, and Leigh Ann Eliseo.
   Areas most interested in agenting: Nonfiction, politics, sports, current events, science, fitness, women's issues, music, business and history, fiction, literary fiction, commercial fiction.
   Areas not interested in agenting: Poetry, screenplays, children's.
   Best way to initiate contact: Query letter with SASE enclosed. No faxes, no e-mails.
   Commission: 15%.
   Representative titles: *Tuesdays with Morrie* by Mitch Albom (Doubleday); *Body for Life* by Bill Phillips (HarperCollins); *Isaac's Storm* by Erik Larson (Crown).

BLEECKER STREET ASSOCIATES, INC.

532 LaGuardia Place, #617, New York, NY 10012
212-677-4492   fax: 212-388-0001

Agent: Agnes Birnbaum
   Place of birth: Budapest, Hungary, but have lived most of my life in the United States.
   Education: Educated in Europe and America.
   Career history: Spent 16 years as an Editor before starting my own agency in 1984. Was Senior Editor at Pocket Books and NAL; Editor in Chief of Award Books, later a part of Berkley.
   Hobbies/personal interests: Reading, classical music, movies, theater, travel.
   Areas most interested in agenting: Nonfiction: History, biography, science, investigative reporting, health, women's issues, popular psychology, nature and outdoor writing, true adventure, New Age/spirituality. Fiction: Mystery and suspense thrillers, women's novels.
   Areas not interested in agenting: Poetry, science fiction, Westerns, children's books, film/TV scripts, plays, professional and academic books.
   If not agenting, what would you be doing? I'd still be an editor.
   Best way to initiate contact: With a short letter about the book and the author. An SASE is a must. No faxes or e-mails, please.
   Reading-fee policy: We have no reading fee.
   Client representation by category: Nonfiction, 75%; Fiction, 25%.

B

Commission: 15% on domestic sales; 25% on foreign and film/TV if a co-agent is used (who gets 10% commission)—it's 15% on foreign and film/TV if Bleecker is the sole agent.

Titles sold last year: 60.

Rejection rate (all submissions): 90% (alas!).

Most common mistakes authors make: They call or fax; send handwritten, ungrammatical letters; they tell you the book is great because their husband/mother/children all loved it.

Description of the client from Hell: Writers with unreasonable and unrealistic expectations; people who don't know the market they're writing for; someone who is unprofessional—late in delivery of work, refuses to make editorial changes, falls apart from rejection of critiques. The person who asks for a personal meeting prior to sending in material for professional evaluation.

Description of a dream client: The writer with talent and creative new ideas. Writers who are passionate about their work, are willing to self-promote, and understand the pros and cons of the business behind the books.

Why did you become an agent? I love books. I enjoyed being an editor and I wanted to go into business for myself. This was the logical next profession that still involved reading and writers.

What can writers do to enhance their chances of getting you as agent? They can send a great short letter (an art form in itself)—a writer who knows how to convince me the idea is salable by listing facts instead of adjectives. Authors who have proven expertise on the topics of their books and are familiar with the market for them, know the competition, and can point out how their books are wonderfully different.

How would you describe what you actually do for a living? Wonderful fun—I really enjoy what I do. And I think I'm good at it. I'm good at the negotiating process, good at helping writers shape their work. Bleecker has an excellent track record with first-time authors, for example.

What do you think about editors? I like them. I used to be one so I can relate to their problems and points of view. It's helpful when an agent who was once on the other side of the desk can anticipate the objections in the deal-making process and have the answers handy in advance.

What do you think about publishers? They can be too tough on writers. However, ultimately I think that publishers and authors share a common goal: a terrific book that is also successful.

Comments: I wish that beginning writers read more on the topic of the genre they themselves are working in. Bestselling authors are especially worthwhile to dissect and study—there are inevitably good reasons why someone attracts a large following.

Representative titles: *Boys into Men: Raising African-American Male Teenagers* by Nancy Boyd-Franklin, Ph.D., and A. J. Franklin, Ph.D. (Dutton/Plume); *The Women's Pharmacy* by Julie Catalano (Dell); *Strange Skies* by Patricia Barnes-Svarney and Thomas Svarney (Fireside/Touchstone); *Bright Minds—Poor Grades* by Michael Whitley, Ph.D. (Perigee/Putnam); *The Encyclopedia of the Occult* by Brad Steiger (Gale); *How Hitler Could Have Won WWII* by Bevin Alexander (Crown); *Ophelia Speaks* by

Sara Shandler (Harper); *The Irish Manor House Murder* by Dicey Deere (St. Martins); *Angel's Crime* by Preston Pairo (NAL); *Smart Guide to Time Management* by Lisa Rogak (Wiley); *Her Father's Daughter* by Mollie Poupeney (Random House).

B

BOOKENDS, LLC

136 Long Hill Road, Gillette, NJ 07933
908-604-2652
www.bookends-inc.com

Agents: Jessica Faust, Jacky Sach

Born: Faust: March 24, 1971, Minnesota. Sach: June 9, 1964, United Kingdom.

Education: Faust: B.A. in Journalism, Marquette University. Sach: B.A. in English, Oneonta, New York.

Career history: Faust: Berkley Publishing: 1994–1998 (Associate Editor); Macmillan Publishing 1998–1999 (Senior Editor). Sach: Berkley Publishing/Penguin Putnam: 1986–2000.

Hobbies/personal interests: Faust: Walking my dog, running, travel, cooking, gardening, yard sales, flea markets. Sach: Playing with my dog and cats, reading, running, cooking, gardening, backpacking, camping, outdoor enthusiast.

Areas most interested in agenting: Faust: Romance and mysteries, women's fiction, nonfiction, business, relationships, self-help, psychology, parenting, pets, health. Sach: Literary fiction, mysteries, spirituality, self-help, suspense/thriller fiction.

Areas not interested in agenting: Faust: Children's, science fiction, fantasy. Sach: Children's, science fiction and fantasy, textbooks and religion.

If not agenting, what might you be doing? Faust: I would be an editor. I spent seven years in publishing as an acquisitions editor and I loved every minute of it. There is no doubt in my mind that if I were to leave agenting, it would only be because I've made a decision to re-join a publishing house. Sach: Writing, editing, service work of some capacity, or traveling.

Best way to initiate contact: Query letters are accepted via snail mail and e-mail. However, if you know the material you are submitting fits a category our agency represents, feel free to send along a partial. Always include a brief query letter, outlining your book and giving your credentials as a writer, a synopsis of the book, and an SASE. The agency does not accept e-mail attachments and will only look at short letters.

Client representation by category: Nonfiction, 60%; Fiction, 40%.

Commission: 15% English language; 20% British and foreign translation; 15% television, movie, and so on.

Number of titles sold last year: Approximately 25.

Rejection rate (all submissions): 80%.

Most common mistakes authors make: Faust: Not including a cover letter. I don't know how many times I'll request a manuscript after getting an e-mail or snail mail query, only to receive the material and nothing else. I get hundreds of submissions and queries a month and can't always remember which I've requested and which were just sent to me. It is important to remind me in a short letter not only that I've requested your material, but who you are, what your background is, and a brief two-sentence synopsis of your book. Sach: Clients forget that we look at hundreds of submissions and cannot always keep track of random communications and submissions. I appreciate a potential client who is clear with every piece of communication with me, detailing who the client is, what the client is sending me, conversations we may have had, dates submissions were sent, and titles of submissions.

Description of the client from Hell: Faust: Clients from Hell already know everything there is to know and don't need an editor. They usually think the book is perfect just as they wrote it and will refuse to accept any editorial suggestions their agent or editor might make. In addition, their primary goal is to be a star, and they expect their editor and agent to make them one, without doing any work themselves. Sach: Clients from Hell think they have written the perfect book that needs no help whatsoever and are resistant to changes and input from editors and agents. These clients also think that everything should be dropped immediately for them and have no understanding of time and patience. The client from Hell is egotistical, self-centered, and impatient.

Description of a dream client: Faust: My dream clients understand the need for an editor or an agent. They know that their book is not perfect and relish the look of a second pair of eyes, someone who isn't so close to the characters that she can't see their flaws. They take the time to know the industry and ask questions of things they don't understand. Dream clients write because they love to write, not just because they want to be published. And whether they are published or not, they are always writing. Sach: My dream clients understand the symbiotic relationship between writers and agents/editors. The clients are open to suggestion and change and want their books to be the best they can be. The clients rely on the hard-earned experience and knowledge of their editors and agents, while communicating their own ideas, dreams, and suggestions. Dream clients are patient and eager to learn and grow. Dream clients want thriving/positive relationships with their agents and strive first and foremost to make the best books possible. Dream clients also are willing to learn about the publishing industry. I believe that knowledgeable clients are good clients. Dream clients are writers at heart. They are most interested in writing; getting published is a wonderful benefit but not the reason they write. Most of all, these client write, write, write!

How did you become an agent? Faust: In 1999, Jacky Sach and I were sitting in her Brooklyn apartment discussing our jobs and careers when, out of the blue, I wondered if she would ever consider starting a business. Boom! Five months later we were the proud owners of BookEnds, LLC, a book packaging company. After just a short year in business, we were proud to say we had sold 10 books, but for some reason neither of us felt we were getting what we wanted from the business. That's when it hit us. What we really missed was working with the authors. We missed the romance and intrigue (literally) of working on fiction and nonfiction and helping authors craft the work they created. That's when we decided it was time to present ourselves as agents. We'd already had a number of requests for representation, so in 2001 we made it official. Sach: I'll rely on my partner's (Jessica Faust's) words for this one. Well said!

Why did you become an agent? Faust: I really love working with authors. I love helping them shape the book, and I love brainstorming during its inception. While I was able to achieve these things as an editor, I felt hemmed in by the confines of the publishing house. As an agent, I can take on almost any project that interests me because I have a huge variety of publishing houses to offer it to. Sach: I love reading and I love representing writers. I love the idea of helping someone fulfill a dream and build a career in writing. I also enjoy the creative input I have as an agent.

What can writers do to enhance their chances of getting you as their agent? Faust: I'm looking for writers with new and terrific ideas. While I'll always consider looking at a writer who describes her work as the next Nora Roberts, I would much rather find that writer whom everyone else describes as "the next of." I want to find a mystery series with a detective that no one has thought of and a romance I lose myself in and can't put down. For nonfiction writers, I'm looking for authors with a platform. I want people who have ideas of their own and who speak and write and promote those ideas. To them, books are just another platform, not the only platform. Sach: Originality.

How would you describe what you do for a living? Faust: I am an advocate for authors. It is my job to coach authors (as needed) through writing the book and then negotiate the contract and deal with the publishing house on their behalf. Sach: Author advocate.

What do you think about editors? Faust: Since I was an editor for many years, I think they are wonderful. I have a good relationship with many editors, and 90 percent of them do their job out of love. They love books and they love helping authors shape their manuscript. Unfortunately, editors are often restrained by the confines of the company they work for. Not all publishing houses handle cozy mysteries or historical romances, and for that reason editors are not always able to take on a project they love. It is a frustrating job at times, and editors are often given a bad rap for these reasons. Sach: I think today's editors are extremely overworked. A large percentage of them are wonderful, dedicated, hardworking individuals who have an honest desire to find a great writer and develop that writer's career—not just for the bestseller status but also for the joy of producing something notable. I believe that many talented editors are out there.

What do you think about publishers? Faust: They are businesspeople and while what they deal with is often considered art, the publishers themselves only look at it from a business perspective. This is an important thing for all writers to remember. Sach: There are fewer publishers left, as consolidation becomes more frequent—I wish there were more publishers! I wish the bottom line didn't weigh as heavily as it does. I wish writing as an art were more appreciated. But all in all, I do think publishers are doing a good job of getting writers out there. Although I do wish there were more opportunities for new writers and the publishers were more willing to take big chances. . . . I also think many publishers feel this way themselves.

What were your favorite films last year? Faust: Unfortunately, I'm not much of a movie buff. *Gladiator,* was that last year? Sach: *Billy Elliot* and *Traffic.*

Do you watch the *Sopranos?* Faust: No. Sach: No.

Comments: Faust: There are so many amazing writers out there with wonderful stories to tell, but those who really hit home with me are the writers who are doing it from the heart. They are writing about something they know and writing because of their love for writing. I love being an agent and I'm looking forward to, more than anything, working with and meeting so many new and terrific writers and helping them make their dreams come true. Sach: What rocks my world is when I know I am reading the truth; when the truth just rings out from the plate, whether it's a novel or a nonfiction work, honesty speaks to me. That moment when you read something and you know it is absolutely right, completely perfect . . . nothing is more beautiful than that.

Representative titles: *Out of Lawndale* by Libby Fischer Hellmann (Berkley); *Critical Lives: Che Guevara* by Eric Luther with Ted Henken, M.A. (Alpha); *How Queer!! Parenting in the Gay, Lesbian, Bisexual and Transgendered Community* by Arlene (Ari) Ishtar Lev (Berkely); *CSW-R, CASAS Streetwise Guide to Publicity* by Sandra Beckwith (Adams Media); *Court TV's You Be the Judge* by Patrick Sauer (Warner).

B

PAMELA K. BRODOWSKY LITERARY AGENCY

RR 5, Box 5391 A, Moscow, PA 18444
570-689-2692
e-mail: pmlbrod.aol.com

Agent: Pamela K. Brodowsky
   Born: October 1967, Midland Park, New Jersey.
   Education: Business.
   Career history: Sales and marketing, business consultant, literary agent.
   Hobbies/personal interests: Literature, film, art, and classical music.
   Areas most interested in agenting: Fiction: Romance, thrillers, mystery, suspense. Nonfiction: Women's issues, self-help.
   Areas not interested in agenting: Science fiction, poetry.
   Best way to initiate contact: Send a query letter with SASE; enclose the first 15 pages of the manuscript. Please do not send full, unsolicited manuscripts.
   Client representation by category: Nonfiction, 10%; Fiction, 85%; Children's, 5%.
   Commission: 15%.
   Number of titles sold last year: 10.
   Rejection rate (all submissions): 95%.
   Description of the client from Hell: A person who listens to you when you're talking, but doesn't hear what you're saying.
   Description of the dream client: A writer who has the determination and ability to succeed. A true professional. One who knows it's not as easy as 1-2-3.
   Most common mistakes authors make: Queries that don't provide me with enough information; bad grammar; they don't enclose an SASE with the query letter.
   What can writers do to enhance their chances of getting you as their agent? A well-written query letter is a good place to start.
   Why did you become an agent? There is only one answer to this questions and that is I have a great love for the written word.
   If not agenting, what might you be doing? I would likely be a sales executive.
   How would you describe what you do for a living? Challenging—and I love a challenge.
   What do you think about editors? I think most are underpaid.
   What do you think about publishers? I think they are the cores of our apples.

What were your favorite films last year? *Chocolat, Pearl Harbor.*
Do you watch the *Sopranos?* No.
Comments: I think it's terrible that this world is filled with people who are capable of killing one another without a second thought. Life is precious; live it to the fullest today, because there is no making up for lost time tomorrow.

B

ANDREA BROWN LITERARY AGENCY, INC.

PO Box 1027, Montara, CA 94037
650-728-1783   fax: 650-728-1732
e-mail: ablitag@pacbell.net

Agents: Andrea Brown; Laura Rennert, Associate Agent
Born: Rennert: December 16, 1964, Bethesda, Maryland.
Education: Brown: B.A. in Journalism and English, Syracuse University. Rennert: B.A., Cornell University; M.A., University of Virginia; Ph.D. in English Literature, University of Virginia.
Career history: Brown: Editorial Assistant, Dell; Editorial Assistant, Random House; Assistant Editor (all children's books), Knopf; started agency in 1981. Rennert: Faculty member in English department of universities in the United States and in Japan for eight years. Freelance editor for four years. Associate Agent at Andrea Brown Literary Agency for four years.
Hobbies/personal interests: Brown: Golf, theater, gardening, travel, my cats.
Areas most interested in agenting: Brown: Easy-readers, anything humorous, science activity books, high-tech nonfiction for all ages. Rennert: Picture books, middle-grade and young adult fiction, historical fiction, photography; I am also looking for talented illustrators who are also writers.
Areas not interested in agenting: Brown: Don't send adult books; we specialize in children's books and still get flooded with adult proposals. No rhyming picture books. Rennert: I am an omnivorous reader and an omnivorous agent. We do, however, represent primarily children's books.
If not agenting, what might you be doing? Brown: I've been an agent so long now, I can't imagine doing anything else, though it's often so frustrating these days. Rennert: If I weren't an agent, I would continue my career as a professor of English Literature and as a scholar.
Best way to initiate contact: Brown: Query letter with SASE only. Rennert: A query letter and four chapters of work or a query and a complete picture book manuscript.
Client representation by category: Brown: Children's, 99% (Nonfiction, 50%; Fiction, 50%). Rennert: Nonfiction, 3%; Fiction, 2%; Children's, 95%.
Commission: 15% domestic; 20% foreign.
Number of titles sold last year: Brown: Not for public consumption—more than last year.
Rejection rate (all submissions): Brown: 95%.
Most common mistakes authors make: Brown: Faxing queries. I hate that. Or long calls, asking lots of questions before I'm interested. And calling after I've already said no.

Or re-sending with minor changes after we have rejected it. It closes the door on any future interest I may have in the writer. Rennert: The most common mistakes are not knowing the comparables and competition. If you are going to write picture books, for example, then you should be reading *a lot* of picture books.

Description of the client from Hell: Brown: People who have to talk to their agent on a daily basis, always think their work is perfect as it is and that the editor is always wrong. Rennert: The client from Hell wants frequent phone updates and constant hand-holding. Because we specialize in children's books, we have more clients and make more deals than adult agents. The sheer volume of manuscripts and deals with which we are involved takes up much of our time during and after business hours, and the client from Hell is one who doesn't understand that much of our time is spent on the business of promoting and selling books.

Description of the dream client: Brown: Authors who work hard and take their career seriously; they respect that an agent has many clients to represent, but still remember to mention that they appreciate the time and effort taken on their behalf. Rennert: My dream client is one who is devoted to the craft of writing, who welcomes editorial input and who is willing to revise and, if necessary, revise again. My dream clients understand that the work of selling books takes a lot of time and dedication, and they welcome e-mail updates and communication, interspersed with the occasional phone call.

Why did you become an agent? Brown: I fell into the children's book field and loved it. I loved working with authors and illustrators and creating good books for kids. I saw that authors needed more representation in the changing children's books field, and I was the first to represent both children's book authors *and* illustrators. That was 1981, and now authors need agents more than ever. Rennert: I became an agent because of my love of the written word and of books. I wanted to be passionate about what I do and to work with people who are passionate about what they do.

What can writers do to enhance their chances of getting you as their agent? Brown: Doing their homework in the children's book field as to appropriate age group, category, length, and so on. If writers come off as knowledgeable and professional (and can write and think commercially), I'm more likely to take them on. Writing well is not enough. Rennert: If writers can move me to laughter or to tears, then I usually think very carefully about taking them on as clients. I look for writers with whom I can have a long-term relationship and with whom I can grow.

How would you describe what you do for a living? Rennert: I am involved in the creative process, working with writers to help them realize the full potential of their vision and to perfect their craft. I use my relationships with publishers to help find the best home for each writer's work, and then I negotiate the best deal possible for my authors.

What do you think about editors? Brown: Editors are the writer's best friend (other than their agent). They are hard-working, caring people who really want to create excellent, beautiful books, and don't get enough appreciation.

Comments: Brown: Unfortunately, everyone thinks it is easy to write for children. Actually, it is the toughest form of writing to do, especially picture books. In a few words, a writer must tell a perfect story with a fresh writing voice. It takes rare talent to pull it off well. It's more important to write from the child within you than to have three children and think you can write. Many people make this mistake. A children's writer must have the passion and voice to get published. Name brands sell, and it's tougher than ever to get a new writer published. Good writing is not enough. Writers must think in a commercial way and plan to promote their books. And don't waste your time trying to get an agent if you just have one picture book. Agents need writers committed to a long-term career writing for children.

Representative titles: *"K" Is for Kitten* by Niki Leopold, illustrated by Susan Jeffers (Penguin/Putnam); *Escape from Heart* by Lynette Stark (Harcourt); *Paul McCartney: I Saw Him Standing There* by Jorie Gracen (Billboard Books/Watson Guptil); *How People Learned to Fly* by Fran Hodgkins, illustrated by Tru Kelley (HarperCollins); *Christmas John* by Margaret Raven (Farrar Straus & Giroux); *The First Day* by Ellen Jackson (Millbrook Press).

CURTIS BROWN LTD.

Ten Astor Place, New York, NY 10003
212-473-5400

Agents: Ellen Geiger, Elizabeth Harding, Ginger Knowlton, Laura Blake Peterson, Douglas Stewart, Mitchell Waters

The following information pertains to ELLEN GEIGER:
Born: New York, New York.
Education: Graduate Degree in Anthropology.
Career history: Former PBS Executive before becoming a literary agent.
Hobbies/personal interests: Tennis, reading, growing perfect tomatoes, travel, film, theater, arts.
Areas most interested in agenting: Nonfiction of all kinds, especially narrative, and high-quality commercial and literary fiction, cutting-edge issues, journalists, Asia and Asian-American subjects, religion, science, history.
Areas not interested in agenting: Romance, New Age, children's, poetry, cookie-cutter thrillers, right-wing propaganda.
Best method to initiate contact: Query letter with SASE, sample chapters (if novel) or proposal (if nonfiction).
If not agenting, what would you be doing? I'll always be an agent.
Client representation by category: Nonfiction, 75%; Fiction, 25%.
What is your commission structure? 15% domestic; 20% Canadian/overseas.
Rejection rate (all submissions): 95%.
Most common mistakes authors make: Sending a whole manuscript with a query letter without being requested, sloppy mistakes and typos in proposals, calling repeatedly for status reports, telling me what a great *film* their book will make.
Description of the client from Hell: Someone who can't be pleased, no matter what happens. An overanxious author who calls or e-mails all the time; suspicious authors who can't trust their agents.
Description of the dream client: A writer who is talented, patient, hard working, self-confident. A writer with a track record of some sort. A genius who is also a nice person.

How did you become an agent? I was mentored into the business by a top agent.

Why did you become an agent? It's immensely satisfying to bring good work to the public.

What can writers do to enhance their chances of getting you as an agent? Write a dynamite query letter, have some expertise on the subject (if nonfiction) or a publishing track record (if fiction).

How would you describe what you actually do for a living? Among other clichés: mine for gold, storm the barricades, pour oil on the waters, throw caution to the winds, tilt at windmills.

What do you think about editors? They are under tremendous pressure to justify their acquisitions before their Editorial Boards, so submissions need to be truly excellent. They are also seriously understaffed and cannot do the kind of in-depth editing and hand-holding they'd like to do.

What do you think about publishers? They should all tithe at the shrine of St. Oprah for popularizing literature and creating new readers.

Comments: I love it when unusual books become hits, like *Tuesdays with Morrie* or *Longitude*. This happens often enough in publishing to give me hope.

Representative titles: *Body RX* by Dr. Scott Connelly (Putnam); *Lillian Gish* by Charles Affron (Scribner); *God at the Edge* by Niles Goldstein (Bell Tower); *Murder with Puffins, Flamingos, etc.* by Donna Andrews (St. Martin's Press).

The following information pertains to ELIZABETH HARDING:

Education: B.A. in English, University of Michigan (Ann Arbor).

Areas most interested in agenting: Children's literature.

Best method to initiate contact: Query letter or sample chapters.

Client representation by category: Children's, 100%.

Commission: 15% domestic; 20% foreign; 15% dramatic.

The following information pertains to GINGER KNOWLTON:

Born: Before the 1960s in Princeton, New Jersey.

Education: Questionable, navy brat quality.

Career history: I worked in a factory assembling display cases in Mystic, Connecticut, for a time. Gained numerous pounds one summer working in a bakery in Mendocino, California. I've taught preschool and I directed an infant and toddler child-care center. That means I organized a lot of fundraisers. I started working at Curtis Brown in 1986.

Areas most interested in agenting: Middle grade and teenage novels.

Areas not interested in agenting: I prefer to remain open to all ideas.

Best method to initiate contact: A simple, straightforward letter with a return envelope works well.

If not agenting, what might you be doing? I love my job, but if I had the luxury of not having to work, I would play tennis even more than I already do; I would tend my gardens more fastidiously; and I would spend more time playing with others.

Client representation by category: Nonfiction, 5%; Fiction, 5%; Children's, 90%.

Commission: 15% domestic; 20% foreign.

Rejection rate (all submissions): 98%.

Most common mistakes authors make: Expecting an answer within a week, but mostly poor quality writing.

Description of the client from Hell: Happy to report that I still don't have firsthand experience with a "client from Hell," so once again I will refrain from describing one (for fear of a self-fulfilling prophecy).

Description of a dream client: Professional authors who respect my job as I respect theirs, who will maintain an open dialogue so we may learn from each other and continue to grow, who are optimistic and enthusiastic, and who continue to write books worthy of publication.

How did you become an agent? I asked Dad for money for graduate school. He offered me a job at Curtis Brown instead.

What do you think about editors? I have a lot of respect for editors and I think they have an incredibly difficult job. As in all professions, some are more gifted than others.

The following information pertains to LAURA BLAKE PETERSON:

Education: B.A., Vassar College.

Career history: 1986–present, Curtis Brown, Ltd.

Hobbies/personal interests: Gardening, pets, regional equestrian competitions.

Areas most interested in agenting: Exceptional fiction, narrative nonfiction, young adult fiction, anything outstanding.

Areas not interested in agenting? Fantasy, science fiction, poetry.

Best way to initiate contact: The best way is through a referral from either a client of mine or an editor with whom I work.

Client representation by category: Nonfiction, 40%; Fiction, 40%; Children's, 20%.

Commission: 15% domestic; 20% foreign.

Rejection rate (all submissions): 98%.

Common mistakes authors make: Calling, rather than sending a query letter.

Description of the client from Hell: Authors who call incessantly, preventing me from accomplishing anything on their behalf.

Description of the dream client: A talented writer who knows the idiosyncrasies of the publishing business yet nonetheless remains determined to be a part of it; a writer with the skills and patience to participate in an often frustrating and quirky industry.

Why did you become an agent? I love language. I can't imagine a better job than helping to bring a skilled writer to the attention of the book-buying public.

If not agenting, what might you be doing? Teaching, gardening, who knows?

What can writers do to enhance their chances of getting you as an agent? Do their homework. Find out what I (or whoever they're contacting) like to read and represent, what books I've sold in the past, etc. Read this survey!

The following information pertains to DOUGLAS STEWART:

Born: 1971, Wisconsin.

Education: B.A., Vassar College.

Areas most interested in agenting: Literary fiction, serious nonfiction.

Areas not interested in agenting: Romance, how-to, health, children's, spirituality.

Best way to initiate contact: Query letter and one sample chapter (fiction), or just a query letter (nonfiction).

Client representation by category: Nonfiction, 50%; Fiction, 50%.

Rejection rate (all submissions): 98%.

Representative titles: *Shadow Baby* by Alison McGhee (Harmony Books); *Lit Life* by Kurt Wenzel (Random House); *Mountain City* by Gregory Martin (FSG/North Point); *Ghostwritten* by David Mitchell (Random House); *Humanity* by Jonathan Glover (Yale University Press); *The Colors of Nature* by Alison Deming and Laucet Savog (Milkweed).

The following information pertains to MITCHELL WATERS:

Born: June 19, 1957, Brooklyn, New York.

Education: M.A. in English Literature, Fordham University.

Hobbies/personal interests: Tennis, theater, opera.

Areas most interested in agenting: Literary fiction, narrative nonfiction, mystery, suspense, health, social sciences, gay and lesbian fiction, nonfiction.

Areas not interested in agenting: Science fiction, romance.

Best way to initiate contact: Query letter.

Client representation by category: Nonfiction, 60%; Fiction, 35%; Children's, 5%.

Commission: 15% domestic sales.

Number of titles sold last year: 25.

Rejection rate (all submissions): 95%.

Most common mistakes authors make: Frequent follow-up phone calls.

Why did you become an agent? To be an advocate for talented writers.

If not agenting, what might you be doing? Teaching literature.

What can writers do to enhance their chances of getting you as an agent? Be patient, but remind me they are there.

PEMA BROWNE LTD.

71 Pine Road, HCR Box 104B, Neversink, NY 12765
845-985-2936, 845-985-2062

Agents: Pema Browne (Pema rhymes with Emma), Perry Browne

Education: Pema: Moore College of Art, University of Pennsylvania; Barnes Foundation. Perry: B.A. in English/Communications, Syracuse University.

Career history: Pema: Artist/Painter; exhibited widely, in three N.Y. city shows; art buyer. Perry: Radio/TV DJ; commercials.

Hobbies/personal interests: Travel.

Areas most interested in agenting: Solid adult literary fiction and nonfiction. Children's, all genres from novelty, picture books, novels, to nonfiction.

Areas not interested in agenting: Poetry, pornography, photography, science fiction.

Best way to initiate contact: One-page query letter with SASE (no checks).

Reading-fee policy: No reading fee.

Client representation by category: Nonfiction, 35%; Fiction, 30%; Children's, 35%.

Commission: 15% manuscripts; 20% author/illustrations; 30% illustrations; 10% screenplays.

Number of titles sold last year: 28.

Rejection rate (all submissions): 99%.

Description of the client from Hell: We do not handle anyone who would fit that description.

Description of a dream client: Authors who have integrity and professionalism and continue to polish their skills. Those who present well-thought-out proposals and neat manuscripts.

Representative titles: *Soul Echoes: The Healing Power of Past Life Therapy* by Thelma Freedman Ph.D. (Citadel Press); *Get the Job You Want in 30 Days, Revised Special Edition* by Gary Joseph Grappo (Berkley); *A Perfect Mismatch* by Catherine Blair (Regnery Romance/Kensington); *Dead Man's Rock* by Linda Cargill (YA Horror Suspense/Cora Verlag); *The Beast Within* by Susan Scott (Cora Verlag); *Magical Math Series* by Lynette Long, Ph.D. (John Wiley & Sons); *Happy Birthday,* illustrated by John Sandford (HarperCollins); *It's Not My Job* by Ted Lish, illustrated by Charles Jordan (Munchweiler Press).

SHEREE BYKOFSKY ASSOCIATES, INC.

16 West 36th Street, New York, NY 10018
212-244-4144

Agent: Sheree Bykofsky

Born: September 1956, Queens, New York.

Education: B.A., State University of New York, Binghamton; M.A. in English and Comparative Literature, Columbia University.

Career history: Executive Editor/Book Producer, the Stonesong Press (1984–1996); Freelance Editor/Writer (1984); General Manager/Managing Editor, Chiron Press, 1979–1984. Author and co-author of a dozen books, most notably *The Complete Idiot's Guide to Getting Published* (Alpha/Macmillan).

Hobbies/personal interests: Tournament Scrabble, poker, racquetball, movies, bridge.

Areas most interested in agenting: Popular reference, adult nonfiction (hardcovers and trade paperbacks), quality fiction (highly selective).

Areas not interested in agenting: Genre romances, science fiction, Westerns, occult and supernatural, children's books.

If not agenting, what would you be doing? Writing and editing.

Best way to initiate contact: Send a well-written, detailed query letter with an SASE. Please, no phone calls.

Reading-fee policy: No reading fee.

Client representation by category: Nonfiction, 80%; Fiction, 20%.

Commission: 15%.

Number of titles sold last year: 100.

Rejection rate (all submissions): 90%.

Most common mistakes authors make: Excessive hubris; not explaining what the book is about; paranoia (we're not going to steal your idea); sloppy grammar, punctuation, and spelling.

Description of the client from Hell: I only take on an author if I feel we can work well together.

Description of a dream client: One who is not only a talented writer but also who is a professional in every sense—from writing the proposal to promoting the book. Also, writers who appreciate my hard work on their behalf. I love when authors read my book *The Complete Idiot's Guide to Getting Published.*

How did you become an agent? I managed a small textbook publishing company. Then I was a book producer and author, then an agent.

Why did you become an agent? It suits me, and I feel I have the talent and experience to do it well.

Comments: In addition to being an agent, I have been a book packager and an author. This gives my clients and me a perspective that most agents do not have. Often, I match my clients with publishers' ideas.

Representative titles: *Niche and Grow Rich* by Jennifer Basye Sander and Peter Sander; *365 Ways to Become a Millionaire Without Being Born One* by Brian Koslow (Dutton); *Love Types: Discover Your Romantic Style and Find Your Soul Mate* by Alexander Avila (Avon); *Multicultural Manners* by Norine Dresser (Wiley); *Race Manners* by Bruce Jacobs (Arcade); *The Bearded Lady* by Sharlee Dieguez (Hill Street); *The Complete Idiot's Guide to Getting Published* by Sheree Bykofsky (Alpha/Macmillan); *Dealers, Healers, Brutes & Saviors* by Gerald and Susan Meyers (Wiley); *In All the Wrong Places* by Donna Anders (Pocket); *22 Ways to Creating a Meaningful Work Place* by Tom Terez (Adams); *Breast Cancer Survival Manual* by John Link, M.D. (Holt); *Create Your Own Luck* by Azriela Jaffe (Adams); *The Baghavad Gita for Westerners* by Jack Hawley (New World Library); *The Toltec Way* by Susan Gregg (Renaissance); *Christmas Windows in New York: A Pictorial Look at 100 Years of Christmas Windows* by Sheryll Bellman (Rizzoli).

CARLISLE & COMPANY

24 East 64th Street, New York, NY 10021
212-813-1881   fax: 212-813-9567

Agent: Emma Joanne Parry
  Born: September 11, 1973, Malmesbury, England.
  Education: St. Catherine's College, University of Cambridge, St. Mary's Convent, Cambridge.
  Career History: Ogilvy and Mather Account Executive; Gillon Aitken Associates Ltd. London.
  Hobbies/personal interests: Travel, film, theater, and contemporary art.
  Areas most interested in agenting: Serious nonfiction and literary fiction.
  Areas not interested in agenting: Children's books, plays, film scripts.
  Best way to initiate contact: By letter.
  Client representation by category: Nonfiction, 50%; Fiction, 50%.
  Commission: 15% home; 20% abroad.

Number of titles sold last year: 45.
Rejection rate (all submissions): 99%.
Do you watch the *Sopranos?* Yes.
Representative titles: *Leaving Reality Behind: A History of the Internet* by Adam Wishart (Ecco/HarperCollins); *Captives* by Linda Cohey (Pantheon/Random House); *The Impressionist* by Hori Kunzru (Dutton/Plume); *Angel Rock* by Darren Williams (Knopf); *The Bash Dyslexicon* by Mark Crispin (W. W. Norton).

C

MARIA CARVAINIS AGENCY, INC.

1350 Avenue of the Americas, Suite 2905, New York, NY 10019
212-245-6365   fax: 212-245-7196
e-mail: mcamariacarvainisagency.com

Agents: Maria Carvainis, President; Frances Kuffel, Executive Vice President
Born: Carvainis: March 24, 1946, Brisbane, Australia. Kuffel: 1956, Missoula, Montana.
Education: Carvainis: B.A., City College of New York, 1967. Kuffel: B.A. in Religious Studies and B.A. in English, University of Montana; M.F.A. in Creative Writing, Cornell University.
Career history: Maria Carvainis established the Maria Carvainis Agency, Inc., in 1977 and the agency has expanded and been profitable ever since. Prior to 1977, she worked for 10 years in the publishing industry as an Editor and then Senior Editor at Macmillan Publishing, Basic Books, Avon Books, and Crown Publishing. She has been active in the Association of Authors' Representatives, serving as a Board Member, Treasurer, and Chair of the AAR Contracts Committee, and currently is a member of the AAR Royalty Committee.
Hobbies/personal interests: Carvainis: Reading literary fiction, biographies, and mysteries; gardening, gourmet cooking, wine appreciation, and international travel. Maria is a Conservator of the New York Public Library, Member of Literary Partners, President of the Bidwell House Museum, and devotee of vintage English cars, especially Bentleys. Kuffel: Writing, reading.
Areas most interested in agenting: The agency represents both fiction and nonfiction, with special interest in general fiction/mainstream, literary fiction, mystery and suspense, thrillers, historicals, young adult, contemporary women's fiction, biography and memoirs, business, psychology, and popular science. Kuffel: Narrative nonfiction, history and biography, memoir, science, literary fiction; high-end, historical fiction.
Areas not interested in agenting: Carvainis: Science fiction. Kuffel: Westerns.
If not agenting, what would you be doing? Carvainis: I have never considered an alternative profession. Kuffel: I'd get to read books and have a social life.
Best way to initiate contact: Carvainis: An articulate and succinct query letter with SASE. Include a one- or two-paragraph description of the project, mention writing credits, if any, and describe where your project fits in the marketplace. In addition, identify what material is available: complete manuscript, sample chapters, or synopsis. Kuffel: A one-page query letter describing the project, with pertinent autobiographical information and an SASE.
Reading-fee policy: No reading fee.

Client representation by category: Carvainis: Nonfiction, 40%; Fiction, 60%. Kuffel: Nonfiction, 33%; Fiction, 66%.

Commission: 15% domestic, 20% foreign.

Number of titles sold last year: Confidential.

Rejection rate (all submissions): Carvainis: 99%, but new original writers should never be discouraged by the statistics. Kuffel: 99%.

Most common mistakes authors make: Carvainis: Some writers view their queries as form letters. They claim more for their project than it delivers. Kuffel: Query letters should be concise; address the plot, not the meaning of the project in question; limit autobiographical remarks to what really applies; and show a real understanding both of what the marketplace is and how the project (and the author) really stand in relation to it.

Description of a dream client: Carvainis: A writer who is intelligent, has original ideas, and is informed about the marketplace, in addition to having the ability to write and willingness to rewrite. Kuffel: Dream clients are talented, first and foremost. They listen to my advice and consider it well before disagreeing with it (although, of course, dream clients always agree). They trust my taste, experience, and abilities.

How did you become an agent? Carvainis: I wanted to be an entrepreneur and used my 10 years of editorial experience to do so. Kuffel: I dropped out of a Ph.D. program in English and my parents suggested, kindly, that at 30 years of age I might want to get a job. I didn't know what to do, but I liked books so I applied for some jobs in publishing. My first offer—as her assistant—was from a literary agent and eventually I began handling subrights and building a list.

Why did you become an agent? Carvainis: After 10 years on the corporate side of the desk, I found myself more identified with the authors and their interests than with the corporate mission. Furthermore, I wanted to be an independent businessperson, responsible only to my clients and myself. I was willing to take a risk for greater personal and financial rewards and have had the satisfaction of helping many writers fulfill their aspirations and establish careers. Kuffel: I like books. I wanted to help writers. I had a chance to do it and I took advantage of it.

What can writers do to enhance their chances of getting you as an agent? Writers should be able to crystallize the originality of their work. Clarity is a sign of competence and confidence.

How would you describe what you actually do for a living? Carvainis: I believe that I am a long-term business partner with the writer to build a successful career. Each writer has unique strengths. My job is to complement the author. Authors vary in how much creative direction they need. Authors who are still building a readership can often benefit from editorial direction as they shape the next project. The role of agents always involves vigorously trying to sell projects they represent because they believe in the author. After the sale, it is all about negotiating the best contract and protecting the author's rights. Kuffel: I'm a matchmaker, a fine-points-stickler, and a policeman. This means I size a project up against the marketplace, work with the author to present the best and most competitive project possible, and then exploit my editorial contacts in finding the right home for the writer and the book. When I've been successful in that, I make sure the contracts are as advantageous for the writer as possible, that the editor and publisher are doing their jobs, regarding the book, and that all avenues of income related to the book are exploited. So part of the job is very expansive, and the other is very narrow.

What do you think about editors? Carvainis: Editors today vary tremendously in their abilities. Because the corporate structure uses agents as readers or screeners of material, the editor is primarily in an acquisition role, often spending more time in meetings than in working with authors and manuscripts. Kuffel: I think they're smart and talented. I also think that, increasingly, they work in and, often, against the corporate environments of which they are a part. It's not just that the bottom line is being examined, it is also a growing lack of vision and volition that's filtering down from parent companies, the focus of which is wildly different from books.

What do you think about publishers? Carvainis: There is tremendous confusion in the industry among publishers. The great uncertainty is whether the traditional role of a publisher has value or whether a publisher is simply a content provider. And the emergence of electronic commerce and the electronic book, combined with globalized consolidation, seems at times to totally preoccupy them. Kuffel: My reservations are similar to those I expressed about editors, but publishers are often the entities invoked to excuse lack of vision, commitment, and/or advocacy on the parts of other members of the publishing "team."

What were your favorite films last year? Carvainis: *Crouching Tiger, Hidden Dragon.* Kuffel: *Wonder Boys; Bridget Jones' Diary; The Anniversary Party; Hedwig and the Angry Itch.*

Do you watch the *Sopranos*? Carvainis: Yes—on video. Kuffel: I don't even have time for the Weather Channel.

Representative titles: Carvainis: *A Summer to Remember* by Mark Balogh (Delacorte); *Fame: The Power and Cost of a Fantasy* by Sue Erikson Bloland (Viking); *The Guru Guide to the Knowledge Economy* by Joseph H. and Jimmie T. Boyett (John Wiley & Sons); *Envy* by Sandra Brown (Warner Books); *Trophy Widow* by Michael Kahn (TOR/Forge); *Paint It Black* by P. J. Parrish (Kensington). Kuffel: *The Devil's Hearth* by Phillip DePoy (St. Martin's Press); *The Floating World* by Cynthia Gralla (Ballantine); *The Puppeteer's Apprentice* by D. Anne Love (Margaret McEdlerry Books); *Last Breath* by Peter Stark (Ballantine); *Princess Naughty and the Voodoo Cadillac* by Fred Willard (Longstreet Press).

MARTHA CASSELMAN, LITERARY AGENT

PO Box 342, Calistoga, CA 94515
707-942-4341

Agent: Martha Casselman

Born: New York City.

Education: B.A. in English and Education, Jackson College of Tufts University; Radcliffe Publishing Procedures Course.

Career history: Magazines, Editorial Assistant, Copyeditor, Editor (*Good Housekeeping, Show* magazine, *Holiday* magazine); Freelance Editor and Reader (Book-of-the-Month Club, Viking, etc.)—in New York before moving to California in 1976.

Hobbies/personal interests: Can you believe—reading? (Belongs to a reading group.)

Areas most interested in agenting: Food books, some nonfiction, other exciting books too wonderful to turn away.

Areas not interested in agenting: Poetry, textbooks, religion, fiction, children's, or full scripts.

If not agenting, what would you be doing? It changes. I can't remember not being an agent.

Best way to initiate contact: Write a brief letter (with SASE), and be straightforward about what other contacts are being made; make proposal/query so good it's impossible for me not to go after it (but expect long-distance return calls to be collect if you make a query by phone). Reminder: No return postage means no response. Sorry.

Reading-fee policy: No reading fee.

Client representation by category: Nonfiction, 98%; Fiction, 2%.

Commission: 15%, plus some copying, overnight mail expenses; 20% if using subagents.

Number of titles sold last year: Confidential.

Rejection rate (all submissions): 99%.

Most common mistakes authors make: Not doing their marketing homework: What are the other books out there? Do an evaluation, neither knocking nor overpraising. How is this book going to get readers/buyers, with all the other books in competition with it?

Description of the client from Hell: My sympathies are increasingly with authors, except when authors simply don't want to listen to reality (please don't shoot the messenger—when it's me, anyway).

Why did you become an agent? An accident; also, there were almost no publishing jobs (except for editors) in 1979.

If not agenting, what might you be doing? Reading the newspaper.

How would you describe what it is you actually do for a living? Do you have a week or two?

How did you become an agent? Just an accident, but a pretty wise one.

Do you watch the *Sopranos?* No (no cable).

CASTIGLIA LITERARY AGENCY

1155 Camino Del Mar, Suite 510, Del Mar, CA 92014
Golden direct line: 858-454-4983   fax: 858-755-7063

Agents: Julie Castiglia, Winifred Golden

Education: Castiglia: Educated in England.

Career history: Castiglia: Published writer (three book titles—hundreds of magazine articles, essays, poetry in literary anthologies), Freelance Editor Agent (past 14 years).

Hobbies/personal interests: Castiglia: Traveling, hiking, skiing, gardening, animals, decorative arts, books.

Areas most interested in agenting: Castiglia: Mainstream, literary, ethnic fiction. Nonfiction: Psychology, science and health, biography, women's issues, niche books, contemporary issues, narrative nonfiction, how-to. Golden: Mainstream fiction and nonfiction, literary and ethnic fiction, narrative nonfiction, pop culture, true crime, suspense, science fiction.

C

Areas not interested in agenting: Castiglia: Horror and science fiction; formula romance. Golden: Poetry, romance, fantasy.

Best way to initiate contact: Query letter with SASE.

Reading-fee policy: No reading fee.

Client representation by category: Nonfiction, 50%; Fiction, 50%.

Commission: 15% domestic

Number of titles sold last year: 25

Rejection rate (all submissions): 95%.

Why did you become an agent? Castiglia: I've always loved books and knew the publishing business well, having sold my own three books and edited other writers' work. It was a natural step.

What can writers do to enhance their chances of getting you as an agent? The Castiglia Agency: We prefer potential clients to be referred by editors, professional writers, or clients. Otherwise, the query letter has to knock our socks off.

Representative titles: *Harlem Redux* by Persia Walker (Simon & Schuster); *Oracle of Love* by Lee Ann Richards (Three Rivers/Random House); *Dogz in the Hood* by Melinda Roth (St. Martin's); *Story Book Style* by Doug Keister and Arrol Gellner (Penguin); *Ready to Roll* by Doug Keister and Arrol Gellner (Penguin); *The Graceful Parent: How to Raise a Gentle and Loving Child* by Eve Dreyfus, M.D. (Ten Speed); *Healing the Brain* by Dr. Curt Freed and Simon LeVay (Times Books/Holt); untitled novel by April Sinclair, author of *Coffee Will Make You Black* (Hyperion); *Youth in Revolt* by C. D. Payne (Doubleday); *Sunday You Learn How to Box* by Bill Wright (Scribners); *The Ethics of Star Trek* by Judith Barad, Ph.D., with Ed Robertson (HarperCollins); *Young Black Rich and Famous: Ball, Hip Hop and the Redefinition of the American Dream* by Todd Boyd, Ph.D. (Doubleday).

WM CLARK ASSOCIATES

325 West 13th Street, New York, NY 10014
212-675-2784   fax: 646-349-1658
www.wmclark.com   e-mail: wcquery@wmclark.com

Agent: William Clark

Born: Roanoke, Virginia.

Education: College of William and Mary.

Career history: Virginia Barber Agency (1992–1993); William Morris Agency (1993–1997).

Areas most interested in agenting: Mainstream literary fiction and quality nonfiction, especially memoirs, popular culture, and current events.

Areas not interested in agenting: Horror, science fiction, fantasy, children's or young adult, how-to.

If not agenting, what would you be doing? I would be a Buddhist monk.

Best way to initiate contact: E-mail queries (to wcquery@wmclark.com). E-mail queries should include a general description of the work, a synopsis/outline, biographical information, and publishing history, if any. I will respond whether or not I am interested in your work or idea, or if I feel it is not right for me.

Client representation by category: Nonfiction, 40%; Fiction, 60%.

Number of titles sold last year: 28.

Rejection rate (all submissions): 95%.

Commission: 15% domestic, 20% foreign.

Description of the client from Hell: I have no clients from Hell.

Description of the dream client: Clients who understand their role in the publication of the book, beyond actually writing the book.

Representative titles: *River Town* by Peter Hessler (HarperCollins); *Light House* by William Monahan (Riverhead); *Born to Rent* by David Eddie (Riverhead); *Gig* by Marisa Bowe, John Bowe, and Sabin Streeter (Crown); *The Heat of Lies* by Jonathan Stone (St. Martin's Press); *Tha Doggfather* by Snoop Dogg (William Morrow); *God, Dr. Buzzard, and the Bolito Man* by Cornelia Bailey, with Christena Bledsoe (Doubleday); *Mark Hampton: The Art of Friendship* by Duane Hampton; *The Official Bjork* by Bjork (Bloombury); *Stardust Melodies* by Will Friewald (Pantheon).

CLAUSEN, MAYS & TAHAN LITERARY AGENCY

249 West 34th Street, New York, NY 10001
212-239-4343   fax: 212-239-5248
e-mail: CMTassist@aol.com

Agents: Stedman Mays, Mary M. Tahan

Education: Mays: M.A. in English, University of Virginia. Tahan: M.A. in Near East Studies, New York University.

Areas most interested in agenting: Mostly nonfiction: women's issues, relationships, men's issues, parenting, spirituality, religion, history, memoirs, biography, autobiography, true stories, medical, health/nutrition, psychology, how-to, business/financial, fashion/beauty, style, humor, novels (both genre and literary); rights for books optioned for TV movies and feature films.

Areas not interested in agenting: Although the majority of our list is nonfiction, we are actively looking for novels.

Best way to initiate contact: A query letter (containing proposed book concept and author bio) or brief proposal (containing the following sections: Concept, Market Analysis, Competition, Publicity, Author's Credentials, and Outline), including self-addressed stamped envelope for return of materials. Do not fax queries or proposals.

Reading-fee policy: No reading fees.

Client representation by category: Nonfiction, 95%; Fiction, 5%.

Commission: 15%.

Rejection rate (all submissions): 95%.

Description of a dream client: An author with a vision who listens to constructive suggestions. (It is also important for an author to be willing to promote the book aggressively, resourcefully, and creatively. Publishers look for authors skilled at generating publicity.)

Why did you become an agent? Love publishing—learn with every book.

Representative titles: *The Okinawa Program* by Bradley Willcox, M.D., Craig Willcox, Ph.D., and Makoto Suzuki, M.D. (Clarkson Potter); *The Science and Art of Tracking* by Tom Brown (Berkeley); *The Naked Civil Servant* (Penguin) and *Resident Alien: The New York Diaries* (Alyson), both titles by Quentin Crisp; *The Power of Apology* by Beverly Engel (John Wiley & Sons); *Does This Make Me Look Fat?* by Leah Feldon (Villard/Random House); *The Rules* and *The Rules II* (Warner Books) and *The Rules for On-Line Dating* (Pocket Books), all titles by Ellen Fein and Sherrie Schneider; *The Official RENT-A-HUSBAND Guide to a Safe, Problem-Free Home* by Kaile R. Warren Jr. and Jane Craig (Broadway/Doubleday); *What the IRS Doesn't Want You to Know: A CPA Reveals the Tricks of the Trade* by Martin Kaplan and Naomi Weiss (Villard—revised annually); *How to Write a Movie in 21 Days* by Viki King (HarperCollins).

RUTH COHEN, INC.

PO Box 2244, La Jolla, CA 92038
858-456-5805

Agent: Ruth Cohen

Areas most interested in agenting: *Very selective* women's fiction (contemporary themes of modern women), mysteries (different settings with fascinating characters), juvenile literature (quality picture books, middle-grade fiction/nonfiction, young-adult novels, thrillers (no drugs or Mafia).

Areas not interested in agenting: Films, scripts, poetry, books in rhyme or verse, science fiction, Westerns, how-to books.

Best way to initiate contact: Send a query letter (must send a SASE), which also includes the opening 10 to 15 pages of the manuscript. *Please, no unsolicited full manuscripts.*

Reading-fee policy: No reading fee. Charge for foreign mailings and copying manuscripts.

Client representation by category: Nonfiction, 5%; Fiction, 60%; Children's, 35%.

Commission: 15% domestic; 20% foreign.

Number of titles sold last year: 56.

Description of the client from Hell: There aren't really any clients from Hell. There are clients who grow disappointed and who despair of the publishing world as it merges and alters and leaves fewer opportunities for new writers to succeed in work they love—writing.

Description of a dream client: Clients who understand that our combined efforts generally will advance both our careers, and that patience and stamina are the preferred attributes for getting published well—now and always.

Comments: Keep trying—and keep trying to detach yourself from your own writing so that you can view it objectively. Then reassess, revise, rework, and resubmit.

FRANCES COLLIN, LITERARY AGENT

PO Box 33, Wayne, PA 19087-8033
610-254-0555

Agent: Fran Collin

Areas not interested in agenting: Cookbooks, gardening books, illustrated books (coffee-table books, that is).

If not agenting, what would you be doing? Haven't a clue.

Best way to initiate contact: Query letter by mail with SASE, unless recommended by editors, writers (clients), or other professionals, in which case, telephone. No faxes please. No e-mail unless invited to do so.

Client representation by category: Nonfiction, 49%; Fiction, 49%; Textbooks, 1%; Poetry, 1%.

Commission: 15% on U.S. deals; 20% on foreign, translation, film, and permissions.

Rejection rate (all submissions): 99.44/100%.

How did you become an agent? Went for an interview to a large agency as a secretary and never looked back.

Why did you become an agent? I discovered that I could be paid for introducing my writer friends to editors—that is, I found that there was a profession devoted to my avocation.

COLLINS McCORMICK LITERARY AGENCY

10 Leonard Street, New York, NY 10013
212-219-2894   fax: 212-219-2895
www.collinsmccormick.com   e-mail: info@collinsmccormick.com

Agents: Nina Collins, David McCormick, Leslie Falk, Britt Carlson
   Education: Barnard College, Reed College.
   Areas most interested in agenting: Literary and commercial fiction; narrative nonfiction; nonfiction in the areas of health, psychology, history, women's issues, sports.
   Areas not interested in agenting: Science fiction, fantasy, romance.
   Best way to initiate contact: Query letter.
   Client representation by category: Nonfiction, 50%; Fiction, 50%.
   Commission: 15%; 20% foreign.
   Number of titles sold last year: 20.
   Rejection rate: 90%.

DON CONGDON ASSOCIATES, INC.

156 Fifth Avenue, Suite 625, New York, NY 10010-7002
fax: 212-727-2688
e-mail: congdon@veriomail.com

Agents: Don Congdon, Michael Congdon, Susan Ramer, Cristina Concepcion
   Areas not interested in agenting: Romance, how-to, textbooks.
   Best way to initiate contact: Send a query letter with SASE.
   Client representation: Nonfiction, 55%; Fiction, 44%; Children's, 1%.
   Commission: 15% domestic; 19% foreign.
   Most common mistakes authors make: Not sending an SASE, sending material as an attachment to e-mail instead of copying and pasting it to the e-mail (which we require for

security reasons), not providing enough description of the work(s), not revealing the query is being sent simultaneously to other agents.

Representative titles: *Me Talk Pretty One Day* by David Sedaris (Little Brown); *From the Dust Returned* by Ray Bradbury (HarperCollins); *The Envy of the World* by Ellis Cose (Simon & Schuster); *The Gravity of Sunlight* by Rosa Shand (Soho Press).

CREATIVE MEDIA AGENCY INC.

240 West 35th Street, Suite 500, New York, NY 10001
212-560-0909

Agent: Paige Wheeler
  Born: 1967 in Richmond, Virginia.
  Education: Boston University.
  Career history: Euromoney Publications, London; Harlequin/Silhouette Books; Artists Agency Inc.; Creative Media Agency Inc.
  Areas most interested in agenting: Fiction: commercial fiction, women's fiction, romance, mysteries, thrillers. Nonfiction: popular reference, self-help, how-to, pop culture, women's issues.
  Areas not interested in agenting: Horror, sci-fi, fantasy, Westerns, children's, biographies.
  Best way to initiate contact: Send a query letter with an SASE.
  Reading-fee policy: No reading fee.
  Client representation by category: Nonfiction, 40%; Fiction, 60%.
  Commission: 15% domestic, 20% foreign.
  Rejection rate (all submissions): 90%.
  Description of the client from Hell: Uncooperative, impatient—doesn't understand the nature of publishing.
  Description of a dream client: Cooperative, patient, brilliant, willing to work as a partner to build a solid career.
  Why did you become an agent? It is a great combination of many talents. You are an editor, salesperson, and businessperson simultaneously.
  Representative titles: *Targeting the Job You Want* by Kate Wendleton (Career Press); *Cosmically Chic* by Greg Polkosnik (Andrews McMeel); *Made in America: The People Behind the Brands That Made America Great* by John Gove (Berkley); *A Star to Sail By* by Susan Delaney (Onyx/NAL); *Qualified for Murder* by Roberta Islerb (Berkley); *Once Upon a Time in Great Britain* by Melanie Wentz (St. Martin's Press); *Compass of Health* by Kihyon Kim (New Page Press).

CROSSMAN LITERARY AGENCY

65 East Scott, Suite 12J, Chicago, IL 60610
312-664-6470   fax: 312-664-7137
e-mail: crossmanla@aol.com

Agent: Nancy Crossman
   Career history: V.P.; Editorial Director; Associate Publisher, Contemporary Books, Inc.
   Areas most interested in agenting: General nonfiction, self-help, gift books.
   Areas not interested in agenting: Children's or young adult titles; fiction; poetry.
   Best way to initiate contact: Query with synopsis and SASE.
   Reading-fee policy: No reading fee.
   Commission: 15%.
   Number of titles sold last year: 25.
   Most common mistakes authors make: Not doing their marketing and competition homework.
   Description of a dream client: Dream clients are professional, work as team players, are talented, and are passionate about their work.
   Why did you become an agent? After 16 years as the director of a publishing house, I left so that I could work on a variety of projects that personally interested me.
   What can writers do to enhance their chances of getting you as an agent? Be patient and have a good sense of humor.
   Representative titles: *The Cake Mix Doctor* by Anne Byrn (Workman); *Breast Fitness: An Optimal Exercise and Health Plan for Reducing Your Risk of Breast Cancer* by Drs. Anne McTiernan, Julie Gralow, and Lisa Talbott (St. Martin's Press); *The Pocket Parent* by Gail Reichlin and Caroline Winkler (Workman); *The New Success Rules for Women* by Susan Abrams (Prima); *A Golfer's Education* by Darren Kilfara (Algonquin Books).

RICHARD CURTIS ASSOCIATES, INC.

171 East 74th Street, New York, NY 10021
212-772-7363

Agent: Richard Curtis
   Born: June 23, 1937.
   Education: B.A. in American studies, Syracuse University; M.A. in American studies, University of Wyoming.
   Career history: Foreign Rights Manager, Scott Meredith Literary Agency (1959–1966); freelance author (1967–1975); started own agency (1975); incorporated Richard Curtis Associates, Inc. (1979); first President of Independent Literary Agents Association (1980); Treasurer (1991–1995) and President (1995–1997) of Association of Authors' Representatives.
   Hobbies/personal interests: Watercolor painting, softball, racquetball, classical music.
   Areas most interested in agenting: Commercial nonfiction, including business, history, biography, narrative nonfiction, celebrity biographies, medical, sports. Literary and commercial fiction. Thrillers, science fiction, romance, pop culture. The media and entertainment. Software/multimedia.
   Areas not interested in agenting: Everything not in the previous categories.
   If not agenting, what would you be doing? A pianist, an artist, a catcher for the New York Mets, a linebacker for the New York Giants, a volleyball player on a California beach, a psychotherapist, a rabbi, a playwright.

Best way to initiate contact: One-page query letter, plus no more than a one-page synopsis of proposed submission. Must be accompanied by an SASE, or we won't reply. No faxed queries, no e-mail queries. No submission of material unless specifically requested. If requested, submission must be accompanied by an SASE, or we assume you don't want your submission back.

Reading-fee policy: No reading fee.

Client representation by category: Nonfiction, 75%; Fiction, 25%.

Commission: 15% on basic sale to domestic publisher; 15% on dramatic rights (movies, television, audio, multimedia); 20% on British and foreign publication rights.

Number of titles sold last year: Approximately 150.

Rejection rate (all submissions): 99.9%.

Most common mistakes authors make: Phone queries instead of a letter. Want to see us before we've read material. Don't proofread their work.

Description of the client from Hell: High PITA factor. PITA stands for Pain In The Ass. Divide commissions earned into time dealing with complaints.

Description of a dream client: Low PITA factor.

Why did you become an agent? Love authors, love publishers, love books, love being in the middle.

How would you describe what you actually do for a living? When asked if she knew what her daddy did for a living, my (then) little daughter said, "He's a book sender." I'm not sure I've heard a better description. But I do think of myself more as an artists' manager than an agent in the old 10-percenter sense.

How did you become an agent? An employment agent sent me to an agency when I graduated, and having fallen in, I never wanted to get out.

What do you think about editors? They have become as disenfranchised as authors. Which is why I love them as much as I love authors.

What do you think about publishers? It's become an impossible profession.

Comments: The average published book today has the shelf life of a tomato. That's because the distribution system, making books fully returnable for credit, is completely outmoded. Now electronic delivery of text, as well as print on demand presses, have created the potential for an exciting alternative publishing industry. To meet that demand, Richard Curtis has launched e-reads, an online publisher/book retailer, to reissue previously published books. Contact info@e-reads.com.

Representative titles: *Hardcover* by Dan Simmons (St. Martin's); *Pocoverse* by Robert Metzger (Ace); *Suspicion of Vengeance* by Barbara Parker (Dutton).

LIZA DAWSON ASSOCIATES

240 West 35th Street, New York, NY 10001
Liza Dawson: 212-465-9071; Rebecca Kurson: 212-629-9212

Agents: Liza Dawson, Rebecca Kurson.
Born: Dawson: 1955. Kurson: 1970.

Education: Dawson: B.A. in History, Duke University; graduate of Radcliffe's Publishing Procedure Course, 1977. Kurson: B.A. in English, University of Chicago; M.A. in Writing, New York University.

Career history: Dawson: Founded Liza Dawson Associates in 1998 after 20 years as an Executive and Senior Editor at William Morrow and G. P. Putnam. Kurson: Worked in editorial department at Farrar, Straus and Giroux from 1995 to 1999. With Liza since June 1999.

Hobbies/personal interests: Dawson: Local and national politics, archaeology, gardening, lassoing lively kids.

Areas most interested in agenting: Dawson: Literary, as well as intelligent, commercial fiction with a distinctive voice. This would include domestic dramas, fiction written by African Americans, speculative fiction, historicals, sophisticated thrillers, as well as stories set in Asia, India, and the Middle East. In nonfiction, I am interested in academics, specifically historians, psychologists and sociologists; doctors who have a fresh angle on popular subjects, journalists who have found their niche, media personalities, true crime written with flair, business books, travel, parenting, and memoirs. Kurson: Nonfiction: Narratives about nature or science, anything about animals, vegetarian lifestyle, cutting-edge journalism, memoirs. Fiction: Literary.

Areas not interested in agenting: Dawson: Poetry, Westerns, romances, science fiction. Kurson: Commercial fiction, romance, sci-fi, New Age, business.

If not agenting, what would you be doing? Dawson: Digging for ancient treasure in Italy. Kurson: Teaching.

Best method to initiate contact: Dawson: Query letter with an SASE. Kurson: Recommendation from an editor or a query letter with SASE.

Reading-fee policy: Dawson: No reading fee. Kurson: No reading fee.

Client representation by category: Dawson: Nonfiction, 55%; Fiction, 45%. Kurson: Nonfiction, 60%; Fiction, 39%; Children's, 1%.

Commission: 15% domestic; 20% foreign

Number of titles sold last year: Dawson: 40. Kurson: 15.

Rejection rate (all submissions): Dawson: 99%. Kurson: 99%.

Most common mistakes authors make: Dawson: Not targeting submissions appropriately, sending out hundreds of form letters, gushing about how personally satisfying the writing experience has been.

Description of the client from Hell: Dawson: A talented author with no ambition.

Description of a dream client: Dawson: A brilliant, funny, focused, fearless workaholic with lots of friends in the media.

Why did you become an agent? Dawson: It combines all my passions. Reading, gossip, business-advise-dispensing, and matchmaking. Kurson: It's thrilling to work with writers.

What can writers do to enhance their chances of getting you as an agent? Dawson: Write a businesslike letter that cogently describes why a publisher might find the work appealing. Kurson: They might have publishing credentials from magazines or literary journals, or a particular expertise.

How would you describe what you actually do for a living? Kurson: Eating lunch and making pitches over the phone. Lots of line editing.

What do you think about editors? Dawson: Most editors are heroic. They work seven days a week, edit more than they're given credit for, and care deeply about their authors.

What do you think about publishers? Dawson: Almost every publisher has a different corporate philosophy about the best way to make money. Is it through a few big authors? Is it by developing a brand name? Is it by trying to get the attention of the media? Each publisher and each editor has a particular strength, and each has different needs. My job is to figure out which house is right for an author at the particular time I'm submitting a manuscript. You can't talk about publishers as if they were a monolithic entity.

What were your favorite films last year? Kurson: *Our Song, Memento,* and *Best in Show.*

Do you watch the *Sopranos?* Kurson: I live in Jersey—of course.

Comments: Kurson: E-mail submissions are dreadful.

Representative titles: Dawson: *Back Roads* by Tawni O'Dell (Viking); *In Transit* by Olympia Dukakis (HarperCollins); *Darjeeling and Pastry* by Bharti Kirchner (St. Martin's Press); *My Dog Bit Me, I Think* by John Callahan (Ballantine); *Life or Debt* by Stacy Johnson (Ballantine Hardcover); *Blood Junction* by Caroline Carver (Warner Hardcover); *The Inscription* by Pam Binder (Pocket Books); *Taverna* by Tom Stone (Simon & Schuster). Kurson: *Last Things* by David Searcy (Viking); *Edinburgh* by Alexander Chee (Welcome Rain); *Even Dogs Go Home to Die* by Linda St. John (HarperCollins); *Banyard's Folly* by Paul Collins; *Grace* by Jane Roberts Wood (Dutton).

DeFiore and Company, Author Services

853 Broadway, Suite 1715, New York, NY 10003
212-505-7979   fax: 212-505-7779
e-mail: submissions@defioreandco.com

Agent: Brian DeFiore

Born: August 16, 1956, New York City.

Education: B.A. in English, Queens College.

Career history: 1981–1988, Editor, St. Martin's Press; 1988–1990, Senior Editor, Dell Publishing; 1990–1992, VP, Editorial Director, Delacorte Press; 1992–1997, VP, Editor in Chief, Hyperion; 1997–1998, Senior Vice President, Random House Trade Books; Publisher, Villard.

Hobbies/personal interests: Movies, theater, cooking, being a good dad.

Areas most interested in agenting: Commercial fiction, suspense fiction, modern fiction, business books, finance books, self-help, inspiration, health, memoir, biography, entertainment, cooking, sports, psychology.

Areas not interested in agenting: Romance, science fiction, poetry.

If not agenting, what would you be doing? I'd be a psychotherapist.

Best way to initiate contact: By query, either by letter or e-mail. The query should be kept to one page and should describe the book and the author's credentials for writing it, including not only educational background, if that is important, but the life experiences important to the writing of the book. If sending via e-mail, please do not use attachments—which I will not open (because of possible virus infection).

Reading-fee policy: We do not charge reading fees.

Client representation by category: Nonfiction, 66%; Fiction, 33%.

Commission: 15% domestic; 20% foreign.

Number of titles sold last year: 15.

Rejection rate (all submissions): 95%.

Most common mistakes authors make: There are two: First is to pitch me several different sorts of projects at once, as if that demonstrates a broad range. That actually gives the impression of someone who does not have a passionate idea or direction. It is much more effective for writers to make one strong pitch for the project that they love the most. After I'm excited by that and want to take the client on, I'll want to hear about others. The second mistake is when people argue with me over an initial negative reaction instead of questioning why I had it. For example, if I say I don't want to take a project on because there are too many similar books in the market, instead of arguing that I'm mistaken and that your book is different, take a step back and think: This is the reaction a professional had to my material. What can I add to the proposal to demonstrate that this book is unique?

Description of the client from Hell: Someone who hears but doesn't listen and who refuses to accept the reality of what the publishing business is, versus some fantasy about what it should be.

Description of a dream client: Someone whose ideas turn me on and whose skill with words inspires me. Someone who has a unique perspective on the world or on the tiniest piece of it. Writers who understand that they must take an active role in the process of publishing their work, but do not insist on controlling it—who are willing to work hard and keep the faith.

How did you become an agent? After 15 years in training as an Editor, Editor in Chief, and Publisher of major New York publishing houses, I started up the business myself early in 1999, in New York's Union Square.

Why did you become an agent? After 15 years on the publishing side of things, as first an Editor, then Editor in Chief, then Publisher, I was getting frustrated with having my work life become more about corporate infighting and posturing than about creative development of material and the building of authors' careers. I thought I'd have more fun and creative satisfaction on this side of the business.

What can writers do to enhance their chances of getting you as an agent? Write a very persuasive query letter that demonstrates competence, creativity, and wherewithal. Then, if I respond to the query, demonstrate a high level of business and personal courtesies. Agents and their clients have a very intense and intimate relationship. If the early contact seems strained, difficult, unreasonably demanding—then I may well take a "life is too short" attitude toward taking the client on.

How would you describe what you actually do for a living? I nurture the creative spirit in writers, work with them on shaping their material into a form most attractive to the modern publishing world, then I find the most effective way of presenting their work to the media community and negotiate the best deal possible. Then I handle all business affairs relating to the work—including management of the finances and making sure that the publisher is holding up its end of the bargain and doing its job effectively and properly.

D

What do you think about editors? Having been one myself for most of my career, I have great respect for what they do and great sympathy for the difficulty they have in working inside complex corporate structures. They are overworked, understaffed, and often unappreciated, but they are the lifeblood of any publishing operation. These days corporations give much more clout to their sales and marketing people than they do their editors—without honoring the fact that they would have little to sell or market unless their editors brought in great material.

What do you think about publishers? I think that the people who constitute "publishers" are for the most part good, professional people who respect good writing, have good intentions, and are creative and enthusiastic supporters of authors and their work. I think that, these days, the huge corporate structures, in which most individual publishing companies are but a small piece, foster an environment in which, too often, the most creative and powerful executives have to focus their energies on the survival of their divisions rather than on the careers of individual authors. That's unfortunate.

Comments: Despite the fact that we've seen enormous changes in the publishing industry in the past few years—and that those changes seem to me just the beginning of cataclysmic changes to come—I think that this is actually a good time for writers and for creative material. While big publishing companies keep consolidating and trimming costs and staff, small presses are thriving, Internet book sellers are exploding, books are being sold through every sort of retailer, new online magazines (and print magazines) enter the market every month, new beautiful superstores open all the time. And most important, more and more books are being sold everywhere. The problems of the industry have to do with the distribution of profit, not with whether a huge profitable market exists. It does. I'm a firm believer in the power of the free marketplace, and I believe that the industry shake-ups will continue and that the publishing industry as we know it may be unrecognizable 10 years from now, but that as long as people demand to read good books—and every indication is that that demand is *increasing*—then the industry will reshape itself to meet the demands of that market. Whether that new shape will include only one enormous foreign-owned publishing company or thousands of small ones, it's impossible to say—but whatever happens, good writing will be read and authors will need strong, intelligent representation in order to maneuver the new landscape of the business.

Representative titles: *Mr. Fix-It Introduces You to Your Home* by Lou Manfredini (Ballantine); *You Got Nothing Coming: Notes of a Prison Fish* by Jimmy Lerner (Broadway); *Shooting Doctor Jack* by Norman Green (HarperCollins); *A Burning Homeland* by Richard Yancey (Simon & Schuster); *Morning by Morning: The Education of Three Black Men* by Paula Penn-Nabrit (Villard); *Temptations* by Michael and Ellen Albertson (Simon & Schuster); *Life Is Not a Stress Rehearsal* by Loretta LaRoche (Broadway).

JOELLE DELBOURGO ASSOCIATES, INC.

450 Seventh Avenue, Suite 3004, New York, NY 10123
fax: 212-279-8863
www.Delbourgo.com   e-mail: info@Delbourgo.com

Agent: Joelle Delbourgo

Education: B.A. Magna Cum Laude, Phi Beta Kappa Williams College (double major in History and English Literature); M.A. with Honors in English Literature from Columbia University.

Career history: Fall 1999 to present, President and Founder of Joelle Delbourgo Associates, Inc. 1996–1999, HarperCollins (1996–1997, Vice President, Editorial Director; 1997–1999, Senior Vice President, Editor in Chief and Associate Publisher; 1980–1996 held various positions from Senior Editor to Vice President, Editor in Chief of Hardcover and Trade Paperback; 1976–1980, various editorial positions at Bantam Books).

Areas most interested in agenting: Serious nonfiction, including history, psychology, women's issues, medicine and health, business, thesis-based books and interdisciplinary approaches to nonfiction subjects, literary fiction, some commercial fiction, some historical fiction. I handle some high-end lifestyle and fine art titles. I'm interested in serious thinkers and original ideas.

Areas not interested in agenting: No category fiction (including romance, Westerns, science fiction, and fantasy), very few thrillers, no children's books or technical books.

Best way to initiate contact: By writing an intelligent query letter, one page preferably in a readable type, that shows that you've done your homework.

Client representation by category: Nonfiction, 80%; Fiction, 20%.

Commission: 15% domestic; 20% on foreign and film.

Number of titles sold last year: 15.

Rejection rate (all submissions): 90%.

Description of the client from Hell: The client who approaches me by phone, sends materials in minuscule type without an SASE or by disc, calls to find out if the package has arrived, won't take no for an answer. Clients with a smattering of publishing knowledge that makes them second-guess the agent every step. In truth, I avoid these clients.

Description of a dream client: The client who has been thinking about the idea or book for a long time; who is passionate, committed, serious, respectful, and works hard over the long term to do right by the book. The client who understands that this is a partnership, between agent and client at first, and then with the editor and publisher. My role is to guide, advise, cheer, facilitate, boost egos, and be there when the going gets rough.

Most common mistakes authors make: Pretending they know me when they don't, not sending an SASE, writing letters telling me how many other agents have rejected them already or how little they know about the process. Good-bye!

What can writers do to enhance their chances of getting you as their agent? Read books and articles about publishing to gain an understanding of the process. *Be professional.* Listen to advice, and understand that it comes from years of experience. Be kind. I am impressed by serious credentials or life experience, and, of course, it helps if the author has already established a platform, has contacts, media experience, been published previously, or won awards and/or grants.

Why did you become an agent? I had put in 25 years on the corporate side, climbing the ladder from Editorial Assistant to many years as a top executive. I loved the publishing process, but it also grinds you down. I wanted to get back to what got me into publishing in the first place: working with writers and editors again. I also wanted to work for a company in which I could set the tone, one that is professional and generous and respect-ful, and the best way to do it seemed to be to create it myself!

If not agenting, what might you be doing? I would be a college professor or dean, per-haps, or a writer myself. Anything that involves life as learning. Publishing has been a con-tinuous graduate school for me and has allowed me to hone my skills and knowledge, while pushing the envelope in those areas I'm curious about. My authors are often pioneers in their fields, and I get a firsthand education working with them. It really works both ways.

How would you describe what you do for a living? That's always tough to do. I see myself as helping to shape the culture, by choosing to support and develop ideas I find exciting, bodies of information that need to be shared, and literary experiences that will touch readers' hearts and minds. I like being a catalyst in people's lives, occasionally helping them to live their dreams. I am a muse, mother, therapist, advocate, CEO, and friend. Sometimes I wish I had something like that in my life!

How did you become an agent? I left a high-level job I loved and the next day sat down and worked for eight hours, trying to figure out how to translate my deep experi-ence into a company that specialized in literary management and some consulting. I am really an editor and publisher in drag; agenting allows me to continue having the conver-sations I've always loved to have, but from a different vantage point, which I think is im-measurably valuable to authors.

What do you think about editors? I'm nuts about them. Occasionally, you meet those who aren't smart or good at their job, but most are exceptional. They love what they do and live every day in the hope that they'll discover something wonderful, something worthy, something that can sell. I love the older, wiser, experienced ones, who have per-fected their craft, but I'm also very impressed with the taste and talents of the many young editors in the business who have the ear of their management and take their re-sponsibilities very seriously.

What do you think about publishers? They face a very tough challenge. I have a great deal of compassion for them (especially since I've been one!). There's enormous pressure to make margins that simply don't exist for the most part in publishing. It's an antiquated formula. And not many other businesses have to define every single "product" as distinct from every other every day. There is some franchise publishing, of course, but most publishers have to strike some balance between reducing books to formulas and highlighting what makes each one special, and that message has to be translated down the line, every step of the way, to booksellers and to the consumer.

What were your favorite films last year? I loved *Divided We Fall,* a Czech film; *Greenfingers;* and *The Others;* the latter was absolutely different.

Do you watch the *Sopranos?* No, I just didn't get into it.

Comments: I get really irritated by all the gloom and doom about publishing. It's true that the traditional world of book publishing is shrinking, but it's equally true that there are marvelous new opportunities if you keep your eyes open. I'm fascinated with the op-portunity that university presses have, for example, to develop what the "big" firms call "mid-list," or by the new trade lists being developed by McGraw-Hill, which was for-merly thought of primarily as a business publisher, and Rodale Books, which is expand-ing beyond direct mail. While I'm a realist, my philosophy is to think positively and go where the opportunity is. I hate it when people don't agree with me, but, hopefully, I'm right about books more often then I'm wrong; no one "owes" you anything. You want to sell books because they are good and because someone at the publishing house has a vision for how to bring them to market. When it works correctly, it's a beautiful thing.

DH LITERARY, INC.

PO Box 990, Nyack, NY 10960
212-753-7942
e-mail: dhendin@aol.com

Agent: David Hendin

Born: December 16, 1945.

Education: B.S. in Biology, Education, University of Missouri, 1967; M.A. in Journalism, University of Missouri, 1967.

Career history: United Feature Syndicate/United Media; Senior Vice President and Chief Operating Officer of United Feature Syndicate; President and Chief Operating Officer of World Almanac, Pharos Books (1970–1993). Author of 11 nonfiction books, including *Death as a Fact of Life* (Norton, Warner), *The Life Givers* (Morrow), and co-author of *The Genetic Connection* (Morrow, Signet).

Hobbies/personal interests: Archaeology.

Areas most interested in agenting: Strong nonfiction. I also represent comic strips and columns for newspaper syndication (very selectively).

Areas not interested in agenting: Fiction submissions By Referral Only.

If not agenting, what would you be doing? Excavating ruins in the Middle East or teaching journalism at a university (both of which I've done).

Best way to initiate contact: E-mail: dhendin@aol.com

Reading-fee policy: No reading fee. We're members of the AAR.

Client representation by category: Nonfiction, 85%; Fiction, 10%; Textbooks, 5%.

Commission: 15%.

Number of titles sold last year: 15.

Rejection rate (all submissions): 99.9%.

Most common mistakes authors make: Send too much material before being asked; don't write a good query letter; don't enclose SASE; start the query by telling me they have 14 unpublished projects. . . .

Description of the client from Hell: I have no clients from Hell.

Description of a dream client: Great ideas, prompt delivery, at least a passing interest in the business side of publishing.

Why did you become an agent? I have been a newspaper columnist, book author, and President of a publishing company. Becoming an agent was the next logical extension of my professional life—not to mention that some of my best friends are writers!

Comments: Writers—send me your fabulous ideas. I have a relatively small number of clients and love to work on projects I like.

Representative titles: *Age of Anxious Anxiety* by Tom Tiede (Grove/Atlantic); *Doc in the Box* by Elaine Viets (Dell); *Miss Manners' History of American Etiquette* by Judith Martin (W. W. Norton & Co.).

D

DHS Literary, Inc.

2528 Elm Street, Suite 350, Dallas, TX 75226
214-363-4422   fax: 214-363-4423
e-mail: submissions@dhsliterary.com

Agents: David Hale Smith, Seth Robertson

Born: Smith: July 9, 1968. Robertson: March 4, 1974.

Education: Smith: B.A. in English, Kenyon College, 1990. Robertson: B.A. in English, B.A. in Spanish, University of Virginia, 1996.

Career history: Smith: Copyeditor, one year, Southwest NewsWire, Inc., Dallas; Assistant Agent/Agent, three years. Dupree/Miller & Associates, Dallas; founded DHS Literary Agency, March 1994. Robertson: English teacher, one year, Instituto Norteamericano, Santiago, Chile; started at DHS Literary in January 1998.

Hobbies/personal interests: Smith: Reading, writing, camping, hiking, travel. Robertson: Reading, writing, travel, photography.

Areas most interested in agenting: Smith: Mainstream fiction: thrillers, suspense, mystery, historical fiction. Literary fiction. Business nonfiction. Multicultural interests. Pop culture, music, film and television, technology. General nonfiction and gift books. Robertson: Nonfiction: Narrative nonfiction, biography, true crime, pop culture, travel/adventure, health, humor, music. Fiction: Literary fiction, thrillers, suspense, mysteries.

Areas not interested in agenting: Smith: Short stories, poetry. Robertson: Romance, fantasy, poetry.

If not agenting, what would you be doing? Smith: I am in awe of good writers, and I have always wanted to be one. I know some pretty good stories, and I plan on taking a crack at writing them down someday. I would also like to sail around the world with my family one day.

Best way to initiate contact: E-mail queries to submissions@dhsliterary.com. No file attachments please. No snail mail queries accepted.

Reading-fee policy: No reading fee.

Client representation by category: Nonfiction, 65%; Fiction, 35%.

Commission: 15% domestic sales; 25% on foreign (via subagents).

Number of titles sold last year: 42.

Rejection rate (all submissions): 99%.

Most common mistakes authors make: The biggest mistake we see people making is coming on too strong without backing up their claims of "sure-fire" success. We think that people must be aggressive to get noticed in this business—but if you're all style and no substance, it is a waste of everybody's time. Another common blunder we see is just a general lack of preparedness. Spend some time learning about the business before contacting agents and publishers.

Description of the client from Hell: Unprofessional people who think that once they have an agent, their role in placing and selling their work is finished. We had a client who made the mistake of thinking this agency was his personal secretarial and counseling firm, without ever realizing that all the time we spent talking to him and doing his busy-work was time we couldn't spend selling his stuff. He is no longer a client.

Description of a dream client: A professional in every phase of the business, who believes that the agent–author relationship is a team endeavor. A successful publishing experience is the result of a collaborative effort. We work extremely hard for our clients—and we work even harder for those who make it easier for us to do our job by working with us, not against us.

Why did you become an agent? Smith: I have always loved books, reading good ones, and talking about them with other people—that's the best part of the job. When I learned that agents get to see the good stuff even before the publishers do, that's where I wanted to be. Robertson: I love being able to work with books in a variety of ways. As an agent, I have the opportunity not only to make sales pitches and negotiate contracts, but also to brainstorm and work creatively with our clients.

What might you be doing if you weren't an agent? Robertson: I would probably still be working with writers and books, perhaps as an editor.

What can writers do to enhance their chances of getting you as an agent? See our description of the "dream client." We actually have an "Ideal Client Profile": talented, passionate, professional, progressive thinker, articulate communicator, and financially independent. If you fit that profile, we want to hear from you.

How would you describe what it is you do for a living? We manage the careers of professional writers.

Representative titles: *Critical Space* by Greg Rucka (Bantam); *The Origin Diet* by Elizabeth Somer (Henry Holt); *Life Makeovers* by Cheryl Richardson (Broadway); *Never Count Out the Dead* by Boston Teran (Minotaur/St. Martin's).

SANDRA DIJKSTRA LITERARY AGENCY

PMB 515, 1155 Camino Del Mar, Del Mar, CA 92014-2605
858-755-3115 ext. 18   fax: 858-792-1494
e-mail: sdla@dijkstraagency.com

Agent: Sandra Dijkstra
  Born: New York, New York.
  Education: B.A. in English, Adelphi; M.A. in Comparative Literature, UC Berkeley; Ph.D. in French Literature, UC San Diego.
  Career history: University professor, literary agent.
  Hobbies: Reading, films.
  Areas most interested in agenting: Quality fiction (commercial and literary); narrative nonfiction; history; psychology; health; business; spiritual; self-help; children's literature (commercial and literary).
  Areas not interested in agenting: Westerns, romances, fantasy, poetry, science fiction, screenplays.
  If not agenting, what would you be doing? I would be an editor and/or college professor.
  Best way to initiate contact: *We no longer accept unsolicited manuscripts.* We will only consider those manuscripts recommended to us by our authors, published professionals, and contacts.
  Reading-fee policy: No reading fee.

Client representation by category: Nonfiction, 50%; Fiction, 40%; Children's, 10%.
Commission: 15% domestic and film; 20% foreign.
Number of titles sold last year: 40.
Rejection rate (all submissions): 70%–80%.
Description of the client from Hell: The client from Hell is never satisfied and has expectations that exceed all possibilities of realization.
Description of a dream client: Dream clients trust their agents, ask the right questions, and offer useful support material. They do not e-mail and/or call daily. These clients call on need and keep us apprised of progress. These clients are professionals who understand that we are their partners and advocates and help us to represent their best interests.
Why did you become an agent? To publish books that make a difference and to help writers realize their dreams.
What do you think about editors? Overworked and underpaid. They are, by and large, dedicated and passionate about authors and books.
What do you think about publishers? In a perfect world, they would have more support, more money, and more time! Publishers should be "making public the book, in the fullest sense," which they do only some of the time.
Comments: Many writers and readers continue to believe in the importance of words and thoughts and messages and stories—all of which make us more civilized!
What are some common mistakes authors make? Incessant phoning to check on the status of their submissions.
What can writers do to enhance their chances of getting you as an agent? They should try to find a bookseller, author, or publisher to recommend them to us. They should also try to publish their work in magazines—forcing us to chase them!
How would you describe what you actually do for a living? I read and hope to fall in love. I talk on the phone and prepare editors to fall in love (and then pay for the privilege to publish what they've fallen in love with). I support talent with all my heart and brainpower.
Representative titles: *The Bonesetter's Daughter* by Amy Tan (Putnam); *The Seven Stories of Love: And How to Choose Your Happy Ending* by Marcia Millman (William Morrow); *The Diary of V* by Debra Kent (Warner Books); *The Twentieth Wife* by Indu Sundaresan (Pocket Books); *Racing the Antelope: What Animals Teach Us About Running and Life* by Bern Heinrich (HarperCollins); *Red Poppies* by Alai, translated by Howard Goldblatt (Houghton Mifflin).

Jim Donovan Literary

4515 Prentice, Suite 109, Dallas, TX 75206
214-696-9411

Agent: Jim Donovan
   Born: December 6, 1954.
   Education: B.S., University of Texas.
   Career history: In books since 1981 as a bookstore Manager; chain-store Buyer; published writer (*Dallas: Shining Star of Texas,* 1994, Voyageur Press; *The Dallas Cowboys*

Encyclopedia, 1996, Carol Publishing; *Elvis Immortal,* 1997, Legends Press; *Custer and the Little Bighorn,* 2001, Voyager Press); Freelance Editor; Senior Editor, Taylor Publishing, six years. Literary Agent since 1993.

Areas most interested in agenting: Any book with something fresh to say, whether it's fiction or nonfiction.

Areas not interested in agenting: Children's, poetry, short stories, romance, religious/spiritual, technical books, computer books.

If not agenting, what would you be doing? A publisher.

Best way to initiate contact: Nonfiction: Query with synopsis and SASE. Fiction: Query with 2–5 page synopsis, first 30–40 pages, and SASE.

Reading-fee policy: No reading fee.

Client representation by category: Nonfiction, 75%; Fiction, 25%.

Commission: 15%.

Number of titles sold last year: About 24.

Rejection rate (all submissions): 97%.

Most common mistakes authors make: The top 10 query letter turnoffs: (1) Don't use a form letter that begins with "To whom it may concern" or "Dear editor." (2) Don't say your writing is better than bestselling writers'. (3) Don't mention your self-published books unless they've sold several thousand copies. (4) Don't refer to your "fiction novel." (5) Don't brag about how great or how funny your book is. (6) Don't quote rave reviews from your relatives, friends, or editors whom you've paid. (7) Don't tell the agent how you're positive your book will make both of you rich. (8) Don't say it's one of five novels you've finished. (9) Don't tell the editor that he'll be interested because it will make a great movie. (10) Don't ask for advice or suggestions (if you don't think it's ready, why should they?).

What do you think about editors? Editors are the miners of the publishing world—they spend days and nights digging through endless layers of worthless material for the occasional golden nugget. Anything the agent or the writer can do to make their job easier is greatly appreciated, so I stress that to potential writers.

Comments: Most aspiring authors don't want to put in the time and effort necessary to become published—they think that if they attend enough writers' conferences and read enough books on how to become published that somehow, through some form of osmosis or alchemy, they will become published. I'm not interested in working with someone who doesn't understand that the key to publication is revision . . . and more revision . . . and more revision.

Representative titles: *Unitas* by Dan McGraw (Doubleday); *The Patriot-Trader* by Michael Kauffman (Random House); *Sales Proposals for Dummies* by Bob Kantin (Hungry Minds); *The Undefeated* by Jim Dent (St. Martin's); *The Burning* by Tim Madigan (St. Martin's); *Lazy Days at Lahinch* by Tony Finn (Sleeping Bear Press).

DUNHAM LITERARY, INC.

156 Fifth Avenue, Suite 625, New York, NY 10010-7002
212-929-0994   fax: 212-929-0904
www.dunhamlit.com

D

Agents: Jennie Dunham; Donna H. Lieberman

Born: Dunham: April 1969. Lieberman: April 30, 1957, New York City.

Education: Dunham: Magna Cum Laude, Anthropology major, Princeton University. Lieberman: B.A., Brandeis University; J.D., New York Law School.

Career history: Dunham: One year at John Brockman Associates, one year at Mildred Marmur Associates, six years at Russell & Volkening, started Dunham Literary in August 2000. Lieberman: I became affiliated with Dunham Literary in the spring of 2001, after more than 15 years of experience as an attorney. I also have freelance experience (writing and editing) for Aspen Law and Business Panel Publishing (formerly Prentice Hall).

Hobbies/personal interests: Dunham: Book arts and paper making, movies, photography, Old English, language and linguistics, feminist/women's studies, travel, science, history, health, religion and spirituality. I'm an animal lover, but I'm partial to dogs (I have a Newfoundland). I also collect first printings of first editions of books. Lieberman: Reading (of course), theater, music, travel.

Areas most interested in agenting: Dunham: Quality fiction, nonfiction, and children's. Lieberman: Quality fiction, mysteries, American and European history.

Areas not interested in agenting: Dunham: Romance, science fiction, poetry, horror, Westerns, and individual short stories. Also, we don't represent plays or screenplays (but we do represent books into movies and plays). Lieberman: Westerns, individual short stories, poetry.

Best way to initiate contact: Write a letter describing the project and the author's qualifications for the project and enclose the customary self-addressed, stamped envelope for a response. If the project seems as if we might be interested, we will request it. Please do not send sample material unless requested. We have lots of information on our Web site about submissions and what we're interested in. Lieberman: Write a query letter describing the manuscript/project and the author's qualifications and enclose the customary self-addressed, stamped envelope for a response. Please do not send sample material unless requested. (See the Web site for details.)

Client representation by category: Fiction, 25%; Nonfiction, 25%; Children's, 50%.

Commission: 15% domestic, motion picture, and other dramatic contracts; 20% foreign contracts.

Number of titles sold last year: 40.

Rejection rate (all submissions): We reject the vast majority of query letters sent to us, but we read each one and respond usually within a week. So many people write to us with books about topics that we don't handle. Just doing this little bit of research will substantially increase a writer's chance of finding the right match with an agent.

Description of the client from Hell: Dunham: A client who says one thing and does another, who doesn't trust an agent's advice, who doesn't know or pay attention to the market, whose writing needs editing, and who tries to tell agents how to handle their business.

Description of the dream client: Dunham: A client who is productive, dedicated, talented, successful, interesting, and pleasant and is a good client. It's also good if the client wins awards and is a self-promoter. Lieberman: An individual whose work I love and who is a responsible, practical grown-up with a sense of humor.

Most common mistakes authors make: Dunham: In this day of computers, it's a mistake to send a form query letter without a specific person's name in the salutation. Also, sometimes writers address agents familiarly as if they knew them, which really should be reserved for people who do know them personally. The grammar, spelling, and punctuation should all be correct. It's really best to send the query letter in writing, rather than to call first and ask to send it. That does not constitute a solicited manuscript. It's a big turn-off to call and try to pitch a project on the phone or to try to interview the agent before making the submission. Lieberman: As unexciting as it may be to write a query letter, if the letter isn't well written and interesting, I'm not going to believe that the manuscript is. Also, at the risk of sounding harsh, please don't tell me how much your friends liked your manuscript—they're your friends.

What can writers do to enhance their chances of getting you as an agent? Dunham: Professionalism, good writing, good ideas, and the willingness to work with an agent to manage the writer's career make me enthusiastic about a client. More people try to write bestsellers than good books, and if they concentrated on writing a good book, they'd be closer to having a bestseller. We look closely at a writer's previous experience and credentials, especially previously published magazine pieces and books. Lieberman: A well-written letter that conveys what makes your project or manuscript unique and that you are someone who can really write is a great way to introduce yourself. Also, always mention previous publications, award nominations and grants, and other credentials.

Why did you become an agent? Dunham: As an agent, I like helping authors to bring their books to the world. In this sense I like to think of myself as a midwife of creativity or someone who can make a writer's dream come true. I like the variety of book projects I handle as an agent. I receive great satisfaction in protecting authors by negotiating contracts for them. Ever since my first job as an agent, I knew that this was what I wanted for a career. Lieberman: I love books. My idea of hell is a place without them. So, after years as a lawyer, I decided that it was time to represent writers and to do my best to make sure that stories I love to read get published.

If not agenting, what would you be doing? Dunham: Maybe I would be an anthropologist or a professor of English, folklore, or communications. Maybe I would work as a book conservator or bookbinder. Maybe I would become a rare book dealer. Lieberman: I am a lawyer, and I have also considered editing or, if I win the lottery, starting my own small press.

How would you describe what you do for a living? Dunham: Mostly, I am a businessperson. An agent has three main responsibilities to clients: (1) To submit projects and solicit offers, (2) To negotiate contracts on behalf of clients, and (3) To receive and distribute payments appropriately. That's not all agent does, but those are the basics. Equally important are the roles an agent doesn't play for clients. An agent is not a banker who gives loans, an agent is not an accountant who prepares taxes for clients, and an agent is not a therapist or parent. But the agent is often the one stable person in the client's career. I also feel that I'm a midwife to creativity, in that I can listen to the client's idea of the project and pitch it to publishers so that the publisher sees the success the project could have from the client's creativity. Lieberman: I read lots of manuscripts, write letters, make phone calls, and try to find and sell precious gems.

How did you become an agent? Dunham: The way things usually happen: by mistake. I thought I wanted to be an editor, but I got offered a position at an agency. I decided to take it because at least it was a foot in the door. I loved it, and I've never looked back.

D

Lieberman: I started out reading manuscripts on a freelance basis, and decided I wanted to do this for real when I found myself doing work I was excited about and working with a terrific person.

What do you think about editors? Dunham: Editors are advocates within their companies for the books they work on. They also play an integral role in the creative process of helping an author shape a book. Good editors can help authors produce their best work. On the other hand, an editor who is really a frustrated writer is not necessarily the best creative partner for an author. Lieberman: I think an editor who loves a particular manuscript is an invaluable resource and an advocate for that author within the publishing company.

What do you think about publishers? Dunham: Publishers have distribution channels that are extremely useful to authors. When publishers get behind a book, they have the contacts to get visibility for a book. And publishers give a book credibility because they, as experts in the business, have chosen each book as worthy of their resources and investment. All of these are important for increasing the sales of a book. Lieberman: They manufacture and sell my favorite product. I would like to see them do more to promote new authors.

What were your favorite films last year? Dunham: *O Brother, Where Art Thou?; Chocolat; Shrek; Harry Potter and the Sorcerer's Stone.* Lieberman: *Croupier, A.I.* (Yes, I'm one of the people who really liked it.)

Do you watch the *Sopranos*? Dunham: No, as a matter of fact I do not watch the *Sopranos*. I tend to watch the Discovery Channel, the Learning Channel, and the History Channel. Lieberman: No—I've yet to get cable.

Comments: Lieberman: Hmm. Possibly that there are a lot of people who write well, but very few whose writing goes to that next level, where characters live and breathe and the story simultaneously takes me out of myself and gives me a better understanding of what matters to me. The writers whose work is in the second category are doing some of the most important work in the world.

Representative titles: *Living Dead Girl* by Tod Goldberg (Soho); *Native New York* by Evan Pritchard (Council Oak Books); *Molly* by Nancy Jones (Crown); *365 Goddess* by Patricia Telesco (HarperSanFrancisco); *Magick Made Easy* by Patricia Telesco (HarperSanFrancisco); *Enemy Glory* by Karen Michalson (Tor); *Letters of Intent,* edited by Meg Daly and Anna Bondoc (Free Press); *Hands on Feet* by Michelle Kluck (Running Press); *Hidden Witness* by Jackie Napolean Wilson (St. Martin's Press); *The Wonderful Wizard of Oz* (pop-up) by Robert Sabuda (Little Simon); *Molly and the Magic Wishbone* by Barbara McClintock (Farrar, Straus & Giroux); *Who Will Tell My Brother?* by Marlene Carvell (Hyperion); *Bittersweet* by C. Drew Lamm (Clarion); *Lincoln,* illustrated by David Johnson (Scholastic); *The Young Naturalist's Handbook of Butterflies and Beetles* by Robert Sabuda and Matthew Reinhart (Hyperion); *Animal Popposites* by Matthew Reinhart (Little Simon); *Clever Beatrice,* illustrated by Heather Solomon (Atheneum).

HENRY DUNOW LITERARY AGENCY

22 West 23rd Street, New York, NY 10023
212-645-7606   fax: 212-645-7614
e-mail: dunowlit@rcn.com

Agents: Henry Dunow, Jennifer Carlson, Kyung Cho

   Career history: Curtis Brown, Ltd., Harold Ober Associates; Henry Dunow Literary Agency, founded 1997.

   Areas most interested in agenting: Quality fiction and nonfiction.

   Areas not interested in agenting: Science fiction.

   Best way to initiate contact: Query LETTER, not e-mailed query.

   Reading-fee policy: No fee.

   Client representation by category: Nonfiction, 40%; Fiction, 60%.

   Commission: 15% domestic; 20% foreign.

   Rejection rate (all submissions): 95%.

   Comments: Keep your mind on the work, not on the market.

   Representative authors: Robert Hellenga, William Kotzwinkle, Elizabeth McCracken, Susan Power, Kirkpatrick Sale, Melanie Thernstrom, Marianne Wiggins, Heidi Jularits, Aimee Bender, Jean Thompson, Marisa Silver, David Schickler, Stephen Amidor, Kevin Baker.

D

JANE DYSTEL LITERARY MANAGEMENT, INC.

One Union Square West, Suite 904, New York, NY 10003

212-627-9100

www.dystel.com

Agent: Jane Dystel

   Education: B.A., New York University. Attended, but did not graduate from, Georgetown Law.

   Career history: Permissions Editor at Bantam Books; Managing & Acquisitions Editor at Grosset & Dunlap; Publisher of *World Almanac* and founder of World Almanac publications; Partner at Acton and Dystel Inc.; Partner at Acton, Dystel, Leone and Jaffe; Founder and Owner of Jane Dystel Literary Management, Inc.

   Hobbies/personal interests: Golf, cooking, ice-skating, travel, Jewish studies.

   Areas most interested in agenting: Literary and commercial fiction; serious nonfiction.

   Areas not interested in agenting: Poetry.

   If not agenting, what would you be doing? I'd be in some area of law or public service.

   Best way to initiate contact: Submit a query letter accompanied by an outline and a couple of sample chapters (with SASE). E-mail queries are accepted, but no attachments.

   Reading-fee policy: No reading fee.

   Client representation by category: Nonfiction, 80%; Fiction, 20%.

   Commission: 15%.

   Number of titles sold last year: 85.

   Rejection rate (all submissions): 95%.

   Most common mistakes authors make: Flashy, self-important letters full of hype and cuteness. Authors who refer to their work as "fictional novels." Most common and costly mistakes have to do with bad grammar, sloppy presentation, illegible material (exotic fonts or single spacing), and lack of proofreading.

What gets you excited? Intelligent, well-written queries that show originality.

Description of the client from Hell: Someone who calls incessantly, wanting updates and hand-holding. Someone who whines about everything. Someone who is dishonest and unpleasant.

Description of a dream client: Someone who is talented and asks intelligent questions. Someone who is patient and understanding of the fact that selling books can be a slow process. Writers who take rejection in their stride.

Why did you become an agent? Having worked in many other areas of publishing, it seemed like an exciting new field to explore. I was intrigued by the increasing importance of the agent–author relationship in the publishing world.

Comments: People should read more and read better books.

Representative titles: *Simplify Your Work Life* by Elaine St. James; *Keep It Simple, Stupid* by Judge Judy (Sheindlin); *Water Carry Me* by Thomas Moran; *Taken for a Ride* by Bill Vlasic and Brad Stertz; *The Eight Human Talents* by Gurmukh; *The Sparrow* by Mary Russell; *The Italian Country Table* by Lynne Rosetto Kasper; *Pride* by Lorene Cary; *China Boy* by Gus Lee; *The Will* by Reed Arvin; *Bobby Flay Cooks American* by Bobby Flay; *Kushiel's Dart* by Jacqueline Carey; *Fargo Rock City* by Chuck Klosterman.

E

ANN ELMO AGENCY, INC.

60 East 42nd Street, New York, NY 10165
212-661-2880

Agent: Lettie Lee
  Areas most interested in agenting: Nonfiction, romance, juvenile.
  Areas not interested in agenting: Poetry.
  Best way to initiate contact: Query letter.
  Commission: 15%, no reading fee.

ERRATA LITERARY, INC.

PO Box 99, Chalfont, PA 18914
252-996-646   fax: 215-996-9946
www.Computerdesk.com/errata   e-mail: errata@pipeline.com

Agent: Elizabeth Ann Joyce
  Born: March 16, 1942 (identical twin), Hackensack, New Jersey.
  Education: Associates in Business Administration, Bergen Community College, 1981.
  Career history: Accounting, 1960–1978; Atlantic Aviation, 1979–1985; Paralegal, 1986–1996; Literary Agent 1996–2002. Have had a long and varied career in television/radio and print work as a model for ads and commercials, while bringing up two sons as a single mom. In 1991, established my own column for a Pennsylvania newspaper, *The Metaphysical Corner*.
  Hobbies/personal interests: Travel, gardening, music, movies, writing, friends, alternative medicine, meditation group, yoga.

Areas most interested in agenting: A wide variety of narrative nonfiction historic research, sociology, science, self-help, memoirs, biography, how-to books, art coffee-table books, fiction, science fiction, mysteries, a well-written literary novel, commercial suspense and mystery, children's books (prepublished books from other countries).

Areas not interested in agenting: Romance novels, poetry, cookbooks, textbooks, horror, erotica, porn, essays.

Best way to initiate contact with you: I prefer e-mail or telephone but will always need a query letter with a synopsis and chapter outline, including SASE. A referral from a friend always works.

Client representation by category: Nonfiction 80%, Fiction 15%, Children's 5%.

Commission: 15% domestic; 20% foreign, client provides submission materials and postage with a minimum of $250 deposit for advance expenses, photocopies, and mailings.

Number of titles sold last year: 8

Rejection rate (all submissions): 20–40%

Description of the client from Hell: We do not tolerate this type of client. But clients from Hell are those who think their book should sell overnight, constantly call for updates, overrate their writing skills, demand quick responses from editors, do not believe in editing, and will not listen to any constructive advice or critique.

Description of the dream client: A good, clear, descriptive, and talented writer. Dream clients are considerate, patient, accept critique well, and apply what they learn. Talented professionals and creative writers who understand this is teamwork and an ongoing project. They will take the time to educate themselves about the publishing process, and somehow their presence makes you want to smile.

Common mistakes authors make: Sending me their book in a bound spiral format. No SASE. A letter or outline that does not talk about the book but about themselves. A sloppy submission with coffee stains on the papers. Dogeared pages. Does not know and does not follow the basic manuscript preparation guidelines.

What can writers do to enhance their chances of getting you as their agent? Keep on working and submitting. Write me a clever query letter that causes me to react. Make me chuckle, make me smile, make me want to pick up the phone and call you. For fiction: Have a creative concept that is timely and well researched. Show me your passion for the book by submitting a great proposal and loving your subject matter.

Why did you become an agent? My husband, a writer and journalist, collects first editions and is an avid reader. We have more than 4,000 inscribed books in our home. I love to read and write, and the agent idea sort of became enticing.

If not agenting, what might you be doing? Writing my own book or producing a screenplay.

How would you describe what you do for a living? The creating and sales of worthwhile, informative books. Creating a book takes inner depth and understanding of the circumstances of events around you. To be able to set a description down on paper that touches the heart and mind of another is as much an art as a gallery of Sergeant paintings.

How did you become an agent? Our dear friend, Adrian Gilbert, asked me to submit his book, *Signs in the Sky*, when he visited the United States. He thought I knew the right contacts and that I have a talent for sales. I submitted it to my friend Patty Gift at Harmony Books, and it sold right away. I was hooked.

What do you think about editors? They are the ones who truly have the insight and power to pull the creativity out of the author. They tighten up the work and make it presentable to the public. A good editor can make a poorly written book almost a masterpiece. They are the power behind the author.

What do you think about publishers? They can be a bit nearsighted and hesitant to take a chance on a new idea. But we would be nowhere without them. Many of them have the real talent to provide the finishing touches to the book, to get the work out to the mass public in a presentable and informative way. Most of them are very overworked.

What were your favorite films last year? *A Beautiful Mind, In the Bedroom.*

Do you watch the *Sopranos?* YES! We have all the series video taped.

Representative titles: *Signs in the Sky* by Adrian Gilbert (Three Rivers Press-Random House); *GIZA The Truth* by Chris Olgivie-Herald and Ian Lawton (Invisible Cities Press); *Genesis Unveiled* by Ian Lawton (Invisible Cities Press); *The Holy Kingdom* by Adrian Gilbert (Invisible Cities Press); *Moses, Pharaoh of Egypt* by Ahmed Osman (Inner Traditions Press).

Comments: Please visit our Web site to get a better idea of the books Errata Literary, Inc., represents (www.computerdesk.com/errata). We also have a list of guidelines on how to prepare your presentation for submission to an agent. It's a good rehearsal before it goes out to the publisher. Errata will not accept a submission without a book proposal (for nonfiction), a synopsis (for fiction), and a complete chapter outline. Skip the dedications and acknowledgments, as they are the last to be written. Many people talk constantly about how they are going to write their book. They ask me about ideas over and over. I say to them, don't tell me about it, just write the book. *Man was given a mind to speak and write. The power of words is what makes our character. What we think and what we say is who we are.*

FARRIS LITERARY AGENCY

PO Box 570069, Dallas, TX 75357-0069
972-203-8804
e-mail: farris1@airmail.net

Agents: Michael D. Farris, Susan Morgan Farris

Born: Michael: June 30, 1955, Baton Rouge, Louisiana. Susan: September 23, 1958, Dallas, Texas.

Education: Michael: B.A. in Political Science, University of Texas at Arlington; J.D. (Cum Laude), Texas Tech University School of Law. Susan: B.A. (Cum Laude) in English, Stephen F. Austin State University; J.D., Texas Tech University School of Law.

Career history: Michael: Attorney since 1983, freelance Editor. Susan: Attorney since 1983, freelance Editor, college Instructor.

Hobbies/personal interests: Michael: Reading, travel, movies, sports. Susan: Gardening, traveling, reading.

Areas most interested in agenting: Fiction: Thrillers, suspense, mysteries, romance, mainstream, horror, action/adventure, literary, Christian, Westerns. Nonfiction: How-to, law, true crime, self-help, current affairs, popular culture, women's issues, biography, history, political, travel, sports, theater/film, spiritual, inspirational.

Areas not interested in agenting: Poetry, fantasy, New Age, occult, gay/lesbian, erotica, science fiction, technical, computer.

Best way to initiate contact: Send a one-page query letter with SASE or an e-mail query letter.

Commission: 15% domestic; 20% foreign.

Description of the client from Hell: Those who fail to follow through on what they need to do, but who make outrageous demands on others.

Description of the dream client: Clients who write well, tell a good story, are articulate and personable, and allow agents to do their job.

Common mistakes authors make: Failing to proofread and/or not knowing how to properly use the English language.

What can writers do to enhance their chances of getting you as their agent? Have more than one book in them, and be able to sell themselves as well as their writing.

Why did you become an agent? Michael: I have loved reading my entire life. I decided to do something that combines my legal training and skills with that love. Susan: With my English degree and love of literature, it was a natural progression to add "literary agent" to "attorney at law."

If not agenting what might you be doing? Lounging on a beach in Hawaii.

How would you describe what you do for a living? As a start-up agency, we hope to be able to help people tell their stories to the world.

How did you become an agent? As a start-up agency, we're still in the process of becoming agents. Thus far, it has required a lot of research into the world of publishing, which adds to a base of knowledge from our backgrounds as attorneys. The other steps have included learning all we can about writing, both creative and other forms, and a lot of reading.

What do you think about editors? Editors are all looking for that next great writer. We hope to be able to help them find several.

What do you think about publishers? Publishing has become a bottom line–oriented business. We'd like to help with their bottom lines by bringing them talented new writers.

What were your favorite films last year? *Memento, A Beautiful Mind, O Brother, Where Art Thou?, Oceans Eleven, The Man Who Wasn't There.*

Do you watch the *Sopranos?* No.

Comments: The only ones who accomplish their dreams are those who dare to dream. So dream.

F

THE FLORIDA LITERARY AGENCY, INC.

808 Normandy Trace Road, Tampa, FL 33602
813-221-7305
www.agentflorida.com

Agent: Kevin A. DiTanna

Education: University of Tampa (undergraduate); University of Florida (law school).

Career history: For the past five years, I have practiced business, corporate, and real estate law in Tampa, Florida, concentrating on negotiating and drafting favorable, yet fair, contracts for and on behalf of my clients.

Hobbies/personal interests: Sports (Florida Gator and Tampa Bay Buccaneer football), movies, books, and travel.

Areas most interested in agenting: Screenplays and manuscripts written by young, hungry, talented writers. Scripts that can be converted into low-budget films and scripts with well-developed, interesting characters and a never-been-done-before story line.

Areas not interested in agenting: It would be foolish for me to place a limitation on the types of work I wish to represent. There's probably a niche for every type of book in the world. If you disagree, visit Barnes & Noble sometime. Having said this, I must admit, I'm not a huge science fiction fan.

Best way to initiate contact: An author should begin by sending (via U.S. mail—not e-mail) a well-written query letter to me that contains enough detail to describe the work, but not so much that it takes me all day to read it. Include a resume of the author's personal history and background. I like to know a little bit about a person before I begin to represent that individual. To ensure a written response from me, include an SASE. I like, and intend, to respond to all query letters. However, I am not willing to deplete my life savings to keep the U.S. mail system in business. If interested in your work, I will contact you via letter, phone call, or e-mail and will ask that you send me a draft of your work.

Client representation by category: Nonfiction, 10%; Fiction, 80%; Children's, 10%.

Commission: 15% domestic; 25% foreign sales.

Number of titles sold last year: Judge me not for what I have accomplished in the past, but for what I am about to accomplish in the future (and I'll do the same for you.)

Rejection rate (all submissions): 95%. What can I say? Most of what I'm sent isn't quite what I'm looking for. At the same time, most of what I see on TV or at the movies, or what I read in published books, ain't all that great either.

Description of the client from Hell: Clients from Hell are those who: (a) call me on a daily basis (I'll let you know when there is good news, believe me), (b) refuse to take my advice when offered (I don't offer unless I feel it will ultimately improve the content of work that authors have submitted to me), (c) fail to proofread their work a million times before submitting it to me, (d) stop writing after finishing one piece of work and expect to have that one piece published or produced, or (e) *doubt my ability as an agent.*

Description of the dream client: Talented individuals, preferably who live in the state of Florida, who are under the age of 35, in the early stages of their writing career, who have an unquenchable thirst for success, but who are patient enough to understand that production of their work will take an incredible amount of time and effort. Those who are responsive to constructive criticism, yet feel strongly about what they have written. Those willing to revise as instructed (or at least willing to consider it). Those who understand the power of the written word and who are confident enough to indulge in the process of writing. Most important, though, my dream client is someone who is driven to write—not for money or fame, but for the love of the craft.

Common mistakes authors make: Not having a script finished prior to seeking my representation. Sending an unsolicited screenplay or manuscript. Asking about how many or which books, movies, or authors I've represented in the past. Come on, people. Think about it. If you were well known enough to be asking those kinds of questions, you wouldn't be looking in this book, would you? Submitting a screenplay or manuscript without thoroughly proofreading it first.

What can writers do to enhance their chances of getting you as an agent? I like screenplays and manuscripts written for mainstream America. Well-drafted, informative query letters that emit the authors' passion for their work go a long way with me, as do following the instructions listed previously.

Why did you become an agent? I truly enjoy receiving and reviewing the work of an up-and-coming author—one whose work shows incredible potential. I love the evaluation and discovery process. In addition, I feel that my suggestions on improving a piece of work can increase the chances of getting a piece of work produced. Most important, I like the result of seeing writers I've helped reach their ultimate goal.

If not agenting, what might you be doing? Teaching a writing class.

How would you describe what you do for a living? In a few simple words—evaluating, convincing, and selling. From the moment I receive a query letter from a potential author, I evaluate and attempt to predict the potential success of the subject work. I'm an author's harshest critic. I must be inspired, and I have to believe in the author's vision. Once I've found a project that I feel could be worth pursuing, I have to convince myself that it truly is something that is marketable. Then I have to convince the author that I'm the right agent for the job. Once an author and I come to an agreement about representation, I provide my constructive comments about how, in my opinion, the body of the work can be improved and expect the author to prepare a rewrite (over and over again) until that person can't rewrite it again. Then I have the author rewrite it one more time. When I finally believe a piece of work is ready to be submitted, I begin the unenviable task of trying to convince someone else—namely, publishers, editors, and production companies—that the project is worth producing. In the end, I do what it takes to get the work produced.

How did you become an agent? Prior to becoming an agent, I practiced law for over five years. I parlayed this into incorporating and owning my own agency.

What do you think about editors? For the most part, they're honest, hard-working, overworked, intelligent people who can make or break the success of a body of work. Great editors work well with agents and authors to make the overall production a success.

What do you think about publishers? They are, quite simply, the ultimate arbiters of an author's work. It doesn't matter how much you, my mother, or I love an author's work. If we can't convince a publisher, producer, or editor to get on board, the work won't get to the next stage. It always amazes me how one publisher loves a certain piece of work, while others "wouldn't touch it with a 10-foot pole." In the end, there's a symbiotic relationship between a publisher, agent, and writer. We all need each other. Then again, agents and authors are all subject to the golden rule—that is, he with the gold makes the rules—and let's face it, publishers are the ones with the gold.

What were your favorite films last year? *Vanilla Sky* and *A Beautiful Mind.*

Do you watch the *Sopranos?* Occasionally.

Comments: Getting a manuscript published or a screenplay produced is no picnic. If it were, we'd all be driving in limousines on our way to our next movie premiere or book signing. An author's job is to write. An agent's job is to convince and sell. You do your job, and do it well, and I'll do mine. Together, with a hell of a lot of hard work and a little bit of luck, maybe we'll be successful in our venture. Rejection, while humbling, is part of the publishing and production game. If 25 agents tell you your script is no good, get back on your feet and send it to 25 more. There's always a place in this world for talent.

You've just got to find that certain place, and you can't give up trying to find it. If your first masterpiece can't find a home, keep writing. People who were born to write never stop writing, regardless of how discouraging it becomes. You've got to believe that sooner or later your luck will change. And when it does, there's no greater feeling than that of accomplishment.

F

THE FOGELMAN LITERARY AGENCY

7515 Greenville Avenue, Suite 712, Dallas, TX 75231
214-361-9956   fax: 214-361-9553
www.Fogelman.com   e-mail: fogel@aol.com

Agents: Evan M. Fogelman, Linda M. Kruger, Kim Leak
  Born: Fogelman: May 1, 1960. Kruger: May 16, 1967. Leak: 1974, Dallas, Texas.
  Education: Fogelman: B.A. with Honors, Tulane University, 1982; J.D., Tulane University, 1985; Stanford Publishing Course. Kruger: B.A. in Media Theory and Criticism, University of Texas at Austin, 1989. Leak: University of North Texas
  Career history: Fogelman: Entertainment attorney, book reviewer, author publicist. Kruger: Has been with the agency since its inception. Leak: Flight attendant, marketing, print design.
  Hobbies/personal interests: Fogelman: Enjoying the company of my wife and children, laughter, French bulldogs, distance running, history, issues of constitutional law, investing. Kruger: Walking, dogs, reading, home projects, movies. Leak: Reading, black jack, water-skiing, love attending live music performances and sporting events.
  Areas most interested in agenting: Fogelman: Romantic suspense, mysteries, romance with humor/idiosyncrasy, thrillers, all matter of nonfiction, business subjects. Leak: Mystery, suspense, memoir, biographies, true crime.
  Areas not interested in agenting: Fogelman: Anything not listed previously. Kruger: Poetry, short stories, true Westerns, science fiction, historical fiction, action adventure, New Age, mysteries. Leak: Historical romance, science fiction, children's.
  If not agenting, what would you be doing? Fogelman: I'd be in the oil business. Book deals are often a lot like wildcat oil wells, actually. Kruger: Taking way too many pictures of my two Labs.
  Best way to initiate contact: Fogelman: E-mail or snail mail. Kruger: A query letter with SASE will be responded to within five business days. Published authors are invited to call. No unsolicited material, please. Please check out our Web site at www.Fogelman.com. Leak: E-mail.
  Reading-fee policy: No reading fee.
  Client representation by category: Fogelman: Nonfiction, 50%; Fiction, 50%. Kruger: Nonfiction, 10%; Fiction, 90%. Leak: Nonfiction, 25%; Fiction, 75%.
  Commission: 15% domestic, including all agency-negotiated subsidiary-rights deals; 10% foreign.
  Number of titles sold last year: Fogelman: 75-plus; Kruger: 50-plus.
  Rejection rate (all submissions): 99.5%.

Most common mistakes authors make: Fogelman: Seeking representation too early in the process. If you're a new novelist, finish the book first. If you're a nonfiction writer, do a formal proposal first. Kruger: When writers cannot tell me what type of a book they have written. One writer described his book as (and this is an actual quote), "A non-genre erotic contemporary mainstream men's fantasy action/adventure romantic sexual comedy novel, or, if you really need a category, call it Romance Novel, Male Division." In helping writers categorize their books, I always ask one question: If you had one copy of your manuscript and you had to put it on one bookshelf at the bookstore, where would it go? Also, I hate unsolicited material.

What can writers do to enhance their chances of getting you as an agent? Kruger: Research the agency and know what I am looking for and what types of work I represent. Our Web site really helps!

Description of the client from Hell: Fogelman: Authors who would rather complain to me about how unfair publishing is instead of finishing their book; authors who scream for all the rest of us to make our deadlines, yet demand an extension on every contracted manuscript delivery date. Kruger: A writer who does not realize that this is a creative, yet professional, business.

Description of a dream client: Fogelman: Authors who loves to write more than they like to tell others, "I'm a writer." Kruger: Someone who keeps the lines of communication open. This is a two-way relationship. As for the creative process, my dream client creates characters and then releases those characters to tell the story.

How did you become an agent? Kruger: I met Evan Fogelman when he opened the doors to the agency. His enthusiasm and love of the business were contagious and my schooling and background made agenting second nature for me. Fogelman: As an entertainment lawyer, I started negotiating book deals and became enthralled. Leak: I chose to follow my passion after finding the perfect mentors, Evan and Linda.

Why did you become an agent? Fogelman: I completely enjoy the crossroads of art and commerce. Kruger: There are many reasons I became an agent, but what keeps me in this business is the chance to work with such creative individuals. This is an exciting business, one unlike any other profession. The atmosphere of our agency is always entertaining and challenging. I wouldn't change a thing. Leak: It is truly my passion to read an author's art in its rawest form and then take it to publication.

If not agenting, what might you be doing? Leak: Learning to fly planes—aviation enthusiast!

How would you describe what you actually do for a living? Kruger: I wear many hats. I'm an editor, a listener, a cheerleader, a reader, a salesman, a negotiator. At times, I am a pit bull and at other times, I let silence work for me. Fogelman: Well, it's rather like the oil business: Plan for hitting paydirt and carve up a royalty and rights pie!

What do you think about editors? Kruger: As long as they are acquiring my clients' books, I love them. Fogelman: What—are you a comedian? I love editors. Without them, I wouldn't have a job. Leak: What Evan and Linda said.

What do you think about publishers? Kruger: As long as they're publishing my clients' books, I love them. Fogelman: I like Linda's answer. Leak: What Evan and Linda said. . . .

F

What were your favorite films last year? Fogelman: *O Brother, Where Art Thou?*. Kruger: Films? Who has time to watch movies when I have so many wonderful books from my clients to read?! Actually, I just rented *O Brother, Where Art Thou?,* and loved it. Leak: Just bring me Mark Wahlburg!!!

Do you watch the *Sopranos*? No. But I watch my wife watching the *Sopranos*—now that's interesting!! Kruger: No. Leak: No, but *Six Feet Under* was a welcome HBO newcomer.

Comments: Fogelman: Spending four hours each day in a chat room will do very little to help turn your book into a screenplay. Remember, writing is better than a regular-type job—that's one of the reasons you got into it, right? Share what you do with your children—they will look at reading in a whole new way. Kruger: I've heard it said that there are those who are compelled to write and those who love to write. My clients are compelled to write—and I love what they write.

Representative titles: The Agency's clients include Terri Brisbin, Lisa Cach, Alice Duncan, Anne Eames, Elizabeth Eliot, Jane Graves, Leann Harris, Candice Hern, Victoria Chancellor, Caroline Rose Hunt, Joni Johnston, Karon Karter, April Kihlstrom, Sylvie Kurtz, Karen Leabo, Delia Parr, Pam McCutcheon, Laurel O'Donnell, Gwen Pemberton, Susan Plunkett, Louise B. Raggio, Laura Renken, Larry Shriner, Teresa Southwick, Crystal Stovall, Katherine Sutcliffe, RaeAnne Thayne, Ronda Thompson, and Cathy Yardley.

FORTHWRITE LITERARY AGENCY

23852 West Pacific Coast Highway, #701, Malibu, CA 90265
310-456-5698   fax: 310-456-6589

Agent: Wendy Keller
  Born: Chicago, Illinois.
  Education: Arizona State University.
  Career history: Agent since 1988, founded ForthWrite 1989.
  Hobbies/personal interests: Reading, gardening, languages.
  Areas most interested in agenting: Business (sales, management, marketing, finance), self-help, pop psych, health/alternative health, metaphysical/perennial wisdom.
  Areas not interested in agenting: Everything but those listed previously as interests! No juvenile fiction.
  Best way to initiate contact: E-mail query first.
  Reading-fee policy: No reading fee.
  Client representation by category: Nonfiction, 100%.
  Commission: 15% life of property; 20% foreign we place.
  Number of titles sold last year: 11.
  Rejection rate (all submissions): 99.999%.
  Most common mistakes authors make: (1) Telling me their book is better than anything ever published so far! (2) Not recognizing that there have to be more than three other people in the United States interested in their topic for me to sell it.
  Description of the client from Hell: I don't take on "clients" from Hell! But there are apparently thousands of unpublished "authors" from Hell! They're the ones who didn't

research their topic before writing; who don't understand that there are competitive books; *or* who start their query letter with "I'm a bestseller to be!"

Description of a dream client: My list of authors.

Why did you become an agent? Because fresh, hot ideas excite me.

If not agenting, what might you be doing? Playing chess in the Rose Garden with my joint chiefs of staff, to take a breather from running the world.

How did you become an agent? An angel of unsolicited submissions left a pile of hopeful authors' magnum opuses on my desk.

What can writers do to enhance their chances of getting you as an agent? Research your competition and be prepared to adapt your concept if necessary to make it worth more money.

How would you describe what you actually do for a living? I spend 5,000 hours each day on the phone, sleep a while, and then go back to my desk.

What do you think about editors? I think the world would come to a screeching halt without their dedication to content.

What do you think about publishers? I love every single one who sends accurate checks by their due date.

Do you watch the *Sopranos?* Never.

Comments: If you're a writer who wants to get published and you've spent the time to read this book, write your idea, and know how your book contributes to this crowded market, good for you. But if you haven't done your research—that is, you don't know *who* will buy your book and why—buy this guide. But before you discourage yourself and waste our time and yours, find out what your book contributes: Is it new? Different? Better? More? How does it compare with all the other similar books? Why will anyone buy it? Why? Find an agent when you can answer that question because you won't before.

Representative titles: *If You're Going Through Hell, Don't Stop!* by Trevor Romain (Celestial); *The Power Path: Merging Shamanism with Business* by Jose and Lena Sterans (New World Library); *Air Rage: Crisis in the Skies* by Andrew Thames (Greenwood); *Funosophy* by Nancy Zwiers (Conari Press).

JEANNE FREDERICKS LITERARY AGENCY, INC.

221 Benedict Hill Road, New Canaan, CT 06840
voice/fax: 203-972-3011
e-mail: jfredrks@optonline.net

Agent: Jeanne Fredericks

Born: April 19, 1950.

Education: B.A., Mount Holyoke College, 1972; Radcliffe Publishing Procedures Course; M.B.A., New York University Graduate School of Business Administration, 1979.

Career history: Assistant to Editorial Director and Foreign/Subsidiary Rights Director, Basic Books (1972–1974); Managing Editor and Acquisitions Editor, Macmillan (1974–1980); Editorial Director, Ziff-Davis Books (1980–1981); Literary Agent, Susan P. Urstadt Agency (1990–1996); Acting Director, Susan P. Urstadt Agency (1996–1997); established own agency, February 1997. Member of AAR.

Hobbies/personal interests: Family activities, tennis, skiing, swimming, N.I.A., yoga, reading, cooking, traveling, crew, gardening, casual entertaining, antiquing, pets.

Areas most interested in agenting: Practical, popular reference by authorities, especially in health, sports, science, business, cooking, parenting, travel, antiques and decorative arts, gardening, women's issues.

Areas not interested in agenting: Horror, occult fiction, true crime, juvenile, textbooks, poetry, essays, plays, short stories, science fiction, pop culture, computers and software guides, politics, pornography, overly depressing or violent topics, memoirs that are more suitable for one's family or that are not compelling enough for the trade market, romance, manuals for teachers.

If not agenting, what would you be doing? A trade book publisher or a writer.

Best way to initiate contact: Please query (with SASE) by mail, with outline, description of project, author biography, sample writing. No phone calls. No fax. E-mail queries should be short and without attachments.

Reading-fee policy: No reading fee.

Client representation by category: Nonfiction, 98%; Fiction, 2%.

Commission: 15% domestic (20% movie, TV, video); 20% foreign (if direct); 25% foreign (if with co-agent).

Number of titles sold last year: 20.

Rejection rate (all submissions): 95%.

Most common mistakes authors make: Calling me to describe their proposed books and giving far too much detail. I'd much rather see that potential clients can write well before I spend valuable phone time with them. Also, claiming to have the only book on a subject when a quick check on the Internet reveals that there are competitive titles.

Description of the client from Hell: Arrogant, pushy, self-centered, unreliable writers who don't understand publishing or respect my time, and who vent their anger in an unprofessional way.

Description of a dream client: Creative, cooperative, professional writers who are experts in their fields and who can offer information and guidance that are new and needed by a sizable audience.

Why did you become an agent? I enjoy working with creative writers who need my talents to find the right publishers for their worthy manuscripts and to negotiate fair contracts on their behalf. I'm still thrilled when I open a box of newly published books by one of my authors, knowing that I had a small role in making it happen. I'm also ever hopeful that the books I represent will make a difference in the lives of many people.

What can writers do to enhance their chances of getting you as an agent? Show me that they have thoroughly researched the competition and can convincingly explain why their proposed books are different, better, and needed by large, defined audiences. Be polite, patient, and willing to work hard to make their proposals ready for submission.

What do you think about editors? Having been on the editorial side of publishing for about 10 years, I have great respect for the demands on the time of a busy editor. I therefore try to be targeted and to the point when I telephone them and provide them with a one-page pitch letter that gives them the essence of what they need to make a proposal to management. I also make sure that the proposals I represent are focused, complete, and professional to make it easy for an editor to grasp the concept quickly and have a good sense of what the book will be like and why it will sell well. With few exceptions, editors value the creativity and hard work of authors and are intelligent and well meaning. Since they are often overwhelmed with manuscripts, paperwork, and meetings, though, they sometimes neglect some of their authors and need an agent's nudging and reminders.

Representative titles: *From Storebought to Homemade* by Emyl Jenkins (QVC); *How to Invest in Real Estate* by Carolyn Janik (Kiplinger); *The Art and Craft of Pounding Flowers* by Laura Martin (QVC); *Mother-Daughter Jewish Cooking* by Evelyn and Judi Rose (William Morrow & Co.); *Getting Ready for Baby* by Helene Tragos Stelian (Chronicle); *The Internet Legal Guide* by Dennis Powers (John Wiley & Sons); *The Complete Idiot's Guide to Homeschooling* by Marsha Ransom.

SARAH JANE FREYMANN LITERARY AGENCY

59 West 71st Street, Suite 9B, New York, NY 10023
212-362-9277   fax: 212-501-8240

Agent: Sarah Jane Freymann

Born: London, England.

Education: Although educated mostly in New York, I went to a French school, the Lycée Français, which is why I am fluent in many languages; and I traveled a great deal from a very early age.

Career history: My first job was with the United Nations; I also worked as a model and as an editor.

Hobbies/personal interests: Spiritual journeys; adventures of all kinds that generate insight, growth, a greater appreciation for our world, passion, an inquisitive mind, and a gentle heart; wonderful food, laughter, and long walks shared with good friends; listening to my daughter's beautiful voice.

Areas most interested in agenting: Nonfiction: Spiritual, psychology, self-help; women's/men's issues; health (conventional and alternative); cookbooks; narrative nonfiction; natural science, nature; memoirs, biography; cutting-edge current events; multicultural issues; popular culture. Fiction: Quality mainstream and literary fiction.

Areas not interested in agenting: Science fiction, fantasy, horror, genre romance, genre mysteries, screenplays, anything channeled.

If not agenting, what would you be doing? Teaching Proprioceptive Writing; working with children and adolescents; cultivating a quiet haven in a garden by the sea.

Best way to initiate contact: Via e-mail (no attachments), or by fax. We prefer not to accept any unsolicited mail.

Reading-fee policy: No reading fee.

Client representation by category: Nonfiction, 85%; Fiction, 15%.

Commission: 15% domestic; 20% foreign.

Rejection rate (all submissions): 85%.

Most common mistakes authors make: Please do not call us and attempt to describe your work over the telephone. E-mail your query letter and let us know if you have submitted to more than one agent at a time.

Description of the client from Hell: I wouldn't know—we've never had one.

Description of a dream client: Someone who is not only a natural storyteller and writes beautifully, with passion and intelligence, but who is also a nice human being—a "mensch." Someone with a sense of humor. Writers who have the patience and willingness to rewrite and rework their material if necessary. And last, but not least, clients who have the confidence not to call us too often and who realize that if we spend all our time talking to them on the phone, we won't have that time to spend selling their work.

Why did you become an agent? Probably in the genes. I'm a natural matchmaker and a physician's daughter. I like to think that thanks to my intervention, this author and that publisher met, formed a relationship, and that I am the midwife to this wonderful book.

What can writers do to enhance their chances of getting you as an agent? Submit a strong, clear, well-written query letter that sells both the book and its author, with the promise of substance rather than hype.

How would you describe what you actually do for a living? I'm a treasure hunter constantly in search of hidden gems and undiscovered talent; I'm an editor who helps clients shape their manuscripts and proposals; I'm a matchmaker, a deal-maker, and a negotiator; and finally, I'm a believer with the conviction that books (in whatever form they're published) are still our most powerful magic.

What do you think about editors? I love editors. They are intelligent, surprisingly idealistic, well informed, incredibly hardworking, devoted to their books and to their authors, and among my dearest friends.

What do you think about publishers? As of this writing, so much has changed. Our challenge now is to balance "business as usual" with an appropriate response to these extraordinary times; to create books that reach across borders and transcend differences, while also safeguarding our freedom of speech and of thought. I believe that by this common bond, we are all—author, agent, publisher, and reader—united.

What were your favorite films last year? *Himalaya, You Can Count on Me, Before Night Falls, Pollack, Hedwig and the Angry Itch,* and *Amores Perros.*

Do you watch the *Sopranos?* You bet!! As well as *The West Wing* and *OZ.*

Comments: Even though agents have had to respond to the current realities of the publishing world accordingly, we remain the bridge between the creative and the commercial; between the world of the writer and the world of the publisher. This makes an agent's job pretty tricky, because we have to be aware of how the industry works: know which editors are looking for what kinds of books. . . . What the competition is. . . . What the sales possibilities are. . . . And how to pitch the publisher in an arresting and compelling way. But at the same time, we still have to be willing to be seduced: by a writer's passion, by an extraordinary story, by memorable characters, by powerful ideas. We have to be willing to take a chance on a project or a writer we believe in. This requirement to be both a clear-headed businessperson and a dreamer is a balancing act, but in order to represent clients in the best way possible, it's necessary.

Representative titles: *Pam Anderson Cooks Smart* by Pam Anderson (Houghton Mifflin); *In Search of the Golden Moon Bear: The Mystery of a New Species* by Sy Montgomery (Simon & Schuster); *Yoga Body, Buddha Mind* by Cyndi Lee (Riverhead); *A Big Free Happy Unusual Life: Self-Expression and Creativity for Those Who Have Time for*

Neither by Nina Wise (Broadway Books); *Great Food the John Ash Way* by John Ash, with Amy Mintzer (Clarkson Potter); *Asian Grill* by Su-Mei Yu (Morrow); *The Mother/Daughter Sacred Circle: Reconnecting Through Spirit* by Celia Straus (Ballantine); *The Teen Health Book: A Parent's Guide to Their Adolescent's Health and Well-Being* by Ralph I. Lopez, M.D. (W. W. Norton); *Estate Gardens and Retreats* by Melba Levick (Rizzoli); *I'm Almost Always Hungry* by Lora Zarubin (Abrams).

MAX GARTENBERG, LITERARY AGENT

521 Fifth Avenue, Suite 1700, New York, NY 10175
212-292-4354   fax: 212-535-5033
e-mail: gartenbook@att.net

Agent: Max Gartenberg
  Born: New York City.
  Education: B.A., New York University; M.A., Brown University.
  Career history: As an English major with a graduate degree, I drifted into college teaching, then realized that I wanted to be where the action was, not where it had been in the past. I was living in the Midwest when that lightning bolt struck—about the same time I had to go to New York on family business. The rest is commentary.
  Areas most interested in agenting: Although I will occasionally take on a new novelist whose talent seems to me superior, fiction writers might be well advised to look elsewhere. I am most interested in solid nonfiction—books that present fresh and significant information or viewpoints—regardless of subject area, whether for trade, paperback, or reference.
  Areas not interested in agenting: I am not interested in category fiction, novelty books, and personal memoirs.
  Contact methods: With a one- or two-page, first-class letter describing any relevant background information, accompanied by an SASE if the writer wishes any sort of reply. I usually don't read sample pages or chapters if these are included. And I am absolutely turned off by cold calls and faxed queries.
  Reading-fee policy: No reading fee.
  Commission: 15% on initial sale; thereafter, 10% on sales in the United States, 15–20% elsewhere.
  Rejection rate (all submissions): 95%.
  Most common mistakes authors make: What most turns me off is a solicitation that tells me almost nothing about the writer or his material but requests detailed information about myself and my services, which is readily available in such books as the *Writer's Guide.*
  What gets you excited? A sense that the writer knows his subject, has reviewed the literature that has come before, and has written a book that is genuinely fresh and new.
  Description of the client from Hell: Clients who demand unceasing attention, who are never satisfied with the deal I bring them (they always have friends whose agents got

G

twice as much), who deliver their manuscript late and in such disorder that the publisher rejects it and demands return of the advance—and who, on top of everything, blame me for the mess. This is not an imaginary character.

Description of a dream client: A writing professional who can be counted on to produce a well-made, literate, enlightening, and enjoyable book with a minimum of *Sturm und Drang*. Fortunately, this is not an imaginary character, either.

Why did you become an agent? I love good books. They are the pillars of our civilization. It is a privilege to work with those who create them.

Representative titles: *Encyclopedia of Environmental Studies* by William Ashworth and Charles E. Little (Facts on File); *The Life and Art of Charles Addams* by Linda H. Davis (Random House); *The Rail* by Howard Owen (Permanent Press).

THE SEBASTIAN GIBSON AGENCY

PO Box 13350, Palm Desert, CA 92255-3350
760-322-2446   fax: 760-322-3857

Agent: Sebastian Gibson
   Born: December 8, 1950.
   Education: B.A. (Cum Laude), UCLA; L.L.B. (Magna Cum Laude), University College Cardiff, Great Britain; J.D., University of San Diego School of Law.
   Career history: Author of two novels, six screenplays, the lyrics and music to a stage musical, and hundreds of copyrighted songs. Author of published legal articles in both the United States and England. Performed as a stage musician on tour in the United States and Europe, and in a national television special. Obtained law degrees in both the United States and Great Britain. Practiced law in San Diego for four years, subsequently in England and the Middle East, and in 1984 began the Law Offices of Sebastian Gibson in Palm Springs, California. Presently practice law and represent literary and entertainment clients from law offices in Palm Springs, California.
   Hobbies/personal interests: Reading well-written books, traveling to book fairs, discovering new talent.
   Areas most interested in agenting: All categories of fiction, particularly novels with interesting characters and well-woven plots. Especially interested in psychological thrillers, historical novels, mystery/suspense and action/adventure or espionage with romance subplots and interesting twists, crime/police with humorous/gritty elements, medical dramas, women's fiction, sagas, and any well-written novel with unusual characters. Nonfiction with unusual approaches or written by celebrities, cookbooks or photography with a novel twist, humorous diet books, controversial issues, biographies, current affairs, "kiss and tell" books, and women's issues. What really gets us excited is when we read something fresh and new, with a genre all its own, or a story told in a way that has never been told before. If it grabs our imagination, it will grab the imagination of a publisher and the buying public as well.

Areas not interested in agenting: Poetry, textbooks, essays, short stories, how-to books, books in verse, computer, gardening, pornography, autobiographies by noncelebrities, drug recovery.

If not agenting, what would you be doing? Sipping piña coladas on a beach in Greece, far away from telephones, car phones, beepers, pagers, and computers.

Best way to initiate contact: Fiction: Send query letter or book proposal with outline and the first three chapters or up to 50 pages with an SASE. Proposals and sample chapters without postage will be trashed. No disks, please. Sample chapters should already be edited and without typographical errors or incorrect grammar.

Reading-fee policy: No reading fee as such. We do, however, request a bush-league, small potato, hardly worth mentioning but ever so popular contribution to our efforts of $20 per submission, which in the past has been used to pay for guard dogs to keep other agents away from our authors, to send those delightfully tacky pens and coasters that publishers like so much, and to pay for all those cocktails at the pools in Palm Springs and Las Vegas where we do our reading (eat your hearts out, you agents who winter in New York). Seriously, each year we receive more and more submissions, and to give each one the time it deserves increases our overhead dramatically. Now, unfortunately, we have also had to purchase haz-mat outfits for all of our staff, body armor, and air testing technology and that's just for the guard dogs. We are now requiring that each submission bear the words on the outside of your envelope "check enclosed." This is to entice our staff to take the chance on opening your submission. Submissions without these words on the outside of the envelope are subject to immediate destruction, without return of the contents. If you do not have a rich aunt, a trust fund, or a three-car garage and cannot afford this fee, we suggest you contact another agent, as we are extremely choosy and now, as you can tell, also somewhat paranoid about opening the mail.

Client representation by category: Nonfiction, 30%; Fiction, 60%; Children's, 10%.

Commission: 20% domestic; 30% foreign (split with foreign agents).

Rejection rate (all submissions): 99.9%

Most common mistakes authors make: Sending first drafts, no SASE, faxing queries, incessant calls, autobiographies, and travel memoirs of trips to Orlando or Tijuana.

Description of the client from Hell: We don't have any over-demanding clients with unrealistic expectations. Five years ago we buried them all alive in killer anthills in the desert. Recently, one was dug up and found to still be typing away.

Description of a dream client: Bestselling authors who leave their present uncaring agent for the personal care our agency can provide.

Why did you become an agent? With my background in music and literature, as well as interests in Europe and the law, it was a natural progression to add a literary agency to our law firm.

Comments: Sadly, as this book goes to print, the world is a different place than it was only months before. While it's difficult to predict what the world will be like months from now, there will always be the need for good books. Writers, however, more than ever, should not be tempted to write only books using the events of the day as their backdrop, but rather must take into consideration the mood of the population and strive to produce works that will entice the buyers at your local bookstore and hold their interest until the last page.

IRENE GOODMAN LITERARY AGENCY

521 Fifth Avenue, New York, NY 10175
212-682-1978   fax: 212-490-6502

Agent: Irene Goodman

Born: November 29, 1949, Detroit, Michigan.

Education: B.A., University of Michigan, 1971; M.A., University of Michigan, 1973.

Career history: Editorial Assistant at T. Y. Crowell, 1975–1976; Assistant at Kirby McCauley Agency, 1976–1978; established own agency in 1978.

Hobbies/personal interests: Theater, opera, cooking, Nantucket, the Berkshires, Doonesbury, figure skating (watching, not doing), politics, movies, hanging out with small children, watching cooking shows on weird cable channels.

Areas most interested in agenting: All types of women's fiction, romance novels, mysteries, and thrillers.

Areas not interested in agenting: Literature, esoteric nonfiction, techno-thrillers, macho genre books, psychobabble, feminist diatribes. I don't handle children's books because I like to leave something sacred.

If not agenting, what would you be doing? When I was in my 20s, I was considering two career options: pursuing an advanced degree in medieval studies or studying gourmet cooking in Paris. The third option was to come to New York and go into book publishing, which is obviously what I did.

Best way to initiate contact: By referral, or by sending a query that is as good as the best page in your manuscript.

Reading-fee policy: No reading fee.

Client representation by category: Nonfiction, 5%; Fiction, 95%.

Commission: 15% domestic; 10% foreign. Foreign rights are handled by Danny Baron, International.

Number of titles sold last year: 40.

Rejection rate (all submissions): 98%.

Most common mistakes authors make: They don't tell me enough about their book, or they try to send things I don't handle.

Description of the client from Hell: Someone who wants me to be mother, psychiatrist, best friend, sounding board, loan officer, editor, accountant, and lawyer—all rolled into one. I am none of those things in my work. What I am is an agent.

Description of a dream client: I have several real dream clients. It is my privilege to work with them. Here's what they all have in common: They work hard, they don't whine, they have a terrific sense of humor, they are intelligent, they have lives and expect me to have one, and—oh, yes—they have talent. They are responsible for themselves, they know how to say thank you, they know how to laugh at themselves (and at me occasionally, when I deserve it), and they like to give people the benefit of the doubt. They enrich my life and give as much back to me as I give to them.

Why did you become an agent? I became an agent because it was my destiny. That sounds pompous, but consider this: I don't like working in large companies because I can't tolerate the politics. I like to be a part of a working community, but I also need to fly solo. Autonomy is stimulating to me; it motivates me to get things done. I love making deals, I love books, and I love having an equal partnership with a very talented author. Bureaucracy makes me crazy, and I love being in a position where I can cut through it.

How would you describe what you do for a living? I am a career manager. I nurture projects into fruition, sell them for as much money as they will command, and then work with the author to build on each success.

How did you become an agent? I started out working for a publisher, saw what agents did, and said to myself, "I could do that." So I did.

What do you think about editors? They are underpaid and overworked. Some of my best friends are editors. Really.

What do you think about publishers? Oh, they're okay. Just don't think that because they're a big company, they know what they're doing.

What were your favorite films last year? *Erin Brockovich, Billy Elliot, Meet the Parents.*

Do you watch the *Sopranos?* Bada Bing!!

Representative titles: *The Last Chance Café* by Linda Lael Miller (Pocket); *Star Light, Star Bright* by Katherine Stone (Mira); *Between Friends* by Debbie Macomber (Mira); *Miss Match* by Leslie Carroll (first novel—Ballantine); *Married for a Month* by Susan Mallery (Pocket).

G

GRAYBILL & ENGLISH, LLC

1920 N Street, NW, Suite 620, Washington, DC 20036-1619
202-861-0106   fax: 202-457-0662
www.GraybillandEnglish.com

Agents: Nina Graybill, Jeff Kleinman, Elaine English, Lynn Whittaker

Born: Kleinman: September 28, 1965, Cleveland, Ohio. Whittaker: October 24. English: October 10, 1949, Asheville, North Carolina.

Education: Graybill: George Washington Law School, 1987. Kleinman: B.A. with High Distinction in English/Modern Studies, University of Virginia; M.A. in Italian Language/Literature, University of Chicago. Whittaker: Undergraduate in English and Political Science at University of Georgia; M.A. in English, University of Georgia; graduate work in Political Science at MIT and Harvard. English: Undergraduate in Latin (Magna Cum Laude) at Randolph Macon Woman's College; J.D., National Law Center at George Washington University.

Career history: Graybill: I am an attorney specializing in publishing and entertainment law and a literary agent. Graybill & English began in 1997. Prior to becoming a lawyer, I was a freelance editor and writer, working on presidential and congressional investigations and commissions, the final one being the House-Senate Iran-Contra Committee in 1987. I am also the co-author of six cookbooks. Kleinman: After graduating from the University of Virginia, I lived in Italy for about three years, studying the Italian Renaissance. Previously an Associate at the art and literary law firm of Kaufman & Silverberg in Washington, D.C., I am now counsel to the law firm of Graybill & English. Whittaker: Many years as an Editor and Publications Director in academic and educational publishing, several years a Publisher and Editor in Chief of a small press, co-author of two women's history books. English: After pursuing careers in teaching, social services, and personnel management, I completed law school and began working as an attorney for a public interest organization, Reporters Committee for Freedom of the Press, on open government and media issues. I then joined a small firm with a publishing law/agenting practice. For more than 15 years in private practice, I have concentrated on media and publishing issues. Recently, I decided to expand my legal practice to include agenting of commercial fiction.

Hobbies/personal interests: Graybill: Reading, cooking, antiques, design and architecture, art. Kleinman: Art, history, horses (train dressage and event horses). English: Reading, hiking, natural photography.

Areas most interested in agenting: Graybill: Narrative nonfiction, very readable serious nonfiction (e.g., health, psychology, science, culture and race, history, politics), some light nonfiction, literary/commercial fiction, and limited mystery and suspense. Kleinman: Prescriptive nonfiction, health, parenting, aging, nature, pets, how-to, and so on. Narrative nonfiction, especially books with a historical bent, but also travel, nature, ecology, politics, military, espionage, cooking, romance, equestrian, pets, memoir, biography. Fiction: very well written, character-driven novels; some science fiction and fantasy, suspense, thrillers; otherwise mainstream commercial and literary fiction. Whittaker: Creative and narrative nonfiction of all kinds; serious nonfiction, especially history and biography; nature and science writing; literary fiction; mysteries; how-to/self-help; celebrity. Subjects of particular interest include women's stories and issues, U.S. history, multicultural and African-American subjects, race relations, dogs, sports, health/nutrition, psychology, business/career, pop culture, writing. Also, academics who can write for the trade market. English: Women's fiction, including romances (single title, both contemporary and historical).

Areas not interested in agenting: Graybill: Children's, genre fiction (except some mysteries and suspense), poetry, New Age, spirituality, screenplays, stage plays. Kleinman: Mysteries, romance, Westerns, children's poetry, plays, screenplays. Whittaker: Children's/young adult, romance, Westerns, science fiction, screenplays, and scripts. English: No Westerns, time travel, or paranormal romances and no nonfiction.

If not agenting, what would you be doing? Graybill: I am also an attorney, a sometime cookbook writer, and a part-time interior design consultant. Kleinman: If I weren't an agent, I'd probably be practicing intellectual property law. English: Simply practicing law.

Best way to initiate contact: Graybill: Query letter, with a one-page synopsis and sample chapters for fiction, and a proposal or detailed explanation of the book and a bio for nonfiction, and an SASE. Kleinman: Written or e-mail. Nonfiction: Cover letter, proposal, including author credentials and sample chapter and/or outline. Fiction: Cover letter and the first few pages of the novel. Whittaker: A query letter that outlines book and author credentials, sent by regular mail or e-mail (no attachments please). Okay to send sample of up to 30 pages with mailed query letter. I also love to meet writers at writing conferences and to hear from writers who have heard me speak on panels. And I love getting referrals. English: Query letter with one-page synopsis (can be sent by regular mail or e-mail, no attachments please). Will make final decision without reading full manuscript.

Reading-fee policy: AAR members; no reading fee.

Client representation by category: Nonfiction, 80%; Fiction, 20%.

Commission: 15% domestic; 25% first serial; 20% foreign.

Rejection rate (all submissions): 95%.

Most common mistakes authors make: Graybill: Overhyped letters about how wonderful they and their certain-to-be bestselling book are; query letters and first pages (even paragraphs) of a manuscript that are full of typos, grammatical errors, misspellings (which to me indicates a lack of professionalism). Kleinman: Groveling—agents are professionals, and they expect writers to act professionally as well; providing too much information—telling me too much about the project, rather than being able to succinctly summarize it; and sending me a poorly formatted, difficult-to-read manuscript. Whittaker: Handing me a list of 10 books they're writing and asking me to choose which ones I'd like to see. Querying me about types of books I don't represent. English: Rushing their manuscripts to an agent or editor before they have completed editing, critiquing, and proofreading.

Description of the client from Hell: Graybill: I try to spot these coming and step aside: Writers with an overblown sense of their talent and value, writers who don't want to put in the time and hard work a proposal or a manuscript requires. I don't mind big egos or artistic temperament, I just ask that there be some valid underpinnings for them. Kleinman: Clients from Hell don't listen, don't incorporate suggestions, and believe that the world "owes" them a bestseller.

Description of the dream client: Graybill: Dream clients are enthusiastic; eager to make their work even better; considerate; prompt; and very, very talented. Kleinman: Someone who writes beautifully; who has marketing savvy and ability; who is friendly, accessible, easy to work with, and fun to talk to and can follow directions and guidance without taking offense, realizing that an agent's job is to help make the end product even better than it already was.

How did you become an agent? Kleinman: My law firm shared offices with an agency, and I did several book contracts. Gradually, I started reading manuscripts, talking to writers, and before long, there I was—a literary agent. English: Deliberate decision made after intensive study of market.

Why did you become an agent? Graybill: I became a lawyer/agent because I wanted to combine my interest and background in books and writing with my new law degree. Kleinman: Agentry is a great marriage of law and writing—both of which I'm very interested in. Whittaker: I've loved to read all my life and believe in the power of books to affect people's lives. I like the combination of solitary work (reading, thinking, evaluating, editing) and social interaction (with writers, editors, booksellers, and others in the book

G

world). I love my clients and enjoy learning from them, making them happy by selling their work, and giving them whatever advice and support they need to develop their careers. I also really enjoy the eclectic variety of books I share with my clients. English: Because I love books, enjoy working with authors, and wanted to contribute, in even a small way, to the creative process by which the reading public is entertained.

What can writers do to enhance their chances of getting you as an agent? Graybill: If writers are referred by someone I know, I will look at their project a little more closely than I might a stranger's. But mostly, I am interested in a query letter offering a fresh treatment of an intriguing topic by someone with the appropriate credentials to write such a book. In the case of fiction, I look for writers who, their natural talent aside, have read many, many good books in their area of interest, such as literary fiction or mysteries, and who have studied fiction writing enough—through reading, courses, workshops, writing groups—to understand the demands of their chosen type of fiction. Kleinman: *Enhance your credentials.* Get published. Show me (so I can show a publisher) that you're a good risk for publication. If you don't have any eye-opening credentials, then be sure that the writing is as strong and as fresh as you can make it. Whittaker: Most of all, be good writers. Also, have books on topics I love. Teach me about something new. English: Know their target market and have a well-written, solid manuscript, with an inventive plot, good pacing, strong dialogue, and realistic, strong characters.

How would you describe what you actually do for a living? Kleinman: Soothe egos.

What do you think about editors? Graybill: I really admire strong, hands-on editors who understand what a book and its author are about and only seek to make it better, and those who stay actively involved throughout the entire process, from acquisition through launch. Kleinman: I think that too often they're overworked and underpaid, and often don't have the time to really "connect the dots" in a manuscript or a proposal—so it's crucial that we (the writer and I) connect the dots for them.

What do you think of publishers? Graybill: I've never heard any writers say that their publishers did enough to promote their books. I am distressed about the takeover of so many publishers by a few conglomerates because the competition among publishers is far less intense and the emphasis is on trendy books that sell in huge numbers at the expense of smaller but worthwhile books. Kleinman: Probably by the time this book comes out, there will only be one publisher left.

Comments: Kleinman: From personal experience, I know how frustrating it can be to work with literary agents; your manuscript disappears for months at a time, only to return to you with a polite little "Sorry, not for us" scrawled on your original cover letter. Or an agent agrees to take you on, and a year goes by with no word—only to have your manuscript returned to you with "Sorry, I'm just not enthusiastic enough about this one." Was it submitted to publishers? If not, just what was your agent doing for the past year? Who knows? Don't expect that from me. My turnaround time, at the moment, is about two months for fiction solicited manuscripts and about three weeks for nonfiction proposals.

Representative titles: *The 50 Greatest Women in Broadcasting* by American Women in Radio & Television (Andrews McMeel); *Herblock: A Cartoonist's Life* by Herbert Block (Times Books/Random House); *Madam Secretary: A Biography of Madeleine Albright* by Thomas Blood (Thomas Dunne/St. Martin's Press); *The Lost Ships* by Dr. Mensun Bound (Simon & Schuster); *Mom I Want a Pet* by Mary Jane Checchi (St. Martin's

Press); *The Anxiety Cure: An Eight Step Program* by Robert DuPont, Elizabeth DuPont Spencer, and Caroline DuPont (John Wiley & Sons); *The Messenger: A Biography of Elijah Muhammad* by Karl Evanzz (Pantheon); *From Nero's Nagging Mother to Catherine's Stable of Studs: A Treasury of Royal Scandals* by Michael Farquhar (Penguin); *Stirring the Mud: On Swamps, Bogs, and Human Imagination* by Barbara Hurd (Beacon Press); *If Men Were Angels* by Karaim Reed (Norton); *The Complete Guide to African-American Baby Names* by Linda Keister (Dutton); *Meltdown on Main Street: Why Small Business Is Leading the Revolution Against Big Government* by Richard Lesher (Dutton); *The Buying of the President* by Charles Lewis (Avon); *When Divas Confess* by Marcia Lieberman and Paul Griffiths (Universe/Rizzoli); *Fathering Words: The Making of an African American Writer* by Ethelbert Miller (Thomas Dunne Books/St. Martin's); *The Encyclopedia of Heaven* and *The Encyclopedia of Hell* by Miriam Van Scott (St. Martin's Press); *Radio Priest: Charles Coughlin, the Father of Hate Radio* by Donald Warren (The Free Press).

ASHLEY GRAYSON LITERARY AGENCY

1342 18th Street, San Pedro, CA 90732
310-548-4672   fax: 310-514-1148

Agents: Ashley Grayson, Carolyn Grayson, Dan Hooker

Born: C. Grayson: Los Angeles, California. Hooker: Los Angeles, California.

Education: A. Grayson: B.S. in Physics. C. Grayson: B.A. in English, Wellesley College; M.B.A. in Marketing, UCLA. Hooker: B.A. in Spanish, UCLA.

Career history: A. Grayson: Computer sales, Management Consultant, Literary Agent. C. Grayson: Market Research Analyst; Consultant and Managing Editor for marketing consulting firm. Hooker: Several jobs before coming to agenting. Agenting the past 10 years. Published writer of about a dozen short stories and articles.

Hobbies/personal interests: C. Grayson: Reading, gardening, travel, snorkeling, golf, investing, wine, cooking. Hooker: Writing, reading, checking out bookstores wherever I go, sports, strange low-budget movies.

Areas most interested in agenting: A. Grayson: Commercial and literary fiction, historical novels, suspense, thrillers, young adult, science fiction. I read widely and would be happy to have a top-of-category work in just about any area. I am willing to read an occasional published book in German for possible sale in the U.S./UK markets. I am also the agent for a number of entertainment companies and Web sites that wish to spin their properties into books. C. Grayson: Mainstream commercial fiction. Some literary fiction. Women's fiction: mainstream and romance (historical and contemporary). Mystery, suspense, thrillers, crime and true crime, horror. Children's and young adult fiction. Would like to take on more nonfiction: travel, gardening, cooking, health, some self-help, how-to, pop culture, bio/autobiographies, creative nonfiction. Hooker: Commercial fiction; mysteries; thrillers; suspense; hard science fiction; contemporary fantasy; horror; young adult and middle-grade; quality fiction by outstanding new voices. Nonfiction: Popular subjects and treatment with high commercial potential.

Areas not interested in agenting: The agency is not interested in representing poetry, screenplays, short stories, novellas, action/adventure, war books, novelty, New Age, psychic phenomena, textbooks, or books about religion. A. Grayson: I believe I can obtain an optimal business deal for virtually any book on any topic if one or more buyers can be identified. I am unlikely to be an effective crusader to locate a single publisher for narrow-focused works on politics or diet and health, in addition to the above list. C. Grayson: No memoirs. Hooker: Not interested in epic fantasy.

If not agenting, what would you be doing? A. Grayson: I would probably be running a software or Net-based company. C. Grayson: Ad agency executive; landscape architect; interior designer; living on the beach in Hawaii. Hooker: Writing, which I do anyway, as time permits.

Best way to initiate contact: Published authors can fax or call to discuss their needs. An intelligent query letter is the best way for an unpublished writer to apply. C. Grayson: By referral or query letter with synopsis and SASE. Hooker: Concise query letter that tells me about your book and about your writing background.

Reading-fee policy: No reading fee.

Client representation by category: A. Grayson: Nonfiction, 15%; Fiction, 65%; Children's, 20%. C. Grayson: Nonfiction, 10%; Fiction, 50%; Children's, 40%. Hooker: Nonfiction, 5%; Fiction, 75%; Children's, 20%.

Commission: 15% U.S. and Canada; 20% international; 10% film/TV plus subagent/legal fees.

Number of titles sold last year: More than 100. C. Grayson: Difficult to answer because we sell most of the foreign rights for clients' works ourselves, so we have sold some books six or more times in a year.

Rejection rate (all submissions): Greater than 95%. Hooker: 99%.

Most common mistakes authors make: A. Grayson: Unrealistic and outrageous claims for the quality of the work or the potential audience for the work are frequent. Errors of grammar in cover letters are surprisingly common. C. Grayson: Query letters that are too much hype and/or contain too little information about the book(s). Giving incomplete information regarding previous works. Do not query more than one person in our agency! Do not send your query by certified mail with signature required. And there is no need to send one sheet of paper in a 9" × 13" envelope.

Description of the client from Hell: A. Grayson: Of course, we don't represent any clients from Hell, but such a person is more interested in the celebrity of being an author than in actually writing books. Those who feel that grammar and spelling are for the little people to fix; who call after working hours, are late on delivery, or want to borrow money. Anyone who won't work on the next book until the first (or second) one sells. Anyone who calls up weekly and asks, "How about a book about (insert the news event of the week)—would that be worth a lot of money?" Any clients who also want to second-guess their agent. C. Grayson: Those who try to do my job, call three times a day, think they are my only clients.

Description of a dream client: C. Grayson: Those who keep writing wonderful books; are in command of their craft; are willing to accept editorial advice, either from us and/or from editors; are creative, respectful, loyal, and dependable. A. Grayson: Dream clients always have a few ideas simmering for the next book or two. They always listen to input and feedback, but ultimately decide what to do and how to do it because the clients both respect the market and uphold their standards of art and technique. We seek productive authors with a proven audience whose works we can sell in multiple territories and across different media: books to film and TV.

Why did you become an agent? A. Grayson: I love to read books and sell new ideas. The real reason I became an agent is that Judy-Lynn Del Rey (the late founder of the Del Rey imprint at Random House) told me in 1976 that I should. She had great insight—I'm still having a great time. C. Grayson: The joy of discovering new talent and seeing the books in print. Hooker: As an aspiring writer, I wanted to learn about the publishing business, but I didn't want to move to New York to work in a publishing house. I found a good agency near my home, and they gave me a chance. Turned out I really liked agent stuff.

What can writers do to enhance their chances of getting you as an agent? Hooker: Develop your own "voice," one that can only be identified as yours, and tell the reader about life and people in that voice. Be dedicated and patient. Don't overhype your marketability; I can figure that out. Be more than good—be damn good.

Comments: A. Grayson: Our international success in selling clients' rights is excellent; we generally attend all the major rights fairs and have sold our clients' works in more than 16 languages. Hooker: I always like to connect with talented writers who aren't afraid to express their unique perspectives on this world of ours. Determination and a professional attitude are absolute requirements, too.

Representative titles: *Hokkaido Popsicle* by Isaac Adamson (HarperCollins); *The Return of Buzz* by Buzz Aldrin and John Barnes (Tor); *Merchants of Souls* by John Barnes (Tor); *Move Your Stuff, Change Your Life* by Karen Rauch Carter (Simon & Schuster); *The Playmaker* by J. B. Cheaney (Knopf Books for Young Readers); *Monsters of Morely Manor* by Bruce Coville (Harcourt); *The Fat White Vampire Blues* by Andrew Fox (Ballantine); *Virginia Bound* by Amy Butler Greenfield (Clarion); *Something More* by Winnie Griggs (Dorchester); *Wizards of the Game* by David Lubar (Philomel); *But I Don't Feel Too Old to Be a Mommy* by Doreen Nagle (Health Communications); *The Grave* by Christopher Pike (Pocket/Archway); *The Ink Drinker* by Eric Sanvoisin and Martin Matje (Delacorte Press); *For Love or Country* by Kerrelyn Sparks (Forge); *Wheelers* by Ian Stewart and Jack Cohen (Warner); *Expanded Orgasm* by Patricia Taylor, Ph.D. (Sourcebooks); *The Dragon Delasangre* by Alan F. Troop (ROC); *The Boy with the Lampshade on His Head* by Bruce Wetter (Atheneum).

G

SANFORD J. GREENBURGER ASSOCIATES, INC.

55 Fifth Avenue, New York, NY 10003
212-206-5000   fax: 212-463-8718
www.Greenburger.com

Agents: Heide Lange, Vice President; Faith Hamlin, Beth Vesel, Theresa Park, Elyse Cheney, Daniel Mandel, Peter Harrison McGuigan, Julie Barer

Best way to initiate contact: Query letter with SASE.

Client representation by category: Nonfiction, 60%; Fiction, 40%.

Commission: 15% domestic; 20% international.

Number of titles sold last year: Hundreds.

The following information pertains to HEIDE LANGE:

Born: July 21, 1949.

Education: B.A., Hunter College, CUNY.

Career history: I started working at the agency while attending college. As Sanford Greenburger's assistant, I was fortunate to learn the business from a "publishing gentleman" with an international reputation, and it's been my home for 28 years. My books have generally reflected my background, interests, and stages in my life. Married, two children, I've handled general nonfiction, from art, which was my college major (*Drawing on the Right Side of the Brain* was my first bestseller), to relationships and sex (*The G Spot*), pregnancy and childbirth, parenting, women's health and other issues, current events, controversy, biographies, memoirs, journalism, some general reference, how-to, self-improvement.

Hobbies/personal interests: Reading, gardening, bicycling, rollerblading, and any other activities I can share with the family before our children go off to college (in a flash it seems).

Areas most interested in agenting: See above and representative titles below, but basically, if authors are passionate about and experienced in the subject they are writing about, I'm prepared to be enticed by it.

Areas not interested in agenting: Category fiction, children's books.

Why did you become an agent? The fact that I love to read was really my entry into this business, and sometimes I still can't believe I can make money doing what I love. That, and the clients I can help to realize their dreams, makes this very gratifying work.

Representative titles: *Let Me Hear Your Voice: A Family's Triumph Over Autism* by Catherine Maurice (Knopf); *Emotional Wisdom* by Jean Grasso Fitzpatrick (Viking); *Raising Your Spirited Child* by Mary Kurcinka (HarperCollins); *Swim with the Dolphins: How Women Can Succeed in Corporate America on Their Own Terms* by Connie Glaser and Barbara Smalley (Warner); *The Multi-Orgasmic Man: How Any Man Can Experience Multiple Orgasms and Dramatically Enhance His Sexual Relationship* by Mantak Chia and Douglas Abrams Arava (HarperSanFrancisco); *The Random House Word Menu* by Stephen Glazier (Random House); *Life's Big Instruction Book: The Almanac of Indispensable Information* by Carol Madigan and Ann Elwood (Warner); *Lauren Groveman's Kitchen: Nurturing Foods for Family and Friends* by Lauren Groveman (Chronicle); *Italian Food and Drink: An A to Z Guide* by John Mariani (Broadway Books); *A Cold Stay in Hell: One Woman's Tale of Courage and Survival on Mount McKinley* by Ruth Ann Kocour, as told to Michael Hodgson (St. Martin's); *Rains All the Time: A Social History of Weather in the Pacific Northwest* by David Laskin (Sasquatch Books); *Darwin's Orchestra: An Almanac of Nature in History and the Arts* by Michael Sims (Holt).

The following information pertains to FAITH HAMLIN:

Education: Speech Therapy and Psychology, Boston University.

Career history: Mother of two; bookstore Buyer/manager; Sales Rep for several publishers; Sales Manager for Macmillan, Atheneum, Scribner, Free Press; agent for 14 years.

Areas most interested in agenting: Most nonfiction, especially health, medical, psychology, parenting, women's issues, sports, biography/autobiography, business, science, humor, the arts, and books by journalists. Especially looks for experts in their fields.

Areas not interested in agenting: General fiction.

Representative titles: Adult: *Healing ADD; Healing Anxiety and Depression* (Putnam); *Healing the Hardware of the Soul* (Free Press); *Change Your Brain, Change Your Life* by Daniel Amen, M.D. (Crown); *Dr. Folkman's War* by Robert Cooke (Random House); *Book of the Seasons* by Anthony Aveni (Oxford University Press); *The Eureka Effect* by David Perkins (Norton); *Organizing from the Inside Out* by Julie Morgenstern (Holt); *Skyscrapers* by Roger Shepherd (McGraw Hill); *Preserving the World's Great Cities* by Anthony Tung (Clarkson Potter); *Wondrous Contrivances* by Merritt Ierley (Clarkson Potter); *Plane Insanity* by Elliot Hester (St. Martin's); *Andy Warhol* by Wayne Koestenbaum (Penguin Lives); *The Long Tomorrow: From Aging to Immortality* by Michael R. Rose (Viking); *Loose Balls, The Curse of Rocky Colavito, Our Tribe* by Terry Pluto (Simon & Schuster); *Great Feuds in Medicine, Great Feuds in Science* by Hal Hellman (Wiley); *Is Our Food Safe?* by Warren Leon and Caroline Smith DeWaal (Harmony/Three Rivers). Children's: *Martin's Big Words* by Doreen Rappaport (Hyperion); *You Can't Take a Balloon* (series) *into the Metropolitan Museum, the National Gallery, the Museum of Fine Arts* by Robin Preiss Glasser and Jacqueline Preiss Weitzman (Dial).

The following information pertains to BETH VESEL:

Education: B.A. in English, with a minor in Political Science, UC Berkley; graduate work in Comparative Literature, UC Berkley.

Career history: Agent at Greenburger since 1988. Worked for Gloria Loomis prior to that.

Areas most interested in agenting: Entertaining literary fiction, original, relevant serious psychology.

Areas not interested in agenting: Category/genre fiction.

Why did you become an agent? Because I love books and care about authors.

If not agenting, what might you be doing? I would be a writer.

Representative titles: *Kiddie Drug Madness* by Larry Diller (Basic Books); *The Unraveling* by Martin Roper (Henry Holt); *Finding Your Own North Star* by Martha Beck (Crown); *Transference* by Keith Ablow (St. Martin's).

The following information pertains to THERESA PARK:

Education: B.A., University of California, Santa Cruz; J.D., Harvard Law School.

Career history: Previously an attorney with Cooley Godward (Palo Alto, California); joined Sanford J. Greenburger Associates in 1994.

Areas most interested in agenting: Commercial fiction; serious nonfiction, including cultural studies, science, history, multicultural/cross-cultural issues, memoir, social narrative, serious psychology, event-driven narrative works, Asian-American work.

Areas not interested in agenting: Science fiction, humor, diet books.

If not agenting, what might you be doing? I don't know—I love being an agent so much that I can't imagine doing anything else right now.

What can writers do to enhance their chances of getting you as their agent? Be professional; send concise, effective query letters.

Why did you become an agent? I love books, I love to work with people, and I love to do deals! Also, with my background as a transfunctional lawyer, it seemed like the

G

right area of publishing to get into. One of the best things about being a lawyer was having clients—I enjoy getting to know people and working closely with them on their manuscripts and proposals; the personal reward of watching a client's career blossom is the best part of my job.

Representative titles: *The Notebook, Message in a Bottle, A Walk to Remember, The Rescue* by Nicholas Sparks (Warner Books); *Remaking Eden: Cloning and Beyond in a Brave New World* by Lee Silver (Avon Books); *The Eighth Continent: Life, Death, and Discovery in the Lost World of Madagascar* by Peter Tyson (Morrow); *Bloodlines: From Ethnic Pride to Ethnic Terrorism* by Vamik Volkan, M.D. (Farrar, Straus & Giroux); *The Family Virtues Guide* by Linda Kavelin Popv with Dan Popv and John Kaelin (Dutton Signet); *The Simple Living Guide* (Broadway Books) and *Simple Loving: A Path to Deeper, More Sustainable Relationships* by Janet Luhrs (Viking/Penguin); *Handyman* by Linda Nichols (Delacorte); *My Spy: Memoir of a CIA Wife* by Bina Cay Kiyonaga (Avon Books); *Voodoo Science: The Road from Foolishness to Fraud* by Robert L. Park (Oxford University Press); *Dante's Inferno* by Sarah Lovett (Simon & Schuster); *P.E.A.C.E.* by Guy Holmes (Simon & Schuster).

The following information pertains to DAN MANDEL:

Education: B.S., Cornell University.

Career history: Associate, Diane Cleaver, Inc.

Areas most interested in agenting: Fiction, new media, politics, and popular culture.

If not agenting, what might you be doing? I would, of course, be a writer.

Representative titles: *Penny Dreadful* and *Kiss Me* by Will Christopher Baer (Viking); *A Gentleman's Game* by Tom Coyne (Grove/Atlantic); *Wormwood* by D. J. Levien (Miramax Books); *The Fundamentals of Play* by Caitlin Macy (Random House); *The Dice Man* by Luke Rhinehart (Overlook Press); *The Soulful Sounds of Alton Brown* by James Ellis Thomas (Simon & Schuster); *Sharkman Six* by Owen West (Simon & Schuster); *The Guerrilla Girls' Bedside Companion to the History of Western Art* (Penguin); *Speaking in Spanglish* by Ed Morales (St. Martin's Press); *Westside* by William Shaw (Simon & Schuster)

The following information pertains to JULIE BARER

Education: B.A., Vassar College.

Areas most interested in agenting: Literary fiction, narrative and serious nonfiction, including science, biography, memoir, and history.

Areas not interested in agenting: Self-help, diet, parenting, horror, romance, humor.

Best way to initiate contact: Send a well-written query letter with an SASE.

Why did you become an agent? I'm a voracious reader, and I love books. I also love working closely with writers, helping edit and shape their projects, and finding their books the right home. Being an agent lets me be a part of the process that brings books to the world, and that's very exciting.

If not agenting, what might you be doing? I can't imagine doing anything else right now, but someday I'd love to have my own bookstore.

Representative titles: *The Best of Animals: Stories* by Lauren Grodstein (Persea Books); *The Winter Zoo* by John Beckman (Henry Holt); *An Everyday Savior* by Kathryn

Larrabee (4 Walls 8 Windows); *Live from New York: The KGB Bar Fiction Anthology,* edited by Rebecca Donner (St. Martin's Press).

The following information pertains to PETER HARRISON MCGUIGAN:
  Areas most interested in agenting: Narrative nonfiction, science, adventure, and literary and controversial fiction.
  What can writers do to enhance their chances of getting you as their agent? Have patience.
  Representative titles: *No Apparent Danger* by Victoria Bruce (HarperCollins); *Sonic Boom* by John Alderman (Perseus); *The Official Iron Chef Companion* (Beverly Books); *A Brief History of the Smile* by Angus Trumble (Basic Books); *The Bird Conservation Handbook* by American Bird Conservatory (W. H. Freeman).

FREDERICK GREY AGENCY, LLC

6214 Bayshore Boulevard, Tampa, FL 33611-5024
813-624-9466   fax: 813-839-0986
e-mail: drgrey@tampabay.rr.com

Agent: Lawrence Grey, M.D.
  Born: April 5, 1955, New York City.
  Education: B.A. (Magna Cum Laude), Hofstra University; Medical degree, SUNY Downstate Medical Center, New York City; Postgraduate medical training in surgery, urology, and pathology. Board certified in surgery, 1988. Additional studies in literature and foreign language.
  Career history: I practiced medicine for about a dozen years, privately, eventually becoming a leader in my area of expertise, surgical reconstruction of male genitalia, and surgical and pharmacological correction of erectile dysfunction. I made a fortune and got extremely bored. I continue to practice medicine, but strictly on a pro bono basis at the time of this writing. I have authored three novels and edited many more, written numerous medical articles and several short stories and have done a great deal of ghost writing. Finally, I have done marketing on a corporate level with substantial success.
  Hobbies/personal interests: Writing; working on a fourth novel. I still do ghost writing and editing. I am an instrument-rated, multi-engine pilot, and owner of twin-engine aircraft. I am a companion to my wonderful wife (first wife!), Muriel Lavallee-Grey, M.D., and our two beloved Doberman Pinschers, Sam and Stormy.
  Areas most interested in agenting: I like commercial fiction, horror, hardcore murder mysteries, and medical thrillers. I will review and consider any quality fiction. In the area of nonfiction, I accept only medical and health-related subjects, but no quackery or books about enemas to cure brain cancer.
  Areas not interested in agenting: No porno. No hate books. No feminist manifestos. No historical novels. No fundamental religious stuff.
  If not agenting, what would you be doing? I would continue to do the other things I do and do them more.

G

Best way to initiate contact: Fiction: Query letter, 3-page synopsis, first 50 pages. Nonfiction: Solid, well-constructed proposal.

Client representation by category: Nonfiction, 15%; Fiction, 85%.

Commission: 15% domestic; 20% foreign.

Number of titles sold last year: 22.

Rejection rate (all submissions): 90%.

Most common mistakes authors make: They call, they nag, they impose, they compare themselves to Hemingway, they push, they prod, they poke, they compare themselves to Henry Miller, they pester, they pound, and so on. But even if these are the most common mistakes, they are rare enough that my job is still a pleasure. And most prospective clients are rather nice.

Description of the client from Hell: Gargantuan ego, minuscule talent, immature, demanding, impulsive; they phone often, fax multiple pages at a time, and suffer with halitosis and flatulence. They are middle-aged, single, live with their parents, pick their nose, and don't like dogs. Have not had one of these yet, but I know it will happen.

Description of a dream client: The dream client has talent, patience, trust, maturity, character, wings, and so on.

How did you become an agent? The forces of nature nudged me into the publishing business.

Why did you become an agent? I love books, reading, learning, and other people who love books, reading, and learning. The excitement of finding smashing new talent makes each day worthwhile.

What do you think about editors? Underloved, maybe underpaid. It's a tough job and I'm glad they do it.

What can writers do to enhance their chances of getting you as an agent? Follow instructions, have manners, communicate in writing, and accept constructive criticism. Do not send form letters or pages stained with coffee or body fluids.

If not agenting, what might you be doing? Just what I'm doing.

Do you watch the *Sopranos*? No.

Representative titles: I consider this information to be confidential and so state in my contracts.

Comments: Strictly self-serving, fundamentally dishonest, ass-kissing people suck. There are a lot of them. Some are very successful. You know how they got there. Understanding, kind people with goodness (not greatness) rock everyone's world. So do people who put people before money. They are fairly rare, but I know some. Dogs rock my world, as do other animals, and nature.

THE CHARLOTTE GUSAY LITERARY AGENCY

10532 Blythe Avenue, Los Angeles, CA 90064
fax: 310-559-2639
mediastudio.com/gusay

Agent: Charlotte Gusay
   Education: B.A. in English Literature/Theater; M.A. in English.

Career history: Taught in secondary schools for several years. Interest in filmmaking developed. Founded (with partners) a documentary film company in the early 1970s. Soon became interested in the fledgling audio-publishing business. Became the Managing Editor for the Center for Cassette Studies/Scanfax, producing audio programs, interviews, and documentaries. In 1976 founded George Sand, Books, in West Hollywood, one of the most prestigious and popular bookshops in Los Angeles. It specialized in fiction and poetry, sponsored readings and events. Patronized by the Hollywood community's glitterati and literati, George Sand, Books, was the place to go when looking for the "best" literature and quality books. It was here that the marketing of books was preeminent. It closed in 1987. Two years later the Charlotte Gusay Literary Agency was opened.

Hobbies/personal interests: Gardens and gardening, magazines (a magazine junkie), good fiction, reading, anything French, anything Greek.

Areas most interested in agenting: I enjoy both fiction and nonfiction. Prefer commercial, mainstream—but quality—material. Especially like books that can be marketed as film material. Also, material that is innovative, unusual, eclectic, nonsexist. Will consider literary fiction with crossover potential. TCGLA is a signatory to the Writers' Guild and so represents screenplays and screenwriters selectively. I enjoy unusual children's books and illustrators, but have begun to limit children's projects.

Areas not interested in agenting: Does not consider science fiction or horror, poetry or short stories (with few exceptions), or the romance genres per se.

If not agenting, what would you be doing? I would write a book called *Zen and the Art of Gardening with a Black Thumb* (I'm kidding!). I would travel to Istanbul and become a foreign agent. I would finish all of Proust. I would re-read Jane Austen. Work on my French. Study Greek. Play the piano. Tap dance.

Best way to initiate contact: Send one-page query letter with SASE. Then if we request your material (book, proposal, whatever it is), note the following guidelines: For fiction: Send approximately the first 50 pages and a synopsis, along with your credentials (i.e., list of previous publications, and/or list of magazine articles, and/or any pertinent information, education, and background.) For nonfiction: Send a proposal consisting of an overview, chapter outline, author biography, sample chapters, marketing and audience research, and survey of the competition. Important note: Material will not be returned without an SASE. Second important note: Seduce me with humor and intelligence.

Reading-fee policy: No reading fee. No editorial fees. When a client is signed, the client and I share 50/50% out-of-pocket expenses. In certain cases, I charge a nominal processing fee—especially when considering unsolicited submissions—decided upon as and when queries arrive in my office.

Client representation by category: Nonfiction, 40%; Fiction, 15%; Children's, 10%; Books to Film/Screenplays, 35%.

Commission: 15% books; 10% screenplays.

Most common mistakes authors make: Clients must understand the role of agents and that agents represent only the material they feel they can best handle. Potential clients must understand that any given agent may or may not be an editor, a sounding board, a proposal writer, or a guidance counselor. Because of the enormous amount of submissions, queries, and proposals, the agent most often has only the time to say yes or no to your project. Above all, when clients don't understand why in the world I can't respond to a multiple submission with regard to their "900-page novel" within a few days, all I can do is shake my head and wonder if that potential client realizes I am human.

Description of the client from Hell: The one who does not understand the hard work we do for our clients. Or the one who refuses to build a career in a cumulative manner, but rather goes from one agent to the next and so on. Or clients who circulate their manuscripts without cooperating with their agents. Or those who think it all happens by magic. Or those who do not understand the nuts and bolts of the business.

Description of the dream client: The one who cooperates. The one who appreciates how hard we work for our clients. The one who submits everything on time, in lean, edited, proofed, professional copies of manuscripts and professionally prepared proposals. Clients who understand the crucial necessity of promoting their own books until the last one in the publisher's warehouse is gone. Those who work hard on their book selling in tandem with the agent. The author–agent relationship, like a marriage, is a cooperative affair, and it's cumulative. The dream client will happily do absolutely whatever is necessary to reach the goal.

How did you become an agent? With a great entrepreneurial spirit, cold calls, seat-of-the pants daring, 12 years in the retail book business (as founder and owner of a prestigious book shop in L.A.), and 20 years of business experience, including producing films and editing spoken-word audio programs; agenting is the most challenging and rewarding experience I've ever had.

Why did you become an agent? I became an agent because I know how to sell books and movies. Above all, I am knowledgeable and experienced, and I love agenting.

How would you describe what you actually do for a living? My job is essentially that of a bookseller. I sell books. To publishers, producers, and ultimately to the retail book trade. Sometimes, I develop a book idea. Sometimes, I develop someone's story, help the writer get a proposal written. I've even written proposals myself because I believed strongly in the book, or the person's story, or the salability of an idea. For fiction writers with potential, I sometimes make cursory suggestions, but most often I help them to find a professional editor to work on their novel *before* it is submitted to a publishing house.

What do you think about editors? Editors are overworked and underpaid. Therefore, if you wish to have the best chance of having your work accepted, you must do their work for them and don't complain. That is the reality of the editor's milieu. Editors are usually very smart. Most always, if they're any good, they are temperamental, and they know their particular publisher's market. If interested, they know how to make your work fit into their list. Do what your editor (and agent) tells you. No argument.

What do you think about publishers? Publishers are having a very difficult time these days. The "conglomeratizing" of the publishing business is extremely worrisome and publishers are feeling the pressure. However, publishers are always looking for the next great writer, the next great book, and a way to make both successful. (That means making money.)

What were your favorite films last year? Recent films and not-so-recent films I liked: *Something About Mary, Shakespeare in Love*. A few of my all-time favorite films are *Runaway Train, The English Patient, Rebel Without a Cause, Woman in the Dunes*.

Do you watch the *Sopranos?* I subscribed to HBO so I could watch the *Sopranos.* I watched it a few times. It's very clever. I prefer to listen to Mozart or Wheezer or watch a movie.

Comments*:* Be professional. Be courteous. Be patient. Understand that we are human. Pay careful attention to the kinds of projects we represent. Query us only if you feel your project fits with our agency profile. Know what we are overworked, always swamped with hundreds of queries. Know that we love and understand writers. Take us to lunch. Send flowers (just kidding).

Representative titles: *Imperial Mongolian Cooking: Recipes from the Kingdoms of Genghis Khan* by Marc Cramer (Hippocrene Publishers). Films: *Love Groucho: Letters from Groucho Marx to His Daughter Miriam,* edited by Miriam Marx Allen (Faber & Faber, Straus & Giroux U.S., and Faber & Faber U.K.), sold to CBS; *A Place Called Waco: A Survivor's Story* by David Thibodeau and Leon Whiteson (Public Affairs/ Perseus Book Group), sold to Fox; *Baby Love: The Private Files of an Adoption Attorney* by Randi G. Barrow, Esq. (Penguin/Putnam); *Rio L.A.: Tales from the Los Angeles River* by Patt Morrison, with photographs by Mark Lamonica (Angel City Press); *Vintage!: The Ultimate Guide to Selected Resale and Vintage Shopping in North America & Online with Style Tips from Fashion Experts, Hollywood Costume Designers and Film and Tele- vision Stars* by Diana Eden and Gloria Lintermans (Really Great Books Publishers).

REECE HALSEY AGENCY/REECE HALSEY AGENCY, NORTH

8733 Sunset Boulevard, Suite 101, Los Angeles, CA 90069
310-652-2409   fax: 310-652-7593

Reece Halsey Agency, North:
98 Main Street #704, Tiburon, CA 94920
415-789-9191   fax: 415-789-9177
e-mail: bookgirl@worldnet.att.net

Agents: Kimberley Cameron, Dorris Halsey (North)

Education: Halsey: Educated in France. Cameron: Marlborough School, Humboldt State University, Mount St. Mary's College.

Career history: Halsey: Worked with her husband, Reece, who was head of the liter- ary department at William Morris. They opened this office in 1957. Cameron: Former publisher, Knightsbridge Publishing Company. Has been working with Dorris Halsey since 1993.

Hobbies/personal interests: Reading for the sheer pleasure of it.

Areas most interested in agenting: Literary fiction, writing that we feel is exceptional in its field.

Areas not interested in agenting: Children's fiction, poetry.

If not agenting, what would you be doing? Reading.

Best way to initiate contact: Ms. Halsey works with referrals only. Please send an SASE with all queries to Kimberley Cameron at Reece Halsey North.

H

Reading-fee policy: No reading fee.

Client representation by category: It depends completely on the material we decide to represent. It changes often. The most accurate breakdown is Nonfiction, 30%; Fiction, 70%.

Commission: 15% domestic; 20% foreign.

Number of titles sold last year: We don't feel this should be public information.

Rejection rate (all submissions): 98%.

Most common mistakes authors make: We are always impressed by politeness, in a well-written letter or otherwise. Their most costly mistake is using too many rhetorical adjectives to describe their own work.

Description of the client from Hell: One who calls too often and asks, "What's new?"

Description of a dream client: A patient author who understands the publishing business and knows what it takes to get a book sold.

Why did you become an agent? We both love books and what they have to teach us. We both understand how important and powerful the written word is and appreciate what it takes to be a good writer.

Note: Dorris Halsey has the distinguished honor of representing the Aldous Huxley Estate. HarperCollins is publishing all his works, marking the centennial of his birth (1894–1963). Dorris has sold many celebrity biographies, nonfiction works, and fiction to most major houses and smaller houses, including Knightsbridge.

Comments: This business, especially today, is all uphill. We work extremely hard at what we're doing, and the love of books is what keeps us going. I don't think many agents do what they do every day for the money. We feel an exceptional amount of responsibility for our authors, and I just wish they could see and hear what we do for them. We have the highest regard for the process of writing and do the best we can with the material in our hands. What more can one do?

JEANNE K. HANSON LITERARY AGENCY

6708 Cornelia Drive, Edina, MN 55435
voice/fax: 952-920-8819
e-mail: jkhlit@aol.com

Agent: Jeanne K. Hanson

Born: August 12, 1944.

Education: B.A. in Philosophy and English, Wellesley College; M.A.T. in English and Education, Harvard; M.A. in Journalism, University of Minnesota; Radcliffe Publishing Course.

Career history: Teacher for 2 years; Journalist for 15 years; Literary Agent for 16 years.

Hobbies/personal interests: Running, reading, weight lifting.

Areas most interested in agenting: Nonfiction books written by journalists, science books for the general public written by protesters.

Areas not interested in agenting: Genre fiction; celebrity books; memoirs; self-help.

If not agenting, what would you be doing? Probably being a writer.

Best way to initiate contact: Query letter with a table of contents and 1–3 pages of sample writing from the book.

Client representation by category: Nonfiction, 98%; Fiction, 2%.

Commission: 15% with no extra fees.

Number of titles sold last year: 20.

Rejection rate (all submissions): 99%.

Most common mistakes authors make: Large multiple submissions (agents can just tell); self-absorbed authors who may be a little nuts, even.

Description of the client from Hell: Someone who is really late delivering the book to the publisher; someone who sends me a proposal sealed so tightly with layers and layers of paper and tape that it takes forever to open it!

Description of a dream client: A great journalist who understands how to write for an audience and how to analyze trends; a professor who really, really knows something really interesting and can write about it in a way that doesn't sound like a classroom lecture.

How did you become an agent? I wrote a book and liked my agent.

Why did you become an agent? Because I love books and love doing deals for them that make everybody happy!

What can writers do to enhance their chances of getting you as an agent? Have a great idea.

How would you describe what you actually do for a living? Getting to yes.

What do you think about editors? Nice.

What do you think about publishers? O.K.

Representative titles: *Cancer Club* by Christine Clifford (Putnam); *Frolicking Fauna* by Roger Knutson (W. H. Freeman).

THE HARDY AGENCY

3020 Bridgway, #204, Sausalito, CA 94965
415-898-2414

H

Agents: Michael Vidor, Anne Sheldon

Born: Vidor: December 20, 1949, Michigan. Sheldon: 1958, California.

Education: Vidor: B.A., Western Michigan/Wayne State. Sheldon: West Valley College/ San Jose State.

Career history: Vidor: Marketing and Advertising; co-founded the Hardy Agency in 1990. Sheldon: Publisher, Enchanté Publishing; Publishing and Marketing Consultant; co-founded the Hardy Agency, 1990.

Hobbies/personal interests: Vidor: Sailing, photography, travel, Baja. Sheldon: Music, film, gardening, cooking.

Areas most interested in agenting: Fiction: Contemporary to commercial. Nonfiction: History, sociology, contemporary issues, pop culture.

Areas not interested in agenting: Vidor: No children's, romance, science fiction, Westerns, mysteries.

If not agenting, what might you be doing? Vidor: Promoting and marketing books, perhaps selling pencils. Sheldon: I'd be a landscape architect, or I'd live on the beach somewhere.

Best way to initiate contact: Query letter and first two chapters.

Client representation by category: Nonfiction, 20%; Fiction, 80%.

Commission: 15% domestic, 20% foreign and film.

Number of titles sold last year: 8.

Rejection rate (all submissions): 99%.

Most common mistakes authors make: Vidor: Talking too much rather than showing me through their work. Sheldon: Sending us material that doesn't fall into a category we represent and not knowing what our submission requirements are. Not working to further their own career and having nothing to tell us about what they've accomplished.

Description of the client from Hell: Vidor: Writers who don't understand how the business works and would expect me to execute on their behalf, based on their misguided perceptions. Authors who write simply for the money. Impatient individuals with emotional triggers. Sheldon: One who mistakes publishing as an easy business and doesn't recognize the amount of work done by those who are ultimately successful.

Description of the dream client: Vidor: Hardworking, dedicated to the craft and to promoting oneself. Professional in every sense of the word. Sheldon: One who has become an expert on the publishing business and who has done the work, from both a publishing and a marketing standpoint.

How did you become an agent? Vidor: Fell in love with my partner. Sheldon: It was the result of an epiphany.

Why did you become an agent? Vidor: Combination of passion for the arts, a writer's super-ego, and masochistic tendencies. Sheldon: Because I love great books.

What can writers do to enhance their chances of getting you as an agent? Vidor: Have good interpersonal skills and a working knowledge of the business. Sheldon: They should make sure the work is complete and polished. They should be fully engaged in moving their career forward; attending conferences, belonging to a writer's group, placing short stories in literary journals, entering contests, and getting nominated for awards. Then tell us about those things.

How would you describe what you do for a living? Vidor: I promote writing and the translation of art. Sheldon: I steer the careers of writers.

What do you think about editors? Vidor: Tough job. Good ones are few and far between. Sheldon: Great editors are priceless. But the success or failure of any book is the responsibility of its author.

What do you think about publishers? Vidor: The same. Most have little real desire to be the gatekeeper of an essence of life: the written word. Sheldon: Publishing is an industry in constant flux. Some publishers are amazingly great, some are merely printers. All of them offer something; the key is knowing what that is and approaching the right publishers for any given project. Not all of publishing resides in New York.

What were your favorite films last year? Vidor and Sheldon: *Traffic, Snatch, Sexy Beast, 3000 Miles from Graceland, Blow, O Brother, Where Art Thou?*.

Do you watch the *Sopranos?* Vidor and Sheldon: Yes, and *Six Feet Under.*

Comments: Vidor: Never give up. Do the right thing. The truth will set you free. Move forward or die. "Our contemporary Western society, in spite of its material, intellectual and political progress, is increasingly less conductive to mental health, and tends to undermine the inner security, happiness, reason and the capacity for love in the individual; it tends to turn him into an automaton who pays for his human failure with increasing mental sickness, and with despair hidden under a frantic drive for work and so-called pleasure" (Erich Fromm). "Let us be kinder to one another" (Aldous Huxley's last words).

Representative titles: *Pay It Forward* by Catherine Ryan Hyde (Simon & Schuster/film to Warner Brothers); *Defending Andy* by Marilyn Azevedo (Health Communications); *Electric God* by Catherine Ryan Hyde (Simon & Schuster/film to Propaganda Film); *Walter's Purple Heart* by Catherine Ryan Hyde (Simon & Schuster).

THE JOY HARRIS LITERARY AGENCY

156 Fifth Avenue, Suite 617, New York, NY 10010
fax: 212-924-6609

Agent: Joy Harris
  Areas most interested in agenting: Literary fiction and narrative nonfiction.
  Areas not interested in agenting: Romance, science fiction.
  Best way to initiate contact: Send a query letter via mail with a sample chapter.
  Client representation by category: Nonfiction, 50%; Fiction, 50%.
  Rejection rate (all submissions): 95%.
  Do you watch the *Sopranos?* Yes.
  Representative titles: *Ahab's Wife* by Sena Geter Naslund (HarperCollins); *Jund & Juliet* by Julian Gough (Random House); *The Kennedy Men* by Larry Leamer (Harper-Collins); *Getting a Life* by Helen Simpson (Viking).

H

JOHN HAWKINS & ASSOCIATES

71 West 23rd Street, Suite 1600, New York, NY 10010
212-807-7040   fax: 212-807-9555

Agents: J. Warren Frazier, Anne Hawkins, William Reiss, Elly Sidel
  Born: Reiss: September 14, 1942.
  Education: Frazier: Princeton. Reiss: B.A., Kenyon College. Sidel: B.A., Bennington College. Hawkins: A.B., Bryn Mawr College.
  Career history: Reiss: Freelance Researcher; Editorial Assistant to Lombard Jones (a graphic designer and Editor); Encyclopedia Editor, Funk & Wagnall's Standard Reference Library; Literary Agent. Sidel: I have had a long, varied career in publishing, film, and television, as well as raising two children as a single mom and working as a certified chemical-dependency counselor at Hazeldon in Minnesota. Also Vice President of Movies and Mini-Series, Warner Brothers Television Director of Special Projects, CBS Entertainment,

New York; Vice President of Production, 20th Century Fox Film Corporation; Senior Editor, Bantam Books; Manager of Subsidiary Rights, Bantam Books, and so on.

Hobbies/personal interests: Sidel: Reading; going to the ballet, movies, theater; hanging out; playing with friends and family; walking; swimming; politics; travel. Hawkins: Music, collecting tribal art, hiking, gardening—almost any excuse to be outdoors.

Areas most interested in agenting: Frazier: Fiction: Literary and commercial, mysteries, suspense. Nonfiction: Biography, travel, natural history, science. Reiss: Biographies, nonfiction historical narratives, archaeology, science fiction and fantasy, mysteries and suspense, true-crime narrative, natural history, children's fiction, adult fiction. Sidel: Fiction: Literary and commercial fiction, including mysteries, suspense, and novels touching women's issues and family issues. Nonfiction: Narrative nonfiction, including spirituality, biography, women's and family issues, recovery, natural history, current events and popular culture; prescriptive nonfiction, including spirituality, relationship issues, and popular culture.

Areas not interested in agenting: Frazier: Romance. Reiss: Romance novels, poetry, plays. Sidel: Cookbooks, children's, science fiction, romance. Hawkins: Genre men's military, horror, romance, and juvenile fiction; "how-to" nonfiction. Fiction: children's books, romance, horror, Westerns. Nonfiction: cookbooks, "how-to." Other: poetry, plays, screenplays.

If not agenting, what might you be doing? Hawkins: Hard to say, since I really love being a literary agent. Other dream jobs might be working as a curator in a major museum or running an experimental nursery for exotic trees, shrubs, and perennials. Sidel: Travel around the world.

Best way to initiate contact: Frazier: Letter with personality, one-half page synopsis of book with first 3–4 chapters. Reiss: Telephone or send a letter describing project, with a few sample pages to provide a sense of writing style. Sidel: Through a personal or professional referral; concise query letter, brief author bio. Include e-mail address and/or SASE, one-page synopsis, opening chapter(s) of book (no more than 50 pages).

Reading-fee policy: No reading fee.

Client representation by category: Frazier: Nonfiction, 50%; Fiction, 50%. Hawkins: Nonfiction, 40%; Fiction, 60%.

Commission: 15% domestic; 20% foreign.

Rejection rate (all submissions): 95%.

Most common mistakes authors make: Sidel: Someone who is too pushy and aggressive and won't take no for an answer. Hawkins: Two extremes here—the under-promoter and the over-promoter. The under-promoter throws together a sloppy query package with a rambling, unconvincing letter and/or sample chapters riddled with errors. The over-promoter makes extravagant claims about the project—"a sure pick for Oprah's Book Club" or "guaranteed to be a #1 national bestseller." It's hard to take either seriously.

Description of the client from Hell: Sidel: Someone with unrealistic expectations.

Description of a dream client: Sidel: A talented, flexible, creative professional writer who understands that this is a process. Someone with a sense of humor and a Pulitzer Prize. Hawkins: Dream clients take the trouble to educate themselves about the realities of the publishing business and enter the process armed with good sense, good manners, and good humor.

Why did you become an agent? Sidel: A good way to integrate all of my professional and personal experience, use my contacts, and work with ideas and smart, creative people, as well as earn a living.

What can writers do to enhance their chances of getting you as an agent? Hawkins: As a practical matter, projects directly referred by people I know always rise to the top of the pile, since they are more likely to be a good fit with my taste and areas of expertise. But there's also the occasional cold-call query letter that shows so much personality, intelligence, and professionalism that I'm predisposed to like the sample materials. An agent and an author work together for a long time, and I want to feel that I will enjoy representing writers as much as their work.

Do you watch the *Sopranos?* Sidel: You bet!!

Representative titles: *Confessions of an Ugly Stepsister* by Gregory Maguire (Regan Books/Harper); *Copper Elephant* by Adam Rapp (Front Street); *Hart's War* by John Katzenbach (Ballantine); *Trespassing* by John Hanson Mitchell (Perseus Books); *Earless Living* by Rhonda Britten (Dutton); *The Muse Asylum* by David Czuchlewski (Putnam); *Body of Knowledge* by Steve Giegerich (Scribner).

HEACOCK LITERARY AGENCY

707 Seventh Street, Tularosa, NM 88352
505-585-2475
e-mail: GraceBooks@aol.com

Agent: Rosalie Grace Heacock Thompson
 Born: Girard, Kansas.
 Education: B.A. in Fine Arts/Literature (Cum Laude), California State University, Northridge, 1971; M.A. in Humanities (Magna Cum Laude), California State University, Dominguez Hills, 1991.
 Career history: Editor, Green Hut Press, Valencia, California, 1975; Editor, Kids & Company, Los Angeles, California, 1977; Heacock Literary Agency, founded in 1978, by James B. Heacock and Rosalie Grace Heacock Thompson.
 Areas most interested in agenting: Well-written books.
 Areas not interested in agenting: Science fiction, horror, true crime, category fiction.
 Best way to initiate contact? Please send a query letter with self-addressed, stamped envelope enclosed. Letters without return postage cannot be answered, as we receive around 250 queries per week. Prefer no multiple queries, please.
 Client representation by category: Nonfiction, 80%; Fiction, 5%; Children's, 5%.
 Commission: 15% domestic; 25% foreign.
 Number of titles sold last year: 16.
 Rejection rate (all submissions): 98%.
 How did you become an agent? Two good friends (living abroad) could not get an agent and asked me to submit their work. I found the process so fascinating that I could not resist plunging into the field of literary representation.

H

Why did you become an agent? I became an agent because I cherish ideas, have a keen curiosity, and love good books.

What can writers do to enhance their chances of getting you as their agent? It is a matter of timing, which is beyond the writer's control. If my list is full (which is approaching at this time), I will reluctantly reject good material so that I may perform a better service for those currently under representation. This has nothing to do with the author, but rather with timing.

What do you think about editors? I respect them and appreciate their dedication.

RICHARD HENSHAW GROUP

127 West 24th Street, 4th Floor, New York, NY 10011
212-414-1172   fax: 435-417-5208

Agent: Rich Henshaw

    Born: September 18, 1964, New York, New York.

    Education: B.A., Franklin and Marshall College.

    Career history: Independent since 1995; 1987–1995, Agent and Director of Foreign Rights, Richard Curtis Associates; 1992–1995, Partner in the Content Company, an agency specializing in new media.

    Hobbies/personal interests: My family, books, cooking, wine, travel, skiing.

    Areas most interested in agenting: Mainstream and genre fiction, including mysteries and thrillers, science fiction, fantasy, horror, historical, literary, and women's and romance. Nonfiction areas of interest are business, celebrity biography, computer, current events, health, history, how-to, movies, popular culture, popular reference, popular science, psychology, self-help, cooking, and sports. I am also interested in working with books that lend themselves to adaptation to alternative media formats.

    Areas not interested in agenting: Fiction: children's, young adult, Westerns, poetry, short stories. Nonfiction: coffee table books, cookbooks, scholarly books.

    If not agenting, what would you be doing? I might start my own publishing company.

    Best way to initiate contact: Query letter and first 50 pages (with SASE) for fiction. Query letter (with SASE) for nonfiction. I also accept queries by e-mail, not to exceed one page. My e-mail address is submissions@Henshaw.com.

    Reading-fee policy: No reading fee.

    Client representation by category: Nonfiction, 30%; Fiction, 70%.

    Commission: 15% domestic; 20% foreign.

    Number of titles sold last year: 18.

    Rejection rate (all submissions): 97%.

    Most common mistakes authors make: No SASE. Unpolished manuscripts. Bound manuscripts. Slick queries that say little about the characters, plot, subject, or style of the work.

    Description of the client from Hell: Blames agent for all pitfalls in the publishing process. Never expresses gratitude or appreciation for a job well done.

Description of a dream client: Informed, courteous, loyal, professional.

Why did you become an agent? Since I wrote my first (terrible) short story in college and attempted to market it, I've been fascinated by the creative process involved in writing and the manner in which books and other intellectual property are commercially exploited. I've always been an agent and I can't imagine doing anything else.

Representative titles: *Peg Allen's Community Cookbook* by Peg Allen (Clarkson Potter); *The Well-Trained Mind* by Susan Wise Bauer and Jessie Wise (W. W. Norton); *The Shadow Dancer* by Margaret Coel (Berkley Prime Crime); *Bad Lawyer* by Stephen Solomita (Penzler/Carroll and Graf); *The Singing of the Dead* by Dana Stabenow (St. Martin's Press); *Nothing Gold Can Stay* by Dana Stabenow (Dutton); *Silk and Song* by Dana Stabenow (Warner/I Publish).

THE JEFF HERMAN AGENCY, LLC

332 Bleecker Street, Suite G-31, New York, NY 10014
212-941-0540   fax: 212-941-0614
www.jeffherman.com   e-mail: jeff@jeffherman.com

Agents: Jeff Herman, Deborah Levine Herman

Born: J. Herman: December 17, 1958, Long Island, New York. D. L. Herman: October 4, 1958, Long Island, New York.

Education: J. Herman: Liberal Arts, B.S., Syracuse University, 1981. D. L. Herman: Too much. B.A., Ohio State University; Master's of Journalism, Ohio State University Graduate School in a dual degree with the College of Law. Got Juris Doctorate, passed the bar, and have been in recovery ever since.

Career history: J. Herman: Publicity Department—Schocken Books, Account Executive for a public relations agency, founded my own PR agency, founder of literary agency in 1988. D. L. Herman: An Assistant Attorney General for Ohio, private litigator—civil matters, writer neophyte, rejection-letter expert (recipient), ghostwriter, author, book proposal/book doctor/literary agent/rejection-letter expert (purveyor).

Hobbies/personal interests: J. Herman: Eating, sleeping, walking, staring at nothing. D. L. Herman: My three children, low-brow entertainment, yard sales, antiques, flea markets, oil painting, karaoke, gossip magazines, celebrities, spiritual development, horses, my pets.

Areas most interested in agenting: J. Herman: I could answer this, but by tomorrow, I'll change my mind. D. L. Herman: Popular culture, unique nonfiction. I like books that usher in the trends rather than trail behind.

Areas not interested in agenting: J. Herman: As above. D. L. Herman: Anything pompous, judgmental, or boring. Autobiographies are difficult to place, but they can be used as the backdrop for exceptional projects. No matter how wonderful or tragic your life might be, it will take a lot for it to compete as straight autobiography.

If not agenting, what would you be doing? J. Herman: I'd get a job with Fed Ex.

Best way to initiate contact: J. Herman: Letters, e-mails, faxes. D. L. Herman: Query letter sent to my attention through our Midwest office: PO Box 307540, Columbus, OH 43230.

H

Reading-fee policy: J. Herman: As per AAR rules, we don't charge any.

Client representation by category: J. Herman: Nonfiction, 90%; Children's Textbooks, 10%. D. L. Herman: Nonfiction, 95%.

Commission: 15% on domestic sales; still 10% for foreign.

Number of titles sold last year: 25.

Rejection rate (all submissions): In the high 90s.

Most common mistakes authors make: J. Herman: Muddying their pitch. Putting their expectations beyond their value. D. L. Herman: Asking me to sell myself to them. I'm too busy. Being rude or demanding on the phone. We all answer phones to cover each other. Those of you who try to get past our screening process by behaving like royalty might just find yourself talking to me and pitching yourself right into embarrassment. Another mistake is to try to pitch by phone unless we know you or are related to you. This is a hard-copy business; follow protocol.

Description of the client from Hell: J. Herman: There are several archetypes that come to mind, such as: manic egomaniacs who really don't have much to sell other than their own wind, people who nag me so that I either have to fire them or make them a close relative. People who interminably obsess about what others were "supposed" to do for them or did to them. D. L. Herman: Those who view their writing as a destination and not a process. We can each be messengers of the greater light. The trick is to know when to get out of the way. There are no real clients from Hell because, if they are too arrogant to accept direction, I send them back to the Universe for further polishing and education.

Description of a dream client: J. Herman: They know how to punch a hole through unfortunate circumstances and walk through to the other side. And they know how to see and embrace a good thing. D. L. Herman: Those who listen to and finds their own inner voice. This is where the best writing is found. A person like this understands that time and space are not always what we want them to be. Sometimes the Universe has its own agenda.

How did you become an agent? J. Herman: I started by pitching manuscripts written by my public relations clients. I would just cold-call publishers and get editors on the phone. I didn't know that made me a literary agent until much later.

Why did you become an agent? J. Herman: I have a weak back and strong eyes. D. L. Herman: To learn to become a writer. Then I married Jeff Herman to ensure representation. He still makes me put it in writing!

What can writers do to enhance their chances of getting you as an agent? J. Herman: Don't give up. D. L. Herman: Focus on writing from a business perspective. If no one would ever buy your book, how can we possibly sell it for you? If your project is well-thought-out and commercially meaningful, you have as much chance as anyone else does.

How would you describe what you actually do for a living? J. Herman: I help get books published.

What do you think about editors? J. Herman: That's a tough job, because there are so many people they have to answer to, so many people they have to cover for, so many they have to appease, and so many details to attend to. They are underappreciated.

What do you think about publishers? J. Herman: Ask me again next year.

Comments: J. Herman: Seriously, none of this is rocket science. Please enjoy what you do, and educate yourself about what it takes to succeed.

Representative titles: *The Aladdin Factor* by Mark Victor Hansen and Jack Canfield (Berkley*); Blackroots: An African American Guide to Tracing the Family Tree* by Tony Burroughs (Simon & Schuster); *Driving Your Woman Wild in Bed* by Staci Keith (Warner Books); *Pocket Guide to Saints* by Annette Sandoval (Dutton); *Getting Your Kid Off Ritalin* by David Stein, Ph.D. (Jossey-Bass); *The Angry Child* by Timothy Murphy (Random House); *The Complete Idiot's Guide to Investing Like a Pro* by Ed Koch and Debra DeSalvo (Macmillan); *E-Fear: Protecting Yourself in the Digital World* by Ira Winkler (Prentice Hall); *The Unauthorized Story of the Beatles' Get Back Sessions* by Doug Sulpy (St. Martin's Press); *The 10 Habits of Naturally Slim People* by Jill Podjasek (Contemporary); *Southern Invincibility: Why the South Lost the Civil War* by Wiley Sword (St. Martin's Press); Words of Wisdom: Selected Quotes From His Holiness the Dalai Lama* (book and calendar) by Margaret Gee (Andrews McMeel); *Exploring Meditation* by Susan Shumsky (Career Press); *Born to Be Wild: Freeing the Spirit of the Hyper-Active Child* by Kristi Boylan (Penguin/Putnam); *Tom Hopkin's Complete Guide to Sales Success* by Tom Hopkins (Warner Books); *The Toastmaster's Guide to Public Speaking* by Michael Aun and Jeff Slutsky (Dearborn).

JULIE HILL MEDIA AND LITERARY AGENCY

PO Box 1313, La Jolla, CA 92038
fax: 208-975-6958
e-mail: Hillagent@aol.com

Agent: Julie Hill

Education: B.A., University of Arizona; graduate work, UCLA; University of California, Berkeley, Publishing Program.

Career History: I come to agenting from writing. I have written for magazines and Internet sites such as Citysearch/Microsoft, and I wrote a nonfiction book some years ago. I also learned book publicity during my career as an author, and the tutelage of Arielle Ford of the Ford Group prepared me well for understanding what authors must do to market their work.

Hobbies/personal interests: Art, fine cuisine, horticulture, long-distance travel.

Areas most interested in agenting: Nonfiction of any kind, especially how-to, self-help. I have had a fair number of successes with art and architecture books and would like to represent more experts in those fields. Travel and health books are always welcome.

Areas not interested in agenting: Poetry, screenplays, large coffee-table books, cookbooks.

If not agenting, what would you be doing? Writing.

Best way to initiate contact: Send a book proposal with a market analysis and an SASE.

Client representation by category: Nonfiction, 100%.

Commission: 15% domestic; 20% foreign.

Number of titles sold: 22.

Rejection rate: 90%.

Description of the client from Hell: They call to chat. Want their lawyer to read everything.

Description of the dream client: They have a perfectly finished and researched book proposal and know they must market their work after publication, with or without a hired publicist.

Why did you become an agent? After I published my book, I understood how tough and how much fun being a published author is—I like making authors happy and successful.

Representative titles: *Art and Healing* by Barbara Ganim (Three Rivers/Random House); *Visual Journaling* by Barbara Ganim and Susan Fox (The Theosophical Press/Quest Books); *American Gargoyles, Spirits in Stone* by Darlene Crist and Robert Llewellyn (Clarkson Potter/Random House); *Café Life Rome* by Joe Wolff and Roger Paperno (Interlink Books).

HORNFISCHER LITERARY MANAGEMENT, INC.

PO Box 50067, Austin, TX 78763-0067

fax: 512-472-0077

Agent: Jim Hornfischer

Born: 1965, Massachusetts.

Education: J.D./M.B.A., University of Texas at Austin; B.A., Colgate University.

Career history: President, Hornfischer Literary Management, Inc., founded 2001; Agent, Literary Group International, 1993–2001; Editorial positions, McGraw-Hill General Books Division and HarperCollins Adult Trade Division, 1987–1992.

Hobbies/personal interests: Books. What else is there? (Okay, there's sports, too, and maybe music, and the occasional movie.)

Areas most interested in agenting: All types of high-quality narrative nonfiction, biography and autobiography, current events, U.S. history, military history, world history, political and cultural subjects, science, medicine/health, business/management/finance, academic writing and research that has a general-interest audience. Quality literary and commercial mainstream fiction.

Areas not interested in agenting: Poetry, genre mysteries, genre science fiction, genre romances.

Best way to initiate contact: A smartly tailored personal letter that suggests professionalism and/or accomplishment, together with 30–50 pages of good material that supports your optimism. With nonfiction, submit a full proposal that includes a thorough overview of the book and its market, author bio/c.v., chapter summaries, and two sample chapters. With fiction, please send a one-page synopsis and the first 30–35 pages of the manuscript.

Reading-fee policy: No.

Client representation by category: Nonfiction, 95%; Fiction, 5%.

Commission: 15% domestic; 20% foreign.

Number of titles sold last year: 15.

Rejection rate (all submissions): The same parade-drenching number as the rest of them.

Description of the dream client: Thinks big, drinks from glasses that are half full, writes even grocery lists with narrative momentum, keeps an open ear for useful advice, and runs with it in brilliant and surprising ways.

Common mistakes authors make: Succumbing to "Hollywood fever" by insisting on making their pitch in person or via telephone. Demanding an editorial critique of their work. (Agents can't spend time providing gratis critiques; reading time is simply too scarce.) Requiring us to audition for the role of their agent before we're even remotely interested. Not enclosing return postage, then becoming indignant over lack of response.

What can writers do to enhance their chances of getting you as their agent? Grasp the rudiments of the business (even if as an artist you'd prefer not to bother), temper your ambition with patience and a long view, and refine and improve your craft continuously.

Why did you become an agent? Getting a good book published, especially one that might not otherwise have been, can be rewarding in a life-affirming sort of way.

If not agenting, what might you be doing? Practicing law and suing the tar out of those who take advantage of innocent, hard-working writers.

How would you describe what you actually do for a living? My wife always tells me that I shatter dreams for a living, because I send back so many rejections. I prefer to think that for those writers for whom I do useful work, I make them.

What do you think about editors? They're the heart and soul of their companies, and management should listen to them more closely. To the smart ones, anyway.

What do you think of publishers? The good ones are patrons to their authors, believe in those authors, and make the market for their authors' work. But most publishers are under financial pressures that have little to do with publishing, and hence sometimes lose the all-important long-term view of an author's career development.

Representative titles: *Flags of Our Fathers* by James Bradley, with Ron Powers (Bantam); *Age of Gold: The California Gold Rush and the New American Dream* by H. W. Brands (Doubleday); *Tom and Huck Don't Live Here Anymore* by Ron Powers (St. Martin's); *My Life Has Stood a Loaded Gun* by Theo Padnos (Talk/Miramax); *A Good Forest for Dying* by Patrick Beach (Doubleday); *The Wars He Fought* by Kareem Abdul Jabbar, with Michael Hurd (Doubleday); *Why Things Break* by Mark Eberhart (Scribner); *The History of the Republican Party* by Lewis Gould (Random House); *Desperate Hours: The Epic Rescue of the Andrea Doria* by Richard Goldstein (Wiley); *The Bullet Meant for Me* by Jan Reid (Broadway); *The First American: The Life and Times of Benjamin Franklin* by H. W. Brands (Doubleday); *The "Jewish Threat": Antisemitic Politics of the U.S. Army* by Joseph Bendersky (Basic); *The Man Who Flew the Memphis Belle* by Col. Robert K. Morgan (USAF, Ret.), with Ron Powers (Dutton); *What to Do When Your*

H

Baby Is Premature by Joseph A. Garcia-Prats, M.D., and Sharon Simmons Hornfischer, R.N., B.S.N. (Crown); *Latter Days: An Insider's Guide to Mormonism* by Coke Newell (St. Martin's).

IMPRINT AGENCY, INC.

611 Broadway, Suite 731, New York, NY 10012
212-420-7910
e-mail: imprintagency@earthlink.net

Agent: Stephany Evans
 Born: October 11, 1957, West Chester, Pennsylvania.
 Education: Communications/theater arts, Elizabethtown College, Elizabethtown, PA. Assorted art (drawing, painting), writing, and filmmaking classes at various NYC schools and institutions.
 Career history: Co-founder/producer/actress Zemmel theater company, NYC. Assorted acting gigs in theater and film. Assistant to Editorial Direct, S&S Audio; Editor of alternative health/personal growth magazine *Free Spirit,* have done freelance editing in a wide range of categories, and ghostwritten books in the spiritual category. Began agenting with Sandra Martin/Paraview; founded own agency in 1993.
 Hobbies/personal interests: Painting, mosaics, flea-marketing, restoring several old adobe houses in West Texas, traveling, going to the movies.
 Areas most interested in agenting: I have eclectic tastes, but have especially enjoyed working with spirituality, New Age, alternative health/healing, parenting, psychology/transpersonal psychology, women's issues, popular reference; and would love to find some really good fiction—either literary or commercial.
 Best way to initiate contact: Query letter via e-mail or letter (with SASE). Please do not send full proposals or manuscripts via e-mail.
 Client representation by category: Nonfiction, 95%; Fiction, 5%.
 Commission: 15% domestic; 20% foreign (when using a subagent).
 Number of titles sold last year: 26.
 Rejection rate (all submissions): Because a large number of the submissions I receive are referrals, my rejection rate is fairly low, about 75–80%, compared with the somewhat average 90%.
 Description of the client from Hell: Writers with unrealistic notions about the potential of their projects and also about what a publisher can/will do for them. Loose cannons who do end-arounds the agent, firing off calls, e-mails, or letters to their editors when feeling insecure. Those who send their material in bits and pieces or who fail to update on important teaching/promotional work they are doing.
 Description of the dream client: One who supplies all necessary info in a timely way without incessant micro-updates; one who is a lovely person, as well as being a terrific writer with a fresh, interesting point of view.

Most common mistakes authors make: Expecting the agent to be a mind-reader and not supplying crucial information about their background or marketing platform; or, not caring about their presentation—spelling, grammar, typos, single-spaced type. Or, not disclosing that they have sent their work to several agents at once, or, worse, have already sent their material to several publishers on their own. Or, they have no idea of what the competition is for their book.

What can writers do to enhance their chances of getting you as an agent? They should do all of their homework—have a timely concept in a beautifully organized package. Know their competition, and have a great platform in place. And be nice.

Why did you become an agent? I have been an avid reader all my life and after dabbling in several areas of the arts, while growing sicker and sicker of waitressing and bartending, found that this is the first job that never bores me. I love being among the first to hear an author's new idea, and I also love the people who make up the publishing industry.

If not agenting, what might you be doing? Making art, establishing a gallery to show and sell other artists' work, traveling . . . reading, maybe publishing?

Representative titles: *Wide Awake: Buddhism for the Next Generation* by Diana Winston (Perigee); *Dancing on Quicksand: A Transforming Friendship in the Age of Alzheimer's* by Marilyn Mitchell (Johnson Books); *Ina May's Birth Bible* by Ina May Gaskin (Bantam Dell); *Unconditional Bliss: Finding Happiness in Times of Hardship* by Raphael Cushnir (Quest Books); *Cheapskates' Guide to Spas in America* by Nathaniel Altman (Kensington); *Beyond the Numbers: Lessons in Business and Life* by James H. Warsaw, with Skip Berry (Davies-Black); *Encyclopedia of the Harlem Renaissance* by Aberjhani and Sandra L. West (Facts on File); *The Pagan Book of Halloween* by Gerina Dunwich (Penguin Compass); *Horses Don't Lie: What Horses Teach Us About Our Natural Capacity for Awareness, Confidence, Courage, and Trust* by Chris Irwin, with Bob Weber (Marlow & Company); *Exploring Feng Shui: Ancient Secrets & Modern Insights for Love, Joy and Abundance* by Shawne Mitchell (New Page Books).

INTELLECTUAL PROPERTY MANAGEMENT GROUP

PO Box 503, Kensington, MD 20895-0503
fax: 815-550-0842
www.ipmg.net   e-mail: nyc_dc_la_sf@yahoo.com

Agents: Christina Arneson, Jon Russell (Associate); Elizabeth Russell (Associate)

Born: Arneson: 1965, Spokane, Washington. J. Russell: 1958, Tipton, Indiana. E. Russell: 1961, Tipton, Indiana.

Education: Arneson: Florida State University and New York University. J. Russell: University of Minnesota. E. Russell: Earlham College, University of California Los Angeles, and San Francisco Law School.

Career history: Arneson: I stared out at Putnam in Subsidiary Rights. I was later recruited to work at the new imprint started by Disney, Hyperion. I worked at Simon &

Schuster for a while, but have spent the better part of my career as an agent. Jon Russell and his sister Elizabeth Russell work part time assisting Christina. They cover the East and West Coast (and in-between), searching for quality fiction and nonfiction, as well as assisting her with Web site design and administrative tasks.

Hobbies/personal interests: All of us are interested in book packaging, marketing, e-commerce, reading, cooking, biking, tennis, sailing, traveling, and "thinking outside the box."

Areas most interested in agenting: Literary fiction and commercial/mass market non-fiction; Latina/Latino fiction and nonfiction, health and science nonfiction.

Areas not interested in agenting: Genre fiction, poetry, and children's literature.

Best way to initiate contact: Via e-mail only! If you don't or can't submit via e-mail, we will be of little use to you. We are working from the four corners of the United States and need to have all initial contacts transmittable via the Internet.

Client representation by category: Nonfiction, 65%; Fiction, 20%; Textbooks, 1%; Other, 14%.

Commission: 15%.

Number of titles sold last year: 27.

Rejection rate (all submissions): 98%.

Description of the client from Hell: Well, we hate to include anyone in this category because we know that they are just trying to protect their own interests or don't know any better, but there are some annoyances we can mention: people who think we're going to steal their idea so they behave coyly, prospective clients who find our home numbers and call us, people who use all caps in e-mails, egotistical people who believe editors at large publishing houses should be able to make snap decisions as to whether their literary property should be acquired, not realizing that the editor has to sell a manuscript internally to dozens of people, ranging from marketing, to legal, to subsidiary rights, as well as to other senior editorial staff members—it's a long process.

Description of the dream client: Someone who writes well and sells even better.

Most common mistakes authors make: They should quickly get to the point and quite often don't. We also need the truth without elaboration. When you tell us about your potential market in a book proposal, give realistic numbers. We want researched market numbers, rather than vague descriptions like "a book for those retiring in the next five years." How many are retiring in five years and what percentage of that number are likely to buy the book and why?

What can writers do to enhance their chances of getting you as an agent? Know your market. This is the most important piece of information we can give writers. You have to know exactly who they are, how many of them are out there, where they buy books, how many books they buy, how often they read . . . all of that information is absolutely crucial in this market. You also have to have a good idea what you are getting into. We want clients who know that their responsibility is in marketing their own book, because regardless of who publishes your work, you will need to work if you want to realize your full potential.

Why did you become an agent? Helping people get their work published, recognized, and purchased is a very rewarding experience.

If not agenting, what might you be doing? We would write more books ourselves.

How would you describe what you do for a living? Network, read, *research,* handhold, predict the future, find solutions, network some more.

How did you become an agent? Christina started her agency as a hobby, something she could do while her kids were babies. When her first author (a previously unpublished 24-year-old) was nominated for the National Book Award, she thought, "Oh, this is easy." It's a good thing she had that early validation in literary property sales, as there have been some tough years.

What do you think about editors? Editors are in a tough position right now. Rather than being able to rely on their strength—being a good editor—their job now requires them to read the minds of the marketing and sales people. It's not about the "really good book," it's about the "really good sell."

What do you think about publishers? We love smaller publishers and choose to work with them first. The larger houses are very frustrating unless the client is an established author.

What were your favorite films last year? *You Can Count on Me, Billy Elliot, Pearl Harbor, Gladiator, La Verite 2,* and *The Closet.*

Do you watch the *Sopranos?* Isn't it required?

Comments: We don't know if editors are reading this, but we would love to make a blanket statement that you really need to check the letters your assistants are sending out. We can't tell you how many submissions we've received back with copies of interoffice (confidential) material, editors' notes, readers' reports, and typos in rejection letters. We received a rejection letter for Christina's now published book *How to Aggravate a Man,* which she had compared to Nora Hayden's *How to Satisfy a Man.* The letter we got back rejected Nora's book!!!—and the letter came from her own publisher. We once got an interoffice memo with a list of how much advance money should be paid out for books according to who the agent is, having nothing to do with the book or its quality. That was quite frightening.

JCA LITERARY AGENCY

27 West 20th Street, Suite 1103, New York, NY 10011
fax: 212-807-0461

Agents: Peter Steinberg, Jeff Gerecke, Tony Outhwaite

Areas most interested in agenting: Literary fiction, narrative nonfiction, history, science, true crime, thrillers, mysteries, commercial fiction.

Areas not interested in agenting: Children's books, romance.

Best way to initiate contact: Query letter with first 50 pages, synopsis, SASE.

Client representation by category: Nonfiction, 40%; Fiction, 60%.

Most common mistakes authors make: Sending out a work before it's ready—that is, sending out an early draft. You only get one shot.

J

What can writers do to enhance their chances of getting you as an agent? Get their work published in magazines and journals before coming to me.

Do you watch the *Sopranos?* Yes.

THE KARPFINGER AGENCY

357 West 20th Street, New York, NY 10011
212-691-2690

Agent: Olivia B. Blumer
  Born: Long Island.
  Education: Goucher College.
  Career history: Doubleday—Editorial, Rights, Publicity (10 years); Atheneum, Rawson, Scribner, Macmillan—Rights Director (5 years); Warner—Rights and Editorial (9 years); Agent 5 years.
  Hobbies/personal interests: Tennis, gardening, travel, flea markets, cooking, poker, reading.
  Areas most interested in agenting: Quality fiction, some food, gardening, self-help. Inspiration, how-to, narrative nonfiction, memoir, quality nonfiction, and nature.
  Areas not interested in agenting: Science fiction, poetry, children's.
  If not agenting, what might you be doing? Gardening, antiquing/junking, travel, reading for pleasure.
  Best way to initiate contact: Via mail (letter of inquiry).
  Client representation (by category): Nonfiction, 75%; Fiction, 25%.
  Commission: 15% domestic; 20% foreign.
  Number of titles sold last year: 12.
  Rejection rate (all submissions): 90+%.
  What are some common mistakes writers make? Fiction: I hate plot summaries; give me the big picture. Think Macro. Nonfiction: Someone who hasn't researched the competition or analyzed the market.
  Description of the client from Hell: Whiny, unprofessional; never says, "And how are you?"; calls constantly for no reason, just attention.
  Description of the dream client: Dream clients treat their career like a job; in other words, they are professional. Are considerate of my boundaries, that is, don't call me constantly, don't call me at home, are self-reliant, have a sense of humor.
  Why did you become an agent? Ran out of patience with corporate life. Agenting is more creative, with fewer meetings and less time wasted. I wanted to invest in myself.
  How would you describe what you do for a living? I'm a matchmaker who turns into a marriage counselor after the contract is signed.
  What do you think about editors? Some good, some bad. All are under the gun.
  What do you think about publishers? Some good, some bad. Wish there were more up-and-coming small presses.
  Representative titles: *A Year by the Sea* by Anderson (Doubleday/Broadway); *Hot Sour Salty Sweet* by Alford (Artisan/Workman); *Let Evening Come* by Morrison (Doubleday); *Mirabilis* by Cokal (Blue Hen/Putnam); *The Ice Child* by Duguid McGregor.

K

Natasha Kern Literary Agency, Inc.

PO Box 2908, Portland, OR 97208-2908
503-297-6190
www.natashakern.com

Agent: Natasha Kern

Education: University of North Carolina, Chapel Hill; Columbia University, New York; graduate work, New York University.

Career history: Publicist and Editor for New York publishers and Acquisitions Editor for New York agents prior to founding her own agency in 1986.

Hobbies/personal interests: Gardening, travel, animals and birds, yoga, new physics, performing arts, history, geology, and, of course, storytelling and reading.

Areas most interested in agenting: Fiction: Commercial and literary, mainstream women's, romances, historicals, thrillers, suspense, mysteries and inspirational fiction; magical realism. Nonfiction: Investigative journalism, health, science, women's issues, parenting, spirituality, psychology, business, self-help, gardening, current issues, gay topics, animals/nature, controversial subjects, and narrative nonfiction.

Areas not interested in agenting: Fiction: Horror and fantasy, true crime, short stories, children's or young adult. Nonfiction: Sports, cookbooks, poetry, coffee-table books, computers; technical, scholarly or reference; stage plays, scripts, screenplays, or software.

If not agenting, what would you be doing? I did everything else I ever wanted to do before becoming an agent. Agenting is truly a calling for me, and I would not be as happy doing anything else. It is a case of "Do what you love (and are good at) and the money follows." I also have a deep commitment to bringing new knowledge, new ideas, and new writing into the world. I believe storytelling is powerful and a great book truly can change the world.

Best way to initiate contact: Send a one-page query letter with an SASE. Include a brief summary, genre, submission history (publishers/agents), estimated word count, your writing credits, information about how complete the project is, name of past or present agent (if any). For nonfiction, include your credentials for writing your book, your targeted audience, and whether a proposal is available. Do not send sample chapters or manuscripts unless requested.

Reading-fee policy: No reading fee charged.

Client representation by category: Nonfiction, 40%; Fiction, 60%.

Commission: 15% domestic and film; 20% foreign.

Number of titles sold last year: 41.

Rejection rate (all submissions): 99% unsolicited; 85% solicited partials, proposals, and manuscripts. From 4,000 queries every year, approximately 10 writers are accepted for representation. Write a good query! We are selective, but we do want to find successful writers of the future.

Most common mistakes authors make: Not describing their material or project adequately. Querying by fax, phone, or e-mail. Sending unrequested material. Exaggerated claims or credentials. Comparing themselves favorably to current bestselling authors. Lack of professionalism. Omitting the end from a synopsis.

K

Description of the client from Hell: I do not have any clients like this. All of my clients are people I respect and admire as individuals, as well as writers. They are committed to their own success, and I am committed to helping them to achieve it. They understand the complex tasks involved in agenting, including sales, negotiations, editorial, arbitration, foreign and film rights, and so forth, and we work as a team to ensure the best outcome for their work. Usually, problem clients who are difficult to work with are identified before a contract is signed.

Description of a dream client: One who participates in a mutually respectful business relationship, is clear about needs and goals, and communicates about career planning. If we know what you need and want, we can help you to achieve it. A dream client has a gift for language and storytelling, a commitment to a writing career, a desire to learn and grow, and a passion for excellence. This client understands that many people have to work together for a book to succeed and that everything in publishing takes far longer than one imagines. Trust and communication are truly essential. How wonderful that so many of my clients are dream clients.

Why did you become an agent? When I left New York, I knew that I wanted to stay in publishing. However, editorial work was not sufficiently satisfying by itself. I knew I could acquire and develop salable properties and that my background gave me expertise in sales and running a company. I wanted to work with people long-term and not just on a single project or phase of one. Plus, I had an entrepreneurial temperament and experience negotiating big-money deals from raising venture capital for high-tech firms. When I developed literary projects for other agents that did not sell, I knew I could sell them myself—so I did. I've never regretted that decision. Agenting combined my love of books, my affinity for deal making, and my preference for trusting my own intuition. I sold 28 books the first year the agency was in business.

What can writers do to enhance their chances of getting you as an agent? In nonfiction, the author's passionate belief in the subject, as well as expertise and a defined audience, are appealing. A client who is willing to listen, learn, and work hard to succeed. If there are writing problems, I will get this author help, in order to produce a salable proposal. In fiction, I look for a wonderful, fresh, authorial voice, a page-turning plot that really does keep me up at night after a long day, well-structured chapters, and imaginative prose. A writer who can pull me into another point of view and another world I don't want to leave. In fiction, the writing is everything. We are glad to encourage promising writers who still need to master some aspects of craft, if they are willing to work with an editor.

How would you describe what you actually do for a living? Unpublished writers often think an agent's job is sales and negotiations. I am often involved in a book's development from the initial concept through preparation of a proposal; editorial advice; selection of appropriate editors; submissions; negotiations; troubleshooting publication problems, including reviewing publicity planning, distribution concerns, creating a Web site, and working with private publicists; long-term career planning and strategies; handling an author's financial affairs, auditing royalty statements, collecting unpaid moneys, dealing with tax documents and legal issues of many kinds; subsidiary sales, including foreign rights, film rights, audio, video, and other rights; handling career crises or conflicts with publishers; assisting authors in earning a livelihood with their writing; provid-

K

ing expertise at writers' conferences; educating clients about the publishing industry and its vicissitudes; keeping in touch with editors and their acquisitions interests or concerns about clients; attending industry events like Book Expo; meeting personally with clients, editors, and others in the industry; answering hundreds of e-mails each week; talking on the phone a lot; reading the work of clients and prospective clients and keeping up with trends; working with office staff and upgrading corporate procedures and technical support; supervising the bookkeeper and accountants; arranging articles and interviews for trade publications, and so on. It's a long day.

What do you think about editors? Editors are indispensable, and every writer should be blessed with a good one. It is one of my primary goals to match each client with the editor who is perfect for him or her. I often succeed and the result is magical, like all great collaborations: Fred Astaire and Ginger Rogers, Maxwell Perkins and Thomas Wolfe, Gilbert and Sullivan. Writers are more successful in great partnerships. No one can be objective about his or her own work or realistically expect to recognize all of his or her own flaws. Most artistic endeavors require a coach—a voice coach, a dance teacher, a master painter. Writing is no exception. There are gifted editors, both private editors and those at publishing houses, who can turn a strong manuscript into a great one, a gifted author into a bestselling one. I want all my clients to have that opportunity.

What do you think about publishers? They are going to have some interesting times ahead in the volatile new world of publishing, with challenges at every turn. Developing new talent and valuing the writers who are creating their long-term success would seem to be prerequisites for meeting these challenges. We keep up with changes in the industry like e-books and POD and also work with new emerging presses, as well as major publishers. We can help authors to understand the publisher's point of view (and vice versa) in all situations so that a win-win deal will result.

Comments: Believe in yourself and your own gifts. Keep in mind that the challenge for every writer is twofold—to have something to say and to have the mastery of the craft to say it well. Study and practice plotting, pacing, point of view, and so forth—so you can express exactly what you want to say. Nothing is more important than being true to your own artistic vision and understanding the requirements of the medium you have chosen to express it, whether you are writing a symphony, a haiku, or a novel. Keep in mind that in imitating other writers, you can only be second-rate at being them. Expressing your own inner thoughts, feelings, and stories in your own way is the only path to real success. Your world, your history, your experiences, your insights cannot be duplicated by anyone else. Bring us in to share your vision, your imagination. No one can do it better than you can, because the truth of your uniqueness is what you are here to offer everyone else. It is what moves us and takes us outside of our own lives when we read what you have written.

Representative titles: *American Apartheid: The Jim Crow Story* by Jerrold Packard (St. Martin's Press); *Biological Exuberance* by Bruce Bagemihl (St. Martin's Press); *Healthy Baby/Toxic World* by Melody Milam Potter and Erin Milam (New Harbinger); *Hope Is the Thing with Feathers* by Christopher Cokinos (Tarcher); *Identity Is Destiny* by Laurence Ackerman (Berrett-Koehler); *The Ecological Garden* by Toby Hemenway (Chelsea Green); *The Quiet Game* by Greg Iles (Dutton); *Daughter of God* by Lewis Perdue (Forge/TOR);

K

The Nephilim by Lynn Marzulli (Zondervan); *The Sacred Bedroom* by Jon Robertson (New World Library); *Water Touching Stone* by Eliot Pattison (St. Martin's); *Ribbon of Years* by Robin Hatcher (Tyndale); *The Hunger for Ecstasy* by Jalaja Bonheim (Rodale); *Biocosm* by Jim Gardner (Inner Ocean); *Diamonds* by Nick Kublicki (Sourcebooks).

KIDDE, HOYT & PICARD

335 East 51st Street, New York, NY 10022
212-755-9461   fax: 212-223-2501

Agents: Kay Kidde; Zarinah Jones, Assistant Agent
  Born: Kidde: August 30, 1930. Jones: May 19, 1976, Bronx, New York.
  Education: Kidde: Chatham Hall, Virginia, 1948; B.A., Vassar College, 1952. Jones: Weshoun School, Pennsylvania, 1994.
  Career history: Kidde: Has taught, worked as Editor, Senior Editor at NAL, Putnam/ Coward McCann, Harcourt. Jones: I worked with the Managing Editor of Books, Inc., then in the marketing department of Little Brown & Co.
  Hobbies/personal interests: Kidde: Published poet, writer; ocean swimming, sailing. Jones: Travel, appreciating nature.
  Areas most interested in agenting: Kidde: Mainstream/literary fiction, mainstream nonfiction, romantic fiction, mystery. Jones: Love stories and books that can help people to improve their lives.
  Areas not interested in agenting: Kidde: Male adventure, porn, science fiction, young adult, juvenile, poetry, unpublished short stories. Jones: Books about war, politics, and sports.
  Best way to initiate contact: Write a query letter (with SASE). We are currently not representing unpublished authors.
  Reading-fee policy: No reading fee. Author is responsible for photocopying, some long-distance telephone and fax expenses, and postage expenses for manuscripts being returned to the author.
  Client representation by category: Nonfiction, 25%; Fiction, 75%.
  Commission: 15% for new clients.
  Number of titles sold last year: 15.
  Rejection rate (all submissions): 95% or more.
  Most common mistakes authors make: Kidde: They push too hard, overwrite, and lack professionalism. Jones: Some call every few days expecting priority treatment, not realizing the volume of similar requests we get here. Patience is always appreciated.
  Description of the client from Hell: The prospective client from Hell is one who is pushy, loud, not a stylist, unpublished.
  Description of the dream client: Pleasant, respectful, a fine stylist, imaginative.
  How did you become an agent? Kidde: I started as an editor and found myself more on the author's side. Jones: I started book publishing in college and after college at Radcliff Publishing Course. After that, I was sure agenting was the right position for me.
  Why did you become an agent? Kidde: Because I love good books. Jones: I wanted to be a part of the book-making process on the creative side.

K

What can writers do to enhance their chances of getting you as an agent? Kidde: Give us breathing space, cordiality, and let the work speak for itself. Jones: Some previous publishing experiences (magazines, newspapers, journals).

If not agenting, what would you be doing? Kidde: I would devote more time to my own writing, especially poetry. Jones: This is exactly what I always wanted to do. If I could not do this, I might be an editor or go back to school full time.

How would you describe what you actually do for a living? Kidde: Help to get good authors of value out there. Jones: Besides helping to run a small business, I handle calls from perspective authors, read query letters and submissions, and respond to each one. I also handle the concerns of our authors.

What do you think about editors? I admire many of them.

What do you think of publishers? I admire many, but feel they're selling out to commercialism only, in some cases.

Do you watch the *Sopranos?* Kidde: No. Jones: No.

What were your favorite films last year? Jones: *Unbreakable* is still on my mind. I also enjoyed *The Mists of Avalon* (TV movie on TNT)

Comments: Kidde: I love a good story and a well-told novel with people in it to whom I can look up, who are witty and sympathetic, admirable.

Representative titles: *Elvis Live at Five* by John Paxson (Thomas Dunne/St. Martin's); *Officer of the Court* by Lelia Kelly (Kensington); *A Novel About Little John* by Michael Cadnum (Viking); *The Lost Diaries of Iris Week* by Janice Law (St. Martin's).

THE KNIGHT AGENCY

PO Box 550648, Atlanta, GA 30355
Deidre: 404-816-9620; Pamela: 706-485-8564   fax: 404-237-3439
e-mail: deidremk@aol.com, pamelaharty@aol.com

Agents: Deidre Knight, Pamela Harty

Born: Harty: Atlanta, Georgia.

Career history: Knight: Background in film production and marketing/sales. Established the Knight Agency in 1996. Member of the AAR, the Author's Guild, and Romance Writers of America. Harty: Background in sales and business management. Joined the Knight Agency in 2000. Associate member of the AAR.

Hobbies/personal interests: Knight: Music, playing Hammond organ and keyboard, reading, travel, and films. Harty: Reading, travel, biking, movies, and my family.

Areas most interested in agenting: Knight: Romance and women's fiction; most areas of nonfiction, including personal finance, business, parenting, careers, religion, music, pop culture, health, self-help, narrative nonfiction, and popular reference. Harty: Nonfiction, especially business, health, parenting, self-help, African-American narrative nonfiction, and religion, especially Christian living. In fiction, seeking romance (single title, contemporary, historical, and inspirational).

Areas not interested in agenting: Knight: Science fiction, fantasy, mystery, action-adventure, New Age, occult. Harty: New Age, poetry, sports, science fiction, fantasy, and occult.

K

If not agenting, what would you be doing? Knight: Something entrepreneurial and creative, such as running a small press or a film production company. Music management has always appealed to me, too. Harty: I can't imagine doing anything else, but if I had to pick, I would be an artist whose paintings sold for big money.

Best way to initiate contact: Send a one-page query letter with SASE prior to submitting material. Queries without return postage cannot be answered, nor can we accept e-mail queries with attached documents. Please do not call or fax.

Reading-fee policy: No reading fee.

Client representation by category: Nonfiction, 50%; Fiction, 50%.

Commission: 15% domestic; 20–25% foreign.

Number of titles sold last year: Knight: 40; Harty: 14.

Rejection rate (all submissions): 99%.

Most common mistakes authors make: Calling or faxing rather than sending a query letter. Interviewing me up front about my qualifications. Querying me about categories I don't represent. Forgetting return postage with their query letter. Boasting about having written "the next bestseller." Submitting work that isn't their best or isn't as well developed as it needs to be.

Description of the client from Hell: Calls and e-mails constantly for updates. Faxes incessantly, most often with needless information. Isn't receptive to my input and suggestions. Rude and unappreciative, never thanking me for my hard work. Generally doesn't respect my time. Impatient with the publishing process.

Description of a dream client: Hardworking, reliable, loyal, and informed. Respectful of my time and efforts on his or her behalf. Appreciative of what I do. Receptive to feedback. A team player. Dream clients are realistic in their publishing goals and committed to a long-term process of building a career.

How did you become an agent? Knight: My husband is a writer, and I became aware of the agenting profession through him. For a long time I thought this would make a terrific career for me, and in 1996 I decided to make "the leap." It's gone very well for me and has proved to be the right career choice. Now my husband has me for an agent, which is an added benefit!

Why did you become an agent? Knight: I've always been a salesperson, as well as a voracious reader. Agenting combines both of those qualities perfectly. Harty: Deidre and I (we're sisters) were raised by parents who loved to read, and they really instilled that passion in us. Deidre and I have always known that one day we would work together, so when she started the agency, I knew that eventually there would be a place for me. Last year, the time was finally right. This is my "dream come true" job. I get to read a lot, sell a lot, and work with people who love and support me!

What can writers do to enhance their chances of getting you as an agent? Present a nonfiction proposal that is thoroughly conceived and well-written, including market analysis and promotional opportunities, full chapter outlines, and competition. I'm open to a very wide range of nonfiction ideas, so send me a well-developed proposal and show me why it will sell—you'll grab my attention. In fiction, I'm looking for strong writers of romance, women's fiction, and commercial fiction. I also love books that combine both literary and commercial elements (think Alex Garland's *The Beach* or Donna Tartt's *The Secret History*).

How would you describe what you actually do for a living? Knight: I've often told people that I am the "Jerry Maguire of books." I look for terrific books and authors, then represent them to appropriate publishers, with the end goal of finding the right match. I negotiate all elements of the author's deal and thoroughly review and negotiate his or her contract. I then serve as that author's liaison with his or her publishing house and editor in all business-related matters, including negotiating future offers. More important, I help plan that author's career well beyond the first book. Our mutual goal is to develop a successful writing career, not merely to publish a single book.

Do you watch the *Sopranos*? Knight: I tape every episode and even own the season one box set. I must say that season three was a study in aimless plotting and lost opportunities. Let's hope season four is better! Harty: Never miss an episode—and wasn't the season finale pitiful?

Representative titles: Knight: *Beyond Success* by Brian Biro (Penguin Putnam); *True North* by Beverly Brandt (St. Martin's Press); *Lone Rider* by Lauren Bach (Warner Books); *A Beginner's Guide to Day Trading Online* by Toni Turner (Adams Media); *Healing Hearts* by Cheryl Wolverton (Harlequin); *How'dja Get That Job? Over 100 Careers in the Music Business* by Tanja Crouch (Barron's); *Simply Living* by Cecil Murphey (Westminster John Knox Press); *Kiss of the Highlander* by Karen Marie Moning (Bantam Dell); *Lone Rider* by Lauren Bach (Warner). Harty: *How to be Your Own Publicist* by Jessica Hatchigan (NTC/McGraw Hill); *Getting Honest with God* by Mark Littleton (Inner Varsity Press); *Foundation for Love* by Doreen Rainey (BET); *Orly: The True Account of the Disaster That Shaped Atlanta* by Ann Uhry Abrams (Hill Street Press).

LINDA KONNER LITERARY AGENCY

10 West 15th Street, Suite 1918, New York, NY 10011
212-691-3419

Agent: Linda Konner
  Born: Brooklyn, New York.
  Education: B.A. in Modern Languages, Brooklyn College; M.A.T. in Sociology and Urban Education, Fordham University.
  Career history: 1976–1981, Editor at *Seventeen* magazine; 1981–1983, Managing Editor, and 1983–1985, Editor in Chief at *Weight Watchers Magazine;* 1985–1986, Entertainment Editor at *Redbook;* 1986–1993, Entertainment Editor at *Woman's World* magazine; 1996–present, Literary Agent. Author of eight books.
  Hobbies/personal interests: Movies, theater, travel, exploring New York City.
  Areas most interested in agenting: Nonfiction only: Especially health, self-help, fitness and nutrition, relationships, parenting, pop psychology, celebrities, how-to, career, personal finance, African American
  Areas not interested in agenting: Fiction, children's, illustrated books
  If not agenting, what would you be doing? Writing books; in particular, a book I can't sell for the life of me, called *Apartners: Living Apart and Loving It* (my honey of 24 years and I are not married and don't live together).
  Best way to initiate contact: Send a brief query letter along with SASE.

K

Reading-fee policy: No reading fee.

Client representation by category: Nonfiction, 100%.

Commission: 15% domestic, 25% foreign (my foreign rights subagents collect 15%).

Number of titles sold last year: About 16.

Rejection rate (all submissions): 90%.

What gets you excited? See description of a dream client.

Description of the client from Hell: Clients from Hell don't follow through. Say they will turn in a proposal promptly/do a rewrite promptly/come up with ideas for the next book but then never do. Shmooze endlessly with me on the phone, either out of loneliness or to get my help coming up with a new idea. Think that "fun" multicolored proposals with lots of (needless) visuals are great (they do not save an otherwise poor idea or poor writing).

Description of a dream client: Those who write well and have a steady stream of good, commercial nonfiction ideas. Are experts in their field (or have access to one). Not afraid to think big. They have a sense of the marketplace—what's happening in the publishing world and what is likely to sell. They follow directions. Turn things around promptly. Keep phone conversations brief and to the point. Appreciate the efforts I'm making on their behalf.

Why did you become an agent? I wanted a change from book writing. I had successfully sold and negotiated contracts for several books of my own and my friends (often getting better deals for myself than my agents had gotten), and I enjoyed the process. Also, I had always had many more good book ideas than I ever had the time to write myself, and now I can see some of my ideas (such as *The Wedding Dress Diet*) blossom into books written by other talented people, who may be good writers but don't have a concrete book idea at the moment.

Representative titles: *Date Like a Man . . . to Get the Man You Want* (HarperCollins); *The Force Program: Six Questions That Will Change Your Life* by Joseph Nowinski, Ph.D. (Rodale); *Power Surge: How to Look Good and Feel Great After 40* by Ann Kearney-Cooke, Ph.D., and Florence Isaacs (Pocket).

BARBARA S. KOUTS, LITERARY AGENT

PO Box 560, Bellport, NY 11713
631-286-1278

Agent: Barbara S. Kouts

Born: October 24, 1936.

Education: B.A. in English, New York University; M.A. in English, SUNY at Stony Brook.

Career history: Freelance editorial work at book publishers and magazines; began working in literary agency 1980; founded own agency in 1991.

Hobbies/personal interests: Walking, swimming, reading, bicycle riding, gardening, spending time with my family and friends.

Areas most interested in agenting: Children's, literary novels, psychology, parenting, interpersonal relationships. Mysteries. Novels with depth in ideas and characters. Health, sports, and gardening.

Areas not interested in agenting: Science fiction and romance novels.

If not agenting, what would you be doing? Traveling, sailing around the world, working with children, reading, and writing.

Best way to initiate contact: Query letter and description of project (with SASE).

Reading-fee policy: No reading fee (only photocopying expenses).

Client representation by category: Nonfiction, 20%; Fiction, 20%; Children's, 60%.

Commission: 15%.

Number of titles sold last year: Lost count!

Rejection rate (all submissions): 90% of new submissions and queries.

Most common mistakes authors make: Calling on the phone over and over again to find out about everything! Constantly! Sending sloppy and unprofessional work!

What gets you excited? They are professional in all aspects of their query letter and phone conversations. Real pros stand out!

Description of the client from Hell: Expecting much too much—instant reads, instant dollars, instant attention! A feeling of nontrust, quibbling over everything.

Description of a dream client: Hardworking, reliable, consistent in writing, willing to rewrite and revise, kind and considerate. Upbeat and cheerful.

How did you become an agent? Studied English literature, studied editorial procedures. Worked for a book publisher and a magazine publisher.

Why did you become an agent? Great love of books! And good reads! I love to see a manuscript turn into a published book.

How would you describe what you actually do for a living? I work for writers to better their careers. I work to serve writers.

What do you think about editors? I admire a good editor, and there are many in the field now.

What do you think about publishers? A good publisher publishes good books, books of fine quality!

Comments: Keep on writing—never give up! "To one's own self be true." Hakuna matata.

Representative titles: *Dancing on the Edge* by Han Nolan; *Sacajawea* by Joseph Bruchac; *Cinderella Skeleton* by Robert San Souci; *Froggy's First Christmas* by Jonathan London.

IRENE KRAAS AGENCY

256 Rancho Alegre, Santa Fe, NM 87508
505-438-7715   fax: 505-438-7783

Agent: Irene W. Kraas

Born: August 16, is this necessary?

Education: B.A. in Psychology; M.Ed. in Educational Psychology.

Career history: Career Counselor; Management Consultant and Trainer to business, universities, and government; Literary Agent (1990–present).

Hobbies/personal interests: Reading, hiking, and enjoying life.

Areas most interested in agenting: At the moment, the agency is looking for psychological thrillers, mysteries, and sci-fi. Material by unpublished authors will be accepted in

K

those areas only. Published authors seeking representation may contact me regarding material in any area except children's picture books and chapter books.

Areas not interested in agenting: Any other than those listed previously. For published authors, please send query or call.

If not agenting, what would you be doing? I've done what I've wanted all along and this is the ultimate. However, if I had to choose, I would be a rich publisher and publish all those great books that I've had rejected!

Best way to initiate contact: Send me a short cover letter, the first 50 pages of a completed manuscript, and return postage. Please, no query letters!!

Reading-fee policy: No reading fee.

Client representation by category: Nonfiction, 5%; Fiction, 95%; Children's, 20%.

Commission: 15%.

Number of titles sold last year: Varies from year to year.

Rejection rate (all submissions): 99%.

Most common mistakes authors make: No cover letter or no return postage. Envelope too small. I can ignore everything if it's a great manuscript.

Description of the client from Hell: I'll take the fifth, thanks.

Description of a dream client: Great writers who trust me to do the very best for them.

Why did you become an agent? I went from 20 years in business consulting to becoming the great American writer to agenting. I love using my business acumen in helping first-time authors get a break.

How would you describe what you actually do for a living? I read, read, read. Then sell, sell, sell.

What do you think about editors? Mostly, they are top-notch people interested in good writing.

What do you think about publishers? Well, let's just say they don't always see the picture clearly and don't always have the writer's best interests in mind. But that's why we have agents!

Do you watch the *Sopranos*? Yes.

Representative titles: *Dogs with Jobs* by Chris Farran (Avon); *Wars You've Never Heard Of* by Chelsea Quinn Yarbro (TOR); *St. Germain 15 + 16* by Chelsea Quinn Yarbro (Warner); *Acoma Passage Way* by Kimberley Griffiths Little (Random House); *A Matter of Profit* by Hilari Bell (Avon); *The Fixer* by Jon Wierz (Kensington).

LAURA LANGLIE, LITERARY AGENT

275 President Street, Apartment 3, Brooklyn, NY 11231
fax: 718-858-6161
e-mail: ljlangliel@aol.com

Agent: Laura Langlie
  Born: January 21, 1964, Minneapolis, Minnesota.
  Education: University of Iowa.
  Career history: Associate Production Manager at Kensington; Editorial Subrights, Production, Publicity, etc., Carroll & Graf; Kidde, Hoyt & Picard Literary Agency, Agent.

Hobbies/personal interests: Going to the movies and the theater. Cooking and ice-skating.

Areas most interested in agenting: I'm most enthusiastic about representing a book that appeals to me as a reader. Any good story well told, whether it be a romance, mystery, or literary novel, truly excites me. The same can be said for nonfiction. I look for books about a fascinating time, event, or person—something unique or an established subject revisited in a new fashion.

Areas not interested in agenting: Male adventure, military novels, most science fiction, poetry, and erotica.

Best way to initiate contact: Send me a brief query letter, accompanied by an SASE. Make sure you tell me about your book—what's the hook?—why is it worthwhile?—and about yourself.

Client representation by category: Nonfiction, 50%; Fiction, 25%; Children's, 25%.
Commission: 15%.
Number of titles sold last year: 30.
Rejection rate (all submissions): 90%.

Description of the client from Hell: My clients from Hell are unrealistic, not open to suggestions on how to improve their work, those who don't realize that once a book is accepted, their work is only just beginning.

Description of the dream client: My dream clients are optimistic, eager, and willing to work hard with me to reach their goals.

Common mistakes authors make: They don't tell me enough about themselves in their query letter. Remember to address why you're the right author for this book.

What can writers do to enhance their chances of getting you as their agent? Be a pleasant, patient, straightforward person. No one wants to work hard for someone who's unpleasant and difficult.

Why did you become an agent? I enjoy helping people. There's nothing more satisfying than making a deal on an author's behalf and seeing it work out in the end for all three parties.

If not agenting, what might you be doing? I'd be involved in publishing in some capacity. I've been reading *Publishers Weekly* since I was in high school.

How would you describe what you do for a living? I'm a matchmaker. Sometimes it works; sometimes the matches result in a divorce. On the whole, however, I've got a pretty good track record.

How did you become an agent? I was asked if I wanted to become an agent. At that time, I was working as a freelance editor and thought to take advantage of the opportunity. I always enjoyed my relationships with authors. It appears that it was what I was meant to do.

What do you think about editors? Editors are really partners with agents. A good editor is a true find. An editor's enthusiasm and dedication can make all the difference to a book's success.

What do you think about publishers? I think it's a tough market for publishers today. Books have never been a big moneymaking industry, but since many publishers are now owned by large corporations, there's considerable pressure on the publishing divisions to deliver a profit. I like working with a variety of publishers. Often, smaller publishers can surprise you with their creativity and passion for what they do.

L

What were your favorite films last year? *The Princess Diaries,* of course. I also liked *The Deep End, Legally Blonde,* and *Gosford Park.*

Do you watch the *Sopranos?* Yes, I just subscribed to HBO.

Comments: What "rocks my world" is to help clients realize their dreams.

Representative titles: *Shadow of an Angel* by Mignon F. Ballard (St. Martin's Press/Berkley); *Much Obliged* by Jessica Benson (Zebra); *The Princess Diaries, Princess in the Spotlight, Princess in Love* by Meg Cabot (HarperCollins); *Mutiny and Murder in the Pacific* by Joan Druett (Algonquin); *The Lobotomist* by Jack El-Hai (John Wiley and Sons); *Chasing the Devil's Tail* by David Fulmer (Poisoned Pen Press); *The Doctor and the Dead Man's Chest* by Robin Hathaway (Thomas Dunne Books/St. Martin's Press); *Tigers of the Snow* by Jonathan Neale (Thomas Dunne Books/St. Martin's Press); *Lost at Sea* by Jonathan Neale (Houghton Mifflin); *Fire and Ice* by Eric Pinder (Algonquin); and *Good Bad Women* by Elizabeth Woodcraft (Kensington).

MICHAEL LARSEN—ELIZABETH POMADA LITERARY AGENTS

1029 Jones Street, San Francisco, CA 94109-5023
415-673-0939
www.larsen-pomada.com   e-mail: larsenpoma@aol.com

Agents: Michael Larsen, Elizabeth Pomada

Born: Larsen: January 8, 1941, New York, New York. Pomada: June 12, 1940, New York, New York.

Education: Larsen: City College of New York, 1965. Pomada: Cornell University, 1962.

Career history: Larsen: Worked at Bantam, William Morrow, and Pyramid (now part of Berkley). Pomada: Worked at Holt, David McKay, and the Dial Press. Members: AAR. Sold books to more than 100 publishers. Started Northern California's oldest literary agency in 1972. Written or co-authored 15 books. Larsen wrote *How to Write a Book Proposal; Literary Agents: What They Do, How They Do It;* and *How to Find and Work with the Right One for You,* and, with Jay Conrad Levinson and Rick Frishman, co-authored *Guerrilla Marketing for Writers: 100 Weapons for Selling Your Work.* I speak at the Learning Annex and writers' conferences, including Maui and Santa Barbara. I present seminars on "Get Paid to Write Your Book! 3 Steps to Writing an Irresistible Book Proposal," "Guerrilla Marketing for Writers," "3 Ways to Make Yourself Irresistible to Any Agent or Publisher," "Taking the Guesswork Out of Publishing: 15 Ways to Test-Market Your Books to Guarantee Their Success."

Hobbies/personal interests: Larsen: Reading books between covers without the phone ringing, jazz and classical music, France, movies and other media, technology and the future. (After all, it is where I'm going to spend the rest of my life.) Pomada: France, traveling and writing about it; and reading for pleasure.

Areas most interested in agenting: General fiction and nonfiction. Larsen: Beautiful writing, new ideas with social or esthetic value, anything that large and medium-sized houses will buy, how-to's, self-help, business, technology, trends, visions of the future, health, spirituality, pop culture, history, architecture, illustrated books. Pomada: Nonfiction: books for women, travel, food, the arts, and narrative nonfiction, including memoirs and biographies. Fiction: General, women's, historical and contemporary, commercial, literary, thrillers, suspense, and genre: romance, mystery, fantasy; Westerns and science fiction, but only if they break out of the category and sweep me away.

Areas not interested in agenting: Articles, short stories, poetry, screenplays, children's and young adult, textbooks, stories of abuse, books that will only interest small houses. Agents and editors want to look forward to working with the books and authors they take on. This makes them less receptive to books that are only depressing. Like the readers they are surrogates for, agents and editors like happy endings or a positive slant on a depressing subject. If possible, don't sell a problem; sell a solution.

Best way to initiate contact: Fiction: Elizabeth is eager to see the first 10 pages of a completed novel, followed by a 2-page synopsis after you have gotten feedback from people who know writing. Please include an SASE, and your daytime phone number. Nonfiction: Michael's book on proposals describes what we need to see. If your book will be aimed at a wide national audience and will depend on your promotional efforts to keep selling, please mail your title and promotion with an SASE or e-mail them as a letter, not as an attachment. If it's a serious or narrative book, please send the first three chapters followed by a 2-page synopsis, an SASE, and your daytime phone number.

Client representation by category: Nonfiction, 70%; Fiction, 30%.

Commission: 15% domestic, which includes film and most expenses; foreign 20%, except Asia 30%.

Number of titles sold last year? 15–20.

Rejection rate (all submissions): More than 90%.

Description of the client from Hell: We have an eccentric California approach to agenting. We like to handle books we like by writers we like and sell them to editors we like. So we don't even have a client from Heck.

Description of the dream client: Dream clients are alchemists who have a clear vision of their literary and financial goals, which they pursue with relentlessness tempered by passion, professionalism, optimism, and grace; make nothing in their lives more important than achieving their goals; have a steady stream of brilliant ideas they can transform into gold: write exquisite prose that gives us, the editors and the book buyers who read it, chills; understand that agents and writers don't sell books; books sell themselves; understand that publishing a book is an imperfect process that will create problems so they make the best of any situation by taking the long view as well as the short view; are lifelong learners about writing, publishing and their field; are motivated more by love than money, by art than commerce; inspire passion and excellence in everyone who comes into contact with them and their work; believe that the right book will change the world and use their literary gifts to make a difference as well as a living; balance their personal and professional lives without sacrificing one to the other; call us when they have a problem; understand that as writers, we endure the same problems they do, so we try to balance truth and charity; understand that since they are free to leave us at any time, we always have an incentive to keep them satisfied.

Most common mistakes authors make: Not following the advice in this book.

What can writers do to enhance their chances of getting you as an agent? Come as close as they can to the ideal of the dream client. Check our Web site or send a #10 SASE for our free brochure "3 Ways to Make Yourself Irresistible to Any Agent or Publisher" to find out about us. There are 1,200 agents out there. Tell us why you want us.

L

Why did you become an agent? We love books, and we love helping writers make their work 100 percent and then reap the rewards and recognition they deserve.

If not agenting, what would you be doing? Larsen: Writing. Pomada: Traveling the world and writing about it.

How would you describe what you do for a living? We are *mediators* between you and the marketplace, *scouts* who know what publishers want, *midwives* who help you give birth to your ideas and make sure your work is ready before submitting it, *matchmakers* who arrange working marriages between you and the best possible editor and publisher for your books, *negotiators* who hammer out the best contract for you, *advocates* between you and your publisher throughout the publication process, and *mentors* who advise you about publishing, promotion, your writing, and your career—an *oasis* of encouragement when you need it.

How did you become an agent? Larsen: The Symbionese Liberation Army made me an agent. When the SLA kidnapped Patricia Hearst, I sold a book about it in four phone calls and thought, "Gee, this looks easy. I should do it for a living!" Pomada: When we moved to San Francisco, I registered with an employment agency that specialized in writers. The owner couldn't find me a job, but she had all these manuscripts and didn't know what to do with them. We did.

What do you think about editors? People become editors for the same reason they become agents: because they like books and people. We wouldn't be agents if we didn't know a lot of wonderful editors who are dedicated to acquiring good books, editing them well, and being the in-house agent for the books they buy by stirring up as much enthusiasm for their books as they can inside and outside of the house. Editors are the ultimate middle-people, trying to please publishers, authors, agents, and themselves. The overworked and underpaid editors who do this, while balancing art and commerce so they can keep their jobs, deserve to be regarded as the heroes of the business.

What do you think about publishers? Consolidation, conglomerization, technology, and the globalization of culture and commerce are transforming the industry, but no one knows into what. Competition, stockholders, and rising costs force the six conglomerates that dominate the industry to be more concerned about the bottom line than about supporting new writers while they build the audience for their books. This creates opportunities for small and niche publishers, university presses, and self-publishers.

Do you watch the *Sopranos?* No.

Comments: You have at least 17 options for getting your books published (they're listed on our Web site). Large and medium-sized houses are only one of them, but they are the only way that agents can make a living. More than 90 percent of agents must find new writers to make a living. But even though they can't make a living saying no, they reject more than 90 percent of the material they receive. Despite this paradoxical situation, we think it's easier than ever to get an agent. What's getting harder is writing something strong enough to convince large and medium-sized houses to take a chance on it. If you can, it will be easier than ever for you to find an agent and a publisher, because the more challenging publishing becomes, the easier it is to sell books that meet that challenge. If you want to be published by a large or medium-sized house, follow these steps: Learn how agents and publishers work. Read what you love to read and write what you love to read. Read competitive books so you can use the one you love as models. You can only write as well as you read.

L

Accept the bad news that you won't get your proposal or manuscript right by yourself and be glad about the good news: You don't have to. Understand that publishing is based on relationships. Build on- and off-line networks of publishing people and professionals in your field who can help you with feedback on your idea, your work, finding an agent, promotion, sources of information, and connections to other potential members of your networks. Come up with a new idea or an exciting new twist on an old one. Write the manuscript for a novel or a proposal for a nonfiction book. Whether you're writing fiction or nonfiction, prepare a promotion plan. Revise your work as often as needed. Share it with many readers: friends and family, potential buyers, literate readers, authors of books like yours, experts on the subject, and a devil's advocate who can spot whatever needs to be improved or removed. Approach agents or publishers the way their listings in directories recommend. Do everything you can for your books. Look at your career, not as being based on 1 book but based on 10 or 20, each better than the last. You are the most important person in the publishing process because you make it go. If you are writing to meet the needs of the marketplace and you can promote your books, now is the best time ever to be a writer. There are more subjects for you to write about, more ways to build your networks and learn about writing and publishing, more books and authors to serve as models for you to emulate, more options for getting your books published, and more ways to promote your books and profit from them than ever. Proceed as if success is inevitable. Persistence rewards talent.

Representative titles: *Guerrilla Creativity: Make Your Message Irresistible with the Power of Memes* by Jay Conrad Levinson, the 18th book in the Guerrilla series; *The Silver Wyrm* by Katharine Kerr, the 13th volume in the Deverry Series (Daw); *Way of the Peaceful Warrior: A Book that Changes Lives,* the revised 20th anniversary edition, with a new afterword by Dan Millman (H. J. Kramer/New World Library); *Aces: True Stories of Victory and Valor in the Skies of World War II* by William Yenne (Berkley); *The Amazing Dad: More Than 400 Ways to Wow Your Kids* by Giovanni Livera and Ken Preuss (Perigee); *Enlightened Office Politics: Understanding, Coping with, and Winning the Game—Without Losing Your Soul* by Michael and Deborah Dobson (AMACOM); *Goddess Initiation: A Practical Celtic Program for Soul Healing, Self-Fulfillment and Wild Wisdom* by Francesca de Grandis (HarperSanFrancisco); *Guerrilla Publicity: 34 Golden Rules to Boost Your Profits* by Jay Conrad Levinson, Rick Frishman, and Jill Lublin, the 19th book in the Guerrilla Marketing Series (co-agent) (Adams Media Corporation); *The Money Dragon* by Pam Chun, the first of a two-volume series of historical novels based on her family (Sourcebooks); *Tomorrow's Child,* a short story by Lisa Mason, to Universal Pictures.

JAMES LEVINE COMMUNICATIONS, INC.

307 Seventh Avenue, Suite 1906, New York, NY 10001
212-337-0934
www.jameslevine.com

West Coast Office:
112 Auburn Street, San Rafael, CA 94901
415-785-1582

L

Agents: James A. Levine, Arielle Eckstut (West Coast Office), Daniel Greenberg, Stephanie Kip Rostan, Miek Coccia

Born: Levine: April 20, 1946. Eckstut: August 25, 1970. Greenberg: October 13, 1970. Rostan: March 7, 1973. Coccia: July 10, 1979.

Education: Levine: B.A., Amherst College; M.A. C. Phil. (English Literature), University of California, Berkeley; Ed.D., Harvard University. Eckstut: B.A., University of Chicago. Greenberg: B.A. (History), University of Wisconsin at Madison. Rostan: Phillips Academy; B.A. (English/Creative Writing), Princeton. Coccia: New York University (Gallatin School of Individualized Study).

Career history: Levine: Spent much of my career doing what I do now: putting together ideas, people, and money; identifying, nurturing, and marketing talent; creating projects that make a difference. As an entrepreneur in the not-for-profit and academic sectors, including a decade as Vice President at the Bank Street College of Education in New York City, I channeled people's expertise into a variety of media: print, software, video, multimedia, and audio. Eckstut: Pastry chef prior to becoming literary agent. Greenberg: Penguin Books and then in Italy with the Roberto Santachiara Literary Agency. Rostan: Editor, Bantam Books and then Book Producer, iVillage.com. Coccia: Student.

Hobbies/personal interests: Levine: Jazz, sports (playing them), photography, travel, hiking, voracious reading in a wide range of areas. More than twenty years as founder/director of The Fatherhood Project, a nonprofit research and educational initiative now located at the Families and Work Institute in New York City. Have written seven books, most recently *Working Fathers: New Strategies for Balancing Work and Family*, two software manuals, and more than one hundred articles for leading magazines. Also produced the PBS documentary *Fatherhood U.S.A.* Eckstut: Working with writers as an agent at James Levine Communications has fostered my own writing, and I have co-authored two books: *Pride and Promiscuity: The Lost Sex Scenes of Jane Austen* and *Satchel Sez: The Wit and Wisdom of Leroy "Satchel" Paige*, with an introduction by Bob Costas. I also love to cook, bake, and make art (I have a design background). I'm also an avid moviegoer and former member of an improvisational theatre group. Greenberg: When I'm not standing in the middle of the room on one leg balancing 1,500 page manuscripts on my head (my all time favorite hobby!), I'm watching movies, cooking meals, riding my bicycle, or doing yoga. Rostan: Red Sox baseball fan, green belt in karate, travel, writing, animals. Coccia: Art and film. And foreigners.

Areas most interested in agenting: Levine: I love the challenge of working with smart people who have great ideas. Eckstut: First, great writing. Second, great recipes. Greenberg: For fiction, any piece of solid writing interests me, no matter what the genre. I also look at credentials and publishing history. I keep my eyes open for a sharp sense of humor. Rostan: Commercial and literary fiction, including mystery/suspense and women's fiction, smart self-help, psychology. Coccia: In fiction, I tend to enjoy literary novels with a darker edge and a unique writing style, with gay fiction a plus. In nonfiction, interested in humor, pop culture, and science, but willing to work on anything that catches my eye.

Areas not interested in agenting: Levine: Anything that's poorly written. Eckstut: Romance, children's, true crime, academic, and professional books. Greenberg: Romances. Rostan: Business, cookbooks, science fiction, children's, academic. Coccia: Romance, self-help, military/FBI thrillers.

L

If not agenting, what would you be doing? Levine: Writing and working in some other organizational setting to develop people's talent. Eckstut: Industrial designer? Director? Chef? Who knows! Greenberg: Impossible to conceive of such a scenario. Rostan: Writing (can't say whether it would be published!) and traveling everywhere. Coccia: Something in the art or film world.

Best way to initiate contact: Fill out the easy-to-use submission form on our Web site, www.jameslevine.com. It's listed under How We Work/Submission.

Client representation by category: Nonfiction, 80%; Fiction, 20%.

Commission: 15%.

Rejection rate: 99%.

Most common mistakes authors make: Send a whole manuscript, unsolicited, with no SASE, then keep calling—wanting to know why they have not gotten their manuscript back. Forget to explain who they are, why they're qualified to write, and, most important, who the audience is for their work.

Description of the client from Hell: Calls all the time for unnecessary reasons and never once says thanks.

Description of a dream client: Organized, thoughtful, easy to get along with, conscientious, reliable, cordial, and fun!

Why did you become an agent? We feel passionately about feeling passionately about the projects we take on. Levine: I was an agent before I ever knew I was an agent. Eckstut: Pure luck. Greenberg: I enjoy working with talented and interesting people. There is also nothing quite as exciting as the huge deal! Rostan: To be involved in the creative process of bringing books to market and the business aspects of making deals. Coccia: Fell into it, but found I enjoy it, because my interests are always changing and agenting gives me the opportunity to constantly be working on something new that I'm passionate about.

What can writers do to enhance their chances of getting you as their agent? Send us chocolate. (Just kidding.) Be organized and easy to work with—this will go a long way with your editor, too.

What were your favorite films last year? Levine: *You Can Count on Me, Heartbreakers, O Brother Where Art Thou?* Greenberg: I'm a big fan of the *Royal Tenenbaums.* Eckstut: *The Royal Tenenbaums, Amelie, Shackleton's Antarctic Adventure.* Rostan: *The Lord of the Rings, A Beautiful Mind, Moulin Rouge.*

Representative titles: *Our Dumb Century* by The Onion (Crown); *Crossing the Chasm* by Geoffrey Moore (HarperBusiness); *Queen Bees & Wannabes* by Ross Wiseman (Crown); *Non-Campus Mentis* by Anders Henriksson (Workman); *Chicken* by David Henry Sterry (Regan); *Resurrecting Mingus* by Jenoyne Adams (Simon &Schuster); *Act Natural* by Ken Howard (Random House); *Piloting Palm* by Andrea Butter and David Pogue (Wiley); *Fruitflesh* by Gayle Brandeis (HarperSanFrancisco); *CNBC 24/7 Trading* (Wiley); *The Root Worker* by Rainelle Burton (Overlook); *Customers.com* by Patricia Seybold (Crown); *The Common Thread* by Martha Manning (Morrow); *Why God Won't Go Away* by Andrew Newberg, M.D., Eugene D'Aquili, M.D., Ph.D., and Vince Rause (Ballantine); *Raising Fences: A Black Man's Love Story* by Michael Datcher (Riverhead); *Reinventing Medicine* by Larry Dossey, M.D. (HarperSanFrancisco); *How to Quit Golf: A 12-Step Program* by Craig Brass (Dutton); *Room Redux* by Joanne Eckstut and Sheran

L

James (Chronicle); *How to Raise a Family on Less Than Two Incomes* by Denise Topel-nicki (Broadway); *The Complete Cancer Survival Guide* by Peter Teeley and Philip Bashe (Doubleday); *Run Catch Kiss* by Amy Sohn (Simon & Schuster); *Undoing Depression* by Richard O'Connor (Little, Brown); *Satchel Sez: The Wit, Wisdom and World of Leroy "Satchel" Paige* by David Sterry and Arielle Eckstut (Crown); *The Quest for Immortality: Science at the Frontiers of Aging* by S. Jay Olshansky and Bruce Carnes (W.W. Norton).

PAUL S. LEVINE LITERARY AGENCY

1054 Superba Avenue, Venice, CA 90291-3940
310-450-6711   fax: 310-450-0181
e-mail: pslevine@ix.netcom.com

Agent: Paul S. Levine
Born: March 16, 1954, New York.
Education: B.Comm., Concordia University, Montreal; M.B.A., York University, Toronto; J.D., USC.
Career history: Attorney for more than 20 years.
Areas most interested in agenting: Commercial fiction and nonfiction.
Areas not interested in agenting: Science fiction fantasy and horror, children's and young adult books.
If not agenting, what would you be doing? Practicing entertainment law.
Best way to initiate contact: Query by snail mail (with SASE), e-mail, fax.
Reading-fee policy: No reading fee.
Client representation by category: Nonfiction, 60%; Fiction, 40%.
Commission: 15%.
Number of titles sold last year: 30.
Rejection rate (all submissions): 95%.
Most common mistakes authors make: Writing bad query letters.
What gets you excited? See description of a dream client.
Description of the client from Hell: One who calls, faxes, e-mails, or otherwise tries to contact me every day. One who constantly needs reassurance that each rejection letter does not mean the client's project lacks merit and that the client is an awful person.
Description of a dream client: The opposite of above.
Why did you become an agent? I have loved the book business ever since I started practicing law in 1980. My first client was a major book publisher.
What can writers do to enhance their chances of getting you as an agent? Contact me in a professional manner. Be referred by an existing client, colleague, or friend.
How would you describe what you actually do for a living? I represent writers—book authors, screenwriters, television writers, and writer-producers.
What do you think about editors? I love them.
What do you think about publishers? I love them, too.
Comments: I always tell my clients that the only thing that I know how to write is a contract—I envy writers who can actually write.

L

THE LITERARY GROUP INTERNATIONAL

270 Lafayette Street, Suite 1505, New York, NY 10012
212-274-1616   fax: 212-274-9876
www.theliterarygroup.com   e-mail: litgrpfw@aol.com

Agents: Frank Weimann, Andrew Stuart

Hobbies/personal interests: Weimann: Ice hockey.

Areas most interested in agenting: Weimann: Categories include sports, science, how-to, mystery, romance, suspense, African-American subjects, politics, memoirs, history. All types of high-quality narrative nonfiction, current events, military history, U.S. history, world history, political subjects, science, medicine/health, business/management/ finance, academic writing and research that has a general-interest audience. Quality literary and mainstream fiction.

Areas not interested in agenting: Poetry, science fiction.

If not agenting, what would you be doing? Weimann: This is all I ever wanted to do.

Best way to initiate contact: The ideal way to initiate contact is by sending us a clear, concise, compelling query letter.

Reading-fee policy: No reading fee.

Client representation by category: Weimann: Nonfiction, 65%; Fiction, 35%; Children's, 5%.

Commission: 15% domestic; 20% foreign.

Number of titles sold last year: Weimann: 75.

Rejection rate (all submissions): Weimann: 99%.

Most common mistakes authors make: The most common mistake is to insist on meeting with us. It is what's on the page that counts, not a wonderful personality.

Description of the client from Hell: The worst thing a client can do, in my mind, is to constantly bombard the agency and/or publisher with needless phone calls.

Description of a dream client: Most of our authors fit into this category. Dream clients are willing to put their faith and confidence into our hands and trust that we will do what is in their best interest.

How did you become an agent? My first client, Thomas "Hollywood" Henderson, asked me to represent him after publishers loved his story and hated the proposal I wrote for him.

Why did you become an agent? Very simple—I don't have the ability to write books, but have the ability to help those who can.

How would you describe what you do for a living? I have the greatest job in the world.

What can writers do to enhance their chances of getting you as their agent? It is important to us that a writer is willing to rely on our experience and take career suggestions from us.

What do you think about editors? I believe editors are the most overworked and underpaid people in the creative arts.

What do you think about publishers? Where would we be without them?

Representative titles: *The Darwin Awards: Evolution in Action* by Wendy Northcutt (E. P. Dutton); *Flags of Our Fathers* by James Bradley (Bantam Doubleday Dell); *October*

L

Sky by Homer Hickam (Dell); *It's Only a Game* by Terry Bradshaw (Pocket); *Russell Rules* by Bill Russell (Penguin); *Access to Power* by Robert Ellis (Pinnacle Books); *The Mystery Kiss* by Judith Landsdowne (Zebra Books); *A Thousand Goodbyes* by Jim Huber (Thomas Nelson); *Seven Prayers That Can Change Your Life* by Len Felder (Andrews McMeel); *God Don't Like Ugly* by Mary Monroe (Kensington Books); *Britney Spears' Heart to Heart* by Britney Spears and Lynn Spears (Three Rivers Press).

Toni Lopopolo Literary Management

8837 School House Lane, Coopersburg, PA 18036
215-679-0560   fax: 215-679-0561
e-mail: LopopoloBooks@aol.com

Agent: Toni Lopopolo

Born: July 18, Los Angeles.

Education: M.A.

Career history: 1972–1973, Publicity Associate, Bantam Books; 1973–1975, Paperback Marketing Manager, Houghton-Mifflin; 1975–1981, Executive Editor, Macmillan; 1981–1990, Executive Editor, St. Martin's Press; 1990–present, Literary Agency.

Hobbies/personal interests: Reading, house restoration, my dogs, opera, antiques.

Areas most interested in agenting: Nonfiction, psychology, self-help, family and parenting, interior decor and collecting, narrative nonfiction, personal spirituality, animals, and other of today's most important subjects. Fiction: mysteries with interesting, ethnic protagonists, Latino writers, quirky novels.

Areas not interested in agenting: Try me.

If not agenting, what might you be doing? I'd like to go back to teaching.

Best way to initiate contact: Terrific query letter and excellent credentials.

Client representation by category: Nonfiction, 80%; Fiction, 20%.

Commission structure: 15% domestic; 20% foreign.

Number of titles sold last year: 14.

Rejection rate (all submissions): 95%.

Common mistakes authors make: Fiction writers who have not mastered the skills that make up the craft of book-length fiction; phoning to tell me their "idea" for a book; wannabe writers who have not done their homework such as learning how to write a query letter and enclose an SASE, who do not have the credentials or the platform for the nonfiction subject they propose; those who balk at writing a proposal; fiction writers who send a 10-page synopsis, and much more.

Description of the client from Hell: The terminally insecure.

Description of the dream client: The true professional writers who trust and believe in their agent and themselves.

How did you become an agent? It was a natural segue after 20 years in book publishing.

Why did you become an agent? Becoming an agent was a natural follow-up to a long publishing career. The love of good books.

How would you describe what you do for a living? I search for talented writers and manage their careers. This includes a lot of editing.

L

What can writers do to enhance their chances of getting you as their agent? For nonfiction, submitting an excellently crafted proposal, for fiction, writers who have mastered the skills that make up the craft of book-length fiction and the craft of meticulous self-editing. Writers who have done their homework in how to correctly submit to an agent and who show strong self-confidence are welcome.

If not agenting, what would you be doing? I'd be refurbishing fixer-upper houses. I love the process. Plus, I'd have more than three dogs. And reading already published books by the hundreds.

What do you think about editors? Because I worked as an editor for many years, I am very empathetic to their workload and plight in the machinery of a publishing house. Many are great talents.

What do you think about publishers? It is daunting to walk into a bookstore and see the thousands of books sitting on the shelves. These books live or die with little help from the publishers who put them there. Conglomerate publishing has not helped the old sink-or-swim philosophy and that's discouraging, but we press on, don't we? And, as long as publishers publish and readers keep reading, agents will sell books.

What were your favorite films last year? *Sixth Sense, Traffic, My Dog Skip.*

Do you watch the *Sopranos?* Every episode several times. And then compare reactions and notes with family members and friends. I even know the song Uncle Junior sang in the last episode of 2001. "Core Ingrato!"

Representative titles: *Self-Promotion for Creative People* by Lee Silber (Crown); *Real-Life Home Schooling* by Rhonda Barfield (Pocket Books); *Five Steps to Emotional Healing* by Gloria Arenson (Simon & Schuster); The Starletta Duval mystery series (*Green Money* and *Reckless Eyeballin';* Ballantine).

LOWENSTEIN ASSOCIATES INC.

121 West 27th Street, Suite 601, New York, NY 10001
212-206-1630   fax: 212-727-0280

Agents: Barbara Lowenstein, Nancy Yost, Eileen Cope, Dorian Karchmar

   Born: Lowenstein: New York. Yost: California. Karchmar: October 9, 1969, New York City.

   Education: Yost: B.A. in Comparative Literature, UNLV. Cope: Degrees in Political Science and Journalism. Karchmar: B.A. in English, Wesleyan University; M.F.A. in Creative Nonfiction, University of Iowa.

   Career history: Lowenstein: 25 years as head of Lowenstein Associates. Yost: Most recent: Agent, Lowenstein (since 1990); Contracts Department, Random House; Editor, Avon Books. Cope: Was an Editor with the Putnam Berkley Group. Karchmar: Prior to Lowenstein Associates in the beginning of 1999, I taught creative writing while completing an M.F.A. at the University of Iowa. Prior to that, I worked in publicity and promotion for four years at rock and jazz record labels.

   Hobbies/personal interests: Lowenstein: Adventure travel. Yost: Reading, snorkeling/scuba, rollerblading, movies, opera, antiquing. Karchmar: Music, reading (I'm a news junkie), art, history, hiking, cooking, and gardening.

L

Areas most interested in agenting: Lowenstein: Fiction: literary and commercial fiction, African-American. Nonfiction: health and women's issues, narrative travel, adventure travel, current affairs, science, biography, African-American. Yost: Crime fiction, women's fiction, popular science, culture, natural sciences, women's issues, some health, "how-to," nonfiction, light reference, up-market thrillers, and commercial fiction. Cope: Literary and multicultural fiction, comparative religions, psychology, ethics, contemporary social issues, contemporary ethnic and cultural issues, Asian studies, anthropology, sexuality, politics, and the arts (particularly music, theater, and art history). Karchmar: Literary fiction with commercial potential; narrative nonfiction—the subject matter is far less important to me than the quality of the prose and the rendering of the storyline; women's fiction; psychological suspense/thrillers; the arts.

Areas not interested in agenting: Yost: No Westerns, sci-fi, political nonfiction, no textbooks. Cope: All category fiction, children's, and young adult. Karchmar: Westerns, science fiction, romance, children's/young adult.

If not agenting, what would you be doing? Lowenstein: Extreme sports. Yost: I'd either be raising puppies between scuba classes or be a personal shopper for shoes. Karchmar: Writing and teaching.

Best way to initiate contact: Lowenstein: Query letter with SASE. Yost: The old way (sorry!)—by query letter. Cope: Please send a query letter and c.v. with an SASE. Karchmar: Query letter with SASE. If nonfiction, go ahead and enclose the proposal if it's finished.

Reading-fee policy: No reading fee.

Number of titles sold last year: 40–50.

Client representation by category: Lowenstein: Nonfiction, 75%; Fiction, 25%. Yost: Nonfiction, 25%; Fiction, 75%. Cope: Nonfiction, 60%; Fiction, 40%. Karchmar: Nonfiction: 50%; Fiction: 50%.

Commission: 15% U.S.; 20% foreign; 15% film.

Rejection rate (all submissions): Lowenstein: 90%. Yost: 95%. Karchmar: 95%.

Most common mistakes authors make: Yost: Sending material that (a) I don't represent, (b) is in rough draft and needs extensive revisions. Karchmar: Trying to get an agent too early in their career and their development as a writer.

Description of the client from Hell: Lowenstein: One who doesn't deliver or delivers an unpublishable manuscript. Yost: It's all in the attitude—some symptoms, though, include over-aggressive phone calls, incomplete communication of desires, opinions leading to resentment and miscommunication, unrealistic expectations, phoning at home on weekends, surly manners.

Description of a dream client: Lowenstein: Delivers a great proposal, is professional, and then delivers a terrific book; cooperates with the publisher and brings something to the process of marketing; is good on television and is willing to work like Hell to get the book sold without driving everyone nuts! Yost: Creative, industrious, knowledgeable about one's area of "expertise"/genre. Oh, you can be currently on the bestseller list, and your brother is head of Ingram, Barnes & Noble, and Borders, while your father is head of a major movie studio and wants to produce all of your books. Karchmar: Approaches authorship as an art and a profession; entrepreneurial; willing to revise a proposal or manuscript until it's as strong as possible; has a grasp of the basic "rules" of the industry; sense of humor; has good promotional contacts and is not shy about using them.

L

M

How did you become an agent? Yost: As an editor, I was "recruited" by my current employer with the promise of being able to play in everyone's backyard instead of just one. Karchmar: I realized during graduate school that agenting would be a good way for me to bring together my intellectual and professional strengths. Moved back to NYC after receiving my M.F.A., found a job as an assistant at Lowenstein Associates, and acted like I knew what I was doing until, eventually, I did know what I was doing. I also worked extremely hard.

Why did you become an agent? Lowenstein: Love books. Yost: I love books, and I like to help authors find the right "fit" for a good career. Also, I love the challenge of always getting better and knowing there's always more to learn—about the business of publishing and life in general. Karchmar: I love reading, editing, and helping good books get into the world; I get to be involved with a project from inception through publication and beyond, and it's a good outlet for my need to be intensely involved in whatever I do.

What can writers do to enhance their chances of getting you as an agent? Yost: Writing marketable books—that is, know your genre; and any referrals by published writers/editors/industry professionals are useful, too. Karchmar: Take your career as far as you can yourself before trying to get an agent: publish in magazines/literary journals; enter and place in contests; develop your credentials/promotionals platform (especially for nonfiction) You need to show that you've already had some success with your writing—that an agent should take a gamble on you.

How would you describe what you actually do for a living? Yost: Part salesperson, part editor, part lawyer, part therapist, part pit-bull, part cheerleader.

What do you think about editors? Yost: Hardworking (overworked!) and, mostly, very dedicated to books.

What do you think about publishers? Yost: That answer depends on the house.

Comments: Yost: Not enough room in your book for my rants!!

Representative titles: *Achievement Matters: Getting Your Child the Best Education Possible* by Hugh Price; *Secrets of the Baby Whisperer* by Tracy Hogg/Milinda Blau (Ballantine); *10 Good Choices That Empower Black Women's Lives* by Grace Cornish (Crown); *Emotional Alchemy* by Tara Bennett-Goleman (Harmony); *Into the Arms of Strangers: Stories of the Kindertransport* by Mark Jonathan Harris (Bloomsbury); *Good Girl's Guide to Bad Girl's Sex* by Barbara Keesling (M. Evans); *The Reed Reader* by Ishmael Reed (Basic); *Healing Lazarus* by Lewis Richmond (Pocket); *Writ of Execution* by Perri O'Shaughnessy (Delacorte); *The Promise in a Kiss* by Stephanie Laurens (Morrow); *A Finer End* by Deborah Crombie (Bantam); *Searching for Intruders* by Stephen Byler (Morrow); *Insect Dreams* by Marc Estrin (Blue Hen); *Daughter of the Game* by Tracy Grant (Morrow); *Sunday's Silence* by Gina Nahai (Harcourt); *Letters for Emily* by Camron Wright (Pocket).

DONALD MAASS LITERARY AGENCY

160 West 95th Street, Suite 1B, New York, NY 10025
fax: 212-866-8181
e-mail: dmla@mindspring.com

M

Agents: Donald Maass, Jennifer Jackson, Michelle Brummer

Born: Maass: 1953, Columbus, Georgia. Jackson: 1971, Cambridge, New York. Brummer: 1972, Zama, Japan.

Education: Maass: B.A., St. Lawrence University, 1975; Jackson: B.A., St. Lawrence University, 1993. Brummer: B.A., University of Georgia, 1995.

Career history: Maass: 1977–1978, Editor, Dell Publishing; 1979, Agent, Scott Meredith Literary Agency, Inc.; 1980, founded Donald Maass Literary Agency. Jackson: 1993–present, Donald Maass Literary Agency. Brummer: 1995–1996, Assistant Store Manager, B. Dalton Super Store, and Assistant Publicist. L. Cade: 1996–1997, Editorial Assistant; 1997–1998, Assistant Agent; 1998–1999, Assistant Agent and Rights Associate.

Hobbies/personal interests: Maass: Reading, theater, sailing, squash, antiques, stock market. Jackson: Cooking, cross-stitch, books, writing, Web-page design, RPGs. Brummer: Books, film, travel, photography, and creating mosaics.

Areas most interested in agenting: Maass: Fiction specialist. Concentration in science fiction, fantasy, mystery, suspense, horror, frontier, mainstream, and literary. Jackson: Fiction specialist in all genres, especially romance, women's fiction, mystery, suspense, thrillers, science fiction, and fantasy. Brummer: Fiction: literary, mainstream, science fiction, fantasy, horror, and historical romances.

Areas not interested in agenting: Maass: Pop psychology, how-to, true crime, humor/novelty, juvenile. Jackson: Nonfiction, poetry, and children's books.

If not agenting, what would you be doing? Maass: Oh, Lord, it's too late to think about that now. Brummer: In a different world, I would own an independent bookstore.

Best way to initiate contact: Send a concise, one-page query letter (with SASE) that includes a description of the book and any prior book or short story credits.

Reading-fee policy: No reading fee.

Client representation by category: Fiction, 100%. Jackson: Nonfiction, 1%; Fiction, 99%.

Commission: 15% domestic; 20% foreign.

Number of titles sold last year: Maass: 75. Jackson: 30.

Rejection rate (all submissions): 99%.

Most common mistakes authors make: Long summaries. You need only three things to hook me on your story: setting, protagonist, problem. Brevity is also good in your bio and career plans.

Description of a dream client: Patient, passionate, dedicated to craft, writes for the joy of it, works well with others, enjoys the publishing game.

Why did you become an agent? Maass: I love books, and I believe that fiction matters. Brummer: Of course, I love books, so discovering new authors is as exciting as it is rewarding. It is wonderful to be part of the process of bringing books to print. Jackson: It grew very naturally out of my love for books and storytelling. I've never looked back.

Comments: Maass: I currently serve on the Board of Directors of the AAR. Interested writers may want to read my book *The Career Novelist,* published in 1996 by Heinemann. Brummer: While writing is a creative process, publishing is a business. If you view it as such, your professional relationships with others in publishing (e.g., editors, agents, publicists) will be more fruitful.

Representative titles: *The Pillars of the World* by Anne Bishop (Penguin/Putnam/ Roc); *Devlin's Luck* by Patricia Bray (Bantam Spectra); *Shadowside* by Linda Castillo (Penguin Putnam); *The Impertinent Miss Bancroft* by Karla Hocker (Kensington); *Blood & Ivory* by P. C. Hodgell (Meisha Merlin); *Children of Cthulhu* by John Pelan and Benjamin Adams (Del Rey); *Annie's Attic* by Patricia Rosemoor (Harlequin Blaze); *Ensign Longknife: Mutineer* by Mike Shepherd (Penguin Putnam/Ace); *Tides of Passion* by Tracy Sumner (Kensington); *Saving Souls* by Lucy Taylor (Penguin Putnam/Oryx).

CAROL MANN AGENCY

55 Fifth Avenue, New York, NY 10003
Mann: 212-206-5635; Esersky: 212-206-5637; Fitzgerald: 212-206-5636

Agents: Carol Mann, Gareth Esersky, Jim Fitzgerald

Born: Mann: July 23, 1949, Cambridge, Massachusetts. Esersky: June 3, 1951, Hanover, New Hampshire. Fitzgerald: El Paso, Texas.

Education: Mann: University High, Chicago; Smith College. Esersky: B.A., Goucher College; M.A. (and Ph.D. studies), Tufts University. Fitzgerald: Jesuit High School, El Paso; Regis College, Denver; University of Colorado, Boulder.

Career history: Mann: Teacher, the Brearley School; educational marketing, Avon Books. Esersky: Editor (Dell, Putnam Berkley, Simon & Schuster), Author (*Please Read This for Me* [Morrow]; *List Yourself for Pregnancy; List Yourself for Parenting* [Andrews McMeel]); and Book Packager. Fitzgerald: Teacher (Indian High School, Santa Fe); Editor (*New York Times,* Doubleday, St. Martin's Press); Author (four books, ranging from *The Ronald Reagan Paperdoll Book* to *The Joys of Smoking*); Book Packager/Designer; Agent.

Hobbies/personal interests: Mann: Tennis, film, social history. Fitzgerald: Member of the National Railroad Historical Society; model railroading; crossword puzzles; photo slide shows; collages (manual and electronic); poetry (both read and written); singer Hazel Dickens, Metallica, and Spanish Prayer in Colonial America. Esersky: Yoga; creative nonfiction; film and theater; family life.

Areas most interested in agenting: Mann: Fiction: Authors Paul Auster, Marita Golden. Nonfiction: history, psychology, health and fitness, alternative medicine, sociology, anthropology, political science, American social history, popular culture, biography, memoir, true crime. Esersky: Parenting, popular psychology, inspiration/religion, narrative nonfiction, self-discovery, Judaica, health, nutrition, popular culture. Fitzgerald: Fiction: First-time authors, such as Douglas Coupland and Rachel Resnick; Spanish authors, such as Ray Loriga and Alberto Fueguet. Nonfiction: Music, biography, socio-pop culture; alternative travel books; anthropology; memoir; Buddhism and enlightened thought; and last but not least, humor (HA-HA).

Areas not interested in agenting: Mann: Any genre fiction (i.e., romance, historicals, mysteries, etc.), children's books, and/or illustrated books. Esersky: Politics and history, fiction, children's books, illustrated books. Fitzgerald: Health; gardening; mysteries, how-to, self-help, cookbooks.

If not agenting, what would you be doing? Esersky: Be an editor, do research, or write. Fitzgerald: Working in conjunction with Jesuits or raising money for a Kurt Cobain Memorial in Rio de Janeiro.

Best way to initiate contact: With a query letter and SASE. No phone or fax queries. No unsolicited manuscripts (query first). Esersky: Query letter with description of proposed work and author information; SASE. No unsolicited manuscripts; query first. Fitzgerald: With a query letter and SASE. No phone, fax, or e-mail queries. No unsolicited manuscripts. (Query letters first.)

Reading-fee policy: No reading fee.

Client representation by category: Mann: Nonfiction, 85%, Fiction, 15%. Esersky: Nonfiction, 80%, Fiction, 20%. Fitzgerald: Nonfiction, 60%; Fiction, 30%; other, 10%.

Commission: 15%.

Number of titles sold last year: Fitzgerald: 15.

Rejection rate (all submissions): Fitzgerald: 98%.

Description of the client from Hell: Fitzgerald: Clients who fail to communicate all the information that they may know. The biggest example is if a particular property has been shopped before and to whom.

Description of a dream client: Mann: Nonfiction: Those who have extensive experience and credentials in their field and are willing to self-promote. Fiction: Stronger writers who have previously had their work published by a (big or small) trade house and/or in a serious literary journal, *Granta, Paris Review, Story,* and so forth. Esersky: Nonfiction: Someone with strong credentials and experience who is a willing self-promoter. An articulate, positive, interested individual who is willing to do the work it takes to get successfully published. Fitzgerald: Writers who are honest, who trust in you, communicate, deliver when expected, don't expect a million dollars, don't complain, are realistic, read other books in their genre, and look ahead.

Why did you become an agent? Fitzgerald: Having been an editor within a house for over two decades, I saw the book publishing business going the way of the television and movie businesses. Talent was being bought and not employed. Editors were no longer expected to be championed for ideas; they were not lauded for excellent line work or editorial skills, but for their financial acumen instead. Their business smarts and savvy were valued more by the house. It was time to get out and return to do what I did best and that is preparing the idea and letting others market and sell it.

What can writers do to enhance their chances of getting you as an agent? Esersky: Generate good, thoughtful, persuasive proposals; know your market and do research about the publishing industry (a little knowledge can go a long way).

Comments: Mann: If you want to write professionally (i.e., for a living), know your market, learn about the process, and be willing to self-promote as you would in any job. Fitzgerald: In five years the traditional publishing business will be half of what it is now. The Internet and the electronic by-products thereon are the new information and enjoyment sources that people are not only gravitating toward but enjoying more. Ask yourself, what do you enjoy more? A good movie or a good book? It is important for publishers to continue to change and remain ahead of the curve. Yes, there will be books, but will they only be instructional manuals for the DVDs that are pocketed in the back? Will the virtual reality experience overcome all the others? Will we even recognize the language that we

M

are now using? @ used to be seen only on ledger sheets designating the exact cost of something. What does it now represent? The electric language world is now here. Notice how the syntax of what you write by hand is completely different from when you use a keyboard. The challenge for everyone involved in this game is to stay creative and ahead of the accountants.

Representative titles: *Bringing Heaven Down to Earth* by Rabbi Tzvi Freeman (Adams Media); *Easy to Love, Difficult to Discipline* by Dr. Becky Bailey (Morrow); *Just Plain Folks* by Lorrain Johnson and Sue Coleman; *Meditation Made Easy* by Lorin Roche (HarperSanFrancisco); *Meditation Secrets for Women* (HarperSanFrancisco); *Monica's Untold Story* by Anonymous; *Radical Healing* by Dr. Rudolph Ballantine (Harmony); *Stop Cancer Before It Starts* by the American Institute for Cancer Research (St. Martin's Press); *The Fire of Discontent* by Jeffrey Jones (Hazeldon); *Timbuktu* by Paul Auster (Holt). Mann: *The Unexpected Legacy of Divorce* by Dr. Judith Wallerstein (Hyperion); *E=MC²* by David Bodanis (Walker); *The Last Days: A Son's Story of Sin and Segregation at the Dawn of the New South* by Charles Marsh (Basic); *The Protein Power Lifeplan* by Drs. Mike and Mary Dan Eades (Warner); *The Holocaust Kid* by Sonia Pilcer (Persea); *Escape Your Shape* by Edward Jackowski, Ph.D. (Pocket Books); *Peaceful Parents, Peaceful Kids* by Naomi Drew (Kensington). Fitzgerald: *Hell's Angel* by Sonny Barger (William Morrow); *Digital Hustlers* by Casey Kait and Stephen Weiss (Regan/HarperCollins).

MANUS & ASSOCIATES LITERARY AGENCY, INC.

375 Forest Avenue, Palo Alto, CA 94301
650-470-5151   fax: 650-470-5159
www.ManusLit.com   e-mail: ManusLit@ManusLit.com

Agents: Janet Wilkens Manus, Jillian W. Manus, Jandy Nelson, Stephanie Lee, Laura Bradford

Born: Janet Wilkens Manus: Hartford, Connecticut. Jillian Manus: April 26—That's all you get, in New York City. Nelson: November 25, 1965, New York. Lee: August 6, Palo Alto, California. Bradford: February 6, San Francisco, California.

Education: Janet Wilkens Manus: B.A. and M.A. Jillian Manus: NYU Film School and life. Nelson: B.A., Cornell University; M.F.A., Brown University. Lee: B.A. in Literature, Stanford University. Bradford: B.A. in Literature, UC San Diego.

Career history: Janet Wilkens Manus: Formerly, Foreign Rights Agent for British and foreign publishers; East Coast Rep for the *Guinness Book of World Records*. Jillian Manus: TV agent at ICM, Director of Development at Warner Bros. and Universal Studios, VP of Production for Dino Delaurentis, VP of Media Acquisitions at Trender AG in Zurich, Associate Publisher of two national magazines dealing in entertainment and technology sections. Nelson: I worked in academic teaching, creative writing, and drama and worked in theater and film, doing everything from stage management to dramatizing. Lee: I worked in this office during college and never left. Bradford: Bookstore Manager, Career Counselor, Creative Magazine Editor.

Hobbies/personal interests: Janet Wilkens Manus: Travel, arts, football, interrelating with three adult daughters, two grandsons, and husband. Jillian Manus: Yoga, old movies,

M

classic literature, boxing, ballet, gymnastics, critiquing, movies, waterskiing; all sports, political efforts, child rearing, and children's health and welfare. Nelson: Books, film, theater, hiking, traveling, festivity, poetry. Lee: Movies, books, music, pop culture, sculpture, kitsch, camping. Bradford: Travel, writing, books, skiing, swimming, football games, adopting causes, caffeine, competition. I once jumped out of an airplane.

Areas most interested in agenting: Janet Wilkens Manus: True crime with TV/film potential; issue-based true crime; parenting; food books (cookbooks and food memoirs); unique mysteries. Jillian Manus: Women's commercial literary fiction, fiction that I can successfully sell into the movie/TV marketplace, health and nutrition, sports, prescriptive self-help and self-esteem, biographies/memoirs, dramatic narrative fiction, politics, parenting, high-concept suspense/thrillers, child rearing. Nelson: Literary fiction, multicultural fiction, memoirs, thrillers, commercial fiction, women's fiction; narrative nonfiction; women's issues; intelligent, prescriptive self-help; health; pop culture. Lee: Commercial literary fiction, dark/quirky fiction, prescriptive self-help memoirs, narrative nonfiction, Gen X/Gen Y issues, young voices. Bradford: Commercial fiction, mysteries, sexy thrillers, historicals, contemporary romance, memoirs, prescriptive self-help, health issues.

Areas not interested in agenting: Janet Wilkens Manus: Romance, science fiction, poetry, espionage, textbooks, computer books, Westerns, magazine articles. Jillian Manus: Romantic novels, horror, sci-fi/fantasy, children's, Westerns, textbooks, cookbooks, craft books, travel, poetry, magazine queries and articles, computers, technology. Nelson: Romance, fantasy, sci-fi, Westerns, horror, poetry, children's, cookbooks, craft books, screenplays. Lee: Romance, fantasy, science fiction, Westerns, horror, children's, poetry, screenplays, mystery, magazine articles, gift books, cookbooks. Bradford: Screenplays, poetry, magazine articles, gift books, fantasy, science fiction, horror, children's, cookbooks.

If not agenting, what would you be doing? Janet Wilkens Manus: Secret service agent, educator. Jillian Manus: I would love to be a teacher, an honest politician, a child psychologist, or an Olympic gymnast. Nelson: Teaching, climbing Mt. Everest, being a rock star! Lee: Writing, editing, filmmaking, or launching a new magazine. Bradford: I don't know, can I be James Bond?

Best way to initiate contact: Fiction: Send a compelling pitch letter with the first 30 pages and an SASE. Nonfiction: Send a compelling pitch letter and bio, and an SASE. Please do not query call.

Reading-fee policy: No reading fee.

Client representation by category: Janet Wilkens Manus: Nonfiction, 70%; Fiction, 30%. Lee: Nonfiction, 40%; Fiction, 60%; Bradford: Nonfiction, 25%; Fiction, 75%. Jillian Manus: Nonfiction, 60%; Fiction, 40%. Nelson: Nonfiction, 50%; Fiction, 50%.

Commission: 15% for domestic publication and worldwide motion pictures and TV; 25% for foreign publication, only if co-agented.

Number of titles sold last year: A lot!

Rejection rate (all submissions): 95%.

Most common mistakes authors make: Janet Wilkens Manus: Calling instead of writing with their bio and proposal (nonfiction) or three chapters (fiction). Jillian Manus: They call instead of introducing themselves and their projects in queries. Nelson: They call instead of querying.

M

Description of a dream client: Janet Wilkens Manus: A talented writer who is a team player. Jillian Manus: A great writer who works well in a team effort. Nelson: An awesome and disciplined writer with a delightful disposition. Lee: An enthusiastic and well-rounded writer who plays well with others. Bradford: Communicative, productive, ambitious, filled with enthusiasm and originality.

How did you become an agent? Janet Wilkens Manus: My husband (a publishing lawyer) talked me into it. Jillian Manus: My mother talked me into it! Nelson: I badgered Jillian Manus. Lee: I badgered Jandy Nelson. Bradford: I badgered Stephanie Lee.

Why did you become an agent? Janet Wilkens Manus: I love books and think it is a wonderful calling. Jillian Manus: Because I love working with writers, as I truly respect their dedication and craft. Nelson: To work with writers and to help bring writing into the world that will move, enrich, inspire, and delight the reading public. Lee: Because books are magical and working with writers is equally so. Bradford: I started as a writer. Actually, I had just begun tiptoeing my way through the publishing world, trying to find a place to plant myself, when I met an agent at a conference. She told me what it was that agents did and whammo! I was hooked. Nothing else would feel this right.

What can writers do to enhance their chances of getting you as an agent? Fiction: We rely on the quality of the writing. Nonfiction: It is helpful for a nonfiction writer to have a platform and additional avenues of distribution, such as lecture circuits, seminars, and so forth.

How would you describe what you actually do for a living? Janet Wilkens Manus: I keep my eyes open, nurture, and enjoy. Jillian Manus: I search, nurture, sell, and celebrate. Nelson: Rejoicing in writers and their words. Lee: Treasure hunting. Bradford: I search for diamonds in the rough.

What do you think about editors? Janet Wilkens Manus: A talented and caring editor means everything. Jillian Manus: I think savvy editors are worth their weight in gold. Nelson: They are the wizards behind the curtains.

What do you think about publishers? Janet Wilkens Manus: I respect them for having a tough time in the present climate of publishing. Jillian Manus: I respect and pity them at the same time. Bradford: Keeping an eye on the bottom line in a subjective and charged creative atmosphere is a formidable job and one I do not envy.

Representative titles: *Catfish and Mandala* by Andrew Pham (Farrar, Straus & Giroux); *Getting It Right: How Working Mothers Successfully Take Up the Challenge of Life, Family, and Career* by Dr. Laraine Zappert (Pocket Books); *The World of Normal Boys* by K. M. Soehnlien (Kensington); *Breast Cancer Beyond Convention: Alternative Therapies for Women with Breast Cancer* ed. by Mary Tagliaferri, Debu Tripathy, and Isaac Cohen (Pocket Books); *Life's an Open Book: Bibliotherapy a Novel Approach to Living* (Riverhead); *The Territory of Men: One Woman's Trespass* by Joelle Fraser (Random House); *Dream of the Walled City* by Lisa Huang Fleischman (Pocket Books); *The One-Minute Millionaire* by Mark Victor Hansen and Robert Allen (Harmony/Three Rivers); *The Last City Room* by Al Martinez (St. Martin's Press); *Matt Makes a Run for the Border* by Texas icon, chef Matt Martinez (Lebhar-Friedman). *Cane River* by Lalita Tademy (Warner); *Forgive for Good* by Dr. Frederick Luskin (HarperCollins); *Business Plan for the Body* by Jim Karas (Three Rivers).

M

MARCH TENTH, INC.

4 Myrtle Street, Haworth, NJ 07641
201-387-6551

Agent: Sandra Choron

Born: March 10, 1950, New York City.

Education: B.A., Lehman College, New York.

Career history: As an Editor, Publisher, Author, and Book Producer, I have had experience in all aspects of book publishing at both large (Dell) and small (Hawthorn) firms.

Hobbies/personal interests: Popular culture, music, folk art, painting.

Areas most interested in agenting: Popular culture, history, general nonfiction, music, commercial fiction, fine fiction, self-help (those without credentials need not apply), biography, new trends, novelties.

Areas not interested in agenting: Genre fiction, techno-thrillers, politics, personal memoirs of people who never did anything interesting, special interest, picture books, short fiction, poetry.

If not agenting, what would you be doing? Writing.

Best way to initiate contact: Submit a query letter (with SASE).

Reading-fee policy: No reading fee.

Client representation by category: Nonfiction, 90%; Fiction, 10%.

Commission: 15% domestic; 20% foreign or dramatic rights.

Number of titles sold last year: 20.

Rejection rate (all submissions): 90%.

Most common mistakes authors make: They fail to describe the project in a concise way. They fail to state their credentials. I don't like being hyped. Facts and sales ammunition are great, but if there are three exclamation points in your first paragraph, my BS-detector goes crazy!

Description of the client from Hell: Someone who is convinced that "everyone" will buy his book.

Description of a dream client: Tall, dark . . .

How did you become an agent? It's a long story. . . .

Why did you become an agent? As an editor, my interests always exceeded the capabilities of any one publisher. Agenting allows me great range and flexibility.

What can writers do to enhance their chances of getting you as an agent? Know your audience.

How would you describe what you actually do for a living? I make books happen.

What do you think about editors? They come in too many shapes and sizes to generalize.

What do you think about publishers? See above.

What were your favorite films last year? Home movies of my vacation in Mexico; *Being John Malkovich.*

Do you watch the *Sopranos?* Fuggetaboudit.

Comments: Publishing a book is an incredibly gratifying experience. It can also be unbelievably grueling. Enter at your own risk.

Representative titles: *Song* by Bruce Springsteen (Avon); *Sex* by John Waters and Bruce Hainley (Thames and Hudson); *If: Questions for the Game of Life* (series) by Evelyn

McFarlane and James Saywell (Villard); *We Shall Overcome* by Dave Marsh (Simon & Schuster); *And My Shoes Keep Walking Back to You* by Kathi Goldmark (Chronicle); *Bitch Slap!* by Darius James (Feral House).

M

MARGRET MCBRIDE LITERARY AGENCY

7744 Fay Avenue, Suite 201, La Jolla, CA 92037
858-454-1550   fax: 858-454-2156
www.mcbrideliterary.com   e-mail: staff@mcbridelit.com

Agent: Margret McBride
   Career history: Random House, Ballantine Books, Warner Books.
   Areas most interested in agenting: Commercial fiction/nonfiction and business.
   Areas not interested in agenting: Children's books, poetry, genre and category romance, scientific/professional (nontrade) books, textbooks, magazine articles.
   If not agenting, what would you be doing? I would be a Prima ballerina.
   Best way to initiate contact: Write a query letter. Visit our Web site for the submission process.
   Reading-fee policy: No reading fee.
   Client representation by category: Nonfiction, 85%; Fiction, 15%.
   Commission: 15% domestic; 25% foreign.
   Number of titles sold last year: We have had as many as six books at one time on the *Business Week* bestseller list.
   Rejection rate (all submissions): We take only very few spectacular new works.
   Most common mistakes authors make: Asking to meet before we review the project. Assuming that the people who work for me do not talk to me at least 20 times a day!
   Description of the client from Hell: I wouldn't know, I don't allow myself to go there.
   Description of a dream client: An author who remembers he is writing a book for readers to love, enjoy, inform, and possibly help.
   How did you become an agent? Everyone I know in publishing told me I should be one so I took a chance.
   Why did you become an agent? I'm addicted to great ideas. Also as a way of getting revenge. My mother used to warn me that no one was ever going to pay me for just reading books all day.
   What can writers do to enhance their chances of getting you as an agent? Demonstrate they are willing and capable of promoting their books—with enthusiasm!!
   How would you describe what you actually do for a living? I take nice people and turn them into monsters.
   If not agenting, what would you be doing? I would be a senator or governor of California first, then president of the United States. So U.S. citizens can be grateful that I became an agent.
   What do you think about editors? Hardworking, brilliant, and should get more credit for their work. Every publisher's catalogue should list the editor who championed the book through the process.

M

What do you think about publishers? Need to adapt a new way of learning what the public wants so they won't be so surprised when books sell millions of copies because of a "fluke." Market research is the one missing ingredient. Publishers as a whole are really special people who do their work because they really want to make the world think from time to time. They want to make a difference. They should all be named for saints when they move on.

Do you watch the *Sopranos?* Two times—Too violent.

Comments: Publishers should give incentives to the PR department so that they will feel motivated not to take *no* for an answer. This is the one weak link at most publishers. More time needs to be spent on making authors more promotable. A publisher will spend half a million dollars on an author and never suggest media training.

Representative titles: *Thirteen Senses* by Victor Villasenor; *Incriminating Evidence* by Sheldon Siegel; *High Five* by Ken Blancherd and Sheldon Brules; *Fish!* by Stephen C. Ludien, John Christian, and Harry Paul; *Fierce Conversations* by Susan Scott; *Whoever Makes the Most Mistakes Wins* by Richard Faism, Ph.D., and Ralph Keyes; *Step Wars* by Grace Gabe and Jane Cysma; *Mind Like Water* by Jan Ballard.

McIntosh and Otis, Inc.

353 Lexington Avenue, 15th Floor, New York, NY 10016
212-687-7400

Agents: Juvenile Department: Tracey Adams; Adult Department: Eugene Winick, Sam Pinkus, Elizabeth Winick, Evva Pryor—Motion picture/television department.

Career history: McIntosh and Otis, Inc., has been representing authors since 1927 and has one of the oldest juvenile departments in the country.

Areas most interested in agenting: Material that is fresh, original, and special in some way.

Best way to initiate contact: Adult and juvenile fiction or nonfiction, send a query letter and sample chapter (include SASE). For picture books, send the entire manuscript.

Reading-fee policy: No reading fee.

Commission: 15%.

Sally Hill McMillan & Associates

429 East Kingston Avenue, Charlotte, NC 28203
704-334-0897   fax: 704-334-1897
e-mail: mcmagency@aol.com

Agent: Sally McMillan

Education: M.A. in English, University of Carolina-Charlotte.

Career history: After teaching English a few years, I started my own publishing career in the marketing department of UNC Press, Chapel Hill, in 1974. Then I started up a small

M

publishing company, East Woods Press, and ran it from 1977–1987, sold it to Globe Pequot Press, stayed on as editor from 1987–1990, began my own literary agency in 1990.

Hobbies/personal interests: Travel, French language, cruising, reading.

Areas most interested in agenting: Southern fiction, women's mainstream fiction, mystery/suspense, health, psychology, history, Americana.

Areas not interested in agenting: Romance, science fiction, fantasy, children's books, cookbooks.

Best way to initiate contact: Fiction: Query with SASE. Nonfiction: Proposal with SASE.

Client representation by category: Nonfiction, 70%; Fiction, 30%.

Commission: 15%; 20% on co-agented subrights sales.

Description of the client from Hell: Although I don't have any clients from Hell, I imagine one to be someone who thinks only of herself and is not appreciative of the time and effort I and others expend on her behalf. I find that my more successful clients are those who understand the business from multiple points of view, including mine, and realize that they need to care for and feed their agent in order to be cared for and fed in return.

Description of the dream client: My dream clients are those who are considerate of my time, listen to and follow my advice, provide all information requested and offer more if needed, work hard to promote their books, work even harder to write the best books possible, and are ambitious and realistic about their careers.

Most common mistakes authors make: Calling and asking to take me to lunch before sending me their work, sending the wrong kind of projects to me.

What can writers do to enhance their chances of getting you as their agent? Follow my advice about the dream client.

Why did you become an agent? I love working directly with writers and found that running a growing press meant that I had to give that up more and more. As an agent, I get to be as proactive as I want to be in shaping a book. I also love the flexibility of the job and the variety of work experience that goes along with it.

If not agenting, what might you be doing? I would be writing or teaching if I weren't so consumed by other people's writings and teachings.

How would you describe what you do for a living? I play matchmaker all day long and help make people's dreams come true. It's a wonderfully satisfying job.

How did you become an agent? Some of my former authors asked me to place their books. I did it for love and got hooked.

What do you think about editors? Most editors I know care very much about writers and are often frustrated because they cannot make things happen for them.

What do you think about publishers? Most publishers I know have the finest intentions. I know from experience that they have a very difficult job and an enormous responsibility.

Comments: I don't claim to have created it, but my favorite advice to writers is "Perseverance rewards talent."

Representative titles: *Friendship Cake, The Things I Know Best, Garden of Faith,* and *A Clean Heart* by Lynne Hinton (HarperSanFrancisco); *Fire in the Rock* by Joe Martin (Ballantine); *Home Across the Road* by Nancy Peacock (Bantam); *Sins of the Brother, Dog*

M

Island, and *A Clean Kill* by Mike Stewart (Putnam); *Don't Let Your Mind Stunt Your Growth* by Bryan Robinson (New Harbinger); *Wedding Etiquette for Divorced Families* by Martha Woodham (Contemporary/McGraw Hill); *20,000 Secrets of Tea* by Victoria Zak (Dell).

CLAUDIA MENZA LITERARY AGENCY

1170 Broadway, Suite 807, New York, NY 10001
212-889-6850

Agent: Claudia Menza

Career history: 1969–1973, Assistant Editor, *Evergreen Review;* 1973–1983, various titles, Managing Editor before leaving, Grove Press; 1983–present, President, Claudia Menza Literary Agency; published writer; member, Academy of American Poets; member, Italian American Writers Association; member, P.E.N.

Areas most interested in agenting: African-American fiction and nonfiction, photography books, general nonfiction that concerns social and political issues.

Areas not interested in agenting: Science fiction, poetry, plays, mysteries, thrillers, memoir, romance, textbooks, children's books.

If not agenting, what would you be doing? Being a publisher.

Best way to initiate contact: Query letter, outline, and 20-page sample if nonfiction. Query letter and 50-page sample if fiction. SASE must be included with both. No phone calls.

Reading-fee policy: No reading fee.

Client representation by category: Nonfiction, 50%; Fiction, 50%.

Commission: 15% on all rights represented, except in case of a co-agent being used (film, dramatic, or foreign rights) and then it's 20%.

Rejection rate (all submissions): 80%.

Most common mistakes authors make: Calling to solicit interest in their manuscripts. Calling us to see if we've either received or read their manuscripts. Not including an SASE with submissions. Asking if they can deliver the manuscript in person.

What can writers do to enhance their chances of getting you as an agent? Be understanding about our time; we receive between 10 and 20 manuscripts per day.

Description of the client from Hell: A client who calls several times a week for updates on a book's submission status or calls with questions several times a week instead of saving all questions for one call. A client who makes unreasonable requests of a publisher: a 15-city author tour when sales don't warrant it; a full-page ad in the *New York Times* when a book has sold 5,000 copies; a car to take the author to a meeting with a publisher (yes, someone actually has requested that); a six-figure advance for a second book when the first book sold 5,000 copies.

Description of a dream client: Writers who keep in mind the realities of the publishing business; who make their phone calls short, unless a long call is warranted; who trust what the agent is telling them and don't try to convince the agent to do something that is not in the their best interests. After all, why hire a professional if you don't want to follow that person's advice? Having said that, dream clients also come up with imaginative ideas as to how best to promote their work and themselves.

Why did you become an agent? I love books. I love writers.

How would you describe what you do for a living? Represent the work of writers and manage their careers. Help them to develop into the kinds of writers they want to be.

Representative titles: *Some Sunday* by Margaret Johnson (Dafina Books/Kensington); *Shades of Jade* by Gloria Mallette (Strivers Row/Random House); *Trophy Man* by Joy McElroy, M.D. (Simon & Schuster); *Inc. Yourself 10th Edition* by Judith H. McQuown (Career Press); *Black Theater in the African Continuum* by Paul Carter Harrison et al. (Temple University Press); *Stagolee* by Cecil Brown (Ballantine/One World/Random House).

DORIS S. MICHAELS LITERARY AGENCY, INC.

1841 Broadway, Suite 903, New York, NY 10023
212-265-9474   fax: 212-265-9480
www.dsmagency.com

Agents: Doris S. Michaels; Faye Bender

Born: Michaels: May 1955, Lodi, California.

Education: B.A. in English and German Literature, University of California at Santa Cruz; M.A.T. in German and English, University of California at Berkeley; Certificate in Computer Technology, Columbia University; Certificate in Book and Magazine Publishing, Summer Publishing Institute, New York University. Bender: B.A., Wellesley College.

Career history: Acquisitions Editor for Prentice Hall, 1982–1984; Technology Consultant and Trainer for PHINET and Prudential-Bache, 1984–1987; International Information Center Manager for Union Bank of Switzerland, based in Zurich, 1987–1992; independent Literary Agent based in NYC, 1994–present. Bender: Associate, Nicholas Ellison, Inc.

Hobbies/personal interests: Reading, music, especially listening to classical music and playing the violin. Sports, especially mountain biking, skiing, and swimming. Computers. Bender: Hiking, camping, archaeology.

Areas most interested in agenting: Fiction: commercial fiction, literary fiction, women's fiction, novels with strong screen potential. Adult nonfiction (hardcovers and trade paperbacks): Biographies, business, classical music, sports, women's issues. Multimedia electronic works for computers. Bender: Commercial fiction, literary fiction, women's fiction, serious nonfiction, politics, popular culture, biography.

Areas not interested in agenting: Science fiction, fantasy, mysteries, thrillers, romances, Westerns, occult and supernatural, horror stories, poetry, textbooks, religion, film scripts, cookbooks, diet books, short stories, articles, humor, professional manuals. Bender: Any genre work, religion, poetry.

If not agenting, what would you be doing? Touring as a concert violinist. Bender: I'd be working on an archaeological dig in Central America or ensconced in the purgatory that is graduate school.

Best way to initiate contact: E-mail: mail@dsmagency.com. Please, no calls.

Reading-fee policy: No reading fee.

Client representation by category: Nonfiction, 50%; Fiction, 50%.

Commission: 15%.

Number of titles sold last year: 30.

N

Rejection rate (all submissions): 98%.

Most common mistakes authors make: They send an unprofessional query letter. Bender: Typos in a query letter, calling to confirm receipt (chances are, we received it).

Description of the client from Hell: I only work with clients with whom I can develop a good working relationship. Bender: An author who doesn't appreciate the enormous amount of work that goes into getting a book published.

Description of a dream client: Someone who has talent, understands the publishing process, appreciates the hard work I do, and listens carefully. Bender: Someone who has the talent to develop a fresh idea and the insight to think of me.

How did you become an agent? After attending New York University's Summer Publishing Institute, I began my own agency in 1994.

Why did you become an agent? I enjoy reading good fiction and the process of helping talented writers get published.

How would you describe what you actually do for a living? I seek out talented writers and help them get published. I work closely with them to help them grow and build their careers. My time is spent maintaining the connections that I have with some of the industry's top editors, reading the projects of my clients and projects from potential clients, and giving my best efforts to ensure the production of high-quality work and the most professional image possible for my agency.

What do you think about editors? The best editors are those who respond in a timely manner to submissions. They are willing to negotiate contracts to ensure the best deal possible for all parties concerned. They are passionate about their projects, and they are willing to work closely with both the author and me as a team to help build the author's career.

Representative titles: Michaels: *Cycles: How We'll Live, Work and Buy* by Maddy Dychtwald (Free Press); *How to Be a Great Boss* by Jeffrey H. Fox (Hyperion); *The Neatest Little Guide to Do-It-Yourself Investing* by Jason Kelly (Plume); *Safety Net* by Kathleen Sindell (John Wiley & Sons); *Quantum Leading* by Hamilton Beazley (John Wiley & Sons). Bender: *In the River Sweet* by Patricia Henley (Pantheon); *Blue Cats and Chartreuse Kittens* by Patricia Duffy (Henry Holt & Co.); *Pink Think: Or How to Become a Woman in Many Uneasy Lessons* by Lynn Peril (W. W. Norton); *Yell-Oh Girls!* by Vickie Nam (HarperCollins); *Shacking Up: The Smart Woman's Guide to Living in Sin Without Getting Burned* by Stacy and Wynne Whitman (Broadway Books).

JEAN V. NAGGAR LITERARY AGENCY

216 East 75th Street, 1E, New York, NY 10021
212-794-1082

Agents: Jean V. Naggar, Anne Engel, and Alice Tasman

Born: Tasman: May 26, 1967, Philadelphia, Pennsylvania.

Education: Naggar: B.A., with Honors, London University. Engel: Bachelor of Laws, London University. Tasman: B.A., Brown University, 1989; M.F.A., Sarah Lawrence College, 1994.

Career history: Naggar: Writer, Editor, Translator, Book Reviewer. Engel: 20 years as an Editor in British publishing houses. Tasman: Jean V. Naggar Literary Agency in subrights and agenting my own list from 1995–present.

Hobbies/personal interests: Naggar: Parenting, reading, music, business, travel, cooking. Wide-ranging other interests that do not include sports and politics. Engel: Looking at cities, cooking, and entertaining.

Areas most interested in agenting: Naggar: Fiction: strong, well-written mainstream fiction, literary fiction, contemporary, suspense, historical fiction, mysteries. Nonfiction: biography, literary autobiography or memoirs, science for the layperson, psychology, and sophisticated self-help. Engel: Science, biography, exclusively nonfiction. Tasman: Literary/commercial nongenre fiction, literary thrillers, multicultural nonfiction, celebrity biographies.

Areas not interested in agenting: Naggar: Sports, politics, category fiction, most science fiction, KGB/South American drug-cartel espionage. Engel: Fiction, children's books, coffee-table books, children's books. Tasman: Science fiction, fantasy fiction, romance, self-help.

If not agenting, what would you be doing? Tasman: Working in the production office of a film company, or maybe I'd be teaching high school English.

Best way to initiate contact: Naggar: Query letter. Engel: An enthusiastic, balanced letter. Tasman: Query letter.

Reading-fee policy: No reading fee.

Client representation by category: Naggar: Nonfiction, 45%; Fiction, 45%; Children's, 10%. Engel: Nonfiction, 100%. Tasman: Nonfiction, 10%; Fiction, 90%;

Commission: 15% domestic; 20% international. Tasman: 15% of advance; 10% of subrights sales. Kuffel: 15% domestic; 20% international.

Number of titles sold last year: Naggar: 47. Tasman: 6, it was my first year agenting.

Rejection rate (all submissions): 96%. Tasman: 75%.

Most common mistakes authors make: Naggar: Not doing any background research on agents before contacting; asking, Do you want to see my work? without describing it; calling every five minutes to check up on things—a sure precursor of the client from Hell! Tasman: Too many calls before we've agreed to take them on.

Description of the client from Hell: Naggar: An author who has chosen me as an agent but never quite trusts me. Tasman: Clients who ask to read and/or write their submission letters. Unpublished authors who ask if they can quit their jobs. An unemployed client. An unpublished author who is banking on a six-figure advance.

Description of a dream client: Naggar: Talented, appreciative, intelligent, knowledgeable. Tasman: A client who lets you do your job; a relationship based in trust and faith. A client who isn't afraid to move on to the next project. Clients who don't nag; who are patient and realize that their job is temporarily finished—now it's my turn to roll up your sleeves; get to it.

How did you become an agent? Tasman: I was getting my M.F.A. at Sarah Lawrence College. I worked as an intern for the Wendy Weil Agency. I was extremely interested in books and film. Wendy strongly suggested I look for a job in subrights, which is where I started at this agency.

Why did you become an agent? Naggar: I love reading and respect writers. I enjoy being an advocate for writers I respect. Tasman: I love books and people. I thought I wanted to be a writer, but realized that I am much more effective and happy being part of someone else's creative process.

What can writers do to enhance their chances of getting you as an agent? Tasman: Give me time to thoroughly assess their work! Naggar: Present themselves well, have patience to wait out my heavy reading schedule, and make no early outrageous claims for their work.

How would you describe what you actually do for a living? Tasman: I represent writers; I am the liaison between a writer and a publisher. I read manuscripts, edit manuscripts, pitch manuscripts to editors, and place them with the appropriate publishing house. Naggar: Indulge my reading enthusiasms and then enlist the world to take pleasure with me! Read and negotiate strong contracts. Supervise and set in motion every possible venue to enhance a client's career.

What do you think about editors? Tasman: I am grateful for editors They're vital.

What do you think about publishers? Tasman: Ditto.

Comments: Tasman: How difficult it is to find a home for literary fiction and good quality fiction in general!

Representative titles: *Lucky in the Corner* by Carol Anshaw (Houghton Mifflin); *The Shelters of Stone* by Jean M. Auel (Crown); *China Run* by David Ball (Simon & Schuster); *In the Yikes Zone: A Conversation with Fear* by Mermer Blakeslee (Plume); *Drastic* by Maud Casey (Morrow); *Self-Coaching: How to Heal Anxiety and Depression* by Joe Luciani (Wiley); *The Associate* by Phillip Margolin (HarperCollins); *Wild Justice* by Phillip Margolin (HarperCollins); *Fiona Range* by Mary McGarry Morris (Viking); *Greenwichtown* by Joyce Palmer (St. Martin's Press); *Rashomon Gate* by Ingrid Parker (St. Martin's Press); *Nectar* by Lily Prior (Ecco Press/HarperCollins); *Eyes of the Albatross* by Carl Safina (Holt); *Saving Your Brain* by Jeff Victoroff (Bantam Dell).

THE CRAIG NELSON COMPANY

115 West 18th Street, Fifth Floor, New York, NY 10011
212-929-3242   fax: 212-929-3667
e-mail: litagnt@aol.com

Agent: Craig Nelson

Born: February 6, 1955, Marion, Indiana.

Career history: Twenty years in the book industry, previously Executive Editor and Vice President of Random House, Hyperion, and HarperCollins.

Hobbies/personal interests: Third World travel, being frightened.

Areas most interested in agenting: Dramatic nonfiction, storytelling, history, biography, current affairs, psychology and science, literary fiction with an "outsider" perspective.

Areas not interested in agenting: Category mystery, romance, sci-fi, fantasy, domestic dramas, and excessively fanciful New Age/spiritual tomes.

If not agenting, what would you be doing? I'd give up all my real estate and pare down to the absolute essentials, and put them in a box. Then I'd wander the globe, just me and my box.

Best way to initiate contact: Query first (e-mail preferred; fax forbidden). If snail mail, include an SASE.

Reading-fee policy: No reading fee.

Client representation by category: Nonfiction, 75%; Fiction, 25%.

Commission: 15% domestic, 20% foreign.

Number of titles sold last year: 15.

Rejection rate (all submissions): I'd guess 1,000 to 1.

Most common mistakes authors make: Most novice writers don't do the research to find out what agents work in their category, not realizing that publishing is a very specialized business. I don't know anything about the mass-market original mysteries, romance, and other category fiction, and I don't know anything about children's literature, cookbooks, or scientific and technical publications, so I can't work in those fields.

Why did you become an agent? As a book company Editor I had 15 bestsellers, and every single one of them did great things for their authors, agents, and publishers . . . but not for their editor.

What can writers do to enhance their chances of getting you as an agent? In nonfiction, follow the rules of attention-grabbing journalism (well outlined in James Stewart's book *Follow the Story*). In fiction, do something groundbreaking, so that when it's published two years from now, it'll be fresh and original.

How would you describe what you actually do for a living? (1) Convince authors to make their manuscripts salable. (2) Convince publishers to take a chance. (3) Provide a haven in a heartless world. (4) Remember that "life is just a bowl of cherries," . . . and so forth and so on.

New Brand Agency Group

A Division of Alter-Entertainment LLC
370 Jefferson Drive, Suite 204, Deerfield Beach, FL 33442
954-764-3331   fax: 954-725-6461
www.literaryagent.net   e-mail: AgentNB@aol.com

Agent: Mark Ryan
  Born: March 17, 1971.
  Education: Psychology, Ambassador University.
  Career history: Before becoming an agent, I spent seven years as a success coach for various populations: executives, developmentally delayed adults; the homeless; and disadvantaged youth (abused and neglected teens, including jailed offenders). During that time, I led workshops, facilitated groups, engaged in private sessions, and wrote behavior modification programs. This period of my life was fulfilling, but I still hadn't found an outlet for my other passion: publishing. I had always thought that a degree in English or journalism, or an M.F.A. degree, was a prerequisite for being successful (as an agent,

editor, or author). Don't misunderstand . . . these things are helpful. But it is more important that you have an understanding of, and appreciation for, human nature (including your own) and the human condition; as well as an understanding of, and appreciation for, history and popular culture. Five years as an agent have shown me that these are the things that make a great agent, editor, or writer. My experience has also shown me that the greatest agents, editors, and writers haven't always lived easy lives, as some might think. Rather, they have followed their hearts—living more out of love than fear—which often means a great deal of pain and struggle before one's "greatness" is ever realized (all the components of a great story, incidentally). Some other things I did along the way, before becoming an agent: weed-puller, lawn cutter, actor (Baltimore Orioles commercial— age 10), bag-boy, prep cook, aircraft parts painter, telemarketer, door-to-door sales, logging foreman, and assistant chemist/metallurgist.

Hobbies: My wife and soul mate (they are the same person, by the way); new ideas and new experiences; people and people-watching; movies; participating at writers' conferences, leadership conferences, and spirituality conferences.

Areas most interested in agenting: Fiction and nonfiction with bestseller or high commercial potential . . . projects with national and/or international appeal likely to sell more than 100,000 copies. Fiction: adult and/or young adult (thrillers, mysteries, suspense, light horror, mainstream, light literary). Nonfiction: popular culture; success/leadership; psychology/self-help; relationships (interpersonal and romantic); spirituality; gift/novelty.

Areas not interested in agenting: Star-Trek novels; anything with the work *intergalactic* in it; genre romance; hard-core science fiction and fantasy; nonfiction sports; erotica; technical writing; poetry (just because I read it, doesn't mean I'd try to sell it); knitting; regional books; short story collections; personal manifestos. Also, books accompanied by query letters that say "Just read it!" or "Send me 20 dollars and I'll send you my manuscript."

Best way to initiate contact: Visit the New Brand Web site (www.literaryagent.net) and review the sample queries posted there. I've spent a great deal of time to provide a content-rich environment. Take advantage of it. Then e-mail your query by clicking on the link provided. You will receive a response directly from me within a day or two if I'm interested. As far as I know, New Brand is the first agency to accept electronic queries only.

Client representation by category: Nonfiction, 50%; Fiction, 25%; Children's, 25% (no picture books).

Commission: 15% domestic; 20% foreign.

Number of titles sold last year: Enough that I've stopped counting.

Rejection rate (all submissions): 99.5%.

Description of the client from Hell: I've heard stories from other agents, but I am proud of all of my clients. A big part of my decision to begin working with an author is based on whether I like, trust, and respect the author, not just the work itself.

Description of the dream client: Has long-term publication goals and studies the industry before seeking representation. Perceives the author–agent relationship as a partnership. Rewards my enthusiasm and hard work with trust and patience.

Most common mistakes authors make: Many writers don't understand that the most experienced agents have seen/heard tens of thousands of pitches (e-mail, letter, phone, and person-to-person at writer's conferences). As a result these agents are able to sense, immediately, if you know what you're talking about. Make sure you are ready, before you present both yourself and your work.

What can writers do to enhance their chances of getting you as an agent? Imagine me sitting in front of 1,000 submissions (the total number of submissions I receive each month), with the intent of selecting one new author for representation. Realize that some of those submissions are from authors who have been previously represented by other agents; already published books with major publishing houses; self-published and sold tens of thousands of copies; paid professional editors thousands of dollars for editing; strong promotional platforms (radio, TV, newspaper, magazines, workshops, and seminars, extensive client mailing lists); M.F.A. degrees; a background in publishing (previously agents, editors, etc.). Once you understand the level of competition, take it very seriously and be sure you are doing everything you can to become the best in your genre. Spend time in places where you will grow—bookstores, workshops, critique groups, reading groups, conferences, and so on. Network and build your promotional platform. Read (or at least skim) many books on craft and marketing. Study your market and target your submissions. Remember that neatness and spelling do count. Finally, keep writing. Regularly. Distinctly. Then find an agent who believes in you—with the knowledge, connections, and energy to make things happen.

Why did you become an agent? I became an agent so I could get my own books published. Along the way I discovered that the lifestyle of a successful agent is just as rewarding as the lifestyle of a successful author. And it allows you to spend time with more people. So now I am living two lives, although agenting is my primary focus.

If not agenting, what might you be doing? It's just not an option. I was born to be an agent.

How would you describe what it is you do for a living? Agents sell books. And the best agents use every tactic (within reason, conscience, and the law), to get it done. In short, agents also: view the author–agent relationship as a partnership; help authors discover and develop their niches; help massage proposals and books into clean, tight, marketable copy; offer strong contacts with publishers; add credibility to their authors' work because of their experience; are aware of the tastes and eccentricities of individual editors and publishers; give authors new book ideas; are energetic and persistent; return calls and correspondence promptly; sort out unexpected catastrophes; help develop speaking platforms and offer other marketing support; are always learning, stretching, growing; aren't afraid to fight for their authors.

How did you become an agent? Through fate or Divine intervention (depending on your own particular beliefs), I met Eric Alterman, the founder of New Brand Agency. I was looking to learn more about publishing since I was an aspiring author. And Eric gave me an opportunity to do just that by making me a partner. During the four years that followed, Eric left me alone to manage New Brand (which let me find and earn my wings), while he established several technology companies. In June 2001 I bought out the agency.

What do you think about editors? Editors want to be involved in developing the next bestseller as badly as you and I. If they receive a project they think and feel will be successful, they will buy it.

What do you think about publishers? Publishers pay my bills. I like them a lot.

N

Comments: Choose your agent carefully. Remember, if you have mastered your craft, you will have several agents to choose from. When you do have several agents interested, talk with them to determine which one is most worth developing a long-term relationship with. By the way, editors do the same thing with agents. I figured that out early on when an editor told me, "I invited you to lunch to see what you are all about. I want to know if I should develop a relationship with you." I wasn't offended because I was there for the same reason (not every editor is exceptional). So, when you are speaking with agents, look for the following three things. Trust—the best agents are open, sincere, reliable, and, contrary to popular opinion, character-centered. Passion—the best agents only work on projects they are passionate about and with authors they are passionate about (in part, because they couldn't live with themselves if they didn't and because it lets them pitch each project with genuine enthusiasm). Competence—the best agents have a strong track record; they are familiar with protocol; they can quickly spot properties with potential to become bestsellers; and they are focused (they don't handle 30 different types of books). Believe in yourself, and don't settle for anything less than the best.

Representative titles: *24/7* and *Flash 5* by Jim Brown (Ballantine); *The Marriage Plan: How to Marry Your Soul Mate in a Year or Less* by Aggie Jordan, Ph.D. (Broadway/ Bantam); *The Body of Christopher Creed* by Carol Plum-Ucci (Harcourt Brace/Paramount); *The Finnegan Zwake Mystery Series* by Michael Dahl (Pocket/Scholastic); *The Young Shakespeare Mystery Series* (Hyperion); *The Misfits, Inc. Mystery Series* by Mark Delaney (Peachtree); *The Crisis Counselor* by Jeff Caponigro (Contemporary); *Eat or Be Eaten* by Phil Porter (Prentice-Hall); *Father to Son* by Harry Harrison (Workman); *The Walrus Was Paul: The Great Beatle Death Clues of 1969* by Gary Patterson (Simon & Schuster); *The Dog's Drugstore* by Dr. Richard Redding and Myrna Weibel, D.V.M. (St. Martin's Press); *The Women's Guide to Legal Issues* by Nancy Jones (Renaissance); *The Husband Book* by Harry Harrison (Andrews McMeel); *The Scooter Spy Mystery Series* by Michael Dahl (Pocket); various mysteries by Rae Foley (Simon & Schuster); various young adult novels by Susan Rottman (Peachtree/Penguin).

New England Publishing Associates, Inc.

PO Box 5, Chester, CT 06412
860-345-7323   fax: 860-345-3660
www.nepa.com   e-mail: nepa@nepa.com

Agents: Elizabeth Frost-Knappman, Edward W. Knappman
Born: EFK: October 1, 1943. EWK: November 17, 1943.
Education: EFK: B.A. in Anthropology, George Washington University, 1965; graduate work at University of Wisconsin and New York University. EWK: B.A. in History, George Washington University, 1965; M.S. in Journalism, Columbia University, 1966.
Career history: EFK: Senior Editor, William Morrow; Senior Editor, Doubleday; Editor, William Collins & Sons (London); Associate Editor, Natural History Press. Author of *Courtroom Drama Vols. 1–3: Women's Suffrage in America, Women's Rights on Trial: 101 Historic Trials from Anne Hutchinson to The Virginia Military Institute Cadets;*

World Almanac of Presidential Quotations, ABC-CLIO History of Women's Progress in America, and *The Quotable Lawyer.* EWK: Publisher of Facts on File; Executive Vice President of Facts on File. Editor of *Great World Trials, Great American Trials, American Jobs Abroad* (with V. Harlow), and *Sex, Sin, and Mayhem.*

Hobbies/personal interests: EFK: Swimming, knitting, gardening, and tennis. EWK: Reading in the areas of history and politics.

Areas most interested in agenting: EFK: Women's subjects, science, biographies, current events, literature. EWK: Reference, history, business, information, self-help, biographies, narrative nonfiction.

Areas not interested in agenting: Personal memoirs, fiction, children's books, screenplays.

If not agenting, what would you be doing? EFK: Traveling. EWK: Traveling.

Best way to initiate contact: Send a well-thought-out proposal with a sample chapter and resume. Check our submission guidelines page at www.nepa.com and follow them.

Reading-fee policy: No reading fee.

Client representation by category: Adult nonfiction, 95%.

Commission: 15%, unless co-agents must be employed for dramatic or foreign rights.

Number of titles sold last year: 65.

Rejection rate (all submissions): 95%.

Most common mistakes authors make: It's important to put in the time and effort to perfect a proposal. The key is to carefully research your competition, not just in the bookstores, but in the libraries, union catalog, and *Books in Print.*

Most common mistakes authors make: Make substitutions in materials; call too soon for a decision; treat the competition too cavalierly.

Description of the client from Hell: There are no clients from Hell, just nervous ones.

Description of a dream client: Professional, flexible about revisions, patient, friendly.

How did you become an agent? In 1982 EFK found it easier to be a parent while working from home, starting a new business.

Why did you become an agent? After many years as an editor (EFK) and publisher (EWK), we wanted to start our own business and move midway between Boston and New York City. Our combined literary agency, book-producing business, and consulting operations allow us to do this. What started as a small business in 1983 has grown to a good-sized one, with five employees to serve clients.

What can writers do to enhance their chances of getting you as an agent? Follow our guidelines for preparing proposals; request a sample proposal if you need a model; make certain your qualifications match the book you wish to write; make your sample chapters the best literary quality you can.

How would you describe what you actually do for a living? Read, edit, query editors, submit your work to publishers, negotiate the best possible sale and contracts, make subsidiary rights sales (foreign, dramatic), do all bookkeeping for the life of your book, problem solve day in, day out.

What do you think about editors? Editors are well read, hardworking, underpaid people who are under constant pressure to turn a profit for the conglomerates that employ them.

What do you think about publishers? Working with most publishers today is like dealing with the Department of Agriculture. No one has sufficient power, efficiency is not at a premium, and decisions are made by committee. So authors would be wise not to try to go it alone.

Comments: The world of publishing has changed so radically in the last 30 years that the business is difficult for authors, agents, and editors alike. Presses want the same genre or brand-name books. Advances are less competitive than ever before. Fortunately, each year start-ups and new imprints emerge to breathe new life into our industry, taking more chances on a first book or a writer without a "platform." Still, our advice to authors is, Don't give up your day job.

Representative titles: *Book of Management Wisdom* (Wiley); *Cigars, Whiskey, & Winning* (Prentice Hall); *Dust* (University of California Press); *Eudora Welty: A Writer's Life* (Doubleday); *How to Live Well Off Your Investments* (Adams); *Ice Blink: The Tragic Fate of Sir John Franklin's Lost Polar Expedition; Penguin Dictionary of American English Usage* (Penguin); *Susan Sontag: The Making of an Icon* (Norton); *The ASPCA Complete Pet Care Manual* (Penguin); *Every Heart Attack Is Preventable* (Lifeline-Regnery); *The Feel Good Curriculum* (Perseus); *The Urban Tree Book* (Crown); *How to Stop Heartburn* (Wiley); *Wireless Rules* (McGraw Hill); *Contrary Winds: Bering Steller & the Russian Discovery of America* (William Morrow); *Women of the Civil War* (Routledge); *Jack London's Women* (University of Massachusetts Press)

THE RICHARD PARKS AGENCY

138 East 16th Street, Suite 5B, New York, NY 10003
212-254-9067

Agent: Richard Parks
   Education: B.A., Duke University; M.A., University of North Carolina.
   Career history: Curtis Brown, Ltd. (1970–1978); United Artists Corporation (1978–1981); Alexander, Smith & Parks (1981–1988); The Richard Parks Agency (1989–present).
   Best way to initiate contact: Fiction: by referral only. Nonfiction: by referral or query letter with SASE.
   Reading-fee policy: No reading fee.
   Client representation by category: Nonfiction, 50%; Fiction, 50%.
   Commission: 15% domestic, 20% foreign.
   Most common mistakes authors make: No calls, e-mail, or faxed queries, please.

JAMES PETER ASSOCIATES, INC.

PO Box 358, New Canaan, CT 06840
fax: 203-972-1759

Agent: Gene Brissie
   Born: New York City.
   Education: Princeton University.

Career history: Farrar, Straus and Giroux; Simon & Schuster; G. P. Putnam's Sons; Contemporary Books; Prentice Hall; James Peter Associates.

Hobbies: Reading, music, history, pop culture, science, sports.

Areas most interested in agenting: All nonfiction areas.

Areas not interested in agenting: Children's books, YA, poetry.

Best way to initiate contact: Query letter with SASE.

Client representation by category: Nonfiction, 100%.

Commission: 15% domestic; 20% foreign.

Number of titles sold last year: 35–40.

Description of the client from Hell: An author who views the writer/publisher relationship as an adversarial one.

Description of the dream client: An author who writes a solid proposal and delivers a good manuscript, on time.

What can writers do to enhance their chances of getting you as an agent? The most salable authors have a strong understanding of the marketplace and they know what has a good chance of selling.

Why did you become an agent? I worked on the other side of the desk as an editor, editor in chief, and publisher for close to 25 years, and I wanted to try this side. I know how to sell to editors and publishers.

If not agenting, what would you be doing? I'd be a publisher.

How would you describe what you do for a living? I help mold proposals, submit and sell them to editors and publishers, negotiate the contracts, and collect and dispense the proceeds for a group of very talented authors.

How did you become an agent? I was fortunate to buy JPA from its founder, Bert Holtje, one of the best.

What do you think about editors? I love them.

What do you think about publishers? I love them.

Do you watch the *Sopranos?* Not regularly; I've seen it a few times.

Representative titles: *Nothing to Fear: Lessons in Leadership from Franklin Delano Roosevelt* by Alan Axelrod (Prentice Hall); *The Encyclopedia of Submarines* by Wilbur Cross (Facts on File); *The Penguin Dictionary of American Folklore* by Harry Oster and Alan Axelrod (Penguin); *Unsolved Mysteries of Science* by John Malone (John Wiley & Sons); *Encyclopedia of the American West* (3 volumes), Zenda Inc. (Macmillan); *Walkin' a Line: A Journey from the Past to the Present Along the Mason Dixon Line* by William Ecenbarger (M. Evans & Co.); *Hepatitis C: The Silent Killer* by Carol Turkington (Contemporary Books); *The Complete Idiot's Guide to Latino History and Culture* by Danilo Figueredo (Alpha Books).

PINDER LANE & GARON-BROOKE ASSOCIATES, LTD.

159 West 53rd Street, Suite 14-E, New York, NY 10019
212-489-0880
e-mail: pinderl@interport.net

Agents: Dick Duane, Nancy Coffey (Consulting Agent), Robert Thixton

Career history: Duane: Agent since 1960, co-owner; also packages feature films, handles movie tie-ins, and has an extensive advertising background. Thixton: Agent since 1975, co-owner. Coffey: Agent since 1992; previously Editorial Adviser to Editor in Chief at Putnam Berkley Publishing; Editorial Director, Ballantine Books and Avon Books.

Areas most interested in agenting: In general, any intriguing well-written book, either fiction or nonfiction. Fiction: Commercial and literary fiction, including thrillers, technothrillers, adventure, romance, science fiction/fantasy, and some young adult fiction. Nonfiction: personal lifestyle, including cookbooks, pop culture, historical biographies, investigative reporting, and natural history.

Areas not interested in agenting: None.

Best way to initiate contact: A one-page query letter briefly describing the author's work. A positive response can be expected within four weeks of submission of a query. There will be no response if the agency is not interested in seeing further material. No unsolicited manuscripts accepted.

Reading-fee policy: No charge for requested material.

Client representation by category: Nonfiction, 25%; Fiction, 75%.

Commission: 15% domestic; 30% foreign.

Number of titles sold last year: 20.

Rejection rate (all submissions): 95%.

Most common mistakes authors make: Telling the agency that they are considering several other agencies, and they will "let you know." Our agency doesn't audition, and that type of potential client will not be signed. Any material submitted to our agency must be on an exclusive basis while we take the time to read and evaluate a manuscript.

Description of the client from Hell: Authors who call asking why their books haven't sold after a very short submission time. An author who does not know the state of the publishing industry, who does not do research "on the shelves" in bookstores. The market is very tough out there, and writers should be as objectively tough on their manuscripts as publishers are when they respond to a submission.

Description of a dream client: Authors who listen to their agents concerning rewrites and editorial work and who know the state of the publishing marketplace. An author who will rewrite and edit, regardless of how many times it is required, knowing that it is critical to have the manuscript in the best possible shape before submitting it to publishers. An author who understands that not all books are sold the "first-time out."

Why did you become an agent? The agents at Pinder Lane & Garon-Brooke Associates, Ltd., have an enduring love of literature in all its forms. To be able to nurture a writer's career strikes us as the most desirable job anyone, anywhere, could have.

What can writers do to enhance their chances of getting you as an agent? They should listen to comments our agents make about their work without becoming defensive. A willingness to listen to suggestions in order to make a manuscript better and salable is the only attitude possible and is often the deciding factor in whether or not a client is signed.

What do you think about editors? In today's changing publishing world, many editors' jobs go beyond what their traditional editorial efforts have been in the past.

Comments: The future of book publishing will be so closely aligned to other media that agents will have to have expertise in all fields of films, television, Internet, electronic, and other new media in order to negotiate the best contracts for their clients. Because our agents have cross-media experience in all areas of publishing, promotion, advertising, and other related fields, we feel Pinder Lane & Garon-Brook Associates, Ltd., is uniquely positioned as a literary/media agency for the publishing industry.

Representative titles: *An Army of Children* by Evan H. Rhodes (Bastei Lube); *Threshold, Fertile Group and Reaper* by Ben Mezrich (HarperCollins); *Getting to the Good Part* and *Scenes from a Sistah* by Lolita Files (Warner Books); *Jealousy* by Nancy Friday (M. Evans & Co.); *Kennedy Weddings, Jackie—The Clothes of Camelot* and *Jackie and Diana—Maidens, Mothers, Myths* by Jay Mulvaney (St. Martin's Press); *The Gemini Man, Nobody's Safe,* and *The 4 Phase Man* by Richard Steinberg (Doubleday); *Protect & Defend* and *Invasion* by Eric Harry (Berkley); *Shattered Bone* and *The Third Consequence* by Chris Stewart (M. Evans & Co.); *The Ladies of Covington Send Their Love* and *Gardens of Covington* by Joan Medlicott (Tom Dunne); *The Sixth Fleet Series* by David Meadows (Berkely).

P

PMA LITERARY AND FILM MANAGEMENT, INC.

45 West 21st Street, 6th Floor, New York, NY 10010
212-929-1222
www.pmalitfilm.com   e-mail: queries@pmalitfilm.com

Agents: Peter Miller, Kate Garrick
   Born: Miller: Atlantic City, New Jersey. Garrick: Virginia Beach, Virginia, July 21, 1977.
   Education: Miller: B.A., Monmouth College. Garrick: B.A. in English Literature (Summa Cum Laude), Florida State University; M.A. in English Literature, New York University.
   Career history: Miller: Founded Writers House, a literary agency, 1972; founded the Peter Miller Agency, 1974; incorporated agency in 1981; founded PMA Literary and Film Management, Inc., 1992. Founded 21st Century Lion, Inc. (a production company) in 1996. Have now been in business for almost 30 years. Garrick: Entire career spent with PMA.
   Hobbies/personal interests: Miller: Traveling, gourmet food and wine, reading, fishing, playing with my daughters (Liseanne and Margo). Garrick: Movies, cooking, swimming, books.
   Areas most interested in agenting: Miller: Action/suspense fiction, thrillers and legal thrillers, history, serious journalism, current events, pop culture. Garrick: Literary fiction, general nonfiction, especially history and pop culture, fringe fiction and nonfiction.
   Areas not interested in agenting: Miller: Poetry, pornography, children's books. Garrick: Cookbooks, children's books, poetry.
   What might you be doing if you weren't an agent? Miller: A publisher or film producer, executive at a film studio.

P

Best way to initiate contact: Miller: Send a query to my attention, detailing the essence of the book and why it is commercial, along with a biography of the author. Garrick: Send a query letter by regular mail or e-mail with a synopsis and a bio.

Reading-fee policy: No.

Client representation by category: Miller: Nonfiction, 20%; Fiction, 60%; Screenplays, 30%. Garrick: Nonfiction, 20%; Fiction, 80%.

Commission: Miller: Domestic 15%; film rights 10–15%; foreign rights 20–25%. Garrick: Domestic: 15%; Film: 10–15%; Foreign: 20–25%.

Number of titles sold last year: Miller: 20. Garrick: One novel.

Rejection rate (all submissions): Miller: 90–95%. Garrick: 95%.

Most common mistakes authors make: Miller: Many authors express a negative attitude toward agents and the publishing industry in general. What a way to win your potential agent's confidence! Garrick: Sending me too much material or following up too soon or too often while being aggressive. It makes me wary of working with them.

Description of the client from Hell: Miller: The client who sends you a handwritten manuscript and calls you every day to see if you have read it.

Description of a dream client: Miller: Clients who trust your judgment and let you work for them. After all, I've been selling books for almost 30 years and I've sold over 800, so I must be doing something right. Garrick: The writer who delivers a professional product on time and who understands my limitations.

Why did you become an agent? Miller: I had always wanted to be involved with films and I figured out early on that a great way to find properties was in the book world. I'm glad it happened this way because I think I'm good at it. I love my work. Garrick: I love books and writing, and I feel this gives me an opportunity to put that passion to a practical use.

What can writers do to enhance their chances of getting you as an agent? Miller: Submit a professional, well-thought-out query letter with a polished synopsis and/or manuscript presentation. Garrick: Send me their very best work and do their research. Find out what I'm looking for and what I've done.

How would you describe what you actually do for a living? Miller: Dealmaker.

If not agenting , what might you be doing? Garrick: Teaching or possibly working as an editor.

What do you think of editors? Miller: They're brilliant, God-like, and I highly respect them.

What do you think about publishers? Miller: Publishers are in the business to make money!

What were your favorite films last year? Garrick: *Sexy Beast, Ghost World, Magnolia* (that was 2000), *Crouching Tiger* (also 2000).

Do you watch the *Sopranos?* Garrick: If I'm near a TV with HBO, yes, but normally no.

Comments: Miller: Writers, write *on!*

Representative titles: *Miss Julia Takes Over* by Ann Ross (Viking); *Satin Doll* by Karen E. Quinones Miller (Simon & Schuster); *Brothers* by Freddie Lee Johnson, III (One World/Ballantine); *The New York Cabbie Cookbook* by Mary Ellen Winston and Holly Garrison (Running Press); *Dream in Color* by Darlene Johnson (HarperCollins);

The Unwanted by Kien Nguyen (Little Brown); *No Finish Line: The Marla Runyan Story* by Marla Runyan (G. P. Putnam's Sons); *Buddha's Child* by former South Vietnam Prime Minister Nguyen Cao Ky and Marvin J. Wolf (St. Martin's Press); *Chocolate for a Woman's Blessings* by Kay Allenbaugh (Fireside, Simon & Schuster); *Walking to Canterbury* by Jerry Ellis (Ballantine); *Quilts Are Forever* by Kathy Lamancusa (Fireside and Simon & Schuster); *Kursk Down!* by Clyde Burleson (Warner Books); *Tolkien on Leadership* by Joe Tye (Prentice Hall); *Final Verdict: The Simple Truth in the Killing of JFK* by Vincent Bulgliosi (W. W. Norton); *The Secret Universe of Names* by Roy Feinsen (Overlook Press). Garrick: *A Little Piece of Sky* by Nicole Bailey-Williams (Doubleday).

AARON PRIEST LITERARY AGENCY

708 Third Avenue, 23rd Floor, New York, NY 10017
212-818-0344   fax: 212-573-9417

Agents: Lisa Erbach Vance, Paul V. Cirone

Born: Vance: Chicago, Illinois. Cirone: June 4, 1974, Brooklyn, New York.

Education: Vance: B.A. in English Literature, Northwestern University, Academic honors. Cirone: B.A. in English, New York University.

Career history: Vance: Management Trainee at Random House, Inc. Foreign Rights Associate at Crown Publishing Group. Cirone: Five-year Assistant and apprentice to Molly Friedrich.

Hobbies/personal interests: Cirone: Audiophile, weight training, films, and, of course, reading.

Areas most interested in agenting: Vance: Novels—literary and/or commercial and narrative nonfiction. I'm particularly interested in women's fiction and bold, riveting thrillers. I also love historical novels and mystery/suspense with truly unique plots and characters. I'm always hungry for thoughtful books—beyond the previous categories. I'm more interested in quality than category. Cirone: Literary fiction, multicultural, gay and lesbian, Latin American, and African-American fiction among others. Narrative-driven nonfiction; I love "magical realism" and some horror as well. Also, historical fiction and literary thrillers.

Areas not interested in agenting: Vance: Genre romance, cozy mysteries, horror, fantasy/science fiction, "New Age"—fiction or nonfiction, poetry, screenplays, young adult/children's, health/diet, how-to. Cirone: Genre mystery, genre romance, commercial thrillers, self-help books, prescriptive nonfiction.

If not agenting, what might you be doing? Cirone: I might be an English teacher, still in school, or a disc jockey.

Best method to initiate contact: Vance: Query letter that includes a good synopsis of the work and/or a statement about the themes the book explores—no longer than 2–3 pages. Include first chapter, if desired. An SASE is not required. If I'm interested, I will respond within three weeks. I will not respond if not interested. Cirone: Query letter.

Reading-fee policy: No reading fee.

Client representation by category: Vance: Nonfiction, 15%; Fiction, 85%. Cirone: Nonfiction, 20%; Fiction, 80%.

Commission: Vance: 15%. Domestic sales; 10% on all foreign sales (plus additional 10% for foreign sub-agents). Cirone: 15%.

Number of titles sold last year: Cirone: Sold my first novel in July 2000.

Rejection rate (all submissions): Vance: 99%. Cirone: 90%.

Most common mistakes authors make: Vance: An unfocused description or not enough description of the work. Gimmicks or excessive cuteness; let your personality shine through, but please don't play games with me. Microscopic type size in query letters.

Description of the client from Hell: Vance: One who is demanding—as opposed to cooperative. One who is paranoid—publishing is not a conspiracy against writers!

Description of a dream client: Vance: One who takes editorial suggestions well. One who understands that successful publication requires a team effort—that the author's job doesn't end when the manuscript is accepted. One whose creativity doesn't stop with the written word. One who is positive. Cirone: One who is amenable to some editorial guidance, is personable, and is passionate about writing.

How did you become an agent? Vance: Years of working as Aaron Priest's assistant, plus a background in foreign rights. Cirone: I began as an intern at Aaron Priest and worked my way through the ranks.

Why did you become an agent? Vance: A passion for books, coupled with a desire to be as involved in publishing as possible. An agent has to understand all aspects of the business and know a lot of people—it's challenging, thrilling, and great fun! Cirone: Because I love to read and because after five years of being an apprentice to Molly Friedrich, I was inspired to try my hand at it.

How would you describe what you actually do for a living? Vance: I see myself as a career-builder. I am dedicated to those who are dedicated to writing, and my objective is to see the "big picture" for my clients, as well as manage the details. I'm looking for writers who are ready and ripe for growth, whether they are already published or not. Cirone: An agent is responsible for shepherding writers toward publication, to get them the right relationship with the most appropriate editors/publishers.

What do you think about editors? Cirone: I think some are fiercely intelligent, passionate about books, and crucial to a book's publication.

What do you think about publishers? Cirone: I think publishers are obviously corporate-minded, so that can be frustrating. But for the most part, I have to believe that they have the books' best interests in mind.

Representative titles: Vance: *Tell No One* by Harlan Coben (Delacorte); *The Magic of Ordinary Days* by Ann Howard Creel (Viking); *Acid Test* by Ross LaManna (Ballantine); *Mother to Mother* by Sindiwe Magma (Beacon); new mystery series by G. M. Ford (Avon); Cirone: *Peace Like a River* by Leif Enger (Grove Atlantic).

SUSAN ANN PROTTER, LITERARY AGENT

110 West 40th Street, Suite 1408, New York, NY 10018
212-840-0480

Agent: Susan Ann Protter

Career history: Associate Director, Subsidiary Rights Dept., Harper & Row Publishers, Inc.; founded Susan Ann Protter Agency in 1971.

Hobbies/personal interests: Sailing, film, opera, travel, languages.

Areas most interested in agenting: Suspense fiction, including mysteries and thrillers; women's fiction; science fiction; exotic fiction. Nonfiction: (by recognized experts only); general and women's health; parenting; how-to; popular science and medicine; alternative medicine; history and biography.

Areas not interested in agenting: Star Trek, Star Wars, romance, Westerns, children's books, high fantasy, dark fantasy, horror and textbooks.

Best way to initiate contact: One-page query letter with SASE (no e-mail), which gives overview, brief synopsis, author's background. If interested, will request first 30 pages and outline with an SASE. No reply without SASE.

Reading-fee policy: No reading fee.

Client representation by category: Nonfiction, 45%; Fiction, 55%.

Commission: 15%.

Number of titles sold last year: 20.

Rejection rate (all submissions): 97%. The agency can accommodate very few new authors; prior publication is an asset.

Most common mistakes authors make: Spend the first paragraph of their letter apologizing for taking up your time or telling you that they are unaware of the proper way to write a manuscript.

Comments: As an agent, I am looking for writers with whom I believe I will be able to connect for the long haul. The author and agent need to share a sense of joined vision and goals. Without that, they are unlikely to succeed as a team.

Representative titles: *The Cat on the Bus* by Lydia Adamson (Signet); *Life and Death on Your Own Terms* by L. L. Basta, M.D. (Prometheus); *The Pickup Artist* by Terry Bisson (TOR); *Perfect Planet, Clever Species* by William Burger, Ph.D. (Prometheus); *Dreams and Nightmares* by Ernest Hartmann, M.D. (Perseus); *Mass Hate* by Neil Kressel, Ph.D. (Plenum); *Stack and Sway* by Neil J. and Dorit F. Kressel, J.D. (Westview/ Perseus); *Daughter of the Fifth Moon* (Signet); *Sew Fast, Sew Easy* by Elissa K. Meyrich (St. Martin's); *Spaceland* by Rudy Rucker (TOR).

SUSAN RABINER LITERARY AGENCY, INC.

240 West 35th Street, Suite 500, New York, NY 10001-2506
fax: 212-279-0932
e-mail: susan@rabiner.net

Agents: Susan Rabiner, Howard Boyer, Susan Arellano

Career history: Former Editorial Director and Vice President of Basic Books, the serious nonfiction division of HarperCollins Publishers, Senior Editor at Pantheon Books, St. Martin's Press, Oxford University Press.

Areas most interested in agenting: Serious nonfiction: history, science, biography, business, economics, politics, law, psychology.

Areas not interested in agenting: Fiction, self-help, New Age, and memoir.

Best way to initiate contact: E-mail a query, snail mail a proposal

Client representation by category: Nonfiction, 95%; Textbooks, 5%.

Commission: 15% domestic; 20% foreign.

Number of titles sold last year: 15.

Why did you become an agent? I became an agent after 25 years as an Editor because I felt that authors needed help conceptualizing their projects editorially before they showed them to publishers.

Representative titles: *The Chinese in America* by Iris Chang (Viking-Penguin); *Atom: A Space Odyssey* by Lawrence Krauss (Little Brown & Co.); *Philosophy from the Inside* by Colin McGrinn (HarperCollins); *Winning the Talent Wars* by Bruce Tulgan (W. W. Norton); *Hirohito and the Making of Modern Japan* by Herb Bix (HarperCollins); *Tragedy and Triumph: The Story of Postwar Europe* by Will Hitchcock (Broadway Books); *The Seven Sins of Memory* by Daniel Schacter (Houghton Mifflin).

HELEN REES LITERARY AGENCY

123 North Washington Street, Boston, MA 02114-2113

617-723-5232, ext. 233   fax: 617-723-5211

e-mail: reesliterary@aol.com

R

Agents: Helen Rees; Barbara Rifkind; Ann Collette

Born: October 2, 1936.

Education: B.A. in History, George Washington University.

Career history: Director of Office of Cultural Affairs, City of Boston (1978–1982); Literary Agent (1983–present).

Hobbies/personal interests: Horseback riding, opera, theater, hiking.

Areas most interested in agenting: Literary fiction, history, psychology, business. Rifkind: History, business, science and biography. Collette: Literary fiction, thrillers, commercial fiction, psychology.

Areas not interested in agenting: Children's books, young adult, science fiction, poetry, cookbooks, gardening books, photography.

Best way to initiate contact: Query letter (with SASE) with three chapters and a synopsis.

Reading-fee policy: No reading fee.

Client representation by category: Nonfiction, 65%; Fiction, 15%; Other, 20%.

Commission: 15% domestic; 20% foreign.

Number of titles sold last year: 20.

Rejection rate (all submissions): 85%.

Most common mistakes authors make: In a query letter, they unrealistically hype their material.

Description of the client from Hell: Someone who sends a manuscript over and calls an hour later to see if I've read it.

Description of a dream client: Someone who listens and is talented.

Representative titles: *It's Your Ship* by D. Michael Abrashoff (Warner); *As the Future Catches Us* by Juan Enriquez Cabot (Crown); *Shouting Fire* by Alan Dershowitz (Little Brown & Co.); *Supreme Injustice* by Alan Dershowitz (Oxford University Press); *PWC Guide to New Taxi Law* by Price Waterhouse Cooper (Ballantine); *Harm's Way* by Anna Salter (Basic Books); *Giants of Enterprise* by Richard S. Tedlow (Harper Business); *Buying Dad* by Harlyn Aizley (Alyson Publications).

REGAL LITERARY INC.

52 Warfield Street, Montclair, NJ 07043
973-509-5767   fax: 973-509-0259

Agent: Joseph Regal
  Born: 1968.
  Education: B.A. English, magna cum laude, Columbia College, Columbia University.
  Career history: I started my own agency in 2002, after 11 years at Russell & Volkening (the last 6 as the Senior Agent). Before I was an agent, I was briefly a professional musician.
  Hobbies/personal interests: Music (classical, rock, funk, blues, jazz, etc.), sports (basketball, tennis), art, photography, science, philology, spirituality, travel, design.
  Areas most interested in agenting: I am interested in good stories, whether fiction (commonly called "literary") or nonfiction. I am especially interested in cultures with which I am unfamiliar—be they Pakistani, Greek, Irish, Thai, inner city Cleveland, or the American South. In nonfiction, those stories tend to be narratives from science, history, and memoir—even photobooks and cookbooks. I look for voice more than subject.
  Areas not interested in agenting: No genre—romance, science fiction, or horror. Nor do I handle self-help, diet books, or prescriptive nonfiction.
  If not agenting, what might you be doing? I'd be a musician, physicist, or priest.
  Best method to initiate contact: Send a query letter with SASE, and if it's fiction, include a synopsis and the first five pages.
  Client representation by category: Nonfiction, 50%; Fiction, 50%.
  Commission: 15%.
  Number of titles sold last year: 20.
  Rejection rate (all submissions): 99%.
  Most common mistakes authors make: Because of the tremendous drain on our time and resources, the little things mean a lot when agents look at query letters. It is truly astounding how many people send poorly written letters, rife with typos and grammatical errors. Why would we show your work more respect than you show it? If you can't write a good letter, we're not going to be too enthusiastic about the prospects for the book.
  Description of the client from Hell: There is no client from Hell. The relationship between author and agent is like any other: It flourishes when there are clear ground rules that each party respects. If boundaries are transgressed, it is up to one party to communicate that to the other. While no one's perfect (including me), this system almost always works.

Description of a dream client: Dream clients show me the same respect, patience, enthusiasm, and care that I show them and their work.

How did you become an agent? Pretty much by accident; I was singing in a band in New York City and needed a day job. Since I loved books, I wanted to get into publishing and was lucky enough to land at a very fine agency. I had planned to remain an assistant, but within my first year, I fell in love with three novels the other agents were rejecting and was allowed to offer my assistance to the writers. I sold all three (eventually) and found myself hooked.

Why did you become an agent? I love books, and the next best thing to being a mother is being a midwife. I enjoy getting involved in every stage of the publishing process and find it very satisfying to think that I have made a contribution through my advocacy of writers I admire.

What can writers do to enhance their chances of getting you as their agent? Write a really good book or nonfiction proposal. Sometimes it helps if there is something unique about you that makes a difference if we're on the fence—a fascinating career, the support of a famous writer, incredible life experiences, being a 25-year-old ex-cover girl—but in the end, it's all about the writing.

How would you describe what you actually do for a living? I juggle. At any given moment, I'm a talent scout, editor, psychologist, art consultant, lawyer, or salesman.

What do you think about editors? I don't have any thoughts about editors as a group. As with any group, there are good, bad, and indifferent editors. I do know it's not an easy job balancing the needs of your publishing house, your authors, and your passions.

What do you think about publishers? I think the publishing industry is slightly out of touch with the real world. When all you do is read books for a living, you can lose sight of how the average reader comes to books and how little time most people have for reading. This is manifested in different ways, but most obviously in marketing and publicity. In what other industry would the newest, least experienced employees be in charge of promoting a product? Of course, that's if the product is actually promoted, which quite often it isn't—especially if it's literary fiction, which needs the most promotion but often gets the least. Publishers need to re-imagine the whole promotional structure; a sea change is possible, but only if people believe it is possible.

What were your favorite films last year? To tell the truth, I don't get out much. I spend most of my time reading, though I do love film. I'm not sure there's a lot worth going out to see. I did really enjoy *Memento*.

Do you watch the *Sopranos*? Who wants to know?

Comments: It's a very exciting time for books. I feel that the threat of electronic publishing has helped awaken publishers from their collective slumber. Because of e-books and the Internet, everyone has begun to think about publishing in a slightly different way. I don't think most publishers or agents (including me) have grasped fully what the information revolution will mean—certainly not the end of books, as some fear—but there is a lot of energy now, and positive things are happening. One of the most cheering aspects is that publishers have begun to realize how important it is that they establish themselves as a brand, an arbiter of quality, in a world where any author can put his or her work online and invite people to read it and buy it. If the means of delivery and distribution begins to slip away, it ironically places a greater emphasis on some of the old-fashioned aspects of publishing, editorial work in particular. One nice benefit has been a slight renaissance in the publishing of literary fiction, but there are bound to be other unexpected results. Where does that leave you? Do good work. Strive for excellence. Take pleasure in the work itself. The world will still recognize quality; it's only a question of how long it takes.

Representative titles: *Warriors of God* by James Reston Jr. (Doubleday); *Veiled Courage* by Cheryl Benard (Broadway); *Hollow Ground* by Stephen Marion (Algonquin); *The Watermelon King* by Daniel Wallace (Houghton Mifflin); *Dirt Music* by Tim Winton (Scribner); *The First Americans* by Dr. James Adovasio and Jake Page (Random House); *Across the Nightingale Floor* by Lian Hearn (Riverhead); *Song and Dance* by Alan Shapiro.

JODY REIN BOOKS, INC.

7741 South Ash Court, Littleton, CO 80122
303-694-4430
www.jodyreinbooks.com

Agent: Jody Rein

Career history: Spent 13 years in publishing at Contemporary Books (Senior Editor), Bantam Doubleday Dell(Executive Editor), and Morrow/Avon Books (Executive Editor). Incorporated Jody Rein Books in 1994.

Areas most interested in agenting: Very commercial nonfiction written by people who have both media contacts/experience and true expertise in their chosen subject matter. Serious and compelling narrative nonfiction. An amazing work of literary fiction by an award-winning short-story writer.

Areas not interested in agenting: Category fiction (mystery, romance, science fiction, horror, etc.), poetry, children's books.

Best way to initiate contact: A recommendation from someone I trust. A one-page query letter.

Reading-fee policy: No reading fee.

Client representation by category: Nonfiction, 85%; Fiction, 15%.

Commission: 15%.

Number of titles sold last year: 7.

Rejection rate (all submissions): 90–95%.

Most common mistakes authors make: Fax me; e-mail me; send me something I know nothing about; call me; say, "I can write about anything!"; say, "Well, I don't really know if this has been done before . . ."

Description of the client from Hell: Not someone I would do business with! (An author who expects a perfect publishing experience but doesn't expect to do any work on his own.)

Description of a dream client: Those with a fabulous idea and the requisite writing experience, life experience, education, and passion to pull it off. Plus, media experience and contacts. Plus, a real willingness to do whatever they can to work with the agent and publisher to make their book a bestseller. Plus, respect for themselves, for the book, for the publisher, and for me.

Why did you become an agent? I had been in the publishing business at an executive level for 13 years when I moved to Denver. I love this business. Being an agent was the only way to stay in the business, working with the top professionals in New York—and still live in the Rocky Mountains.

Comments: You can find good agents anywhere in the country, but make sure you protect yourself by doing adequate research. Ask the agent who wants to represent you if she has New York experience, how you would work together, and so on. But don't ask these questions until she has offered to represent you. If she doesn't want to sell your work, it doesn't matter what her experience is.

Representative titles: *Skeletons on the Zahara* by Dean King (Little Brown); *Guernica* by Russell Martin (Dutton); *The Seashell on the Mountain Top* by Allan Cutler (Penguin/Putnam); *8 Simple Rules for Dating My Teenage Daughter* by W. Bruce Camfron.

THE AMY RENNERT AGENCY

98 Main Street #302, Tiburon, CA 94920
415-789-8955   fax: 415-789-8944

Agent: Amy Rennert
  Born: Brooklyn, New York.
  Career history: Editor-in-Chief of *San Francisco Focus* magazine and *Women's Sports* magazine.
  Areas most interested in agenting: Narrative nonfiction, especially memoirs; business; pop culture; health; adventure; sports; psychology; food; wine; and travel. Literary fiction, mysteries, suspense.
  Areas not interested in agenting: Religious fundamentalism, gag gifts, romance novels, science fiction.
  Best way for a client to initiate contact: Query with a cover letter and a proposal for nonfiction with one sample chapter; cover letter, and 50–75 pages of sample writing for fiction. We don't need to see a query letter first.
  Reading-fee policy: No reading fee.
  Client representation by category: Nonfiction, 75%; Fiction, 20%; Children's, 5%.
  Commission: 15% domestic; 20% foreign.
  Number of titles sold last year: 26.
  Rejection rate (all submissions): 95%.
  Most common mistakes authors make: Some common mistakes include not taking enough care in writing a good cover letter, not enclosing a self-addressed envelope (of appropriate size with appropriate postage) for return of materials wanted back, sending out manuscripts that aren't the absolutely best material they can produce, and faxing over revised pages three days after the package has arrived.
  Description of dream client: Dream clients write like a dream and are professional in all dealings. They learn a little or a lot about the publishing business before a approaching the agency. Dream clients don't need money desperately right now, but are interested in a

writing career and let their hard work lead them in the right direction. The dream client has talent, patience, and perseverance.

Why did you become an agent? For the opportunity to bring books that matter into the world, so that I could use both my editorial and my business skills, so that I didn't have to work for anybody else, and so that I could help writers achieve their dreams while realizing my own.

What do you think about editors? I think that most of them care about books. They are smart and market savvy and are too pressured by the bottom line these days. I wish, and they wish, too, that they had more time to edit books.

Representative titles: *Blood Washes Blood* by Frank Viviano (Pocket Books); *A Slant of Sun* (Norton) and *Into the Tangle of Friendship* (Houghton Mifflin) by Beth Kephart; *Anatomies: A Novella and Stories* by Anndee Hochman (Picador); *Salon.com's Wanderlust,* edited by Don George (Villard); *Red House* by Sarah Messer (Viking); *Waiting: True Confessions of a Waitress* (HarperCollins); *The Rebel Rules: Daring to Be Yourself in Business* by Chip Conely (Simon & Schuster/Fireside); *The Mother's Guide to Sex* by Anne Semans and Cathy Winks (Times Books); *A Bright Red Scream* by Marilee Strong (Viking); *Harvests of Joy* by Robert Mondavi (Harcourt Brace); *Muhammed Ali: Ringside,* edited by John Miller and Aaron Kenedi (Bulfinch); *The Poison Sky: A Jack Liffey Mystery* by John Shannon (Berkley).

R

THE ANGELA RINALDI LITERARY AGENCY

PO Box 7877, Beverly Hills, CA 90212-7665
310-842-7665 fax: 310-837-8143
e-mail: e2arinaldi@aol.com

Agent: Angela Rinaldi

Career history: Editor at NAL/Signet, Pocket Books, Bantam, Manager Book Publishing, the *Los Angeles Times.*

Areas most interested in agenting: Literary and commercial fiction, narrative nonfiction, prescriptive and pro-active self-help, business, finance, and career.

Areas not interested in agenting: Cookbooks, category romance, Westerns, science fiction, young adult, poetry, screenplays, children's, sports, coffee-table books, software.

Best way to initiate contact: Fiction: send first three chapters with brief synopsis; Nonfiction: query first or send proposal. Please allow 4 to 6 weeks' response time. Please do not fax queries, do not messenger letters, and do not send certified mail. Please remember to include SASE and return postage.

Client representation by category: Nonfiction, 60%; Fiction, 40%.

Commission: 15% domestic; 20% foreign.

Representative titles: *Who Moved My Cheese?* by Dr. Spencer Johnson (Putnam); *The Seventh Sin* by Eben Paul Perison (NAL/Signet); *Blind Spot* by Stephanie Kane (Bantam); *The Thyroid Solution* by Dr. Ridha Arem (Ballantine *The Starlite Drive In* by Marjorie Reynolds (William Morrow); *Stepwives* by Lynn Oxhorn Ringwood, Louise

Oxhorn, and Marjorie Krausz (Simon & Schuster). *Enlightened Golf* by Dr. Joseph Parent (Doubleday); *Before Your Pregnancy* by Amy Ogier and Dr. Lisa Mazzallo (Ballantine).

ANN RITTENBERG LITERARY AGENCY, INC.

1201 Broadway, Suite 708, New York, NY 10001
212-684-6936   fax: 212-684-6929
e-mail: ARLAInc@banet.net

Agent: Ann Rittenberg
 Born: 1957, New York, New York.
 Education: B.A., Eckerd College.
 Career history: 1979–1980, *St. Petersburg Times;* 1980–1986, Editor, Atheneum Publishers; 1986–1992, Agent, Julian Bach Agency; 1992–present, President, Ann Rittenberg Literary Agency, Inc.
 Hobbies/personal interests: Gardening, travel, ballet/theater, entertainment, cabaret, New York.
 Areas most interested in agenting: Literary fiction, upmarket contemporary women's fiction, biography/autobiography/memoir, cultural history, social history, and serious narrative nonfiction.
 Areas not interested in agenting: Sci-fi, genre fiction, romance, how-to, gift books.
 If not agenting, what would you be doing? Traveling the world, playing tennis and golf, studying art and languages, writing literary criticism—in other words, pursuing leisure activities! There's no other job I'd want to have.
 Best way to initiate contact: Write me a letter.
 Client representation by category: Nonfiction, 50%; Fiction, 50%.
 Commission: 15% domestic, 15% film (split with subagent), 20% foreign.
 Number of titles sold last year: 25.
 Rejection rate (all submissions): 98%.
 Most common mistakes authors make: When writers say, "I've just finished a novel . . . ," I wonder why they haven't put it through another draft before approaching agents. I also don't like letters that focus more on marketing than they do on the work.
 Description of the client from Hell: Those who don't want to revise their work until after it's sold to a publishing house. Those who never call, then complain about lack of attention.
 Description of a dream client: All of my clients are dream clients. They are hardworking, enthusiastic, dedicated to writing, convinced that the work comes first, conscious that the author–agent relationship flourishes when it is a partnership based on mutual respect and trust.
 Why did you become an agent? When I worked in a publishing house, I saw that it wasn't politic to put the author's needs before the needs of the publicity department, the sales department, the rights department, even the book-ordering department. That didn't seem right to me, and I became an agent so that I could advocate for authors.
 What can writers do to enhance their chances of getting you as an agent? Keep their letters short.

How would you describe what you actually do for a living? Advocating for authors, with all that entails: Coping with an avalanche of paperwork and a cacophony of telephone calls, faxes, and e-mails; meeting editors, film producers, and foreign publishers and staying current with their interests and the demands of the marketplace. I also spend a lot of time talking to clients so I can get to know them and their hopes and needs, as well as their work, and I strategize about when to submit work, how to get the best work out of a writer, how to raise a writer's profile, and how to get the publishers to focus on how to best publish each book I represent.

What do you think about editors? I think they are smart, wonderful, creative, caring people who are swamped by work and the demands of the corporations so many of them work for.

What do you think about publishers? They're too big and are inefficient as a result of streamlining and merging in a quest for economic efficiency. Some of them are too small, and while they can give personal attention at every stage in a way that the big publishers can't, their distribution arrangements can be a source of frustration.

Representative titles: *A Short History of Rudeness* by Mark Caldwell (Picador); *Altars in the Street* by Melody Chavis (Harmony); *Every Day* by Elizabeth Richards (Pocket); *First Cut: A Season in the Human Anatomy Lab* by Albert Howard Carter III (Picador); *Rescue* by Elizabeth Richards (Pocket); *Shizuko's Daughter* by Kyoko Mori (Holt); *Someone Else's Child* by Nancy Woodruff (Simon & Schuster); *The Poetry of Sight* by Avis Berman (Clarkson Potter/Crown); *Mystic River* by Dennis Lehare (William Morrow & Co.).

R

JUDITH RIVEN, LITERARY AGENT/EDITORIAL CONSULTANT

250 West 16th Street, #4F, New York, NY 10011
212-255-1009
e-mail: Rivenlit@att.net

Agents: Judith Riven; Deborah Jurkowitz, Associate

Education: B.A.; M.A. in English Literature.

Career history: Majority of experience as an Acquiring Editor for several major trade publishers. Independent Agent since mid-1993.

Areas most interested in agenting: Medical/health—both conventional and alternative; natural history (am particularly interested in the Southwest), food, social issues, narrative nonfiction, senior fiction—quirky approaches to traditional subjects.

Areas not interested in agenting: Gratuitous violence, genre fiction other than mysteries.

Best way to initiate contact: E-mail brief query. NO ATTACHMENTS. No faxes.

Reading-fee policy: None.

Client representation by category: Nonfiction, 95%; Fiction, 5%.

Commission: 15% of all moneys; 10% of foreign (foreign agent commissions at 15% for a total of 25%).

Number of titles sold last year: 15.

Rejection rate (all submissions): 95%.

Most common mistakes authors make: Trumpeting their great abilities instead of letting the material and their credentials and experience speak for themselves.

Description of the client from Hell: Writers who are unwilling to listen—and to hear feedback on their work. Anyone who believes that working hurriedly is more important than working thoroughly.

Description of a dream client: Most of my clients are dream clients. I try to represent people whose work I admire and who share a vision of working collaboratively, who have high aspirations and realistic goals and are willing to commit themselves to achieving them.

Why did you become an agent? It was a natural evolution from being an acquisitions editor. As publishing became more corporate, I found I wanted the ability to work more independently. I have always loved publishing and agenting. I was offered the perfect situation to continue working with the author helping to shape ideas and negotiate book deals.

What can writers do to enhance their chances of getting you as an agent? Very thoughtfully and carefully develop their proposal before getting in touch with me.

How would you describe what you do for a living? I get to work with many wonderful and special people who are excited about and committed to what they're doing, whether they're cancer researchers, psychologists, chefs, entomologists, or novelists, and I represent their ideas to another group of exceptional people: editors.

What do you think of editors? Most are seriously smart, very committed, and enormously overworked. They have a broad and deep perspective on what's happening in the marketplace.

What do you think about publishers? They're in a more and more difficult situation. The large ones tend to get bogged down in corporate bureaucracy. The smaller ones are hard pressed to compete both in acquiring and getting their books into the marketplace.

What were your favorite films last year? It was a bad year for films.

Do you watch the *Sopranos?* Devotedly.

Representative titles: *Going Through Ghosts* by Mary Sojouner (Scribner); *Waiting for Bebe* by Lourdes Alcanic (Ballantine); *Wired* by Linda Rosenkrantz (Henry Holt & Co.).

B. J. ROBBINS LITERARY AGENCY

5130 Bellaire Avenue, North Hollywood, CA 91607
fax: 818-760-6616
e-mail: Robbinsliterary@aol.com

Agent: B. J. Robbins

Born: New York City.

Education: B.A. (Magna Cum Laude with Highest Distinction) in English, Phi Beta Kappa, University of Rochester.

Career history: Worked in book publishing for 15 years before moving to L.A. and opening my agency in 1992. Started in publicity at Simon & Schuster and M. Evans before going to Harcourt, where I spent 7 years, in New York and San Diego, in jobs ranging from Publicity Manager to Marketing Director and Senior Editor.

Hobbies/personal interests: Basketball (I play in a mom's league), baseball (which I don't play); does shopping with my teenage daughter count as a hobby?

Areas most interested in representing: I look for projects that are fresh and original and have literary merit, whether they're novels or narrative nonfiction. I also look for experts who can impart important information in a unique way.

Areas not interested in agenting: I don't do most genre fiction: romance, science fiction, fantasy, horror, westerns, techno-thrillers, anything apocalyptic. No screenplays, poetry, children's books. No books about dating.

Best way to initiate contact: Don't call, fax, or e-mail. Send a short cover letter accompanied by a small sample of your writing (first three chapters or so for fiction, a proposal for nonfiction) with an SASE .

Client representation by category: Nonfiction, 50%; Fiction, 50%.

Commission: 15% domestic; 20% foreign.

Rejection rate (all submissions): 95%.

Description of the client from Hell: Clients who don't understand how the business works, who have unrealistic expectations, who call constantly or at inappropriate times. Fortunately, I have eliminated all clients from Hell and have developed excellent CFH radar.

Description of the dream client: All of mine fit this category. They behave professionally; they know how publishing works, even if they're first-timers, because they've taken the time to do their homework.

Most common mistakes authors make: The list is long, but here are a few pet peeves, including random chapters instead of the first three; telling me we're going to make a million dollars; any kind of gimmick; calling your work a "fiction novel" or, for that matter, a "nonfiction novel"; not including return postage; having spelling and grammatical errors in the cover letter; including a synopsis/outline longer than three pages.

What can writers do to enhance their chances of getting you as an agent? Write a simple, straightforward cover letter that includes a brief description of your work, the reasons why you are soliciting my agency, and a short bio. I also like to see a sample of your writing, so include 50 pages or so and an SASE.

Why did you become an agent? I had just moved to L.A. and was looking for a way to use my varied publishing experience in order to continue to work with writers while working for myself.

If not agenting, what might you be doing? I'd sing torch songs in a seedy San Francisco nightclub and do stand-up on the side. I'd really learn how to play the piano. Oh, and I'd work on my hook shot.

What do you think about editors? All the editors I work with are exceptionally smart, work hard, and really care about authors.

What do you think about publishers? Same as above.

Do you watch the _Sopranos?_ Yes.

Representative titles: _Snow Mountain Passage_ by James D. Houston (Knopf); _The Last Summer_ by John Hough Jr. (Simon & Schuster); _The Drums of Quallah Battoo_ by Charles Corn (Dutton); _Quickening_ by Laura Catherine Brown (Random House); _Katie.com_ by Katherine Tarbox (Dutton); _Please Please Please_ by Renee Swindle (Dial Press).

R

R

LINDA ROGHAAR LITERARY AGENCY, INC.

133 High Point Drive, Amherst, MA 01002
413-256-1921   fax: 413-256-2636
www.lindaroghaar.com   e-mail: LRoghaar@aol.com

Agent: Linda L. Roghaar

Born: September 11, 1947, Winchester, Massachusetts.

Education: B.A. in Religion, Miami University (Ohio), 1969; M.A. in Liberal Studies, Vanderbilt University, 1997.

Career history: I've worked in publishing since 1974, first as a Book-Seller and Bookstore Manager, then as a publisher's Sales Rep. Established the agency in 1997.

Areas most interested in agenting: I am a generalist.

Areas not interested in agenting: Children's, horror, science fiction.

If not agenting, what would you be doing? Selling books in another division of the publishing industry.

Best way to initiate contact: Query letter with SASE or an e-query.

Reading-fee policy: No reading fee.

Client representation by category: Nonfiction, 90%; Fiction, 10%.

Commission: 15% domestic, 20% foreign.

Rejection rate (all submissions): 98%.

Most common mistakes authors make: Calling me to tell me about the book. Sending an incomplete, confusing package, not enough postage, or a metered envelope.

Description of a dream client: Writers who are friendly, patient, organized. A sense of humor always helps, along with a realistic perspective of their place in publishing. Those who have thought through the idea (for nonfiction) or polished the manuscript (for fiction) before contacting me.

How did you become an agent? I've been an entrepreneur for so long! I researched the industry, wrote a business plan, and opened my doors. My 25 years of experience in the publishing business have been invaluable in my everyday dealings with writers and publishers.

Why did you become an agent? I love making the connection between writer and publisher and seeing worthy projects find their way into print. Years ago, I made that connection between the bookstore customer and a book, and then for many years as a publisher's rep between publisher and bookseller. Now, it's between writer and publisher, and that is a natural progression for me. I really love my work!

What can writers do to enhance their chances of getting you as an agent? Present the material in a clear, complete package.

What do you think about editors? Overall, a delightful and interesting group of people who deal remarkably well with the frustrations of their jobs.

What do you think about publishers? I divide publishers into two groups: The Big Guys (maybe by the time you read this, it will be One Big Guy) and the Independents. The Big Guys: They can really get things done and continue to produce quality lists. My biggest frustration with them is this—they want something new and different, but with a track record. They are less likely to take chances and therefore miss some very good opportunities. The Independents: They publish some of the most interesting and important books today and now, finally, get better review attention. The quality of their production is excellent, and each book gets a lot of in-house attention. My frustrations are less precise, less timely publishing schedules; long lead times to decide on a manuscript; smaller advances. Generally, though, at all publishing houses people are overworked, a bit frantic, and totally committed to their work.

Representative titles: *Crooked Heart* by Cristina Sumners (Bantam); *Waddle On: The Penguin Plan* by John The Penguin Bingham (Rodale); *She's Leaving Home: Letting Go as My Daughter Goes to College* by Connie Jones (Andrews McMeel); *Led by the Spirit: Discerning God's Will in Our Lives* by Debra Famington (Jossey Bass).

THE ROSENBERG GROUP

2800 Harlanwood Drive, Fort Worth, TX 76109
817-921-5173
www.rosenberggroup.com

Agent: Barbara Collins Rosenberg

Born: The Bronx, New York.

Education: B.A. in Theater and English, Montclair State University.

Career history: Senior Acquisitions Editor for eight years at Harcourt; agent since June 1998.

Areas most interested in agenting: Romance, women's fiction, mystery, literary fiction, sports fiction. Any commercial nonfiction, college textbooks for first- and second-year courses.

Areas not interested in agenting: Inspirational, and paranormal, science fiction, espionage, children's, scholarly.

If you weren't agenting, what might you be doing? Something to do with books and ideas.

Best way to initiate contact: Query letter via snail mail. *Faxed and e-mail queries will not be addressed.*

Client representation by category: Nonfiction, 50%; Fiction, 40%. Textbooks, 10%.

Commission: 15% domestic.

Number of titles sold last year: 32.

Rejection rate (all categories): 95%.

Most common mistakes authors make: Soliciting multiple products in multiple genres in multiple writing forms.

Description of the client from Hell: I have been in publishing for too long to allow the "client from Hell" through our door.

Description of the dream client: Dream clients have done their research and spent the time to hone their craft before seeking representation.

How did you become an agent? I have always thought of publishing as an accidental career.

Why did you become an agent? I am fascinated and challenged by the marketplace. I am driven by the wonderful sense of dignity that comes when you find that special project.

What can writers do to enhance their chances of getting you as their agent? Make a conscious effect to understand the sales, marketing, and promotion sides of commercial publishing. Know where their book fits in the market.

How would you describe what it is you actually do for a living? I help authors navigate the treacherous waves of a writer's career.

What do you think about editors? They're overworked and underpaid.

What do you think about publishers? We are very optimistic. We think there will be more opportunities for writers in the next five years from publishers of all sizes, than there ever have been before.

What were your favorite films last year? *The Anniversary Party, The Closet, Memento, Bridgett Jones' Diary.*

Do you watch the *Sopranos?* I never miss it.

Comments: Please check our Web site before querying us: www.rosenberggroup.com.

Representative titles: Fiction: *The Rag and Bone Shop* by Jeff Rackham, Ph.D. (Zoland); *The Promise* by Dee Davis (Leisure); *Law Dogs* by J. Lee Butts (Berkley). Nonfiction: *My Twice Loved Life: A Memoir* by Donald M. Murraq (Ballantine); *Doing College* by Sherrie Nist, Ph.D., and Jodi Holschhub, Ph.D. (Ten Speed Press). College Textbooks*: Alternative Currents: Perspectives from Cyberspace and the Popular Press* by Carol Lea Clark (Houghton Mifflin); *The Curious Writer* by Bruce Balknser, Ph.D. (Allyn & Bacon).

R

RITA ROSENKRANZ LITERARY AGENCY

440 West End Avenue, Suite 15D, New York, NY 10024-5358
212-873-6333

Agent: Rita Rosenkranz

Career history: Editor at various New York publishing houses before becoming an agent in 1990.

Areas most interested in agenting: All areas of nonfiction, with emphasis on biography, business, parenting, cooking, current affairs, cultural issues, health, history, how-to, self-help, theater/film, popular culture, religious/inspirational, science, women's issues.

Areas not interested in agenting: Fiction and children's books.

Best way to initiate contact: Send an outline/proposal with an SASE. I do not accept queries by e-mail or fax. I consider simultaneous queries and submissions.

Client representation by category: Nonfiction, 98%; Fiction, 1%; Children's, 1%.

Commission: 15% on domestic sales; 20% on foreign sales.

Number of titles sold last year: 40.

Rejection rate (all submissions): 95%.

Representative titles: *Flowers, White House Style* by Dottie Temple and Stan Finegold (Simon & Schuster); *Wolf Pack* by Steven T. Smith (John Wiley & Sons); *Work Naked: Eight Essential Principles for Peak Performance in the Virtual Workplace* by Cynthia C. Froggatt (Jossey-Bass); *Appetizer Atlas* by Arthur L. Meyer and Mick Vann

(John Wiley & Sons*); My Mother's Charms: Timeless Gifts and Family Wisdom* by Kathleen Oldford (HarperSanFrancisco).

CAROL SUSAN ROTH, LITERARY REPRESENTATION

1824 Oak Creek Drive, Suite 416, Palo Alto, CA 94304
650-323-3795
e-mail: carol@authorsbest.com

Agent: Carol Susan Roth
  Born: October 22, 1947, New Brunswick, New Jersey.
  Education: B.A., New York University; M.A., East West Counseling and Psychotherapy; California Institute of Integral Studies, San Francisco; Stanford University Professional Publishing Program, Mark Victor Hansen, "Building Your Speaking and Publishing Empire."
  Career history: Trained as a psychotherapist specializing in motivational training seminars. More than a decade producing and promoting public events (100+) with the "who's who" in personal growth, spirituality, health, and business (bestselling authors, including John Gray, Scott Peck, Bernie Siegal, Thomas Moore). In 1987, produced the first Spirituality and Business Conference—"The Heart of Business"—with more than a dozen multimillionaire entrepreneurs who had followed their hearts to great success.
  Hobbies/personal interests: Warm-water sailing, Siddha yoga, the Dalai Lama.
  Areas most interested in agenting: 100% Nonfiction only; My specialty is spirituality, health, personal growth, business. I represent many first-time authors, as well as clients who have been published before and several who have been published with 20 to 30 books each.
  Areas not interested in agenting: Sorry, *no fiction/no channeling,* or any book written by an author without credentials, groundbreaking new content, charisma, and dedication to making it a bestseller.
  If not agenting, what would you be doing? Book development, marketing strategy, and promotion for authors (which I also do now).
  Best way to initiate contact: Please send your query and proposal with several sample chapters and a marketing plan with SASE. Also, your media kit, seminar brochures, videos. Please don't send e-mail files.
  Reading-fee policy: No reading fee. Consulting available for proposal development, marketing strategy, and promotion. I also refer out to book doctors/ghostwriters.
  Client representation by category: Nonfiction, 100%.
  Commission: 15%. I arrange for the publisher to set up separate accounts so that the author is paid directly.
  Number of titles sold last year: 17.
  Rejection rate (all submissions): 95%.
  Most common mistakes authors make: They don't realize that publishing is a fiercely competitive business, that their book is seen as a product by editors. Publishers

now are more interested in the ability of authors to promote themselves and their work than even in the book concept itself!

Description of the client from Hell: An author without credentials, exciting new content, or charisma who thinks that becoming a bestselling author is a hobby.

Description of a dream client: My clients! They have hearts. They inspire and educate me. Hardworking—willing to do whatever it takes—brilliant and fun.

Why did you become an agent? I promoted many authors on their way to the bestseller lists. It was thrilling. I find it even more exciting to work directly with authors, collaborating with them to develop their work and their careers.

What can writers do to enhance their chances of getting you as an agent? Be original! Be willing to work hard to develop your celebrity and your audience. Love yourself, your work, your world.

How would you describe what you actually do for a living? I'm a visionary, confidante, developer, coach, cheerleader, matchmaker, and marketer.

What do you think about editors? I deeply respect great editors. They are the vital link in bringing my clients' work to the public.

What do you think about publishers? Publishers all have their own personality or flavor. It's great fun identifying and matching what they want with my authors' expertise.

Comments: I want to make you a star if you have a great message that serves humanity on this beautiful blue pearl Earth.

Representative titles: *Two Questions* by Michael Ray (Scribner); *Healing Zen* by Ellen Birx (Viking); *Yoga RX* by Larry Payne (Broadway); *Kindling the Celtic Spirit* by Mar Freeman (HarperSanFrancisco); *Changewave Investing 2.0* by Tobin Smith (Doubleday/ Currency); *Investing in Biotech* by Jim McCamant (Perseus); *Extreme Success* by Frank McKinney (John Wiley & Sons); *Power Yoga for Dummies* by Doug Swenson (Hungry Minds); *Networking for Dummies* by Donna Fisher (Hungry Minds); *Advertising for Dummies* by Gary Dahl (Hungry Minds); *Career Change for Dummies* by Carol McMelland (Hungry Minds); *Drums for Dummies* by Jeff Strong (Hungry Minds).

THE PETER RUBIE LITERARY AGENCY

240 West 35th Street, Suite 500, New York, NY 10001
212-279-1776
www.prlit.com

Agents: Peter Rubie; Associate Agents: Jennifer Dechiara and June Clark

Born: Rubie: May 3, 1950.

Education: Rubie: Journalism degree, NCTJ, England.

Career history: Rubie: Fleet Street newspapers (England); BBC radio news (England); Fiction Editor, Walker & Co. (New York City); book doctor (New York City); literary agent; published novelist, and nonfiction writer. Adjunct Professor at New York University.

Hobbies/personal interests: Rubie: Movies, chess, politics/world affairs, music, science.

Areas most interested in agenting: Pop culture, business, history, pop science, strong narrative nonfiction, Judaica, New Age, children's books, literate thrillers, literate crime novels, literate science fiction and fantasy, literary fiction. We intend to bridge the gap between traditional publishing and e-publishing.

If not agenting, what would you be doing? Writing full time.

Best way to initiate contact: Query letter with SASE and a proposal.

Reading-fee policy: No reading fee.

Client representation: Nonfiction, 75%: Fiction, 25%.

Commission: 15% domestic; 20% foreign.

Number of titles sold last year: Rubie: 50.

Rejection rate (all submissions): 95%.

Most common mistakes authors make: Overly cute approach, putting form over substance, unrealistic view of publishing, and being unprofessional.

Description of the client from Hell: Unprofessional, unreal expectations, no knowledge of the publishing industry, calls every day for news, does not listen to advice, and a control freak.

Description of a dream client: Dream clients know the market and how to present their material; take editorial input well; have patience. They call every six weeks or so, work with the agent as part of an effective team; are responsive, responsible, and thoroughly professional.

Why did you become an agent? To help discover new talent and help further the careers of established writers. As a writer, I try to be the sort of agent I would like to have.

Comments: I wish more writers considered themselves professionals and looked at their careers accordingly. To understand my philosophy of writing, read my book *The Elements of Storytelling* (John Wiley, 1996).

Representative titles: *Toward Rational Exuberance* by Mark Smith (Farrar, Straus & Giroux); *How to Keep Your Cool with Your Kids* by Lou Makarowski (Perigee); *On Night's Shore* by Randall Silvis (St. Martin's Press); *Jew Boy* by Alan Kaufman (Fromm); *Glass Harmonica* by Louise Marley (ACE); *The Emperor and the Wolf* by Stuart Galbrayth (Farber); *Soupy Sez* by Soupy Sales and Charles Sazberg (M. Evans & Co.); *Hope's End* by Stephen Chambers (TOR); *Einstein's Refrigerator* by Steve Silverman (Andrews McMeel); *Jaco* by Bill Milkaoski (Backbeat).

THE SAGALYN LITERARY AGENCY

4825 Bethesda Avenue, Suite 302, Bethesda, MD 20814
301-718-6440
e-mail: agency@sagalyn.com

Agent: Raphael Sagalyn

Areas most interested in agenting: Adult fiction and nonfiction.

Areas not interested in agenting: Cookbooks, children's, screenplays, poetry.

Best way to initiate contact: Send a query letter outlining your professional experience and a brief synopsis by e-mail.

Representative titles: *The Fortune Tellers* by Howard Kurtz (Free Press); *The Breach* by Peter Baker (Scribner); *The Future of Success* by Robert Reich (Knopf); *The Mind of the CEO* by Jeffrey Clarten (Basic Books); *The Cutout* by Francine Mathews (Bantam).

VICTORIA SANDERS & ASSOCIATES

241 Avenue of the Americas, New York, NY 10014
212-633-8811
e-mail: queries@victoriasanders.com

Agent: Victoria Sanders
  Born: Hollywood, California.
  Education: B.F.A., New York University, 1983; J.D., Benjamin N. Cardozo School of Law, 1988.
  Career history: WNET/Channel 13 (PBS); Simon & Schuster Inc.; Carol Mann Agency; Charlotte Sheedy Agency; founded own agency in 1992.
  Areas most interested in agenting: Fiction: literary and commercial. Nonfiction: history, biography, politics, sociology, psychology. Special interests: African-American, Latin, women's, gay and lesbian work.
  Areas not interested in agenting: Hard science, children's, textbooks, and poetry.
  If not agenting, what would you be doing? A producer.
  Best way to initiate contact: Only accepting e-mail queries. Send query to queries@victoriasanders.com.
  Reading-fee policy: No reading fee.
  Client representation by category: Nonfiction, 50%; Fiction, 50%.
  Commission: 15% straight; 20% if co-agented foreign; 20% film; and TV commission is 15%.
  Number of titles sold last year: 22.
  Rejection rate (all submissions): 90%.
  Most common mistakes authors make: Rambling queries, typos, no SASE, multiple books printed in a letter.
  Description of the client from Hell: Negative personality.
  Description of the dream client: Hardworking, dedicated writers with their head screwed on tight.
  What can writers do to enhance their chances of getting you as an agent? Well written, attention grabbing letter. Knowledge of other authors we represent and reason why they believe they would fit in well.
  How would you describe what you actually do for a living? I am an advocate for writers.
  How did you become an agent? After law school I worked in the contracts/legal department of Simon & Schuster for almost three years. I was very unhappy in the corporate world but loved publishing. I went into agenting because I felt that writers have historically been treated poorly.
  Why did you become an agent? It's the best of both worlds. I get to read manuscripts and negotiate deals. I came from L.A. and film and, after getting a law degree, realized

that the best part of the entertainment business was in bridging the gap between the writer or artist and the producer or publisher. I love being the representative and friend of my clients.

What do you think about editors? They are incredibly smart, dedicated, and mostly underpaid group.

What do you think about publishers? A few great ones still exist.

What were your favorite films last year? *Erin Brockovich; Notting Hill,* because Julia Roberts is fabulous.

Do you watch the *Sopranos?* Oh, yeah.

Representative titles: *Leaving* by Richard Dry (St. Martin's Press); *Can't Stop, Won't Stop: Portraits of Hip Hop Generation* by Jeff Chang (St. Martin's Press); *Jim and Louella* by Dr. Bertice Berry (Doubleday); *The Harold Cruse Reader,* edited by W. Derasni Cobb (Dutton).

SCHIAVONE LITERARY AGENCY, INC.

236 Trails End, West Palm Beach, FL 33413-2135
voice/fax: 561-966-9294
e-mail: profschia@aol.com

Agent: James Schiavone, Ed.D.

Born: New York City.

Education: B.S., M.A., New York University; Ed.D., Nova University; Professional Diploma, Columbia University.

Career history: Professor Emeritus of Developmental Skills at the City University of New York; Literary Agent.

Areas most interested in agenting: Celebrity biography; autobiography; memoirs; nonfiction. Fiction: mainstream, commercial, and literary; thrillers and mysteries; romances, historical. Children's: all genres of fiction and nonfiction.

Areas not interested in agenting: Poetry; short stories.

If not agenting, what would you be doing? Teaching graduate courses in the psychology of reading; writing nonfiction.

Best way to initiate contact: Queries only via post. Include brief bio-sketch, synopsis, previous books published. Nonfiction: Send full-blown proposal. No response without SASE. No phone calls, faxes. One-page e-mail queries are acceptable, absolutely NO attachments.

Reading-fee policy: No reading fee.

Client representation by category: Nonfiction, 51%; Fiction, 41%; Children's, 5%; Textbooks, 3%.

Commission: 15% domestic; 20% foreign.

Number of titles sold last year: 17.

Rejection rate (all submissions): 90%.

Most common mistakes authors make: Failure to query first; no SASE; send unsolicited manuscript; expect agency to download entire manuscript via e-mail; make initial contact via phone/fax.

Description of a dream client: One who is a published, successful author.

How did you become an agent? It was a natural segue from academia.

Why did you become an agent? I have enjoyed a lifetime love of books and reading. I served as a reading specialist in schools and colleges and authored five trade books and three textbooks. I enjoy representing creative people and helping them to sell their work.

How would you describe what you actually do for a living? Sell creative work of authors/clients to major publishing houses; negotiate contracts; handle business details—enabling authors to concentrate on the craft of writing.

What do you think about editors? I have been fortunate in working with the best editors in the industry. Generally, they are conscientious, indefatigable, and sincere in bringing an author's work to press. Agenting would be impossible without them.

What do you think about publishers? They are the backbone of the industry. I am grateful for the serious consideration they give to my highly selective submissions.

Comments: While I prefer working with authors published by major houses, I do encourage submissions from highly creative, talented first-time authors.

SUSAN SCHULMAN—A LITERARY AGENCY

454 West 44th Street, New York, NY 10036
212-713-1633   fax: 212-581-8830
2 Bryan Plaza, Washington Depot, CT 06794
860-868-3700   fax: 860-868-3704
e-mail: Schulman@aol.com

Agent: Susan Schulman

Areas most interested in agenting: Books for, by, and about women; psychology, popular culture, and contemporary history, business, and health-related topics, Children's books.

Areas not interested in agenting: Romance, fantasy, and humor.

Best way to initiate contact: The best contact is through personal recommendation or a letter of inquiry, including a synopsis of the work and an SASE.

Reading-fee policy: No reading fee. We are a member of the AAR.

Commission: 15% new clients; 20% for foreign sales.

Rejection rate (all submissions): I regret that most submissions are returned for work or forwarded to another agent. About 3% of the unsolicited submissions become active.

Client Representation by category: Nonfiction, 60%; Fiction, 20%; Children's, 20%.

Most common mistakes authors make: The most common mistakes are calling to inquire about their letter of inquiry or to pitch their project over the phone, and failure to include SASE. The larger mistakes include unfinished work, unpolished writing, and ill-prepared proposals.

Why did you become an agent? I love business and I love to read. Literary representation is like Christmas to me. Each new package offers the potential to enjoy the read and to sell it so others may as well.

What can writers do to enhance their chances of getting you as an agent? We appreciate writers who have done their homework—writers who have taken the time to educate themselves on the publishing industry and a bit about the process of literary representation. We seek enthusiastic self-starters.

Representative titles: *Why Is This Happening to Me Again?* by Alan Down (Simon & Schuster); *Corporate (IR) Responsibilities* by Lawrence Mitchell (Yale University Press); *True Balance* by Sonia Choquette (Random House); *Into the A, B, Sea* by Deborah Rose (Scholastic Press); *Boys and Girls Learn Differently* by Michael Gurian (Jossey-Bass).

SCOVIL CHICHAK GALEN LITERARY AGENCY, INC.

381 Park Avenue South, Suite 1020, New York, NY 10016
fax: 212-679-6710
e-mail: russellgalen@scglit.com, annaghosh@scglit.com

Agents: Russell Galen; Anna Ghosh
  Born: Ghosh: Bristol, United Kingdom.
  Education: Ghosh: Woodstock, International School, India; B.A., Hampshire College, Massachusetts.
  Areas most interested in agenting: Ghosh: Literary nonfiction, history, biography, memoir, popular culture, psychology, science, adventure, art, food, spirituality, Asian/African/Latino/Native American interest, women's fiction, historicals and literary fiction.
  Areas not interested in agenting: Ghosh: Children's books.
  Best way to initiate contact: Ghosh: Please send a well-written query letter that briefly describes the project, its audience, and the author's qualifications. For fiction, a sample chapter may be included. No phone calls. Due to high volume, e-mails may not receive a reply if we're not interested.
  Client representation by category: Nonfiction, 60%; Fiction, 40%.
  Commission: 15% domestic; 20% for international sales inclusive of any subagents.
  Representative titles: *In the Hand of Dante* by Nick Tosches (Little Brown); *Ship Wrecker* by Paul Garrison (HarperCollins); *The Pillars of Creation* by Terry Goodkind (TOR); *The Mansions of the Moon* by Benson Bobrick (Simon & Schuster); *In the Blink of an Eye: The Cause of the Most Dramatic Event in the History of Life* by Dr. Andrew Parker (Perseus); *Comic Wars: How Two Tycoons Battled Over the Marvel Comics Empire—And Both Lost* by Dan Raviv (Broadway); *A Plague Odyssey* by Edward Marriott (Henry Holt); *House of Light* by Joyce Carl Thomas (Hyperion); *Life Someplace Else* by J. California Cooper (Doubleday); *Life Inside* by Mindy Lewis (Pocket); *Good as Any* by Timothy Westmoreland (Harcourt Brace); *Queenmaker* by India Edghill (St. Martin's); *Guide to Vastu Living* by Kathleen Cox (Pocket); *Interfaith Weddings* by Reverend Susanna Macomb (Pocket); *The Naked Savage* by Madhusree Mukerjee (Houghton Mifflin).

SEBASTIAN LITERARY AGENCY

172 E. Sixth Street, #2005, St. Paul, MN 55101-1978
651-224-6670
e-mail: harperlb@aol.com

Agent: Laurie Harper

Born: September 1954.

Education: Business and finance, with pre-law studies.

Career history: The literary agency was founded in 1985. It evolved simultaneously with the closing of my small Bay Area regional publishing company (Sebastian Publishing), which published gift books, selling to B. Dalton, Waldenbooks, and independents throughout the West Coast. After I placed books with other publishers for authors I could not publish, I discovered my strengths as an agent. I briefly experienced the author's side of publishing by writing a media biography of a legendary radio personality (*Don Sherwood: The Life and Times of the World's Greatest Disc Jockey,* Prima Publishing, 1989), which enjoyed 12 weeks on the *San Francisco Chronicle*'s bestseller list. Prior to publishing, I was in banking (operations and lending) with a major California bank for eight years. I frequently consult with authors.

Hobbies/personal interests: Reading; games; outdoor activities, including skiing, sailing, rollerblading, shooting hoops, bike riding.

Areas most interested in agenting: Narrative nonfiction across a broad spectrum, though not family memoirs; consumer reference; health/nutrition/medical issues; psychology/sociology, current affairs/journalism, business (management, careers, business stories), and various books/topics that target mainstream educated readers.

Areas not interested in agenting: Mainstream fiction is being nominally considered, though it is not a big part of my list. No genre fiction. No poetry, children's, original screenplay material, gift books, religious, academic, or scholarly.

If not agenting, what would you be doing? I would most likely be in contract law, perhaps working for the Authors Guild.

Best way to initiate contact: Please note that I am taking on few new clients at this time. Send a query letter explaining the project, who you are, and why you are doing this book. Feel free to include the proposal, outline, and a sample chapter. And, of course, the SASE. I do not want phone calls unless the author has been referred to me by a client or colleague.

Reading-fee policy: No reading fee or editorial fee. I do charge my clients a one-time $100 fee, which is a nominal contribution to phone and postage expenses incurred prior to a first sale.

Client representation by category: Nonfiction, 99%; Fiction, 1%.

Commission: 15% domestic; 20% foreign.

Number of titles sold last year: It usually averages about 20.

Rejection rate (all submissions): 95%. The majority of new clients come from referrals from my clients or industry professionals and colleagues. However, every submission is read and considered on its own merit.

Most common mistakes authors make: It is a costly mistake to use anything other than the current year's resource material when exploring potential agents, due to the constant changes in the industry. It is also counterproductive to query without providing the agent with sufficient orientation and information. We are reading the proposal cold. The author has to make it make sense; give it a proper framework. Demonstrate that you know the market for your book; what's been published, how your book fits into the scheme of things. You must answer the obvious questions: Who cares? Why? Are these book-buying people? How many are there? Can anyone find them? What do you specifically have to offer a publisher who would invest in this project? Publishing is, after all, first and foremost a business . . . not an endowment for the arts or for hobbyists.

Description of the client from Hell: The first thing has to be unrealistic expectations; financial and promotional expectations that are simply not realistic for as-yet-unproved authors. For previously unpublished authors, it's understandable that they don't know the industry, but it is incumbent upon prospective authors to inform themselves on the basics. Attend some conferences; do some reading; talk to other published authors. I'm happy to coach an author about strategy or problem solving, to help plan out a realistic publishing career path, but the agent can't be in charge of teaching Publishing 101. Another difficulty comes if the author expects the agent to perform miracles: We can't sell what isn't salable. It is the author's responsibility to consider and reflect upon the feedback given by agents and publishers and to use that to improve the manuscript's potential for publication. I expect my clients to be mature professional adults, capable of approaching this process positively and constructively. No whining allowed.

Comments: The challenge facing every author and publisher (and therefore agent) is how to reach a readership, how to get people to buy this particular book. It isn't a matter of "Put it out there and they will come." Accordingly, my decisions about which authors to partner with are based on many elements. Aside from the book itself, I consider the talents of the writer and what the writer brings to the marketing and promotion of that book. I also have to balance my overall client list. And, certainly, I evaluate the timing of your book for the specific category and market. The best advice I can give a writer is to only write the books you have to write, that book for which you have passion, skill, and ability to promote and market over many years. As an agent I am focused on books and authors that can compete at a national level for readers' precious attention.

Representative titles: *The Ten Smartest Decisions a Woman Can Make After Forty* by Tina Tessina, Ph.D. (Renaissance Books); *Bald in the Land of Big Hair: A True Story* by Joni Rogers (HarperCollins); *The Other Side of Eden: Life with John Steinbeck* by Nancy Steinbeck (Prometheus); *Latticework: The New Investing* (Texere) and *The Essential Warren Buffett* by Robert Hagstrom (Wiley); *A Dance for Emilia* by Peter S. Beagle (Dutton); *The Third Age: 6 Principles for Growth and Renewal After Forty* by William Sadler, Ph.D. (Perseus); *Too Nice for Your Own Good* by Duke Robinson (Warner); *Executive Thinking* by Leslie Kossoff (Davies-Black Publishing); *Natural Beauty from the Garden* by Janice Cox (Henry Holt); *Champions of Silicon Valley* by Charles Sigismund (Wiley).

S

THE SEYMOUR AGENCY

475 Miner Street, Canton, NY 13617
315-386-1831   fax: 315-386-1037
theseymouragency.com   e-mail: mseymour@slic.com

Agent: Mary Sue Seymour
  Born: September 21, 1952.

Education: B.S., State University of Potsdam, New York; postgraduate work with Potsdam State, Ithaca College.

Career history: Taught 11 years in the public school system; professional artist; currently teach part time; freelance writer published in several national magazines.

Hobbies/personal interests: Piano, reading, alpine skiing, swimming, hiking, camping in the Adirondacks(!).

Areas most interested in agenting: Christian romance, Christian self-help, romance, Westerns, and general nonfiction.

Areas not interested in agenting: Short stories, screenplays, poetry

If not agenting, what would you be doing? Writing and painting

Best way to initiate contact: Short query letter and first 50 pages of novel or nonfiction proposal summary.

Reading-fee policy: No.

Client representation by category: Nonfiction, 40%; Fiction, 50%; Children's, 5%; Textbooks, 5%.

Commission: 12.5% published authors; 15% unpublished.

Number of titles sold last year: Several.

Rejection rate (all submissions): 95%.

Description of the client from Hell: Never had one.

Description of the dream client: Dream clients are those who write a lot, use suggestions, are enthusiastic about their writing, appreciate what we try to do for them, and send us books we can sell.

How did you become an agent? We listed ourselves in a writer's guide and sold a four-book contract with our first submission. I guess it was just meant to be.

Why did you become an agent? I love books—reading and learning—and I enjoy each of the diverse challenges of publishing. Books are fundamental to our society, and I take pride in being part of their contribution. There is enormous satisfaction from creating a successful team—making the right match between author and publisher, negotiating a fair contract that promotes a successful venture, and assisting in every way to build long-lasting relationships.

What can writers do to enhance their chances of getting you as an agent? Being professionally polite, and a sense of humor doesn't hurt either.

Common mistakes authors make? Send a fax—Include no SASE and expect me to call them—try to write a snappy cover letter without actually describing their project. For example, is it fiction or nonfiction? If it's fiction, what genre is it?

How would you describe what you actually do for a living? Attend conferences such as the RWA Step Back in Time Conference held in Williamsburg, Virginia, in 1999, the Romantic Times Convention held in Toronto in 1999, Ottowa Romance Writers Brunches in 1999 and 2000, and the Fiction from the Heartland Writers Conference in Kansas City in 2001. Work seven days a week, try to keep our clients feeling good about themselves, work with contracts and royalties, and keep accurate records of all of the above.

What do you think about editors? Editors are professionals who know their stuff. They work long hours and bring too much work home (any is too much).

What were your favorite films last year? I don't watch movies. I like to exercise, be outside, and read good books, such as Max Lucapo's Christian writings.

Do you watch the *Sopranos*? I don't watch television.

Comments: Writing comes from deep within ourselves—it's a reflection of us as people. We write about our friends, our experiences, and our own thoughts. Therefore, it's not surprising that when our novel is rejected, we take it personally. It means we're not "good" people. We've opened up our innermost thoughts to strangers, and these people denied their worth. I can understand why so many writers feel this way. But the reality of the situation is, writing is a business and business is about making money. If agents reject your work, they feel that their companies can't make money on it. If editors reject your work, they feel that their companies can't make money on it. But just because a book isn't a moneymaker doesn't mean it's bad. I've seen some intriguing toys developed for Christmas marketing that I wouldn't want my name on. Yet they made a lot of money. Separate your self-esteem from commercialism. They're two different things. Thousand of musicians are out of work in this country, but that doesn't diminish the quality of their music. Not all writers get their books published, but no one can distinguish who will and who won't.

Representative titles: *The Everything Golf Instruction Book* by Mary Lawrence (Adams Media); *The Everything Kids Math Puzzle Book* by Meg and Glenn Clemens (Adams Media); untitled historical romance by Betty Davidson (Berkley/Jove); *Black Soldiers, White Wars* by Betty Alt (Greenwood); untitled Christmas Anthology Novella by Tori Phillips (Harlequin); *Search for Last Chance* by Audra McWilliams (Thorndike Press).

THE ROBERT E. SHEPARD AGENCY

4111 18th Street, Suite 3, San Francisco, CA 94114
415-255-1097
www.shepardagency.com   e-mail: query@shepardagency.com

Agent: Robert Shepard

Education: B.A., M.A. in English, University of Pennsylvania.

Career history: I've spent 19 years in and around the publishing world. For nearly 9 of them, I worked in the trade division of Addison-Wesley, a respected publisher that has since been merged-and-acquired out of existence. My work on the editorial, sales, and marketing sides of publishing and later as a consultant has given me a good understanding of the "business" side, as well as excellent working relationships with scores of acquisitions editors. But after more than eight years in my own practice as an agent, I'm especially proud of the close rapport I've established with authors—one reason I've chosen to keep my agency small. With dozens of books in print, I'm now working with several clients for the second or third time.

Hobbies/personal interests: Hiking, biking, trains, raptors, and diagramming sentences.

Areas most interested in agenting: I represent only nonfiction, and under that heading I've cultivated two separate categories of books. The first consists of works driven by an exceptionally strong, unified, literary narrative—books intended to make complex ideas accessible to a wider public; to shed new light on aspects of history, society, or popular culture; or to provide fresh insights into people, places, or concepts we may think of as commonplace. On this side of the practice, my subject headings include history, contemporary affairs and politics, science for laypeople, sexuality, urbanism, and sports. The other general category of books I represent tends to be driven less by narrative and more by hard information; on this side, I have a core interest in personal finance and investing, business, and series-oriented works in travel, music, and popular culture. It's safe to say that I'm interested in neither the most commercial nor the most abstruse kinds of books; but I'm happy to represent works that change readers' minds, that may require a somewhat more intellectually curious audience, or about which someone might say, "I never thought this would be an interesting subject, but this book was a super read!"

Areas not interested in agenting: I never handle fiction, poetry, screenplays, or textbooks, and in general I'm not interested in autobiographical works—even when they relate in some way to my regular categories. (In other words, I most likely wouldn't represent a book on your sailing trip through the South Pacific, during which you played the clarinet; but I might represent a history of that region—or a biography of Benny Goodman). Robert E. Shepard Agency titles are usually aimed at a broad audience, so that highly specialized works (such as ones that examine religious writings in detail, or whose intended readers are mainly in a single profession) are not appropriate. As a general rule, I'm also not interested in works on New Age spirituality, self-help, or recovery.

If not agenting, what would you be doing? It could go one of three ways: Either I would go back and get that Ph.D. and write papers on 19th-century authors who were extremely prominent in their day but who paradoxically have become totally obscure (probably due to bad marketing), or I would be conducting a symphony orchestra, or I would be riding trains somewhere in an attempt to escape my job as publisher of a distinguished literary nonfiction house. I'm not picky.

Best way to initiate contact: Never call or fax; neither will speed consideration of your proposal. I encourage authors to mail a query letter or proposal or to e-mail a relatively brief query describing the proposed work, its intended audience, and the author's own credentials and reason for writing on this subject. Don't just refer me to a Web site; I want to see how you present your ideas in the succinct form demanded by a query letter, whether by mail or e-mail. Please do not attach any computer files to e-mail messages; for security purposes, they'll be deleted. If you use regular mail, always enclose a postage-paid return envelope capable of holding everything you sent me, without which you will not receive a reply.

Reading-fee policy: No reading fee.

Client representation by category: Nonfiction, 100%.

Commission: 15% domestic, 20% for "subagented" foreign rights.

Number of titles sold last year: 10. I have deliberately kept the practice small in order to devote time to my clients. I am happy to see proposals from new authors or from authors whose previous works may have been in genres other than general nonfiction. However, your credentials and expertise should be suited to the kind of book you're proposing.

Rejection rate (all submissions): 99%.

Most common mistakes authors make: A big one is failing to share the proposal with a friend, another writer, or a trusted adviser before sending it out. Authors who work in a vacuum risk losing perspective. In the many months you've been working on your book proposal—and very often they really do take that long to write—has your focus shifted inadvertently? Have you failed to discuss some aspect of your topic that an agent or editor might find fascinating—simply because you're too immersed in writing to realize you'd missed it? Have you cited a date or name incorrectly, making yourself look careless even though you really do know your facts? A trusted adviser, particularly one with experience in writing books, can help you improve your proposal or even catch mistakes before you send it to agents. Not to sound like the English teacher I sometimes think I should have been, but bad spelling and grammar often guarantee rejection slips, too. Proofread your work, and if you don't trust your proofreading skills, find someone you do trust to help you. I also counsel authors to avoid proposal clichés. A big one is "there's no competition for my book." You should always try to find works that others might consider competitive, and then describe what's new, different, and better about yours. Finally, there are two important housekeeping issues: Always enclose a return envelope large enough to hold your material, with the proper postage (without which you won't get a response); and always provide your return address.

Description of the client from Hell: One who's good at selling an agent or editor on a book but doesn't want to actually write it. Writing is tough and an agent tries to help, but in the end the responsibility is the author's.

Description of a dream client: Those who are passionate about writing, passionate about their subjects, and appreciative when things go right.

Why did you become an agent? I love books and believe they can and should still be central to our cultural life, even in an era when they're being joined by new sources of entertainment and information all the time. But the consolidations of leading publishers during the 1990s resulted in the loss of many editors, the very people who traditionally worked the closest with authors, helped them craft better books, and made sure that the marketing got done. The vast majority of today's editors are as talented and dedicated as ever but find themselves with more books to edit and less time to spend with authors. So although authors create the intellectual property that fuels our culture, they can feel lost in the publishing shuffle, confused by business aspects of their writing careers, and even disillusioned by the paradoxical demand of publishers to write "fresh" books that nonetheless don't deviate much from the constraints of established categories. I see my role as an agent as that of a mentor and advocate for my clients and their work, as a diplomat who can moderate the author–publisher relationship, as a business adviser who watches over royalty statements, and, in the end, as someone who helps authors feel good about the writing experience, so they can write more books in the future. The good news is that when everything works as it should, the wealth of media outlets available to us in the Internet age means books can be more, rather than less, influential.

What can writers do to enhance their chances of getting you as an agent? Go to a good independent bookstore. It's essential for authors to have some perspective on their work, and that means knowing all about books that are similar, or that an agent might mistake as being similar, and (in another vein) being able to talk about authors you respect whose work is in some ways akin to yours. There's nothing more helpful to me than a short overview that answers questions like these: Why did you write this book? What need does it fill? What audience do you envision? What are some books like yours, even if they are terrible (and say why)? Why are you the right person to write this book? What would you like your work to achieve that hasn't been achieved before? Browsing in bookstores, and buying and reading a few recent works, can be very helpful as you answer those questions. I recommend libraries, too, but it's essential to stay current.

Representative titles: *Wine and War: The French, the Nazis, and the Battle for France's Greatest Treasure* by Don and Petie Kladstrup (Broadway Books); *Talking Money: Everything You Need to Know About Your Finances and Your Future* by Jean Chatzky (Warner Books); *Word Freak: Heartbreak, Triumph, Genius and Obsession in the World of Competitive Scrabble* by Stefan Fatsis (Houghton Mifflin); *Between Sodom and Eden: A Gay Journey Through Today's Changing Israel* by Lee Walzer (Columbia University Press); *Legacy of the Prophet: Despots, Democrats, and the New Politics of Islam* by Anthony Shadid (Westview Press); *The Uncle Book: Everything You Need to Know to Be a Kid's Favorite Relative* by Jesse Cogan (Marlow & Co.); *Sidewalk Critic: Lewis Mumford's Writings on New York,* edited by Robert Wojtowicz (Princeton Architectural Press); *Your Employee Stock Options* by Alan Unger and Mark Sakanashi (HarperCollins).

WENDY SHERMAN ASSOCIATES, INC.

450 Seventh Avenue, Suite 3004, New York, NY 10123
212-279-9027   fax: 212-279-8863
e-mail: wendy@wsherman.com

Agent: Wendy Sherman
  Born: New York City.
  Education: Bachelor Degree in Special Education.
  Career history: Opened this agency in 1999. Was previously with the Aaron Priest Agency. Vice President Executive Director at Henry Holt, Vice President Associate Publisher at Owl Books, Vice President Sales and Subsidiary Rights (1988–1999). Also worked at Simon & Schuster and Macmillan.
  Hobbies/personal interests: Reading, skiing, walking, traveling.
  Areas most interested in agenting: Quality fiction, thrillers, suspense, narrative non-fiction,
  Areas not interested in agenting: Genre fiction such as science fiction, fantasy, horror, mysteries, romance, and children's books.
  If not agenting, what would you be doing? I could be back in corporate publishing, but choose not to pursue that career path.
  Best way to initiate contact: Query letter via regular mail to agency.
  Reading-fee policy: No.
  Client representation by category: Nonfiction, 50%; Fiction, 50%.
  Commission: 15% domestic; 20% foreign.
  Number of titles sold last year: 14.
  Rejection rate (all submissions): 99%.
  Most common mistakes authors make: The most common mistake is not properly targeting the right agent. Writers should do their research as to who seems to be a good fit for their material. I would also have to say that prospective clients should have some patience. We receive 100+ submissions per week and read them all. In addition, it's important to re-

member that what counts is finding the right agent—one who really sees the potential for the book—not just finding any agent. We do accept e-mail queries, but do not open attachments. I like to be informed if other agencies are being queried at the same time. Once we ask to read the manuscript, we prefer exclusivity for a reasonable time period.

Description of the client from Hell: The client from Hell is unreasonably demanding and doesn't trust my judgment and experience.

Description of a dream client: All of my clients (so far) are dream clients. They have faith in my experience, appreciate my efforts on their behalf, and have been supportive of my launching a new agency. My clients have been well rewarded with excellent contracts with wonderful publishers.

How did you become an agent? After leaving Henry Holt, I had the opportunity to work for the Aaron Priest Agency. I had thought about agenting for some time, and it seemed like the perfect way to make the change from working for a publisher to becoming an agent.

Why did you become an agent? 20+ years as a publisher led me to this career. I sold subsidiary rights for most of my career and love selling and negotiating. I opened this agency because I wanted to be able to offer my clients the benefit of my publishing experience, while enjoying the opportunities and challenges associated with owning one's own business.

How would you describe what you actually do for a living? I find new writers and bring them to the attention of the best possible/most enthusiastic editor. I also work with previously published writers who, for whatever reason, are interested in what we have to offer.

What do you think about editors? More than ever, editors have a very tough job. They not only have to find manuscripts they want to publish, but then convince in-house colleagues in editorial, marketing, and sales to support the acquisitions.

What do you think about publishers? It's tougher than ever for publishers to make money these days. We need to work together and have mutually respectful and collaborative relationships.

Comments: For me, being an agent is the best of all worlds. I get to work with writers I care about and help make their dreams come true. In my role as an agent I have been able to expand upon my relationships with editors and publishers. I am always looking for the next amazing novel or nonfiction project. While most of our new clients come from referrals, we consider every query we receive and in spite of the enormous amount of material we have to decline, I never lose my optimism that I'll find something wonderful. The challenge as an agent is to take on what you feel strongly about and what you are confident you can sell. Not just take on clients to say you have them. That said, we are very selective.

Representative titles: Fiction: *What About the Love Part* (Stories) by Stephanie Rosenfeld (Ballantine); *Househusband* by Ad Hudler (Ballantine); *A Quiet Storm* by Rachel Howzell Hall (Simon & Schuster); *Crawling at Night* by Nani Power (Grove/Atlantic); *The Silver Star* by Howard Bahr (Henry Holt). Nonfiction: *Still with Me* by Andrea King Collier (Simon & Schuster); *Cliffs of Despair* by Tom Hunt (Random House); *The Sunday Game* by Alan Eisenstock (Pocket Books); *Back in the Day—Growing Up* *with Tupac Shakur* by Darrin Bastfield (Ballantine/One World); *The Invincible Executive* by Tom Schweich (Contemporary/McGraw Hill).

JACQUELINE SIMENAUER LITERARY AGENCY, INC.

PO Box A.G., Mantoloking, NJ 08738
941-597-9964   fax: 732-262-0825

Agents: Jacqueline Simenauer, Fran Pardi
    Born: Simenauer: February 23, 1949, New York. Pardi: 1949, Pittsburgh, Pennsylvania.
    Education: Simenauer: Fordham University. Pardi: B.A. in English.
    Career history: Simenauer: Editor, World Wide Features, Inc.; President, Psychiatric Syndication Service, Inc.; freelance writer and co-author: *Beyond the Male Myth* (Times Books); *Husbands and Wives* (Times Books); *Singles: The New Americans* (Simon & Schuster); *Not Tonight Dear* (Doubleday); *Singles Guide to Cruise Vacations* (Prima Publishing). Pardi: Strong journalism background; freelance writer, and editor.
    Hobbies/personal interests: Simenauer: Cruising the world. Pardi: Music, reading, dance, theater.
    Areas most interested in agenting: Simenauer: I like a wide range of strong commercial nonfiction books that includes medical, health/nutrition, popular psychology, how-to/self-help, parenting, women's issues, spirituality, men's issues, relationships, social sciences, fashion, beauty, business, computers, reference. Pardi: Cookbooks, medical books, and fiction.
    Areas not interested in agenting: Poetry, crafts, children's books.
    If not agenting, what would you be doing? Simenauer: Become an entrepreneur. Pardi: Probably sitting on a beach or in front of a fireplace reading published books, as opposed to unpublished books.
    Best way to initiate contact: Simenauer: I prefer a query letter with SASE. Pardi: Query letter with SASE.
    Reading-fee policy: No reading fee.
    Client representation by category: Nonfiction, 95%; Fiction, 5%.
    Commission: 15%.
    Rejection rate (all submissions): Simenauer: 95%. Pardi: 98%.
    Most common mistakes authors make: Simenauer: Call and tell you that other agents are interested and want to know what you will do for them if they decide to go with you (and this is before you have even had a chance to see their material). Pardi: Cute gimmicks or self-platitudes. What's on the paper is the only thing that matters.
    Description of the client from Hell: Simenauer: One who keeps calling for all sorts of reasons. Doesn't send SASE, yet demands material back. Calls collect. Calls with long-winded query and expects you to make a decision over the phone. Sends in handwritten, illegible query. Pardi: The one who thinks I can read 250 pages a minute and keeps calling back to check on status. This is one case where the squeaky wheel does not get oiled. It just gets annoying.
    Description of a dream client: Simenauer: Sends in a terrific outline—well-written, great idea, easy to work with. Follows through. Has patience and loyalty. Pardi: The one

S

who trusts that I will do everything in my power to represent the book without being badgered.

Why did you become an agent? Simenauer: I have been an articles editor, journalist, freelance writer, and co-author. Agenting seemed the next step. Pardi: I sort of fell into it, but quickly realized that it does satisfy my "readaholic" compulsion. The only time I am not reading is when I am driving (although I do manage to absorb a few paragraphs at traffic lights).

Comments: Simenauer: I think my background as a freelance writer and co-author makes me even more sympathetic to struggling writers. I understand what it feels like to see your name on a book jacket and appear on a major TV show, and if I can help you achieve your dream, then it becomes mine as well. But understand that it takes a great deal of perseverance to go from an idea to a proposal strong enough to get the attention of the publishing world. I hear good ideas all day long, yet few ever go anywhere. Pardi: I love to be surprised when I read a manuscript, and I love to become emotionally involved. Also, I am a little partial to Pittsburgh Steelers fans.

MICHAEL SNELL LITERARY AGENCY

PO Box 1206, Truro, MA 02666-1206
508-349-3718

Agents: Michael Snell, President; Patricia Snell, Executive Vice President

Born: Michael: August 16, 1945, Denver, Colorado. Patricia: March 6, 1951, Boston, Massachusetts.

Education: Michael: B.A., DePauw University, Phi Beta Kappa. Patricia: Fine Arts, Pratt Institute.

Career history: Michael: Editor, Wadsworth Publishing Company (1967–1978); Executive Editor, Addison-Wesley (1978–1979); Owner, Michael Snell Literary Agency (1979–present). Patricia: Financial Officer; Editor; Executive V.P., H. Michael Snell, Inc. (1986–present).

Hobbies/personal interests: Michael: Tennis, golf, shell-fishing, fishing, gardening. Patricia: Tennis, organic vegetable and flower gardening.

Areas most interested in agenting: Nonfiction books that offer readers genuine, tangible benefits, especially practical, applied self-help and how-to titles in all areas: health and fitness, parenting, relationships, sex, travel, gardening, sports, psychology, communication, writing and publishing, pet care, and training. Michael specializes in business, management, leadership, finance, computers, technology, entrepreneurship, motivation, careers at all levels, from professional/reference to low-level how-to. Both Michael and Patricia emphasize books by women for women on all subjects, from workplace issues and entrepreneurship and management to dating, marriage, relationships, communication, sex, and parenting.

Areas not interested in agenting: Personal memoirs, science fiction, children's books, noncommercial fiction.

If not agenting, what would you be doing? Almost any creative career (painting, sculpture, fiction-writing, teaching) where something solid and valuable arises from

S

applying skill and endures long after you die. Then, again, it's nice to get paid for your accomplishments.

Best way to initiate contact: New authors can obtain a brochure, "How to Write a Book Proposal," by sending an SASE. We also urge prospective clients to read our 1997 book *From Book Idea to Bestseller* (Prima Publishing). Keep query letters concise and focused: your topic, your credentials, and your intended audience. Always include an SASE for response. We only consider new clients on an exclusive basis.

Reading-fee policy: No, we work strictly on a commission basis.

Client representation by category: Nonfiction, 90%; Fiction, 10%.

Commission: 15% of all income from primary and subsidiary rights, with higher percentages arranged for developmental editing, rewriting, line editing, collaborating, and ghostwriting.

Number of titles sold last year: 51.

Rejection rate (all submissions): 93%.

Most common mistakes authors make: Authors who do not respect the etiquette that multiple queries are okay, but multiple submissions are not. Too many ambitious would-be authors engage in their quest for an agent as if they were looking for a plumber rather than for a mentor and friend. They forget that we invest valuable time, expertise, and resources every minute we spend reacting to, critiquing, developing, editing, and shaping a project. Manipulation, playing one agent off against another, while gaining value from both, usually backfires. It certainly derails the crucial building of a trusting relationship.

Description of the client from Hell: Subject experts who assume expertise in writing and publishing and do not appreciate that they can learn from our 40 years of book development experience. Eager authors who do not take the time to develop the full potential of their books and grow impatient with the inherently slow, deliberate nature of book publishing. Writers so intent on making money that they forget that bestsellers benefit readers' lives first and foremost and make money only when they solve problems and change readers' lives. Hastiness, inattention to detail, manipulativeness, greediness, dishonesty and lack of integrity, and humorlessness drive us crazy, just as they drive any businessperson crazy.

Description of a dream client: Any writers, regardless of their background and areas of expertise, who take time to listen and learn about project development and publishing; who take time to develop and write a valuable book proposal and manuscript; who enter into a relationship with us in a spirit of partnership; who work hard but patiently; who, above all, maintain a sense of perspective and humor. Dream clients display all the traits we expect from friends and family: trust, honesty, integrity, respect, and a genuine caring. Without those qualities, no relationship can flourish. With them, all the hard work can pay off for all concerned—author, agent, editor, and publisher.

How did you become an agent? I reached a point after 13 years as an Editor working for a corporation where more time was consumed in organizational politics and meetings than in working with writers, words, and manuscripts. Skills gained in publishing enabled us to hang out our own shingle, focus on authors and their books, and broaden our interests and relationships. Now, in a sense, we work with and for 200 authors and 50 different publishing houses.

Why did you become an agent? A lifelong love of writing and books, a belief that books can make a big difference in people's lives. In business terms, good books satisfy needs, provide tangible benefits, and solve problems. In a human sense, a successfully published book brings the same personal satisfaction a parent gets from the birth of a child or a gardener from a bountiful harvest. How amazing to do work that brings constant, daily joy! Agenting satisfies all three major needs: personal, financial, and spiritual (in the broadest sense of the word).

What can writers do to enhance their chances of getting you as an agent? Approach us with enthusiasm and confidence, but also with a certain amount of humility. Ask vital questions about your project and listen closely to our answers. If you want to know about our credentials and track record, read our book *From Book Idea to Bestseller* (Prima), where you'll not only learn about our approach, but will also meet over 50 of our clients in the book's examples. Treat us as you would any potential business partner, but bear in mind that publishing is a people business, where success hinges on qualities you cannot put in a contract: loyalty, trustworthiness, and love. Love? Yes, when we (or an editor) fall in love with a book, we (or the publisher) will work our tails off to help make it succeed.

How would you describe what you actually do for a living? Three words: development, development, development. A query arrives, we send back developmental advice. A proposal results, we offer suggestions for developing its full potential. We sell the book to a publisher, we develop the author's relationship with an editor. Even after a client has published 3 or 5 or 30 books, development and continued growth dominate our daily activities. Marketing and contract negotiation are the easy parts. Adding value takes a whale of a lot of time and energy.

What do you think about editors? These days, fewer editors actually edit. They often function as traffic cops, buying projects and putting them into production. To deal with that trend, we and our authors must fill the gap, shouldering responsibility for developmental editing. Still, we love editors. Without them, we could not generate income for ourselves and our writers. Everything we say about relationship-building between an agent and client applies to agent–editor and author–editor relationships.

What do you think about publishers? The huge houses have become more bureaucratic and slow. The newer, more entrepreneurial houses are quicker, more personal, more aggressive. Both the conglomerate and the independent offer pros and cons to authors. Still, it has gotten more difficult to find the right home for the right book.

What were your favorite films last year? *Crouching Tiger, Hidden Dragon; You Can Count on Me; Das Boot* (four-hour version); *Traffic; Best in Show; Wonder Boys.*

Do you watch the *Sopranos?* We have never taped anything with our VCR, with the sole exception of all three *Sopranos* seasons.

Comments: You want to hear us rant and rave? Push either of these "Hot Buttons": Marketing and Technology. Increasingly, the marketing folks at publishing companies carry all the clout, giving thumbs up or thumbs down to a book an editor loves and wants to buy. But these people couldn't land or hold a marketing position with a real business. They wouldn't recognize a well-written manuscript if it whacked them upside the head; they assume a writer's next book will sell less than her first book; they judge a book by its cover; they market what they do publish with all the skill and enthusiasm of toothpaste salespeople. If someone made us king of the world, we'd give smart, experienced editors with good judgment and instincts all the decision-making power, and we'd tell the marketing department to get creative, get to work, and sell their butts off. Technology! Fax! E-mail! Hurry, hurry, hurry, I need it yesterday! Oh, all these machines are fine, they make a writer's job a lot easier, but a computer does not make a writer one IQ point smarter, and a fax or e-mail message does not make a communication one iota more urgent. If we could wave a magic wand, we'd make all aspiring book authors type their queries and proposals and manuscripts on old standard upright typewriters (with carbon paper!). The queries would get shorter, the proposals more concise, the manuscripts more carefully crafted. Okay, that's extreme. But don't let your machines seduce you into thinking you no longer need to slow down, take your time, think about it, and do it right. Machines may make you speedier, but they do not add quality, just quickness and quantity. P.S. If you're not having fun in this crazy business, you really ought to be doing something else with your life.

Representative titles: *The Power of a Good Fight* by Lynne Eisaguirre (Macmillan); *Windows MCSE for Dummies* by Glenn Weadock (Hungry Minds); *Business Writing Makeovers* by Hawley Roddick (Adams); *How to Say It to Your Dog* by Janine Adams (Prentice Hall); *Bulletproof Presentations* by Mike Campbell (Career Press); *Complete Idiot's Guide to Starting a Restaurant* by Howard Cannon (Alpha Books); *The Moonlighters' Daytrading Bible* by David Rye (Entrepreneur); *Business Models and Plans* by Don Debelak (Entrepreneur); *Upgrading & Repairing Your Personal Computer* by Glenn Weadock (Sybex); *Great Party!* by Anne Stuart-Hamilton (Prentice Hall); *Speed Dreams: A Guide to Nascar Tracks* by Jay Ahuja (Kensington); *An Innovator's Tale* by Craig Hickman (Wiley); *As Told by Water* by David James Duncan (Sierra); *How to Say It to the One You Love* by Paul Coleman (Prentice Hall).

S

SPECTRUM LITERARY AGENCY, INC.

320 Central Park West, Suite 1-D, New York, NY 10025
212-362-4323

Agent: Lucienne Diver
  Education: Degree in English/Writing and Anthropology (Summa Cum Laude), State University of New York, Potsdam.
  Hobbies/personal interests: Hobbies: reading, writing, painting, mandolin, theater. Personal interests: forensics, anthropology.
  Areas most interested in agenting: Fantasy, science fiction, mysteries, romance, suspense. Primarily adult commercial fiction.
  If not agenting, what would you be doing? I considered going to graduate school for forensic anthropology. Publishing won out.
  Best way to initiate contact: Query letter with brief synopsis and SASE.
  Reading-fee policy: No reading fee.

Most common mistakes authors make: The biggest turn-off is ego. Authors convinced that their first novels will break all sales records the first week on the shelves are likely to be disappointed and difficult to work with. One very basic mistake is the failure to include an SASE with a submission. Most agencies and publishing houses will not even look at material that does not come with a response envelope. Many writers underestimate the importance of the cover letter, which is, after all, the first impression the reader gets.

Description of the client from Hell: Has unrealistic expectations (first novel will break all sales records and be made into a major motion picture grossing billions). It happens, but not daily.

Description of a dream client: Someone who has taken the time to learn something of the business and who can make informed decisions.

Why did you become an agent? I love books, was always excited by the prospect of a job in publishing, and love working with intelligent, creative people.

Spencerhill Associates, Ltd.

24 Park Row, PO Box 374, Chatham, NY 12037
518-392-9293
e-mail: ksolem@klsbooks.com

Agent: Karen Solem
Born: New York, New York.
Education: B.A., Wheaton College, 1972.
Career history: 25 years in corporate publishing. Editor-in-Chief of Silhouette Books; Editor-in-Chief and Associate Publisher at Harper Paperback.
Hobbies/personal interests: Equestrian sports, gardening.
Areas most interested in agenting: Women's fiction, romance, mystery, thrillers—basically commercial fiction and some commercial nonfiction.
Areas not interested in agenting: Science fiction.
Best way to initiate contact: Query with sample chapters and synopsis with an SASE.
Client representation by category: Nonfiction, 20%; Fiction, 80%.
Commission: 15% for adult; 10% for Y/A; 20% foreign.
Number of titles sold last year: Over 100.
Rejection rate (all submissions): 95%.
Description of the client from Hell: Someone who has no understanding of the way this business works; who does not have reasonable and realistic goals, who is overdemanding and difficult with editors or publishers.
Description of the dream client: My dream client would be someone who has a career plan, but who tempers that with an understanding of the business and a realistic view of the market. Someone who's a self-starter and self-motivator.
Most common mistakes authors make: Show me too much across a broad range—that shows me they are not focused and disciplined about their work.

What can writers do to enhance their chances of getting you as an agent? Be focused, have a solid career plan and a vision for their work.

Why did you become an agent? I spent nearly 25 years on the other side of the desk, working for publishers—this was an opportunity to help the author and advocate for them exclusively. I've been with Writer's House for over 6 years and am now starting my own agency.

Representative titles: *Final Proof* by Cathy Palmer (Tyndale); *Best of Sisters* by Karen Stone (Mira); *On the Edge* by Lynn Erickson (Berkley); *The Dixie Belle's Guide to Love* by Luanne Jones (Avon); *Maggie Needs an Alibi* by Kasey Michaels (Kensington).

PHILIP G. SPITZER LITERARY AGENCY

50 Talmage Farm Lane, Easthampton, NY 11937
631-329-3650   fax: 631-329-3651
e-mail: spitzer516@aol.com

Agent: Philip Spitzer
  Born: August 6, 1939, New York City.
  Education: M.A., New York University Graduate Institute of Book Publishing; M.A. in French, University of Paris, France.
  Career history: New York University Press, 1961–1962; McGraw Hill Book Company, trade sales, Sales Promotion Manager, art book department, 1963–1966; John Cushman Associates/Curtis Brown Ltd. Literary Agency, 1966–1969; Philip G. Spitzer Literary Agency, 1969–present.
  Hobbies/personal interests: Sports and travel.
  Areas most interested in agenting: Fiction: literary and suspense. Quality nonfiction, including sports, biography, current events.
  Areas not interested in agenting: Most category fiction, most how-to.
  If not agenting, what might you be doing? Book sales representative.
  Best way to initiate contact: Query letter with SASE.
  Reading-fee policy: No reading fee.
  Client representation by category: Nonfiction, 40%; Fiction, 60%.
  Commission: 15% domestic; 20% foreign.
  Number of titles sold last year: 25.
  Rejection rate (all submissions): 95%.
  Most common mistakes authors make: Telephoning is a mistake.
  Description of the client from Hell: Daily phone calls; impossible to satisfy; if book doesn't sell—either to publisher or subsequently in bookstores—agent is to blame.
  Description of the dream client: Informed, respectful, and loyal.
  Why did you become an agent? An opportunity to work closely with both authors and publishers.
  Do you watch the *Sopranos*? No.
  Representative titles: *Screwball* by Dave Ferrell (Morrow); *The Blue Edge of Midnight* by Jonathon King (Dutton); *The Poet and the Murderer* by Simon Worrall (Dutton);

The Burying Field by Kenneth Abel (Putnam); *City of Bones* by Michael Connelly (Little Brown); *Joli Blon's Bounce* by James Lee Buvke (Simon & Schuster).

STEELE-PERKINS LITERARY AGENCY

26 Island Lane, Canandaigua, NY 14424
fax: 716-396-3579
e-mail: pattiesp@aol.com

Agent: Pattie Steele-Perkins
   Education: B.A. in English, Nazareth College; M.S. in Communications, Syracuse University, New House School.
   Career history: 15 years as a literary agent.
   Areas most interested in agenting: Romance and women's fiction.
   Areas not interested in agenting: Science fiction, paranormal, children's books.
   Best way to initiate contact: Through the mail. Send a synopsis and three chapters with an SASE.
   Client representation by category: Fiction, 100%.
   Commission: 15%.
   Most common mistakes authors make: They send their work before it's ready.
   Description of the client from Hell: The unpublished author who calls every day and e-mails twice a day.
   Description of the dream client: The published author who is so busy writing books she doesn't know I'm alive except at contract time.
   What can writers do to enhance their chances of getting you as an agent? Writers should study the marketplace and submit work to those agents who specialize in the author's genre.
   What do you think about editors? Editors love books and are in constant search of "The Book."

STIMOLA LITERARY AGENCY

210 Crescent Avenue, Leonia, NJ 07605
voice/fax: 201-944-9886
e-mail: LtryStudio@aol.com

Agent: Rosemary B. Stimola
   Born: November 6, 1952, Queens, New York.
   Education: B.A. in Elementary Education; M.A. in Applied Linguistics; Ph.D. in Linguistics and English Psych; All from NYU.
   Career history: Teacher, children's bookseller, freelance editor, education consultant, agent.
   Hobbies/personal interests: Beach combing.

Areas most interested in agenting: Preschool through young adult fiction/nonfiction.

Areas not interested in agenting: Adult fiction.

Best way to initiate contact: E-mail query.

Client representation by category: Children's, 90%; Other, 10%.

Commission: 15%.

Number of titles sold last year: 12.

Rejection rate (all submissions): 90% or more.

Description of the client from Hell: Desperate for money, has unrealistic expectations and a major ego.

Description of the dream client: Talented, flexible, and realistic.

Most common mistakes authors make: "I've published for adults so I can certainly write for children."

What can writers do to enhance their chances of getting you as their agent? Referrals through editors, other clients, or agents.

Why did you become an agent? I like it, it likes me.

If not agenting, what might you be doing? Working as an editor.

How would you describe what you actually do for a living? I make the best possible deal for a book and then work collaboratively with a writer, editors, and others to produce the best possible book.

How did you become an agent? Editors kept referring clients to me even before I had formalized the studio!

What do you think about editors? A mixed bag . . . from the sublime to the absurd.

What do you think about publishers? Too bottom line–oriented right now; often view P&Ls as a firm predictor of future sales.

What were your favorite films last year? *O Brother, Where Art Thou?; Chocolat; Billy Elliot.*

Do you watch the *Sopranos?* Every single week.

Comments: No need to make things more difficult than necessary. I love dealing with straight shooters who answer calls and don't waste their time or mine.

Representative titles: *The Beacon Hill Boys* by Ken Mochizuki (Scholastic Press); *If I Were in Charge, The Rules Would Be Different* by James Proimos (Scholastic Press); *Who Is Baseball's Greatest Pitcher?* by Jeff Kisseloff (Carus Publishing); *Sweet Talkin' Board Book Series* by Jackie Reinach (Random House); *The Learning Tree* by Marcia Vaughan (Lee & Low Books).

STRATEGIC SOLUTIONS, INC. LITERARY AGENTS

17820 Pheasant Lane, Little Rock, AR 72206
501-888-4702   fax: 501-888-8589
e-mail: strategicsolns@aol.com

Agents: Marissa J. Carter, Bonnie S. Hibschman

Born: Carter: March 2, 1952, London, England. Hibschman: August 14, 1951, Michigan City, Indiana.

Education: Carter: B.A. in Biochemistry, Oxford University, 1974; Ph.D. in Chemistry, Brandeis University, 1985. Hibschman: B.S. in Education (English), Eastern Illinois University, 1974; Persuasive, Expository and Technical Writing, University of Arkansas at Little Rock, 1999.

Career history: Carter: Scientist for more than 25 years (R&D, manufacturing, sales, marketing, technical writing); Writer and Editor since 1999. Hibschman: Teacher for three years, sales and marketing for years when not cooking, cleaning, coaching, chauffeuring, sewing, or working on fundraising projects for two terrific daughters throughout their school years. I've written all my life, but finally turned it into a writing/editing business degree in 1999.

Hobbies/personal interests: Carter: Technology, travel, aviation, and playing foosball with Bonnie in the lunch hour. Hibschman: Writing, movies, reading, talking with interesting people.

Areas most interested in agenting: Carter: Thrillers (especially espionage and technothrillers), military adventure, spiritual novels, science fiction, science and technology, general business, exposés (especially David and Goliath stories), investigative crime, and biographic material (especially scientists). Hibschman: Exposés, autobiographies, contemporary events, literary and mainstream fiction, human interest, and spiritual understanding.

Areas not interested in agenting: Carter: Children's books, erotica, sports, cooking, art books, Westerns, and *please* no more stories about drugs, trafficking, and gangs. Hibschman: Historical nonfiction, cooking, erotica, children's books, arts, and pets.

Best way to initiate contact: Send a query letter, including a bio. For fiction: send first three chapters, plus synopsis; nonfiction: outline, plus first three chapters.

Client representation by category: Carter: Nonfiction, 65%; Fiction, 25% Textbooks, 10%. Hibschman: Nonfiction, 75%; Fiction, 15%; Other, 10%.

Commission: 15% domestic; 20% foreign rights.

Rejection rate (all submissions): Carter: We reject a very high percentage of manuscripts on the first go-around, although several have subsequently been accepted after considerable rework. Hibschman: Nearly all first-time submissions need some work to be ready for representation. If an author is serious and wants to pursue publication, critiques are valuable tools that can help an author with the "weak" spots. Even though I might like a manuscript, the first submission is usually rejected with comments on improvement.

Description of the client from Hell: Carter: Those who don't do their homework, demand to be constantly updated, and don't follow up on our suggestions in a timely manner. We try to screen out these types ahead of time, but if you see any lifeless bodies on the front page of the *Arkansas Democratic Gazette,* you'll know our screening process broke down. Hibschman: Funny you should ask. A client who sends a genre that we do not represent, who tells me how to do my job, who demands answers that cannot be given, who tries to throw monkey wrenches into the timeline, who doesn't have the foggiest idea about the processes involved, or who throws a temper tantrum on the phone.

Description of the dream client: Carter: Someone who takes our suggestions to heart and goes the extra mile; a good writer who wants to put in the time to become a great writer; someone who is patient and understands that the publishing process can be a long and arduous course. Hibschman: Imaginative, witty, creative; a person who takes great pains and pleasure in the craft and has a unique, developed style; a person who can incorporate constructive criticism, knowing that improvement and enhancement of the writing is the goal; a person who understands that less is sometimes more.

What are common mistakes authors make? Carter: Sending manuscripts in single-spaced format, not properly paginated, and with weird scene/chapter formats. Sending a "circular"-type query letter, indicating this is the hottest bestseller since *Gone with the Wind,* and little else. Hibschman: Sending an e-mail saying, "I have a bestseller," but saying nothing about the book or the author.

What can writers do to enhance their chances of getting you as an agent? Carter: Following proper protocol: learn to write an attention-getting query letter, and include supplementary material in the appropriate format. What really impresses me is when authors have researched their market and indicate how their work fits in, AND have had their work well edited.

Why did you become an agent? Carter: A combination of things: I was tired of the corporate scene and constant travel and frustrated with other agents dismissing my books with a curt "not for us." I wanted a completely different career. I wanted to be an agent who was approachable and who could nurture writing talent . . . a writing coach, I guess. Hibschman: I'm happiest when working with words, someone else's or my own. It was a natural progression, like learning to swim after wading in the pond.

If not agenting, what might you be doing? Carter: Probably inventing new and exotic pyrotechnic mixtures and plastics in my garage laboratory. Hibschman: Finishing the gazebo in my backyard that was started about five years ago.

How would you describe what you do for a living? Carter: I write, read, and edit all kinds of written material, talk on the phone, deal with morons, run down to Office Depot and the Post Office, and learn the idiosyncrasies of computer programs. Once in a while I yell "Yahoo!" when I discover fresh talent. Hibschman: Grading papers on a grander scale—but the writers actually like to write.

How did you become an agent? Carter: My business partner and I founded an editing, writing, and translation company in 2000. We began acquiring clients in the course of our editing and writing activities, and several urged us to become literary gatekeepers and represent them. We decided to start literary agent activities in the fall of 2001, with the premise of helping promising writers any way we could. We haven't looked back. Hibschman: We were editing one of the best manuscripts we'd ever seen, and when we sent it back to the author, he asked, "Well . . . why don't you represent it for me? I don't see any reason to find someone else when I already like to work with you." We looked at each other, lightbulbs flashing in our brains as if to say, "Hello? Are you listening? Pay attention." And we said in unison, "Why not?"

What do you think about editors? Carter: Overworked and underpaid . . . they have my sympathies. With the little time they have, it's a wonder they find the time to talk to anyone. Hibschman: If they'd rather be doing something else, then they better go do it. It's an occupation that's either in the bones or isn't.

What do you think about publishers? Carter: Becoming more and more focused on the bottom line . . . which is okay, but I would like to see publishers take more risks with first-time authors who have something to say in a fresh and imaginative way. Seeing the same authors again and again on the bestseller lists bothers me a lot. While some bestselling material is good, a lot of it isn't. Publishers are hyping money-making big-time authors and lowering the standards of publishing at the same time. Perversely, the bar is set even higher for new authors. Most authors will reach a certain number of books and become stale because they are on the deadline treadmill. I find it sad that sales and marketing have triumphed over good editorial judgment. Hibschman: They are human beings, covering the spectrum of human behavior. No one's perfect. Everyone makes a few mistakes along the way.

What were your favorite films last year? Carter: *Spy Game, Pearl Harbor, Thirteen Days.* Hibschman: The crop was rather sparse. But Robert Redford, *Spy Game,* could come to my house for dinner (or breakfast, or lunch, or brunch)—at his convenience.

Do you watch the *Sopranos?* Carter: Nope. Hibschman: Uh-uh!

Comments: Carter: Rissy's diatribes: "Service" has become an oxymoron; lack of ethics and corruption in the corporate world and in government; the almighty dollar, and those dedicated to chasing it; jingoism usurping human rights, diversity, and tolerance of others. Whatever happened to "Love thy neighbor as thyself"? Hibschman: A few disturbances in the business are: Seeing the same authors in the top 20, year after year, even if their writing has gone downhill (and some whose writing started on a downhill slide and never recovered). Publishers who wouldn't give an excellent new author a break, even if their lists have been drenched in soggy soup for years. Editors of publishing houses who won't respond to submissions; who guard their offices, identities, and phone numbers like Fort Knox. Sometimes, it takes a new agent to discover a new author of bestseller magnitude. Fresh eyes are valuable assets. Oh, and publishers who send back pithy letters that an editor is no longer on their staff, even when the editor left the day before.

ROBIN STRAUS AGENCY, INC.

229 East 79th Street, New York, NY 10021
212-472-3282

Agent: Robin Straus

Education: B.A., Wellesley College; M.B.A., New York University.

Career history: Little, Brown, Editorial; Doubleday, Subsidiary Rights; Random House, Subsidiary Rights; Wallace & Sheil Agency, Agent; founded Robin Straus Agency in 1983. American representative for Andrew Nurnberg Associates Ltd., Jonathan Clowes Ltd., and Margaret Hanbury, out of London.

Areas most interested in agenting: General high-quality fiction and nonfiction.

Areas not interested in agenting: Genre fiction: science fiction, mysteries, romances, horror. No screenplays or books for children.

Best way to initiate contact: Letter, sample material, biographical information, and prior submission history, SASE (stamped, no metered postage) essential. No material will be returned without an SASE.

Reading-fee policy: No reading fee.

Client representation by category: Nonfiction, 65%; Fiction, 30%; Children's, 5% (only those written by our adult book writers).

Commission: 15% domestic, 20% foreign.

Number of titles sold last year: Authors represented include: Thomas Flanagan, fiction; Andrew Hacker, nonfiction; J. G. Ballard, fiction; Brian Aldiss, fiction; Frederick Turner, nonfiction; James Villas, cookbook; David Burnham, nonfiction; Alex Garland, fiction; Theodore Zeldin, nonfiction; Colin Eisler, nonfiction; Thomas Lickona, nonfiction; Antony Beevor, nonfiction; Michele Hernandez, nonfiction; Stephen Fox, nonfiction; Gustaw Herling, fiction and nonfiction; Anne Willan, cookbooks; Sheila Kohler, fiction, Peter Watson, nonfiction; David Doubilet, nonfiction and photography.

Rejection rate (all submissions): 99.5%.

Most common mistakes authors make: Faxing material, and a long synopsis (sample pages tell us much more).

THE JOHN TALBOT AGENCY, INC.

540 West Boston Post Road, PMB 266, Mamaroneck, NY 10543 -3437
914-381-9463
www.johntalbotagency.com

Agent: John Talbot

Education: B.A., DePauw University.

Career history: I am a Literary Agent and former book Editor with 16 years of experience in corporate book publishing. Prior to becoming an Agent, I spent seven years as a Senior Editor with the Putnam Berkley Group, where I edited such *New York Times* bestselling authors as Tom Clancy, W. E. B. Griffin, and Jack Higgins, as well as rising literary stars like Tom Perrotta, author of *Election* (Putnam), the novel upon which the Matthew Broderick movie was based, and Fred Haefele, author of *Rebuilding the Indian: A Memoir* (Riverhead). I published national bestsellers in hardcover, trade paperback, and mass market paperback, along with five *New York Times* Notable Books. I began my career at Simon & Schuster and worked at Pocket Books and Putnam Berkley before moving on to the Anita Diamant Literary Agency and then forming my own agency. I represent clients who write in all genres, with literary fiction, narrative nonfiction, and suspense being my areas of emphasis. I am a member of the Authors Guild.

Hobbies/personal interests: Sailing, boating, and related water sports. I am a published poet and have had a novel optioned for film. Church is a growing influence in my life.

Areas most interested in agenting: I am most enthusiastic about agenting literary fiction, narrative nonfiction, and novels of suspense. In fiction, I am looking for the fresh and occasionally edgy voice, no matter the subject or genre. Writers with minority backgrounds and unusual experiences and perspectives interest me, as do, perhaps conversely, writers of what Sue Miller calls domestic realism. Previous publication in literary journals and magazines is a big plus. Narrative nonfiction can cover almost any subject, but adventure and personal journey are particular interests of mine. *Rebuilding the Indian* (see above) is a good example of both. Newspaper and magazine experience can be helpful in this area; many books are generated from concepts first tried out in articles.

Areas not interested in agenting: I do not represent children's books, science fiction, fantasy, Westerns, poetry, or screenplays.

If not agenting, what would you be doing? Perhaps writing or teaching, but at this point in my life I couldn't realistically see myself doing anything else—I love my job just the way it is, and I've worked hard to make it that way.

Best way to initiate contact: Clients for both fiction and nonfiction should send a query letter, outline, and 10 sample pages to my attention, along with a self-addressed, stamped envelope for reply, with enough postage for the material to be returned if you want it returned. Do not send postmarked envelopes, as the postmark will not be valid outside your area. Please do not send original manuscripts or artwork.

Reading-fee policy: I do not charge reading fees.

Client representation by category: Nonfiction, 30%; Fiction, 70%.

Commission: 15% on all domestic sales, including film and subsidiary sales. Commissions on foreign rights sales vary; they are usually 20%, but can go to 25%, depending on co-agent.

Number of titles sold last year: I sold approximately 25 titles last year.

Rejection rate (all submissions): My acceptance rate for cold queries has been 1 in 500.

Most common mistakes authors make: A phone pitch or queries by fax or e-mail. Labeling fiction as mainstream. Telling me you have several more unpublished novels. Sending an obvious form letter. Telling me about your personal life and writing habits instead of describing the book itself. Suggesting your own marketing plans and cover design. Including parts of other agents' or editors' rejection letters. Using referrals from people I don't know.

Description of the client from Hell: Clients from Hell don't respect my time. They fail to recognize the publisher's justly proprietary attitude toward marketing, book design, and other facets of publication. They won't take suggestions for change, no matter how small or well-reasoned; complain about writing; and treat being published as a right instead of the opportunity and privilege that it is.

Description of a dream client: Dream clients respect my personal and professional lives. They trust me. They are open to input from their editor. They love to read and they love to write. They are enthusiastic about their ideas and about what they do.

Why did you become an agent? Becoming an agent was a natural progression from being an editor. It's the same type of work, but I'm able to spend less time in meetings and more time working with authors. I can also handle a more eclectic range of material, and I get to work with editors throughout the industry who share my passions and enthusiasms.

What can writers do to enhance their chances of getting you as an agent? Try to respect my time. Make sure your proposal is clear, succinct, and well organized. Make sure the rest of your material is finished and ready to go if I'm interested.

How would you describe what you actually do for a living? I help authors manage their careers for the long term. I find and put projects that I'm passionate about into the hands of equally enthusiastic editors.

What do you think about editors? Editors without a doubt are the hardest working and most idealistic people in book publishing.

What do you think about publishers? Publishers represent the best opportunity for gifted writers to get wide distribution, readership, and money in what is an often difficult business.

What were your favorite films last year? *Apocalypse Now Redux; Legally Blonde; The Score.*

Do you watch the *Sopranos?* I do watch the *Sopranos* and have been a fan since the first episode.

Comments: A large part of success comes with a proper attitude. The most successful authors I know enjoy the process of learning and got into the business for the pleasure and challenge of writing. Impatience, mistrustfulness, and competitiveness with other writers can be very damaging to a career. Focus on your own content, find your own best voice, and enjoy the ride. This can be a wonderful business.

Representative titles: Fiction: *Frontera Street* by Tanya Maria Barrientos (NAL); *Deep Sound Channel* and *Thunder in the Deep* by Joe Buff (Bantam); *SexGeek* by Gary S. Kadet (Forge); *Render Safe* by Jodie Larsen (Berkley); *Lily of the Valley* and *Around Again* by Suzanne Strempek Shea (Pocket Books); *Forgive the Moon* by Maryanne Stahl (NAL); *Burden* by Tony Walters (St. Martin's Press). Nonfiction: *The Dr. Atkins' Age-Defying Diet Revolution* by Sheila Buff (St. Martin's Press); *Girlfriends' Secrets: Insider Info, Extraordinary Tips, and True Confessions About Cosmetic Surgery* by Charlee Ganny (Renaissance); *The Encyclopedia of Pirates and Piracy* by David Jacobs (Facts on File); *The Complete Idiot's Guide to Fantasy Football* by Michael Zimmerman (Macmillan); *Inez: A Memoir* by Clarence Major (John Wiley & Sons); *Doomsday: End of the World Scenarios* by Richard Moran (Macmillan).

T

SUSAN TRAVIS LITERARY AGENCY

1317 North San Fernando Boulevard, #175, Burbank, CA 91504
818-557-6538

Agent: Susan Travis

Education: B.A., English Literature, University of California, Berkeley.

Career history: Prior to establishing my agency in 1995, I spent four years with the Margret McBride Literary Agency, most recently as an Associate Agent. Before joining the Margret McBride Agency, I worked in the Managing Editorial Department of Ballantine Books, New York.

Areas most interested in agenting: I represent fiction and nonfiction and truly enjoy working on both. For fiction, I am currently representing literary and mainstream fiction and am interested in reading just about anything, provided the writing is good and there is depth to the work. My nonfiction interests encompass a wide area. In the past, I've handled cookbooks, self-help/psychology, health, and business. I would like to receive more nonfiction submissions for books targeted at a general audience, not those aimed at an exclusive or limited market.

Areas not interested in agenting: I do not represent children's or young-adult works, poetry, screenplays, science fiction, fantasy, or horror.

Best way to initiate contact: Fiction: A query letter that gives a brief synopsis or overview of the project and any pertinent information about the author. The letter should be concise. My interest is usually piqued more by a description of the underlying themes in a project rather than a blow-by-blow plot summary. The first 15–20 pages of the manuscript may be enclosed with the query. Nonfiction: A query letter giving a brief overview of the project and a brief description of the author's credentials or expertise. Or, a complete proposal may be sent. If the manuscript is complete, the author should query first rather than sending the entire manuscript. An SASE with correct postage must be enclosed for a reply and return of material.

Reading-fee policy: No reading or marketing fees.

Client representation by category: Nonfiction, 70%; Fiction, 30%.

Commission: 15% domestic, 20% foreign.

Rejection rate (all submissions): 95%.

Most common mistakes authors make: Verbal/telephone queries seldom work. If authors are trying to market writing, then they must let the writing speak for itself. Authors have to make the effort to pitch their work using the written word. One of the most costly mistakes an author can make is to market work prematurely. I usually base decisions on an as-is basis, not on the hidden potential. Unpolished manuscripts can rarely compete with those by authors who have taken the extra time to polish their projects and make a professional submission.

Description of a dream client: Dream clients are those who are professional, businesslike yet friendly, who appreciate input and advice but don't require constant hand-holding.

SCOTT TREIMEL

434 Lafayette Street, New York, NY 10003
fax: 212-505-0664
e-mail: MeScottyT@earthlink.net

Agent: Scott Treimel

Career history: Curtis Brown, Scholastic, United Features Syndicate, Warner Brothers, HarperCollins Children's Books.

Best way to initiate contact: First-class mail.

Commission: 15–20% domestic; 20–25% foreign.

Rejection Rate (all submissions): 97%; most new clients have already published at least one book.

Representative titles: *Shattering Glass* by Gail Giles (Roaring Books Press); *The Difference Between Babies & Cookies* by Mary Hauson (Harcourt); *Tribes* by Arthur Slade (Random House); *How They Got Over* by Eloise Greenfield; *Look What the Cat Dragged In* by Gary Hogg (Dutton); *Aunt Lucy Went to Buy a Hat* by Alica Low (HarperCollins).

UNITED TRIBES

240 West 35th Street, #500, New York, NY 10001
212-244-4166
e-mail: janguerth@aol.com

Agent: Jan-Erik Guerth
　Born: 1965, in a Volkswagen Beetle.
　Education: M.Ph. in Cultural Studies, New York University.
　Career history: Comedian (one of five funny Germans!), journalist, radio producer, film distributor, before discovering my true passion—publishing.
　Areas most interested in agenting: Only nonfiction—including "Spirituality in Everyday Life"; ethical, social, gender, and cultural issues; comparative religion; self-help and wellness; science and arts; history and politics; nature and travel; and any fascinating future trends and other serious nonfiction.
　Areas not interested in agenting: Depends on each project, but most certainly not agriculture, animals, military/war, sports, and needlework.
　Best way to initiate contact: Outline with one sample chapter, resume, and SASE.
　Reading-fee policy: No reading fee.
　Client representation by category: Nonfiction, 100%.
　Commission: 15%; 20% on foreign rights sales.
　Description of the client from Hell: Has two little horns on forehead, hides bushy tail and horse's hoof, and smells of sulfur and roses.
　Description of a dream client: Has been reported missing.

THE RICHARD R. VALCOURT AGENCY, INC.

177 East 77th Street PPHC, New York, NY 10021

Agent: Richard R. Valcourt
　Born: November 29, 1941, Fall River, Massachusetts.
　Education: B.A., Roger Williams College; M.A., New York University; ABD, City University Graduate School; L.L.B., LaSalle Extension University.
　Career history: Radio-television Journalist (1961–1980); Program Administration, City University of New York (1980–1995); Instructor, Department of Political Science, Hunter College (1981–1995); founded Richard Valcourt Agency (1995), Consulting Faculty, American Military University (1996–present). Editor in Chief, *International Journal of Intelligence* (1998–present), Executive Editor (1986–1998).
　Areas most interested in agenting: Now represent exclusively professional and scholarly works in international relations, national security, and related aspects of United States government and politics.
　Areas not interested in agenting: All works not included in the above category.
　Best way to initiate contact: Letter of inquiry (with SASE), brief biography, summary of material.

Reading-fee policy: No reading fee. May charge for photocopying, mailing, and phone calls if excessive.

Client representation by category: Nonfiction, 100%.

Commission: 15% domestic, 20% foreign.

Rejection rate (all submissions): 99.5%.

What can writers do to enhance their chances of getting you as an agent? Be experienced practitioners, academics, or journalists in the fields I represent.

THE VINES AGENCY, INC.

648 Broadway, Suite 901, New York, NY 10012
212-777-5522   fax: 212-777-5978
e-mail: JV@vinesagency.com

Agent: James C. Vines

Born: May 1, 1966, Huntsville, Alabama.

Education: Auburn University.

Career history: Raines & Raines, Literary Agent, 1989–1992; Virginia Barber Literary Agency, Literary Agent, 1993–1995; The Vines Agency, Inc., Literary Agent, 1995–present.

Hobbies/personal interests: Sailing, music.

Areas most interested in agenting: Quality commercial fiction, thrillers, women's fiction, quality commercial nonfiction, adventure, relationship books.

Areas not interested in agenting: If it's well written, I want to see it.

If not agenting, what would you be doing? I am an agent because I can't be anything else.

Best way to initiate contact: Query letter with one-page letter describing the story, along with SASE.

Reading-fee policy: No reading fees whatever.

Client representation by category: Nonfiction, 50%; Fiction, 50%.

Commission: 15% domestic, 20% foreign.

Number of titles sold last year: 30.

Rejection rate (all submissions): I reject 80% of the "over the transom" submissions I receive.

Most common mistakes authors make: Writing 12-page cover letters (single-spaced); sending chapters from the middle of the novel, claiming "those are the best"; and calling to see if I've had a chance to read the material yet.

Description of the client from Hell: I do not represent hellish clients.

Description of a dream client: See my list of authors under "Representative titles."

How did you become an agent? I had met some brilliant authors who needed a good business manager, and I couldn't find anything else in this world nearly as exciting as helping them to develop their careers.

Why did you become an agent? I love great authors and want to help them reach their goals.

What can writers do to enhance their chances of getting you as an agent? Write on subjects about which you are passionate. Research the marketplace to make sure the same book hasn't already been written by somebody else. Don't pack your manuscript in plastic "peanuts" that will require us to vacuum the office after opening the box containing your manuscript.

How would you describe what you actually do for a living? I identify the largest and best audience for a book and then arrange deals on the author's behalf with the publishers and film producers best positioned to deliver that book to its audience.

What do you think about editors? I love editors, if they're good.

What do you think about publishers? The right publisher for the right author is a dream come true.

Comments: Please don't write for the money because if you do write for the money, you'll be intolerable once you finally get it.

Representative titles: *The Warmest December* by Bernice L. McFadden (Dutton/ Plume); *The Surrendered Wife* by Laura Doyle (Simon & Schuster); *The Fourth Wall* by Beth Saulnier (Warner Books); *Naked Came the Phoenix* by Marcia Talley et al. (St. Martin's Press); *Meltdown* by James Powlik (Delacorte); *Miami Twilight* by Tom Coffey (Pocket Books); *California Fire and Life* by Don Winslow (Knopf Publishing); *Hunting with Hemingway* by Hilary Hemingway (Riverhead Books); *America the Beautiful* by Moon Unit Zappa (Scribner); *Cross Dressing* by Bill Fitzhugh (HarperCollins); *The Bottoms* by Joe Lansdale (Warner Books & New Line Cinema).

STEPHANIE VON HIRSCHBERG LITERARY AGENCY, LLC

565 Fifth Avenue, 18th Floor, New York, NY 10017
212-486-8216   fax: 212-865-1494

Agent: Stephanie von Hirschberg

Born: December 18, 1950, Pretoria, South Africa.

Education: B.A. in English, Comparative Literature (Magna Cum Laude), Finch College; M.A. in English Literature, St. John's University.

Career history: I began my career as an Editor at Doubleday, working on fiction and general nonfiction. In 1984, I joined *New Woman* magazine because I wanted to do more hands-on editorial work. For the next 14 years, I worked on all kinds of stories—psychology, celebrities, finance, health, careers. I wrote articles, surveys, a book review column, and an alternative health column. I also freelanced as a book editor. In 1994, I received the Editor of the Year award from the American Society of Journalists and Authors, in recognition of my support of writers. I am co-author of the off-Broadway play *We Are Your Sisters,* an adaptation of a biography of African-American women in the nineteenth century. In 1998, I moved to *Reader's Digest* to work on narrative and dramatic nonfiction stories. I launched my literary agency in 1999.

Hobbies/personal interests: Reading, animals, ecology, jazz.

Areas most interested in agenting: Psychology, medicine, mind-body practices, self-help, religion (ecumenical), mythology, biography, nature, environmental issues, animals, true-life adventure, teen girls, literary fiction, mainstream women's fiction.

V

Areas not interested in agenting: Children's books, horror.

If not agenting, what would you be doing? I'd probably be a farmer (organic foods only) and run a small publishing company out of my barn.

Best way to initiate contact: Send a query letter with an SASE; for novels, please include a 10–15 page sample.

Reading-fee policy: No reading fee.

Client representation by category: Nonfiction, 75%; Fiction, 25%.

Commission: 15%; 25% if a co-agent is involved (e.g., for film or foreign rights).

Number of titles sold last year: 3.

Rejection rate (all submissions): 98%.

Most common mistakes authors make: Not doing enough homework about the competition and similar books. Poorly written queries and proposals.

Description of a dream client: Someone who is talented, highly motivated, appreciates editorial suggestions, and has a sense of humor and a positive, realistic outlook.

Why did you become an agent? I love books and the whole, crazy business of publishing. Also, I enjoy being a catalyst—developing talent, bringing great stories and ideas into the world, making dreams come true.

What can writers do to enhance their chances of getting you as an agent? Recommendations from writers I've worked with, from established writers, and from directors of writing workshops count for a lot.

Representative titles: *Secrets of the Tsil Café* by Thomas Fox Averill (Blue Hen/Penguin/Putnam); *Book of Cain* by Herb Chapman (Carroll & Graf); *The Best Food Processor Cookbook Ever* by Norene Gilletz (Whitecap Canada).

WALES LITERARY AGENCY, INC.

PO Box 9428, Seattle, WA 98109-0428
206-284-7114
e-mail: waleslit@aol.com

Agent: Elizabeth Wales

Born: March 30, 1952.

Education: A.B, Smith College; graduate work in English and American Literature, Columbia University.

Career history: Worked in the trade sales departments at Oxford University Press and Viking Penguin; worked in city government and served a term on the Seattle school board; also worked as a Bookseller and Publisher's Representative.

Areas most interested in agenting: A wide range of narrative nonfiction and literary fiction titles. Especially interested in nonfiction projects that could have a progressive cultural or political impact. In fiction, looking for talented mainstream storytellers, both new and established. Especially interested in writers from the Northwest, Alaska, the West Coast, and what have become known as the Pacific Rim countries.

Areas not interested in agenting: Children's books, almost all genre projects (romance, historicals, true crime, horror, action/adventure), how-to, self-help.

Best way to initiate contact: Send query letter with writing sample(s) and a brief description of the book project with SASE to the agency for consideration.

Reading-fee policy: No reading fee.

Client representation by category: Nonfiction, 60%; Fiction, 40%.

Commission: 15% domestic.

Number of titles sold last year: 14.

Rejection rate (all submissions): Most of our projects and authors come from referrals, but several times a year we "discover" a beauty of a book from the submissions pile.

Why did you become an agent? For the adventure and the challenge; also, I am a generalist—interested in variety.

Comments: I am particularly interested in writers who are dedicated to writing and/or who have a particularly compelling story to tell.

Representative titles: *Midnight to the North* by Sheila Nickerson (Tarcher/Penguin Putnam); *Rides, an Autobiography* by K. Lake (Algonquin); *Fateful Harvest* by Duff Wilson (HarperCollins); *Skipping Towards Gomorrah: Sin in America* by Dan Savage (Dutton).

T. C. WALLACE, LTD.

425 Madison Avenue, Suite 1001, New York, NY 10017
212-759-8600   fax: 212-759-9428
e-mail: tcwallace@mindspring.com

Agent: Tom C. Wallace

Born: December 13, 1933, Vienna, Austria.

Education: B.A., Yale, 1955; M.A. in History, 1957.

Career history: Editor, 1959–1987; literary agent 1987–present.

Hobbies: History, biography, memoir, thrillers, and good fiction.

Areas most interested in agenting: Serious nonfiction (history, biography, memoir). Fiction (literary novels, thrillers).

Areas not interested in agenting: Self-help books and "pop" nonfiction in general.

Best way to initiate contact: A brief, but intelligent, letter.

Reading-fee policy: No.

Commission: 15% domestic, 20% foreign and translation.

Number of titles sold last year: 10.

Client representation by category: Nonfiction, 75%; Fiction, 25%.

JOHN A. WARE LITERARY AGENCY

392 Central Park West, New York, NY 10025

Agent: John A. Ware

Born: May 21, 1942.

Education: B.A. in Philosophy, Cornell University; graduate work in English Literature, Northwestern University.

Career history: Editor, eight years, Doubleday & Company; Literary Agent, one year, James Brown Associates/Curtis Brown Ltd.; founded John A. Ware Literary Agency in 1978.

Hobbies/personal interests: Music, choral singing and blues bands, Italy, and running.

Areas most interested in agenting: Biography and history; investigative journalism, social commentary, and contemporary affairs; bird's eye views of phenomena; literary and suspense fiction; Americana and folklore; nature and science.

Areas not interested in agenting: Technothrillers and women's romances, men's action-adventure; how-to's, save the area of medicine and health; guidebooks and cookbooks; science fiction, personal memoirs, reference, and young adult.

If not agenting, what would you be doing? Teaching philosophy or working as a sportswriter, or in some position in race relations.

Best way to initiate contact: Query letter only with SASE.

Reading-fee policy: No reading fee. Only for Xeroxing, authors' copies of galleys and books, and unusual mailing expenses—for example, messengers.

Client representation by category: Nonfiction, 80%; Fiction, 20%.

Commission: 15% on all sales, save foreign, which are 20%.

Rejection rate (all submissions): 90%.

Description of the client from Hell: Untrusting, and accordingly, nudging.

Description of a dream client: Dream clients are professional at all aspects of their chosen writing area; trusting; in possession of a sense of humor.

Why did you become an agent? I like working with writers, editorially and otherwise, outside the corporate realms of meetings and red tape, inside of which I worked as an editor.

Do you watch the *Sopranos?* Yes.

Comments: In what remains of our genteel world of books, I would encourage a shoring up of the realm of common courtesy, returning phone calls, saying please and thank you, and so forth and so on.

Representative titles: *Ada Blackjack* (biography) by Jennifer Niven (Hyperion); *Metaplanetary,* a novel by Tony Daniel (HarperCollins); *Every Drop for Sale* by Jeff Rothfader (Putnam); *The Heart of Addiction* by Lance M. Dodes, M.D. (HarperCollins); *The Immortal Class* by Travis Hugh Culley (Vintage); *The Water and the Blood,* a novel by Nancy E. Turner (Judith Regan/HarperCollins); *Gilded City* by M. H. Dunlop (Morrow/Avon).

WATERSIDE PRODUCTIONS, INC.

The Waterside Building, 2191 San Elijo Avenue, Cardiff-by-the-Sea, CA 92007-1839
760-632-9190   fax: 760-632-9295
www.waterside.com

Agents: David Fugate, Margot Maley, Matthew Wagner

Education: Fugate: B.A. in Literature, University of California, San Diego. Maley: Literature, University of California, San Diego. Wagner: B.A. in Literature/Creative Writing, University of California, Santa Cruz.

Career history: Fugate: Agent with Waterside Productions since 1994. Maley: Literary Agent with Waterside since 1992. Wagner: I've been a Library Clerk, a Bookbinder, a Bookstore Clerk, and a Buyer. I've been a Literary Agent for eight years.

Hobbies/personal interests: Fugate: Biking, cooking, reading, running. Wagner: Yoga, tennis, golf, lots of reading.

Areas most interested in agenting: Fugate: Computer books and compelling nonfiction in many areas, including business, technology, sports, and pop culture. Wagner: Computer books, Internet-specific programming titles, sports, culture and technology, general how-to, business, and management. Maley: Computer books, business, technology, parenting, health and fitness and online courses.

Areas not interested in agenting: Fugate: Fiction, New Age, children's, religious, romance, poetry, short stories. Maley: Fiction, New Age, religious. Wagner: Fiction, poetry, self-help.

If not agenting, what would you be doing? Fugate: I would be the sixth man for some mediocre professional basketball team in Greece, or a nomadic ski bum, or a project-development person at Miramax, or on the editorial side of the publishing industry. Maley: I would be leading safaris in East Africa. Wagner: Editor, publisher, or packager. I would love to run a bookstore someday.

Best way to initiate contact: Query letter or proposal.

Reading-fee policy: No reading fee.

Client representation by category: Fugate: Nonfiction, 100%. Maley: Nonfiction, 100%. Wagner: Nonfiction, 95%; Textbooks, 5%.

Commission: 15% domestic, 20% film, 25% foreign.

Number of titles sold last year: Fugate: 110. Maley: 110. Wagner: 100.

Rejection rate (all submissions): 95%.

Most common mistakes authors make: Fugate: Not researching their market thoroughly. Maley: A poorly written proposal or query letter or too many phone calls to check on the status of their proposal. Wagner: Telling me the book is sure to sell several million copies because the market is everyone. Insufficient market research.

Description of the client from Hell: Fugate: The client from Hell is unprofessional, confrontational, and fails to meet deadlines. Maley: A rude, arrogant, pushy, and impatient person who has completely unrealistic expectations. Wagner: What they said!

Description of a dream client: Fugate: Talented writers who are professional, maintain positive relationships with their editors, and look to resolve problems in a positive way. Maley: A great writer with good ideas who meets deadlines and is friendly and pleasant to deal with. Wagner: Professional, open-minded, creative, honest, and disciplined.

Why did you become an agent? Fugate: I like books, words, and ideas. Maley: Growing up, I always seemed to have either a book or a phone in my hand. Wagner: Probably because I can talk really fast. Also, I love books and like dealing with writers and publishers. It helps to be on the cutting edge.

Comments: Fugate: Please visit our Web site at www.waterside.com for information about our authors, publishers we work with, and the Waterside Publishing Conference, held annually in San Diego.

Representative titles: Maley: *Dreamweaver Magic* by Al Sparber (New Riders Press); *A+ Certification for Dummies* by Ron Gilster (Hungry Minds, Inc.); *The Digital Photog-*

raphy Bible by Ken Milburn (Hungry Minds, Inc.); *Inside Business Incubators and Corporate Ventures* by Sally Richards (Wiley); *John Chambers and the Cisco Way* by John K. Waters (Wiley); *Fed Up! Dr. Oliver's Ten Step No Diet Fitness Plan* by Dr. Wendy Oliver (Contemporary Books). Wagner: *KISS Guide to Windows* by Rich Levin (Dorling Kindersly); *Poor Richard's Building Online Communities* by Margy Levine Young (Top Floor Publishing); *PCs for Dummies* by Dan Gookin (Hungry Minds). Fugate: *The JavaScript Bible* by Danny Goodman (Hungry Minds); *The Flash 6 Bible* by Rob Reinhardt (Hungry Minds); *Inside XML* by Steven Holzner (New Riders); *Hack Attacks Revealed* by John Chirillo (Wiley Technical Publishing).

WIESER & WIESER, INC.

25 East 21st Street, New York, NY 10010
212-260-0860

Agents: Olga B. Wieser, Jake Elwell
  Born: Elwell: July 23, 1964, Milton, Massachusetts.
  Education: Elwell: B.A., Lake Forest College.
  Career history: O. Wieser: NYU Press; Agent since 1975. Elwell: House painter; high school English teacher; Wieser & Wieser: Assistant, 1989–1994; Agent, 1994–present.
  Hobbies/personal interests: Elwell: Antiques, book collecting, hockey, fishing, travel.
  Areas most interested in agenting: O. Wieser: Well-written, challenging books of all kinds. Strong commercial and literary fiction; holistic, medical, and psychological issues are of particular interest. Elwell: Commercial fiction, including mysteries, historicals, military, suspense, romance. Nonfiction backed by a strong author profile: history, true crime, biography, Americana, books about New England.
  Areas not interested in agenting: O. Wieser: Category romance; historicals. Elwell: Science fiction, self-published books that did poorly.
  If not agenting, what would you be doing? O. Wieser: Writing. Elwell: Teaching, traveling, trying to be a writer, painting houses.
  Best way to initiate contact: Through a referral from someone we know well or by mail with a well-presented outline and opening 50 pages with SASE. Please, no phone or faxed queries.
  Reading-fee policy: No reading fee.
  Client representation by category: Nonfiction, 45%; Fiction, 50%; Children's, 5%.
  Commission: 15% domestic; 20% foreign.
  Number of titles sold last year: 50.
  Rejection rate (all submissions): 97%.
  Most common mistakes authors make: Showing material that is incomplete in planning or presentation. Pitches that try to shock or impress with coolness. We avoid faxed proposals, spiral (or otherwise) bound manuscripts, and solicitations that include past rejection letters from agents and editors (yes, it happens!) like the plague.
  Description of the client from Hell: Pitches numerous, disparate ideas and expects reaction/action on all of them. Never is satisfied.

Description of a dream client: Knowledgeable of the realities of publishing (good and bad). Appreciative, receptive to our input, resourceful, and trustworthy.

Why did you become an agent? O. Wieser: There's no job more rewarding, enriching, and exciting. Elwell: I like working in an entrepreneurial setting, and I love books. And there's nothing like playing a role in bringing a book to life.

Representative titles: *Diamond Jim Brady* by H. Paul Jeffers (John Wiley & Sons); *Inferno: The Firebombing of Japan* by Edwin P. Hoyt (Madison Books); *Forgotten Eagle: The Story of Wiley Post* by Bryan and Frances Sterling (Carroll & Graf); *Encyclopedia of the Negro Leagues* by Thom Loverro (Facts on File); *History of the Popes* by Charles Coulombe (Citadel); *A Rogue for Christmas* by Kate Huntington (Zebra); *Sea of Grey* by Dewey Lambdin (St. Martin's Press); *Terminal Run* by Michael DiMercurio (NAL); *Turbulence* by John J. Nance (Putnam); *Tragic Wand* by James Tucker (NAL).

WRITERS HOUSE LLC

21 West 26th Street, New York, NY 10010
212-685-2400   fax: 212-685-1781

Agents: Steven Malk, Susan Ginsburg, Michele Rubin, Albert J. Zuckerman, Merrilee Heifetz, Amy Berkower, Jennifer Lyons, Susan Cohen, Simon Lipskar, Jodi Reamer

Born: Ginsburg: New York. Lebowitz: Baltimore, Maryland. Lyons: August 30, 1961, New York City. Cohen: June 27, 1958.

Education: Ginsburg: Yale University. Zuckerman: D.F.A. in Dramatic Literature, Yale. Heifetz: B.A., Sarah Lawrence College. Lyons: B.A., Sarah Lawrence College; M.A., Middlebury College. Cohen: B.A., Princeton University.

Career history: Ginsburg: Editor in Chief, Atheneum; Executive Editor, St. Martin's; Executive Editor, Simon & Schuster/Pocket Books. Zuckerman: Naval officer; Foreign Service officer, U.S. State Department; Assistant Professor of Playwriting, Yale Drama School; winner of Stanley Drama Prize for best new American play of 1964; author of two published novels and of *Writing the Blockbuster Novel;* writer for *The Edge of Night* on TV; Broadway producer. Heifetz: Teaching writing to children; Literary Agent. Lyons: Began as an Assistant to Joan Daves. Became Director in 1995. I also work as a senior Writer's House Agent. Cohen: 20 years at Writer's House.

Hobbies/personal interests: Zuckerman: Helping writers; tennis, antique textiles and furniture. Heifetz: Cooking, art, sports. Lyons: Dance, rare books, travel.

Areas most interested in agenting: Ginsburg: Fiction: commercial fiction of any type and literary fiction that is accessible. Nonfiction: broad range of topics chosen purely by interest and marketability. Narrative nonfiction, women's issues, science, biography/autobiography, cookbooks. Zuckerman: Fiction: wonderful novels of all kinds, especially those accessible and attractive to a large readership. Nonfiction: history, biography, narrative nonfiction. Lyons: Literary and commercial fiction, memoir and anthology, narrative nonfiction, parenting, illustrated packaged international authors, literary estates. Cohen: Children's books; both authors and illustrators; adults, selected number of nonfiction projects.

Areas not interested in agenting: Ginsburg: Children's books, science fiction. Zuckerman: Scholarly, professional. Heifetz: Men's adventure. Lyons: Romance, limited science fiction. Cohen: Science fiction, fantasy, educational, inspirational, academic, financial, business.

If not agenting, what would you be doing? Heifetz: Living in Italy. Lyons: I would work in the arts, perhaps as a curator of a literary series such as the one at Symphony Space or the 92nd Street Y. I would also teach.

Best way to initiate contact: Ginsburg: Through written correspondence—query letter (with SASE). Zuckerman: An interesting, intelligent letter (with SASE). Heifetz: Letter (with SASE). Lyons: Send a query letter and three sample chapters. Cohen: Query letter.

Reading-fee policy: No reading fee.

Client representation by category: Agency as a whole has about 500 clients. Ginsburg: 40–50 clients; Nonfiction, 60%; Fiction, 40%. Zuckerman: About 70 clients; Nonfiction, 50%; Fiction, 50% Heifetz: Nonfiction, 10%; Fiction, 80%; Children's, 10%. Lyons: Nonfiction, 50%; Fiction, 45%, Children's, 5%. Cohen: Nonfiction, 15%; Fiction, 5%; Children's, 80%.

Commission: 15% domestic and film; 20% foreign.

Number of titles sold last year: Agency: More than 400. Lyons: 65. Cohen: 100.

Rejection rate (all submissions): 50%. Cohen: 90%.

Most common mistakes authors make: Lyons: They call too often, demand too much too quickly, and are anxious about everything. They try to be "cute" instead of being straightforward. They send submissions in strange formats and colors. No need for that. Cohen: Telling me they were referred by someone I've never heard of, sending photos of themselves, sending unprofessional illustrations with their stories.

Description of the client from Hell: Heifetz: I don't have any. Lyons: A writer who doesn't have any sense of boundaries and who has not bothered to learn the very basics of publishing. I expect professional behavior. I don't do well with demanding and ungrateful people. Working together is a partnership and requires mutual respect.

Description of a dream client: Heifetz: Talented, professional, pleasant to deal with, prolific. Lyons: A writer who is professional. I work with authors who are well prepared, polite, and understanding of the process. A good client understands that agenting is a tough business and that agents only have limited amounts of time during the day to be interrupted. Authors should be focused on what they are writing about.

How did you become an agent? Lyons: My father is a publisher. He began the Lyons Press about 15 years ago. Prior to that, he was an English professor and nonfiction editor at Crown Publishing. He introduced me to publishing at an early age, and I had the bug. Also, I met Joan Daves, who represented six Nobel Prize–winning authors, right after graduate school. She immediately took me into the company, which is a part of Writer's House, LLC. Cohen: I started at an entry-level position, became an agent's assistant, and after learning how to represent authors, started doing so.

Why did you become an agent? Heifetz: I like reading and I like writers. Lyons: I like the combination of reading, writing, doing publicity and legal work, and working with authors.

How would you describe what you actually do for a living? Cohen: I help authors navigate the world of trade publishing.

Comments: Well-known clients are: Octavia E. Butler, Nora Roberts, F. Paul Wilson, Tim Willocks, Ridley Pearson, Ann Martin, Francine Pascal, James Howe, Bruce Sterling, Joan D. Vinge, Cynthia Voigt, Colin Wilson, Robin McKinley, Ed Humes, Robert

Anton Wilson, Lora Brody, Jane Feather, Ken Follett, Michael Lewis, Stephen Hawking, V. C. Andrews, Linda Howard, Paula Danziger, Banana Yoshimoto, Barbara Delinsky, Eileen Goudge, Sydney Omarr, David Berlinski, Jessica Harris, Leigh and Leslie Keno, Neil Gairman, Laurell Hamilton, Rosanne Cash.

Representative titles: *The Universe in a Nutshell* by Stephen Hawking (Bantam); *Coast Road* by Barbara Delinsky (Simon & Schuster, first in a three-book mystery series); *Inner Harbor* by Nora Roberts (Berkley); *Inside Intel* by Tim Jackson (Dutton); *Monitor* by James DeKay (Walker); *American Gods* by Neil Gaiman (Avon); *Style and the Man* by Alan Flusser (Harper); *Sunflower* by Martha Powers (Simon & Schuster); *The First Wives' Club* by Olivia Goldsmith (Simon & Schuster); *The Hammer of Eden* by Ken Follett (Crown); *The Swan Maiden* by Susan King (Penguin Putnam); *Tired of Nagging (30 Days to Positive Parenting)* by Virginia Stowe with Andrea Thompson; *Next* by Michael Lewis (Knopf). Cohen: *MacLean Trilogy* by Janice Johnson (Harlequin); *The World* by Roni Schotter (Atheneum); *The Pickle Museum* by Debbie Tilley (Harcourt); *Irish Anthology* by Kathleen Krull (Hyperion); *Looking for Mr. Right* by Bradley Trevor Greive; *Captain Underpants* by Dave Pilkey.

THE ZACK COMPANY, INC.

243 West 70th Street, Suite 8D, New York, NY 10023-4366
www.zackcompany.com

Agent: Andrew Zack

Born: 1966, Massachusetts.

Education: B.A. in English and Political Science, University of Rochester, 1988.

Career history: I began my publishing career on the retail side as the Evening Manager of an independent bookstore in Massachusetts. While attending the University of Rochester in Rochester, New York, I continued working on the retail side at the university's Barnes & Noble bookstore. Later, I served as an Editor on several student publications, including two years as the Managing Editor of the university yearbook, *Interpres.* I graduated in 1988 with a B.A. and the summer following attended the Radcliffe Publishing Course at Harvard University, an intensive publishing "boot camp" led by numerous publishing veterans. In September of 1988, I began work at Simon & Schuster Trade Division as a Foreign Rights Assistant, where I worked with S&S's foreign subagents in the licensing of foreign editions. Not long thereafter, I moved to Warner Books as an Editorial Assistant. While there, I edited a number of titles and began acquiring on my own. I next worked at Donald I. Fine, Inc., as an Assistant Editor and Rights Associate. Within six months, I was promoted to Associate Editor and Rights Manager. I acquired numerous titles and sold subsidiary rights to the entire Fine list, including serial, book club, reprint, large print, film, and television. I also served as liaison with Fine's British and foreign subagents. The Berkley Publishing Group was my next home, my having been recruited as an Editor. I was eventually responsible for more than 40 titles and brought a number of first-time authors to the list. I left Berkley during a corporate downsizing and entered the world of freelance. As a freelance Editor, I worked with a number of different clients, including several literary agencies and major publishers such as the Berkley Publishing

Group, Donald I. Fine, Inc., Avon Books, Dell Publishing, and Tom Doherty Associates. I also reviewed for *Kirkus* and the Book-of-the-Month Club. I became a Literary Agent in September of 1993, joining the then recently formed Scovil Chichak Galen Literary Agency as a full Agent. I launched the Andrew Zack Literary Agency in March of 1996, which I then incorporated as the Zack Company, Inc., in May 1997.

Hobbies/personal interests: Indoor rowing, biking, film, investing, computers, jazz, reading, racquetball.

Areas most interested in agenting: Serious narrative nonfiction; history and oral history, particularly military history and intelligence services history; politics and current affairs works by established journalists and political insiders or pundits; science and technology and how they affect society, by established journalists, science writers, or experts in their fields; biography/autobiography/memoir by or about newsworthy individuals, individuals whose lives have made a contribution to the historical record; personal finance and investing; parenting by established experts in their field; health and medicine by doctors or established medical writers; business by nationally recognized business leaders or established business writers, for example, from *The Wall Street Journal;* relationship books by credentialed experts, that is, psychiatrists, psychologists, and therapists with prior publishing credits. Commercial fiction (but not "women's fiction"); thrillers in every shape and form—international, serial killer, medical, scientific, computer, psychological, military, legal; mysteries and not-so-hard-boiled crime novels; action novels, but not action/adventure; science fiction and fantasy, preferably hard science fiction or military science fiction (I was a huge Robert Heinlein fan when I was younger) and big, elaborate fantasies (not coming-of-age fantasies) that take you to a new and established world; horror novels that take you on a roller-coaster ride; historical fiction (but not Westerns).

Areas not interested in agenting: Women's fiction, romance novels, and anything that is intended primarily for a woman reader; genre horror novels, Westerns, religious works, Christian fiction or nonfiction, gay or lesbian fiction; humor (unless by an established humorist/columnist/comedian); any work of nonfiction in a specialized field that is not by a qualified expert in the field; anything that is supposed to be a novel but is less than 65,000 words; previously self-published books that have sold less than 20,000 copies; any novel featuring drug dealers or drug conspiracies or using AIDS as a weapon; medical thrillers about the evils of HMOs.

If not agenting, what would you be doing? I would likely still be an editor, or I might have gone to law school and pursued a career in entertainment law.

Best way to initiate contact: First, visit our Web site at www.zackcompany.com and see our Submission Guidelines. For nonfiction, I prefer a query letter with a resume and 1–2 pages describing the project. For fiction, I prefer a query letter that includes some publishing history (including title, publisher, and year), if any, and a two- or three-paragraph summary of the work. Keep in mind that if your query letter is poorly written, contains typos or spelling errors, and doesn't engage me, then I will expect no more of your book and will not request it.

Reading-fee policy: No reading fee.

Client representation by category: Nonfiction, 35%; Fiction, 65%. (I want more nonfiction by leading authorities in their areas of expertise.)

Z

Commission: 15% domestic, 20% foreign.

Rejection rate (all submissions): 99.95%.

Most common mistakes authors make: Calling instead of writing; writing a query letter for a work of fiction that doesn't describe the book! My Web site contains an article on how to write a good query letter.

Description of the client from Hell: Clients from Hell have probably published two or three, or maybe three or four, books. These are likely fiction but might be nonfiction. They have "fired" their previous agent because their career is going nowhere and that is, of course, the agent's fault. They are looking for an agent who can "make things happen"; and just to make sure those things happen, they call a minimum of three or four times a week for updates. They regularly pitch ideas to their old editors, to the point where those editors call me and ask me to stop my clients from doing this constantly. These clients are convinced that their ideas are future bestsellers and can't understand why no one agrees with them. They want instant feedback from me or their editors and never once consider that I may have other clients or that the editors may have books on production schedules ahead of theirs. These clients send proposals via e-mail and don't understand why there isn't an instant response (the one downside to e-mail is that it creates a presumption that because it's almost instantaneous in delivery, the reply to it should be instantaneous). Bottom line: Clients from Hell believe that their needs outweigh everyone else's—their agent's, their editor's, their publicist's, and the needs of all the other authors with whom those people may be working.

Description of a dream client: Dream clients act like professionals. They prepare their material according to publishing standards. They keep me updated on the progress of the work and on their career. They send me an updated biography when something significant happens, as well as copies of reviews of published books if the reviews reach them before getting to my office. They call with news, or fax or e-mail me with news, but generally are aware that time spent "chatting" is time that could be spent selling their works. And, of course, they are *New York Times* bestselling authors.

Why did you become an agent? I had been in the publishing business as an editor and subsidiary rights salesperson for a number of years. I had the opportunity to move into representation with a start-up firm that held a lot of promise. It seemed to be the next, natural step in my career.

How would you describe what you actually do for a living? I represent authors in the sale of their works to publishers, film studios, audio companies, and so on. That means reviewing materials to see if I believe there is a market for them, locating the best markets for them, concluding the sale, negotiating the contract on behalf of my client, and continuing to follow up with the buyer to ensure that the process goes well and that the buyer is using the best efforts to make the work a success.

What do you think about editors? In today's publishing world, editors have become more like product managers. Because of the demands on them to meet with marketing, publicity, and art departments, there is little time to brainstorm with their authors, to help develop the work. In addition, technology has made it mechanically easier to write books, which has resulted in an explosion in the number of books that are submitted. The sheer amount of reading required has made it that much more difficult for editors to look for "diamonds in the rough." Instead, they are looking for more "perfect" books that need little editorial work.

What do you think about publishers? Publishers today are looking for the biggest bang for their buck. They seem more willing to spend $100,000–$1 million on a book and put a big push behind it than to spend $10,000–$25,000 on several books and advertise and promote these books. I would guess that even with a $100,000 advance, publishers are going to do a lot less to push a book than an author might want. Publishers are loath to spend money to make money and will only invest heavily in promotion if a large advance is involved. This forces agents and authors to seek larger and larger advances that frequently do not earn out, which in some cases means the publisher loses money. When the publisher loses money, that means it is less likely to take risks and, strangely enough, it is the smaller books that are seen as risks, not the big-money books. This makes it more and more difficult for first-time authors to be sold, unless publishers perceive the author as the "next big thing." In the end, if authors are not the "next big thing," and the publisher loses money on their books, it is very likely those authors will have a very difficult time selling their second book. A vicious cycle is at work, but it is generally one that was started by publishers and can only be ended by publishers.

Do you watch the *Sopranos*? Yes, as well as *The West Wing, ER, Stargate: SG-1, Sex and the City, Six Feet Under, Frasier, Will and Grace,* and *Fanscape.*

Comments: The agent–author relationship is a business partnership. Agents have their role and authors have their role. Neither is an employee of the other. Interestingly enough, I never hear about agents or authors hiring each other, but I hear about them firing one another all the time. Agents, obviously, are businesspeople. Authors need to be businesspeople, too. Authors should do their best to be as informed as possible about the nature of the publishing business. They should subscribe to *Publishers Weekly,* or at least read it in the library every week. They should talk to their local independent bookseller (and if they really want to learn a few things, they should get a part-time job working in a bookstore). My best client is an educated client. I find that the hardest thing about the agent–author relationship is communication. E-mail has become an important mode of communication for me. It's quick and easy and almost instantaneous as a form of communication. Authors should be able to ask their agents all the questions they want, and if an author's agent disagrees with that, it's time to find another agent. But authors also need to recognize that every minute spent on the phone with them is a minute that could be spent selling their projects. As long as authors understand the job they have and the job agents have in the author–agent relationship, the business partnership will flourish and be profitable.

Representative titles: Please visit my Web site at: www.zackcompany.com.

SUSAN ZECKENDORF ASSOCIATES, INC.

171 West 57th Street, New York, NY 10019
212-245-2928

Agent: Susan Zeckendorf
  Born: New York City.

Education: B.A., Wellesley College; M.Ed., Columbia Tercheri College.

Areas most interested in agenting: Mysteries, literary fiction, biography, social history, mainstream fiction, science, music.

Areas not interested in agenting: Romance, science fiction, poetry, young adult, children's books.

Best way to initiate contact: Query letter with SASE.

Client representation by category: Nonfiction, 50%; Fiction, 50%.

Commission: 15% U.S.; 20% foreign.

Rejection rate (all submissions): 95%.

Representative titles: *The Hard Scrabble Chronicles* by Lawie Morrow (Berkeley); *Secrets of the Night* by Una Mary Parker (Headline); *The First Four Hundred: Mrs. Astor's New York in the Gilded Age* by Jerry E. Patterson (Rizzoli).

PART THREE

Road Maps to
Your Success

The Battle of the UNs (Unagented/Unsolicited Submissions)

Jeff Herman

Most major publishing houses claim to have policies that prevent them from even considering unagented/unsolicited submissions. *Unagented* means that a literary agent did not make the submission. *Unsolicited* means that no one at the publisher asked for the submission.

It's possible that you, or people you know, have already run into this frustrating roadblock. You may also be familiar with the rumor that it's more difficult to get an agent than it is to get a publisher—or that no agent will even consider your work until you *have* a publisher. On the surface, these negatives make it seem that you would have a better shot at becoming a starting pitcher for the Yankees or living out whatever your favorite improbable fantasy might be.

But, as you will soon learn, these so-called policies and practices are often more false than true, especially if you develop creative ways to circumvent them.

I have dubbed the previous obstacle course the Battle of the UNs. If you're presently unagented/unsolicited, you're one of the UNs. Welcome! You're in good company. Nobody is born published. There is no published author who wasn't at one time an UN. Thousands of new books are published each year, and thousands of people are needed to write them. You can be one of them.

In this chapter I'll show you how to win the Battle of the UNs. But first let me clarify an important distinction. When I use the word *win* here, I don't mean to say that you'll necessarily get your work published. What I mean is: You'll gain reasonable access to the powers-that-be for your work, and you'll learn how to increase the odds—dramatically—that your work will in fact be acquired.

Please be realistic. For every published writer, there are, at minimum, several thousand waiting in line to get published. "Many are called, but few are chosen."

It's completely within your power to maximize your chances of getting published. It's also within your power to minimize those chances. There are reasons why some highly talented people habitually underachieve, and those reasons can often be found within them. If you fail, fail, and fail, you should look within yourself for possible answers. What can you do to turn it around? If you find some answers, then you haven't failed at all, and the lessons you allow yourself to learn will lay the groundwork for success in this and in other endeavors.

Having an agent greatly increases the likelihood that you will be published. For one thing, on the procedural level, established agents can usually obtain relatively rapid (and serious) consideration for their clients. One basic reason for this is that editors view agents as a valuable screening mechanism—that is, when a project crosses the editor's desk under an agent's letterhead, the editor knows it's undergone vetting from someone in the industry who is familiar with the applicable standards of quality and market considerations.

I usually recommend that unpublished writers first make every attempt to get an agent before they start going directly to the publishers. It's significantly easier to get an agent than it is to get a publisher—not the other way around. Most agents I know are always on the lookout for fresh talent. Finding and nurturing tomorrow's stars are two of our functions.

However, one of my reasons for writing and researching this book is to reveal to you that as a potential author, not having an agent does not necessarily disqualify you from the game automatically. Before I show you ways to win the Battle of the UNs, I'd like you to have a fuller understanding of the system.

YOU ARE THE EDITOR

Imagine that you're an acquisitions editor at one of America's largest publishing firms in New York City. You have a master's degree from an Ivy League college and you, at least, think you're smarter than most other people. Yet you're earning a lot less money than most of the people who graduated with you. Your classmates have become lawyers, accountants, bankers, and so forth, and they all seem to own large, well-appointed apartments or homes—whereas you, if you fall out of bed, might land in the bathtub of your minuscule New York flat.

On the other hand, you love your job. For you, working in publishing is a dream come true. As in other industries and professions, much of your satisfaction comes from advancement—getting ahead.

To move up the career ladder, you'll have to acquire at least a few successful titles each year. To find these few good titles, you'll be competing with many editors from other publishers and perhaps even with fellow editors within your own firm. As in any other business, the people who make the most money for the company will get the choice promotions and the highest salaries. Those who perform less impressively will tend to be passed over. (Of course, being a good editor and playing politics well are also important.)

There are two tried-and-true sources for the titles that publishers acquire: literary agents and direct solicitations.

Literary Agents

As an editor on the move, you'll cultivate relationships with many established literary agents. You'll want them to know what you like and what you don't like. And, by showing these agents you're disposed to acquiring new titles to build your position in the company, you'll encourage these agents to send you projects they think are right for you.

When you receive material from agents, you usually give it relatively fast consideration—especially if it's been submitted simultaneously to editors at other houses, which is usually the case. When something comes in from an agent, you know it's been screened and maybe even perfected. Established agents rarely waste your time with shoddy or inappropriate material. They couldn't make a living that way because they'd quickly lose credibility with editors.

Direct Solicitations

If you're an ambitious editor, you won't just sit back passively and wait to see what the agents might bless you with. When you're resourceful, the opportunities are endless. Perhaps you'll contact your old American history professor and ask her to do a book showcasing her unique perspectives on the Civil War.

Or maybe you'll contact that young, fresh fiction writer whose short story you just read in a leading literary journal. You might even try reaching that veteran United States senator who just got censured for sleeping with his young aides.

One place you'll tend *not* to use is the "slush pile." This is the room (more like a warehouse) where all the unagented/unsolicited submissions end up. Looking through the slush pile isn't a smart use of your limited time and energy. The chances that anything decent will be found there are much less than 1 percent. You have less-than-fond memories of your first year in the publishing business, when, as an editorial assistant (which was basically an underpaid secretarial job), one of your tasks was to shovel through the slush. Once in a great while, something promising could be found; but most of the stuff wasn't even close. At first, you were surprised by how unprofessional many of the submissions were. Many weren't addressed to anyone in particular; some looked as if they had been run over by Mack trucks; others were so poorly printed they were too painful for tired eyes to decipher—the list of failings is long.

No, the slush pile is the last place—or perhaps no place—to find titles for your list.

Now you can stop being an editor and go back to being whoever you really are. I wanted to show you why the system has evolved the way it has. Yes, though it's rational, it's cold and unfair, but these qualities aren't unique to publishing.

You're probably still wondering when I'm going to get to that promised modus operandi for winning the Battle of the UNs. Okay, we're there.

OUT OF THE SLUSH

The following steps are intended to keep you out of the infamous slush pile. Falling into the slush is like ending up in jail for contempt of court; it's like being an untouchable in India; it's like being Frank Burns on *M*A*S*H*. My point is that nobody likes the Slushables. They're everyone's scapegoat and nobody's ally.

Once your work is assigned to the slush pile, it's highly unlikely that it will receive effective access. Without access, there can be no acquisition. Without acquisition, there's no book.

Let's pretend that getting published is a board game. However, in this game you can control the dice. Here are several ways to play.

Get the Names!

If you submit to nobody, it will go to nobody. Sending it to "The Editors," "Gentlemen," or the CEO of a $100-million publishing house equals sending it to no one.

Use the directory in this book to get the names of the suitable contacts.

In addition to using this directory, there are two other proven ways to discover who the right editors may be:

1. Visit bookstores and seek out recent books that are in your category. Check the acknowledgments section of each one. Many authors like to thank their editors here (and their agents). If the editor is acknowledged, you now have the name of someone who edits books like yours. (Remember to call to confirm that the editor still works at that publishing house.)
2. Simply call the publisher and ask for the editorial department. More often than not, a young junior editor will answer the phone with something like, "Editorial." Like people who answer phones everywhere, these people may sound as if they are asleep, or they may sound harried, or even as if they're making the most important declaration of their lives. Luckily for you, publishers plant few real secretaries or receptionists in their editorial departments, since it's constantly reconfirmed that rookie editors will do all that stuff for everyone else—and for a lot less money! Hence, real editors (although low in rank) can immediately be accessed.

Returning to the true point of this—once someone answers the phone, simply ask, "Who edits your business books?" (Or whatever your category is.) You can also ask who edited a specific and recent book that's similar to yours. Such easy but vital questions will bring forth quick and valuable answers. Ask enough times and you can build a list of contacts that competes with this book.

Don't Send Manuscripts Unless Invited to Do So!

Now that you're armed with these editors' names, don't abuse protocol (editors yell at *me* when you do—especially when they know where you've gotten their names). Initiate contact by sending a letter describing your work and encouraging the editor to request it. This letter, commonly referred to as a query letter, is in reality a sales pitch or door-opener. (Please see the material in this book about query letters for a full overview of this important procedure.) In brief, the letter should be short (less than $1\frac{1}{2}$ pages), easy to read and to the point, personalized, and well printed on good professional stationery. Say what you have, why it's hot, why you're a good prospect, and what's available for review upon request.

In addition to the letter, it's okay to include a resume/bio that highlights any writing credits or relevant professional credentials; a brief summary (2–3 pages) if the book is nonfiction, or a brief synopsis if it's fiction; a photo, if you have a flattering one; and promotional materials. Be careful: At this stage your aim is merely to whet the editor's appetite; you don't want to cause information overload. Less is more.

Also include a self-addressed stamped envelope (SASE). This is an important courtesy; without it, you increase your chances of getting no response. Editors receive dozens of these letters every week. Having to address envelopes for all of them would be very time-consuming. And at 37 cents a pop, it's not worth doing. The SASE is generally intended to facilitate a response in the event of a negative decision. If the editor is intrigued by your letter, he may overlook the missing SASE and request to see your work—but don't count on it.

You may be wondering: If I have the editor's name, why not just send her my manuscript? Because you're flirting with the slush pile if you do. Even though you have the editor's previously secret name, you're still an UN, and UNs aren't treated kindly. An editor is inundated with reams of submissions, and her problem is finding good stuff to publish. If you send an unsolicited manuscript, you'll just be perceived as part of that problem. She'll assume you're just another slushy UN who needs to be sorted out of the way so she can go on looking for good stuff. A bad day for an editor is receiving a few trees' worth of UN manuscripts; it deepens her occupational neurosis.

On the other hand, a professional letter is quite manageable and is, at least, likely to be read. It may be screened initially by the editor's assistant, but will probably be passed upstairs if it shows promise.

If the editor is at all intrigued by your letter, she will request to see more material, and you will have earned the rank of being solicited. Even if your work is not ultimately acquired by this editor, you will have at least challenged and defeated the UNs' obstacle course by achieving quality consideration. Remember: Many people get published each year without the benefits of being agented or initially solicited.

It's okay, even smart, to query several editors simultaneously. This makes sense because some editors may take a very long time to respond or, indeed, may never respond. Querying editors one at a time might take years. If more than one editor subsequently requests and begins considering your work, let each one know that it's not an exclusive. If an editor requests an exclusive, that's fine—but give him a time limit (4 weeks is fair).

Don't sell your work to a publisher before consulting everyone who's considering it and seeing if they're interested. If you do sell it, be sure to give immediate written and oral notification to everyone who's considering it that it's no longer available.

The query-letter stage isn't considered a submission. You only need to have follow-up communications with editors who have gone beyond the query stage, meaning those who have requested and received your work for acquisition consideration. If you don't hear back from an editor within 6 weeks of sending her your letter, it's safe to assume she's not interested in your work.

If you send multiple queries, don't send them to more than one editor at the same house at the same time. If you don't hear back from a particular editor within 6 weeks of your submission, it's probably safe to query another editor at that house. One editor's reject is another's paradise; that's how both good and bad books get published.

We've just covered a lot of important procedural ground, so don't be embarrassed if you think you've forgotten all of it. This book won't self-destruct (and now, presumably, you won't either).

Cold Calls Breed Cold Hearts

One more thing: It's best not to cold-call these editors. Don't call them to try to sell them your work. Don't call them to follow up on query letters or submissions. Don't call them to try to change their minds.

Why? Do you like it when someone calls you in the middle of your favorite video to sell you land in the Nevada desert, near a popular nuclear test site?

Few people like uninvited and unscheduled sales calls. In some businesses, such as public relations, calling contacts is a necessary part of the process—but not in publishing. Furthermore, this business is based on hard copy. You may be the greatest oral storyteller since Uncle Remus, but if you can't write it effectively and engagingly, nobody will care. You'll end up soliciting their hostility. Of course, once they *are* interested in you on the basis of your hard copy, your oral and physical attributes may be of great importance to them.

On the other hand, some people are so skilled on the telephone that it's a lost opportunity for them not to make maximum use of it as a selling method. If you're one of these extremely rare and talented people, you should absolutely make use of whatever tools have proved to work best for you.

Everything I've said is my opinion. This is a subjective industry, so it's likely—no, it's for certain—that others will tell you differently. It's to your advantage to educate yourself to the fullest extent possible (read books, attend workshops, and so forth)—and in the end, to use your own best instincts about how to proceed. I'm confident that my suggestions are safe and sound, but I don't consider them to be the beginning and the end. The more you know, the simpler things become; the less you know, the more complex and confusing they are.

BREAKING THE RULES

Taken as a whole, this book provides a structure that can be considered a set of guidelines, if not hard-and-fast rules. Some people owe their success to breaking the rules and swimming upstream—and I can certainly respect that. Often such people don't even know they're breaking the rules; they're just naturally following their own unique orbits (and you'll find a few illustrations of this very phenomenon elsewhere in these essays). Trying to regulate such people can often be their downfall.

On one hand, most of us tend to run afoul when we stray from established norms of doing business; on the other hand, a few of us can't succeed any other way (Einstein could have written an essay about that). If you're one of those few, hats off to you! Perhaps we'll all learn something from your example.

Keep reading!

Write the Perfect Query Letter

Deborah Levine Herman

Jeff Herman

The query is a short letter of introduction to publishers or agents, encouraging them to request to see your fiction manuscript or nonfiction book proposal. It is a vital tool, often neglected by writers. If done correctly, it can help you to avoid endless frustration and wasted effort. The query is the first hurdle of your individual marketing strategy. If you can leap over it successfully, you're well on your way to a sale.

The query letter is your calling card. For every book that makes it to the shelves, thousands of worthy manuscripts, proposals, and ideas are knocked out of the running by poor presentation or inadequate marketing strategies. Don't forget that the book you want to sell is a product that must be packaged correctly to stand above the competition.

A query letter asks the prospective publisher or agent if she would like to see more about the proposed idea. If your book is fiction, you should indicate that a manuscript or sample chapters are available on request. If nonfiction, you should offer to send a proposal and, if you have them, sample chapters.

The query is your first contact with the prospective buyer of your book. To ensure that it's not your last, avoid common mistakes. The letter should be concise and well written. You shouldn't try to impress the reader with your mastery of all words over three syllables. Instead, concentrate on a clear and to-the-point presentation with no fluff. Think of the letter as an advertisement. You want to make a sale of a product, and you have very limited space and time in which to reach this goal.

The letter should be only one page long if possible. It will form the basis of a query package that will include supporting materials. Don't waste words in the letter describing material that can be included separately. Your goal is to pique the interest of an editor who has very little time and probably very little patience. You want to entice her to keep reading and ask you for more.

The query package can include a short resume, media clippings, or other favorable documents. Do not get carried away, or your package will quickly come to resemble junk mail. Include a self-addressed stamped envelope (SASE) with enough postage to return your entire package. This will be particularly appreciated by smaller publishing houses and independent agents.

For fiction writers, a short (1- to 5-page), double-spaced synopsis of the manuscript will be helpful and appropriate.

Do not waste money and defeat the purpose of the query by sending an unsolicited manuscript. Agents and editors may be turned off by receiving manuscripts of 1,000+ pages that were uninvited and that are not even remotely relevant to what they do.

The query follows a simple format (which can be reworked according to your individual preferences): (1) lead; (2) supporting material/persuasion; (3) biography; and (4) conclusion/pitch.

YOUR LEAD IS YOUR HOOK

The lead can either catch the editor's attention or turn him off completely. Some writers think getting someone's attention in a short space means having to do something dramatic. Editors appreciate cleverness, but too much contrived writing can work against you. Opt instead for clear conveyance of thoroughly developed ideas and get right to the point.

Of course, you don't want to be boring and stuffy in the interest of factual presentation. You'll need to determine what is most important about the book you're trying to sell, and write your letter accordingly.

You can begin with a lead similar to what you'd use to grab the reader in an article or a book chapter. You can use an anecdote, a statement of facts, a question, a comparison, or whatever you believe will be most powerful.

You may want to rely on the journalistic technique of the inverted pyramid. This means that you begin with the strongest material and save the details for later in the letter. Don't start slowly and expect to pick up momentum as you proceed. It will be too late.

Do not begin a query letter like this: "I have sent this idea to 20 agents/publishers, none of whom think it will work. I just know you'll be different, enlightened, and insightful, and will give it full consideration." There is no room for negatives in a sales pitch. Focus only on positives—unless you can turn negatives to your advantage.

Some writers make the mistake of writing about the book's potential in the first paragraph without ever stating its actual idea or theme. Remember, your letter may never be read beyond the lead, so make that first paragraph your hook.

Avoid bad jokes, clichés, unsubstantiated claims, and dictionary definitions. Don't be condescending; editors have egos, too, and have power over your destiny as a writer.

SUPPORTING MATERIAL: BE PERSUASIVE

If you are selling a nonfiction book, you may want to include a brief summary of hard evidence, gleaned from research, that will support the merit of your idea. This is where you convince the editor that your book should exist. This is more important for nonfiction than it is for fiction, where the style and storytelling ability are paramount. Nonfiction writers must focus on selling their topic and their credentials.

You should include a few lines showing the editor what the publishing house will gain from the project. Publishers are not charitable institutions; they want to know how they can get the greatest return on their investment. If you have brilliant marketing ideas or know of a well-defined market for your book where sales will be guaranteed, include this rather than other descriptive material.

In rereading your letter, make sure you have shown that you understand your own idea thoroughly. If it appears half-baked, the editors won't want to invest time fleshing out your thoughts. Exude confidence so that the editor will have faith in your ability to carry out the job.

In nonfiction queries, you can include a separate table of contents and brief chapter abstracts. Otherwise, it can wait for the book proposal.

YOUR BIOGRAPHY IS NO PLACE FOR MODESTY

In the biographical portion of your letter, toot your own horn, but in a carefully calculated, persuasive fashion. Your story of winning the third-grade writing competition (it was then that you knew you wanted to be a world-famous writer!) should be saved for the documentary done on your life after you reach your goal.

In the query, all you want to include are the most important and relevant credentials that will support the sale of your book. You can include, as a separate part of the package, a resume or biography that will elaborate further.

The separate resume should list all relevant and recent experiences that support your ability to write the book. Unless you're fairly young, your listing of academic accomplishments should start after high school. Don't overlook hobbies or non-job-related activities if they correspond to your book story or topic. Those experiences are often more valuable than academic achievements.

Other information to include: any impressive print clippings about you; a list of your broadcast interviews and speaking appearances; and copies of articles and reviews about any books you may have written. This information can never hurt your chances and could make the difference in your favor.

There is no room for humility or modesty in the query letter and resume. When corporations sell toothpaste, they list the product's best attributes and create excitement about the product. If you can't find some way to make yourself exciting as an author, you'd better rethink your career.

HERE'S THE PITCH

At the close of your letter, ask for the sale. This requires a positive and confident conclusion with such phrases as "I look forward to your speedy response." Such phrases as "I hope" and "I think you will like my book" sound too insecure. This is the part of the letter where you go for the kill.

Be sure to thank the reader for his or her attention in your final sentence.

FINISHING TOUCHES

When you're finished, reread and edit your query letter. Cut out any extraneous information that dilutes the strength of your arguments. Make the letter as polished as possible so that the editor will be impressed with you, as well as with your idea. Don't ruin your chances by appearing careless; make certain your letter is not peppered with typos and misspellings. If you don't show pride in your work, you'll create a self-fulfilling prophecy; the editor will take you no more seriously than you take yourself.

Aesthetics are important. If you were pitching a business deal to a corporation, you would want to present yourself in conservative dress, with an air of professionalism. In the writing business, you may never have face-to-face contact with the people who will determine your future. Therefore, your query package is your representative.

If editors receive a query letter on yellowed paper that looks as if it's been lying around for 20 years, they will wonder if the person sending the letter is a has-been or a never-was.

You should invest in a state-of-the-art letterhead—with a logo!—to create an impression of pride, confidence, and professionalism. White, cream, and ivory paper are all acceptable, but you should use only black ink for printing the letter. Anything else looks amateurish.

Don't sabotage yourself by letting your need for instant approval get the best of you. Don't call editors. You have invited them to respond, so be patient. Then prepare yourself for possible rejection. It often takes many nos to get a yes.

One more note: This is a tough business for anyone—and it's especially so for greenhorns. Hang in there.

QUERY TIPS

If you have spent any time at all in this business, the term *query letter* is probably as familiar to you as the back of your hand. Yet no matter how many courses you've attended and books you've read about this important part of the process, you may still feel inadequate when you try to write one that sizzles. If it's any consolation, you're far from being alone in your uncertainties. The purpose of the query letter is to formally introduce your work and yourself to potential agents and editors. The immediate goal is to motivate them to promptly request a look at your work, or at least a portion of it.

In effect, the letter serves as the writer's first hurdle. It's a relatively painless way for agents and editors to screen out unwanted submissions without the added burden of having to manhandle a deluge of unwanted manuscripts. They are more relaxed if their inboxes are filled with 50 unanswered queries, as opposed to 50 uninvited 1,000-page manuscripts. The query is a very effective way to control the quality and quantity of the manuscripts that get into the office. And that's why you have to write good ones.

The term *query letter* is part of the lexicon and jargon of the publishing business. This term isn't used in any other industry. I assume it has ancient origins. I can conjure up the image of an English gentleman with a fluffy quill pen composing a most civilized letter to a prospective publisher for the purpose of asking for his work to be read and, perchance, published. Our environments may change, but the nature of our ambitions remain the same.

Let's get contemporary. Whenever you hear the term *query letter,* you should say to yourself "pitch" or "sales" letter. Because that's what it is. You need the letter to sell.

QUERY LETTER TIPS

- *Don't be long-winded.* Agents/editors receive lots of these things, and they want to mow through them as swiftly as possible. Ideally, the letter should be a single page with short paragraphs. (I must admit I've seen good ones that are longer than a page.) If you lose your reader, you've lost your opportunity.
- *Get to the point; don't pontificate.* Too many letters go off on irrelevant detours, which makes it difficult for the agent/editor to determine what's actually for sale—other than the writer's soapbox.
- *Make your letter attractive.* When making a first impression, the subliminal impact of aesthetics cannot be overestimated. Use high-quality stationery and typeface. The essence of your words is paramount, but cheap paper and poor print quality will only diminish your impact.
- *Don't say anything negative about yourself or your attempts to get published.* Everyone appreciates victims when it's time to make charitable donations, but not when it's time to make a profit. It's better if you can make editors/agents think that you have to fight them off.

Q & A: MORE QUERY LETTER TIPS

Q: *Why can't I bypass the query hurdle by simply submitting my manuscript?*

A: You may—and no one can litigate against you. But if you submit an unsolicited manuscript to a publisher, it's more likely to end up in the so-called slush pile and may never get a fair reading. If it's sent to an agent, nothing negative may come of it. However, most agents prefer to receive a query first.

Sending unsolicited nonfiction book proposals is in the gray zone. Proposals are much more manageable than entire manuscripts, so editors/agents may not particularly mind. But you may want to avoid the expense of sending unwanted proposals. After all, the query is also an opportunity for you to screen out those who clearly have no interest in your subject. Also, you shouldn't be overly loose with your ideas and concepts.

These pointers, in combination with the other good information in this book and all the other available resources, should at least give you a solid background for creating a query letter that sizzles.

The Knockout Nonfiction Book Proposal

JEFF HERMAN

The nonfiction book proposal is very similar to a sales brochure; viewed as such, and given its due and primary importance in the process of editorial acquisition and book publishing in general, mastery of proposal writing will give you more than a mere leg up: It will invariably make the difference between success and failure.

Before agents and publishers will accept a work of fiction (especially from a newer writer), they require a complete manuscript. However, nonfiction projects are different: A proposal alone can do the trick. This is what makes nonfiction writing a much less speculative and often more lucrative endeavor (relatively speaking) than fiction writing.

You may devote five years of long evenings to writing a 1,000-page fiction manuscript, only to receive a thick pile of computer-generated rejections. Clearly, writing nonfiction doesn't entail the same risks. On the other hand, writing fiction is often an emotionally driven endeavor in which rewards are gained though the act of writing and are not necessarily based on rational, practical considerations. Interestingly, many successful nonfiction writers fantasize about being fiction writers.

Fiction writing, whether it be pulp or literary, is one of the most creative things a person can do. And there is a market for fiction: Millions of Americans read fiction voraciously. As is covered elsewhere in this book, the fiction market has a category structure through which agents and publishers can be approached.

Nevertheless, as an author, you should understand that writing nonfiction is the easier road to getting published.

As you'll learn, the proposal's structure, contents, and size can vary substantially, and it's up to you to decide the best format for your purposes. Still, the guidelines given here serve as excellent general parameters. In addition, a topnotch excellent model proposal is featured later in this chapter.

APPEARANCE COUNTS

- Your proposal should be printed in black ink on clean, letter-sized (8½" × 11"), white paper.
- Avoid slick-surfaced computer paper. Be sure to type or print out your manuscript on bond paper—and to separate and trim the pages if they are generated from a fanfold tractor-fed printer.
- Letter-quality printing is by far the best. Make sure the ribbon or toner or ink cartridge is fresh and that all photocopies are dark and clear enough to be read easily. Be wary of old manual typewriters—have the proposal retyped on up-to-date equipment if necessary. Publishing is an image-driven business, and you will be judged, perhaps unconsciously, on the physical and aesthetic merits of your submission.
- Always double-space, or you can virtually guarantee reader antagonism—eyestrain makes people cranky.
- Make sure your proposal appears fresh and new and hasn't been dog-eared, marked-up, and abused by previous readers. No editor will be favorably disposed if she thinks that everyone else on the block has already sent you packing. You want editors to suppose that you have lots of other places you can go, not nowhere else to go.
- Contrary to common practice in other industries, editors prefer not to receive bound proposals. If an editor likes your proposal, she will want to photocopy it for her colleagues, and your binding will only be in the way. If you want to keep the material together and neat, it's best to use a paper clip; if it's a lengthy proposal, maybe it will work best to clip each section together separately.

THE TITLE PAGE

The title page should be the easiest part, but it can also be the most important, since, like your face when you meet someone, it's what is seen first.

Try to think of a title that's attractive and effectively communicates your book's concept. A descriptive subtitle, following a catchy title, can help to achieve both goals. It's very important that your title and subtitle relate to the book's subject, or an editor might make an inaccurate judgment about your book's focus and automatically dismiss it. For instance, if you're proposing a book about gardening, don't title it *The Greening of America*.

Examples of titles that have worked very well are:

How to Win Friends and Influence People by Dale Carnegie
Think and Grow Rich by Napoleon Hill
Baby and Child Care by Dr. Benjamin Spock
How to Swim with the Sharks Without Being Eaten Alive by Harvey Mackay

And, yes, there are notable exceptions: An improbable title that went on to become a perennial success is *What Color Is Your Parachute?* by Richard Bolles. Sure, you may gain freedom and confidence from such exceptional instances, and by all means let your imagination graze during the brainstorming stage. However, don't bet on the success of an arbitrarily conceived title that has nothing at all to do with the book's essential concept or reader appeal.

A title should be stimulating and, when appropriate, upbeat and optimistic. If your subject is an important historic or current event, the title should be dramatic. If a biography, the title should capture something personal (or even controversial) about the subject. Many good books have been handicapped by poorly conceived titles, and many poor books have been catapulted to success by good titles. A good title is good advertising. Procter & Gamble, for instance, spends thousands of worker-hours creating seductive names for its endless array of soap-based products.

The title you choose is referred to as the "working title." Most likely, the book will have a different title when published. There are two reasons for this: (1) A more appropriate or arresting title (or both) may evolve with time; and (2) the publisher has final contractual discretion over the title (as well as over a lot of other things).

The title page should contain only the title; your name, address, and telephone number—and the name, address, and phone number of your agent, if you have one. The title page should be neatly and attractively spaced. Eye-catching and tasteful computer graphics and display-type fonts can contribute to the overall aesthetic appeal.

OVERVIEW

The overview portion of the proposal is a terse statement (one to three pages) of your overall concept and mission. It sets the stage for what's to follow. Short, concise paragraphs are usually best.

BIOGRAPHICAL SECTION

This is where you sell yourself. This section tells who you are and why you're the ideal person to write this book. You should highlight all your relevant experience, including media and public-speaking appearances, and list previous books, articles, or both, published by or about you. Self-flattery is appropriate—so long as you're telling the truth. Many writers prefer to slip into the third person here, to avoid the appearance of egomania.

MARKETING SECTION

This is where you justify the book's existence from a commercial perspective. Who will buy it? For instance, if you're proposing a book on sales, state the number of people who earn their livings through sales; point out that thousands of large and small companies are sales-dependent and spend large sums on sales training, and that all sales professionals are perpetually hungry for fresh, innovative sales books.

Don't just say something like "My book is for adult women and there are more than 50 million adult women in America." You have to be much more demographically sophisticated than that.

COMPETITION SECTION

To the uninitiated, this section may appear to be a set-up to self-destruction. However, if handled strategically, and assuming you have a fresh concept, this section wins you points rather than undermines your case.

The competition section is where you describe major published titles with concepts comparable to yours. If you're familiar with your subject, you'll probably know those titles by heart; you may have even read most or all of them. If you're not certain, check *Books in Print*—available in virtually every library—which catalogues all titles in print in every category under the sun. Don't list everything published on your subject—that could require a book in itself. Just describe the leading half-dozen titles or so (backlist classics, as well as recent books) and *explain why yours will be different.*

Getting back to the sales-book example, there is no shortage of good sales books. There's a reason for that—a big market exists for sales books. You can turn that to your advantage by emphasizing the public's substantial, insatiable demand for sales books. Your book will feed that demand with its unique and innovative sales-success program. Salespeople and companies dependent on sales are always looking for new ways to enhance sales skills (it's okay to reiterate key points).

PROMOTION SECTION

Here you suggest possible ways to promote and market the book. Sometimes this section is unnecessary. It depends on your subject and on what, if any, realistic promotional prospects exist.

If you're proposing a specialized academic book such as *The Mating Habits of Octopi,* the market is a relatively limited one, and elaborate promotions would be wasteful. But if you're proposing a popularly oriented relationship book along the lines of *The Endless Orgasm in One Easy Lesson,* the promotional possibilities are also endless. They would include most major electronic broadcast and print media outlets, advertising, maybe even some weird contests. You want to guide the publisher toward seeing realistic ways to publicize the book.

CHAPTER OUTLINE

This is the meat of the proposal. Here's where you finally tell what's going to be in the book. Each chapter should be tentatively titled and clearly abstracted. Some successful proposals have fewer than 100 words per abstracted chapter; others have several hundred words per chapter. Sometimes the length varies from chapter to chapter. There are no hard-and-fast rules here; it's the dealer's choice. Sometimes less is more; at other times a too-brief outline inadequately represents the project.

At their best, the chapter abstracts read like mini-chapters—as opposed to stating "I will do . . . and I will show . . ." Visualize the trailer for a forthcoming movie; that's the tantalizing effect you want to create. Also, it's a good idea to preface the outline with a table of contents. This way, the editor can see your entire road map at the outset.

SAMPLE CHAPTERS

Sample chapters are optional. A strong, well-developed proposal will often be enough. However, especially if you're a first-time writer, one or more sample chapters will give you an opportunity to show your stuff and will help dissolve an editor's concerns about your ability to actually write the book, thereby increasing the odds that you'll receive an offer—and you'll probably increase the size of the advance, too.

Nonfiction writers are often wary of investing time to write sample chapters since they view the proposal as a way of avoiding speculative writing. This can be a shortsighted position, however, for a single sample chapter can make the difference between selling and not selling a marginal proposal. Occasionally, a publisher will request that one or two sample chapters be written before he makes a decision about a particular project. If the publisher seems to have a real interest, writing the sample material is definitely worth the author's time, and the full package can then be shown to additional prospects, too.

Many editors say that they look for reasons to reject books and that being on the fence is a valid reason for rejecting a project. To be sure, there are cases where sample chapters have tilted a proposal on the verge of rejection right back onto the playing field!

Keep in mind that the publisher is speculating that you can and will write the book upon contract. A sample chapter will go far to reduce the publisher's concerns about your ability to deliver a quality work beyond the proposal stage.

WHAT ELSE?

There are a variety of materials you may wish to attach to the proposal to further bolster your cause. These include:

- Laudatory letters and comments about you.
- Laudatory publicity about you.
- A headshot (but not if you look like the Fly, unless you're proposing a humor book or a nature book).
- Copies of published articles you've written.
- Videos of TV or speaking appearances.
- Any and all information that builds you up in a relevant way, but be organized about it—don't create a disheveled, unruly package.

LENGTH

The average proposal is probably between 15 and 30 double-spaced pages, and the typical sample chapter an additional 10 to 20 double-spaced pages. But sometimes proposals reach 100 pages, and sometimes they're 5 pages total. Extensive proposals are not a handicap.

Whatever it takes!

MODEL SUCCESSFUL NONFICTION BOOK PROPOSAL

What follows is a genuine proposal that won a healthy book contract. It's excerpted from *Write the Perfect Book Proposal* by Jeff Herman and Deborah Adams (John Wiley & Sons) and includes an extensive critique of its strongest and weakest points. All in all, it's an excellent proposal and serves as a strong model.

The book is titled *Heart and Soul: A Psychological and Spiritual Guide to Preventing and Healing Heart Disease* and is written by Bruno Cortis, M.D. This project was sold to the Villard Books division of Random House. Every editor who saw this proposal offered sincere praise. Ironically, several of these editors regretted not being able to seek the book's acquisition. From the outset I was aware this might happen. The past few years have given us numerous unconventional health and healing books—many of which are excellent. Most publishers I approached felt that their health/spirituality quota was already full and that they would wind up competing with themselves if they acquired any more such titles.

Experienced agents and writers are familiar with the market-glut problem. In many popular categories it's almost endemic. If you're prepared for this reality from the outset, there are ways to pave your own road and bypass the competition. Dedicated agents, editors, and writers want to see important books published, regardless of what the publishers' lists dictate. Furthermore, it is not necessary for every publisher to want your book (though that is the proven way to maximize the advance). In the end, you need only the right publisher and a reasonable deal. Let's look at the title page from the book proposal.

HEART AND SOUL

(This is a good title. It conjures up dramatic images similar to a soulful blues melody. And it has everything to do with what this proposal is about. The subtitle is scientific and provides a clear direction for the patients.)

**Psychological and Spiritual Guide to
Preventing and Healing Heart Disease
by
Bruno Cortis, M.D.
Book Proposal**

**The Jeff Herman Agency, Inc.
Midwest Editorial Office
731 East Broad Street
Columbus, OH 43205
telephone: 212-941-0540**

(The title page is sufficient overall. But it would have been better if the software had been available to create a more striking cover sheet. To a large degree, everything does initially get judged by its cover.)

OVERVIEW

(One minor improvement here would have been to shift the word "Overview" to the center of the page—or otherwise styling the typeface for such headings and subheadings throughout the proposal to make them stand out from the body text.)

Heart disease is the number-one killer of Americans over the age of 40. The very words can sound like a death sentence. Our heart, the most intimate part of our body, is under siege. Until now, most experts have advised victims of the disease, as well as those who would avoid it, to change avoidable risk factors, like smoking, and begin a Spartan regimen of diet and exercise. But new research shows that risk factors and lifestyle are only part of the answer. In fact, it is becoming clear that for many patients, emotional, psychological, and even spiritual factors are at least as important, both in preventing disease and in healing an already damaged heart.

(This is a powerful lead paragraph. The author knows a lot of books are out there about heart disease. The first paragraph of the overview immediately distinguishes this book proposal and draws attention to "new research." Anything that is potentially cutting edge is going to catch the eye of a prospective publisher.)

Like *Love, Medicine, and Miracles* by Bernie Siegel, which showed cancer patients how to take charge of their own disease and life, *Heart and Soul* will show potential and actual heart patients how to use inner resources to form a healthy relationship with their heart, actually healing circulatory disorders and preventing further damage.

(The preceding paragraph contains the central thesis for the project, and it is profoundly important. In retrospect, this could have worked exceedingly well as the first paragraph of the proposal, thereby immediately setting the stage. This is a clever comparison to a highly successful book. It indicates an untapped market that has already proved itself in a similar arena. Instead of merely making unsubstantiated claims based on the success of Dr. Siegel's work, the author shows what this book will do to merit the same type of attention.)

The author, Bruno Cortis, M.D., is a renowned cardiologist whose experience with hundreds of "exceptional heart patients" has taught him that there is much more to medicine than operations and pills.

(It is good to bring the author's credentials into the overview at this juncture. A comparison has been made with a highly successful and marketable doctor/author—which will immediately raise questions as to whether this author has similar potential. The author anticipates this line of editorial reasoning and here makes some strong statements.)

Dr. Cortis identifies three types of heart patients:
- Passive Patients, who are unwilling or unable to take responsibility for their condition. Instead, these patients blame outside forces, withdraw from social contacts, and bewail their fate. They may become deeply depressed and tend to die very soon.
- Obedient Consumers, who are the "A" students of modern medicine. Following doctors' orders to the letter, these patients behave exactly as they are supposed to, placing their fates in the hands of the experts. These patients tend to die exactly when medicine predicts they will.
- Exceptional Heart Patients, who regard a diagnosis of heart disease as a challenge. Although they may have realistic fears for the future, these patients take full responsibility for their situation and actively contribute to their own recovery. While they may or may not follow doctors' orders, these patients tend to choose the therapy or combination of therapies that is best for them. They often live far beyond medical predictions.

(This is an exceptional overview—especially where it defines the three patient types.)

It is Dr. Cortis's aim in this book to show readers how to become exceptional heart patients, empowering them to take responsibility for their own health and well-being.

(The remaining paragraphs of this overview section show a highly focused and well-thought-out plan for the book. The writing collaborator on this project had to condense and assimilate boxes and boxes of material to produce this concise and to-the-point overview that leaves no questions unanswered. Although it took a great deal of effort for the writer to write such a good proposal, there is no struggle for the editor to understand exactly what is being proposed and what the book is going to be about.)

Although Dr. Cortis acknowledges the importance of exercise, stress management, and proper nutrition—the standard staples of cardiac treatment—he stresses that there is an even deeper level of human experience that is necessary in order to produce wellness. Unlike other books on heart disease, *Heart and Soul* does not prescribe the same strict diet and exercise program for everyone. Instead it takes a flexible approach, urging readers to create their own unique health plan by employing psychological and spiritual practices in combination with a variety of more traditional diet and exercise regimens.

While seemingly revolutionary, Dr. Cortis's message is simple: You can do much more for the health of your heart than you think you can. This is true whether you have no symptoms or risk factors whatsoever, if you have some symptoms or risk factors, or if you actually already have heart disease.

MARKET ANALYSIS

Heart and Soul could not be more timely. Of the $1\frac{1}{2}$ million heart attacks suffered by Americans each year, nearly half occur between the ages of 40 and 65. Three-fifths of these heart attacks are fatal. While these precise statistics may not be familiar to the millions of baby boomers now entering middle age, the national obsession with oat bran, low-fat foods, and exercising for health shows that the members of the boomer generation are becoming increasingly aware of their own mortality.

(The writer would be well advised to ease off the use of the term baby boomer. It is so often used in book proposals that many editors are undoubtedly sick of it—and some have said so. It might have been better merely to describe the exceptional number of people in this pertinent age bracket—without attempting to sound trendy. Good use of facts, trends, and the public's receptivity to what some would characterize as an unorthodox treatment approach.)

This awareness of growing older, coupled with a widespread loss of faith in doctors and fear of overtechnologized medicine, combine to produce a market that is ready for a book emphasizing the spiritual component in healing, especially in reference to heart disease.

Most existing books on the market approach the subject from the physician's point of view, urging readers to follow doctor's orders to attain a healthy heart.

There is very little emphasis in these books on the patient's own responsibility for wellness or the inner changes that must be made for the prescribed regimens to work. Among the best known recent books are:

(Not a big deal in this instance—but ordinarily it would be better to have identified this portion of the proposal as the competition section and set it off under a separate heading.)

Healing Your Heart, by Herman Hellerstein, M.D., and Paul Perry (Simon & Schuster, 1990). Although this book, like most of the others, advocates proper nutrition, exercise, cessation of smoking, and stress reduction as the road to a healthy heart, it fails to provide the motivation necessary to attain such changes in the reader's lifestyle. Without changes in thinking and behavior, readers of this and similar books will find it difficult, if not impossible, to follow the strict diet and exercise program recommended.

In Heart Talk: Preventing and Coping with Silent and Painful Heart Disease (Harcourt Brace Jovanovich, 1987), Dr. Peter F. Cohn and Dr. Joan K. Cohn address the dangers of "silent" (symptomless) heart disease. While informative, the book emphasizes only one manifestation of heart disease and does not empower readers with the motivational tools needed to combat that disease.

(This section is termed the market analysis, which in this proposal actually departs from the approach of the typical marketing section of most proposals. Instead of telling the publisher how to sell the book, the writing collaborator [see the About the Authors section further on] shows special insight into the target audience. The key is that this analysis is not merely a statement of the obvious. This type of in-depth analysis of the potential reader can be very persuasive.)

The Trusting Heart, by Redford Williams, M.D. (Times Books, 1989), demonstrates how hostility and anger can lead to heart disease, while trust and forgiveness can contribute to wellness. While these are important points, the holistic treatment of heart disease must encompass other approaches as well. The author also fails to provide sufficient motivation for behavioral changes in the readers.

(The author does a good job of demonstrating the invaluable uniqueness of this particular project—especially important when compared with the strong list of competitors.)

The best book on preventing and curing heart disease is Dr. Dean Ornish's *Program for Reversing Heart Disease* (Random House, 1990). This highly successful book prescribes a very strict diet and exercise program for actually reversing certain types of coronary artery disease. This still-controversial approach is by far the best on the market; unfortunately, the material is presented in a dense, academic style not easily accessible to the lay reader. It also focuses on Dr. Ornish's program as the "only way to manage heart disease," excluding other, more synergistic methods.

(The writer collaborator directly analyzed the competition, highlighting the most relevant books on the market without listing each one directly. Although you do not want to present the editor with any unnecessary surprises, if there are too many similar books out in your particular subject area, you might want to use this approach. The writer confronts the heaviest competition directly by finding specific distinguishing factors that support the strength of his proposed project.)

APPROACH

Heart and Soul will be a 60,000- to 70,000-word book targeted to health-conscious members of the baby boom generation. Unlike other books on heart disease, it will focus on the "facts of the connection between the mind and the body as it relates to heart disease, showing readers how to use that connection to heal the heart." The book will be written in an informal but authoritative style, in Dr. Cortis's voice. It will begin with a discussion of heart disease and show how traditional medicine fails to prevent or cure it. Subsequent chapters will deal with the mind–body connection, and the role in healing of social support systems, self-esteem, and faith. In order to help readers reduce stress in their lives, Dr. Cortis shows how they can create their own "daily practice" that combines exercise, relaxation, meditation, and use of positive imagery. Throughout the book, he will present anecdotes that demonstrate how other Exceptional Heart Patients have overcome their disease and gone on to lead healthy and productive lives.

In addition to a thorough discussion of the causes and outcomes of coronary artery disease, the book will include tests and checklists that readers may use to gauge their progress, and exercises, ranging from the cerebral to the physical, that strengthen and help heal the heart. At the end of each chapter readers will be introduced to an essential "Heartskill" that will enable them to put the advice of the chapter into immediate practice.

Through example and encouragement *Heart and Soul* will offer readers a variety of strategies for coping with heart disease, to be taken at once or used in combination. Above all an accessible, practical book, *Heart and Soul* will present readers with a workable program for controlling their own heart disease and forming a healthy relationship with their hearts.

(This is a good summary statement of the book.)

ABOUT THE AUTHORS

Bruno Cortis, M.D., is an internationally trained cardiologist with more than 30 years' experience in research and practice. A pioneer of cardiovascular applications of lasers and angioscopy, a Diplomate of the American Board of Cardiology, contributor of more than 70 published professional papers, Dr. Cortis has long advocated the need for new dimensions of awareness in health and the healing arts. As a practicing physician and researcher, his open acknowledgment of individual spirituality as the core of health puts him on the cutting edge of those in traditional medicine who are beginning to create the medical arts practices of the future.

(This is a very good description of the author. The writing collaborator establishes Dr. Cortis as both an expert in his field and a compelling personality. All of this material is relevant to the ultimate success of the book.)

Dr. Cortis has been a speaker at conferences in South America, Japan, and Australia, as well as in Europe and the United States. His firm, Mind Your Health, is dedicated to the prevention of heart attack through the development of human potential. Dr. Cortis is the cofounder of the Exceptional Heart Patients program. The successful changes he has made in his own medical practice prove he is a man not only of vision and deeds, but an author whose beliefs spring from the truths of daily living.

(A formal vita follows in this proposal. It is best to lead off with a journalistic-style biography and follow up with a complete and formal resume—assuming, as in this case, the author's professional credentials are inseparable from the book.)

Kathryn Lance is the author of more than 30 books of nonfiction and fiction (see attached publications list for details). Her first book, *Running for Health and Beauty* (1976), the first mass-market book on running for women, sold half a million copies. *The Setpoint Diet* (1985), ghosted for Dr. Gilbert A. Leveille, reached the *New York Times* bestseller list for several weeks. Ms. Lance has written widely on fitness, health, diet, and medicine.

(Though she wasn't mentioned on the title page, Lance is the collaborator. This brief bio and the following resume reveal a writer with virtually impeccable experience. Her participation served to ensure the editors that they could count on the delivery of a high-quality manuscript. Her bio sketch is also strong in its simplicity. Her writing credits are voluminous, but she does not use up space here with a comprehensive listing. Instead she showcases only credits that are relevant to the success of this particular project. Comprehensive author resumes were also attached as addenda to the proposal package.)

HEART AND SOUL
by
Bruno Cortis, M.D.
Chapter Outline

(Creating a separate page [or pages] for the entire table of contents is a useful and easy technique to enable the editor to gain a holistic vision for the book before delving into the chapter abstracts. In retrospect, we should have had one here.)

(The following is an exceptional outline because it goes well beyond the lazy and stingy telegraph approach that many writers use, often to their own detriment. [Telegrams once were a popular means of communication that required the sender to pay by the word.] Here each abstract reads like a miniature sample chapter unto itself. It proves that the writers have a genuine command of their subject, a well-organized agenda, and superior skills for writing about it. Together they are a darn good team. Whatever legitimate reasons a publisher may have had for rejecting this proposal, it had nothing to do with its manifest editorial and conceptual merits. Some writers are reluctant to go this editorial distance on spec. However, if you believe in your project's viability and you want to maximize acquisition interest and the ultimate advance, you'll give the proposal everything you've got.)

Contents

Introduction: Beating the Odds: Exceptional Heart Patients
(See sample chapter.)

CHAPTER ONE. YOU AND YOUR HEART
Traditional medicine doesn't and can't "cure" heart disease. The recurrence rate of arterial blockage after angioplasty is 25–35 percent, while a bypass operation only bypasses the problem, but does not cure it. The author proposes a new way of looking at heart disease, one in which patients become responsible for the care and well-being of their hearts, in partnership with their physicians. Following a brief, understandable discussion of the physiology of heart disease and heart attack, further topics covered in this chapter include:

(This is a good technique for a chapter abstract. The writer organizes the structure as a listing of chapter topics and elaborates with a sample of the substance and writing approach that will be incorporated into the book. The editor cannot, of course, be expected to be an expert on the subject, but after reading this abstract will come away with a good sense of the quality of the chapter and the depth of its coverage.)

Heart disease as a message from your body. Many of us go through life neglecting our bodies' signals, ignoring symptoms until a crisis occurs. But the body talks to us and it is up to us to listen and try to understand the message. The heart bears the load of all our physical activity as well as our mental activity.

Stress can affect the heart as well as any other body system. This section explores the warning signs of heart disease as "messages" we may receive from our hearts, what these messages may mean, and what we can do in response to these messages.

Why medical tests and treatments are not enough. You, the patient, are ultimately responsible for your own health. Placing all faith in a doctor is a way of abdicating that responsibility. The physician is not a healer; rather, he or she sets the stage for the patient's body to heal itself. Disease is actually a manifestation of an imbalance within the body. Medical procedures can help temporarily, but the real solution lies in the patient's becoming aware of his own responsibility for health. This may involve changing diet, stopping smoking, learning to control the inner life.

(Although the abstracts are directed to the editor who reviews the proposal, the writer incorporates the voice to be used in the book by speaking directly to the reader. This is an effective way to incorporate her writing style into the chapter-by-chapter outline.)

Getting the best (while avoiding the worst) of modern medicine. In the author's view, the most important aspect of medicine is not the medication but the patient/physician relationship. Unfortunately, this relationship is often cold, superficial, professional. The patient goes into the medical pipeline, endures a number of tests, then comes out the other end with a diagnosis, which is like a flag he has to carry for life. This view of disease ignores the patient as the *main* component of the healing process. Readers are advised to work with their doctors to learn their own blood pressure, blood sugar, cholesterol level, and what these numbers mean. They are further advised how to enlist a team of support people to increase their own knowledge of the disease and learn to discover the self-healing mechanisms within.

How to assess your doctor. Ten questions a patient needs to ask in order to assure the best patient–doctor relationship.

Taking charge of your own medical care. Rather than being passive patients, readers are urged to directly confront their illness and the reasons for it, asking themselves: How can I find a cause at the deepest level? What have I learned from this disease? What is good about it? What have I learned about myself? Exceptional heart patients don't allow themselves to be overwhelmed by the disease; rather, they realize that it is most likely a temporary problem, most of the time self-limited, and that they have a power within to overcome it.

Seven keys to a healthy heart. Whether presently healthy or already ill of heart disease, there is a great deal readers can do to improve and maintain the health of their hearts. The most important component of such a plan is to have a commitment to a healthy heart. The author offers the following seven keys to a healthy heart: respect your body; take time to relax every day; accept, respect, and appreciate yourself; share your deepest feelings; establish life goals; nourish your spiritual self; love yourself and others unconditionally. Each of these aspects of heart care will be examined in detail in later chapters.

Heartskill #1: *Learning to take your own pulse.* The pulse is a wave of blood sent through the arteries each time the heart contracts; pulse rate therefore provides important information about cardiac function. The easiest place to measure the pulse is the wrist: place your index and middle finger over the underside of the opposite wrist. Press gently and firmly until you locate your pulse. Don't use your thumb to feel the pulse, because the thumb has a pulse of its own. Count the number of pulse beats in fifteen seconds, then multiply that by four for your heart rate.

This exercise will include charts so that readers can track and learn their own normal pulse range for resting and exercising, and be alerted to irregularities and changes that may require medical attention.

(The inclusion of this technique shows how specific and practical information will be included in the book—important for a nonfiction book proposal. Editors look for what are called the program aspects of a book, because they can be used in promotional settings—and may also be the basis for serial-rights sales to magazines.)

CHAPTER TWO. YOUR MIND AND YOUR HEART

This chapter begins to explore the connection between mind and body as it relates to heart disease. Early in the chapter readers will meet three Exceptional Heart Patients who overcame crushing diagnoses. These include Van, who overcame a heart attack (at age 48), two open-heart surgeries, and "terminal" lung cancer. Through visualization techniques given him by the author, Van has fully recovered and is living a healthy and satisfying life. Goran, who had a family history of cardiomyopathy, drew on the support and love of his family to survive a heart transplant and has since gone on to win several championships in an Olympics contest for transplant patients. Elaine, who overcame both childhood cancer and severe heart disease, is, at the age of 24, happily married and a mother. The techniques used by these Exceptional Heart Patients will be discussed in the context of the mind–body connection.

(The authors do not save the good stuff for the book. If you have interesting case studies or anecdotes, include them in your abstracts: The more stimulating material you can include, the more you can intrigue your editor. In general, this chapter-by-chapter synopsis is exceptionally detailed in a simplified fashion, which is important for this type of book.)

How your doctor views heart disease: Risk factors v. symptoms. Traditional medicine views the risk factors for heart disease (smoking, high blood cholesterol, high blood pressure, diabetes, obesity, sedentary lifestyle, family history of heart disease, use of oral contraceptives) as indicators of the likelihood of developing illness. In contrast, the author presents these risk factors as *symptoms* of an underlying disease, and discusses ways to change them. Smoking, for example, is not the root of the problem, which is, rather, fear, tension, and stress. Smoking is just an outlet that the patient uses to get rid of these basic elements, which he or she believes are uncontrollable. Likewise high cholesterol, which is viewed by the medical establishment as largely caused by poor diet, is also affected by stress. (In a study of rabbits on a high-cholesterol diet, narrowing of arteries was less in rabbits that were petted, even if the diet remained unhealthful.) Other elements besides the traditional "risk factors," such as hostility, have been shown to lead to high rates of heart disease.

A mind/body model of heart disease. It is not uncommon to hear stories like this: They were a very happy couple, married 52 years. Then, suddenly, the wife developed breast cancer and died. The husband, who had no previous symptoms of heart disease, had a heart attack and died two months later. All too often there is a very close relationship between a traumatic event and serious illness. Likewise, patients may often become depressed and literally will themselves to die. The other side of the coin is the innumerable patients who use a variety of techniques to enlist the mind–body connection in helping to overcome and even cure serious illnesses, including heart disease.

Rethinking your negative beliefs about heart disease. The first step in using the mind to help to heal the body is to rethink negative beliefs about heart disease. Modern studies have shown that stress plays a most important role in the creation of heart disease, influencing all of the "risk factors." Heart disease is actually a disease of self, caused by self, and is made worse by the belief that we are its "victims." Another negative and incorrect belief is that the possibilities for recovery are limited. The author asserts that these beliefs are untrue, and that for patients willing to learn from the experience, heart disease can be a path to recovery, self-improvement, and growth.

The healing personality: tapping into your body's healing powers. Although the notion of a "healing personality" may sound contradictory, the power of healing is awareness, which can be achieved by anyone. The author describes his own discovery of spirituality in medicine and the realization that ultimately the origin of disease is in the mind. This is why treating disease with medicine and surgery alone does not heal: because these methods ignore the natural healing powers of the body/mind. How does one develop a "healing personality"? The starting point is awareness of the spiritual power within. As the author states, in order to become healthy, one must become spiritual.

Writing your own script for a healthy heart. Before writing any script, one must set the stage, and in this case readers are urged to see a cardiologist or physician and have a thorough checkup. This checkup will evaluate the presence or absence of the "risk factors" and assess the health of other body organs as well. Once the scene is set, it is time to add in the other elements of a healthy heart, all of which will be explored in detail in the coming chapters.

Making a contract with your heart. We see obstacles only when we lose sight of our goals. How to make (either mentally or on paper) a contract with one's heart that promises to take care of the heart. Each individual reader's contract will be somewhat different; for example, someone who is overweight might include in the contract the desire that in six months she would weigh so much. The point is to set realistic, achievable goals. Guidelines are provided for breaking larger goals down into small, easily achievable, steps. Creating goals for the future makes them a part of the present in the sense that it is today that we start pursuing them.

What to say when you talk to yourself. In the view of the author, the greatest source of stress in life is negative conversations we have with ourselves. These "conversations," which go on all the time without our even being aware of them, often include such negative suggestions as "When are you going to learn?" "Oh, no, you stupid idiot, you did it again!" When we put ourselves down, we reinforce feelings of unworthiness and inadequacy, which leads to stress and illness. Guidelines are given for replacing such negative self-conversation with more positive self-talk, including messages of love and healing.

Heartskill #2: *Sending healing energy to your heart.* In this exercise, readers learn a simple meditation technique that will help them get in touch with their natural healing powers and begin to heal their hearts.

CHAPTER THREE. THE FRIENDSHIP FACTOR: PLUGGING INTO YOUR SOCIAL SUPPORT SYSTEM

Heart disease is not an isolated event, and the heart patient is not an isolated human being. Among the less medically obvious "risk factors" involved in coronary disease is social isolation. In this chapter the author discusses the importance of maintaining and strengthening all the social support aspects of the patient's life, including family, friendship, community, and sex. He shows how intimacy and connection can be used not just for comfort but also as actual healing tools.

Sexual intimacy: the healing touch. Following a heart attack, many patients may lose confidence due to a fear of loss of attractiveness or fear of death. Citing recent studies, the author points out that there is a difference between making sex and making love. The desire for sex is a human need and is not limited to healthy people. Anybody who has had a heart problem still has sexual needs and ignoring them may be an additional cause of stress. Guidelines for when and how to resume sexual activity are offered. Other topics covered in this chapter include:

* *Keeping your loved ones healthy, and letting them keep you healthy*
* *How you may be unwittingly pushing others out of your life*
* *The art of nondefensive, nonreactive communication*

- *Accepting your loved ones' feelings and your own*
- *How to enlist the support of family and friends*
- *Joining or starting your own support group*
- Heartskill #3: *Mapping your social support system*

CHAPTER FOUR. OPENING YOUR HEART: LEARNING TO MAKE FRIENDS WITH YOURSELF

In addition to enlisting the support of others, for complete healing it is necessary for the patient to literally become a friend to himself or herself. This may entail changing old ways of thinking and responding, as well as developing new, healthier ways of relating to time and other external stresses. In this chapter the author explores ways of changing Type A behavior, as well as proven techniques for dealing with life's daily hassles and upsets. An important section of the chapter shows readers how to love and cherish the "inner child," that part of the personality that needs to be loved, to be acknowledged, and to have fun. Equally important is the guilt that each of us carries within, and that can lead not only to unhealthy behaviors but also to actual stress. The author gives exercises for learning to discover and absolve the hidden guilts that keep each of us from realizing our true healthy potential. Topics covered in this chapter include:

A positive approach to negative emotions
Checking yourself out on Type A behavior: a self-test
Being assertive without being angry
Keeping your balance in the face of daily hassles and major setbacks
Making a friend of time
Identifying and healing your old childhood hurts
Letting go of hurts, regrets, resentments, and guilt
Forgiving yourself and making a new start
The trusting heart
Heartskill #4: *Forgiveness exercise*

CHAPTER FIVE. IDENTIFYING AND ELIMINATING STRESS IN YOUR LIFE

The science of psychoneuroimmunology is beginning to prove that the mind and body are not only connected, but also inseparable. It has been demonstrated that changes in life often precede disease. Lab studies have shown that the amount of stress experienced by experimental animals can induce rapid growth of a tumor that would ordinarily be rejected. For heart patients, the fact of disease itself can become another inner stress factor that may worsen the disease and the quality of life. One out of five healthy persons is a "heart reactor," who has strong responses under stress that induce such unhealthful physiological changes as narrowing of the coronary arteries, hypertrophy of the heart muscle, and high blood pressure. In this chapter the author shows readers how to change stress-producing negative beliefs into constructive, rational beliefs that reduce stress. Included are guidelines to the five keys for controlling stress: diet, rest, exercise, attitude, and self-discipline.

Why you feel so stressed-out
Where does emotional stress come from and how does it affect your heart?
Your stress signal checklist
Staying in control
Calculating your heart-stress level at home and on the job
Stress management
Heartskill #5: *Mapping your stress hotspots*

CHAPTER SIX. YOUR FAITH AND YOUR HEART

As the author points out, there are few studies in the field of spirituality and medicine, because physicians, like most scientists, shy away from what is called "soft data." Soft data are anything outside the realm of physics, mathematics, etc.: the "exact sciences." As a physician, the author has grown ever more convinced of the body's natural healing power, which is evoked through mind and spirit. No matter how "spirit" is defined, whether in traditional religious terms or as a component of mind or personality, the truth is that in order to become healthy, it is necessary to become spiritual.

In a 10-month study of 393 coronary patients at San Francisco General Hospital, it was proven that the group who received outside prayer in addition to standard medical treatment did far better than those who received medical treatment alone. Those in the experimental group suffered fewer problems with congestive heart failure, pneumonia, cardiac arrests, and had a significantly lower mortality rate. This chapter explores the possible reasons for this startling result and illuminates the connection between spirit and health.

The difference between spirituality and religion. A discussion of the differences between traditional views of spirituality and the new holistic approach that sees mind, body, and spirit as intimately connected and interdependent.

Faith and heart disease. The healing personality is that of a person who takes care of his own body. He may also use such other "paramedical" means to get well as physical exercise, a proper diet, prayer, meditation, positive affirmations, and visualization techniques. The author surveys these techniques that have been used for centuries to contribute to the healing of a wide variety of diseases. Other topics exploring the connection between faith and a healthy heart include:

Tapping into your personal mythology
Forgiving yourself for heart disease
Keeping a psychological-spiritual journal
Heartskill #6: *Consulting your inner adviser*

CHAPTER SEVEN. PUTTING IT ALL TOGETHER: HOW TO DEVELOP YOUR OWN DAILY PRACTICE FOR A HEALTHY HEART

Daily Practice as defined by the author is a personalized program in which readers will choose from among the techniques offered in the book to create their own unique combination of mental and physical healing exercises. Each component of the daily practice is fully explained. The techniques range from the familiar—healthful diet and exercise—to the more spiritual, including prayer, meditation, and visualization. Included are examples of each of these techniques as practiced by Exceptional Heart Patients.

The benefits of daily practice
Meditation: how to do it your way
Stretching, yoga, and sensory awareness
Hearing with the mind's ear, seeing with the mind's eye
The psychological benefits of exercise
Healthy eating as a meditative practice
The healing powers of silent prayer
Creating your own visualization exercises
Creating your own guided-imagery tapes
Using other types of positive imagery
Heartskill #7: *Picking a practice that makes sense to you*

CHAPTER EIGHT. LEARNING TO SMELL THE FLOWERS

In our society, pleasure is often regarded as a selfish pursuit. We tend to feel that it is not as important as work. And yet the key element in health is not blood pressure, or cholesterol, or blood sugar; instead it is peace of mind and the ability to enjoy life. Indeed, this ability has been proven to prevent illness. In this chapter the author focuses on the ability to *live* in the moment, savoring all that life has to offer, from the simple physical pleasures of massage to the more profound pleasures of the spirit. Topics covered in this chapter include a discussion of Type B behavior, which can be learned. The secrets of this type of behavior include self-assurance, self-motivation, and the ability to relax in the face of pressures. The author shows how even the most confirmed Type A heart patient can, through self-knowledge, change outer-directed goals for inner ones, thus achieving the emotional and physical benefits of a Type B lifestyle. Other topics discussed in this chapter include:

Getting the most out of the present moment
Taking an inventory of life's pleasures
Counting down to relaxation
Hot baths, hot showers, hot tubs, and saunas
Touching; feeding the skin's hunger for human touch
Pets, plants, and gardens as healing helpers
Heartskill #8: *Building islands of peace into your life*

CHAPTER NINE. CREATING YOUR FUTURE

The heart may be viewed in many different ways: as a mechanical pump, as the center of circulation, as the source of life. The author suggests viewing the heart above all as a spiritual organ, the center of love, and learning to figuratively fill it with love and peace. A *positive* result of heart disease is the sudden knowledge that one is not immortal, and the opportunity to plan for a more worthwhile, fulfilling life in the future. In this final chapter, Dr. Cortis offers guidelines for setting and achieving goals for health—of mind, body, and spirit. For each reader the goals, and the means to achieve them, will be different. But as the author points out, this is a journey that everyone must take, patients as well as doctors, readers as well as the author. No matter how different the paths we choose, we must realize that truly "our hearts are the same."

The Art of Happiness
Choosing your own path to contentment
Goals chosen by other exceptional heart patients
Developing specific action steps
Reinforcing and rethinking your life goals
Finding your own meaning in life and death
Heartskill #9: *Helping others to heal their hearts*

RECOMMENDED READING

APPENDIX I. For Friends and Family: How to Support an Exceptional Heart Patient

APPENDIX II. On Finding or Starting a Self-Help Group

APPENDIX III. About the Exceptional Heart Patient Project

AUTHOR'S NOTES

ACKNOWLEDGMENTS

INDEX

(Appendixes are always a valuable bonus.)

(It is great to be able to include an actual endorsement in your proposal package. Quite often, writers state those from whom they intend to request endorsements—but do not actually have them lined up. Perhaps unnecessary to say, but valuable to reiterate, is that editors and agents are not overly impressed by such assertions. They do, however, nod with respect to those authors who demonstrate that they can deliver on their claims. The inclusion of at least one such blurb creates tremendous credibility.)

GERALD G. JAMPOLSKY, M.D.
Practice Limited to Psychiatry
Adults and Children

April 1, 1998

Mr. Jeff Herman
The Jeff Herman Agency, Inc.
140 Charles Street, Suite 15A
New York, NY 10014

Dear Jeff:
You may use the following quote for Bruno's book:

> *"Dr. Bruno Cortis writes from the heart—for the heart. This is a much-needed and very important book."*

Gerald Jampolsky, M.D.
Coauthor of *Love Is the Answer*

With love and peace,

Jerry

Gerald Jampolsky, M.D.

(The author, Dr. Cortis, is very well connected in his field. He solicited promises from several prominent persons to provide cover endorsements like this one. Having these promises to provide such blurbs at the time I marketed the proposal further enhanced the agency's sales position.)

Rejected . . . Again

The Process and the Art of Perseverance

JEFF HERMAN

Trying to sell your writing is in many ways similar to perpetually applying for employment; it's likely you will run into many walls. And that can hurt. But even the Great Wall of China has a beginning and an end—for it's simply an external barrier erected for strategic purposes. In my experience, the most insurmountable walls are the ones in our own heads. Anything that is artificially crafted can and will be overcome by people who are resourceful and determined enough to do it.

Naturally, the reality of rejection cannot be completely circumvented. It is, however, constructive to envision each wall as a friendly challenge to your resourcefulness, determination, and strength. There are many people who got through the old Berlin Wall because for them it was a challenge and a symbol—a place to begin, not stop.

The world of publishing is a potentially hostile environment, especially for the writer. Our deepest aspirations can be put to rest without having our achieved peace or satisfaction. But it is within each of us to learn about this special soil and blossom to our fullest. No rejection is fatal until the writer walks away from the battle, leaving the written work behind, undefended and unwanted.

WHY MOST REJECTION LETTERS ARE SO EMPTY

What may be most frustrating are the generic word-processed letters that say something like: "not right for us." Did the sender read any of your work? Did that person have any personal opinions about it? Could she not have spared a few moments to share her thoughts?

As an agent, it's part of my job to reject the vast majority of the submissions I receive. And with each rejection, I know I'm not making someone happy. On the other hand, I don't see spreading happiness as my exclusionary purpose. Like other agents and editors, I make liberal use of the generic rejection letter.

Here's why: Too much to do, too little time. There just isn't sufficient time to write customized, personal rejection letters. To be blunt about it, the rejection process isn't a profit center; it does consume valuable time that otherwise could be used to make profits. The exceptions to this rule are the excessive-fee-charging operations that make a handsome profit with each rejection.

In most instances, the rejection process is "giveaway" time for agents and editors since it takes us away from our essential responsibilities. Even if no personal comments are provided with the rejections, it can require many hours a week to process an ongoing stream of rejections. An understaffed literary agency or publishing house may feel that it's sufficiently generous simply to assign a paid employee the job of returning material as opposed to throwing it away. (And some publishers and literary agencies do in practice simply toss the greater portion of their unsolicited correspondence.) Agents and editors aren't Dear Abby, though many of us wish we had the time to be.

Therefore, your generic rejection means no more and no less than that particular agent/editor doesn't want to represent/publish you and (due to the volume of office correspondence and other pressing duties) is relaying this information to you in an automated, impersonal way. The contents of the letter alone will virtually never reveal any deeper meanings or secrets. To expect or demand more than this might be perceived as unfair by the agent/editor.

KNOW WHEN TO HOLD, KNOW WHEN TO FOLD

It's your job to persevere. It's your mission to proceed undaunted. Regardless of how many books about publishing you've read, or how many writers' conferences you've attended, it's up to no one but you to figure out how and when to change your strategy if you want to win at the book-publishing game.

If your initial query results are blanket rejects, then it may be time to back off, reflect, and revamp your query presentation or overall approach. If there are still no takers, you may be advised to reconceive your project in light of its less-than-glorious track record. Indeed, there might even come a time for you to use your experience and newfound knowledge of what does and doesn't grab attention from editors and agents—and move on to that bolder, more innovative idea you've been nurturing in the back of your brain.

AN AUTHENTIC SUCCESS STORY

Several years ago, two very successful, though unpublished, gentlemen came to see me with a nonfiction book project. My hunch was that it would make a lot of money. The writers were professional speakers and highly skilled salespeople, so I arranged for them to meet personally with several publishers, but to no avail.

All told, we got more than 20 rejections—the dominant reason being that editors thought the concept and material weak. Not ones to give up, and with a strong belief in their work and confidence in their ability to promote, the authors were ultimately able to sell the book for a nominal advance to a small Florida publishing house—and it was out there at last, published and in the marketplace.

As of this writing, *Chicken Soup for the Soul,* by Jack Canfield and Mark Victor Hansen, has sold millions of copies and has been a *New York Times* bestseller for several years straight. Furthermore, this initial success has generated many bestselling sequels.

We all make mistakes, and the book rascals in New York are definitely no exception. Most important, Canfield and Hansen didn't take no for an answer. They instinctively understood that all those rejections were simply an uncomfortable part of a process that would eventually get them where they wanted to be. And that's the way it happened.

A RELENTLESS APPROACH TO SELLING YOUR BOOK

I once heard a very telling story about Jack Kerouac, one from which we can all learn something. Kerouac was a notorious literary figure who reached his professional peak in the 1950s. He's one of the icons of the Beat Generation and is perhaps best remembered for his irreverent and manic travel-memoir-as-novel *On the Road.*

Sales Tales from the Beat Generation

The story begins when Kerouac was a young and struggling writer, ambitiously seeking to win his day in the sun. He was a charismatic man and had acquired many influential friends. One day Kerouac approached a friend who had access to a powerful publishing executive. Kerouac asked the friend to hand-deliver his new manuscript to the executive, with the advice that it be given prompt and careful consideration.

When the friend handed the manuscript to the executive, the executive took one glance and began to laugh. The executive explained that two other people had hand-delivered the very same manuscript to him within the last few weeks.

What this reveals is that Kerouac was a master operator. Not only did he manage to get his work into the right face, but also he reinforced his odds by doing it redundantly. Some might say he was a manipulator, but his works were successfully published, and he did attain a measure of fame in his own day, which even now retains its luster.

. . . AND FROM THE BEATEN

I will now share a very different and more recent story. It starts in the 1940s, when a bestselling and Pulitzer Prize–winning young-adult book was published. Titled *The Yearling,* this work was made into an excellent movie starring Gregory Peck. The book continues to be a good backlist seller.

In the 1990s, a writer in Florida, where *The Yearling*'s story takes place, performed an experiment. He converted the book into a raw double-spaced manuscript and changed the title and author's name—but the book's contents were not touched. He then submitted the entire manuscript to about 20 publishers on an unagented/unsolicited basis. I don't believe the submissions were addressed to any specific editors by name.

Eventually, this writer received many form rejections, including one from the book's actual publisher. Several publishers never even responded. A small house in Florida did offer to publish the book.

What is glaringly revealed by this story? That even a Pulitzer Prize–winning novel will never see the light of day if the writer doesn't use his brain when it's time to sell the work.

How to Beat Yourself—And How Not To

People who are overly aggressive do get a bad rap. As an agent and as a person, I don't like being hounded by salespeople—whether they're hustling manuscripts or insurance policies. But there are effective ways to be heard and seen without being resented. Virtually anyone can scream loud enough to hurt people's ears. Only an artist understands the true magic of how to sell without abusing those who might buy. And we all have the gift to become artists in our own ways.

Here's an example of what not to do:

It's late in the day and snowing. I'm at my desk, feeling a lot of work-related tension. I answer the phone. It's a first-time fiction writer. He's unflinchingly determined to speak endlessly about his work, which I have not yet read. I interrupt his meaningless flow to explain courteously that while I will read his work, it's not a good time for me to talk to him. But he will not let me go; he's relentless. Which forces me to be rude and cold as I say "Bye" and hang up. I then resent the thoughtless intrusion upon my space and time. And I may feel bad about being inhospitable to a stranger, whatever the provocation.

Clearly, the previous scenario does not demonstrate a good way to initiate a deal. I'm already prejudiced against this writer before reading his work.

Here's a more effective scenario:

Same conditions as before. I answer the telephone. The caller acknowledges that I must be busy and asks for only 30 seconds of my time. I grant them. He then begins to compliment me; he's heard I'm one of the best, and so forth. I'm starting to like this conversation; I stop counting the seconds. Now he explains that he has an excellent manuscript that he is willing to give me the opportunity to read and would be happy to send it right over. He then thanks me for my time and says good-bye. I hang up, feeling fine about the man; I'll give his manuscript some extra consideration.

In conclusion, relentless assertiveness is better than relentless passivity. But you want your style to be like Julie Andrews's singing voice in *The Sound of Music,* as opposed to a 100-decibel boom box on a stone floor.

The Literary Agency
from A to Z
How Literary Agents Work

JEFF HERMAN

Literary agents are like stockbrokers, marketing or sales directors, or real-estate agents: They bring buyers and sellers together, help formulate successful deals, and receive a piece of the action (against the seller's end) for facilitating the partnership.

Specifically, literary agents snoop the field for talented writers, unearth marketable nonfiction book concepts, and discover superior fiction manuscripts to represent. Simultaneously, agents cultivate their relationships with publishers.

When an agent detects material she thinks she can sell to a publisher, she signs the writer as a client, works on the material with the writer to maximize its chances of selling, and then submits it to one or more appropriate editorial contacts.

The agent has the contacts. Many writers don't know the most likely publishers; even if the writers do have a good overview of the industry and some inside contacts, the typical agent knows many more players and also knows which editors like to see what material. And the agent may even be aware of finesse elements such as recent shifts in a publisher's acquisition strategy.

HOW AGENTS WORK FOR THEIR CLIENTS

A dynamic agent achieves the maximum exposure possible for the writer's material, which greatly enhances the odds that the material will be published—and on more favorable terms than a writer is likely to yield.

Having an agent gives the writer's material the type of access to the powers-that-be that it might otherwise never obtain. Publishers assume that material submitted by an agent has been screened and is much more likely to fit their needs than is the random material swimming in the slush pile.

If and when a publisher makes an offer to publish the material, the agent acts on the author's behalf and negotiates the advance (the money paid up front), table of royalties, control of subsidiary rights, and many other important and marginal contract clauses that may prove to be important down the line. The agent acts as the writer's advocate with the publisher for as long as the book remains in print or licensing opportunities exist.

The agent knows the most effective methods for negotiating the best advance and other contract terms and is likely to have more leverage with the publisher than the writer does.

There's more to a book contract than the advance-and-royalty schedule. There are several key clauses that you, the writer, may know little or nothing about, but would accept with a cursory perusal in order to expedite the deal. Striving to close any kind of agreement can be intimidating if you don't know much about the territory; ignorance is a great disadvantage during a negotiation. An agent, however, understands every detail of the contract and knows where and how it should be modified or expanded in your favor.

Where appropriate, an agent acts to sell subsidiary rights after the book is sold to a publisher. These rights can include: serial rights, foreign rights, dramatic and movie rights, audio and video rights, and a range of syndication and licensing possibilities. Often, a dynamic agent will be more successful at selling the subsidiary rights than the publisher would be.

THE AGENT'S PERSPECTIVE

No agent sells every project she represents. Even though authors are signed on the basis of their work's marketability, agents know from experience that some projects with excellent potential are not necessarily quick-and-easy big-money sales. And, yes, each and every agent has at least on occasion been as bewildered as the author when a particularly promising package receives no takers. Some projects, especially fiction, may be marketed for a long time before a publisher is found (if ever).

THE AUTHOR'S EXPECTATIONS

What's most important is that you, the author, feel sure the agent continues to believe in the project and is actively trying to sell it.

For his work, the agent receives a commission (usually 15 percent) against the writer's advance and all subsequent income relevant to the sold project.

Although this is an appreciable chunk of your work's income, the agent's involvement should end up netting you much more than you would have earned otherwise. The agent's power to round up several interested publishers to consider your work opens up the possibility that more than one house will make an offer for it, which means you'll be more likely to get a higher advance and also have more leverage regarding the various other contractual clauses.

The writer–agent relationship can become a rewarding business partnership. An agent can advise you objectively on the direction your writing career should take. Also, through her contacts, an agent may be able to get you book-writing assignments you would never have been offered on your own.

Scout for the Best Agent for You

There are many ways to get an agent; your personal determination and acumen as a writer will be two of your most important assets. The best way to gain access to potential agents is by networking with fellow writers. Find out which agents they use and what's being said about whom. Maybe some of your colleagues can introduce you to their agents or at least allow you to drop their names when contacting their agents. Most agents will be receptive to a writer who has been referred by a current and valued client.

This book features a directory of literary agencies, including their addresses, the names of specific agents, and agents' specialty areas, along with some personal remarks and examples of recent titles sold to publishers.

Query First

The universally accepted way to establish initial contact with an agent is to send a query letter. Agents tend to be less interested in—if not completely put off by—oral presentations. Be sure the letter is personalized: Nobody likes generic, photocopied letters that look like they're being sent to everyone.

Think of the query as a sales pitch. Describe the nature of your project and offer to send additional material—and enclose a self-addressed stamped envelope (SASE). Include all relevant information about yourself—along with a resume if it's applicable. When querying about a nonfiction project, many agents won't mind receiving a complete proposal. But you might prefer to wait and see how the agent responds to the concept before sending the full proposal.

For queries about fiction projects, most agents prefer to receive story-concept sheets, plot synopses, or both; if they like what they see, they'll request sample chapters or ask you to send the complete manuscript. Most agents won't consider manuscripts for incomplete works of fiction, essentially because few publishers are willing to do so.

If you enclose an SASE, most agents will respond to you, one way or another, within a reasonable period of time. If the agent asks to see your material, submit it promptly with a polite note stating that you'd like a response within 4 weeks on a nonfiction proposal, or 8 weeks on fiction material. If you haven't heard from the agent by that time, write or call to find out the status of your submission.

Circulate with the Flow

You're entitled to circulate your material to more than one agent at a time, but you're obligated to let each agent know that such is the case. If and when you do sign with an agent, immediately notify other agents still considering your work that it's no longer available.

At least 200 literary agents are active in America, and their individual perceptions of what is and isn't marketable will vary widely—which is why a few or even several rejections should never deter writers who believe in themselves.

BUYER AND SELLER REVERSAL

When an agent eventually seeks to represent your work, it's time for her to begin selling herself to you. When you're seeking employment, you don't necessarily have to accept the first job offer you receive; likewise, you do not have to sign immediately with the first agent who wants you.

Do some checking before agreeing to work with a particular agent. If possible, meet the agent in person. A lot can be learned from in-person meetings that can't be gathered from telephone conversations. See what positive or negative information you can find out about the agent through your writers' network. Ask the agent for a client list and permission to call certain clients. Find out the agent's specialties.

Ask for a copy of the agent's standard contract.* Most agents today will want to codify your relationship with a written agreement; this should protect both parties equally. Make sure you're comfortable with everything in the agreement before signing it. Again, talking with fellow writers and reading books on the subject are excellent ways to deepen your understanding of industry practices.

When choosing an agent, follow your best instincts. Don't settle for anyone you don't perceive to be on the level, or who doesn't seem to be genuinely enthusiastic about you and your work.

SELF-REPRESENTATION: A FOOL FOR A CLIENT?

Agents aren't for everyone. In some instances, you may be better off on your own. Perhaps you actually do have sufficient editorial contacts and industry savvy to cut good deals by yourself. If so, what incentive do you have to share your income with an agent?

Of course, having an agent might provide you the intangible benefits of added prestige, save you the hassles of making submissions and negotiating deals, or act as a buffer through whom you can negotiate indirectly for tactical reasons.

You might also consider representing yourself if your books are so specialized that only a few publishers are potential candidates for them. Your contacts at such houses might be much stronger than any agent's could be.

ATTORNEYS: LITERARY AND OTHERWISE

Some entertainment/publishing attorneys can do everything an agent does, though there's no reason to believe they can necessarily do more. A major difference between the two is that the lawyer may charge you a set hourly fee or retainer, or any negotiated combination thereof, instead of an agency-type commission. In rare instances, writer–publisher disputes might need to be settled in a court of law, and a lawyer familiar with the industry then becomes a necessity.

BOTTOM-LINE CALCULATIONS

The pluses and minuses of having an agent should be calculated like any other business service you might retain—it should benefit you more than it costs you. Generally speaking, the only real cost of using an agent is the commission. Of course, using the wrong agent may end up causing you more deficits than benefits, but even then you may at least learn a valuable lesson for next time.

Your challenge is to seek and retain an agent who's right for you. You're 100 percent responsible for getting yourself represented and at least 50 percent responsible for making the relationship work for both of you.

More Questions and Answers About Agents, Editors, and the Publishing Industry

Jeff Herman

In the course of my ongoing participation in publishing workshops, seminar presentations, and panels at writers' conferences, certain questions arise time and again. Many of these requests for information go straight to the heart of the world of book publishing.

The following questions are asked from the gut and replied to in kind. In order to be of value to the author who wishes to benefit from an insider view, I answer these serious queries in unvarnished terms, dispensing with the usual sugarcoating in order to emphasize the message of openness and candor.

Q: Is it more difficult to get an agent than it is to get a publisher?

A: I believe it's substantially easier to get an agent than it is to get a publisher.

The primary reason for this is that no agent expects to sell 100 percent of the projects she chooses to represent. Not because any of these projects lack merit (though some of them may), but because only so many titles are published per year—and many excellent ones just won't make the cut. This is especially true for fiction by unknown or unpublished writers, or for nonfiction in saturated categories. As a result, many titles will be agented but never published.

Naturally, a successful agent prefers to represent projects that she feels are hot and that publishers will trample each other to acquire. But few, if any, agents have the luxury of representing such sure-bet projects exclusively. In fact, the majority of their projects may be less than "acquisition-guaranteed," even though they are of acquisition quality. The agent assumes that many of these projects will eventually be sold profitably, but probably doesn't expect all of them to be. Every experienced agent knows that some of the best cash cows were not easily sold.

Make no mistake—it's not easy to get a reputable agent. Most agents reject 98 percent of the opportunities that cross their desks. They accept for representation only material they believe can be sold to a publisher. That is, after all, the only way for them to earn income and maintain credibility with publishers. If an agent consistently represents what a publisher considers garbage, that will become her professional signature—and her undoing as an agent.

But don't despair. This is a subjective business, composed of autonomous human beings. One agent's reject can be another's gold mine. That's why even a large accumulation of rejections should never deter you as a writer. Some people get married young, and some get married later!

Q: Is there anything I can do to increase my odds of getting an agent?
A: Yes.

First consider the odds quoted in the previous answer. The typical agent is rejecting 98 percent of everything he sees. That means he's hungry for the hard-to-find 2 percent that keeps him in business. If you're not part of that 2 percent, he'll probably have no use for you or your project. Your challenge is to convince him that you're part of that select 2 percent.

Q: What do agents and editors want? What do they look for in a writer? What can I do to become that kind of writer?
A: Let's back up a step or two and figure out *why* agents want to represent certain projects and *why* editors want to buy them. This industry preference has little to do with quality of writing as such.

Many highly talented writers never get published. Many mediocre writers do get published—and a number of them make a lot of money at it. There are reasons for this. The mediocre writers are doing things that more than compensate for their less-than-splendid writing. And the exceptional writers who underachieve in the publishing arena are (regardless of their talents) most likely doing things that undermine them.

In other words, being a good writer is just part of a complex equation. Despite all the criticism the educational system in the United States has received, America is exceedingly literate and has a mother lode of college graduates and postgraduates. Good, knowledgeable writers are a dime a dozen in this country. *Profitable* writers, however, are a rare species. And agents and editors obviously value them the most. Once more: Being an excellent writer and a financially successful writer don't necessarily coincide. Ideally, of course, you want to be both.

To maximize your success as a writer, you must do more than hone your ability to write; you must also learn the qualifiers and the disqualifiers for success. Obviously, you wish to employ the former and avoid the latter. Publishing is a business, and agents tend to be the most acutely business-oriented of all the players. That's why they took the risk of going into business for themselves (most agents are self-employed).

If you wish, wear your artist's hat while you write. But you'd better acquire a business hat and wear it when it's time to sell. This subtle ability to change hats separates the minority of writers who get rich from the majority who do not. In my opinion, rich writers didn't get rich from their writing (no matter how good it is); they got rich by being good at business.

Many good but not-so-wealthy writers blame various internal or external factors for their self-perceived stagnation. My answer to them is: Don't blame anyone, especially yourself. To lay blame is an abdication of power. In effect, when you blame, you become a car with an empty gas tank, left to the elements. The remedy is to fill the tank yourself. Learn to view mistakes, whether they be yours or those of the people you relied upon, as inconvenient potholes—learning to move around them will make you an even better driver. Remember the old credo: Only a poor workman blames his tools.

Observe all you can about those who are successful—not just in writing, but in all fields—and make their skills your skills. This is not to insist that making money is or should be your first priority. Your priorities, whatever they are, belong to you. But money is a widely acknowledged and sought-after emblem of success.

If an emphasis on personal gain turns you off, you may, of course, pursue other goals. Many successful people in business find the motivation to achieve their goals by focusing on altruistic concepts—such as creating maximum value for as many people as possible. Like magic, money often follows value even if it wasn't specifically sought. If you're unfortunate enough to make money you don't want, there's no need to despair: There are many worthy parties (including charities) that will gladly relieve you of this burden.

Here are specific ways to maximize your ability to get the agent you want:

• *Don't start off by asking what the agent can do for you.* You're a noncitizen until the agent has reason to believe that you may belong to that exclusive 2 percent club the agent wants to represent. It's a mistake to expect the agent to do anything to sell herself to you during that initial contact. You must first persuade her that you're someone who's going to make good money for her business. Once you've accomplished that, and the agent offers you representation, you're entitled to have the agent sell herself to you.

• *Act like a business.* As you're urged elsewhere in this book, get yourself a professional letterhead and state-of-the-art office equipment. While rarely fatal, cheap paper and poor-looking type will do nothing to help you—and in this business you need all the help you can give yourself.

Virtually anyone—especially the intellectually arrogant—is apt to be strongly affected on a subliminal level by a product's packaging. People pay for the sizzle, not the steak. There is a reason why American companies spend billions packaging, naming, and advertising such seemingly simple products as soap. We would all save money if every bar of soap were put into a plain paper box and just labeled "Soap." In fact, the no-frills section does sell soap that way—for a lot less. But few people choose to buy it that way. Understand this human principle, without judging it, and use it when packaging yourself.

• *Learn industry protocol.* I never insist that people follow all the rules. As Thomas Jefferson wisely suggested, a revolution every so often can be a good thing. But you should at least know the rules before you break them—or before you do anything.

For instance: Most agents say they don't like cold calls. I can't say I blame them. If my rejection rate is 98 percent, I'm not going to be enthusiastic about having my ear talked off by someone who is more than likely part of that 98 percent. Just like you, agents want to use their time as productively as possible. Too often, cold calls are verbal junk mail. This is especially true if you are a writer selling fiction; your hard copy is the foot you want to get through the door.

Speaking for myself, most cold calls have a neutral effect on me (a few turn me off, and a few rouse my enthusiasm). I try to be courteous, because that's how I would want to be treated. I will allow the caller to say whatever he wants for about one minute before I take over to find out what, if anything, the person has in the way of hard copy. If he has some, I invite him to send it with an SASE. If he doesn't have any, I advise him to write some and then send it. Usually, I don't remember much about what he said on the phone; I may not even remember that he called. But that doesn't matter; it's the hard copy that concerns me at first. This is the way it works with most agents. We produce books, not talk.

An agent's time is an agent's money (and therefore his clients' money). So don't expect any quality access until the agent has reason to believe you're a potential 2 percenter. If you're the CEO of General Motors, for instance, and you want to write a book, then all you need to do is call the agent(s) of your choice and identify yourself; red carpets will quickly appear. But the vast majority of writers have to learn and follow the more formalized procedures.

• As explained elsewhere in this book, view the query letter as a sales brochure. The best ones are rarely more than $1^1/_2$–2 pages long and state their case as briefly and efficiently as possible.

Here are the most common query mistakes:

1. Long, unfocused paragraphs.
2. Pontificating about irrelevancies (at least, matters that are irrelevant from the agent's perspective).
3. Complaining about your tribulations as a writer. We all know it's a tough business, but nobody likes losers—least of all, shrewd agents. Always be a winner when you're selling yourself, and you'll be more likely to win.

Most agents are hungry for that golden 2 percent, and they dedicate a great deal of time shoveling through mounds of material looking for it. You must be the first to believe that you are a 2 percenter, and then you must portray yourself that way to others. Reality begins in your own head and is manifested primarily through your own actions—or lack thereof.

Every agent and editor has the power to reject your writing. But only you have the power to be—or not to be—a writer.

Q: Should I query only one agent at a time?
A: Some of my colleagues disagree with me here, but I recommend querying 5 to 10 agents simultaneously, unless you already have your foot in the door with one. I suggest this because some agents will respond within 10 days, while others may take much longer or never respond at all. Going agent by agent can eat up several months of valuable time before a relationship is consummated. And then your work still has to be sold to a publisher.

To speed up this process, it's smart to solicit several agents at a time, though you should be completely upfront about it. If you go the multiple-submissions route, be sure to mention in your query letters to each agent that you are indeed making multiple submissions (though you needn't supply your agent list).

When an agent responds affirmatively to your query by requesting your proposal or manuscript, it's fine then to give the agent an exclusive reading. However, you should impose a reasonable time frame—for instance, 2 weeks for a nonfiction proposal and 4 weeks for a large manuscript. If it's a nonexclusive reading, make sure each agent knows that's what you want. And don't sign with an agent before talking to all the agents who are reading your work. (You have no obligation to communicate further with agents who do not respond affirmatively to your initial query.)

Most agents make multiple submissions to publishers, so they should be sensitive and respectful when writers have reason to use the same strategy agents have used with success.

Q: How do I know if my agent is working effectively for me? When might it be time to change agents?

A: As I remarked earlier, agents don't necessarily sell everything they represent, no matter how persistent and assertive they may be. In other words, the fact that your work is unsold doesn't automatically mean that your agent isn't doing his job. To the contrary, he may be doing the best job possible, and it may be incumbent upon you to be grateful for these speculative and uncompensated efforts.

Let's say 90 days pass and your work remains unsold. What you need to assess next is whether your agent is making active and proper attempts to sell your work.

Are you receiving copies of publisher rejection letters regarding your work? Generally, when an editor rejects projects submitted by an agent, the work will be returned within a few weeks, along with some brief comments explaining why the project was declined. (In case you're wondering, the agent doesn't have to include an SASE; the editors *want* agent submissions.) Copies of these rejection letters should be sent to you on a regular basis as the agent receives them. While no one expects you to enjoy these letters, they at least document that your agent is circulating your work.

If you have received many such rejection letters within these 90 days, it's hard to claim that your agent isn't trying. If you've received few or none, you might well call the agent for a status report. You should inquire as to where and when your work has been submitted, and what, if anything, the results of those submissions have been. In the end, you will have to use your own best judgment as to whether your agent is performing capably or giving you the run-around.

If it ever becomes obvious that your agent is no longer seriously trying to sell your work (or perhaps never was), you should initiate a frank discussion with the agent about what comes next. If the agent did go to bat for you, you should consider the strong possibility that your work is presently unmarketable and act to preserve the agent relationship for your next project. Remember, if your work remains unsold, your agent has lost valuable time and has made no money.

If the evidence clearly shows that your agent has been nonperforming from day one, then your work has not been tested. You should consider withdrawing it and seek new representation.

Agent-hopping by authors is not rampant, but it's not uncommon either. Often the agent is just as eager as you—or more so—for the break-up to happen. One veteran colleague once told me that when he notices he hates to receive a certain client's phone calls, then it's time to find a graceful way to end the relationship.

The wisdom of agent-jumping must be assessed on a case-by-case basis. The evidence shows that many writers have prospered after switching, while others have entered limbo or even fallen far off their previous pace.

Before you decide to switch agents, you should focus on why you are unhappy with your current situation. It may be that if you appeal to your agent to discuss your specific frustrations—preferably in person, or at least by phone—many or all of them can be resolved, and your relationship will be given a fresh and prosperous start.

Agents are not mind readers. You only have one agent, but your agent has many clients. It is therefore mostly your responsibility as a writer client to communicate your concerns and expectations effectively to your agent. Your relationship may require only occasional adjustments, as opposed to a complete break-up.

Q: Who do agents really work for?

A: Themselves! Always have and always will.

True, agents serve their clients, but their own needs and interests always come first. Of course, this is the way it is in any business relationship (and in too many personal ones). You should never expect your lawyer, accountant, or stockbroker (and so on) to throw themselves into traffic to shield you from getting hit.

As long as the interests of the agent and the writer are in harmony, everything should work out well. However, on occasion the writer may have expectations that could be detrimental to the agent's own agenda (not to mention state of mind). Writers must never lose sight of the truth that publishers are the agent's most important customers. Only a foolish agent would intentionally do serious damage to her relationships with individual editors and publishing houses. It should be further noted that there is, therefore, a fine line that an agent will not cross when advocating for her clients.

Q: What do agents find unattractive about some clients?

A: Agents are individuals, so each will have his own intense dislikes. But, generally speaking, a certain range of qualities can hamper any and all aspects of an agent's professional association with a client—qualities that often have similarly negative effects in realms other than publishing. Here's a litany of displeasing client types and their characteristics.

- *The Pest.* Nobody likes a nag, whether at home or at the office. A squeaky wheel may sometimes get the grease—not that anyone likes the effect—but more often this person gets the shaft.
- *The Complainer.* Some people can never be satisfied, only dissatisfied. It seems to be their mission in life to pass along their displeasure to others. These folks are never any fun—unless you're an ironic observer.
- *The BS Artist.* These clients believe everything even remotely connected with themselves is the greatest—for example, their fleeting ideas for books should win them

millions of dollars up front. Of course, if they actually produce the goods, then the BS part of the term doesn't apply to them.

- *The Screw-Up.* These clients miss trains, planes, and deadlines. Their blunders can create major hassles for those who count on them.
- *The Sun God.* Some people believe they are more equal than others and will behave accordingly. It's a real pleasure to see Sun Gods humbled.
- *The Liar.* Need I say more?

Sometimes these wicked traits combine, overlap, and reinforce themselves in one individual to create what an agent may rate as a veritable client from hell. Enough said on this subject for now, except that I would be remiss if I did not insist that no trade or professional class is immune to this nefarious syndrome—not even literary agents.

Q: How does someone become an agent?

A: For better or worse, anyone in America can declare himself an agent—at any time. But what people say and what they do are different things. Legitimate literary agents earn most or all of their income from commissions. The less-than-legitimate agencies most often depend on reading and management fees for their cash, with few, if any, actual book sales to their credit.

Most agents earn their stripes by working as editors for publishers. But that is by no means the only route, nor is it necessarily the most effective training ground. Good agents have emerged from a variety of environments and offer a broad range of exceptional credentials. What's most important is the mix of skills they bring to their agenting careers, such as: (1) Strong relationship skills—the ability to connect with people and earn their confidence. (2) Sales and marketing skills—the ability to get people to buy from them. (3) Persuasion and negotiating skills—the ability to get good results in their dealings. (4) An understanding of the book market and of what publishers are buying. (5) An ability to manage many clients and projects at the same time.

Q: Who owns book publishing?

A: Many decades ago, book-publishing entities were customarily founded by individuals who had a passion for books. Though they obviously had to have business skills to make their houses survive and thrive, money was not necessarily their primary drive (at least, not in the beginning), or they would have chosen more lucrative endeavors.

The vestiges of these pioneers can be found in the family names still extant in the corporate designations of most of today's publishing giants. But apart from the human-sounding names, these are very different companies today. Much of the industry is owned by multinational, multibillion-dollar conglomerates that have priorities other than the mere publication of books. The revenues from book operations are barely noticeable when compared with such mass-market endeavors as movies, TV/cable, music, magazines, sports teams, and character licensing. Stock prices must rise, and shareholders must be optimally satisfied for these firms to feel in any way stable.

Q: How does this type of ownership affect editors and the editorial-acquisition process?

A: This rampant corporate ownership translates into an environment in which book editors are pressured to make profitable choices if their careers are to prosper. At first look, that doesn't sound radical or wrongheaded, but a downside has indeed developed—editors are discouraged from taking risks for literary or artistic rationales that are ahead of the market curve or even with an eye toward longer-term development and growth of a particular writer's readership.

The bottom line must be immediately appeased by every acquisition, or the nonperforming editor's career will crumble. The editor who acquires blockbusters that the culturally elite disdain is an editor who is a success. The editor whose books lose money but are universally praised by critics is an editor who has failed.

Of course, the previous comparison is extreme. Most editors are not single-minded money-grubbers and do their best to acquire meaningful books that also make commercial sense. Where the cut becomes most noticeable is for the thousands of talented fiction writers who will never write big money-makers. While slots still exist for them, large publishers are increasingly reluctant to subsidize and nurture these marginally profitable writers' careers. Commercially speaking, there are better ways to invest the firm's resources.

Q: What, if any, are a writer's alternatives?

A: Yes, the big kids are dominant on their own turf and intend to extend their claim to as much of book country as they can. But this isn't the end of the story. The heroes are the thousands of privately owned "Mom and Pop" presses from Maine to Alaska who only need to answer to themselves. Every year, small presses, new and old, make an important contribution to literate culture with books that large publishers won't touch. It's not uncommon for some of these books to become bestsellers. University presses also pump out important (and salesworthy) books that would not have been published in a rigidly commercial environment.

Q: Is there anything positive to say about the current situation?

A: I don't mean to imply that the corporate ownership of the bulk of the book industry is absolutely bad. Indeed, it has brought many benefits. Publishers are learning to take better advantage of state-of-the-art marketing techniques and technologies and have more capital with which to do it. The parent entertainment and communications firms enable the mainstream commercial publishers to cash in on popular frenzies, as with dinosaur mania, the latest and most salacious scandals, fresh interest in the environment or fitness, or celebrity and other pop-culture tie-ins, such as *Gump* and *Madonna* books.

The emergence of superstores enables more books to be sold. The stores create very appealing environments that draw much more traffic than conventional old-style bookstores. Many people who hang out at the superstores were never before motivated to go book shopping. But once they're in one of these well-stocked stores—whether at the bookshelves, ensconced in a reading-seat, or perched by a steaming mug at an in-store cafe—they're likely to start spending.

The unfortunate part is that many small independent bookshops cannot compete with these new venues. However, many others are finding clever ways to hang on, by accenting special reader-interest areas or offering their own individual style of hospitality.

Q: How profitable is publishing?

A: One way to measure an industry's profitability is to look at the fortunes of those who work in it. By such a measure, the book business isn't very profitable, especially when compared to its twentieth-century sisters in entertainment and information industries: movies, television, music, advertising, and computers. Most book editors require a two-income family if they wish to raise children comfortably in New York or buy a nice home. The vast majority of published authors rely upon their day jobs or spouse's earnings.

A handful of authors make annual incomes in the six and seven figures, but it's often the movie tie-ins that get them there and in turn push even more book sales.

A fraction of book editors will climb the ranks to the point at which they can command six-figure incomes, but most never attain this plateau. Almost all of those writers just starting in the business earn barely above the poverty level for their initial publishing endeavors—if that.

A well-established literary agent can make a lot of money. The trick is to build a number of backlist books that cumulatively pay off healthy commissions twice a year, while constantly panning for the elusive big-advance books that promise short-term (and perhaps long-term) windfalls.

In many ways, the agents are the players best positioned to make the most money. As sole proprietors, they're not constrained by committees and can move like lightning. When everything aligns just right, the agent holds all the cards by controlling access to the author (product) and the publisher (producer).

The publishing companies themselves appear at least adequately profitable, averaging about 5 to 10 percent return on revenues (according to their public balance sheets). The larger companies show revenues of between $1 billion and $2 billion, sometimes nudging higher.

These are not sums to sneeze at. But most of those sales derive from high-priced non-bookstore products like textbooks and professional books. Large and midsize publishers alike are dependent upon their cash-cow backlist books for much of their retail sales. These books entail virtually no risk or investment, since their customer base is essentially locked in for an indefinite period, and the publisher has long ago recouped the initial investment. Many backlist books are legacies from editors and business dynamics that current employees may know nothing about.

The real risk for the current regime is their *frontlist*, which is the current season's crop. Large houses invest tens of millions of dollars to acquire, manufacture, market, and distribute anywhere from 50 to a few hundred "new" books. A small number of big-ticket individual titles will by themselves represent millions of dollars at risk. Most titles will represent less than $50,000 in risk on a pro-rata basis.

In practice, most of these frontlist titles will fail. The publisher will not recoup its investment and the title will not graduate to the exalted backlist status. But like the fate of those innumerable turtle eggs laid in the sand, it's expected that enough spawn will survive to generate an overall profit and significant backlist annuities well into the future.

In the fairness of a broader picture, it is known that most motion pictures and television shows fail, as do most new consumer products (such as soap or soft drinks) that have engendered enormous research-and-development costs. It's the ones that hit—and hit big—that make the odds worth enduring for any industry.

Scams and Book Doctors, in That Order

Jeff Herman

Publishing scams have become an epidemic. I read somewhere that writers are getting ripped off for more than $50 million a year, and some scam artists have even gone to jail.

Let's start by looking at ethics. I don't like ethics. They're like organized religion—prone to promoting arrogance, subjective judgment, and hypocrisy. I do like honesty. Honesty's best defense is the fast and consistent enforcement of consequences against those people who harm others.

The best defense is not to be a victim in the first place. Without becoming a paranoid lunatic, you must accept that bad deeds are hovering around waiting to happen. Sometimes, you may be tempted into being a perpetrator. That's why houses have glass windows and why the universe can't stay angry, or else we'd all have to go to Hell. It's more likely, however, that you'll be a victim, not a "do-er," on any given day; though it's hoped you'll be neither. Both extremes may be mostly, or completely, within your power to be or not to be. For instance, I'll never understand why women jog by themselves in Central Park when it's dark out. And I'll never understand why writers send fat checks to virtual strangers.

To what extent should society protect its citizens from making stupid choices? I've seen smart men and women date and marry morons, with predictably disastrous results. I've done enough stupid things in my life to qualify for the Infra-Mensa society many times over. How about you? Should someone have stopped us? And if we were stopped, might we not have been even more stupid the next time?

Basically, I'm praising stupidity as a natural right and gift. It's unnatural to overly protect people from themselves. We all see what happens to individuals who are excessively parented or to entire communities that are enabled to subsist in perpetual poverty and social decay.

So what about writers who get scammed? Well, they should stop doing it.

- They should stop sending money to get people to "read" their work, since there are several hundred real agents who will do that for free.
- They should stop smoking and stop eating other fat mammals.
- They should stop giving money to unproven strangers who promise to get them published, since there are several hundred real agents who will do that on a contingency.
- They should wear seatbelts, especially when in New York taxis.
- They should stop giving money to unproven strangers who promise to "fix" the work, especially since there are at least dozens of real former book editors who can genuinely fix your work.
- They should stop maintaining balances on their credit cards.
- They should always ask for evidence of ability whenever asked for money.

If we, as writers, walk the above line, then parasitic acts could not exist and thrive. We would not need more laws, more people working for government, or any ethics. Such things only exist in the absence of honesty and in the dissonance that follows.

As a service, I have attached information about specific "Book Doctor" organizations and individuals that I'm familiar with and trust. These are people who either have deep experience working as real editors at real publishers, have "doctored" many manuscripts to the point of publication, or both. Retaining their skills will often make the difference between getting a deal or being a "close call."

This is the first time I've had this list, so I welcome additional referrals, or self-referrals, for the next edition.

I endorse none of these people or the expectations they might create. I simply want you to have a safe place to turn if you need and are ready to receive help.

The following is an actual pitch letter from a fee-charging agency, with only the names and other identifying information changed. Such correspondence is typical of the alluring invitations writers often receive in response to their agent submissions.

If a writer chooses to explore this route, I strongly advise following these preliminary steps:

1. Ask for references. You're being asked to shell out hundreds of dollars to a virtual stranger. Get to know those who would eat your money.
2. Ask for a list of titles sold. Find out whether the so-called agency actually has an agenting track record. Or is this particular operation just a high-priced reading service with an agency façade?
3. Better yet, call or write to non–fee charging agents and ask them to recommend book doctors, collaborative writers, or editorial freelancers whom they use to shape and develop their own clients' works, or see the "Book Doctor" section in this book. This may be a better place to spend your money.

BEWARE OF SHARKS!

The following correspondence is genuine, though all names and titles have been altered. My purpose for exposing these ever-so-slightly personalized form letters isn't to condemn or ridicule anyone. I simply wish to show how some subsidy publishers hook their clients.

Shark House Publishers

Mr. Bourne Bate
Brooklyn Bridge
East River, NY 00000

Dear Mr. Bate:

Your manuscript *A Fish's Life* is written from an unusual perspective and an urgent one. In these trying economic times that have created despair and anguish, one must give thought to opportunities, and this upbeat and enthusiastic book makes us realize that those opportunities are out there! My capsule critique: Meticulous aim! With a surgeon's precision we're taught how to work through everything from raising money to targeting areas. There is a sharp eye here for all of the nuances, studded with pointers and reasoning, making it a crucial blueprint.

What can I say about a book like this? It stopped me in my tracks. I guess all I can do is thank you for letting me have the opportunity to read it.

The editors who read this had a spontaneous tendency to feel that it was imbued with some very, very good electricity and would be something very special for our list and saw such potential with it that it was given top priority and pushed ahead of every other book in house. The further problem is that publishing being an extremely rugged business, editorial decisions have to be based on hard facts, which sometimes hurt publishers as much as authors. Unfortunately, we just bought several new nonfiction pieces . . . yet I hate to let this one get away. Publishing economics shouldn't have anything to do with a decision, but unfortunately, it does and I was overruled at the editorial meeting.

Still I want you to know that this is a particularly viable book and one that I really would love to have for our list. Furthermore, this might be picked up for magazine serialization or by book clubs because it is so different. Our book *Enraptured* was serialized six times in *International Inquirer* and sold to Andorra. *The Devil Decided* sold well over 150,000 copies, and we have a movie option on it. *Far Away,* serialized in *Places* magazine and *Cure Yourself,* was taken by a major book club.

I really want this book for our list because it will fit into all the areas that we're active in. Therefore, I'm going to make a proposition for you to involve yourself with us. What would you think of the idea of doing this on a cooperative basis? Like many New York publishers these days, we find that sometimes investors are interested in the acquisition of literary properties through a technique that might be advantageous under our tax laws. There is no reason that the partial investor cannot be the writer, if that person so chooses. Tax advantages may accrue.

I'd be a liar if I promised you a bestseller, but I can guarantee that nobody works as hard promoting a book as we do: We nag paperback, book club, magazine, and foreign publishers with our zeal and enthusiasm. We do our PR work and take it seriously because this is where we're going to make the money in the long run. One of our authors hired a top publicist on his own for $50,000. He came limping back to us, saying they didn't do the job that we did, and which we don't charge for. This made our office feel very proud of all our efforts.

I feel that your book deserves our efforts because it is something very special. Think about what I've written to you, and I will hold the manuscript until I hear from you. I truly hope that we can get together because I really love this book and believe it is something we can generate some good action for vis-à-vis book clubs, foreign rights, etc., because it is outstanding and has tremendous potential.

Sincerely,

Eda U. Live

Eda U. Live
Executive Editor

The writer of *A Fish's Life* wrote back to Shark House (all names have been changed) and informed the vanity press that he did not want to pay any money to the publisher to have his book published. The vanity house responded with the following letter. This publisher has probably learned from experience that some exhausted writers will return to them with open wallets after fruitless pursuit of a conventional commercial publishing arrangement.

SHARK HOUSE PUBLISHERS

Mr. Bourne Bate
Brooklyn Bridge
East River, NY 00000

Dear Mr. Bate:

I have your letter in front of me and I want you to know that I think very highly of the book. Before I go any further, I want to tell you that it is a topnotch book and it hits the reader.

In order for us to do a proper job with a book, there is a great deal of PR work involved and this is very costly. To hire an outside agent to do a crackerjack job would cost you upward of $50,000. Yet here we do not charge for it because it is part of our promotion to propel a book into the marketplace, and it is imperative that this be done. The author has to be booked on radio and TV, stores have to be notified, rights here and abroad have to be worked on, reviewers contacted, autograph parties arranged, and myriad details taken care of.

In view of this, why did I ask you to help with the project? I think the above is self-explanatory, especially when we are in the midst of a revolution between books and television. Publishers are gamblers vying for the same audience. Just because a publisher loves a book is no guarantee that the public is going to love it. In times when bookstores are more selective in the number of books they order, the best of us tremble at the thought of the money that we must put out in order to make a good book a reality.

Be that as it may, I have just come from another editorial meeting where I tried to re-open the case for us, but unfortunately, the earlier decision stands.

As a result, I have no choice but to return the manuscript with this letter. I would also like to tell you that you must do what the successful writers do. Keep sending it out. Someone will like it and someone will buy it.

I wish you every success. Live long and prosper.

Sincerely,

Eda U. Live

Eda U. Live
Executive Editor

INDEPENDENT EDITORS GROUP

The Independent Editors Group is a professional affiliation of highly select, diverse, experienced freelance editors/book doctors who work with writers, editors, and agents in trade book publishing. They are: Sally Arteseros, Maureen Baron, Carolyn Blakemore, Deborah Chiel, Paul De Angelis, Joyce Engelson, Jerry Gross, Susan Leon, Richard Marek, Joan S. Pollack, James O'Shea Wade, and Genevieve Young.

Years of distinguished tenure at major publishing houses made them eminently qualified to provide the following editorial services on fiction and nonfiction manuscripts.

- In-depth evaluations and detailed critiques
- Problem-solving
- Plot restructure
- Developmental and line editing
- Reorganization, revision, and rewriting
- Book proposals and development
- Ghostwriting and collaboration

If any editor is unavailable, referrals will be made to other appropriate IEG members. Inquiries are welcomed; please do not send manuscripts. Fees, references, and resumes are available from editors on request.

Whenever you have a project calling for freelance editorial expertise, get in touch with the best editors in trade book publishing today to solve your manuscript problems.

Sally Arteseros

2 Fifth Avenue, Suite 10-T
New York, NY 10011
Fax: 212-982-2053

Edits all kinds of fiction; literary, commercial, women's, historical, contemporary, inspirational. A specialist in short stories. And in nonfiction: biography, autobiography, memoir, psychology, anthropology, business, regional books, and academic books. Editor at Doubleday for more than 25 years.

Maureen Baron

150 West 87th Street, #6C
New York, NY 10024
212-787-6260

Former Vice President/Editor in Chief of NAL/Signet Books continues to work with established and developing writers in all areas of mainstream fiction and nonfiction. Specialties: medical novels and thrillers; women's issues; health matters; African American fiction; biography; memoirs. Knows the market and has good contacts. Book club consultant.

Carolyn Blakemore

242 East 19th Street
New York, NY 10003
Fax: 212-228-6835

A hardcover book Editor for more than 30 years, specializing in commercial fiction, history, and biography, research, and outlines. Has worked with S. M. Alsop, Barbara T. Bradford, James Dickey, Kitty Carlisle, Kitty Kelley, Joseph Lash, John D. MacDonald, Alexandra Ripley, John Toland, Thomas Fleming, Lawrence Grobel, and William Morris.

Deborah Chiel

180 West End Avenue, #23
New York, NY 10023
Fax: 212-362-1104

Freelance writer, book doctor, and Editor whose ghostwriting credits include a major work of alternative medicine for a leading New York oncologist and a legal thriller inspired by a real-life corporate courtroom battle. Also coauthored a glitzy romantic novel and has written more than a dozen novelizations based on feature film and television scripts.

Paul De Angelis Book Development

PO Box 97
Cornwall Bridge, CT 06754
Fax: 860-672-6861

Manuscript evaluations, rewriting or ghostwriting, and editing. Thirty years' experience in key positions at St. Martin's Press, E. P. Dutton, and Kodansha America. Special expertise in history, current affairs, music, biography, literature, translations, popular science. Authors worked with: Delany sisters, Mike Royko, Peter Guralnick, Barbara Pym, Alexander Dubcek.

Joyce Engelson

1160 Fifth Avenue, #402
New York, NY 10029
Fax: 212-860-9095

Sympathetic, hands-on editing; goal: commercial publication. Forty years' experience. Concentrations: thrillers, mysteries, literary and first novels; health, psychology, mind/body, women's issues, American history, pop culture, sports, comedy ("best sense of humor in the biz"—try me!). Authors include Richard Condon, Norman Cousins, Gael Greene. And me.

Jerry Gross

63 Grand Street
Croton-on-Hudson, NY 10520-2518
Fax: 914-271-1239

More than 40 years of specific, problem-solving critiquing, line editing, restructuring, and rewriting of mainstream and literary fiction and nonfiction manuscripts and proposals. Specialties: male-oriented escape fiction, popular psychology, and pop culture. My goal is to make the manuscript as effective and salable as possible.

Susan Leon

21 Howell Avenue
Larchmont, NY 10538
Fax: 914-833-1429

Editor specializing in preparation of book proposals and collaborations, including two *New York Times* bestsellers. Fiction: All areas—commercial, literary, historical, and women's topics. Nonfiction: history, biography, memoir, autobiography, women's issues, family, lifestyle, design, travel, food. Also, law, education, information, and reference guides.

Richard Marek

29 East 9th Street
New York, NY 10003
Fax: 212-420-1819

Former President and Publisher of E. P. Dutton specializes in editing and ghostwriting. Edited Robert Ludlum's first nine books, James Baldwin's last five, and Thomas Harris's *The Silence of the Lambs*. As ghostwriter, collaborated on six books, among them a novel that sold 225,000 copies in hardcover and more than 2 million in paperback.

Joan S. Pollack

890 West End Avenue, #14B
New York, NY 10025
Fax: 212-666-4219

Specializing in autobiography, biography, memoirs, and fiction; any manuscripts with a narrative line. Collaborative ghosting of celebrity biographies—for example, Douglas Fairbanks, Jr., *The Salad Days* (Doubleday) and *A Hell of a War* (St. Martin's Press); Jack Benny and Joan Benny, *Sunday Nights at Seven* (Warner Books).

James O'Shea Wade

1565 Baptist Church Road
Yorktown Heights, NY 10598
Voice/fax: 914-962-4619

With 30 years' experience as Editor in Chief and Executive Editor for major publishers, including Crown/Random House, Macmillan, Dell, and Rawson-Wade, I edit and ghostwrite in all nonfiction areas and specialize in business, science, history, biography, and military. Also edit all types of fiction, prepare book proposals, and evaluate manuscripts.

Genevieve Young

30 Park Avenue
New York, NY 10016
Fax: 212-683-9780

Detailed analysis of manuscripts, including structure, development, and line editing. Areas of special interest include biography, autobiography, medicine, animals, modern Chinese history, and all works with a story line, whether fiction or nonfiction.

Ten Signs of a
Scam Book Doctor

JERRY GROSS

Working with an expert, ethical book doctor can often make the difference between being published or remaining unpublished. Conversely, working with an unqualified, unethical book doctor can often be hazardous—even fatal—to your career.

You've worked hard to save the money to hire a book doctor. Make sure that the book doctor you hire will turn out to be a good investment. Here are 10 signs that someone who claims to be a professional book doctor may be trying to scam you.

1. *A scam book doctor states that you can't get published unless you hire a book doctor.* You may hear that editors and publishers demand that a manuscript be professionally edited before they will consider it for publication, or that agents won't take on a client unless the writer first works with a book doctor to polish the manuscript.

Not true. Agents and editors still take on manuscripts that need a lot of work, but, to be candid, they don't do it too often because they are usually overworked and overwhelmed by the volume of material submitted to them. That's why working with a good book doctor can at least improve your odds of being accepted by an agent and an editor.

2. *A scam book doctor guarantees, or at least implies, that his editing will get you accepted by an agent.*

Not true! No reputable book doctor can make this statement because no book doctor can persuade an agent to represent a project that the agent does not like, believe in, or see as commercially viable. Beauty is in the eye of the beholder, and editors and agents often see a manuscript's potential through very different eyes.

3. *A scam book doctor guarantees, or strongly implies, that once she's edited your manuscript, an agent will definitely be able to sell it.*

Not true. The vagaries, shifts of taste, and trends in the publishing marketplace are such that agents themselves cannot be sure which manuscripts will be salable.

4. *A scam book doctor admits (or you discover) that he has a "financial arrangement" with the person or company who referred you to him.* In plain English, this means that he kicks back part of his fee for the referral.

This is inarguably unethical. There should be no financial relationship between the book doctor and the referring party. If one exists, it can adversely affect the honesty and integrity of his evaluation, his line editing of your manuscript, or both.

5. *A scam book doctor does not guarantee that she will edit your manuscript personally.*
Since you are hiring the editor for her specific expertise, insist that she guarantee in writing that she will edit the manuscript herself. If she won't do this, look elsewhere for an editor.

6. *A scam book doctor tells you that he can't take on your project, but will subcontract it.*
However, he won't tell you who will edit it, and he won't provide you with that editor's background, samples of that editor's work, or any references. And he does not give you the right to accept or refuse the editor he suggests.

If you do decide to work with another editor because the one you wanted is overbooked or otherwise unavailable, then you have every right to know as much about the person recommended by him as you know about the editor making the recommendation. You also have every right to decide whether you want to work with the editor whom he recommends.

7. *A scam book doctor won't provide references from authors or agents she's worked with.*
Obviously, the editor won't provide you with names of dissatisfied clients, but you can learn a lot by gauging the enthusiasm (or lack of it) with which the client discusses working with the book doctor. Ask questions: "Was she easy and friendly to work with?"; "Was she receptive to ideas?"; "Was she available to discuss her approach to line-editing, critique of the manuscript, or both?"; "Did you feel that you got good value for your money?"

8. *A scam book doctor won't provide samples of his editing or critiques.*
Engaging in a book doctor without seeing how he line-edits or problem-solves a manuscript is akin to buying oceanfront property in Arizona from a real estate salesman on the phone or on the Web. Talk is cheap, but good editing is expensive. Make sure you are buying the expertise you need; demand to see samples of the editor's work. If he balks, hang up the phone!

9. *A scam book doctor sends you an incomplete Letter of Agreement* that does not specify all the costs you will incur, what she will do for each of her fees, a schedule of payment, and a due date for delivery of the edited or critiqued manuscript.

Every one of your contractual obligations to each other should be spelled out clearly in the Letter of Agreement before you sign it. If changes are agreed upon during the course of the author–editor relationship, these changes should either be incorporated into a new

Letter of Agreement that both parties sign or be expressed in rider clauses added to the Agreement that are initialed by both editor and author. There should be no hidden or "surprise" costs at the time of the final payment to the book doctor.

10. *A scam book doctor wants the entire fee before he begins to work.*

There are many different kinds of payments possible when an author hires an editor; the most common is half the fee paid on signing the Letter of Agreement and the other half when the work is completed. Full payment before the editorial work has begun is not an option. Hang up immediately if the book doctor demands such an arrangement.

A final caution: Be convinced that you are hiring the right book doctor before signing the Letter of Agreement. Not only your money, but also your career is at stake!

Book Doctors
The Real Deal

Susan Schwartz

Most writers are aware that publishers have become much more business-oriented and competitive in this age of consolidation. What these writers may not know is that the movers and shakers in the publishing industry increasingly rely on independent editors—sometimes called "book doctors"—to transform promising material into publishable books and magazine articles and provide writers with their professional expertise.

Words into Print is one of three currently thriving alliances of top New York publishing professionals who provide independent editorial services to publishers, literary agents, book packagers, content providers, and—most important—directly to writers. In addition to our affiliation with such organizations as ASJA, the Author's Guild, the Women's National Book Association, PEN, and the NWU, Words into Print also offers a Web site (www.wordsintoprint.org) that lists our members and their e-mail addresses, credentials, and recently completed projects. It also provides direct links to related sites. A writer accessing our Web site can approach any editor directly or send a general query to determine which editor or editors are best suited to and available for a particular project.

The editors affiliated with Words into Print have diverse publishing backgrounds. Some of us specialize in fiction, some in nonfiction; some are terrific proposal writers; some are conscientious line editors; some of us function as project developers, matching subjects with appropriate writers and, from there, finding agents and in some cases publishers to handle projects. We offer ghostwriting and other collaborative services, as well as general consultation to writers.

Independent editors who make up groups such as Words into Print can save writers time and heartache by steering them in the right direction at the outset. We work hard for the writers who hire us, as we shape their material, give advice, and meet regularly with the on-staff professionals who make today's publishing decisions. By tapping our expertise, writers acquire the tools they need to navigate the submission and publishing process. While we can't guarantee that every writer's project will find an agent or result in a sale to a publisher, our track record speaks for itself in the number of projects that come our way, are rewritten or reshaped, and then are sold.

If you are engaging a freelance editor or "book doctor," here are some questions to consider:

- Does the editor have on-staff experience? The best book doctors spent decades on staff at major New York publishers and have inside knowledge of what publishers are looking for, how they view manuscripts and proposals, and what it takes to make them notice yours.
- Does the editor's experience mesh with the kind of project you are attempting to publish? Does that person's initial comments about your project make sense? The best editors don't necessarily tell writers what they want to hear; they evaluate material with a clear idea of the competition and marketing climate facing the project and can often suggest ways to reshape and restructure to enhance marketability.
- Is the editor a member of an independent editors' group, such as Words into Print, or affiliated with one of the established professional writers' groups (ASJA, the Author's Guild, the Women's National Book Association, PEN, and the NWU)? Belonging to at least one of these groups is a mark of professionalism.
- How many projects did the editor complete in the past year, and what kind of assignments were they? The best independent editors receive assignments from a wide variety of sources: literary agents, publishers, other editors, and directly from writers who contact them via personal recommendation or over the Internet.
- What specifically does the editor's fee include? Many independent editors charge a reading or consultation fee up front to determine your project's needs. After making that determination, the editor negotiates fees, depending on the time and level of editing the project requires. Some editors charge by the hour; others offer a "package deal."
- What other services can the editor provide? Not only do independent editors have the expertise to help you shape a project, but also, once an agent is on board, that editor can be helpful in guiding the project through the submission process to successful publication and beyond. One of my clients calls me her "secret weapon" in dealing with her agent and her publisher. I'm often called upon to interpret everything from a rushed agent phone call to baffling letters she receives from her on-staff editor (a former colleague of mine). While it was her agent who brought us together several projects ago, neither the agent nor the editor has any idea that I'm still involved behind the scenes, nor do they need to. In this case, I work for the author, helping her get the most out of the professionals involved in her book's success.

In an increasingly competitive marketplace, the difference between capturing a publisher's attention and being relegated to the "slush pile" often rests on the kind of professional polish and presentation that only industry professionals can provide. Independent editors' groups, such as Words into Print, provide the services that writers need *before* they approach agents or publishers with their projects. We have the credentials and the track record vital to getting writers' work noticed and gaining entry into the sometimes baffling, always formidable publishing world.

Susan A. Schwartz, former Editor at Doubleday, Facts On File, and Contemporary Books and currently a member of the independent editors' group Words into Print (www.wordsinto print.org), has served as a book doctor and ghostwriter for the past four years.

WiP is an alliance of top New York publishing professionals who have pooled our talents and resources to provide a broad range of editorial services. Whatever your needs, we can help you realize your writing and publishing goals. Working with authors, publishers, literary agents, book packagers, and content providers worldwide, our members are available to:

- Develop book proposals and other editorial projects
- Evaluate, critique, troubleshoot, and "doctor" manuscripts
- Line-edit and rewrite text for all media
- Coauthor and ghostwrite for commercial, professional, and academic markets
- Write original text for books, magazines, Web sites, and corporate publications
- Manage illustrated projects, from conception to delivery of art and text on disk
- Advise writers on the publishing process
- Offer referrals to literary agents, book packagers, and publishers
- Offer referrals for other publishing services, including graphic design, research (text and photo), translation, copyediting, proofreading, and indexing

WiP's members specialize in the following subject areas:

Nonfiction: alternative health, anthologies, anthropology, architecture, art, autobiography, biography, business, cookbooks, crafts, criticism, cultural issues, current affairs, divorce, education, film/television, geography, health/fitness, history, humor, illustrated books, journalism, Judaica, law, lifestyle, memoir, music, nature, parenting, performing arts, philosophy, photography, politics, popular culture, psychology, reference, religion, science, self-help, social issues, spirituality, theater, travel/adventure, true crime, women's studies.

Fiction: action, adventure, literary novels, mysteries, poetry, popular novels, short stories, suspense, thrillers, young adult.

Brief profiles of our members, along with contact information, follow. We welcome all queries and contacts to individual members or to our group e-mail or mailing address, but please do not send unsolicited manuscripts. With our diverse backgrounds and experience, we can match you with the right editor for you. Our client lists, resumes, references, portfolios, and fees are available upon request. For the best in the business, look no further. The editors at **WiP** look forward to working with you!

WORDS INTO PRINT MEMBERS

Bonny V. Fetterman Popular and scholarly nonfiction: biography/memoir, history, Judaica. General social sciences with special expertise in Jewish history, literature, and culture; biblical studies; anthologies; and translations.

Penelope Franklin General nonfiction, including autobiography/memoir, diaries and letters, women's issues, travel, art, history, psychology, humor, health, natural history, food, paranormal phenomena, anthologies.

Ruth Greenstein Literary fiction, illustrated nonfiction, biography, memoir, social and cultural issues, travel and adventure, nature, religion and spirituality, health, psychology, visual and performing arts, architecture, media tie-ins, anthologies, reference, poetry.

Paul D. McCarthy Commercial and literary fiction, serious and popular nonfiction, popular reference, screenplays, and other creative material for Internet and media publication.

Diane O'Connell Autobiography/memoir, self-help, psychology, health/fitness, parenting, divorce, education, film, theater, journalism, crafts, cooking, narrative nonfiction, and young adult and mainstream fiction.

Susan A. Schwartz Ghostwriting: fitness, memoirs. Editing: popular nonfiction (health, parenting, business, relationships, memoirs); popular reference books (all subjects); book proposals and assessments; corporate and marketing publications (histories, biographies, conference materials); Web site content; fiction (women's fiction; medical, legal, and political thrillers; general categories).

Katharine Turok Literary and popular fiction, biography/memoir, general nonfiction, film and theater, translations, photography, poetry, psychology, travel, women's issues, art and architecture, reference, anthologies.

Daniel Zitin Fiction: most popular genres, including literary novels, mysteries, thrillers, and novels of action and suspense.

THE ASSOCIATION OF AUTHOR REPRESENTATIVES (AAR)

Attached here is the Canon of Ethics from the Association of Author Representatives (AAR). Even though I make fun of ethics as a ruling concept and don't know which high horse imposed the use of the word *Canon* in this instance, these are excellent guidelines that all agents should follow and that clients should expect and demand that agents follow.

Membership within the AAR implies complete compliance with these guidelines. The AAR is not an agency of enforcement or endorsement. It can simply grant or deny membership in the organization. It's not a so-called trade group. It could be seen as a collective "study" group composed of people who share common pursuits and mutual interests—in this case, book agenting.

Many good agents have chosen to be nonaffiliated with the AAR, including yours truly, for various reasons. In my case, I do a number of "packaged" deals, and my wife does a number of collaboration or "work-for-hire" arrangements, which puts us outside the narrow membership parameters. Excellent agencies that do other "things" beyond simple agenting will not be members for the same reason.

Therefore, membership in the AAR is a pretty good indication of legitimacy. But nonmembership, in and of itself, may indicate nothing.

About the AAR

The AAR was formed in 1991 through the merger of the Society of Authors' Representatives (founded in 1928) and the Literary Agents Association (founded in 1977).

The AAR's objectives include keeping agents informed about conditions in publishing, the theater, the motion picture and television industries, and related fields; encouraging cooperation among literary organizations; and assisting agents in representing their author-clients' interests.

To qualify for membership in the AAR, an agent must meet professional standards specified in the organization's bylaws and agree to its **Canon of Ethics.**

The AAR cannot regulate the commissions, fees, services, or other competitive business practices of its members.

Membership Qualifications

Membership in the AAR is restricted to agents whose primary professional activity for the two years preceding application for membership in the AAR has been as an authors' representative or a playwrights' representative.

To qualify for membership, the applicant for membership in the literary branch of the AAR must have been the agent principally responsible for executed agreements concerning the grant of publication, translation, or performance rights in 10-different literary properties during the 18-month period preceding application.

Alternatively, if the applicant is a dramatic agent, the agent must have been principally responsible for executing agreements for the grant of rights for at least five stage productions before live audiences (in First Class theaters, off-Broadway theaters, LORT theaters, or major institutional theaters in New York City) during the preceding two-year period. At least one such grant must have used either the Approved Production Contract of the Dramatists Guild, Inc., or have been a grant for the production of the play off-Broadway in New York City.

Member agents must conduct their business in such a manner as to be in compliance with legal and fiduciary duties to their clients, and each member agent must agree, in writing, to adhere to the AAR's Canon of Ethics.

Associate members are full-time employees of a sponsoring agent member. They do not themselves qualify for full membership, but are actively engaged in the selling of rights to literary or dramatic properties.

The previous qualifications are merely a digest of some of the requirements for membership. The full requirements are set forth in the Bylaws of the Association of Authors' Representatives, Inc.

Canon of Ethics

1. The members of the Association of Authors' Representatives, Inc., are committed to the highest standard of conduct in the performance of their professional activities. While affirming the necessity and desirability of maintaining their full individuality and freedom of action, the members pledge themselves to loyal service to their clients' business and artistic needs and will allow no conflicts of interest that would interfere with such service. They pledge their support to the Association itself and their principles of honorable coexistence, directness, and honesty in their relationships with their co-members. They undertake never to mislead, deceive, dupe, defraud, or victimize their clients, other members of the Association, the general public, or any person with whom they do business as a member of the Association.

2. Members shall take responsible measures to protect the security and integrity of clients' funds. Members must maintain separate bank accounts for money due their clients so that there is no commingling of clients' and members' funds. Members shall deposit funds received on behalf of clients promptly upon receipt and shall make payments of domestic earnings due clients promptly, but in no event later than 10 business days after clearance. Sums under $50 shall be paid within a reasonable time of clearance. However, on stock and similar rights, statements of royalties and payments shall be made

not later than the month following the member's receipt, each statement and payment to cover all royalties received to the 25th day of the previous calendar month. Payments for amateur rights shall be made not less frequently than every six months. A member's books of account must be open to the client at all times with respect to transactions concerning the client.

3. In addition to the compensation for agency services that is agreed upon between a member and a client, a member may, subject to the approval of the client, pass along charges incurred by the member on the client's behalf, such as copyright fees, manuscript retyping, photocopies, copies of books for use in the sale of other rights, long-distance calls, special messenger fees, etc. Such charges shall be made only if the client has agreed to reimburse such expenses.

4. A member shall keep each client apprised of matters entrusted to the member and shall promptly furnish such information as the client may reasonably request.

5. Members shall not represent both buyer and seller in the same transaction. Except as provided in the next sentence, a member who represents a client in the grant of rights in any property owned or controlled by the client may not accept any compensation or other payment from the acquirer of such rights, including but not limited to so-called packaging fees, it being understood that the member's compensation, if any, shall be derived solely from the client. Notwithstanding the foregoing, a member may accept (or participate in) a so-called packaging fee paid by an acquirer of television rights to a property owned or controlled by a client if the member: (a) fully discloses to the client at the earliest practical time the possibility that the member may be offered such a "packaging fee," which the member may choose to accept; (b) delivers to the client at such time a copy of the Association's statement regarding packaging and packaging fees; and (c) offers the client at such time the opportunity to arrange for other representation in the transaction. In no event shall the member accept (or participate in) both a packaging fee and compensation from the client with respect to the transaction. For transactions subject to the Writers Guild of America (WGA) jurisdiction, the regulations of the WGA shall take precedence over the requirements of this paragraph.

6. Members may not receive a secret profit in connection with any transaction involving a client. If such profit is received, the member must promptly pay over the entire amount to the client. Members may not solicit or accept any payment or other things of value in connection with their referral of any author to any third party for any purpose, provided that the foregoing does not apply to arrangements made with a third party in connection with the disposition of rights in the work of a client of the member.

7. Members shall treat their clients' financial affairs as private and confidential, except for information customarily disclosed to interested parties as part of the process of placing rights, as required by law, or, if agreed with the client, for other purposes.

The AAR believes that the practice of literary agents charging clients or potential clients for reading and evaluating literary works (including outlines, proposals, and partial or complete manuscripts) is subject to serious abuse that reflects adversely on our profession. For that reason, members may not charge clients or potential clients for reading and evaluating literary works and may not benefit, directly or indirectly, from the charging for such services by any other person or entity. The term *charge* in the previous sentence includes any request for payment other than to cover the actual cost of returning materials.

Self Publishing = Maybe Vanity = No (Probably)

Jeff Herman

Many books in print have sold hundreds of thousands of copies but will never appear on any lists, nor will they ever be seen in a bookstore, nor will the authors ever care. Why? Because these authors are self-publishers and make as much as a 90 percent profit margin on each copy they sell.

Their initial one-time start-up cost to get each of their titles produced may have been $15,000, but after that, each 5,000-copy print run of a hardcover edition costs about $1.25 per unit. The authors sell them for $25 each. When they do a high-volume corporate sale, they're happy to discount the books 20 percent or more off the $25 list price.

Now, we said that no bookstores are in the picture. Then how and where are the authors selling their books? The answer to this question is also the answer to whether or not it makes sense for you to self-publish. Most self-publishers achieve financial success with:

1. A well-linked Web site designed to sell and upsell.
2. A well-oiled corporate network, which translates into frequent high-volume orders by companies that distribute the book in-house as an educational tool or distribute them at large as a sales vehicle (customized printings are no problem).
3. Frequent public speaking events where backroom sales happen.
4. Frequent and self-generated publicity that's designed to promote the books and leads people to the Web site, a toll free number, or both.

Obviously, most of us don't have this kind of in-house infrastructure, which brings us back to the most important question: How will you sell copies of your self-published book? If you don't have a realistic answer in place, then self-publishing may not be a viable option after all, or at least your initial expectations have to be reoriented.

Why can self-publishers make so much money? Because they get to keep it. Here's how a conventional book publisher's deal gets divided up:

- Start with a trade paperback listed at $20.
- $10 goes to the retailer.
- $1.50 goes to the author.
- The first $15,000 goes to set the book up.
- $1.00 goes to printing each copy.
- $? Corporate overhead. (If the publisher overpaid on the advance, then this number goes higher.)
- $?? Publisher's profit. (This is a real wild card. If a publisher is an inefficient operation, then any profit may be out of reach. If too few books sell, there are only losses, no matter how lean and mean the publisher may be.)

A secondary source of no-overhead revenues for both publishers and self-publishers is ancillary rights, which includes exports, translations, and audio editions.

What's clear is that the published author makes a tiny fraction of the per-unit sale versus what the self-publisher makes. But the publisher also absorbs all the risks. And then there's the distribution factor . . .

WHAT'S DISTRIBUTION AND WHY DO SELF-PUBLISHERS HAVE A TOUGH TIME WITH IT?

Because everyone else does, too. Distribution is the process that gets books onto shelves, theoretically. Strong distribution does not ensure that bookstores will elect to stock the title. Too many books are published, compared to the quantity and quality of shelf space to accommodate them. You can have a big-name publisher and an invisible book. Distribution only generates the potential for the book to be available in stores, and nonexistent distribution deletes that potential.

All established book publishers have proven distribution channels in place, consisting of warehouses, fulfillment and billing operations, and traveling or regional salespeople who pitch the stores.

Smaller-sized presses may not be able to afford all of that, so they'll pay a 15 percent commission to a large house to handle it for them, or they will retain an independent distributor that does nothing but distribute for small presses.

Brick and mortar bookstores are not eager to open accounts with self-publishers. It's too much of a hassle. Same goes for independent distributors.

Several brilliant self-publishing consultants have devised ways to bypass these distribution obstacles. Look for their books in the "Suggested Resources" section of this book.

Vanity publishing is for morons. I don't mean to be insulting. It's just that you end up spending so much more than necessary, all for the illusion that you've been published in the conventional sense. In truth, the only thing you'll get out of the deal are boxes of expensive books that were probably not edited or well produced.

Hiring qualified editors, consultants, and so on, to help you make the best self-published book possible does not fall under the vanity label.

When the Deal Is Done

How to Thrive After Signing a Publishing Contract

JEFF HERMAN

Congratulations! You've sold your book to an established publishing house. You've gained entry to the elite club of published authors. You'll discover that your personal credibility is enhanced whenever this achievement is made known to others. It may also prove a powerful marketing vehicle for your business or professional practice.

Smell the roses while you can. Then wake up and smell the coffee. If your experience is like that of numerous other writers, once your book is actually published, there's a better-than-even chance you'll feel a bit of chagrin. Some of these doubts are apt to be outward expressions of your own inner uncertainties. Others are not self-inflicted misgivings—they are most assuredly ticked off by outside circumstances.

Among the most common author complaints are: (1) Neither you nor anyone you know can find the book anywhere. (2) The publisher doesn't appear to be doing anything to market the book. (3) You detest the title and the jacket. (4) No one at the publishing house is listening to you. In fact, you may feel that you don't even exist for them.

As a literary agent, I live through these frustrations with my clients every day, and I try to explain to them at the outset what the realities of the business are. But I never advocate abdication or pessimism. There are ways for every author to substantially remedy these endemic problems. In many cases this means first taking a deep breath, relaxing, and reaching down deep inside yourself to sort out the true source of your emotions. When this has been accomplished, it's time to breathe out, move out, and take charge.

What follows are practical means by which each of these four most common failures can be preempted. I'm not suggesting that you can compensate entirely for what may be a publisher's defaults; it's a tall order to remake a clinker after the fact. However, with lots of smarts and a little luck you can accomplish a great deal.

A PHILOSOPHY TO WRITE BY

Let me introduce a bit of philosophy that applies to the writer's life, as well as it does to the lives of those who are not published. Many of you may be familiar with the themes popularized by psychotherapists, self-awareness gurus, and business motivators that assert the following: To be a victim is to be powerless—which means you don't have the ability to improve your situation. With that in mind, avoid becoming merely an author who only complains and who remains forever bitter.

No matter how seriously you believe your publisher is screwing up, don't fall into the victim trap. Instead, find positive ways to affect what is or is not happening for you.

Your publisher is like an indispensable employee whom you are not at liberty to fire. You don't have to work with this publisher the next time, but this time it's the only one you've got.

There are a handful of perennially bestselling writers, such as John Grisham, Anne Rice, Mary Higgins Clark, and Michael Crichton, whose book sales cover a large part of their publisher's expense sheet. These writers have perhaps earned the luxury of being very difficult, if they so choose (most of them are reportedly quite the opposite).

But the other 99.98 percent of writers are not so fortunately invested with the power to arbitrate. No matter how justified your stance and methods may be, if you become an author with whom everyone at the publishing house dreads to speak, you've lost the game.

The editors, publicists, and marketing personnel still have their jobs, and they see no reason to have you in their face. In other words: Always seek what's legitimately yours, but always try to do it in a way that might work *for* you, as opposed to making yourself persona non grata till the end of time.

Attacking Problem No. 1: Neither You Nor Anyone You Know Can Find the Book Anywhere

This can be the most painful failure. After all, what was the point of writing the book and going through the whole megillah of getting it published if it's virtually invisible?

Trade book distribution is a mysterious process, even for people in the business. Most bookstore sales are dominated by the large national and regional chains, such as Waldenbooks, B. Dalton, Barnes & Noble, and Crown. No shopping mall is complete without at least one of these stores. Publishers always have the chain stores in mind when they determine what to publish. Thankfully, there are also a few thousand independently owned shops throughout the country.

Thousands of new titles are published each year, and these books are added to the seemingly infinite number that are already in print. Considering the limitations of the existing retail channels, it should be no surprise that only a small fraction of all these books achieves a significant and enduring bookstore presence.

Each bookstore will dedicate most of its visual space to displaying healthy quantities of the titles it feels are safe sells: books by celebrities and well-established authors, or books that are being given extra-large printings and marketing budgets by their publishers, thereby promising to create demand.

The rest of the store will generally provide a liberal mix of titles, organized by subject or category. This is where the backlist titles reside and the lower-profile newer releases try to stake their claims. For instance, the business section will probably offer two dozen or so sales books. Most of the displayed titles will be by the biggest names in the genre, and their month-to-month sales probably remain strong, even if the book was first published several years ago.

In other words, probably hundreds of other sales books were written in recent years that, as far as retail distribution is concerned, barely made it out of the womb. You see, the stores aren't out there to do you any favors. They are going to stock whatever titles they feel they can sell the most of. There are too many titles chasing too little space.

It's the job of the publisher's sales representative to lobby the chain and store buyers individually about the merits of her publisher's respective list. But here, too, the numbers can be numbing. The large houses publish many books each season, and it's not possible for the rep to do justice to each of them. Priority will be given to the relatively few titles that get the exceptional advances.

Because most advances are modest, and since the average book costs about $20,000 to produce, some publishers can afford to simply sow a large field of books and observe passively as some of them sprout. The many that don't bloom are soon forgotten, as a new harvest dominates the bureaucracy's energy. Every season, many very fine books are terminated by the publishing reaper. The wisdom and magic these books may have offered are thus sealed away, disclosed only to the few.

I have just covered a complicated process in a brief fashion. Nonetheless, the overall consequences for your book are in essence the same. Here, now, are a few things you may attempt in order to override such a stacked situation. However, these methods will not appeal to the shy or passive:

- *Make direct contact with the publisher's sales representatives.* Do to them what they do to the store buyers—sell 'em! Get them to like you and your book. Take the reps near you to lunch and ballgames. If you travel, do the same for local reps wherever you go.
- *Make direct contact with the buyers at the national chains.* If you're good enough to actually get this kind of access, you don't need to be told what to do next.
- *Organize a national marketing program aimed at local bookstores throughout the country.*

  There's no law that says only your publisher has the right to market your book to the stores. (Of course, except in special cases, all orders must go through your publisher.) For the usual reasons, your publisher's first reaction may be "What the hell are you doing?" But that's okay; make the publisher happy by showing her that your efforts work. It would be wise, however, to let the publisher in on your scheme up front.

  If your publisher objects—which she may—you might choose to interpret those remarks simply as the admonitions they are, and then proceed to make money for all. This last observation leads to ways you can address the next question.

Attacking Problem No. 2: The Publisher Doesn't
Appear to Be Doing Anything to Market the Book

If it looks as if your publisher is doing nothing to promote your book, then it's probably true. Your mistake is being surprised and unprepared.

The vast majority of published titles receive little or no marketing attention from the publisher beyond catalog listings. The titles that get big advances are likely to get some support, since the publisher would like to justify the advance by creating a good seller.

Compared to those in other Fortune 500 industries, publishers' in-house marketing departments tend to be woefully understaffed, undertrained, and underpaid. Companies like Procter & Gamble will tap the finest business schools, pay competitive salaries, and strive to nurture marketing superstars. Book publishers don't do this.

As a result, adult trade book publishing has never been especially profitable, and countless sales probably go unmade. The sales volumes and profits for large, diversified publishers are mostly due to the lucrative—and captive—textbook trade. Adult trade sales aren't the reason that companies like Random House can generate more than $1 billion in annual revenues.

Here's What You Can Do:

Hire your own public relations firm to promote you and your book. Your publisher is likely to be grateful and cooperative. But you must communicate carefully with your publishing house.

Once your manuscript is completed, you should request a group meeting with your editor and people from the marketing, sales, and publicity departments. You should focus on what their marketing agenda will be. If you've decided to retain your own PR firm, this is the time to impress the people at your publishing house with your commitment and pressure them to help pay for it. At the very least, the publisher should provide plenty of free books.

Beware of this common problem: Even if you do a national TV show, your book may not be abundantly available in bookstores that day—at least, not everywhere. An obvious answer is setting up 800 numbers to fill orders, and it baffles me that publishers don't make wider use of them. There are many people watching *Oprah* who won't ever make it to the bookstore, but who would be willing to order then and there with a credit card. Infomercials have proved this.

Not all talk or interview shows will cooperate, but whenever possible you should try to have your publisher's 800 number (or yours) displayed as a purchasing method, in addition to the neighborhood bookstore. If you use your own number, make sure you can handle a potential flood.

If retaining a PR firm isn't realistic for you, then do your own media promotions. There are many good books in print about how to do your own PR. (A selection of relevant titles may be found in this volume's "Suggested Resources" section.)

Attacking Problem No. 3: You Detest the Title and Jacket

Almost always, your publisher will have final contractual discretion over title, jacket design, and jacket copy. But that doesn't mean you can't be actively involved. In my opinion, you had better be. Once your final manuscript is submitted, make it clear to your editor that you expect to see all prospective covers and titles. But simply trying to veto what the publisher comes up with won't be enough. You should try to counter the negatives with positive alternatives. You might even want to go as far as having your own prospective covers professionally created. If the publisher were to actually choose your version, the house might reimburse you.

At any rate, don't wait until it's after the fact to decide you don't like your cover, title, and so forth. It's like voting: Participate or shut up.

Attacking Problem No. 4: No One at the Publishing House Seems to Be Listening to You

This happens a lot—though I bet it happens to certain people in everything they do. The primary reasons for this situation are either (1) that the people you're trying to access are incompetent; (2) that you're not a priority for them; or (3) that they simply hate talking to you.

Here are a few things you might try to do about it:

- *If the contact person is incompetent, what can that person really accomplish for you anyway?* It's probably best to find a way to work around this person, even if he begins to return your calls before you place them.
- *The people you want access to may be just too busy to give you time.* Screaming may be a temporary remedy, but eventually, they'll go deaf again. Obviously, their time is being spent somewhere. Thinking logically, how can you make it worthwhile for these people to spend more time on you? If being a pain in the neck is your best card, then perhaps you should play it. But there's no leverage like being valuable. In fact, it's likely that the somewhere else they're spending their time is with a very valuable author.
- *Maybe someone just hates talking to you.* That may be this person's problem. But, as many wise men and women have taught, allies are better than adversaries. And to convert an adversary is invaluable. Do it.

CONCLUSION

This essay may come across as cynical. But I want you to be realistic and be prepared. Many publishing success stories are out there, and many of them happened because the authors made them happen.

For every manuscript that is published, probably a few thousand were rejected. To be published is a great accomplishment—and a great asset. If well tended, it can pay tremendous dividends.

Regardless of your publisher's commitment at the outset, if you can somehow generate sales momentum, the publisher will most likely join your march to success and allocate a substantial investment to ensure it. In turn, the publisher may even assume all the credit. But so what? It's to your benefit.

Writing Micro Fiction

Dennis E. Hensley

I have had more than 100 short stories published in everything from popular slicks to prestigious literary quarterlies. That sounds impressive until you learn that I've been at it for 30 years, averaging only 3 or 4 short story sales per year. Meanwhile, I've also written 7 novels, 26 nonfiction books, and more than 3,000 newspaper and magazine articles. Do you see a pattern here?

I've never found writing short fiction to be easy. Developing a plot, establishing a setting, creating believable characters, infusing realistic dialogue, and presenting a logical resolution to the story's crisis—all within 2,000 to 5,000 words—is a challenge. But if that's bad, an even greater challenge is trying to write the "micro" short story (750–1,250 words), currently popular in Sunday school take-home papers, literary digests, and regional periodicals.

My first micro was called "Could Beethoven Have Made It in Nashville?" (*Stereo,* Spring, 1973). It was a 1,000-word comedy with a simple premise: If Ludwig van Beethoven were alive today and tried to get a job as a musician in Nashville, Tennessee, would anyone hire him?

What made the story work was its simplicity. There was one setting (a country music recording studio), only two characters (Beethoven and the studio engineer), and one basic joke (a talented man is out of his element). The comedy came from the fact that Beethoven had long hair like modern musicians, and he wore long, black coat-tails like Johnny Cash. He looked the part. Yet he couldn't deliver the goods. The comedic format was formed around the dialogue between the two men, both talented artists but neither one having a clue as to what the other one was talking about. Very little author narrative was required.

The micro story is wedged within very strict framing. The setting usually is limited to one spot (a classroom, a library alcove, the backseat of a taxi). Walk-on characters may be needed, but the central characters are usually limited to just two people (dad with son, boss and new employee, doctor seeing patient). The plot must be confined to one problem or crisis that can be resolved without extenuating circumstances or plot complications.

Writing micro fiction is like playing with a toy telescope. If you look into the small aperture, you see a wide panorama of distant scenes brought into close view (the novel, the traditional short story). However, if you turn the telescope around and look into the wide aperture, you see very small images and a very limited field of vision (the micro story).

Ideas for micro plots are often derived from "scenes," "snatches of conversation," or "real life lessons" heard or witnessed on the run. The idea for my 950-word story "The Competition" (*Challenge,* February 15, 1976) came from two overlapping events at my church.

Our church custodian had retired that year. At his farewell dinner, he said that in his youth he had planned to be a preacher. He received a scholarship to a Bible college, but had a farm accident and broke his hip. He had to forfeit the scholarship and remain bedridden. He felt it was the worst thing that could ever have happened to him. However, he fell in love with the nurse who came by to check on him each afternoon. They married, raised a family, and had a marvelous life together. He said his accident turned out to be the best "break" he'd ever had.

About this same time, our church sponsored a statewide youth talent rally, with prizes ranging from savings bonds to college scholarships. A young trumpet player from our church took second place in the instrumental performance category. He was devastated. Someone else received the scholarship he so desperately wanted. I heard him say, "This is the worst thing that could ever have happened to me" . . . and with that, I had the basis of my micro story.

I opened the story at the competition with the old custodian wishing the young musician good luck. The boy then performed well, but finished second.

He couldn't face his friends or family, so he retreated to the church basement.

The old man followed him, told him his own "worse thing ever" story and how it became his "best thing ever" story. They took a moment to pray together for the boy to have a right attitude toward competition. The story ended with the old man reminding the boy that he was only a junior and he still had next year in which to compete for a scholarship. The boy lifted the trumpet, gave it a practice toot, and the story was over.

Again, we see one setting (a church), two characters (the boy and the custodian), and one plot lesson (learning to see defeat in a broader context). This micro story must be that concise. Its dialogue must be crisp, to the point, and must always provide necessary information or move the plot forward. Adjectives and adverbs must be eliminated through the use of visual nouns ("mansion" or "shack" rather than "house") and action verbs ("slapped" or "tapped" rather than "touched"). The plot conflict must be created at the onset of the story. The ending must evoke a reader response (a laugh, a nod of agreement, a wince of surprise).

Interestingly enough, although I find short fiction very challenging, I continue to write it. It is the best practice I know for learning how to make each word count. That discipline carries over into everything else I write. The scenes in my novels are more plot-intensive if I think "micro." The dialogue in my interviews is more distilled and pertinent if I think "micro." Even my feature reporting is better if I think in a micro mentality—keep to the facts, limit the scope, get to the crux of the problem immediately, and don't leave the reader baffled at the end.

And . . . that's the short of it, friends!

The Secrets of Ghostwriting and Collaboration Success

TONIANNE ROBINO

Thousands of people in the world have valuable information to share or incredible stories to tell. But only a few of them have the ability or the time to write their own books. That's where you—the professional writer—come into the picture. If you're a strong, clear writer, have the ability to organize thoughts and ideas into a logical order, and can put your ego in the back seat, you may have what it takes to be a successful ghostwriter or collaborator.

The life of a professional writer has its share of pains, but it also has an ample amount of perks. To begin with, it provides a means of escape from the Monday through Friday, 9 to 5 grind. The pay is good, and as you improve your skills and broaden your network, it gets better. In addition to being paid to learn and write about interesting people, philosophies, and methods, being a professional writer puts you in touch with a wide array of fascinating people. I've had the chance to interview some of the planet's most brilliant people and to explore the work of trendsetters and pioneers in the fields of business, psychology, health, fitness, relationship building, astrology, and metaphysics. I have been flown to Paris to meet with leaders in the field of innovation, wined and dined at some of New York's most exclusive restaurants, and collected agates on the Oregon coast, all in the name of "work." If this sounds appealing, keep reading.

WHAT'S THE DIFFERENCE BETWEEN GHOSTWRITING AND COLLABORATING?

One of the most common questions I'm asked is "What's the difference between a ghostwriter and a collaborator?" The answer can vary from project to project. But, typically, a ghostwriter gathers the author's original materials and research and turns them into a book, based on the author's specifications (if the book will be self-published) or the publisher's specifications (if the book has been sold through the proposal process). Theoretically, although ghostwriters do conduct interviews and undertake additional research, they do not contribute their own thoughts or ideas to the content of the book.

In reality, the boundaries of the ghostwriter are not always so clear. As a ghostwriter, I have created 80 percent of the exercises in a number of self-help books, provided many original ideas for content, and "given away" plenty of great title ideas. I don't regret these choices because they felt right and, in the cases mentioned, I was being fairly paid for my ideas, as well as for my services. My being generous with my contributions also made my clients happy and helped to build the foundation of my business. But don't take this too far. For one thing, it's not always a wise choice—particularly if you're giving away original ideas that are perfect for your own book. For another thing, the author you're working with may not appreciate this type of input from you. Do not overstep your boundaries as a ghostwriter by adding your own thoughts to a book, unless the author specifically asks you to do this.

In my more naïve days, and following two glasses of Chardonnay, I made the mistake of sharing my unsolicited input with the author of a health book that I was ghostwriting. In the midst of my enthusiasm, I started brainstorming ideas that she might use to illustrate some of the book's major points. Suddenly, she sprung out of her chair, pointed at me, and declared, "Let's get something straight. This is MY book!" Ouch! I *was* offering ideas without being asked, but on the other hand, I was only suggesting. Even so, take the word of an initiate and tread softly on your client's turf.

Nowadays, if an author wants me to contribute my own ideas and create original material to support the book, I work with that person as a collaborator and generally receive a coauthor credit, either on the cover or on the title page. Getting credit isn't the most important thing when you're starting out, but if you want to publish your own books in the future, stringing together a list of credits can give you a considerable advantage.

If a book cover says "by John Doe *and* Jane Smith," they were probably equal collaborators. That can mean:

- they're both experts and one or both of them wrote the book,
- they're both experts and they hired a ghostwriter to write the book, or
- the first author is the expert and the second is a professional writer.

If a book cover says "by John Doe *with* Jane Smith," Jane probably wrote the book. It could also mean that Jane was a contributor to the book.

Whether you will be serving as a ghostwriter or a collaborator should be clarified up front. Which way to go depends on the project and the people involved. Some of my clients want me to be a "ghost" because they want exclusive cover credit, or they want people to think they wrote their own book. (If this bothers you, now would be a good time to bail out.) Other clients say, "I'm not a writer. This is my material, but I don't want to pretend I wrote this book," or "You deserve credit for what you're doing." On the flip side of the coin, you may be willing to write some books that you don't want your name on. Let's hope this is not because you haven't done a good job! Perhaps you're trying to establish yourself in a particular field of writing and may not want to be linked with projects outside of your target area. That's a judgment call, and you're the best one to make it.

BEING "INVISIBLE" HAS ITS ADVANTAGES

Years ago, after signing my first contract to ghostwrite a book about personal development, I called a friend to share the great news. But instead of being happy for me, she said, "That's not fair. Why should you write a book and not get any credit for it? You teach that stuff in your seminars. Why don't you write the book yourself?" She was also upset that I wouldn't divulge the name of the "mystery author."

She had no way of knowing how challenging it can be to publish your first book flying solo. The author whom I was writing for was well-known and regularly spoke to huge crowds of people all around the world. He had created the perfect platform for this book and was in the prime position to make it a success. He had been previously published and his depth of knowledge in this topic was far greater than my own.

For me, it was a chance to learn more about one of my favorite topics from one of the best sources available. It was also a chance to slip into the publishing world through the back door. I dashed in and never looked back. Once I completed that book, the author referred me to a friend who hired me to write a book about her spiritual journey. She, in turn, introduced me to a professional speaker who wanted to self-publish a book on personal coaching, but could never find the time to write it. And so it goes. If you do a good job, one book can easily lead to the next.

Besides that, being invisible has its advantages. I can zip into the grocery store in purple sweatpants, hair in a ponytail on top of my head, and not a stitch of make-up, and nobody notices or cares! I can kiss my husband in public without camera flashes going off around us, and nobody shows up at my door uninvited, except my mother-in-law.

WHEN CREDIT IS DUE

After you've ghostwritten your first book or two, you'll have more confidence in yourself and your abilities. You will probably start fantasizing (if you haven't already) about seeing your name on the cover, instead of tucked into the acknowledgments section—if that! My name didn't even appear in the first few books that I wrote. Beginning with the fourth book, I asked for a credit in the acknowledgments. Since then, I've been thanked for being a wordsmith, editorial adviser, writing coach, editor, and a "great friend." At least, that was a step in the right direction. However, as much as I relish my anonymity, I also look forward to the day when I'm writing more of my own books than other people's! For that reason, most of the professional writing that I do now is as a collaborator/coauthor.

TEN STEPS TO SUCCEEDING AS A PROFESSIONAL WRITER

There are a number of things to consider before quitting your job and striking out as a professional writer. Writing is a constant process and no matter how good a writer may be, that individual can always get better. Another point to consider is that being a great writer doesn't ensure your success. Writing is a business, and the more you learn about running a business, the better off you'll be. If you're stagnating in a job you abhor, reframe your situation so that you see it as an opportunity to continue earning an income while you make the transition to your writing career. Meanwhile, focus on polishing your writing and interpersonal skills and learn as much about operating a business as you can. The more you learn now, the fewer mistakes you'll make later.

1. Assess Your Writing Skills

Now is the time to be as objective about your writing as possible. Regardless of where you believe you could or should be along your writing path, what counts at the moment is where you are *right now*. What writing experience do you have? Have you taken any writing courses? Does your writing flow from one thought logically to the next, or does it need to be better organized? Is your writing smooth and conversational, or does it sound stiff or overly academic? What sorts of positive and negative comments have you received about your writing? Have you had anything published? If not, get going!

If you're too close to your writing to be objective, hire an editor, book doctor, or writing coach to give you some forthright feedback. This assessment will help you to learn where you excel and where you should focus your efforts for improvements. The good news is that there's a market for writers at all points on the professional spectrum. You may not be ready to take on your first book, but you could be qualified to ghostwrite an article, collaborate on a chapter, or polish someone else's work. Begin at your current skill level and commit to a path of improvement. By doing this, you will increase your abilities and your income.

2. Make Your First List

Everyone knows at least a few experts. Whether the experts in your life are doctors, professors, psychologists, interior decorators, photographers, archaeologists, or magicians, chances are that some of them have a goal to write a book. Unless these people are good writers and have a lot of free time, which very few experts have, their book will remain on their "wish list" until someone like you shows up to help them. So begin to make a "potential author" list by answering the following questions. For each question, list as many names as you can think of.

Do you know people who are pioneers or experts in their field?

Do you know people who are famous, either in general or in their area of expertise?

Who are the experts, celebrities, or trendsetters whom your friends or associates know?

Once you've made your list, number the names, starting with number one for the person you would most like to work with. Resist the urge to contact these people until you have professionally prepared for your meeting, by learning more about them and taking Steps 3 and 4.

3. Prepare a Professional Package

Put together a promotional package for yourself, or hire a professional to help you do it. This package should include your resume or bio, the services you offer, and a variety of writing samples, showing different styles and topics. You might also insert a page of testimonials from people you have helped with your writing skills or from teachers and coaches who can attest to your abilities. If you've been published, include clean copies of a few of your best clips. If you haven't, enclose a few essays that demonstrate your ability to write clearly and deliver a message effectively.

When you send out your promotional package, enclose a personal pitch letter. Basically, you are telling people what you believe they have to offer the world through their experience or expertise. You're also telling them why you are the perfect person to write the article, manuscript, or book proposal.

4. Set Your Rates

Some writers enclose a Rate Sheet in their promotional package, but I don't recommend it. I *do* recommend that you make a rate sheet for your own reference. This will be your guide when you are deciding what to charge your clients. Since every project is a little different, don't commit to a price until you estimate how much time and money it will take for you to do the job well.

Calculate how fast you can write final copy, by keeping track of the actual hours spent writing, editing, and proofreading an article or sample chapter. When the piece is completed to your satisfaction, follow this formula:

Total number of words in final copy

Divided by

Total number of hours to complete final copy

Equals:

Your average speed per hour

The idea isn't to race. This exercise is designed to give you a reality check. If you don't know your average speed for producing final copy, you won't be able to create realistic deadline schedules and you'll have no idea how much you're earning for a day of work.

While you may be able to speed through a first draft, the chapter isn't finished until you've edited, polished, and proofread it.

In addition to estimating your actual writing time, build in time for research, interviews, and meetings with the author. You should also estimate the amount of postage, phone charges, faxes, audio tapes, transcription services, and anything else that will be money out of your pocket. Once you've done your homework, you can present the client with a Letter of Agreement (see Closing the Deal, Step 7) that includes what you will charge and what they will get for your fee.

Writers' rates vary wildly. I was paid $10,000 for the first few books that I ghostwrote, and this is still a great starter rate for a nonfiction book ranging from 70,000 to about 85,000 words. You may not be able to charge this much the first time or two, but with each publication that you add to your list, you can inch up your price. When you reach the point where you are earning $15,000 or more on a book, you will be in the company of some of the most successful ghostwriters. The average fee to write a book proposal can range from $1,000 up to $8,000 or more. When you turn writing into a full-time adventure and write several proposals and books each year, while perhaps editing others, you'll be well on your way to ongoing financial and publishing success!

Many times, if you are working as a "writer for hire," you are paid a flat fee and do not receive royalties from book sales. If you are ghostwriting the book, you may be able to negotiate for royalties. (Royalties for ghostwriting can range from 10 percent of the author's royalties to 50 percent.) If you're a collaborator, in most cases you're entitled to a percentage of the book sales. However, many contracts state that the writer does not begin to receive royalties until the publisher has recouped the initial advance for the book. In some cases, the writer's royalties do not begin until the author has recouped the amount invested in the writer. The bottom line is that most ghostwriters don't receive a dime in royalties until thousands of books have been sold. I suggest that you charge what you're worth up front and think of royalties as icing on the cake.

5. Polish Your Interpersonal Skills

Unfortunately, some of the best writers are not comfortable talking to people or selling themselves to potential clients. If you see this as a possible pitfall in building your business, make it a priority to develop your interpersonal skills. Plenty of books, tapes, and seminars address personal development, communication skills, networking, and conflict resolution. Devote yourself to learning how to be more comfortable and effective in your interactions with others.

Practice listening closely to what your client is saying, without interrupting. Growing up in an Italian family with everyone talking at once, I had no problem paying attention to what my clients were saying. (If you can listen to three people at once, you can easily hear one at a time!) However, mastering the discipline to keep my mouth shut until it was my turn to talk was another matter entirely. While interjecting and simultaneous talking is considered par for the course in some settings, many people are offended by interruptions and consider them rude. If you have an exciting idea or pertinent question on the tip of your tongue, jot it down, and wait until your clients complete their thoughts, before chiming in.

Learn how to communicate with your clients in a way that is open and caring. For example, rather than telling an author that the file of notes she sent you was so disorganized that dealing with it was like "stumbling blindfolded through a maze," tell her you appreciate her ability to think of so many things at once. Then tell her what you want her to do. "Please put all of your notes under specific category headings, so I can keep all of your great ideas organized." The rule is to think before you speak. There are usually better ways to communicate a thought than the first words that pop into your head or out of your mouth!

Another skill that is essential for a ghostwriter and important for a collaborator is learning how to keep your ego in check. It's not uncommon for a writer to start feeling attached to a project and have a desire for greater freedom or control of the content or writing style. Remind yourself that this book is not yours. Your day will come, and working as a professional writer is paving the way for that to happen.

One of the surest ways to nip your ghostwriting career in the bud is to break the code of confidentiality that you have with the author of the book. Degrees of "invisibility" differ by project, but if the author doesn't want anyone to know you are writing the book, zip your lips. Other than perhaps your spouse, there is no one, and I mean *no one,* that you should tell. You can say you're writing a book, and you can divulge the general topic, but that has to be the end of the conversation. To this day, my best friends have no idea who I've ghostwritten books for—except in the cases where the authors have publicly acknowledged me for my participation.

Finally, one of the most beneficial interpersonal skills that a writer or anyone else can possess is a sense of humor. Things are bound to go wrong somewhere along the way, and being able to laugh together with your client will ease tension and stress and make the project a whole lot more fun. It's also valuable to learn to laugh at yourself. My father always said, "If you can look at yourself in the mirror at the end of the day and laugh, you'll make it in life." Oftentimes, when I write a book I create a blooper file, just for my own entertainment. This file contains all of the funny, startling, and obscene typos that I find when I proofread my work.

Keep in mind that there are scores of great writers in the world. Why would an author choose to work with someone who's cranky, arrogant, or self-absorbed if it's possible to work with someone equally talented who is also pleasant, down to earth, and fun?

6. Know When to Run!

Some day, in the not too distant future, you will have a chance to write a book that you know in your gut is not a good match. This might be because it's a topic that bores your pants off, the point of view is in direct opposition to your own beliefs, or the material is leagues away from your scope of knowledge, experience, or ability for comprehension. In spite of all this, you may be tempted to leap into this "opportunity." Maybe your rent is due, the phone company is threatening to disconnect you, or maybe you just can't wait any longer to write your first book. Before you rationalize this decision or override your instincts, take a step back and think about it for at least two days before you commit. For instance, I should have failed Algebra class, but my professor gifted me with the lowest passing grade. Even so, when I was offered a chance to ghostwrite *Understanding the Intrigue of Calculus,* I was tempted to do it. Fortunately, two bounced check notices (caused by my math errors) snapped me back to reality, and I graciously declined the offer.

Aside from making a good match with a topic, it is imperative that you feel good about the book's author. It usually takes about nine months to write a book and doing it with someone else can be compared to having a baby together—minus the sex. If you like each other, it can be a wonderful journey filled with creative energy. If you don't like each other, it can be a recurring nightmare that doesn't go away when you wake up.

Years ago, I took on the daunting task of "saving a book." The complete manuscript was due in three months and the author's writing team had mysteriously jumped ship. When I spoke with the author for the first time, she was both friendly and enthusiastic, but she also seemed a little desperate. I ignored my instincts, and two days later I was sitting in her apartment discussing the book. Several things happened that day, and each one of them should have set off warning flares in my mind. To begin with, the author's materials were in complete disarray. (No problem, I told myself. I'm a great organizer.) Second, in between telling me how important it is to speak to our mates with respect, she was berating her husband for his lack of photocopying abilities and sundry other things that he couldn't do right to save his life. (She's just stressed out, I justified.) And third, as I leafed through the disheveled stacks of unnumbered pages, I came across a few very cryptic and angry-sounding notes from the writing team that had bailed out. (I reassured myself that even if others had failed, I would not.)

These rationalizations would soon come back to bite me. And not just once. As it turned out, nine writers had attempted to complete this manuscript before I was contacted. Four writers quit, one writer had a nervous breakdown, three of them disappeared into thin air, and another had his phone disconnected. Ironically, the week the book was released, I had the pleasure of meeting one of the writers who had wisely run for her life. We traded our "Crazy-Author Horror Stories" over steaming plates of fried rice and laughed until tears streamed down our cheeks. At that point it was funny, but not a moment before! If you connect with an author who enters the scene waving red flags, run for your life!

7. Close the Deal

Verbal agreements are not enough. If you're working with a publishing house, the author or the author's agent will usually have a contract for you to sign. Make sure you understand this agreement before you sign it. Don't be afraid to ask questions. These contracts are written in "legalese" and can be daunting the first time you encounter one. If you're working with an author who plans to self-publish, create a "letter of agreement" that specifies exactly what services you are providing, the fees involved, the date of delivery, and any other considerations that should be put into writing. This document should be signed by both you and the author; it will help to prevent assumptions or other misunderstandings concerning your business agreement.

8. Capture the Author's Voice

Whether you're working as a ghostwriter or a collaborator, one of your jobs is to capture the voice of the author. Simply put, you want to write in a way that makes it sound like the author is talking. It shouldn't sound like another author whose style you admire, and it most certainly should not sound like you!

Practice reading a few paragraphs from a favorite book, and then write a few of your own, mimicking the author's voice. Do this with a wide variety of authors, and over time, you will develop an "ear" for others' voices.

One of the best ways to write in the author's voice is to conduct taped interviews with the author and have them transcribed onto computer disk. You can cut and paste the pertinent information into each chapter, in the author's own words, and then smooth it out and expand it as needed.

9. Create and Keep Deadlines

There are nearly as many methods of meeting deadlines as there are writers. I tend to take a very methodical approach, dividing up the work into equal parts, circling my "days off," and carefully penciling each chapter deadline on my desk calendar. (I can't help it, I was born this way.) Other writers would go mad with this approach. One of the best writers I know creates 10 percent of the book the week she signs the contract and the other 90 percent the month before the manuscript is due. I couldn't even conceive of this approach and would never have believed it could be done if I hadn't witnessed it personally. The secret is to find out what works best for you. But don't kid yourself. Very few writers can write a great book in less than six months. At least until you settle into your own rhythm, pace yourself. Set reasonable deadlines and find a way to stay accountable to those dates.

Staying accountable to my own deadline schedule was initially much harder than I thought it would be. (There are so many tempting diversions in life!) Frequently, when I was supposed to be writing, I was toying with an art project, combing the forest floor in search of gourmet mushrooms, or just staring out the window. My sense of urgency wasn't ignited until my cash flow began to dwindle. That was when I discovered my motivation. Food, shelter, electricity. It may sound like common sense, but for me it was an "aha" moment. I *do* have some built-in motivation, but it's keeping my cash flow going that moves me from the sunroom to my office each day.

Linking your productivity with your payments works very well. Ask for one-third of your fee up front. This assures you that the author is serious and provides income so you can focus on the book. Schedule your second payment of one-third to coincide with turning in 50 percent of the manuscript. The final one-third is slated for the date you deliver the final manuscript to the author. If you feel you need more deadlines, divide your fee into four or more payments, each contingent on completing a certain amount of work.

10. Ask for Referrals

I don't have a business card that says "writer." I don't advertise my writing or editing services, and networking requires an hour's drive from the sanctuary of my forest home into the nearest city—which translates into: I rarely do it. By all sensible accounts, I shouldn't be making it as a ghostwriter. And yet I am, and have been for more than a decade. The secret to my success is word of mouth marketing. My clients are happy with my work and me, so they hire me again. They also tell their friends and associates about me, and the wheel continues to spin, seemingly of its own volition.

I know there are many more approaches to marketing, but I've learned that personal referrals usually provide clients whom I want to work with**.** It's possible for a satisfied client to refer you to an author whom you'd rather eat glass than work with, but most of the time, personal referrals increase your chances of connecting with authors and projects that are interesting and appealing.

When you've completed your work and satisfied your client, ask for referrals. If you've delivered the goods, they'll be happy to brag about you to their friends and associates who "just can't seem to find the right writer."

MAINTAIN YOUR BRIDGES

After the manuscript is complete, the author will be busy with promotional plans and getting back to regular business. You will be focusing on your next project. It's easy to get caught up in the day-to-day happenings and neglect to maintain the bridges that you've already built.

Make it a point to connect with satisfied clients from time to time. Hearing from you will help them think of you for future projects and will increase the likelihood that they'll remember to refer you to someone else. Every couple of months, send a card, a funny e-mail, or an upbeat fax. I phone previous clients only on occasion, and when I do, I call them at their office and keep it short. You want to be the person they look forward to hearing from, not the one who won't go away!

Publishing Abroad

Mark Schreiber

When my sister wrote her first novel, for young adults, I suggested an alternative way to submit it to publishers, since not all U.S. houses have young adult lists and since most agents—including my own—don't handle young adult fiction. So instead I showed it to my Dutch publisher, who not only bought the manuscript, but had it translated and in print within a year, far quicker than some American publishers take to bring a book to market. And my sister now has a three-book deal with HarperCollins.

While it isn't necessarily always easier to publish abroad, agents aren't ubiquitous in other countries, and author–editor relationships, like European architecture, harken back to a less corporatized world. Even in Germany, home of the largest publishing conglomerates, many small to medium-sized houses don't insist on agented submissions. And everyone, from Brazil to Japan, reads books in English.

Now, of course, most English-language books sold abroad have already been published here, but there are exceptions, as my sister's case has proved. Many foreign publishers lack the resources to acquire bestsellers, and not all American bestsellers do well in other countries. Conversely, some books that failed to take off in the United States find a more receptive audience abroad. If your book deals with Ireland or Mexico, for example, you might find more enthusiasm for your work in those countries than you would here. Even books set in America—such as my sister's novel—might pique a foreign editor's interest, given the global appetite for all things American.

Children's books, or other books that rely on illustrations or photographs, may be easier to sell when publishers in different countries agree to share the production costs. In such cases translation costs are minimal, and images transcend language barriers. A Dutch friend of mine has written a children's book chronicling the trade between the Netherlands and Japan. She was unable to find a Dutch publisher willing to bear the expenses of a four-color book, so she approached Japanese publishers for a coproduction.

In addition, if you or your parents were born abroad, you might wish to try that country first. For instance, many of the large U.S. houses such as Simon & Schuster and Little Brown have independent subsidiaries in Australia. And Australian fiction lists tend heavily toward Australian writers and themes. So if you or your parents are Australian, you might receive a more sympathetic reading in Sydney than in New York.

One good resource for foreign publishers is the *Literary Marketplace*. Another is international book fairs. The biggest is in Frankfurt, and the largest for children's books is in Bologna. Although they aren't open to the public and aren't specifically for writers, many writers do find a way to attend. Other annual book fairs, in London, Antwerp, and other cities, may be more accessible and you might schedule a vacation to coincide with them. Attendance isn't necessary, however; you can obtain information on foreign publishers and their lists by visiting the fairs' Web sites or reading reports about them in *Publishers Weekly* and other trade journals.

It's always better to approach editors with outlines or queries, rather than sending the entire manuscript. If a foreign publisher shows interest, be sure to sell only the rights for that language, and request that the contract be in English and payment in dollars. Unlike U.S. deals, which remain in effect until the book goes out of print or the copyright expires, many foreign contracts are for specific terms, such as seven years, after which the author is at liberty to resell the rights.

Fiction Dictionary

Jamie M. Forbes

In book publishing, people describe works of fiction as they relate to categories, genres, and other market concepts, which, coming from the mouths of renowned industry figures, can make it sound as if there's a real system to what is actually a set of arbitrary terminology. Categories are customarily viewed as reflecting broad sectors of readership interest. Genres are either subcategories (classifications within categories) or types of stories that can pop up within more than one category—though *genre* and *category* are sometimes used interchangeably.

For instance, suspense fiction (as a broad category) includes the jeopardy story genre (typified by a particular premise that can just as easily turn up in a supernatural horror story). Or, again within the suspense fiction category, there's the police procedural (a subcategory of detective fiction, which is itself a subcategory of suspense that is often spoken of as a separate category). The police procedural can be discussed as a distinct genre with its own special attributes; and there are particular procedural genre types, such as those set in the small towns of the American plains or in a gritty urban environment. As a genre-story type, tales of small-town American life also surface in the context of categories as disparate as literary fiction, horror stories, Westerns, and contemporary and historical romance.

As we can see, all of this yakety-yak is an attempt to impose a sense of order onto what is certainly a muddy creative playing field.

The following listing of commonly used fiction descriptives gives an indication of the varieties of writing found within each category. This is not meant to be a strict taxonomy. Nor is it exhaustive. The definitions associated with each category or genre are fluid and personalized in usage and can seem to vary with each author interview or critical treatise, with each spate of advertising copy or press release, or they can shift during the course of a single editorial conference. One writer's "mystery" may be a particular editor's "suspense," which is then marketed to the public as a "thriller."

Then, too, individual authors do come up with grand, original ideas that demand publication and thereby create new categories or decline to submit to any such designation. But that's another story—maybe yours.

ACTION-ADVENTURE

The action-oriented adventure novel is best typified in terms of premise and scenario trajectory. These stories often involve the orchestration of a journey that is essentially exploratory, revelatory, and (para)military. There is a quest element—a search for a treasure in whatever guise—in addition to a sense of pursuit that crosses over into thrillerdom. From one perspective, the action-adventure tale, in story concept if not explicit content, traces its descent from epic-heroic tradition.

In modern action-adventure we are in the territory of freebooters, commandos, and mercenaries—as well as suburbanites whose yen for experience of the good life, and whose very unawareness in the outback, takes them down dangerous trails. Some stories are stocked with an array of international terrorists, arms-smugglers, drug-dealers, and techno-pirates. Favorite settings include jungles, deserts, swamps, and mountains—any sort of badlands (don't rule out an urban environment) that can echo the perils that resound through the story's human dimension.

There can be two or more cadres with competing aims going for the supreme prize—and be sure to watch out for lots of betrayal and conflict among friends, as well as the hitherto unsuspected schemer among the amiably bonded crew.

Action-adventures were once thought of as exclusively men's stories. No more. Writers invented new ways to do it, and the field is now open.

COMMERCIAL FICTION

Commercial fiction is defined by sales figures—either projected (prior to publication, even before acquisition) or backhandedly through actual performance. Commercial properties are frontlist titles, featured prominently in a publisher's catalog and given good doses of publicity and promotion.

An agent or editor says a manuscript is commercial, and the question in response is apt to be: How so? Many books in different genres achieve bestseller potential after an author has established a broad-based readership and is provided marketing support from all resources the publisher commands.

Commercial fiction is not strictly defined by content or style; it is perhaps comparative, rather than absolute. Commercial fiction is often glitzier, more stylishly of the mode in premise and setting; its characters strike the readers as more assuredly glamorous (regardless of how highbrow or lowlife).

A commercial work offers the publisher a special marketing angle, which changes from book to book or season to season—this year's kinky kick is next year's ho-hum. For a new writer in particular, to think commercially is to think ahead of the pack and not jump on the tail-end of a bandwagon that's already passed. If your premise has already played as a television miniseries, you're way too late.

Commercial works sometimes show elements of different categories, such as detective fiction or thrillers, and may cut across or combine genres to reach out toward a vast readership. Cross-genre books may thus have enticing hooks for the reading public at large; at the same time, when they defy category conventions they may not satisfy genre aficionados. If commercial fiction is appointed by vote of sales, most popular mysteries are commercial works, as are sophisticated bestselling sex-and-shopping oh-so-shocking wish-it-were-me escapades.

CRIME FICTION

Related to detective fiction and suspense novels, in subject matter and ambiance, are stories centered on criminal enterprise. Crime fiction includes lighthearted capers that are vehicles in story form for the portrayal of amusingly devious aspirations at the core of the human norm. Crime stories can also be dark, black, *noir,* showing the primeval essence of tooth-and-nail that brews in more than a few souls.

Some of the players in crime stories may well be cops of one sort or another (and they are often as corrupt as the other characters), but detection per se is not necessarily the story's strong suit. It is just as likely that in the hands of one of the genre's masters, the reader's lot will be cast (emotionally, at least) in support of the outlaw characters' designs.

DETECTIVE FICTION

Varieties of detective fiction include police procedurals (with the focus on formal investigatory teamwork); hard-boiled, poached, or soft-boiled (not quite so tough as hard-boiled); and the cozy (a.k.a. tea-cozy mysteries, manners mysteries, manor house mysteries).

Detectives are typically private or public pros; related professionals whose public image, at least, involves digging under the surface (reporters, journalists, computer hackers, art experts, psychotherapists, and university academics, including archaeologists); or they may be rank amateurs who are interested or threatened via an initial plot turn that provides them with an opportunity (or the necessity) to assume an investigatory role.

The key here is that the detective story involves an ongoing process of discovery that forms the plot. Active pursuit of interlocking clues and other leads is essential—though sometimes an initial happenstance disclosure will do in order to kick off an otherwise tightly woven story.

The manifold denominations of modern detective fiction (also called mysteries, or stories or novels of detection) are widely considered to stem from the detective tales composed by the nineteenth-century American writer Edgar Allan Poe. Though mysterious tracks of atmosphere and imagery can be traced in the writings of French symbolists (Charles Baudelaire was a big fan of Poe), the first flowering of the form was in Britain, including such luminaries as Arthur Conan Doyle, Agatha Christie, and Dorothy L. Sayers. Indeed, in one common usage, a traditional mystery (or cozy) is a story in the mode initially established by British authors.

The other major tradition is the American-grown hard-boiled detective story, with roots in the tabloid culture of America's industrial growth and the associated institutions of yellow journalism, inspirational profiles of the gangster-tycoon lifestyle, and social-action exposés.

The field continues to expand with infusions of such elements as existentialist character conceits, the lucidity and lushness of magic-realists, and the ever-shifting sociopolitical insights that accrue from the growing global cultural exchange.

Occasionally, detective fiction involves circumstances in which, strictly speaking, no crime has been committed. The plot revolves around parsing out events or situations that may be construed as strange, immoral, or unethical (and are certainly mysterious), but which are by no means considered illegal in all jurisdictions.

FANTASY FICTION

The category of fantasy fiction covers many of the story elements encountered in fables, folktales, and legends; the best of these works obtain the sweep of the epic and are touched by the power of myth. Some successful fantasy series are set within recognizable museum-quality frames, such as those of ancient Egypt or the Celtic world. Another strain of fantasy fiction takes place in almost-but-not-quite archaeologically verifiable regions of the past or future, with barbarians, nomads, and jewel-like cities scattered across stretches of continent-sized domains of the author's imagination.

Fair game in this realm are romance, magic, and talking animals. Stories are for the most part adventurous, filled with passion, honor, vengeance—and *action*. A self-explanatory subgenre of fantasy fiction is termed sword-and-sorcery.

HORROR

Horror has been described as the simultaneous sense of fascination and terror, a basic attribute that can cover significant literary scope. Some successful horror writers are admired more for their portrayal of atmosphere than for attention to plot or character development. Other writers do well with the carefully paced zinger—that is, the threat-and-delivery of gore; in the hands of skilled practitioners, sometimes not much more is needed to produce truly terrifying effects.

The horror genre has undergone changes—there is, overall, less reliance on the religiously oriented supernatural, more utilization of medical and psychological concepts, more sociopolitical and cultural overtones, and a general recognition on the part of publishers that many horror aficionados seek more than slash-and-gore. Not that the readers aren't bloodthirsty—it is just that in order to satisfy the cravings of a discerning audience, a writer must create an augmented reading experience.

The horror itself can be supernatural in nature, psychological, paranormal, or techno (sometimes given a medical-biological slant that verges on sci-fi), or can embody personified occult/cultic entities. In addition to tales of vampires, were-creatures, demons, and ghosts, horror has featured such characters as the elemental slasher/stalker (conceived with or without mythic content), a variety of psychologically tormented souls, and just plain folks given over to splatterhouse pastimes. Whatever the source of the horror, the tale is inherently more gripping and more profound when the horrific beast, force, or human foe has a mission, is a character with its own meaningful designs and insights—when something besides single-minded bloodlust is at play.

At times, the horror premise is analogous to a story of detection (especially in the initial setup); often the horror plot assumes the outlines of the thriller (particularly where there is a complex chase near the end); and sometimes the horror-story scenario ascribes to action-adventure elements. However, rather than delineating a detailed process of discovery (as in a typical mystery) or a protracted hunt throughout (as in the thriller), the horror plot typically sets up a final fight to the finish (until the sequel) that, for all its pyrotechnics and chills, turns on something other than brute force.

LITERARY FICTION

The term *literary* describes works that feature the writer's art expressed at its most refined levels; literary fiction describes works of literature in such forms as the novel, novella, novelette, short story, and short-shorts (also known as flash fiction). In addition to these fictional formats, literary works include poetry, essays, letters, dramatic works, and superior writing in all nonfiction varieties, covering such areas as travel, food, history, current affairs, and all sorts of narrative nonfiction, as well as reference works.

Literary fiction can adhere to the confines of any and all genres and categories, or suit no such designation. A work of fiction that is depicted as literary can (and should) offer the reader a multidimensional experience. Literary can designate word selection and imagery that is careful or inspired or that affects an articulated slovenliness. A literary character may be one who is examined in depth or is sparsely sketched to trenchant effect. Literature can postulate philosophical or cultural insights and portray fresh ideas in action. Literary works can feature exquisitely detailed texture or complete lack of sensory ambiance.

Structurally, literary fiction favors story and plot elements that are individualistic or astonishingly new, rather than tried-and-true. In some cases the plot as such does not appear important, but beware of quick judgment in this regard: Plotting may be subtle, as in picking at underlying psychology or revelation of character. And the plot movement may take place in the reader's head, as the progressive emotional or intellectual response to the story, rather than demonstrated in external events portrayed on paper.

To say that a work is literary can imply seriousness. Nonetheless, many serious works are not particularly sober, and literary reading should be a dynamic experience—pleasurably challenging, insightful, riveting, fun. A work that is stodgy and boring may not be literary at all, for it has not achieved the all-important aim of being fine reading.

Obviously, a book that is lacking with respect to engaging characters, consciousness of pace, and story development, but that features fancy wordplay and three-page sentences, is hardly exemplary of literary mastery. Though such a work may serve as a guidepost of advanced writing techniques for a specialized professional audience, it is perhaps a more limited artifice than is a slice-and-dice strip-and-whip piece that successfully depicts human passion and offers a well-honed story.

Commercial literature, like commercial fiction in general, is essentially a back-definition; commercial literature indicates works of outstanding quality written by authors who sell well, as opposed to just plain literature, which includes writers and works whose readership appeal has not yet expanded beyond a small core. Noncommercial literary works are staples of the academic press and specialized houses, as well as of selected imprints of major trade publishers.

When a literary author attracts a large readership or manages to switch from the list of a tiny publisher to a mammoth house, the publisher might decide a particular project is ripe for a shot at the big-time and slate the writer for substantial attention, accompanied by a grand advance. If you look closely, you'll note that literary authors who enter the commercial ranks are usually not just good writers: Commercial literary works tap into the cultural pulse, which surges through the editorial avenues into marketing, promotion, and sales support.

In day-to-day commercial publishing discourse, to call a piece of work *literary* simply means it is well written. As a category designation, literary fiction implies that a particular book does not truly abide by provisos of other market sectors—though if the work under discussion does flash some category hooks, it might be referred to in such catch-terms as a literary thriller or literary suspense.

MAINSTREAM FICTION

A mainstream work is one that can be expected to be at least reasonably popular to a fairly wide readership. In a whim of industry parlance, to various people in publishing the label *mainstream* signifies a work that is not particularly noteworthy on any count—it's a work of fiction that's not literary, according to circumscribed tastes, and not something easily categorized with a targeted, predictable base of readership. Maybe not particularly profitable, either, especially if the publishing house is bent on creating bestsellers. A mainstream work may therefore be seen as a risky proposition, rather than a relatively safe bet.

Let this be a cautionary note: In some publishing minds, a plain-and-simple mainstream book signifies midlist, which equals no sale. In a lot of publishing houses, midlist fiction, even if it's published, gets lost; many commercial trade houses won't publish titles they see as midlist (see **Midlist Fiction**).

A mainstream work may be a good read—but if that's all you can say about it, that's a mark against its prospects in the competitive arena. When a story is just a good story, the publisher doesn't have much of a sales slant to work with; in publishing terms that makes for a dismal enough prognosis for an editor or agent to pass.

If a manuscript has to sell on storytelling merits or general interest alone, it most likely won't sell to a major publisher at all. If mainstream fiction is what you've got, you, the writer, are advised to return to the workshop and turn the opus into a polished piece with a stunning attitude that can be regarded as commercial, or redesign the story line into a category format such as mystery, suspense, or thriller. A mainstream mystery or mainstream thriller may contain characters who aren't too wacko and milieus that aren't overly esoteric. Such works are eminently marketable, but you might suppress the mainstream designation in your query and just call your work by its category or genre moniker.

If you've got the gifts and perseverance to complete a solid story, and you find yourself about to say it's a mainstream book and no more, you'll be further along faster if you work to avoid the midlist designation. Think commercially and write intrepidly.

Please note: Many editors and agents use the term *mainstream fiction* more or less synonymously with commercial fiction (see **Commercial Fiction**).

MIDLIST FICTION

Midlist books are essentially those that do not turn a more-than-marginal profit. That they show a profit at all might testify to how low the author's advance was (usually set so the publisher can show a profit based on projected sales). Midlist books may be category titles, literary works, or mainstream books that someone, somewhere believed had commercial potential (yet to be achieved).

The midlist is where no one wants to be: You get little if any promotion, few reviews, and no respect. Why publish this kind of book at all? Few publishers do. A midlist book was most likely not intended as such; the status is unacceptable unless the writer is being prepped for something bigger and is expected to break through *soon*. When a writer or series stays midlist too long, they're gone—the publishers move on to a more profitable use of their resources.

If the publishers don't want you, and the readers can't find you, you're better off going somewhere else, too. (See **Commercial Fiction** or any of the other category designations.)

MYSTERY

Many people use the term *mystery* to refer to the detective story (see **Detective Fiction**). When folks speak of traditional mysteries, they often mean a story in the British cozy mold, which can be characterized—but not strictly defined—by an amateur sleuth (often female) as protagonist, a solve-the-puzzle story line, minimal body count (with all violence performed offstage), and a restrained approach to language and tone. Sometimes, however, a reference to traditional mysteries implies not only cozies, but also includes stories of the American hard-boiled school, which are typified by a private eye (or a rogue cop), up-front violence as well as sex, and vernacular diction.

On the other hand, mysteries are seen by some to include all suspense fiction categories, thereby encompassing police procedurals, crime capers, thrillers, and even going so far afield as horror and some fantasy fiction.

In the interests of clarity, if not precision, here we'll say simply that a mystery is a story in which something of utmost importance to the tale is unknown or covert at the outset and must be uncovered, solved, or revealed along the way. (See **Crime Fiction**, **Detective Fiction**, **Fantasy Fiction**, **Horror**, **Suspense Fiction**, and **Thriller**.)

ROMANCE FICTION

The power of love has always been a central theme in literature, as it has in all arts, in all life. For all its importance to the love story genre, the term *romance* does not pertain strictly to the love element. The field can trace its roots through European medieval romances that depicted knights-errant and women in distress, which were as much tales of spiritual quest, politics, and action as love stories. The Romantic movement of the nineteenth century was at its heart emblematic of the heightened energy lent to all elements of a story, from human passion, to setting, to material objects, to psychological ramifications of simple acts.

Thanks to the writers and readers of modern romances, they've come a long way from the days of unadulterated heart-stopping bodice-rippers with pampered, egocentric heroines who long for salvation through a man. Today's romance most often depicts an independent, full-blooded female figure in full partnership with her intended mate.

Modern romance fiction is most assuredly in essence a love story, fueled by the dynamics of human relationships. From this core, writers explore motifs of career and family, topical social concerns, detective work, psychological suspense, espionage, and horror, as well as historical period pieces (including European medieval, Regency, and romances set in the American West) and futuristic tales. Romance scenarios with same-sex lovers are highlighted throughout the ranks of vanguard and literary houses, though this theme is not a priority market at most trade publishers or romance-specialist presses.

Among commercial lead titles tapped for bestseller potential are those books that accentuate the appeal of romance within the larger tapestry of a fully orchestrated work. (See also **Women's Fiction**.)

SCIENCE FICTION

Take humankind's age-old longings for knowledge and enlightenment and add a huge helping of emergent technology, with the twist that science represents a metaphysical quest—there you have the setup for science fiction. Though the basic science fiction plot may resemble that of action-adventure tales, thrillers, or horror stories, the attraction for the reader is likely to be the intellectual or philosophical questions posed, in tandem with the space-age glitter within which it's set. In terms of character interaction, the story line should be strong enough to stand alone when stripped of its technological trimmings.

In the *future fiction* genre, the elements of science fiction are all in place, but the science tends to be soft-pedaled, and the story as a whole is character-based. In a further variation, the post-apocalyptic vision presents the aftermath of a cataclysm (either engendered by technology or natural in origin) that sets the survivors loose on a new course that demonstrates the often-disturbing vicissitudes of social and scientific evolution. Such scenarios are generally set in the not-too-distant future, are usually earth-based, or are barely interstellar, with recognizable (but perhaps advanced) technology as the norm.

Purity of genre is at times fruitless to maintain or define. Is Mary Shelley's *Frankenstein* a science fiction tale or a horror story, or is it primarily a literary work? Is Jules Verne's *20,000 Leagues Under the Sea* science fiction or a technothriller—or a futuristic action-adventure?

Stories of extraterrestrial exploration, intergalactic warfare, and other exobiological encounters are almost certain to be placed within the science fiction category, until the day when such endeavors are considered elements of realism.

SUSPENSE FICTION

Suspense fiction embraces many literary idioms, with a wide range of genres and subdivisions categorized under the general rubric of suspense. Indeed, in broad terms, all novels contain suspense—that is, if the writer means for the reader to keep reading and reading, and reading on . . . way into the evening and beyond.

Suspense fiction has no precise formula that specifies certain character types tied to a particular plot template. It is perhaps most applicable for a writer to think of suspense as a story concept that stems from a basic premise of situational uncertainty. That is: Something horrible is going to happen! Let's read! Within suspense there is considerable latitude regarding conventions of style, voice, and structure. From new suspense writers, editors look for originality and invention and new literary terrain, rather than a copycat version of last season's breakout work.

However, that said, writers should note that editors and readers are looking for works in which virtually every word, every scene, every blip of dialog serves to heighten suspense. This means that all imagery—from the weather to social setting, to the food ingested by the characters—is chosen by the writer to induce a sense of unease. Each scene (save maybe the last one) is constructed to raise questions or leave something unresolved. Every sentence or paragraph contains a possible pitfall. A given conversational exchange demonstrates edgy elementals of interpersonal tension. Everything looks rosy in one scene? Gotcha! It's a setup to reveal later what hell lurks underneath. Tell me some good news? Characters often do just that, as a prelude to showing just how wrong things can get.

The *jeopardy* story (or, as is often the case, a *woman-in-jeopardy* story) reflects a premise, rather than being a genre per se. A tale of jeopardy—a character under continuous, increasing threat and (often) eventual entrapment—can incorporate what is otherwise a psychological suspense novel, a medical thriller, an investigatory trajectory, or a slasher-stalker spree.

Additional subdivisions here include *romantic suspense* (in which a love relationship plays an essential or dominant role (see **Romance Fiction**), *erotic suspense* (which is not necessarily identical to neurotic suspense), and *psychological suspense* (see immediately following).

Suspense, Psychological

When drifts of character, family history, or other psychodynamics are central to a suspense story's progress and resolution, the tale may aptly be typified as psychological. Sometimes superficial shticks or gimmicks suffice (such as when a person of a certain gender turns out to be cross-dressed—surprise!), but such spins work best when the suspense is tied to crucial issues the writer evokes in the characters' and readers' heads and then orchestrates skillfully throughout the story line.

There are, obviously, crossover elements at play here, and whether a particular work is presented as suspense, psychological suspense, or erotic suspense can be more of an advertising-copywriting decision than a determination on the part of editor or author.

THRILLER

The thriller category is exemplified more by plot structure than by attributes of character, content, or story milieu. A thriller embodies what is essentially an extended game of pursuit—a hunt, a chase, a flight worked fugue-like through endless variations.

At one point in the history of narrative art, thrillers were almost invariably spy stories, with international casts and locales, often set in a theater of war (hot or cold). With shifts in political agendas and technical achievement in the real world, the thriller formula has likewise evolved. Today's thriller may well involve espionage, which can be industrial or political, domestic or international. There are also thrillers that favor settings in the realms of medicine, the law, the natural environs, the human soul, and the laboratory; this trend has given rise to the respective genres of legal thriller, medical thriller, environmental thriller, thrillers with spiritual and mystical themes, and the technothriller—assuredly there are more to come.

The thriller story line can encompass elements of detection or romance and certainly should be full of suspense, but these genre-specific sequences are customarily expositional devices or may be one of many ambient factors employed to accentuate tension within the central thriller plot. When you see a dust jacket blurb that depicts a book as a mystery thriller, it likely connotes a work with a thriller plot trajectory that uses an investigatory or detective-work premise to prepare for the chase.

WESTERN FICTION

The tradition of Western fiction is characterized as much by its vision of the individualist ethic as it is by its conventional settings in the frontier milieu of the American West during the period from the 1860s to the 1890s, sometimes extending into the early 1900s. Though the image of the lone, free-spirited cowpoke with an internalized code of justice has been passed down along the pulp-paper trail, it has long been appreciated by historians that the life of the average itinerant ranch-hand of the day was anything but glamorous, anything but independent.

Whatever the historical record, editors by and large believe readers don't want to hear about the lackluster aspects of saddle tramps and dust-busting ruffians. Nevertheless, there have been inroads by books that display the historically accurate notions that a good chunk of the Western scene was inhabited by women and men of African American heritage, by those with Latino cultural affinities, by Asian expatriates, and by European immigrants for whom English was a second language, as well as by a diversity of native peoples.

Apart from the traditional genre Western, authors are equipped for a resurgence in a variety of novels with Western settings, most notably in the fields of mystery, crime, action-adventure, suspense, and future fiction. Among the newer Western novels are those replete with offbeat, unheroic, and downright antiheroic protagonists; and the standardized big-sky landscape has been superseded by backdrops that go against the grain.

Family sagas have long included at least a generation or two who drift, fight, and homestead through the Western Frontier. In addition, a popular genre of historical romance is set in the American West (see **Romance Fiction**).

Many contemporary commercial novels are set in the Western United States, often featuring plush resorts, urban and suburban terrain, as well as the remaining wide country. The wide variety of project ideas generated by writers, as well as the reader response to several successful ongoing mystery series with Western elements, indicates a lively interest out there.

WOMEN'S FICTION

When book publishers speak of women's fiction, they're not referring to a particular genre or story concept (even if they think they are). This category—if it is one—is basically a nod to the prevalence of fiction readers who are women. Women's fiction is a marketing concept. As an informal designation, women's fiction as a matter of course can be expected to feature strong female characters and, frequently, stories offered from a woman's perspective.

As for the writers of books in this category—many (if not most) are women, but certainly not all of them are; the same observation applies to readers. Men can and do read these works, too—and many professional male writers calculate potential readership demographics (including gender) as they work out details of story and plot.

In essence, what we've got is storytelling that can appeal to a broad range of readers, but may be promoted principally to the women's market. It makes it easier to focus the promotion and to pass along tips to the publisher's sales representatives.

Many women writers consider their work in abstract compositional terms, regardless of whom it is marketed to. Other women writers may be publicized as cultural pundits, perhaps as feminists, though they don't necessarily see their message as solely women-oriented. Are they women writers or simply writers? So long as sales go well, they may not even care.

Some women writers adopt the genderless pose of the literary renegade as they claw their way through dangerous domains of unseemly characterization, engage in break-through storytelling techniques, and explore emergent modes of love. (After all, how can a force of nature be characterized by sex?) Any and all of these female wordsmiths may find themselves publicized as women authors.

Romantic fiction constitutes one large sector of the women's market, for many of the conventions of romance tap into culturally significant areas of the love relationship of proven interest to women bookbuyers.

Descriptive genre phrases pop in and out of usage; some of them trip glibly from the tongue and are gone forevermore, while others represent established literary norms that endure: kitchen fiction, mom novels, family sagas, domestic dramas, historical romances, chick lit, lipstick fiction, erotic thrillers. When these popular titles are written, promoted, or both, in ways intended to pique the interest of women readers, whatever else they may be, they're automatically women's fiction.

The Author–Agent Agreement

JEFF HERMAN

The author–agent relationship is a business relationship. Substantial sums and complex deals may be involved. It's to everyone's advantage to explicitly codify the rules and parameters of the relationship in a brief, plain-English agreement. It's true that the author–agent relationship can become unusually cozy. Still, there's no reason why even the best of friends can't have written business agreements without diminishing their mutual trust and affection. From at least one perspective, explicitly written agreements can be seen to go hand in hand with—and serve to underscore or amplify—existing bonds of confidence, faith, and friendship.

Some agents prefer oral understandings and handshakes, but most use a standard written agreement. It's unlikely that any two agencies will use the same agreement, but most agreements overlap each other closely in their intent and spirit.

Several aspects of the author–agent arrangement are covered by the typical agreement. Here are some of the major points of consideration, along with some key questions you might reflect on as you peruse the materials your prospective agent has submitted to you:

1. Representation

What precisely will the agency be representing? Will it be a per-project representation? Or will it include all future works as well? Will it automatically cover all nonbook sales, such as magazine or newspaper articles? The extent of the representation should be spelled out so that there are no memory lapses or misunderstandings down the line.

2. *Agency Commission*

The agency will receive a commission for all sales it makes against the work's advance and on any subsequent income derived from royalties and the licensing of various rights. According to a recent study by the Authors' Guild, most agencies charge new clients 15 percent for domestic sales. Many agencies charge 20–30 percent for foreign sales, since the commission often has to be split with local subagents (the agent in the foreign country who actually expedites the sale).

3. *Duration and Potential Termination of the Agreement*

When does the agreement end? How can the author or agency act to terminate the agreement? What happens after it's terminated?

Are agency agreements negotiable? Probably. It's a case-by-case situation. Don't be afraid to question, or attempt to reword, some aspects of the agreement. It will be better if such discussions are held in a friendly manner, directly between you and the agent. As a cautionary note: It is a common observation that the involvement of third parties—especially lawyers—can backfire and ignite issues that are irrelevant to the traditional ground rules of the author–agent understanding. It's fine to consult a lawyer, but you should be the point person.

The following is the standard agreement that I use with my clients. It's provided for your reference. It's not the only way an agreement can be or should be.

SAMPLE LETTER OF AGREEMENT

This Letter of Agreement between THE JEFF HERMAN AGENCY, LLC, ("Agency") and _____ ("Author"), entered into on *(date)*, puts into effect the following terms and conditions:

REPRESENTATION

- The Agency is hereby exclusively authorized to seek a publisher for the Author's work, hereby referred to as the "Project," on a per-project basis. The terms and conditions of this Agreement will pertain to all Projects the Author explicitly authorizes the Agency to represent, through oral and written expression, and that the Agency agrees to represent. Separate Agreements will not be necessary for each single project, unless the terms and conditions differ from this Agreement.

COMMISSION

- If the Agency sells the Project to a publisher, the Agency will be the Agent-of-Record for the Project's income-producing duration and will irrevocably keep 15 percent of all the Author's income relevant to sold Project. The due Agency commission will also pertain to all of the Project's subsidiary rights sales, whether sold by the Agent, Author, or Publisher. In the event the agency uses a subagent to sell foreign or film rights, and the subagent is due a commission, the Agency commission for such will be 10 percent, and the subagent's commission will not be more than 10 percent. All

Project income will be paid by the publisher to the Agency. The Agency will pay the Author all due monies within a reasonable time, upon receipt and bank clearance, with full accounting provided. The Agency will not be required to return any legitimately received commissions should the Author–Publisher contract be terminated or if the Author's work is unacceptable to the Publisher. There will be an Agency Clause in the Author–Publisher contract stating the Agency's status, the wording of which shall be subject to Author approval. These terms will be binding on the Author's estate in the event of his/her demise.

EXPENSES

- The Agency will be entitled to receive reimbursement from the Author for the following specific expenses relevant to its representation of the Project: Manuscript/proposal copying costs; long-distance telephone calls and faxes between Author and Agency; necessary overnight deliveries and local messenger costs; postage and handling for manuscripts, foreign shipping and communications costs. An itemized accounting and records of all such items will be maintained by the Agency and will be shown to the Author. No significant expenses (in excess of $25.00) will be incurred without the Author's prior knowledge and consent. The Agency will have the option to either bill the Author for these expenses, regardless of whether or not the Project in question is sold to a publisher, or to charge such expenses against the Author's account.

PROJECT STATUS

- The Agency agrees to forward to the Author copies of all correspondence received from publishers in reference to the Author's Project(s).

REVISIONS

- This Agreement can be amended or expanded by attaching Rider(s) to it, if all parties to this Agreement concur with the terms and conditions of the Rider(s) and sign them.

TERMINATION

- This Agreement can be terminated in writing by any party to it by writing to the other parties, at any time following its execution. However, the Agency shall remain entitled to due commissions that may result from Agency efforts implemented prior to the termination of this Agreement and will remain entitled to all other due monies as stated in this Agreement. Termination of the Agency representation of one or more Author Projects will not imply termination of this Agreement, unless such is specifically requested in writing.

Signatures below by the parties named in this Agreement will indicate that all parties concur with the terms and conditions of this Agreement.

<table>
<tr><td>_____</td><td>_____</td></tr>
<tr><td>THE JEFF HERMAN AGENCY, INC.</td><td>AUTHOR</td></tr>
<tr><td></td><td>Social Security No.:</td></tr>
<tr><td></td><td>Date of birth:</td></tr>
</table>

Specific project(s) being represented at this time:

Q & A

Q: If you, Mr. Herman, were the writer, what are some of the key points that would most concern you about an agent's agreement?

A: If I were a writer, I would prefer to see the following incorporated into my agreement with the literary agency:

1. I would want the representation to be on a per-project basis. I would not want to be automatically obligated to be represented by the agent on my next project.
2. I would want a liberal termination procedure. If at any point after signing the agreement I change my mind, I want the ability to immediately end the relationship.

Of course, I realize that the agent will be entitled to his commission relevant to any deals I accept that result from his efforts on the project's behalf—even if the deal is consummated after my termination of the agent.

The Collaboration Agreement

Jeff Herman

Any book that is written by two or more writers is a collaborative effort. Such collaborative endeavors are predominately nonfiction works, though collaborative fiction is by no means unheard of (typically, a novel featuring a celebrity author that is for the most part written by someone else, or two bestselling novelists looking to synergize their reader base). There are several reasons why a writer might choose to collaborate with another, as opposed to writing the book alone.

The most common reasons are:

- A person may have the essential expertise, professional status, and promotability to author a book, but may lack time, ability, interest, or any combination of these, to do the actual writing. Therefore, retaining someone to do the writing is a sensible— even preferable—alternative.
- Some nonfiction projects, especially academic or professionally oriented ones, cover a broad range of material, and few individuals may have the requisite depth to write the book unilaterally. Therefore, two or more writers with complementary specializations may team up. For exceptionally technical books, such as medical texts, there can be several collaborators.

Many writers earn handsome incomes writing other people's books. When they are collaborative writers, their names are flashed along with the primary author of the project (and given second billing, usually preceded by "and," "with," or "as told to"). If they are true ghostwriters, they may well have the same level of input and involvement as collaborators, but will generally receive no public recognition for their work (other than perhaps a subtle pat on the back in the acknowledgments section).

WHAT ARE COLLABORATION AGREEMENTS?

As with any business relationship, it's wise for the collaborators to enter into a concise agreement (written in plain English) that spells out all the terms and conditions of the relationship—especially each party's respective responsibilities and financial benefits.

A collaboration agreement can run from 1 to more than 20 pages, depending on how much money is at issue and the complexity of the other variables. Most of the time we in the industry can keep these agreements down to an easy-to-read 2 pages. It's probably not necessary to go to the expense of retaining a lawyer for this task. If you have an agent, he can probably draw up an agreement for you or at least show you several samples.

The following is a sample collaboration agreement that is similar to ones used by many of my clients.

(*Disclaimer:* This sample collaboration agreement is intended only as a reference guide.)

SAMPLE COLLABORATION AGREEMENT

This collaboration agreement (Agreement), entered into on [*date*], by and between John Doe (John) and Jane Deer (Jane), will put into effect the following terms and conditions, upon signing by both parties.

(1) Jane will collaborate with John in the writing of a book about [*subject or brief description goes here*].

(2) In consultation with John, Jane will prepare a nonfiction book proposal and sample chapter for the purpose of selling the book to a publisher.

(3) Jane and John will be jointly represented by [*name of literary agent/agency*].

(4) John will be the book's spokesperson. John's name will appear first on the cover and in all publicity, and his name will be more prominently displayed than Jane's.

(5) Following the sale of the project proposal to a publisher, if, for any reason, Jane does not wish to continue as a collaborator, she shall be entitled to [*monetary amount goes here*] against the book's first proceeds in consideration of her having written the successful proposal, and she will forfeit any future claims against the book and any connection thereto.

(6) Jane's and John's respective estates will be subject to the terms and conditions of this Agreement, in the event of either's demise.

(7) John agrees to indemnify and hold Jane harmless from any liability, claim, or legal action taken against her as a result of her participation in the book proposal or book. Such exoneration includes but is not limited to costs of defending claims, including reasonable counsel fees. John agrees that any funds derived from sale of the proposal or book may be utilized to pay such claims.

(8) This Agreement can be amended or expanded by attaching riders to it, if such riders are signed by Jane and John.

(9) No other claims or representations are made by either party; both agree that this Agreement fully integrates their understanding. No other representations, promises, or agreements are made except as may be in writing and signed by the party to be held responsible.

(10) Jane shall receive the first [*monetary amount goes here*] of the book's proceeds when sold to a publisher. John shall receive the next [*monetary amount goes here*]. All income thereafter shall be evenly received (50/50). All subsidiary rights income shall be split 50/50.

(11) John will own the book's copyright.

(12) John will be responsible for paying expenses relevant to the preparation of the proposal (photocopying; telephone; deliveries; travel, etc.). Upon the book's sale to a publisher and the receipt of the first part of the advance, John will be reimbursed for 50 percent of these expenses by Jane. John and Jane will equally split (50/50) costs relevant to writing the book following its sale to a publisher.

JANE DEER   JOHN DOE

_____   _____

Q & A

Q: What about agent representation if it's a collaborative effort?
A: There are two possibilities:

1. *The same agent will represent both parties.* However, this requires the agent to be equal in her dealings with both parties. For instance, the agent should avoid tilting toward John while he's negotiating the collaboration agreement with Jane. What I do is provide both parties with accurate advice and then step aside as they—hopefully—work things out between themselves and then come back to me with all issues resolved.

    More important: the agent should not "double-dip." In other words, my commission will only pertain to the work's income. I will not touch any money that one collaborator may pay to the other, even if such payments exceed the work's advance.
2. Some collaborations can be coagented. Each collaborator may already have a different agent. Or it may be felt that there will be a conflict of interest for the same agent to represent both parties.

    When this happens, both agents will negotiate the collaboration agreement with each other in behalf of their respective clients. All parties will then work out a strategy to determine which agent is to be out front selling and negotiating the deal. Each agent will receive a commission only against her client's respective share.

As with any other business relationship, collaboration agreements generally have the best chance to produce a productive and successful outcome when they reasonably and realistically reflect the rights, responsibilities, special talents, and good interests of all involved parties.

Making It Happen

Deborah Levine Herman

Nothing is better than having your first book published. You may want to believe that spouses, friends, children, and world peace are more important, but when you see your name and your words in print it is nothing short of ego ecstasy.

Your publisher gives you a release date and you wait expectantly for the fanfare, but unless you're well known already (and remember, this is your first book), chances are your publisher will devote only modest publicity to your book.

It will be exciting if you are asked to do radio or television interviews, but do not expect Oprah fresh out of the gate. There are exceptions, of course, but it's important for you to know that most books don't receive extensive publisher support. It may not seem logical that a publisher would take you all the way to the mountain and not help you climb your way to the top, but it is the reality of the business. The reality is that the destiny of your book remains largely in your hands. With the right combination of drive, know-how, and chutzpah, you can make it happen for yourself.

IDEAS FOR MAKING IT HAPPEN

Here are some ideas for making it happen.

You can always hire a publicist. If you have the means, there are many publicists who can help you promote your book and who will do a lot of the work for you. You will have many great bragging opportunities when you work it into conversations that your *publicist* is setting your book tour.

Publicists are expensive and don't always deliver. You may want to check out our book *Make It Big Writing Books* to become publicist-savvy. This book contains interviews with top publicists, as well as some great promotion ideas. You can also read about how some bestselling authors made it to the top.

If you don't take the publicist route, you can do many things for yourself. Work with your publisher's publicity department. Its staff members may not invest their time and resources, but they should support your efforts.

As soon as you know the approximate date your book will be released to the bookstores, start your campaign. Ask your publicity department for review copies of your book and create a target list of possible magazines, newsletters, Web sites, and newspapers that might want to review your book. Don't sit on this. Magazines work months in advance. If your book is coming out in April, you should be contacting magazines as early as you possibly can; six months in advance isn't too soon. March is way too late. If you can't get review copies, you should still find ways to query the magazines. You may be able to get copies of your book covers and provide sample chapters.

It will be helpful for you to create an attractive publicity packet. You will need a biography of yourself, a good photograph, a copy of the book cover or the material your publisher uses to sell your book to the bookstores, a news release about your book, and any other relevant information. Do not forget to put in contact information. Book endorsements are also great, if you have them.

This packet can be used for magazines and any other print media, as well as for television and radio. If you want to spare some expense, create a one-page information sheet that you can fax to prospects whom you also contact by phone. Lists of radio stations are available in the reference department of your public library. Radio interviews can be done by phone. The key is to create a hook that will entice radio producers to use you on their shows. Think in terms of a short explanatory sentence that captures the essence of your book in as few words as possible.

For book signings, contact the promotions person at the bookstores you target. If you plan to visit various cities on a self-designed book tour, contact bookstores and local media well in advance so they can publicize the event. Maximize your visit to each city with a coordinated plan that will help promote your signing.

If your book is fiction, you can arrange for events in which you read portions of your book for an audience. Venues are available beyond the bookstores, but you will need to be creative in determining what they are.

If your book is nonfiction, create a topic stemming from your book that can be the subject of a workshop or lecture. Many venues are available that could help you publicize the event. Don't worry if you don't make money through lectures. If you are part of a seminar company, the exposure it will give your book in the promotional materials alone will be valuable.

Be creative. Don't let your ego trick you into believing you are above the hard work it takes to make a book successful. Roll up your sleeves. If you are passionate about your book, you are the one who can best "make it happen."

Time Management

Deborah Levine Herman

It is probably more difficult for writers who do not have a separate day job to manage time and to meet deadlines. If you are a full-time writer, you are not confined to a structured day and have to be self-disciplined and self-motivated.

If you are by nature a methodical writer who keeps an orderly home and an efficient calendar, is always prompt, and never misses appointments, I truly envy you. If you are like me, all of the above require great effort and are probably much more challenging than writing itself.

I love any kind of creative endeavor and am passionate about writing. I am also easily distracted. If I am not under deadline, I work at home and am just as likely to wallpaper my house as I am to write a book proposal, query letter, or fiction piece. As you know, there are many things writers can be doing between assignments to further their careers. You can write, research, plan, or promote existing projects. You can also promote yourself to gain a forum for your ideas and future projects. Unfortunately, I sometimes like to procrastinate to the point that I am not even aware of how much time I may be wasting.

I do not recommend the unofficial Deborah Herman method of kamikaze writing. As my career has developed, I have been learning to improve my time-management techniques. I am a work in progress, but I can share what works for me.

TIME MANAGEMENT TECHNIQUES

If writing is what you do, you need to treat it as a job. It is fine if you want to think about it all the time and define yourself by it. But it is important for you to delineate between the work of writing and your life. Otherwise, you will wind up looking at the basic activities of life management as something akin to playing hooky from what you really "should" be doing. There are even times when I view housework as a treat because I am stealing time from my work. For anyone who knows me, that is truly a pitiful concept.

You need to set up a schedule that allows you to leave your work behind. If you commit to a deadline, you must evaluate approximately how many work hours you will need to do the job. Some people write quickly and prolifically, and some write as if they are constipated. You have to be honest in determining how much time you will need for actual writing and how much time you will need to pace, twist your hair, or play solitaire on your PC until you are able to focus. You don't need to feel guilty if you have some writing rituals, but be sure to consider them part of your overall schedule.

It is best if you schedule your writing and writing-related activities at the same time every day. Writing is a very concentration-intensive activity so you may not be able to devote eight straight hours to it. If you can be productive for two hours, that may be enough time per day. If you need to do more, I suggest you work in two-hour blocks with a substantial break in between them. You need to listen to your own writing rhythms. Sometimes I can work for 2 to 3 hours that seem like 1 hour, and other times 1 hour can seem like 10. As long as you set aside the same time each day, you will be consistently productive and will use your time well.

When you finish your writing or writing-related activities for the day or business week, forget about them. Have a life. Have fun. Get some exercise. Stretch. Take care of your home and laundry. Do the things everyone else does to create balance. Writing takes a lot out of you emotionally, physically, and mentally. You do not want to use up your energy all at once, or you will become miserable and will no longer love to write. If you do not love to write, get out of the business. Writing is not glamorous. Sometimes it can be tedious and grueling. But if you can't imagine doing anything else with your life, make sure to be good to yourself so that you can be effective.

Do not wait for inspiration to strike before you write. If you have chosen writing as a profession, you need to be professional. You can't just wait for the right mood to strike before you get down to business. If you wake up feeling a little down, don't give into it. Kick yourself in the rear and get to your desk or computer.

Do not listen to your inner voice if it tells you your work stinks. Nothing will mess up your writing schedule more than your little inner demons. Go to work anyway, or you will never make any progress. The unfortunate thing about writing is that we do not get the kind of instant feedback we would get at a standard job. If we do a good job, no one is there to tell us so, and we do not believe our friends and family anyway. If we do a bad job, we may not know it and will still not believe anyone who tells us so. We work in a vacuum. So plod along. You will get the feedback you need when you obtain contracts for your work or when you hand in the completed manuscripts to your publisher.

The irony about writing as a profession is that we need such strong egos and are probably among the least-secure members of the human population. So view yourself as a business producing a product. As long as it meets acceptable standards for the marketplace, do not worry if it is not perfect. Once you relax about the work, you will see how much more productive you can be. You may even find you enjoy the process and produce higher-quality work. If you relax within the schedule you have created, you give yourself the chance to develop your craft and hone your skills and voice. Whether you are a ghostwriter, a novelist, or a specialist in nonfiction, you will develop a signature style. You can't do this if you are so uptight that you can't breathe.

So managing your time is really a state of mind. There are many books that will teach you specific techniques for organization, calendar usage, and time management to the minute. But for writers, the most important factor is how you feel about your writing, your career, and your life. If you seek balance and want to be productive, you will create a system that works for you. If you want to drive yourself crazy and wind up drinking yourself to an early grave so that you can be immortalized as an "arteest," let your time manage you. I vote for balance. I love to be free-spirited and eccentric. It is my most comfortable persona. But when I am under deadline, I do not think the anxiety is worth it. I also do not think it is worth it if my house is ready to be condemned, my children are running away to Grandma's, and my husband is ready to commit justifiable homicide. So take control of your time and see what a difference it will make.

The Path to Publication in the New Millennium

Morris Rosenthal

Imagine sending a query letter offering an unfinished manuscript to eight publishers and receiving four positive responses within the week. Or, out of the blue, the managing editor of a major imprint contacting you to ask whether you need a publisher for your work? These scenarios may sound like an advertisement in a writer's magazine intended to separate you from your money, but they actually happened to me, thanks to the Internet.

Why Publish on the Internet?

The vast majority of writers today have exchanged their typewriters for personal computers, but their sole focus remains sending that double-spaced manuscript off to New York City with an SASE. That's a shame, because by simply skipping down an extra item in the File menu of your word processor, you can save that document as HTML, a form ready for instant publication on the Internet. "Why should I give my work away for free?" you argue. "What if someone steals it?"

Your primary challenge, as an unpublished writer, is getting people to read your work and respond to it. After all, you need to convince editors and agents that you really know your market, but how can you do that if your market has never heard of you? Whether you write plumbing books or poetry, an audience for your work exists on the Internet, and if you can fix people's leaky pipes or hearts, they will show their appreciation. The main pay-offs of Web publishing for the unknown writer are reader feedback and traffic (visitors to your site).

Testimonial e-mails from visitors to your site can carry real weight with an acquisitions editor. In fact, McGraw-Hill used excerpts from nine such letters as a marketing tool on the back cover of my first published book, *The Hand-Me-Down PC*. Feedback from Web surfers is valuable for another reason; this audience isn't tied to you by friendship or blood. Even criticism is useful because these people *are* your market, and compliments from Mom are rarely as uplifting as those from a complete stranger. Traffic on your site can be used to prove that you do have an audience and, even more important for smaller publishers, that you know how to promote yourself. By the way, a copyright is a copyright, so if someone does plagiarize your work, take it as a compliment and threaten to sue.

WHAT TO PUT ON YOUR SITE

Building a Web site is something that anyone can do. Before you rush out and buy the latest book on the subject, try setting up a free Web site using one of the online providers, such as Geocities, which will lead you through the process step by step. This doesn't have to be your permanent site. In fact, there are many good reasons to host your site on a commercial server for anywhere from $10 to $50 per month. The main point is to get started. Unlike paper publishing, Web publishing is flexible by its very nature. If you make a spelling mistake, want to change something you said, add a picture, or even close down the site, you can do it instantly any time of the day or night!

The critical components (2 Cs) for any Web site are content and contact—content is the work you want people to see and contact is the means through which they can react to it, normally e-mail. As I said, it only takes one click of the mouse to save your manuscript in Web format, but you might want to produce material specifically targeted for the Web. Many people who surf the Web are looking for answers, so if you write nonfiction, you could offer to answer readers' e-mailed questions about your subject of expertise. This can take some time, but you will definitely learn what your audience is interested in rather than what you think they are interested in. This "hands-on" experience really carries weight with editors.

For example, back in 1995, I signed up for a $14.95/month Internet account with a national service that was later acquired by AOL. Learning that it came with space for a Web site, I posted a short guide titled "Troubleshooting and Repairing Clone PCs," which I had previously written for some co-op students I had trained. My primary motivation in posting the computer material was to attract people to read the short fiction and poetry I had also posted on the site. People who didn't find an answer to their problems but who thought I might be able to help them began sending me questions. Recognizing that this was "content," I began adding a new question and answer to the Web site each night. This section of the site, titled "The Midnight Question," became the most popular draw during the years that I maintained it and had a large number of repeat visitors. That original short guide and the material from the "Midnight Question" became the core of my first published book.

Many journalists now depend on the Internet for material to fill out their articles, and the questions and answers I posted on my site brought me two generous helpings of free publicity. The first was a front-page story in *The Investor's Business Daily,* which described me as a "Digital Age Dear Abbey" and the second was an interview and a link on the *Dateline MSNBC* site, which sent 10,000 visitors to my site in a single day. These cases may be extreme, but I continue to receive regular exposure in both online and traditional publications due to material I have posted online.

When it comes to fiction and poetry, you have little choice other than to publish whole works on the Web. In some documented cases, individuals began by Web publishing a novel, responded to reader demand by self-publishing their own books, and eventually landed real publishing contracts, but this kind of success is rare. Publishing fiction and poetry on the Internet is less likely to bring an unknown author the kind of instant exposure that can result from a well-planned information site, but the feedback, when it comes, is all the more welcome for that reason. The modest successes I've experienced with fiction on the Web, like having a short story picked up for a printed zine or adopted onto a genre site, have worked wonders for my bruised fiction ego.

Once I got an e-mail from a guy with a corporate return address, asking if I could send him my online novel, which was then posted in twenty-six individual HTML documents, as a Word file. I wrote back asking why he wanted the novel in Word format when he could already get it in any Web browser. He replied, "Nothing sinister, I'm reading it at the office and if it's in Word, I can act like I'm working."

GETTING PEOPLE TO COME TO YOUR SITE

"Even if you build it, they won't come unless you tell them it's there!"

MORRIS ROSENTHAL—MARCH 21, 2000

From Fortune 500 ghost sites to Aunt Millie's home page with pictures of the cat, the Web is crowded with sites that nobody visits. As you have read in many sections of this book, publishing is a business, and in business you can't escape from marketing. The good news is that on the Web, the only type of marketing you need is free, as long as you provide the labor. This marketing of your site can be broken into three basic areas: search engines and directories, link trading (including Web rings), and discussion groups.

Search engines and directories, once very different beasts, have been integrated to the point where I'll treat them as one subject. Examples of these are Yahoo, Altavista, Infoseek, Excite, Lycos, Webcrawler, Snap, and so on. The pure search engine concept is one in which you type certain key words into a box and the search engine returns some or all of the sites containing those key words in one combination or another, depending on the search conditions you apply. A pure directory is a hierarchical catalog in which you choose a general subject, like "Arts and Humanities," and continually narrow down your search in layer after layer of categories until you reach "Bronze casting techniques in Ancient Greece." The key is for you to get listed in the major search engines and directories, and not to get taken in by an ad for a service that will list you in 1,000 search engines for $19.95. Most search traffic is directed by a handful of search engines and directories, primarily those listed herein. Make sure that you submit to any search engines and directories that *you* use, and just hope that your potential readers think the same way.

If you want to be published, you must undertake one exercise in market research: Try to put yourself in the shoes of your target audience and search the Web for the sort of work you hope to publish. You'll quickly get a feel for the type of key words you should include on your pages, not to mention valuable insight into the "competition," which makes up an important part of any sales pitch to a traditional publisher. You may be astounded by the number of sites that already offer almost exactly what you planned to be first with. But don't be discouraged: In publishing, the bigger the existing market, the more likely a publisher will want to produce another title for it. Competing with other Web sites will help you hone your skills for the big battle, which is competing with other books.

Getting listed in search engines is easy. Simply go to the search engine site, look for a link that says "Submit your URL" or "Add your site," and click on it. This will bring you to a submissions page where you type in the address of your new Web page. Take note of any search engine you visit so that you can return in two weeks to see if it listed you, and resubmit if it didn't. Repeat as needed. Directories take a little more thought and persistence. You need to carefully choose which category you want to be listed in, and again, the best way to do this is to pretend you are a potential reader looking for whatever it is you write about. Directory entries are handled by human beings rather than by automated software, so only a small number of submissions are ever actually looked at. Sound familiar? Some directories even offer a guaranteed consideration of your site for a flat fee, around $100, but Yahoo is the only one I would even consider paying, and then only for a commercial site.

A link is essentially an address holder that shows up in most browsers as an underlined word or phrase. Link exchanges work on the old principle of "You scratch my back, I'll scratch yours." You find another site with content related to your own site, and you and the other webmaster negotiate an exchange of links via e-mail. When visitors to your site click on a link you have made to another site, they're gone. I'm not a big fan of link exchanges because they can easily get out of hand to the point where your site is no more than a revolving door. If you provide good content and make sure you are listed in the big search engines, people who maintain "all links" sites, essentially small targeted directories, will eventually find and link you. WebRings, on the other hand, are a nice way to join an online community of people who share your writing interests. For an index of WebRings and how to join, visit www.webring.com.

Discussion groups and news groups are a highly targeted way to announce the existence of your site. There are tens of thousands of public news or use groups, not to mention those discussion groups hosted on individual sites. Odds are, somebody out there is interested in what you are doing. It was by way of a technology discussion group that I received an unsolicited offer from a major imprint to publish a book based on my online material, although I eventually turned them down in favor of McGraw-Hill. The editor was apparently in the habit of checking the group for new trends or potential material, and a message I had posted to the group about new online material brought her to my site.

This Is the Future

Maybe you secretly hate your computer, though you avoid thinking about it while you're working for fear it will read your mind and trash your documents. There will always be room for a small number of eccentrics whose quirks are part and parcel of their attraction, but it's a tough role to break in with. The Internet is the future, and a Web strategy will be an integral part of any query letter in the coming years. The best way to learn about the Web and its potential is to get online and experiment with it. Even if you never post material to the Internet, you will need to understand how the publishing industry uses this tool.

Lest you think, "This is all great and fine for writing about technology, but what about my special field?" let me relate a final anecdote. For the past couple of years, I've worked on translations of my great-grandmother's Hebrew books. I wanted to get a short piece published about how she came to learn Hebrew in 1860s Latvia. This is definitely not "high tech" stuff. A Web search conducted with Altavista turned up a list of possible publications, and I sent queries to those that listed e-mail addresses for the editor. I submitted the article, via e-mail, to the most enthusiastic of the three or four responses, where it was accepted for publication in the next issue. The edited copy was sent for my approval, via e-mail, and the only time paper or postage entered the process was when the publisher sent me five complimentary copies of the magazine.

Once you have a Web site of your own, you'll wonder how you lived without one. For example, you can access your own material from any Internet-connected computer in the world! No more missed opportunities because the dog ate the manuscript and the editor you met on vacation wants to see it yesterday. I have written and submitted material for publication from a friend's computer on the other side of the Atlantic. With e-mail, you'll never worry about missing a phone call. A popular Web site can actually pay! You can sell self-published books to people for less than the cost of the inkjet cartridge they would use up printing it, or you can sell yourself as a consultant, speaker, writer, and so on. Last but not least, you can sign up as an AMAZON associate, referring your visitors to AMAZON.COM for books you suggest, have reviewed, or have written. Currently, AMAZON is putting more than $100 per month into my pocket, which more than pays the freight for a commercial Web site.

The State of Book Publishing, Today and Tomorrow

Jeff Herman

For several years the big question for everyone in publishing has been: "How will the Internet affect the book business?"

I'm going to go out on a limb here and say that new technologies don't and won't matter, because it's all about delivery and production systems. It has nothing to do with the evolution of the creative process or the measure of America's appetite for reading books. Whether you're composing your verse with a chisel on a limestone tablet or orally dictating to a computer that will immediately generate your hard copy (or cyber copy), it's still all about creating.

Cassettes and LPs quickly disappeared when CDs appeared. But the producers, distributors, and artists remained the same. Napster did threaten to overthrow the status quo by enabling consumers to acquire products without having to pay, but that was obviously illegal and unsustainable.

One day consumers may routinely buy and read books without touching a piece of paper (*Star Trek*'s Captain Picard was deemed eccentric for his tendency to read books the "old-fashioned" way). Yet what hasn't been clearly explained is why this, in and of itself, is revolutionary.

A revolution is when the existing power structure is abruptly overthrown and replaced by something much different. Do we see that happening? It's true that anyone with a computer can virtually self-publish his or her book in cyberspace. But then how do you get people to know about it and motivate them to buy it? Online self-publishing saves you the trouble and expense of printing and storing thousands of copies in your garage, all on spec, but one hundred thousand words written by WHO? is likely to be forever lost in cyberspace.

The only really important issue is working out a reasonable compensation structure for writers, as publishers shift their front- and backlists to electronic "books."

We need to pay closer attention to the fallout from the "globalization" of America's publishing infrastructure, which began more than 10 years ago and has managed to consolidate the largest piece of the publishing pie into a few hands, most of which are as American as a Volkswagen. Independently owned "boutique" houses will always emerge and thrive, but they can act only from the margins. The sky hasn't fallen, but the atmosphere is different.

In the past, most books were acquired not so much for their immediate success, but because it was hoped they would nourish the "backlist," which was the surest way for a publisher to bolster its existence into the future. But that isn't today's publishing model. The large houses and the bookstore chains want megaselling, supernova brands, not a smorgasbord of delicacies. You can almost see these words written across the proverbial transoms of editors' offices: "Only bestselling writers need apply."

This is not to suggest that the midlist book is dead; far from it. Publishers can't afford to kill the midlist. But they are disrespecting it by refusing to adequately support it. The race is on to consolidate resources and place bets on the Derek Jeters of publishing. That's what gets noticed and rewarded by the corporate overlords.

But here's a silly little secret: If large houses stopped betting the farm on flaky blockbusters and mostly concentrated on feeding their healthy backlists with smart midlist acquisitions, they would be much more profitable today and tomorrow, and many more writers could make decent money from writing. And there would be a lot more good books to sell, buy, and read.

Yet an even more systemic issue pre-exists today's regime: We are a nation of readers. Tens of millions of us avidly read *People Magazine* and many other mass-market publications each week. But only a tiny fraction of this dedicated readership routinely buys books. What a shame, especially for writers, since an expanding market would mean more book contracts.

Why? There are many reasons, but I believe the most important one is historical. Two hundred years ago only a few people could actually read, and the vast majority of the population was functionally illiterate. Furthermore, only a few people could actually afford to buy books. It follows that book publishing, at its very genesis, could and would only serve the nation's most affluent and educated layer, which formed a narrow slice of the whole.

Things are much different today, and most of us are decent and active readers. But publishing as an institution has never caught up with the fact that the "rest of us" now read and have a few bucks. In fact, the most profitable book sectors, like mass-market romance, are treated as proletarian baggage, even though they subsidize many of the million-dollar acquisition mistakes made by the "smart" people.

The day that book publishers can see the *National Enquirer* as a role model instead of a joke, editors will all be earning healthy six-figure incomes, bookstores will be as common as drugstores, and many more writers will actually be writing during the day.

Web Sites for Authors

One of the most valuable aspects of the World Wide Web for writers is that it provides the opportunity to explore the world of publishing. This annotated list of Web sites offers descriptions of some of the most useful sites for writers. For your convenience, sites are grouped according to the following categories:

- Anthology Resources
- Children's Literature Resources
- E-Publishing Resources
- Funding Resources
- Horror Resources
- Mystery Resources
- Poetry Resources
- Romance Resources
- Science Fiction Resources
- Screenwriting Resources
- Western Resources
- General Resources

ANTHOLOGY RESOURCES

ANTHOLOGIES ONLINE
http://www.anthologiesonline.com

Writers will find more than great articles and frequent postings of calls for manuscripts. From Chicken Soup to Horror, anthology publishers post their calls for writers. Subscribers have advance notice of calls for manuscripts and may apply for a free promotional page.

The site has a comprehensive, up-to-date list of paying markets for writers of science fiction, fantasy, horror, and slipstream. One page lists all markets; other pages break out markets by pro, semi-pro, anthologies, and contests, as well as by print and electronic formats. Listings include summaries of guidelines and indications of markets' "aliveness," plus Web site URLs.

CHILDREN'S LITERATURE RESOURCES

CHILDREN'S BOOK COUNCIL
http://www.cbcbooks.org/

"CBC Online is the Web site of the Children's Book Council—encouraging reading since 1945." It provides a listing of articles geared toward publishers, teachers, librarians, booksellers, parents, authors, and illustrators—all those who are interested in the children's book field.

THE SOCIETY OF CHILDREN'S BOOK WRITERS AND ILLUSTRATORS
http://www.scbwi.org/

This Web site "has a dual purpose: It exists as a service to our members, as well as offering information about the children's publishing industry and our organization to non-members." It features a listing of events, awards and grants, publications, information for members, information on how to become a member, and a site map.

VERLA KAY'S WEBSITE
http://www.verlakay.com

This site is packed with information to assist writers of children's stories. Whether you are a beginner or a multipublished writer, there is something here for you. A chat room with nightly chats with other children's writers, online workshops and transcripts of past workshops, a Getting Started page, and a Published Writers page are just some of the features of this award-winning Web site.

WRITE4KIDS.COM
http://www.write4kids.com/

"Whether you're published, a beginner, or just someone who's always dreamt of writing for kids," here you'll find a free library of how-to information, opportunities to chat with other children's writers and illustrators, links to research databases, articles, tips for beginners, secrets for success as a children's writer, message boards, a children's writing survey, the chance to ask questions of known authors, and the opportunity to register in the Web site's guestbook to receive free e-mail updates filled with news and tips. The site also features a listing of favorite books, Newberry Medal winners, Caldecott Award winners, current bestsellers, and a link to its own children's bookshop.

E-PUBLISHING RESOURCES

BOOKBOOTERS.COM

http://www.bookbooters.com

Bookbooters Press is a full-service digital publisher specializing in the electronic and print-on-demand publication of high-quality works of fiction and nonfiction. Through our Web site, www.bookbooters.com, customers may securely purchase titles by some of today's bestselling authors in e-book, CD-ROM, and paperback formats. The Authors Area includes a community area to meet other authors and to submit manuscripts for consideration by our team of professional acquisition editors.

eKIDna eBOOKS

http://www.ekidna.com.au

eKIDna eBooks is a small but growing publisher of e-books for children at home and at school. Based in Australia, eKIDna has strong ties with North American e-book publishers and is concentrating on its educational list for early English reading. Paying high royalties, it is a writer-friendly site limited mostly by its difficulty in finding illustrators who are willing to work for royalty-only; so if you are an illustrator, too—or can take an illustrator with you—your chances of quick publication are immensely advanced.

eNOVEL

http://www.enovel.com

eNovel.com, the world's biggest e-book site, is a publisher and retailer of books written by authors who are trying to launch their writing careers. Writers may publish for free and sell their books as an e-book, a print-on-demand book, or an audio book. Every book published is subject to eNovel.com's proprietary rating system, which allows readers to determine which book is their favorite overall and within each genre. eNovel.com's marketplace also affords writers an opportunity to chat, link their author Web site to eNovel.com, comment on books, and send out press releases for purposes of public relations.

JACOBYTE BOOKS

http://www.jacobytebooks.com

Jacobyte Books is a publisher of fiction and nonfiction works. We are a commercial nonsubsidy organization that pays 40 percent royalties to our authors. Our secure online bookstore offers books in every genre, available in print-on-demand paperback, on disk, and as downloads in the following formats: PDF, SoftBook, HieBook, and HTML.

MYSTIC-INK

http://www.mystic-ink.org

Mystic-Ink is a nonsubsidy publishing house and one of the first online communities connecting readers and writers. Readers discover great books and participate in discussion forums with many of their favorite authors. Writers find a supportive environment and promotional tools to advance their work into the digital world. Mystic-Ink is now under the direction of the Electronic Literature Institute, Inc., an educational nonprofit organization that was formed to raise awareness of alternative forms of reading.

XC PUBLISHING

http://www.xcpublishing.com

XC Publishing is a royalty-paying electronic publisher of high-quality original science fiction, fantasy, romance, and mystery electronic books. Authors can count on solid editorial support and a long shelf life for their titles. The site also offers book-related extras, as well as several book review e-mail newsletters. The site includes author's guidelines and a sample contract.

ZANDER EBOOKS

http://www.zanderebooks.com

Zander eBooks is a royalty-paying electronic publisher and e-book seller offering a high-quality selection of fiction, nonfiction, and children's e-books in the widest variety of formats available. Customers can choose from HTML, Adobe PDF, Microsoft Reader, Palm/Pocket PC, Franklin Reader, RocketBook, and paperback editions of our titles. A portion of the proceeds from each e-book sale is donated to reforestation programs, in an effort to educate the public about the ecological benefits of e-books.

FUNDING RESOURCES

ADJUNCTNATION: GRANTS

http://www.adjunctnation.com/preview/grants.index.php3

The At-a-Glance Guide to Grants offers information about grants, including a glossary of terms in grant forms, sample contracts, links to grant-related sites, a database of funding opportunities, and related agencies, foundations, and organizations. The site also includes a tutorial section with information on how to write a proposal and how to win a grant.

ART DEADLINES LIST

http://www.xensei.com/users/adl

The Art Deadline is a "monthly newsletter providing information about juried exhibitions and competitions, call for entries/proposals/papers, poetry and other writing contests, jobs, internships, scholarships, residencies, fellowships, casting calls, auditions, try-outs, grants, festivals, funding, financial aid, and other opportunities for artists, art educators, and art students of all ages. Some events take place on the Internet."

BookZone

http://www.bookzone.com

This site offers information on writing, marketing, business, and legal issues for publishing professionals. It features forums, publishing news, and online subscriptions to journals "at the guaranteed lowest prices on the Web. For design, development, e-commerce solutions, promotion, and exposure, BookZone is the busiest and best Web host for publishers, authors, and other publishing professionals."

Foundation Center, The

http://fdncenter.org/

The Foundation Center Web site is dedicated to assisting writers in finding grants. It offers "over 200 cooperating sites available in cities throughout the United States. Of particular note is its large online library, with a wonderful interactive orientation to grant seeking. You'll even find application forms for several funding sources here."

FundsforWriters.com

http://www.chopeclark.com/fundsforwriters.htm

FundsforWriters specializes in leading writers to grants, awards, contests, fellowships, markets, and jobs. The two Web sites and three newsletters provide a weekly abundance of sources for writers to reference and put checks in the bank. The other sites teach you how to write. FundsforWriters tells you where to make a living doing it.

National Writers Union

http://www.nwu.org/

The union for freelance writers working in U.S. markets offers grievance resolution, industry campaigns, contract advice, health and dental plans, member education, job banks, networking, social events, and much more.

Western States Arts Federation

http://www.westaf.org/

The WSAF is a "nonprofit arts service organization dedicated to the creative advancement and preservation of the arts. Focused on serving the state arts agencies, arts organizations, and artists of the West, WSAF fulfills its mission by engaging in innovative approaches to the provision of programs and services and focuses its efforts on strengthening the financial, organizational, and policy infrastructure of the arts in the West."

HORROR RESOURCES

DARKECHO HORROR
http://www.darkecho.com/darkecho/index.html

Dark Echo Horror features interviews, reviews, a writers' workshop, dark links, and a newsletter. Articles relate to topics such as the perception and psychology of the horror writer, the "best" horror, and reviews of dark erotica. The site also offers information and links to fantasy writing.

HORROR WORLD
http://pluto.spaceports.com/~mot/index.html

Horror World offers information about horror fiction, book reviews, new authors, horror movies, author message boards, HorrorNet chat room, and a reference guide and critique of horror fiction that features some 500 authors and 2,500 novels. The site also includes exclusive author interviews, book and chapbook reviews, and horror news.

HORROR WRITERS ASSOCIATION
http://www.horror.org/

The Horror Writers Association (HWA) was formed to "bring writers and others with a professional interest in horror together, and to foster a greater appreciation of dark fiction in general." Bestower of the Bram Stoker Awards, HWA offers a newsletter, late-breaking market news, informational e-mail bulletins, writers' groups, agents, FAQ, and links.

ONLINE CLASSIC HORROR AND FANTASY FICTION
http://home6.swipnet.se/~w-60478/

The Classic Horror and Fantasy Page aims to "collect links to every work of classic horror and fantasy fiction available on the Internet. The main purpose of this page is not to display the works themselves, but rather to direct the reader to other sites where the works are housed." Some of the authors and works that the site includes are Sir Richard Burton, *The Arabian Nights,* 1850 (translation); Johann Wolfgang von Goethe, *Faust,* 1808; and Edgar Allan Poe, *Collected Works.*

MYSTERY RESOURCES

AMERICAN CRIME WRITERS LEAGUE
http://www.acwl.org

The American Crime Writers League was established "by a group of writers who wanted a private forum for exchanging ideas, complaining about almost anything, and trying to understand this decidedly wacky business." The site includes information about interviews, conference information, agents' home telephone numbers, reviews, interviews, and more.

CLOCKTOWER BOOKS
http://www.clocktowerfiction.com/

Clocktower Fiction aims to "provide free quality original fiction for avid readers." Clocktower Fiction publishes *Outside: Speculative and Dark Fiction,* which is a freelance, paying, online publication that is published three times a year. The site provides links to grammar, writing, and other writers' resources and covers a variety of genres, including mystery, science fiction, macabre, suspense thrillers, and noir fiction.

CLUELASS HOME PAGE
http://www.cluelass.com

The ClueLass Home Page offers awards for mystery fiction and nonfiction, information about conferences and conventions, and mystery groups for writers and fans. It includes information about markets, other contests, reference material, and online support, as well as listings of mystery magazines and newsletters, an international directory of mystery booksellers and publishers, and factual links about crime, forensics, and investigation.

THE MYSTERIOUS HOME PAGE
http://cluelass.com/MystHome/index.html

The Mysterious Home Page is "a guide to mysteries and crime fiction on the Internet." The site offers newsgroups, mailing lists, information on conferences and conventions, publishers, book dealers, interactive fiction, reviews, and electronic mysteries.

MYSTERY AND DETECTIVE FICTION SITES
http://userpages.umbc.edu/~lharris/Mystery.htm

The Mystery and Detective Fiction Sites page offers a listing of resources from Animals in Mysteries to True Crime. Other focus areas of the site include authors' interviews and articles, characters, chat lines, conventions, discussion groups, newsletters, e-zines, mailing lists, online mysteries, publishers, reviews, and bookstores.

MYSTERY ON-LINE
http://www.webinspect.com/mystery.htm

Mystery On-Line is a site that is a work-in-progress of a mystery novel on the Web. Amateur and published writers may submit chapters for the Mystery On-Line continuing story. Each month a new chapter is selected and published on the site from the submissions. The site also includes mystery writing links, book reviews, and a link to the online bookstore.

MYSTERY WRITERS OF AMERICA

http://www.mysterywriters.org

Mystery Writers of America "helps to negotiate contracts, watches development in legislation and tax law, sponsors symposia and mystery conferences, and publishes books." The site includes mystery links, awards, a calendar of events, writers' discussions, and a new online mystery every day. It was established to promote and protect "the interests and welfare of mystery writers and to increase the esteem and the literary recognition given to the genre."

THE MYSTERY WRITERS' FORUM

http://www.zott.com/mysforum

The Mystery Writers' Forum consists of "mystery writers and aspiring mystery authors who are sharing our trials, tribulations, and research problems and triumphs on a supportive, threaded bulletin board system." The site includes a bookstore, Internet links, and cyber crime references.

SHORT MYSTERY FICTION SOCIETY

http://www.thewindjammer.com/smfs/

The Short Mystery Fiction Society "seeks to actively recognize writers and readers who promote and support the creative art form of short mysteries in the press, in other mystery organizations, and through awards." The site offers a newsletter and other resources.

SISTERS IN CRIME INTERNET CHAPTER

http://www.sinc-ic.org

Sisters in Crime is a Web site that vows to "combat discrimination against women in the mystery field, educate publishers and the general public as to inequities in the treatment of female authors, raise awareness of their contribution to the field, and promote the professional advancement of women who write mysteries." The site includes information about local chapters of Sisters in Crime and offers mystery links and online bookstores.

POETRY RESOURCES

ACADEMY OF AMERICAN POETS, THE

htt3p://www.poets.org/index.cfm

The Academy of American Poets Web site offers news regarding contest opportunities and winners, an online poetry classroom, the first-ever poetry book club, events calendars, and a search feature to find a specific poet or poem. Users can also listen to an author read a poem in RealAudio. The "My Notebook" feature allows visitors to keep a file of favorite poems or readings from the site. There are also discussion group and literary links sections.

ALIENFLOWER

http://www.sonic.net/web/alienflower/

AlienFlower is a site that offers poetry essays and virtual art, a discussion forum, literary links, video poetry readings, and more.

ATLANTIC UNBOUND POETRY PAGES

http://www.theatlantic.com/unbound/poetry

The Atlantic Unbound Poetry Pages are brought to you from the *Atlantic Monthly,* a literary magazine. The Web site offers reviews of new poetry, a discussion forum, and the Audible Anthology, which is a collection of poetry sound files, poetry articles, links, and poetry from the *Atlantic Monthly* online zine. It is a searchable site and offers poetry and literature links.

ELECTRONIC POETRY CENTER

http://wings.buffalo.edu/epc/

There are perhaps more poetry Web sites online than for any other literary genre, so picking one representative site is really quite pointless. But we do recommend the Electronic Poetry Center at the University of New York at Buffalo, which is the heart of the contemporary poetry community online, having been around since the early days of gopher space—practically the Dark Ages in computer time. Of particular note are the active and well-respected poetics mailing list, the large collection of audio files, and an extensive listing of small press poetry publishers.

THE INTERNATIONAL LIBRARY OF POETRY

http://www.poetry.com

The International Library of Poetry Web site offers information about its writing competitions, which focus on "awarding large prizes to poets who have never before won any type of writing competition." The site also includes Internet links, a list of past winners, anthologies of winning poems, and chat rooms.

NATIONAL POETRY ASSOCIATION, THE

http://www.poetryandperformance.org

The National Poetry Association Web site, supported in part by Grants for the Arts and Maya Angelou, offers an online poetry journal called *Poetry USA* and aims to "promote poets and poetry to wider audiences by all possible means, serving both the literary community and the general public." The site is dedicated to the memory of William Burroughs, Allen Ginsberg, Denise Levertov, and Jack Micheline. It includes information about the National Poetry Association's current projects and offers contests for poets.

PERIHELION ROUND TABLE DISCUSSIONS

http://www.webdelsol.com/Perihelion/p-discussion3.htm

The Perihelion Round Table Discussions is a site that brings to the public the thoughts of established poets and editors on issues of the Internet and its effect on poetry and the writing of poetry. There is also a discussion area where readers and visitors may add their insight to the discussions.

POETRY SOCIETY OF AMERICA, THE

http://www.poetrysociety.org/

The Poetry Society of America Web site includes information about the newest developments in the Poetry in Motion project, which posts poetry to seven million subway and bus riders in New York City, Chicago, Baltimore, Portland, and Boston. It also includes news about poetry awards, seminars, the tributes in libraries program, the poetry in public program, and poetry festivals.

POETS & WRITERS

http://www.pw.org/

Poets & Writers is an online resource for creative writers that includes publishing advice, message forums, contests, a directory of writers, literary links, information on grants and awards, news from the writing world, trivia, and workshops.

THE WRITER'S LIFE

http://www.thewriterslife.net

The Writer's Life is an online interactive writing and resource site where published, as well as nonpublished, authors submit their articles/short stories/poetry for publication. It is the site's goal to help writers achieve their dreams and goals of becoming published. The site provides publishing links, author interviews, Literary Link-of-the-Week awards, great writing sites, e-publishing links, freelancing opportunities, conference and workshops information, author quotes, chat, newsletter, in-house writing group, and more.

ROMANCE RESOURCES

ROMANCE WRITERS OF AMERICA

http://www.rwanational.org

Romance Writers of America (RWA) is a national nonprofit genre writers' association–the largest of its kind in the world. It provides networking and support to individuals seriously pursuing a career in romance fiction.

USEFUL LINKS FOR ROMANCE WRITERS AND READERS

http://www.jaclynreding.com/links/

If you're interested in writing fiction, particularly in the romance genre, consider this Web site the launching pad for getting you where you need to go on the Internet. Hundreds of Web sites have been arranged in easy-to-navigate categories, covering all aspects of the craft of writing—from research to publishers to booksellers to bestseller lists—this place has it all. New sites are constantly being added and you can even submit your own favorite sites! Voted one of the 101 BEST WEB SITES FOR WRITERS by Writer's Digest Magazine.

SCIENCE FICTION RESOURCES

SCIENCE FICTION AND FANTASY WRITERS OF AMERICA, INC.
http://www.sfwa.org

The official Web site of the Science Fiction and Fantasy Writers of America offers information about the organization, its members, affiliated publications, an art gallery, and various awards.

SCIENCE FICTION AND FANTASY WRITING WORKSHOP
http://pages.prodigy.com/sfworkshop/

The Science Fiction and Fantasy Workshop was established "to provide workshop experience through the mail, and to put writers in contact with others in the same situation." The site offers a newsletter that includes articles on topics such as world-building, laws of magic, alien creation, working with editors, and a market column.

SFNOVELIST
http://www.sfnovelist.com/index.htm

SFNovelist is "an online writing group dedicated to novelists who write 'hard science' SF." It is a highly structured and organized system of the exchange of science fiction manuscripts for consideration by other writers. Its goals are to "become in the marketplace a premier source of novelists who write 'believable/hard science" SF; garner the attention of SF publishers, SFWA, and other writers' organizations for SF novelists; and develop a cadre of strong novelists, most of whom become published. Behind every great writer is usually a group of fellow writers who are equally serious about their writing, establish a presence at major SF writer conferences and conventions, and provide services and information to members that will help them in their search for self-improvement and in getting published. This includes contacts with other known writers and publishers and sources of distribution and marketing.

SCREENWRITING RESOURCES

HOLLYWOOD CREATIVE DIRECTORY
http://www.hcdonline.com

The Hollywood Creative Directory's mission is to be the preferred and preeminent source of professional and educational information to, for, and about the entertainment industry, not only to the current entertainment industry professional community, but to aspiring professionals as well. HCD publishes the *Producers Directory,* "the phone book to Hollywood," a must-have directory for screenwriters. HCD offers screenwriter and film directories in an online subscription database. The Web site maintains one of the best entertainment job boards for the industry. HCD also publishes many how-to screenwriting books under the imprint of Lone Eagle Publishing, including the bestselling *Elements of Style for Screenwriters* and *How Not to Write a Screenplay.*

HOLLYWOOD SCRIPTWRITER
http://www.hollywoodscriptwriter.com

Hollywood Scriptwriters is an international newsletter that offers articles on craft and business "to give screenwriters the information they need to work at their careers." The site includes low-budget and indie markets available for finished screenplays, as well as a listing of agencies that are currently accepting submissions from readers of Hollywood Scriptwriter. According to Hollywood Scriptwriter, "people like Harold Ramis, Francis Ford Coppola, and Larry Gelbart have generously given of their time, knowledge, and experiences to share with HS's readers."

SCREENWRITERS HOME PAGE, THE
http://home.earthlink.net/~scribbler/

The Screenwriters Home Page offers "articles and interviews by people who work, day in and day out, in the movie business." Its aim is to help "not only with writing, but with the reality of the entertainment world." It includes agent listings, best ways to have your script rejected, professionals' thoughts on screenwriting, and industry news.

SCREENWRITERS & PLAYWRIGHTS HOME PAGE
http://www.teleport.com/~cdeemer/scrwriter.html

The Screenwriters & Playwrights Home Page was "designed to meet the special needs of screenwriters and playwrights." Although the site has been closed, you can download a PDF that has the contents of the old site, including screenwriting basics, marketing tips, screenplay formats, agent listings, pitches and query letters, producer listings, writing for actors, and tips from pros.

SCREENWRITERS RESOURCE CENTER
http://www.screenwriting.com

The Screenwriters Resource Center aims to "provide links to products and services for screenwriters, compiled by the staff at the National Creative Registry." It includes links to many screenwriting sites and offers advice and copyright words of warning for writers posting original work on the Internet.

SCREENWRITERS UTOPIA
http://www.screenwritersutopia.com/

Screenwriters Utopia includes "helpful hints for getting screenplays produced, script development services, and contest information." The site includes a screenwriters' work station, tool kit, agent listings, and creative screenwriting magazines. Interviews with the screenwriters of *Sleepless in Seattle, Blade,* and *The Crow: City of Angels* are featured, and other interviews are archived. The site also includes chat rooms, message boards, a writer's directory, and a free newsletter.

SCREENWRITER'S WEB, THE
http://breakingin.net

The site offers screenwriters and filmmakers tips, tools, and resources to help them get their scripts read and recommended to the movies. Special features: interviews with film pros, screenplay tutorials, script marketing tips, and insider information from an experienced LA screenwriter.

WESTERN RESOURCES

WESTERN WRITERS OF AMERICA, INC.
http://www.westernwriters.org

"WWA was founded in 1953 to promote the literature of the American West and bestow Spur Awards for distinguished writing in the Western field." The site offers information about Old West topics, a listing of past Spur Award winners, and opportunities to learn about WWA and the Spur Award, to apply for membership in WWA, to subscribe to *Roundup Magazine,* or to contact Western authors whose work interests you.

GENERAL RESOURCES

1001 WAYS TO MARKET YOUR BOOKS
http://www.bookmarket.com/1001bio.html

1001 Ways to Market Your Books is a site that offers a book marketing newsletter, consulting services, and book marketing updates. Other topics include success letters, author bios, sample chapters, and tables of contents.

AMERICAN BOOKSELLERS ASSOCIATION
http://www.bookweb.org

The American Booksellers Association is a trade association representing independent bookstores nationwide. The site links members to recent articles about the industry and features Idea Exchange discussion forums.

AMERICAN DIALECT SOCIETY
http://www.americandialect.org/

The American Dialect Society Web site offers discussion lists, a newsletter, and a contacts list. Writers will find the "Dialect in Literature Bibliography" useful, as well as CD-ROM dictionaries and style and grammar guides.

AMERICAN JOURNALISM REVIEW
http://www.ajr.org/

This redeveloped site includes more editorial content, updated links to news industry sites, an improved job search function called "The Employment Section," and other interactive features.

AMERICAN SOCIETY OF JOURNALISTS AND AUTHORS
http://www.asja.org/

The American Society of Journalists and Authors is "the nation's leading organization of independent nonfiction writers." It offers its members professional development aids, such as confidential market information, an exclusive referral service, seminars and workshops, and networking opportunities. The site offers all visitors a newsletter, legal updates from the publishing world, and professional links.

ASSOCIATED WRITING PROGRAMS, THE
http://www.awpwriter.org/

The Associated Writing Programs Web site offers information about the AWP annual conference, a list of writers' conferences, a list of AWP member schools, articles and information on writing and writing programs, and a sample of articles and news from the AWP magazine *The Writer's Chronicle.* Members of AWP enjoy an online conferencing system, career advice, career placement service, a subscription to *The Writer's Chronicle,* and notice of contests and awards.

ASSOCIATION OF AMERICAN PUBLISHERS, INC.
http://www.publishers.org/index.htm

The Association of American Publishers "is the principal trade association of the book publishing industry." The site includes information and registration for annual meetings and conferences, industry news, info about book publishing, industry stats and issues, and copyright data.

ASSOCIATION OF AUTHORS' REPRESENTATIVES, THE
http://www.publishersweekly.com/aar/

The Association of Authors' Representatives is dedicated to "keeping agents informed about conditions in publishing, the theater, the motion picture and television industries, and related fields; encouraging cooperation among literary organizations; and assisting agents in representing their author-clients' interests." Agents must qualify for membership in the AAR by meeting professional standards set forth and by subscribing to its canon of ethics. The Web site includes a list of AAR members, a newsletter, and links.

AUTHOR NETWORK

http://www.author-network.com

Author Network is a flourishing international community for writers. The site includes articles, monthly columns, a newsletter, message board, discussion group, critique service, and thousands of links to other writing sites. The writer in residence, Paul Saevig, provides a regular supply of instructional essays that may help new writers or even established authors. Other material and articles are provided by regular contributors, who are generally published authors themselves. Author Network promotes individual writers and other sites of interest to writers, as well as competitions, conferences, and courses.

AUTHORLINK

http://www.authorlink.com/

This information service for editors, literary agents, and writers boasts more than 165,000 loyal readers per year. Features include a "Manuscript Showcase" that contains 500+ ready to publish, evaluated manuscripts.

AUTHORS GUILD, THE

http://www.authorsguild.org/

For more than 80 years the Guild has been the authoritative voice of American writers . . . its strength is the foundation of the U.S. literary community. This site features contract advice, a legal search, information on electronic rights and how to join the organization, a bulletin index, publishers' row, a listing of board members, and current articles regarding the publishing field. There is also a link for Back-in-print.com, an online bookstore featuring out-of-print editions made available by their authors.

AYLAD'S WRITER'S GROUP

http://www.publication.com/aylad

This site provides a forum for "people to get their work read and critiqued by fellow writers in a friendly atmosphere." The service is free and all writing forms are welcome. The site includes links to other resources for writers.

BLACK WRITERS ALLIANCE

http://www.blackwriters.org/

The Black Writers Alliance is the "first literary arts organization to utilize the power of the online medium to educate, inform, support and empower aspiring and published

Black writers. The Black Writers Alliance (BWA) is dedicated to providing information, news, resources, and support to Black writers, while promoting the Internet as a tool for research and fellowship among the cultural writing community." The site offers users access to its media kit, a forum, a directory of speakers, a photo album, mailing lists, and chat rooms. The Black Writers Alliance is the first online community that has hosted an annual conference for its members.

BOOKLIST

http://www.ala.org/booklist/index.html

Booklist is a "digital counterpart of the American Library Association's *Booklist* magazine." In the site is a current selection of reviews, feature articles, and a searchable cumulative index. Review topics include books for youth, adult books, media, and reference materials. The site also includes press releases, the best books list, and subscription information.

BOOKNOTE

http://www.booknote.com/

Booknote specializes in custom-designed Web sites for authors, book titles, literary agents, and publishers. Its award-winning sites are individually designed to capture the creativity of the unique individuals they feature. Booknote also extensively target markets each site to all relevant special-interest or news groups on the Web, to increase both the person's recognition and World Wide Web sales.

BOOKREPORTER

http://www.bookreporter.com/brc/index.asp

Bookreporter is a site that offers book reviews and a perspectives section that deals with topics such as when a book becomes a movie. It features a daily quote by a famous author.

BOOKTALK

http://www.booktalk.com/

Want to find out how to click with the people who talk books? Booktalk is a site where writers and readers learn more about the publishing industry. Besides an extensive literary agent list, there are articles about how to get published, writing tips from authors, and a bulletin board. The host for many author home pages, Booktalk allows readers to interact with bestselling authors, learn about new releases, read book excerpts, and see what's upcoming. A slushpile section lists conferences and publishing links.

BOOKWIRE

http://www.bookwire.com/bookwire

Partners with *Publishers Weekly, Literary Market Place,* and the *Library Journal,* among others, Bookwire is a site that offers book industry news, reviews, original fiction, author interviews, and guides to literary events. The site features publicity and marketing opportunities for publishers, authors, booksellers, and publicists, and it includes a list of the latest Bookwire press releases.

BookZone

http://www.bookzone.com/

BookZone was created "to increase book sales and profits for publishers." The site features a Super Catalog of books, thousands of book-related links, industry insights and resources, publishing news, and site hosting, development, and online marketing.

Burry Man Writers Center, The

http://www.burryman.com/

With members and visitors in 104 countries, the Burry Man truly is "a worldwide community of writers." Working professionals and beginning writers find exclusive articles on the craft and business of writing, an extensive list of freelance job resources, a vast section focusing on Scotland, and links to more than 3,000 primary sources of information, giving writers the chance to speak to one another and use the Internet to hone their skills.

Coffeehouse for Writers

http://www.coffeehouseforwriters.com/

The Coffeehouse for Writers is an "online writer's colony; a place where writers—from novice to professional—gather to critique, advise, and encourage each other." The site provides links to other resources for writers and a list of suggested books.

E-booksCafe

http://www.topzone.com/ebookscafe/

E-booksCafe is dedicated to helping fellow writers reach out and touch the world through words. It provides an assortment of books to the public in the e-book and POD format in all genres of fiction, as well as nonfiction. It also offers authors worldwide the opportunity to promote and sell their e-books and POD books for free at its site.

Eclectic Writer, The

http://www.eclectics.com/writing/writing.html

This site is an information source for those interested in crime, romance, horror, children's, technical, screen, science fiction, fantasy, mystery, and poetry writing. It features articles, a fiction writer's character chart, resources by genre, reference materials, research, general writing resources, online magazines and journals, writing scams, awards, and a writing-related fun page.

EDITOR'S PEN, THE

http://users.zoominternet.net/~dwlacey/reflections.htm

The Editor's Pen site exists to connect "sites for and about Writers, Editors, and Indexers." It includes links to lists of freelancers and online dictionaries. Other interesting links include an "Edit challenge" and "Quotable words of editorial wisdom."

EDITORIAL EYE, THE

http://www.eeicom.com/eye/

The Editorial Eye Web site consists of a sampler of articles originally printed in the newsletter by the same name. The articles discuss techniques for writing, editing, design, and typography, as well as information on industry trends and employment. The *Eye* has been providing information to publication professionals for 18 years.

ENCYCLOPAEDIA BRITANNICA

http://www.eb.com/

This service is subscription-based and allows the user to search the Encyclopaedia Britannica. New users can try a "sample search."

FORWRITERS.COM

http://www.forwriters.com/

This "mega-site" provides numerous links to writing resources of all kinds. It lists conferences, markets, agents, commercial services, and more. The "What's New" feature allows the user to peruse what links have recently been added under the various categories.

GRANTA

http://www.granta.com/

The Granta Web site offers information about the most current issue of this highly regarded literary journal. The introduction is an explanation and background info about the topic around which the issue is based. The contents of the issue are listed, and visitors to the site may read a sample from the issue, as well as obtain subscription and ordering information. It also offers similar information about back issues and a readers' survey.

HOLLYLISLE.COM

http://hollylisle.com/

HollyLisle.com offers a community of supportive writers helping each other reach their writing goals. Led by full-time novelist Holly Lisle, the community includes crit circles, discussion and research boards, workshops, free real-time writing classes with professional writers and people who can offer their expertise in areas of interest to writers, writing articles, free writing e-books and the award-winning free e-zine *Vision: A Resource for Writers,* plus chapters, cover art, works-in-progress, and surprises for readers.

HYPNOSIS FOR WRITERS

http://pages.globetrotter.net/drknight/kn-write.html

Hypnosis for Writers is a site explaining the benefits of hypnosis for writers to overcome writer's block, generate ideas, improve concentration, end procrastination, increase motivation, enrich characterization, and deal with rejection.

INSCRIPTIONS

http://www.inscriptionsmagazine.com

Inscriptions is the weekly e-zine for professional writers. For the past four years, each jam-packed issue has featured writing and publishing-related articles, interviews with experts, job opportunities, writing contests, paying markets, book reviews, and links. Sign up for the e-mail version and receive more than 70 pages of useful information each week, perfect for the freelancing writer or telecommuting editor. Learn how to earn money for your stories. Find your next job opportunity. Or enter the monthly writing contest and win cash prizes.

LITERARY MARKET PLACE

http://reference.infotoday.com/lmp/us/index_us.asp

The Literary Market Place Web site offers information about publishers, which are categorized by U.S. book publishers, Canadian book publishers, and small presses, as well as literary agents, including illustration and lecture agents. The site also offers trade services and resources.

LOCAL WRITER'S WORKSHOP

http://members.tripod.com/~lww_2/introduction.htm

The Local Writer's Workshop is an Internet forum for works in progress, especially those "in the early stages of revision." The creators of this membership-based site pride themselves on its community ethic.

MIDWEST BOOK REVIEW

http://www.execpc.com/~mbr/bookwatch/

Responsible for *Bookwatch,* a weekly television program that reviews books, videos, music, CD-ROMs, and computer software, as well as five monthly newsletters for community and academic library systems and much more, the Midwest Book Review was founded in 1980. This site features its reviews.

MISC.WRITING

http://www.scalar.com/mw/

"Misc.writing is a Use Net newsgroup that provides a forum for discussion of writing in all its forms—scholarly, technical, journalistic, and mere day-to-day communication." Web site resources include a writer's bookstore and market information.

NATIONAL ASSOCIATION OF WOMEN WRITERS

http://www.naww.org/

The National Association of Women Writers (NAWW) was founded to support, encourage, entertain, motivate, and inspire women writers. NAWW offers a *free* weekly inspirational/how-to e-magazine, an online Member Portfolio, a Member Publications page, a quarterly member publication ("The NAWW Writer's Guide"), a Discussion List, a Member Only Online Critique Group, Daily Inspiration, a Writer's Resource Library, and much more. The NAWW site was voted one of the Top Ten "Best Sites" by *Writer's Digest* for 2001.

NATIONAL WRITERS UNION

http://www.nwu.org/

The National Writers Union is the trade union for freelance writers of all genres. The Web site provides links to various service of the union, including grievance resolution, insurance, job information, and databases.

NEWSLINK

http://newslink.org/

NewsLink offers exceptionally well-organized links to newspapers, broadcasters, and magazines. Users can search by name, or browse by state or national papers, major metros, dailies, nondailies, major networks, subject, or country. NewsLink also has a JobLink feature, where users can post a job or search for a job. The site makes hundreds of updates each week, so you can be sure you are getting up-to-the-minute information.

NOVELIST

http://novelnow.cjb.net/

The Novelist is dedicated to helping novel writers get published, tackling issues such as querying agents and the nature of the business, independent publishers versus the Big Six, and marketing. In the section for writer's conference notes you can read "what went on" at the venues. Includes thousands of links to writer resources, including agents and publishers and an open message board where writers can blow off steam or post news.

PAINTED ROCK

http://www.paintedrock.com/memvis/memvis1.htm

"Painted Rock provides services to nonpublished writers, published writers, and readers." Free features on the site include information on a free 12-week Artist's Way program, message boards, goal writing groups, writing topics, a book discussion group, a research listserv, and *The Rock* online magazine. In addition to their free services, the site offers paid online writing classes, a subscription-based newsletter, and two bookstores, as well as advertising, promotion for authors, and Web site hosting and design.

PARA PUBLISHING

http://www.parapublishing.com/

The Para Publishing Book Writing, Publishing, & Promoting page offers "the industry's largest resources/publications guide," a customized book writing/publishing/promoting information kit, as well as current and back issues of its newsletter. The site also includes research links, a listing of suppliers, and mailing lists.

PEN AMERICAN CENTER

http://www.pen.org/

PEN is an international "membership organization of prominent literary writers and editors. As a major voice of the literary community, the organization seeks to defend the freedom of expression wherever it may be threatened, and to promote and encourage the recognition and reading of contemporary literature." The site links to information about several PEN-sponsored initiatives, including literary awards.

PUBLISHERS WEEKLY

http://publishersweekly.reviewsnews.com/

Publishers Weekly Online offers news about the writing industry, as well as special features about reading and writing in general and genre writing. The site also includes news on children's books, book-selling, interviews, international book industry news, and industry updates.

PURE FICTION

http://www.purefiction.com/start.htm

Based in London and New York, Pure Fiction is a Web site "for anyone who loves to read—or aspires to write—bestselling fiction." The site includes reviews, previews, writing advice, an online bookshop, a writers' showcase, Internet links, and more. It also offers a mailing list.

PUT IT IN INK

http://www.putitinink.com

Put It In Ink brings you articles, tips, books, software, and information about the craft of writing and getting published. Find information about newsletters (both print and online), e-zines, self-publishing and traditional publishing, freelancing, freelance jobs/markets, marketing tips, article writing, ideas to write about, and more.

R. R. BOWKER

http://www.bowker.com/bowkerweb/

R. R. Bowker is a site that offers a listing of books in print on the Web, books out of print, an online directory of the book publishing industry, a data collection center for R. R. Bowker publications, and a directory of vendors to the publishing community.

REJECTION COLLECTION

http://www.rejectioncollection.com/

"Rejected? Don't despair." Visit rejectioncollection.com, where you can share your misery online. Visitors can post their own rejection letters and read rebuffs received by other writers and creative artists. The site also features inspirational stories, sob stories, rants, author and editor interviews, rejection links, and a monthly e-zine, *The Reject's Rag,* as well as a "Rejectioncollector of the Month" contest.

SENSIBLE SOLUTIONS FOR GETTING HAPPILY PUBLISHED

http://www.happilypublished.com/

This site, Sensible Solutions for Getting Happily Published, is "designed to help writers, publishers, self-publishers, and everyone else who cares about reaching readers, including editors, agents, booksellers, reviewers, industry observers and talk show hosts . . . and aims to help books get into the hands of the people they were written for." It includes information about finding a publisher, ways for publishers to raise revenues, the self-publishing option, how to boost a book's sales, and sensible solutions for reaching readers.

SHARPWRITER.COM

http://www.sharpwriter.com/

SharpWriter.Com is a practical resources page for writers of all types—a "writer's handy virtual desktop." Reference materials include style sheets, dictionaries, quotations, and job information. The Office Peacemaker offers to resolve grammar disputes in the workplace.

SHAW GUIDES, INC., WRITERS CONFERENCES & WORKSHOPS
http://www.writing.shawguides.com/
Shaw Guides: Writers Conferences & Workshops is a subscription-based listing of sponsors and the following month's writer's conferences calendar. The Shaw Site for Writer's Conferences allows the user to search for information about 400 conferences and workshops worldwide. An e-mail service can be used to get updates about conferences that meet user criteria for dates, topics, and locations. Other resources include Quick Tips, links to organizations, and information about residencies and retreats.

SMALL PUBLISHERS ASSOCIATION OF NORTH AMERICA
http://www.spannet.org/home.htm
Small Publishers Association of North America is a site for "independent presses, self-publishers, and savvy authors who realize if their books are to be successful, they must make them so." The site offers pages for "fun, facts, and financial gain." It also offers a newsletter.

UNITED STATES COPYRIGHT OFFICE
http://lcweb.loc.gov/copyright/
The United States Copyright Office site allows the user to find valuable information about copyright procedures and other basics. In addition, the user can download publications and forms, then link to information about international copyright laws.

WEB OF ON-LINE DICTIONARIES, A
http://www.geocities.com/WestHollywood/Castro/6101/dic/diction1.html
This index of online dictionaries includes 165 different languages and gives preference to free resources. A new feature allows the user to translate words from any European language to any other.

WEBSTER DICTIONARY
http://www.m-w.com/netdict.htm
Like its paper counterpart, this Web-based dictionary provides definitions to words and phrases sought by users. For word lovers, features like "Word of the Day" and "Word Game of the Day" are included as well.

WELL, THE
http://www.well.com/
The WELL (Whole Earth 'Lectronic Link) is an online gathering place that its creators call a "literate watering hole for thinkers from all walks of life."

WOMEN WHO WRITE

http://members.aol.com/jfavetti/womenww/www.html

Women Who Write is a "collage of women based all over the United States with a passion for writing." The site provides useful links and a large dose of encouragement to women writers of all experience levels.

WOODEN HORSE PUBLISHING

http://www.woodenhorsepub.com/

Wooden Horse Publishing is a complete news and resource site for article writers. Visitors get news about markets, including planned, new, and folding magazines; editor assignments; and editorial changes. The site features a searchable market database of over 3,000 U.S. and Canadian consumer and trade magazines. Entries include full contact information, writer's guidelines, and—only at Wooden Horse—reader demographics and editorial calendars. Newsletter describes new markets and industry trends.

WRITE FROM HOME

http://www.writefromhome.com/

Whether you're a freelance writer, author, or writing from home but employed by a publication, this site strives to offer work-at-home writers tips, information, and resources to help you balance your writing career and children under one roof. You'll also find lots of writing and marketing resources to help you achieve the success you desire. It features a chat room, e-mail discussion list, and a monthly e-zine, featuring articles, markets, guidelines, tips, and more.

WRITELINKS COMMUNICATION CONSULTANTS

http://www.writelinks.com/

The site provides an array of services that include workshops, personalized tutoring, and critique groups. "WriteLinks is designed to be of value to all writers, regardless of their experience, genre, or focus."

WRITER AND MARKET

http://writerandmarket.searchking.com/

Looking to get published or need something to publish? Need an agent or a client? Want to know the latest news in the publishing industry? Bookmark this site—it's got your answers. It maintains an exhaustive listing of every writing resource on the Internet. The site is updated constantly and is always on the lookout for new resources to add.

WRITER'S BBS, THE
http://www.writers-bbs.com/home.shtml

The Writer's BBS is intended for "authors, poets, journalists, and readers" and high-lights writers' chat rooms, discussion forums, and an e-zine for beginning writers called "Fish Eggs for the Soul." It also includes games, personal ads, copyright information, mailing lists, Internet links, an adults-only section, and the online King James Bible.

WRITER'S CENTER, THE
http://www.writer.org/center/aboutwc.htm

The Writer's Center is a Maryland-based nonprofit that "encourages the creation and distribution of contemporary literature." The Web site provides information on the organi-zation's 200+ yearly workshops and links to its publication *Poet Lore and Writer's Carousel.*

WRITERS.COM
http://www.writers.com/

"Writers on the Net is a group of published writers and experienced writing teachers building an online community and resource for writers and aspiring writers." A subscrip-tion to the mailing list provides a description and schedule of classes offered by the site and a monthly newsletter.

WRITERS-EDITORS NETWORK
http://www.writers-editors.com/

The Writers-Editors Network has been "linking professional writers with those who need content and editorial services since 1982." The site features agent listings, articles on marketing tools, and a database of more than 10,000 e-mail addresses of editors and book publishers. The site also links to fabulous how-to e-books of dream jobs for writers.

WRITER'S EXCHANGE
http://www.writers-exchange.com/

The Writer's Exchange is a community designed to share and enrich the lives of writ-ers. The site features articles, writing links, a listing of writing books, jobs/markets, book and software reviews, ask the experts, author interviews, authors' homepages, author ser-vices, announcements, and awards. The site offers a monthly e-zine, which includes book reviews, writing tips, marketing ideas, and Web site reviews.

WRITERS GUILD OF AMERICA

http://www.wga.org/

The WGA West site provides information about the Guild and its services, such as script registration. Other links to writing resources are provided as well.

WRITERS MANUAL

http://www.writersmanual.com/

Writers Manual is an online writer-related information warehouse. It receives information from writers, publishers, and agents worldwide, which includes links, announcements, articles, book reviews, press releases, and more. The site features free writer-related articles, links and resources, recommended books, and a vast job board that lists jobs for traditional and online publishing markets, syndication markets, publishers, grants/fellowships, and contests. The site hosts contests on a monthly basis, including the Writer Critique Contest, in which a published author edits and critiques the writing of one winner.

WRITERSNET

http://www.writers.net/

WritersNet is a site that "helps build relationships between writers, publishers, editors, and literary agents." It consists of two main sections, "The Internet Directory of Published Writers," which includes a list of published works and a biographical statement, and "The Internet Directory of Literary Agents," which lists areas of specialization and a description of the agency. Both are searchable and include contact information. It is a free service that hopes to "become an important, comprehensive matchmaking resource for writers, editors, publishers, and literary agents on the Internet."

WRITERSPACE

http://www.writerspace.com/

"Writerspace specializes in the design and hosting of Web sites for authors. We also provide Web services for those who may already have Web sites but wish to include more interactivity in the way of bulletin boards, chat rooms, contests, and e-mail newsletters." The site features an author spotlight, contests, workshops, mailing lists, bulletin boards, chat rooms, romance links, a guestbook, information on adding your link, Web design, Web hosting, its clients, and rates.

WRITER'S RETREAT, THE

http://www.angelfire.com/va/dmsforever/index.html

The objectives of the Writer's Retreat are "to provide a meeting place for writers everywhere, to provide market information, to list relevant Internet links, to list inspirational and motivational information and quotations for writers of all races, creeds, and backgrounds, and to have and provide fun while doing it!"

WRITERSWEEKLY.COM
http://www.writersweekly.com/

This is the home of the most current paying markets to be found online. WritersWeekly publishes a free weekly e-zine featuring new paying markets and freelance job listings. Serving more readers than any other freelance writing e-zine (60K, as of December 2001), it is dedicated to teaching writers how to make more money writing.

WRITERS WRITE
http://www.writerswrite.com/

This "mega-site" provides myriad resources, including a searchable database of online and print publications in need of submissions. The Writers Write chat room is open 24 hours a day for live discussion.

WRITING CORNER
http://www.writingcorner.com/

Writing Corner is dedicated to the reader and writer alike, providing a one-stop place for author sites, chats, and giveaways, along with articles on all aspects of writing. The weekly "JumpStart" newsletter is designed to motivate writers at every level, while the "Author's Corner" newsletter keeps readers apprised of author events. The site features market information, resource listings, book reviews, and vast archives of writing information for fiction, nonfiction, and corporate writers.

WRITING-WORLD.COM
http://www.writing-world.com/

This site offers more than 250 articles on the craft and business of writing, in such categories as freelancing, fiction, genres, skill-building, children's writing, self-publishing, and more. It features a regularly updated list of writers' contests, a "writers wanted" section, and a free biweekly e-mail newsletter with articles, publishing news, and market information.

YOUCANWRITE.COM
http://www.youcanwrite.com/

YouCanWrite.com is one of Writer's Digest's 101 Best Sites for Writers and is the brainchild of two long-time publishing professionals who know the business from the inside out. Aspiring nonfiction writers can get the real story on what agents and editors look for in a salable manuscript. The site offers a wealth of free information, and its Insider

Guides are practical, fun to read e-books that cover all the bases—from agents to books proposals to contracts.

ZUZU'S PETALS LITERARY RESOURCE, THE
http://www.zuzu.com/

The Zuzu's Petals Literary Resource is a site that focuses on a comprehensive list of writers' resource links and information. It includes a bookstore; discussion forums; its literary magazine, *Zuzu's Petals Quarterly Online;* art news, which reports on news in the literary world; and contests.

Glossary

A

abstract A brief sequential profile of chapters in a nonfiction book proposal (also called a **synopsis**); a point-by-point summary of an article or essay. In academic and technical journals, abstracts often appear with (and may serve to preface) the articles themselves.

adaptation A rewrite or reworking of a piece for another medium, such as the adaptation of a novel for the screen. (*See also* **screenplay**.)

advance Money paid (usually in installments) to an author by a publisher prior to publication. The advance is paid against royalties: If an author is given a $5,000 advance, for instance, the author will collect royalties only after the royalty moneys due exceed $5,000. A good contract protects the advance if it should exceed the royalties ultimately due from sales.

advance orders Orders received before a book's official publication date, and sometimes before actual completion of the book's production and manufacture.

agent The person who acts on behalf of the author to handle the sale of the author's literary properties. Good literary agents are as valuable to publishers as they are to writers; they select and present manuscripts appropriate for particular houses or of interest to particular acquisitions editors. Agents are paid on a percentage basis from the moneys due their author clients.

American Booksellers Association (ABA) The major trade organization for retail booksellers, chain and independent. The annual ABA convention and trade show offers a chance for publishers and distributors to display their wares to the industry at large and provides an incomparable networking forum for booksellers, editors, agents, publicists, and authors.

American Society of Journalists and Authors (ASJA) A membership organization for professional writers. ASJA provides a forum for information exchange among writers and others in the publishing community, as well as networking opportunities. (*See also* **Dial-a-Writer**.)

anthology A collection of stories, poems, essays, and/or selections from larger works (and so forth), usually carrying a unifying theme or concept; these selections may be written by different authors or by a single author. Anthologies are compiled as opposed to written; their editors (as opposed to authors) are responsible for securing the needed reprint rights for the material used, as well as supplying (or providing authors for) pertinent introductory or supplementary material and/or commentary.

attitude   A contemporary colloquialism used to describe a characteristic temperament common among individuals who consider themselves superior. Attitude is rarely an esteemed attribute, whether in publishing or elsewhere.

auction   Manuscripts a literary agent believes to be hot properties (such as possible bestsellers with strong subsidiary rights potential) will be offered for confidential bidding from multiple publishing houses. Likewise, the reprint, film, and other rights to a successful book may be auctioned off by the original publisher's subsidiary rights department or by the author's agent.

audio books   Works produced for distribution on audio media, typically audiotape cassette or audio compact disc (CD). Audio books are usually spoken-word adaptations of works originally created and produced in print; these works sometimes feature the author's own voice; many are given dramatic readings by one or more actors, at times embellished with sound effects.

authorized biography   A history of a person's life written with the authorization, cooperation, and, at times, participation of the subject or the subject's heirs.

author's copies/author's discount   Author's copies are the free copies of their books the authors receive from the publisher; the exact number is stipulated in the contract, but it is usually at least 10 hardcovers. The author will be able to purchase additional copies of the book (usually at 40% discount from the retail price) and resell them at readings, lectures, and other public engagements. In cases where large quantities of books are bought, author discounts can go as high as 70%.

author tour   A series of travel and promotional appearances by an author on behalf of the author's book.

autobiography   A history of a person's life written by that same person, or, as is typical, composed conjointly with a collaborative writer ("as told to" or "with"; *see also* **coauthor**; **collaboration**) or **ghostwriter**. Autobiographies by definition entail the authorization, cooperation, participation, and ultimate approval of the subject.

B

backlist   The backlist comprises books published prior to the current season and still in print. Traditionally, at some publishing houses, such backlist titles represent the publisher's cash flow mainstays. Some backlist books continue to sell briskly; some remain bestsellers over several successive seasons; others sell slowly but surely through the years. Although many backlist titles may be difficult to find in bookstores that stock primarily current lists, they can be ordered either through a local bookseller or directly from the publisher.

backmatter   Elements of a book that follow the text proper. Backmatter may include the appendix, notes, glossary, bibliography and other references, list of resources, index, author biography, offerings of the author's and/or publisher's additional books and other related merchandise, and colophon.

bestseller   Based on sales or orders by bookstores, wholesalers, and distributors, best-sellers are those titles that move in the largest quantities. Lists of bestselling books can be local (as in metropolitan newspapers), regional (typically in geographically keyed trade or consumer periodicals), or national (as in *USA Today*, *Publishers Weekly*, or the *New York Times*), as well as international. Fiction and nonfiction are usually listed separately, as are hardcover and paperback classifications. Depending on the list's purview, additional in-dustry-sector designations are used (such as how-to/self-improvement, religion and spiri-tuality, business and finance); in addition, bestseller lists can be keyed to particular genre or specialty fields (such as bestseller lists for mysteries, science fiction, or romance nov-els, and for historical works, biography, or popular science titles)—and virtually any other marketing category at the discretion of whoever issues the bestseller list (for in-stance African-American interests, lesbian and gay topics, youth market).

bibliography   A list of books, articles, and other sources that have been used in the writ-ing of the text in which the bibliography appears. Complex works may break the bibliog-raphy down into discrete subject areas or source categories, such as General History, Military History, War in the Twentieth Century, or Unionism and Pacifism.

binding   The materials that hold a book together (including the cover). Bindings are generally denoted as hardcover (featuring heavy cardboard covered with durable cloth and/or paper, and occasionally other materials) or paperback (using a pliable, resilient grade of paper, sometimes infused or laminated with other substances such as plastic). In the days when cloth was used lavishly, hardcover volumes were conventionally known as clothbound; and in the very old days, hardcover bindings sometimes featured tooled leather, silk, precious stones, and gold and silver leaf ornamentation.

biography   A history of a person's life. (*See also* **authorized biography**; **autobiogra-phy**; **unauthorized biography**.)

blues (or bluelines)   Photographic proofs of the printing plates for a book. Blues are re-viewed as a means to inspect the set type, layout, and design of the book's pages before it goes to press.

blurb   A piece of written copy or extracted quotation used for publicity and promotional purposes, as on a flyer, in a catalog, or in an advertisement (*see also* **cover blurbs**).

book club   A book club is a book-marketing operation that ships selected titles to sub-scribing members on a regular basis, sometimes at greatly reduced prices. Sales of a work to book clubs are negotiated through the publisher's subsidiary rights department (in the case of a bestseller or other work that has gained acclaim, these rights can be auctioned off). Terms vary, but the split of royalties between author and publisher is often 50%/50%. Book club sales are seen as blessed events by author, agent, and publisher alike.

book contract   A legally binding document between author and publisher that sets the terms for the advance, royalties, subsidiary rights, advertising, promotion, publicity—plus a host of other contingencies and responsibilities. Writers should therefore be thoroughly familiar with the concepts and terminology of the standard book-publishing contract.

book distribution   The method of getting books from the publisher's warehouse into the reader's hands. Distribution is traditionally through bookstores but can include such means as telemarketing and mail-order sales, as well as sales through a variety of special-interest outlets such as health-food or New Age venues, sports and fitness emporiums, or sex shops. Publishers use their own sales forces as well as independent salespeople, wholesalers, and distributors. Many large and some small publishers distribute for other publishers, which can be a good source of income. A publisher's distribution network is extremely important, because it not only makes possible the vast sales of a bestseller but also affects the visibility of the publisher's entire list of books.

book jacket   (*See* **dust jacket**.)

book producer or **book packager**   An individual or company that can assume many of the roles in the publishing process. A book packager or producer may conceive the idea for a book (most often nonfiction) or series, bring together the professionals (including the writer) needed to produce the book(s), sell the individual manuscript or series project to a publisher, take the project through to manufactured product—or perform any selection of those functions, as commissioned by the publisher or other client (such as a corporation producing a corporate history as a premium or giveaway for employees and customers). The book producer may negotiate separate contracts with the publisher and with the writers, editors, and illustrators who contribute to the book.

book review   A critical appraisal of a book (often reflecting a reviewer's personal opinion or recommendation) that evaluates such aspects as organization and writing style, possible market appeal, and cultural, political, or literary significance. Before the public reads book reviews in the local and national print media, important reviews have been published in such respected book-trade journals as *Publishers Weekly*, *Kirkus Reviews*, *Library Journal*, and *Booklist*. A gushing review from one of these journals will encourage booksellers to order the book; copies of these raves will be used for promotion and publicity purposes by the publisher and will encourage other book reviewers nationwide to review the book.

Books in Print   Listings, published by R. R. Bowker, of books currently in print; these yearly volumes (along with periodic supplements such as *Forthcoming Books in Print*) provide ordering information, including titles, authors, ISBN numbers, prices, whether the book is available in hardcover or paperback, and publisher names. Intended for use by the book trade, *Books in Print* is also of great value to writers who are researching and market-researching their projects. Listings are provided alphabetically by author, title, and subject area.

bound galleys   Copies of uncorrected typesetter's page proofs or printouts of electronically produced mechanicals that are bound together as advance copies of the book (compare **galleys**). Bound galleys are sent to trade journals (*see* **book review**) as well as to a limited number of reviewers who work under long lead times.

bulk sales   The sale at a set discount of many copies of a single title (the greater the number of books, the larger the discount).

byline   The name of the author of a given piece, indicating credit for having written a book or article. Ghostwriters, by definition, do not receive bylines.

C

casing   Alternate term for binding (*see* **binding**).

category fiction   Also known as genre fiction. Category fiction falls into an established (or newly originated) marketing category (which can then be subdivided for more precise target marketing). Fiction categories include action-adventure (with such further designations as military, paramilitary, law enforcement, romantic, and martial arts); crime novels (with points of view that range from deadpan cool to visionary, including humorous capers as well as gritty urban sagas); mysteries or detective fiction (hard-boiled, soft-boiled, procedurals, cozies); romances (including historicals as well as contemporaries); horror (supernatural, psychological, or technological); thrillers (tales of espionage, crisis, and the chase), Westerns, science fiction, and fantasy. (*See also* **fantasy**, **horror**, **romance fiction**, **science fiction, suspense fiction**, and **thriller**.)

CD or **computer CD**   High-capacity compact discs for use by readers via computer technology. CD-ROM is a particular variety; the term is somewhere between an acronym and an abbreviation—CD-ROMs are compact computer discs with read-only memory, meaning the reader is not able to modify or duplicate the contents. Many CDs are issued with a variety of audiovisual as well as textual components. When produced by publishers, these are sometimes characterized as books in electronic format. (*See also* **multimedia**.)

children's books   Books for children. As defined by the book-publishing industry, children are generally readers aged 17 and younger; many houses adhere to a fine but firm editorial distinction between titles intended for younger readers (under 12) and young adults (generally aged 12 to 17). Children's books (also called juveniles) are produced according to a number of categories (often typified by age ranges), each with particular requisites regarding such elements as readability ratings, length, and inclusion of graphic elements. Picture books are often for very young readers, with such designations as toddlers (who do not themselves read) and preschoolers (who may have some reading ability). Other classifications include easy storybooks (for younger school children), middle-grade books (for elementary to junior high school students), and young adult (abbreviated YA, for readers through age 17).

coauthor   One who shares authorship of a work. Coauthors all have bylines. Coauthors share royalties based on their contributions to the book. (Compare **ghostwriter**.)

collaboration   Writers can collaborate with professionals in any number of fields. Often a writer can collaborate in order to produce books outside the writer's own areas of formally credentialed expertise (for example, a writer with an interest in exercise and nutrition may collaborate with a sports doctor on a health book). Though the writer may be billed as a coauthor (*see* **coauthor**), the writer does not necessarily receive a byline (in which case the writer is a **ghostwriter**). Royalties are shared, based on respective contributions to the book (including expertise or promotional abilities as well as the actual writing).

colophon   Strictly speaking, a colophon is a publisher's logo; in bookmaking, the term may also refer to a listing of the materials used, as well as credits for the design, composition, and production of the book. Such colophons are sometimes included in the backmatter or as part of the copyright page.

commercial fiction   Fiction written to appeal to as broad-based a readership as possible.

concept   A general statement of the idea behind a book.

cool   A modern colloquial expression that indicates satisfaction or approval, or may signify the maintenance of calm within a whirlwind. A fat contract for a new author is definitely cool.

cooperative advertising (co-op)   An agreement between a publisher and a bookstore. The publisher's book is featured in an ad for the bookstore (sometimes in conjunction with an author appearance or other special book promotion); the publisher contributes to the cost of the ad, which is billed at a lower (retail advertising) rate.

copublishing   Joint publishing of a book, usually by a publisher and another corporate entity such as a foundation, a museum, or a smaller publisher. An author can copublish with the publisher by sharing the costs and decision making and, ultimately, the profits.

copyeditor   An editor, responsible for the final polishing of a manuscript, who reads primarily in terms of appropriate word usage and grammatical expression, with an eye toward clarity and coherence of the material as presented, factual errors and inconsistencies, spelling, and punctuation. (*See also* **editor**.)

copyright   The legal proprietary right to reproduce, have reproduced, publish, and sell copies of literary, musical, and other artistic works. The rights to literary properties reside in the author from the time the work is produced—regardless of whether a formal copyright registration is obtained. However, for legal recourse in the event of plagiarism or other infringement, the work must be registered with the U.S. Copyright Office, and all copies of the work must bear the copyright notice. (*See also* **work-for-hire**.)

cover blurbs   Favorable quotes from other writers, celebrities, or experts in a book's subject area, which appear on the dust jacket and are used to enhance the book's point-of-purchase appeal to the potential book-buying public.

crash   Coarse gauze fabric used in bookbinding to strengthen the spine and joints of a book.

curriculum vitae (abbreviated **c.v.**) Latin expression meaning "course of life"—in other words, the **résumé**.

D

deadline In book publishing, this not-so-subtle synonym is used for the author's due date for delivery of the completed manuscript to the publisher. The deadline can be as much as a full year before official publication date, unless the book is being produced quickly to coincide with or follow up a particular event.

delivery Submission of the completed manuscript to the editor or publisher.

Dial-a-Writer Members of the American Society of Journalists and Authors may be listed with the organization's project-referral service, Dial-a-Writer, which can provide accomplished writers in most specialty fields and subjects.

direct marketing Advertising that involves a "direct response" (which is an equivalent term) from a consumer—for instance, an order form or coupon in a book-review section or in the back of a book or mailings (direct-mail advertising) to a group presumed to hold a special interest in a particular book.

display titles Books that are produced to be eye-catching to the casual shopper in a bookstore setting. Often rich with flamboyant cover art, these publications are intended to pique bookbuyer excitement about the store's stock in general. Many display titles are stacked on their own freestanding racks; sometimes broad tables are laden with these items. A book shelved with its front cover showing on racks along with diverse other titles is technically a display title. Promotional or **premium** titles are likely to be display items, as are mass-market paperbacks and hardbacks with enormous bestseller potential. Check your local bookstore and find a copy of this edition of *Writer's Guide*—if not already racked in display manner, please adjust the bookshelf so that the front cover is displayed poster-like to catch the browser's eye (that's what *we* do routinely).

distributor An agent or business that buys books from a publisher to resell, at a higher cost, to wholesalers, retailers, or individuals. Distribution houses are often excellent marketing enterprises, with their own roster of sales representatives, publicity and promotion personnel, and house catalogs. Skillful use of distribution networks can give a small publisher considerable national visibility.

dramatic rights Legal permission to adapt a work for the stage. These rights initially belong to the author but can be sold or assigned to another party by the author.

dust jacket (also **dustcover** or **book jacket**) The wrapper that covers the binding of hardcover books, designed especially for the book by either the publisher's art department or a freelance artist. Dust jackets were originally conceived to protect the book during shipping, but now their function is primarily promotional—to entice the browser to actually reach out and pick up the volume (and maybe even open it up for a taste before buying) by means of attractive graphics and sizzling promotional copy.

dust-jacket copy   Descriptions of books printed on the dust-jacket flaps. Dust-jacket copy may be written by the book's editor but is often either recast or written by in-house copywriters or freelance specialists. Editors send advance copies (*see also* **bound galleys**) to other writers, experts, and celebrities to solicit quotable praise that will also appear on the jacket. (*See also* **cover blurb**.)

E

editor   Editorial responsibilities and titles vary from house to house (often being less strictly defined in smaller houses). In general, the duties of the editor-in-chief or executive editor are primarily administrative: managing personnel, scheduling, budgeting, and defining the editorial personality of the firm or imprint. Senior editors and acquisitions editors acquire manuscripts (and authors), conceive project ideas and find writers to carry them out, and may oversee the writing and rewriting of manuscripts. Managing editors have editorial and production responsibilities, coordinating and scheduling the book through the various phases of production. Associate and assistant editors edit; they are involved in much of the rewriting and reshaping of the manuscript and may also have acquisitions duties. Copyeditors read the manuscript and style its punctuation, grammar, spelling, headings and subheadings, and so forth. Editorial assistants, laden with extensive clerical duties and general office work, perform some editorial duties as well—often as springboards to senior editorial positions.

Editorial Freelancers Association (EFA)   This organization of independent professionals offers a referral service, through both its annotated membership directory and its job phone line, as a means for authors and publishers to connect with writers, collaborators, researchers, and a wide range of editorial experts covering virtually all general and specialist fields.

el-hi   Books for elementary and/or high schools.

endnotes   Explanatory notes and/or source citations that appear either at the end of individual chapters or at the end of a book's text; used primarily in scholarly or academically oriented works.

epilogue   The final segment of a book, which comes "after the end." In both fiction and nonfiction, an epilogue offers commentary or further information but does not bear directly on the book's central design.

F

fantasy   Fantasy is fiction that features elements of magic, wizardry, supernatural feats, and entities that suspend conventions of realism in the literary arts. Fantasy can resemble prose versions of epics and rhymes or it may be informed by mythic cycles or folkloric material derived from cultures worldwide. Fantasy fiction may be guided primarily by the author's own distinctive imagery and personalized archetypes. Fantasies that involve heroic-erotic roundelays of the death-dance are often referred to as the sword-and-sorcery subgenre.

film rights   Like **dramatic rights**, these belong to the author, who may sell or option them to someone in the film industry—a producer or director, for example (or sometimes a specialist broker of such properties)—who will then try to gather the other professionals and secure the financial backing needed to convert the book into a film. (*See also* **screenplay**.)

footbands   (*See* **headbands**.)

footnotes   Explanatory notes and/or source citations that appear at the bottom of a page. Footnotes are rare in general-interest books, the preferred style being either to work such information into the text or to list informational sources in the bibliography.

foreign agents   Persons who work with their United States counterparts to acquire rights for books from the U.S. for publication abroad. They can also represent U.S. publishers directly.

foreign market   Any foreign entity—a publisher, broadcast medium, etc.—in a position to buy rights. Authors share royalties with whoever negotiates the deal or keep 100% if they do their own negotiating.

foreign rights   Translation or reprint rights that can be sold abroad. Foreign rights belong to the author but can be sold either country-by-country or en masse as world rights. Often the U.S. publisher will own world rights, and the author will be entitled to anywhere from 50% to 85% of these revenues.

foreword   An introductory piece written by the author or by an expert in the given field (*see* **introduction**). A foreword by a celebrity or well-respected authority is a strong selling point for a prospective author or, after publication, for the book itself.

Frankfurt Book Fair   The largest international publishing exhibition—with five hundred years of tradition behind it. The fair takes place every October in Frankfurt, Germany. Thousands of publishers, agents, and writers from all over the world negotiate, network, and buy and sell rights.

Freedom of Information Act   Ensures the protection of the public's right to access public records—except in cases violating the right to privacy, national security, or certain other instances. A related law, the Government in the Sunshine Act, stipulates that certain government agencies announce and open their meetings to the public.

freight passthrough   The bookseller's freight cost (the cost of getting the book from the publisher to the bookseller). It is added to the basic invoice price charged the bookseller by the publisher.

frontlist   New titles published in a given season by a publisher. Frontlist titles customarily receive priority exposure in the front of the sales catalog—as opposed to backlist titles (usually found at the back of the catalog), which are previously published titles still in print.

frontmatter   The frontmatter of a book includes the elements that precede the text of the work, such as the title page, copyright page, dedication, epigraph, table of contents, foreword, preface, acknowledgments, and introduction.

fulfillment house   A firm commissioned to fulfill orders for a publisher—services may include warehousing, shipping, receiving returns, and mail-order and direct-marketing functions. Although more common for magazine publishers, fulfillment houses also serve book publishers.

G

galleys   Printer's proofs (or copies of proofs) on sheets of paper, or printouts of the electronically produced setup of the book's interior—the author's last chance to check for typos and make (usually minimal) revisions or additions to the copy (*see* **bound galleys**).

genre fiction   (*See* **category fiction**.)

ghostwriter   A writer without a byline, often without the remuneration and recognition that credited authors receive. Ghostwriters often get flat fees for their work, but even without royalties, experienced ghosts can receive quite respectable sums.

glossary   An alphabetical listing of special terms as they are used in a particular subject area, often with more in-depth explanations than would customarily be provided by dictionary definitions.

H

hardcover   Books bound in a format that uses thick, sturdy, relatively stiff binding boards and a cover composed (usually) of a cloth spine and finished binding paper. Hardcover books are conventionally wrapped in a dust jacket. (*See also* **binding**; **dust jacket**.)

headbands   Thin strips of cloth (often colored or patterned) that adorn the top of a book's spine where the signatures are held together. The headbands conceal the glue or other binding materials and are said to offer some protection against accumulation of dust (when properly attached). Such bands, placed at the bottom of the spine, are known as footbands.

hook   A term denoting the distinctive concept or theme of a work that sets it apart—as being fresh, new, or different from others in its field. A hook can be an author's special point of view, often encapsulated in a catchy or provocative phrase intended to attract or pique the interest of a reader, editor, or agent. One specialized function of a hook is to articulate what might otherwise be seen as dry albeit significant subject matter (academic or scientific topics; number-crunching drudgery such as home bookkeeping) into an exciting, commercially attractive package.

horror   The horror classification denotes works that traffic in the bizarre, awful, and scary in order to entertain as well as explicate the darkness at the heart of the reader's soul. Horror subgenres may be typified according to the appearance of were-creatures, vampires, human-induced monsters, or naturally occurring life forms and spirit entities— or absence thereof. Horror fiction traditionally makes imaginative literary use of paranormal phenomena, occult elements, and psychological motifs. (*See* **category fiction**; **suspense fiction**.)

how-to books   An immensely popular category of books ranging from purely instructional (arts and crafts, for example) to motivational (popular psychology, self-awareness, self-improvement, inspirational) to get-rich-quick (such as in real estate or personal investment).

hypertext   Works in hypertext are meant to be more than words and other images. These productions (ingrained magnetically on computer diskette or CD) are conceived to take advantage of readers' and writers' propensities to seek out twists in narrative trajectories and to bushwhack from the main path of multifaceted reference topics. Hypertext books incorporate documents, graphics, sounds, and even blank slates upon which readers may compose their own variations on the authored components. The computer's capacities to afford such diversions can bring reader and hypertext literateur so close as to gain entry to each other's mind-sets—which is what good books have always done.

I

imprint   A separate line of product within a publishing house. Imprints run the gamut of complexity, from those composed of one or two series to those offering full-fledged and diversified lists. Imprints as well enjoy different gradations of autonomy from the parent company. An imprint may have its own editorial department (perhaps consisting of as few as one editor), or house acquisitions editors may assign particular titles for release on appropriate specialized imprints. An imprint may publish a certain kind of book (juvenile or paperback or travel books) or have its own personality (such as a literary or contemporary tone). An individual imprint's categories often overlap with other imprints or with the publisher's core list, but some imprints maintain a small-house feel within an otherwise enormous conglomerate. The imprint can offer the distinct advantages of a personalized editorial approach, while availing itself of the larger company's production, publicity, marketing, sales, and advertising resources.

index   An alphabetical directory at the end of a book that references names and subjects discussed in the book and the pages where such mentions can be found.

instant book   A book produced quickly to appear in bookstores as soon as possible after (for instance) a newsworthy event to which it is relevant.

international copyright   Rights secured for countries that are members of the International Copyright Convention (*see* **International Copyright Convention**) and that respect the authority of the international copyright symbol, ©.

International Copyright Convention   Countries that are signatories to the various international copyright treaties. Some treaties are contingent upon certain conditions being met at the time of publication, so an author should inquire before publication into a particular country's laws.

introduction   Preliminary remarks pertaining to a piece. Like a foreword, an introduction can be written by the author or an appropriate authority on the subject. If a book has both a foreword and an introduction, the foreword will be written by someone other than the author; the introduction will be more closely tied to the text and will be written by the book's author. (*See also* **foreword**.)

ISBN (International Standard Book Number)   A 10-digit number that is keyed to and identifies the title and publisher of a book. It is used for ordering and cataloging books and appears on all dust jackets, on the back cover of the book, and on the copyright page.

ISSN (International Standard Serial Number)   An 8-digit cataloging and ordering number that identifies all U.S. and foreign periodicals.

J

juveniles   (*See* **children's books**.)

K

kill fee   A fee paid by a magazine when it cancels a commissioned article. The fee is only a certain percentage of the agreed-on payment for the assignment (no more than 50%). Not all publishers pay kill fees; a writer should make sure to formalize such an arrangement in advance. Kill fees are sometimes involved in work-for-hire projects in book publishing.

L

lead   The crucial first few sentences, phrases, or words of anything—be it a query letter, book proposal, novel, news release, advertisement, or sales tip sheet. A successful lead immediately hooks the reader, consumer, editor, or agent.

lead title   A frontlist book featured by the publisher during a given season—one the publisher believes should do extremely well commercially. Lead titles are usually those given the publisher's maximum promotional push.

letterhead   Business stationery and envelopes imprinted with the company's (or, in such a case, the writer's) name, address, and logo—a convenience as well as an impressive asset for a freelance writer.

letterpress   A form of printing in which set type is inked, then impressed directly onto the printing surface. Now used primarily for limited-run books-as-fine-art projects. (*See also* **offset**.)

libel   Defamation of an individual or individuals in a published work, with malice afore-thought. In litigation, the falsity of the libelous statements or representations, as well as the intention of malice, has to be proved for there to be libel; in addition, financial damages to the parties so libeled must be incurred as a result of the material in question for there to be an assessment of the amount of damages to be awarded to a claimant. This is contrasted to slander, which is defamation through the spoken word.

Library of Congress (LOC)   The largest library in the world is in Washington, D.C. As part of its many services, the LOC will supply a writer with up-to-date sources and bibliographies in all fields, from arts and humanities to science and technology. For details, write to the Library of Congress, Central Services Division, Washington, DC 20540.

Library of Congress Catalog Card Number   An identifying number issued by the Library of Congress to books it has accepted for its collection. The publication of those books, which are submitted by the publisher, are announced by the Library of Congress to libraries, which use Library of Congress numbers for their own ordering and cataloging purposes.

Literary Market Place (***LMP***)   An annual directory of the publishing industry that contains a comprehensive list of publishers, alphabetically and by category, with their addresses, phone numbers, some personnel, and the types of books they publish. Also included are various publishing-allied listings, such as literary agencies, writer's conferences and competitions, and editorial and distribution services. *LMP* is published by R. R. Bowker and is available in most public libraries.

literature   Written works of fiction and nonfiction in which compositional excellence and advancement in the art of writing are higher priorities than are considerations of profit or commercial appeal.

logo   A company or product identifier—for example, a representation of a company's initials or a drawing that is the exclusive property of that company. In publishing usage, a virtual equivalent to the trademark.

M

mainstream fiction   Nongenre fiction, excluding literary or avant-garde fiction, that appeals to a general readership.

marketing plan   The entire strategy for selling a book: its publicity, promotion, sales, and advertising.

mass-market paperback   Less-expensive smaller-format paperbacks that are sold from racks (in such venues as supermarkets, variety stores, drugstores, and specialty shops) as well as in bookstores. Also referred to as rack (or rack-sized) editions.

mechanicals   Typeset copy and art mounted on boards to be photocopied and printed. Also referred to as pasteups.

midlist books   Generally mainstream fiction and nonfiction books that traditionally formed the bulk of a publisher's list (nowadays often by default rather than intent). Midlist books are expected to be commercially viable but not explosive bestsellers—nor are they viewed as distinguished, critically respected books that can be scheduled for small print runs and aimed at select readerships. Agents may view such projects as a poor return for the effort, since they generally garner a low-end advance; editors and publishers (especially the sales force) may decry midlist works as being hard to market; prospective readers often find midlist books hard to buy in bookstores (they have short shelf lives). Hint for writers: Don't present your work as a midlist item.

multimedia   Presentations of sound and light, words in magnetically graven image—and any known combination thereof as well as nuances yet to come. Though computer CD is the dominant wrapper for these works, technological innovation is the hallmark of the electronic-publishing arena, and new formats will expand the creative and market potential. Multimedia books are publishing events; their advent suggests alternative avenues for authors as well as adaptational tie-ins with the world of print. Meanwhile, please stay tuned for virtual reality, artificial intelligence, and electronic end-user distribution of product.

multiple contract   A book contract that includes a provisional agreement for a future book or books. (*See also* **option clause/right of first refusal**.)

mystery stories or **mysteries** (*See* **suspense fiction**.)

N

net receipts   The amount of money a publisher actually receives for sales of a book: the retail price minus the bookseller's discount and/or other discount. The number of returned copies is factored in, bringing down even further the net amount received per book. Royalties are sometimes figured on these lower amounts rather than on the retail price of the book.

New Age   An eclectic category that encompasses health, medicine, philosophy, religion, and the occult—presented from an alternative or multicultural perspective. Although the term has achieved currency relatively recently, some publishers have been producing serious books in these categories for decades.

novella   A work of fiction falling in length between a short story and a novel.

O

offset (offset lithography)   A printing process that involves the transfer of wet ink from a (usually photosensitized) printing plate onto an intermediate surface (such as a rubber-coated cylinder) and then onto the paper. For commercial purposes, this method has replaced letterpress, whereby books were printed via direct impression of inked type on paper.

option clause/right of first refusal   In a book contract, a clause that stipulates that the publisher will have the exclusive right to consider and make an offer for the author's next book. However, the publisher is under no obligation to publish the book, and in most variations of the clause the author may, under certain circumstances, opt for publication elsewhere. (*See also* **multiple contract**.)

outline   Used for both a book proposal and the actual writing and structuring of a book, an outline is a hierarchical listing of topics that provides the writer (and the proposal reader) with an overview of the ideas in a book in the order in which they are to be presented.

out-of-print books   Books no longer available from the publisher; rights usually revert to the author.

P

package   The package is the actual book; the physical product.

packager   (*See* **book producer**.)

page proof   The final typeset copy of the book, in page-layout form, before printing.

paperback   Books bound with a flexible, stress-resistant, paper covering material. (*See also* **binding**.)

paperback originals   Books published, generally, in paperback editions only; sometimes the term refers to those books published simultaneously in hardcover and paperback. These books are often mass-market genre fiction (romances, Westerns, Gothics, mysteries, horror, and so forth) as well as contemporary literary fiction, cookbooks, humor, career books, self-improvement, and how-to books—the categories continue to expand.

pasteups   (*See* **mechanicals**.)

permissions   The right to quote or reprint published material, obtained by the author from the copyright holder.

picture book   A copiously illustrated book, often with very simple, limited text, intended for preschoolers and very young children.

plagiarism   The false presentation of someone else's writing as one's own. In the case of copyrighted work, plagiarism is illegal.

preface   An element of a book's frontmatter. In the preface, the author may discuss the purpose behind the format of the book, the type of research upon which it is based, its genesis, or underlying philosophy.

premium   Books sold at a reduced price as part of a special promotion. Premiums can thus be sold to a bookseller, who in turn sells them to the bookbuyer (as with a line of modestly priced art books). Alternately, such books may be produced as part of a broader marketing package. For instance, an organization may acquire a number of books (such as its own corporate history or biography of its founder) for use in personnel training and as giveaways to clients; or a nutrition/recipe book may be displayed along with a company's diet foods in non-bookstore outlets. (*See also* **special sales**.)

press agent   (*See* **publicist**.)

press kit   A promotional package that includes a press release, tip sheet, author biography and photograph, reviews, and other pertinent information. The press kit can be put together by the publisher's publicity department or an independent publicist and sent with a review copy of the book to potential reviewers and to media professionals responsible for booking author appearances.

price   There are several prices pertaining to a single book: The invoice price is the amount the publisher charges the bookseller; the retail, cover, or list price is what the consumer pays.

printer's error (PE)   A typographical error made by the printer or typesetting facility, not by the publisher's staff. PEs are corrected at the printer's expense.

printing plate   A surface that bears a reproduction of the set type and artwork of a book, from which the pages are printed.

producer   (*See* **book producer**.)

proposal   A detailed presentation of the book's concept, used to gain the interest and services of an agent and to sell the project to a publisher.

public domain   Material that is uncopyrighted, whose copyright has expired, or that is uncopyrightable. The last includes government publications, jokes, titles—and, it should be remembered, ideas.

publication date (or **pub date**)   A book's official date of publication, customarily set by the publisher to fall 6 weeks after completed bound books are delivered to the warehouse. The publication date is used to focus the promotional activities on behalf of the title—so that books will have had time to be ordered, shipped, and be available in the stores to coincide with the appearance of advertising and publicity.

publicist (press agent)   The publicity professional who handles the press releases for new books and arranges the author's publicity tours and other promotional venues (such as interviews, speaking engagements, and book signings).

publisher's catalog   A seasonal sales catalog that lists and describes a publisher's new books; it is sent to all potential buyers, including individuals who request one. Catalogs range from the basic to the glitzy and often include information on the author, on print quantity, and on the amount of money slated to be spent on publicity and promotion.

publisher's discount   The percentage by which a publisher discounts the retail price of a book to a bookseller, often based in part on the number of copies purchased.

Publishers' Trade List Annual   A collection of current and backlist catalogs arranged alphabetically by publisher, available in many libraries.

Publishers Weekly (PW)   The publishing industry's chief trade journal. *PW* carries announcements of upcoming books, respected book reviews, interviews with authors and publishing-industry professionals, special reports on various book categories, and trade news (such as mergers, rights sales, and personnel changes).

Q

quality   In publishing parlance, the word "quality" in reference to a book category (such as quality fiction) or format (quality paperback) is a term of art—individual works or lines so described are presented as outstanding products.

query letter   A brief written presentation to an agent or editor designed to pitch both the writer and the book idea.

R

remainders   Unsold book stock. Remainders can include titles that have not sold as well as anticipated, in addition to unsold copies of later printings of bestsellers. These volumes are often remaindered—that is, remaining stock is purchased from the publisher at a huge discount and resold to the public.

reprint   A subsequent edition of material that is already in print, especially publication in a different format—the paperback reprint of a hardcover, for example.

résumé   A summary of an individual's career experience and education. When a résumé is sent to prospective agents or publishers, it should contain the author's vital publishing credits, specialty credentials, and pertinent personal experience. Also referred to as the curriculum vitae or, more simply, vita.

returns   Unsold books returned to a publisher by a bookstore, for which the store may receive full or partial credit (depending on the publisher's policy, the age of the book, and so on).

reversion-of-rights clause   In the book contract, a clause that states that if the book goes out of print or the publisher fails to reprint the book within a stipulated length of time, all rights revert to the author.

review copy   A free copy of a (usually) new book sent to electronic and print media that review books for their audiences.

romance fiction or **romance novels**   Modern or period love stories, always with happy endings, which range from the tepid to the torrid. Except for certain erotic-specialty lines, romances do not feature graphic sex. Often mistakenly pigeonholed by those who do not read them, romances and romance writers have been influential in the movement away from passive and coddled female fictional characters to the strong, active modern woman in a tale that reflects areas of topical social concern.

royalty   The percentage of the retail cost of a book that is paid to the author for each copy sold after the author's advance has been recouped. Some publishers structure royalties as a percentage payment against net receipts.

S

sales conference   A meeting of a publisher's editorial and sales departments and senior promotion and publicity staff members. A sales conference covers the upcoming season's new books, and marketing strategies are discussed. Sometimes sales conferences are the basis upon which proposed titles are bought or not.

sales representative (sales rep)   A member of the publisher's sales force or an independent contractor who, armed with a book catalog and order forms, visits bookstores in a certain territory to sell books to retailers.

SASE (self-addressed stamped envelope)   It is customary for an author to enclose SASEs with query letters, with proposals, and with manuscript submissions. Many editors and agents do not reply if a writer has neglected to enclose an SASE with correspondence or submitted materials.

satisfactory clause   In book contracts, a publisher will reserve the right to refuse publication of a manuscript that is not deemed satisfactory. Because the author may be forced to pay back the publisher's advance if the complete work is found to be unsatisfactory, the specific criteria for publisher satisfaction should be set forth in the contract to protect the author.

science fiction   Science fiction includes the hardcore, imaginatively embellished technological/scientific novel as well as fiction that is even slightly futuristic (often with an after-the-holocaust milieu—nuclear, environmental, extraterrestrial, genocidal). An element much valued by editors who acquire for the literary expression of this cross-media genre is the ability of the author to introduce elements that transcend and extend conventional insight.

science fiction/fantasy   A category fiction designation that actually collapses two genres into one (for bookseller-marketing reference, of course—though it drives some devotees of these separate fields of writing nuts). In addition, many editors and publishers specialize in both these genres and thus categorize their interests with catchphrases such as sci-fi/fantasy.

screenplay   A film script—either original or one based on material published previously in another form, such as a television docudrama based on a nonfiction book or a movie thriller based on a suspense novel. (Compare with **teleplay**.)

self-publishing   A publishing project wherein an author pays for the costs of manufacturing and selling his or her own book and retains all money from the book's sale. This is a risky venture but one that can be immensely profitable (especially when combined with an author's speaking engagements or imaginative marketing techniques); in addition, if successful, self-publication can lead to distribution or publication by a commercial publisher. Compare with **subsidy publishing**.

self-syndication   Management by writers or journalists of functions that are otherwise performed by syndicates specializing in such services. In self-syndication, it is the writer who manages copyrights, negotiates fees, and handles sales, billing, and other tasks involved in circulating journalistic pieces through newspapers, magazines, or other periodicals that pick up the author's column or run a series of articles.

serial rights   Reprint rights sold to periodicals. First serial rights include the right to publish the material before anyone else (generally before the book is released, or coinciding with the book's official publication)—either for the U.S., a specific country, or for a wider territory. Second serial rights cover material already published, either in a book or another periodical.

serialization   The reprinting of a book or part of a book in a newspaper or magazine. Serialization before (or perhaps simultaneously with) the publication of the book is called first serial. The first reprint after publication (either as a book or by another periodical) is called second serial.

series   Books published as a group either because of their related subject matter (such as a biographical series on modern artists or on World War II aircraft) and/or single authorship (a set of works by Djuna Barnes, a group of books about science and society, or a series of titles geared to a particular diet-and-fitness program). Special series lines can offer a ready-made niche for an industrious author or compiler/editor who is up to date on a publisher's program and has a brace of pertinent qualifications and/or contacts. In contemporary fiction, some genre works are published in series form (such as family sagas, detective series, fantasy cycles).

shelf life   The amount of time an unsold book remains on the bookstore shelf before the store manager pulls it to make room for newer incoming stock with greater (or at least untested) sales potential.

short story   A brief piece of fiction that is more pointed and more economically detailed as to character, situation, and plot than a novel. Published collections of short stories—whether by one or several authors—often revolve around a single theme, express related outlooks, or comprise variations within a genre.

signature   A group of book pages that have been printed together on one large sheet of paper that is then folded and cut in preparation for being bound, along with the book's other signatures, into the final volume.

simultaneous publication   The issuing at the same time of more than one edition of a work, such as in hardcover and trade paperback. Simultaneous releases can be expanded to include (though rarely) deluxe gift editions of a book as well as mass-market paper versions. Audio versions of books are most often timed to coincide with the release of the first print edition.

simultaneous (or multiple) submissions   The submission of the same material to more than one publisher at the same time. Although simultaneous submission is a common practice, publishers should always be made aware that it is being done. Multiple submissions by an author to several agents is, on the other hand, a practice that is sometimes not regarded with great favor by the agent.

slush pile   The morass of unsolicited manuscripts at a publishing house or literary agency, which may fester indefinitely awaiting (perhaps perfunctory) review. Some publishers or agencies do not maintain slush piles per se—unsolicited manuscripts are slated for instant or eventual return without review (if an SASE is included) or may otherwise be literally or figuratively pitched to the wind. Querying a targeted publisher or agent before submitting a manuscript is an excellent way of avoiding, or at least minimizing the possibility of, such an ignoble fate.

software   Programs that run on a computer. Word-processing software includes programs that enable writers to compose, edit, store, and print material. Professional-quality software packages incorporate such amenities as databases that can feed the results of research electronically into the final manuscript, alphabetization and indexing functions, and capabilities for constructing tables and charts and adding graphics to the body of the manuscript. Software should be appropriate to both the demands of the work at hand and the requirements of the publisher (which may contract for a manuscript suitable for on-disk editing and electronic design, composition, and typesetting).

special sales   Sales of a book to appropriate retailers other than bookstores (for example, wine guides to liquor stores). This classification also includes books sold as premiums (for example, to a convention group or a corporation) or for other promotional purposes. Depending on volume, per-unit costs can be very low, and the book can be custom-designed. (*See also* **premium**.)

spine   That portion of the book's casing (or binding) that backs the bound page signatures and is visible when the volume is aligned on a bookshelf among other volumes.

stamping   In book publishing, the stamp is the impression of ornamental type and images (such as a logo or monogram) on the book's binding. The stamping process involves using a die with a raised or intaglioed surface to apply ink stamping or metallic-leaf stamping.

subsidiary rights   The reprint, serial, movie and television, and audiotape and videotape rights deriving from a book. The division of profits between publisher and author from the sales of these rights is determined through negotiation. In more elaborately commercial projects, further details such as syndication of related articles and licensing of characters may ultimately be involved.

subsidy publishing   A mode of publication wherein the author pays a publishing company to produce his or her work, which may thus appear superficially to have been published conventionally. Subsidy publishing (alias vanity publishing) is generally more expensive than self-publishing, because a successful subsidy house makes a profit on all its contracted functions, charging fees well beyond the publisher's basic costs for production and services.

suspense fiction   Fiction within a number of genre categories that emphasize suspense as well as the usual (and sometimes unusual) literary techniques to keep the reader engaged. Suspense fiction encompasses novels of crime and detection (regularly referred to as mysteries—these include English-style cozies; American-style hard-boiled detective stories; dispassionate law-enforcement procedurals; crime stories); action-adventure; espionage novels; technothrillers; tales of psychological suspense; and horror. A celebrated aspect of suspense fiction's popular appeal—one that surely accounts for much of this broad category's sustained market vigor—is the interactive element: The reader may choose to challenge the tale itself by attempting to outwit the author and solve a crime before detectives do, figure out how best to defeat an all-powerful foe before the hero does, or parse out the elements of a conspiracy before the writer reveals the whole story.

syndicated column   Material published simultaneously in a number of newspapers or magazines. The author shares the income from syndication with the syndicate that negotiates the sale. (*See also* **self-syndication**.)

syndication rights   (*See also* **self-syndication**; **subsidiary rights**.)

synopsis   A summary in paragraph form, rather than in outline format. The synopsis is an important part of a book proposal. For fiction, the synopsis portrays the high points of story line and plot, succinctly and dramatically. In a nonfiction book proposal, the synopsis describes the thrust and content of the successive chapters (and/or parts) of the manuscript.

T

table of contents   A listing of a book's chapters and other sections (such as the front-matter, appendix, index, and bibliography) or of a magazine's articles and columns, in the order in which they appear; in published versions, the table of contents indicates the respective beginning page numbers.

tabloid   A smaller-than-standard-size newspaper (daily, weekly, or monthly). Traditionally, certain tabloids are distinguished by sensationalism of approach and content rather than by straightforward reportage of newsworthy events. In common parlance, *tabloid* is used to describe works in various media (including books) that cater to immoderate tastes (for example, tabloid exposé, tabloid television; the tabloidization of popular culture).

teleplay   A **screenplay** geared toward television production. Similar in overall concept to screenplays for the cinema, teleplays are nonetheless inherently concerned with such TV-loaded provisions as the physical dimensions of the smaller screen, and formal elements of pacing and structure keyed to stipulated program length and the placement of commercial advertising. Attention to these myriad television-specific demands are fundamental to the viability of a project.

terms   The financial conditions agreed to in a book contract.

theme   A general term for the underlying concept of a book. (*See also* **hook**.)

thriller   A thriller is a novel of suspense with a plot structure that reinforces the elements of gamesmanship and the chase, with a sense of the hunt being paramount.

Thrillers can be spy novels, tales of geopolitical crisis, legal thrillers, medical thrillers, technothrillers, domestic thrillers. The common thread is a growing sense of threat and the excitement of pursuit.

tip sheet   An information sheet on a single book that presents general publication information (publication date, editor, ISBN, etc.), a brief synopsis of the book, information on relevant other books (sometimes competing titles), and other pertinent marketing data such as author profile and advance blurbs. The tip sheet is given to the sales and publicity departments; a version of the tip sheet is also included in press kits.

title page   The page at the front of a book that lists the title, subtitle, author (and other contributors, such as translator or illustrator), as well as the publishing house and sometimes its logo.

trade books   Books distributed through the book trade—meaning bookstores and major book clubs—as opposed to, for example, mass-market paperbacks, which are often sold at magazine racks, newsstands, and supermarkets as well.

trade discount   The discount from the cover or list price that a publisher gives the bookseller. It is usually proportional to the number of books ordered (the larger the order, the greater the discount), and typically varies between 40% and 50%.

trade list   A catalog of all of a publisher's books in print, with ISBNs and order information. The trade list sometimes includes descriptions of the current season's new books.

trade (quality) paperbacks   Reprints or original titles published in paperback format, larger in dimension than mass-market paperbacks, and distributed through regular retail book channels. Trade paperbacks tend to be in the neighborhood of twice the price of an equivalent mass-market paperback version and about half to two-thirds the price of hardcover editions.

trade publishers   Publishers of books for a general readership—that is, nonprofessional, nonacademic books that are distributed primarily through bookstores.

translation rights   Rights sold either to a foreign agent or directly to a foreign publisher, either by the author's agent or by the original publisher.

treatment   In screenwriting, a full narrative description of the story, including sample dialogue.

U

unauthorized biography   A history of a person's life written without the consent or collaboration of the subject or the subject's survivors.

university press   A publishing house affiliated with a sponsoring university. The university press is generally nonprofit and subsidized by the respective university. Generally, university presses publish noncommercial scholarly nonfiction books written by academics, and their lists may include literary fiction, criticism, and poetry. Some university presses also specialize in titles of regional interest, and many acquire projects intended for commercial book-trade distribution.

unsolicited manuscript   A manuscript sent to an editor or agent without being requested by the editor/agent.

V

vanity press   A publisher that publishes books only at an author's expense—and will generally agree to publish virtually anything that is submitted and paid for. (*See also* **subsidy publishing**.)

vita   Latin word for "life." A shortened equivalent term for *curriculum vitae* (*see also* **résumé**).

W

word count   The number of words in a given document. When noted on a manuscript, the word count is usually rounded off to the nearest 100 words.

work-for-hire   Writing done for an employer, or writing commissioned by a publisher or book packager who retains ownership of, and all rights pertaining to, the written material.

Y

young-adult (YA) books   Books for readers generally between the ages of 12 and 17. Young-adult fiction often deals with issues of concern to contemporary teens.

young readers or **younger readers**   Publishing terminology for the range of publications that address the earliest readers. Sometimes a particular house's young-readers' program typifies books for those who do not yet read; which means these books have to hook the caretakers and parents who actually buy them. In certain quirky turns of everyday publishing parlance, *young readers* can mean anyone from embryos through young adults (and "young" means *you* when you want it to). This part may be confusing (as is often the case with publishing usage): Sometimes *younger adult* means only that the readership is allegedly hip, including those who would eschew kid's books as being inherently lame and those who are excruciatingly tapped into the current cultural pulse, regardless of cerebral or life-span quotient.

Z

zombie (or **zombi**)   In idiomatic usage, a zombie is a person whose conduct approximates that of an automaton. Harking back to the term's origins as a figure of speech for the resurrected dead or a reanimated cadaver, such folks are not customarily expected to exhibit an especially snazzy personality or be aware of too many things going on around them; hence some people in book-publishing circles may be characterized as zombies.

Suggested Resources

SELF-PUBLISHING RESOURCES

All-By-Yourself Self-Publishing
by David H. Li
Premier Publishing
PO Box 341267
Bethesda, MD 20827
e-mail: davidli@erols.com

The Art of Self-Publishing
by Bonnie Stahlman Speer
Reliance Press
60-64 Hardinge Street
Deniliquin, NSW 2710
Australia
e-mail: reliance@reliancepress.com.au

Book Production: Composition, Layout, Editing & Design. Getting It Ready for Printing
by Dan Poynter
Para Publishing
PO Box 8206-240
Santa Barbara, CA 93118-8206
805-968-7277   fax: 805-968-1379
cellular: 805-680-2298
e-mail: DanPoynter@aol.com, 75031.3534@compuserve.com

Business and Legal Forms for Authors and Self-Publishers
by Tad Crawford
Allworth Press
10 East 23rd Street, Suite 210
New York, NY 10010
212-777-8395

*The Complete Guide to Self-Publishing: Everything You Need
to Know to Write, Publish, Promote, and Sell Your Own Book*
by Tom Ross, Marilyn Ross
Writer's Digest Books
1507 Dana Avenue
Cincinnati, OH 45207
513-531-2222   fax: 513-531-4744

The Complete Guide to Successful Publishing
by Avery Cardoza
Cardoza Pub.
132 Hastings Street
Brooklyn, NY 11235
800-577-WINS, 718-743-5229   fax: 718-743-8284
e-mail: cardozapub@aol.com

The Complete Self-Publishing Handbook
by David M. Brownstone, Irene M. Franck
Plume
375 Hudson Street
New York, NY 10014
212-366-2000

*The Economical Guide to Self-Publishing:
How to Produce and Market Your Book on a Budget*
by Linda Foster Radke, Mary E. Hawkins (Editor)
Five Star Publications
PO Box 6698
Chandler, AZ 85246-6698
480-940-8182

Exports/Foreign Rights, Selling U.S. Books Abroad
by Dan Poynter
Para Publishing
PO Box 8206-240
Santa Barbara, CA 93118-8206
805-968-7277   fax: 805-968-1379
cellular: 805-680-2298
e-mail: DanPoynter@aol.com, 75031.3534@compuserve.com

A Guide to Successful Self-Publishing
by Stephen Wagner
Prentice Hall Direct
240 Frisch Court
Paramus, NJ 07652
201-909-6200

How to Make Money Publishing from Home, Revised 2nd Edition:
Everything You Need to Know to Successfully Publish Books,
Newsletters, Web Sites, Greeting Cards, and Software
by Lisa Shaw
Prima Publishing
3000 Lava Ridge Court
Roseville, CA 95661

How to Publish, Promote, and Sell Your Own Book
by Robert Lawrence Holt
St. Martin's Press
175 Fifth Avenue
New York, NY 10010
212-674-5151

How to Publish Your Own Book and Earn $50,000 Profit
by Gordon Burgett
Communication Unlimited
PO Box 6405
Santa Maria, CA 93456
800-563-1454   fax: 805-937-3035
e-mail: gordon@sops.com

How to Self-Publish & Market Your Own Book: A Simple Guide for Aspiring Writers
by Mack E. Smith, Sara Freeman Smith
UR Gems Group
PO Box 440341
Houston, TX 77244-0341
281-596-8330

How to Self-Publish Your Book with Little or No Money!
A Complete Guide to Self-Publishing at a Profit!
by Bettie E. Tucker, Wayne Brumagin
Rainbow's End Company
354 Golden Grove Road
Baden, PA 15005 US
724-266-2346   fax: 724-266-2346

How You Can Become a Successful Self-Publisher in America and Elsewhere
by Paul Chika Emekwulu
Novelty Books
PO Box 2482
Norman, OK 73070
voice/fax: 405-447-9019
e-mail: novelty@telepath.com

Make Money Self-Publishing: Learn How from Fourteen Successful Small Publishers
by Suzanne P. Thomas
Gemstone House Publishing
PO Box 19948
Boulder, CO 80308
800-324-6415

The Prepublishing Handbook:
What You Should Know Before You Publish Your First Book
by Patricia J. Bell
Cat's Paw Press
9561 Woodridge Circle
Eden Prairie, MN 55347
952-941-5053   fax: 952-941-4759
e-mail: catspawpress@aol.com

The Publish It Yourself Handbook (25th Anniversary Edition)
by Bill Henderson (Editor)
W. W. Norton & Company
500 Fifth Avenue
New York, NY 10110
212-354-5500

Publish Your Own Novel
by Connie Shelton, Lee Ellison (Editor)
Intrigue Press
PO Box 27553
Philadelphia, PA 19118
800-996-9783

The Self-Publisher's Writing Journal
by Lia Relova
Pumpkin Enterprises
12 Packet Road
Palos Verdes, CA 90275
e-mail: princesslia@hotmail.com

The Self-Publishing Manual: How to Write, Print & Sell Your Own Book
by Dan Poynter
Para Publishing
PO Box 8206-240
Santa Barbara, CA 93118-8206
805-968-7277   fax: 805-968-1379
cellular: 805-680-2298
e-mail: DanPoynter@aol.com, 75031.3534@compuserve.com

A Simple Guide to Self-Publishing: A Step-by-Step Handbook to Prepare,
Print, Distribute & Promote Your Own Book—3rd Edition
by Mark Ortman
Wise Owl Books
PO Box 29205
Bellingham, WA 98228
360-671-5858
e-mail: publish@wiseowlbooks.com

Smart Self-Publishing: An Author's Guide to Producing a Marketable Book
by Linda G. Salisbury
Tabby House
4429 Shady Lane
Charlotte Harbor, FL 33980-3024
 941-629-7646   fax: 941-629-4270

The Woman's Guide to Self-Publishing
by Donna M. Murphy
Irie Publishing
301 Boardwalk Drive
PO Box 273123
Fort Collins, CO 80527-3123
970-482-4402   fax: 970-482-4402
e-mail: iriepub@verinet.com

INDUSTRY RESOURCES

30 Steps to Becoming a Writer and Getting Published:
The Complete Starter Kit for Aspiring Writers
by Scott Edelstein
Writer's Digest Books
1507 Dana Avenue
Cincinnati, OH 45207
513-531-2222   fax: 513-531-4744

500 Ways to Beat the Hollywood Script Reader:
Writing the Screenplay the Reader Will Recommend
by Jennifer M. Lerch
Fireside
1230 Avenue of the Americas
New York, NY 10020
212-698-7000

1001 Ways to Market Your Books: For Authors and Publishers:
Includes Over 100 Proven Marketing Tips Just for Authors
by John Kremer
Open Horizons
PO Box 205
Fairfield, IA 52556

1,818 Ways to Write Better & Get Published
by Scott Edelstein
Writer's Digest Books
1507 Dana Avenue
Cincinnati, OH 45207
513-531-2222   fax: 513-531-4744

2002 Poet's Market:
1,800 Places to Publish Your Poetry (Poet's Market, 2002)
by Nancy Breen (Editor)
Writer's Digest Books
1507 Dana Avenue
Cincinnati, OH 45207
513-531-2222   fax: 513-531-4744

2002 Childrens Writers & Illustrators Market
by Alice Pope
Writer's Digest Books
1507 Dana Avenue
Cincinnati, OH 45207
513-531-2222   fax: 513-531-4744

2002 Novel & Short Story Writers Market
by Annie Bowling (Editor)
Writer's Digest Books
1507 Dana Avenue
Cincinnati, OH 45207
513-531-2222   fax: 513-531-4744

2002 Writer's Market:
8,000 Editors Who Buy What You Write (Writers Market 2000)
(Electronic version also available.)
by Kirsten Holm (Editor)
Writer's Digest Books
1507 Dana Avenue
Cincinnati, OH 45207
513-531-2222   fax: 513-531-4744

Advice to Writers: A Compendium of Quotes, Anecdotes,
and Writerly Wisdom from a Dazzling Array of Literary Lights
by John Winoker (Compiler)
Vintage Books
299 Park Avenue
New York, NY 10171
212-751-2600

The American Directory of Writer's Guidelines:
What Editors Want, What Editors Buy (3rd edition)
by John C. Mutchler
Quill Driver Books
1831 Industrial Way, #101
Sanger, CA 93657
fax: 559-876-2170
e-mail: sbm12@csufresno.edu

The Art and Science of Book Publishing
by Herbert S. Bailey Jr.
Ohio University Press
Scott Quadrangle
Athens, OH 45701

The Author's Guide to Marketing Your Book:
From Start to Success, for Writers and Publishers
by Don Best, Peter Goodman
Stone Bridge Press
PO Box 8208
Berkeley, CA 94707
800-947-7271   fax: 510-524-8711
e-mail: sbporter@stonebridge.com

An Author's Guide to Publishing
by Michael Legat
Robert Hale Ltd.
Clerkenwell House 45-47
Clerkenwell Green, London
England EC1R 0HT
0171-251-2661

The Big Deal: Hollywood's Million-Dollar Spec Script Market
by Tom Taylor
William Morrow & Company
1350 Avenue of the Americas
New York, NY 10019
212-261-6500

Book Blitz: Getting Your Book in the News: 60 Steps to a Best Seller
by Barbara Gaughen, Ernest Weckbaugh
Best Seller Books
7456 Evergreen Drive
Santa Barbara, CA 93117
800-444-2524

Book Business: Publishing: Past, Present, and Future
by Jason Epstein
W. W. Norton & Company
500 Fifth Avenue
New York, NY 10110
212-354-5500   fax: 212-869-0856

Book Editors Talk to Writers
by Judy Mandell
John Wiley & Sons
605 Third Avenue
New York, NY 10158-0012
212-850-6000   fax: 212-850-6088
e-mail: info@wiley.com

Book Promotion for the Shameless:
101 Marketing Tips that Really Work (3.5 diskette)
by Lorna Tedder
Spilled Candy Publications
PO Box 5202
Niceville, FL 32578-5202
850-897-4644
e-mail: orders@spilledcandy.com

Book Promotion for Virgins: Answers to a New Author's
Questions About Marketing and Publicity
by Lorna Tedder
Spilled Candy Publications
PO Box 5202
Niceville, FL 32578-5202
850-897-4644
e-mail: orders@spilledcandy.com

The Book Publishing Industry
by Albert N. Greco
Allyn & Bacon
75 Arlington Street, Suite 300
Boston, MA 02116
617-848-6000

Book Publishing: The Basic Introduction
by John P. Dessauer
Continuum Publishing Group
370 Lexington Avenue
New York, NY 10017
212-953-5858

Breaking into Print: How to Write and Publish Your First Book
by Jane L. Evanson, Luanne Dowling
Kendall/Hunt Publishing Company
4050 Westmark Drive
PO Box 1840
Dubuque, IA 52004-1840
800-228-0810, 319-589-1000

Business and Legal Forms for Authors and Self-Publishers
by Tad Crawford
Allworth Press
10 East 23rd Street
New York, NY 10010
fax: 212-777-8261
e-mail: groberts@allworth.com

The Career Novelist: A Literary Agent Offers Strategies for Success
by Donald Maass
Heinemann
22 Salmon Street
Port Melbourne, Victoria 3207
Australia
e-mail: customer@hi.com.au

The Case of Peter Rabbit: Changing Conditions of Literature for Children
by Margaret MacKey
Garland Publishing
29 West 35th Street
New York, NY 10001-2299
212-216-7800   fax: 212-564-7854
e-mail: info@taylorandfrancis.com

Children's Writer's & Illustrator's Market, 2000:
800 Editors & Art Directors Who Buy Your Writing & Illustrations
by Alice Pope (Editor)
Writer's Digest Books
1507 Dana Avenue
Cincinnati, OH 45207
513-531-2222   fax: 513-531-4744

Complete Guide to Book Marketing
by David Cole
Allworth Press
10 East 23rd Street
New York, NY 10010
fax: 212-777-8261
e-mail: groberts@allworth.com

The Complete Guide to Book Publicity
by Jodee Blanco
Allworth Press
10 East 23rd Street, Suite 210
New York, NY 10010
212-777-8395

The Complete Guide to Writer's Groups, Conferences, and Workshops
by Eileen Malone
John Wiley & Sons
605 Third Avenue
New York, NY 10158-0012
212-850-6000   fax: 212-850-6088
e-mail: info@wiley.com

The Complete Guide to Writing Fiction and Nonfiction—And Getting It Published
by Patricia Kubis, Robert Howland
Prentice Hall Direct
240 Frisch Court
Paramus, NJ 07652
201-909-6200

A Complete Guide to Writing for Publication
by Susan Titus Osborn (Editor)
ACW Press
5501 North 7th Avenue, # 502
Phoenix, AZ 85013
877-868-9673
e-mail: editor@acwpress.com

The Complete Idiot's Guide to Getting Published
by Sheree Bykofsky, Jennifer Basye Sander
Alpha Books
201 West 103rd Street
Indianapolis, IN 46290
317-581-3500

The Complete Idiot's Guide to Getting Your Romance Published
by Julie Beard
Alpha Books
4500 East Speedway, Suite 31
Tucson, AZ 85712
fax: 800-770-4329

Complete Idiot's Guide to Publishing Children's Books
by Harold D. Underdown, Lynne Rominger
Alpha Books
4500 East Speedway, Suite 31
Tucson, AZ 85712
fax: 800-770-4329

The Copyright Permission and Libel Handbook:
A Step-by-Step Guide for Writers, Editors, and Publishers
by Lloyd J. Jassin, Steve C. Schecter
John Wiley & Sons
605 Third Avenue
New York, NY 10158-0012
212-850-6000   fax: 212-850-6088
e-mail: info@wiley.com

Desktop Publishing & Design for Dummies
by Roger C. Parker
IDG Books Worldwide, Inc.
919 East Hillsdale Boulevard, Suite 400
Foster City, CA 94404-2112
800-762-2974

The Directory of Poetry Publishers: 2001–2002
(Directory of Poetry Publishers, 17th edition)
by Len Fulton (Editor)
Dustbooks
PO Box 100
Paradise, CA 95967
800-477-6110, 530-877-6110   fax: 530-877-0222

Directory of Small Press/Magazine Editors & Publishers
(Directory of Small Press and Magazine Editors and Publishers, 31st edition)
by Len Fulton (Editor)
Dustbooks
PO Box 100
Paradise, CA 95967
800-477-6110, 530-877-6110   fax: 530-877-0222

Editors on Editing: What Writers Need to Know About What Editors Do
by Gerald Gross (Editor)
Grove Press
841 Broadway
New York, NY 10003
212-614-7850

The First Five Pages: A Writer's Guide to Staying Out of the Rejection Pile
by Noah T. Lukeman
Fireside
1230 Avenue of the Americas
New York, NY 10020
212-698-7000

Formatting & Submitting Your Manuscript (Writer's Market Library Series)
by Jack Neff
Writer's Digest Books
1507 Dana Avenue
Cincinnati, OH 45207
513-531-2222   fax: 513-531-4744

From Book Idea to Bestseller: What You Absolutely,
Positively Must Know to Make Your Book a Success
by Michael Snell, Kim Baker (Contributor), Sunny Baker (Contributor)
Prima Publishing
3000 Lava Ridge Court
Roseville, CA 95661

From Pen to Print: The Secrets of Getting Published Successfully
by Ellen M. Kozak
Henry Holt
115 West 18th Street
New York, NY 10011
212-886-9200   fax: 212-633-0748
e-mail: publicity@hholt.com

Get Published: Top Magazine Editors Tell You How
by Diane Gage
Henry Holt
115 West 18th Street
New York, NY 10011
212-886-9200   fax: 212-633-0748
e-mail: publicity@hholt.com

Get Your First Book Published: And Make It a Success
by Jason Shinder, Jeff Herman, Amy Holman
Career Press
3 Tice Road
PO Box 687
Franklin Lakes, NJ 07417
201-848-0310

Getting Your Book Published for Dummies
by Sarah Parsons Zackheim with Adrian Zackheim
Hungry Minds, Inc.
909 Third Avenue
New York, NY 10022

Getting Your Book Published for Dummies
by Sarah Parsons Zackheim
IDG Books Worldwide, Inc.
919 East Hillsdale Boulevard, Suite 400
Foster City, CA 94404-2112
800-762-2974

*Getting Your Manuscript Sold: Surefire Writing and
Selling Strategies That Will Get Your Book Published*
by Cynthia Sterling, M. G. Davidson
Empire Publishing Service
PO Box 717
Madison, NC 27025-0717
fax: 336-427-7372

*How to Be Your Own Literary Agent:
The Business of Getting a Book Published*
by Richard Curtis
Houghton Mifflin Company
222 Berkeley Street
Boston, MA 02116-3764
617-351-5000

How to Get Happily Published (5th edition)
by Judith Appelbaum
HarperCollins
10 East 53rd Street
New York, NY 10022-5299
212-207-7000

How to Publish, Promote, and Sell Your Own Book
by Robert Lawrence Holt
St. Martin's Press
175 Fifth Avenue
New York, NY 10010
212-674-5151

How to Write a Book Proposal
by Michael Larsen
Writer's Digest Books
1507 Dana Avenue
Cincinnati, OH 45207
513-531-2222   fax: 513-531-4744

How to Write a Damn Good Novel
by James N. Frey
St. Martin's Press
175 Fifth Avenue
New York, NY 10010
212-674-5151

How to Write Irresistible Query Letters
by Lisa Collier Cool
Writer's Digest Books
1507 Dana Avenue
Cincinnati, OH 45207
513-531-2222   fax: 513-531-4744

How to Write and Sell Your First Nonfiction Book
by Oscar Collier, Frances Spatz Leighton
St. Martin's Press
175 Fifth Avenue
New York, NY 10010
212-674-5151

How to Write & Sell Your First Novel
by Oscar Collier
Writer's Digest Books
1507 Dana Avenue
Cincinnati, OH 45207
513-531-2222   fax: 513-531-4744

How to Write What You Want and Sell What You Write
by Skip Press
Career Press
3 Tice Road
PO Box 687
Franklin Lakes, NJ 07417
201-848-0310

In the Company of Writers: A Life in Publishing
by Charles Scribner
Scribner
1230 Avenue of the Americas
New York, NY 10020
212-698-7000

The Insider's Guide to Getting an Agent
by Lori Perkins
Writer's Digest Books
1507 Dana Avenue
Cincinnati, OH 45207
513-531-2222   fax: 513-531-4744

The Joy of Publishing
by Nat G. Bodian
Open Horizons
PO Box 205
Fairfield, IA 52556

*Jump Start Your Book Sales: A Money-Making Guide
for Authors, Independent Publishers and Small Presses*
by Marilyn Ross, Tom Ross
Writer's Digest Books
1507 Dana Avenue
Cincinnati, OH 45207
513-531-2222   fax: 513-531-4744

*Kirsch's Guide to the Book Contract:
For Authors, Publishers, Editors and Agents*
by Jonathan Kirsch
Acrobat Books
PO Box 870
Venice, CA 90294
fax: 310-823-8447

Kirsch's Handbook of Publishing Law: For Author's, Publishers, Editors and Agents
by Jonathan Kirsch
Acrobat Books
PO Box 870
Venice, CA 90294
fax: 310-823-8447

Literary Agents: A Writer's Introduction
by John F. Baker
IDG Books Worldwide, Inc.
919 East Hillsdale Boulevard, Suite 400
Foster City, CA 94404-2112
800-762-2974

Literary Agents: What They Do, How They Do It, and How to
Find and Work with the Right One for You, Revised and Expanded
by Michael Larsen
John Wiley & Sons
605 Third Avenue
New York, NY 10158-0012
212-850-6000   fax: 212-850-6088
e-mail: info@wiley.com

Literary Marketplace 2001: The Directory of the American
Book Publishing Industry with Industry Yellow Pages
by R. R. Bowker Staff
R. R. Bowker
630 Central Avenue
New Providence, NJ 07974
888-269-5372
e-mail: info@bowker.com

Making It in Book Publishing
by Leonard Mogel
IDG Books Worldwide, Inc.
919 East Hillsdale Boulevard, Suite 400
Foster City, CA 94404-2112
800-762-2974

Marketing Strategies for Writers
by Michael H. Sedge
Allworth Press
10 East 23rd Street, Suite 210
New York, NY 10010
212-777-8395

Merriam-Webster's Manual for Writers and Editors
Merriam Webster
47 Federal Street
PO Box 281
Springfield, MA 01102
413-734-3134   fax: 413-731-5979
e-mail: mwsales@m-w.com

Negotiating a Book Contract: A Guide for Authors, Agents and Lawyers
by Mark L. Levine
Moyer Bell Ltd.
Kymbolde Way
Wakefield, RI 02879
888-789-1945, 401-789-0074   fax: 401-789-3793
e-mail: sales@moyerbell.com

Nonfiction Book Proposals Anybody Can Write:
How to Get a Contract and Advance Before Writing Your Book
by Elizabeth Lyon
Blue Heron Pub.
1234 SW Stark Street, Suite 1
Portland, OR 97205
fax: 503-223-9474
e-mail: bhp@teleport.com

Novel & Short Story Writer's Market, 2000: 2,000 Places to
Sell Your Fiction (Novel and Short Story Writer's Market, 2000)
by Barbara Kuroff (Editor), Tricia Waddell (Editor)
Writer's Digest Books
1507 Dana Avenue
Cincinnati, OH 45207
fax: 531-531-4744

Poet Power! The Practical Poet's Complete Guide
to Getting Published (and Self-Published)
by Thomas A. Williams
Venture Press
PO Box 1582
Davis, CA 95617-1582
530-756-2309   fax: 530-756-4790
e-mail: wmaster@ggweb.com

The Portable Writers' Conference: Your Guide to Getting and Staying Published
by Stephen Blake Mettee (Editor)
Word Dancer Press
1831 Industrial Way, #101
Sanger, CA 93657
voice/fax: 559-876-2170
e-mail: sbm12@csufresno.edu

*The Prepublishing Handbook: What You Should
Know Before You Publish Your First Book*
by Patricia J. Bell
Cat's Paw Press
9561 Woodridge Circle
Eden Prairie, MN 55347
952-941-5053   fax: 952-941-4759
e-mail: catspawpre@aol.com

Publish to Win: Smart Strategies to Sell More Books
by Jerrold R. Jenkins, Anne M. Stanton
Rhodes & Easton
35 Clark Hill Road
Prospect, CT 06712-1011
203-758-3661   fax: 603-853-5420
e-mail: biopub@aol.com

The Screenwriter's Bible: A Complete Guide to Writing, Formatting, and Selling Your Script
by David Trottier
Silman-James Press
3624 Shannon Road
Los Angeles, CA 90027
323-661-9922   fax: 323-661-9933

Secrets of a Freelance Writer: How to Make $85,000 a Year
by Robert W. Bly
Henry Holt
115 West 18th Street
New York, NY 10011
212-886-9200   fax: 212-633-0748
e-mail: publicity@hholt.com

Self-Editing for Fiction Writers
by Renni Browne, Dave King
HarperCollins
10 East 53rd Street
New York, NY 10022-5299
212-207-7000

A Simple Guide to Marketing Your Book:
What an Author and Publisher Can Do to Sell More Books
by Mark Ortman
Wise Owl Books
24425 Fieldmont Place
West Hills, CA 91307
818-716-9076
e-mail: apweis@pacbell.net

The Shortest Distance Between You and a Published Book
by Susan Page
Broadway Books
841 Broadway
New York, NY 10003
212-614-7850

Telling Lies for Fun & Profit
by Lawrence Block, Sue Grafton (Introduction)
William Morrow & Company
1350 Avenue of the Americas
New York, NY 10019
212-261-6500

This Business of Books: A Complete Overview of the Industry from Concept Through Sales
by Claudia Suzanne, Carol Amato (Editor), Thelma Sansoucie (Editor)
Wambtac
17300 17th Street, #J276
Tustin, CA 92780
800-641-3936   fax: 714-954-0793
e-mail: bookdoc@wambtac

This Business of Publishing: An Insider's View of Current Trends and Tactics
by Richard Curtis
Allworth Press
10 East 23rd Street, Suite 210
New York, NY 10010
212-777-8395

What Book Publishers Won't Tell You:
A Literary Agent's Guide to the Secrets of Getting Published
by Bill Adler
Citadel Press
3300 Business Drive
Sacramento, CA 95820
fax: 916-732-2070

The Whole Picture: Strategies for Screenwriting Success in the New Hollywood
by Richard Walter
Plume
375 Hudson Street
New York, NY 10014
212-366-2000

Writer Tells All: Insider Secrets to Getting Your Book Published
by Robert Masello
Owl Books
115 West 18th Street
New York, NY 10010
212-886-9200

Write the Perfect Book Proposal: 10 Proposals That Sold and Why
by Jeff Herman, Deborah M. Adams
John Wiley & Sons
605 Third Avenue
New York, NY 10158-0012
212-850-6000   fax: 212-850-6088
e-mail: info@wiley.com

Writer's Guide to Book Editors, Publishers, and Literary Agents, 13th Edition
Who They Are! What They Want! and How to Win Them Over!
by Jeff Herman
Prima Publishing
3000 Lava Ridge Court
Roseville, CA 95661

A Writer's Guide to Overcoming Rejection:
A Practical Sales Course for the As Yet Unpublished
by Edward Baker
Summerdale Publishing Ltd.

Writer's International Guide to Book Editors, Publishers, and Literary Agents:
Make the Whole English-Speaking Publishing World Yours with
This One-of-a-Kind Guide
by Jeff Herman
Prima Publishing
3000 Lava Ridge Court
Roseville, CA 95661

The Writer's Legal Guide (2nd edition)
by Tad Crawford, Tony Lyons
Allworth Press
10 East 23rd Street, Suite 210
New York, NY 10010
212-777-8395

The Writer's Market Companion
by Joe Feiertag, Mary Carmen Cupito
Writer's Digest Books
1507 Dana Avenue
Cincinnati, OH 45207
513-531-2222   fax: 531-531-4744

Writer's & Illustrator's Guide to Children's Book Publishers and Agents
by Ellen R. Shapiro
Prima Publishing
3000 Lava Ridge Court
Roseville, CA 95661

The Writer's Legal Companion: The Complete Handbook for the Working Writer
by Brad Bunnin, Peter Beren
Perseus Press
11 Cambridge Center
Cambridge, MA 02142
e-mail: info@perseuspublishing.com

The Writer's Legal Guide (2nd edition)
by Tad Crawford, Tony Lyons
Allworth Press
10 East 23rd Street, Suite 210
New York, NY 10010
212-777-8395

The Writer's Little Instruction Book:
385 Secrets for Writing Well and Getting Published
by Paul Raymond Martin, Polly Keener
Writer's World Press
35 North Chillecothe Road, Suite D
Aurora, OH 44202
330-562-6667   fax: 330-562-1216
e-mail: Writersworld@juno.com

Writing Down the Bones: Freeing the Writer Within
by Natalie Goldberg
Shambhala Publications
PO Box 308
Boston, MA 02117
617-424-0030   fax: 617-236-1563

Writing Successful Self-Help and How-To Books
by Jean Marie Stine
John Wiley & Sons
605 Third Avenue
New York, NY 10158-0012
212-850-6000   fax: 212-850-6088
e-mail: info@wiley.com

Writing the Nonfiction Book
by Eva Shaw, Ph.D.
Rodgers & Nelsen Publishing Company
PO Box 700
Loveland, CO 80537
970-593-9557

*You Can Make It Big Writing Books: A Top Agent Shows
How to Develop a Million-Dollar Bestseller*
by Jeff Herman, Deborah Levine Herman, Julia DeVillers
Prima Publishing
3000 Lava Ridge Court
Roseville, CA 95661

*Your Novel Proposal: From Creation to Contract: The Complete Guide to
Writing Query Letters, Synopses and Proposals for Agents and Editors*
by Blythe Camenson
Writer's Digest Books
1507 Dana Avenue
Cincinnati, OH 45207
513-531-2222   fax: 513-531-4744

E-PUBLISHING RESOURCES

A Cheap and Easy Guide to Self-Publishing E-Books
by Wayne F. Perkins
1st Books Library
2595 Vernal Pike
Bloomington, IN 47404

800-839-8640   fax: 812-339-6554
outside USA and Canada: 812-339-6000

Electronic Publishing: The Definitive Guide
by Karen S. Wiesner
Avid Press
5470 Red Fox Drive
Brighton, MI 48114
810-801-1177
e-mail: cgs@avidpress.com

ePublishing for Dummies
by Victoria Rosenborg
Hungry Minds, Inc.
909 Third Avenue
New York, NY 10022

*The Freelance Writer's E-Publishing Guidebook: 25+ E-Publishing
Home-Based Online Writing Businesses to Start for Freelancers*
by Anne Hart
iUniverse.com
800-376-1736
e-mail: publisher@iuniverse.com

How to Get Your E-Book Published
by Richard Curtis, W. T. Quick
Writer's Digest Books
1507 Dana Avenue
Cincinnati, OH 45207
513-531-2222   fax: 513-531-4744

How to Publish and Promote Online
by M. J. Rose, Angela Adair-Hoy
Griffin Trade Paperback
175 Fifth Avenue
New York, NY 10010
212-647-5151

Official Adobe Electronic Publishing Guide
by Adobe Creative Team
Adobe Press
345 Park Avenue
San Jose, CA 95110-2704
408-536-6000

*U-Publish.Com: How Individual Writers Can Now
Effectively Compete with the Giants of Publishing*
by Dan Snow, Danny O. Poynter
Unlimited Publishing
PO Box 3007
Bloomington, IN 47402
e-mail: publish@unlimitedpublishing.com

What Every Writer *Must* Know About E-Publishing
by Emily A. Vander Veer
Emily A. Vander Veer
e-mail: emily@emilyv.com

Writing.Com: Creative Internet Strategies to Advance Your Writing Career
by Moira Anderson Allen
Allworth Press
10 East 23rd Street, Suite 210
New York, NY 10010
212-777-8395

*Your Guide to Ebook Publishing Success:
How to Create and Profitably Sell Your Writing on the Internet*
by James Dillehay
Warm Snow Publishers
50 Sufi Road
PO Box 75
Torreon, NM 87061
e-mail: service@craftmarketer.com

Index

INSTRUCTIONS FOR CD-ROM DELUXE EDITION USERS

Running the CD   No installation is required. The only files transferred to your hard disk are the ones you choose to copy or install.

Minimum System Requirements

Windows 98; Pentium II 200-MHz; 32 MB RAM

Macintosh OS 8.1; PowerPC-based; 32 MB RAM

Internet Explorer 4.x or Netscape Navigator 4.x

Because there is no install routine, running the CD in Windows or the Macintosh Operating System is a breeze. Whether you are on a PC or Mac, follow these instructions for installation:

1. Insert the CD in the CD-ROM drive.
2. Browse the CD drive from your desktop, or click on the CD icon on your desktop if using a Macintosh.
3. Click on **start_here.html,** and the program will start.

This CD contains:

- **Writer's Desktop Database.** This powerful tool contains the complete 13th edition of Jeff Herman's *Writer's Guide to Book Editors, Publishers, and Literary Agents.*
- **Writer's Guide Helpful Links.** This assortment of Internet links will enable you to tap into valuable writing resources available online.
- **Using the Writer's Desktop Database**   While using the Writer's Desktop Database, check out the powerful Help menu at any time for instructions on every feature or for tips on how to use the program more efficiently.

The following are some basic instructions to help you search the database:

1. From the search page, choose the type of search you wish to perform (Publisher/Agency, Editor/Agent, Published Titles) by clicking on the appropriate tab at top.
2. Next, enter your search criteria into the appropriate fields. For example, if you've written a mystery novel and wish to find a publisher, enter "mystery" into the "Description" or "Interest" fields to find a list of publishers who accept mystery novels.
3. Click on the "Perform Search" button. A list of results will pop up. To view the details of a particular item in the list, click on the underlined publisher or agency name on the left side of the screen.
4. To perform a new search, simply repeat the process from step 1.